Fodor's 2015
SPAIN

D0069140

WELCOME TO SPAIN

Spain conjures images of flamenco dancers, café-lined plazas, white hillside villages, and soaring cathedrals. Beyond these traditional associations, this modern country offers top-notch art museums, inventive cuisine, and exciting nightlife. From the Pyrenees to the coast, its landscapes and varied cultures are worth exploring. Especially enticing is the national insistence on enjoying everyday pleasures. The Spanish live life to its fullest whether they are strolling in the park, pausing for a siesta, lingering over lunch, or dancing until dawn.

TOP REASONS TO GO

★ **Cool Cities:** Barcelona, Madrid, Seville, Granada, Valencia, Bilbao, San Sebastián, and Salamanca.

★ **Amazing Architecture:** From the Moorish Alhambra to Gaudí's eclectic Sagrada Família.

★ **History:** From Segovia's Roman aqueduct to Córdoba's Mezquita, history comes alive.

★ **Superlative Art:** Masterpieces by Goya, El Greco, Picasso, Dalí, and Miró thrill.

★ **Tapas and Wine:** Spain's justly famed small bites pair perfectly with its Riojas.

★ **Beautiful Beaches:** From Barcelona's city beaches to Ibiza's celebrated strands.

Fodor's SPAIN 2015

Publisher: Amanda D'Acierno, *Senior Vice President*

Editorial: Arabella Bowen, *Editor in Chief*; Linda Cabasin, *Editorial Director*

Design: Fabrizio La Rocca, *Vice President, Creative Director*; Tina Malaney, *Associate Art Director*; Chie Ushio, *Senior Designer*; Ann McBride, *Production Designer*

Photography: Melanie Marin, *Associate Director of Photography*; Jessica Parkhill and Jennifer Romains, *Researchers*

Maps: Rebecca Baer, *Senior Map Editor*; Mark Stroud (Moon Street Cartography) and David Lindroth, *Cartographers*

Production: Linda Schmidt, *Managing Editor*; Evangelos Vasilakis, *Associate Managing Editor*; Angela L. McLean, *Senior Production Manager*

Sales: Jacqueline Lebow, *Sales Director*

Marketing & Publicity: Heather Dalton, *Marketing Director*; Katherine Punia, *Senior Publicist*

Business & Operations: Susan Livingston, *Vice President, Strategic Business Planning*; Sue Daulton, *Vice President, Operations*

Fodors.com: Megan Bell, *Executive Director, Revenue & Business Development*; Yasmin Marinaro, *Senior Director, Marketing & Partnerships*

Copyright © 2015 by Fodor's Travel, a division of Random House LLC

Writers: Lauren Frayer, Ignacio Gómez, Jared Lubarsky, Elizabeth Prosser, Joanna Styles, Steve Tallantyre, Suzanne Wales

Editors: Salwa Jabado, Kristan Schiller (*Barcelona editor*)

Editorial Contributors: Penny Phenix, John Rambow

Production Editors: Carolyn Roth, Jennifer DePrima

ISBN 978-0-8041-4278-6

ISSN 0361-9648

All details in this book are based on information supplied to us at press time. Always confirm information when it matters, especially if you're making a detour to visit a specific place. Fodor's expressly disclaims any liability, loss, or risk, personal or otherwise, that is incurred as a consequence of the use of any of the contents of this book.

SPECIAL SALES

This book is available at special discounts for bulk purchases for sales promotions or premiums. For more information, e-mail specialmarkets@penguinrandomhouse.com

PRINTED IN THE UNITED STATES OF AMERICA

10 9 8 7 6 5 4 3 2 1

CONTENTS

CONTENTS

CONTENTS

CONTENTS

ABOUT
THIS GUIDE

Fodor's Recommendations

Everything in this guide is worth doing—
we don't cover what isn't—but exceptional sights, hotels, and restaurants are
recognized with additional accolades.
Fodor's Choice★ indicates our top recommendations; and **Best Bets** call attention to
notable hotels and restaurants in various
categories. Care to nominate a new place?
Visit Fodors.com/contact-us.

Trip Costs

We list prices wherever possible to help
you budget well. Hotel and restaurant
price categories from **$** to **$$$$** are noted
alongside each recommendation. For
hotels, we include the lowest cost of a
standard double room in high season.
For restaurants, we cite the average price
of a main course at dinner or, if dinner
isn't served, at lunch. For attractions,
we always list adult admission fees; dis-
counts are usually available for children,
students, and senior citizens.

Hotels

Our local writers vet every hotel to recom-
mend the best overnights in each price cat-
egory, from budget to expensive. Unless
otherwise specified, you can expect pri-
vate bath, phone, and TV in your room.
For expanded hotel reviews, facilities, and
deals visit Fodors.com.

Top Picks
★ Fodor's Choice

Listings
⊠ Address
⊠ Branch address
☎ Telephone
🖷 Fax
⊕ Website
✉ E-mail
🖾 Admission fee
🕑 Open/closed times
Ⓜ Subway
⊹ Directions or Map coordinates

Hotels & Restaurants
🏨 Hotel
🛏 Number of rooms
🍽 Meal plans
✕ Restaurant
🍸 Reservations
👔 Dress code
🚫 No credit cards
$ Price

Other
⇨ See also
☞ Take note
🏌 Golf facilities

Restaurants

Unless we state otherwise, restaurants are
open for lunch and dinner daily. We men-
tion dress code only when there's a specific
requirement and reservations only when
they're essential or not accepted. To make
restaurant reservations, visit Fodors.com.

Credit Cards

The hotels and restaurants in this guide
typically accept credit cards. If not, we'll
say so.

1

EXPERIENCE
SPAIN

WHAT'S WHERE

Numbers refer to chapters.

2 Madrid. Its boundless energy makes sights and sounds larger than life. The Prado, Reina Sofía, and Thyssen-Bornemisza museums make one of the greatest repositories of Western art in the world. The cafés in the Plaza Mayor and the wine bars in the nearby Cava Baja buzz, and nightlife stretches into the wee hours around Plaza Santa Ana. Sunday's crowded flea market in El Rastro is thick with overpriced oddities.

3 Toledo and Trips from Madrid. From Madrid there are several important excursions, notably Toledo, as well as Segovia and Salamanca. Other cities in Castile–La Mancha and Castile–León worth checking out if you're traveling include León, Burgos, Soria, Sigüenza, and Cuenca. Extremadura, Spain's remote borderland with Portugal, is often overlooked, but has some intriguing places to discover. Highlights include prosperous Cáceres, packed with medieval and Renais-sance churches and palaces; Trujillo, lined with mansions of Spain's imperial age; ancient Mérida, Spain's richest trove of Roman remains; and the Jerte Valley, which turns white in late March with the blossom-ing of its million cherry trees.

4 Galicia and Asturias. On the way to Santiago de Compostela to pay homage to St. James, Christian pilgrims once crossed Europe to a corner of Spain so remote it was called *finis terrae* ("World's End"). Santiago still resonates with mystic importance. In the more mountainous Asturias, picturesque towns nestle in green highlands, and sandy beaches stretch out along the Atlantic. Farther east, in Cantabria, is the Belle Époque beach resort of Santander.

5 Bilbao and the Basque Country. Greener and cloudier than the rest of Spain, and stubbornly independent in spirit, the Basque region is a country within a country, proud of its own language and culture as well as its coastline along the Bay of Biscay—one of the peninsula's wildest and most dramatic.

6 The Pyrenees. Cut by some 23 steep north–south valleys on the Spanish side alone, with four indepen-dent geographical entities—the valleys of Campodrón, Cerdanya, Aran, and Baztán—the Pyrenees has a wealth of areas to explore, with different cultures and languages to match.

Bay of Biscay

Santander

CANTABRIA

Burgos

Palencia

Valladolid

Duero

CASTILE–LEÓN

3

Segovia

Ávila

2

MADRID ✪

Toledo

Aranjuez

Tajo

CASTILE–
LA MANCHA

Alcázar
de San Juan

Guadiana

Ciudad Real

Valdepeñas

órdoba

Jaén

ANDALUSIA

ntequera

Granada

Málaga

COSTA DEL SOL

BASQUE COUNTRY
(EUSKADI)

San
Sebastián

Bilbao

Trevino

5

Logroño

LA RIOJA

Soria

NAVARRE

PYRENEES

6

Huesca

Ebro

Zaragoza

ARAGON

FRANCE

ANDORRA

Girona

CATALONIA

Lleida

COSTA
BRAVA

Barcelona

Tarragona

COSTA
DORADA

Tortosa

Teruel

Cuenca

Júcar

Requena

Castellón
de la Plana

Valencia

COSTA DEL AZAHAR

VALENCIA

Albacete

Segura

Alicante

COSTA BLANCA

MURCIA

Murcia

Lorca

Cartagena

Almería

COSTA DE
ALMERÍA

Melilla

MOROCCO

*Balearic
Sea*

Menorca

Mallorca

BALEARIC
ISLANDS

Ibiza

Formentera

*Mediterranean
Sea*

0   100 miles

0   150 km

WHAT'S WHERE

7 Barcelona. The Rambla in the heart of the Old City is packed day and night with strollers, artists, street entertainers, vendors, and vamps, all preparing you for Barcelona's startling architectural landmarks. Antoni Gaudí's sinuous Casa Milà and unique Sagrada Família church are masterpieces of the Moderniste oeuvre.

8 Catalonia, Valencia, and the Costa Blanca. A cultural connection with France and Europe defines Catalonia. The citrus-scented, mountain-backed plain of the Levante is dotted with Christian and Moorish landmarks and extensive Roman ruins. Valencia's signature dish, paella, fortifies visitors touring the city's medieval masterpieces and exuberant modern architecture. The Costa Blanca has party-'til-dawn resort towns like Benidorm as well as small villages where time seems suspended in centuries past. The rice paddies and fragrant orange groves of the Costa Blanca lead to the palm-fringed port city of Alicante.

9 Ibiza and the Balearic Islands. Ibiza still generates buzz as a summer playground for clubbers from all over, but even this isle has its quiet coves. Alternatively, much of Ibiza's rave-all-night crowd chooses neighboring Formentera as their chill-out daytime destination. Mallorca has some built-up and heavily touristed pockets, along with long vistas of pristine, rugged mountain beauty. On comparatively serene Menorca, the two cities of Ciutadella and Mahón have remarkably different histories, cultures, and points of view.

10 Andalusia. Eight provinces, five of which are coastal (Huelva, Cádiz, Málaga, Granada, and Almería) and three of which are landlocked (Seville, Córdoba, and Jaén), compose this southern autonomous community known for its Moorish influences. Highlights are the haunting Mezquita of Córdoba, Granada's romantic Alhambra, and seductive Seville.

11 Costa del Sol and Costa de Almería. With more than 320 days of sunshine a year, the Costa is especially seductive to Northern Europeans eager for a break from the cold. As a result, vast holiday resorts sprawl along much of the coast, though there are respites: Marbella, a longtime glitterati favorite, has a pristine Andalusian old quarter, and villages such as Casares seem immune to the goings-on along the water.

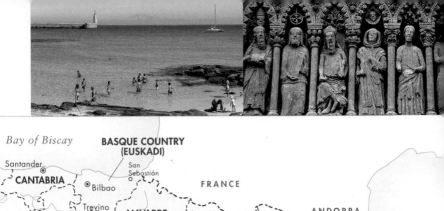

Bay of Biscay

BASQUE COUNTRY (EUSKADI)

Santander

CANTABRIA

Bilbao

San Sebastián

FRANCE

ANDORRA

Trevino

NAVARRE

Burgos

Logroño

LA RIOJA

Palencia

Soria

Valladolid *Duero*

CASTILE–LEÓN

Segovia

Ávila

MADRID ✪

Toledo

Aranjuez

CASTILE–LA MANCHA

Alcázar de San Juan

Ciudad Real

Valdepeñas

Guadiana

Tajo

Teruel

ARAGON

Zaragoza

Huesca

Lleida

Tarragona

CATALONIA

Girona

7

COSTA BRAVA

Barcelona

Tortosa

COSTA DORADA

Cuenca

8

Castellón de la Plana

Requena

Valencia

COSTA DEL AZAHAR

VALENCIA

Júcar

Albacete

Segura

Alicante

COSTA BLANCA

MURCIA

Murcia

Cartagena

Lorca

Córdoba

10

Jaén

ANDALUSIA

Antequera

Granada

Almería

COSTA DE ALMERÍA

11

Málaga

COSTA DEL SOL

Balearic Sea

Menorca

Mallorca

BALEARIC ISLANDS

9

Ibiza

Formentera

Mediterranean Sea

Melilla

MOROCCO

0   100 miles

0   150 km

SPAIN PLANNER

When to Go

Summer in Spain is hot, and temperatures can hit 100°F (38°C). Although air-conditioning is the norm in hotels and museums, walking and exploring can be uncomfortable, particularly in Andalusia. In August, major cities empty out, with Spaniards migrating to the beach—expect huge traffic jams August 1 and 31. Many small shops and some restaurants shut down; most museums remain open.

Winters are mild and rainy along the coasts and bitterly cold elsewhere. Snow is rare except in the mountains, where you can ski December through March in the Pyrenees and at resorts near Granada, Madrid, and Burgos.

May and October are optimal for visiting Spain, as it's generally warm and dry. May has more hours of daylight; October is the harvest season, which is especially colorful in the wine regions.

Spring has spectacular fiestas, particularly Valencia's Las Fallas in March and Seville's Semana Santa (Holy Week), a week from mid-March to mid-April, followed by the Feria de Abril (April Fair), showcasing horses, bulls, and flamenco. April in southern Spain is warm but still cool enough to make sightseeing comfortable.

Getting Here

Most flights into Spain go to Madrid or Barcelona, though Málaga in Andalusia is popular with carriers traveling from the United Kingdom and other European countries; Girona is a busy hub for the no-frills carriers bringing holiday travelers to nearby Barcelona or the beaches of the Costa Brava. You can also travel by ferry from the United Kingdom to northern Spain, by ferry or catamaran from Morocco to southern Spain, or on a cruise: Barcelona is Spain's main port of call, but others include Málaga, Cádiz, Gibraltar, Valencia, A Coruña, and destinations in the Balearic Islands. From France or Portugal you can drive or take a bus.

Getting Around

Once in Spain, you can travel by bus, car, or train. Buses are often faster than local trains, and bus fares tend to be lower. Service is extensive, though less frequent on weekends.

For rail travel, the local-route RENFE trains are economical and run on convenient schedules; the AVE, Spain's high-speed train, is wonderfully fast—it can go from Madrid to Seville or to Barcelona in under three hours. ■TIP→ Rail passes like the Eurailpass must be purchased before you leave for Europe.

Large, chain car-rental companies all have branches in Spain, though the online outfit Pepe Car (⊕ www.pepecar.com) may have better deals. Its modus operandi: the earlier you book, the less you pay. In Spain, most vehicles have manual transmissions; if you order a compact, make sure it has air-conditioning. ■TIP→ If you don't want a stick shift, reserve well in advance and specify automatic transmission.

A few rules of the road: children under 12 may not ride in the front seat, and seat belts are mandatory for all passengers. ■TIP→ Follow speed limits. Rental cars are frequently targeted by police monitoring speeding vehicles, and speed cameras are common.

For more travel info, see the Travel Smart Spain chapter.

Restaurant Basics

Most restaurants in Spain don't serve breakfast (*desayuno*); for coffee and carbs, head to a bar or *cafetería*. Outside major hotels, where room rates often include morning buffets, breakfast in Spain is usually limited to coffee and toast or a roll. Lunch (*comida* or *almuerzo*) traditionally consists of an appetizer, a main course, and dessert, followed by coffee and perhaps a liqueur. Between lunch and dinner the best way to snack is to sample a variety of *tapas* (appetizers) at a bar. Dinner (*cena*) is somewhat lighter than lunch, with perhaps only one course. In addition to an à la carte menu, most restaurants offer a daily fixed-price menu (*menú del día*), including two courses, wine, and dessert at an attractive price. It's traditionally a lunch thing but is increasingly offered at dinner in popular tourist destinations.

Hotel Basics

There are many types of lodgings in Spain, from youth hostels (different from an *hostal,* which is a budget hotel) to boutique hotels and modern high-rises and various options in between. Among the most popular lodgings in Spain are the paradores—government-run, upscale hotels, many of them in historic buildings or visit-worthy locations. Rates are reasonable, considering that most paradores have four- or five-star amenities, including a restaurant serving regional specialties. *(See "A Night with History" In Focus feature for more information.)*

Do I Have to Eat So Late?

Many of the misunderstandings for visitors to Spain concern mealtimes. The Spanish eat no earlier than 1:30 pm for lunch, preferably after 2 pm, and not before 9 pm for dinner. Dining out on the weekend can begin at 10 pm or even later. In areas with heavy tourist traffic, some restaurants open a bit earlier.

Siesta?

Dining is not the only part of Spanish life with a bizarre timetable. Outside major cities most shops shut in the afternoons from 2 to 5 pm, when shopkeepers go home to eat the main meal of the day and perhaps snooze for a while. It's best to work this into your plans on an "if you can't beat them, join them" basis, taking a quick siesta after lunch in preparation for a long night out on the town.

Smoking?

As of January 1, 2010, smoking is entirely forbidden in bars, cafés, and restaurants. The considerable smoking population has resigned itself to the ban but, weather permitting, outdoor tables fill up first—and fast.

Travel Times by Train

FRANCE

ANDORRA

PYRENEES

COSTA BRAVA

San Sebastián
Irún
< 1hr 55mn >
< 25mn >
< 55mn >
Vitoria-Gasteiz
Pamplona
< 50mn > Logroño
Castejón
< 1hr 50mn >
Soria
< 1hr 45mn >
Huesca
< 45mn >
Girona
< 1hr 15mn >
< 2hr 40mn >
< 1hr 20mn >
< 45mn >
Zaragoza
< 1hr 15mn >
Lleida
< 30mn >
< 35mn >
Barcelona
< 1hr 55mn >
Teruel
< 2hr 20mn >
Tortosa
Tarragona
< 3hr 5mn >
Cuenca
< 2hr 50mn >
< 1hr 15mn >
< 2hr 5mn >
< 3hr 25mn >
Castellón de la Plana
< 1hr 40mn >
< 45mn >
Valencia
< 1hr 35mn >
< 1hr >
Albacete
< 1hr 35mn >
< 1hr 45mn >
Alicante
< 4hr 45mn >
Murcia
< 1hr >
< 1hr >
< 2hr 20mn >
Lorca
< 45mn >
Cartagena
Almería

TRAVEL TIMES

Destination	Fastest Times
Madrid to Barcelona	2 hrs 30 mins
Madrid to Bilbao	4 hrs 57 mins
Madrid to Seville	2 hrs 20 mins
Madrid to Granada	4 hrs 25 mins
Madrid to Santander	4 hrs 25 mins
Madrid to Valencia	1 hrs 38 mins
Madrid to Santiago de Compostela	5 hrs 30 mins
Barcelona to Bilbao	6 hrs 20 mins
Barcelona to Valencia	2 hrs 59 mins
Seville to Granada	3 hrs 10 mins

SPAIN TODAY

Politics

Since the advent of democracy in 1976, Spanish politics has been dominated by the two largest parties: the Partido Socialista Obrero Español (PSOE) socialist party and right-wing Partido Popular (PP) party. In the 2011 national, regional, and local elections, the PSOE—in power since 2004—was handed widespread defeats, giving the opposition right PP outright majorities in 8 of the 13 regions that were up for grabs, and, nationally, installing PP party leader Mariano Rajoy as prime minister.

The electorate soured on the austerity measures the PSOE had adopted to cope with the country's considerable economic problems—not the least of them the highest unemployment rate in the euro zone—but the PP government has taken many measures even further: It raised income taxes, introduced labor reforms that make it easier for employers to fire workers, weakened the system of collective bargaining (thus lowering wages), and reduced both the numbers and salaries of public-sector, public-health, and education employees. The months following the election turned the spotlight on the *indignados*—the "indignant ones"—who gathered in Occupy Wall Street–style protests against the cutbacks in major cities nationwide; demonstrations have continued sporadically since then.

An important element of PP policy is its opposition to any further devolution of powers to Spain's autonomous regions, which are responsible for their own education, welfare, and health care budgets—and where chronic borrowing and overspending have contributed significantly to the nation's economic crises. Rajoy's determined centralism has only added fuel to separatist sentiments, especially in Catalonia, where parties advocating outright independence won the regional elections in late 2012. In 2013, the regional parliament set the date for an independence referendum in 2015, although this is unlikely to go ahead because it's unconstitutional.

The Economy

The introduction of the euro in January 2002 brought about a major change in Spain's economy, as shopkeepers, hoteliers, restaurateurs, and real estate agents all rounded prices up in an attempt to make the most of the changeover from the old currency, and the country became markedly more expensive. This did little to harm Spain's immense tourism machine, at least until the recession began to take its toll in 2009. A weaker euro and an improvement in global economic conditions brought the hospitality industry bouncing back in 2012 and 2013; this reflected, in some measure, a return on the government's €1.5 billion loan to "de-seasonalize" the industry (reducing its dependence on the summer beach-bound holiday market) and expand both the eco-friendly and the upscale cultural components of the Spanish travel experience. With the economy staging a slow recovery (the economy shrank by some 1.2% in 2013), tourism remains a bright spot: Spain's 60-million-plus visitors contribute around 12% annually to the country's GDP.

Religion

The state-funded Catholic Church, closely tied to the right-wing PP and with the national Cadena Cope radio station as its voice, continues to hold considerable social and political influence in Spain, with members of secretive groups such as

Opus Dei and the Legionarios de Cristo holding key government and industry positions.

Despite the church's influence, at street level Spain has become a secular country, as demonstrated by the fact that 70% of Spaniards supported the decidedly un-Catholic 2005 law allowing gay marriage. And although more than 75% of the population claims to be Catholic—attendance at Mass has been bolstered over the last decade by strongly Catholic South American and Eastern European immigrants—less than 20% go to church on a regular basis.

More than 1 million Muslims reside in Spain, making Islam the country's second-largest religion.

The Arts

Spain's devotion to the arts is clearly shown by the attention, both national and international, paid to its annual Principe de Asturias prize, where Prince Felipe hands out accolades to international high achievers such as Philip Roth and Annie Leibovitz, and to homegrown talent such as the golfer José María Olazábal and writer Antonio Muñoz Molina, who has taught at the City University of New York.

Film is at the forefront of the Spanish arts scene. Acclaimed director Pedro Almodóvar notched another triumph in 2013 with his comic take on air travel in *I'm So Excited!*, starring Spanish leads Antonio Banderas and Penelope Cruz (who also teamed up with her husband, Javier Bardem, under the direction of Ridley Scott for *The Counselor*).

In contrast, Spanish music continues to be a rather local affair, though the summer festival scene, including the Festival Internacional de Benicàssim and WOMAD (World of Music and Dance), serves up top names to revelers who come from all over Europe to soak up music in the sun.

While authors such as Miguel Delibes, Rosa Montero, and Maruja Torres flourish in Spain, few break onto the international scene, with the exception of Arturo Pérez Reverte, whose books include *Captain Alatriste* and *The Fencing Master*, and Carlos Ruiz Zafón, author of the acclaimed *Shadow of the Wind*, *The Angel's Game*, and *Prisoner of Heaven*. Spain's contribution to the fine arts is still dominated by three names: the Mallorca-born artist Miquel Barceló; the Basque sculptor Eduardo Chillida, who died in 2002; and the Catalan abstract painter Antoni Tàpies, who died in 2012.

Sports

With Real Madrid and FC Barcelona firmly established as international brands, and La Liga recognized as one of the world's most exciting leagues, soccer remains the nation's favorite sport. The national soccer team, known as La Roja ("The Red One"), is the only team in the world to have won the European Cup twice and the World Cup in succession. La Roja was a serious contender for its second successive World Cup in summer 2014, but was eliminated early in the group stages. After *fútbol*, what rivets the Spanish fan's attention are cycling, tennis, basketball, and motorcycle racing. Alberto Contador, who won the 2012 Vuelta de España; Rafael Nadal, the first tennis player to hold Grand Slam titles on clay, grass, and hard court; brothers Pau and Marc Gasol, who play for the Los Angeles Lakers and the Memphis Grizzlies respectively; and Marc Márquez who in 2013 was the youngest winner ever of MotoGP, are national heroes.

WHAT'S NEW IN SPAIN

Kicks

Since 2009, when FC Barcelona brought home every trophy a Spanish soccer club could acquire—the domestic Triple Crown (La Liga, King's Cup, and Supercopa), the UEFA European Champions League cup, and the FIFA Club World Championship—Barça has remained the acknowledged best fútbol team in the world. Archrival Real Madrid denied them the King's Cup in 2011 and La Liga in 2012, a situation that reversed itself in 2013. In 2014, the capital's other soccer club, Atlético de Madrid, won the title for the first time in 18 years. Both Madrid teams contested the final for the UEFA Champions League.

Art: Ups and Downs

There were a variety of ups for the arts in 2013: the Reina Sofía Museum in Madrid received record numbers of visitors for its Salvador Dalí exhibition; the Patios in Córdoba were awarded UNESCO Intangible Cultural Heritage of Humanity status; and Granada celebrated the thousandth anniversary of the kingdom of Al-Andalus. On the downside, the government raised the I.V.A. tax from 8% to 21% on all cultural events, resulting in an all-time low for attendance figures at cinemas and theaters, and museum visits dropped because of fewer national tourists.

Getting Around

There are plenty of regional air connections in Spain these days, but the national railway's high-speed AVE trains are stiff competition: prices are about the same, but with trips like Madrid–Barcelona clocking in at 2 hours and 30 minutes, the AVE is the fastest, most comfortable way to go. Spain now has more high-speed track in service or under construction than any other country in Europe, although construction on several AVE routes (for example, Madrid–Galicia and Granada–Seville) has slowed down considerably after cutbacks in funding. ⇨ *See the Train Map and the Travel Smart Spain chapter for details.*

No Bull?

In 2010 the Catalan Parliament narrowly approved a bill to ban bullfighting in the region (a similar ban has been in force on the Canary Islands since 1991); the more conservative regions of Madrid, Valencia, and Murcia reacted with proposals to give the "sport" the legal status of a protected cultural heritage. The national parliament presented and passed this proposal in 2013. Like anything that even remotely touches on the question of Spanish identity, this is a politically hot issue; animal-rights activists have an uphill battle ahead.

Holy Ground

A work in progress since 1882, Gaudí's Sagrada Família church in Barcelona was formally consecrated in November 2010 by Pope Benedict XVI. Still a long way from a fully functioning house of worship—construction is expected to take at least until 2026—the church remains a major tourist attraction *(⇨ see Chapter 7).*

MAKING THE MOST OF YOUR EUROS

Way back when, people traveled to Europe because it was cheap. That's not so today, but don't let that stop you from going—you just need to think creatively about how to spend your money.

Save Before You Go

Online research and trip planning. The more research you do, the better prepared you'll be to save. Sometimes you can save money by purchasing a package deal or a tour.

Money matters. Know the exchange rate, and your credit card and ATM card fees. When you call your bank and credit card company for this information, be sure to let them know when and where you're traveling so they don't flag your card. Change any PINs to four digits.

Save on Lodgings

Rent an apartment or house. One of the most costly parts of a vacation is lodging. Not only can renting an apartment be cheaper than a hotel, but access to a kitchen lowers food costs. Many rental sites let you book for less than a week; typically, these flats can sleep five on some combination of beds and fold-out sofas, and often have Wi-Fi connectivity.

Stay off the beaten path. If your vacation is for more than a couple of days, consider staying outside the pricey, heavily touristed areas. If public transportation is easy and cost-effective, as it is in Madrid and Barcelona, then you'll get to know an off-the-beaten-path neighborhood with its less expensive local eateries, and still be able to see the sights.

Sight-See, Don't Sight-Spend

Pass or no pass? Buying a multisite or museum pass can make sense if your plans include heavy sightseeing rather than just hitting top spots; some can also save time, since many passes also allow you to skip long lines.

Book tickets online. Go online for advance-purchase tickets for sites and performances. You might get discounts, or beat the lines with time-specific entry for sites like the Prado in Madrid, Barcelona's Sagrada Família, or Granada's Alhambra.

Research schedules. Find out which sites have discounted hours; most museums offer lower-priced or free tickets one afternoon or evening a week.

Save on Transportation

Take public transit instead of taxis. Madrid, Barcelona, Valencia, and Bilbao all have excellent, inexpensive, and easy-to-navigate metro and bus systems; local bus service elsewhere around the country is usually easy to use as well. Don't automatically buy bulk tickets or a pass, though, without first doing the math.

Avoid expensive airport transport. Research alternatives before you go, to prevent hailing a pricey taxi on arrival. Public transit isn't always your best option since some metros may be well connected but hard to navigate with heavy luggage. Check destinations for cost-effective, privately operated shuttle services to and from the airport.

Compare airlines and train travel. Low-cost Europe-based airlines such as Ryanair, easyJet, and Vueling can get you around Europe cheaply, but the fast trains in Spain can also be quick and inexpensive.

Book ahead. RENFE offers considerable discounts if you book ahead; tickets are available up to six months in advance of travel. If there are four of you, consider booking a "table ticket" (*mesa,* denoted by an *M*), which offers big discounts on regular prices.

SPAIN
TOP ATTRACTIONS

La Alhambra, Granada

(A) Nothing can prepare you for the Moorish grandeur of Andalusia's greatest monument. The palace unfolds in a series of sumptuous courtyards and gardens, with softly playing fountains, delicate stone tracery, and exquisite motifs in ceramic tile. (⇨ Chapter 10)

Toledo

(B) El Greco's city (the fourth centenary of his death was 2014), an hour southwest of Madrid, is often described as Spain's spiritual capital, and past inhabitants—including Jews, Romans, and Muslims—have all felt its pull. Perched on a ridge above the Río Tajo, Toledo is a tapestry of medieval buildings, churches, mosques, and synagogues threaded by narrow, cobbled streets and squares. (⇨ Chapter 3)

La Sagrada Família, Barcelona

(C) The symbol of Barcelona, Antoni Gaudí's extraordinary unfinished cathedral should be on everyone's must-see list.

The iconic pointed spires, with organic shapes that resemble honeycombed stalagmites, are visible from almost any point in the city, and it's well worth taking a tour round them if you're fit and don't mind heights. (⇨ Chapter 7)

Guggenheim, Bilbao

(D) All swooping curves and rippling forms, the architecturally innovative museum—one of Frank Gehry's most breathtaking projects—was built on the site of the city's former shipyards and inspired by the shape of a ship's hull. The Guggenheim's cachet is its huge spaces: there's room to stand back and admire works such as Richard Serra's monumental steel forms; sculpture by Miquel Barceló and Eduardo Chillida; and paintings by Anselm Kiefer, Willem de Kooning, and Mark Rothko. (⇨ Chapter 5)

Museo del Prado, Madrid

(E) One of the world's greatest museums, the Prado holds masterpieces by Italian and Flemish painters, but its jewels are the works of Spaniards: Goya, Velázquez, and El Greco. *(⇨ Chapter 2)*

Mérida's Roman Ruins

(F) In the center of a somewhat drab modern town is the largest Roman city on the Iberian Peninsula. Ogle the fabulously preserved Roman amphitheater with its columns, statues, and tiered seating, or the humbler, yet equally beguiling, 2nd-century house with mosaics and frescoes. *(⇨ Chapter 3)*

Cuenca's Hanging Houses

(G) Cuenca is all honey-color buildings, handsome mansions, ancient churches, and earthy local bars. Seek out the famous Casas Colgadas, or "Hanging Houses," with their facades dipping precipitously over a ravine. Dating from the 15th century, the balconies appear as an extension of the rock face. *(⇨ Chapter 3)*

San Lorenzo de El Escorial

(H) This giant palace-monastery (with no fewer than 2,673 windows), built by the megalomaniac Felipe II, makes visitors stop in their tracks. The exterior is austere, but inside the Bourbon apartments and library are lush with rich, colorful tapestries, ornate frescoes, and paintings by such masters as El Greco, Titian, and José de Ribera. *(⇨ Chapter 2)*

Mezquita, Córdoba

An extraordinary mosque, the Mezquita is famed for its thicket of red-and-white-stripe columns resembling a palm grove oasis interspersed with arches and traditional Moorish embellishments. It's a fabulous, massive monument that comprises a whole block in the center of Córdoba's tangle of ancient streets and squares. *(⇨ Chapter 10)*

SPAIN'S TOP EXPERIENCES

Get Festive

Plan your visit, if you can, to coincide with one of Spain's virtually countless fairs and festivals. With the possible exception of the Italians, nobody does annual celebrations like the Spanish: fireworks, solemn processions, historical reenactments, pageants in costume, and street carnivals of every description fill the calendar. The most famous fair of all is Seville's **Feria de Abril** (April Fair), when sultry señoritas dance in traditional flamenco garb, and the cream of society parades through the streets in horse-drawn carriages. Second only to Rio in terms of revelry and costumes, Spain's pre-Lenten **Carnaval** inspires serious partying: Santa Cruz de Tenerife, in the Canary Islands, is legendary for its annual extravaganza of drinking, dancing, and dressing up—the more outrageous the better—but Cadíz, on the Atlantic coast, and Sitges, south of Barcelona, have blowouts nearly as good; celebrations typically carry on for 10 days. For Barcelona's **Festa de Sant Jordi**, honoring St. George, the city's patron saint, tradition dictates that men buy their true love a rose, and women reciprocate by buying their beau a book; on that day (April 23) the city streets are filled with impromptu book and flower stalls. In the **Semana Santa** (Holy Week: mid-March to mid-April), the events of the Passion are recalled in elaborate processions of hooded and gowned religious brotherhoods carrying elaborate floats through the streets from local churches to cathedrals in cities all over Spain; the most impressive take place in Seville, Málaga, and Cartagena in Murcia. And did we mention fireworks? The fiesta of **Las Fallas de San José**, in Valencia (around March 19), is a week of rockets, firecrackers, pinwheels, and processions in traditional costume, culminating on the Nit del Foc (Night of the Fire), when hundreds of huge papier-mâché figures are dispatched in a spectacular pyrotechnic finale.

Dance 'til Dawn

A large part of experiencing Spain doesn't begin until the sun sets or end until it rises again. The Spaniards know how to party and the nightlife is, well, an essential part of life. If you really want to experience the ultimate party, head to the island of **Ibiza**, in the Balearic Islands, in the summer, but otherwise any of the big cities can pretty much guarantee late-night fun.

Visit a Market

Mercados (markets) are the key to delicious local cuisine and represent an essential part of Spanish life, largely unaffected by competition from supermarkets and hypermarkets. You'll find fabulous produce sold according to whatever is in season: counters neatly piled with shiny purple eggplants, blood-red peppers, brilliant orange cantaloupes, fresh figs, and cornucopias of mushrooms and olives. While cities and most large towns have daily fruit and vegetable markets from Monday through Saturday, Barcelona might be the best city for market browsers, with its famed **Boqueria** as well as smaller mercados in lovingly restored Moderniste buildings, with wrought-iron girders and stained-glass windows, all over the city. Take the opportunity to get a culinary education—but be warned: the vendors are in the business of selling food, and can get cranky with rubberneckers.

Get Outdoors

Crisscrossed with mountain ranges, Spain has regions that are ideal for walking, mountain biking, and backpacking, and mountain streams throughout the country offer trout- and salmon-fishing

opportunities. Perhaps the best thing about exploring Spain's great outdoors is that it often brings you nearer to some of the finest architecture and cuisine in Iberia. The 57,000-acre **Parque Nacional de Ordesa y Monte Perdido,** in the Pyrenees, is Spain's version of the Grand Canyon, with waterfalls, caves, forests, meadows, and more. The **Sierra de Gredos,** west of Madrid, in Castile and León, bordering Extremadura, is a popular destination for climbing and trekking. Hiking is excellent in the interior of Spain, in the **Alpujarras Mountains** southeast of Granada and in the **Picos de Europa** in the north. The pilgrimage road to Santiago de Compostela, known as **El Camino de Santiago,** has been drawing devotees and adventurers for more than 1,000 years; it traverses the north of Spain from either Roncesvalles in Navarra or the Aragonese Pyrenees to Galicia. The **Doñana National Park,** in Andalusia, is one of Europe's last tracts of true wilderness, with wetlands, beaches, sand dunes, marshes, 150 species of rare birds, and countless kinds of wildlife, including the endangered imperial eagle and lynx.

Try Some Wine

Spain is one of the world's biggest wine-producing countries, with local specialties found in just about every region. For the most famous, sample still and sparkling wines in the Penedès in Catalonia; sip oak-aged reds in La Rioja; taste the Ribera del Duero reds in Castile-León (and decide for yourself if they're better than those in La Rioja); or try the different types of sherry in Jerez de la Frontera in Andalusia. Slightly off the beaten wine track are Galician wines led by white albariño, Córdoba's sherries, and Murcia's little-known reds and whites. Book a tour in a *bodega* (wine cellar) and prepare to raise your glass. ¡*Salud!*

Lordly Lodgings

A quintessential experience for visitors to Spain is spending a night, or several, in one of the government-run hotels called **paradores**. The settings are unique—roughly half of the 94 paradores are important cultural properties from the 12th to the 18th century: restored castles, Moorish citadels, monasteries, ducal palaces, and the like—and most are furnished in the style of the region. Every parador has a restaurant that serves local specialties.

Hit the Beach

Virtually surrounded by bays, oceans, gulfs, straits, and seas, Spain is a beach-lover's dream as well as an increasingly popular destination for water-sports enthusiasts. Oceanfront—8,000 km (5,000 miles) of it, not counting the islands—is Spain's most important hospitality asset, and sun worshippers can choose from long sweeps of beach on sheltered bays to tiny crescents of sand in rocky inlets that only boats can reach. There are 12 *costas* (designated coastal areas) along the Mediterranean, and seven more along the Atlantic from Portugal around to France. One of the great things about Spanish sands is that some of the best are literally extensions of the cities you otherwise come to Spain for—so you can spend a morning in the surf and sun, then steep yourself in history or art for an afternoon, and finish the day with a great meal and an evening of music. Among the best city beaches are **La Concha** (San Sebastián), **Playa de la Victoria** (Cadiz), Barcelona's string of beaches, **Playa de los Peligros** (Santander), and **El Cabanyal** (Valencia).

SPAIN'S TOP MUSEUMS

In the Golden Age of Empire (1580–1680), Spanish monarchs used Madrid's wealth not only to finance wars and civil projects but also to underscore their own grandeur by collecting and commissioning great works of art. That national patrimony makes Spain a museum-lover's paradise—all the more so for the masterworks of modern painting and sculpture that have been added since, and for the museum buildings themselves, many of them architecturally stunning.

Madrid

Centro de Arte Reina Sofía, Madrid. The modern collection focuses on Spain's three great modern masters: Picasso, Dalí, and Miró. The centerpiece is Picasso's monumental *Guernica.* (⇨ *Chapter 2*)

Museo del Prado, Madrid. In a magnificent neoclassical building on one of Madrid's most elegant boulevards, the Prado, with its collection of Spanish and European masterpieces, is frequently compared to the Louvre. (⇨ *Chapter 2*)

Museo Thyssen-Bornemisza, Madrid. This mass of artwork was purchased by the Spanish government in 1993 from the Baron Thyssen-Bornemisza. Among the some 1,600 paintings in the collection are works by Dürer, Rembrandt, Titian, and Caravaggio—and important pieces from the impressionist and early modern periods. (⇨ *Chapter 2*)

Catalonia and Valencia

Museu Picasso, Barcelona. Five elegant medieval and early-Renaissance palaces in the Gothic Quarter house this collection of some 3,600 works by Picasso, who spent the early years of his career (1895–1904) in Barcelona. (⇨ *Chapter 7*)

Museu Nacional d'Art de Catalunya, Barcelona. MNAC has the finest collection of Romanesque frescoes and devotional

sculpture in the world, most rescued from abandoned chapels in the Pyrenees. Taking the fragile frescoes off crumbling walls, building supports for them in the same intricate shapes as the spaces they came from (vaults, arches, windows), and rehanging them was an astonishing feat of restoration. (⇨ *Chapter 7*)

Fundació Miró, Barcelona. Designed by Miró's friend and collaborator, architect Lluís Sert, this museum was the artist's gift to the city that shaped his career. It houses some 11,000 of Miró's works: oils, sculpture, textiles, drawings, and prints. (⇨ *Chapter 7*)

Museo de Bellas Artes, Valencia. At the edge of the city's Royal Gardens, the MBA is one of the finest smaller collections in Spain. It houses masterworks by Ribalta, Velázquez, Ribera, and Goya, and a gallery devoted to 19th-century Valencian painter Joaquin Sorolla. (⇨ *Chapter 8*)

Northern Spain

Museo Guggenheim, Bilbao. Frank Gehry's museum is a work of art in its own right, the first great building of the 21st century. Even its detractors now hail it for the transformative impact it has had on what was once a grimy industrial city. Inside, the galleries showcase international and Spanish art by modern and contemporary painters and sculptors. It's easy to combine a visit of several days to Bilbao with a trip to Barcelona. (⇨ *Chapter 5*)

Southern Spain

Museo de Bellas Artes, Seville. Rivaled only by the Prado in terms of Spanish art, the MBA collection includes works by Murillo, Zurbarán, and El Greco, and Gothic art, baroque religious sculpture, and Sevillian art from the 19th and 20th centuries. (⇨ *Chapter 10*)

FAQ

What are my lodging options in Spain? For a slice of Spanish culture, stay in a parador; to indulge your pastoral fantasies, try a *casa rural* (country house), Spain's version of a bed-and-breakfast. On the other end of the spectrum are luxurious high-rise hotels along the coastline and chain hotels in the major cities. Traveling with your family? Consider renting an apartment or go for a family room deal in a hotel.

Do I need to book hotels beforehand, or can I just improvise once I'm in Spain? In big cities or popular tourist areas it's best to reserve well ahead. In smaller towns and rural areas, you can usually find something on the spot, except when local fiestas are on—for those dates you may have to book months in advance.

How can I avoid looking like a tourist in Spain? Ditch the white tennis shoes and shorts for a start, and try to avoid baseball caps. A fanny pack will betray you instantly; a *mochila*—an all-purpose cloth or leather bag with a long shoulder strap, bought locally—will serve you better.

Do shops really close for siesta? In general, shops close from 2 to 5 pm, particularly in small towns and villages. The exceptions are supermarkets and large department stores, which tend to be open from 9 am to 9 pm in the center of Madrid and Barcelona, and at major resorts stores often stay open all day.

How much should I tip at a restaurant? You won't find a service charge on the bill, but the tip is included. For stellar service, leave a small sum in addition to the bill, between 5% and 10%. If you're indulging in tapas, just round the bill to the nearest euro.

If I only have time for one city, should I choose Barcelona or Madrid? It depends on what you're looking for. Madrid will give you world-class art and much more of a sense of a workaday Spanish city, while cosmopolitan Barcelona has Gaudí, Catalan cuisine, and its special Mediterranean atmosphere.

Can I get dinner at 7 pm, or do I really have to wait until the Spanish eat at 9 pm? If you really can't wait, head for the most touristy part of town; there you should be able to find bars and cafés that will serve meals at any time of day. But it won't be nearly as good as the food the Spaniards are eating a couple of hours later. You might be better off just dining on tapas.

How easy is it to cross the border from Spain into neighboring countries? Spain, Portugal, and France are members of the EU, so borders are open. Good trains connect Madrid and Lisbon (from about €40), and Madrid and Paris (from about €160). American citizens need only a valid passport to enter Morocco; ferries run regularly to Tangier from Tarifa (€35 one way, €129 with a car) and Algeciras (€22 one way, €115 with a car).

Can I bring home the famous Ibérico ham, Spanish olives, almonds, or baby eels? Products you can legally bring into the United States include olive oil, cheese, olives, almonds, wood-smoked paprika, and saffron. These products must be declared at customs. Ibérico ham, even vacuum-sealed, is not legal, so you may not get past customs agents and their canine associates. If caught, you risk confiscation and fines. And don't even think about trying to bring back *angulas* (eels).

For more help on trip planning, see the Travel Smart Spain chapter.

QUINTESSENTIAL SPAIN

La Siesta

The unabashed Spanish pursuit of pleasure and the unswerving devotion to establishing a healthy balance between work and play is nowhere more apparent than in the midday shutdown. In the two-salary, 21st-century Spanish family, few people still observe the custom of going home for lunch, and fewer still take the classic midday snooze—described by novelist Camilo José Cela as "*de padrenuestro y pijama*" (with a prayer and pajamas). The fact remains, however, that most stores and businesses close from about 2 to 5 pm.

El Fútbol and the Tortilla de Patata

The Spanish National Fútbol League and the *tortilla de patata* (potato omelet) have been described as the only widely shared phenomena that bind the nation together. Often referred to as *tortilla española* to distinguish it from the French omelet (a thin envelope of egg, often filled with cheese) or the flat, all-dough Mexican tortilla filled

with meat, the Spanish potato omelet is a thick, cake-shape mold of potatoes (and sometimes onions) bound with egg and ideal for breakfast, snacks, or full meals. In the right chef's hands, the tortilla can be elevated to a gourmet delicacy, but even in a hole-in-the-wall tapas bar, you can't go too far wrong.

In the case of the soccer league, the tie that binds often resembles tribal warfare, as bitter rivalries centuries old are played out on the field. Some of these, such as the Real Sociedad (San Sebastián)–Athletic Bilbao feud, are fraternal in nature, brother Basques battling for boasting rights, but others, such as the Madrid–Barcelona face-offs, are as basic to Spanish history as Moros y Cristianos (a reenactment of the battle between the Moors and the Christians). The beauty of the game is best appreciated in the stadiums, but local sports bars, many of them official fan clubs

f you want to get a sense of Spanish culture and indulge in some of its
pleasures, start by familiarizing yourself with the rituals of Spanish life.
These are a few things you can take part in with relative ease.

of local teams, are where you see fútbol
passions at their wildest.

El Paseo

One of the most delightful Spanish customs is *el paseo* (the stroll), which traditionally takes place during the early
evening and is common throughout the
country but particularly in *pueblos* and
towns. Given the modern hamster-wheel
pace of life, there is something appealingly
old-fashioned about families and friends
walking around at a leisurely pace with
no real destination or purpose. Dress is
usually formal or fashionable: elderly
señoras with their boxy tweed suits, men
with jackets slung, capelike, round the
shoulders, teenagers in their latest Zara
gear, and younger children in their Sunday
best. El paseo provides everyone with an
opportunity to participate in a lively slice
of street theater.

Sunday Lunch

The Spanish love to eat out, especially on
Sunday, the traditional day when families make an excursion of a long leisurely
lunch—often, depending on the time
of year, at an informal seaside restaurant (*chiringuito*) or a rural *venta* (meal
for sale). The latter came into being in
bygone days when much of the seasonal
work, particularly in southern Spain, was
done by itinerant labor. Cheap, hearty
meals were much in demand, and some
enterprising country housewife saw the
opportunity to provide ventas; the idea
soon spread. Ventas are still a wonderfully
good value today, not just for the food but
also for the atmosphere: long, scrubbed
wooden tables; large, noisy Spanish families; and a convivial informality. Sunday
can be slow. So relax, and remember that
all good things are worth waiting for.

GREAT ITINERARIES

MADRID AND THE SOUTH

CAPITAL CITY TO THE ALHAMBRA, 10 DAYS

Days 1–3: Madrid
Start the day with a visit to either the **Prado**, the **Museo Thyssen-Bornemisza,** or the **Centro de Arte Reina Sofía**. Then head to the elegant **Plaza Mayor**—a perfect jumping-off point for a tour of the Spanish capital. To the west, see the **Plaza de la Villa, Palacio Real** (the Royal Palace), **Teatro Real** (Royal Theater), and the royal convents; to the south, wander around the maze of streets of **La Latina** and **El Rastro** and try some local tapas.

On Day 2, visit the sprawling **Barrio de las Letras,** centered on the Plaza de Santa Ana. This was the favorite neighborhood of writers during the Spanish golden literary age in the 17th century, and it's still crammed with theaters, cafés, and good tapas bars. It borders the Paseo del Prado on the east, allowing you to comfortably walk to any of the art museums in the area. If the weather is pleasant, take an afternoon stroll in the **Parque del Buen Retiro.**

For your third day in the capital, wander in **Chueca** and **Malasaña,** the two neighborhoods most favored by young *madrileños*. Fuencarral, a landmark street that serves as the border between the two, is one of the city's trendiest shopping enclaves. From there you can walk to the **Parque del Oeste** and the **Templo de Debod**—the best spot from which to see the city's sunset. Among the lesser-known museums, consider visiting the captivating **Museo Sorolla**, Goya's frescoes and tomb at the

Ermita de San Antonio de la Florida, or the **Real Academia de Bellas Artes de San Fernando** for classic painting. People-watch at any of the terrace bars in either Plaza de Chueca or Plaza 2 de Mayo in Malasaña. (⇨ *Chapter 2*)

Logistics: If you're traveling light, the subway (Metro Line No. 8) or the bus (No. 200) will take you from the airport to the city for €5. A taxi will cost around €30. Once in the center consider walking or taking the subway rather than cabbing it in gridlock traffic.

Days 4 and 5: Castilian Cities
There are several excellent options for half- or full-day side trips from Madrid to occupy Days 4 and 5. **Toledo** and **Segovia** are two of the oldest Castilian cities—both have delightful old quarters dating back to the Romans. There's also **El Escorial**, which houses the massive monastery built by Felipe II. Two other nearby towns also worth visiting are **Aranjuez** and **Alcalá de Henares.** (⇨ *Chapter 3*)

Logistics: Toledo and Segovia are stops on the high-speed train line (AVE), so you can get to either of them in a half hour from Madrid. To reach the old quarters of both cities take a bus or cab from the train station or take the bus from Madrid; busing is also the best way to get to El Escorial. Reach Aranjuez and Alcalá de Henares via the intercity train system.

Day 6: Córdoba or Extremadura
Córdoba, the capital of both Roman and Moorish Spain, was the center of Western art and culture between the 8th and 11th century. The city's breathtaking **Mezquita** (mosque), which is now a cathedral, and the medieval **Jewish Quarter** bear witness to the city's brilliant past. From Madrid you could also rent a car and visit the lesser-known cities north of **Extremadura,**

such as **Guadalupe** and **Trujillo**, and over-nighting in **Cáceres**, a UNESCO World Cultural Heritage city, and returning to Madrid the next day. (⇨ *Chapter 10 for Córdoba and Chapter 3 for Extremadura*)

Logistics: The AVE train will take you to Córdoba from Madrid in under two hours. An alternative is to stay in Toledo, also on the route heading south, and then head to Córdoba the next day, although you need to return to Madrid by train first. Once in Córdoba, take a taxi for a visit out to the summer palace at Medina Azahara.

Days 7 and 8: Seville

Seville's **Cathedral**, with its tower La Giralda, **Plaza de Toros Real Maestranza,** and **Barrio de Santa Cruz** are visual feasts. Forty minutes south you can sip the world-famous sherries of **Jerez de la Frontera,** then munch jumbo shrimp on the beach at **Sanlúcar de Barrameda.** (⇨ *Chapter 10*)

Logistics: From Seville's AVE station, take a taxi to your hotel. After that, walking and hailing the occasional taxi are the best ways to explore the city. A rental car is the best option to reach towns beyond Seville.

> ### TIP
>
> Spain's modern freeways and toll highways are as good as any in the world—with the exception of the signs, which are often hard to decipher as you sweep past them at the routine speed of 120 kph (74.5 mph).

Days 9 and 10: Granada

The hilltop **Alhambra** palace, Spain's most visited attraction, was conceived by the Moorish caliphs as heaven on earth. Try any of the city's famous tapas bars and tea shops, and make sure to roam the magical, steep streets of the **Albayzín,** the ancient Moorish quarter. (⇨ *Chapter 10*)

Logistics: The Seville–Granada leg of this trip is best accomplished by renting a car—Antequera makes a good quick stop on the way. However, the Seville-to-Granada trains (four daily, just over 3 hours, €30) are an alternative. Another idea is to head first from Madrid to Granada, and then from Granada via Córdoba to Seville.

GREAT ITINERARIES

BARCELONA AND THE NORTH

GAUDÍ, THE NORTH COAST, AND GALICIA, 16 DAYS

Days 1–3: Barcelona

To get a feel for Barcelona, begin with **La Rambla** and **Boquería** market. Then set off for the **Gothic Quarter** to see the **Catedral de la Seu, Plaça del Rei**, and the Catalan and Barcelona government palaces in **Plaça Sant Jaume.** Next, cross Via Laietana to the **Born-Ribera** (waterfront neighborhood) for the Gothic **Santa Maria del Mar** and nearby **Museu Picasso.**

Make Day 2 a Gaudí day: visit the **Temple Expiatori de la Sagrada Família,** then **Park Güell.** In the afternoon see the **Casa Milà** and **Casa Batlló,** part of the Manzana de la Discòrdia on Passeig de Gràcia. **Palau Güell,** off the lower Rambla, is probably too much Gaudí for one day, but don't miss it. *(⇨ See "Gaudí: Architecture Through the Looking Glass" in Chapter 7)*

On Day 3, climb **Montjuïc** for the **Museu Nacional d'Art de Catalunya,** in the hulking **Palau Nacional.** Investigate the **Fundació Miró, Estadi Olímpic,** the **Mies van der Rohe Pavilion,** and **CaixaForum** exhibition center. At lunchtime, take the cable car across the port for seafood in **Barceloneta** and then stroll along the beach. *(⇨ Chapter 7)*

Logistics: In Barcelona, walking or taking the subway is better than cabbing it.

Day 4: San Sebastián

San Sebastián is one of Spain's most beautiful—and delicious—cities. Belle Époque buildings nearly encircle the tiny bay, and tapas bars flourish in the old quarter. Not far from San Sebastián is historic **Pasajes de San Juan.** *(⇨ Chapter 5)*

Logistics: Take the train from Barcelona to San Sebastián (5 hours) first thing in the morning. You don't need a car in San Sebastián proper, but visits to cider houses in Astigarraga, Chillida Leku on the outskirts of town, and many of the finest restaurants around San Sebastián are possible only with your own transportation or a taxi (the latter with the advantage that you won't get lost). The freeway west to Bilbao is beautiful and fast, but the coastal road is recommended at least as far as Zumaia.

Days 5 and 6: The Basque Coast

The Basque coast between San Sebastián and Bilbao has a succession of fine beaches, rocky cliffs, and picture-perfect fishing ports. The wide beach at **Zarautz,** the fishermen's village of **Getaria,** the **Zuloaga Museum in Zumaia,** and **Bermeo's** port and fishing museum should all be near the top of your list. *(⇨ Chapter 5)*

Days 7 and 8: Bilbao

Bilbao's Guggenheim Museum is worth a trip for the building itself, and the **Museum of Fine Arts** has an impressive collection of Basque and Spanish paintings. Restaurants and tapas bars are famously good in Bilbao. *(⇨ Chapter 5)*

Logistics: In Bilbao, use the subway or the Euskotram, which runs up and down the Nervión estuary.

Days 9 and 10: Santander and Cantabria

The elegant beach town of **Santander** has an excellent summer music festival every August. Nearby, **Santillana del Mar** is one of Spain's best Renaissance towns, and the museum of the **Altamira Caves** displays reproductions of the famous underground Neolithic rock paintings discovered here.

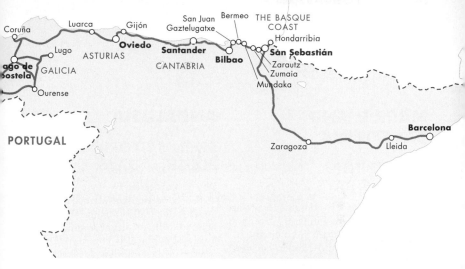

Exploring the **Picos de Europa** will take you through some of the peninsula's wildest reaches, and the port towns along the coast provide some of Spain's most pristine beaches. (⇨ *Chapter 4*)

Days 11–13: Oviedo and Asturias

The coast road through **Ribadesella** and the cider capital **Villaviciosa** to **Oviedo** is scenic and punctuated with tempting beaches. Oviedo, its **Cathedral,** and the simplicity of its pre-Romanesque churches are worlds away from the richness of Córdoba's Mezquita and Granada's Alhambra. (⇨ *Chapter 4*)

Logistics: The A8 coastal freeway gets you quickly and comfortably to Oviedo and just beyond. From there, go west into Galicia via the coastal N634—a slow but scenic route to Santiago.

Days 14–16: Santiago de Compostela and Galicia

Spain's northwest corner, with **Santiago de Compostela** at its spiritual and geographic center, is a green land of bagpipes and apple orchards. The albariño wine country, along the Río Miño border with Portugal, and the *rías* (estuaries), full of delicious seafood, will keep you steeped in *enxebre*—Gallego for "local specialties and atmosphere." (⇨ *Chapter 4*)

> **TIP**
>
> Be prepared for bilingual traffic signs and local spellings that do not match your map, which probably adheres to the "traditional" Castilian spelling.

Logistics: The four-lane freeways AP9 and A6 whisk you from Lugo and Castro to Santiago de Compostela and to the Rías Baixas. By car is the only way to tour Galicia. The AC862 route around the upper northwest corner and the Rías Altas turns into the AP9 coming back into Santiago.

GREAT ITINERARIES

MADRID AND BARCELONA

SPAIN'S TOP CITIES, 6 DAYS

Combining Spain's two largest and greatest cities on a six-day itinerary gives you the chance to take in the contrasts of Imperial Madrid and Moderniste Barcelona. Both cities are vibrant, energetic cultural centers showcasing some of Europe's greatest art and architecture as well as Spanish gastronomy at its best. You can also get a taste for Spain's late-night fun, sample its colorful markets, and stay at some of the country's best lodgings. However, Madrid and Barcelona feel very different, and you'll find huge contrasts in their landscapes, culture, and ambience. By visiting them both you'll get a good idea of the many facets that make up Spain.

For what to do on your days in Madrid, see the Madrid and the South itinerary above. For Barcelona, see the Barcelona and the North itinerary above.

Logistics: Take the high-speed train (AVE) from Madrid to Barcelona (journey time is 2 hours and 30 minutes). For the return journey, fly from Barcelona to Madrid Barajas Airport in time to catch your flight home.

ANDALUSIA

SPAIN'S GLORIOUS SOUTH, 7 DAYS

Day 1: Córdoba
Córdoba's breathtaking **Mezquita** (mosque), now a cathedral, is an Andalusian highlight, and the medieval **Jewish Quarter** is lovely to explore. If you're here during May, visit the **Festival de los Patios** (Patio Festival). (⇨ *Chapter 10*)

Days 2–3: Seville
The city that launched Christopher Columbus to the New World, **Seville** is a treasure trove of sights. Start with the **Cathedral** and climb the Giralda Tower for great views of the city. Move on to the richly decorated **Alcázar,** still an official royal residence, with its many beautiful patios. The **Jewish Quarter** in Santa Cruz is a charming labyrinth of alleyways and squares. In the afternoon, cross to **Triana** over the Guadalquivir River and lose yourself in the quiet streets, which are the birthplace of many a flamenco artist. (⇨ *Chapter 10*)

Logistics: Take the high-speed train (AVE) to Seville from Córdoba (45 minutes). Seville is a compact city and easy to navigate so it's best to explore on foot.

Day 4: Jerez de la Frontera and Ronda via Arcos de la Frontera
Jerez de la Frontera is the world's sherry headquarters and home to some of the greatest bodegas. Visit Domecq, Harvey, or Sandeman, and, if you have time, watch the world's finest dancing horses at the prestigious Royal Andalusian School of Equestrian Art. The lovely clifftop village of **Arcos de la Frontera,** one of Andalusia's prettiest *pueblos blancos* (white villages), makes a great stop on the way to **Ronda.**

Barcelona

PORTUGAL

Córdoba
ANDALUSIA
Seville ○ Granada
Arcos de la Frontera
Jerez de Málaga
la Frontera Ronda
COSTA DEL SOL

Mediterranean Sea

One of the oldest towns in Spain, Ronda is famed for its spectacular position and views; get the best photo from the Juan Peña El Lebrijano Bridge. (⇨ *Chapter 10*)

Logistics: Rent a car in Seville and take the highway to Jerez de la Frontera before making your way to Ronda via Arcos de la Frontera. If you have time, stop off in the lovely village of Grazalema.

Day 5: Málaga

Start your exploration of the capital of the **Costa del Sol, Málaga,** with the **Roman theater,** Moorish **Alcazaba,** and Gothic **Cathedral.** Stroll down to the Muelle Uno on the port for views of the city skyline and **Gibralfaro** castle before returning to the center to visit the **Museo Picasso** and browse the shops in Larios and surrounding streets. (⇨ *Chapter 11*)

Logistics: Leave Ronda early and enjoy the scenic drive to Málaga via the A354. In Málaga, explore on foot, leaving your car in a central lot or at your hotel.

Days 6–7: Granada

Allow a good half day to visit the hilltop **Alhambra** palace and Generalife gardens (⇨ *Alhambra: Palace-Fortress in Chapter 10*). From there, walk down to the city center to the **Cathedral** and **Capilla Real,** the shrine of Isabella of Castile and Ferdinand of Aragón. Finish your day with some

TIP

Rent a car with a GPS navigation system to help you find your way from one Andalusian city to the next. Help with navigating is also useful in the cities themselves.

tapas at one of the many famous tapas bars. On Day 7, walk up to the Albayzín, the ancient Moorish quarter, for a leisurely wander around the narrow streets. Take your time in the Plaza de San Nicolás and admire the magnificent views of the Alhambra and Sierra Nevada before you leave. (⇨ *Chapter 10*)

Logistics: The drive to Granada from Málaga takes about one hour and 15 minutes. Granada is best explored on foot so leave your car at the hotel.

HISTORY YOU CAN SEE

Ancient Spain

The story of Spain, a romance-tinged tale of counts, caliphs, crusaders, and kings, begins long before written history. The Basques were among the first here, fiercely defending the green mountain valleys of the Pyrenees. Then came the Iberians, apparently crossing the Mediterranean from North Africa around 3000 BC. The Celts arrived from the north about a thousand years later. The seafaring Phoenicians founded Gadir (now Cádiz) and several coastal cities in the south three millennia ago. The parade continued with the Greeks, who settled parts of the east coast, and then the Carthaginians, who founded Cartagena around 225 BC and dubbed the then-wild, forested, and game-rich country Ispania, after their word for rabbit: *span*.

What to See: Near Barcelona, on the Costa Brava, rocket yourself back almost 3,000 years at **Ullastret**, a settlement occupied by an Iberian people known as the Indiketas. On a tour, actors guide groups through the homes and fortifications of some of the peninsula's earliest inhabitants, the defensive walls attesting to the constant threat of attack and the bits of pottery evidence of the settlement's early ceramic industry. Not far away in **Empúries** are ruins of the Greek colony established in the 6th century BC. At the **Museo de Cádiz** in Andalusia, you can view sarcophagi dating back to the 1100 BC founding of the city.

The Roman Epoch

Modern civilization in Iberia began with the Romans, who expelled the Carthaginians and turned the peninsula into three imperial provinces. It took the Romans 200 years to subdue the fiercely resisting Iberians, but their influence is seen today in the fortifications, amphitheaters, aqueducts, and other ruins in cities across Spain, as well as in the country's legal system and in the Latin base of Spain's Romance languages and dialects.

What to See: Segovia's nearly 3,000-foot-long **Acueducto Romano** is a marvel of Roman engineering. Mérida's Roman ruins are some of Spain's finest, including its **bridge, theater,** and **outdoor amphitheater.** Tarragona was Rome's most important city in Catalonia, as the **walls, circus,** and **amphitheater** bear witness, while Zaragoza boasts a **Roman amphitheater** and a **Roman fluvial port** that dispatched flat-bottomed riverboats loaded with wine and olive oil down the Ebro.

1100 BC	Earliest Phoenician colonies are formed, including Cádiz, Villaricos, Almuñecar, and Málaga. Natives include Basques in the Pyrenees, Iberians in the south, and Celts in the northwest.
237 BC	Carthaginians land in Spain.
206 BC	Romans expel Carthaginians from Spain and gradually conquer peninsula.
AD 74	Roman citizenship extended to all Spaniards.

419	Visigothic kingdom established in central and northern Spain, with capital at Toledo.
711–12	Visigothic kingdom overthrown by invading Muslims (Moors), who create an emirate, with the capital at Córdoba.
813	Discovery of remains of St. James; the cathedral of Santiago de Compostela is built and becomes a major pilgrimage site.
1085–1270	Main years of the Reconquest.
1478	Spanish Inquisition begins.

The Visigoths and Moors

In the early 5th century, invading tribes crossed the Pyrenees to attack the weakening Roman Empire. The Visigoths became the dominant force in central and northern Spain by AD 419, establishing their kingdom at Toledo and eventually adopting Christianity. But the Visigoths, too, were to fall before a wave of invaders. The Moors, an Arab-led Berber force, crossed the Strait of Gibraltar in AD 711 and swept through Spain in an astonishingly short time, launching almost eight centuries of Muslim rule. The Moors brought with them citrus fruits, rice, cotton, sugar, palm trees, glassmaking, and the complex irrigation system still used around Valencia. The influence of Arabic in modern Spanish includes words beginning with "al," such as *albóndiga* (meatball), *alcalde* (mayor), *almohada* (pillow), and *alcázar* (fortress), as well as prominent phonetic characteristics ranging from the fricative *j* to, in all probability, the lisping *c* (before *e* and *i*) and *z*. The Moorish architecture and Mudejar Moorish-inspired Gothic decorative details found throughout most of Spain tell much about the splendor of the Islamic culture that flourished here.

What to See: Moorish culture is most spectacularly evident in Andalusia, derived from the Arabic name for the Moorish reign on the Iberian Peninsula, al-Andalus, which meant "western lands." The fairy-tale **Alhambra** palace overlooking Granada captures the refinement of the Moorish aesthetic, while the earlier 9th-century **Mezquita** at Córdoba bears witness to the power of Islam in al-Andalus.

Spain's Golden Age

By 1085, Alfonso VI of Castile had captured Toledo, giving the Christians a firm grip on the north. In the 13th century, Valencia, Seville, and finally Córdoba—the capital of the Muslim caliphate in Spain—fell to Christian forces, leaving only Granada in Moorish hands. Nearly 200 years later, the so-called Catholic Monarchs—Ferdinand of Aragón and Isabella of Castile—were joined in a marriage that would change the world. Finally, on January 2, 1492, 244 years after the fall of Córdoba, Granada surrendered and the Moorish reign was over.

The year 1492 was the beginning of the nation's political golden age: Christian forces conquered Granada and unified all of current-day Spain as a single kingdom; in what was, at the time, viewed

1479–1504	Isabella and Ferdinand rule jointly.	ca. 1520 –1700	Spain's Golden Age.
1492	Granada, the last Moorish outpost, falls. Christopher Columbus, under Isabella's sponsorship, discovers the islands of the Caribbean, setting off a wave of Spanish exploration. Ferdinand and Isabella expel Jews and Muslims from Spain.	1605	Miguel de Cervantes publishes the first part of *Don Quixote de la Mancha*.
1516	Ferdinand dies. His grandson Carlos I inaugurates the Habsburg dynasty.	1618–1648	Thirty Years' War: a dynastic struggle between Habsburgs and Bourbons.
1519–22	First circumnavigation of the world by Ferdinand Magellan's ships.	1701–14	War of the Spanish Succession. Claimants to the throne are Louis XIV of France, Holy Roman Emperor Leopold I, and electoral prince Joseph Ferdinand of Bavaria.

as a measure promoting national unity, Jews and Muslims who did not convert to Christianity were expelled from the country. The departure of educated Muslims and Jews was a blow to the nation's agriculture, science, and economy from which it would take nearly 500 years to recover. The Catholic Monarchs and their centralizing successors maintained Spain's unity, but they sacrificed the spirit of international free trade that was bringing prosperity to other parts of Europe. Carlos V weakened Spain with his penchant for waging war, and his son, Felipe II (Phillip II), followed in the same expensive path, defeating the Turks in 1571 but losing the "Invincible Spanish Armada" in the English Channel in 1588.

What to See: Celebrate Columbus's voyage to America with **festivities in Seville, Huelva, Granada, Cádiz, and Barcelona,** all of which display venues where "The Discoverer" was commissioned, was confirmed, set out from, returned to, or was buried. Wander through the somber **El Escorial,** a monastery northwest of Madrid commissioned by Felipe II in 1557, finished in 1584, and the last resting place of most of the Habsburg and Bourbon kings of Spain since then.

War of the Spanish Succession

The 1700–14 War of the Spanish Succession ended with the fall of Barcelona, which sided with the Habsburg Archduke Carlos against the Bourbon Prince Felipe V. El Born market, completed in 1876, covered the buried remains of the Ribera neighborhood where the decisive battle took place. Ribera citizens were required to tear down a thousand houses to clear space for the Ciutadella fortress, from which fields of fire were directed, quite naturally, toward the city the Spanish and French forces had taken a year to subdue. The leveled neighborhood, then about a third of Barcelona, was plowed under and forgotten by the victors, though never by barcelonins.

What to See: In Barcelona, the **Fossar de les Moreres cemetery,** next to the Santa María del Mar basilica, remains a powerful symbol for Catalan nationalists who gather there every September 11, Catalonia's National Day, to commemorate the fall of the city in 1714.

Spanish Civil War

Spain's early-19th-century War of Independence required five years of bitter guerrilla fighting to rid the peninsula of Napoleonic troops. Later, the Carlist

1756–63	Seven Years' War: Spain and France versus Great Britain.
1808	Napoléon takes Madrid.
1809–14	The Spanish War of Independence: Napoleonic armies thrown out of Spain.
1834–39	First Carlist War: Don Carlos contests the crown; an era of upheaval begins.
1873	First Spanish Republic declared. Three-year Second Carlist War begins.
1898	Spanish-American War: Spain loses Cuba, Puerto Rico, and the Philippines.

1936–39	Spanish Civil War; more than 600,000 die. General Francisco Franco wins and rules Spain for the next 36 years.
1977–78	First democratic election in 40 years; new constitution restores civil liberties and freedom of the press.
1992	Olympic Games held in Barcelona.
2000	Juan Carlos celebrates 25 years as Spain's king.
2002	Spain bids farewell to the peseta, adopts the euro (EU common currency).

wars set the stage for the Spanish Civil War (1936–39), which claimed more than half a million lives. Intellectuals and leftists sympathized with the elected government; the International Brigades, with many American, British, and Canadian volunteers, took part in some of the worst fighting, including the storied defense of Madrid. But General Francisco Franco, backed by the Catholic Church, got far more help from Nazi Germany, whose Condor legions destroyed the Basque town of Gernika (in a horror made infamous by Picasso's monumental painting *Guernica*), and from Fascist Italy. For three years, European governments stood by as Franco's armies ground their way to victory. After the fall of Barcelona in January 1939, the Republican cause became hopeless, and Franco's Nationalist forces entered Madrid on March 27, 1939.

What to See: Snap a shot of **Madrid's Plaza Dos de Mayo,** in the Malasaña neighborhood, where officers Daoiz and Velarde held their ground against the superior French forces at the start of the popular uprising against Napoléon. The archway in the square is all that remains of the armory Daoiz and Velarde defended to the death. Trace the shrapnel marks on

HIDDEN MEANINGS

What's *not* there in Spain can be just as revealing as what is. For example, there are no Roman ruins in Madrid, as it was founded as a Moorish outpost in the late 10th century and was not the capital of Spain until 1560, a recent date in Spanish history. Likewise, Barcelona has no Moorish architecture—the Moors sacked Barcelona but never established themselves there, testifying to Catalonia's medieval past as part of Charlemagne's Frankish empire. Al-Andalus, the 781-year Moorish sojourn on the peninsula, was farther south and west.

the wall of the **Sant Felip Neri church** in Barcelona, evidence of the 1938 bombing of the city by Italian warplanes under Franco's orders. East of Zaragoza, **Belchite** was the scene of bloody fighting during the decisive Battle of the Ebro. The town has been left exactly as it appeared on September 7, 1937, the day the battle ended.

2004	Terrorist bombs on Madrid trains claim almost 200 lives; the conservative Partido Popular loses the general election and the socialist PSOE under Prime Minister José Luis Zapatero comes to power.
2005	Parliament legalizes gay marriage, grants adoption and inheritance rights to same-sex couples.
2007	Parliament passes a bill formally denouncing Franco's rule, and ordering Franco-era statues and plaques removed from streets and buildings.
2009	Spain enters recession for the first time since 1993; unemployment hits 19.4%, with nearly 5 million people jobless.
2010	Spain wins the FIFA soccer World Cup.
2011	PP wins in a landslide parliamentary election; Mariano Rajoy becomes prime minister.
2012	Spain continues in recession with unemployment at an all-time high of 26%. Economic recovery isn't forecast until 2015 at the earliest.

LANGUAGES OF SPAIN

Spanish

One of the questions you might be asking yourself as you plan your trip to a non-English-speaking country is how useful your high school Spanish will be. Well, you don't need to be fluent to make yourself understood pretty much anywhere in Spain. With immigrants in substantial numbers, many from Latin America, people in Spain are generally quite tolerant of variations on the "standard" language known as *castellano*, or Castilian Spanish—the official language of the country, by royal decree, since

1714. The Spanish you learned in school is a Romance language descended from Latin, with considerable Arabic influence—the result of the nearly eight centuries of Moorish presence on the Iberian Peninsula. The first recorded use of Spanish dates to the 13th century; in the 15th century, Antonio de Nebrija's famous grammar helped spread Spanish throughout the empire's sprawling global possessions. Pick up a Spanish phrase book, dust off that Spanish accent your high school language instructor taught you, and most Spaniards will understand your earnest request for directions to the subway—and so will some 400 million other Spanish speakers around the world.

Spain's Other Languages

What Spaniards speak among themselves is another matter. The country has a number of other significant language populations, most of which predate Castilian Spanish. These include the Romance languages Catalan and Gallego (or Galician-Portuguese) and the non-Indo-European Basque language, Euskera. A third tier of local dialects includes Asturiano (or Bable); Aranese; the variations of Fabla Aragonesa (the languages of the north-central community of Aragón); and, in Extremadura, the provincial dialect, Extremaduran.

Catalan is spoken in Barcelona, in Spain's northeastern autonomous community of Catalonia, in southern France's Roussillon region, in the city of L'Alguer on the Italian island of Sardinia, and in Andorra (where it is the national language). It is derived from Provençal French and is closer to Langue d'Oc and Occitan than to Spanish. Both **Valenciano** and **Mallorquín,** spoken respectively in the Valencia region and in the Balearic Islands, in the Mediterranean east of Barcelona, are considered dialects of Catalan.

Gallego is spoken in Galicia in Spain's northwestern corner and more closely resembles Portuguese than Spanish.

Euskera, the Basque language, is Spain's greatest linguistic mystery. Links to Japanese, Sanskrit, Finnish, Gaelic, and the language of the lost city of Atlantis have proven to be false leads or pure mythology. The most accepted theory on Euskera suggests that it evolved from a language spoken by the aboriginal inhabitants of the Iberian Peninsula and survived in isolation in the remote hills of the Basque country. Euskera is presently spoken by about a million inhabitants of the Spanish and French Basque provinces.

Asturiano (or Bable) is a Romance language (sometimes called a dialect) spoken in Asturias and in parts of León, Zamora, Salamanca, Cantabria, and Extremadura by some 700,000 people.

Aranés (or Occitan), derived from Gascon French, is spoken in Catalonia's westernmost valley, the Vall d'Arán.

Fabla aragonesa is the collective term for all of Aragón's mountain dialects—some 15 of them in active use and all more closely related to Gascon French and Occitan than to Spanish.

Extremaduran, a Spanish dialect, is spoken in Extremadura.

25

Immerse yourself in the storied settings of paradores like Santiago de Compostela (left) and Sigüenza (above).

A NIGHT WITH HISTORY

Spain's nearly 100 paradores have one thing in common: heritage status. More often than not they also have killer views. Plan a trip with stays at a number of these remarkable hotels and experience the splendors of Spanish history and culture around the country. Spaniards themselves love the paradores and make up about 65 percent of visitors.

For nearly a century, the Spanish government has been in the hotel business—to universal acclaim from foreign and domestic travelers. The state-run hotels, called *paradores*, come in two types. About a third of them are modern resorts, built in the last few decades. The majority are splendid restorations—ducal palaces, hilltop castles, monasteries and convents, and Arab fortresses: the repositories of Spain's cultural heritage, with a new lease on life. Interiors have museum-quality period decor but the amenities are thoroughly modern. The historic paradores make wonderful romantic getaways, but they can also be surprisingly family-friendly stopovers.

PAY LESS, GET MORE
The accommodations and cuisine at most paradores are as good and, in many cases, vastly superior to those of four- and five-star hotels—usually at comparable or lower prices. And most paradores have magnificent settings: depending on where you stay, for instance, you might have a balcony with views of the Alhambra, or perhaps you'll be able to see snow-peaked mountains or vistas of the sweeping Spanish plains from your bedroom.

FROM ROYAL HUNTING LODGE TO FIRST PARADOR

An advocate for Spanish tourism in the early 20th century, King Alfonso XIII was eager to develop a country-wide hotel infrastructure that would cater to local and overseas travelers. He directed the Spanish government to set up the Royal Tourist Commission to mull it over, and in 1926, commissioner Marquis de la Vega Inclán came up with the parador ("stopping place") idea and searched for where to build the first such inn. His goal was to find a setting that would reflect both the beauty of Spain and its cultural heritage. He nominated the wild Gredos Mountains, where royalty came to hunt and relax, a few hours west of Madrid.

King Alfonso XIII

By October of 1928, the Parador de Gredos opened at a spot chosen by King Alfonso himself, amid pine groves, rocks, and the clear waters of Avilá. In 1937, this parador is where the fascist Falange party was established, and a few decades later, in 1978, it's where national leaders drafted the Spanish Constitution.

SPAIN'S PARADOR CHAIN

When Alfonso gave his blessing to the establishment of Spain's first parador, he probably didn't realize that he was sitting on a financial, cultural, and historical gold mine. But after it opened, the Board of Paradores and Inns of Spain was formed and focused its energies on harnessing historical, artistic, and cultural monuments with lovely landscapes into a chain—an effort that has continued to this day.

The number of state-run paradores today approaches nearly 100, with the latest two being the Parador La Granja on the grounds of the royal summer home of Carlos III and Isabel de Farnesio in Segovia, and the Parador Cruz de Tejeda in the Canary Islands.

PILLOW TALK

Grace Kelly

Given that many paradores were once homes and residences to noble families and royalty, it's no surprise that they've continued to attract the rich and famous. Italian actress Sophia Loren stayed at the Parador de Hondarribia, as did distinguished Spanish writer José Cela, and Cardona's castle and fortress was the backdrop for the Orson Welles movie *Falstaff*.

Topping the list, though, may be the Parador de Granada: President Johnson, Queen Elizabeth, and actress Rita Hayworth all stayed here. Additionally, Grace Kelly celebrated some of her honeymoon trip with Prince Rainier of Monaco in these hallowed halls, and many Spanish intellectuals and artists have also gotten cozy in this charming, sophisticated abode.

WHAT TO EXPECT

Walk where famous people have walked in the Parador de Granada's courtyard.

Paradores have been restored to provide modern amenities, within their classic settings, so you can count on some luxuries. Some have swimming pools, while others have fitness rooms and/or saunas. Most paradores have access to cable TV, though English channels may be limited to the basics; movies may be available via a pay-per-view service. Laundry facilities are available at almost all of the paradores, and most have Wi-Fi.

As with most lodgings, it's always advised to reserve in advance.

Lodging at the paradores is generally equivalent to a four-star hotel and occasionally a five-star. The dining is another feature, though, that sets the paradores apart. The food is generally very good and traditionally inspired: paradores pride themselves on their use of fresh produce and regional cuisine.

Cost: Prices at the paradores vary, depending on location and time of year. In general, one-night stays range from €95 to €250, though the Parador de Granada will hit your wallet for at least 80 euros more per night. July through September and Easter Week tend to be the most expensive times.

DISCOUNTS

If you're 55 or over, or aged 18 to 30, you're eligible for the *Días dorados* (Golden Days) or *Escapada joven* (Young Escape) discounts of 10% on parador room tariffs from Sunday to Thursday and 5% on Friday and Saturday plus a 30% discount on breakfast. Or there's the *Especial 2 noches* with at least 10% discount on two nights in half-board (includes breakfast and dinner) accommodation. To qualify for discounts you must book online or by phone.

PARADORES WORTH VISITING

With its Spanish plateresque façade, the Parador de León adorns the Plaza de San Marcos.

PARADOR DE CANGAS DE ONIS, *Chapter 4.* This beautiful former monastery is in the mountains of Picos de Europa.

PARADOR DE GRANADA, *Chapter 10.* Within the walls of Alhambra, this former monastery is Spain's most popular, and most expensive, parador.

PARADOR DE HONDARRIBIA, *Chapter 5.* This 10th-century castle-cum-fortress in the heart of Hondarribia looks severe from the outside but is elegant and lovely inside, with sweeping views of the French coastline.

PARADOR HOSTAL SAN MARCOS, *Chapter 3.* Pure luxury sums up this five-star monastery, with arguably the best restaurant in the parador network.

PARADOR DE PLASENCIA, *Chapter 3.* This Gothic convent lies in the heart of Plasencia's beautiful old quarters.

PARADOR DE SANTILLANA GIL BLAS, *Chapter 4.* Santillana de Mar may be one of the most beautiful villages in Spain; this parador in the mountains is perfect for peace and quiet.

PARADOR DE SANTIAGO DE COMPOSTELA, *Chapter 4.* This 15th-century hospital is one of the most luxurious and beautiful of the parador chain.

PARADOR DE SIGÜENZA, *Chapter 3.* This sprawling 12th-century Moorish citadel is arguably the finest architectural example of all the parador castles.

■ TIP➜ If you plan to spend at least five nights in the paradores, the "five-night card" offers excellent savings. You can purchase and use the card (€550) at any parador except Granada every day of the year apart from Easter week, May 1–4, Oct. 31–Nov. 1 and Dec. 5–7. Note that the card does not guarantee a room; you must make reservations.

PARADOR INFORMATION

For more information about paradores, consult the official parador website, ⊕ *www.parador.es/en,* or call ☎ *34 902/547979.*

MADRID

WELCOME TO MADRID

TOP REASONS TO GO

★ **Hit the Centro Histórico:** The Plaza Mayor on any late night when it's almost empty is the place that best evokes the glory of Spain's Golden Age.

★ **Stroll down museum row:** Find a pleasant mix of art and architecture in the Prado, the Reina Sofía, and the Thyssen, all of which display extensive and impressive collections.

★ **Nibble tapas into the night:** Indulge in a *madrileño* way of socializing. Learn about the art of tapas and sample local wines while wandering among the bars of Cava Baja.

★ **Relax in the Retiro gardens:** Visit on a Sunday morning, when it's at its most boisterous, to unwind and take in the sun and merrymaking.

★ **Burn the midnight oil:** When other cities turn off their lights, madrileños swarm to the bars of the liveliest neighborhoods—Malasaña, Chueca, Lavapiés, and more—and stretch the party out until dawn.

1 Palacio, La Latina, and Sol. Palacio and La Latina have the city's highest concentration of aristocratic buildings and elegant yet affordable bars and restaurants, and Sol has some of the city's busiest streets and oldest shops.

2 Barrio de las Letras. This area is where all the major Spanish writers eventually settled. There's still a bohemian spirit here, good nightlife, and some of the city's trendiest hotels.

3 Chueca, Malasaña, and Chamberí. These neighborhoods offer eclectic, hip restaurants, shops run by young proprietors and landmark cafés. The triangle between Fuencarral, Gran Vía, and Corredera Baja has become known as the Triball area.

2

GETTING ORIENTED

Madrid is composed of 21 districts, each broken down into several neighborhoods. The most central district is called just that, Centro. Within this district you'll find all of Madrid's oldest neighborhoods: Palacio, Sol, La Latina, Lavapiés, Barrio de las Letras, Malasaña, and Chueca. Other well-known districts, which we'll call neighborhoods for the sake of convenience, are Salamanca, Retiro, Chamberí (north of Centro), Moncloa (east of Chamberí), and Chamartín. The city of Madrid dates back to the 9th century, but its perimeter wasn't enlarged by much until the mid-19th century, when an urban planner knocked down the wall built in 1625 and penciled new neighborhoods in what were formerly the outskirts. This means that even though there are now more than 3.3 million people living in a sprawling metropolitan area, the almond-shaped historic center is a concentrated area that can pleasantly be covered on foot.

4 Embajadores. The two areas in the Embajadores neighborhood, Rastro and Lavapiés, are full of winding streets. The Rastro bustles every Sunday with its flea market; Lavapiés is the city's multicultural beacon, with plenty of low-budget restaurants.

5 Salamanca and Retiro. Salamanca has great designer shops and sophisticated and expensive restaurants. Retiro, so called for its proximity to the park of the same name, holds some of the city's most expensive buildings.

6 Chamartín and Tetuán. These are two of the newer neighborhoods. They don't have much artistic value, but remain mostly ungentrified and have plenty of personality.

EATING AND DRINKING WELL IN MADRID

Spain's capital draws the finest cuisine, from seafood to rice dishes, from all over the Iberian Peninsula, but Madrid's most authentic local fare is based on the roasts and stews of Castile, Spain's mountain-studded central tableland.

(top left) A selection of tapas, including smoked ham and roasted peppers (top right) A hearty clam and beans stew (bottom left) Ingredients for a classic cocido madrileño

With a climate sometimes described as *nueves meses de invierno y tres de infierno* (nine months of winter and three of hell) it's no surprise that classic Madrid cuisine is winter fare. Garlic soup, partridge stew, and roast suckling pig and lamb are standard components of Madrid feasts, as are baby goat and chunks of beef from Ávila and the Sierra de Guadarrama. *Cocido madrileño* (a powerful winter stew) and *callos a la madrileña* (stewed tripe) are favored local specialties, while *jamón ibérico de bellota* (acorn-fed Ibérico ham)—a specialty from *la dehesa*, the rolling oak parks of Extremadura and Andalusia—has become a Madrid staple. Summer fare borrows heavily from Andalusian cuisine while minimalist contemporary cooking offers lighter postmodern alternatives based on traditional ingredients and recipes.

TAPAS

Itinerant grazing from tavern to tavern is especially important in Madrid, beneficiary of tapas traditions from every corner of Spain. The areas around Plaza Santa Ana, Plaza Mayor, and Cava Baja buzz with excitement as groups arrive for a glass of wine or two accompanied by anything from *boquerones* (pickled anchovies) or *aceitunas* (olives) to *raciones* (small plates) of *calamares* (squid) or *albóndigas* (meat balls).

2

SOUPS

Sopa de ajo, garlic soup, also known as *sopa castellana,* is cooked with *pimentón* (paprika), a bay leaf, stale bread, and an egg or two for flavor and texture. A warming start to a winter meal, bits of ham or chorizo may be added, while a last-minute visit to the oven crisps the surface sprinkling of Manchego cheese. Often eaten during Lent as an ascetic but energizing fasting dish, garlic soup appears in slightly different versions all over Spain. *Caldo* (chicken or beef broth), a Madrid favorite on wet winter days, is often offered free of charge in traditional bars and cafés with an order of anything else.

STEWS

Cocido madrileño is a Madrid classic, a winter favorite of broth, garbanzo beans, vegetables, potatoes, sausage, pork, and hen simmered in earthenware crocks over coals. *Estofado de perdiz* is a red-leg partridge stewed slowly with garlic, onions, carrots, asparagus, and snow peas before being served in an earthenware casserole that keeps the stew piping hot. *Estofado de judiones de La Granja* (broad-bean stew) is another Madrid favorite: pork, quail, clams, or ham stewed with onions, tomato, carrots, bay leaves, thyme, and broad beans from the Segovian town of La Granja de San Ildefonso.

ROASTS

Asadores (restaurants specializing in roasts) are an institution in and around Madrid, where the *cochinillo asado,* roast piglet, is the most iconic specialty. From Casa Botín in Madrid to Mesón de Cándido in Segovia and Toledo's Adolfo Restaurant *(⇨ Chapter 3),* madrileños love their roasts. Using milk-fed piglets not more than 21 days old, oak-burning wood ovens turn out crisp roasts tender enough to carve using the edge of a plate. Close behind is the *lechazo,* or milk-fed lamb, that emerges from wood ovens accompanied by the aromas of oak and Castile's wide meseta: thyme, rosemary, and thistle.

WINES

The traditional Madrid house wine, a simple Valdepeñas from La Mancha south of the capital, is giving way to designer wines from Castile–La Mancha, El Bierzo, Ribera del Duero, and new wine-producing regions popping up all over the peninsula. Traditional light-red wines lack the character to properly accompany a cocido or a roast, whereas many of these new wines combine power and an earthy complexity capable of matching central Spain's harsh continental climate and hearty cuisine.

Updated by Ignacio Gómez

Madrid—the Spanish capital since 1561—celebrates itself and life in general around the clock. A vibrant crossroads, Madrid has an infectious appetite for art, music, and epicurean pleasure, and it's turned into a cosmopolitan, modern urban center while fiercely preserving its traditions.

The modern city spreads east into the 19th-century grid of the Barrio de Salamanca and sprawls north through the neighborhoods of Chamberí and Chamartín, but the Madrid you should explore thoroughly on foot is right in the center, in Madrid's oldest quarters, between the Royal Palace and the midtown forest, the Parque del Buen Retiro. Wandering around this conglomeration of residential buildings with ancient red-tile rooftops, punctuated by redbrick Mudejar churches and grand buildings with gray-slate roofs and spires left by the Habsburg monarchs, you're more likely to grasp what is probably the city's major highlight: the buzzing bustle of people who are elated when they're outdoors.

Then there are the paintings—the artistic legacy of one of the greatest global empires ever assembled. King Carlos I (1500–58), who later became Emperor Carlos V (or Charles V), made sure the early masters of all European schools found their way to Spain's palaces and this collection was eventually placed in the Prado. Between the Prado, the contemporary Reina Sofía, the eclectic Thyssen-Bornemisza collection, and Madrid's smaller artistic repositories—the Real Academia de Bellas Artes de San Fernando, the Convento de las Descalzas Reales, the Sorolla Museum, the Lázaro Galdiano Museum, and the CaixaForum—there are more paintings than you could admire in a lifetime.

The attractions go beyond the well-known baroque landmarks. Now in the middle of an expansion plan, Madrid is making sure that some of the world's best architects will leave their imprint on the city. This is certainly the case with Jacques Herzog and Pierre de Meuron, who are responsible for the CaixaForum arts center, which opened in 2008 across from the Botanical Garden. Major renovations of the Museo del Prado and the Centro Reina Sofía are by Rafael Moneo and Jean Nouvel, respectively. Looming towers by Norman Foster and César Pelli have changed the city's northern landscape. Other projects include the

Madrid-Río project, which has added new green spaces along the banks of the Manzanares River; the controversial and sustainable Museum of Art and Architecture that Argentinean architect Emilio Ambasz plans to build across from the Prado; the new Royal Collection Museum, expected to open sometime in 2015, by Tuñón and Mansilla; and the daring renovation of the whole area of Paseo del Prado, which has been entrusted to Portuguese architect Alvaro Siza, although after several delays this project seems to have come to a halt due to the downturn in the economy and political wrangling over the detail.

PLANNING

WHEN TO GO

Madrid is hot and dry in summer—with temperatures reaching 95°F to 105°F in July and August—and chilly in winter, with minimum temperatures in the low 30s or slightly less in January and February, though snow in the city is rare. **The most pleasant time to visit is spring, especially May,** when the city honors its patron saint. June and September through December are also good.

The Festival de Otoño (Autumn Festival), from mid-May to early June, blankets the city with pop concerts, poetry readings, flamenco, and ballet and theater from world-renowned companies.

If you can, avoid Madrid in July and August—especially August, even though fares are better and there are plenty of concerts and open-air activities; many locals flee to the coast or to the mountains, so many restaurants, bars, and shops are closed.

MADRID AVG. TEMPS.

JAN.	FEB.	MAR.	APR.	MAY	JUNE
48°F/9°C	52°F/11°C	59°F/15°C	64°F/18°C	70°F/21°C	81°F/27°C
JULY	AUG.	SEPT.	OCT.	NOV.	DEC.
88°F/31°C	86°F/30°C	77°F/25°C	66°F/19°C	55°F/13°C	48°F/9°C

PLANNING YOUR TIME

Madrid's most valuable art treasures are all on display within a few blocks of Paseo del Prado. This area is home to the Prado Museum, with its astounding selection of masterworks by Diego Velázquez, Francisco de Goya y Lucientes, El Greco, and others; the Centro de Arte Reina Sofía, with an excellent collection of contemporary art; and the Thyssen Museum, with a singular collection that stretches from the Renaissance to the 21st century. Each can take a number of hours to explore, so it's best to alternate museum visits with less overwhelming attractions. If you're running short on time and want to pack everything in, replenish your energy at any of the tapas bars or restaurants in the Barrio de las Letras (behind the Paseo del Prado, across from the Prado Museum).

Any visit to Madrid should include a walk in the old area between Puerta del Sol and the Royal Palace. Leave the map in your back pocket as you come across the Plaza Mayor, the Plaza de la Villa, and the

Plaza de Oriente, and let the streets guide you to some of the oldest churches and convents standing. The Royal Palace makes a good start and end point.

GETTING HERE AND AROUND
AIR TRAVEL
Madrid's Barajas Airport is Europe's fourth largest. Terminal 4 (T-4) handles flights from 32 carriers, including American Airlines, British Airways, and Iberia. All other U.S. airlines use Terminal 1.

AIRPORT TRANSFERS Airport terminals are connected by bus service and also to the metro (Línea 8) and take you to the city center in 30 to 45 minutes for around €5 (€1.50–€2 plus a €3 airport supplement). For €5 there's also a convenient bus to Avenida de América (note that bus drivers don't take bills greater than €20), where you can catch the subway or a taxi to your hotel. In 2014, taxis began charging a flat fee of €30 from the airport to anywhere in the city center.

BUS TRAVEL
Buses are generally less popular than trains, though they're sometimes faster. Madrid has no central bus station: most of southern and eastern Spain (including Toledo) is served by the Estación del Sur. Estación de Avenida de América and Estación del Sur have subway stops (Avenida de América and Méndez Álvaro).

Red city buses (€1.50 for a one-way ticket) run from about 6 am to 11:30 pm.

Bus Stations Estación del Avenida de América ⊠ *Av. de América 9, Salamanca* Ⓜ *Av. de América.* **Estación del Sur** ⊠ *Méndez Álvaro s/n, Atocha* ⊕ *www.estaciondeautobuses.com* Ⓜ *Méndez Álvaro.* **Intercambiador de Moncloa** ⊠ *Princesa 89, Moncloa* Ⓜ *Moncloa.*

BIKE TRAVEL
Madrid launched an electric-bicycle sharing program in summer 2014. There is a network of 1,600 bikes distributed in 124 stations across the city. Locals can purchase a yearly membership but visitors can pay per ride, buying a ticket at each service station. The bikes can be borrowed from, and returned to, any station in the system. Occasional users pay €2 for the first half hour and €4 for each successive half hour.

CAR TRAVEL
Driving in Madrid is best avoided because parking and traffic are nightmares, but many of the nation's highways radiate from Madrid, including the A6 (Segovia, Salamanca, Galicia); the A1 (Burgos and the Basque Country); the A2 (Guadalajara, Barcelona, France); the A3 (Cuenca, Valencia, the Mediterranean coast); the A4 (Aranjuez, La Mancha, Granada, Seville); the A42 (Toledo); and the A5 (Talavera de la Reina, Portugal). The city is surrounded by ring roads (M30, M40, and M50), from which most of these highways are easily picked up. There are also toll highways (marked R2, R3, R4, and R5) that bypass major highways, and the A41, a toll highway connecting Madrid and Toledo.

SUBWAY TRAVEL

The metro costs from €1.50 to a maximum of €2, depending on how far you're traveling within the city; you can also buy a 10-ride Metrobus ticket (€12.20) or a daily ticket for €8.40 that can also be used on buses. The **Abono Turístico** (Tourist Pass) allows unlimited use of public buses and the subway for one to seven days. Buy it at tourist offices, metro stations, or select newsstands. The metro runs from 6 am to 1:30 am, though a few entrances close earlier. *(⇨ See the metro map in this chapter.)*

Subway Information Metro Madrid ☎ *902/444403* ⊕ *www.metromadrid.es.*

TAXI TRAVEL

Taxis work under three different tariff schemes. Tariff 1 is for the city center from 6 am to 9 pm; meters start at €2.40. There is a fixed taxi fare of €30 to or from the airport from the city center. Supplements include €3 to or from bus and train stations. Tariff 2 is from 9 pm to 6 am in the city center (and 6 am to 10 pm in the suburbs); the meter runs faster and charges more per kilometer. Tariff 3 runs at night beyond the city limits. All tariffs are listed on taxi windows.

Taxi Services Radio Taxi Gremial ☎ *91/447–5180.* **Radioteléfono Taxi** ☎ *91/547–8200.* **Tele-Taxi** ☎ *91/371–2131.*

TRAIN TRAVEL

Madrid is the geographical center of Spain, and all major train lines depart from one of its two main train stations (Chamartín and Atocha) or pass through Madrid (the third train station, Norte, is primarily for commuter trains). Though train travel is comfortable, for some destinations buses run more frequently and make fewer stops; this is true for Segovia and Toledo, unless you take the more expensive high-speed train.

Commuter trains to El Escorial, Aranjuez, and Alcalá de Henares run frequently. The best way to get a ticket for such trains is to use one of the automated reservation terminals at the station (they're in the *cercanías* area), but you can buy tickets online for the high-speed AVE regional lines. You can reach Segovia from the Atocha station in a half hour, the same time it takes you to get to Toledo. If you return the same day, the ticket may cost less than €22. The AVE stations in Toledo and Segovia are outside the city, meaning once there you'll have to take either a bus or a taxi to get to their old quarters.

The AVE line can get you to Barcelona in less than three hours. If you buy the ticket more than two weeks ahead and are lucky enough to find an online fare (with discounts up to 60% off the official fare), you may pay less than €50 each way for tickets that will often carry some change and cancellation restrictions. Otherwise expect to pay between €106 and €128 each way—the more expensive being the nonstop service.

For more information about buying train tickets, see the Travel Smart chapter.

Train Information Estación Chamartín ⊠ *C. Agustín de Foxá s/n, Chamartín* ☎ *91/315–9976* Ⓜ *Chamartín.* **Estación de Atocha** ⊠ *Glorieta del Emperador*

Carlos V, Atocha ☎ *91/528–4630* Ⓜ *Atocha.* **Estación de Príncipe Pío (Norte)** ✉ *Paseo de la Florida s/n, Moncloa* ☎ *902/240202 for RENFE* Ⓜ *Príncipe Pío.*

DISCOUNTS AND DEALS

The **Madrid Card** gives you free entry to 50 museums and monuments, and lets you skip the lines for many attractions. It's available in increments of one, two, three, or five days, and can be purchased at ⊕ *www. madridcard.com,* at tourist offices, and at some museums and hotels.

SIDE TRIPS

Madrid is an excellent jumping-off point for exploring other historically significant sites. The massive monastery of El Escorial is probably the best destination if you want to stick close to Madrid, but the high-speed train makes it easy to venture farther, to two destinations that should be on everybody's list: Toledo and Segovia. Other options worth exploring are Ávila (1½ hours away by AVE) and Salamanca (2½ hours away by AVE). Any of these four destinations *(⇨ all detailed in Chapter 3)* make great day trips, except Salamanca, for which you really need an overnight to experience fully; Toledo would optimally get an overnight as well, but you can do it in a day if time is limited.

TOURS
BIKE TOURS

Although biking in the city can be risky because of the heavy traffic and madrileños' disregard for regulations, the city parks and the surrounding towns are good for enjoyable rides.

Contact Information Bike Spain. This company rents bikes and organizes guided tours in Madrid and all over Spain. Bike rentals cost from €12–€17 for half-day and all-day bike rentals and €115 for an all-day guided trip to El Escorial. Bike Spain also organizes bike tours for the tourist office within the Official Guided Tours program every Saturday at 10 am and Sunday at 4 pm in English. Tours in Spanish take place Saturday afternoon and Sunday morning. ☎ *91/559–0653, 677/356586 (ask for Pablo)* ⊕ *www.bikespain.info* 🖃 *From €12.* **Bravo Bike.** For guided biking tours in Madrid (€31) or to rent bikes (€20 a day, or less if you rent for a few days), check out Bravo Bike. It also offers multiday guided and self-guided bike tours near Madrid, in Toledo, Aranjuez, Chinchón, and Segovia, as well as tours along the pilgrimage route to Santiago de Compostela and Andalusia, among others. ☎ *91/758–2945* ⊕ *www.bravobike. com* 🖃 *From €31.*

BUS TOURS

Contact Information Julià Tours. This tour company offers half- and full-day trips to sites outside Madrid, including Toledo, El Escorial, and Segovia. ☎ *91/769–0707* ⊕ *www.juliatravel.com* 🖃 *From €50.* **Madrid City Tours.** These popular tourist buses make 1½-hour circuits of the city (there is a Historic Madrid tour and a Modern Madrid tour) with recorded English commentary. There are one- and two-day passes allowing you to get on and off at various attractions. ☎ *902/024758* ⊕ *www.madridcitytour.es* 🖃 *From €21.* **Plaza Mayor tourist office.** Madrid's city hall tourist office runs about 40 popular bus, cycling, and walking tours a week, under the Madrid Guided Tours program. There are tours in English every day, with various departure points. ☎ *91/588–2906* ⊕ *www.esmadrid.com* 🖃 *From €5.90.*

WALKING TOURS

Contact Information Asociación Nacional de Guías de Turismo. This tour operator offers custom history and art walks by certified travel guides. 🖀 *91/542–1214* ⊕ *www.apit.es.* **Carpetania Madrid.** This company offers custom tours, as well as literary walks on the life and works of some of Spain's classical and contemporary authors. 🖀 *91/531–1418, 657/847685* ⊕ *www. carpetaniamadrid.com* 🖃 *From €100 for up to 10 people (2-hr walk).*

2

EXPLORING MADRID

The real Madrid is not to be found along major arteries like the Gran Vía and the Paseo de la Castellana. To find the quiet, intimate streets and squares that give the city its true character, duck into the warren of villagelike byways in the downtown area that extends 2 km (1 mile) from the Royal Palace to the Parque del Buen Retiro and from Plaza de Lavapiés to the Glorieta de Bilbao. Broad *avenidas*, twisting medieval alleys, grand museums, stately gardens, and tiny, tile taverns are all jumbled together, creating an urban texture so rich that walking is really the only way to soak it in.

■**TIP→** Petty street crime is a serious problem in Madrid, and tourists are frequent targets. Be on your guard, and try to blend in by keeping cameras concealed, avoiding obvious map reading, and securing bags and purses, especially on buses and subways and outside restaurants.

PALACIO, LA LATINA, AND SOL

The narrow streets of Madrid's old section, which includes the Palacio, La Latina, and Sol neighborhoods—part of Madrid's greater Centro district—wind back through the city's history to its beginnings as an Arab fortress. As elsewhere in Madrid, there is a mix of old buildings and new ones: the neighborhoods here might not be as uniformly ancient as those in the nearby cities of Toledo and Segovia (or as grand), but the quiet alleys make for wonderful exploring.

Beyond the most central neighborhoods, Madrid also has several other sites of interest scattered around the city. Moncloa and Casa de Campo are the neighborhoods to the north and east of Palacio—that is, you can easily walk to the Templo de Debod or visit Goya's tomb if you're in the vicinity of the Royal Palace.

PALACIO

Madrid's oldest neighborhood, Palacio is the home of the imposing Royal Palace. This is where the military post set by Mohamed I— the first foundation in Madrid—stood in the 9th century. The quarter, which borders the Plaza Mayor on the east, is full of winding streets with plenty of good restaurants and cafés and many of the city's most traditional shops.

TOP ATTRACTIONS

Monasterio de la Encarnación (*Monastery of the Incarnation*). Once connected to the Royal Palace by an underground passageway, this Augustinian convent now houses less than a dozen nuns. Founded in 1611 by

Madrid Metro

La Granja · Ronda del la Communicación · La Moralia · Marqués de la Falla · Valtava · Reyes Catolicos · **10 Hospital del Norte**

Las Tablas · Palas de Rey · Maria Tudor · Manuel de Falla
Montecarmelo · Álvarez de Villaamil · Antonio Saura · Virgen del Cortijo

9 Mirasierra · Herrera Oria · Tres Olivos · Blasco Ibáñez · Fuente de la Mora · **1 Pinar de Chamartin**

7 Pitis · Lacoma · Barrio del Pilar · Begoña · Bamloú · Manoteras · Hortaleza · Parque de Santa María

Avda. Ilustación · Peñagrande · Ventilla · Valdeacederas · **Chamartín** · San Lorenzo · Campo de las Naciones · **Aeropuerto T4**

Estación de Aravaca 2 · Antonio Machado · Valdezarza · Tetuán · Duque de Pastrana · Mar de Cristal · Canillas · Aeropuerto · **8 Barajas**

Francos Rodríguez · Estrecho · Cuzco · **Plaza Castilla** · Pío XII · Esperanza

Berna · **Guzmán el Bueno 6** · Alvarado · Santiago Bernabéu · **Colombia** · Concha Espina · Arturo Soria · **5 Alameda de Osuna**

Avenida de Europa · Metropolitano · Islas Filipinas · **Cuatro Caminos 1** · Prosperidad · El Capricho

Campus de Somosaguas · Ciudad Universitaria · **Canal** · Ríos Rosas · **Nuevos Ministerios** · Rep. Argentina · Cruz del Rayo · Canillejas

Dos Castillas · **Moncloa** · Quevedo · Iglesia · Alonso Cano · Alfonso XIII · Torre Arias

Bélgica · **Argüelles** · **San Bernardo** · **Gregorio Marañón 7** · **9 Avda. de América** · Cartagena · P. de las Avenidas · Suanzes

Pozuelo Oeste · Ventura Rodríguez · **4 Bilbao** · **2** · Rubén Darío · B. de la Concepción · Ciudad Lineal

Somosaguas Centro · **Pl. de España** · **Noviciado** · **Tribunal** · **Alonso Martínez** · Quintana · **Pueblo Nuevo**

Somosaguas Sur · **3** · Colón · **N. de Balboa** · El Carmen · Ascao · García Noblejas

Prado del Rey · Lago · Santo Domingo · Chueca · Serrano · Lista · **Diego de León** · La Elipa · Simancas

Colonia de los Ángeles · **Callao** · **Gran Vía** · Velázquez · **Ventas** · La Almudena · San Blas

Prado de la Vega · **Príncipe Pío** · Puerta de Ángel · **Goya** · **Manuel Becerra** · Alsacia · Las Musas

Ciudad de la imagen · **Colonia Jardín 10** · **Opera** · **Sol** · Sevilla · Banco de España · Ave. de Guadalajara · Estadio Olimpi

3 Puerta de Boadilla · Batán · La Latina · Tirso de Molina · Banco de España · Retiro · O'Donnell · Barrio del Puer

Casa de Campo · Puerta de Ángel · Pta. de Toledo · **Príncipe de Vergara** · Coslada Centra

Aviación Española · Lucero · Alto de Extremadura · Lavapiés · Antón Martín · Ibíza · **6** · La Rambla

Cuatro Vientos · Campamento · Marqués de Vadillo · Atocha · Atocha Renfe · **6 Sainz de Baranda** · San Fernando

Joaquín Vilumbrales · Laguna · Urgel · Pirámides · Palos de la Frontera · Menéndez Pelayo · Estrella · Jarama

Parque Lisboa · Carpetana · **Acacias** · Conde de Casal · Vinateros · Henares

Alcacón Central **12** · Empalme · **Embajadores** · **Pacífico** · Artilleros · **Hospital d Henares 7**

Parque Oeste · **Oporto** · Opañel · **Plaza Elíptica** · Delicias · Puente de Vallecas · Pavones

Universidad Rey Juan Carlos · **Puerta del Sur** · Usera · **Legazpi** · Méndez Alvaro · Valdebernardo · Vicálvaro

San Nicasio · Vista Alegre · **Aluche** · Carabanchel · A.Planetario · Nueva Numancia · San Cipriano

Móstoles Central · Eugenia de Montijo · Abrantes · Portazgo · Puerta de Arganda

Leganés Central · San Francisco · Pan Bendito · Almendrales · Buenos Aires · Rivas Urbanizaciones

Pradillo · San Fermín-Orcasur · Hospital 12 de Octubre · Alto de Arenal · Rivas Vaciamadrid

Carabanchel Alto · Ciudad de los Ángeles · La Poveda

Hospital de Móstoles · **La Peseta 11** · Villaverde Bajo Croce · Miguel Hernández · **9 Arganda del Rey**

Manuela Móstoles · El Carrascal · San Cristóbal · Sierra de Guadalupe

Loranca · **12** · Hospital Severo Ochoa · El Bercial · **3 Villaverde Alto** · Villa de Vallecas

Hospital de Fuenlabrada · Casa del Reloj · Julian Besteiro · Los Espartales · Congosto

Parque Europa · Fuenlabrada Central · El Casar · La Gavia

Juan de la Cierva · Getate Central · Las Suertes

Conservatorio · **Valdecarros 1**

Arroyo Culebro · Parque de los Estados

KEY

- **1** *Metro Terminals*
- ○ *Metro Stations*
- ▣ *Transfer Stations*
- ┼┼ *Railway Lines*
- • *Train Stations*

Queen Margarita de Austria, the wife of Felipe III, it has several artistic treasures, including a reliquary where a vial with the dried blood of St. Pantaleón is said to liquefy every July 27. The ornate church has superb acoustics for medieval and Renaissance choral concerts. ⊠ *Pl. de la Encarnación 1, Palacio* 🕾 *91/454–8800 for tourist info office* 💶 *€7, €10 combined ticket with Monasterio de las Descalzas Reales* ⊙ *Tues.– Sat. 10–2 and 4–6:30, Sun. 10–3; last tickets sold 45 mins before closing* Ⓜ *Ópera.*

Monasterio de las Descalzas Reales (*Monastery of the Royal Discalced, or Barefoot, Nuns*). This 16th-century building was restricted for 200 years to women of royal blood. Its plain, brick-and-stone facade hides paintings by Francisco de Zurbarán, Titian, and Pieter Brueghel the Elder—all part of the dowry the novices had to provide when they joined the monastery—as well as a hall of sumptuous tapestries crafted from drawings by Peter Paul Rubens. The convent was founded in 1559 by Juana of Austria, one of Felipe II's sisters, who ruled Spain while he was in England and the Netherlands. It houses 33 different chapels—the age of Christ when he died and the maximum number of nuns allowed to live at the monastery at the same time—and more than 100 sculptures of Jesus as a baby. About 30 nuns (not necessarily of royal blood) still live here, cultivating their own vegetables in the convent's garden. ■ TIP➜ You must take a tour in order to visit the convent; it's conducted in Spanish only. ⊠ *Pl. de las Descalzas Reales 3, Palacio* 🕾 *91/454–8800* 💶 *€7, €10 combined ticket with Monasterio de la Encarnación* ⊙ *Tues.–Sat. 10–2 and 4–6:30, Sun. 10–15; last tickets sold 1 hr before closing* Ⓜ *Sol.*

RAINY-DAY TREAT

Chocolatería Valor. Despite what the ads say, Madrid is not always sunny. If you hit a rainy or a chilly day, walk along the western side of the Monasterio de las Descalzas Reales until you see, on your left, the Chocolatería Valor. Inside you'll find the thick Spanish version of hot chocolate, perfect for dipping crispy churros. ⊠ *C. Postigo de San Martín 7, Palacio* Ⓜ *Callao.*

Fodor's Choice
★

Palacio Real. Emblematic of the oldest part of the city and intimately related to the origins of Madrid—it rests on the terrain where the Muslims built their defensive fortress in the 9th century—the Royal Palace awes visitors with its sheer size and monumental presence that unmistakably stands out against the city's silhouetted background. The palace was commissioned in the early 18th century by the first of Spain's Bourbon rulers, Felipe V. Outside, you can see the classical French architecture on the graceful **Patio de Armas:** Felipe was obviously inspired by his childhood days at Versailles with his grandfather Louis XIV. Look for the stone statues of Inca prince Atahualpa and Aztec king Montezuma, perhaps the only tributes in Spain to these pre-Columbian American rulers. Notice how the steep bluff drops west to the Manzanares River—on a clear day, this vantage point commands a view of the mountain passes leading into Madrid from Old Castile; it's easy to see why the Moors picked this spot for a fortress.

Inside, 2,800 rooms compete with each other for over-the-top opulence. A two-hour guided tour in English winds a mile-long path through

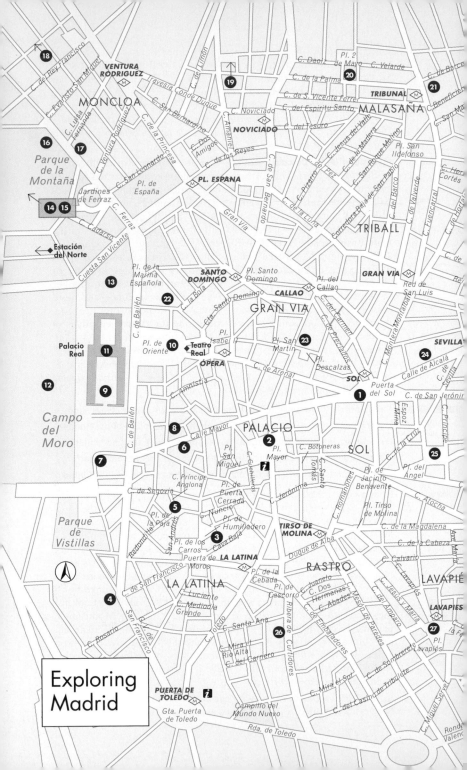

Exploring
Madrid

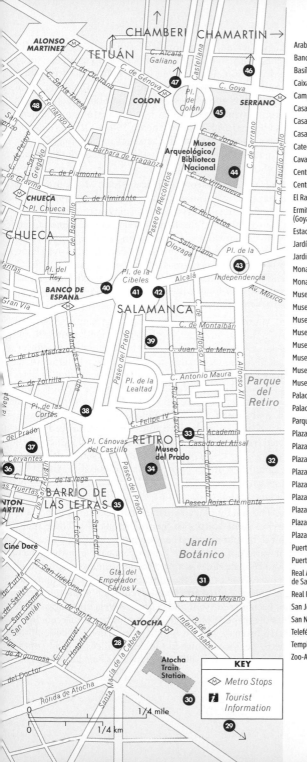

the palace; highlights include the **Salón de Gasparini,** King Carlos III's private apartments, with swirling, inlaid floors and curlicued stucco wall and ceiling decoration, all glistening in the light of a 2-ton crystal chandelier; the **Salón del Trono,** a grand throne room with the royal seats of King Juan Carlos and Queen Sofía; and the **banquet hall,** the palace's largest room, which seats up to 140 people for state dinners. No monarch has lived here since 1931, when Alfonso XIII was deposed after a Republican electoral victory. The current king and queen live in the far simpler Zarzuela Palace on the outskirts of Madrid; this palace is used only for official occasions.

Also worth visiting are the **Museo de Música** (Music Museum), where five stringed instruments by Antonio Stradivari form the world's largest such collection; the **Painting Gallery,** which displays works by Spanish, Flemish, and Italian artists from the 15th century on; the **Armería Real** (Royal Armory), with historic suits of armor and frightening medieval torture implements; and the **Real Oficina de Farmacía** (Royal Pharmacy), with vials and flasks used to mix the king's medicines. ⊠ *C. Bailén s/n, Palacio* ☎ *91/454–8800* 🖾 *€10, €17 with guided tour; €3.40 Royal Armory only; €2 Painting Gallery only* ⊙ *Apr.–Sept., daily 10–8; Oct.–Mar., daily 10–6* Ⓜ *Ópera.*

Plaza de la Villa. Madrid's town council met in the medieval-looking complex here from the Middle Ages until 2009, when it moved to the new city hall headquarters in the post-office building at Plaza Cibeles, leaving the space to house city hall offices. The oldest building is the **Casa de los Lujanes,** on the east side—it's the one with the Mudejar tower. Built as a private home in the late 15th century, the house carries the Lujanes crest over the main doorway. Also on the plaza's east end is the brick-and-stone **Casa de la Villa,** built in 1629, a classic example of Madrid design, with clean lines and spire-topped corner towers. Connected by an overhead walkway, the **Casa de Cisneros** was commissioned in 1537 by the nephew of Cardinal Cisneros. It's one of Madrid's rare examples of the flamboyant plateresque style, which has been likened to splashed water. ⊠ *Palacio* ⊙ *Free guided tour in Spanish Mon. at 5; otherwise closed to the public* Ⓜ *Sol, Ópera.*

Plaza de Oriente. The stately plaza in front of the Royal Palace is surrounded by massive stone statues of Spanish monarchs. These sculptures were meant to be mounted on the railing on top of the palace, but Queen Isabel of Farnesio, one of the first royals to live in the palace, had them removed because she was afraid their enormous weight would bring the roof down. (Well, that's the *official* reason; according to palace insiders, the queen wanted the statues removed because her own likeness had not been placed front and center.) A Velázquez drawing of King Felipe IV is the inspiration for the statue in the plaza's center. It's the first equestrian bronze ever cast with a rearing horse. The sculptor, Italian artist Pietro de Tacca, enlisted Galileo Galilei's help in configuring the statue's weight so it wouldn't tip over. ⊠ *Palacio* Ⓜ *Ópera.*

WORTH NOTING

Arab Wall. The remains of the Moorish military outpost that became the city of Madrid are visible on Calle Cuesta de la Vega. The sections of wall here protected a fortress built in the 9th century by Emir Moham-med I. In addition to being an excellent defensive position, the site had plentiful water and was called *Mayrit*, Arabic for "source of life" (this is the likely origin of the city's name). All that remains of the *medina*—the old Arab city that formed within the walls of the fortress—is the neighborhood's crazy quilt of streets and plazas, which probably follow the same layout they did more than 1,100 years ago. ⊠ *Cuesta de la Vega, Palacio* Ⓜ *Ópera.*

Campo del Moro (*Moors' Field*). Below the Sabatini Gardens but acces-sible only by an entrance on the far side is the Campo del Moro. Enjoy the clusters of shady trees, winding paths, and lawn leading up to the Royal Palace. Inside the gardens is a **Museo de Carruajes** (Carriage Museum), displaying royal carriages and equestrian paraphernalia from the 16th through 20th century. ⊠ *Paseo Virgen del Puerto s/n, Palacio* Ⓜ *Príncipe Pío.*

Catedral de la Almudena. The first stone of the cathedral, which adjoins the Royal Palace, was laid in 1883 by King Alfonso XII and the result-ing edifice was consecrated by Pope John Paul II in 1993. Built on the site of the old church of Santa María de la Almudena (thought to be the city's main mosque during Arab rule), the new cathedral was intended to be Gothic in style, with needles and spires; funds ran low, so the design was simplified into the existing, more austere classical form. The cathedral has a wooden statue of Madrid's female patron saint, the Virgin of Almudena, reportedly discovered after the Chris-tian Reconquest of Madrid. Legend has it that when the Arabs invaded Spain, the local Christian population hid the statue of the Virgin in a vault carved in the old Roman wall that encircled the city. When the Christians reconquered Madrid in 1085, they looked for it, and after nine days of intensive praying—others say it was after a procession honoring the Virgin—the wall opened up to show the statue framed by two lighted candles. Its name is derived from the place where it was found: the wall of the old citadel (in Arabic, *al mudeyna*). ⊠ *Bailén 10, Palacio* ☎ *91/542-2200* 💷 *Free* ☉ *Daily 9–9* Ⓜ *Ópera.*

San Nicolás de los Servitas (*Church of St. Nicholas of the Servitas*). This church tower is one of the oldest buildings in Madrid. There's some debate over whether it once formed part of an Arab mosque. It was more likely built after the Christian Reconquest of Madrid in 1085, but the brickwork and the horseshoe arches are evidence that it was crafted by either Mudejars (Moorish workers) or Spaniards well versed in the style. Inside, exhibits detail the Islamic history of early Madrid. ⊠ *Pl. de San Nicolás, Palacio* ☎ *91/559–4064* 💷 *Donation suggested* ☉ *Mon. 8:30–1:30 and 5:30–9, Tues.–Sat. 8:30–9:30 am and 6:30–9 pm, Sun. 10–2; groups by appointment* Ⓜ *Ópera.*

LA LATINA
Officially part of the Palacio neighborhood, this bustling area bordered by Calle de Segovia to the north; Calle Toledo to the east; Plaza de la Cebada to the south; and Calle Bailén, with its imposing Basílica de San Francisco, to the west, has created a reputation of its own. It now houses some of the city's oldest buildings, plenty of sloping streets, and some of the best spots for tapas, especially on the Cava Baja and Cava Alta, and the area around Plaza de la Paja.

TOP ATTRACTIONS
Cava Baja. The epicenter of the fashionable and historic La Latina neighborhood—a maze of narrow streets that extend south of Plaza Mayor and across Calle Segovia—this is a diagonal street crowded with excellent tapas bars and traditional restaurants. Its lively atmosphere spills over onto nearby streets and squares, including Almendro, Cava Alta, Plaza del Humilladero, and Plaza de la Paja. ⊠ *La Latina* Ⓜ *La Latina.*

Plaza de la Paja. At the top of the hill, on Costanilla San Andrés, the Plaza de la Paja was the most important square in medieval Madrid. The plaza's jewel is the **Capilla del Obispo** (Bishop's Chapel), built between 1520 and 1530; this was where peasants deposited their tithes, called *diezmas*—literally, one-tenth of their crop. The stacks of wheat on the chapel's ceramic tiles refer to this tradition. Architecturally, the chapel marks a transition from the blocky Gothic period, which gave the structure its basic shape, to the Renaissance, the source of the decorations. It houses an intricately carved polychrome altarpiece by Francisco Giralta, with scenes from the life of Christ. To visit the chapel (🕒 *Tues. 9:30–12:30, Thurs. 4–5:30*) reserve in advance (🖀 *91/559–2874* ✉ *reservascapilladelobispo@archimadrid.es*).

The chapel is part of the complex of the domed church of **San Andrés,** one of Madrid's oldest, which was severely damaged during the civil war. For centuries the church held the remains of Madrid's male patron saint, San Isidro Labrador (now with his wife's remains, at the Real Colegiata de San Isidro, on nearby Calle Toledo). St. Isidore the Laborer was a peasant who worked fields belonging to the Vargas family—the 16th-century **Vargas Palace** forms the eastern side of the Plaza de la Paja. According to legend, St. Isidro worked little but had the best-tended fields thanks to many hours of prayer. When Señor Vargas came to investigate, Isidro made a spring of sweet water spurt from the ground to quench his master's thirst. A hermitage (Ermita de San Isidro), now on Paseo de la Ermita del Santo, west of the Manzanares River, was built next to the spring in 1528. Every May 15 there's a procession followed by festivities in the meadow next to the hermitage. In olden days, the saint's remains were paraded through the city in times of drought. ⊠ *La Latina* Ⓜ *La Latina.*

WORTH NOTING
Basílica de San Francisco el Grande. In 1760 Carlos III built this impressive basilica on the site of a Franciscan convent, allegedly founded by St. Francis of Assisi in 1217. The dome, 108 feet in diameter, is the largest in Spain, even larger than that of St. Paul's in London. The seven main doors were carved of American walnut by Casa Juan Guas. Three

chapels adjoin the circular church, the most famous being that of **San Bernardino de Siena,** which contains a Goya masterpiece depicting a preaching San Bernardino. The figure standing on the right, not looking up, is a self-portrait of Goya. The 16th-century Gothic choir stalls came from La Cartuja del Paular, in rural Segovia Province. ⊠ *Pl. de San Francisco, La Latina* ☎ *91/365–3800* ☎ *€3 guided tour* ☉ *June–Sept., Tues.–Fri. 10:30–12:30 and 5–7; Oct.–May, Tues.–Fri. 10:30–12:30 and 4–6* Ⓜ *Puerta de Toledo, La Latina.*

SOL

In this small neighborhood built in the 16th century, the Plaza del Sol used to mark the city's geographic center. The square has been renovated a number of times, the last renovation taking place in 2005–09, and it's no longer the city center—as the city keeps growing, that center has been displaced to the east. It encompasses, among other sites, the monumental Plaza Mayor, and also the popular pedestrian shopping area in between the Plaza Mayor and Callao.

Plaza Mayor. Austere, grand, and often surprisingly quiet compared with the rest of Madrid, this public square, finished in 1620 under Felipe III—whose equestrian statue stands in the center—is one of the largest in Europe, measuring 360 feet by 300 feet. It's seen it all: *autos-da-fé* ("trials of faith," i.e., public burnings of heretics); the canonization of saints; criminal executions; royal marriages, such as that of Princess María and the King of Hungary in 1629; bullfights (until 1847); masked balls; and all manner of other events. Special events still take place here.

This space was once occupied by a city market, and many of the surrounding streets retain the charming names of the trades and foods once headquartered there. Nearby are Calle de Cuchilleros (Knifemakers' Street), Calle de Lechuga (Lettuce Street), Calle de Fresa (Strawberry Street), and Calle de Botoneros (Buttonmakers' Street). The plaza's oldest building is the one with the brightly painted murals and the gray spires, called Casa de la Panadería (Bakery House) in honor of the bread shop over which it was built; it is now the tourist office. Opposite is the Casa de la Carnicería (Butcher Shop), now a police station.

The plaza is closed to motorized traffic, making it a pleasant place to sit at one of the sidewalk cafés, watching alfresco artists, street musicians, and madrileños from all walks of life. Sunday morning brings a stamp and coin market. Around Christmas the plaza fills with stalls selling trees, ornaments, and nativity scenes. ⊠ *Sol* Ⓜ *Sol.*

QUICK BITES

Mercado de San Miguel. Near the Plaza Mayor, the most exciting, and interactive, addition to the Madrid tapas scene is this old market, which has been converted into a gourmet nirvana. Open till the wee hours of the night, the swanky, bustling stalls are usually filled with a mix of madrileños and tourists sampling plates of Manchego cheese with a good Rioja or Ribera del Duero red wine, or perhaps less traditional fare such as oysters with Champagne, Austrian pastries, crackers topped with Russian caviar, Andalusian shrimp paired with sherry, and much more. ⊠ *Pl. de San Miguel*

s/n, Palacio ⊕ *www.mercadodesanmiguel.es* ⊙ *Mon.–Wed. and Sun. 10 am–midnight, Thurs.–Sat. 10 am–2 am* Ⓜ *Ópera.*

Puerta del Sol. Crowded with people but pedestrian-friendly, the Puerta del Sol is the nerve center of Madrid. The city's main subway interchange is below, and buses fan out from here. A brass plaque in the sidewalk on the south side of the plaza marks Kilometer 0, the spot from which all distances in Spain are measured. The restored 1756 French-neoclassical building near the marker now houses the offices of the regional government, but during Franco's reign it was the headquarters of his secret police, and it's still known colloquially as the Casa de los Gritos (House of Screams). Across the square are a bronze statue of Madrid's official symbol, a bear with a *madroño* (strawberry tree), and a statue of King-Mayor Carlos III on horseback. ⊠ *Sol* Ⓜ *Sol.*

Gourmet Experience. El Corte Inglés, Spain's largest department store, has opened up a gourmet food court, a gastronomic enclave with top-quality offerings, on the ninth floor of its main building in Callao. It makes for a good quick stop if your feet hurt after strolling along the Gran Vía or even nearby Sol. The space has some well-known local food brands such as La Máquina (seafood) or Imanol (tapas), as well as other international options (hamburgers, Mexican, etc.), but the undisputed star is StreetXO, the take-away food stall from David Muñoz, Madrid's current top chef and the mastermind behind the acclaimed DiverXO (⇨ *see Where to Eat*). This spot not only pays tribute to Asian-cuisine street vendors, but also offers glimpses of David Muñoz's inventive fusion cuisine at affordable prices. Try his version of a club sandwich with ricotta cheese, fried quail egg, and the Japanese spice mixture sichimi togarashi. Grab your tray, and perhaps a cocktail from Juanillo Club (another of the stalls), and try to find an empty spot on the terrace, which offers panoramic views of the city, including the Royal Palace. ⊠ *Pl. de Callao 1, Sol* ✛ *Located on the 9th fl. of El Corte Inglés. Take the 2nd entrance walking down Callao on Calle Carmen and across from Fnac.*

Real Academia de Bellas Artes de San Fernando (*St. Ferdinand Royal Academy of Fine Arts*). Designed by José Churriguera in the waning baroque years of the early 18th century, this museum showcases 500 years of Spanish painting, from José Ribera and Bartolomé Esteban Murillo to Joaquín Sorolla and Ignacio Zuloaga. The tapestries along the stairways are stunning. It displays paintings up to the 18th century, including some by Goya. Guided tours, by very qualified and amenable guides, are available on Tuesday, Thursday, and Friday at 11, except during August. The same building houses the **Instituto de Calcografía** (Prints Institute), which sells limited-edition prints from original plates engraved by Spanish artists. Check listings for classical and contemporary concerts in the small upstairs hall. ⊠ *Alcalá 13, Sol* ☎ *91/524–0864* ⊕ *www.realacademiabellasartessanfernando.com* ▤ *€6 (free Wed.)* ⊙ *Tues.–Sun. 9–3* Ⓜ *Sol.*

MONCLOA

A large neighborhood extending to the northwest of Madrid, Moncloa includes high-class residential areas, such as Puerta de Hierro o Aravaca; more urban ones, such as Arguelles, the city's largest university campus; and some of the city's best parks: Casa de Campo, Parque del Oeste (with the Templo de Debod gardens), and la Dehesa de la Villa.

Ermita de San Antonio de la Florida (Goya's tomb). Built between 1792 and 1798 by the Italian architect Francisco Fontana, this neoclassical church was financed by King Carlos IV, who also commissioned Goya to paint the vaults and the main dome: he took 120 days to complete his assignment, painting alone except for a little boy who stirred his pigments. This gave him absolute freedom to depict events of the 13th century (e.g., St. Anthony of Padua resurrecting a dead man) as if they had happened five centuries later with naturalistic images never before used to paint religious scenes. Opposite the image of the frightening dead man on the main dome, Goya painted himself as a man covered with a black cloak. The frescoes' third-restoration phase ended in 2005, and visitors can now admire them in their full splendor. Goya, who died in Bordeaux in 1828, is buried here (without his head, since it was stolen in France), under an unadorned gravestone. ⊠ *Glorieta de San Antonio de la Florida 5, Moncloa* ☎ *91/542–0722* ⊡ *Free* ⊘ *Tues.–Sun. 10–8* Ⓜ *Príncipe Pío.*

Museo del Traje (*Costume Museum*). This museum traces the evolution of dress in Spain, from old royal burial garments (very few of which remain) through the introduction of French fashion by Felipe V to the 20th-century creations of couturiers such as Balenciaga and Pertegaz. The 18th century claims the largest number of pieces. Explanatory notes are in English, and the museum has a superb restaurant. To get here, from Moncloa take Bus No. 46 or walk along the northeastern edge of Parque del Oeste. ⊠ *Av. Juan de Herrera 2, Moncloa* ☎ *91/549–7150* ⊕ *museodeltraje.mcu.es* ⊡ *€3 (free Sat. after 2 and Sun.)* ⊘ *Tues.–Sat. 9:30–7, Sun. 10–3* Ⓜ *Ciudad Universitaria.*

FAMILY **Teleférico.** Kids love this cable car, which takes you from the Rosaleda gardens in the Parque del Oeste to the center of Casa de Campo in about 10 minutes. ■ TIP→ This is not the best way to get to the zoo and theme park if you're with children because the walk from the cable car is at least 2 km (1 mile), and you'll probably need to ask for directions. You're better off riding the Teleférico out and back, then taking the bus to the zoo. ⊠ *Estación Terminal Teleférico, Paseo de Pintor Rosales, at C. Marques de Urquijo, Moncloa* ☎ *91/541–1118* ⊕ *www.teleferico. com* ⊡ *€4 one-way, €5.80 round-trip* ⊘ *Apr.–Sept., daily noon–dusk; Oct.–Mar., weekends noon–dusk* Ⓜ *Arguelles.*

Templo de Debod. This 4th-century BC Egyptian temple was donated to Spain in thanks for its technical assistance with the construction of the Aswan Dam. The western side of the small park around the temple is the best place to watch Madrid's outstanding sunsets. ⊠ *Paseo de Pintor Rosales, Moncloa* ☎ *91/765–1008* ⊡ *Free* ⊘ *Oct.–Mar., Tues.–Fri. 9:45–1:45 and 4:15–6:15, weekends 10–2; Apr.–Sept., Tues.–Fri. 10–2 and 6–8, weekends 10–2* Ⓜ *Plaza de España, Ventura Rodríguez.*

The Puerta del Sol, Madrid's central transportation hub, is sure to be passed through by every visitor to the city.

FAMILY **Zoo-Aquarium.** One of the most comprehensive zoological parks in Europe, Madrid's zoo houses a large variety of animals (including rarities such as an albino tiger) that are grouped according to their geographical origin. It also has a dolphinarium and a wild bird reservoir that hold entertaining exhibitions twice a day on weekdays and more often on weekends—check times on arrival and show up early to get a good seat. ■ TIP→ Reduced ticket prices are available by booking online. The zoo is in the Casa de Campo, a large park right outside the western part of the city. ■ TIP→ Though the nearest metro stop is Casa de Campo it's best reached via subway to Príncipe Pío and then Bus No. 33. ⊠ *Casa de Campo s/n, Moncloa* ☎ *902/345–014* ⊕ *www.zoomadrid.com* 🎟 *€22.90* 🕐 *Feb. and Mar., weekdays 11–6, weekends 10:30–7; Apr.–Aug., weekdays 10:30–7 (until 7:30 July and Aug.), weekends 10:30–9; Sept. and Oct., weekdays 11–6:30, weekends 10:30–7:30; Nov.–Jan., weekdays 11–6, weekends 10:30–6* Ⓜ *Casa de Campo, Príncipe Pío then Bus No. 33.*

BARRIO DE LAS LETRAS

The Barrio de las Letras, long favored by tourists for its clean-cut looks and its fun places to hang out, was named for the many writers and playwrights from the Spanish Golden Age (16th and 17th centuries) who set up house within a few blocks of Plaza Santa Ana. Once a shelter to *los madrileños castizos*—the word *castizo* means "authentic"—it is fast becoming one of the favored living areas of Spanish and foreign professionals affluent enough to pay the soaring real estate prices and willing to withstand the chaos of living within these lively and creative

The vertical outdoor garden is a stunning element of the CaixaForum cultural center. The sculpture in front of the building is changed periodically.

enclaves. Calle de las Huertas (full of bars and clubs), is pedestrian-only, making the neighborhood even more attractive for walking around and socializing.

TOP ATTRACTIONS

CaixaForum. Swiss architects Jacques Herzog and Pierre de Meuron, who transformed a former London power station into that city's Tate Modern, performed a similar feat here. Their conversion of this early-20th-century power station has created a stunning arts complex fit to become the fourth point in Madrid's former triangle of great art institutions—the Prado, the Reina Sofía, and the Thyssen-Bornemisza museums. Belonging to one of the country's wealthiest foundations (La Caixa), the structure seems to float on a newly created, sloped public plaza, with a tall vertical garden designed by French botanist Patrick Blanc on its northern side contrasting with a geometric rust-color roof. Inside, the huge exhibition halls display ancient as well as contemporary art, including a sample of La Caixa's own collection. The restaurant on the fourth floor has good views. ⊠ *Paseo del Prado 36, Barrio de las Letras* ☎ *91/330–7300* ✉ *Free* ◷ *Daily 10–8* Ⓜ *Atocha.*

Fodor'sChoice
★
Museo Thyssen-Bornemisza. Opened in 1992, the Thyssen occupies spacious galleries filled with natural light in the late-18th-century Villahermosa Palace (itself finished in 1771). This ambitious collection of almost 1,000 paintings traces the history of Western art with examples from every important movement, from the 13th-century Italian Gothic through 20th-century American pop art. The works were gathered from the 1920s to the 1980s by Swiss industrialist Baron Hans Heinrich Thyssen-Bornemisza and his father. At the urging of his wife, the baron

donated the entire collection to Spain in 1993, and a renovation in 2004 increased the number of paintings on display to include the baroness's personal collection (considered of lesser quality). Critics have described the museum's paintings as the minor works of major artists and the major works of minor artists, but the collection still traces the development of Western humanism as no other in the world.

One of the high points is Hans Holbein's *Portrait of Henry VIII* (purchased from the late Princess Diana's grandfather, who used the money to buy a Bugatti sports car). American artists are also well represented; look for the Gilbert Stuart portrait of George Washington's cook, and note how closely the composition and rendering resemble the artist's famous painting of the Founding Father. Two halls are devoted to the impressionists and post-impressionists, including many works by Camille Pissarro and a few each by Pierre-Auguste Renoir, Claude Monet, Edgar Degas, Vincent van Gogh, and Paul Cézanne. Find Pissarro's *Saint-Honoré Street in the Afternoon, Effect of Rain* for a jolt of mortality, or Renoir's *Woman with a Parasol in a Garden* for a sense of bucolic beauty lost.

Within 20th-century art, the collection is strong on dynamic German expressionism, with some works by Georgia O'Keeffe and Andrew Wyeth along with Edward Hoppers, Francis Bacons, Robert Rauschenbergs, and Roy Lichtensteins. The temporary exhibits can be fascinating and in summer are sometimes open until 11 pm. A rooftop restaurant serving tapas and drinks is open in the summer until past midnight. You can buy tickets in advance online. ⇨ *See "The Art Walk" box for how to include the Museo Thyssen-Bornemisza as a part of an art-theme Paseo del Arte excursion.* ⊠ *Paseo del Prado 8, Barrio de las Letras* ☎ *91/369–0151* ⊕ *www.museothyssen.org* ⊠ *Permanent collection €10 (free Mon.), temporary exhibition €11, combined €17; €25.60 combined Paseo del Arte ticket for the Prado, Reina Sofía, and Thyssen-Bornemisza* ⊗ *Mon. noon–4, Tues.–Sun. 10–7* Ⓜ *Banco de España.*

Plaza Santa Ana. This plaza was the heart of the theater district in the 17th century—the Golden Age of Spanish literature—and is now the center of Madrid's thumping nightlife. A statue of 17th-century playwright Pedro Calderón de la Barca faces the **Teatro Español,** where playwrights such as Félix Lope de Vega, Tirso de Molina, Pedro Calderón de la Barca, and Ramón del Valle-Inclán released some of their plays. (Opposite the theater and off to the side of a hotel is the diminutive **Plaza del Ángel,** with one of Madrid's best jazz clubs, the **Café Central.**) One of Madrid's most famous cafés, **Cervecería Alemana,** is on Plaza Santa Ana and is still catnip to writers and poets. ⊠ *Barrio de las Letras* Ⓜ *Sevilla.*

WORTH NOTING

Banco de España. This massive 1884 building, Spain's central bank, takes up an entire block. It's said that part of the nation's gold reserves are held in vaults that stretch under the Plaza de la Cibeles traffic circle all the way to the fountain. (Some reserves are also stored in Fort Knox, in the United States.) The bank is not open to visitors, but the architecture is worth viewing. ⊠ *Paseo del Prado s/n, at Pl. de la Cibeles, Barrio de las Letras* Ⓜ *Banco de España.*

Casa de Cervantes. A plaque marks the private home where Miguel de Cervantes Saavedra, author of *Don Quijote de la Mancha,* committed his final words to paper: *"Puesto ya el pie en el estribo, con ansias de la muerte"* ("One foot already in the stirrup and yearning for death"). The Western world's first runaway best seller and still one of the most widely translated and read books in the world, Cervantes's spoof of a knightly novel playfully but profoundly satirized Spain's rise and decline while portraying man's dual nature in the pragmatic Sancho Panza and the idealistic Don Quixote, ever in search of wrongs to right. ⊠ *Calle Cervantes and Calle León, Barrio de las Letras* Ⓜ *Antón Martin, Sevilla.*

Casa de Lope de Vega. Considered the Shakespeare of Spanish literature, Fray Lope Félix de la Vega Carpio (1562–1635) is best known as Lope de Vega. A contemporary and adversary of Cervantes, he wrote some 1,800 plays and enjoyed great success during his lifetime. His former home is now a museum with an intimate look into a bygone era: everything from the whale-oil lamps and candles to the well in the tiny garden and the pans used to warm the bedsheets brings you closer to the great dramatist. The space also accommodates poetry readings and workshops. There is a 45-minute guided tour in English starting every half hour (reservations are necessary) that runs through the playwright's professional and personal life—including his intense love life—and also touching on 17th-century traditions. Don't miss the Latin inscription over the door: *"Parva Propia Magna / Magna Aliena Parva"* ("Small but mine big / Big but someone else's small"). ⊠ *Calle Cervantes 11, Barrio de las Letras* ☎ *91/429–9216* ⮻ *Free* ☉ *Tues.–Sun. 10–3 (last tour at 2)* Ⓜ *Antón Martin, Sevilla.*

CHUECA, MALASAÑA, AND CHAMBERÍ

Once known primarily for thumping nightlife and dodgy streets, these two Madrid neighborhoods have changed significantly in the past decade. Money from city hall and from private investors was used to renovate buildings and public zones, thereby drawing prosperous businesses and many professional and young inhabitants. The triangle area created by Fuencarral, Gran Vía, and Corredera Baja is becoming more gentrified and is known as Triball.

CHUECA

Chueca has been completely transformed by the gay community. Noisy bars and overcrowded nightclubs are still a trademark of the area, but it now also makes for pleasant daytime walks and has many inexpensive restaurants, hip shops, great cultural life, and inviting summer terraces.

Casa Longoria. A Moderniste palace commissioned in 1902 by the businessman and politician Javier González Longoria, the Casa Longoria was built by a disciple of Gaudí. The winding shapes, the plant motifs, and the wrought-iron balconies are reminiscent of Gaudí's works in Barcelona. The building's jewel is its main iron, bronze, and marble staircase, which is unfortunately off-limits to tourists because the building is now in private hands. ⊠ *Fernando VI 4, Chueca* Ⓜ *Alonso Martínez, Chueca.*

Cisne Azul. Walking past the Cisne Azul you may wonder why such a bland-looking bar is crowded with locals in a neighborhood that's obsessed with style. The reason is simple: wild mushrooms. In Spain there are more than 2,000 different species, and here they bring the best from the province of León, grill them on the spot with a bit of olive oil and serve them in a variety of ways: with a fried egg yolk, scallops, foie gras, and so on. We suggest you elbow yourself up to the bar and order the popular *mezcla de setas* (mushroom sampler) with a fried egg yolk. ⊠ *Gravina 19, Chueca* ☎ *91/521-3799* Ⓜ *Chueca.*

Mercado de San Antón. Following the successful transformation of the Mercado de San Miguel, near the Plaza Mayor, the city completely refurbished another old neighborhood food market into a more cosmopolitan enclave. Above the traditional market you can join the madrileños, glasses of wine, cider, or vermouth in hand, scarfing down small servings of international food—think sushi, Greek, Italian—and tapas (seafood options are particularly noteworthy) from the fancy food stalls. On the third level is a casual restaurant (La Cocina de San Antón) and a large terrace, perfect for indulging in a cold daiquiri or a caipirinha on a hot summer night. ⊠ *Augusto Figueroa 24, Chueca* ☎ *913/300730* ⊕ *www.mercadosananton. com* ⊙ *Mon.–Sat. 10–10; restaurant Sun.–Thurs. 10 am–midnight, Fri. and Sat. 10 am–1:30 am* Ⓜ *Chueca.*

MALASAÑA

Famous for being the epicenter of La Movida, the countercultural movement that united rockers, punks, artists and other creative tribes in the 1980s, this neighborhood maintains the same bubbling and transgressive spirit. There are lots of bars, terraces, and shops, mostly by young designers; happening squares such as the Plaza del 2 de Mayo, Plaza de Comendadoras, and Plaza de San Ildefonso; and arguably the city's best nightlife.

TOP ATTRACTIONS

Centro de Conde Duque. Built by Pedro de Ribera in 1717–30 to accommodate the Regiment of the Royal Guard, this imposing building has gigantic proportions (the facade is 250 yards long) and was used as a military academy and an astronomical observatory in the 19th century. A fire damaged the upper floors in 1869, and after some decay it was partially renovated and turned into a cultural and arts center, with temporary art exhibitions in some of its spaces, including the public and historical libraries. In summer, concerts are held outside in the main plaza. ⊠ *Conde Duque 9 and 11, Malasaña* ☎ *915/885–834* ⊕ *www. condeduquemadrid.es/en* ⊙ *Tues.–Sat. 10–2 and 5:30–9, Sun. 10:30–2 exhibitions only* Ⓜ *San Bernardo.*

QUICK
BITES

La vita e'bella. For an inexpensive lunch on a pleasant day, stop here for any of its savory take-away dishes—strombolis, calzones, pizzas, arancini, or pastas—and enjoy your meal with other young madrileños, sitting on a bench at the nearby and bustling Plaza de San Ildefonso or Plaza de Juan Pujol. ⊠ *C. Espíritu Santo 13 or Pl. de San Ildefonso 5, Malasaña* 🕾 *91/521-4108* Ⓜ *Tribunal, Noviciado.*

WORTH NOTING

Museo de Historia. Founded in 1929 in a former 17th-century hospice, this museum houses paintings, drawings, pictures, ceramics, furniture, and other objects illustrating Madrid's history. Exhibits are separated into four major historic periods—Empire, Enlightment, Industrial Revolution, and Modern Times. The museum's collection of around 40,000 items (some of which are in storage at the Centro Conde Duque and brought here only for temporary exhibitions) span the five centuries since Felipe II brought the royal court to Madrid. The restored ornamented facade—a baroque jewel by Pedro de Ribera—and the painstakingly precise, nearly 18-foot model of Madrid—a project coordinated by León Gil de Palacio in 1830—are the two stand-out exhibits you should not miss. ⊠ *Fuencarral 78, Malasaña* 🕾 *91/701-1863* ⊕ *www.madrid.es/museodehistoria* 🎟 *Free* ⊙ *Tues.–Sun. 9:30–8* Ⓜ *Tribunal.*

Plaza del 2 de Mayo. On this unassuming square stood the Monteleón Artillery barracks, where some brave Spanish soldiers and citizens fought Napoléon's invading troops on May 2, 1808. The arch that now stands in the middle of the plaza was once at the entrance of the old barracks, and the sculpture under the arch represents captains Daoiz and Velarde. All the surrounding streets carry the names of that day's heroes. The plaza, now filled with spring and summer terraces, makes a good place to stop for a drink. One of the most popular cafés, Pepe Botella, carries the demeaning nickname the people of Madrid gave to Joseph Bonaparte, Napoléon's brother, who ruled Spain from 1808 to 1813: *Botella* ("bottle" in English) is a reference to his falsely alleged fondness for drink. ⊠ *Malasaña* Ⓜ *Noviciado, Tribunal.*

CHAMBERÍ
Chamberí is a large area to the north of Chueca and Malasaña. It's mostly residential but has a few lively spots, especially the streets around Plaza de Olavide.

Museo Sorolla. See the world through the exceptional eye of Spain's most famous impressionist painter, Joaquín Sorolla (1863–1923), who lived and worked most of his life at the home and garden he designed. Entering this diminutive but cozy domain is a little like stepping into a Sorolla painting because it's filled with the artist's best-known works, most of which shimmer with the bright Mediterranean light and color of his native Valencia. ⊠ *General Martinez Campos 37, Chamberí* 🕾 *91/310-1584* ⊕ *museosorolla.mcu.es* 🎟 *€3 (free Sun.)* ⊙ *Tues.–Sat. 9:30–8, Sun. 10–3* Ⓜ *Rubén Darío, Gregorio Marañón.*

You can rent rowboats at the lake in the Parque del Buen Retiro; it's a great way to cool off in the summer.

EMBAJADORES

Bordering the old city wall (torn down in the mid-19th century) to the south, Embajadores included most of Madrid's old industrial areas in the 17th and 18th centuries, when it housed, among others, beer, glass, and car factories. That industrial past is now long gone and now it's a residential area with some historical buildings and some of the city's liveliest areas, such as Rastro and Lavapiés. Purse snatching and petty crime are not uncommon in these two areas, so be alert.

RASTRO

The Rastro area in Embajadores traces back to the last third of the 16th century, when it marked the lower part of the old city's wall. The old slaughterhouses of this quarter (and all the other businesses related to that trade) are the origins of today's flea market, which spreads all over the neighborhood on Sunday. It gets quite busy on the weekends, especially on Sunday mornings.

El Rastro. Named for the *arrastre* (dragging) of animals in and out of the slaughterhouse that once stood here and, specifically, the *rastro* (blood trail) left behind, this site explodes into a rollicking flea market every Sunday from 9 to 3, with dozens and dozens of street vendors with truly bizarre bric-a-brac ranging from costume earrings to sent postcards to thrown-out love letters. There are also more formal shops where it's easy to turn up treasures such as old iron grillwork, a marble tabletop, or a gilt picture frame. The shops (not the vendors) are also open during the week, allowing for quieter and more serious bargaining. Even so, people-watching on Sunday is the best part: for serious browsing and bargaining, any *other* morning is a better time to turn up treasures. ✉ *Ribera de los Curtidores s/n, Embajadores* Ⓜ *La Latina, Puerta de Toledo.*

LAVAPIÉS

Housed along its sloping narrow streets, Lavapiés has the highest concentration of immigrants—mostly Chinese, Indian, and North African—in Madrid, and as a result the area has plenty of ethnic markets and inexpensive restaurants as well as bustling crowds, especially in the Plaza de Lavapiés. The area also has the highest number of *corralas* still standing, a type of building (now protected by the city after many years of abandonment) which was popular in Madrid in the 17th century. In the corralas, all the apartments are connected to a central patio, which serves as the community's social hub.

TOP ATTRACTIONS

Fodor's Choice
★
Centro de Arte Reina Sofía (*Queen Sofía Art Center*). Spain's National Museum of Contemporary Art houses works by all the major 20th-century Spanish painters and sculptors. The permanent art collection features 1,000 works on four floors (the second and fourth floors of the Sabatini building and the ground and first floors of the Nouvel annex) and, despite concentrating on painting, puts a much higher emphasis on other art forms such as photography and cinema. The new collection breaks from the traditional habit of grouping works by major artistic movement and individual artist: instead, the current director has chosen to contextualize the works of the great modern masters—Picasso, Miró, and Salvador Dalí—and of other big local names, such as Juan Gris, Jorge Oteiza, Pablo Gargallo, Julio Gonzalez, Eduardo Chillida, and Antoni Tàpies, into broader narratives that attempt to explain better the evolution of modern art. This means, for instance, that in the first room of the collection (201), you'll find a selection of Goya's *Disasters of War* engravings (the proto-romantic and proto-surrealist great master serving as a precursor of the avant-garde movements of the 20th century) next to one of the first movies ever made, *Employees Leaving the Lumière Factory,* by the Lumière brothers. And you will find that the Picassos or Dalís are not all displayed together in a single room, but scattered around the 38 rooms of the permanent collection.

The museum's showpiece is Picasso's *Guernica*, in Room 206 on the second floor. The huge black-and-white canvas—suitably lighted and without distracting barriers—depicts the horror of the Nazi Condor Legion's bombing of the ancient Basque town of Gernika in 1937, during the Spanish Civil War. The work, something of a national shrine, was commissioned from Picasso by the Republican government for the Spanish pavilion at the 1937 World's Fair in an attempt to gather sympathy for the Republican side during the civil war. The museum rooms adjacent to *Guernica* now reconstruct the artistic significance of the Spanish participation in the World's Fair, with works from other artists such as Miró, Josep María Sert, and Alexander Calder. *Guernica* did not reach Madrid until 1981, as Picasso had stipulated in his will that the painting return to Spain only after democracy was restored.

The fourth floor in the Sabatini building is devoted to art created after World War II, and the Nouvel annex displays paintings, sculptures, photos, videos, and installations from the last quarter of the 20th century.

The museum was once a hospital, but today the classical granite austerity of the space is somewhat relieved (or ruined, depending on your point of view) by the playful pair of glass elevator shafts on its facade. Three separate buildings joined by a common vault were added to the original complex in 2005—the first contains an art bookshop and a public library, the second a center for contemporary exhibitions, and the third an auditorium and restaurant-cafeteria. The latter, although expensive, makes an excellent stop for refreshments, be it a cup of tea or coffee, a snack, or even a cocktail, and in summer there's also a popular snack bar set up in the gardens. ⇨ *See "The Art Walk" box for how to include the Centro de Arte Reina Sofía as part of an art-theme Paseo del Arte excursion.* ✉ *Santa Isabel 52, Embajadores* ☎ *91/467–5062* 🌐 *www.museoreinasofia.es* 🎫 *€8 (free Mon. and Wed.–Sat. after 7 pm, Sun. 3–7); €25.60 combined Paseo del Arte ticket for the Prado, Reina Sofía, and Thyssen-Bornemisza* ⏲ *Mon. and Wed.–Sat. 10–9, Sun. 10–7 (after 2:30 only the temporary exhibition can be visited)* Ⓜ *Atocha.*

WORTH NOTING

Plaza Lavapiés. The heart of the historic Jewish barrio, this plaza at the top of Calle de la Fe remains a multicultural neighborhood hub. To the east is the Calle de la Fé (Street of Faith), which was called Calle Sinagoga until the expulsion of the Jews in 1492. The church of **San Lorenzo** at the end was built on the site of the razed synagogue. Legend says Jews and Moors who chose baptism over exile had to walk up this street barefoot to the ceremony to demonstrate their new faith. ✉ *Embajadores* Ⓜ *Lavapiés.*

SALAMANCA AND RETIRO

By the mid-19th century, city officials decided to expand Madrid beyond the 1625 wall erected by Felipe IV. The result was a handful of new, well-laid-out neighborhoods.

SALAMANCA

The Salamanca neighborhood, one of the new areas included in the program of city expansions which started in the second half of the 19th century, was originally supposed to provide shelter for the working classes. However, it soon became a favorite location for the bourgeois, the upper class, and the aristocracy. Currently it draws a more mixed crowd but still houses most of the city's expensive restaurants and luxury shops.

Museo Arqueológico (*Museum of Archaeology*). After being closed for more than six years, this newly renovated museum, enclosed in a massive neoclassical building, reopened in spring 2014 with three large floors filled with Spanish relics, artifacts, and treasures ranging from ancient history to the 19th century. Among the highlights are *La Dama de Elche*, a bust of a wealthy, 5th-century-BC Iberian woman (notice that her headgear is a rough precursor to the mantillas and hair combs still associated with traditional Spanish dress); the ancient Visigothic votive crowns discovered in 1859 near Toledo, which are believed to date back to the 7th century; and the medieval ivory crucifix of

Continued on page 91

CLOSE UP

The Art Walk (Paseo del Arte)

Picasso's *Guernica*, in the Centro de Arte Reina Sofía

Any visit to Madrid should include a stroll along Paseo del Prado, lined with some world-class museums (whose architecture as well as art are worth admiring), and some wandering in the adjoining Barrio de las Letras, the old literary neighborhood that is now a happening area full of restaurants. You can tour the area in about two hours, longer if you visit the Prado, lounge in any of the Barrio de las Letras's charming tapas bars, or take a stroll in Retiro Park.

■ **TIP→** The Paseo del Arte (Art Walk) pass allows you to visit the Prado, the Reina Sofía, and the Thyssen-Bornemisza for €21.60. You can buy it at any of the three museums, and you don't have to visit all of them on the same day.

The Paseo del Prado stretches from the Plaza de la Cibeles to Plaza del Emperador Carlos V (also known as Plaza Atocha) and is home to Madrid's three main art museums—the Prado, the Reina Sofía, and the Thyssen-Bornemisza—as well as the CaixaForum, an art institution with fabulous

temporary exhibitions. In earlier times the Paseo marked the eastern boundary of the city, and in the 17th century it was given a cleaner neoclassical look. A century later, King Carlos III designed a leafy nature walk with glorious fountains and a botanical garden to provide respite to madrileños during the scorching summers.

The stretch of the Paseo del Prado from Plaza Cánovas del Castillo north to Cibeles houses some notable buildings, but it's the southern end of the Paseo that shouldn't be missed. Start your walk on Plaza Cánovas del Castillo, with its Fuente de Neptuno (Fountain of Neptune); on the northwestern corner is the **Museo Thyssen-Bornemisza.** To your left, across from the plaza, is the elegant Ritz hotel, alongside the obelisk dedicated to all those who have died for Spain, and across from it on the right is the **Museo del Prado,** the best example of neoclassical architecture in the city and one of the world's best-known museums. It was enlarged in 2007 with the addition of what's

2

widely known as "Moneo's cube," architect Rafael Moneo's steel-and-glass building that now encloses the cloister of the old Monasterio de los Jerónimos. The monastery, of which now only the church stands, is easily dwarfed by the museum, but this is by far the oldest building in this part of the city, dating to 1503, and was at one time the core of the old **Parque del Buen Retiro** (the park stretched as far as the Paseo del Prado until the 19th century, when Queen Isabel II sold a third of its terrain to the state) and the reason for the park's name: the monastery is where the Habsburg kings would temporarily "retire" from their mundane yet overwhelming state affairs. The park, always bustling, especially on the weekends, is a great place to finish off a day or to unwind after some intense sightseeing.

To the right of the Prado, across from the Murillo Gate, is the **Jardín Botánico,** also a wonderful place to relax with a book or to sketch under the shelter of a leafy exotic tree. Across the street is the sloping plaza that leads to the **CaixaForum,** an impressive arts exhibition center.

The Paseo del Prado ends on the Glorieta del Emperador Carlos V, a traffic circle where you'll find the **Estación de Atocha,** a train station resembling the overturned hull of a ship, and, to the west of the plaza, across from Calle Atocha, in the building with the exterior glass elevators, the **Centro de Arte Reina Sofía,** Madrid's modern art museum and the current home of Picasso's *Guernica.*

West of the Paseo del Prado is the lively Barrio de las Letras neighborhood, full of charming and historic streets and popular bars for a snack or a sit-down meal after museum sightseeing—from the Paseo del Prado, just take Calle Huertas, Calle Lope de Vega, or any of the other cross streets from Calle Alameda or Calle San Pedro. Along Calle Lope de Vega are the excellent tapas bars La Dolores and El Cervantes. Near here, at the corner of Calle León and Calle Cervantes is the Casa de Cervantes, where, as the plaque on the wall attests, the author of *Don Quijote* died on April 23, 1616 (he was buried in the convent and church of the Trinitarias Descalzas, also on Calle Lope de Vega, but his remains were misplaced in the 17th century). Down the street, at No. 11, is the Casa de Lope de Vega, where the "Spanish Shakespeare," Fray Lope Félix de la Vega Carpio, lived and worked. Walk Calle León until it merges with Calle Prado, then make a left and end your tour of this neighborhood at Plaza de Santa Ana, the Barrio de las Letras's lively main square, also crowded with bars, including the Cervecería Alemana, one of Ernest Hemingway's favorite hangouts while he was in Madrid (it's a fine place to sip a beer, *but for dining check our restaurant reviews later in the chapter*).

If you feel the need to wear out your walking shoes a little more, take Calle Príncipe and then Calle Sevilla to Calle Alcalá, make a right, and head down until you reach **Plaza de la Cibeles,** then walk up to the **Puerta de Alcalá** and enter the **Parque del Buen Retiro** through the entrance on that square.

EL PRADO:
MADRID'S BRUSH WITH GREATNESS

One of the world's top museums, the Prado is to Madrid what the Louvre is to Paris, or the Uffizi to Florence: a majestic city landmark and premiere art institution that merits the attention of every traveler who visits the city.

Approaching its 200th anniversary, the Prado, with its unparalleled collection of Spanish paintings, is one of the most visited museums in the world. Foreign artists are also well represented—the collection includes masterpieces of European painting such as Hieronymus Bosch's *Garden of Earthly Delights*, *The Annunciation* by Fra Angelico, *Christ Washing the Disciples' Feet* by Tintoretto, and *The Three Graces* by Rubens—but the Prado is best known as home to more paintings by Diego Velázquez and Francisco de Goya than anywhere else.

Originally meant by King Charles III to become a museum of natural history, the Prado nevertheless opened, in 1819, as a sculpture and painting museum under the patronage of his grandchild, King Philip VII. For the first bewildered *madrileños* who crossed the museum's entrance back then, there were only about 300 paintings on display. Today there are more than 3 million visitors a year and, since the 2007 opening of the gleaming new addition by Spanish architect Rafael Moneo, known as the Jerónimos building, the displayed collection is 2,000-plus paintings, and still growing (the whole collection is estimated at about 8,000 canvases, plus 1,000 sculptures).

WHEN TO GO
The best time to visit the Prado is early in the morning, when the museum first opens, to beat the rush.

HUNGRY?
If your stomach rumbles during your visit, check out the café/restaurant in the foyer of the new building.

CONTACT INFORMATION
✉ Paseo del Prado s/n, 28014 Madrid
☎ (+34) 91 330 2800.
🌐 www.museodelprado.es

HOURS OF OPERATION
🕐 Mon.–Sat. 10 AM–8 PM, Sun. 10 AM–7 PM, Closed Monday, New Year's Day, Good Friday, Fiesta del Trabajo (May 1), and Christmas.

ADMISSION
🎫 €14. Free Mon. to Sat. 6 PM–8 PM, Sun. 5PM. To avoid lines, buy tickets in advance online.

The Trinity by El Greco, 1577. Oil on canvas.

THE COLLECTION

With works from the Middle Ages to the 19th century, the Prado's painting collection—though smaller than that of the Louvre and St. Petersburg's Hermitage—may arguably be the world's most captivating for the quality of the masterworks it features.

The Prado's origins can be traced back to the royal collections put together by the successive Hapsburg kings, who were not all equally adept at governing but who all had a penchant for the arts. Throughout the 16th and 17th centuries they amassed troves of paintings from Spanish and foreign painters and spread them among their many palaces. This meant that the bulk of the Prado's collection grew out of the rulers' whim and therefore doesn't offer, like some of its peers, an uninterrupted vision of the history of painting. This shortcoming turned into a blessing, though, as the kings' artistic "obsessions" are the reason you'll find such extensive collections of paintings by Velázquez, Titian, and Rubens (in the latter case, it was Phillip IV who, when Rubens died, sent

(top) A Velázquez statue graces the museum's old entrance. (bottom) Visitors now enter via a new $202 million wing, designed by Rafael Moneo.

representatives to Antwerp to bid for the artist's best works).

The collection starts with the Spanish Romanesque (12th and 13th century), and features important Italian (Veronese, Tintoretto, Titian), Flemish (Van Dyck, Rubens), and Dutch (Bosch, Rembrandt) collections, as well as scores of works by the great Spanish masters (Velázquez, Goya, Ribera, Zurbarán, Murillo, and others). The Jerónimos building made it possible to add some new works from 19th-century Spanish painters (Rosales, Fortuny, Madrazo, and more).

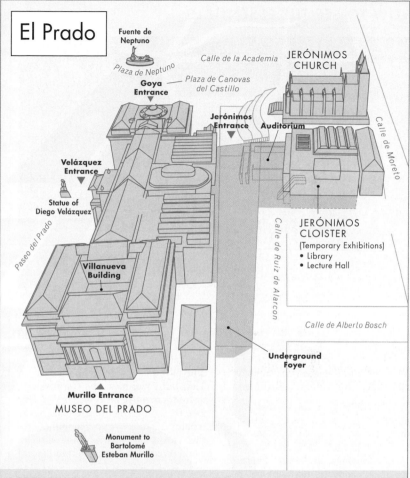

El Prado

Fuente de Neptuno

Plaza de Neptuno

Calle de la Academia

JERÓNIMOS CHURCH

Goya Entrance

Plaza de Canovas del Castillo

Jerónimos Entrance   Auditorium

Calle de Moreto

Velázquez Entrance

Statue of Diego Velázquez

Paseo del Prado

Villanueva Building

Calle de Ruiz de Alarcon

JERÓNIMOS CLOISTER
(Temporary Exhibitions)
• Library
• Lecture Hall

Calle de Alberto Bosch

Underground Foyer

Murillo Entrance

MUSEO DEL PRADO

Monument to Bartolomé Esteban Murillo

GETTING IN

The museum has two ticket-selling points and four entrance points. **The best thing to do is buy your tickets online**: you'll avoid the usually long lines; you can also reserve an audio guide (pick it up in the main foyer in the Jerónimos building) at the same time. If you don't buy tickets online, **another time-saving option is the two vending machines** outside the Goya entrance.

All in-person ticket sales are at the Goya entrance, on the north side of the museum, either at the main entrance at street level, or on the upper level: street level is ticket sales for temporary exhibitions and where you collect tickets bought online if you didn't print them out at home; the upper level gives access to the permanent collection. If you've purchased tickets for the temporary exhibition, you must access the museum through the Jerónimos entrance. **With online tickets printed at home, or a Museum Pass, you can enter at any entrance.**

HOW TO SEE THE ESSENTIALS

Inside the Jerónimos cloister.

Don't let the Prado's immense size intimidate you. You can't see it all in a day, but if you zero in on some of the museum's masterpieces, you can have a rich experience without collapsing.

With 2,000 paintings distributed among dozens of galleries, the question immediately arises: what should I see? Let's face it: while the Prado has sculptures, drawings, and other treasures spanning centuries, its "why-go"—its "must-go"—is its paintings. Most of the attention, all of it deserved, goes to the Spanish historical headliners: Diego Velázquez, El Greco, and Francisco de Goya, and on a lesser scale, Pedro Ribera, Bartolomé Murillo, and Francisco de Zurbarán. Most of these artists' works are on display on the first floor of the Villanueva building.

A QUICK TOUR

If you want to focus on the essentials—which will take about an hour and a half—enter the museum through the Goya entrance on the upper level: to the left and right, after you enter, are the galleries devoted to Renaissance and Baroque Italian painting (Titian, Tintoretto, Verónes, and Caravaggio). From there move onto Rubens (gallery 24), then on to the long spinal gallery (rooms 25 to 29) that accommodates the works of Ribera and Murillo. Make a required detour to the adjacent

THE JERÓNIMOS CLOISTER

On the second floor of the new addition is the restored cloister of San Jerónimo el Real, the medieval church now adjacent to the museum. There, in one of the quietest corners of the Prado, you'll find a collection of 16th-century sculptures by Milanese bronze artists Leone and Pompeo Leoni. While you take it all in, ponder the fact that during Moneo's expansion, the 3,000 blocks of stone that make up this cloister had to be dismantled, restored, and reassembled in their original positions.

galleries (rooms 9A-10A) on the east side to admire the elongated spiritual figures of El Greco, and the folkloric characters and penetrating self-portraits of Rembrandt (room 7). Head back to the main corridor, where you'll find 46 of Velázquez's masterful works, and which will also take you past Gallery 12, home to the museum's most famous canvas: Velázquez's *Las Meninas.* Make sure, also, to see Goya's two *Majas*—one fully dressed, the other nude—displayed next to each other in Gallery 36, and his famous subtle royal composition *The Family of Charles IV* (Gallery 32). Then head down to the ground floor to see some of Goya's best known works (*Second of May, 1808* and *Third of May 1808*, as well as *Saturn Devouring One of His Sons,* and the gory Black Paintings (all in rooms 64-67).

The airy upper-level galleries.

Once you exit the Goya galleries downstairs you'll be facing the 12 new galleries (60 to 75) devoted to the 19th-century Spanish painters: if you're curious about Joaquín Sorolla and haven't had a chance to visit the museum dedicated to his work, stop at galleries 60 and 60A to see some of his colorful art. Otherwise, cross the main foyer and stop at gallery 56 to take in Hieronymus Bosch's triptych *The Garden of Earthly Delights,* before heading toward the Velázquez exit or toward the Jerónimos building and its small but bustling café/restaurant for a well-deserved break.

THE PRADO ONLINE

The Prado has followed the example many other big-name museums and enhanced its website in an attempt to make the collection more accessible, even if you can't be there in person. The site includes an online gallery of more than 1,000 paintings (3,000 if you speak Spanish), and offers audio commentary and in-depth analysis of some paintings, among other things. It now has an official app, The Prado Guide app allows you to explore all of the museum's masterpieces and plan your visit in advance. If you're hungry for more, check out the 14 paintings scanned and displayed in super-high definition on Google Earth—search for Prado 3D, activate the tag "3D Buildings," and enjoy the technological feat!

MONEO'S DAZZLING EXPANSION

In 2007 Spanish architect Rafael Moneo's gleaming new addition to the Prado opened, bringing the museum into a new era. Moneo's red stucco "cube" envelopes the Cloister of the Jerónimos behind the old Villanueva building, but the bulk of the new premises are under the street in a vast steel-and-glass wedge-shape foyer that houses the temporary exhibitions plus some state-of-the-art add-ons: a café/restaurant, a bookshop with print-on-demand services, and a 400-seat auditorium. The new building has enabled the Prado to double its exhibition space to a total of 16,000 square meters (52,800 square feet) and to showcase more than 400 hundred new paintings—mostly from the Romanesque and the 19th century—that until the addition had laid hidden on huge steel shelves in the museum's underground vaults.

THREE GREAT MASTERS

FRANCISCO DE GOYA 1746–1828
Goya's work spans a staggering range of tone, from bucolic to horrific, his idyllic paintings of Spaniards at play and portraits of the family of King Carlos IV contrasting with his dark, disturbing "black paintings." Goya's attraction to the macabre assured him a place in posterity, an ironic statement at the end of a long career in which he served as the official court painter to a succession of Spanish kings, bringing the art of royal portraiture to unknown heights.

Francisco de Goya

Goya found fame in his day as a portraitist, but he is admired by modern audiences for his depictions of the bizarre and the morbid. Beginning as a painter of decorative Rococo figures, he evolved into an artist of great depth in the employ of King Charles IV. The push-pull between Goya's love for his country and his disdain for the enemies of Spain yielded such masterpieces as *Third of May 1808*, painted after the French occupation ended. In the early 19th century, Goya's scandalous *The Naked Maja* brought him before the Spanish Inquisition, whose judgment was to end his tenure as a court painter.

DIEGO VELÁZQUEZ 1599–1660
A native of Seville, Velázquez gained fame at age 24 as court painter to King Philip IV. He developed a lifelike approach to religious art in which both saints and sinners were specific people rather than generic types. The supple brushwork of his ambitious history paintings and portraits was unsurpassed. Several visits to Rome, and his friendship with Rubens, made him the quintessential baroque painter with an international purview.

Diego Velázquez

DOMENIKOS THEOTOKOPOULOS (AKA "EL GRECO") 1541–1614
El Greco's art was one of rapture and devotion, but beyond that his style is almost impossible to categorize. "The Greek" found his way from his native Crete to Spain through Venice; he spent most of his life in Toledo. His twisted, elongated figures imbue both his religious subjects and portraits with a sense of otherworldliness. While his palette and brushstrokes were inspired by Italian Mannerism, his approach to painting was uniquely his own. His inimitable style left few followers.

Domenikos Theotokopoulos

SIX PAINTINGS TO SEE

SATURN DEVOURING ONE OF HIS SONS (1819)
FRANCISCO DE GOYA Y LUCIENTES
In one of fourteen nightmarish "black paintings" executed by Goya to decorate the walls of his home in the
later years of his life, the mythological God Kronos,
or Saturn, cannibalizes one of his children in order to
derail a prophecy that one of them would take over his
throne. *Mural transferred to canvas.*

Saturn Devouring One of His Sons

THE GARDEN OF DELIGHTS OR LA PINTURA DEL MADROÑO (1500)
HIÉRONYMUS BOSCH
Very little about the small-town environment of the
Low Countries where the Roman Catholic Bosch lived
in the late Middle Ages can explain his thought-pro-
voking, and downright bizarre, paintings. His depictions of mankind's sins and virtues, and the heavenly
rewards or demonic punishments that await us all,
have fascinated many generations of viewers. The
devout painter has been called a "heretic," and compared to Salvador Dalí for his disturbingly twisted renderings. In this three-panel painting, Adam and Eve
are created, mankind celebrates its humanity, and hell
awaits the wicked, all within a journey of 152 inches!
Wooden Triptych.

The Garden of Delights

LAS MENINAS (THE MAIDS OF HONOR) (1656-57)
DIEGO VELÁZQUEZ DE SILVA
Velázquez's masterpiece of spatial perspective occupies
pride-of-place in the center of the Spanish baroque galleries. In this complex visual game, *you* are the king and
queen of Spain, reflected in a distant hazy mirror as the
court painter (Velázquez) pauses in front of his easel to
observe your features. The actual subject is the Princess
Margarita, heir to the throne in 1656. *Oil on canvas.*

Las Meninas

STILL LIFE (17th Century; no date)
FRANCISCO DE ZURBARÁN
Best known as a painter of contemplative saints,
Zurbarán, a native of Extremadura who found success working with Velázquez in Seville, was a peerless
observer of beauty in the everyday. His rendering of
the surfaces of these homely objects elevates them to
the stature of holy relics, urging the viewer to touch
them. But the overriding mood is one of serenity and
order. *Oil on canvas.*

Still Life

2

IN FOCUS EL PRADO: MADRID'S BRUSH WITH GREATNESS

DAVID VICTORIOUS OVER GOLIATH (1599)
MICHELANGELO MERISI (CARAVAGGIO)

Caravaggio used intense contrasts between his dark and light passages (called *chiaroscuro* in Italian) to create drama in his bold baroque paintings. Here, a surprisingly childlike David calmly ties up the severed head of the giant Philistine Goliath, gruesomely featured in the foreground plane of the picture. The astonishing realism of the Italian painter, who was as well known for his tempestuous personal life as for his deftness with a paint brush, had a profound influence on 17th century Spanish art. *Oil on canvas*.

David Victorious over Goliath

THE TRINITY (1577)
DOMENIKOS THEOTOKOPOULOS (EL GRECO)

Soon after arriving in Spain, Domenikos Theotokopoulos created this view of Christ ascending into heaven supported by angels, God the Father, and the Holy Spirit. It was commissioned for the altar of a convent in Toledo. The acid colors recall the Mannerist paintings of Venice, where El Greco was trained, and the distortions of the upward-floating bodies show more gracefulness than the anatomical contortions that characterize his later works. *Oil on canvas*.

The Trinity

PICASSO AND THE PRADO

The Prado contains no modern art, but one of the greatest artists of the 20th century had an important history with the museum. **Pablo Picasso** (1891–1973) served as the director of the Prado during the Spanish civil war, from 1936 to 1939. The Prado was a "phantom museum" in that period, Picasso once noted, since it was closed for most of the war and its collections hidden elsewhere for safety.

Picasso with his wife
Jacqueline Roque

Later that century, the abstract artist's enormous *El Guernica* hung briefly on the Prado's walls, returning to Spain from the Museum of Modern Art in 1981. Picasso had stipulated that MoMA give up his anti-war masterpiece after the death of fascist dictator Francisco Franco, and it was displayed at the Prado and the Casón del Buen Retiro until the nearby Reina Sofia was built to house it in 1992.

Picasso in his atelier

2

Ferdinand and Sancha. There is also a replica of the early cave paintings in Altamira (access to the real thing, in Cantabria Province, is highly restricted). ■ TIP→ Consider getting the multimedia guide offering select itineraries to make a visit more manageable. ⊠ *C. Serrano 13, Salamanca* ☎ *91/577-7912* ⊕ *www.man.es* ⊠ *€3* ☉ *Tues.–Sat. 9:30–8, Sun. 9:30–3* Ⓜ *Colón.*

Museo Lázaro Galdiano. This stately mansion of writer and editor José Lázaro Galdiano (1862–1947), a 10-minute walk across the Castellana from the Museo Sorolla, has decorative items and paintings by Bosch, El Greco, Murillo, and Goya, among others. The remarkable collection comprises five centuries of Spanish, Flemish, English, and Italian art. Bosch's *St. John the Baptist* and the many Goyas are the stars of the show, with El Greco's *San Francisco de Assisi* and Zurbarán's *San Diego de Alcalá* close behind. ⊠ *C. Serrano 122, Salamanca* ☎ *91/561–6084* ⊕ *www.flg.es* ⊠ *€6 (free last hr)* ☉ *Mon. and Wed.–Sat. 10–4:30, Sun. 10–3* Ⓜ *Gregorio Marañón.*

Plaza Colón. Named for Christopher Columbus, this plaza has a statue of the explorer (identical to the one in Barcelona's port) looking west from a high tower in the middle of the square. Behind Plaza Colón is **Calle Serrano,** the city's premier shopping street (think Gucci, Prada, and Loewe). Stroll in either direction on Serrano for some window-shopping. ⊠ *Salamanca* Ⓜ *Colón.*

RETIRO

The Retiro holds the city's best-known park, Parque del Buen Retiro, and the neighborhood's borders extend both to the east and west of Madrid's green lung. The area between the western side of the park and the Paseo del Prado, which used to be part of the park until it was sold to the Estate and built during the rule of Isabel II, showcases some of the city's most exclusive, expensive, and sought-after real estate. The area on the opposite side of the park is livelier, with many quality tapas bars and less expensive restaurants.

TOP ATTRACTIONS

Fodor'sChoice ★ **Museo del Prado** (Prado Museum). ⇨ *See "El Prado: Madrid's Brush with Greatness." See "The Art Walk" for a way to include the Museo del Prado as part of an art-theme Paseo del Arte excursion. A combined ticket for the Prado, Reina Sofía, and Thyssen-Bornemisza costs €21.60.*

FAMILY
Fodor'sChoice ★ **Parque del Buen Retiro** (*The Retreat*). Once the private playground of royalty, Madrid's crowning park is a vast expanse of green encompassing formal gardens, fountains, lakes, exhibition halls, children's play areas, outdoor cafés, and a **Puppet Theater** featuring free slapstick routines that even non–Spanish speakers will enjoy. Shows take place on Saturday at 1 and on Sunday at 1, 6, and 7. The park is especially lively on weekends, when it fills with street musicians, jugglers, clowns, gypsy fortune-tellers, and sidewalk painters, along with hundreds of Spaniards out for some jogging, rollerblading, bycicling, or just a walk. The park holds a book fair in May and occasional flamenco concerts in summer. From the entrance at the Puerta de Alcalá, head straight toward the center and you can find the **Estanque** (lake), presided over by a grandiose equestrian statue of King Alfonso XII, erected by his

mother. Just behind the lake, north of the statue, is one of the best of the park's many cafés.

The 19th-century **Palacio de Cristal** (Crystal Palace), southeast of the Estanque, was built to house exotic plants from the Philippines, a Spanish possession at the time. This airy marvel of steel and glass sits on a base of decorative tile. Next door is a small lake with ducks and swans. Along the Paseo del Uruguay at the park's south end is the **Rosaleda** (Rose Garden), bursting with color and heavy with floral scents for most of the summer. West of the Rosaleda, look for a statue called the **Ángel Caído** (Fallen Angel), which madrileños claim is the only one in the world depicting the prince of darkness before (during, actually) his fall from grace. ⊠ *Puerta de Alcalá, Retiro* ⌑ *Free* Ⓜ *Retiro.*

WORTH NOTING

Estación de Atocha. A steel-and-glass hangar, Madrid's main train station was built in the late 19th century by Alberto Palacio Elissague, the architect who became famous for his work with Ricardo Velázquez in the creation of the Palacio de Cristal (Crystal Palace) in Madrid's Retiro Park. Closed for years, and nearly torn down, Atocha was restored and refurbished by Spain's internationally acclaimed architect Rafael Moneo. ⊠ *Paseo de Atocha s/n, Retiro* ☎ *91/420–9875* Ⓜ *Atocha.*

Jardín Botánico (*Botanical Garden*). Just south of the Prado, the gardens provide a pleasant place to stroll or sit under the trees. True to the wishes of King Carlos III, they hold many plants, flowers, and cacti from around the world. ⊠ *Pl. de Murillo 2, Retiro* ☎ *91/420–3017* ⊕ *www. rjb.csic.es* ⌑ *€3* ⊘ *May–Aug., daily 10–9; Apr. and Sept., daily 10–8; Mar. and Oct., daily 10–7; Nov.–Feb., daily 10–6* Ⓜ *Atocha.*

Museo Naval. Anyone interested in Patrick O'Brian's painstakingly detailed naval novels or in old vessels and war ships will be interested in the 500 years of Spanish naval history displayed in this museum. The collection, which includes documents, maps, weaponry, paintings, and hundreds of ship models of different sizes, is best enjoyed by those who speak some Spanish. Beginning with Queen Isabella and King Ferdinand's reign and the expeditions led by Christopher Columbus and the conquistadors, exhibits also reveal how Spain built a naval empire that battled Turkish, Algerian, French, Portuguese, and English armies and commanded the oceans and the shipping routes for a century and a half. Moving to the present day, the museum covers Spain's more recent shipyard and naval construction accomplishments. Guided tours, in Spanish only, are offered on Thursday at 11:15 and weekends at 11:30. ⊠ *Paseo del Prado 5, Retiro* ☎ *91/523–8789* ⊕ *www.armada.mde.es/ museonaval* ⌑ *Free* ⊘ *Tues.–Sun. 10–6* Ⓜ *Banco de España.*

Palacio de Cibeles. This ornate building on the southeast side of Plaza de la Cibeles, built at the start of the 20th century and formerly called Palacio de Comunicaciones, is a massive stone compound of French, Viennese, and traditional Spanish influences. It first served as the city's main post office and, after renovations, it is now the City Hall's main building housing the office of the mayor of Madrid, several exhibition halls, an elegant restaurant with two terraces on the sixth floor—with panoramic views of the city—and a breakfast and tapas bar on the second floor. ✉ *Pl. de Cibeles, Retiro* ☎ *902/197197* ◷ *Weekdays 8:30 am–9:30 pm, Sat. 8:30–2* Ⓜ *Banco de España.*

Plaza de la Cibeles. A tree-lined walkway runs down the center of Paseo del Prado to the grand Plaza de la Cibeles, where the famous Fuente de la Cibeles (Fountain of Cybele) depicts the nature goddess driving a chariot drawn by lions. Even more than the officially designated bear and arbutus tree of Madrid's coat of arms, this monument, beautifully lighted at night, has come to symbolize Madrid—so much so that during the civil war, patriotic madrileños risked life and limb to sandbag it as Nationalist aircraft bombed the city. ✉ *Retiro* Ⓜ *Banco de España.*

Puerta de Alcalá. This triumphal arch was built by Carlos III in 1778 to mark the site of one of the ancient city gates. You can still see the bomb damage inflicted on it during the civil war. ✉ *C. de Alcalá s/n, Retiro* Ⓜ *Retiro.*

Real Fábrica de Tapices. Tired of the previous monarchs' dependency on the Belgian and Flemish thread mills and craftsmen, King Felipe V decided to establish the Royal Tapestry Factory in Madrid in 1721. It was originally housed near Alonso Martínez, and moved to its current location in 1889. Some of Europe's best artists collaborated in the factory's tapestry designs. The most famous was Goya, who produced 63 cartoons (rough plans), some of which can be seen at the Prado. It's said that he put so much detail into them that the craftsmen complained he'd made their work miserable. The factory, still in operation, applies traditional weaving techniques from the 18th and 19th centuries to modern and classic designs—including Goya's. Textiles are available for sale (you can suggest your own design) at skyrocketing prices: €1,000 per square meter (10¾ square feet) for carpets, €9,000–€12,000 per square meter for tapestries. The factory also runs a training center that teaches traditional weaving techniques to unemployed teenagers, who later become craftspeople. ✉ *Fuenterrabía 2, Retiro* ☎ *91/434–0550* ⊕ *www.realfabricadetapices.com* 🎫 *€4* ◷ *Weekdays 10–2; guided tour every 30 min starting at 10* Ⓜ *Atocha.*

San Jerónimo el Real. Ferdinand and Isabella used this church and cloister as a *retiro*, or place of meditation—hence the name of the nearby park. The building was devastated in the Napoleonic Wars, then rebuilt in the late 19th century. ✉ *Moreto 4, behind Museo del Prado, Retiro* ☎ *91/420–3578* ◷ *Daily 10–1 and 5–8:30* Ⓜ *Banco de España, Atocha.*

CHAMARTÍN AND TETUÁN

CHAMARTÍN

This large neighborhood, which extends to the north of the city from Avenida de América, wasn't annexed to Madrid until 1948. During the following decades, and due to the construction of new sites such as the Chamartín Train Station and the National Auditorium of Music, it has been gaining popularity among madrileños as a good and lively place to live.

A typical evening scene: beer and tapas on the terrace of one of Madrid's many tapas bars

TETUÁN

As the city of Madrid was growing it also needed to expand its boundaries to annex what in the second half of the 19th century were still rough areas mostly inhabited by the working classes who came to the city for work and couldn't afford to live closer to the center. One such area is the neighborhood of Tetúan, which extends very differently on both sides of Bravo Murillo, one of the city's longest streets. Its eastern side is more developed, with plenty of office buildings and commercial real estate. The western side is more residential, with a higher immigrant population.

WHERE TO EAT

Spain in general has become a popular foodie pilgrimage, and Madrid showcases its strengths with a cornucopia of cuisines, cutting-edge style, and celebrated chefs who put the city on par with Europe's most renowned dining capitals.

Top Spanish chefs fearlessly borrow from other cuisines and reinvent traditional dishes. The younger crowd, as well as movie stars and artists, flock to the casual Malasaña, Chueca, and Latina neighborhoods for the affordable restaurants and the tapas bars with truly scintillating small creations. When modern cuisine gets tiresome, seek out such local enclaves as Casa Ciriaco, Casa Botín, and Casa Paco for unpretentious and hearty home cooking.

The house wine in basic Madrid restaurants is often a sturdy, uncomplicated Valdepeñas from La Mancha. A Rioja or a more powerful, complex Ribera del Duero, the latter from northern Castile, normally accompanies serious dining. Ask your waiter's advice; a smooth Rioja, for example, may not be up to the task of accompanying a cocido or roast suckling pig. After dinner, try the anise-flavored liqueur (*anís*) produced outside the nearby village of Chinchón.

The best tapas areas in Madrid are in the Chueca, Latina, Sol, Santa Ana, Salamanca, and Lavapiés neighborhoods. Trendy La Latina has a concentration of good tapas bars in Plaza de la Paja and on Cava Baja, Cava Alta, and Almendro streets. Chueca is colorful and lively, and the tapas bars there reflect this casual and cheerful spirit in the food and interior design. The bars around Sol are quite traditional (many haven't changed in decades), but the constant foot traffic guarantees customers (and means the bars don't always have to strive for better food and service). In touristy Santa Ana, avoid the crowded and usually pricey tapas bars in the main plaza and go instead to the ones on the side streets. The tapas bars in the Salamanca neighborhood are more sober and traditional, but the food is often excellent. In Lavapiés, the neighborhood with the highest concentration of immigrants, there are plenty of tapas bars serving Moroccan, African, and Asian-inspired food.

Use the coordinate (✥ B2) at the end of each listing to locate a site on the corresponding map.

WHAT IT COSTS IN EUROS

	$	$$	$$$	$$$$
RESTAURANTS	under €16	€16–€22	€23–€29	over €29

Prices in the reviews are the average cost of a main course or equivalent combination of smaller dishes at dinner or, if dinner is not served, at lunch.

PALACIO, LA LATINA, AND SOL

PALACIO

$$ SPANISH 🍴 **La Bola.** First opened as a *botellería* (wine shop) in 1802, La Bola slowly developed into a tapas bar and then into a full-fledged restaurant. The traditional setting is the draw: the bar is original, and the dining nooks, decorated with polished wood, Spanish tile, and lace curtains, are charming. Amazingly, the restaurant belongs to its founding family, with the seventh generation currently in training. Try the house specialty: *cocido a la madrileña* (a hearty meal of broth, garbanzo beans, vegetables, potatoes, and pork). [$] *Average main: €21* ✉ *Bola 5, Palacio* ☎ *91/547–6930* 🌐 *www.labola.es* 💳 *No credit cards* 🕒 *Closed Sun. in Aug. No dinner weekends* [M] *Ópera* ✥ *B3.*

$$ SPANISH 🍴 **Taberneros.** Madrileños favor this refined bar primarily for the wine. There are wine racks and decanters exhibited all around, and knowledgeable waiters are more than happy to guide guests through their wide selection of local brands. The food is on a par, with a menu that includes such local specialties as croquetas, artichoke salad, chickpea and octopus stew, and beef tartare, as well as Asian-inspired dishes like the Dragon's Eyes (a rice cake filled with chicken and vegetables

BEST BETS FOR MADRID DINING

Fodor's Choice★	By Price	
		Le Petit Bistrot, p. 100
		Mercado de la Reina,
Arzábal, $$, p. 109	**$**	p. 102
Asiana, $$$$, p. 100		Puerto Lagasca, p. 109
Casa Benigna, $$$,	Arabia, p. 100	Sacha, p. 111
p. 111	Bazaar, p. 101	Sudestada, p. 112
Casa Paco, $$$, p. 97	Home Burger, p. 101	Ten Con Ten, p. 109
DiverXO, $$$$, p. 111	La Musa, p. 102	Triciclo, p. 100
Goizeko Wellington, $$$,	Nueva Galicia, p. 98	
p. 105	Pulcinella, p. 102	**$$$**
La Terraza—Casino de		El Pescador, p. 104
Madrid, $$$$, p. 98	**$$**	Goizeko Wellington,
Las Tortillas de Gabino,	Álbora, p. 104	p. 105
$$, p. 103	Arrocería Gala, p. 98	
Mercado de la Reina, $$,	Arzábal. p. 109	**$$$$**
p. 102	Casa Ciriaco, p. 96	DiverXO, p. 111
Santceloni, $$$$, p. 103	La Castela, p. 110	La Terraza—Casino de
Sergi Arola Gastro, $$$$,	La Gamella, p. 110	Madrid, p. 98
p. 103	Las Tortillas de Gabino,	Ramon Freixa, p. 109
Zalacaín, $$$$, p. 111	p. 103	Viridiana, p. 110

in a curry sauce) or tuna loin in soy sauce. Wine by the glass and a weekly lunch menu are also available. Show up early or be prepared to wait. $ *Average main: €18* ⊠ *Santiago 9, Palacio* ☎ *91/542–2460* ☽ *No lunch Mon.* Ⓜ *Ópera* ✦ *C4.*

LA LATINA

$$$ ✕ **Casa Botín.** The *Guinness Book of Records* calls this the world's old-
SPANISH est restaurant (est. 1725), and Hemingway called it the best. The lat-ter claim may be a bit over the top, but the restaurant *is* excellent and extremely charming (and so successful that the owners opened a "branch" in Miami, Florida). There are four floors of tile and wood-beam dining rooms, and, if you're seated upstairs, you'll pass centuries-old ovens. Musical groups called *tunas* (mostly made up of students dressed in medieval costume) often come by to perform. The specialties are *cochinillo* (roast pig) and *cordero* (roast lamb). It's rumored Goya washed dishes here before he made it as a painter. $ *Average main: €23* ⊠ *Cuchilleros 17, off Pl. Mayor, La Latina* ☎ *91/366–4217* ⊕ *www. botin.es* Ⓜ *Tirso de Molina* ✦ *C5.*

$$ ✕ **Casa Ciriaco.** One of Madrid's most traditional restaurants—host to a
SPANISH long list of Spain's who's who, from royalty to philosophers, painters, and bullfighters—serves up simple home cooking in an unpretentious environment. You can get a carafe of Valdepeñas or a split of Rioja reserve to accompany the *perdiz con judiones* (partridge with broad beans). The *pepitoria de gallina* (hen in an almond sauce) is another

favorite. $ *Average main: €17* ⊠ *C. Mayor 84, La Latina* ☎ *91/559–5066* ⊗ *Closed Wed. and Aug.* Ⓜ *Ópera* ✛ *B4.*

$$ ✕ **Casa Lucas.** Quieter than most of its boisterous street neighbors, this
SPANISH small quaint bar with just a few tables offers a short but creative selection of local wines and homemade tapas. Some of the food favorites include the *Carinena* (grilled pork sirloin with caramelized onion), *Madrid* (scrambled eggs with onion, *morcilla* [blood pudding], and pine nuts in a tomato base), and *huevos a la Macarena* (eggs in puff pastry with mushrooms, fried artichokes, fried ham, béchamel, and pine nuts). Since it gets packed easily, try to drop by early both at lunch and dinner times. $ *Average main: €21* ⊠ *Cava Baja 30, La Latina* ☎ *91/365–0804* ⊗ *No lunch Wed.* Ⓜ *La Latina* ✛ *C5.*

$$$ ✕ **Casa Paco.** This Castilian tavern wouldn't have looked out of place
STEAKHOUSE two or three centuries ago, and today you can still squeeze past the
Fodor'sChoice old, zinc-top bar, crowded with madrileños downing Valdepeñas, and
★ into the tiled dining rooms. Feast on thick slabs of red meat, sizzling on plates so hot the meat continues to cook at your table. The Spanish consider overcooking meat a sin, so expect looks of dismay if you ask for your meat *bien hecho* (well done); opt for *al punto* (medium) or *poco hecha* (medium rare), instead. You order by weight, so remember that a *medio kilo* is more than a pound. To start, try the *pisto manchego* (La Mancha version of ratatouille) or the Castilian *sopa de ajo* (garlic soup). $ *Average main: €23* ⊠ *Puerta Cerrada 11, La Latina* ☎ *91/366–3166* ⌂ *Reservations essential* ⊗ *Closed 1st wk of Aug. No dinner Sun.* Ⓜ *Tirso de Molina* ✛ *C5.*

$$ ✕ **El Almendro.** Getting a weekend seat in this rustic old favorite is quite
SPANISH a feat, but drop by any other time and you'll be served ample *raciones* (bigger tapas portions meant to be shared) such as the *roscas* (round hot bread filled with various types of cured meats), *huevos rotos* (fried eggs with homemade potato chips), *pistos* (sautéed vegetables with a tomato base) or *revueltos* (scrambled eggs: a favorite preparation is the Habanero, with fava beans and blood pudding). Note that drinks and food need to be ordered separately (a bell rings when your food is ready and you collect it by the small window). $ *Average main: €21* ⊠ *Almendro 13, La Latina* ☎ *91/365–4252* Ⓜ *La Latina* ✛ *C5.*

$$$ ✕ **El Landó.** This *castizo* (authentic or highly traditional) restaurant with
SPANISH dark wood-paneled walls lined with bottles of wine serves classic Spanish food. Specialties of the house are *huevos estrellados* (fried eggs with potatoes and sausage), grilled meats, a good selection of fish (sea bass, haddock, grouper) with many different sauces, and steak tartare. As you sit down for your meal, you'll immediately be served a plate of bread with tomato, a salad, and Spanish ham. Check out the pictures of famous celebrities who've eaten at this typically noisy landmark; they line the staircase that leads to the main dining area. $ *Average main: €26* ⊠ *Pl. Gabriel Miró 8, La Latina* ☎ *91/366–7681* ⌂ *Reservations essential* ⊗ *Closed Sun., Easter, and Aug.* Ⓜ *La Latina* ✛ *B5.*

$$ ✕ **Juana la Loca.** This tempting spot serves sophisticated and unusual
SPANISH tapas that can be as pricey as they are delightful. They have sumptuous creations such as *fideuà con butifarra de calamar* (a paella-type dish cooked with thin macaroni-shape pasta instead of rice and served with

calamari sausage) or *huevo confit-
ado trufado* (poached egg with truffle), yet customers also rush to the
counter for their version of the classic *tortilla de patatas*—here made
with caramelized onions, sweeter
and juicier than the ones you might
find elsewhere. If you drop by the
bar during the weekend, go early,
when the tapas are freshest. On weekdays, order from the menu. $ *Av-
erage main: €21* ⊠ *Pl. Puerta de Moros 4, La Latina* ☎ *91/364–0525*
⊘ *No lunch Mon.* Ⓜ *La Latina* ✛ *B5.*

<table>
<tr><td></td><td></td><td>

DEALS AND DISCOUNTS

Most restaurants offer a fixed-
price *menú del día* for lunch that
includes a starter, main course,
dessert, wine, and coffee.
</td></tr>
</table>

$$ | ✕ **Txirimiri.** It's easy to locate this Basque tapas place by the crowds
TAPAS | that gather at its door, which may make this hot spot uncomfortable at
times, but the food is worth being jostled a bit. Among the highlights
are the Unai hamburger (fried in tempura with foie gras), the Span-
ish omelet—one of the city's best—the crayfish and cuttlefish black
risotto, the *croquetas de cocido* (made with the meat from the popular
Madrilenian stew), or the bull's tail sandwich. Arrive early and you may
be lucky enough to get one of the tables in the back. $ *Average main:
€21* ⊠ *Humilladero 6, La Latina* ☎ *91/364–1196* Ⓜ *La Latina* ✛ *C5.*

SOL

$$$$ | ✕ **La Terraza—Casino de Madrid.** This rooftop terrace just off Puerta del
ECLECTIC | Sol is in one of Madrid's oldest, most exclusive clubs (the *casino* is a
Fodor's Choice | club for gentlemen, not gamblers; it's members only, but the restaurant
★ | is open to all). When it opened the food was inspired and overseen by
celebrity chef Ferran Adriá, but as the years have gone by, chef Fran-
cisco Roncero has built a reputation of his own. Try any of the light
and tasty mousses, foams, and liquid jellies, or indulge in the unique
tapas—experiments of flavor, texture, and temperature, such as the
salmon *ventresca* in miso with radish ice cream or the spherified sea
urchin. There's also a sampler menu. $ *Average main: €38* ⊠ *Alcalá 15,
Sol* ☎ *91/521–8700* ⊕ *www.casinodemadrid.es* ⌾ *Reservations essen-
tial* ⊘ *Closed Sun., Mon., and Aug.* Ⓜ *Sol* ✛ *E3.*

$ | ✕ **Nueva Galicia.** This small family-run bar and restaurant has long been
SPANISH | one of the best values in the center of Madrid—it's two blocks from
the Puerta del Sol—and you can eat inside or, during summer, at tables
on the pedestrian-only side street. It's usually noisy and serves simple
food, but a starter, main course, dessert, and a full bottle of wine can be
consumed for a ridiculously low price, or you can choose to share some
of the larger portions (*raciones*) of octopus, cuttlefish, *lacón* (cooked
ham with Galician potatoes), or *pisto* (a Spanish ratatouille). If you're
heading out, you can get a sandwich to go. $ *Average main: €9* ⊠ *Cruz
6, Sol* ☎ *91/522–5289* ▬ *No credit cards* ⊘ *Closed Sun. and Aug.* Ⓜ *Se-
villa* ✛ *E4.*

BARRIO DE LAS LETRAS

$$ | ✕ **Arrocería Gala.** Hidden on a back street not far from Calle Atocha
MEDITERRANEAN | and the Reina Sofía, this cheerful Mediterranean restaurant is usually
packed, thanks to the choice of paellas, fideuás, risottos, and hearty

chickpea and bean stews—all served with salad, dessert, and wine. Tables of four or fewer must order the same type of rice. The front dining area is modern and festive; the back room incorporates trees and plants in a glassed-in patio. It has an affordable prix fixe lunch menu on weekdays. [$] *Average main: €16* ✉ *Moratín 22, Barrio de las Letras* ☎ *91/429–2562* ✍ *Reservations essential* ▭ *No credit cards* ⏲ *Closed Mon.* [M] *Antón Martín* ✥ *F5.*

2

$$ ITALIAN 🍴 **Come Prima.** There are fancier and more expensive Italian restaurants in the city but none as warm or authentic as this one. Decorated with black-and-white photos of Italian actors and stills from movies, the interior is divided into three areas; the bistrolike front, with green-and-white checkered tablecloths, is the most charming. Portions are large, eye-catching, and tastefully presented. The risottos are popular, especially the Zucchine (with zucchini and king prawns) and the Selvático (with porcini mushrooms and Parmesan). The menu also features innovative fresh pastas like liver- or pumpkin-filled ravioli and a pappardelle with white-truffle cream and egg yolk. [$] *Average main: €20* ✉ *C. Echegaray 27, Barrio de las Letras* ☎ *91/420–3042* ✍ *Reservations essential* ⏲ *Closed Mon. No dinner Sun.* [M] *Antón Martín* ✥ *E5.*

$ TAPAS 🍴 **El Cervantes.** Clean, unspoiled despite the very touristy area, and very popular among locals, this spot—usually cramped on the weekends—serves plenty of hot and cold tapas and one of the best and most refreshing draft beers in the city. It has a long menu with praised choices such as the *pulpo a la gallega* (octopus with potatoes, olive oil, and paprika), the *empanada* (tuna-stuffed pastry puff), the *piquillo* peppers stuffed with cod and shrimp or any of the *tostas* (toast topped with ingredients like mushroom, shrimp, etc.), which you can also order in a sampler, or the mixed grill. [$] *Average main: €13* ✉ *Pl. de Jesús 7, Barrio de las Letrasa* ☎ *91/429–6093* ⏲ *No dinner Sun.* [M] *Antón Martín* ✥ *F4.*

$$ TAPAS 🍴 **Estado Puro.** At this hypersleek dining space (with a great summer terrace) cooking wizard Paco Roncero reinvents popular dishes such as *patatas bravas* (here served with a layer of alioli on top and filled with spicy sauce), Spanish omelet (with the basic potatoes and onions topped with egg foam and served in a martini glass) or *soldaditos de Pavía* (battered cod with Romesco sauce). Don't skip dessert: his version of the almond-based Tarta de Santiago cake is highly recommended. There is another location nearby, on Plaza del Angel 9, that is also open daily. [$] *Average main: €16* ✉ *Pl. Cánovas del Castillo 4, Barrio de las Letras* ☎ *91/330–2400* [M] *Banco de España* ✥ *F4.*

$ TAPAS 🍴 **La Dolores.** Usually crowded and noisy, this is a great choice for a quick bite and for a glass of one of the best draft beers in Madrid. It certainly doesn't have a wide variety of food, but some of the tapas that you'll find on display on the counter have long become staples among local customers: white tuna belly (*ventresca*), smoked cod on bread, and the wittily named "marriage," a combination of fresh red and white anchovies marinated in either olive oil or vinegar—which you can also enjoy at one of the few tables in the back. [$] *Average main: €15* ✉ *Pl. de Jesús 4, Barrio de las Letras* ☎ *91/429–2243* [M] *Antón Martín* ✥ *F5.*

$ MEDITERRANEAN 🍴 **La Finca de Susana.** This is one of the best bargains in the city. A diverse crowd is drawn to this loftlike space for the grilled vegetables, oven-cooked *bacalao* (salt cod) with spinach, and the caramelized duck with plums and couscous. The hardwood floor is offset by warm colors, and one end of the dining room has a huge bookcase lined with wine bottles. Arrive by 1 for lunch and 8:30 for dinner or be prepared to wait. *[$] Average main: €10 ✉ C. Arlabán 4, Cortes ☎ 91/369–3557 🌐 www.lafinca-restaurant.com ✍ Reservations not accepted [M] Sevilla ✥ E4.*

$$ FRENCH 🍴 **Le Petit Bistrot.** After more than a decade of working in French restaurants and hotels in different parts of the world, Carlos Campillo and his wife Frédérique Sévèque took on a challenge converting what was once a bullfighting-themed tavern into a Parisian bistro. Though some elements, such as the long brass-topped bar, hint at its castizo origins, there's much that's truly French here in addition to the food, including the servers, the wine, and the French aperitifs. Specialties include onion soup, escargot, Brie fritters, duck breast with orange juice, and the chateaubriand steak with butter, tarragon, and vinegar. On Sunday and holidays brunch is also served. *[$] Average main: €16 ✉ Pl. de Matute 5, Barrio de las Letras ☎ 91/429–6265 🌐 www.lepetitbistrot.net 🕘 Closed Mon. No dinner Sun. and Wed. [M] Anton Martín ✥ E5.*

$$ TAPAS 🍴 **Triciclo.** A contemporary Spanish reinvention of a French bistro, this is a lively tapas bar with a more relaxed adjacent restaurant for those not used to fighting for space at the counter. The décor is informal, with tall tables in the bar and some sculptures of tricycles which allude to the restaurant's name, but it's the food which has quickly helped establish a reputation in the neighborhood and beyond. The menu has three parts: less elaborate dishes, such as the grilled and smoked crayfish; more intricate dishes from all over Spain such as the purple-garlic soup and the deer venison tenderloin with couscous; and some selected fare from all over the world, like the salt-baked duck breast. Note that you can choose a full, half, or one-third portion (the equivalent of a tapa) of each dish, and order wine by the glass. *[$] Average main: €16 ✉ Santa María 28, Barrio de las Letras ☎ 91/024–4798 🌐 www.eltriciclo.es 🕘 Closed Sun. [M] Antón Martín ✥ F5.*

CHUECA, MALASAÑA, AND CHAMBERÍ

CHUECA

$ MOROCCAN 🍴 **Arabia.** Pass through the heavy wool rug hanging at the entrance and you may feel as if you've entered Aladdin's cave, decorated as this restaurant is with adobe, wood, brass, whitewashed walls, and lavish palms. Full of young, boisterous madrileños, this is a great place to try elaborate Moroccan dishes like stewed lamb with honey and dry fruits or vegetarian favorites such as couscous with milk and pumpkin. To start, order the best falafel outside of Morocco or the yogurt cucumber salad. Reservations are essential on the weekend. *[$] Average main: €9 ✉ Piamonte 12, Chueca ☎ 91/532–5321 🕘 Closed Mon. No lunch Tues.–Fri. [M] Chueca ✥ F2.*

$$$$ ECLECTIC Fodor's Choice ★ 🍴 **Asiana.** Young chef Jaime Renedo surprises even the most jaded palates in this unique setting—his mother's Asian antiques furniture store, which used to be a ham-drying shed, where seats are amid a Vietnamese bed, a life-size Buddha, and other merchandise for sale. Renedo brings to his job a contagious enthusiasm for cooking and experimentation

as well as painstaking attention to detail, and the eclectic 15-dish fixed sampler menu (€85, and the only menu on offer) perfectly balances Spanish, East Asian, Peruvian, and Japanese cooking traditions. If you're willing to forfeit exclusiveness but want to indulge in a milder version of the chef's creations, try the adjacent and much more affordable Asiana Next Door. [$] *Average main: €85* ✉ *Travesía de San Mateo 4, Chueca* ☎ *91/310–4020, 91/310–0965* 🌐 *www.restauranteasiana.com* ✍ *Reservations essential* ⏲ *Closed Sun.–Thurs. and Aug. No lunch* [M] *Tribunal* ✥ *E1.*

$ MEDITERRANEAN 🍴 **Bazaar.** The owners of the successful central restaurant La Finca de Susana expanded their repertoire by opening this Chueca spot serving low-priced, creative Mediterranean food of reasonable quality in a trendy environment. Resembling an old-fashioned convenience store, its square upper floor has large windows facing the street, high ceilings, and hardwood floors; the downstairs is larger but less interesting. Standout dishes include the tuna *rosbif* (roasted and sliced thinly, like beef) with mango chutney and the tender ox with Parmesan and arugula. For dessert, a popular choice is the *chocolatísimo* (chocolate soufflé). To get a table, arrive by 1 for lunch and by 8:30 for dinner. [$] *Average main: €10* ✉ *C. Libertad 21, Chueca* ☎ *91/523–3905* ✍ *Reservations not accepted* [M] *Chueca* ✥ *F2.*

$ SPANISH 🍴 **El Bocaíto.** Perhaps a bit too rustic-looking—complete with decorative tiles of matadors and flamenco dancers on the walls—for the hipster neighborhood where it's located, this spot nonetheless has always been a landmark with a very faithful following, including many of the local movie stars who live in its vicinity. It has three dining areas and around 100 tapas on the menu, including 15 to 20 types of *tostas* (toast topped with prawns, egg and garlic, pâté with caviar, cockles, and so on), a good selection of cured meats, and surely some of the best *pescaíto frito* (deep-fried whitebait) in the city. [$] *Average main: €13* ✉ *Libertad 6, Chueca* ☎ *91/532–1219* ⏲ *Closed Sun. and Aug.* [M] *Chueca* ✥ *F3.*

$ AMERICAN 🍴 **Home Burger.** If you're getting nostalgic after days of traveling across Spain, don't miss out on this mishmash of two deeply ingrained American concepts—the hamburger and the diner—with a European twist. The result is a very affordable menu, favored by Chueca and Malasaña hipsters, that includes your traditional beef hamburgers but also plenty of unusual offerings, such as the Tandoori burger; the Mexican, with chicken, avocado, and a salsa made with red chiles; the Caprichosa, with Brie and onion jam; or the vegetarian options with falafel or soy. They are clearly doing it right—there are now three other locations in Madrid, all centrally located: at Espíritu Santo 12 and Calle Silva 25 in Malasaña, and at Calle Cruz 7 in Barrio de las Letras. [$] *Average main: €13* ✉ *San Marcos 26, Chueca* ☎ *91/522–9728* 🌐 *www.homeburgerbar.com* ✍ *Reservations essential* [M] *Chueca* ✥ *D1.*

$ SPANISH 🍴 **La Tita Rivera.** Just a block from a Fuencarral street that embodies youthful and rebellious energy, this place has an industrial vibe enhanced by the exposed pipes of the beer tanks. It has a varied menu that includes chicken and pork burritos but the highlights here are the small tapas *casis* ("almost"), as in "falling short of a whole meal": dinner rolls filled with all sorts of ingredients such as calamari and alioli, a cod omelet, marinated pork with pungent Asturian cheese, and even strawberries with cream cheese. The bar has a much sought-after quiet terrace in the back where you can indulge in a cold glass of Galician beer or, if in a more daring mood, an unusual mojito—with the owners' homemade herb liquor. [$] *Average main: €11* ✉ *Pérez Galdós 4, Chueca* ☎ *91/522–1890* [M] *Chueca* ✣ *E2.*

$$ TAPAS Fodor's Choice ★ 🍴 **Mercado de la Reina.** Plentiful and inexpensive tapas and succulent larger portions—think scrambled eggs with a variety of meats and vegetables, tasty local cheeses, and salads—make this large, tastefully decorated bar-restaurant a handy stop for people who want to refuel without having to sit through a long meal. There's also a more formal dining area with long tables where groups can share some of the more elaborate meat and fish options and an outdoor terrace. A lounge downstairs—with an extensive gin menu—accommodates those who want to keep the night rolling. [$] *Average main: €17* ✉ *Gran Vía 12, Chueca* ☎ *91/521–3198* [M] *Banco de España* ✣ *E3.*

$ ITALIAN 🍴 **Pulcinella.** Tired of not being able to find a true Italian restaurant in the city, owner Enrico Bosco opened this homey trattoria filled with memorabilia of Italian artists. Always bustling and frequented by families and young couples, it seems like a direct transplant from Naples. Superb fresh pastas; the best pizzas and focaccias in the city, cooked in a brick oven; and the homemade tiramisù are the standout dishes. The branch across the street, Cantina di Pulcinella, belongs to the same owners and serves the same food. [$] *Average main: €13* ✉ *Regueros 7, Chueca* ☎ *91/319–7363* 🌐 *www.gruppopulcinella.com* ✍ *Reservations essential* [M] *Chueca* ✣ *F1.*

MALASAÑA

$ SPANISH 🍴 **Bodega de la Ardosa.** Done up like an Irish pub, with large wooden barrels serving as tables, this charming bar (owned by a select club) has more than a century of history. There's great vermouth and draft beer, along with food specialties such as *salmorejo* (a thick, cold tomato soup similar to gazpacho), a juicy tortilla de patatas made by the owner's mother, and croquetas with various fillings, including béchamel and prawns (*carabineros*) and strong, aromatic goat cheese from the North (Cabrales). Tables at the back (you have to dip under the counter to get there) are quieter. Expect to hear a good selection of jazz. [$] *Average main: €13* ✉ *Colón 13, Malasaña* ☎ *91/521–4979* [M] *Tribunal* ✣ *E2.*

$ MEDITERRANEAN 🍴 **La Musa.** The trendy, elegant vibe and creative menu of unique salads and tapas (try the *bomba,* a potato filled with meat or vegetables in a spinach sauce, or the huge marinated venison brochette) draw a stylish young crowd. Breakfast is served during the week, and there's a good fixed-price lunch menu. The second, bigger location (at Costanilla de San Andrés 12, on Plaza de la Paja in La Latina) has a larger and more international menu with additions like hummus, lobster tempura, and California rolls, to name a few, and a trendy, white-brick, vaulted basement with vintage decor frequented by many of the movie actors living in the neighborhood. Show up early or expect to wait. [$] *Average main: €10* ✉ *Manuela Malasaña 18, Malasaña* ☎ *91/448–7558* 🌐 *www.grupolamusa.com* ✍ *Reservations not accepted* [M] *Bilbao* ✣ *D1.*

$ ✕ **Mui.** You won't find stale tapas piled up on rickety counters at this
TAPAS   popular and tastefully decorated spot: instead, selections are prepared
on the spot. There are traditional dishes like spicy patatas bravas; *gildas* (skewers) of yellow pepper with anchovies and olives; grilled pork
ear; bull's tail stew and blood pudding, as well as more sophisticated
fare like steak tartare, or oysters served in various ways (with a Champagne reduction sauce, with thistle and artichokes, etc.). It also has a
lounge area on the top floor for those wanting to extend the night out
in true madrileño style. $ *Average main: €12* ⊠ *Ballesta 4, Malasaña*
☎ *91/522–5786* ☯ *Closed Sun. and Mon.* ✛ *D2.*

CHAMBERÍ

$$ ✕ **Las Tortillas de Gabino.** Few national dishes raise more intense debates
TAPAS   among Spaniards than the tortilla de patata. A deceivingly simple dish,
Fodor's Choice   it has many variations: some like it soft with the eggs runny, others
★   prefer a spongy, evenly cooked result. At this lively restaurant you'll
find crowds of Spaniards gobbling up one of the city's finest traditional
versions of the tortilla, as well as some unconventional ones—potatoes
with octopus, potato chips with salmorejo, tortillas with garlic soup,
with codfish and leek stew, with truffles (when available), and with a
potato mousse, to name just a few—that are best enjoyed when shared
by everyone at the table. The menu includes plenty of equally succulent non-egg choices and a green-apple sorbet that shouldn't be missed.
$ *Average main: €16* ⊠ *Rafael Calvo 20, Chamberí* ☎ *91/319–7505*
⊕ *www.lastortillasdegabino.com* ☯ *Closed Sun.* Ⓜ *Rubén Darío* ✛ *E1.*

$$$$ ✕ **Santceloni.** An enduring star of the city's contemporary cuisine, this
MEDITERRANEAN   top-notch restaurant managed to survive the sudden death of its founder,
Fodor's Choice   star chef Santi Santamaría, garnering even greater acclaim under the
★   leadership of Santamaría's successor and best disciple, Óscar Velasco.
In a sophisticated environment, where the service, the tableware, and
the wine suggestions are as impeccable as the food, Velasco makes
exquisite combinations of Mediterranean ingredients accompanied by
a comprehensive and unusual wine list. Go with an appetite and lots of
time (a minimum of three hours) because a meal here is ceremonious. If
you're a meat lover, make sure you try the *jarrete* (veal shank). Cheese
aficionados swoon over the cheese sampler offered before dessert. $ *Average main: €53* ⊠ *Paseo de la Castellana 57, Chamberí* ☎ *91/210–8840*
⊕ *www.restaurantesantceloni.com* ⌕ *Reservations essential* ☯ *Closed
Sun., Easter wk, and Aug. No lunch Sat.* Ⓜ *Gregorio Marañón* ✛ *H1.*

$$$$ ✕ **Sergi Arola Gastro.** Celebrity chef Sergi Arola—Ferran Adrià's most
ECLECTIC   popular disciple—vaulted to the top of the Madrid dining scene at
Fodor's Choice   La Broche, then left (in 2007) to go solo. The result is a smaller, less
★   minimalist though equally modern bistro space crafted to enhance the
dining experience, 30 customers at a time. At the height of his career
and surrounded by an impeccable team—which now also includes a talented and talkative bartender in the lounge—Arola offers two sampler
menus ranging from five courses (€105) to eight (€135) in the namesake
"Sergi Arola" menu, as well as some limited à la carte options. The
choices include some of the chef's classic surf-and-turf dishes (such as
rabbit filled with giant scarlet shrimp) and nods to his Catalonian roots
(sautéed broad beans and peas with blood sausage). The wine list has

more than 600 labels, mostly from small producers, all available by the glass. $ *Average main: €40* ✉ *Zurbano 31, Chamberí* ☎ *91/310–2169* ⊕ *www.sergiarola.es* ✍ *Reservations essential* ☉ *Closed Sun. and Mon.* Ⓜ *Alonso Martínez* ✛ *G1.*

EMBAJADORES

LAVAPIÉS

$$ ✕**Casa Lastra.** Established in 1926, this Asturian tavern is popular with
SPANISH Lavapiés locals. The rustic, half-tile walls are strung with relics from the Asturian countryside, including wooden clogs, cowbells, sausages, and garlic. Specialties include *fabada* (Asturian white beans stewed with sausage), *fabes con almejas* (white beans with clams), and *queso de Cabrales* (aromatic cheese made in the Picos de Europa). Great hunks of bread and Asturian hard cider complement the hearty meals; desserts include tangy baked apples. There's an inexpensive prix fixe lunch menu on weekdays. $ *Average main: €17* ✉ *Olivar 3, Lavapiés* ☎ *91/369–0837* ☉ *Closed Wed. and July. No dinner Sun.* Ⓜ *Tirso de Molina, Antón Martín* ✛ *E5.*

SALAMANCA AND RETIRO

SALAMANCA

$$ ✕**Álbora.** The owners of this sleek restaurant also produce cured hams
TAPAS and top-notch canned foods, and these quality ingredients are included in a menu that manages to be both traditional and creative. The dining areas include an avant-garde, street-level tapas bar and a more refined restaurant on the second floor. The former, with a large countertop and tall tables lined up along the wall, is a good option if you don't want to sit through a long meal, and quite popular. It has simple staples, among them the cured meats (salchichón, chorizo, lomo, or Iberian ham), and also plenty of more elaborate fare, such as roasted scallops with cream of lobster and spider crab, risotto with mussels, or the Bilbao-style pisto. It serves half portions and has a good selection of wines by the glass, and great gin and tonics. $ *Average main: €17* ✉ *Jorge Juan 33, Salamanca* ☎ *91/781–6197* ⊕ *www.restaurantealbora.com* Ⓜ *Velázquez* ✛ *H1.*

$$$ ✕**El Pescador.** Owned by the proprietors of the best fish market in
SEAFOOD town, this seafood restaurant with a warm modern interior welcomes guests with an impressive window display of fresh seafood—red and white prawns, blue crabs, lobsters, oysters, barnacles, crayfish, and the renowned Galician Carril clams are just some of what you might see. The selection of exceedingly fresh white fish (including turbot, sole, grouper, and sea bass) can be prepared oven-cooked, grilled, battered, or fried in olive oil with garlic and cayenne pepper. In addition to the dining room, there is a large wooden counter where you can snack while sipping an Albariño made especially for the restaurant. $ *Average main: €25* ✉ *José Ortega y Gasset 75, Salamanca* ☎ *91/402–1290* ⊕ *www.marisqueriaelpescador.net* ✍ *Reservations essential* ☉ *Closed Sun.* Ⓜ *Lista* ✛ *H1.*

$$ ✕**Estay.** A buzzing two-story bar and restaurant with classic and refined
SPANISH furnishings, this spot has quickly become a landmark in the Salamanca

neighborhood. It is frequented by a very varied clientele—the city's posh crowd mingles with families—all in search of its creative and yet traditional food. The tapas menu is plentiful and diverse, with specialties like the *tortilla española con atún y lechuga* (Spanish omelet with tuna and lettuce), *raba*s (fried calamari), or fried Brie, and the desserts are unusually diverse and savory. There is a dish of the day for €13, and a few tapas samplers. Ⓢ *Average main: €20* ✉ *Hermosilla 46, Salamanca* ☎ *91/578–0470* ◷ *Closed Sun.* Ⓜ *Velázquez* ✛ *H1.*

$$$
SPANISH
Fodor'sChoice
★
✕**Goizeko Wellington.** Aware of the more sophisticated palate of Spain's new generation of diners, the owners of the traditional madrileño dreamland that is Goizeko Kabi opened this other restaurant that shares the virtues of its kin but has none of its stuffiness. The menu here delivers the same quality fish, house staples such as the *kokotxas de merluza* (hake jowls) either grilled or sautéed with herbs and olive oil, and the *chipirones en su tinta* (line-caught calamari cooked in its own ink); as well as pastas, a superb lobster and crayfish risotto, and some hearty bean stews. The interior of the restaurant is warm and modern with citrus-yellow walls. Ⓢ *Average main: €28* ✉ *Hotel Wellington, Villanueva 34, Salamanca* ☎ *91/577–6026* ⚒ *Reservations essential* ◷ *Closed Sun. No lunch Sat. in July and Aug.* Ⓜ *Retiro, Príncipe de Vergara* ✛ *H2.*

$
TAPAS
✕**Jurucha.** If you're shopping in the Serrano area, this is the place to go for a quick bite at a good price and a cold draft beer. It will never win a design award (its look is indistinguishable even from other bars on the same street) but gaze at the tapas on display on its long counter and you'll understand why locals love it so much. Highlights include the *gambas con alioli* (prawns with a garlic-mayo sauce), fried *empanadillas* (small empanadas), egg or ham croquetas, and the omnipresent Spanish omelet. If you find the usually crowded counter a bit too uncomfortable, there are tables in the back. Ⓢ *Average main: €15* ✉ *Ayala 19, Salamanca* ☎ *91/575–0098* ◷ *Closed Sun and Aug.* Ⓜ *Serrano* ✛ *H1.*

$$$$
JAPANESE
✕**Kabuki Wellington.** This elegant Japanese dining spot serves the kind of superbly fresh sushi and sashimi you'll find in other parts of the world, but where it really excels is in chef Ricardo Sanz's Spanish-based combinations. Examples include a dish with sea bass carpaccio (*usuzukuri*) on top of black-skinned potatoes from the Canary Islands and Canarian green mojo sauce; beef bone-marrow nigiri sushi (honoring the classic cocido madrileño); and oxtail with teriyaki sauce. For dessert, don't miss the reinvented hot chocolate with crispy churros. Ⓢ *Average main: €31* ✉ *Hotel Wellington, Velázquez 6, Salamanca* ☎ *91/575–4400* ⊕ *www.restaurantekabuki.com* ◷ *Closed Sun. No lunch Sat.* Ⓜ *Retiro, Príncipe de Vergara* ✛ *H2.*

$$$
SEAFOOD
✕**La Trainera.** With its nautical theme and maze of little dining rooms, this informal restaurant is all about fresh seafood—the best that money can buy. Crab, lobster, shrimp, mussels, and a dozen other types of shellfish are served by weight in *raciones* (large portions). Many Spanish diners share several plates of these shellfish as their entire meal, but the grilled hake, sole, or turbot makes an unbeatable second course. To accompany the legendary *carabineros* (giant scarlet shrimp), skip the listless house wine and go for a bottle of Albariño from the southern Galician coast. Ⓢ *Average main: €27* ✉ *Lagasca 60, Salamanca*

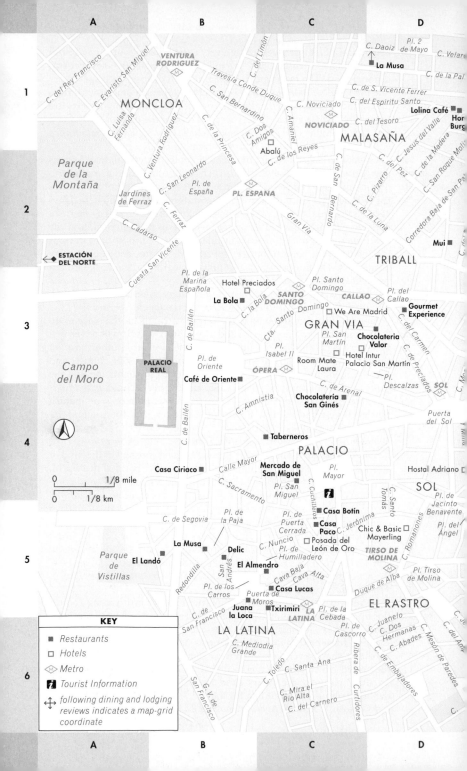

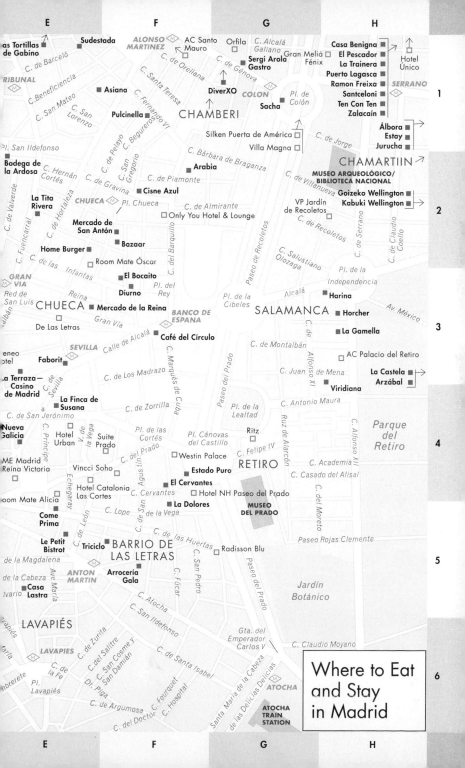

Where to Eat
and Stay
in Madrid

☎ *91/576–8035* ⊕ *www.latrainera.es* ⊘ *Closed Sun. and Aug.* Ⓜ *Serrano* ✣ *H1.*

$$ ✕ **Puerto Lagasca.** Old-style tapas bars with floors littered with prawn
TAPAS tails and olive pits are still in the majority in the city, but there's a
new breed that has more in common with the city's upscale restaurants, though with prices that don't leave you gasping for air when the
check arrives. Puerto Lagasca, with dishes based on what's in season,
is one of the best tapas bars in its league, where diners can share traditional appetizers like salmorejo, roasted peppers, fresh anchovies, a
tomato and tuna salad, and good assortment of meat and fish options—
among the latter, a good pick is the fried-fish sampler. Note that it also
serves half portions. Ⓢ *Average main: €17* ⊠ *Lagasca 81, Salamanca*
☎ *91/576–4111* ⊕ *puertolagasca.com* ⊘ *No dinner Sun.* Ⓜ *Nuñez de
Balboa* ✣ *H1.*

$$$$ ✕ **Ramon Freixa.** Celebrity-chef Ferran Adrià once stated that his dream
SPANISH was to cook for only one guest at a time, and Ramon Freixa, a Catalan and another among the handful of chefs who are raising the bar of
Spanish cuisine, gets close to Adrià's fantasy at this small restaurant
with only seven tables. The experience in the baroque-inspired setting is
best enjoyed by true connoisseurs, considering that some of the dishes
are so sophisticated and intricate they're served on up to three different
plates. "Less is more" is definitely not the motto here, as dishes like the
"deconstructed tomato"—10 different varieties of tomato cooked in 10
different ways—proves, but if you have the wallet, this is a delicious
adventure. Ⓢ *Average main: €40* ⊠ *Hotel Selenza, Claudio Coello 67,
Salamanca* ☎ *91/781–8262* ⊕ *www.ramonfreixamadrid.com* ⊜ *Reservations essential* ⊘ *Closed Sun. and Mon.* Ⓜ *Serrano* ✣ *H1.*

$$ ✕ **Ten Con Ten.** Sophisticated upscale madrileños and local celebrities
SPANISH all flock to this bustling Asturian-inspired restaurant that's lately on
everyone's must-do list. It is a positive balance between two sometimes
very clashing elements: PR buzz and food quality. Located at the core
of the city's main shopping district, it displays a retro bourgeois look
with two well defined spaces: a massive rectangular bar area with some
tall wooden tables—usually crowded during the after-work hours by
posh businessmen sipping fancy cocktails—and a classier dining room
at the back. The menu is long and eclectic but where it stands out
is in those dishes with local roots: the fried rice with queen scallops
(*zamburiñas*), the roasted octopus, the monkfish hamburger, or the
Asturian beans (*verdinas*) with quail. Reserve well in advance and go
for lunch if you want to avoid noise and bustle. Ⓢ *Average main: €22*
⊠ *Ayala 6, Salamanca* ☎ *91/575–9254* ⊕ *www.restaurantetenconten.
com* Ⓜ *Serrano* ✣ *H1.*

RETIRO

$$ ✕ **Arzábal.** The only thing typical about this popular tapas bar—so
TAPAS popular that it now has two locations on the same block (the other on
Fodor's Choice the corner of Menéndez Pelayo)—are the Iberian hams hanging from
★ the ceiling and the paper tablecloths; the quality and sophistication of
the food, however, stand well out and above the crowd. Go to the bar
for a quick bite, like fresh salty anchovies with bread and tomato, fried
artichokes, or a bowl of salmorejo accompanied by a cold beer or a glass

of wine. At the handful of tables, hungry locals share more elaborate fare: think sautéed rice with truffle and wild mushrooms, quail with sautéed onions, or a tomato-and-white tuna-belly salad. Note that it also serves half portions of many dishes. $ *Average main: €16* ⊠ *Dr. Castelo 2, Retiro* ☎ *91/557–2691* ⊕ *H3.*

$$$$ ✕ **Horcher.** The faithful continue to fill this traditional shrine to fine
GERMAN dining, once considered Madrid's best restaurant and still worth seeking out. Wild boar, venison, hare, partridge, and wild duck, as well as unique burgers (monkfish, swordfish, or the juicy German-style, made with beef and veal) are standard options. Ox stroganoff with noodles and a Pommery mustard sauce, pork chops with sauerkraut, and *baumkuchen* (a chocolate-covered fruit-and-cake dessert) reflect the restaurant's Germanic roots. The dining room is decorated with brocade and antique Austrian porcelain; an ample selection of French and German wines rounds out the menu. $ *Average main: €39* ⊠ *Alfonso XII 6, Retiro* ☎ *91/522–0731* ⊕ *www.restaurantehorcher.com* ⌣ *Reservations essential* 🏛 *Jacket and tie* ⊗ *Closed Sun., Easter wk, and Aug. No lunch Sat.* Ⓜ *Retiro* ⊕ *H3.*

$$ ✕ **La Castela.** Traditional taverns with tin-top bars, beer and vermouth
TAPAS cooled with stainless-steel coils, and uberefficient waiters are a dying breed in Madrid, but this one, just a couple of blocks from the Retiro park, is one of the best. It's always busy with locals clamoring over plates of sautéed wild mushrooms, fresh salty anchovies served with a cucumber and tomato salad (*pipirrana*), or clams in an Andalusian white wine sauce. You can stop for a quick bite at the bar—they'll serve you a free tapa with every drink—or enjoy heartier choices, such as the chickpea and king prawn stew, in the homey dining room at the back. $ *Average main: €18* ⊠ *C. Doctor Castelo 22, Retiro* ☎ *91/574–0015* ⊕ *www.lacastela.com* ⌣ *Reservations essential* ⊗ *Closed Sun.* Ⓜ *Ibiza* ⊕ *H3.*

$$ ✕ **La Gamella.** Classic American dishes—Caesar salad, regular or gour-
AMERICAN met hamburgers, steak tartare—as well as fusion Mediterranean-American options are the heart of the reasonably priced menu at this perennially popular dinner spot. The sophisticated rust-red, blue, and yellow dining room, batik tablecloths, and oversize plates are complemented by attentive service. The lunchtime menú del día is a good value, as is the Sunday American-style brunch. $ *Average main: €21* ⊠ *Alfonso XII 4, Retiro* ☎ *91/532–4509* ⊕ *www.lagamella.com* ⊗ *No dinner Sun.* Ⓜ *Retiro* ⊕ *H3.*

$$$$ ✕ **Viridiana.** A black-and-white color scheme punctuated with prints
ECLECTIC from Luis Buñuel's classic film, the restaurant's namesake, is the hallmark of this relaxed, somewhat cramped bistro. Iconoclast chef Abraham Garcia says "market-based" is too narrow a description for his creative menu, which changes every two weeks: standards include *foie de pato con chutney de frutas* (duck liver with fruit chutney) and *huevos sobre mousse de hongos* (eggs on a mushroom mousse with black truffle). The wine choices can be overwhelming, so ask for help, and save room for one of the creative desserts such as the coconut *pannacota* with sour chocolate, or the Abraham's sorbet with firewater. $ *Average main: €30* ⊠ *Juan de Mena 14, Retiro* ☎ *91/531–1039* ⊕ *www.*

restauranteviridiana.com ♠ *Reservations essential* ⊘ *Closed Sun. and Easter* Ⓜ *Retiro* ✛ *G3.*

$$$$ ✕ **Zalacaín.** This restaurant, decorated in dramatic dark wood, gleaming
BASQUE silver, and apricot hues, introduced nouvelle Basque cuisine to Spain
Fodor's Choice in the 1970s and has since become a Madrid classic. It's particularly
★ known for using the best and freshest seasonal products available as
well as for having the best service in town. Making use of ingredients
such as various fungi, game, and hard-to-find seafood, the food here
tends to be unusual—it's not one of those places where they cook with
liquid nitrogen, yet you won't find these dishes elsewhere. $ *Average
main: €34* ✉ *Alvarez de Baena 4, Salamanca* ☎ *91/561–4840* ⊕ *www.
restaurantezalacain.com* ♠ *Reservations essential* 🏛 *Jacket and tie*
⊘ *Closed Sun., Easter wk, and Aug. No lunch Sat.* Ⓜ *Gregorio Marañón* ✛ *H1.*

CHAMARTÍN AND TETUÁN

CHAMARTÍN

$$$ ✕ **Casa Benigna.** Owner Don Norberto takes gracious care in what he
SPANISH does, providing a carefully chosen and health conscious menu and
Fodor's Choice painstakingly selected wines to devoted customers. Evidence of crafts-
★ manship is alive in every corner of the casual and understated hide-
away, from the best rice in the city (cooked with extra-flat paella pans
especially manufactured for the restaurant) to the ceramic plates from
Talavera, but the star attraction is the chef and his astounding knowl-
edge of food (he has his own brand of tuna, olive oil, and balsamic
vinegar). He generously talks (and often sings) to his guests without
ever looking at his watch. $ *Average main: €26* ✉ *Benigno Soto 9,
Chamartín* ☎ *91/416–9357* ♠ *Reservations essential* ⊘ *Closed Christ-
mas wk, Easter wk, and Aug. No dinner Sun. and Mon.* Ⓜ *Concha
Espina, Prosperidad* ✛ *H1.*

$$ ✕ **Sacha.** Playful sketches decorate the walls of this French bistro–style
SPANISH restaurant filled with oversize antique furniture. The cuisine is provin-
cial Spanish with a touch of imagination. The *lasaña de erizo de mar*
(sea urchin lasagna), *arroz con setas y perdiz* (rice with mushrooms and
partridge), and the *Villagodio* (a thick, grilled cut of beef) are just some
of the house specialties. The small terrace, secluded and sheltered by
trees, is popular in the summer. $ *Average main: €22* ✉ *Juan Hurtado
de Mendoza 11, Chamartín* ☎ *91/345–5952* ♠ *Reservations essential*
⊘ *Closed Sun., Easter, and Aug.* Ⓜ *Cuzco* ✛ *G1.*

TETUÁN

$$$$ ✕ **DiverXO.** When you ask a madrileño about a remarkable food expe-
ECLECTIC rience—something that stirs the senses, not just feeds the appetite—
Fodor's Choice David Muñoz's rather austere venue is often the first name you'll hear.
★ With a wide-ranging background that includes stints at London's Nobu
and Hakkasan, this young, cheerful chef has an uncanny ability to
mix and tamper with traditions and techniques without transgressing
them. Witness his Spanish tortilla: a dough ball filled with potato and
caramelized onions with a side of bean purée and Mexican chili sauce,
reminiscent of both the Spanish omelet and Chinese dim sum. The

restaurant serves only three sampler menus—the most challenging is an 11-dish proposal, for €120. Getting a table at this food shrine is akin to buying a ticket for the Super Bowl, so call well ahead—you can make reservations up to a month in advance. (As of this writing, the restaurant will move to a nearby and more flamboyant location, the NH Eurobuilding, sometime in summer 2014.) $ *Average main: €35* ⊠ *Pensamiento 28, Tetuán* 🕾 *91/570–0766* ⊕ *diverxo.com* ⌲ *Reservations essential* ⊘ *Closed Sun. and Mon.* Ⓜ *Tetúan* ✛ *G1.*

$$ ✕ **Sudestada.** Before Estanis Carenzo and Pablo Giudice, the two Argen-
ASIAN FUSION   tinians who own this place, brought their pungent and tongue-tingling curries into the city, madrileños were used to rather soulless understandings of South Asian food. They alone reeducated the palates of scores of local diners with Vietnamese, Thai, Malaysian, and Laotian recipes in a venue that resembles a neat, upscale dinner, with leather benches and wood floors. The short menu comprises clients' favorites—like the pork and crab spring rolls and the braised beef cheeks in a red curry sauce—to which they add some daily specials. They also have three different sampler menus. Try a Tom Collins with lychees and lemon to accompany your meal. $ *Average main: €22* ⊠ *Ponzano 85, Tetuán* 🕾 *91/533–4154* ⊘ *Closed Sun. and Mon.* Ⓜ *Ríos Rosas* ✛ *E1.*

WHERE TO STAY

Madrid kicked off the new millennium with a hotel boom, and the last decade has seen its number of hotel rooms nearly double. From 2009 to 2010 alone, the number of hotel rooms available increased by 4,000, and the failed bids to host the Olympic Games pushed up the total amount to about 900 hotels and 86,000 rooms by early 2014.

Plenty of the new arrivals are medium-price chain hotels that try to combine striking design with affordable prices. A step higher is the handful of new hotels that lure the hip crowd with top-notch design and superb food and nightlife. These have caused quite a stir in the five-star range and forced some of the more traditional hotels—long favored by dignitaries, star athletes, and artists—to enhance their food and service. Meanwhile, hostals and small hotels have shown that low prices can walk hand in hand with good taste and friendly service.

The Gran Vía, a big commercial street and Madrid's equivalent to Broadway in New York, cuts through many neighborhoods. During the day it has a good feel of Madrid's hustle and bustle and nightlife energy, but it does lose a bit of its charm when the stores are closed.

Use the coordinate (✛ B2) at the end of each listing to locate a site on the corresponding map.

BEST BETS FOR MADRID LODGING

Having trouble deciding where to stay in Madrid? Fodor's writers have selected some of their favorites in the lists below. Details are in the full reviews.

2

Fodor's Choice★

AC Palacio del Retiro, $$$$, p. 119

AC Santo Mauro, $$$$, p. 118

De las Letras, $$, p. 116

Hostal Adriano, $, p. 116

Hotel Urban, $$$$, p. 116

Only You Hotel & Lounge, $$$, p. 118

Room Mate Alicia, $$, p. 117

Room Mate Óscar, $, p. 118

Villa Magna, $$$$, p. 119

By Price

$

Abalú, p. 118

Chic & Basic Mayerling, p. 115

Hostal Adriano, p. 116

Room Mate Óscar, p. 118

We Are Madrid, p. 115

$$

Hotel Catalonia Las Cortes, p. 116

Hotel NH Paseo del Prado, p. 116

Hotel Preciados, p. 116

Room Mate Alicia, p. 117

Silken Puerta de América, p. 120

$$$

Hotel Único, p. 119

Only You Hotel & Lounge, p. 118

Radisson Blu, p. 117

$$$$

AC Santo Mauro, p. 118

Hotel Urban, p. 116

Orfila, p. 119

Westin Palace, p. 118

By Experience

MOST CHARMING

Abalú, $, p. 118

AC Santo Mauro, $$$$, p. 118

Hostal Adriano, $, p. 116

Hotel Intur Palacio San Martín, $$, p. 114

Orfila, $$$$, p. 119

Room Mate Alicia, $$, p. 117

Room Mate Laura, $, p. 115

Hotel Único, $$$, p. 119

MOST HISTORIC

Hotel Intur Palacio San Martín, $$, p. 114

Ritz, $$$$, p. 120

Westin Palace, $$$$, p. 118

BEST DESIGN

Abalú, $, p. 118

De las Letras, $$, p. 116

Hotel Urban, $$$$, p. 116

ME Madrid Reina Victoria, $$$, p. 117

Only You Hotel & Lounge, $$$, p. 118

Room Mate Alicia, $$, p. 117

Room Mate Laura, $, p. 115

Room Mate Óscar, $, p. 118

Hotel Único, $$$, p. 119

Silken Puerta de América, $$, p. 120

Villa Magna, $$$$, p. 119

Vincci Soho, $$, p. 118

BEST FOR FAMILIES

Abalú, $, p. 118

Suite Prado, $, p. 117

VP Jardín de Recoletos, $$, p. 119

We Are Madrid, $, p. 115

MOST CENTRAL

Hotel Intur Palacio San Martín, $$, p. 114

Hotel Urban, $$$$, p. 116

Posada del León de Oro, $$, p. 115

Radisson Blu, $$$, p. 117

Ritz, $$$$, p. 120

Room Mate Alicia, $$, p. 117

Room Mate Laura, $, p. 115

Westin Palace, $$$$, p. 118

BEST FOR HIPSTERS

Abalú, $, p. 118

Chic & Basic Mayerling, $, p. 115

De las Letras, $$, p. 116

Hostal Adriano, $, p. 116

Hotel Urban, $$$$, p. 116

ME Madrid Reina Victoria, $$$, p. 117

Posada del León de Oro, $$, p. 115

Room Mate Óscar, $, p. 118

BEST VIEWS

ME Madrid Reina Victoria, $$$, p. 117

Westin Palace, $$$$, p. 118

BEST FOR BUSINESS TRAVELERS

AC Palacio del Retiro, $$$$, p. 119

AC Santo Mauro, $$$$, p. 118

WHERE SHOULD I STAY?

	Neighborhood Vibe	Pros	Cons
Palacio and Sol	Anchored by the locally flavored Plaza Mayor, this historic quarter is full of narrow streets and taverns.	Has the most traditional feel of Madrid neighborhoods; lodging and dining of all sorts, including many inexpensive (though usually undistinguished) hostals and old-flavor taverns.	Can be tough to navigate; many tourist traps.
Barrio de las Letras (including Carrera de San Jerónimo and Paseo del Prado)	A magnet for tourists, this classic literary nest has several pedestrian-only streets. Most of the exciting new hotels are here.	Renovated Plaza Santa Ana and Plaza del Ángel; the emergence of posh hotels and restaurants; conveniently between the oldest part of the city and all the major art museums.	Noisy, especially around Plaza Santa Ana; some bars and restaurants overpriced due to the tourists.
Chueca and Malasaña	Vibrant and bustling, this is where you want to be if you're past your twenties but still don't want to be in bed before midnight.	These barrios burst with a bit of everything: busy nightlife, alternative shops, charming cafés, and fancy and inexpensive local and international restaurants.	Extremely loud, especially on the weekends; dirtier than most other neighborhoods.
Chamberí, Salamanca, and Retiro	Swanky, posh, and safe, these are the neighborhoods many high-end hotels and restaurants call home.	Quiet at day's end; plenty of good restaurants; home to the upscale shopping (Salamanca) and residential (Salamanca and the eastern side of Retiro) areas.	Blander and with less character (except for the expensive area of Retiro, which is also less lively) than other districts; expensive.

Prices in the reviews are the lowest cost of a standard double room in high season. Hotel reviews have been shortened. For full information, visit Fodors.com.

WHAT IT COSTS IN EUROS				
	$	$$	$$$	$$$$
HOTELS	under €125	€125–€174	€175–€225	over €225

Prices are for two people in a standard double room in high season.

PALACIO, LA LATINA, AND SOL

PALACIO

$$ ⊞ **Hotel Intur Palacio San Martín.** In an unbeatable location across from
HOTEL   one of Madrid's most celebrated monuments (the Convent of Descalzas), this hotel, once the U.S. embassy and later a luxurious residential building crowded with noblemen, still exudes a kind of glory. **Pros:**

charming location; spacious rooms. **Cons:** average-quality restaurant. [$] *Rooms from: €160* ✉ *Pl. de San Martín 5, Palacio* ☎ *91/701–5000* 🌐 *www.intur.com* 🛏 *94 rooms, 8 suites* 🍴 *No meals* [M] *Ópera, Callao* ✥ *C3.*

$ HOTEL 🏨 **Room Mate Laura.** On Plaza de las Descalzas, this hotel is in an old apartment building that's been refurbished following the company's mantra of good distinctive design without burning a hole in the customer's pocket. **Pros:** friendly service; kitchenettes make this ideal for long stays. **Cons:** only the best rooms have views of the convent; no restaurant; some bathrooms need to be revamped. [$] *Rooms from: €110* ✉ *Travesía de Trujillos 3, Palacio* ☎ *91/701–1670* 🌐 *www.roommatehotels.com* 🛏 *36 rooms* 🍴 *No meals* [M] *Ópera* ✥ *C3.*

$ RENTAL 🏨 **We Are Madrid.** A good option among the apartment offerings that have sprouted around Madrid in the last couple of years, offering studios or one-bedroom apartments that accomodate three or five people. **Pros:** good value; well-stocked apartments. **Cons:** studios only have sofa beds; only the one-bedroom apartments have an oven in the kitchen; minimum three-day stay on weekends, and two-day stay on weekdays. [$] *Rooms from: €100* ✉ *Costanilla de los Ángeles 16, Palacio* ☎ *91/126–9106* 🌐 *www.wearemadrid.net* 🛏 *3 studios, 3 apartments* 🍴 *No meals* [M] *Gran Vía, Sol* ✥ *C3.*

LA LATINA

$$ HOTEL 🏨 **Posada del León de Oro.** This beautifully refurbished late-19th-century guesthouse is nestled in one of the most happening streets of the city. **Pros:** unbeatable location; lively atmosphere; family rooms can fit four people. **Cons:** double rooms facing the inside courtyard are quite small; rooms on the first floor and those facing the street can get noisy on weekends. [$] *Rooms from: €140* ✉ *Cava Baja 12, La Latina* ☎ *91/119–1494* 🌐 *www.posadadelleondeoro.com* 🛏 *27 rooms* 🍴 *No meals* [M] *La Latina* ✥ *C5.*

SOL

$ HOTEL 🏨 **Ateneo Hotel.** Spacious rooms are offered in this restored 18th-century building, once home to the Ateneo—a club founded in 1835 to promote freedom of thought. **Pros:** sizeable rooms; triple and quadruple rooms available. **Cons:** though now pedestrianized and safe (thanks to the police station), the street still attracts some sketchy characters; noisy area. [$] *Rooms from: €95* ✉ *Montera 22, Sol* ☎ *91/521–2012* 🌐 *www.hotel-ateneo.com* 🛏 *38 rooms, 6 suites* 🍴 *Breakfast* [M] *Gran Vía, Sol* ✥ *E3.*

$ HOTEL 🏨 **Chic & Basic Mayerling.** A former textile wholesaler's premises is now a small boutique hotel, just a few blocks off Plaza Mayor and Plaza Santa Ana, and it lives up to the franchise name by offering sleek minimalism at just the right value. **Pros:** some rooms accommodate up to three people; nice terrace; free Wi-Fi; comfortable beds; great location. **Cons:** rooms are smallish by U.S. standards; white walls show dirt; services are spartan. [$] *Rooms from: €100* ✉ *Conde de Romanones 6, Sol* ☎ *91/420–1580* 🌐 *www.chicandbasic.com* 🛏 *22 rooms* 🍴 *Breakfast* [M] *Tirso de Molina* ✥ *D5.*

$$ HOTEL Fodor's Choice ★ **De Las Letras.** Modern-pop interior design seamlessly respects and accents the original details of this 1917 building on the bustling Gran Vía. **Pros:** young vibe; gym with personal trainers; happening rooftop bar. **Cons:** lower rooms facing noisy Gran Vía could be better insulated. [$] *Rooms from: €142* ✉ *Gran Vía 11, Sol* ☎ *91/523–7980* 🌐 *www.hoteldelasletras.com* 🛏 *103 rooms, 7 suites* 🍴 *No meals* [M] *Banco de España* ✣ *E3.*

$ HOTEL Fodor's Choice ★ **Hostal Adriano.** Tucked away on a street with dozens of bland competitors a couple of blocks from Sol, this hotel really stands out for its price and quality. **Pros:** friendly service; great value; charming touches. **Cons:** short on facilities. [$] *Rooms from: €65* ✉ *De la Cruz 26, 4th fl., Sol* ☎ *91/521–1339* 🌐 *www.hostaladriano.com* 🛏 *22 rooms* 🍴 *No meals* [M] *Sol* ✣ *D4.*

$$ HOTEL **Hotel Preciados.** In a 19th-century building on the quieter edge of one of Madrid's main shopping areas, this hotel is both charming and convenient. **Pros:** conveniently located; good-size bathrooms; free Wi-Fi; happening bar/restaurant. **Cons:** expensive breakfast; bustling area. [$] *Rooms from: €160* ✉ *C. Preciados 37, Sol* ☎ *91/454–4400* 🌐 *www.preciadoshotel.com* 🛏 *95 rooms, 6 suites* 🍴 *No meals* [M] *Callao* ✣ *B3.*

BARRIO DE LAS LETRAS

$$ HOTEL **Catalonia Puerta del Sol.** The regal cobblestone corridor leading to the reception desk, the atrium with walls made partly of original granite blocks, and the magnificent main wooden staircase presided over by a lion statue best reveal this building's 18th-century origins. **Pros:** grand, quiet building; spacious rooms. **Cons:** street looks a bit scruffy. [$] *Rooms from: €130* ✉ *C. Atocha 23, Barrio de las Letras* ☎ *91/369–7171* 🌐 *www.hoteles-catalonia.es* 🛏 *63 rooms* 🍴 *No meals* [M] *Tirso de Molina* ✣ *D4.*

$$ HOTEL **Hotel Catalonia Las Cortes.** A late-18th-century palace a few yards from Plaza Santa Ana, formerly owned by the Duke of Noblejas, this hotel retains a good part of its aristocratic past. **Pros:** tastefully decorated rooms; big walk-in shower; triple rooms available; great location. **Cons:** common areas are rather dull. [$] *Rooms from: €140* ✉ *Prado 6, Barrio de las Letras* ☎ *91/389–6051* 🌐 *www.hoteles-catalonia.com* 🛏 *64 rooms, 10 suites* 🍴 *No meals* [M] *Sevilla, Antón Martín* ✣ *E4.*

$$ HOTEL **Hotel NH Paseo del Prado.** Once the residence of a count, this hotel a block from the Prado is a reasonable yet luxurious alternative to the five-star establishments that populate the area. **Pros:** sizable and elegant bathrooms; good location. **Cons:** you'll have to upgrade if you want good views; extra fee for in-room Wi-Fi. [$] *Rooms from: €150* ✉ *Pl. Cánovas del Castillo 4, Barrio de las Letras* ☎ *91/330–2400* 🌐 *www.nh-hoteles.es* 🛏 *114 rooms, 1 suite* 🍴 *No meals* [M] *Banco de España* ✣ *F4.*

$$$$ HOTEL Fodor's Choice ★ **Hotel Urban.** This is the hotel that best conveys Madrid's new cosmopolitan spirit, with its stylish mix of authentic ancient artifacts and daring sophistication. **Pros:** excellent restaurant and happening bar; rooftop swimming pool. **Cons:** some rooms are small; rooms near the elevator can be noisy. [$] *Rooms from: €240* ✉ *C. de San Jerónimo 34,*

CLOSE UP

Lodging Alternatives

If you want a home base that's roomy enough for a family and comes with cooking facilities, consider a furnished rental. These can save you money, too. Apartment rentals are increasingly popular in Madrid. Rentals by the day or week can be arranged, though prices may rise for short stays. Prices range from €100 to €300 per day depending on the quality of

the accommodations, but perfectly acceptable lodging for four can be found for around €175 per night. These are just a few of the apartment rental agencies that Fodorites are using these days: ⊕ www.niumba. com; ⊕ www.spain-select.com/ en_US; ⊕ www.habitatapartments. com/madrid-apartments; ⊕ www. apartinmadrid.com.

Barrio de las Letras ☎ 91/787–7770 ⊕ *www.derbyhotels.com* ➥ *96 rooms, 7 suites* ⊙ *No meals* Ⓜ *Sevilla* ✛ *E4.*

$$$
HOTEL
🏨 **ME Madrid Reina Victoria.** In an unbeatable location, this ultramodern hotel retains a few reminders of the era when bullfighters would convene here before setting off to Las Ventas—a few bulls' heads hang in the lounge and some abstract pictures of bullfighting are scattered around, but the old flair has been superseded by cutting-edge amenities. **Pros:** modern vibe and high-tech gadgetry; trendy bars and restaurant; great location. **Cons:** the need to preserve some of the building's historical features makes some rooms rather small. Ⓢ *Rooms from: €185* ✉ *Pl. Santa Ana 14, Barrio de las Letras* ☎ 91/531–4500 ⊕ *www.memadrid. com* ➥ *182 rooms, 9 suites* ⊙ *No meals* Ⓜ *Sol* ✛ *E4.*

$$$
HOTEL
🏨 **Radisson Blu.** The Radisson chain may not be Scandinavian anymore, but this outpost across from the Prado retains the austere lines of its lineage, counterbalanced by painstaking attention to detail. **Pros:** terrific location; wide array of services. **Cons:** some standard rooms are rather small; pricey breakfast. Ⓢ *Rooms from: €190* ✉ *Moratín 52, Barrio de las Letras* ☎ 91/524–2626 ⊕ *www.radissonblu.com/pradohotel-madrid* ➥ *54 rooms, 6 suites* ⊙ *No meals* Ⓜ *Atocha* ✛ *G5.*

$$
HOTEL
Fodor'sChoice
★
🏨 **Room Mate Alicia.** The all-white lobby with curving walls, ceiling, and lamps, and the fancy gastrobar facing Plaza Santa Ana set the hip mood for the mostly young urbanites who stay in this former trench coat factory. **Pros:** great value; chic design; laid-back atmosphere; unbeatable location. **Cons:** standard rooms are small; some might not care for the zero-privacy bathroom spaces. Ⓢ *Rooms from: €130* ✉ *Prado 2, Barrio de las Letras* ☎ 91/389–6095 ⊕ *www.room-matehoteles.com* ➥ *34 rooms, 3 suites* ⊙ *No meals* Ⓜ *Sevilla* ✛ *E5.*

$
HOTEL
🏨 **Suite Prado.** Popular with Americans, this stylish apartment hotel is near the Prado, the Thyssen-Bornemisza, and the Plaza Santa Ana tapas area. **Pros:** large rooms; great for families and longer stays. **Cons:** a bit noisy; some of the kitchens could use revamping. Ⓢ *Rooms from: €110* ✉ *Manuel Fernández y González 10, Barrio de las Letras*

☎ *91/420–2318* 🌐 *www.suiteprado.com* 🛏 *18 apartments* 🍴 *Multiple meal plans* [M] *Sevilla* ✣ *F4.*

$$ HOTEL 🏨 **Vincci Soho.** Faithful to its surname, this hotel seems as if it's been transplanted from London or New York into one of Madrid's busiest neighborhoods—everything on the ground floor emphasizes urban elegance and imagination. **Pros:** stylish; central location; great breakfast buffet; sheltered quiet courtyard. **Cons:** standard rooms are rather small and some can be noisy. [$] *Rooms from: €140* ✉ *Prado 18, Barrio de las Letras* ☎ *91/141–4100* 🌐 *www.vinccihoteles.com* 🛏 *167 rooms* 🍴 *No meals* [M] *Sevilla, Antón Martín* ✣ *F4.*

$$$$ HOTEL 🏨 **Westin Palace.** Built in 1912, Madrid's most famous grand hotel is a Belle Époque creation of Alfonso XIII and has hosted the likes of Salvador Dalí, Marlon Brando, Rita Hayworth, and Madonna. **Pros:** grand hotel with tons of history; weekend brunch with opera performances. **Cons:** standard rooms face a backstreet; pricey in-room Internet. [$] *Rooms from: €230* ✉ *Pl. de las Cortés 7, Barrio de las Letras* ☎ *91/360–8000* 🌐 *www.palacemadrid.com* 🛏 *467 rooms, 45 suites* 🍴 *No meals* [M] *Banco de España, Sevilla* ✣ *F4.*

CHUECA, MALASAÑA, AND CHAMBERÍ

CHUECA

$$$ HOTEL Fodor'sChoice ★ 🏨 **Only You Hotel & Lounge.** The Ibizan owners of this hotel bring that island's mix of glamour, energy, and cutting-edge music and design to one of Madrid's most happening neighborhoods, Chueca. **Pros:** great location; affable service; plenty of amenities; late check-out (for example, if you check in at 6 pm you won't have to leave until 6 pm the next day). **Cons:** the bed area in the rooms is a bit cramped; you'll need to pay a bit more to get rooms with views of Barquillo Street. [$] *Rooms from: €190* ✉ *Calle Barquillo 21, Chueca* ☎ *91/005–2222* 🌐 *www.onlyyouhotels.com/en* 🛏 *70 rooms* 🍴 *No meals* ✣ *F2.*

$ HOTEL Fodor'sChoice ★ 🏨 **Room Mate Óscar.** Bold, bright, and modern, the flagship Room Mate is undeniably hip and glamorous. **Pros:** friendly staff; hip guests; fashionable facilities. **Cons:** noisy street; may be *too* happening for some. [$] *Rooms from: €100* ✉ *Pl. Vázquez de Mella 12, Chueca* ☎ *91/701–1173* 🌐 *www.room-matehoteles.com* 🛏 *69 rooms, 6 suites* 🍴 *Breakfast* [M] *Chueca* ✣ *E2.*

MALASAÑA

$ HOTEL 🏨 **Abalú.** Each of the lodging options in this hotel, in the heart of one of the city's youngest and liveliest neighborhoods, is a small oasis of singularity. **Pros:** unique room decoration; charming café. **Cons:** rooms smaller than average; Wi-Fi is not free. [$] *Rooms from: €95* ✉ *Pez 19, Malasaña* ☎ *91/531–4744* 🌐 *www.hotelabalu.com* 🛏 *8 rooms, 8 suites, 12 apartments* 🍴 *Breakfast* [M] *Noviciado* ✣ *C1.*

CHAMBERÍ

$$$$ HOTEL Fodor'sChoice ★ 🏨 **AC Santo Mauro.** Once the Canadian embassy, this turn-of-the-20th-century mansion is now an intimate luxury hotel, an oasis of calm a short walk from the city center. **Pros:** quite private; sizable rooms with comfortable beds; good restaurant; exclusive quiet gardens. **Cons:**

pricey breakfast; not in the historic center. $ *Rooms from: €280* ⊠ *Zurbano 36, Chamberí* ☎ *91/319–6900* ⊕ *www.ac-hotels.com* ⇆ *51 rooms* ❧⚭*No meals* Ⓜ *Alonso Martínez, Rubén Darío* ✛ *F1.*

$$$$
HOTEL

⛩ **Orfila.** Hidden away on a leafy little residential street not far from Plaza Colón, this elegant 1886 town house has every comfort of the larger five-star Madrid hotels, but in more intimate surroundings. **Pros:** quiet street; refined interiors; attentive service; free Wi-Fi. **Cons:** all rooms except for the suites have bathtubs and no stand-alone showers; small TVs. $ *Rooms from: €270* ⊠ *Orfila 6, Chamberí* ☎ *91/702–7770* ⊕ *www.hotelorfila.com* ⇆ *20 rooms, 12 suites* ❧⚭*No meals* Ⓜ *Alonso Martínez* ✛ *G1.*

SALAMANCA AND RETIRO

SALAMANCA

$$$$
HOTEL

⛩ **Gran Meliá Fénix.** A Madrid institution, this hotel is a mere hop from the posh shops of Calle Serrano. **Pros:** close to shopping; great breakfast buffet; quadruple rooms accommodate two adults and two children available; exclusive wellness center. **Cons:** rather small bathrooms; below-average restaurant. $ *Rooms from: €230* ⊠ *Hermosilla 2, Salamanca* ☎ *91/431–6700* ⊕ *www.solmelia.com* ⇆ *214 rooms, 11 suites* ❧⚭*No meals* Ⓜ *Colón* ✛ *H1.*

$$$
HOTEL

⛩ **Hotel Único.** Discreetly tucked away in the midst of the Salamanca shopping district, this is a gem of a boutique hotel. **Pros:** great interior design; personalized service; Ramon Freixa restaurant. **Cons:** rooms facing the street can be noisy; fewer facilities than some of the larger hotels. $ *Rooms from: €220* ⊠ *Claudio Coello 67, Salamanca* ☎ *91/781–0173* ⊕ *www.unicohotelmadrid.com* ⇆ *44 rooms, 5 suites* ❧⚭*No meals* ✛ *H1.*

$$$$
HOTEL
Fodor's Choice
★

⛩ **Villa Magna.** There are luxury hotels in Madrid with grander history or more cutting-edge design, yet none walks along that slippery border between the classic and the modern with as much ease and grace as the Villa Magna. **Pros:** attentive service; rooms larger than the Madrid average; right in the main shopping area; great restaurants (Tse Yang and Villa Magna). **Cons:** expensive room service; the exterior looks rather dull. $ *Rooms from: €325* ⊠ *Paseo de la Castellana 22, Salamanca* ☎ *91/587–1234* ⊕ *www.villamagna.es* ⇆ *150 rooms* ❧⚭*No meals* ✛ *G1.*

$$
HOTEL

⛩ **VP Jardín de Recoletos.** This boutique apartment hotel offers great value on a quiet street just a couple blocks from the Retiro Park and Madrid's main shopping area. **Pros:** spacious rooms with kitchens; good restaurant; free Wi-Fi. **Cons:** the garden closes at midnight and when crowded can be noisy $ *Rooms from: €160* ⊠ *Gil de Santivañes 6, Salamanca* ☎ *91/781–1640* ⊕ *www.recoletos-hotel.com* ⇆ *36 rooms, 7 suites* ❧⚭*No meals* Ⓜ *Colón* ✛ *H2.*

RETIRO

$$$$
HOTEL
Fodor's Choice
★

⛩ **AC Palacio del Retiro.** A palatial early-20th-century building, once owned by a noble family with extravagant habits (the elevator carried their horses up and down from the rooftop exercise ring), this spectacular hotel epitomizes tasteful modern style. **Pros:** spacious, stylish rooms;

within walking distance of the Prado; bathrooms stocked with all sorts of complimentary products. **Cons:** pricey breakfast; lower rooms facing the park can get noisy. [$] *Rooms from: €265* ✉ *Alfonso XII 14, Retiro* ☎ *91/523–7460* ⊕ *www.ac-hotels.com* ☞ *50 rooms, 8 suites* ⦿ *No meals* Ⓜ *Retiro* ✛ *H3*.

$$$$ ⦿ **Ritz.** Alfonso XIII, about to marry Queen Victoria's granddaughter,
HOTEL encouraged and personally supervised the construction of this hotel—the most exclusive in Spain—for his royal guests, and he performed the opening ceremony in 1910. **Pros:** old-world flair; lovely tearoom and summer terrace; excellent location. **Cons:** what's classic for some may feel stuffy and outdated to others. [$] *Rooms from: €295* ✉ *Pl. de la Lealtad 5, Retiro* ☎ *91/701–6767* ⊕ *www.ritzmadrid.com* ☞ *167 rooms* ⦿ *No meals* Ⓜ *Banco de España* ✛ *G4*.

CHAMARTÍN

$$ ⦿ **Silken Puerta de América.** Inspired by Paul Eluard's *La Liberté*, whose
HOTEL verses are written across the facade, the owners of this hotel granted an unlimited budget to 19 of the world's top architects and designers; the result is 12 hotels in one, with floors by Zaha Hadid, Norman Foster, Jean Nouvel, David Chipperfield, and others. **Pros:** an architect's dreamland; top-notch restaurant and bars. **Cons:** less-than-convenient location; the distinctive interior design doesn't always get the required maintenance. [$] *Rooms from: €170* ✉ *Av. de América 41, Chamartín* ☎ *91/744–5400* ⊕ *www.hotelpuertamerica.com* ☞ *282 rooms, 33 suites* ⦿ *No meals* Ⓜ *Avenida de América* ✛ *G1*.

PERFORMING ARTS

As Madrid's reputation as a vibrant, contemporary arts center has grown, artists and performers have been arriving in droves. Consult the daily listings and Friday city-guide supplements in any of the leading newspapers—*El País, El Mundo,* or *ABC,* all of which are fairly easy to understand even if you don't read much Spanish.

Seats for the classical performing arts can usually be purchased through your hotel concierge, on the Internet, or at the venue itself.

TICKETS

El Corte Inglés. You can buy tickets for major concerts here. ☎ *902/400222* ⊕ *www.elcorteingles.es/entradas*.

Entradas.com ☎ *902/221622* ⊕ *www.entradas.com*.

FNAC. This large retail media store also sells tickets to musical events. There is a second location on Paseo de la Castellana 79 in the Cuatro Caminos neighborhood. ✉ *Preciados 28, Sol* ☎ *91/595–6100* ⊕ *www. fnac.es*.

Tel-Entrada ☎ *902/101212* ⊕ *www.telentrada.com*.

DANCE AND MUSIC PERFORMANCES

In addition to concert halls listed here, the Convento de la Encarnación and the Real Academia de Bellas Artes de San Fernando museum *(⇨ Exploring Madrid)* hold concerts.

Auditorio Nacional de Música. This is Madrid's main concert hall, with spaces for both symphonic and chamber music. ⊠ *Príncipe de Vergara 146, Salamanca* ☎ *91/337–0140* ⊕ *www.auditorionacional.mcu.es.*

Centro de Conde Duque. This massive venue is best known for its summer live music concerts (flamenco, jazz, pop), but it also has free and often interesting exhibitions, lectures, and theater performances. ⊠ *Conde Duque 11, Centro* ☎ *91/588–5834* ⊕ *www.esmadrid.com/condeduque.*

Círculo de Bellas Artes. Concerts, theater, dance performances, art exhibitions, and events are all part of the calendar here. It also has an extremely popular café and a rooftop restaurant-bar with great views of the city. ⊠ *Marqués de Casa Riera 2, Centro* ☎ *902/422442* ⊕ *www.circulobellasartes.com.*

La Casa Encendida. Film festivals, art shows, dance performances, and weekend events for children are held here. ⊠ *Ronda de Valencia 2, Lavapiés* ☎ *91/506–3875* ⊕ *www.lacasaencendida.com.*

Matadero Madrid. The city's newest and biggest arts center is in the city's old slaughterhouse—a massive early-20th-century neo-Mudejar compound of 13 buildings—and has a theater, multiple exhibition spaces, workshops, and a lively bar. ⊠ *Paseo de la Chopera 14, Legazpi* ☎ *91/517–7309* ⊕ *www.mataderomadrid.org.*

Teatro Real. This resplendent theater is the venue for opera and dance performances. Built in 1850, this neoclassical theater was long a cultural center for madrileño society. A major restoration project has left it filled with golden balconies, plush seats, and state-of-the-art stage equipment. ⊠ *Pl. de Isabel II, Palacio* ☎ *91/516–0660* ⊕ *www.teatro-real.com.*

FILM

Of Madrid's 60 movie theaters, only 12 show foreign films, generally in English, with original sound tracks and Spanish subtitles. These are listed in newspapers under *"v.o."* for *"versión original"*—that is, "undubbed."

Cine Doré. A rare example of Art Nouveau architecture in Madrid, the hip Cine Doré shows movies from the Spanish National Film Archives and eclectic foreign films for €2.50 per session (you frequently get a short film or two in addition to a feature). Showtimes are listed in newspapers under "Filmoteca." The neon pink–trim lobby has a sleek café-bar and a bookshop. ⊠ *Santa Isabel 3, Embajadores* ☎ *91/369–1125* ⊙ *Tues.–Sun. 4 shows daily, starting at 5:30 pm (winter) or 6 pm (summer)* Ⓜ *Antón Martín.*

Filmoteca Cine Doré. The excellent, classic v.o. movies at this theater change daily. ⊠ *Santa Isabel 3, Lavapiés* ☎ *91/369–1125.*

Ideal Yelmo Cineplex. This is your best bet for new releases. ⊠ *Doctor Cortezo 6, Centro* ☎ *902/220922* ⊕ *www.yelmocines.es.*

FLAMENCO

Although the best place in Spain to find flamenco is Andalusia, there are a few venues in Madrid. Note that *tablaos* (flamenco venues) charge around €35–€45 for the show only (with a complimentary drink included), so save money by dining elsewhere. If you want to dine at the tablaos anyway, note that three of them—Carboneras, Corral de la Moreriá, and Café de Chinitas—also offer a show-plus-fixed-menu option that's worth considering.

Café de Chinitas. It's expensive, but the flamenco is the best in Madrid. Make reservations because shows often sell out. The restaurant opens at 8 and there are performances at 8 and 10:30 Monday through Saturday. ⊠ *Torija 7, Palacio* 🕾 *91/559–5135* ⊕ *www.chinitas.com.*

Casa Patas. Along with tapas, this well-known space offers good, relatively authentic (according to the performers) flamenco. Prices are more reasonable than elsewhere. Shows are at 10:30 Monday through Thursday, and at 9 and midnight on Friday and Saturday. ⊠ *Canizares 10, Lavapiés* 🕾 *91/369–0496* ⊕ *www.casapatas.com.*

Corral de la Morería. Dinner à la carte and well-known visiting flamenco stars accompany the resident dance troupe here. Since Morería opened its doors in 1956, celebrities such as Frank Sinatra and Ava Gardner have left their autographed photos for the walls. Shows last for about an hour and a half and are nightly at 8:30 and 10:30. ⊠ *Morería 17, on C. Bailén, La Latina* ✛ *Cross bridge over C. Segovia and turn right* 🕾 *91/365–8446* ⊕ *www.corraldelamoreria.com.*

Las Carboneras. A prime flamenco showcase, this venue rivals Casa Patas as the best option in terms of quality and price. Performers here include both the young, less commercial artists and more established stars on tour. The show is staged at 8:30 and 10:30 Monday through Thursday and at 8:30 and 11 Friday and Saturday. ⊠ *Pl. del Conde de Miranda 1, Centro* 🕾 *91/542–8677* ⊕ *www.tablaolascarboneras. com* ⊗ *Closed Sun.*

NIGHTLIFE

Nightlife—or *la marcha*—reaches legendary heights in Madrid. It's been said that madrileños rarely sleep, largely because they spend so much time in bars, socializing in the easy, sophisticated way that's unique to this city. This is true of young and old alike, and it's not uncommon for children to play on the sidewalks past midnight while multigenerational families and friends convene over coffee or cocktails at an outdoor café. For those in their thirties, forties, and up who don't plan on staying out until sunrise, the best options are the bars along the Cava Alta and Cava Baja, Calle Huertas near Plaza Santa Ana, and Moratín near Antón Martín. Those who want to stay out till the wee hours have more options: Calle Príncipe and Calle De la Cruz—also in Santa Ana—and the Plaza de Anton Martín, especially the scruffier streets that lead onto Plaza Lavapiés. The biggest night scene—with a mixed crowd—happens in Malasaña, which has plenty of trendy hangouts on both sides of Calle San Vicente Ferrer, on Calle La Palma, and on the

Continued on page 128

THE ART OF BULLFIGHTING

Whether you attend is your choice, but love it or hate it, you can't ignore it: bullfighting in Spain is big. For all the animal-rights protests, attempted bans, failed censures, and general worldwide antipathy, there are an astounding number of fans crowding Spain's bullrings between March and October.

CONTROVERSIAL ENTERTAINMENT

SPORT VS. ART

Its opponents call it a blood sport, its admirers—Hemingway, Picasso, and Goya among them—an art form. And the latter wins when it comes to media placement: you won't find tales of a star matador's latest conquest in the newspaper with car racing stories; you'll spy bullfighting news alongside theater and film reviews. This is perhaps the secret to understanding bullfighting's powerful cultural significance and why its popularity has risen over the past decade.

Bullfighting is making certain people very, very rich, via million-dollar TV rights, fight broadcasts, and the 300-plus bull-breeding farms. The owners of these farms comprise a powerful lobby that receives subsidies from the EU and exemption from a 1998 amendment to the Treaty of Rome that covers animal welfare. The Spanish Ministry of Culture also provides considerable money to support bullfighting, as do local and regional governments.

The Spanish media thrive on it, too. The matador is perhaps Spain's last remaining stereotypical hombre, whose popularity outside the ring in the celebrity press is often dramatically disproportionate to what he achieves inside it.

SOME HISTORY

How bullfighting came to Spain isn't completely clear. It may have been introduced by the Moors in the 11th century or via ancient Rome, where human vs. animal events were warm-ups for the gladiators.

Historically, the bull was fought from horseback with a javelin, to train and prepare for war, like hunting and jousting. Religious festivities and royal weddings were celebrated by fights in the local plaza, where noblemen would compete for royal favor, with the populace enjoying the excitement. In the 18th century, the Spanish introduced the practice of fighting on foot. As bullfighting developed, men started using capes to aid the horsemen in positioning the bulls. This type of fighting drew more attention from the crowds, thus the modern *corrida*, or bullfight, took root.

THE CASE AGAINST BULLFIGHTING

Animal welfare activists aggressively protest bullfighting: they argue that the bulls die a cruel death, essentially being butchered alive, and that the horses used as shields sometimes die or are injured.

Activists have had little success in banning bullfights on a national level, and the sport is as popular as ever in the south of Spain and Madrid. In Catalonia, however, a final vote was cast in 2010 that outlawed bullfighting in Barcelona and the rest of Catalonia as of 2012.

SUITING UP

Matadors are easily distinguished by their spectacular and quite costly *traje de luces* (suit of lights), inspired by 18th-century Andalusian clothing. This ensemble can run several thousand dollars, and a good matador uses at least six of them each season. The matador's team covers the cost.

The custom-made jacket (*chaquetilla*) is heavily embroidered with silver or golden thread.

Matadors use two kinds of capes: the *capote*, which is magenta and gold and used at the start to test the ferocity of the bull, and the red cape or *muleta*, used in the third stage.

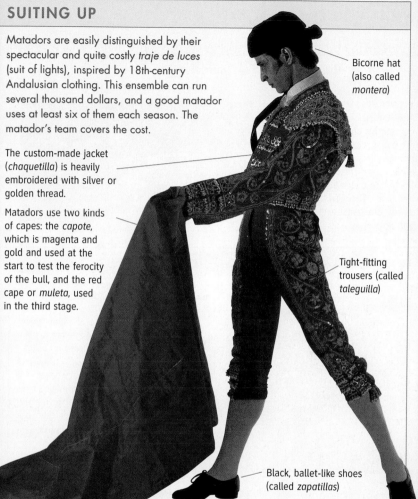

Bicorne hat (also called *montera*)

Tight-fitting trousers (called *taleguilla*)

Black, ballet-like shoes (called *zapatillas*)

OTHER BULLFIGHTING TERMS

Alguacilillo—the title given to the two men in the arena who represent the presiding dignitary and apply his orders.

Banderilleros—the torero's team members who place a set of banderillas (barbed sticks mounted on colored shafts) into the bull's neck.

Corrida de toros—bullfight (literally, running of the bulls); sometimes just referred to as *corrida*.

Cuadrilla—the matador's team of three *banderilleros* and two *picadors*.

Matador—matador literally means "killer."

Paseíllo—the parade that the participants make when they enter the bullring.

Picador—lancers mounted on horseback.

Presidente—the presiding dignitary.

Varas—lances.

WHAT YOU'LL SEE

Modern-day bullfights in Spain follow a very strict ritual that's played out in three stages (*"tercios"* or *"thirds"*).

1st STAGE: TERCIO DE VARAS

After the procession of the matador and his *cuadrilla* (entourage), the bull is released into the arena. A trumpet sounds and the *picadors* (lancers on horseback) encourage the bull to attack the heavily padded horse. They use the lances to pierce the bull's back and neck muscles.

2nd STAGE: TERCIO DE BANDERILLAS

Three *banderilleros* (team members) on foot each attempt to plant barbed sticks mounted on colored shafts into the bull's neck and back. These further weaken the enormous ridges of the bull's neck and shoulder in order to make it lower its head. Rather than use capes, the banderilleros use their bodies to attract the bull.

3rd STAGE: TERCIO DE MUERTE (DEATH)

The matador reenters with his red cape and, if he so chooses, dedicates the bull to an individual, or to the audience. The *faena* (work), which is the entire performance with the *muleta* (cape), ends with a series of passes in which the matador attempts to maneuver the bull into a position so he can drive his sword between the shoulder blades and through the heart.

Lancers astride heavily padded horses parade around the bullring near the beginning of a fight.

AUDIENCE PARTICIPATION

The consummate bullfighting fan is both passionate and knowledgeable. Audiences are in fact part of the spectacle, and their responses during the event is often an indicator of the quality of the corrida. For instance, during the *tercio de varas*, or first third of the fight, when the matador performs with art and courage, he will be rewarded with an ovation. If a picador is overzealous in stabbing the bull and leaves it too weak to fight, the crowd will boo him with whistles.

Similarly, the *estocada*, the act of thrusting the sword by the matador, can generate disapproval from the crowd if it's done clumsily and doesn't achieve a quick and clean death. A *trofeo* (literally a "trophy" but in practical terms the ear of a bull) is the usual indicator of a job well done. When the records of bullfights are kept, trofeos earned by the matador are always mentioned. If the crowd demands, the matador takes a lap of victory around the ring. If more

than or about half the spectators petition the presidente by waving handkerchiefs, the presidente is obliged to award the matador one bull's ear. The best trofeo is the two ears and the tail of a single bull, awarded only on memorable days.

■ **TIP→** When buying tickets for a bullfight, it's usually worth the extra cost for seats in the shade (*sombra*) rather than the cheaper one in the sun (*sol*) because bullfighting season coincides with summer. Seats in areas that get sun and then shade are called *sol y sombra*. Take a cushion with you, or rent one for €1.40, so you're not sitting on the hard concrete. Buy your tickets well in advance—call ☎ 902/150025 or go online to ⊕ www.taquillatoros.com.

STARGAZING

It's not uncommon for local Spanish celebrities to attend bullfights, and during the most prestigious summer carnival, the San Isidro in Madrid, King Juan Carlos often makes an appearance.

streets that come out onto Plaza 2 de Mayo, and on the refurbished and adjacent Triball area. Also big is nearby Chueca, where tattoo parlors and street-chic boutiques break up the endless alleys of gay and lesbian bars, discothèques, and after-hours clubs.

> **BEST BETS FOR ENTERTAINMENT**
>
> ■ **Best flamenco:** Café de Chinitas
>
> ■ **Best jazz venue:** Café Central
>
> ■ **Best salsa:** Azúcar

Most of the commendable cafés you'll find in Madrid can be classified into two main groups: the ones that have been around for many years (Café del Círculo, Café de Oriente), where writers, singers, poets, and discussion groups still meet and where conversations are usually more important than the coffee itself; and the new ones (Faborit, Diurno, Delic, Anglona), which are tailored to hip and hurried urbanites and tend to have a wider product selection, modern interiors, and Wi-Fi.

PALACIO, LA LATINA, AND SOL

PALACIO
BARS AND NIGHTCLUBS
Marula Café. Popular for its quiet summer terrace under the Puente de Segovia arches, its unbeatable electro-funk mixes, and for staying open into the wee hours, this is a cleverly designed narrow space with lots of illuminated wall art. ⊠ *C. Caños Viejos 3, Palacio* ☎ *91/366–1596.*

CAFÉS
Café de Oriente. This landmark spot has a magnificent view of the Royal Palace and its front yard. Inside, the café is divided into two sections—the left one serves tapas and raciones; the right serves more elaborate food. The café also has a splendid terrace that's open when the sun is out. ⊠ *Pl. de Oriente 2, Palacio* ☎ *91/547–1564* Ⓜ *Ópera.*

DISCOS
Charada. A few blocks from the Royal Palace, this is one of the sleekest clubs in the city, with a huge LED screen on the ceiling, professional barmen serving cocktails until 6 am, lots of house and funk music, and a crowd mostly in its late thirties. ⊠ *C. de la Bola 13, Palacio* ☎ *91/541–9291* ⊘ *Closed Mon.–Thurs.*

Reina Bruja. Magical and chameleonlike thanks to the use of LED lighting and the undulating shapes of the columns and walls, this is the place to go if you want a late-night drink—it opens at 11 and closes at 5:30 am—without the thunder of a full-blown disco. ⊠ *Jacometrezo 6, Palacio* ☎ *91/445–6886* ⊘ *Closed Sun.–Wed.*

LA LATINA
BARS AND NIGHTCLUBS
El Viajero. You can get food here, but this place is best known among the madrileños who swarm La Latina on the weekends for its middle-floor bar, which is usually filled by those looking for a drink between lunch and dinner. There's also a fabulous, semi-hidden terrace that tends to

be packed. ⊠ *Pl. de la Cebada 11, La Latina* ☎ *91/366–9064* ۞ *Closed Sun. night and Mon.*

CAFÉS

Anglona. A good option if you're in La Latina, this small café serves a variety of hot chocolates (with cognac, caramel, mint, and more) and imported teas, as well as some sweets, including chocolate cake, carrot cake, and custard crème mille-feuille. At night, sip mojitos or caipirinhas and take in the scene-setting jazz or bossa nova. ⊠ *Príncipe de Anglona 3, La Latina* ☎ *91/365–0587* ۞ *Closed Mon.* Ⓜ *La Latina.*

Delic. This warm, inviting café is a hangout for Madrid's trendy crowd. Besides the *patatitas con mousse de parmesano* (potatoes with a Parmesan mousse) and zucchini cake, homesick travelers will find carrot cake, brownies, and pumpkin pie among the offerings. ⊠ *Costanilla de San Andrés 14, Pl. de la Paja, La Latina* ☎ *91/364–5450* ۞ *Closed Sun. evening, Mon., and Tues.* Ⓜ *La Latina.*

SOL

BARS AND NIGHTCLUBS

Costello. A multispace that combines a café and a lounge, this place caters to a relaxed, conversational crowd; the bottom floor is suited to partygoers, with the latest in live and club music. On weekdays, it also features theater and stand-up comedy. ⊠ *Caballero de Gracia 10, Sol* ☎ *91/522–1815* ⊕ *www.costelloclub.com.*

CAFÉS

Café del Círculo (*La Pecera*). Spacious and elegant, with large velvet curtains, marble columns, hardwood floors, painted ceilings, and sculptures scattered throughout, this eatery inside the famous art center Círculo de Bellas Artes feels more like a private club than a café. Expect a bustling, intellectual crowd. ⊠ *Marqués de Casa Riera 2, Sol* ☎ *91/522–5092* Ⓜ *Banco de España, Sevilla.*

Chocolatería San Ginés. Gastronomical historians suggest that the practice of dipping explains Spaniards' lasting fondness for superthick hot chocolate. Only a few of the old places where this hot drink was served exclusively (with crispy churros), such as this chocolatería, remain standing. It's open virtually 24 hours a day (9:30 am to 7 am weekdays; 9 am to 7 am, weekends) and is the last stop for many a bleary-eyed soul after a night out. ⊠ *Pasadizo de San Ginés (enter by Arenal 11), Sol* ☎ *91/365–6546* Ⓜ *Sol.*

Faborit. A chain spot bold enough to open next door to Starbucks had better serve some great coffee, and for less money; Faborit does, and offers a warm, high-tech environment to boot. Whether your feet hurt and the sun is blazing, or it's chilly out and you're tired of shivering, indulge in a mug of cappuccino with cream or a chai cappuccino. The main café is two blocks from the Puerta del Sol, but there are also now branches on Paseo del Prado, near the CaixaForum, across from the Palace Hotel, and on San Bernardo, just a block off Gran Vía. ⊠ *Alcalá 21, Sol* ☎ *91/521–8616* Ⓜ *Sevilla.*

DISCOS

Cocó Madrid. Dizzyingly colorful, this club has a large dance floor, a bar specializing in fancy cocktails, and different house-music sessions (among them the famous electronic-music Mondo sessions on Thursday and Saturday) which cater to the city's most glamorous and refined. ⊠ *Alcalá 20, Sol* ☏ *91/445–7938* ⊕ *www.cocomadrid.com* ☉ *Closed Mon.–Wed.*

El Sol. Madrid's oldest disco, and one of the hippest clubs for all-night dancing to an international music mix, is open until 5:30 am. There's live music starting at around midnight, Thursday through Saturday. ⊠ *Jardines 3, Sol* ☏ *91/532–6490.*

Joy Eslava. A downtown disco in a converted theater, this is a long-established standby. ⊠ *Arenal 11, Sol* ☏ *91/366–3733.*

BARRIO DE LAS LETRAS

BARS AND NIGHTCLUBS

Café Central. Madrid's best-known jazz venue is chic, and the musicians are often internationally known. Nightly performances are usually from 9 to 11 pm. ⊠ *Pl. de Ángel 10, Barrio de las Letras* ☏ *91/369–4143* ⊕ *www.cafecentralmadrid.com.*

La Piola. With a bohemian spirit and a shabby-chic interior—a second-hand couch, a handful of tables, and a brass bar—this small place, which serves some cold, basic staples during the day (like salmorejo and empanadas) and cocktails at night, is a magnet for people who want to get away from the bustle of the Santa Ana area. ⊠ *León 9, Barrio de las Letras* ☏ *679/744–898* ☉ *Closed Sun.*

The Roof. This is two different spaces connected by an elevator that could easily be confused for a dance floor. The bottom lounge takes up most of the ground floor of the chic ME Madrid, including the reception area; the exclusive rooftop terrace in the same hotel is one of the Madrid's essential summer venues and offers an unbeatable 360-degree view of the city. ⊠ *ME Madrid, Pl. de Santa Ana 14, Barrio de las Letras* ☏ *91/445–6886.*

DISCOS

Azúcar. Salsa has become a fixture in Madrid; check out the most spectacular moves here. ⊠ *Atocha 107, Barrio de las Letras* ☏ *91/429–6208* ⊕ *www.azucarsalsadisco.com.*

CHUECA, MALASAÑA, AND CHAMBERÍ

CHUECA

BARS AND NIGHTCLUBS

Bar Cock. Resembling a room at a very exclusive club (with all the waiters in suits), this bar with a dark wood interior and cathedral-like ceilings serves about 20 different cocktails (hence the name). It caters to an older, more classic crowd. ⊠ *Reina 16, Chueca* ☏ *91/532–2826.*

Del Diego. Arguably Madrid's most renowned cocktail bar, this family-owned place is frequented by a variety of crowds, from movie directors

to moviegoers. ✉ *C. de la Reina 12, Chueca* ☎ *91/523–3106* ⊕ *www. deldiego.com* ⊗ *Closed Sun.*

El Intruso. Easy to miss (it's located inside a building just a block off Fuencarral), this is one of the Malasaña's best lounges. There are live DJs and bands almost every night playing good funk music to a 30-plus crowd. ✉ *Augusto Figueroa 3, Chueca* ⊕ *www.intrusobar.com* ⊗ *Closed Mon.*

Museo Chicote. This landmark cocktail bar–lounge is said to have been one of Hemingway's haunts. Much of the interior can be traced back to the 1930s, but modern elements (like the in-house DJ) keep this spot firmly in the present. ✉ *Gran Vía 12, Chueca* ☎ *91/532–6737* ⊗ *Closed Sun.*

CAFÉS

Café Belén. The handful of tables here are rarely empty on weekends, thanks to the candlelit, cozy atmosphere—it attracts a young, mixed, postdinner crowd. Weekdays are mellower. ✉ *Belén 5, Chueca* ☎ *91/308–2747.*

Diurno. A Chueca landmark, this restaurant-café, DVD rental stop, and take-out spot is spacious, with large windows facing the street, sleek chairs and couches, and lots of plants. Diurno serves healthy snacks and sandwiches along with some indulgent desserts, as well as strawberry mojitos and other cocktails. From 5 pm onwards it becomes a restaurant with a short but varied menu, and also offers a copious brunch on weekends. ✉ *San Marcos 37, Chueca* ☎ *91/522–0009* Ⓜ *Chueca.*

MALASAÑA
BARS AND NIGHTCLUBS

La Realidad. Artists, musicians, aspiring filmmakers—they all flock to this bar with the free-spirited vibe for which Malasaña is famous. Locals come here to chat with friends over tea, delve into their Macs or, later in the day, sip an inexpensive gin and tonic. ✉ *Corredera Baja de San Pablo 51, Malasaña.*

Martínez Bar. True to its name, this place plays homage to the old classic bars that are now a dying breed in the city. It serves coffee, tea, and even an inexpensive Sunday brunch, but folks come here for the cocktails. There are more than 50 brands of gin here, homemade spice-based liquors, and the hard-to-find madrileño artisan-brewed beer, Cibeles. ✉ *Barco 4, Malasaña* ☎ *91/080–2683.*

Santa María. A good option if you are looking to have a drink in the Gran Vía (Triball) area and enjoy some jazz. In a space that mixes vintage design with artsy touches, you'll mingle with a chic bohemian crowd, and choose from a good variety of cocktails—including one bearing the club's name (made with mixed-berry juice with vodka or gin). ✉ *Ballesta 6, Malasaña* ☎ *91/166–0511.*

CAFÉS

Café la Palma. There are four different spaces here: a bar in front, a music venue for intimate concerts (a bit of everything: pop, rock, electronic, hip-hop), a chill-out room in the back, and a café in the center room. Don't miss it if you're in Malasaña. ⊠ *La Palma 62, Malasaña* ☎ *91/522–5031* ⊕ *www.cafelapalma.com.*

Lolina Café. Diverging in its spirit and style (think vintage furniture and pop art wallpaper) from the classier baroque cafés of the neighborhood, this hectic spot attracts the young and techno-savvy with its free Wi-Fi and good assortment of teas, chocolates, cakes, and drinks. ⊠ *Espíritu Santo 9, Malasaña* ☎ *667/201169* Ⓜ *Tribunal.*

DISCOS

Teatro Barceló. A landmark enclave that until 2013 carried the legendary label Pachá in its name, it's been running for over three decades with the same energetic vibe and the blessing of the local crowd. ⊠ *Barceló 11, Malasaña* ☎ *91/447–0128* ☉ *Closed Sun.–Wed.*

CHAMBERÍ

BARS AND NIGHTCLUBS

Le Cabrera. Diego Cabrera, the former barman at Gastro, one of Madrid's best restaurants, has developed a reputation as one of Spain's cocktail beacons. The interior pays homage to the craft (cocktail shakers line walls) and the space gets packed on the weekends. Choose one of the many unique creations, such as the Guaracha (made with berry-flavored vodka, lemon, and mint leaves) or the Tangerine (made with gin, St-Germain, tangerine juice, lime juice, and rosemary sugar), or one of the many cocktail classics. ⊠ *Bárbara de Braganza 2, Chamberí* ☎ *91/319–9457* ☉ *Closed Sun.*

LAVAPIÉS

BARS AND NIGHTCLUBS

Coquette. This is the most authentic blues bar in the city, with live music Tuesday to Thurday at 11, barmen with jeans and leather jackets, and bohemian executives who've left their suits at home and parked their Harley-Davidsons at the door. ⊠ *Torrecilla del Leal 18, Lavapiés* ☎ *91/530–8095.*

CAFÉS

Gau&Café. Along with the theater on the neighborhood's main plaza, the reconstruction of the Escuelas Pías—an 18th-century religious school burnt down during the Spanish civil war and now turned into a university center—is one of Lavapiés's modern highlights. The rooftop has a hidden café with a wide selection of teas and coffee, and its large terrace, open year-round, has great views. It opens at 3:30 pm on weekdays (6 pm June–August, because days are so hot) and at 8 pm on Saturday. ⊠ *Escuelas Pías, Tribulete 14, 4th fl., Lavapiés* ☎ *91/528–2594* ☉ *Closed Sun.* Ⓜ *Lavapiés.*

SALAMANCA AND RETIRO

SALAMANCA

BARS AND NIGHTCLUBS

Eccola Kitchen. A large, stylish club frequented by an upscale crowd mostly in their forties and fifties, Eccola Kitchen is the place to go for an early drink in Salamanca. The space is divided up into several different areas with comfortable leather couches, and the extensive drink menu includes cocktails as well as shooters with eccentric ingredients like Siberian or Korean ginseng. ⊠ *Diego de León 3, Salamanca* ☎ *91/563–2473* ☾ *Closed Sun.*

RETIRO
BARS AND NIGHTCLUBS

Gin Room. Extravagantly decorated, this hot spot between Retiro Park and the Prado is a favorite with posh madrileños. The drinks menu includes about a dozen unusual brands of gin, including the exclusive Citadelle Réserve, here served with lemongrass and edible gold foil. The big attraction here, though, isn't just the gin and tonic, but the dedication with which it's served. ⊠ *Academia 7, Retiro* ☎ *699/755988* ☾ *Closed Sun.*

Ramsés. A multispace venue across from Retiro Park designed by Philippe Starck with two restaurants, a club in the basement, and a bar at street level, this spot is perfect for an early though expensive cocktail, before or after dinner, preferably during the week. Order a Ramsés (black vodka, absinthe, and cranberry juice) and enjoy the parade of the glamorous see-and-be-seen set. ⊠ *Pl. de la Independencia 4, Retiro* ☎ *91/435–1666.*

CAFÉS

Harina. Steps from Retiro Park, this airy all-white café uses house-baked artisanal bread for sandwiches and *bocadillos* (a sandwich on a small loaf of bread), including the classic Iberian ham with tomato. A short lunch menu, scrumptious cakes, and several types of breakfast are also served. The terrace, open from mid-March to early fall, gets busy. ⊠ *Pl. de la Independencia 10, Retiro* ☎ *91/522–8785.*

DISCOS

Golden Boite. This happening spot is hot from midnight on. ⊠ *Duque de Sesto 54, Retiro* ☎ *91/573–8775* ⊕ *www.golden-boite.es.*

CHAMARTÍN AND TETUÁN

CHAMARTÍN
DANCE

69 Pétalos. Five minutes from Plaza de Castilla, this is a popular disco among people in their thirties; there's an eclectic music vibe—pop, hip-hop, swing, electronic—and on-stage performances by actors, go-go dancers, and musicians. ⊠ *Alberto Alcocer, 32, Chamartín* ☾ *Closed Sun.–Wed.*

DISCOS

Skynight. On the top floor of the ultramodern Silken Puerta de América Hotel (⇨ *see Where to Stay*), the Skynight gets really lively on the weekends, with scores of well-off madrileños elbowing their way to the exclusive gin-and-tonic bar, which also offers good views of the western part of the city. ⊠ *Silken Puerta de América Hotel, Av. de América 41, Chamartín* ☎ *91/744–5400* ☾ *Closed Sun.*

TETUÁN
DISCOS
New Garamond. At this popular venue you'll find plenty of space to dance (under the gaze of the go-go girls) but also quieter nooks where you can chat and sip a drink. ⊠ *Rosario Pino 20, Tetuán* ⊙ *Closed Sun.–Wed.*

SPORTS AND THE OUTDOORS

RUNNING

Madrid's best running spots are the Parque del Buen Retiro, where the main path circles the park and others weave under trees and through gardens, and the Parque del Oeste, with more uneven terrain but fewer people. The Casa de Campo is crisscrossed by numerous, sunnier trails.

SOCCER

Fútbol is Spain's number one sport, and Madrid has four teams: Real Madrid, Atlético Madrid, Rayo Vallecano, and Getafe. The two major teams are Real Madrid and Atlético Madrid. For tickets, either call a week in advance to reserve and pick them up at the stadium or stand in line at the stadium of your choice.

Estadio Santiago Bernabeu. Home to Real Madrid, the stadium seats 85,400. ⊠ *Paseo de la Castellana 140, Chamartín* ☎ *91/398–4300* ⊕ *www.realmadrid.es.*

Estadio Vicente Calderón. Atlético Madrid plays at this stadium, which is on the edge of the Manzanares River south of town. ⊠ *Virgen del Puerto 67, Arganzuela* ☎ *91/366–4707, 90/253–0500 for tickets* ⊕ *www. clubatleticodemadrid.com.*

SHOPPING

Spain has become one of the world's design centers. You'll have no trouble finding traditional crafts, such as ceramics, guitars, and leather goods, albeit not at countryside prices (think Rodeo Drive, not outlet mall). Known for contemporary furniture and decorative items as well as chic clothing, shoes, and jewelry, Spain's capital has become stiff competition for Barcelona. Keep in mind that many shops, especially those that are small and family-run, close during lunch hours, on Sunday, and on Saturday afternoon. Shops generally accept most major credit cards.

Madrid has three main shopping areas. The first, the area that stretches from Callao to Puerta del Sol (Calle Preciados, Gran Vía on both sides of Callao, and the streets around the Puerta del Sol), includes the major department stores (El Corte Inglés and the French music-and-book chain FNAC) and popular brands such as H&M and Zara.

The second area, far more elegant and expensive, is in the eastern Salamanca district, bounded roughly by Serrano, Juan Bravo, Jorge Juan (and its blind alleys), and Velázquez; the shops on Goya extend as far as Alcalá. The streets just off the Plaza de Colón, particularly Calle Serrano and Calle Ortega y Gasset, have the widest selection of designer goods—think Prada, Loewe, Armani, and Louis Vuitton—as well as other mainstream and popular local designers (Purificación García, Pedro del Hierro, Adolfo Domínguez, or Roberto Verino). Hidden within Calle Jorge Juan, Calle Lagasca, and Calle Claudio Coello is the widest selection of smart boutiques from renowned Spanish designers, such as Sybilla, DelPozo, or Dolores Promesas.

Finally, for hipper clothes, Chueca, Malasaña, and what's now called the Triball (the triangle formed by Fuencarral, Gran Vía, and Corredera Baja, with Calle Ballesta in the middle) are your best bets. Calle Fuencarral, from Gran Vía to Tribunal, is the street with the most shops in this area. On Fuencarral you can find name brands such as Diesel, Gas, and Billabong, but also local brands such as Homeless, Adolfo Domínguez U (selling the Galician designer's younger collection), and Custo, as well as some makeup stores (Madame B and M.A.C). Less mainstream and sometimes more exciting is the selection you can find on nearby Calles Hortaleza, Almirante, and Piamonte and in the Triball area.

PALACIO AND SOL

PALACIO
CERAMICS

Antigua Casa Talavera. This is the best of Madrid's many ceramics shops. Despite the name, the finest wares sold here are from Manises, near Valencia, but the blue-and-yellow Talavera ceramics are also excellent. ⊠ *Isabel la Católica 2, Palacio* ☎ *91/547–3417.*

Cántaro. Shop here for traditional handmade ceramics and pottery. ⊠ *Flor Baja 8, Palacio* ☎ *91/547–9514* ⊕ *www.ceramicacantaro.com.*

SOL
BOOKS

Casa del Libro. At this shop not far from the Puerta del Sol you'll find an impressive collection of English-language books, including translated Spanish classics. It's also a good source for maps. Its discount store nearby, on Calle Salud 17, sells English classics. ⊠ *Gran Vía 29, Sol* ☎ *90/202–6402.*

BOUTIQUES AND FASHION

Custo. Brothers Custodio and David Dalmau are the creative force behind the success of this chain, whose eye-catching T-shirts can be found in the closets of such stars as Madonna and Julia Roberts. They have expanded their collection to incorporate pants, dresses, and accessories, never relinquishing the traits that have made them famous: bold colors and striking graphic designs. ⊠ *Mayor 37, Sol* ☎ *91/354–0099* ⊠ *Fuencarral 29, Chueca* ☎ *91/360–4636* ⊠ *Serrano 16, Salamanca* ☎ *91/577–2663.*

Seseña. The area around Sol is more mainstream, with big names such as Zara and H&M, and retail media and department stores (e.g., FNAC, El Corte Inglés), but there are some interesting isolated stops such as

Bustling El Rastro flea market takes place every Sunday from 10 to 2; you never know what kind of treasures you might find.

Seseña, which, since the turn of the 20th century, has outfitted international celebrities in wool and velvet capes, some lined with red satin. ⊠ *De la Cruz 23, Sol* ☎ *91/531–6840.*

DEPARTMENT STORES

El Corte Inglés. Spain's largest department store carries the best selection of everything, from auto parts to groceries, electronics, lingerie, and designer fashions. It also sells tickets for major sports and arts events and has its own travel agency, a restaurant (usually the building's top floor), and a great gourmet store. Madrid's biggest branch is the one on the corner of Calle Raimundo Fernández Villaverde and Castellana, which is not a central location. Try instead the one at Sol-Callao (split into three separate buildings), or the ones at Serrano or Goya (each of these has two independent buildings). ⊠ *Preciados 1, 2, and 3, Sol* ☎ *91/379–8000, 90/112–2122 for general info, 90/240–0222 for tickets* ⊕ *www.elcorteingles.es* ⊠ *C. Goya 76 and 85, Salamanca* ☎ *91/432–9300* ⊠ *Princesa 41, 47, and 56, Moncloa* ☎ *91/454–6000* ⊠ *C. Serrano 47, Salamanca* ☎ *91/432–5490* ⊠ *Callao 2, Sol* ☎ *91/379–8000* ⊠ *Raimundo Fernández Villaverde 79, Cuatro Caminos* ☎ *91/418–8800.*

MUSIC

José Ramírez. This company has provided Spain and the rest of the world with guitars since 1882, and its store includes a museum of antique instruments. Prices for new ones range from €122 to €227 for children and €153 to about €2,200 for adults, though some of the top concert models easily break the €10,000 mark. ⊠ *C. de la Paz 8, Sol* ☎ *91/531–4229.*

BARRIO DE LAS LETRAS

BOUTIQUES AND FASHION

Eduardo Rivera. Just a block off Plaza de Santa Ana, this is the flagship store of a young Spanish designer with clothes and accessories for both men and women. He's known for modernizing the look of Spain's current vice president, Soraya Sáenz de Santamaría. ⊠ *Pl. del Ángel 4, Barrio de las Letras* ☎ *91/843–5852* ⊕ *www.eduardorivera.es.*

FLEA MARKETS

El Rastro. On Sunday morning, Calle de Ribera de Curtidores is closed to traffic and jammed with outdoor booths selling everything under the sun—this is its weekly transformation into El Rastro flea market. Crowds get so thick that it takes a while just to advance a few feet amid the hawkers and gawkers. Be careful: pickpockets abound here, so hang on to your purse and wallet, and be especially careful if you bring a camera. The flea market sprawls into most of the surrounding streets, with certain areas specializing in particular products. Many of the goods are wildly overpriced. But what goods! El Rastro has everything from antique furniture to exotic parrots and cuddly puppies, pirated CDs of flamenco music, and keychains emblazoned with symbols of the CNT, Spain's old anarchist trade union. Practice your Spanish by bargaining with the vendors over paintings, colorful Gypsy oxen yokes, heraldic iron gates, new and used clothes, and even hashish pipes. They may not lower their prices, but sometimes they'll throw in a handmade bracelet or a stack of postcards to sweeten the deal. Plaza General Vara del Rey has some of the Rastro's best antiques, and the streets beyond—Calles Mira el Río Alta and Mira el Río Baja—have some truly magnificent junk and bric-a-brac. The market shuts down shortly after 2 pm, in time for a street party to start in the area known as La Latina, centered on the bar El Viajero in Plaza Humilladero. Off the Ribera are two *galerías,* courtyards with higher-quality, higher-price antiques shops. All the shops (except for the street vendors) are open during the week. ⊠ *C. de Ribera de Curtidores, Barrio de las Letras* ☉ *Sun. 9–3.*

FOOD AND WINE

David Cabello. Named after the current owner, this liquor store has been in the family for more than 100 years. It's rustic and a bit dusty and looks like a warehouse rather than a shop, but David knows what he's selling. Head here for a good selection of Rioja wines (some dating as far back as 1920) and local liqueurs, including anisettes and *pacharan,* a fruity liquor made with sloes (the wild fruit of the blackthorn tree, similar to plums). ⊠ *Cervantes 6, Barrio de las Letras* ☎ *91/429–5230.*

González. This traditional food store has a secret in back—a cozy and well-hidden bar where you can sample most of its fare: canned asparagus; olive oil; honey; cold cuts; smoked anchovies, salmon, and other fish; and a good selection of Spanish cheeses and local wines. It also serves good, inexpensive breakfasts. ⊠ *León 12, Barrio de las Letras* ☎ *91/429–5618.*

Mariano Aguado. Behind Plaza Santa Ana, this is a charming 150-year-old wine store with a broad range of wines and fine spirits. ⊠ *Echegaray 19, Barrio de las Letras* ☎ *91/429–6088.*

CHUECA, MALASAÑA, AND CHAMBERÍ

CHUECA

BOUTIQUES AND FASHION

Chueca shelters some local name brands (Hoss, Adolfo Domínguez, and Mango) on Calle Fuencarral and has a multifloor and multistore market (Mercado de Fuencarral) selling modern outfits for younger crowds at No. 45 on the same street.

Jesús del Pozo. This prominent designer died in 2011 and it's now Josep Font who extends its creative legacy with modern clothes for both sexes. It's an excellent, if pricey, place to try on some classic Spanish style. ⌧ *Lagasca 19, Chueca* ☎ *91/219–4038* ⊕ *www.jesusdelpozo.com.*

L'Habilleur. A fancy outlet selling samples and end-of-season designer clothes, this is a good place to find big discounts. ⌧ *Pl. de Chueca 8, Chueca* ☎ *91/531–3222.*

Lemoniez. After more than 20 years in the fashion industry, Basque designer Fernando Lemoniez finally took the plunge and opened his own boutique, in what used to be a fruit shop. Women of all ages can be found browsing the feminine silk and chiffon dresses and gathering insight from Lemoniez himself, who often drops by the store on Saturday morning. ⌧ *Argensola 17, Chueca* ☎ *91/308–4821.*

Pez. A favorite among fashion-magazine editors, this store, on the corner of Calle Fernando VI, features a very chic and seductive European collection—especially Parisian and Scandinavian. ⌧ *Regueros 15, Chueca* ☎ *91/308–6677.*

Próxima Parada. The highly energetic owner of this store enthusiastically digs into racks looking for daring garments from Spanish designers in her quest to modernize her customers' look. The store also sells some original clothespins made by art school students. ⌧ *Conde de Xiquena 9, Chueca* ☎ *91/310–3421.*

Roberto Torretta. This designer, with a celebrity following, makes sophisticated and elegant clothes for the urban woman. ⌧ *Almirante 10, Chueca* ☎ *91/435–7989* ⊕ *www.robertotorretta.com.*

FOOD AND WINE

Poncelet. You can find more than 120 different cheeses from all over Spain as well as almost 300 others from nearby countries such as France, Portugal, Italy, and Holland at Poncelet. Marmalades, wines, and items to help you savor your cheese are also available. ⌧ *Argensola 27, Alonso Martínez* ☎ *91/308–0221* ⊕ *www.poncelet.es.*

MALASAÑA

BOOKS

J&J. A block off San Bernardo, this is a charming café and bookstore run by a woman from Alabama and her Spanish husband. The store stocks a good selection of used books in English. ⌧ *Espíritu Santo 47, Malasaña* ☎ *91/521–8576* ⊕ *www.jandjbooksandcoffee.com.*

BOUTIQUES AND FASHION

Jocomomola. At Sybilla's younger and more affordable second brand, Jocomomola, you'll find plenty of informal, provocative, and colorful pieces, as well as some accessories. ⊠ *Colón 4, Malasaña* ☎ *91/575–0005.*

Mango. The Turkish brothers Isaac and Nahman Andic opened their first store in Barcelona in 1984. Today, Mango has stores all over the world, and the brand rivals Zara as Spain's most successful fashion venture. Mango's target customer is the young, modern, and urban woman. In comparison with Zara, Mango has fewer formal options and favors bohemian sundresses, sandals, and embellished T-shirts. ⊠ *Fuencarral 70, Malasaña* ☎ *91/523–0412* ⊕ *www.mango.com* ⊠ *Fuencarral 4, Bilbao* ☎ *91/445–7811* ⊠ *C. Goya 83, Salamanca* ☎ *91/435–3958* ⊠ *Hermosilla 22, Salamanca* ☎ *91/576–8303.*

Uno de 50. This is a good place for hip original and inexpensive (less than €200) costume jewelry—mostly made from leather and a silver-plated tin alloy—and accessories by Spanish designer Concha Díaz del Río. ⊠ *Fuencarral 17, Malasaña* ☎ *91/523–9975* ⊕ *www.unode50.com* ⊠ *Ayala 26, Salamanca* ☎ *91/577–2610.*

Zara. Young professionals who want the latest look without the sticker shock hit Zara for hip clothes that won't last more than a season or two. The store's minimalist window displays are hard to miss; inside you'll find the latest looks for men, women, and children. Zara is self-made entrepreneur Amancio Ortega's textile empire flagship, and you will find locations all over the city. Its clothes are considerably cheaper in Spain than in the United States or the United Kingdom. There are also two outlet stores in Madrid—in the Gran Vía store and in Calle Carretas—both called Lefties. If you choose to try your luck at the outlets, keep in mind that Monday and Thursday are when new deliveries arrive. ⊠ *Gran Via 34, Triball* ☎ *91/521–1283.* ⊠ *Serrano 23, Salamanca* ☎ *91/436–3158* ⊠ *Carretas 6, Sol* ☎ *91/522–6945* ⊠ *Conde de Peñalver 16, Salamanca* ☎ *91/781–9788* ⊠ *Princesa 58, Moncloa* ☎ *91/549–1616*

CHAMBERÍ

BOOKS

Booksellers. Just across from the Iglesia subway exit, Booksellers has a large selection of books in English; there's another branch nearby, at Calle Fernandez de la Hoz 40. ⊠ *Santa Engracia 115, Chamberí* ☎ *91/702–7944.*

LAVAPIÉS

MUSIC

Percusión Campos. This percussion shop–workshop where Canarian Pedro Navarro crafts his own *cajones flamencos,* or flamenco box drums, is hard to find but his pieces are greatly appreciated among professionals. Prices range between €80 and €210 and vary according to the quality of woods used. ⊠ *Olivar 36, Lavapiés* ☎ *91/539–2178.*

SALAMANCA

BOUTIQUES AND FASHION

Salamanca is the area with the most concentrated local fashion offering, especially on Calles Claudio Coello, Lagasca, and the first few blocks of Serrano. You'll find a good mix of mainstream designers, small-scale exclusive boutiques, and multibrand stores. Most mainstream designer stores are on Calle Serrano.

The top stores for non-Spanish fashions are mostly scattered along Ortega y Gasset, between Nuñez de Balboa and Serrano, but if you want the more exclusive local brands, head to the smaller designer shops unfolding along Calles Claudio Coello, Jorge Juan, and Lagasca. Start on Calle Jorge Juan and its alleys, and then move north along Claudio Coello and Lagasca toward the core of the Salamanca district.

Adolfo Domínguez. This Galician designer creates simple, sober, and elegant lines for both men and women. Of the eight other locations in the city, the one at Calle Fuencarral 5, a block away from Gran Vía, is geared toward a younger crowd, with more affordable and colorful clothes. ⊠ *C. Serrano 5, Salamanca* ☎ *91/577–4744* ⊕ *www. adolfodominguez.com.*

Hoss. The three young female designers working for Hoss and their hip and fashionable clothes are gaining a growing acceptance with younger fashionistas. ⊠ *C. Serrano 18, Salamanca* ☎ *91/781–0612* ⊠ *Fuencarral 16, Chueca* ☎ *91/524–1728.*

Josep Font. This young but renowned Catalonian designer sells his seductive clothes a few blocks from the customary shopping route in the Salamanca neighborhood. Worth the detour, his clothes are distinctive and colorful, with original shapes and small, subtle touches such as ribbons or flounces that act as the designer's signature. ⊠ *Don Ramón de la Cruz 51, Salamanca* ☎ *91/575–9716* ⊕ *www.josepfont.com.*

Loewe. This posh store carries high-quality designer purses, accessories, and clothing made of butter-soft leather in gorgeous jewel-like colors. The store on Calle Serrano 26 displays the women's collection; men's items are a block away, on Serrano 34. Prices can hit the stratosphere. ⊠ *C. Serrano 26 and 34, Salamanca* ☎ *91/577–6056* ⊕ *www.loewe.com* ⊠ *Gran Vía 8, Chueca* ☎ *91/522–6815.*

Nac. You'll find a good selection of Spanish designer brands (Antonio Miró, Hoss, Josep Font, Jocomomola, and Ailanto) at Nac. The store on Calle Génova is the biggest of the four in Madrid. ⊠ *C. Génova 18, Chamberí* ☎ *91/310–6050* ⊕ *www.nac.es* ⊠ *Lagasca 117, Salamanca* ☎ *91/561–3035.*

Pedro del Hierro. This madrileño designer has built himself a solid reputation for his sophisticated but uncomplicated clothes for both sexes. ⊠ *C. Serrano 24, 29, and 40, Salamanca* ☎ *91/575–6906.*

Purificación García. For women searching for contemporary all-day wear, this is a good choice. There's another branch at Claudio Coello 95. ⊠ *C. Serrano 28, Salamanca* ☎ *91/435–8013.*

Sybilla. One of Spain's best-known female designers, with fluid dresses and hand-knit sweaters that are sought after by anyone who is fashion savvy, including Danish former supermodel and now editor and designer Helena Christensen. ⊠ *Jorge Juan 12, at end of one of two cul-de-sacs, Salamanca* ☎ *91/578–1322* ⊕ *www.sybilla.es.*

CERAMICS

Cerámica El Alfar. You'll find pottery from all over Spain here. ⊠ *Claudio Coello 112, Salamanca* ☎ *91/411–3587* ⊕ *www.ceramicaelalfar.es.*

Sagardelos. Specializing in modern Spanish ceramics from Galicia, this store stocks breakfast sets, coffeepots, and objets d'arts. ⊠ *Conde Aranda 2, Salamanca* ☎ *91/310–4830* ⊕ *www.sargadelos.com.*

FOOD AND WINE

Lavinia. One of the largest wine stores in Europe, with a large selection of bottles, books, and bar accessories, as well as a restaurant where you can sample products. ⊠ *José Ortega y Gasset 16, Salamanca* ☎ *91/426–0604* ⊕ *www.lavinia.es.*

Mantequerías Bravo. In the middle of Salamanca's shopping area, this store sells Spanish wines, olive oils, cheeses, and hams. ⊠ *Ayala 24, Salamanca* ☎ *91/576–7641.*

SIDE TRIP FROM MADRID

EL ESCORIAL

50 km (31 miles) northwest of Madrid.

Outside Madrid in the foothills of the Sierra de Guadarrama, El Escorial, commissioned by Felipe II and built over 20 years in the late 16th century, is severe, rectilinear, and unforgiving—it is one of the most gigantic yet simple architectural monuments on the Iberian Peninsula. The Royal Monastery is in the town of San Lorenzo del Escorial, about one hour away from Madrid, and it makes a great half-day side trip from the capital.

GETTING HERE AND AROUND

El Escorial is easily reached by car, train, bus, or organized tour from Madrid. If you plan on taking public transportation, the bus is probably the best option. Herranz's line nos. 661 (through Galapagar) and 664 (through Guadarrama) depart a few times every hour (less frequently on the weekends) from Bay 30 at the *intercambiador* (station) at Moncloa. The 50-minute ride leaves you within a five-minute walk of the monastery. You can also take the cercanías C-8a from either Atocha or Chamartín, but it runs less frequently than the buses and stops at the town of El Escorial, from which you must either take Bus No. L4 (also run by Herranz) to San Lorenzo de El Escorial (where the monastery is) or a strenuous, long walk uphill.

Local tourist office. To get to the local tourist office, cross the arch that's across from the visitors' entrance to the monastery. ⊠ *C. Grimaldi 4, San Lorenzo de El Escorial* ☎ *91/890–5313.*

EXPLORING

Real Monasterio de San Lorenzo de El Escorial (*Royal Monastery of St. Lawrence of Escorial*). Felipe II was one of history's most deeply religious and forbidding monarchs—not to mention one of its most powerful—and the great granite monastery that he had constructed in a remarkable 21 years (1563–84) is an enduring testament to his character.

Felipe built the monastery in the village of San Lorenzo de El Escorial to commemorate Spain's crushing victory over the French at Saint-Quentin on August 10, 1557, and as a final resting place for his all-powerful father, the Holy Roman Emperor Carlos V. He filled the place with treasures as he ruled the largest empire the world had ever seen, knowing all the while that a marble coffin awaited him in the pantheon below. The building's vast rectangle, encompassing 16 courts, is modeled on the red-hot grille upon which St. Lawrence was martyred—appropriately, as August 10 is that saint's day. (It's also said that Felipe's troops accidentally destroyed a church dedicated to St. Lawrence during the battle and sought to make amends.) The building and its adjuncts—a palace, museum, church, and more—can take hours or even days to tour. Easter Sunday's candlelight midnight mass draws crowds, as does the summer tourist season.

The monastery was begun by the architect Juan Bautista de Toledo but finished in 1584 by Juan de Herrera, who would eventually give his name to a major Spanish architectural school. It was completed just in time for Felipe to die here, gangrenous and tortured by the gout that had plagued him for years, in the tiny, sparsely furnished bedroom that resembled a monk's cell more than the resting place of a great monarch. It's in this bedroom—which looks out, through a private entrance, into the royal chapel—that you most appreciate the man's spartan nature. Spain's later Bourbon kings, such as Carlos III and Carlos IV, had clearly different tastes, and their apartments, connected to Felipe's by the Hall of Battles, and which can be visited only by appointment, are far more luxurious.

Perhaps the most interesting part of the entire Escorial is the **Panteón de los Reyes** (Royal Pantheon), a baroque construction room from the 17th century that contains the body of every king since Carlos I except three—Felipe V (buried at La Granja), Ferdinand VI (in Madrid), and Amadeus of Savoy (in Italy). The body of Alfonso XIII, who died in Rome in 1941, was brought to El Escorial in January 1980. The rulers' bodies lie in 26 sumptuous marble-and-bronze sarcophagi that line the walls (three of which are empty, awaiting future rulers). Only those queens who bore sons later crowned lie in the same crypt; the others, along with royal sons and daughters who never ruled, lie nearby, in the **Panteón de los Infantes,** built in the latter part of the 19th century. Many of the royal children are in a single circular tomb made of Carrara marble.

Another highlight is the monastery's surprisingly lavish and colorful **library,** with ceiling paintings by Michelangelo's disciple Pellegrino Tibaldi (1527–96). The imposing austerity of El Escorial's facades makes this chromatic explosion especially powerful; try to save it for last. The library houses 50,000 rare manuscripts, codices, and ancient books, including the diary of St. Teresa of Ávila and the gold-lettered, illuminated Codex Aureus. Tapestries woven from cartoons by Goya, Rubens, and El Greco cover almost every inch of wall space in huge sections of the building, and extraordinary canvases by Velázquez, El Greco, Jacques-Louis David, Ribera, Tintoretto, Rubens, and other masters, collected from around the monastery, are displayed in the **Museos Nuevos** (New Museums). In the **basilica,** don't miss the fresco above the choir, depicting heaven, or Titian's fresco, *The Martyrdom of St. Lawrence,* which shows the saint being roasted alive. ✉ *San Lorenzo de El Escorial* ☎ *91/890–5904, 91/890–5905* 🎟 *€10, €17 with guided tour* 🕒 *Oct.–Mar., Tues.–Sun. 10–6; Apr.–Sept., Tues.–Sun. 10–8.*

WHERE TO EAT

$$$ SPANISH 🍴 **Charolés.** Some go to El Escorial for the monastery; others go for Charolés. It's a landmark that attracts a crowd of its own for its noble bearing, with thick stone walls and vaulted ceilings, wooden beams and floors, and stuffy service; its summer terrace a block from the monastery; and its succulent dishes, such as the heavy beans with clams or mushrooms, and the game meats served grilled or in stews. The four-course mammoth *cocido* (broth, chickpeas, meats, and a salad) on Monday, Wednesday, and Friday tests the endurance of even those with the heartiest appetites. [$] *Average main: €25* ✉ *C. Floridablanca 24* ☎ *91/890–5975.*

$$ SPANISH 🍴 **La Horizontal.** Away from town and surrounded by trees in what used to be a mountain cabin, this family-oriented restaurant is coveted by madrileños, who come here to enjoy the terrace in summer and the cozy bar area with a fireplace in winter. It has a good selection of fish and rice dishes, but the meats and seasonal plates are what draw the large following. Take Paseo Juan de Borbón, which surrounds the monastery, exit through the arches and pass the *casita del infante* (Prince's Quarters) on your way up to the Monte Abantos, or get a cab at the taxi station on Calle Floridablanca. [$] *Average main: €20* ✉ *C. Horizontal s/n* ☎ *91/890–3811* 🕒 *No dinner Mon.–Wed. Oct.–Apr.*

TOLEDO AND TRIPS FROM MADRID

WELCOME TO TOLEDO AND TRIPS FROM MADRID

TOP REASONS TO GO

★ **See El Greco's Toledo:** El Greco's paintings, previously displayed around the world, returned to Toledo in 2014 for the 400th anniversary of the painter's death. Museums have been renovated and El Greco–theme tourist trails link the sites in the stunning city that the Greek-born painter chose to call home.

★ **Be mesmerized by Cuenca's "hanging houses":** Las Casas Colgadas seem to defy gravity, clinging to a cliffside with views over Castile–La Mancha's parched plains.

★ **See Salamanca's old and new cathedrals:** The cathedrals are a fascinating dichotomy—the intricate detail of the new contrasts with the simplicity of the old.

★ **Visit Segovia's aqueduct:** Amazingly well preserved, this still-functioning 2,000-year-old Roman aqueduct is unforgettable.

★ **Get stuck in a time warp:** The walled city of Cáceres is especially evocative at dusk, with its skyline of ancient spires, towers, and cupolas.

1 Castile–La Mancha. Toledo, once home to Spain's famous artist El Greco, is a major destination outside Madrid. Other highlights of the area include lovely Cuenca with its "hanging houses" architecture and Almagro with its splendid parador.

2 Castile–León. There are several worthy destinations in the northern Castile, including medieval Segovia, with its famed Roman aqueduct and Alcázar, and the walled city of Ávila. Farther north is Salamanca, dominated by luminescent sandstone buildings, and the ancient capitals of Burgos and León. Burgos, an early outpost of Christianity, brims with medieval architecture, and you'll see a multitude of nuns roaming its streets. León is a fun university town with some of its Roman walls still in place.

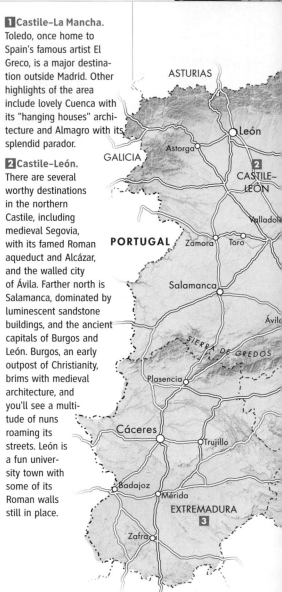

3 Extremadura. Green valleys and pristine mountain villages, along with cities like Cáceres and Trujillo, are the main attractions in upper Extremadura, while the Jerte Valley has stunning natural settings with remote villages that seem to have stopped short of the 20th century. Southern Extremadura reveals the influence of Portugal and Andalusia, and the early Roman capital of Lusitania at Mérida is one of Iberia's finest compendiums of Roman ruins. The *dehesa*, southwestern Spain's rolling oak forest and meadowland, is prime habitat for the semiwild Iberian pig and covers much of southern Extremadura.

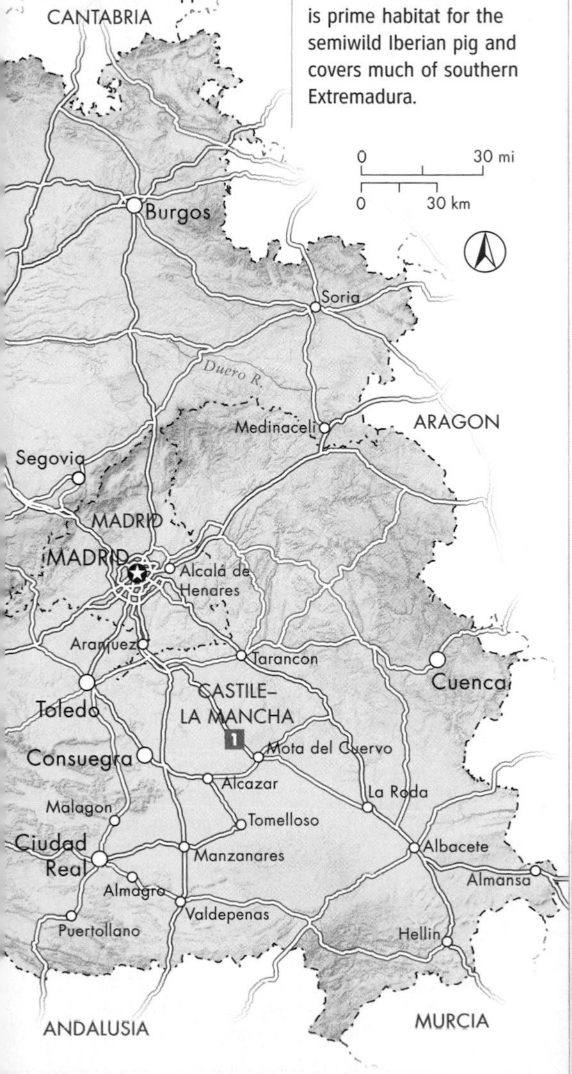

CANTABRIA
0
30 mi
0
30 km
Burgos
Soria
Duero R.
Medinaceli
ARAGON
Segovia
MADRID
MADRID
Alcalá de Henares
Aranjuez
Tarancon
Cuenca
Toledo
CASTILE–LA MANCHA
1
Mota del Cuervo
Consuegra
Alcazar
La Roda
Malagon
Tomelloso
Ciudad Real
Manzanares
Albacete
Almansa
Almagro
Valdepenas
Puertollano
Hellin
ANDALUSIA
MURCIA

GETTING ORIENTED

Castile–La Mancha and Castile–León are like parentheses around Madrid, one north and one south. The name "Castile" refers to the great east–west line of castles and fortified towns built in the 12th century between Salamanca and Soria. Segovia's Alcázar, Ávila's fully intact city walls, and other bastions are among Castile's greatest monuments. Extremadura, just west of Madrid, covers an area of 41,602 square km (16,063 square miles) and consists of two provinces: Cáceres to the north and Badajoz to the south, divided by the Toledo Mountains. To the west, this region borders Portugal; to the south, Andalusia; and to the east, Castile–La Mancha.

EATING AND DRINKING WELL IN CASTILE AND EXTREMADURA

In Spain's central *meseta,* an arid, high plateau, the peasant cooking provides comfort and energy. Roast lamb, pork, and goat are staples, as are soups, stews, and dishes made from scraps, such as the classic *migas de pastor,* shepherd's bread crumbs.

(top left) Roast lamb with potatoes (top right) A simple dish of migas is an excellent way to use up leftover bread. (bottom left) Pisto manchego incorporates a variety of stewed vegetables.

Classic Castilian dishes are *cordero* (lamb) and *cochinillo* (suckling pig) roasted in wood ovens, and other prized entrées include *perdiz en escabeche* (marinated partridge), and *perdices a la Toledana* (stewed partridge, Toledo-style). Broad-bean dishes are specialties in the areas around Ávila and La Granja (Segovia), while *trucha* (trout) and *cangrejos de río* (river crayfish) are Guadalajara specialties. Some of Castile's most exotic cuisine is found in Cuenca, where a Moorish influence appears in such dishes as *gazpacho pastor* (shepherd's stew), a stew made with an assortment of meats. Wild mushrooms are used to enhance aromas in meat dishes and stews or are served on their own in earthenware dishes.

DON QUIXOTE FOOD

Cervantine menus are favorites at taverns and inns throughout Quixote country southeast of Madrid. Both *gachas manchegas* (a thick peasant porridge based on fried legume flour and pork) and *duelos y quebrantos* (scrambled eggs and bacon) are mentioned in *Don Quixote* as typical offerings on late-15th-century rural menus.

3

LAMB

Roast lamb, *cordero asado,* is a favorite dish throughout Castile. A *lechazo,* or milk-fed lamb, should be two to three weeks old and have been carefully protected from bumps and bruises by his shepherd. It's handled with great delicacy all the way to the wood oven where it's roasted slowly on low heat. The forequarters are considered better than the hindquarters, and the left side is more tender, as lambs tend to lie on their right sides, which toughens the meat.

PARTRIDGE

Perdices a la Toledana, partridge prepared in the Toledo way, is one of Castile–La Mancha's most sought-after gastronomical delicacies. Toledo partridges are neither *estofadas* (stewed) nor *escabechadas* (marinated) but, rather, cooked on low heat in wine with vinegar. Up to a dozen wild partridges stew for hours with white wine, olive oil, onions, garlic, and bay leaves until the sauce has nearly evaporated. October to February is the hunting season for partridge and the best time to try this local favorite with fresh birds.

VEGETABLE STEW

La Mancha, the arid and windswept area southeast of Madrid, has its moist vegetable-growing pockets along the Tajo River. *Pisto manchego* is the classic vegetable stew, with ham and chorizo added for protein and flavor. Onions,

green peppers, eggplant, ripe tomatoes, olive oil, chorizo, and ham are the ingredients in this Castilian favorite typically served in an earthenware vessel.

MIGAS DE PASTOR

Translated as "shepherd's bread crumbs," this dish is made with hardened bread that's been softened with water, then broken up and fried in olive oil with lots of garlic and sometimes eggs, as well as bacon, chorizo, peppers, sardines, or squash if available.

GAZPACHO PASTOR (SHEPHERD'S STEW)

Andalusian gazpacho is a cold soup, but in La Mancha, especially in and around Cuenca, gazpacho is a thick stew made of virtually everything in the barnyard, and served very hot. Partridge, hare, rabbit, hen, peppers, paprika, and *tortas gazpacheras* (flatbread made especially for this dish) complete the stew.

CASTILIAN WINES

In Toledo, Carlos Falcó (aka Marqués de Griñón) has developed excellent Dominio de Valdepusa wines using petit verdot and syrah grapes. In Ribera del Duero, winemakers from Pingus and Protos to Pago de Carraovejas offer full-bodied wines using tempranillo grapes, while El Bierzo northwest of León has good values and earthy wines made with the local mencía grape.

Updated by
Lauren Frayer

Madrid, in the center of Spain, is an excellent jumping-off point for exploring, and the high-speed train puts many destinations within easy reach. The Castiles, which bracket Madrid to the north and south, and Extremadura, bordering Portugal, are filled with compelling destinations, steeped in tradition.

For all the variety in the towns and countryside around Madrid, there's something of an underlying unity in Castile—the high, wide meseta of gray, bronze, and (briefly) green. This central Spanish steppe is divided into what was historically known as Old and New Castile, the former north of Madrid, the latter south (known as "New" because it was captured from the Moors a bit later). Occasionally, elderly Spaniards may still refer to the Castiles as "Old" or "New"—labels that persisted through the Franco years—but most people nowadays prefer Castilla y León or Castile–León for the area north of Madrid and Castilla y La Mancha or Castile–La Mancha for the area to the south.

Over the centuries, poets and others have characterized Castile as austere and melancholy. Gaunt mountain ranges frame the horizons; gorges and rocky outcrops break up flat expanses; and the fields around Ávila and Segovia are littered with giant boulders. Castilian villages are built predominantly of granite, and their solid, formidable look contrasts markedly with the whitewashed walls of most of southern Spain.

The very name Extremadura, widely accepted as "the far end of the Duero," as in the Duero River, expresses the wild, remote, isolated, and end-of-the-line character of the region bordering Portugal. With its poor soil and minimal industry, Extremadura never experienced the kind of modern economic development typical of other parts of Spain, and it's still the country's poorest province, but for the tourist, this otherworldly, lost-in-time feel is unforgettable. No other place in Spain has as many Roman monuments as Mérida, capital of the vast Roman province of Lusitania, which included most of the western half of the Iberian Peninsula. Mérida guarded the Vía de la Plata, the major Roman highway that crossed Extremadura from north to south, connecting Gijón with Seville. The economy and the arts declined after the Romans left, but the region revived in the 16th century, when explorers and conquerors of the New World—from Francisco Pizarro and Hernán Cortés to Francisco de Orellana, first navigator of the Amazon—returned to their birthplace. These men built the magnificent palaces that now glorify towns such as Cáceres and Trujillo, and they turned the remote monastery of Guadalupe into one of the great artistic repositories of Spain.

PLANNING

WHEN TO GO

July and August can be brutally hot, and November through February can get bitterly cold, especially in the Sierra de Guadarrama. May and October, when the weather is sunny but relatively cool, are the two best months to visit central Spain.

Spring in Extremadura is the ideal season, especially in the countryside, when the valleys and hills are covered with a dazzle of wildflowers. If you can time it right, the stunning spectacle of cherry-blossom season in the Jerte Valley and La Vera takes place around mid-March. Fall is also a good time for Extremadura, though there may be rain starting in late October.

PLANNING YOUR TIME

Madrid is an excellent hub for venturing farther into Spain, but with so many choices, we've divided them into must-see stand-alone destinations, and those that are worthy stops if you're traveling on to other parts of the country. Some are day trips; others are best overnight.

Must-see, short-trip destinations from Madrid are **Toledo, Segovia** (with **Sepúlveda**), **Sigüenza,** and **Salamanca.** Salamanca should be an overnight trip, because it's farther, and it also has fun nightlife.

Otherwise, if you're traveling to other areas in Spain, we suggest the following stopover destinations:

If you're on your way to Salamanca, stop in **Ávila** (buses go direct to Salamanca without stopping, but most trains stop in **Ávila**).

If you're on your way to Santander or Bilbao, stop in **Burgos.**

If you're on your way to Asturias, stop in **León.**

If you're on your way to Lugo and A Coruña, in Galicia, stop in **Villafranca del Bierzo** or **Astorga.**

If you're on your way to Córdoba or Granada, stop in **Almagro.**

If you're on your way to Valencia, detour to **Cuenca.** Most trains, including the new high-speed AVE to Valencia, will go through Cuenca.

Extremadura is a neglected destination, even for Spanish tourists, but it's a beautiful part of the country, with fascinating cities like Cáceres (a UNESCO World Heritage site) and Trujillo. You can get a lightning impression of Extremadura in a day's drive from Madrid. It's about 2½ hours from Madrid to **Jerte**; from there, you can take the A66 south to **Cáceres,** then head east to **Trujillo** on the N521. Split your time evenly between Cáceres and Trujillo. If you have more time, spend a day exploring the Roman monuments in Mérida, and do some world-famous bird-watching in the **Parque Natural de Monfragüe,** near **Plasencia.** If you can, visit the **Monasterio de Yuste,** where Spain's founding emperor Carlos V died in 1558.

FESTIVALS

Central Spain is the land of festivals, and it's the best place to find an authentic, truly Spanish vibe. Cuenca's Easter celebration and Toledo's Corpus Christi draw people from all over Spain, if not the world. During the pre-Lenten carnival, León and nearby La Bañeza are popular party centers. Expect crowds and book accommodations in advance. Gastronomic festivals abound.

Capeas. From early to mid-September the town fills with bullfighting aficionados from across the country for 12 days of bull-running and bullfighting events with young bulls—but with a proviso that no harm should come to them (they are returned to their pastures when it's all over). ⊠ *Segura de León* ⊕ *www.seguradeleon.com.*

Celebración del Cerdo y Vino. This September festival celebrates pork and wine, with innumerable pork products prepared in public demonstrations. ⊠ *Cáceres* ☎ *927/255765 for tourist office* ⊕ *www.ayto-caceres.es.*

Feria del Queso. Trujillo's cheese festival, in early May, brings together Spain's finest artisanal cheese makers, with hundreds of varieties to taste and buy. The event is understandably popular with foodies. ⊠ *Trujillo* ☎ *927/321450* ⊕ *www.feriadelquesotrujillo.es.*

Festival de Teatro Clásico. In Mérida, the highlight of the cultural calendar is this annual festival, held in the Roman theater from early July to mid-August. It features opera as well as classical drama, and celebrated its 60th year in 2014. ⊠ *Mérida* ☎ *924/009480* ⊕ *www.festivaldemerida.es.*

Fiesta de San Juanin Coria. This ancient festival in late June is a celebration of bulls and bullfighting that has endured for centuries. ⊠ *Coria* ☎ *927/508000* ⊕ *www.coria.org.*

Los Escobazos. On December 7, the city is filled with bonfires to celebrate this festival, dedicated to the Virgen de la Concepción, during which locals play-fight with torches made out of brooms. ⊠ *Jarandilla de la Vera* ☎ *927/560460 for tourist office* ⊕ *www.jarandilla.com.*

WOMAD Cáceres. The World of Music, Arts and Dance in early May draws crowds of around 75,000. Main stages are set up in the magical surroundings of this ancient city's plazas for free concerts, and other events include shows staged in the Gran Teatro, children's events, and a grand procession. ⊠ *Cáceres* ⊕ *www.womap.es or www.womad.org/festivals/caceres.*

GETTING HERE AND AROUND
AIR TRAVEL

The only international airport in Castile is Madrid's Barajas; Salamanca, León, and Valladolid have domestic airports, but the economic crisis has led to a reduction in traffic and they receive very few flights these days. Extremadura's only airport is Badajoz, which receives domestic flights from Madrid, Barcelona, and Bilbao. The nearest international airports are Madrid and Seville.

BUS TRAVEL

Bus connections between Madrid and Castile are excellent. There are several stations and stops in Madrid; buses to Toledo (1 hour) leave every half hour from the Estación del Sur, and buses to Segovia (1¼ hours) leave every hour from La Sepulvedana's headquarters, near Príncipe Pío. Larrea sends buses to Ávila (1¾ hours) from the Estación del Sur. ALSA and Movelia have service to León (4½ hours). Auto Res serves Cuenca (2¾ hours) and Salamanca (3 hours). Buses to Burgos (2½ hours) are run by Continental Auto.

From Burgos, buses head north to the Basque Country; from León, you can press on to Asturias. Service between towns is not as frequent as it is to and from Madrid, so you may find it quicker to return to Madrid and make your way from there. Reservations are rarely necessary.

Buses to Extremadura's main cities can be reached from Madrid and are reliable. The first bus of the day on lesser routes often sets off early in the morning, so plan carefully to avoid getting stranded. Some examples of destinations from Madrid are: Cáceres (7 daily), Guadalupe (2 daily), Trujillo (12 daily), and Mérida (8 daily). For schedules and prices, check the tourist offices or contact the Auto Res bus line. Note that it's best to avoid taking the bus at rush hour, as journeys can be delayed by more than an hour.

CAR TRAVEL

Major divided highways—the A1 through A6—radiate out from Madrid, making Spain's farthest corners no more than five- to six-hour drives, and the capital's outlying towns are only minutes away. If possible, avoid returning to Madrid on major highways at the end of a weekend or a holiday. The beginning and end of August are notorious for traffic jams, as is Semana Santa (Holy Week), which starts on Palm Sunday and ends on Easter Sunday. Side roads vary in quality but provide one of the great pleasures of driving around the Castilian countryside: surprise encounters with historical monuments and spectacular vistas.

If you're heading from Madrid to Extremadura by car, the main gateway, the six-lane A5, moves quickly. The A66, or Vía de la Plata, which crosses Extremadura from north to south, is also effective. The fastest way heading from Portugal is the (Portuguese) A6 from Lisbon to Badajoz (not to be confused with the Spanish A6, which runs northwest from Madrid to Galicia). The main roads are well surfaced and not too congested. Side roads—particularly those that cross the wilder mountainous districts, such as the Sierra de Guadalupe—can be both poorly paved and marked, but afford some of the most spectacular vistas in Extremadura.

Mileage from Madrid:

Madrid to Burgos is 243 km (151 miles).

Madrid to Cáceres is 299 km (186 miles).

Madrid to Cuenca is 168 km (105 miles).

Madrid to Granada is 428 km (266 miles).

Madrid to Léon is 334 km (208 miles).

Madrid to Salamanca is 212 km (132 miles).

Madrid to Segovia is 91 km (57 miles).

Madrid to Toledo is 88 km (55 miles).

Madrid to Ávila is 114 km (71 miles).

The Travel Smart chapter has contact info for major car rental agencies.

TRAIN TRAVEL

All the main towns in Castile–León and Castile–La Mancha are accessible by multiple daily trains from Madrid, with tickets ranging from about €10 to €30, depending on train speed (the high-speed AVE service costs more), the time of day, and the day of the week. Several towns make feasible day trips: there are commuter trains from Madrid to Segovia (30 minutes), Guadalajara (30 minutes), and Toledo (30 minutes). Trains to Toledo depart from Madrid's Atocha station; trains to Salamanca, Burgos, and León depart from Chamartín; and both stations serve Ávila, Segovia, El Escorial, and Sigüenza, though Chamartín may have more frequent service. Trains from Segovia go only to Madrid, but you can change at Villalba for Ávila and Salamanca.

For Extremadura, trains from Madrid stop at Monfragüe, Plasencia, Cáceres, Mérida, Zafra, and Badajoz, running as often as six times daily. The journey from Madrid to Cáceres takes about four hours. Within the province there are services from Badajoz to Cáceres (3 daily, 1 hour 55 minutes), to Mérida (5 daily, 40 minutes), and to Plasencia (2 daily, 2 hours 40 minutes); from Cáceres to Badajoz (3 daily, 1 hour 55 minutes), to Mérida (5 daily, 1 hour), to Plasencia (4 daily, 1 hour 10 minutes), and to Zafra (2 daily, 2 hours 10 minutes); from Plasencia to Badajoz (2 daily, 3 hours), to Cáceres (4 daily, 1 hour 10 minutes), and to Mérida (4 daily, 2 hours 10 minutes). Note that several cities have separate train stations for normal versus AVE high-speed rail service; the newer AVE stations are often farther from town centers.

RESTAURANTS

This is Spain's authentic heartland, bereft of touristy hamburger joints and filled instead with the country's most traditional *tavernas,* which attract Spanish foodies from across the country. Some of the most renowned restaurants in this region are small and family-run, while a few new avant-garde spots in Extremadura serve up modern architecture as well as experimental fusion dishes.

HOTELS

Many of the oldest and most attractive paradores in Castile are in quieter towns such as Almagro, Ávila, Cuenca, León, and Sigüenza. Those in Toledo, Segovia, and Salamanca are modern buildings with magnificent views and, in the case of Segovia, have wonderful indoor and outdoor swimming pools. There are plenty of pleasant alternatives to paradores, too, such as Segovia's Hotel Infanta Isabel, Salamanca's Hotel Rector, and Cuenca's Posada San José, a 16th-century convent. In Extremadura the paradores occupy buildings of great historic or architectural interest. *Hotel reviews have been shortened. For full information, visit Fodors.com.*

WHAT IT COSTS IN EUROS				
	$	**$$**	**$$$**	**$$$$**
estaurants	under €13	€13–€17	€18–€22	over €22
lotels	under €91	€91–€125	€126–€180	over €180

Restaurant prices are the average cost of a main course or equivalent combination of smaller dishes at dinner. Hotel prices are the lowest cost of a standard double room in high season.

TOURS

In summer the tourist offices of Segovia, Toledo, and Sigüenza organize Trénes Turísticos (miniature tourist trains) that glide past all the major sights; contact local tourist offices for schedules.

A great way to really get to know Extremadura is by bike, and you can cut down on the map reading by following the ancient Roman road, the Vía de la Plata: it runs through Extremadura from north to south along A66, dividing it in two, and passes by such villages as Plasencia, Cáceres, Mérida, and Zafra. Parts of the Vía are still preserved and good for bicycling. Note that the region north of the province of Cáceres, including the Jerte Valley, La Vera, and the area surrounding Guadalupe, is mountainous and uneven: be prepared for a bumpy and exhausting ride. (One ambitious Vía hiker created the unofficial website ⊕ *www. theviadelaplata.com*, which has helpful information in English). The regional government has also opened a Vía Verde, or "green way" path along disused railroads, which goes from Logrosán (a couple of miles southwest of Guadalupe) to Villanueva de la Serena (east of Mérida and near Don Benito). This path is a roughly cleared track, more like a nature trail for hikers and bikers, and closed to motor vehicles. Check ⊕ *www.viasverdes.com* for maps of this and other trails.

Contacts Equiberia. Horseback tours, ranging from one to 10 days, offer a unique way to experience the gorges, fields, and forests of the Sierra de Guadarrama. ✉ *Navarredonda de Gredos, Ávila* ☎ *689/343974* ⊕ *www.equiberia.com* 💷 *From €80 per day.* **Hidden Trails.** Based in Vancouver, Canada, this company offers weeklong horseback tours of the Gredo Mountains on the border of Cáceres province. Prices include accommodations and meals. ☎ *888/987–2457 from U.S. or Canada (888/9–TRAILS), 604/323–1141 from U.S. or Canada* ⊕ *www.hiddentrails.com* 💷 *From €950.* **Valle Aventura.** Hiking, horseback-riding, cycling, and kayaking trips in the Jerte Valley can be organized with this company. Prices may not include meals. ☎ *636/631182* ⊕ *www.valleaventura. com* 💷 *Day tours from €213.*

CASTILE–LA MANCHA

Castile–La Mancha is the land of Don Quixote, Cervantes's chivalrous hero. Some of Spain's oldest and most traditional cities are found here, steeped in culture and legend, and often not much visited by tourists. The architecture of Toledo and Cuenca are definite highlights, but the stark plains and villages are also enchanting, with open expanses rarely seen in Western Europe.

TOLEDO

88 km (55 miles) southwest of Madrid.

Fodor's Choice   Long the spiritual capital of Spain, Toledo is perched atop a rocky
★   mount with steep golden hills rising on either side and is bound on three
sides by the Río Tajo (Tagus River). When the Romans arrived here in
192 BC, they built their fortress (the Alcázar) on the highest point of
the rock. Later, the Visigoths remodeled the stronghold.

In the 8th century, the Moors arrived and strengthened Toledo's reputation as a center of religion and learning. Unusual tolerance was
extended to those who practiced Christianity (the Mozarabs) and to the
city's exceptionally large Jewish population. Today, the Moorish legacy
is evident in Toledo's strong crafts tradition, the mazelike streets, and
the predominance of brick (rather than the stone of many of Spain's
historical cities). For the Moors, beauty was to be savored from within
rather than displayed on the surface. Even Toledo's cathedral—one
of the most richly endowed in Spain—is hard to see from the outside,
largely obscured by the warren of houses around it.

Alfonso VI, aided by El Cid ("Lord Conqueror"), captured the city in
1085 and dubbed himself emperor of Toledo. Under the Christians,
the town's strong intellectual life was maintained, and Toledo became
famous for its school of translators, who taught Arab medicine, law,
culture, and philosophy. Religious tolerance continued, and during the
rule of Pedro the Cruel (so named because he allegedly had members
of his own family murdered to advance his position), a Jewish banker,
Samuel Levi, became the royal treasurer and one of the wealthiest men
in the booming city. By the early 1600s, however, hostility toward Jews
and Arabs had grown as Toledo developed into a bastion of the Catholic Church.

Under Toledo's long line of cardinals—most notably Mendoza, Tavera,
and Cisneros—Renaissance Toledo emerged as a center of the humani-
ties. Economically and politically, however, Toledo began to decline
at the end of the 15th century. The expulsion of the Jews from Spain
in 1492, as part of the Spanish Inquisition, eroded Toledo's economic
prowess. When Madrid became the permanent center of the Spanish
court in 1561, Toledo lost its political importance, and the expulsion
from Spain of the converted Arabs (Moriscos) in 1601 meant the departure of most of the city's artisan community. The years the painter El
Greco spent in Toledo—from 1572 to his death in 1614—were those
of the city's decline, which is greatly reflected in his works. In the late
19th century, after hundreds of years of neglect, the works of El Greco
came to be widely appreciated, and Toledo was transformed into a
major tourist destination. Today, Toledo is conservative, prosperous,
proud—and a bit provincial. Its winding streets and steep hills can be
exasperating, especially when you're searching for a specific sight. Take
the entire day to absorb the town's medieval trappings and expect to
get a little lost.

GETTING HERE AND AROUND

The best way to get to Toledo from Madrid is the high-speed AVE train. The AVE leaves from Madrid at minimum nine times daily from Atocha station and gets you there in 30 minutes. Buses leave every half hour from Plaza Elíptica and take 1¼ hours.

TOURS

Cuentame Toledo. The name translates as "Tell me about Toledo" and that's just what they do. The company offers free tours (in English and Spanish) of Toledo's historic center at 5 pm daily, plus a range of other paid tours of the city's monuments, best-kept secrets, subterranean passageways, and urban legends. There are also El Greco–themed tours, nighttime ghost tours, and other routes that include visits to ancient Arab baths. ⊠ *Corral de Don Diego 5* ☏ *925/210767, 608/935856* ⊕ *www.cuentametoledo.com* 🖃 *Free or €12, depending on the tour.*

FAMILY **Toledo TrainVision.** The tourist train chugs past many of Toledo's main sights, departing from the Plaza de Zocodover every hour on the hour during the week, and every 30 minutes on weekends. The tour takes 45–50 minutes and has recorded information in 13 languages—including English, Spanish and French—plus children's versions in those three languages too. Buy tickets at the kiosk in Plaza de Zocodover. ⊠ *Pl. de Zocodover* ☏ *625/301890* 🖃 *€5.10, includes audio tour* ☉ *Apr.–Sept., Mon.–Thurs. 10–7:30, Fri.–Sun. 10 am–11:30 pm; Oct.–Mar., Mon.–Thurs. 10–5, Fri.–Sun. 10–6:30.*

Toledo Xperiences. Lola Torres is a local woman with 20 years' experience as a Toledo tour guide. She can help arrange tours for families or groups, with themes ranging from gastronomy to Jewish history to El Greco, in English, French, and Spanish. ☏ *699/458406* 🖃 *Tours are customized so prices vary; call for details.*

ESSENTIALS

Visitor Information Provincial Tourist Office ⊠ *Subida de la Granja s/n* ☏ *925/248232* ⊕ *www.diputoledo.es.* **Toledo.** There are also smaller branches at the AVE train station and Ayuntamiento (town hall). ⊠ *Pl. de Zocodover 6* ☏ *925/267666, 687/854965, 925/254030, 925/239121* ⊕ *www.toledo-turismo.com.*

TOP ATTRACTIONS

Alcázar. Originally a Moorish citadel (*alcázar* is Arabic for "fortress") and occupied from the 10th century until the Reconquest, Toledo's Alcázar is on a hill just outside the walled city, dominating the horizon. The south facade—the building's most severe—is the work of Juan de Herrera, of El Escorial fame, while the east facade incorporates a large section of battlements. The finest facade is the northern, one of many Toledan works by Covarrubias, who did more than any other architect to introduce the Renaissance style here. The building's architectural highlight is Covarrubias's Italianate courtyard, which, like most other parts of the building, was largely rebuilt after the civil war, when the Alcázar was besieged by the Republicans. Though the Nationalists' ranks were depleted, they held onto the building. General Francisco Franco later turned the Alcázar into a monument to Nationalist bravery. The Alcázar now houses the **Museo del Ejército** (Military Museum),

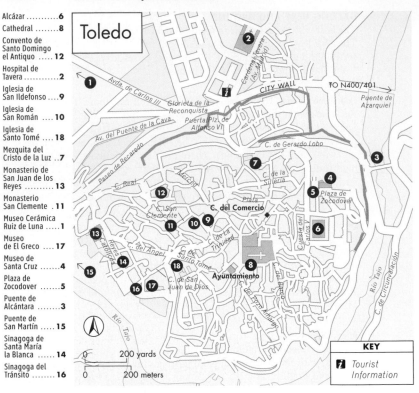

which was formerly in Madrid. ■TIP→ Be sure to keep your ticket— it's needed when you exit the museum. ⊠ *Cuesta de los Capuchinos* ☎ *925/238800* ⊕ *www.museo.ejercito.es* 🎫 *€5, €8 with audio guide (in five languages); free Sun. 10–3. Additional fee may be charged for temporary exhibitions* ⊙ *Thurs.–Tues. 11–5. Last tickets sold 30 mins before closing.*

Calle del Comercio. Near Plaza de Zocodover, this is the town's narrow and busy pedestrian thoroughfare. It's lined with bars and shops and shaded in summer by awnings.

Fodor's Choice ★   **Cathedral.** One of the most impressive structures in all of Spain, this is a must-see on any visit to the city. The elaborate structure owes its impressive Mozarabic chapel, with an elongated dome crowning the west facade, to Jorge Manuel Theotokópoulos. The rest of the facade, however, is mainly early 15th century; it features a depiction of Mary presenting her robe to Ildefonsus, Toledo's patron saint, a Visigoth who was archbishop of the city in the 7th century. Chartres and other Gothic cathedrals in France inspired the cathedral's 13th-century architecture, but the squat proportions give it a Spanish feel, as do the weight of the furnishings and the elaborate choir in the center of the nave. Immediately to your right as you enter the building is a beautifully carved plateresque doorway by Covarrubias, marking the entrance to the Treasury. The latter houses a small Crucifixion by the Italian painter Cimabue and an extraordinarily intricate late-15th-century monstrance by Juan del Arfe, a silversmith of German descent; the ceiling is an excellent example of Mudejar (11th- to 16th-century Moorish-influenced) workmanship.

From here, walk around to the ambulatory; off to the right side is a chapter house with a strange mixture of Italianate frescoes by Juan de Borgoña. In the middle of the ambulatory is an exemplary baroque illusionism by Narciso Tomé known as the *Transparente,* a blend of painting, stucco, and sculpture. Finally, off the northern end of the ambulatory, you'll come to the exquisite sacristy and several El Grecos, including one version of *El Espolio* (*Christ Being Stripped of His Raiment*), the first recorded instance of the painter in Spain. Before leaving the sacristy, look up at the colorful and spirited late-baroque ceiling painting by the Italian Luca Giordano. ⊠ *Calle Cardenal Cisneros 1* ☎ *925/222241* ⊕ *www.catedralprimada.es* 🎟 *€8 for cathedral and museums, €11 to also include tower* ☉ *Mon.–Sat. 10–6:30, Sun. and holidays 2–6:30.*

Hospital de Tavera. Architect Alonso de Covarrubias's last work, this hospital lies outside the city walls, beyond Toledo's main northern gate. A fine example of Spanish Renaissance architecture, the building also houses the **Museo de Duque de Lema** in its southern wing. The most important work in the museum's miscellaneous collection is a painting by the 17th-century artist José Ribera. The hospital's monumental chapel holds El Greco's *Baptism of Christ* and the exquisitely carved marble tomb of Cardinal Tavera, the last work of Alonso de Berruguete. Descend into the crypt to experience some bizarre acoustical effects. A full ticket includes the hospital, museum, old pharmacy, and Renaissance patios. A partial ticket includes everything except the museum. Guided tours are available at 45-minute intervals. ⊠ *Calle Duque de Lerma 2 (also known as Calle Cardenal Tavera)* ☎ *925/220451* ⊕ *www.fundacionmedinaceli.org* 🎟 *€4.50 full ticket, €3.50 partial ticket* ☉ *Mon.–Sat. and holidays 10–1:30 and 3–5:30, Sun. 10–1:30. Ticket office closes 45 mins before the museum.*

Fodor's Choice ★ **Iglesia de San Ildefonso** (*San Ildefonso Church, The Jesuits*). Sometimes simply called "Jesuitas," for the religious order that founded it, the Iglesia de San Ildefonso is named for Toledo's patron saint, a local bishop in the 7th century. It was finally consecrated in 1718, after taking 150 years to build the baroque stone facade with giant Corinthian columns. Its semispherical dome is one of the icons of Toledo's skyline. This impressive building deserves a visit, and a climb up its tower (€2.50) affords the best views over all of Toledo. ⊠ *Pl. Juan de Mariana 1* ☎ *925/251507* 🎟 *€2.50* ☉ *Daily 10–5:45 (until 6:45 in summer).*

Iglesia de Santo Tomé (*Santo Tomé Church*). Not to be confused with the marzipan shop of the same name, the real Santo Tomé is a chapel topped with a Mudejar tower, and built specially to house El Greco's most famous painting, *The Burial of Count Orgaz.* The painting portrays the benefactor of the church being buried with the posthumous assistance of St. Augustine and St. Stephen, who have appeared at the funeral to

DID YOU KNOW?

The Alcázar of Toledo has dominated the city since at least the 3rd century. It is the setting for an important scene of Nationalist lore: during the Spanish Civil War, the Nationalist Colonel Moscardü was defending the building against overwhelming Republican forces. The Republicans held his son hostage, demanding the Alcázar be surrendered. To his son's entreaties to "Surrender or they will shoot me," the father replied, "Then commend your soul to God and die like a hero."

thank the count for his donations to religious institutions named after the two saints. Though the count's burial took place in the 14th century, El Greco painted the onlookers in contemporary 16th-century costumes and included people he knew; the boy in the foreground is one of El Greco's sons, and the sixth figure on the left is said to be the artist himself. Santo Tomé is Toledo's most-visited church besides the Cathedral so to avoid crowds in summer, plan to visit as soon as the building opens. ⊠ *Pl. del Conde 4, Calle Santo Tomé* ☎ *925/256098* ⊕ *www. santotome.org* ✑ *€2.50* ⊙ *Daily 10–5:45 (until 6:45 Mar.–mid-Oct.).*

Fodor's Choice
★ **Monasterio San Clemente.** Founded in 1131, this is Toledo's oldest convent—and it's still in use. About 20 nuns live here, producing their own sweet wine and some of the best marzipan around. Tucked away in the city's historic quarter, the impressive complex includes ruins of a mosque, on which a chapel was built in the Middle Ages. Also here are the preserved ruins of an Islamic house and courtyard, with an ancient well and Arab baths, and a Jewish house from the same period. Free tours, twice daily, include a visit to the kitchen where the Mother Superior usually lets you sample some sweets. Skip the tourist marzipan shops and buy the real stuff here. There's also an adjacent cultural center with rotating history exhibits. ⊠ *Calle San Clemente* ☎ *925/253080* ✑ *termas@consorciotoledo.org* ⊙ *Tues.–Sat. 11–1:30 and 4–6:30, Sun. Mass at noon. Tours: Tues.–Sat. at 11 and 5, Sun. at 11.*

Fodor's Choice
★ **Museo de El Greco** (*El Greco Museum*). This house that once belonged to Peter the Cruel's treasurer, Samuel Levi, is said to have later been El Greco's home, though there's little historical evidence to prove the artist lived here. Nevertheless, the interior is decorated to resemble a "typical" house of El Greco's time. The house is now incorporated into a revamped El Greco museum with several of the artist's paintings, including a panorama of Toledo with the Hospital of Tavera in the foreground, and works of several of El Greco's students (including his son) and other 16th- and 17th-century artists. Medieval caves have been excavated at the site, and there's a beautiful garden in which to take refuge from Toledo's often-scorching summer heat. The impressive museum complex has become a centerpiece for Toledo tourism since the "El Greco 2014" festival, marking the 400th anniversary of the artist's death. ⊠ *Paseo del Tránsito s/n* ☎ *925/223665* ⊕ *museodelgreco. mcu.es or www.elgreco2014.com* ✑ *€3 (free Sat. after 2)* ⊙ *Tues.–Sat. 9:30–6:30 (until 8 Apr.–Sept.), Sun. and holidays 10–3. Last tickets sold 15 mins before closing.*

Museo de Santa Cruz. In a beautiful Renaissance hospital with a stunning classical-plateresque facade, this museum is open all day without a break (unlike many of Toledo's other sights). Aside from some small renovations in early 2013, the light and elegant interior has changed little since the 16th century. Works of art have replaced the hospital beds, and among the displays is El Greco's *Assumption* of 1613, the artist's last known work. A small **Museo de Arqueología** (Museum of Archaeology) is in and around the hospital's delightful cloister. ⊠ *Calle Cervantes 3* ☎ *925/221036* ✑ *Free* ⊙ *Mon.–Sat. 10–7, Sun. and holidays 10–2:30.*

Plaza de Zocodover. Toledo's main square was built in the early 17th century as part of an unsuccessful attempt to impose a rigid geometry on the chaotic Moorish streets. Over the centuries, this tiny plaza has hosted bullfights, executions by the Spanish Inquisition, and countless street fairs. Today it's home to the largest and oldest marzipan store in town, Santo Tomé. You can catch inner-city buses here, and the tourist office is on the south side of the plaza.

Fodor's Choice
★

Sinagoga del Tránsito (*Museo Sefardí, Sephardic Museum*). Financed by Samuel Levi, this 14th-century rectangular synagogue is plain on the outside, but spectacular on the inside, with walls embellished in intricate Mudejar decoration, and both Hebrew and Arabic inscriptions glorifying God, Peter the Cruel, and Levi himself. It's a rare example of architecture reflecting Arabic as the lingua franca of medieval Spanish Jews. It's said that Levi imported cedars from Lebanon for the building's construction, à la Solomon when he built the First Temple in Jerusalem. This is one of only three synagogues still fully standing in Spain (two in Toledo, one in Córdoba), from an era when there were hundreds— though more are in the process of being excavated. Adjoining the main hall is the **Museo Sefardí,** a small but excellent museum of Jewish culture in Spain. ⊠ *Calle Samuel Levi 2* ☎ *925/223665* ⊕ *museosefardi. mcu.es* 🖾 *€3 (free Sat. afternoon)* ⊙ *Tues.–Sat. 9:30–6:30 (until 8 Apr.– Sept.), Sun. and holidays 10–3.*

WORTH NOTING

Convento de Santo Domingo el Antiguo (*Convento de Santo Domingo de Silos; Santo Domingo Convent*). A few minutes' walk north of San Román, this 16th-century convent church is where you'll find the earliest of El Greco's Toledo paintings as well as the crypt where the artist is believed to be buried. The friendly nuns at the convent will show you around its odd little museum, which includes documents bearing El Greco's signature. ⊠ *Pl. Santo Domingo el Antiguo* ☎ *925/222930* 🖾 *€2.50* ⊙ *Mon.–Sat. 11–1:30 and 4–7, Sun. and holidays 4–7.*

Iglesia de San Román. Hidden in a virtually unspoiled part of Toledo, this early-13th-century Mudejar church is now the **Museo de los Concilios y de la Cultura Visigótica,** with exhibits of statuary, manuscript illustrations, jewelry, and an extensive collection of frescoes. The church tower is adjacent to the ruins of Roman baths. ⊠ *Calle San Roman* ☎ *925/227872* 🖾 *Free* ⊙ *Tues.–Sat. 10–2:30 and 4–7, Sun. and holidays 10–2:30.*

Mezquita del Cristo de la Luz (*Mosque of Christ of the Light*). This mosque-chapel is nestled in a park above the city's ramparts. Originally a tiny Visigothic church, the chapel was transformed into a mosque during the Moorish occupation. The Islamic arches and vaulting survived, making this the most important relic of Moorish Toledo. The chapel got its name when Alfonso VI's horse, striding triumphantly into Toledo in 1085, fell to its knees out front (a white stone marks the spot). It was then discovered that a candle had burned continuously behind the masonry the whole time the Muslims had been in power. Allegedly, the first Mass of the Reconquest was held here, and later a Mudejar apse was added. Archaeological excavations are underway to reveal the remnants of a Roman house in the yard nearby. ⊠ *Cuesta de Carmelitas Descalzos 10* ☎ *925/254191* ⌨ *€2.50* ☉ *Daily 10–2 and 3:30–5:45 (until 6:45 Mar.–mid-Oct.).*

Monasterio de San Juan de los Reyes. This convent church in western Toledo was erected by Ferdinand and Isabella to commemorate their victory at the Battle of Toro in 1476. (It was also intended to be their burial place, but their wish changed after Granada was recaptured from the Moors in 1492, and their actual tomb is in that city's Capilla Real.) The building is largely the work of architect Juan Guas, who considered it his masterpiece and asked to be buried here himself. In true plateresque fashion, the white interior is covered with inscriptions and heraldic motifs. ⊠ *San Juan de los Reyes 2* ☎ *925/223802* ⊕ *www.sanjuandelosreyes.org* ⌨ *€2.50* ☉ *Daily 10–5:45 (until 6:45 Apr.–Sept.).*

Museo Cerámica Ruiz de Luna. Most of the region's pottery is made in Talavera de la Reina, 76 km (47 miles) west of Toledo. At this museum you can watch artisans throw local clay, then trace the development of Talavera's world-famous ceramics, chronicled through about 1,500 tiles, bowls, vases, and plates dating back to the 15th century. It's closed on Monday, and there's a small admission fee. ⊠ *Calle San Agustín el Viejo 13, Pl. de San Augustín, Talavera de la Reina* ☎ *925/800149* ⌨ *€0.60* ☉ *Tues.–Fri. 9–3:15, Sat. 9:45–2 and 3:45–7, Sun. 10–2:30.*

Puente de Alcántara. Roman in origin, this is the city's oldest bridge. Next to it is a heavily restored castle built after the Christian capture of 1085 and, above this, a vast and severe military academy, a typical example of fascist architecture under Franco. From the other side of the Tagus River, the bridge offers unparalleled views of Toledo's historic center and the Alcázar. ⊠ *Calle Gerardo Lobo.*

Puente de San Martín. This pedestrian bridge on the western edge of Toledo dates back to 1203 and has splendid horseshoe arches.

QUICK BITES

Teteria Dar Al-Chai. If the maze of Toledo's streets exhausts you, unwind at this Arabian tea house–bar. Just south of San Juan de los Reyes on Calle de los Reyes Católicos, it has plush couches, low tables, and colorful tapestries. The selection of common teas is delightful, but why not try one from the special list: mixed and brewed in-house, they feature a blend of flowers, dried fruit, and spices such as cardamom. Excellent fruit smoothies, crepes, and sandwiches are also available. It's open all day, until 10 pm, on weekdays, but opens at 4 pm on weekends. The tea shop also offers rotating exhibitions of Middle Eastern–theme furniture, artwork, clothing, and handbags for sale. ⊠ *Pl. Barrio Nuevo 5* ☎ *925/225625.*

Sinagoga de Santa María La Blanca. Founded in 1203, Toledo's second synagogue is nearly two centuries older than the more elaborate Tránsito, just down the street. Santa María's white interior has a forest of columns supporting capitals with fine filigree workmanship. ⊠ *Calle de Reyes Católicos 4* ☎ *925/227257* ⌨ *€2.50* ☉ *Daily 10–5:45 (until 6:45 Apr.–Sept.).*

WHERE TO EAT

$$$$ SPANISH Fodor's Choice ★ 🍴 **Adolfo Restaurant.** King Juan Carlos I declared Adolfo's partridge stew the best in Spain. Steps from the cathedral but discreetly hidden, this restaurant has an intimate interior with a coffered ceiling that was painted in the 14th century. From the entryway you can see game, fresh produce, and traditional Toledan recipes being prepared in the kitchen, which combines local tastes with Nueva Cocina tendencies. The *tempura de flor de calabacín* (tempura-battered zucchini blossoms in a saffron sauce) makes for a tasty starter, and what better to finish a meal than a Toledan specialty, *delicias de mazapán* (marzipan sweets). The restaurant runs its own winery and is affiliated with the Toledo culinary arts school. [$] *Average main: €50* ✉ *Calle del Hombre de Palo 7* ☎ *925/227321, 639/938140* 🌐 *www.adolforestaurante.com* ✍ *Reservations essential* ⏲ *No dinner Sun.*

$ SPANISH 🍴 **Bar Ludeña.** Locals and visitors come together at this famous tapas bar to have a beer and share the typical Toledan *carcamusas,* a meat stew with peas and tomatoes served in a hot dish. A couple of steps from the Zocodover square, the bar is famous for heaping plates of free tapas that come with your drink—helping make it a favorite for students, too. [$] *Average main: €12* ✉ *Pl. de la Magdalena 10* ☎ *925/223384* ⏲ *Closed Wed.*

$$ TAPAS 🍴 **Cafe Club Legendario.** As its name suggests, this cocktail bar is legendary—for its Cuban-rum mojitos—and it offers a quite shady spot for breakfast or a quick bite midday, when salads, toasts, and tapas are on the menu. The bar and restaurant are housed in a 17th-century palace, tucked away in Toledo's historic old quarter, and there are several semiprivate rooms for groups and birthday parties. It's open right through from 10 am to midnight. [$] *Average main: €15* ✉ *Pl. de San Vicente 4* ☎ *925/252356, 691/434436.*

$$$ SPANISH Fodor's Choice ★ 🍴 **La Flor de la Esquina.** This charming, rustic, local restaurant and wine bar across from the San Ildefonso Church has a cozy dining room, but the best place to sit is outside, at one of a handful of tables on the Plaza del Padre, with views of Toledo's cathedral spires. There are several daily three-course menus offering very good value (€18 to €30 per person, including local wines). There's also a tapas tasting menu if you want to sample everything. Be sure to try the ample *surtido de ibéricos jamón* (ham) platters and the *medallones de foie de pato con crema de balsámico y frambuesa* (medallions of duck liver with balsamic-vinegar crème and raspberries). [$] *Average main: €20* ✉ *Pl. del Padre Juan de Mariana 2* ☎ *627/945020* 🌐 *www.laflordelaesquina.com.*

WHERE TO STAY

$ HOTEL 🏨 **Hacienda del Cardenal.** Built in the 18th century (restored in 1972) as a summer palace for Cardinal Lorenzana, this quiet and beautiful 3-star hotel is fully outfitted with antique furniture and other nice touches. **Pros:** lovely courtyard; convenient dining. **Cons:** restaurant often full; parking is pricey. [$] *Rooms from: €85* ✉ *Paseo de Recaredo 24* ☎ *925/224900* 🌐 *www.hostaldelcardenal.com* 🛏 *27 rooms* 🍽 *Breakfast.*

$$ HOTEL 🏨 **Hotel Pintor El Greco Sercotel.** Next door to the painter's house, this former 17th-century bakery is now a chic, contemporary hotel managed

Toledo's Santa María la Blanca synagogue is a fascinating symbol of cultural cooperation: built by Islamic architects, in a Christian land, for Jewish use.

by the Sercotel chain. **Pros:** parking garage adjacent. **Cons:** street noise in most rooms; elevator goes to the second floor only. $ *Rooms from: €100 ⊠ Alamillos del Tránsito 13* ☎ *925/285191, 902/141515* ⊕ *www. hotelpintorelgreco.com* ↝ *60 rooms* ❍| *Multiple meal plans.*

SHOPPING

The Moors established silverwork, damascene (metalwork inlaid with gold or silver), pottery, embroidery, and marzipan traditions here. A turn-of-the-20th-century art school next to San Juan de los Reyes keeps some of these crafts alive. For inexpensive pottery, stop at the large stores on the outskirts of town, on the main road to Madrid.

La Encina de Ortega. Named after a massive, 200-year-old oak tree on the Ortega family's property, this gourmet shop sells local wines, olive oil, chocolate, coffee, pâté, and especially, selected jamón ibérico made from pigs raised on the family farm. Owner José María Ortega has garnered local fame for inventing a special ham-cutting method. You can watch him at work in his shop, and perhaps pick up supplies for a picnic. The store is closed Saturday afternoon and all day Sunday, and for a siesta on weekday afternoons. ⊠ *Calle La Plata 22* ☎ *925/102072* ⊕ *www.laencinadeortega.com.*

Santo Tomé Marzipan. Since 1856, Santo Tomé has been Spain's most famous maker of marzipan—a Spanish sweet made from sugar, honey, and almond paste. Visit the main shop on the Plaza de Zocodover, or take a tour of the old convent-turned-factory where it's actually made, on Calle Santo Tomé 3. Call ahead to book tours. You can also order online. ⊠ *Pl. de Zocodover 7* ☎ *925/221168, 925/223763* ⊕ *www. mazapan.com.*

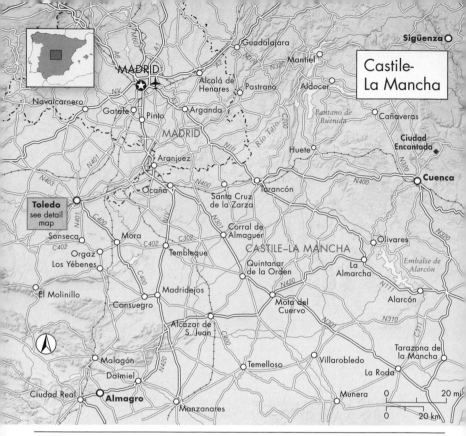

ALMAGRO

215 km (134 miles) south of Madrid.

The center of this noble town contains the only preserved medieval theater in Europe, which stands beside the ancient Plaza Mayor, where 85 Roman columns form two colonnades supporting green-frame, 16th-century buildings. Near the plaza are granite mansions embellished with the heraldic shields of their former owners and a splendid parador in a restored 17th-century convent.

GETTING HERE AND AROUND

Almagro can be reached by train from Madrid, with one service per day departing from Atocha or Chamartin stations for the 2½-hour journey, but it's probably best to have a rental car. The drive south from the capital takes you across the plains of La Mancha, where Don Quixote's adventures unfolded.

ESSENTIALS

Visitor Information Almagro ✉ *Pl. Mayor 1* ☎ *926/860717* ⊕ *www.ciudad-almagro.com.*

EXPLORING

Corral de Comedias. Standing almost as it did in 1628 when it was built, this theater has wooden balconies on four sides and the stage at one end of the open patio. During the golden age of Spanish theater—the time of playwrights Pedro Calderón de la Barca, Cervantes, and Lope de Vega—touring actors came to Almagro, which prospered from mercury mines and lace making. The Corral is the site of an international theater festival (🌐 *www.festivaldealmagro.com*) each July. Festival tickets may be purchased with a credit card through Tele-Entrada (☎ *926/882458*) or with cash (after mid-May) at Palacio de los Medrano on San Agustín 7. ✉ *Pl. Mayor 18* ☎ *926/861539* 🎟 *Audio tour €3, dramatized tour €4* 🕐 *Apr.–June and Aug.–Sept., weekdays 10–2 and 5–8, weekends 10–1 and 5–7; July, daily 10–2 and 6–9; Oct.–early Dec. and Mar., weekdays 10–2 and 4–7, Sat. 10–1 and 4–6, Sun. 10–1 and 4–7; early Dec.–Feb., daily 10–2 and 4–7.*

Museo Nacional del Teatro. This museum displays models of the Roman amphitheaters in Mérida (Extremadura) and Sagunto (near Valencia), both still in use, as well as costumes, pictures, and documents relating to the history of Spanish theater. ✉ *Calle del Gran Maestre 2* ☎ *926/261014, 926/261018* 🌐 *museoteatro.mcu.es* 🎟 *€3 (free Sat. afternoon and Sun. morning)* 🕐 *Sept.–June, Tues.–Fri. 10–2 and 4–7, Sat. 11–2 and 4–6, Sun. and holidays 11–2; July–Aug., Tues.–Fri. 10–2 and 6–9, Sat. 11–2 and 6–8, Sun. 11–2.*

WHERE TO EAT AND STAY

$$$$ SPANISH Fodor's Choice ★

🍴 **El Corregidor.** Several old houses stuffed with antiques make up this fine restaurant and tapas bar. You can enjoy your meal alfresco in the beautiful garden or terrace, or take refuge in the air-conditioned dining room. The menu centers on rich local fare, including game, fish, and spicy Almagro eggplant, a local delicacy. Opt for the full-blown *menú de degustación* (€50) if you're up for seven savory tapas; the cheaper *menú Manchego gastronómico* (€30) is a three-course meal of more traditional, regional specialties, including pisto manchego and ravioli *de cordero* (lamb-stuffed ravioli). There's also a wine bar, hotel, and spa. [$] *Average main: €24* ✉ *Calle Jerónimo Ceballos 2* ☎ *926/860648* 🌐 *www.elcorregidor.com* 🕐 *Closed Mon. No dinner Sun.*

$$$ HOTEL Fodor's Choice ★

🏨 **Parador de Almagro.** Five minutes from the Plaza Mayor of Almagro, this parador is a finely restored 16th-century Franciscan convent with cells, cloisters, and patios. **Pros:** pretty indoor courtyards; outdoor pool; ample parking. **Cons:** bathrooms need fixing up. [$] *Rooms from: €135* ✉ *Ronda de San Francisco 31* ☎ *926/860100* 🌐 *www.parador.es* 🛏 *54 rooms* 🍽 *Some meals.*

CUENCA

168 km (105 miles) southeast of Madrid, 150 km (93 miles) northwest of Valencia.

Fodor's Choice ★

Though somewhat isolated, Cuenca makes a good overnight stop if you're traveling between Madrid and Valencia, or even a worthwhile detour between Madrid and Barcelona. The delightful old town is one of the most surreal looking in Spain, built on a sloping, curling finger of rock with precipitous sides that plunge down to the gorges of the Huécar and Júcar rivers. Because the town ran out of room to expand, some medieval houses dangle right over the abyss and are now a unique architectural attraction: the Casas Colgadas (Hanging Houses). The old town's dramatic setting grants spectacular gorge views, and its cobblestone streets, cathedral, churches, bars, and taverns contrast starkly with the modern town, which sprawls beyond the river gorges.

GETTING HERE AND AROUND

From Madrid, buses leave for Cuenca about every two hours from Conde de Casal. From Valencia, four buses leave every four to six hours, starting at 8:30 am. A high-speed AVE train leaves Madrid approximately every hour and stops in Cuenca (after about 55 minutes) on its way to Valencia. Slower, cheaper trains also run several times daily between Cuenca and Valencia, Madrid, Albacete, and Alicante, on the coast.

ESSENTIALS

Visitor Information Cuenca ⊠ *Av. Cruz Roja 1* ☎ *969/241050* ⊕ *www.turismocuenca.com.*

EXPLORING

Cuenca has 14 churches and two cathedrals—but visitors are allowed inside only about half of them. The best views of the city are from the square in front of a small palace at the very top of Cuenca, where the town tapers out to the narrowest of ledges. Here, gorges are on either side of the precipice, and old houses sweep down toward a distant plateau in front. The lower half of the old town is a maze of tiny streets, any of which will take you up to the Plaza del Carmen. From here the town narrows and a single street, Calle Alfonso VIII, continues the ascent to the Plaza Mayor, which passes under the arch of the town hall.

Fodor's Choice **Casas Colgadas** (*Hanging Houses*). As if Cuenca's famous Casas Col-
★ gadas, suspended impossibly over the cliffs below, were not eye-popping enough, they also house one of Spain's finest and most curious museums, the **Museo de Arte Abstracto Español** (Museum of Spanish Abstract Art)—not to be confused with the Museo Municipal de Arte Moderno, which is next to the Casas Colgadas. Projecting over the town's eastern precipice, these houses originally formed a 15th-century palace, which later served as a town hall before falling into disrepair in the 19th century. In 1927 the cantilevered balconies that had once hung over the gorge were rebuilt, and in 1966 the painter Fernando Zóbel decided to create (inside the houses) the world's first museum devoted exclusively to abstract art. The works he gathered are almost all by the remarkable generation of Spanish artists who grew up in the 1950s and were forced to live abroad during the Franco regime. The major names include Carlos Saura, Eduardo Chillida, Lucio Muñoz, Manuel Millares, Antoni Tàpies, and Zóbel himself. ■ TIP➜ The museum has free smartphone audio guides, which can be downloaded from the website. ⊠ *Calle de los Canónigos* ☎ *969/212983* ⊕ *www.march.es/arte/cuenca* 🖾 *€3* 🕙 *Tues.–Fri. 11–2 and 4–6, Sat. 11–2 and 4–8, Sun. 11–2:30.*

Convento de las Carmelitas Descalzas. A short walk north of San Miguel is the Menendez Pelayo University, originally a convent used in the 17th

Cuenca's precarious Casas Colgadas (Hanging Houses) are also home to the well-regarded Museum of Abstract Art.

century and still called Convento de las Carmelitas Descalzas. If you've reached this far, you've climbed Cuenca and are at the highest elevation the town has to offer. You can't explore inside the convent, but it's worth the climb for beautiful views across Cuenca. ⊠ *Calle del Trabuco*.

Museo Diocesano Catedralicio (*Diocesan Museum of Sacred Art*). In what were once the cellars of the Bishop's Palace, this museum's beautiful collection includes a jewel-encrusted, Byzantine diptych of the 13th century; a Crucifixion by the 15th-century Flemish artist Gerard David; a variety of carpets from the 16th to 18th centuries; and two small El Grecos. From the Plaza Mayor, follow the signs on Calle del Obispo Valero toward the Casas Colgadas. ⊠ *Calle Obispo Valero 1* ☎ *969/224210* ⊕ *museodiocesanodecuenca.blogspot.com.es* ✉ *€5 combined ticket with cathedral* ☉ *Tues.–Sat. 11–2 and 4–6 (5–8 June–Sept.), Sun. and holidays 11–2.*

Plaza San Nicolás. Calle San Pedro shoots off from the northern side of Plaza Mayor and just off Calle San Pedro, clinging to the western edge of Cuenca, is this pleasingly dilapidated square. Nearby, the unpaved Ronda del Júcar hovers over the Júcar gorge and commands remarkable views.

Fodor's Choice ★ **Puente de San Pablo.** The 16th-century stone footbridge over the Huécar gorge was fortified with iron in 1903 for the convenience of the Dominican monks of San Pablo, who lived on the other side. If you don't have a fear of heights, cross the narrow bridge to take in the vertiginous view of the river below and the equally thrilling panorama of the Casas Colgadas. It's by far the best view of the city. A path from the bridge descends to the bottom of the gorge, landing you by the bridge that you crossed to enter the old town. If you've read the popular English novel *Winter in Madrid,* you'll recognize this bridge from the book's final scene.

Santa María La Mayor Cathedral. This cathedral looms large and casts an enormous shadow in the evening throughout the adjacent Plaza Mayor. Built during the Gothic era in the 12th century, atop ruins of a conquered mosque, the cathedral's massive triptych facade has lost all its Gothic origins thanks to the Renaissance. Inside are the tombs of the cathedral's founding bishops, an impressive portico of the Apostles, and a Byzantine reliquary. ✉ *Pl. Mayor* ☎ *969/224626* 🎟 *€3.80, includes audio guide (free 1st Mon. of month)* 🕓 *Daily 10–1 and 4–6 (until 7 June–Oct.).*

OFF THE BEATEN PATH

Ciudad Encantada (*Enchanted City*). Not a city at all, the Ciudad Encantada, 35 km (22 miles) north of Cuenca, is a series of large and fantastic mushroomlike rock formations erupting in a landscape of pines. This commanding spectacle, deemed a "site of national interest," was formed over thousands of years by the forces of water and wind on limestone rocks. Of the formations that are named, the most notable are *Cara* (Face), *Puente* (Bridge), *Amantes* (Lovers), and *Olas en el Mar* (Waves in the Sea)—some of them take some imagination. You can stroll through this enchanted city in less than two hours; you'll need a car to get here. You can also call the friendly hiking guides at Serranía Activa (☎ *969/237992 or 661/059440* 🌐 *www.serraniactiva.com*) to arrange to hike, bike, or hanglide over the area.

WHERE TO EAT

Much of Cuenca's cuisine is based on wild game: partridge, lamb, rabbit, and hen. *Trucha* (trout) from the adjacent river is the fish of choice, and it turns up in many main courses and soups. In almost every town restaurant, you can find Cuenca's pâté, *morterualo,* a mixture of wild boar (*jabalí*), rabbit, partridge, hen, liver, pork loin, and spices, as well as *galianos,* a thick stew served on wheat cake. For dessert, try the almond-based confection called *alajú,* which is enriched with honey, nuts, and lemon, and *torrijas,* made of bread dipped in milk, fried, and sprinkled with powdered sugar.

$$$$ SPANISH Fodor's Choice ★

🍴 **El Figón de Huécar.** A private family tavern for more than 20 years, this intimate restaurant is widely regarded as the No. 1 dining spot in Castile–La Mancha. Its bright, airy dining room is within a medieval stone house, with views of the city. Specialty dishes include *pichón* (dove) stuffed with a basket of quail eggs; "old wine" veal with potatoes *al montón* (fried with garlic); Huécar cold vegetable mousse; or fish "melodies" with potato confit and vegetables. The menú del día (€25 or €36) is a good value. [$] *Average main: €25* ✉ *Ronda de Julián Romero 6* ☎ *969/240062, 629/063366* 🌐 *www.figondelhuecar.es* ✍ *Reservations essential* 🕓 *Closed Mon. No dinner Sun.*

$$ TAPAS Fodor's Choice ★

🍴 **La Ponderosa.** Famous for Cuenca's finest tapas and *raciones*, this place on the bustling Calle de San Francisco is always full and buzzing too. *Chuletillas de lechal* (suckling lamb chops), *huevos fritos con pócima secreta* (fried eggs with a "secret potion"), *setas* (wild mushrooms), *mollejas* (sweetbreads), and a carefully selected list of wines all add up to a superior tapas experience. It's a standing-room-only joint, so if you want to sit, you'll have to come early and find a place on the terrace. $\boxed{\$}$ *Average main: €15* ✉ *Calle de San Francisco 20* ☎ *969/213214* ⌨ *Reservations not accepted* ۞ *Closed Sun. and July.*

WHERE TO STAY

$ 🏨 **Cueva del Fraile.** Surrounded by dramatic landscapes, this comforting
HOTEL and family-friendly out-of-town 3-star hotel occupies a 16th-century
FAMILY building. Pros: beautiful interior garden terrace; outdoor swimming pool and tennis courts. Cons: the relatively remote location, 7 km (4½ miles) from Cuenca, means you'll need your own car. $\boxed{\$}$ *Rooms from: €60* ✉ *Ctra. Cuenca-Buenache, Km 7* ☎ *969/211571* ⊕ *www. hotelcuevadelfraile.com* ⤴ *75 rooms* ۞ *Closed Jan.* ¶○¶ *Breakfast.*

$ 🏨 **Hostal Cánovas.** Near Plaza España, in the heart of the new town, this
B&B/INN is one of Cuenca's best bargains, and though the lobby's not impressive, the inviting rooms more than compensate. Pros: low prices even during the high season. Cons: it's quite a walk up the hill to the center of the city's old quarter. $\boxed{\$}$ *Rooms from: €50* ✉ *Calle Fray Luis de León 38* ☎ *969/213973* ⊕ *www.hostalcanovas.com* ⤴ *17 rooms* ¶○¶ *No meals.*

$$$ 🏨 **Parador de Cuenca.** The rooms are luxurious and serene at the exqui-
HOTEL sitely restored 16th-century convent of San Pablo, pitched on a preci-
Fodor'sChoice pice across a dramatic gorge from Cuenca's city center, with views of
★ the hanging houses. Pros: great views of the hanging houses and gorge. Cons: expensive breakfast not always included in room rate. $\boxed{\$}$ *Rooms from: €176* ✉ *Subida a San Pablo* ☎ *969/232320* ⊕ *www.parador.es* ⤴ *63 rooms* ¶○¶ *Breakfast.*

$ 🏨 **Posada San José.** Part of a 17th- to 18th-century convent, the inn
B&B/INN clings to the top of the Huécar gorge in Cuenca's old town and most
FAMILY of the traditionally furnished rooms here have balconies or terraces
Fodor'sChoice over the river. Pros: cozy historical rooms; stunning views of the gorge.
★ Cons: built to 17th-century proportions, some doorways are stooped and rooms a bit cramped. $\boxed{\$}$ *Rooms from: €83* ✉ *Calle Julián Romero 4* ☎ *969/211300, 639/816825* ⊕ *www.posadasanjose.com* ⤴ *31 rooms* ¶○¶ *Breakfast.*

SIGÜENZA

132 km (82 miles) northeast of Madrid.

The ancient university town of Sigüenza dates back to Roman, Visigothic, and Moorish times, and still has splendid architecture and one of the most beautifully preserved cathedrals in Castile. It's one of the rare Spanish towns that are not surrounded by modern development and sprawl. If you're coming from Madrid via the A2, the approach is breathtaking: you pass through hills and ravines before reaching Sigüenza, surrounded by vast agricultural plains. Sigüenza is an ideal base for exploring the countryside by bike. Spain's famous Ruta Don Quixote, a system of hiking and cycling paths named for Cervantes's literary hero, passes through Sigüenza and nearby villages. The tourist office can direct you to Bicicletas del Olmo, which offers bike rentals and trail maps.

GETTING HERE AND AROUND

There are six train departures daily to Sigüenza from Madrid's Cha-martin station, and the journey takes about 1½ hours. Sigüenza's train station is an easy walk from the historic walled center. Buses depart from Madrid's Avenida de America station once a day and take two hours. If you arrive by car, the approach between the A2 highway and Sigüenza is gorgeous. There's ample parking near the train station, but it's best not to venture into the narrow cobblestone streets of the city center with a car.

ESSENTIALS

Bicycle Rental Bicicletas del Olmo. This rental company is an easy walk toward the river from the city center. ⊠ *Ctra. de Moratilla, nave 1* ☎ *949/390754, 605/787650.*

Visitor Information Sigüenza. Guided tours depart daily from the tourist office (in front of the cathedral) at noon and 4:30, and at 5:15 during summer, May through September. Minimum of 10 people required. ⊠ *Calle Serrano Sanz 9* ☎ *949/347007* ⊕ *www.siguenza.es* ⊠ *€7.*

EXPLORING

FAMILY   **Castillo de Sigüenza.** This enchanting castle overlooking wild, hilly coun-tryside from above Sigüenza, is now a parador *(⇨ see Where to Eat and Stay).* The structure was founded by the Romans but rebuilt at various later periods. Most of the current structure was erected in the 14th cen-tury, when it became a residence for the queen of Castile, Doña Blanca de Borbón, who was banished here by her husband, Pedro the Cruel. During the Spanish Civil War (1936–39), the castle was the scene of fierce battles, and much of the structure was destroyed. The parador's lobby has an exhibit on the subsequent restoration, with photographs of the bomb damage. Nonguests can also visit the dining room and common areas. If you've got half an hour or so to spare, there's also a lovely walking path around the hilltop castle, with a 360-degree view of the city and countryside below.

Catedral de Sigüenza. Begun around 1150 and not completed until the early 16th century, Sigüenza's remarkable cathedral combines Spanish architecture dating from the Romanesque period all the way to the Renaissance. The sturdy western front is forbidding but houses a wealth of ornamental and artistic masterpieces. Go directly to the sacristan, the officer in charge of the care of the sacristy, which holds sacred vestments (the sacristy is at the north end of the ambulatory). From there, you can go on a guided tour, which is a must. The late-Gothic cloister leads to a room lined with 17th-century Flemish tapestries. In the north transept is the late-15th-century plateresque sepulchre of Dom Fadrique of Portugal. The Chapel of the Doncel (to the right of the sanctuary) contains Don Martín Vázquez de Arca's tomb, commis-sioned by Queen Isabella, to whom Don Martín served as *doncel* (page) before dying young (at 25) at the gates of Granada in 1486. Tours of the cathedral's catacombs, on weekends only, are run by the Museo Diocesano de Sigüenza *(⇨ see museum listing for details).* ⊠ *Calle Ser-rano Sanz 2* ☎ *619/362715* ⊠ *Free; €4 for tour of chapel, cloister, and tower* ☉ *Daily 9:30–2 and 4:30–8 (closes at 7:30 on Sun.).*

FAMILY **Museo Diocesano de Sigüenza** (*Diocesan Museum of Sacred Art*). In a refurbished early 19th-century house next to the cathedral's west facade, the small Diocesan Museum has a prehistoric section and mostly religious art from the 12th to 18th centuries. It also runs the tours of the burial chambers (catacombs) under the Cathedral—a spooky favorite for kids. ✉ *Pl. Obispo Don Bernardo* ☎ *949/391023* 🌐 *obsigus.e.telefonica.net* 🎫 *Museum €3, catacomb tours €1 (free on the 3rd Wed. of every month)* ⏲ *Mid-Mar.–mid-Jan., Wed., Thurs., and Sun. 11–2 and 4–7, Fri.–Sat. 11–2 and 4–8. Catacomb tours weekends at 1:30 and 7:30.*

Plaza Mayor. The south side of the cathedral overlooks this harmonious, arcaded Renaissance square, commissioned by Cardinal Mendoza. The small palaces and cobblestone alleys mark the virtually intact old quarter. Along Calle Mayor you'll find the palace that belonged to the doncel's family. The plaza hosts a medieval market on weekends. 🌐 *www.siguenza.es.*

FAMILY **Tren Medieval.** Leaving from Madrid's Chamartín station, this delightful medieval-themed train service runs to Sigüenza mid-April through mid-November. The train comes populated with minstels, jugglers, and other entertainers; it's a great activity for children. The ticket price includes the round-trip train ride, guided visit to Siguenza, entry to all monuments/museums and discounts at area restaurants. Check with the Spanish national train company, RENFE, for departure times/dates. Tickets can also be purchased through some travel agencies. ■ **TIP→ Hold onto your ticket after arrival for discounts at area attractions.** ☎ *902/320320* 🌐 *www.renfe.com/ofertas/oferta_tMedieval.html* 🎫 *€30 round-trip.*

WHERE TO EAT AND STAY

$$ TAPAS FAMILY Fodor's Choice ★ 🍴 **Bar Alameda.** If you stop for only one meal in Sigüenza, make it at this renowned tapas bar around the corner from the train station. With some of the best food in Castile-La Mancha, drawing foodies from as far away as Madrid, it's nevertheless a casual neighborhood place. Weekend lunchtimes are packed, with a lively atmosphere and neighborhood children running around the open dining room. Highlights include the setas stuffed with ham, cheese, and olives. There's a superb selection of local wines by the glass as well. [$] *Average main: €15* ✉ *Calle de la Alameda 2* ☎ *949/390553.*

$$$ HOTEL FAMILY 🏨 **Parador de Sigüenza.** This mighty and fantastical 12th-century castle has hosted royalty for centuries, from Ferdinand and Isabella right up to Spain's present king, Juan Carlos I. **Pros:** excellent breakfast buffet. **Cons:** Because part of the castle was destroyed in the Spanish Civil War, much of what's remaining is a neo-medieval replica. [$] *Rooms from: €160* ✉ *Pl. del Castillo* ☎ *949/390100* 🌐 *www.parador.es* 🛏 *81 rooms* 🍽 *Breakfast.*

CASTILE–LEÓN

This is Spain's true heartland, stretching from the sweeping plains of Castile–La Mancha to the rich wine lands of Ribera del Duero, and up to the foot of several mountain ranges: the Sierra de Gredos, Sierra de

Francia, and northward toward the towering Picos de Europa. The area combines two of Spain's old kingdoms, Léon and Old Castile, with their treasures of palaces, castles, and cathedrals. Segovia and Salamanca are cultural highlights, and Ávila remains one of Europe's best-preserved medieval walled cities.

SEGOVIA

91 km (57 miles) north of Madrid.

Fodor's Choice
★
Breathtaking Segovia sits on a ridge in the middle of a gorgeously stark, undulating plain, and is defined by its Roman and medieval monuments, its excellent cuisine, its embroideries and textiles, and its sense of well-being. An important military town in Roman times, Segovia was later established by the Moors as a major textile center. Captured by the Christians in 1085, it was enriched by a royal residence, and in 1474 the half-sister of Henry IV, Isabella the Catholic (married to Ferdinand of Aragón), was crowned queen of Castile here. By that time Segovia was a bustling city of about 60,000 (its population is about 80,000 today), but its importance soon diminished as a result of its taking the losing side of the Comuneros in the popular revolt against the emperor Carlos V. Though the construction of a royal palace in nearby La Granja in the 18th century somewhat revived Segovia's fortunes, it never recovered its former vitality. Early in the 20th century, Segovia's sleepy charm came to be appreciated by artists and writers, among them painter Ignacio Zuloaga and poet Antonio Machado. Today the streets swarm with day-trippers from Madrid—if you can, visit sometime other than in summer, and spend the night.

If you approach Segovia on N603, the first building you see is the cathedral, which seems to rise directly from the fields. In the foreground lies a steep and narrow valley, which shields the old town from view. Only once you descend into the valley do you begin to see the old town's spectacular position, rising on top of a narrow rock ledge shaped like a ship. As soon as you reach the modern outskirts, turn left onto the Paseo E. González and follow the road marked **Ruta Panorámica**—you'll soon descend on the narrow and winding Cuesta de los Hoyos, which takes you to the bottom of the wooded valley that dips to the south of the old town. Above, you can see the Romanesque church of San Martín to the right, the cathedral in the middle, and on the far left, where the rock ledge tapers, the turrets, spires, and battlements of Segovia's castle, known as the Alcázar.

Tourists on a day trip from Madrid generally hit the triumvirate of basic sights: the aqueduct, the Alcázar, and the cathedral. If you have time, an overnight visit will allow you to sample Segovia's renowned food and nightlife in the Plaza Mayor, where you'll see Spaniards of all ages out until the early hours.

GETTING HERE AND AROUND

High-speed AVE trains from Madrid's Chamartin station take just 30 minutes and drop you at the Guiomar station, about 7 km (4 miles) outside Segovia's center. Bus Nos. 11 and 12 are timed to coincide with arriving trains. Bus No. 11 will take you to the foot of the aqueduct

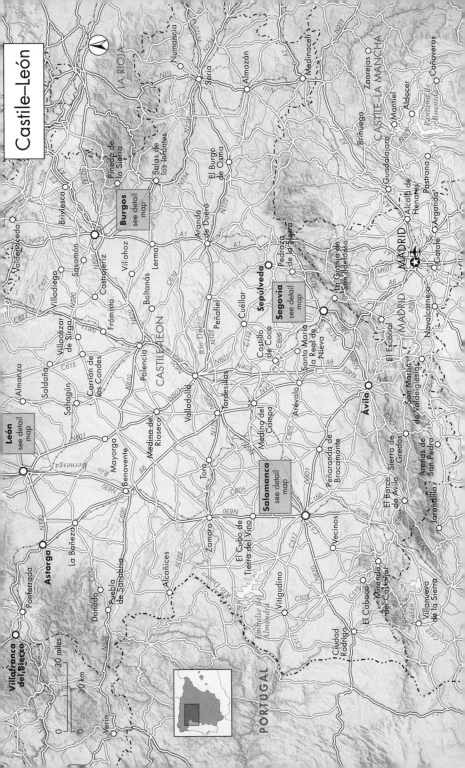

Castile–León

LA RIOJA

CASTILE-LA MANCHA

CASTILE-LEÓN

PORTUGAL

MADRID

Numancia
Soria
Almazán
Medinaceli
Zaorejas
Mantiel
Aldocer
Cañaveras

Pinedo de la Sierra
Salas de los Infantes
El Burgo de Osma
Brihuega
Guadalajara
Alcalá de Henares
Pastrana
Arganda

Valdenebro
Briviesca
Villalhoz
Lerma
Aranda de Duero
La Granja de San Ildefonso
El Escorial
Navalcarnero
Getafe

Burgos see detail map

Sasamón
Castrojeriz
Baltanás
Peñafiel
Cuéllar
Pedraza de la Sierra
Santa María la Real de Nieva
San Martín de Valdeiglesias

Villadiego
Frómista
Castillo de Coca

Sepúlveda

Segovia see detail map

Carrión de los Condes
Palencia
Tordesillas
Arévalo

Villacázar de Sirga
Saldaña
Medina de Rioseco
Valladolid
Medina del Campo

Ávila

Almanza
Sahagún
Mayorga
Benavente
Toro
Peñaranda de Bracamonte
Sierra de Gredos
Arenas de San Pedro

León see detail map

Zamora
Salamanca see detail map
El Barco de Ávila
El Cubo de Tierra del Vino
Vecinos
Jarandilla

Astorga
La Bañeza
Alcañices
Puebla de Sanabria
Donado
Viñigudino
Miranda del Castañar
Villanueva de la Sierra

Ponferrada
Verín
Ciudad Rodrigo
El Cabaco
El Sabao

Villafranca del Bierzo

Embalse de Almendra

30 miles
30 km

after about a 15-minute ride, and No. 12 drops you near the bus station. Urbanos de Segovia operates the 13 inner-city bus lines and one tourist line, which are a better option for getting around than struggling through the narrow streets (and problematic parking) with a car. Segovia's central bus station is five minutes' walk from the aqueduct, along the car-free Paseo de Ezequiel Gonzalez.

ESSENTIALS

Bus Contacts Bus Station ✉ *Paseo de Ezequiel Gonzalez* ☎ *921/427705* ⊕ *www.urbanosdesegovia.com.* **Urbanos de Segovia** ☎ *902/330080* ⊕ *www. urbanosdesegovia.com.*

Visitor Information Segovia. There are two tourist offices in Segovia, one at the entrance to the city, just under the Roman aqueduct, and one in Plaza Mayor. In addition, there's a tourist info kiosk at the bus station. The info below is for the reception center near the aqueduct—the first office you'll encounter on entering the city. The friendly, multi-lingual guides there can also help you book accommodations in Segovia. ✉ *Azoguejo 1* ☎ *921/466720, 921/466721* ⊕ *www. segoviaturismo.es or www.turismodesegovia.com.*

EXPLORING

Fodor's Choice **Acueducto Romano.** Segovia's Roman aqueduct ranks with the Pont du ★ Gard in France as one of the greatest surviving examples of Roman engineering, and it's the city's main sight to see. If you take the AVE in from Madrid on a day trip, the inner-city bus drops you right there. Stretching from the walls of the old town to the lower slopes of the Sierra de Guadarrama, it's about 2,952 feet long and rises in two tiers— above what is now the Plaza del Azoguejo, whose name means "highest point"—to a height of 115 feet. The raised section of stonework in the center originally carried an inscription, of which only the holes for the bronze letters remain. Neither mortar nor clamps hold the massive granite blocks together, but the aqueduct has been standing since the end of the 1st century AD. Its only damage is from the demolition of 35 of its arches by the Moors—the arches were later replaced on the orders of Ferdinand and Isabella. Steps at the side of the aqueduct lead up to the walls of the old town. ✉ *Pl. del Azoguejo.*

FAMILY **Alcázar.** Possibly dating from Roman times, this castle was considerably **Fodor's Choice** expanded in the 14th century, remodeled in the 15th, altered again ★ toward the end of the 16th, and completely remodeled after being gutted by a fire in 1862, when it was used as an artillery school. The exterior, especially when seen below from the Ruta Panorámica, is certainly imposing, and striking murals and stained-glass windows pepper the interior. Crowned by crenellated towers that seem to have been carved out of icing (it's widely believed that the Walt Disney logo is modeled after this castle's silhouette), the ramparts can be climbed for superb views. The claustrophobia-inducing winding tower is worth the knee-wobbling climb and small extra fee, though the views of the green hillside from below the tower are excellent as well. Inside, you can enter the throne room, chapel, and bedroom used by Ferdinand and Isabella. The intricate woodwork on the ceiling is marvelous, and the first room you enter, lined with knights in shining armor, is a crowd-pleaser, particularly for kids. There's also a small armory museum, included in the same

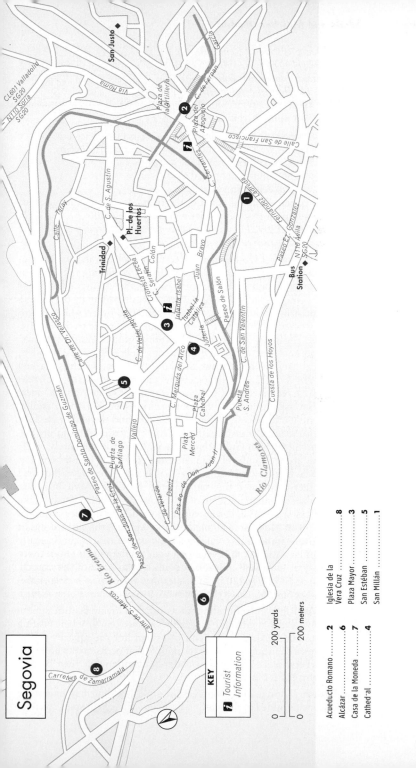

Segovia

KEY

🛈 *Tourist Information*

Acueducto Romano	2
Alcázar	6
Casa de la Moneda	7
Cathed'al	4
Iglesia de la Vera Cruz	8
Plaza Mayor	3
San Estéban	5
San Millán	1

0 ___ 200 yards

0 ___ 200 meters

ticket price. ✉ *Pl. de la Reina Victoria* ☎ *921/460759, 921/460452* ⊕ *www.alcazardesegovia.com* ✑ *€5, €2 to climb the tower (free on 3rd Tues. of every month)* ⊙ *Daily 10–6 (until 7 Apr.–Sept.).*

Casa de la Moneda (*Segovia Mint*). All Spanish coins were minted here from 1455 to 1730. After extensive renovations, the building reopened in 2011 with a celebratory visit

by Spain's queen. Walking down to the riverside complex is pleasant, along a shady path that offers views of the city. ✉ *Calle Fábrica de la Moneda* ☎ *921/420921* ⊕ *www.segoviamint.org* ✑ *Free* ⊙ *Tours must be booked in advance at the tourist office.*

Cathedral. Begun in 1525 and completed 65 years later, Segovia's cathedral was built to replace an earlier one destroyed during the revolt of the Comuneros against Carlos V. It's one of the country's last great examples of the Gothic style. The designs were drawn up by the leading late-Gothicist Juan Gil de Hontañón but executed by his son Rodrigo, in whose work you can see a transition from the Gothic to the Renaissance style. The interior, illuminated by 16th-century Flemish windows, is light and uncluttered, the one distracting detail being the wooden, neoclassical choir. Enter through the north transept, which is marked "Museo"; turn right, and the first chapel on your right has a lamentation group carved in wood by the baroque sculptor Gregorio Fernández. Across from the entrance, on the southern transept, is a door opening into the late-Gothic cloister—both the cloister and the elaborate door leading into it were transported from the old cathedral and are the work of architect Juan Guas. Under the pavement immediately inside the cloister are the tombs of Juan and Rodrigo Gil de Hontañón; that these two lie in a space designed by Guas is appropriate, as the three men together dominated the last phase of the Gothic style in Spain. Off the cloister, a small museum of religious art, installed partly in the first-floor chapter house, has a white-and-gold 17th-century ceiling, a late example of Mudejar *artesonado* work. At night the cathedral is lit up with lovely amber lights, casting a glow on the nearby (and usually crowded) Plaza Mayor. ■TIP➔ **Be on your guard as you enter: there are usually at least half a dozen beggars at the door of the church.** ✉ *Pl. Mayor* ☎ *921/462205* ✑ *Cloister and museum €3 (free cathedral entrance Sun. Mass only)* ⊙ *Daily 9:30–5:30 (to 6:30 Apr.–Sept.).*

Plaza Mayor. Right in front of the cathedral, this lovely historic square comes alive every night and especially on weekends, when visiting madrileños and locals gather at chic cafés that line the square's perimeter. There's a charming gazebo in the middle that occasionally hosts live music. Otherwise it's occupied by children playing while their parents dine nearby. ✉ *Pl. Mayor.*

San Estéban. Though this Romanesque-style building has had some baroque facing added to the interior, the exterior has kept some splendid capitals, as well as an exceptional tower. Due east of the church square is the **Capilla de San Juan de Dios,** next to which is the former pension where the poet Antonio Machado spent his last years in Spain. The family who looked after Machado still owns the building and will show you the poet's Spartan room on request: it has a kerosene stove, iron bed, and round table. ⊠ *Pl. de San Estéban.*

San Millán. Built in the 12th century and a perfect example of the Segovian Romanesque style, this church, a five-minute walk outside town walls, may be the finest in town, aside from the cathedral. The exterior is notable for its arcaded porch, where church meetings were once held. The virtually untouched interior is dominated by massive columns, whose capitals carry such carved scenes as the Flight into Egypt and the Adoration of the Magi. The vaulting on the crossing shows the Moorish influence on Spanish medieval architecture. It's open for Mass only. ⊠ *Av. Fernández Ladreda 26.*

Vera Cruz. Made of local stone that's a warm orange color, this isolated Romanesque church, on northern outskirts of town, off Cuesta de los Hoyos, was built in 1208 for the Knights Templar. Like other buildings associated with this order, it has 12 sides, inspired by the Church of the Holy Sepulchre in Jerusalem. It's about a 45-minute walk outside town (you can see this church on a cliffside from the castle windows), but the trek pays off in full when you climb the bell tower and see all of Segovia silhouetted against the Sierra de Guadarrama. ⊠ *Ctra. de Zamarramia* ☎ *921/431475* ≊ *€2 (free Tues.)* ☉ *Tues. 4–6, Wed.–Sun. 10:30–1:30 and 4–6 (closes at 7 Apr.–Sept.).*

OFF THE BEATEN PATH
Palacio Real de La Granja *(Royal Palace of La Granja).* If you have a car, don't miss the Palacio Real de La Granja in the town of La Granja de San Ildefonso, about 11 km (7 miles) southeast of Segovia (on N601) on the northern slopes of the Sierra de Guadarrama. The palace site was once occupied by a hunting lodge and a shrine to San Ildefonso, administered by Hieronymite monks from the Segovian monastery of El Parral. Commissioned by the Bourbon king Felipe V in 1719, the palace has been described as the first great building of the Spanish Bourbon dynasty. The Italian architects Juvarra and Sachetti, who finished it in 1739, were responsible for the imposing garden facade, a late-baroque masterpiece anchored throughout its length by a giant order of columns. The interior has been badly gutted by fire, but the collection of 15th- to 18th-century tapestries warrants a visit. Even if you don't go into the palace, walk through the magnificent gardens: terraces, ornamental ponds, lakes, classical statuary, woods, and baroque fountains dot the mountainside. On Wednesday, Saturday, and Sunday evenings in the summer (May–September, 6–7 pm), the illuminated fountains are turned on, one by one, creating an effect to rival that of Versailles. The starting time has been known to change on a whim, so call ahead. ⊠ *Pl. de España 15, La Granja* ☎ *921/470019, 921/470020* ⊕ *www. patrimonionacional.es* ≊ *€9 combined ticket, €6 guided tour; €4 fountains only, €3 fountains at night* ☉ *Daily 10–6 (to 8 Apr.–Sept.).*

Segovia's Roman aqueduct, built about 2,000 years ago, is remarkably well preserved.

WHERE TO EAT

$$$$ SPANISH 🍴 **Casa Duque.** This is Segovia's oldest continuously operated restaurant, founded in 1895, still run by the same family, and still located at the same spot on the city's main tourist thoroughfare. The intimate interior has handsome wood beams and a plethora of fascinating bric-a-brac, including wood carvings and coats of armor stashed in every nook and cranny. Roasts and meats are the main specialty here, but the *judiones de La Granja Duque*—enormous white beans from the family farm stewed with sausages or partridge—are also excellent. The local Ribera del Duero wines hold up well with roasts, while setas from the Sierra de Guadarrama add a forest fragrance. Be prepared for wedding parties; if you're lucky, you might get included. [$] *Average main: €30* ✉ *Calle Cervantes 12* ☎ *921/462487, 921/462486* 🌐 *www.restauranteduque.es* ✍ *Reservations essential.*

$$$ SPANISH Fodor's Choice ★ 🍴 **El Fogon Sefardi.** This tavern in Segovia's historic Jewish quarter is owned by the Casa Mudéjar Hospedería hotel, and wins awards, year after year, for the region's best tapas. The menu is exquisite, featuring Segoviano specialities like cochinillo as well as traditional Sephardic Jewish cuisine (though it's not a kosher kitchen). But the tapas are the highlight—the *tostas* are elaborate layers of toasted bread with roasted eggplant, goat cheese, duck liver, or many other gourmet specialties. On summer evenings, the bar area overflows, and waiters pass plates of tapas out the windows to the crowd that spills out onto the area's cobblestone streets. [$] *Average main: €20* ✉ *Calle Judería Vieja 17* ☎ *921/466250.*

$$$$ SPANISH 🍴 **Mesón de Cándido.** Beginning life as an inn near the end of the 18th century, this restaurant was declared a national monument in 1941.

It's one of the first historic buildings you see as you pass under the aqueduct and enter Segovia. Inside, there's a medley of small, irregular dining rooms decorated with a hodgepodge of memorabilia. Amid the dark-wood beams and Castilian knickknacks hang photos of celebrities who have dined here, among them Ernest Hemingway and Princess Grace. The cochinillo, roasted in a wood-fire oven, is a great choice, and partridge stew and roast lamb are also memorable, especially on cold winter afternoons. Ask for a table near a window, with a view of the aqueduct, just a few feet away. It's best to book online. If you don't have time for a full meal, there's also excellent tapas service at the bar. [$] *Average main: €30* ✉ *Pl. de Azoguejo 5* ☎ *921/425911* 🌐 *www.mesondecandido.es* ✍ *Reservations essential.*

$$$$ SPANISH Fodor's Choice ★ 🍴 **Mesón de José María.** With a boisterous bar to set the tone and decibel level, this *mesón* (traditional tavern-restaurant) is definitely hospitable. The owner is devoted to maintaining traditional Castilian specialties while concocting innovations of his own, changing dishes with the seasons. The large, old-style, brightly lighted dining room is often packed, and the waiters are uncommonly friendly. Although it's a bit touristy, it's also popular with locals, and the cochinillo is delicious in any company. [$] *Average main: €35* ✉ *Calle Cronista Lecea 11, off Pl. Mayor* ☎ *921/461111, 921/466017* 🌐 *www.rtejosemaria.com.*

WHERE TO STAY

$ HOTEL 🏨 **Hotel Infanta Isabel.** You'll get great views of the cathedral here, since the hotel is perched on the corner of Plaza Mayor, with its entrance is on a charming albeit congested pedestrian shopping street. **Pros:** boutiquey design; central location; some rooms have balconies overlooking the plaza. **Cons:** some rooms are an odd shape and a bit small; rooms facing the plaza can be noisy on weekends. [$] *Rooms from: €85* ✉ *Pl. Mayor 12* ☎ *921/461300* 🌐 *www.hotelinfantaisabel.com* 🛏 *37 rooms* 🍽 *Multiple meal plans.*

$ HOTEL 🏨 **La Casa Mudejar Hospedería.** Built in the 15th century as a Mudejar palace, this historical property has spacious rooms and a luxury spa that's extremely popular, even with those not staying in the hotel. **Pros:** great location; historic building; wonderful spa. **Cons:** interior design is a little tacky. [$] *Rooms from: €85* ✉ *Calle Isabel la Católica 8* ☎ *921/466250* 🌐 *www.lacasamudejar.com* 🛏 *40 rooms* 🍽 *Multiple meal plans.*

$$$ HOTEL 🏨 **Parador de Segovia.** Architecturally one of the most interesting of Spain's modern paradores (if you like naked concrete), this low building is set on a hill and from its large windows the panorama of Segovia and its aqueduct are spectacular. **Pros:** beautiful views of the city. **Cons:** need a car to get here; rooms not as elegant as in some other paradores—missing the historical elements. [$] *Rooms from: €141* ✉ *Ctra. de Valladolid* ☎ *921/443737* 🌐 *www.parador.es* 🛏 *113 rooms* 🍽 *Multiple meal plans.*

SHOPPING

After Toledo, the province of Segovia is Castile's most important area for crafts. Glass and crystal are specialties of La Granja, and ironwork, lace, and embroidery are famous in Segovia itself. You can buy good lace from the Roma vendors in Segovia's Plaza del Alcázar, but be prepared for some strenuous bargaining, and never offer more than half the opening price. The area around Plaza San Martin is a good place to buy crafts.

Calle Daoíz. Leading to the Alcázar, this street overflows with touristy ceramics, textiles, and gift shops.

Plaza San Martín. Several excellent antiques shops line this small plaza.

SEPÚLVEDA

58 km (36 miles) northeast of Segovia.

A walled village with a commanding position, Sepúlveda has a charming main square, but the main reasons to visit are its 11th-century Romanesque church and a striking gorge with a scenic hiking trail.

GETTING HERE AND AROUND

Sepúlveda is about one hour north of Madrid via a quick drive on the A1 national highway. There are also several buses a day from both Segovia and Madrid. The city is perched on the top of a mountain overlooking a ravine, so you'll likely want transportation up the steep hill. Don't get off the bus or park too soon!

ESSENTIALS

Visitor Information Sepúlveda ✉ *Pl. del Trigo 6* ☎ *921/540237* ⊕ *www. sepulveda.es.*

EXPLORING

El Salvador. This 11th-century church is the oldest Romanesque church in Segovia's province. The carvings on its capitals, probably by a Moorish convert, are quite outlandish. ✉ *Calle Subida a El Salvador 10.*

OFF THE BEATEN PATH

Castillo de Coca. Perhaps the most famous medieval sight near Segovia— and worth a detour between Segovia and Ávila or Valladolid—is the Castillo de Coca, 52 km (32 miles) northwest of the city. Built in the 15th century for Archbishop Alonso de Fonseca I, the castle is a turreted structure of plaster and red brick, surrounded by a deep moat. It looks like a stage set for a fairy tale, and, indeed, it was intended not as a fortress but as a place for the notoriously pleasure-loving archbishop to hold riotous parties. The interior, now occupied by a forestry school, has been modernized, with only fragments of the original decoration preserved. ✉ *C. Antigua Cauca Romana, Coca* ☎ *921/586622, 617/573554* ⊕ *www.castillodecoca.com* ✍ *€2.70* ⊙ *Feb.–Dec., weekdays 10:30–1 and 4:30–6, weekends 11–1 and 4–6 (closes at 7 Apr.– Sept.). Closed 1st Tues. of every month.*

ÁVILA

114 km (71 miles) northwest of Madrid.

In the middle of a windy plateau littered with giant boulders, with the Sierra de Gredos in the background, Ávila can look wild and sinister. Modern development on the outskirts of town partially obscures Ávila's walls, which, restored in parts, look as they did in the Middle Ages. Begun in 1090, shortly after the town was reclaimed from the

Ávila's city walls, which still encircle the old city, have a perimeter of about 2½ km (1½ miles).

Moors, the walls were completed in only nine years—thanks to the daily employment of an estimated 1,900 men. The walls have nine gates and 88 cylindrical towers bunched together, making them unique to Spain in form—they're quite unlike the Moorish defense architecture that the Christians adapted elsewhere. They're also most striking when seen from outside town; for the best view on foot, cross the Adaja River, turn right on the Carretera de Salamanca, and walk uphill about 250 yards to a monument of four pilasters surrounding a cross.

The walls reflect Ávila's importance during the Middle Ages. Populated during the reign of Alfonso VI by Christians, many of whom were nobles, the town came to be known as Ávila of the Knights. Decline set in at the beginning of the 15th century, with the gradual departure of the nobility to the court of Carlos V in Toledo. Ávila's fame later on was largely because of St. Teresa. Born here in 1515 to a noble family of Jewish origin, Teresa spent much of her life in Ávila, leaving a legacy of convents and the ubiquitous *yemas* (candied egg yolks), originally distributed free to the poor but now sold for high prices to tourists. Ávila is well preserved, but the mood is slightly sad, austere, and desolate. It has a sense of quiet beauty, but the silence is dispelled during Fiestas de la Santa Teresa in October; the weeklong celebration includes lighted decorations, parades, singing in the streets, and religious observances.

GETTING HERE AND AROUND
Avilabus (⊕ *www.avilabus.com*) serves the city of Ávila and surrounding villages, though the city itself is easily managed on foot.

ESSENTIALS
Visitor Information Ávila ⊠ *Pl. de la Catedral 4* ☎ *920/211387.*

EXPLORING

Basílica de San Vicente (*Basilica of St. Vincent*). North of Ávila's cathedral, on Plaza de San Vincente, is this much-venerated Romanesque basilica, founded on the supposed site where St. Vincent was martyred in AD303 with his sisters, Sts. Sabina and Cristeta. Construction began in 1130 and continued through the 12th century; the massive church complex was restored in the late 19th and early 20th centuries. The west front, shielded by a vestibule, still has damaged but expressive Romanesque carvings depicting the death of Lazarus and the parable of the rich man's table. The sarcophagus of St. Vincent forms the centerpiece of the basilica's Romanesque interior. The extraordinary, Asian-looking canopy above the sarcophagus is a 15th-century addition. ⊠ *Pl. de San Vicente 1* ☎ *920/225969 for tourist office* ⊕ *www.basilicasanvicente.es* ⌧€2 *(free Sun.)* ⊙ *May–Oct., Mon.–Sat. 10–6:30, Sun. and holidays 10–2 and 4–6; Nov.–Apr., Mon.–Sat. 10–1:30 and 4–6:30, Sun. and holidays 10–2 and 4–6. Closed during Mass.*

Casa de los Deanes (*Deans' Mansion*). This 15th-century building houses the cheerful **Museo Provincial de Ávila,** full of local archaeology and folklore. Part of the museum's collection is housed in the adjacent Romanesque temple of San Tomé el Viejo, a few minutes' walk east of the cathedral apse. ⊠ *Pl. de Nalvillos 3* ☎ *920/211003* ⌧€2 *(free weekends)* ⊙ *June–mid-Oct., Tues.–Sat. 10–2 and 5–8, Sun. 10–2; mid-Oct.–May, Tues.–Sat. 10–2 and 4–7, Sun. 10–2.*

Cathedral (*Catedral de San Salvador*). The battlement apse of Ávila's cathedral forms the most impressive part of the city's walls. Entering the town gate to the right of the apse, you can reach the sculpted north portal (originally the west portal, until it was moved in 1455 by the architect Juan Guas) by turning left and walking a few steps. The present west portal, flanked by 18th-century towers, is notable for the crude carvings of hairy male figures on each side. Known as "wild men," these figures appear in many Castilian palaces of this period. The Transitional Gothic interior, with its granite nave, is heavy and severe. The Lisbon earthquake of 1755 deprived the building of its Flemish stained glass, so the main note of color appears in the beautiful mottled stone in the apse, tinted yellow and red. Elaborate, plateresque choir stalls built in 1547 complement the powerful high altar of circa 1504 by painters Juan de Borgoña and Pedro Berruguete. On the wall of the ambulatory, look for the early-16th-century marble sepulchre of Bishop Alonso de Madrigal, a remarkably lifelike representation of the bishop seated at his writing table. Known as "El Tostado" (the Toasted One) for his swarthy complexion, the bishop was a tiny man of enormous intellect, the author of 54 books. When on one occasion Pope Eugenius IV ordered him to stand—mistakenly thinking him to still be on his knees—the bishop pointed to the space between his eyebrows and hairline, and retorted, "A man's stature is to be measured from here to here!" ⊠ *Pl. de la Catedral s/n* ☎ *920/211641* ⊕ *www.catedralavila.com* ⌧€4 ⊙ *June–mid-Oct., weekdays 10–7:30, Sat. 10–8, Sun. noon–6:30; mid-Oct.–May, weekdays 10–5, Sat. 10–6, Sun. noon–5.*

Convento de San José (*Las Madres*). A cluster of houses joined together, the convent was founded in the late 16th century by St. Teresa of Ávila and is still in use. You can still see the kitchen, cloister, and so-called "devil's staircase," from which Teresa fell and broke her arm in 1577. The complex, just off a pedestrian square four blocks east of the cathedral, also houses the **Museo Teresiano,** with musical instruments used by St. Teresa and her nuns (Teresa specialized in percussion, apparently). ⊠ *Pl. de las Madres 4* ☎ *920/222127* ⊕ *www.sanjosedeavila.es* ⊠ *€1* ⊙ *June–mid-Oct., daily 10–1:30 and 4–7; mid-Oct.–May, daily 10–1:30 and 3–6.*

Convento de Santa Teresa. Inside the south wall on the corner of Calle Dama and Plaza de la Santa, this convent was founded in the 17th century on the site of the saint's birthplace. Teresa's famous written account of an ecstatic vision in which an angel pierced her heart inspired many baroque artists, most famously the Italian sculptor Giovanni Bernini. The convent has a small museum with relics, including one of Teresa's fingers. You can also see the small and rather gloomy garden where she played as a child. ⊠ *Pl. de la Santa 2* ☎ *920/211030* ⊕ *www. teresadejesus.com* ⊠ *Church and reliquary free, museum €2* ⊙ *Church and reliquary daily 9–1 and 3:30–7:30; museum daily 10–1:30 and 3:30–5:30 (10–2 and 4–7 in winter).*

Ermita de San Segundo (*Hermitage of St. Secundus*). At the west end of the town walls, next to the river in a farmyard largely hidden by poplars, this small Romanesque hermitage was founded on the site where the remains of St. Secundus (a follower of St. Peter) were reputedly discovered. It has a realistic-looking marble monument to the saint, carved by Juan de Juni. Inside, a trio of arches and naves symbolizes the Christian trinity—but is rumored to actually be an architectural error. The chapel's caretaker doesn't always adhere to posted visiting hours, and you may have to ask for a key in the adjoining house. Still, it's worth the walk for a look outside. ⊠ *Pl. de San Segundo s/n* ☎ *920/353900 for bishop's office* ⊠ *€1* ⊙ *Daily 11–1 and 4–5.*

Monasterio de la Encarnación. This is the convent where St. Teresa first took orders—scandalously, without her father's permission—and was based for almost 40 years. Its tiny museum has an interesting drawing of the Crucifixion by her teacher St. John of the Cross, as well as a reconstruction of the cell she used when she was a prioress here. The convent is outside the walls in the northern part of town, and is probably worth the walk only to those with a strong interest in St. Teresa's life. ⊠ *Paseo de la Encarnación* ☎ *920/211212* ⊠ *€2* ⊙ *May–Oct., weekdays 9:30–1 and 4–6, weekends 10–1 and 4–6; Nov.–Apr., weekdays 9:30–1:30 and 3:30–6, weekends 10–1:30 and 4–6.*

Real Monasterio de Santo Tomás. A good 10-minute walk from the walls and among housing projects is not where you would expect to find one of the most important religious institutions in Castile. The monastery was founded by Ferdinand and Isabella with the financial assistance of the notorious Inquisitor-General Tomás de Torquemada, who is buried in the sacristy. Further funds were provided by the confiscated property of converted Jews who ran afoul of the Inquisition. Three decorated cloisters lead to the church; inside, a masterly high altar (circa 1506) by Pedro Berruguete overlooks a serene marble tomb by the Italian artist Domenico Fancelli. One of the earliest examples of the Italian Renaissance style in Spain, this influential work was built for Prince Juan, the only son of Ferdinand and Isabella, who died at 19 while a student at the University of Salamanca. After Juan's burial here, his heartbroken parents found themselves unable to return; in happier times they had often attended Mass here, seated in the upper choir behind a balustrade exquisitely carved with their coats of arms. There are free, guided tours at 6 pm on weekends and holidays. The monastery also includes a quirky museum of Asian art, collected by missionaries who traveled to the East. ✉ *Pl. de Granada 1* ☎ *920/352237* 🌐 *www.monasteriosantotomas.com* 🎫 *€4* 🕒 *Mid-Sept.–May, daily 10:30–2 and 3:30–7:30; June–mid-Sept., daily 10:30–9.*

WHERE TO EAT AND STAY

$$$ SPANISH

🍴 **Las Cancelas.** Locals flock to this little tavern for the ample selection of tapas, but you can also push your way through the loud bar area to the dining room. There, wooden tables are heaped with combination platters of roast chicken, french fries, fried eggs, and chunks of home-baked bread. The classic T-bone steak, *chuletón de Ávila,* is enormous and a good value. The succulent cochinillo bursts with flavor. There are 14 hotel rooms available, too; simple, slightly ramshackle arrangements at moderate prices. [$] *Average main: €20* ✉ *Calle de la Cruz Vieja 6* ☎ *920/212249* 🌐 *www.lascancelas.com* 🕒 *Closed early Jan.–early Feb. No dinner Sun.*

$$$$ SPANISH FAMILY

🍴 **Restaurante El Molino de la Losa.** Sitting at the edge of the serene Adaja River, Molino boasts one of the best views of the town walls. The building is a 15th-century mill, the working mechanism of which has been well preserved and provides much distraction for those seated in the animated bar. Lamb is roasted in a medieval wood oven, and the beans from nearby El Barco de Ávila (*judías de El Barco*) are famous. The garden has a small playground for children. Reservations essential for weekend lunches. [$] *Average main: €35* ✉ *Calle Bajada de la Losa 12* ☎ *920/211101, 920/211102* 🌐 *www.elmolinodelalosa.com* 🕒 *No dinner Sun.*

$ HOTEL

🏨 **Palacio de los Velada.** Ávila's top 4-star hotel occupies a beautifully restored 16th-century palace in the heart of the city next to the cathedral, an ideal spot if you like to relax between sightseeing. **Pros:** gorgeous glass-covered patio; great service. **Cons:** some rooms don't have views because the windows are so high. [$] *Rooms from: €90* ✉ *Pl. de la Catedral 10* ☎ *920/255100* 🌐 *www.veladahoteles.com* 🛏 *145 rooms* 🍽 *Multiple meal plans.*

$$ HOTEL FAMILY

🏨 **Parador de Ávila.** This largely rebuilt 16th-century medieval castle is attached to the massive town walls, and a standout feature is its lush garden containing archaeological ruins. **Pros:** gorgeous garden and views; good restaurant; great choice for families. **Cons:** it's a long walk to town—not advised at night. [$] *Rooms from: €100* ✉ *Marqués de Canales de Chozas 2* ☎ *920/211340* 🌐 *www.parador.es* 🛏 *61 rooms* 🍽 *Multiple meal plans.*

SALAMANCA

212 km (132 miles) northwest of Madrid.

Fodor'sChoice ★ Salamanca's radiant sandstone buildings, immense Plaza Mayor, and hilltop riverside perch make it one of the most attractive and beloved cities in Spain. Today, as it did centuries ago, the university predominates, providing an intellectual flavor, a stimulating arts scene, and raging nightlife to match. You'll see more foreign students here per capita than anywhere else in Spain.

If you approach from Madrid or Ávila, your first glimpse of Salamanca will be of the city rising on the northern banks of the wide and winding Tormes River. In the foreground is its sturdy, 15-arch Roman bridge and soaring above it is the combined bulk of the old and new cathedrals. Piercing the skyline to the right is the Renaissance monastery and church of San Estéban. Behind San Estéban and the cathedrals, and largely out of sight from the river, extends a stunning series of palaces, convents, and university buildings that culminates in Plaza Mayor. Despite considerable damage over the centuries, Salamanca remains one of Spain's greatest cities architecturally, a showpiece of the Spanish Renaissance.

GETTING HERE AND AROUND

Salamanca de Transportes (☎ 923/190545) runs 64 municipal buses equipped with lifts for passengers with disabilities, with routes throughout the city of Salamanca. Most visitors would only need to take a bus in order to reach the train and bus stations on the outskirts of the city.

ESSENTIALS

Visitor Information Salamanca Municipal Tourist Office. Salamanca has two tourist offices; this one is the main municipal branch. ✉ *Pl. Mayor 32* ☎ *923/218342* ⊕ *www.salamanca.es.* **Salamanca Regional Tourist Office.** This branch of the Castile–León provincial tourist organization is a good source for information on hiking, cycling, and other activities on the outskirts of Salamanca. In the summer there are also tourist office kiosks open in local bus and train stations. ✉ *Rúa Mayor s/n* ☎ *923/268571, 902/203030.*

EXPLORING

TOP ATTRACTIONS

Fodor'sChoice ★ **Cathedrals.** For a complete exterior tour of Salamanca's old and new cathedrals, take a 10-minute walk around the complex, circling counterclockwise. Nearest the river stands the **Catedral Vieja** (Old Cathedral), built in the late 12th century, one of the most interesting examples of the Spanish Romanesque. Because the dome of the crossing tower has strange, plumelike ribbing, it's known as the Torre del Gallo (Rooster's Tower). The two cathedrals are all part of the same complex, though they have different visiting hours, and you need to enter the Old Cathedral to get to the new one.

The much larger **Catedral Nueva** (New Cathedral) dates mainly from the 16th century, though some parts, including the dome over the crossing and the bell tower attached to the west facade, had to be rebuilt after the Lisbon earthquake of 1755. Work began in 1513 under the direction of the distinguished late-Gothic architect Juan Gil de Hontañón, and, as at Segovia's cathedral, Juan's son Rodrigo took over the work after his father's death in 1526. The New Cathedral's north facade (which contains the main entrance) is ornamental enough, but the west facade is dazzling in its sculptural complexity. Try to visit in late afternoon, when the sun beams off of its surface.

The interior of the New Cathedral is as light and harmonious as that of Segovia's cathedral but larger. It's a triumphant baroque effusion designed by the Churriguera family. The wooden choir seems almost alive with cherubim and saints. From a door in the south aisle, steps descend into the Old Cathedral, where boldly carved capitals supporting the vaulting are accented by foliage, strange animals, and touches of pure fantasy. Then comes the dome, which seems to owe much to Byzantine architecture; it's a remarkably light structure raised on two tiers of arcaded openings. Not the least of the Old Cathedral's attractions are its furnishings, including sepulchres from the 12th and 13th centuries and a curved high altar comprising 53 colorful and delicate scenes by the mid-15th-century artist Nicolás Florentino. In the apse above, Florentino painted an astonishingly fresh Last Judgment fresco.

From the south transept of the Old Cathedral, a door leads into the cloister, which was begun in 1177. From about 1230 until the construction of the main university building in the early 15th century, the chapels around the cloister served as classrooms for university students. In the Chapel of St. Barbara, on the eastern side, theology students answered the grueling questions meted out by their doctoral examiners. The chair in which they sat is still there, in front of a recumbent effigy of Bishop Juan Lucero, on whose head the students would place their feet for inspiration. Also attached to the cloister is a small cathedral museum with a 15th-century triptych of St. Catherine by Salamanca's greatest native artist, Fernando Gallego. ⌧ *Pl. de Anaya and C. Cardenal Pla y Deniel* ☎ *923/217476, 923/281123* ⊕ *www.catedralsalamanca.org* ⌕ *New cathedral free; old cathedral €4.75 (free Tues. 10–noon)* ☉ *New cathedral: Mon.–Sat. 9–1 and 4–6, Sun. 9–1. Old cathedral: Mon.–Sat. 10–12:30 and 4–5:30, Sun. 10–12:30.*

> ### FONSECA'S MARK
>
> Nearly all of Salamanca's outstanding Renaissance buildings bear the five-star crest of the all-powerful and ostentatious Fonseca family. The most famous Fonseca, Alonso de Fonseca I, was the archbishop of Santiago and then of Seville; he was also a notorious womanizer and a patron of the Spanish Renaissance.

Fodor's Choice
★

Plaza Mayor. Built in the 1730s by Alberto and Nicolás Churriguera, Salamanca's Plaza Mayor is one of the largest and most beautiful squares in Spain. The lavishly elegant, pinkish **Ayuntamiento** (city hall) dominates its northern side. The square and its arcades are popular gathering spots for most of Salmantino society, and the many surrounding cafés make this the perfect spot for a coffee break. At night, the plaza swarms with students meeting "under the clock" on the plaza's north side. *Tunas* (strolling musicians in traditional garb) often meander among the cafés and crowds, playing for smiles and applause rather than tips. During local festivals, held several times a year, a cardboard model of a bull

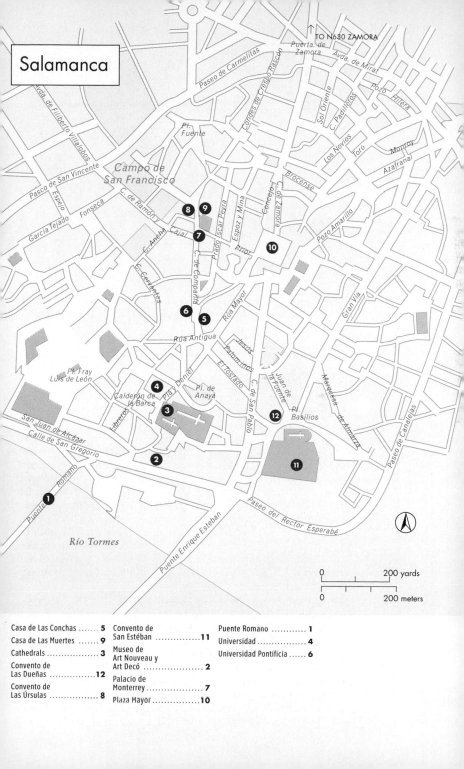

Salamanca

TO N630 ZAMORA

Río Tormes

0   200 yards

0   200 meters

is hoisted up atop the city hall's weathervane—and merriment ensues. ⊠ *Pl. Mayor.*

Universidad. Parts of the university's walls, like those of the cathedral and other structures in Salamanca, are covered with large ocher lettering recording the names of famous university graduates. The earliest names are said to have been written in the blood of the bulls killed to celebrate the successful completion of a doctorate. The **Escuelas Mayores** (Upper Schools) date to 1415, but it was not until more than 100 years later that an unknown architect created their elaborate facade. Above the main door is the famous double portrait of Isabella and Ferdinand, surrounded by ornamentation that plays on the yoke-and-arrow heraldic motifs of the two monarchs. The double-eagle crest of Carlos V, flanked by portraits of the emperor and empress in classical guise, dominates the middle layer of the frontispiece.

Perhaps the most famous rite of passage for new students is to find the single carved frog on the facade. Legend has it that if you spot the frog on your first try, you'll pass all your exams and have a successful university career; for this reason, it's called *la rana de la suerte* (the lucky frog). It can be hard to spot the elusive amphibian, but the ticket booth has posted a clue. The crowd of pointing tourists helps, too. You can then see the beloved frog all over town, on sweatshirts, magnets, pins, jewelry, and postcards.

The interior of the Escuelas Mayores, drastically restored in parts, comes as a slight disappointment after the splendor of the facade. But the *aula* (lecture hall) of Fray Luis de León, where Cervantes, Pedro Calderón de la Barca, and numerous other luminaries of Spain's golden age once sat, is of particular interest. Cervantes carved his name on one of the wooden pews up front. After five years' imprisonment for having translated the *Song of Songs* into Spanish, Fray Luis returned to this hall and began his lecture, "As I was saying yesterday." The Escuelas Menores (Lower Schools) wraps around the patio in front of the Escuelas Mayores. Be sure to check out its serene courtyard. ⊠ *Calle Libreros* ☎ *923/294400, 952/222998* ⊕ *www.salamanca-university.org or www.usal.es* ▣ *€4 (free Mon. morning)* ⊙ *Weekdays 9:30–1:30 and 4–7, Sat. 9:30–1:30 and 4–6:30, Sun. 10–1:30.*

Universidad Pontificia. The ornate, towering complex of the university features a lovely baroque courtyard, but the highlight here is the early-16th-century Escalara Noble (Noble Staircase), which was modeled after San Esteban's Escalera Soto (Grove Staircase) but is larger, taller, and much more stunning. The bottom of each flight is decorated with myriad scenes including games, tournaments, and bullfighting on horseback. From below, it provides one of the best architectural views in Salamanca. Founded in the 13th century as part of the University of Salamanca, the Universidad Pontificia was closed in 1854 after the Spanish government dissolved the University of Salamanca's faculties of theology and canon law in 1854. Reopened in the 1940s, the university continues to teach theology, philosophy, and canon law. Also, from both within and outside the university, take note of the chapel's slightly crocked dome; the Lisbon earthquake of 1755 is to thank.

✉ *Calle Compañía 5* ☎ *923/277100* 💲 *Guided tours €3* ☉ *Wed.–Fri.*
10:30–12:30 and 4–5:30, Sat. 10–1 and 4–5:30, Sun. and holidays
10–1; guided tours every 30 min.

WORTH NOTING

Casa de Las Conchas (*House of Shells*). This house was built around
1500 for Dr. Rodrigo Maldonado de Talavera, a professor of medicine
at the university and a doctor at the court of Isabella. The scallop motif
was a reference to Talavera's status as chancellor of the Order of St.
James (Santiago), the symbol of which is the shell (the shell symbol is
also worn by hikers and pilgrims on the Camino de Santiago de Compostela). Among the playful plateresque details are the lions over the
main entrance, engaged in a fearful tug-of-war with the Talavera crest.
The interior has been converted into a public library. Duck into the
charming courtyard, which has an intricately carved upper balustrade
that imitates basketwork. ✉ *Calle Compañía 2* ☎ *923/269317* 💲 *Free*
☉ *Weekdays 9–9, Sat. 9–2 and 4–7, Sun. 10–2 and 4–7.*

Casa de Las Muertes (*House of the Dead*). Built in about 1513 for the
majordomo of Alonso de Fonseca II, the house takes its name from the
four tiny skulls that adorn its top two windows. Alonso de Fonseca II
commissioned the construction to commemorate his deceased uncle, the
licentious archbishop who lies in the Convento de Las Ursulas, across
the street. For the same reason, the facade also bears the archbishop's
portrait. The small square in front of the house was a favorite haunt of
the poet, philosopher, and university rector Miguel de Unamuno, whose
statue stands here. Unamuno supported the Nationalists under Franco
at the outbreak of the civil war, but he later turned against them. Placed
under virtual house arrest, Unamuno died in the house next door in
1938. During the Franco period, students often daubed his statue red to
suggest that his heart still bled for Spain. You can visit the outside of the
houses, but they're not open to the public. ✉ *Calle de los Bordadores 6.*

Convento de Las Dueñas (*Convent of the Dames*). Founded in 1419, this
convent hides a 16th-century cloister that is the most fantastically decorated in Salamanca, if not in all of Spain. The capitals of its two superimposed Salmantine arcades are crowded with a baffling profusion of
grotesques that can absorb you for hours. As you're wandering through,
take a moment to look down. The interlocking diamond pattern on the
ground floor of the cloister is decorated with the knobby vertebrae of
goats and sheep. It's an eerie yet perfect accompaniment to all the grin-
ning, disfigured heads sprouting from the capitals looming above you.
Don't leave without buying some sweets; the nuns are excellent bak-
ers. ✉ *Pl. del Concilio de Trento s/n* ☎ *923/215442* 💲 *€2* ☉ *Mon.–Sat.*
11–12:45 and 4:30–5:30 .

Convento de Las Úrsulas (*Convent of the Ursulines*). Archbishop Alonso
de Fonseca I lies here, in this splendid Gothic-style marble tomb created by Diego de Siloe during the early 1500s. The building is labeled
on some maps as Convento de la Anunciación. ✉ *Calle de las Úrsulas*
2 ☎ *923/219877* 💲 *€2* ☉ *Tues.–Sun. 11–1 and 4:30–6 (closed last Sun.*
of each month).

Salamanca's central Plaza Mayor was once the venue for the city's bullfights.

Convento de San Esteban (*Convent of St. Stephen*). The convent's monks, among the most enlightened teachers at the university in medieval times, were the first to take Columbus's ideas seriously and helped him gain his introduction to Isabella (hence his statue in the nearby Plaza de Colón, back toward Calle de San Pablo). The complex was designed by one of San Esteban's monks, Juan de Alava. The massive west facade, a thrilling plateresque work in which sculpted figures and ornamentation are piled up to a height of more than 98 feet, is a gathering spot for tired tourists and picnicking locals. The door to the right of the west facade leads you into a golden sandstone cloister with Gothic arcading, interrupted by tall, spindly columns adorned with classical motifs. The church, unified and uncluttered but also dark and severe, allows the one note of color provided by the ornate and gilded high altar of 1692. An awe-inspiring baroque masterpiece by José Churriguera, it deserves five minutes from you to just sit and stare. You can book free guided tours on the website. ⊠ *Pl. Concilio de Trento 1* ☎ *923/215000* ⊕ *www. conventosanesteban.es* 🖭 *€3* ⊗ *Daily 10–2 and 4–7.*

Museo de Art Nouveau y Art Decó. The best thing about this museum is the building it's in, most of which you can tour from the outside. Built at the end of the 19th century, the Casa Lis is a Moderniste building that now houses collections of 19th-century paintings and glass, French and German china dolls, Viennese bronze statues, furniture, jewelry, enamels, and jars. ⊠ *Calle Gibraltar 14* ☎ *923/121425* ⊕ *www. museocasalis.org* 🖭 *€4 (free Thurs. 11–2)* ⊗ *Apr.–Oct. 16, Tues.–Fri. 11–2 and 5–9, weekends 11–9; Oct. 17–Mar., Tues.–Fri. 11–2 and 4–7, weekends 11–8.*

Palacio de Monterrey. Built after 1538 by Rodrigo Gil de Hontañón, the palace was meant for an illegitimate son of Alonso de Fonseca I. As in Rodrigo's other local palaces, the building is flanked by towers and has an open arcaded gallery running the length of the upper level. Such galleries—which in Italy you would expect to see on the ground floor—are common in Spanish Renaissance palaces and were intended to provide privacy for the women of the house and cool the floor below during the summer. Privately owned, the palace is not open to visitors, but you can stroll its grounds. ✉ *Pl. de las Agustinas.*

Puente Romano (*Roman Bridge*). Next to the bridge is an Iberian stone bull, and opposite the bull is a statue commemorating the young hero of the 16th-century novella *The Life of Lazarillo de Tormes and of His Fortunes and Adversities,* a masterpiece of Spanish literature.

WHERE TO EAT

$ TAPAS

🍴 **Bambú.** At peak times, it's standing room only in this jovial basement tapas bar catering to locals and students. The floor may be littered with napkins, and you might have to shout to be heard, but it's the generous tapas and big, sloppy *bocadillos* (sandwiches) that draw the crowds. (There's a dining room in back for which you can make reservations, but the bar is the place to be.) Although paella is usually the exclusive domain of pricey restaurants devoted to the specialty, you can enjoy a *ración* of paella during lunch here, ladled out from a large *caldero* (shallow pan). Another bonus: Even if you just order a drink, you'll be served a liberal helping of the "tapa of the day." [$] *Average main: €12* ✉ *Calle Prior 4* ☎ *923/260092* 🌐 *www.cafeteriabambu.com.*

$$$$ SPANISH Fodor's Choice ★

🍴 **La Hoja 21.** Just off the Plaza Mayor, this upscale restaurant has a glass facade, high ceilings, butter-yellow walls, and minimalist art—signs of an apart-from-the-usual Castilian dining experience. Young chef-owner Alberto López Oliva prepares an innovative menu of traditional fare with a twist, such as *manitas, manzana, y langostinas al aroma de Módena* (pig trotters with prawns and apple slices in Módena vinegar), and *perdiz al chocolate con berza* (partridge cooked in chocolate, served with cabbage). The tasting menus (€30 and €33) are both good values. [$] *Average main: €30* ✉ *Calle San Pablo 21* ☎ *923/264028* 🌐 *www.lahoja21.com* 🕒 *Closed Mon. No dinner Sun.*

$$$ SPANISH Fodor's Choice ★

🍴 **Valencia.** Despite its Mediterranean name, this traditional, family-run restaurant serves up Castilian specialties like garlic soup, partridge salad, local river trout, white asparagus, and suckling lamb. There are weeknight menus and daily specials, too. The tiny front bar is decorated with black-and-white photos of local bullfighters, and is usually packed with locals. There's a dining room out back, but the best place to sit is outdoors on the little square in front, at tables shaded with awnings. What saves this place from being overrun by tourists is that it's on a tiny backstreet that doesn't appear on many maps—but it's actually just steps off the Plaza Mayor. [$] *Average main: €20* ✉ *Calle Concejo 15* ☎ *923/217868* 🌐 *www.restaurantevalencia.com* 🕒 *Closed Nov., Mon., Tues. Sept.–May, and Sun. June–Aug.*

Continued on page 202

Vineyard in Rioja.

THE WINES OF SPAIN

After years of being in the shadows of other European wines, Spanish wines are finally gunning for the spotlight—and what has taken place is nothing short of a revolution. The wines of Spain, like its cuisine, are currently experiencing a firecracker explosion of both quality and variety that has brought a new level of interest, awareness, and recognition throughout the world, propelling them to superstar status. A generation of young, ambitious winemakers has jolted dormant areas awake and even the most established regions have undergone makeovers in order to keep up with these dramatic changes and to compete in the global market. And it's paid off: New 2013 figures show Spain is now the world's biggest wine producer, by land area and volume.

THE ROAD TO GREAT WINE

Frank Gehry designed the visitor center for the Marqués de Riscal winery in Rioja.

Spain has a long wine history dating back to the time when the Phoenicians introduced viticulture, over 3,000 years ago. Some of the country's wines achieved fame in Roman times, and the Visigoths enacted early wine laws. But in the regions under Muslim rule, winemaking slowed down for centuries. Starting in the 16th century, wine trade expanded along with the Spanish Empire, and by the 18th and 19th centuries the Sherry region *bodegas* (wineries) were already established.

In the middle of the 19th century, seeds of change blossomed throughout the Spanish wine industry. In 1846, the estate that was to become Vega Sicilia, Spain's most revered winery, was set up in Castile. Three years later the famous Tío Pepe brand was established to produce the excellent dry fino wines. Marqués de Murrieta and the Marqués de Riscal wineries opened in the 1860s creating the modern Rioja region and clearing the way for many centenary wineries. *Cava*—Spain's white or pink sparkling wine—was created the following decade in Catalonia.

After this flurry of activity, Spanish wines languished for almost a century. Vines were hit hard by phylloxera, and then a civil war and a long dictatorship left the country stagnant and isolated. Just 30 short years ago, Spain's wines were split between the same dominant trio of Sherry, Rioja, and cava, and loads of cheap, watered-down wines made by local cooperatives with little gumption to improve and even less expertise.

Starting in the 1970s, however, a wave of innovation crashed through Rioja and emergent regions like Ribera del Duero and Penedés. In the 1990s, it turned into a revolution that spread all over the landscape—and is still going strong. Today, Spain is the largest wine producer in the world in terms of land area and volume. Europe's debt crisis means domestic wine consumption is down and vintners are doubling their effort to appeal to export markets.

SPANISH WINE CATEGORIES BY AGE

A unique feature of Spanish wines is their indication of aging process on wine labels. DO wines (see "A *Vino* Primer" on following page) show this on mandatory back panels. Aging requirements are longer for reds, but also apply to white, rosé, and sparkling wines. For reds, the rules are as follows:

Vino Joven
A young wine that may or may not have spent some time aging in oak barrels before it was bottled. Some winemakers have begun to shun traditional regulations to produce cutting-edge wines in this category. An elevated price distinguishes the ambitious new reds from the easy-drinking *jóvenes*.

Crianza
A wine aged for at least 24 months, six of which are in barrels (12 in Rioja, Ribera del Duero, and Navarra). A great bargain in top vintages from the most reliable wineries and regions.

Reserva
A wine aged for a minimum of 36 months, at least 12 of which are in oak.

Gran Reserva
Traditionally the top of the Spanish wine hierarchy, and the pride of the historic Rioja wineries. A red wine aged for at least 24 months in oak, followed by 36 months in the bottle before release.

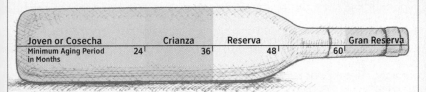

Joven or Cosecha	Crianza	Reserva	Gran Reserva
Minimum Aging Period in Months	24	36	48	60

READING LABELS LIKE A PRO

Term meaning that the wine was bottled at the property

Name of the wine

For some prestigious wines, each bottle is numbered

Alcohol content

Name of the winery

Means the wine was made from vines on a single plot of land

Name of the appellation (look for the expression "Denominación de Origen" displayed in small print just below the appellation's name)

Town where the winery is located

Aging category

Vintage year

ESTATE BOTTLED — SINGLE VINEYARD — PRODUCE OF SPAIN

CONTINO
RIOJA
DENOMINACIÓN DE ORIGEN CALIFICADA
De esta cosecha se han embotellado 117.139 botellas de Reserva
13,5% Vol.   BOT.   75 cl. e
Embotellado en la propiedad
VIÑEDOS DEL CONTINO, S. A.
LAGUARDIA - LASERNA, ESPAÑA
R.E. N.º 5212 VI

RESERVA 2002

A *VINO* PRIMER

Spain offers a daunting assortment of wine styles, regions, and varietals. But don't worry: a few pointers will help you understand unfamiliar names and terms. Most of Spain's quality wines come from designated regions called *Denominaciones de Origen* (Appellations of Origin), often abbreviated as DO. Spain has more than 60 of these areas, which are tightly regulated to protect the integrity and characteristics of the wines produced there.

Beyond international varieties like Cabernet Sauvignon and Chardonnay, the country is home to several high-quality varietals, both indigenous and imported. Reds include Tempranillo, an early-ripening grape that blends and ages well, and Garnacha (the Spanish name for France's Grenache), a spicy, full-bodied red wine. The most popular white wines are the light, aromatic Albariño or Ruedas, and the full-bodied Verdejo.

Rioja wines

❶ The green and more humid areas of the Northwest deliver crisp, floral white albariños in Galicia's Rías Biaxas. In the Bierzo DO, the Mencía grape distills the essence of the schist slopes, where it grows into minerally infused red wines.

❷ Moving east, in the iron-rich riverbanks of the Duero, Tempranillo grapes, here called "Tinto Fino," produce complex and age-worthy

Ribera del Duero reds and hefty Toro wines. Close by, the Rueda DO adds aromatic and grassy whites from local Verdejo and adopted Sauvignon Blanc.

❸ The Rioja region is a winemaker's paradise. Here a mild, nearly perfect vine-growing climate marries limestone and clay soils with Tempranillo, Spain's most noble grape, to deliver wines that possess the two main features of every great region: personality and quality. Tempranillo-based Riojas evolve from a young cherry color and aromas of strawberries and red fruits, to a brick hue, infused with scents of tobacco and leather. Whether medium or

full-bodied, tannic or velvety, these reds are some of the most versatile and food-friendly wines, and have set the standard for the country for over a century.

Nearby, Navarra and three small DO's in Aragón deliver great wines made with the local Garnacha, Tempranillo, and international grape varieties.

❹ Southwest of Barcelona is the region of Catalonia, which encompasses the areas of Penedès and Priorat. Catalonia is best known as the heartland of *cava*,

Chardonnay vines in Navarra.

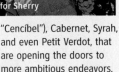

the typically dry, sparkling wine made from three indigenous Spanish varietals: Parellada, Xarel-lo, and Macabeo. The climatically varied Penedès—just an hour south of Barcelona—produces full-bodied reds like Garnacha on coastal plains, and cool-climate varietals like Riesling and Sauvignon Blanc in the mountains. Priorat is a region that has emerged into the international spotlight during the past decade, as innovative winemakers have transformed winemaking practices there. Now, traditional grapes like Garnacha and Cariñena are blended with Cabernet Sauvignon and Syrah to produce rich, concentrated reds with powerful tannins.

❺ The region of **Valencia** is south of Catalonia on the Mediterranean coast. The wines of this area have improved markedly in recent years, with red wines from Jumilla and other appellations finding their way onto the international market. Tempranillo and Monastrell (France's Mourvèdre) are the most common reds. A local specialty of the area is Moscatel de Valencia, a highly aromatic sweet white wine.

❻ In the **central plateau south of Madrid**, rapid investment, modernization, and replanting is resulting in medium bodied, easy drinking, and fairly priced wines made with Tempranillo (here called

Grapes harvested for Sherry

"Cencíbel"), Cabernet, Syrah, and even Petit Verdot, that are opening the doors to more ambitious endeavors.

❼ In sun-drenched Andalusia, where the white albariza limestone soils reflect the powerful sunlight while trapping the scant humidity, the fortified **Jerez** (Sherry) and **Montilla** emerge. In all their different incarnations, from dry finos, Manzanillas, amontillados, palo cortados, and olorosos, to sweet creams and Pedro Ximénez, they are the most original wines of Spain.

JUST OFF THE VINE: NEW WINE DEVELOPMENTS

Beyond Tempranillo: The current wine revolution has recovered many native varieties. Albariño, Godello, and Verdejo among the whites, and Callet, Cariñena, Garnacha, Graciano, Mandó, Manto Negro, Mencía, and Monastrell among the reds, are gaining momentum and will likely become more recognized.

Vinos de Pagos: *Pago*, a word meaning plot or vineyard, is the new legal term chosen to create Spain's equivalent of a *Grand Cru* hierarchy, by protecting quality oriented wine producers that make wine from their own estates.

Petit Verdot: Winemakers in Spain are discovering that Petit Verdot, the "little green" grape of Bordeaux, ripens much easier in warmer climates than in its birthplace. This is contributing to the rise of Petit Verdot in red blends, and even to the production of single varietal wines.

Andalusia's New Wines: For centuries, scorching southern Andalusia has offered world-class Sherry and Montilla wines. Now trailblazing winemakers are making serious inroads in the production of quality white, red, and new dessert wines, something deemed impossible a few years back.

Cult Wines: For most of the past century, Vega Sicilia Unico was the only true cult wine from Spain. The current explosion has greatly expanded the roster: L'Ermita, Pingus, Clos Erasmus, Artadi, Cirsion, Terreus, and Termanthia are the leading names in a list that grows every year.

V.O.S. and V.O.R.S: Sherry's most dramatic change in over a century is the creation of the "Very Old Sherry" designation for wines over 20 years of age, and the addition of "Rare" for those over 30, to easier distinguish the best, oldest, and most complex wines.

Innovative New Blends: A few wine regions have strict regulations concerning the varieties used in their wines, but most allow for experimentation. All over the country, *bodegas* are crafting wines with creative blends that involve local varieties, Tempranillo, and famous international grapes.

Island Wines: In both the Balearic and Canary Islands the strong tourist industry helped to revive local winemaking. Although hard to find, the best Callet and Manto Negro based red wines of Majorca, and the sweet *malvasías* of Lanzarote will reward the adventurous drinker.

SPAIN'S SUPERSTAR WINEMAKERS

Mariano García   Peter Sisseck   Alvaro Palacios   Josep Lluís Pérez

The current wine revolution has made superstars out of a group of dynamic, innovative, and visionary winemakers. Here are some of the top names:

Mariano García. His 30 years as winemaker of Vega Sicilia made him a legend. Now García displays his deft touch in the Ribera del Duero and Bierzo through his four wineries: Aalto, Mauro, San Román, and Paixar.

Peter Sisseck. A Dane educated in Bordeaux, Sisseck found his calling in the old Ribera del Duero vineyards, where he crafted Pingus, Spain's most coveted cult wine.

Alvaro Palacios. In Priorat, Palacios created L'Ermita, a Garnacha wine that is one of Spain's most remarkable bottlings. Palacios also is a champion of the Bierzo region, where he produces wines from the ancient Mencía varietal, known for their vibrant berry flavors and stony minerality.

Josep Lluís Pérez. From his base in Priorat and through his work as a winemaker, researcher, teacher, and consultant, Pérez (along with his daughter Sara Pérez) has become the main driving force in shaping the modern Mediterranean wines of Spain.

MATCHMAKING KNOW-HOW

A pairing of wine with *jamón* and Spanish olives.

Spain has a great array of regional products and cuisines, and its avant-garde chefs are culinary world leaders. As a general rule, you should match local food with local wines—but Spanish wines can be matched very well with some of the most unexpected dishes.

Albariños and the white wines of Galicia are ideal partners for seafood and fish. Dry sherries complement Serrano and Iberico hams, *lomo, chorizo,* and *salchichón* (white dry sauage), as well as olives and nuts. Pale, light, and dry finos and Manzanillas are the perfect aperitif wines, and the ideal companion for fried fish. Fuller bodied amontillados, palo cortados, and olorosos go well with hearty soups. Ribera del Duero reds are the perfect match for the outstanding local lamb. Try Priorat and other Mediterranean reds with strong cheeses and barbecue meats. Traditional Rioja harmonizes well with fowl and game. But also take an adventure off the beaten path: manzanilla and fino are great with sushi and sashimi; Rioja *reserva* fit tuna steaks; and cream sherry will not be out of place with chocolate. *¡Salud!*

WHERE TO STAY

$$$$ HOTEL

Don Gregorio. This upscale boutique hotel has spacious and contemporary rooms in a building with roots in the 15th century. **Pros:** chic, contemporary facilities. **Cons:** restaurant is very expensive; the more casual yet stylish cafeteria is a better bet. [$] *Rooms from: €220* ✉ *Calle San Pablo 80–82* ☎ *923/217015* 🌐 *www.hoteldongregorio.com* 🛏 *17 rooms* 🍴 *Breakfast.*

$$$ HOTEL Fodor's Choice ★

Hotel Rector. From the stately entrance to the high-ceiling guest rooms, this lovely hotel offers a true European experience. **Pros:** terrific value; personal service; good location. **Cons:** parking costs extra; no balconies. [$] *Rooms from: €165* ✉ *Paseo Rector Esperabé 10* ☎ *923/218482* 🌐 *www.hotelrector.com* 🛏 *13 rooms* 🍴 *Multiple meal plans.*

$ B&B/INN Fodor's Choice ★

Microtel Placentinos. This is a lovely little B&B tucked away down a quiet pedestrian street in Salamanca's historic center, near the Palacio de Congresos convention center and a short walk from the Plaza Mayor. **Pros:** some rooms have whirlpool baths; all have free Wi-Fi; only a short walk to bus station. **Cons:** some rooms close to the interior staircase aren't well insulated, and can be noisy. [$] *Rooms from: €75* ✉ *Calle Placentinos 9* ☎ *923/281531* 🌐 *www.microtelplacentinos.com* 🛏 *9 rooms* 🍴 *Breakfast.*

$ HOTEL Fodor's Choice ★

Revolutum Hostel. It feels like a chic design hotel, but with backpacker prices. **Pros:** breakfast included; all rooms have private bathrooms; special rates for families and for stays of longer than five nights. **Cons:** deposit required for towels. [$] *Rooms from: €45* ✉ *Calle Sánchez Barbero 7* ☎ *923/217656* 🌐 *www.revolutumhostel.com* 🛏 *20 rooms* 🍴 *Breakfast.*

NIGHTLIFE AND PERFORMING ARTS

Particularly in summer, Salamanca sees the greatest influx of foreign students of any city in Spain: by day they study Spanish, and by night they fill Salamanca's bars and clubs to capacity.

PERFORMING ARTS

Teatro Liceo. This 732-seat theater, 40 yards from Plaza Mayor, was renovated in 2002, but traces of the old 19th-century theater, built over an 18th-century convent, remain. It hosts classic and modern performances of opera, dance, flamenco, and film festivals. ✉ *Calle del Toro 23, City Center* ☎ *923/218182* 🌐 *www.ciudaddecultura.org.*

NIGHTLIFE

Café Corrillo. This trendy restaurant-bar-café is the main hangout for fans of live music, especially jazz, and top-notch tapas make it a prime haunt for foodies and students alike. Check the website for the concert list and special events like craft beer nights. ✉ *Calle Meléndez 18* ☎ *923/271917* 🌐 *www.cafecorrillo.com.*

Camelot. After 11, a well-dressed crowd, mostly in their 20s and 30s, comes to dance at Camelot, an ancient stone-wall warehouse in one corner of the 16th-century Convento de Las Ursulas. Hours vary, but things generally get going quite late. There's also a sister club called Cubic Club around the corner on Calle Iscar Peira. ✉ *Calle de los Bordadores 3* ☎ *923/219091, 923/212182* 🌐 *www.camelot.es.*

Casino del Tormes. Try your luck at this glitzy, refurbished turn-of-the-20th-century mill on the Tormes River, near the Puente Romano. You'll need your passport to enter. If your pockets go empty or you need a break, browse the surprisingly delightful little museum, where artwork is on display alongside old flour mill equipment. ✉ *Calle La Pesca 5* ☎ *923/281628* ⊕ *www.casinodeltormes.es* ⊙ *Sun.–Thurs. 4 pm–4 am, Fri. and Sat. 8 pm–5 am.*

Gran Café Moderno. After-hours types end the night here, snacking on *churros con chocolate* at daybreak. ✉ *Gran Vía 75–77* ☎ *637/538165, 923/260147* ⊙ *Tues.–Sat. 4 pm–4 am.*

Fodor'sChoice
★

Mesón Cervantes. This upstairs tapas bar draws crowds to its balcony for a drink and unparalleled views of the action below. It's one of the few cafés open early, and a great place to grab your morning coffee and churros before sightseeing. But make sure to double back for a glass of Ribera del Duero and fantastic views of the Plaza Mayor lit up at night. ■ TIP→ Reserve a balcony spot early in the day, and come back to claim your view. ✉ *Pl. Mayor 15, entrance on southeast corner* ☎ *923/217213* ⊕ *www.mesoncervantes.com* ⊙ *Daily 9 am–1:30 am.*

Posada de las Almas. Bask in the romantic glow from stained-glass lamps at this preferred cocktail-and-conversation nightspot for stylish students. Wrought-iron chandeliers hang from the high wood-beam ceilings, harp-strumming angels top elegant pillars, and one entire wall of shelves showcases a somewhat bizarre collection of colorful dollhouses. ✉ *Pl. San Boal 7* ☎ *923/268639* ⊕ *www.posadadelasanimas.com.*

SHOPPING

Artesanía Duende. If you have a car, skip the souvenir shops in Salamanca's center and instead head 35 km (22 miles) through the countryside along the rural SA-300 road to Artesanía Duende, a wooden crafts workshop run by a charming husband-and-wife team. At their home factory, you can see their handicrafts being made. Their music boxes, thimbles, photo frames, and other items are beautifully carved or stenciled with local themes, from the *bailes charros,* Salamanca's regional dance, to the floral designs embroidered on the hems of provincial dresses. With limited open days, it's best to call ahead to schedule a free, personal tour. ✉ *Calle San Miguel 1, Ledesma* ☎ *626/510527, 625/336703, 923/570435* ⊕ *www.creacionesduende.es* ⊙ *Fri.–Sun. 10–8:30.*

Rastro. On Sunday, this flea market—named after the larger one in Madrid—is held just outside Salamanca's historic center. Buses leave from Plaza de España. ✉ *Av. de Aldehuela.*

BURGOS

243 km (151 miles) north of Madrid on A1.

On the banks of the Arlanzón River, this small city boasts some of Spain's most outstanding medieval architecture. If you approach on the A1 from Madrid, the spiky twin spires of Burgos's cathedral, rising above the main bridge, welcome you to the city. Burgos's second pride is its heritage as the city of El Cid, the part-historical, part-mythical hero of the Christian Reconquest of Spain. The city has been known for centuries as a center of both militarism and religion, and even today more nuns fill the streets than almost anywhere else in Spain. Burgos was born as a military camp—a fortress built in 884 on the orders of the Christian king Alfonso III, who was struggling to defend the upper reaches of Old Castile from the constant forays of the Arabs. It quickly became vital in the defense of Christian Spain, and its reputation as an early outpost of Christianity was cemented with the founding of the Royal Convent of Las Huelgas, in 1187. Burgos also became a place of rest and sustenance for Christian pilgrims on the Camino de Santiago. These days, Burgos is also renowned for its cuisine, especially its namesake white cheese and its *morcilla* (blood sausage).

GETTING HERE AND AROUND

Burgos can be reached by train from Madrid, with eight departures daily from Chamartin (about 2½ hours) and by bus, with hourly service from various Madrid stations. Once there, municipal buses cover 45 routes throughout the city, many of them originating in Plaza de España.

ESSENTIALS

Visitor Information Burgos ⊠ *Calle Nuño Rasura 7* ☎ *947/288874* ⊕ *www.turismoburgos.org.*

EXPLORING

TOP ATTRACTIONS

Fodor's Choice ★ **Cathedral.** Start your tour of the city with the cathedral, which contains such a wealth of art and other treasures that the local burghers lynched their civil governor in 1869 for trying to take an inventory of it: the proud citizens feared that the man was plotting to steal their riches. Just as opulent as what's inside is the sculpted Flamboyant Gothic facade of the cathedral. The cornerstone was laid in 1221, and the two 275-foot towers were completed by the middle of the 14th century, though the final chapel was not finished until 1731. There are 13 chapels, the most elaborate of which is the hexagonal Condestable Chapel. You'll find the **tomb of El Cid** (1026–99) and his wife, Ximena, under the transept. El Cid (whose real name was Rodrigo Díaz de Vivar) was a feudal warlord revered for his victories over the Moors; the medieval *Song of My Cid* transformed him into a Spanish national hero.

At the other end of the cathedral, high above the West Door, is the **Reloj de Papamoscas** (Flycatcher Clock), so named for the sculptured bird that opens its mouth as the hands mark each hour. The grilles around the choir have some of the finest wrought-iron work in central Spain, and the choir itself has 103 delicately carved walnut stalls, no two alike. The 13th-century stained-glass windows that once shed a beautiful, filtered light were destroyed in 1813, one of many cultural casualties of Napoléon's retreating troops. ⊠ *Between Pl. del Rey San Fernando and Pl. de Santa María* ☎ *947/204712* ⊕ *www.catedraldeburgos.es* ▤ *€7 (includes audio guide)* ⊙ *Mid-Mar.–Oct., daily 9:30–7:30; Nov.–mid-Mar., daily 10–7. Last admission 1 hr before closing.*

Espolón. The Arco de Santa María frames the city's loveliest promenade, the Espolón. Shaded with black poplars, it follows the riverbank.

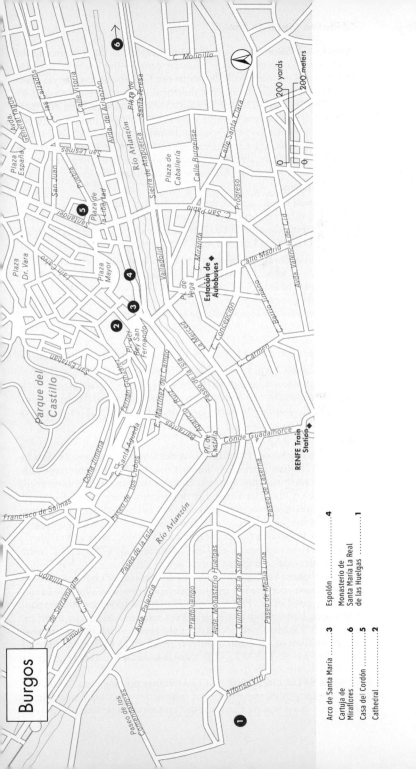

Burgos

Arco de Santa María	3	Espolón	4
Cartuja de Miraflores	6	Monasterio de Santa María La Real de las Huelgas	1
Casa del Cordón	5		
Cathedral	2		

Monasterio de Santa María La Real de Las Huelgas. On the western edge of town, a 1.6-km (1-mile) walk from the center—this convent, founded in 1187 by King Alfonso VIII, is still run by nuns. It has a royal mausoleum, though all but one of the royal coffins were desecrated by Napoléon's soldiers. The one that survived contained clothing that form the basis of the convent's textile museum. Admission includes a guided tour of the monastery, but you can browse the museum at your own pace. ✉ *Calle de Los Compases s/n* ☎ *947/201630 Tues.–Sat. 10:30–1:30 and 4–6:30* 🌐 *www.patrimonionacional.es* 🎫 *€7 for guided tours* 🕒 *Tues.–Sat. 10–2 and 4–6:30, Sun. and holidays 10:30–3.*

WORTH NOTING

Arco de Santa María. Across the Plaza del Rey San Fernando from the cathedral, this is the city's main gate; walk through toward the river and look above the arch at the 16th-century statues of the first Castilian judges, El Cid, King Carlos I, and Spain's patron saint, James.

Cartuja de Miraflores. Founded in 1441, this is an old Gothic monastery, the outside of which is rather plain. Inside, however, is a mass of rich decoration. The Isabelline church has an altarpiece by Gil de Siloe that is said to be gilded with the first gold brought back from the Americas. To get there, follow signs from the city's main gate—it's 3 km (2 miles) to the east, at the end of a poplar- and elm-lined road. ✉ *Ctra. Fuentes Blancas* ☎ *947/252586* 🌐 *www.cartuja.org* 🎫 *Free* 🕒 *Tues.–Sat. 10:15–3 and 4–6, Sun. 11–3 and 4–6; Mass Sun. and holy days at 10:15.*

Casa del Cordón. Ferdinand and Isabella received Columbus in this palace after his second voyage to the New World (1496). It's now a bank, but you can visit the exterior and renaissance courtyard during business hours. ✉ *Pl. de la Libertad and Calle de Santander s/n* 🎫 *Free* 🕒 *Courtyard weekdays 9–2:30.*

WHERE TO EAT AND STAY

$$$ SPANISH 🍴 **Casa Ojeda.** Across from the Casa del Cordón, this popular restaurant—a Castilian classic—is known for inspired Burgos standards, especially roast suckling pig and lamb straight from the 200-year-old wood oven. Other hard-to-resist opportunities are the *alubias rojas ibeas con chorizo, morcilla, y tocino* (red beans with chorizo sausage, blood sausage, and bacon) or the *corazones de solomillo con foie al vinagre de frambuesa* (hearts of beef filet with duck liver and raspberry vinegar). [$] *Average main: €20* ✉ *C. Vitoria 5* ☎ *947/209052* 🌐 *www.restauranteojeda.com* 🕒 *No dinner Sun.*

$$$ HOTEL FAMILY Fodor's Choice ★ 🏨 **Landa Palace.** Family owned and run, this superb hotel, housed in an old castle surrounded by lush gardens, provides supreme luxury at a very good price. **Pros:** stunning indoor-outdoor swimming pool; fireplaces; babysitting available. **Cons:** roads to and from town are busy, and it's not a pedestrian-friendly route; you'll need your own transportation to get here. [$] *Rooms from: €135* ✉ *Ctra. de Madrid-Irún, Km 235* ☎ *947/257777* 🌐 *www.landa.as* 🛏 *13 rooms, 24 suites* 🍽 *Multiple meal plans.*

$ HOTEL 🏨 **Mesón del Cid.** Once home to a 15th-century printing press, this family-run hotel and restaurant has been hosting travelers for generations in light, airy guest rooms that face the cathedral. **Pros:** English-speaking staff; comfy beds; central location. **Cons:** older plumbing, and door handles might break, but the staff is good about remedying any inconveniences. [$] *Rooms from: €60* ✉ *Pl. Santa María 8* ☎ *947/208715* 🌐 *www.mesondelcid.es* 🛏 *55 rooms* 🍴 *Multiple meal plans.*

EL CAMINO

West of Burgos, the N120 to León crosses the ancient Way of St. James, revealing lovely old churches, tiny hermitages, ruined monasteries, and medieval villages across rolling fields. West of León, you can follow the well-worn Camino pilgrimage route as it approaches the giant cathedral in Santiago de Compostela. *See the El Camino de Santiago In Focus feature in Chapter 4 for more information about El Camino.*

NIGHTLIFE

Due to its university students, Burgos has a lively *vida nocturna* (nightlife), which centers on **Las Llanas,** near the cathedral. House wines and *cañas* (small glasses of beer) flow freely through the crowded tapas bars along calles Laín Calvo and San Juan, near the Plaza Mayor. Calle Puebla, a small, dark street off Calle San Juan, also gets constant revelers, who pop into Café Principal, La Rebotica, and Spils Cervecería for a quick drink and bite before moving on. When you order a drink at any Burgos bar, the bartender plunks down a free *pinchito* (small tapa)—a longstanding tradition.

SHOPPING

A good buy is a few bottles of local Ribera del Duero red wines, now strong rivals to those of La Rioja Alta. Burgos is also known for its morcilla and its local cheese, *queso de Burgos,* a mild white variety.

Casa Quintanilla. Founded in 1880, this is a good one-stop spot to pick up some local delicacies, such as morcilla and queso de Burgos. It's closed on Saturday afternoon and all day Sunday. ✉ *Calle Paloma 17* ☎ *947/202535* 🌐 *www.casaquintanilla.es.*

LEÓN

334 km (208 miles) northwest of Madrid, 184 km (114 miles) west of Burgos.

León, the ancient capital of Castile–León, sits on the banks of the Bernesga River in the high plains of Old Castile; today it's a wealthy provincial capital and prestigious university town. The wide avenues of western León are lined with boutiques, and the twisting alleys of the half-timber old town hide the bars, bookstores, and chocolaterías most popular with students.

Historians say that the city was not named for the proud lion that has been its emblem for centuries; rather, they assert that the name is a corruption of the Roman word *legio* (legion), from the fact that the city was founded as a permanent camp for the Roman legions in AD 70. The capital of Christian Spain was moved here from Oviedo in 914 as the Reconquest spread south, and this was the city's richest era.

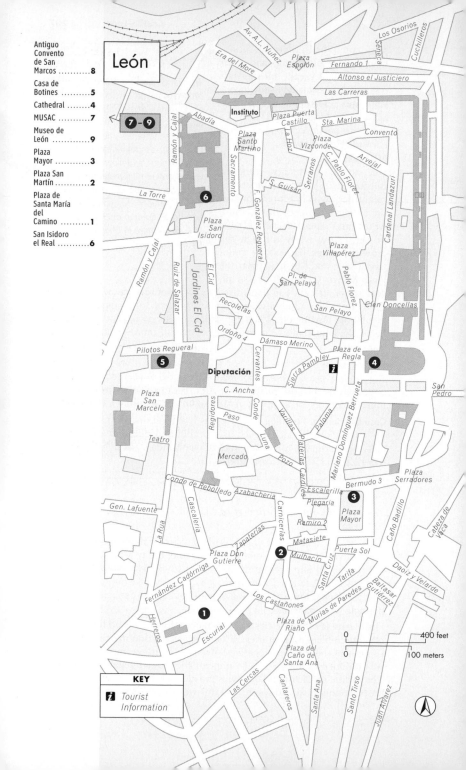

León

KEY

🛈 Tourist Information

As you're wandering the old town, you can still see fragments of the 6-foot-thick ramparts that were once part of the Roman walls. Look down occasionally and you just might notice small brass scallop shells set into the street. The scallop is the symbol of St. James; the town government installed them to mark the path for modern-day pilgrims.

GETTING HERE AND AROUND

León can be reached by train from Madrid, with 10 departures daily from Chamartin station; the journey takes two hours 45 minutes. By bus, ALSA has several departures daily. The company also runs 14 local bus routes around León, but visitors to the city will rarely need them as the historic center is primarily composed of pedestrian-only streets.

ESSENTIALS

Visitor Information León ⊠ *Pl. de San Marcelo 1* ☎ *987/878327* ⊕ *www. leon.es.*

EXPLORING

TOP ATTRACTIONS

Antiguo Convento de San Marcos. Fronted by a large, airy pedestrian plaza, this sumptuous building is now a luxury hotel, the Parador de León *(⇨ see Where to Eat and Stay)*. Originally a home for knights of the Order of St. James, who patrolled the Camino de Santiago, and a stop for weary pilgrims, the monastery you see today was begun in 1513 by the head of the order, King Ferdinand, who thought that knights deserved something better. Finished at the height of the Renaissance, the plateresque facade is a majestic swath of small, intricate sculptures (many depicting knights and lords) and ornamentation—one of the most impressive Renaissance buildings in Spain. Inside, the elegant staircase and a cloister full of medieval statues lead you to the bar, which still has the original defensive arrow slits as windows. As the Anexo Monumental del Museo de León, the convent also displays historic paintings and artifacts. ⊠ *Pl. de San Marcos 7* ☎ *987/245061, 987/237300* ⊕ *www.parador.es* ⊡ *Museum €1* ⊙ *Museum: Oct.–June, Tues.–Sat. 10–2 and 4–7, Sun. 10–2; July–Sept., Tues.–Sat. 10–2 and 5–8, Sun. 10–2.*

Casa de Botines. Just south of the old town, this multigabled, turreted, granite behemoth was designed in the late 1800s by the world-famous Catalan architect Antoni Gaudí (1852–1926). It now houses a bank that's closed to tourists. But the building is gorgeous just from the outside—it's a stark contrast to Gaudí's other, more famous buildings. ⊠ *Calle Legión VII 3.*

Fodor's Choice ★ **Cathedral.** The pride of León is its soaring Gothic cathedral, on the Plaza de Regla. Its upper reaches have more windows than stone. Flanked by two aggressively square towers, the facade has three arched, weatherworn doorways, the middle one adorned with slender statues of the apostles. Begun in 1205, the cathedral has 125 long, thin stained-glass windows, dozens of decorative small ones, and three giant rose windows. The windows depict abstract floral patterns as well as various biblical and medieval scenes; on sunny days, they cast bejeweled streams of light on the beautifully spare, pale sandstone interior. A glass door to the choir gives an unobstructed view of nave windows and the painted altarpiece, framed with gold leaf. The cathedral also contains the sculpted tomb of King Ordoño II, who moved the capital of Christian Spain to León. The museum's collection boasts giant medieval hymnals, textiles, sculptures, wood carvings, and paintings. Look for the carved-wood Mudejar archive, with a letter of the alphabet above each door; it's one of the world's oldest file cabinets. The partial museum visit excludes the museum's best and earliest works: the Romanesque, Gothic, and Renaissance ivory carvings and silversmithery, so opt for the full museum ticket. The absolute highlight is a nighttime guided tour; drop by earlier in the day to find out the current tour times. ■ TIP→ The cathedral is in theory closed to tourists during Sunday Mass; some foreigners have complained of being asked to pay an entrance fee to attend services. ⊠ *Pl. de Regla s/n* ☎ *987/875770* ⊕ *www.catedraldeleon.org* 🖾 *€5, nighttime guided tour €6* ☉ *May–Sept., weekdays 9:30–1:30 and 4–8, Sat. 9:30–noon and 2–6, Sun. 9:30–11 and 2–8; Oct.–Apr., Mon.–Sat. 9:30–1:30 and 4–7, Sun. 9:30–2.*

MUSAC (Museo de Arte Contemparáneo de Castilla y León) (*Museum of Modern Art of Castillo y León*). The inside of this museum reflects contemporary León, while the outside pays homage to the city's history with its own cluster of buildings whose exteriors are cascaded with rectangular stained glass, like its cathedral. This "Museum of the Present" brings art to the people by offering varied workshops and activities for children as well as exhibiting modern creations from all over the globe. Films and concerts also show throughout the year. ⊠ *Av. de los Reyes Leoneses 24* ☎ *987/090000* ⊕ *www.musac.es* 🖾 *€3 (free Sun. 5–9)* ☉ *Tues.–Fri. 11–2 and 5–8, weekends and holidays 11–3 and 5–9.*

Plaza Mayor. This is the heart of the old town, and on Wednesday and Saturday mornings the arcaded plaza bustles with farmers selling produce and cheeses. Many farmers still wear wooden shoes called *madreñas*, designed to walk on mud in this usually wet part of Spain; the odd-looking shoes are raised on three heels, two in front and one in back.

Plaza San Martín. Most of León's tapas bars are in this 12th-century square and the area is called the Barrio Húmedo, or Wet Neighborhood, allegedly because of the large amount of wine spilled here late at night.

WORTH NOTING

Museo de León. This museum displays many important artifacts from the region, covering prehistoric to contemporary times, but pride of place belongs to the Cristo Carrizo (Carrizo Crucifix), a small 11th-century Romanesque ivory carving distinguished by its lifelike expression and powerful presence. Notable are the figure's carefully coiffed hair and beard and the loincloth arranged in sumptuous Byzantine detail. ⊠ *Pl. de Santo Domingo 8* ☎ *987/236405* ⊕ *www.museodeleon.com* 🖾 *€1.20* ☉ *Oct.–June, Tues.–Sat. 10–2 and 4–7, Sun. 10–2; July–Sept. Tues.–Sat. 10–2 and 5–8, Sun. 10–2.*

Plaza de Santa María del Camino. Southwest of the Plaza San Martín, this square used to be called Plaza del Grano (Grain Square) because it was the site of the city's corn and bread market. Also here is the church of **Santa María del Camino,** where pilgrims stop on their way

The multicolor panels on León's MUSAC, the Museum of Contemporary Art, were inspired by the rose window of the city's Gothic cathedral.

west to Santiago de Compostela. The fountain in the middle of the plaza depicts two cherubs clutching a pillar, symbolizing León's two rivers and the capital.

San Isidoro el Real. This sandstone basilica was built into the side of the city wall in 1063 and rebuilt in the 12th century. Adjoining the basilica, the **Panteón de los Reyes** (Royal Pantheon), which has earned the title of the Sistine Chapel of Romanesque art, has vibrant 12th-century frescoes on its pillars and ceiling. The pantheon was the first building in Spain to be decorated with scenes from the New Testament. Look for the agricultural calendar painted on one archway, showing which farming task should be performed each month. Twenty-three kings and queens were once buried here, but their tombs were destroyed by French troops during the Napoleonic Wars. Treasures in the adjacent **Museo de San Isidoro** include a jewel-encrusted agate chalice, a richly illustrated hand-written Bible, and many polychrome wood statues of the Virgin Mary. ⊠ *Pl. de San Isidoro 4* ☎ *987/876161* ⊕ *www.sanisidorodeleon.net* 🖼 *Free; €5 for guided tours of Royal Pantheon and museum* ⊙ *Sept.– June, Mon.–Sat. 10–1:30 and 4–6:30, Sun. 10–1:30; July and Aug., Mon.–Sat. 9–8, Sun. 9–2.*

WHERE TO EAT AND STAY

$$$$
SPANISH
✕**Adonías.** Enter the bar and go up one flight to this softly lit traditional dining room, furnished with rustic tables and colorful ceramics. The cuisine is based on such regional foodstuffs as cured ham, roasted peppers, and chorizo. Try the grilled sea bream or the roast suckling pig and, if you have room, the banana pudding with chocolate sauce. The menu of the day, a great value, includes appetizer, main course, dessert,

and wine. $ *Average main: €32* ✉ *Calle Santa Nonia 16* ☎ *987/206768, 987/252665* ⊕ *www.restauranteadonias.com* ⊘ *Closed Sun.*

$$$ ✕ **Bodega Regia.** Next to the cathedral, this charming and relaxed res-
SPANISH taurant has a restored 14th-century garden patio with lovely stone arches—a great place to appreciate the good food. There's a laid-back bar downstairs and a more formal dining room upstairs. Desserts such as the *pastel de castañas con chocolate caliente* (chestnut cake with hot chocolate) are worth splurging on. Reservations are essential on weekends. $ *Average main: €20* ✉ *Calle Regidores 9–11* ☎ *987/213173* ⊕ *www.regialeon.com* ⊘ *Closed Sun. and 15 days in Jan. and Sept.*

$$$ ✕ **Nuevo Racimo de Oro.** Upstairs from a ramshackle 12th-century tavern
SPANISH in the heart of the old town, this rustic restaurant, once a hostel and hospital for weary pilgrims, now specializes in roast lamb cooked in a wood-burning clay oven. The spicy *sopa de ajo leonesa* (garlic soup) is a classic, and the *solomillo Racimo con micuit de foie al aceite de trufa* (veal filet with duck liver and truffle oil) is criminally good. It's worth saving some room for the *tarta de San Marcos*, a lemon cake served with whipped cream. $ *Average main: €20* ✉ *Pl. de San Martín 8* ☎ *987/214767* ⊕ *www.racimodeoro.com* ⊘ *Closed Wed.*

$ 🏨 **Hotel Paris.** This modest but elegant establishment is both comfort-
HOTEL able and conveniently located. **Pros:** great location; use of in-house spa included in rates. **Cons:** street noise; few staffers speak Eng-lish. $ *Rooms from: €80* ✉ *Calle Ancha 18* ☎ *987/238600* ⊕ *www. hotelparisleon.com* ⮞ *61 rooms* ⦿ *Multiple meal plans.*

$$$$ 🏨 **Parador de León** (*San Marcos Monastery*). This magnificent parador
HOTEL occupies a restored 16th-century monastery and hospital built by King
Fodor's Choice Ferdinand to shelter pilgrims walking the Camino de Santiago. **Pros:**
★ among the most beautiful paradores in Spain; great restaurant. **Cons:** a big difference between the most and the least expensive rooms (this is the place to splurge for the good ones). $ *Rooms from: €230* ✉ *Pl. de San Marcos 7* ☎ *987/237300* ⊕ *www.parador.es* ⮞ *186 rooms, 16 suites* ⦿ *Multiple meal plans.*

NIGHTLIFE

León's most popular hangouts are clustered in Plaza Mayor (mainly couples and families) and Plaza San Martín (college kids). The streets around these plazas (calles Escalerilla, Plegaria, Ramiro 2, Matasiete, and Mulhacén) are packed with tapas bars. In the Plaza Mayor, you might want to start at **Universal, Mesón de Don Quixote, Casa Benito,** or **Bar La Plaza Mayor.** In the Plaza San Martín, the **Latino Bar at No. 10** serves a glass of house wine and your choice of one of four gener-ous tapas.

SHOPPING

Tasty regional treats include roasted red peppers, potent brandy-soaked cherries, and candied chestnuts. You can buy these in food shops all over the city.

Hojaldres Alonso. Part of a local deli chain, this shop near the cathedral is a great place to browse shelves of local goodies (candied nuts, pre-serves), all produced in nearby Astorga. Then head to the café in the back—the focus here is on the baked goods, particularly the *hojaldres* (puff pastries) and *torrijas,* a Castilian version of French toast. The café is a favorite among locals who come for their early evening *merienda* (usually between 6 and 8), Spain's answer to afternoon tea. You can also order online. ✉ *Calle Ancha 7* ☎ *987/252151, 987/616850* ⊕ *www. hojaldresalonso.com.*

Prada a Tope. This restaurant, winery, and gourmet store has a huge estate in the countryside just outside León, but operates a small café and shop in the city—as well as in several other franchises across Spain. Delicacies include chestnuts in syrup, bittersweet figs and pears in wine, jams, and liqueurs. Not enough room in your suitcase? You can also order by mail from their website. ✉ *Calle Alfonso IX* ☎ *987/257221, 987/563366* ⊕ *www.pradaatope.es.*

ASTORGA

46 km (29 miles) southwest of León.

Astorga, where the pilgrimage roads from France and Portugal merge, once had 22 hospitals to lodge and care for ailing travelers. The only one left today is next to the cathedral, which is a huge 15th-century building with four statues of St. James. Astorga is in the area of Maragatos, home to a community with distinct cultural and architectural characteristics, stemming from the region's Celtic and, later, Roman roots.

GETTING HERE AND AROUND
Several buses depart daily from León, about a 45-minute trip to Astorga. If you're driving yourself, there's ample parking and the city is navigable by foot.

ESSENTIALS
Visitor Information Astorga ✉ *Pl. Eduardo de Castro 5* ☎ *987/618222* ⊕ *www.ayuntamientodeastorga.com.*

EXPLORING
Museo de la Catedral. This museum displays 10th- and 12th-century chests, religious silverware, and paintings and sculptures by various Astorgans. ✉ *Pl. de la Catedral* ☎ *987/615820* 🎟 *Cathedral free, museum €3, or €5 combined ticket with Palacio Episcopal* ☉ *May–Sept., Tues.– Sat. 10–2 and 4–8, Sun. 10–2; Oct.–Apr., Tues.–Sat. 11–2 and 4–6, Sun. 11–2.*

FAMILY **Museo del Chocolate** (*Chocolate Museum*). This fascinating museum
Fodor's Choice tells the story of Spain's first chocolate imports: Mexican cacao beans
★ brought back to Spain by the explorer Hernán Cortés. The collection also includes 16th-century hot-chocolate mugs and 19th-century chocolate-production tools. The best part comes at the end, with a chocolate-tasting session. ✉ *Calle José María Gay 5* ☎ *987/616220* ⊕ *www. museochocolateastorga.com* 🎟 *€2.50, €4 combined ticket with the Museo Romano* ☉ *Tues.–Sat. 10:30–2 and 4:30–7, Sun. and holidays 10:30–2; last admission 30 mins before closing.*

FAMILY **Museo Romano** (*Roman Museum*). This small but wonderful and well-
Fodor's Choice organized museum uses the archeological record to show what life was
★ like in Astorga during Roman times, when the city was called Asturica Augusta. A visit here can also be combined with the Ruta Romana,

a walking tour of Roman archaeological remains in Astorga that's organized by the tourist office. ✉ *Pl. San Bartolomé 2* ☎ *987/616937* ⊕ *www.asturica.com* 💶 *€3; €4 combined ticket with Museo del Chocolate; €5 combined ticket with Roman Route* ☉ *Tues.–Sat. 10:30–2 and 4–6, Sun. 10:30–2; Roman Route walking tour daily 11–5, by reservation only.*

Palacio Episcopal (*Archbishop's Palace*). Just opposite Astorga's cathedral is this fairy-tale, neo-Gothic palace, designed for a Catalan cleric by Antoni Gaudí in 1889. Visiting during Astorga's Fiesta de Santa María, the last week of August, is a treat for the senses, when fireworks explode in the sky, casting rainbows of light over Gaudí's ornate, mystical towers. It's also home of the **Museo de Los Caminos** (Museum of the Way), which contains a large collection of folk items, such as the standard pilgrim costume—heavy black cloak, staff hung with gourds, and wide-brimmed hat bedecked with scallop shells—as well as contemporary Spanish art. ✉ *Glorieta Eduardo de Castro s/n, Pl. de la Catedral* ☎ *987/616882* 💶 *€4, or €5 combined ticket with Museo de la Catedral* ☉ *May–Sept., Tues.–Sat. 10–2 and 4–8, Sun. 10–2; Oct.–Apr., Tues.–Sat. 11–2 and 4–6, Sun. 11–2.*

WHERE TO EAT AND STAY

$$$$ ✕ **Restaurante Serrano.** Steps from the cathedral and Palacio Episcopal,
SPANISH   this rustic mesón is quite popular with locals. The menu, which focuses on local products, is often given over to special "gastronomic weeks" that might feature game, wild mushrooms, and pork—there's also a mix of contemporary cuisine and traditional dishes, such as roasted lamb. Don't be surprised by imaginative contemporary adventures, such as duck with chocolate and raspberry sauce. $ *Average main: €38* ✉ *Calle Portería 2* ☎ *987/617866, 646/071736* ⊕ *www.restauranteserrano.es* ☉ *Closed Mon.*

$ 🛏 **Astur Plaza.** This gleaming, well-run hotel on Astorga's Plaza de
HOTEL   España near city hall is a good value. **Pros:** reliable and well-priced hotel. **Cons:** a bit lacking in character; might be better for business travelers than for tourists. $ *Rooms from: €85* ✉ *Pl. de España 2–3* ☎ *987/617665* ⊕ *www.hotelasturplaza.es* 🛏 *32 rooms, 5 suites* ⭐ *Multiple meal plans.*

$ 🛏 **Hotel Vía de la Plata.** A giant slate terrace with views of the coun-
HOTEL   tryside is one major selling point for this pleasing hotel with a tradi-
FAMILY   tional brick-and-stone exterior and lots of sleek, modern details inside. **Pros:** great views and service. **Cons:** weddings virtually take over the hotel on spring weekends, so request a room in a quiet wing, if such a party is in town. $ *Rooms from: €90* ✉ *Calle Padres Redentoristas 5* ☎ *987/619000 for hotel, 987/604165 for spa* ⊕ *www.hotelviadelaplata. com* 🛏 *38 rooms* ⭐ *Multiple meal plans.*

VILLAFRANCA DEL BIERZO

135 km (84 miles) west of León.

After crossing León's grape-growing region, where the complex and full-bodied Bierzo wines are produced, you'll arrive in this medieval village, dominated by a massive and still-inhabited feudal fortress.

Villafranca was a destination in itself for some of Santiago's pilgrims. Visit the Romanesque church of Santiago to see the Puerta del Perdón (Door of Pardon), a sort of spiritual consolation prize for exhausted worshippers who couldn't make it over the mountains. Stroll the streets and seek out the onetime home of the infamous Grand Inquisitor Tomás de Torquemada. On the way out, you can buy wine at any of three local bodegas. From here, you can also visit the area's most famous archaeological site, Las Medulas—the remnants of Roman gold mines.

GETTING HERE AND AROUND

Charter bus trips from León—or better yet, a rental car—remain the best ways to get to this rural region. You'll likely want your own transportation once you get there, to visit Las Medulas, which is several kilometers away. It's also possible to hike or get there by bicycle.

ESSENTIALS

Visitor Information Villafranca del Bierzo. Guided tours depart daily at 11 and 4:30 from the tourist office, next door to the ayuntamiento. Call or go online to reserve, because tours are only given for a minimum of 8 people. ⊠ *Av. Diez Ovelar 10* ☎ *987/540028* ⊕ *www.villafrancadelbierzo.org.*

EXPLORING

FAMILY
Fodor'sChoice
★
Las Medulas. One of northern Spain's most impressive archaeological sites, this sprawling mountainous area of former Roman gold mines is now a UNESCO World Heritage site. Las Medulas, 24 km (15 miles) south of Villafranca del Bierzo, resulted from an ancient mining technique in which myriad tunnels were burrowed through a mountain, then water pumped through them, causing the mountain to collapse. Then miners would sift through the piles of rubble for gold. What's left at Las Medulas is a striking array of half-collapsed mountains of golden clay, with exposed tunnels, nestled in lush green forests. A network of hiking paths weaves through the area. A small archaeology exhibit (open only on weekends) and a visitor center are on site. You can pay to enter some of the tunnels or browse the larger area for free. The visitor center also organizes 3-km (2-mile) walking tours—call ahead to book. ⊠ *Carucedo* ☎ *987/422848, 619/258355* ⊕ *www.fundacionlasmedulas. info* ⊠ *Free; archaeology center €1.20, guided walking tour €2* ⊙ *Visitor center daily 11–2 and 4–6 (until 8 Apr.–Sept.). Archaeology center: Apr.–Sept., weekends 10–1:30 and 4–8; Oct.–Mar., Sat. 10–1:30 and 3:30–6, Sun. 10–2. Tours: Apr.–Sept., daily at 11:30, noon, 5, and 5:30; Oct.–Mar., daily at 11:30, noon, 4, and 4:15.*

WHERE TO STAY

$
B&B/INN
FAMILY
Fodor'sChoice
★
Casa do Louteiro. This charming, rustic inn, in a tiny village near the archaeological site of Las Medulas, was lovingly converted by the owner from a series of medieval ruins. **Pros:** rustic details; friendly staff; fire pit on winter evenings. **Cons:** plenty of hiking and biking nearby, but you'll need a car to get here. $ *Rooms from: €65* ⊠ *Calle Louteiro 6, Orellán* ☎ *652/933419, 652/933971* ⊕ *www.casadolouteiro.es* 🛏 *3 rooms* ¶◎¶ *Multiple meal plans.*

EXTREMADURA

Rugged Extremadura is a find for any lover of the outdoors, so bring your mountain bike (or plan on renting one), hiking boots, and binoculars. The lush Jerte Valley and the craggy peaks of the Sierra de Gredos mark Upper Extremadura's fertile landscape. South of the Jerte Valley is the historical town of Plasencia and the 15th-century Yuste Monastery. In Extremadura's central interior are the provincial capital of Cáceres and the Monfragüe National Park, the province's first and only federally protected park. Lower Extremadura's main towns—Mérida, Badajoz, Olivenza, and Zafra—bolstered by the sizable Portuguese population, have long exuded a Portuguese flavor.

JERTE AND EL VALLE DEL JERTE (JERTE VALLEY)

220 km (137 miles) west of Madrid.

Every spring, the Jerte Valley in northern Extremadura becomes one of Spain's top attractions, famous for its bounty of cherry blossoms. Unsurprisingly, this is where Spain's biggest cherry harvest originates, backed by the snowcapped Gredos mountains. Book ahead for March and April—peak cherry blossom season.

GETTING HERE AND AROUND

You will need a car to get here and explore the valley. For a scenic route, follow N110 southwest from Ávila to Plasencia.

ESSENTIALS

Visitor Information Valle del Jerte ⊠ *Paraje Virgen de Peñas Albas s/n (N110), Cabezuela del Valle* ☎ *927/472558* ⊕ *www.turismovalledeljerte.com.*

EXPLORING

Cabezuela del Valle. Full of half-timber stone houses, this is one of the valley's best-preserved villages. Follow N110 to Plasencia, or, if you have a taste for mountain scenery, detour from the village of Jerte to Hervás, traveling a narrow road that winds 35 km (22 miles) through forests of low-growing oak trees and over the Honduras Pass.

Puerto de Tornavacas (*Tornavacas Pass*). There's no more striking introduction to Extremadura than the Puerto de Tornavacas—literally, the "point where the cows turn back." Part of the N110 road northeast of Plasencia, the pass marks the border between Extremadura and the stark plateau of Castile. At 1,275 meters (4,183 feet) above sea level, it has a breathtaking view of the valley formed by the fast-flowing Jerte River. The valley's lower slopes are covered with a dense mantle of ash, chestnut, and cherry trees, whose richness contrasts with the granite cliffs of Castile's Sierra de Gredos. Cherries are the principal crop. To catch their brilliant blossoms, visit in spring. Camping is popular in this region, and even the most experienced hikers can find some challenging trails. ⊠ *Plasencia.*

WHERE TO EAT AND STAY

$$ ✕ **Restaurante Valle del Jerte.** The service is always cheerful at this small
SPANISH family-run restaurant in a cozy stone house just off the N110 in the village of Jerte. There's a tapas bar and a dining room out back. House

Extremadura

Cherry trees in blossom in the Jerte Valley

specialties include gazpacho, *cabrito* (suckling goat), and local trout from the Jerte River. The homemade, regional desserts are outstanding, with many featuring the Jerte Valley's famed cherries; opt for the *tarta de cerezas* (cherry tart) or the *queso fresco de cabra con miel de cerezo* (goat cheese topped with cherry-flavored honey). There's also an ancient and wonderful wine cellar. $ *Average main: €15* ⊠ *Calle Gargantilla 16, Jerte* ☎ *927/470052, 656/365988* ⊕ *www.donbellota.com.*

$
B&B/INN
FAMILY

Hotel Rural Finca El Carpintero. This restored 150-year-old stone mill and farmhouse has three types of hotel rooms, the best of which has a fireplace, a *salon* (sitting room), and its own entrance. **Pros:** cozy atmosphere; nice grounds with swimming pool; rooms suitable for families; good value. **Cons:** large disparity in quality between rooms and suites. $ *Rooms from: €75* ⊠ *N110, Km 360.5, 9 km (5½ miles) northeast of Jerte* ☎ *927/177089, 659/328110* ⊕ *www.fincaelcarpintero.com* ⤵ *5 rooms, 3 suites* ⦿| *Breakfast.*

$
B&B/INN
FAMILY

La Casería. One of Extremadura's first rural guesthouses, this rambling home, about 10 km (6 miles) southeast of Jerte, is on a spectacular 120-acre working farm, once a 16th-century Franciscan convent. **Pros:** privacy in the cottages; outdoor activities. **Cons:** main lodge often rented out to groups; a bit isolated. $ *Rooms from: €75* ⊠ *N110, Km 378.5, Navaconcejo* ☎ *927/173141* ⊕ *www.lacaseria.es* ⤵ *6 rooms, 3 cottages* ⦿| *Multiple meal plans.*

PLASENCIA

247 km (153 miles) west of Madrid, 79 km (49 miles) north of Cáceres.
Rising dramatically from the banks of the narrow Jerte River and
backed by the peaks of the Sierra de Gredos, this town was founded
by Alfonso VIII in 1180, just after he captured the entire area from the
Moors. Plasencia's motto, *ut placeat Deo et hominibus* ("To give pleasure to God and men"), might well have been a ploy on Alfonso's part
to attract settlers to this wild, isolated place on the southern border of
the former kingdom of León. Partly destroyed during the Peninsular
War of 1808, Plasencia retains far less of its medieval quarter than other
Extremaduran towns, but it still has extensive remains of its early walls
and a smattering of fine old buildings, notably the Casa del Deán. In
addition to being a site for visiting ruins, the city makes a good base
for side trips to Hervás and the Jerte Valley, the Monasterio de Yuste
and Monfragüe Nature Park, or, farther northwest, the wild Las Hurdes
and Sierra de Gata.

GETTING HERE AND AROUND

Trains are the easiest way to get here from Madrid, taking about 2½
hours on a gorgeous scenic route with views of the Gredos mountains.
There are also buses from Madrid, departing at least three times daily.
Once in Plasencia, you can catch city buses every 20 minutes, though
the city is pedestrian-friendly too.

ESSENTIALS

Visitor Information Plasencia ⊠ *Pl. Santa Clara 2* ☎ *927/423843* ⊕ *www.
plasencia.es.*

EXPLORING

Casa del Deán (*Dean's House*). This striking Renaissance building is
now a courthouse and not open to the public, but it's worth a stroll by
to see the outside. The main balcony is an excellent example of Spanish ironwork from that era, supported by neoclassical and Corinthian
columns. ⊠ *Pl. de la Catedral.*

Cathedral. Plasencia's cathedral was founded in 1189 and rebuilt after
1320 in an austere Gothic style that looks a bit incongruous looming
over the town's red-tile roofs. In 1498 the great architect Enrique Egas
designed a new structure, intending to complement or even overshadow
the original, but despite the later efforts of other notable architects of
the time, such as Juan de Alava and Francisco de Colonia, his plans
were never fully realized. The entrance to this incomplete, curious, and
not wholly satisfactory addition is through a door on the cathedral's
ornate but somber north facade. The dark interior of the new cathedral is notable for the beauty of its pilasters, which sprout like trees
into the ribs of the vaulting. You enter the old cathedral through the
Gothic cloister, which has four enormous lemon trees. Off the cloister
stands the building's oldest surviving section, a 13th-century chapter
house, the **chapel of San Pablo,** a late-Romanesque structure with
an idiosyncratic, Moorish-inspired dome. Inside are medieval hymnals
and a 13th-century gilded wood sculpture of the Virgen del Perdón. The
museum in the truncated nave of the old cathedral has ecclesiastical

and archaeological antiques. ✉ *Pl. de la Catedral* ☎ *927/414852, 927/423843* ⊕ *www.diocesisplasencia.org* ✍ *Old cathedral €2, new cathedral free* ☉ *May–Sept., Mon.–Sat. 9–12:30 and 5–6:30, Sun. and holidays 9–11:30; Oct.–Apr., Mon.–Sat. 9–12:30 and 4–5:30, Sun. and holidays 9–11:30.*

Hospital de Santa María. The Renaissance stone facade of this 14th-century building has carvings of shells—an allusion to the Camino de Santiago pilgrimage. Inside, a charming courtyard is lined with Renaissance double arches and filled with orange trees. A former hospital, it now houses the **Museo Etnográfico Textil Provincial Pérez Enciso** (Provincial Ethnographic Textile Museum), with interesting displays of more than 5,000 artifacts, including ancient kitchen tools, textile-manufacturing equipment, and folk dresses. It's the only museum of its kind in Extremadura. ✉ *Pl. del Marqués de la Puebla s/n* ☎ *927/421843* ⊕ *www.brocense.com/textil.asp* ✍ *Free* ☉ *July and Aug., Mon.–Sat. 9:30–2:30; Sept.–June, Wed.–Sat. 11–2 and 5–8, Sun. 11–2.*

Palacio Episcopal (*Bishop's Palace*). Adjacent to Plasencia's cathedral, this former bishop's palace dates back to at least 1400. A coat of arms adorning two upper windows on both sides of the entrance declares that the building was renovated during the tenure of Bishop Don Gutierrez de Vargas Carvajal (who served from 1523 to 1559). The impressive cloister is supported by a series of Renaissance arches. ✉ *Pl. de la Catedral* ✍ *Free* ☉ *Weekdays 9–2.*

FAMILY **Parque de los Pinos.** Walk southeast from the Plaza de San Vicente Ferrer to get to this park, home to peacocks, cranes, swans, pheasants, and monkeys. Full of waterfalls and animals, this is a great spot for children. ✉ *Av. de la Hispanidad s/n* ✍ *Free* ☉ *Daily 10–7 (until 8:30 July and Aug.).*

Plaza de San Vicente Ferrer. Lined with orange trees, this narrow, carefully preserved plaza is at the northwest end of the old medieval quarter. At one end is the 15th-century church of **San Vicente Ferrer,** with an adjoining convent that's now the Parador Plasencia.

Palacio de Mirabel (*Palace of the Marquis of Mirabel*). The north side of the Plaza de San Vicente Ferrer is dominated by the Renaissance Palacio de Mirabel, a two-story, 15th-century palace with a neoclassical interior courtyard surrounded by arches. Pass through the central arch for a view of the courtyard. There are no official visiting hours, but if you knock on the door, the caretaker is often willing to give informal tours. ✉ *Pl. de San Vicente Ferrer s/n* ☎ *927/410701 (try the tourist office if no answer)* ☉ *Mon.–Sat. 10–2 and 4–6 (hrs approximate).*

Plaza Mayor. East of the Plaza de San Vicente Ferrer, at the other end of the Rúa Zapatería, is this cheerful, arcaded square. The mechanical figure clinging to the town-hall clock tower depicts the clock maker and is called the **Mayorga** in honor of his Castilian hometown. Also east of the Plaza de San Vicente you can find a large section of the town's **medieval wall,** on the other side of which is a heavily restored Roman aqueduct.

WHERE TO EAT AND STAY

$$$$ SPANISH 🍴 **La Cocina del Alfonso VIII.** The hotel may be a few decades past its prime, but the restaurant here has long been regionally renowned for its excellent fare, produced mostly with local ingredients. The *ensalada de perdiz* (partridge salad) is a tasty starter, followed perhaps by *bacalao al estilo monacal* (a local monastery's salt-cod recipe) or stuffed leg of lamb with local dandelion greens. Reservations are recommended for Sunday lunch, when locals from across Plasencia gather for a family meal. There's a café and bar adjacent. [$] *Average main: €60* ✉ *Av. Alfonso VIII 32* ☎ *927/410250* 🌐 *www.hotelalfonsoviii.com* 🕒 *No dinner Sun.*

$$$ HOTEL FAMILY 🏨 **Parador de Plasencia.** In a 15th-century Gothic convent, this parador cultivates a medieval environment, with majestic and somber common areas and spacious guest rooms decorated with monastic motifs and heavy wood furniture. **Pros:** successful fusion of old and new; good restaurant; outdoor swimming pool, which is rare in the city center. **Cons:** expensive parking, and free alternative is a long walk away. [$] *Rooms from: €180* ✉ *Pl. San Vicente Ferrer s/n* ☎ *927/425870* 🌐 *www.parador.es* 🛏 *64 rooms, 2 suites* 🍽 *Multiple meal plans.*

SHOPPING

If you're in Plasencia on Tuesday morning, head for the Plaza Mayor and do what the locals have been doing since the 12th century: scout bargains in the weekly market. On the first Tuesday of August, the market is even larger, with vendors from all over the region.

Casa del Jamón. You can stock up here on local charcuterie, sausages, jamón ibérico, cheeses, extremeño wines, and cherry liqueur. There are many branches across Extremadura, or you can order online through its excellent website. It's closed on Sunday and between 2 and 5:30 the rest of the week. ✉ *Calle Sol 18, east of Pl. Mayor* ☎ *927/414271* 🌐 *www.lacasadeljamonplasencia.es.*

LA VERA AND MONASTERIO DE YUSTE

45 km (28 miles) east of Plasencia.

In the north of Extremadura, the fertile La Vera region sits at the foot of the Gredos mountains, which are usually snow-capped through June. With its wildflowers, mountain vistas, and world-famous Yuste Monastery, the area welcomes tourists every spring. One of the souvenirs they're likely to take home is La Vera's famous paprika—*pimentón rojo*. You're likely to see strings of red peppers hanging out to dry on the windowsills of area homes.

GETTING HERE AND AROUND

You'll need a car to get here. Turn left off C501 at Cuacos and follow signs for the monastery (1 km [½ mile]).

ESSENTIALS

Visitor Information Jaraíz de la Vera ✉ *Av. de la Constitución 167* ☎ *927/170587.*

EXPLORING

Fodor's Choice **Monasterio de Yuste** (*Yuste Monastery*). In the heart of La Vera, a region
★ of *gargantas* (steep ravines), rushing rivers, and villages (including the
town of Jaraíz de la Vera), lies the Monasterio de San Jerónimo de
Yuste, founded by Hieronymite monks in the early 15th century. Badly
damaged in the Peninsular War, it was left to decay after the suppres-
sion of Spain's monasteries in 1835, but it has since been restored and
taken over once more by the Hieronymites. Today it's one of the most
impressive monasteries in all of Spain. Carlos V (1500–58), founder
of Spain's vast 16th-century empire, spent his last two years in the
Royal Chambers, enabling the emperor to attend Mass within a short
stumble of his bed. The guided tour also covers the church, the crypt
where Carlos V was buried before being moved to El Escorial (near
Madrid), and a glimpse of the monastery's cloisters. ⊠ *Cuacos de Yuste,
Cáceres* ☎ *927/172197* ⊕ *www.patrimonionacional.es* 🎫 *€9 (free Oct.–
Mar., Wed. and Thurs. 3–6; Apr.–Sept., Wed. and Thurs. 5–8); optional
guided tour €6* ☉ *Daily 10–6 (until 8 Apr.–Sept.).*

Museo del Pimentón (*Paprika Museum*). Tucked away in a 17th-century
row house, this quirky museum tells the history of the locally made
paprika, dubbed "red gold," for which Jaraíz de la Vera is probably
best known nationally. The museum is spread over three floors, with
audiovisual presentations and examples of grinding tools and recipes.
The museum is the centerpiece of the village's annual pepper festival,
held in August. ⊠ *Pl. Mayor 7, Jaraíz de la Vera, Cáceres* ☎ *927/460810*
🎫 *Free* ☉ *Tues.–Sat. 10–2 and 4:30–6:30, Sun. and holidays 10–2.*

WHERE TO STAY

$ 🏨 **Camino Real.** In a village in the highest valley of the Vera, this former
B&B/INN mansion has rustic guest rooms with exposed stone walls and wood-
FAMILY beam ceilings. **Pros:** sprawling terrace with gorgeous views over the
valley; family activities organized; lavish breakfast buffet included.
Cons: those great views of Extremadura's plains also make for cold,
windy winters. $ *Rooms from: €65* ⊠ *Calle Monje 27, Guijo de Santa
Bárbara* ☎ *927/561119* ⊕ *www.casaruralcaminoreal.com* 🍽 *10 rooms*
🍴 *Breakfast.*

$ 🏨 **La Casona.** This rustic estate with spectacular views of the Gredos
B&B/INN mountains has six cozy rooms in the main house, six log-cabin bunga-
FAMILY lows out back, and opportunities for a number of outdoor activities.
Pros: great service; very family-friendly. **Cons:** need your own trans-
portation. $ *Rooms from: €65* ⊠ *Ctra. Navalmoral, EX392, Km 15,
Jaraíz de la Vera* ☎ *927/194145, 629/645930* ⊕ *www.la-casona.es* 🍽 *6
rooms, 6 bungalows* 🍴 *Multiple meal plans.*

SHOPPING

If you like to cook, pick up a tin or two of *pimentón de la Vera* (smoked
sweet paprika), made from the region's prized red peppers, at a deli or
grocery shop in the area.

EN
ROUTE
Parque Natural de Monfragüe. At the junction of the rivers Tiétar and
Tajo, 20 km (12 miles) south of Plasencia on the EX208, is Extremad-
ura's only national park. This rocky, mountainous wilderness is known
for its diverse plant and animal life, including lynx, boar, deer, fox,

black storks, imperial eagles, and the world's largest colony of black vultures. Bring binoculars and head for the lookout point called Salto del Gitano (Gypsy's Leap), on the C524 just south of the Tajo River— vultures can often be spotted wheeling in the dozens at close range. The park's visitor center and main entrance is in the hamlet of Villareal de San Carlos. ⊠ *Ctra. EX208, Villareal de San Carlos* ☎ *927/199134, 927/116498* ⊕ *www.monfrague.com or www.parquedemonfrague.com* ⊙ *Park daily; visitor center Apr.–Oct., weekends 11–7; hrs vary weekdays and Nov.–Mar. (call ahead to check).*

CÁCERES

299 km (186 miles) west of Madrid, 125 km (78 miles) southwest of Monasterio de Yuste.

Fodor's Choice The provincial capital and one of Spain's oldest cities, Cáceres is a pros-
★ perous agricultural town with a vibrant nightlife that draws villagers from the surrounding pueblos every weekend. The Roman colony called Norba Caesarina was founded in 35 BC, but when the Moors took over in the 8th century, they named the city Quazris, which eventually morphed into the Spanish Cáceres. Ever since noble families helped Alfonso IX expel the Moors in 1229, the city has prospered. The pristine condition of the city's medieval and Renaissance quarter is the result of the families' continued occupancy of the palaces erected in the 15th century.

GETTING HERE AND AROUND

Trains from Madrid take about 2½ hours and are the cheapest and easiest way to get to Cáceres. Catch a city bus just outside the train station, which takes you to Plaza Mayor in the historic quarter. The city center is then navigable on foot. If you drive, park on the outskirts as winding, narrow medieval streets are difficult for parking.

TOURS

FAMILY **Los Cuenta Trovas de Cordel.** One of the best ways to see Cáceres is by night. The energetic local guides Vicente and Patxi weave lots of knowledge about Cáceres folklore, legends and ghost stories into their multilingual weekend tours of Cáceres's old quarter, which they present in medieval costume. Call ahead to reserve, or book online. ⊠ *Pl. Mayor* ☎ *667/283187, 667/776205* ⊕ *www.cuentatrovas.blogspot.com.es* ⊠ *€10.*

ESSENTIALS

Bus Station Cáceres ⊠ *Calle Túnez 1* ☎ *927/232550.*

Train Station Cáceres. The train station is an easy 15-minute walk from the city's historic center. ⊠ *Avda. Juan Pablo II 6* ☎ *927/235061, 902/240202.*

Visitor Information Cáceres. The tourist center organizes walking tours of the city, which last about 90 minutes to 2 hours. Call ahead to reserve. The tours, which require a minimum of 10 people, depart from Plaza Mayor daily at 11 and 12:30, with extra tours Monday–Saturday at 4:30 and 5:30 in winter, 5:30 and 6.30 in summer. ⊠ *Pl. Mayor* ☎ *927/010034, 927/217237 for tours.*

The San Mateo church, with the Torre de las Cigüeñas (Tower of the Storks) in the background

EXPLORING

Cáceres Viejo (Old Cáceres), which begins just east of Plaza San Juan, is the best part of town to explore.

TOP ATTRACTIONS

Fodor's Choice **Ciudad Monumental.** On high ground on the eastern side of the Plaza ★ Mayor, the town walls surround one of the best-preserved medieval quarters in Spain. Packed with treasures, Cáceres's Ciudad Monumental (monumental city or old town, also called the *casco antiguo* or Cáceres Viejo) is a marvel: small, but without a single modern building to detract from its aura. The old town is virtually deserted in winter, and occasionally dusted with a light coating of snow—quite a sight to behold.

Museo de Cáceres. The **Casa de las Veletas** (House of the Weather Vanes) is a 12th-century Moorish mansion that is now used as the city's museum. Filled with archaeological finds from the Paleolithic through the Visigothic periods, the art section includes medieval to contemporary painters from El Greco to Tàpies. A highlight is the superb Moorish cistern—the *aljibe*—with horseshoe arches supported by moldy stone pillars. ⊠ *Pl. de las Veletas 1* ☎ *927/010877* ⊕ *museodecaceres. blogspot.com.es* ⊟ *€1.20 (free for EU residents)* ⊗ *Tues.–Sat. 9–3 and 5–8:30 (4–7:30 Oct.–Apr. 13), Sun. 10–3.*

Palacio de Carvajal. Near the cathedral of Santa María stands the elegant Palacio de Carvajal, the only old palace in Cáceres that you can visit, other than the one housing the Museo de Cáceres. There is an imposing granite facade, arched doorway, and tower, and the interior has been restored, complete with period furnishings and art, to look as it did when the Carvajal family lived here in the 16th century. Legend says that King Ferdinand IV ordered the execution of two brothers from the Carvajal family, whom he accused of killing one of his knights. Thirty days later, the king was sued in the Court of God. Judgment was postponed until after the king's death, when the Carvajal brothers were declared innocent. ✉ *Calle Amargura 1 at Pl. Santa María* ☎ *927/255597* ✉ *Free* ⊙ *Weekdays 8 am–9:15 pm, Sat. 10–2 and 5–8, Sun. 10–2.*

Plaza Mayor. On this long, inclined, arcaded plaza you can find several outdoor cafés, the tourist office, and, on breezy summer nights, nearly everyone in town. In the middle of the arcade opposite the old quarter is the entrance to the lively Calle General Ezponda, lined with tapas bars, student hangouts, and discos that keep the neighborhood awake and moving until dawn.

Santa María de Gracia Cathedral. This Gothic church, built mainly in the 16th century, is now the town cathedral. The elegantly carved high altar, dating from 1551, however, is barely visible in the gloom. Follow the lines of pilgrims to the statue of San Pedro de Alcantara in the corner; legend says that touching the stone figure's shoes brings luck to the pilgrims, and the shoes are shiny from all the caressing. A small museum in the back displays religious artifacts. ✉ *Pl. de Santa María s/n* ☎ *927/215313* ✉ *€1* ⊙ *Weekdays 10–2 and 4:30–8, Sat. 9:30–12:50 and 4–6:15, Sun. 9:30–11:50 and 5–6:15 (until 7:15 May–Sept.). Hrs vary Sat. due to weddings.*

Santuario de la Virgen de la Montaña (*Sanctuary of the Virgin of the Mountain*). Just up the hill behind Cáceres's Ciudad Monumental is this 18th-century shrine dedicated to the city's patron saint. The complex is built on a mountain with glorious views of old Cáceres, especially at sunset. The view is worth the 15-minute drive—or even the grueling two-hour walk—despite the rather mundane interior of the church (the golden baroque altar is the only exception). To get here, follow Calle Cervantes until it becomes Carretera de la Montaña; the sanctuary is just off the town tourist map, which you can pick up from the local tourist office. ✉ *Ctra. Santuario Virgin de la Montaña s/n* ✉ *Free* ⊙ *Daily 9–1 and 4–8.*

WORTH NOTING

Palacio de los Golfines de Abajo. The stony severity of this palace seems appropriate when you consider it was once the headquarters of General Franco. The exterior is somewhat relieved by elaborate Mudejar and Renaissance decorative motifs. Some 400 years before Franco, the so-called Catholic Kings purportedly slept here. You can't enter the palace. ✉ *Pl. de los Golfines, Pl. de San Jorge.*

Palacio de los Golfines de Arriba. After you pass through the gate leading to the old quarter, you'll see this palace, dominated by a soaring tower dating from 1515. Only three of the four corner towers remain, adorned with various coats of arms of the families who once lived here. Inside, there are classical collonaded courtyards with Renaissance details, but they're no longer open to the public. Still, the impressive building is worth a stop. ✉ *C. de los Olmos 2.*

Palacio del Capitán Diego de Cáceres. The battlement tower of this palace is also known as the Torre de las Cigüeñas (Tower of the Storks) for obvious reasons. It's now a military residence, but some rooms are occasionally opened up for exhibitions. ⊠ *Pl. San Mateo.*

San Mateo church. Construction on this church began in the 14th century, purportedly over the ruins of

> ### STORKS DROPPING BY
>
> Storks are common in the old quarter of Cáceres, and virtually every tower and spire is topped by nests of storks, considered since the Roman era to be sacred birds emblematic of home, the soul, maternity, spring, and well-being.

a mosque, and took nearly 300 years to finish. The interior is austere, with a 16th-century choir and walls lined with the tombs of prominent Cáceres citizens. The church opens at 10 am most mornings, but check with the tourist office in case of changes. ⊠ *Pl. de San Mateo* ☏ *927/246329* ⊙ *Mon.–Sat. 10–8, Sun. Mass only, at noon and 8 pm.*

Santiago de los Caballeros. The chief building of interest outside the walls of Cáceres' old town, this church was rebuilt in the 16th century by Rodrigo Gil de Hontañón, Spain's last great Gothic architect. The easiest way to reach the church is by exiting the old town on the west side, through the Socorro gate. Inside the church, there is a single nave with ribbed vaults, and a choir stall in the back. The magnificent altarpiece was commissioned in 1557 and made by the Valladolid-based master Alonso de Berruguete. ⊠ *Pl. de Santiago* ⊙ *Daily dawn–dusk.*

WHERE TO EAT

$$$$
SPANISH
Fodor's Choice
★

✕**Atrio.** Off Cáceres's main boulevard, this elegant, modern restaurant (in a hotel of the same name) just might be the best in Extremadura. It specializes in highly refined contemporary cooking, and the menu changes often, but you won't be disappointed with any of the selections, especially if they include venison, partridge, wild mushrooms, or truffles. *Vieiras asadas con trufa negra* (roast scallops with truffle) or *pichón asado* (roast wood pigeon) are two of the signature offerings. Such dishes earned Atrio two Michelin stars. The building is a work of art itself, with modern lines contrasting the surrounding architecture in old Cáceres. This is upscale, high-end dining. You can book online or by phone. Ⓢ *Average main: €60* ⊠ *Pl. de San Mateo 1* ☏ *927/242928* ⊕ *www.restauranteatrio.com* ⌕ *Reservations essential.*

$
EUROPEAN
FAMILY

✕**Chocolat's.** This little chocolate and coffee shop, not far from Plaza San Juan, is the best place in town for breakfast, dessert, or a quick snack. Ⓢ *Average main: €5* ⊠ *Calle Gran Vía s/n* ☏ *927/220158, 608/311204* ▭ *No credit cards.*

$$$$
SPANISH

✕**El Figón de Eustaquio.** A fixture on the quiet and pleasant Plaza San Juan, this restaurant has been run by the same family for nearly 70 years and counting. It's especially popular at lunch—and with good reason. In its jumble of small, old-fashioned dining rooms with wood-beamed ceilings, you'll be served mainly regional delicacies, including *venado de montería* (wild venison) or *perdiz estofada* (partridge stew). Fine Extremaduran wines are also available. Ⓢ *Average main: €30* ⊠ *Pl. San Juan 12–14* ☏ *927/244362, 927/248194* ⊕ *elfigondeeustaquio.com* ⌕ *Reservations essential.*

$ 🍴 **La Tapería.** Hands-down the best tapas in Cáceres—and maybe in
TAPAS Extremadura—are at this tiny taverna that's usually packed with locals.
Fodor's Choice ★ There's a traditional dining room behind the boisterous brick-and-wood bar. The extensive wine list includes lots of bottles from local vineyards, and your drink will come with a heaping plate of tapas. Try the *tostas*—simple toast topped with wonderful combinations of *extremeño* ham, cheese, grilled vegetables, and other hearty ingredients. This is the best value in town, and a very good place to mingle with locals. [$] *Average main: €10* ✉ *Calle Sanchez Garrido 1, bajo* ☎ *927/225147* ⌚ *Closed Mon.*

3

WHERE TO STAY

$ 🏨 **Hotel Iberia.** This budget-friendly hotel is a reliable, quieter alternative
HOTEL to those that are directly on the Plaza Mayor. **Pros:** great value; comes
FAMILY with generous breakfast buffet. **Cons:** the interior style may seem a bit aged if you're not into antiques. [$] *Rooms from: €60* ✉ *Calle Pintores 2* ☎ *927/247634* 🌐 *www.iberiahotel.com* 🛏 *38 rooms* 🍽 *Breakfast.*

$$ 🏨 **Palacio de Oquendo.** This 16th-century palace is now an impressive
HOTEL hotel that rivals the town's parador, at much lower rates. **Pros:** very
Fodor's Choice ★ good value; new design; quiet area close to Plaza Mayor. **Cons:** no parking. [$] *Rooms from: €100* ✉ *Pl. San Juan 11* ☎ *927/215800* 🌐 *www.nh-hotels.com* 🛏 *86 rooms* 🍽 *Multiple meal plans.*

$$$ 🏨 **Parador de Cáceres.** This 14th-century palace in the old town provides
HOTEL a noble setting, with elegant public spaces filled with antiques. **Pros:** good blend of tradition and comfort; fine cuisine and wines. **Cons:** some rooms are basic; old-town location can be confusing to reach by car. [$] *Rooms from: €176* ✉ *Calle Ancha 6* ☎ *927/211759* 🌐 *www.parador.es* 🛏 *39 rooms* 🍽 *Multiple meal plans.*

NIGHTLIFE AND PERFORMING ARTS

Bars in Cáceres stay busy until the wee hours. Nightlife centers on the **Plaza Mayor,** which fills after dinner with families out for a *paseo* (stroll), as well as students swigging *calimocho* (a mix of red wine and Coca-Cola) or *litronas* (liter bottles of beer). **Calle de Pizarro,** south of Plaza San Juan, is lined with cafés and bars.

El Corral de las Cigueñas. There's a hopping nighttime music scene at this charming old-town café with an outdoor patio. In winter months, the club is open only Thursday to Sunday evenings. Hours vary depending on events; call ahead or go online to check concert schedules. ✉ *Cuesta de Aldana 6* ☎ *927/216425, 647/758245* 🌐 *www.elcorralcc.com.*

TRUJILLO

45 km (28 miles) east of Cáceres, 256 km (159 miles) southwest of Madrid.

Trujillo rises up from the boulder-strewn fields like a great granite schooner under full sail. Up above, the rooftops and towers seem medieval. Down below, Renaissance architecture flourishes in squares such as the Plaza Mayor, with its elegant San Martín church. As in Cáceres, storks' nests top many towers in and around the old town—they've become a symbol of Trujillo. Dating back at least to Roman times, the city was captured from the Moors in 1232 and colonized by a number of leading military families.

GETTING HERE AND AROUND

There is no train service to Trujillo, but Avanza Bus (⊕ *www.avanzabus. com*) offers several departures daily from Madrid's Estacion de Sur (3½ hours). Once there, it's best to see Trujillo on foot, as the streets are mostly cobbled or crudely paved with stone (suitable footwear needed). The two main roads into Trujillo leave you at the unattractive bottom end of town. Things get progressively older the farther you climb, but even on the lower slopes—where most of the shops are concentrated—you need walk only a few yards to step into what seems like the Middle Ages.

ESSENTIALS

Visitor Information Trujillo. The tourist office has discount tickets for several museums and tourist sites, and also organizes guided walking tours of the city, at 11 and 4:30. ⊠ *Pl. Mayor* ☏ *927/322677* ⊕ *www.turismotrujillo.com.*

EXPLORING

TOP ATTRACTIONS

Casa Museo de Pizarro. The Pizarro family home is now a modest museum dedicated to the connection between Spain and Latin America. The first floor is a typical home from 15th-century Trujillo, and the second floor is divided into exhibits on Peru and Pizarro's life there. The museum explains the so-called "Curse of the Pizarro," recounting how the conquistador and his brothers were killed in brutal battles with rivals; those who survived never again enjoyed the wealth they had achieved in Peru. ⊠ *Pl. de Santa María and Calle Merced s/n* ☏ *€1.40* ⊗ *Daily 10–2 and 4:30–7:30.*

Castillo. For spectacular views, climb this large fortress, built by the Moors in the 9th century on top of old Roman foundations. To the south are silos, warehouses, and residential neighborhoods. To the north are green fields and brilliant flowers, partitioned by a maze of nearly leveled Roman stone walls, and an ancient cistern. The castle's size underscores the historic importance of now-tiny Trujillo. ⊠ *Cerro Cabeza de Zorro* ☏ *€2* ⊗ *Daily 10–2 and 4–7:30.*

La Villa. This is Trujillo's oldest area, entirely surrounded by its original, albeit much restored, walls. Follow them along Calle Almenas, which runs west from the Palacio de Orellana-Pizarro, beneath the **Alcázar de Los Chaves,** a castle-fortress that was converted into a guest lodge in the 15th century and hosted visiting dignitaries, including Ferdinand and Isabella. Now a college, the building has seen better days. Passing the Alcázar, continue west along the wall to the **Puerta de San Andrés,** one of La Villa's four surviving gates (there were originally seven).

Plaza Mayor. Trujillo's large central square, one of the finest in Spain, is a superb Renaissance creation and the site of the local tourist office. At the foot of the stepped platform on the plaza's north side stands a large, bronze equestrian statue of Francisco Pizarro—the work, surprisingly, of an American sculptor, Charles Rumsey.

Santa María (*Iglesia de Santa María La Mayor*). Attached to a Romanesque bell tower, this Gothic church is the most beautiful in Trujillo. It's only occasionally used for Masses, and its interior has been virtually untouched since the 16th century. The upper choir has an exquisitely carved balustrade, and the coats of arms at each end indicate the seats Ferdinand and Isabella occupied when they came here to worship. Note the high altar, circa 1480, adorned with great 15th-century Spanish paintings. To see it properly illuminated, place a coin in the box next to the church entrance. Climb the tower for stunning views of the town and vast plains stretching toward Cáceres and the Sierra de Gredos. ✉ *Pl. de Santa María* 🎫 *€2 church and exhibits, €1 to climb the tower* 🕓 *Daily 10–2 and 4–7.*

3

WORTH NOTING

Museo de la Coria. Near the Puerta de la Coria and occupying a former Franciscan convent, this museum's exhibits on the relationship between Spain and Latin America are similar to those in the Casa Museo de Pizarro (⇨ *See above*) but with an emphasis on the troops as well as other conquistadors who led missions across the water. The museum is worth visiting just for a look inside the old convent's two-tier central cloister. ✉ *Pl. de Santa María* ☎ *927/659032, 927/321898* 🎫 *Free* 🕓 *Weekends and holidays 11:30–2.*

Palacio de Orellana-Pizarro. Adjacent to the Palacio del Marqués de la Conquista is the former town hall, now a court of law; the alley that runs through this arcaded building's central arch takes you to the Palacio de Orellana-Pizarro, which now serves as a school—one with the most elegant Renaissance courtyard in town. The palace's ground floor, open to visitors, has a deep arched front doorway; on the second story is an elaborate Renaissance balcony bearing the crest of the Pizarro family. Cervantes, on his way to thank the Virgin of Guadalupe for his release from prison, spent time writing in the palace, which once belonged to Juan Pizarro de Orellana, cousin of the Pizarro conquistador who conquered Peru. ✉ *Behind Pl. Mayor* 🎫 *Free* 🕓 *Weekdays 10–1 and 4–6, weekends 11–2 and 4:30–7.*

San Martín. Behind the Pizarro statue, this church is a Gothic structure from the early 16th century, with Renaissance tombs and an old organ. Three of Spanish history's most prominent kings prayed here: Carlos V, Felipe II, and Felipe V. ✉ *Pl. Mayor* 🎫 *€2* 🕓 *Daily 10–2 and 4–7.*

WHERE TO EAT AND STAY

$$$ SPANISH

🍴 **Bizcocho.** A Trujillo institution conveniently located on the Plaza Mayor, Bizcocho specializes in Extramaduran cuisine, with local jamón, queso, and *migas*—breadcrumbs fried with garlic and pork, and moistened with a bit of red wine. The stone and tiled dining room is cozy and cool even in hot Extremadura summers. Reservations are essential on holiday weekends. [$] *Average main: €20* ✉ *Pl. Mayor 11* ☎ *927/322017* 🌐 *www.restaurantebizcochotrujillo.com.*

$$$$ SPANISH Fodor's Choice ★

🍴 **Mesón La Troya.** An institution in these parts, this restaurant has a noisy tapas bar papered with photos of celebrity diners happily posing with its late, great owner, Concha. Opt for a table outside for the best views of the Plaza Mayor, or choose a spot in the charming dining room, which has a barrel-vaulted brick ceiling. The prix-fixe meal includes a starter of *tortilla de patatas* (potato omelet), *chorizo ibérico* (ibérico-pork sausage), and a salad. Notable mains to watch for include the delicious *pruebas de cerdo* (ibérico-pork casserole with garlic and spices). Come hungry: portions are enormous. $ *Average main: €30* ⊠ *Pl. Mayor 10* ☎ *927/321364.*

$
HOTEL
FAMILY
🖭 **Izán Trujillo.** Once a 16th-century convent, this splendid 4-star hotel has a good location, just a short walk from Trujillo's historic center. **Pros:** aesthetically impeccable; friendly and efficient staff. **Cons:** small swimming pool; rooms vary in size. $ *Rooms from: €77* ⊠ *Pl. del Campillo 1* ☎ *927/458900* ⊕ *www.izanhoteles.es* ⇆ *77 rooms, 1 suite* ¶❍¶ *Multiple meal plans.*

$$$
HOTEL
FAMILY
Fodor'sChoice
★
🖭 **Parador de Trujillo.** In yet another of the region's 16th-century convents, this parador is the essence of peace and tranquility, with rooms that are cozy and serene. **Pros:** peace and quiet in the heart of town; swimming pool. **Cons:** expensive; rooms are a bit like monastery quarters—on the small side. $ *Rooms from: €150* ⊠ *Calle Santa Beatriz de Silva 1* ☎ *927/321350* ⊕ *www.parador.es* ⇆ *50 rooms* ¶❍¶ *Breakfast.*

$
HOTEL
Fodor'sChoice
★
🖭 **Posada Dos Orillas.** In the historic center of town, this hotel occupies a 16th-century former stagecoach inn. **Pros:** pleasant interiors; beautiful terrace; good location; good weekend values. **Cons:** no reserved parking. $ *Rooms from: €60* ⊠ *Calle de los Cambrones 6* ☎ *927/659079* ⊕ *www.dosorillas.com* ⇆ *13 rooms* ¶❍¶ *Breakfast.*

SHOPPING

Trujillo is a good place to shop for folk art. Look for multicolor rugs, blankets, and embroidery. There are interesting shops around the Plaza Mayor.

Eduardo Pablos Mateos. This workshop specializes in wood carvings, basketwork, and furniture. Call ahead to schedule a personal tour. ⊠ *Calle de San Judas 3* ☎ *927/321066, 606/174382 (cell phone).*

GUADALUPE

200 km (125 miles) southwest of Madrid, 96 km (60 miles) east of Trujillo.

Guadalupe's monastery is one of the most inspiring sights in Extremadura. Whether you come from Madrid, Trujillo, or Cáceres, the last leg of your journey takes you through beautiful mountain scenery, with the monastery clinging to the slopes. The story of Guadalupe goes back to about 1300, when a local shepherd uncovered a statue of the Virgin, supposedly carved by St. Luke. King Alfonso XI, who often hunted here, had a church built to house the statue and vowed to found a monastery should he defeat the Moors at the battle of Salado in 1340. After his victory, he kept his promise. The greatest period in the monastery's history was between the 15th and 18th centuries, when, under the rule of the Hieronymites, it was turned into a pilgrimage center rivaling Santiago de Compostela in importance. Pilgrims have been coming here since the 14th century, but have been joined in more recent years by a growing number of tourists. Even so, the monastery's isolation—a good two-hour drive from the nearest town—has protected it from

Mérida's excellently preserved Roman amphitheater is the site of a drama festival every July.

commercial excess. The town's residents number only about 2,000. Documents authorizing Columbus's first voyage to the Western Hemisphere were signed here. The Virgin of Guadalupe became the patroness of Latin America, honored by the dedication of thousands of churches and towns in the New World. The monastery's decline coincided with Spain's loss of overseas territories in the 19th century. Guadalupe is also known for its copperware, crafted here since the 16th century.

GETTING HERE AND AROUND
There's no train to Guadalupe, and bus service is sporadic. It's easiest if you have your own car, and park on the outskirts of town. It's small enough to explore on foot, but is hilly and cobblestoned, so wear comfortable shoes.

ESSENTIALS
Visitor Information Guadalupe ⊠ *Pl. Santa María de Guadalupe*
☎ *927/154128* ⊕ *oficinadeturismoguadalupe.blogspot.com.es* ⊗ *Thurs.–Mon..*

EXPLORING
Plaza Mayor (*Plaza de Santa María de Guadalupe*). In the middle of this tiny, irregularly shaped plaza—which is transformed during festivals into a bullring—is a 15th-century fountain, where Columbus's two Native American servants were baptized in 1496.

Fodor's Choice **Real Monasterio de Santa María de Guadalupe** (*Royal Monastery of Our*
★ *Lady of Guadalupe*). Looming in the background of the Plaza Mayor is the late-Gothic facade of Guadalupe's **monastery church,** flanked by battlement towers. The monastery is essentially a whole town in itself. The entrance is to the left of the church. From the large Mudejar cloister,

the required guided tour (they run throughout the day) progresses to the **chapter house,** with hymnals, vestments, and paintings, including a series of small panels by Zurbarán. The ornate 17th-century **sacristy** has a series of eight Zurbarán paintings, from 1638–47. These austere representations of monks of the Hieronymite order and scenes from the life of St. Jerome are the artist's only significant paintings still in the setting they were made for. The tour concludes with the garish, late-baroque **Camarín,** the chapel where the famous *Virgen Morena* (*Black Virgin*) is housed. The dark, mysterious wooden figure hides under a heavy veil and mantle of red and gold; painted panels tell the virgin's life story. Each September 8, the virgin is brought down from the altarpiece and walked around the cloister in a procession with pilgrims following on their knees. Outside, the monastery's gardens have been restored to their original, geometric Moorish style. ✉ *Entrance on Pl. Mayor* ☎ *927/367000* 🌐 *www.monasterioguadalupe.com* 🎟 *€4* 🕒 *Daily 9:30–1 and 3:30–6:30.*

3

WHERE TO EAT AND STAY

$ SPANISH 🍴 **El Mesón Extremeño.** You can't beat the location of this restaurant, within view of the monastery's facade. Pick a table on the plaza outside, or inside in the terra-cotta-tiled dining room. Either way, expect authentic flavors and a hearty meal, particularly if you're a fan of Spain's vast assortment of wild mushrooms. The *menú de la casa* (€9 prix-fixe house menu) includes migas de pastor, sopa de ajo, *chuletillas de cerdo* (pork chops) with green beans, and *solomillo* (filet mignon) topped with aromatic setas of different varieties according to the season. [$] *Average main: €10* ✉ *Pl. Santa María 3* ☎ *927/154327.*

$ SPANISH Fodor's Choice ★ 🍴 **Mesón Cerezo.** This traditional, family-run restaurant right on Plaza Mayor serves up Extremaduran specialties, all with splendid views of the town's main square and monastery. The establishment also offers hotel rooms upstairs. Favorite dishes include cordero or cabrito *asado* (roasted over a wood fire), local jamón, and traditional barbeque. The daily prix-fixe menu is a steal at €8.90, and so are the simple hotel rooms, at about €45. [$] *Average main: €10* ✉ *Pl. Mayor* ☎ *927/154177* 🌐 *www.hostalcerezo2meson.com.*

$ HOTEL Fodor's Choice ★ 🏨 **Hospedería del Real Monasterio.** An excellent and considerably cheaper alternative to the town parador, this inn was built around the 16th-century Gothic cloister of the monastery itself. **Pros:** guests get free monastery admission; excellent restaurant; helpful staff. **Cons:** the monastery's church bells chime around the clock. [$] *Rooms from: €72* ✉ *Pl. Juan Carlos I* ☎ *927/367000* 🌐 *www.hotelhospederiamonasterioguadalupe.com* 🛏 *47 rooms* 🕒 *Closed mid-Jan.–mid-Feb.* 🍽 *Multiple meal plans.*

$$$ HOTEL 🏨 **Parador de Guadalupe.** This exquisite estate, once the 15th-century palace of the Marquis de la Romana, now houses one of Spain's finest paradores. **Pros:** authentic extremeño cooking; stunning architecture. **Cons:** tight parking; long hike from reception to the farthest rooms. [$] *Rooms from: €151* ✉ *Calle Marqués de la Romana 12* ☎ *927/367075* 🌐 *www.parador.es* 🛏 *41 rooms* 🍽 *Multiple meal plans.*

MÉRIDA

76 km (47 miles) south of Cáceres, 191 km (119 miles) north of Seville, 347 km (216 miles) southwest of Madrid.

Mérida has some of the most impressive Roman ruins in Iberia. Founded by the Romans in 25 BC on the banks of the Río Guadiana, the city is strategically located at the junction of major Roman roads from León to Seville and Toledo to Lisbon. Then named Augusta Emerita, it quickly became the capital of the vast Roman province of Lusitania. A bishopric in Visigothic times, Mérida never regained the importance that it had under the Romans, and other than the Roman monuments, which pop up all over town, the city is rather plain.

The glass-and-steel bus station is in a modern district on the other side of the river from the town center. It commands a good view of the exceptionally long **Roman bridge,** which spans two forks of this sluggish river. On the farther bank is the Alcazaba fortress.

Some other Roman sites require a drive. Across the train tracks in a modern neighborhood is the **circo** (circus), where chariot races were held. Little remains of the grandstands, which seated 30,000, but the outline of the circus is clearly visible and impressive for its size: 1,312 feet long and 377 feet wide. Of the existing aqueduct remains, the most impressive is the **Acueducto de los Milagros** (Aqueduct of Miracles), north of the train station. It carried water from the Roman dam of Proserpina, which still stands, 5 km (3 miles) away.

GETTING HERE AND AROUND

There are several buses daily to and from Mérida and Badajoz (1 hour), Sevilla (2½ hours), Cáceres (45 minutes), Trujillo (1½ hours), and Madrid (4½ hours). There are also several daily trains, which take about the same travel time but cost more. Check the RENFE website (⊕ *www.renfe.com*) or tourist office for schedules. Once in Mérida, the city center is navigable by foot or tourist train *(see below).*

ESSENTIALS

Visitor Information Mérida. The tourist office can arrange guided walking tours of Mérida, or call the tour guide association directly (☎ *629/781244*). ✉ *Paseo José Álvarez Sáenz de Buruaga* ☎ *924/330722* ⊕ *www.turismomerida.org.*

EXPLORING

Alcazaba Árabe *(fortress).* To get to this sturdy square fortress, built by the Romans and strengthened by the Visigoths and Moors, continue west from the Museo Nacional de Arte Romano, down Suarez Somontes toward the river and the city center. Turn right at Calle Baños and you can see the towering columns of the **Templo de Diana,** the oldest of Mérida's Roman buildings. To enter the Alcazaba, follow the fortress walls around to the side farthest from the river. Climb up to the battlements for sweeping river views. ✉ *Calle de Graciano* 🎫 *€4 castle only, €12 combined ticket with Roman sites* ☉ *Apr.–Sept., daily 9:30–9; Oct.–Mar., daily 9:30–2 and 4–6:30.*

Basílica de Santa Eulalia. Originally a Visigothic structure, this basilica marks the site of a Roman temple as well as the alleged place where the child martyr Eulalia was burned alive in AD304 for spitting in the face of a Roman magistrate. The site became a focal point for pilgrimages during the Middle Ages. In 1990, excavations surrounding the tomb of the famous saint revealed layer upon layer of Paleolithic, Visigothic, Byzantine, and Roman settlements. You can visit an underground crypt. ✉ *Rambla Mártir Santa Eulalia, Av. de Extremadura 15* ☎ *924/303407* 🔳 *Free; crypt €4* ⊘ *Apr.–Sept., Mon.–Sat. 9:30–2 and 5–7:30; Oct.– Mar., Mon.–Sat. 9:30–2 and 4–6:30.*

Museo Nacional de Arte Romano (*National Museum of Roman Art*). Across the street from the entrance to the Roman sites and connected by an underground passageway is Mérida's superb Roman art museum, in a monumental building designed by the renowned Spanish architect Rafael Moneo. You walk through a series of passageways to the luminous, cathedral-like main exhibition hall, which is supported by arches the same proportion and size (50 feet) as the Roman arch in the center of Mérida, the Arco de Trajano (Trajan's Arch). The exhibits include mosaics, frescoes, jewelry, statues, pottery, household utensils, and other Roman works. Be sure to visit the **crypt** beneath the museum— it contains the remains of several homes and a necropolis that were uncovered while the museum was being built in 1981. ✉ *Calle José Ramón Mélida s/n* ☎ *924/311690, 924/311912* ⊕ *www.museoromano. com* 🔳 *€3* ⊘ *Tues.–Sat. 9:30–6:30 (until 8 Apr.–Sept.), Sun. and holidays 10–3.*

Plaza de España. Mérida's main square adjoins the northwestern corner of the Alcazaba and is highly animated both day and night. The plaza's oldest building is a 16th-century palace, now the Mérida Palace hotel (⇨ *see Where to Stay*). Behind the palace stretches Mérida's most charming area, with Andalusian-style white houses shaded by palms, in the midst of which stands the **Arco de Trajano,** part of a Roman city gate.

Fodor'sChoice ★ **Roman monuments.** Mérida's Roman **teatro** (theater) and **anfiteatro** (amphitheater) are arranged in a verdant park, and the theater—the best preserved in Spain and seating 6,000—is used for a classical drama festival each July. The amphitheater, which holds 15,000 spectators, opened in 8 BC for gladiatorial contests. Next to the entrance to the ruins is the **main tourist office,** where you can pick up maps and brochures. You can buy a ticket to see only the Roman ruins or, for a slightly higher fee, an *entrada conjunta* (joint admission), which also grants access to the Basílica de Santa Eulalia and the Alcazaba. To reach the monuments by car, follow signs to the "Museo de Arte Romano." Parking is usually easy to find. ✉ *Av. de los Estudiantes* ☎ *924/312530* 🔳 *€8 theater and amphitheater; €12 combined admission to Roman sites, basilica, and Alcazaba* ⊘ *Apr.–Sept., daily 9:30–9; Oct.–Mar., daily 9:30–2 and 4–6:30.*

WHERE TO EAT

$
SPANISH
FAMILY
✕ **Cervecería 100 Montaditos.** Don't be put off by the fact that this popular local tavern is part of an international chain. It's still an excellent informal restaurant specializing in both classic and creative *montaditos* (canapés or open sandwiches)—at least 100 of them, topped with anything from tortilla de patatas to jamón ibérico, *mousse de pato* (duck pâté), salmon with julienned garlic and parsley, or wild

mushrooms. With draft beer or a local wine, these light morsels are tasty and excellent value. $ *Average main: €5* ⊠ *Calle Félix Valverde Lillo 3* ☎ *924/318105* ⊕ *www.100montaditos.com.*

$$$$
SPANISH
Fodor'sChoice
★

✕ **Gonzalo Valverde.** With big shoes to fill, this fusion restaurant has taken over the premises of the world famous Michelin-starred Altair. So far, reviews have been outstanding. The kitchen turns out examples of traditional Extremadura classics executed with a modern flair, such as Iberian *porco preto* (free-range pork fed on acorns) with wasabi and setas. The lunchtime menu del día is a great value at €18.90. You can sit in the soaring dining room, reminiscent of an antique wine cellar, or outside on the wood awning–covered terrace with views of the river. $ *Average main: €35* ⊠ *Av. Fernández López 7* ☎ *924/304512* ⊕ *www.gonzalovalverde.com* ⌖ *Reservations essential* ⊗ *No dinner Sun. and Mon.*

$
TAPAS
FAMILY

✕ **La Despensa del Castúo.** For some of the best tapas in Mérida, try this favorite local hangout just 50 meters from the Museo Nacional de Arte Romano. Each tapa costs about €1. One of the specialties is local *morcilla de Guadalupe*, blood sausage made in the nearby town of the same name. It's worth a wait for a table outside. This is a favorite with families, and you'll often see children playing on the terrace during weekend lunches. $ *Average main: €10* ⊠ *Calle Jose Ramon Melida 48* ☎ *924/302251.*

WHERE TO STAY

$$
HOTEL
FAMILY
Fodor'sChoice
★

⌂ **Mérida Palace.** The anchor of the city's Plaza de España, this five-star luxury hotel, now part of the Bluebay chain, has many of the amenities of a sprawling resort, right in the middle of the city. **Pros:** outdoor pool, terrace, and solarium. **Cons:** some front rooms facing the Plaza de España can be noisy in summer. $ *Rooms from: €120* ⊠ *Pl. España 19* ☎ *924/383800, 902/100655* ⊕ *www.hotelmeridapalace.com or www. bluebayresorts.com* ⤳ *76 rooms* ⦿❘ *Multiple meal plans.*

$$$
HOTEL
FAMILY

⌂ **Parador de Mérida.** Also called Parador Vía de la Plata, this spacious hotel exudes an Andalusian cheerfulness, with hints at its Roman and Moorish past. **Pros:** central location; stunning interior courtyard; dazzling light interior. **Cons:** expensive parking; erratic Wi-Fi. $ *Rooms from: €164* ⊠ *Pl. Constitución and Calle Almendralejo, 56* ☎ *924/313800* ⊕ *www.parador.es* ⤳ *81 rooms* ⦿❘ *Multiple meal plans.*

NIGHTLIFE

The many cafés, tapas bars, and restaurants surrounding the Plaza de España and in the Plaza de la Constitución fill with boisterous crowds late into the evening. Calle John Lennon, off the northwest corner of the plaza, is your best bet for late-night dancing, especially in summer.

GALICIA AND ASTURIAS

with Cantabria

WELCOME TO GALICIA AND ASTURIAS

TOP REASONS TO GO

★ **Experience gourmet heaven:** The beautiful Santiago de Compostela is said to contain more restaurants and bars per square mile than any other city in Spain.

★ **Go on rugged hikes:** Spend days in the spectacular Picos de Europa range getting lost in forgotten mountain villages.

★ **Get in on the grapevine:** The Ribeiro region yields Spain's finest white wines.

★ **Enjoy the waterfront activity:** Watch the oyster hawkers at work while dining on a fresh catch on Vigo's Rúa Pescadería.

★ **Discover Santander:** With its intoxicating schedule of live music, opera, and theater performances on the beach and in gardens and monasteries, the city's August festival of music and dance is the perfect backdrop for exploring this vibrant city.

1 Santiago de Compostela and Eastern Galicia. Books and movies have been written about it and millions have walked it, but you don't have to be a pilgrim to enjoy the journey of Camino de Santiago. At the end of the path is Santiago itself, a vibrant university town embedded in hills around the soaring spires of one of Spain's most emblematic cathedrals.

2 The Costa da Morte and Rías Baixas. From Fisterra ("World's End") down to Vigo and the Portuguese border, this area takes in the peaceful seaside towns of Cambados and Baiona, the exquisite beaches of Las Islas Cíes, and the beautifully preserved medieval streets of Pontevedra.

4

Bay of Biscay

COSTA VERDE

uarca · Aviles · Gijón · Villaviciosa · San Vicente de la Barquera · COSTA DE CANTABRIA · Santander · Santoña

Grado · Pola de Siero · Ribadesella · Llanes · Comillas · Laredo

ASTURIAS · Oviedo · Infiesto · **4** · Pendueles · Torrelavega · Castro-Urdiales

Mieres · Cangas de Onís · **5** · Santillana del Mar · CANTABRIA

Cangas de Narcea · Covadonga · PICOS DE EUROPA · Liébana Valley · Potes · **6**

Reinosa

CORDILLERA CANTABRICA

CASTILE-LEÓN

0   20 mi
0   20 km

3 **A Coruña and Rías Altas.** Galicia has more coastline and unspoiled, nontouristy beaches than anywhere else in the country. You can opt for vast expanses of sand facing the Atlantic Ocean or tiny, tucked-away coves, but take note: the water is colder than the Mediterranean, and the region's weather is more unreliable.

4 **Asturias.** Also known as the Senda Costera (Coastal Way), this partly paved nature route between Pendueles and Llanes takes in some of Asturias's most spectacular coastal scenery, including noisy *bufones* (large waterspouts created naturally by erosion) and the Playa de Ballota.

5 **Picos de Europa.** One of Spain's best-kept secrets, the "Peaks of Europe" lie across Asturias, Cantabria, and León. In addition to 8,910-foot peaks, the area has deep caves, excellent mountain refuges, and interesting wildlife. This region is also known for its fine cheeses.

6 **Cantabria.** Santander's wide beaches and summer music-and-dance festival are highlights of this mountain and maritime community. The Liébana Valley, the Renaissance town at Santillana del Mar, and ports and beaches such as San Vicente de la Barquera all rank among northern Spain's finest treasures.

GETTING ORIENTED

The bewitching provinces of Galicia and Asturias lie in Spain's northwest; these rugged Atlantic regions hide a corner of Spain so remote it was once called *finis terrae* (the end of the earth). Galicia is famous for Santiago de Compostela, for centuries a destination for Christian pilgrims seeking to pay homage to St. James. As for Asturias, its verdant hills, sandy beaches, and the massive Picos de Europa mountain range are all part of its pull. To the east, Cantabria borders the Bay of Biscay.

EATING AND DRINKING WELL IN GALICIA AND ASTURIAS

Galicia, Asturias, and Cantabria are famous for seafood and fish so fresh that chefs frown on drowning the inherent flavors in sauces and seasonings. Inland, the Picos de Europa and the mountain meadows are rich in game, sheep, and beef.

(top left) A plethora of seafood delicacies (top right) The classic octopus-and-potato combination (bottom left) The hearty and fortifying caldo gallego

The northern coast of Spain is justly famous for fish and seafood, and specialties include *merluza a la gallega* (steamed hake with paprika sauce) in Galicia, to *merluza a la sidra* (hake in a cider sauce) in Asturias. Look also for Galician seafood treasures such as *vieiras* (scallops) and *pulpo a la gallega* (boiled octopus that's drizzled with olive oil and dusted with salt and paprika). The rainy weather means that bracing stews are a favorite form of sustenance, especially *fabada asturiana* (Asturian bean-and-sausage stew) and Galicia's *caldo gallego* (a thick soup of white beans, turnip greens, ham, and potatoes). Cantabria's cooking is part mountain fare, such as roast kid and lamb or *cocidos* (pork-and-bean stews) in the highlands, and part seafood dishes, such as *sorropotún* (a bonito, potato, and vegetable stew) along the coast.

CABRALES CHEESE

Asturias is known for having Spain's bluest and most pungent cheese, Cabrales, made of raw cow's milk (with goat curd added for a softer consistency). Produced in the Picos de Europa mountains of eastern Asturias, the cheese gets such praise because of the quality of the milk and the dry highland air used to cure it. Cabrales is ideal melted over meat or for dessert with a sweet sherry.

BEANS AND LEGUMES

Fabada asturiana (fava-bean-and-sausage stew) is as well known in Spain as Valencia's paella or Andalusia's gazpacho. A meal in itself, fabada is usually consumed in copious quantities. The secret to great fabada lies in slow simmering while adding small quantities of cold water, and crushing some of the beans so that the creamy paste becomes part of the sauce. Fatback, black sausage, chorizo, and pork chops are added to this powerful dose of protein and vitamin B, and it's cooked on low heat for at least 2½ hours.

VEGETABLES

Turnip greens (*grelo* in Gallego) are a favorite vegetable in Galicia, celebrated in La Festa do Grelo during Carnavales in February. *Lacón con grelos* is a classic Galician specialty combining cured pork shoulder, turnip stalks and greens, potatoes, and chorizo, all boiled for about four hours. The grelo's acidity and the pork shoulder's heavy fat content make the marriage of these two products an ideal union. Similarly, caldo gallego is a powerful mountain or seafarers stew, the whole garden in a pot—including grelos stalks and greens, *alubias* (white beans), and potatoes—with pork for ballast and taste. Traditionally served in earthenware cups called *cuncas,* the diverse ingredients and the fat from the pork make this a fortifying antidote to

the bitter Atlantic climate of Spain's northwest corner.

PULPO A LA GALLEGA

This typical Galician specialty, also known as *polbo á feira,* consists of octopus that's been boiled (traditionally in a copper cauldron), cut into slices, drizzled with olive oil, sprinkled with salt and bittersweet paprika, and served on a wooden plate. A variation is served atop slices of boiled potato; the texture of the potato slices balances the consistency of the octopus.

TO DRINK

The best Galician wine is the fresh, full-bodied, white albariño from Rías Baixas, perfect with seafood. Ribeiro, traditionally sipped from shallow white ceramic cups, or *tazas,* in order to allow aromas to expand, is lighter and fresher. Asturias is known for its *sidra* (hard cider), poured from overhead and quaffed in a single gulp for full enjoyment of its effervescent flavor. Brandy buffs should try Galicia's *queimada* (which some locals claim is a witches' brew), made of potent, grappa-like *orujo* mixed with lemon peel, coffee beans, and sugar in an earthenware bowl and then set aflame and stirred until the desired amount of alcohol is burned off. Orujo is also the basis for several digestifs that Gallegos often sip at the end of a large meal.

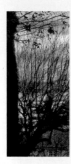

Updated by
Elizabeth
Prosser

Spain's most Atlantic region is en route to nowhere, an end in itself. This magical, remote area is sure to pull at your heartstrings, so be prepared to fall in love. In Gallego they call the feeling *morriña,* a powerful longing for a person or place you've left behind.

Stretching northwest from the lonesome Castilian plains to the rocky seacoast, Asturias and Galicia incorporate lush hills and vineyards, gorgeous *rías* (estuaries), and the country's wildest mountains, the Picos de Europa. Santander and the entire Cantabrian region are cool summer refuges with sandy beaches, high sierras (including part of the Picos de Europa), and tiny highland towns. Santander, once the main seaport for Old Castile on the Bay of Biscay, is in a mountainous zone wedged between the Basque Country and Asturias.

Northwestern Spain is a series of rainy landscapes, stretching from your feet to the horizon. Ancient granite buildings wear a blanket of moss, and even the stone *horreos* (granaries) are built on stilts above the damp ground. Swirling fog and heavy mist help keep local folktales of the supernatural alive. Rather than a guitar, you'll hear the *gaita* (bagpipe), a legacy of the Celts' settlements here in the 5th and 6th centuries BC. Spanish families flock to these cool northern beaches and mountains each summer, and Santiago de Compostela, where a cathedral holds the remains of the apostle James, has drawn pilgrims for 900 years, leaving churches, shrines, and former hospitals in their path. Asturias, north of the main pilgrim trail, has always maintained a separate identity, isolated by the rocky Picos de Europa. This and the Basque Country are the only parts of Spain never conquered by the Moors, so Asturian architecture shows little Moorish influence. It was from a mountain base at Covadonga that the Christians won their first decisive battle against the Moors and launched the Reconquest of Spain. Despite being very much its own region, Cantabria is in spirit much closer to Asturias—with which it shares the Picos de Europa, Castilian Spanish, and similar architecture—than its passionately independent neighbor, the Basque Country.

PLANNING

WHEN TO GO

Galicia can get very hot (more than 90°F [30°C]) between June and September, although summer is the best time for swimming and water sports and for Celtic music festivals. Asturias, in the mountains, is cooler. Galicia can be rainy to the point of saturation—not for nothing is this region called Green Spain—so avoid the area in winter: the rain, wind, and freezing temperatures make driving an arduous experience. Spring and fall are ideal, as the weather is reasonable and crowds are few.

PLANNING YOUR TIME

You can fly into Santiago de Compostela, and a week should be long enough to cover the Santiago area and Galicia's south. From Santiago, you can drive down the PO550 to Cambados, stopping on the way at fishing villages along the Ría de Arousa. If you take the coastal road to Pontevedra, you can spend time there exploring the medieval streets and tapas bars and then drive down to Vigo for a lunch of oysters on Rúa Pescadería. Continue south and arrive before dark at the Baiona parador. Alternatively, travel to A Coruña, and from there head north to some of Spain's loveliest beaches and Viveiro. From here cross into Asturias and spend time in Luarca or Gijón. Another attractive option is getting lost in a small village in the Picos de Europa.

Heading farther east, Santillana del Mar's Renaissance architecture, the Altamira Caves, and the Sardinero Beach at Santander are top spots, while the fishing villages and beaches around Llanes in eastern Asturias, and San Vicente de la Barquera in Cantabria have charming ports and inlets. If you want to delve more deeply into the Picos de Europa and the region's pretty coastline, Asturias and Cantabria merit more than a week's exploration.

FESTIVALS

There's a full calendar of special events in Galicia, including international festivals, major national celebrations, saints' days, and unique local events, some in towns that don't otherwise have much to offer the average traveler.

Carnival. In February and March, on this first major fiesta of the year after Three Kings' Day (January 6), cities, towns, and villages across the region erupt with festive fun, including parades, parties, and wild costumes.

Corpus Christi. During this feast day in June, the town of Ponteareas celebrates flowers and the harvest by carpeting the streets throughout the night with an intricate weave of fresh flowers and leaves, over which a somber parade progresses the following day.

El Día de Santiago (*St. James's Day*). Since it's named for the saint, Santiago is a good place to be on his feast day, June 25, celebrated here with processions, street parties, and spectacular fireworks. It is also one of the few days of the year that the enormous *botafumeiro* (incense burner) is released and swung across the naves of Santiago's Cathedral.

DID YOU KNOW?

Hiking is a popular activity in Galicia: all the better to work off some of those excellent meals.

Festa da Arribada. Celebrating the arrival on March 1, 1493, of the news that the New World had been discovered, the town of Baiona stages a spectacular reenactment on the beach, while the streets go medieval with a costumed procession and artisan market. There's plenty of food and entertainment, and the bars are open all day. It's held on the first weekend in March. ⊕ *www.baiona.org.*

Festa do Chourizo en Sant Anton de Abedes (*St. Anthony of Abedes Sausage Festival*). The town of Verin honors its patron saint every January 17 with a parade and other events dedicated to its *chourizo* (sausage).

Festa do Marisco (*Seafood Festival*). Galicia's famous culinary event, held in O Grove in October, draws crowds to feast on a stunning number of seafood delicacies. ⊕ *www.turismogrove.es.*

Festa do Queixo. Food, folklore, and music are the attractions of this cheese festival, held in the first week of March in Arzüa, near A Coruña. ☎ *981/500000, 981/815001* ⊕ *www.festadoqueixo.org.*

Festa do Viño Albariño (*Albariño Wine Festival*). On the first Sunday of August, the town of Cambados, capital of the Albariño wine region, draws thousands to witness its processions, concerts, cultural events, fireworks, and other revelry honoring local vineyards and wineries—including wine tastings from around 40 different Rias Baixas wineries. The festival goes back to the early 1950s. ⊕ *www.cambados.es.*

Festival Internacional Santander. The city of Santander's big event fills up almost all of August with world-class opera, ballet, classical concerts, and recitals, and attracts top international musicians and dancers. ☎ *942/210508, 942/314853* ⊕ *www.festivalsantander.com.*

Hogueras de San Juan (*San Juan Bonfires*). On the night of June 23, the skies of A Coruña are alight with hundreds of bonfires, notably along the beach, following a day of parades, colorful costumes, and traditional music and dance. ⊕ *www.hoguerassanjuan.com.*

La Folía. San Vicente celebrates this event in late April (the name translates roughly as "folly," and the exact date depends not only on Easter but also on the high tide). Its main attraction is a magnificent maritime procession: the town's colorful fishing fleet accompanies the figure of La Virgen de la Barquera as she is transported in part by boat from her sanctuary outside town to the village church. There she's honored with folk dances and songs before being returned to the sanctuary for another year. ✉ *San Vincente de la Barquera.*

La Reconquista. Marking the anniversary of the expulsion of Napoléon's army on March 28, 1809, Vigo re-creates the events and the atmosphere of that day (which earned it the title "faithful, loyal, and courageous") with battle reenactments, townsfolk in costumes, a 19th-century market, street parties, and lots of food and wine. ⊕ *www.reconquistadevigo.com/en.*

Nuestra Señora del Rosario (*Our Lady of the Rosary*). On August 15, sailors and fishermen in Luarca celebrate the Lady of the Rosary by parading their boats and an image of the Virgin through the harbor, in memory of fishermen who died at sea.

Ortigueira Festival. This major Celtic music festival, which takes place in early or mid-July over four days in the coastal city of Ortigueira, attracts folk musicians from around the world. ☎ *981/422089 for tourist office* ⊕ *www.festivaldeortigueira.com.*

Procesión de las Mortajas (*Procession of the Shrouds*). This late-September event in A Pobra do Caramiñal (A Coruña) dates back to the 15th century. Thousands of people take to the streets, and survivors of illness, bad luck, or bad love parade around town in gratitude for their salvation, preceded by open coffins carried by their families and friends.

Procesión dos Fachós (*Procession of the Scarecrows*). Every January 19, the village of Castro Caldelas, in the Ourense province, commemorates its survival of a 1753 cholera outbreak with a torchlight procession. ⊕ *www.turismourense.com.*

Rapa das Bestas (*Taming of the Beasts*). The beasts that are tamed during this celebration, held in various locations around Galicia over the first weekend in July, are wild horses, which are grappled and subdued by local experts. ⊕ *www.rapadasbestas.es.*

Semana Santa (*Holy Week*). Easter and the rest of Holy Week are observed throughout the region with religious services and colorful processions. Viveiro has a barefoot parade of flagellants illuminated by hundreds of candles. ⊕ *semanasanta.galiciadigital.com.*

GETTING HERE AND AROUND

AIR TRAVEL

The region's domestic airports are in Santander, A Coruña, Vigo, and near San Estéban de Pravia, 47 km (29 miles) north of Oviedo. Santiago de Compostela is a hub for both domestic and international flights. Airport shuttles usually take the form of ALSA buses from the city bus station. Iberia sometimes runs a private shuttle from its office to the airport; inquire when you book your ticket.

BIKE TRAVEL

Cycling the Camino is becoming increasingly popular every year, particularly with international visitors. The official *French Way by Bicycle* booklet, available from **Xacobeo** or from the Santiago tourist office, warns that the approximately 800-km (500-mile) route from the French border to Santiago is a very tough bike trip—bridle paths, dirt tracks, rough stones, and mountain passes. The best time of year to tackle it is late spring or early autumn. The Asturias tourist office's booklet, *Sus Rutas de Montaña y Costa,* available online (⊕ *www.asturias.es*), outlines additional routes. For something a little less arduous, try the final leg of the camino francés, from Sarria to Santiago.

Bike Routes CaminoWays.com. This tour operator can help you bike the Camino with tailor-made packages for individuals and families, child-friendly accommodations if necessary, meals, luggage transfer, and bike rental. ☎ *353/15252886* ⊕ *www.caminoways.com.* **Santiago bike route information** ⊕ *www.caminhodesantiago.com.br/index3.htm.* **Xacobeo** ⊕ *www.xacobeo.es.*

BUS TRAVEL

ALSA runs daily buses from Madrid to Galicia and Asturias. Once here, there is good bus service between the larger destinations in the area, like Santiago, Vigo, Pontevedra, Lugo, A Coruña, Gijón, Oviedo, and Santander, though train travel is generally smoother, faster, and easier. Getting to the smaller towns by bus is more difficult. Galicia-based Monbus offers quick, inexpensive transportation between major cities like Santiago, A Coruña, Vigo, and Pontevedra, as well as smaller towns that may not be easily accessible by train.

Contacts ALSA ☎ *902/422242* ⊕ *www.alsa.es/en.* **Monbus** ☎ *902/292900* ⊕ *www.monbus.es.*

CAR TRAVEL

4

Driving is the best way to get around. The four-lane A6 expressway links the area with central Spain; it takes about five hours to cover the 650 km (403 miles) from Madrid to Santiago, and from Madrid, it's 240 km (149 miles) on the N1 or the A1 toll road to Burgos, after which you can take the N623 to complete the 390 km (242 miles) to Santander.

The expressway north from León to Oviedo and Gijón is the fastest way to cross the Cantabrian Mountains. The AP9 north–south Galician ("Atlantic") expressway links A Coruña, Santiago, Pontevedra, and Vigo, and the A8 in Asturias links Santander to Luarca and beyond. Local roads along the coast or through the hills are more scenic but slower.

TRAIN TRAVEL

RENFE (⊕ *www.renfe.es*) runs several trains a day from Madrid to Santander (4½ hours), Oviedo (7 hours), and Gijón (8 hours), and a separate line serves Santiago (11 hours). Local RENFE trains connect the region's major cities with most of the surrounding small towns, but there may be dozens of stops on the way. Narrow-gauge FEVE trains clatter slowly across northern Spain, connecting Galicia and Asturias with Santander, Bilbao, and Irún, on the French border.

RESTAURANTS

From the humblest of cafeterias to the hautest of dining rooms, chefs in Galicia, Asturias, and Cantabria emphasize the use of fresh, local ingredients. Excellent, cheap meals can be found at smaller, family-run eateries, which usually stick to traditional foods and tend to draw mostly local crowds. Restaurants that stray from the culinary norm— and which also offer top-notch service and elegant surroundings—usually also include a higher price tag.

HOTELS

Expect to feel at home in the region's classic inns: they're usually small, centuries-old, family-owned properties, with plenty that's pleasing, such as gardens, exposed stone walls, and genuinely friendly service. City hotels may not have the same country charm, but they make up for it with professional service, sparkling facilities, and spacious, comfortable rooms. Many big chain hotels may resemble their American counterparts, but you may not be able to assume that they also come with ample parking, big breakfasts, fitness rooms, or other amenities that are more-or-less standard back home. It's a very good idea to book ahead of time May through September, particularly if your stay includes a weekend.

Hotel reviews have been shortened. For full information, visit Fodors. com.

WHAT IT COSTS IN EUROS				
	$	$$	$$$	$$$$
Restaurants	under €13	€13–€17	€18–€22	over €22
Hotels	under €91	€91–€125	€126–€180	over €180

Restaurant prices are the average cost of a main course or equivalent combination of smaller dishes at dinner. Hotel prices are the lowest cost of a standard double room in high season.

SANTIAGO DE COMPOSTELA AND EASTERN GALICIA

The main pilgrimage route of the Camino de Santiago, the camino francés, crosses the Pyrenees from France and heads west across northern Spain. If you drive into Galicia on the A6 expressway from Castile-León, you enter the homestretch, but many people fly into Santiago de Compostela and start exploring from here.

SANTIAGO DE COMPOSTELA

650 km (403 miles) northwest of Madrid.

Fodor's Choice A large, lively university makes Santiago one of the most exciting cities
★ in Spain, and its cathedral makes it one of the most impressive. The building is opulent and awesome, yet its towers create a sense of harmony as a benign St. James, dressed in pilgrim's costume, looks down from his perch. Santiago de Compostela welcomes more than 4.5 million visitors a year, with an extra million during Holy Years (the next will be in 2021), when St. James's Day, July 25, falls on a Sunday.

GETTING HERE AND AROUND
Santiago is connected to Pontevedra (61 km [38 miles]) and A Coruña (57 km [35 miles]) via the AP9 tollway. The N550 is free, but slower. Parking anywhere in the city center can be difficult unless you use one of the numerous car parks around the outside edge of the historical quarter.

Bus service out of Santiago's station is plentiful, with eight daily buses to Madrid (7 to 9 hours) and hourly buses to A Coruña.

High-speed Talgo trains to Madrid take just over six hours; there is daily service to Irún, on the French border, via León and Santander. Trains depart every hour for Galicia's other major towns.

Santiago's center is very pedestrian-friendly, and the distances between attractions are relatively short, so walking is the best and often the only way around town.

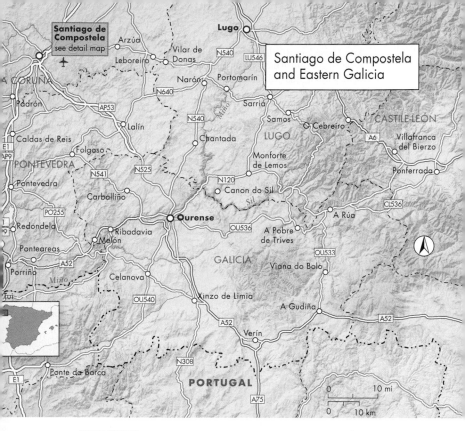

Santiago de Compostela
see detail map

Santiago de Compostela
and Eastern Galicia

Lugo

Arzúa

Vilar de
Donas

N540

LU546

CASTILE-LEÓN

Leboreiro

A CORUÑA

Narón

Portomarín

Padrón

N640

Sarriá

AP53

Samos

Cebreiro

A6

Villafranca
del Bierzo

Lalín

N540

LUGO

Caldas de Reis

E1
AP9

Folgoso

Chantada

Monforte
de Lemos

Ponferrada

PONTEVEDRA

N541

N525

N120

Pontevedra

Carballiño

Canon do Sil

Sil

PO255

Ourense

A Rúa

CL536

Redondela

Ribadavia

OU536

A Pobre
de Trives

Melón

Ponteareas

A52

GALICIA

OU533

Porriño

Celanova

Viana do Bolo

Tui

Miño

OU540

Xinzo de Limia

A Gudiña

A52

A52

Verín

N308

Ponte da Barca

PORTUGAL

E1

A75

0   10 mi

0   10 km

ESSENTIALS

Bike Rentals Bici Total ⊠ *Cuesta de San Marcos 9* ☎ *981/564562* ⊕ *www. bicitotal.es.*

Bus Station Santiago de Compostela ⊠ *Praza de Camilo Díaz Baliño s/n* ☎ *981/542416.*

Tour Information La Asociación Profesional de Guías Turísticos de Galicia. Santiago's association of well-informed guides, which is part of the tourist office, can arrange private walking tours of the city or tours to any place in Galicia. ☎ *981/576698* ⊕ *www.guiasdegalicia.org* ⊠ *From €100 for a general tour, for up to 10 people.*

Train Station Santiago de Compostela ⊠ *Rúa do Hórreo 75* ☎ *902/240505.*

Visitor Information Santiago de Compostela ⊠ *Rúa do Vilar 63* ☎ *981/555129* ⊕ *www.santiagoturismo.com.*

EXPLORING

TOP ATTRACTIONS

Fodor's Choice
★

Casco Antiguo (*Old Town*). The best way to spend your time in Santiago de Compostela is to simply to walk around the casco antiguo, losing yourself in its maze of stone-paved narrow streets and little plazas. The streets hold many old *pazos* (manor houses), convents, and churches.

The most beautiful pedestrian thoroughfares are Rúa do Vilar, Rúa do Franco, and Rúa Nova—portions of which are covered by arcaded walkways called *soportales*, designed to keep walkers out of the rain.

Cathedral. From the Praza do Obradoiro, climb the two flights of stairs to the main entrance of Santiago's cathedral. Although the facade is baroque, the interior holds one of the finest Romanesque sculptures in the world, the **Pórtico de la Gloria.** Completed in 1188 by Maestro Mateo, this is the cathedral's original entrance, its three arches carved with figures from the Apocalypse, the Last Judgment, and purgatory. Below Jesus is a serene St. James, poised on a carved column. Look carefully and you can see five smooth grooves, formed by the millions of pilgrims who have placed their hands here over the centuries. On the back of the pillar, people, especially students preparing for exams, lean forward to touch foreheads with the likeness of Maestro Mateo in the hope that his genius can be shared.

In his bejeweled cloak, St. James presides over the **high altar.** The stairs behind it are the cathedral's focal point, surrounded by dazzling baroque decoration, sculpture, and drapery. Here, as the grand finale of their spiritual journey, pilgrims embrace St. James and kiss his cloak. In the crypt beneath the altar lie the remains of James and his disciples St. Theodore and St. Athenasius.

A pilgrims' mass is celebrated every day at noon. On special, some-what unpredictable occasions, the *botafumeiro* (huge incense burner) is attached to the thick ropes hanging from the ceiling and prepared for a ritual at the end of the pilgrims' mass: as small flames burn inside, eight strong laymen move the ropes to swing the vessel in a massive semicircle across the apse. In earlier centuries, this rite served as an air freshener—by the time pilgrims reached Santiago, they were not, to put it mildly, at their freshest. A botafumeiro and other cathedral treasures are on display in the **museums** downstairs and next door.

On the right (south) side of the nave is the **Porta das Praterías** (Sil-versmiths' Door), the only purely Romanesque part of the cathedral's facade. The statues on the portal were cobbled together from parts of the cathedral. The double doorway opens onto the **Praza das Praterías,** named for the silversmiths' shops that once lined it. ⊠ *Praza do Obra-doiro* 🕾 *902/557812 for cathedral* ⊕ *www.catedraldesantiago.es* 🕾 *Ca-thedral free, museum €6* ☉ *Cathedral daily 7 am–8:30 pm; museum Apr.–Oct., daily 9–8; Nov.–Mar., daily 10–8.*

Cidade da Cultura. More than a decade in the making, Santiago's vast new City of Culture, a controversial striated-stone-and-glass edifice on Mt. Gaiás, has whisked Galician culture into the future. It contains a museum, archive library, performing arts theater, and international arts center. Behind the museum's sweeping facade lie temporary cultural exhibitions. The design of the complex, by the American architect Peter Eisenman, is based on the shape of a scallop shell, the emblem of St. James, and the five medieval caminos that lead pilgrims to Santiago's cathedral. ⊠ *Mt. Gaiás s/n* 🕾 *881/997584* ⊕ *www.cidadedacultura.org* ☉ *Library Tues.–Sun 10–8; museum Tues.–Sun. 11–8.*

Hostal dos Reis Católicos (*Hostel of the Catholic Monarchs*). Facing the cathedral from the left, the hostal was built in 1499 by Ferdinand and Isabella to house the pilgrims who slept on Santiago's streets every night. Having lodged and revived travelers for over 500 years, it's the oldest refuge in the world; it was converted from a hospital to a parador in 1954. The facade bears a Castilian coat of arms along with Adam, Eve, and various saints; inside, the four arcaded patios have gargoyle rainspouts said to be caricatures of 16th-century townsfolk. Behind the lobby is the building's focal point, a Renaissance chapel in the shape of a cross. Thanks to the "Parador Museo" initiative, visitors (as opposed to only guests staying at the parador) can behold these architectural treasures for a small fee (or for free with the purchase of a meal at one of the parador's restaurants). ⊠ *Praza do Obradoiro 1* ☏ *981/582200* ⊕ *www.parador. es* 🎫 *€3* ⊙ *Sun.–Fri. noon–2 and 4–6.*

WORTH NOTING

Cathedral roofs. For excellent views of the city, join one of the tours arranged by Xelmírez Palace that takes you across the *cubiertas*, the granite steps of the cathedral roofs. Call ahead to arrange one in English. Pilgrims made the same 100-foot climb in medieval times to burn their travel-worn clothes below the Cruz dos Farrapos (Cross of Rags). ⊠ *Pazo de Xelmírez, Praza do Obradoiro* ☏ *902/557812* ⊕ *www. catedraldesantiago.es* 🎫 *€12* ⊙ *Tours: Apr.–Oct., daily on the hr 9–8; Nov.–Mar., daily on the hr 10–8.*

Centro Galego de Arte Contemporánea (*Galician Center for Contemporary Art*). On the north side of town, off the Porta do Camino, the CGAC is a stark but elegant modern building that contrasts with the ancient feel of most other places in Santiago. The Portuguese designer Álvaro Siza built the museum of smooth, angled granite, which mirrors the medieval convent of San Domingos de Bonaval next door. Inside, a gleaming lobby of white Italian marble gives way to white-walled, high-ceilinged exhibition halls flooded with light from massive windows and skylights. The museum has a good permanent collection and even better changing exhibits. ⊠ *Rúa Valle Inclán 2* ☏ *981/546619* ⊕ *www.cgac.org* 🎫 *Free* ⊙ *Tues.–Sun. 11–8.*

Museo das Peregrinacións (*Pilgrimage Museum*). North of Acibechería (follow Ruela de Xerusalén) is the Museo das Peregrinacións, with Camino de Santiago iconography from sculptures and carvings to *azabache* (compact black coal, or jet) items. For an overview of the history

Exploring Sites ▼

Casco Antiguo 8

Cathedral 3

Centro Galego
de Arte
Contemporánea 6

Cidade da Cultura 9

Hostal des Reis
Católicos 1

Museo das
Peregrinacións 5

Museo do
Pobo Galego 7

Pazo de Xelmírez 2

Praza da Quintana 4

Hotels & Restaurants ▼

A Barrola 10

Abastos 2.0 8

Adega Abrigadoiro 11

Bierzo Enxebre 7

Carretas 3

Casa Marcelo 1

Don Gaiferos................. 9

Hotel Costa Vella 5

Hotel Monumento
San Francisco 4

La Bodeguilla
de San Roque 6

Parador de Santiago de
Compostela: Hostal dos
Reis Católicos 2

Pazo Cibrán 13

Restaurante Ana 12

KEY

🛈 Tourist Information

❶ Exploring Sites

① Hotels & Restaurants

Santiago de Compostela

of St. James, the cathedral, and the pilgrimage, as well as the Camino's role in the development of the city itself, this is a key visit. ✉ *Rúa de San Miguel 4* ☎ *981/581558* ⊕ *www.mdperegrinacions.com* 💷 *€2.40 (free Sat. 5–8 pm and Sun. all day)* ⏰ *Tues.–Fri. 10–8, Sat. 10:30–1:30 and 5–8, Sun. 10:30–1:30.*

Museo do Pobo Galego (*Galician Folk Museum*). Next door to the CGAC stands the medieval convent of San Domingos de Bonaval. The museum within includes photos, farm implements, traditional costumes, and other items illustrating aspects of traditional Galician life. The star attraction is the 13th-century self-supporting spiral granite staircase that still connects three floors. ✉ *C. San Domingos de Bonaval s/n* ☎ *981/583620* ⊕ *www.museodopobo.es* 💷 *€3 (free Sun.)* ⏰ *Tues.–Sat. 10:30–2 and 4–7:30, Sun. and public holidays 11–2.*

Pazo de Xelmírez (*Palace of Archbishop Xelmírez*). Step into this rich 12th-century building to view an unusual example of Romanesque civic architecture, with a cool, clean, vaulted dining hall. The little figures carved on the corbels in this graceful, 100-foot-long space are drinking, eating, and listening to music with great medieval gusto. Each is different, so stroll around for a tableau of mealtime merriment. ✉ *Praza do Obradoiro* ☎ *902/557812* ⊕ *www.catedraldesantiago.es* 💷 *€6, includes cathedral museum* ⏰ *Tues.–Sat. 11–2 and 4–6, Sun 10–2.*

Praza da Quintana. The wide Praza da Quintana, behind the Santiago cathedral, is the haunt of young travelers and folk musicians in summer. The Porta Santa (Holy Door) is open only during years when St. James's Day falls on a Sunday (the next is 2021).

WHERE TO EAT

$$$
SPANISH

✕**A Barrola.** One of the better options on a street packed with tourist eateries, this seafood-heavy restaurant has polished wood floors and a lively terrace; it's a favorite with the university faculty. The caldo gallego, *santiaguiños* (slipper lobsters), *arroz con bogavante* (rice with lobster), and seafood empanadas are superb, and local delicacies like *angulas* (elvers) and lamprey are served seasonally. If options overwhelm you and you can't decide, you might opt for the *parrillada de pescados* (mixed seafood grill). 💲 *Average main: €20* ✉ *Rúa do Franco 29* ☎ *981/577999* ⊕ *www.restaurantesgrupobarrola.com.*

$$$$
TAPAS
Fodor'sChoice
★

✕**Abastos 2.0.** "From the market to the plate" is the philosophy of Iago Pazos y Marcos Cerqueiro's restaurant. The concept here, to start and finish the day with an empty larder and a blank menu, has quickly grown in reputation. This inventive tapas bar has been transformed from a collection of tiny market stalls adjoining Santiago's food market into a vibrant and contemporary glass-walled space. Ingredients are handpicked in the market each morning and crafted into impeccable dishes bursting with fresh flavors and new ideas. These flavors can be enjoyed in the small 12-seater dining room (reservations highly recommended) or alongside the regulars by simply leaning up against the bar surrounding the exterior. 💲 *Average main: €25* ✉ *Casetas 13–18, Plaza de Abastos s/n* ☎ *981/576145* ⊕ *www.abastosdouspuntocero.es* ⏰ *Closed Sun. and Mon.*

$$ ✕ **Adega Abrigadoiro.** This rustic stone-wall bodega serves some of the
TAPAS best Galician delicacies in town. Its centerpiece, a fully functioning
waterwheel, contrasts with the bodega's central location, a five-min-
ute walk from the Colexio San Xerome. Lean up against a barrel or
sit at one of the long wooden tables and feast on *embutidos* (cold
cuts of meat) and cheeses, accompanied by a selection of wines by the
glass or bottle. $ *Average main: €15* ⊠ *Rúa da Carreira do Conde 5*
☎ *981/563163.*

$ ✕ **Bierzo Enxebre.** Tucked behind the cathedral, this tapas bar special-
SPANISH izes in products from El Bierzo, a region of Castilla and León, either in
the animated bar or in one of the stone walled dining rooms. Visitors
stopping in for a drink at the bar can expect a generous portion of free
tapas, while the menu has a selection of grilled meats, *revueltos* (scram-
bled eggs with a variety of toppings—a regional favorite), cold meats
and cheeses. $ *Average main: €12* ⊠ *Rúa La Troia 10* ☎ *981/581909*
⊕ *www.bierzoenxebre.es* ⊙ *Closed Tues.*

$$$$ ✕ **Carretas.** This casual spot for fresh Galician seafood is around the
SEAFOOD corner from the Hostal dos Reis Católicos. Fish dishes abound, but
the specialty here is shellfish. Start with a plate of melt-in-your-mouth
battered miniscallops, then, for the full experience, order the labor-
intensive *variado de mariscos,* a comprehensive platter of langostinos,
king prawns, crab, and goose barnacles, a white or gray crustacean
found in deep waters. *Salpicón de mariscos* presents the same crea-
tures shelled. For dessert, there's the tastier-than-it-sounds fried milk
pudding. $ *Average main: €25* ⊠ *Rúa das Carretas 21* ☎ *981/563111*
⊕ *www.restaurantesanclemente.com* ⊙ *Closed Sun. and Mon.*

$$ ✕ **La Bodeguilla de San Roque.** This is one of Santiago's favorite spots
TAPAS for *tapeo* (tapas grazing) and *chiquiteo* (wine sampling); it's just a five-
minute walk from the cathedral. The tapas live up to their reputation,
and they're a better choice than the main dishes. The traditional bar
area takes center stage, playing host to locals, pilgrims, and tourists
alike, all gathering for wine, Iberian cured meats, cheeses, and seasonal dishes. It can get crowded, but this only adds to the atmosphere.
$ *Average main: €15* ⊠ *C. San Roque 13* ☎ *981/564379* ⊕ *www.
labodeguilladesanroque.com.*

$$$$ ✕ **Restaurante Ana.** In a converted 200-year-old tannery a short stroll
SPANISH from the city center, chef Ana García offers contemporary Galician cuisine. The tasting menu serves as a mouthwatering introduction, with a
selection of house favorites such as Iberian pork-jowl stew, or scallops
on a bed of pumpkin puree. Wine is more lavishly represented here than
in most other Santiago restaurants; go local with an Albariño from the
Rìas Baixas or a Mencía, and make sure to book a day in advance to
secure one of the six popular tables in the cobbled courtyard, which
has a fountain. $ *Average main: €25* ⊠ *Rúa Olvido 22* ☎ *981/570792*
⊙ *No dinner Sun.*

WHERE TO STAY

$ ▥ **Hotel Costa Vella.** At this classically Galician inn, there's a perfect little
B&B/INN garden and views of red-tile rooftops, the baroque convent of San Francisco, and the green hills beyond (ask for a garden view). **Pros:** charming
views; ideal location; warm, accommodating staff. **Cons:** creaky floors;

Santiago de Compostela's Obradoiro Square

thin walls; no elevator. $ *Rooms from: €82* ✉ *Rúa Porta da Pena 17* ☎ *981/569530* ⊕ *www.costavella.com* ⇱ *14 rooms* †◯† *No meals.*

$$$
HOTEL
🏨 **Hotel Monumento San Francisco.** Contemporary stained-glass windows add a touch of pizzazz to the solemn interior of this converted 13th-century convent, adjoining the church of the same name. **Pros:** superb location in tranquil corner of Santiago's old town; very tidy; easily accessible by car. **Cons:** a bit too quiet at times; mediocre food. $ *Rooms from: €140* ✉ *Campillo San Francisco 3* ☎ *981/581634* ⊕ *www.sanfranciscohm.com* ⇱ *81 rooms* †◯† *No meals.*

$$$$
HOTEL
Fodor's Choice
★
🏨 **Parador de Santiago de Compostela: Hostal dos Reis Católicos.** One of the parador chain's most highly regarded hotels, this 15th-century masterpiece was once a royal hostel and hospital for sick pilgrims. **Pros:** views of Obradoiro square; excellent cuisine; fascinating collection of antiques and paintings. **Cons:** confusing corridors; often filled with people on guided tours; pricey. $ *Rooms from: €284* ✉ *Praza do Obradoiro 1* ☎ *981/582200* ⊕ *www.parador.es* ⇱ *131 rooms, 6 suites* †◯† *Breakfast.*

$
B&B/INN
🏨 **Pazo Cibrán.** This comfortable 18th-century Galician manor house, 7 km (4 miles) from Santiago de Compostela, has six rooms in the main house and five large rooms in the old stable. **Pros:** personal hospitality; authentic and stately country house; delightful gardens. **Cons:** inaccessible without a car; poor local dining options. $ *Rooms from: €75* ✉ *San Xulián de Sales s/n, Vedra* ☎ *981/511515* ⊕ *www.pazocibran. com* ⇱ *11 rooms* †◯† *Breakfast.*

NIGHTLIFE

Santiago's nightlife peaks on Thursday night, because many students spend weekends at home with their families. For up-to-date info on concerts, films, and clubs, pick up the monthly *Compostela Capital Cultural,* available at the main tourist office on Rúa do Vilar, or visit the official tourism website (⊕ *www.santiagoturismo.com*).

> ### IT'S GALLEGO TO ME
>
> In the Gallego language, the Castilian Spanish plaza (town square) is *praza* and the Castilian *playa* (beach) is *praia.* Closer to Portuguese than to Castilian Spanish, Gallego is the language of nearly all road signs in Galicia.

Bars and seafood-themed tapas joints line the old streets south of the cathedral, particularly **Rúa do Franco, Rúa da Raiña,** and **Rúa do Vilar.** A great first stop, especially if you haven't eaten dinner, is **Rúa de San Clemente,** off the Praza do Obradoiro, where several bars offer two or three plates of tapas free with each drink.

BARS

Babel. Popular with students, this bar is a hub for world music, from Galician to Brazilian and Cuban, which it often showcases in concerts during the week. ⊠ *Rúa Calderería 26* ☎ *981/573625.*

Casa das Crechas. Drink to Galicia's Celtic roots here, with live music and Celtic wood carvings hanging from thick stone walls, while dolls of playful Galician witches ride their brooms above the bar. ⊠ *Vía Sacra 3* ☎ *981/560751* ⊕ *www.casadascrechas.com.*

O Beiro. This rustic wine bar attracts a laid-back, professional crowd. It has an excellent selection of wines and small portions of tapas. ⊠ *Rúa da Raiña 3* ☎ *981/581370.*

CAFÉS

Santiago is a great city for coffee drinking and people-watching. Most of the cafés are clustered around the cathedral, in the Casco Antiguo, especially on Rúa Calderería and Rúa do Vilar.

Cafe Bar Derby. Once a gathering place for Galician poets, this remains a serene spot for coffee and pastries. ⊠ *Rúa das Orfas 29* ☎ *981/586417.*

Café Casino. Upholstered armchairs, mirrors, and wood paneling make this atmospheric art-nouveau café feel like an elegant and comfortable library. ⊠ *Rúa do Vilar 35* ☎ *981/577503.*

Iacobus. Cozy Iacobus blends stone walls with contemporary wood trim and light fixtures; there's a glass cache of coffee beans in the floor. Another branch is at Rua Calderería 42. ⊠ *Rúa da Senra 24* ☎ *981/585967* ⊕ *www.iacobuscafe.com.*

PERFORMING ARTS

Auditorio de Galicia. This modern concert hall, north of town, has high-quality classical and jazz programs and a fine art gallery. In residence is the Royal Galician Philharmonic, which has hosted Il Giardino Armonico, the Academy of St. Martin-in-the-Fields, and the Leipzig Gewandhaus Orchestra. ⊠ *Av. Burgo das Nacións s/n* ☎ *981/552290* ⊕ *www.auditoriodegalicia.org.*

Teatro Principal. This venue hosts plays in Spanish, as well as dance performances and film festivals. ✉ *Rúa Nova 22* ☎ *981/542349.*

SHOPPING

Augusto Otero. Founded in 1906, this boutique carries fine handcrafted silver. ✉ *Placa de las Platerías 5* ☎ *981/581027.*

Bolillos. In the fishing town of Camariñas, women fashion exquisite lace collars, scarves, and table linens. This is the best place to buy their work, and watch some of it being crafted. ✉ *Rúa Nova 40* ☎ *981/589776.*

Noroeste. On a tiny lane off Acibechería, Noroeste sells handmade jewelry. ✉ *Ruela de Xerusalén s/n* ☎ *981/577130.*

Sargadelos. Galicia is known throughout Spain for its distinctive blue-and-white ceramics with bold modern designs, made in Sargadelos and O Castro. There is a wide selection at Sargadelos. ✉ *Rúa Nova 16* ☎ *981/581905.*

SPORTS AND THE OUTDOORS

GOLF

Real Aero Club de Santiago. Located 11 km (7 miles) outside Santiago de Compostela, this year-round golf club has an 18-hole course, a putting green, and a golf school. ✉ *Ameixenda, San Mamede de Piñeiro, Ames* ☎ *981/888276, 981/954910* ⊕ *www.aerosantiago.es.*

WATER SPORTS

Turisnorte. These diving experts have information on scuba lessons, equipment rental, guided dives, windsurfing, and parasailing. ✉ *C. Raxoeira 14, Milladoiro* ☎ *981/530009* ⊕ *www.turisnorte.es.*

OURENSE AND LA RIBEIRA SACRA

105 km (65 miles) southeast of Santiago, 95 km (59 miles) east of Vigo.

Despite the uninspiring backdrop of Ourense's new town, Galicia's third-largest city has bubbling thermal springs and an attractive medieval quarter whose animated streets, tapas bars, and plazas come alive, particularly on weekends. A scattering of notable historical monuments includes the colossal arches of the Ponte Vella spanning the River Miño and the 13th-century Cathedral of San Martino. Ourense is a good starting point for exploring the surrounding dramatic landscapes of the Ribeira Sacra (Sacred Riverbank) and Cañon do Sil (Sil River Canyon). This less explored region of interior Galicia is dotted with vineyards, Romanesque churches, and monasteries. Well worth a visit or a short stay is the Parador Estevo, converted from the Benedictine 10th-century Monasterio de Santo Estevo and perched high above the spectacular scenery of the Cañon do Sil.

GETTING HERE AND AROUND

RENFE and Monbus offer frequent services to Ourense from Santiago and Vigo in less than two hours. The A52 links Ourense to Vigo and Pontevedra, and the AG53 with Santiago.

WHERE TO STAY

$ HOTEL **Hotel Carrís Cardenal Quevedo.** Offering stylish city-chic accommodations, this hotel is in a handy location for Ourense's shopping district, restaurants, and lively tapas scene, and is only a five-minute stroll from the historical quarter. **Pros:** well positioned for both shopping district and historical quarter; knowledgeable and friendly staff. **Cons:** expensive breakfast; tight parking space. [$] *Rooms from: €83* ✉ *Rúa Cardenal Quevedo 28–30* ☎ *988/375523, 902/105173* 🌐 *www.carrishoteles.com* 🛏 *37 rooms, 2 suites* 🍴 *Breakfast.*

$ HOTEL Fodor'sChoice ★ **Parador de Santo Estevo.** Clinging to the edge of the Cañon do Sil, this parador, carefully built into the colossal 12th-century Benedictine Monasterio de Santo Estevo, stands out for its atmospheric setting and spectacular vistas. **Pros:** magnificent setting; historical sanctuary surrounded by nature. **Cons:** mediocre food; can get booked up by wedding parties. [$] *Rooms from: €90* ✉ *Monasterio de Santo Estevo, 26 km (16 miles) northeast of Ourense, off CV323 beyond Luintra* ☎ *988/010110* 🌐 *www.parador.es* 🛏 *77 rooms* 🕒 *Closed Dec.–Feb.* 🍴 *No meals.*

LUGO

102 km (63 miles) east of Santiago.

Just off the A6 freeway, Galicia's oldest provincial capital is most notable for its 2-km (1½-mile) **Roman wall.** These beautifully preserved ramparts completely surround the streets of the old town. The walkway on top has good views. The baroque Ayuntamiento has a magnificent rococo facade overlooking the tree-lined **Praza Maior** (Plaza Mayor). There's a good view of the Río Miño Valley from the **Parque Rosalía de Castro,** outside the Roman walls near the cathedral, which is a mixture of Romanesque, Gothic, baroque, and neoclassical styles.

GETTING HERE AND AROUND

RENFE runs eight trains per day to and from A Coruña, a journey of 1½ to 2 hours. Several daily ALSA buses connect Lugo to Santiago de Compostela, Oviedo, and Gijón.

ESSENTIALS

Bus Station Lugo ✉ *Praza do Campo 11* ☎ *982/251658.*

Train Station Lugo ✉ *Pl. Conde de Fontao s/n* ☎ *902/240505.*

Visitor Information Lugo ✉ *Praza do Campo 11* ☎ *982/251658.*

WHERE TO EAT

$$$ SPANISH 🍴 **Mesón de Alberto.** A hundred meters from the cathedral, this cozy venue has excellent Galician fare and professional service. The bar and adjoining *bodega* (winery) serve plenty of cheap *raciónes* (appetizers). The *surtido de quesos gallegos* provides generous servings of four local cheeses; ask for some *membrillo* (quince jelly) to go with them and the brown, crusty corn bread. For dessert, try the *filloas con nata y miel* (flambéed pancakes with cream and honey). The dining room upstairs has an inexpensive set menu. [$] *Average main: €20* ✉ *C. de la Cruz 4* ☎ *982/228310* 🌐 *www.mesondealberto.com* 🕒 *Closed Sun. No dinner Tues.*

THE COSTA DA MORTE AND RÍAS BAIXAS

West of Santiago, scenic C543 leads to the coast. It's windy, rocky, and treacherous—hence its eerie name, the "Coast of Death." Small villages and towns, often surrounded in mist, dot this dramatic stretch of coastline, each with its own collection of legends and traditions. In contrast, the series of wide, quiet estuaries south of here are called the Rías Baixas (Low Estuaries). The hilly drive takes you through a green countryside dappled with vineyards, tiny farms, and Galicia's trademark hórreos, most with a cross at one or both ends. There is plenty to see and do along its coast. You can find Galicia's most popular holiday towns and beaches, and taste exceptional wine and some of Galicia's best food. At its heart lies the medieval charm of handsome Pontevedra; the striking natural port of Vigo dominates a large part of its coastline.

FISTERRA

50 km (31 miles) west of Santiago, 75 km (48 miles) southwest of A Coruña.

There was a time when this lonely, windswept outcrop over raging waters was thought to be the end of the earth—the *finis terrae.* In fact, the official westernmost point of Europe is in Portugal. Despite this, many Camino pilgrims choose to continue the tradition of continuing onto the "end of the earth" from Santiago de Compostela to triumphantly finish at Fisterra's windswept lighthouse, beyond which there is nothing but the boundless expanse of the Atlantic Ocean. Fisterra all but shuts down in winter, but in summer it's a pleasant seaside resort with an attractive harbor.

ESSENTIALS
Visitor Information Fisterra ⊠ *Calle Real 2* ☎ *981/740781.*

EXPLORING
Santa María das Areas. Aside from legends, another draw in this tiny seaside town is its main plaza and the 12th-century church of Santa María das Areas. Romanesque, Gothic, and baroque elements combine in an impressive (but gloomy) facade. ⊠ *Manuel Lago País s/n.*

PONTEVEDRA

135 km (84 miles) southeast of Fisterra, 59 km (37 miles) south of Santiago.

At the head of its ría, Pontevedra is a delightful starting point for exploring the Rías Baixes. Its well-preserved old quarter is a dense network of pedestrian-only streets and handsome plazas flanked with elegant stone buildings, many of which are dressed in cascading flowers in spring and summer. The city got its start as a Roman settlement (its name comes from an old Roman bridge over the Río Lérez). As a powerful base for fishing and international trade, Pontevedra was a major presence in the Atlantic in the 16th century. Nowadays, its streets and plazas are awash with bars and restaurants, and it can get very busy on weekends. It also has the only operating *plaza de toros* (bullring) in Galicia.

GETTING HERE AND AROUND

RENFE and Monbus offer quick, frequent service between Vigo and Pontevedra, a half-hour journey; the same bus and train routes also link Pontevedra to Santiago de Compostela and A Coruña to the north along the AP9.

ESSENTIALS

Bus Station Pontevedra ⊠ *Calle de la Estación s/n* ☎ *986/852408.*

Visitor Information Pontevedra ⊠ *Casa da Luz, Praza da Verdura s/n* ☎ *986/090890.*

EXPLORING

Museo de Pontevedra. Housed in two 18th-century mansions connected by a stone bridge, this museum includes exquisite Celtic jewelry, silver from all over the world, and several large model ships. The original kitchen, with a stone fireplace, is intact; below, you can descend steep wooden stairs to the reconstructed captain's chamber on the battleship *Numancia,* which limped back to Spain after the Dos de Mayo battle with Peru in 1866. Complete the loop by going upstairs in the first building, where there are Spanish, Italian, and Flemish paintings, and some inlay work. ⊠ *Calle Pasantería 2–12* ☎ *986/804100* ⊕ *www. museo.depo.es* 🎫 *Free* ⏲ *Tues.–Sat. 10–9, Sun. 11–2. Closed Dec. 24– Jan. 1 and Jan. 6.*

Basílica de Santa María Mayor. The 16th-century seafarers' basilica has lovely, sinuous vaulting and, at the back of the nave, a Romanesque portal. There's also an 18th-century Christ by the Galician sculptor Ferreiro. ⊠ *Av. de Santa María s/n* ☎ *986/869902* 🎫 *Free* ⏲ *Mon.–Sat. 10–1:30 and 5–9, Sun. 10–2 and 6–9.*

WHERE TO EAT AND STAY

$$$$
SPANISH
✕ **Casa Solla.** Pepe Solla brings Galicia's bounty to his terrace garden restaurant, 2 km (1 mile) outside of town toward O Grove. Try the *menú de degustación* (tasting menu) to sample a selection of regional favorites, such as *lomo de caballa* (grilled mackerel), *caldo gallego de chorizo* (Galician chorizo sausage soup), *merluza con acelga* (cod with chard), or *jarrete de cordero* (sliced lamb shank). Finish off with a selection of Galician cheeses and *torrija con flan de coco y mango* (bread pudding with mango and coconut flan). $ *Average main: €30* ⊠ *Av. Sineiro 7, San Salvador de Poio* ☎ *986/872884* ⏲ *Closed Mon. No dinner Thurs. and Sun.*

$$$
HOTEL
🏨 **Parador de Pontevedra (Casa del Barón).** A 16th-century manor house in the heart of the old quarter, this rather dark parador has guest rooms with recessed windows embellished with lace curtains and large wooden shutters; some face a small rose garden. **Pros:** interesting collection of bric-a-brac; tranquil yet central location. **Cons:** confusing corridors; limited parking; gloomy rooms—a bit haunted house–ish. $ *Rooms from: €155* ⊠ *Rúa Barón 19* ☎ *986/855800* ⊕ *www.parador.es* 🛏 *45 rooms, 2 suites* ⊙| *No meals.*

EN ROUTE

Vineyards of Albariño. Driving west on the PO550, you'll pass vineyards of Albariño. As you wind your way through the small towns around here, you may come across the occasional donkey hauling wagons heaped with grapes. ⊠ *Pontevedra.*

Continued on page 268

EL CAMINO DE SANTIAGO

Traversing meadows, mountains, and villages across Spain, about 100,000 travelers embark each year on a pilgrimage to Galicia's Santiago de Compostela, the sacred city of St. James—they're not all deeply religious these days, though a spiritual quest is generally the motivation. The pilgrims follow one of seven main routes, logging about 19 miles a day in a nearly 500-mile journey. Along the way, they encounter incredible local hospitality and trade stories with fellow adventurers.

A SPIRITUAL JOURNEY

Puente la Reina, a town heavily influenced by the Pilgrim's Road to Santiago de Compostela, owes its foundation to the bridge that Queen Doña Mayor built over the Arga River.

The surge of spiritual seekers heading to Spain's northwest coast began as early as the 9th century, when news spread that the Apostle James's remains were there. By the middle of the 12th century, about 1 million pilgrims were arriving in Santiago each year. An entire industry of food hawkers, hoteliers, and trinket sellers awaited their arrival. They even had the world's first travel guide,

the Codex Calixtinus (published in the 1130s), to help them on their way.

Some made the journey in response to their conscience, to do penance for their sins against God, while others were sentenced by law to make the long walk as payment for crimes against the state.

Legend claims that St. James's body was transported secretly to the area by boat after his martyrdom in Jerusalem in AD 44. The idea picked up steam in 814, when a hermit claimed to see miraculous lights in the sky, accompanied by the sound of angels singing, on a wooded hillside near Padrón. Human bones were quickly discovered at the site, and immediately—and perhaps somewhat conveniently—declared to be those of the apostle (the bones may actually have belonged to Priscillian, the leader of a 4th-century Christian sect).

Word of this important find quickly spread across a relic-hungry Europe. Within a couple of centuries, the road to Santiago had become as popular as the other two major medieval pilgrimages, to Rome and to Jerusalem.

After the 12th century, pilgrim numbers began to gradually decline, due to the dangers of robbery along the route, a growing scepticism about the genuineness of St. James's remains, and the popular rise of science in place of religion.

SCALLOP SHELLS

The scallop shell can be bought at most hostels along the route. After carrying it on the Camino, pilgrims take it home with them as a keepsake.

HOW MANY PILGRIMS TODAY?

By the late 1980s, there were only about 3,000 pilgrims a year, but in 1993 the Galician government launched an initiative called the *Xacobeo* (i.e., Jacobean; the name James comes from the Hebrew word "Jacob"), to increase the number of visitors to the region, and the popularity of the pilgrimage soared. Numbers increased exponentially, and there have been over 100,000 annually since 2006. In holy years, when St. James Day (July 25) falls on a Sunday, the number of pilgrims usually doubles; the most recent holy year was 2010.

WHO WAS ST. JAMES?

After his martyrdom, the Apostle James was revered even more by some and made a saint.

St. James the Great, brother of St. John the Evangelist (author of the Gospel of John and the Book of Revelation), was one of Jesus's first apostles. Sent by Jesus to preach that the kingdom of heaven had come, he crossed Europe and ended up in Spain. Along the way, he saved a knight from drowning in the sea. As legend goes, the knight resurfaced, covered in scallop shells: this is why Camino pilgrims carry this seashell on their journey.

Legend has it that St. James was beheaded by King Herod Agrippa on his return to Judea in AD 44, but that he was rescued by angels and transported in a rudderless stone boat back to Spain, where his lifeless body was encased in a rock. James is said to have resurfaced to aid the Christians in the Reconquista Battle of Clavijo, gaining him the title of Matamoros, or Moor Killer.

When the body of St. James was found people came in droves to see his remains—the Spanish and Portuguese name for St. James is Santiago. The belief arose that sins would be cleansed through the penance of this long walk, an idea no doubt encouraged by the Church at the time.

THE PILGRIMAGE EXPERIENCE

A key Camino stop in La Rioja is the Romanesque-Gothic cathedral Santo Domingo de la Calzada, named for an 11th-century saint who had roads and bridges built along the route.

Not everyone does the route in one trip. Some split it into manageable chunks and take years to complete the whole course. Most, however, walk an average of 19 miles (30 kilometers) a day to arrive in Santiago after a month-long trek. Though not as obvious as Dorothy's yellow-brick road to Oz, the Camino path, which sometimes follows a mountain trail and other times goes through a village or across a field, is generally so well marked that most travelers claim not to need a map (bringing one is highly recommended, however). Travelers simply follow the route markers—gold scallop-shell designs on blue backgrounds posted on buildings or painted on rocks and trail posts.

Walking is not the only option. Bicycles are common along the Camino and will cut the time needed to complete the pilgrimage in half. Arriving in Santiago on horseback is another option, as is walking with a donkey in tow, carrying the bags.

Every town along the route has an official Camino *albergue*, or hostel, often in an ancient monastery or original pilgrim's hospice. They generally accommodate between 40 and 150 people. You can bunk for free—though a donation is expected—in the company of fellow walkers, but may only stay one night, unless severe Camino injuries prevent you from moving on. Be aware that these places can fill up fast. Walkers get first priority, followed by cyclists and those on horseback, with organized walking groups at the bottom of the pecking order. (Sometimes you need to wait until

THE MODERN PILGRIM

The modern pilgrim has technology at his or her fingertips. The official Xacabeo Web site (⊕ www.xacobeo.es/en) can not only help you plan your trip, with detailed route maps and hostel locations, it also has a Xacoblog where you can share videos, photos, and comments, as well as a forum for asking questions and getting feedback. A cell phone application helps you check routes, hostels, and sites to see while you're walking.

PILGRIMAGE ROUTES TO SANTIAGO

after lunch for them to open.) If there is no room at the official albergues, there are plenty of paid hostels along the route. Wherever you stay, get your Pilgrims' Passport, or *credencial*, stamped, as proof of how far you've walked.

A typical day on the Camino involves walking hard through the morning to the next village in time to get a free bed. The afternoon is for catching up with fellow pilgrims, having a look around town, and doing a bit of washing. The Spanish people you meet along the way and the camaraderie with fellow pilgrims is a highlight of the trip for many.

Some albergues serve a communal evening meal, but there is always a bar in town that offers a lively atmosphere and a cheap (8–10 euros) Pilgrim's set menu (quality and fare varies; it consists of three courses plus bread and beverage). Sore feet are compared, local wine is consumed, and new walking partners are found for the following day's stage. Just make sure you get back to the albergue before curfew, around 10 or 11, or you may find a locked door.

On the Camino, all roads lead to the cathedral at Santiago de Compostela.

THE END OF THE LINE

Arriving at the end of the Camino de Santiago is an emotional experience. It is common to see small groups of pilgrims, hands clasped tightly together, tearfully approaching the moss- and lichen-covered cathedral in Santiago's Plaza del Obradoiro. After entering the building through the Pilgrim's Door and hugging the statue of St. James, a special mass awaits them at midday, the highlight of which is seeing the *Botafumeiro*, a giant incense-filled censer, swinging from the ceiling.

Those that have covered more than 62 miles (100 kilometers) on foot, or twice that distance on a bicycle—as evidenced by the stamped passport—can then collect their Compostela certificate from the Pilgrim's office (near the cathedral, at Rúa do Vilar 1). Each day, the first 10 pilgrims to request it are entitled to free meals for three days at the Hostal de los Reyes Catolicos, once a pilgrims' hospice, and now a five-star parador hotel next to the cathedral. Travelers who want to experience more scenery and gain the achievement of going to the "ends of the Earth" continue on to Finisterre, at the western tip of Galicia's Atlantic coast, once thought to be the end of the world.

4

IN FOCUS EL CAMINO DE SANTIAGO

THE CAMINO FRANCÉS (FRENCH WAY)

The most popular of the seven main routes of the Camino de Santiago is the 497-mile (800-kilometer) Camino Francés (French Way), which starts in Spain (in Roncesvalles or Jaca) or in France (in St. Jean de Pied de Port) and

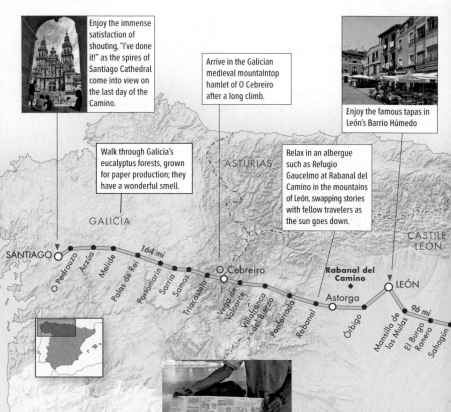

Enjoy the immense satisfaction of shouting, "I've done it!" as the spires of Santiago Cathedral come into view on the last day of the Camino.

Arrive in the Galician medieval mountaintop hamlet of O Cebreiro after a long climb.

Enjoy the famous tapas in León's Barrio Húmedo

Walk through Galicia's eucalyptus forests, grown for paper production; they have a wonderful smell.

Relax in an albergue such as Refugio Gaucelmo at Rabanal del Camino in the mountains of León, swapping stories with fellow travelers as the sun goes down.

Take home a record of your trip.

IF YOU DO IT

The busiest time on the Camino is in the summer months, from June to September, when many Spaniards make the most of their summer holidays journeying the route. That means crowded paths and problems finding a room at night, particularly if you start the Camino on the first few days of any month. This time of year is also very hot. To avoid the intense heat and crowds, many pilgrims choose to start the Camino in April, May, or September. Making the journey in winter is not advised, as Galicia and central Spain can get very cold and you'll face snow in the mountains. September is ideal because the heat has abated somewhat but the sun still rises early and stays out late.

You will need to be fully prepared for tough walking conditions before you set out. The most important part of your equipment is your hiking boots, which should be as professional as your budget allows and well worn in before you hit the trail. Other essentials include a good-quality—and

crosses the high meseta plains into Galicia. The Camino Norte (Northern Way), which runs through the woodlands of Spain's rugged north coast, is also gaining in popularity.

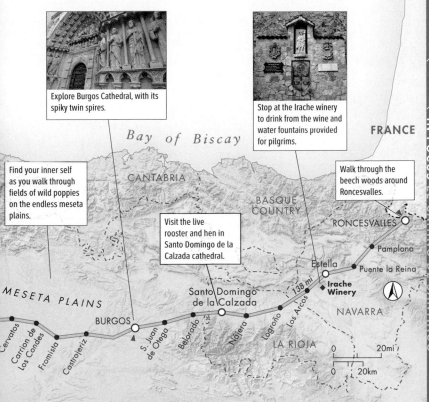

Explore Burgos Cathedral, with its spiky twin spires.

Stop at the Irache winery to drink from the wine and water fountains provided for pilgrims.

Find your inner self as you walk through fields of wild poppies on the endless meseta plains.

Walk through the beech woods around Roncesvalles.

Visit the live rooster and hen in Santo Domingo de la Calzada cathedral.

Bay of Biscay

CANTABRIA

BASQUE COUNTRY

FRANCE

RONCESVALLES

Pamplona

Estella

Puente la Reina

Irache Winery

NAVARRA

MESETA PLAINS

BURGOS

Santo Domingo de la Calzada

Cervatos · Carrion de Los Condes · Fromista · Castrojeriz · S. Juan de Ortega · Belorado · Najera · Logroño · Los Arcos

138 mi

LA RIOJA

0   20mi
0   20km

waterproof (it rains year-round in Galicia)—backpack, sleeping bag, sunscreen, and a medical kit, including Vaseline and blister remedies for sore feet. Don't forget a set of earplugs as well, to keep out the sound of other pilgrims' snores and dawn departures.

To get hold of your *credencial,* or pilgrim's passport, contact one of the Camino confraternity groups. These are not-for-profit associations formed by previous pilgrims to help those who are thinking about doing the Camino (see *www.csj.org. uk/other-websites.htm* for a list of groups). You can also pick up a passport at many of the common starting points, such as the abbey in Roncesvalles, the cathedral in Le Puy, and local churches and Amigos del Camino de Santiago in villages throughout Spain. In some cases, even police stations and city halls have them.

Many albergues throughout Spain also can provide you with a valid *credencial* for a small fee.

HELPFUL WEB SITES
www.xacobeo.es/en
www.caminodesantiago.me
www.csj.org.uk
www.caminoadventures.com
www.caminosantiagodecompostela.com

The Costa
da Morte and
Rías Baixas

O GROVE

31 km (19 miles) northwest of Pontevedra, 75 km (47 miles) south of Santiago.

ESSENTIALS

Visitor Information O Grove ✉ *Praza do Corgo s/n* ☎ *986/731415* ⊕ *www. turismogrove.es.*

EXPLORING

O Grove throws a famous shellfish festival the second week of October, but you can enjoy the day's catch in taverns and restaurants year-round. From O Grove, you can cross a bridge to the island of **A Toxa** (La Toja), famous for its spas—the waters are said to have healing properties. Legend has it that a man abandoned an ailing donkey here and found it up on all fours, fully rejuvenated, upon his return. The island's south side has a palm-filled garden anchored on one side by the **Capilla de San Sebastián,** a tiny church covered in cockleshells.

WHERE TO STAY

$$$ 🏨 **Gran Hotel La Toja.** Extravagant and exorbitant, this classic spa hotel
HOTEL is on the breezy island of La Toja, just across the bridge from O Grove.
Pros: glittering sea views; golf course; excellent services. **Cons:** rooms

can be noisy. $Rooms from: €160$ ⊠ Isla de la Toja ☎ 986/730025 ⊕ www.granhotellatoja.com ⇨ 199 rooms ¡⊙¡ No meals.

SPORTS AND THE OUTDOORS
GOLF
Club de Golf La Toja. Spectacular coastal views and verdant pine forests set the backdrop for players at the 18-hole Club de Golf La Toja. ⊠ Isla de La Toja ☎ 986/730158, 669/444888 ⊕ www.latojagolf.com.

CAMBADOS

34 km (21 miles) north of Pontevedra, 61 km (37 miles) southwest of Santiago.

This breezy seaside town has a charming, almost entirely residential old quarter and is the center for the full-bodied and fruity albariño, one of Spain's best white wines. The impressive main square, **Praza de Fefiñanes**, is bordered by an imposing bodega.

GETTING HERE AND AROUND
Cambados is less than an hour from Santiago de Compostela, to the north, and Vigo and Pontevedra, to the south, via the AP9.

WHERE TO EAT AND STAY
$$$$ ✕ **María José.** From a first-floor spot across from the parador, this long-
SEAFOOD established restaurant produces inventive dishes like scallop salad, mango soup with mascarpone ice cream, or salmon with anchovy mayonnaise. Specialties include *arroz de marisco caldoso* (shellfish, stock, and rice). $ Average main: €25 ⊠ C. San Gregorio 2–1 ☎ 986/542281 ⊙ No dinner Sun.–Tues.

$$$ ☷ **Parador de Cambados (El Albariño).** This airy mansion's rooms are
HOTEL warmly furnished with wrought-iron lamps, area rugs, and full-length wood shutters over small-pane windows. **Pros:** easily accessible; comfortable rooms; excellent dining. **Cons:** Wi-Fi is patchy in some rooms. $ Rooms from: €169 ⊠ Paseo Calzada s/n ☎ 986/542250 ⊕ www.parador.es ⇨ 58 rooms ¡⊙¡ No meals.

SHOPPING
Cucadas. Head to this crafts shop for its large selection of baskets, copper items, and lace. ⊠ Praza de Fefiñáns 8 ☎ 986/542511.

VIGO

31 km (19 miles) south of Pontevedra, 90 km (56 miles) south of Santiago.

Vigo's formidable port is choked with trawlers and fishing boats and lined with clanging shipbuilding yards. The city's gritty exterior gives way to a compact and lively center that clings to a tiered hill rising over an ancient Roman settlement. A jumbled mass of modernist buildings and granite, red-roofed fisherman houses hide the narrow streets of Vigo's appealing *casco vello* (old town). Vigo's highlights can be explored in a few hours.

From 10 to 3:30 daily, on **Rúa Pescadería** in the barrio called La Piedra, Vigo's famed *ostreras*—a group of rubber-gloved fisherwomen who

The coastline of Baiona is one of the first things the crew of Columbus's ship the *Pinta* saw when they returned from their discovery of America.

have been peddling fresh oysters to passersby for more than 50 years—shuck the bushels of oysters hauled into port that morning. Competition has made them expert hawkers who cheerfully badger all who walk by their pavement stalls. When you buy half a dozen (for about €8), the women plate them and plunk a lemon on top; you can then take your catch into any nearby restaurant and turn it into a meal. A short stroll southwest of the old town brings you to the fishermen's barrio of **El Berbés**. **Ribera del Berbés,** facing the port, has several seafood restaurants, most with outdoor tables in summer.

GETTING HERE AND AROUND
A small airport connects Vigo to a handful of destinations, like Madrid and Barcelona, but trains and buses are the best bet for transportation within Galicia. Northbound RENFE trains leave on the hour for Pontevedra, Santiago de Compostela, and A Coruña, making stops at the smaller towns in between. Monbus and ALSA also connect Vigo to the same destinations via the AP9, while AUTNA runs a daily shuttle south to Porto and its international airport, a 2½-hour trip.

ESSENTIALS
Bus Station Vigo ⊠ *Av. de Madrid 57* ☏ *986/373411.*

Train Station Vigo ⊠ *C. Areal s/n* ☏ *902/432343.*

Visitor Information Vigo ⊠ *Estación Marítima de Ría, Oficina 4, C. Cánovas del Castillo 3* ☏ *986/224757.*

EXPLORING

Islas Cíes. The Cíes Islands, 35 km (21 miles) west of Vigo, are among Spain's best-kept secrets. They form a pristine nature reserve that's one of the last unspoiled refuges on the Spanish coast. Starting on weekends in May and then daily June–late September, **Naviera Mar de Ons** (☎ *986/225272* ⊕ *www.mardeons.com*) runs about eight boats from Vigo's harbor (subject to weather conditions), returning later in the day, for the round-trip fare of €18.50 (tickets must be booked in advance on the website). The 45-minute ride brings you to white-sand beaches surrounded by turquoise waters brimming with marine life; there's also great birding. The only way to get around is your own two feet: it takes about an hour to cross the main island. If you want to stay overnight, there's a designated camping area. ⊠ *Estación Marítima* ⊕ *www.campingislascies.com*.

MARCO (*Museum of Contemporary Art*). Housed in a refurbished prison on Vigo's main shopping drag, this gallery hosts intriguing temporary exhibitions along with solo shows of featured artists. ⊠ *C. del Príncipe 54* ☎ *986/113900* ⊕ *www.marcovigo.com* 🎟 *Free* ⊗ *Tues.–Sat. 11–2:30 and 5–9, Sun. 11–2:30.*

Parque del Castro. South of Vigo's old town, this is a quiet, stately park with sandy paths, palm trees, mossy embankments, and stone benches. Atop a series of steps are the remains of an old fort and a *mirador* (lookout) with fetching views of Vigo's coastline and the Islas Cíes. Along its shady western side lies the Castro de Vigo, the remains of Vigo's first Celtic settlement, which dates back to the 3rd century BC. ⊠ *Av. Marqués de Alcedo, between Praza de España and Praza do Rei* 🎟 *Free* ⊗ *Castro de Vigo: May–Sept., Tues.–Sun. 10–1 and 5–8; Oct.– Apr., Tues.–Sun. 10–2 and 4–6.*

WHERE TO EAT AND STAY

$
SPANISH
✗ **Bar Cocedero La Piedra.** This jovial tapas bar is a perfect place to devour the freshest catch from the Rúa Pescadería fisherwomen, and it does a roaring lunch trade with Vigo locals. The chefs serve heaping plates of *mariscos* (shellfish) and scallops with roe at market prices. Fresh and fruity Albariño is the beverage of choice; the chummy, elbow-to-elbow crowd sits at round tables covered with paper, although on a nice day you might want to grab a seat on the terrace to enjoy your oysters and watch the old-town bustle. 💲 *Average main: €10* ⊠ *Rúa Pescadería 3* ☎ *986/431204.*

$$$$
SPANISH
✗ **El Mosquito.** Signed photos from the likes of King Juan Carlos and Julio Iglesias cover the walls of this elegant rose- and stone-wall restaurant, open since 1928. The brother-and-sister team of Ernesto and Carmiña has been at the helm for the last few decades, and specialties include *lenguado a la plancha* (grilled sole) and *navajas* (razor clams). The *tocinillos,* a sugary caramel flan, is also definitely worth trying. The restaurant's name refers to an era when wine arrived in wooden barrels: if mosquitoes gathered at the barrel's mouth, it held good wine. 💲 *Average main: €25* ⊠ *Praza da Pedra 4* ☎ *986/433570* ⊕ *www.elmosquitovigo.com* ⊗ *Closed Sun. and Aug. 15–Sept. 15.*

$
SPANISH
✗ **Fai Bistes.** A rare meat-lovers' paradise in the heart of Vigo's casco vello, Fai Bistes specializes in Galician food with an Italian twist, such

as *chuletón de buey* (T-bone steak) and *chorizo criollo* (sausages) grilled in a coal-fired oven and seasoned lightly with oregano, garlic, and salt. For the complete experience, order the enormous *parrillada mixta* (a mixed grilled meat platter consisting of pork ribs, beef ribs, criollo, roasted chicken, and steak) and accompany it with a glass of Rioja. [$] *Average main: €10* ✉ *Rúa Real 7* ☎ *986/229204* ⏲ *Closed Mon. No dinner Tues.*

$ TAPAS 🍴 **Tapas Areal.** This ample and lively bar flanked by ancient stone and exposed redbrick walls is a good spot for tapas and beer, as well as Albariño and Ribeiro. [$] *Average main: €8* ✉ *C. México 36* ☎ *986/418643* ⏲ *Closed Sun.*

$$$ B&B/INN 🏨 **Rectoral de Cobres.** This good-looking hotel combines contemporary design and handsomely aging rural charm; it was originally built as the village parsonage in 1729. **Pros:** quiet country charm; lots of activities. **Cons:** far from the city—you'll need a car. [$] *Rooms from: €160* ✉ *San Adrián de Cobres, Vilaboa* ☎ *986/673810* 🌐 *www.rectoral.com* 🛏 *8 rooms* 🍽 *No meals.*

NIGHTLIFE

The streets around Praza de Compostela and the pedestrian-only Rúa Montero Ríos, down toward the waterfront, come alive in the early evening for drinks and tapas. Night owls should check out the snazzier cocktail bars in the Areal district (along Rúa Areal and Rúa de Rosalía de Castro), or the pumping rock and indie scene in the Churruca neighborhood (Rúa Rogelio Abalde, Rúa Churruca), from midnight onwards, where you can often stumble across live music.

La Trastienda del Cuatro. Around the corner from Praza de Compostela, this wine bar and restaurant serves fresh and inventive "fusion tapas" and a good selection of wines to a lively, professional crowd. ✉ *Rúa de Pablo Morillo 4* ☎ *986/115881* 🌐 *www.latrastiendadelcuatro.com.*

SHOPPING

There's a large shopping center next to where the cruise ships dock. Close by you'll find A Pedra, the city's main market, where all manner of clothing and electrical goods are for sale. For souvenirs head to the old town, where there is an abundance of artisanal shops selling locally crafted leather, wood, and ceramic goods. On Rúa Cesteiros you can check out Vigo's famous handwoven baskets. Vigo's commercial shopping area is centered on Rúa Principe.

SPORTS AND THE OUTDOORS

There are several horse-riding clubs in the hills around Vigo. The Galician Equestrian Federation is an excellent source of information. And golfers can work on their game at the nearby Ría de Vigo Golf Club.

GOLF

Ría de Vigo Golf Club. The 18-hole Ría de Vigo Golf Club comes with breathtaking views overlooking the estuary and city. ✉ *San Lorenzo Domaio, Moaña, Pontevedra* ☎ *986/327051* 🌐 *www.riadevigogolf.com.*

HORSEBACK RIDING

Federación Hípica Gallega. This group has a list of all riding facilities in Galicia. ✉ *C. Fotógrafo Luís Ksado 17* ☎ *986/213800* 🌐 *www.fhgallega.com.*

Granja O Castelo. The Granjo O Castelo conducts horseback rides along the pilgrimage routes to Santiago from O Cebreiro and Braga (Portugal). ✉ *Castelo 41, Ponte Caldelas, Pontevedra* ☎ *986/425937, 608/381334* 🌐 *www.caminoacaballo.com.*

BAIONA

12 km (8 miles) southwest of Vigo.

At the southern end of the AP9 freeway and the Ría de Vigo, Baiona (*Bayona* in Castilian) is a summer haunt of affluent gallegos. When Columbus's *Pinta* landed here in 1492, Baiona became the first town to receive the news of the discovery of the New World. Once a castle, **Monte Real** is one of Spain's most popular paradores; walk around the battlements for superb views. Inland from Baiona's waterfront is the jumble of streets that make up Paseo Marítima: head here for seafood restaurants and lively cafés and bars. Calle Ventura Misa is one of the main drags. On your way into or out of town, check out Baiona's **Roman bridge.** The best nearby beach is Praia de América, north of town toward Vigo.

GETTING HERE AND AROUND

ATSA buses leave every half hour from Vigo, bound for Baiona and Nigrán. By car, take the AG57 from Vigo to the north or the PO340 from Tui to the southeast.

WHERE TO STAY

$$$$ HOTEL Fodor's Choice ★ 🏨 **Parador de Baiona.** This baronial parador, positioned on a hill within the perimeter walls of a medieval castle, has plush rooms, some with balconies and ocean views toward the Islas Cíes. **Pros:** stupendous medieval architecture; views of the *ría*; luxurious bathrooms. **Cons:** especially pricey for rooms with sea views; occasional plumbing problems. [$] *Rooms from: €290* ✉ *Ctra. de Baiona at Monterreal* ☎ *986/355000* 🌐 *www.parador.es* 🛏 *122 rooms* 🍴 *Breakfast.*

TUI

14 km (9 miles) southeast of Baiona, 26 km (16 miles) south of Vigo.

The steep, narrow streets of Tui, rich with emblazoned mansions, suggest the town's past as one of the seven capitals of the Galician kingdom. Today it's an important border town; the mountains of Portugal are visible from the cathedral. Across the river in Portugal, the old fortress town of Valença contains reasonably priced shops, bars, restaurants, and a hotel with splendid views of Tui.

GETTING HERE AND AROUND

From Vigo, take the scenic coastal route PO552, which goes up the banks of the Miño River along the Portuguese border or, if time is short, jump on the inland A55; both routes lead to Tui.

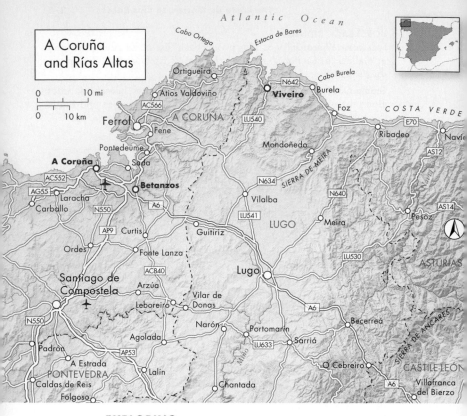

A Coruña
and Rías Altas

0   10 mi
0   10 km

Atlantic Ocean

Cabo Ortega
Estaca de Bares

Ortigueira
Átios Valdoviño
N642   Cabo Burela
Viveiro   Burela
Foz   *COSTA VERDE*

Ferrol
Fene   LU540
A CORUÑA   E70
Ribadeo   Navi

Pontedeume   Mondoñedo   AS12
A Coruña Sada   SIERRA DE MEIRA
AC552
AG55   Betanzos   N634
Laracha   A6   Vilalba   N640
Carballo N550   Pesoz
AP9   Curtis LU541   AS14
Ordes   Guitiriz LUGO   Meira
Fonte Lanza   *ASTURIAS*
AC840   LU530
Santiago de   Arzúa   Lugo
Compostela   Vilar de
          Leboreiro Donas
N550   Narón   A6   Becerreá
          Agolada   Portomarín   SIERRA DE ANCARES
Padrón   LU633 Sarriá
          AP53
A Estrada   Miño   O Cebreiro   *CASTILE-LEÓN*
PONTEVEDRA Lalín   Villafranca
Caldas de Reis   Chantada   A6   del Bierzo
Folgoso

EXPLORING

Cathedral de Santa María de Tui. A crucial building during the medieval wars between Castile and Portugal, Tui's 13th-century cathedral looks like a fortress. The cathedral's majestic cloisters surround a lush formal garden. ⊠ *Pl. de San Fernando* ☎ *986/600511* ⊠ *Free* ⏲ *June–Sept., daily 10:30–2 and 4–9; Oct.–May, daily 10:30–2 and 4–8.*

WHERE TO STAY

$$$
HOTEL
Parador de Tui. This stately granite-and-chestnut hotel on the bluffs overlooking the Miño is filled with local art, and the rooms are furnished with antiques. **Pros:** enticing gardens; varied services; good seafood. **Cons:** a bit of a walk from Tui proper; somewhat pricey. $ *Rooms from: €132* ⊠ *Av. Portugal s/n* ☎ *986/600300* ⊕ *www.parador.es* ⮎ *32 rooms* ⏲ *Closed Dec.–Feb.* ⦿ *No meals.*

A CORUÑA AND RÍAS ALTAS

Galicia's gusty and rainy northern coast has inspired poets to wax, well, poetic. The sun does shine between bouts of rain, though, suffusing town and country with a golden glow. North of A Coruña, the Rías Altas (Upper Estuaries) notch the coast as you head east toward the Cantabrian Sea.

A CORUÑA

57 km (35 miles) north of Santiago.

One of Spain's busiest ports, A Coruña (La Coruña in Castilian) prides itself on being the most progressive city in the region. The weather can be fierce, wet, and windy—hence the glass-enclosed, white-paned galleries on the houses lining the harbor.

GETTING HERE AND AROUND

The A9 motorway provides excellent access to and from Santiago de Compostela, Pontevedra, Vigo, and Portugal, while Spain's north coast and France are accessible along the N634.

Buses run every hour from A Coruña to Santiago. Trains also operate on an hourly basis to Santiago and Pontevedra from the city's San Cristóbal train station; Madrid can be reached in eight hours on high-speed Talgo trains.

Outside the old town, the city's local buses shuttle back and forth between the Dársena de la Marina seafront and more far-flung attractions, such as the Torre de Hércules lighthouse.

ESSENTIALS

Bus Station A Coruña ⊠ *Rúa Caballeros 21* ☎ *981/184335.*

Train Station A Coruña ⊠ *C. Joaquín Planells Riera s/n* ☎ *902/240505.*

Visitor Information A Coruña ⊠ *Oficina de Turismo, Pl. de María Pita 6* ☎ *981/923093* ⊕ *www.turismocoruna.com* ⊠ *Oficina de Turismo Torre de Hércules, Av. Navarra s/n* ☎ *981/923093.*

EXPLORING

TOP ATTRACTIONS

Paseo Marítimo. To see why sailors once nicknamed A Coruña *la ciudad de cristal* (the glass city), stroll the Paseo Marítimo, said to be the longest seaside promenade in Europe. Although the congregation of boats is charming, the real sight is across the street: a long, gracefully curved row of houses. Built by fishermen in the 18th century, they face *away* from the sea—at the end of a long day, these men were tired of looking at the water. Nets were hung from the porches to dry, and fish was sold on the street below. When Galicia's first glass factory opened nearby, someone thought to enclose these porches in glass, like the latticed stern galleries of oceangoing galleons, to keep wind and rain at bay. The resulting emblematic **glass galleries** spread across the harbor and eventually throughout Galicia.

Plaza de María Pita. The focal point of the *ciudad vieja* (old town), this stirring plaza has a north side that's given over to the neoclassical **Palacio Municipal,** or city hall, built 1908–12 with three Italianate domes. The **monument** in the center, built in 1998, depicts the heroine Maior (María) Pita. When England's Sir Francis Drake arrived to sack A Coruña in 1589, the locals were only halfway finished building the defensive Castillo de San Antón, and a 13-day battle ensued. When María Pita's husband died, she took up his lance, slew the Briton who tried to plant the Union Jack here, and revived the exhausted coruñeses, inspiring other women to join the battle.

Torre de Hércules. Much of A Coruña sits on a peninsula, on the tip of which sits this city landmark and UNESCO World Heritage Site—the oldest still-functioning lighthouse in the world. First installed during the reign of Trajan, the Roman emperor born in Spain in AD 98, the lighthouse was rebuilt in the 18th century and looks strikingly modern; all that remains from Roman times are inscribed foundation stones. Scale the 245 steps for superb views of the city and coastline—if you're here on a summer weekend, the tower opens for views of city lights along the Atlantic. Lining the approach to the lighthouse are sculptures depicting figures from Galician and Celtic legends. ✉ *Av. de Navarra s/n* ☏ *981/223730* ⊕ *www.torredeherculesacoruna.es* 🎟 *€3 (free Mon.)* ⊗ *Oct.–May, daily 10–6; June–Sept., daily 10–9.*

WORTH NOTING

Castillo de San Antón. At the northeastern tip of the old town is St. Anthony's Castle, a 16th-century fort that houses A Coruña's **Museum of Archaeology.** The collection includes remnants of the prehistoric Celtic culture that once thrived in these parts, including silver artifacts as well as pieces of the stone forts called *castros.* ✉ *Paseo Alcalde Francisco Vázquez 2* ☏ *981/189850* 🎟 *Free* ⊗ *Sept.–June, Tues.–Sat 10–7:30, Sun. 10–2:30; July and Aug., Tues.–Sat. 10–9, Sun. 10–3.*

Colexiata de Santa María do Campo. Called "St. Mary of the Field" because the building was once beyond the city's walls, this Romanesque beauty dates to the mid-13th century. The facade depicts the Adoration of the Magi; the celestial figures include St. Peter, holding the keys to heaven. Because of an architectural miscalculation the roof is too heavy for its supports, so the columns inside lean outward and the buttresses outside have been thickened. Inside is A Coruña's **Sacred Art Museum,** which holds a collection of gold and silver religious art dating from the 16th century onwards. ✉ *Placa Santa María 1* ☏ *981/203186* ⊗ *Oct.–May, Tues.–Fri. 10–1 and 3:30–5:30, Sat. 10–1; June–Sept., Tues.–Fri. 9–2, Sat. 10–1.*

Iglesia de Santiago. This 12th-century church, the oldest church in A Coruña, was the first stop on the *camino inglés* (English route) toward Santiago de Compostela. Originally Romanesque, it's now a hodgepodge that includes Gothic arches, a baroque altarpiece, and two 18th-century rose windows. ✉ *Pl. de la Constitución s/n.*

BEACHES

Playas Orzán and Riazor. A Coruña's sweeping Paseo Marítimo overlooks two excellent, well-maintained beaches, Playa del Orzán and Playa de Riazor. These long curves of fine golden sand tend to be busy in summer with chattering groups of local families and friends enjoying the milder climate. The area of Playa del Orzán in front of Hotel Meliá Pita is popular with surfers. Cross the Paseo Marítimo for a choice of cafés and restaurants with animated terraces, while on the seafront, kiosks sell ice cream and snacks. Keep in mind that this is the Atlantic, so test the temperature before taking the plunge. There is no natural shade, but you can rent hammocks and parasols. **Amenities:** food and drink; lifeguards; showers; toilets. **Best for:** surfing; swimming; walking. ✉ *Paseo Marítimo.*

WHERE TO EAT AND STAY

$$ ✕ **Adega O Bebedeiro.** Steps from the ultramodern Domus, this tiny res-
SPANISH taurant is beloved by locals for its authentic food. It feels like an old
farmhouse, with stone walls and floors, a fireplace, pine tables and
stools, and dusty wine bottles (*adega* is Gallego for bodega, or wine
cellar). Appetizers such as *pulpo con almejas al ajillo* (octopus with
clams in garlic sauce) are followed by fresh fish at market prices and
an ever-changing array of delicious desserts. Ⓢ *Average main: €17* ✉ *C.
Ángel Rebollo 34* ☎ *981/210609* ☉ *Closed Mon. and 1st wk in Jan.
No dinner Sun.*

$$$$ ✕ **Coral.** The window is an altar of shellfish, with varieties of mol-
SEAFOOD lusks and crustaceans you've probably never seen before. Inside,
wood-panel walls, crystal chandeliers, and 12 white-clad tables help
create an elegant yet casual experience. Specialties include octopus,
spider crab, barnacles, and *turbante de mariscos* (a platter—literally,
a "turban"—of steamed and boiled shellfish). Ⓢ *Average main: €30*
✉ *Callejón de la Estacada 9 at Av. Marina* ☎ *981/200569* ⊕ *www.
restaurantemarisqueriacoral.com* ☉ *Closed Sun.*

$$ ✕ **La Penela.** This contemporary, bottle-green dining room is the perfect
SEAFOOD place to feast on fresh fish while sipping Albariño—try at least a few
crabs or mussels with béchamel, a dish that La Penela's is locally famous
for. If shellfish isn't your speed, the roast veal is also popular. The restaurant occupies a modernist building on a corner of the lively Praza
María Pita. Some tables have views of the harbor, or you can eat in a
glassed-in terrace on the square. Ⓢ *Average main: €15* ✉ *Praza María
Pita 12* ☎ *981/209200* ☉ *Closed last 2 wks of Jan. No dinner Sun.*

$$$ ☷ **Hesperia Finisterre.** A favorite with businesspeople and families, the
HOTEL oldest and busiest of A Coruña's top hotels is only a few minutes walk
from the port, and is bursting with on-site amenities. **Pros:** port and city
views; helpful staff; good leisure activities. **Cons:** inconvenient outdoor
parking; unimpressive breakfast. Ⓢ *Rooms from: €139* ✉ *Paseo del
Parrote 2* ☎ *981/205400* ⊕ *www.hesperia-finisterre.com* ⌁ *92 rooms*
☷❶ *No meals.*

NIGHTLIFE

Begin your evening in the **Plaza de María Pita**: cafés and tapas bars pro-
liferate off its western corners and inland. **Calles Estrella, Franja, Riego
de Agua, Barrera, Galera,** and the **Plaza del Humor** have many bars, some
of which serve Ribeiro wine in bowls. Night owls head for the posh
and pricey clubs around **Praia del Orzán** (Orzán Beach), particularly
along Calle Juan Canalejo. For lower-key entertainment, the old town
has cozy taverns.

Mesón A Roda. Try the tapas (such as pulpo a la gallega, fried cala-
mari, and hearty stewed chicken) in the company of a high-spirited
evening crowd. ✉ *Calle Capitán Troncoso 8* ☎ *981/228671* ⊕ *www.
mesonaroda.com.*

SHOPPING

Calle Real and **Plaza de Lugo** have boutiques with contemporary fashions.
A stroll down **Calle San Andrés,** two blocks inland from Calle Real, or
Avenida Juan Flórez, leading into the newer town, can yield some sartorial

A Coruña is a major port town, but fashionistas might know it as where the first Zara clothing shop opened, back in 1975.

treasures. The local branch of **El Corte Inglés** is on Rúa Ramón y Cajal; it has a full range of sportswear, fashion, and accessories.

Adolfo Dominguez. Galicia has spawned some of Spain's top designers, including this one. ✉ *Av. Finisterre 3* ☎ *981/252539* ⊕ *www. adolfodominguez.com.*

Alfarería y Cerámica de Buño. The glazed terra-cotta ceramics from Buño, a town 40 km (25 miles) west of A Coruña on C552, are prized by aficionados—to see where they're made, drive out to Buño itself, where potters work in private studios all over town. Stop in to this store to see the results. ✉ *C. Barreiros s/n, Malpica de Bergantiños, Buño* ☎ *981/721658.*

José López Rama. Authentic Galician *zuecos* (hand-painted wooden clogs) are still worn in some villages to navigate mud; cobbler José López Rama has a workshop 15 minutes south of A Coruña in the village of Carballo. ✉ *Rúa do Muiño 7, Carballo* ☎ *981/701068.*

SPORTS AND THE OUTDOORS

In A Coruña and the surrounding area there are sports and leisure activities available year-round, including sailing, golf, and hiking. Swimmers and surfers can take advantage of the two kilometers of beach and coastline in the heart of the city.

GOLF

Real Club de Golf de La Coruña. Mackenzie Ross designed this tree-lined course, which has wide fairways and a scattering of lakeside holes. ✉ *La Zapateira s/n* ☎ *981/285200* ⊕ *www.clubgolfcoruna.com.*

HIKING
Nortrek. A one-stop source for advice and equipment for hiking, rock climbing, and skiing. ✉ *C. Inés de Castro 7* ☎ *981/151674.*

WATER SPORTS
Yatesport Coruña. Yachting can be a spectacular way for courageous and experienced sailors to discover hidden coastal sights. Yatesport Coruña rents private yachts and can arrange sailing lessons. The main office is in Vigo. ✉ *Marina Sada, Avenida del Puerto, 18 km (11 miles) east of A Coruña* ☎ *981/620624* ⊕ *www.yatesport.com.*

BETANZOS

25 km (15 miles) east of A Coruña, 65 km (40 miles) northeast of Santiago.

The charming, slightly ramshackle medieval town of Betanzos is still surrounded by parts of its old city wall. An important Galician port in the 13th century, it has silted up since then.

GETTING HERE AND AROUND
From Vigo and other destinations to the south, head north up the AP9; from A Coruña, head east for half an hour along the same motorway.

ESSENTIALS
Visitor Information Betanzos ✉ *Praza de Galicia 1* ☎ *981/776666.*

EXPLORING
Iglesia de San Francisco. The 1292 monastery of San Francisco was converted into a church in 1387 by the nobleman Fernán Pérez de Andrade. His magnificent tomb, to the left of the west door, has him lying on the backs of a stone bear and boar, with hunting dogs at his feet and an angel receiving his soul by his head. ✉ *Pl. de Fernán Pérez Andrade.*

Iglesia de Santiago. The tailors' guild put up the Gothic-style church of Santiago, which includes a Door of Glory inspired by the one in Santiago's cathedral. Above the door is a carving of St. James as the Slayer of the Moors. ✉ *Pl. de Lanzós* ☎ *981/776666 for tourist office.*

VIVEIRO

121 km (75 miles) northeast of Betanzos.

The once-turreted city walls of this popular summer resort are still partially intact. Two festivals are noteworthy here: the **Semana Santa** processions, when penitents follow religious processions on their knees, and the **Rapa das Bestas,** a colorful roundup of wild horses that occurs the first Sunday in July on nearby Monte Buyo.

GETTING HERE AND AROUND
Narrow-gauge FEVE trains connect Viveiro to Oviedo, Gijón, and other points eastward. By car, head east on the AP9 from A Coruña and then take the LU540 to Viveiro.

ESSENTIALS
Visitor Information Viveiro ✉ *Avda. Ramón Canosa s/n* ☎ *982/560079.*

WHERE TO STAY

$$
HOTEL
🖥 **Hotel Ego.** The view of the ría from this hilltop hotel outside Viveiro is unbeatable, and every room has one. **Pros:** hilltop views; relaxing public areas and spa. **Cons:** a little generic; the facade resembles an airport terminal. 💲 *Rooms from: €100* ✉ *Playa de Area 1, off N642, Faro (San Xiao)* ☎ *982/560987* ⊕ *www.hotelego.es* 🛏 *45 rooms* 🍴 *No meals.*

█
OFF THE
BEATEN
PATH
Cerámica de Sargadelos. Distinctive blue-and-white-glazed contemporary ceramics are made at Cerámica de Sargadelos, 21 km (13 miles) east of Viveiro. In July and August it's usually possible to watch artisans work (weekdays 9–1:15) but it's a good idea to call ahead and check first. ✉ *Ctra. Paraño s/n, Cervo* ☎ *982/557841* ⊕ *www.sargadelos.com* 🕒 *Weekdays 9:30–2 and 3–7:30, weekends and holidays 11–2 and 4–7.*

ASTURIAS

As you cross into the Principality of Asturias, the intensely green countryside continues, belying the fact that this is a major mining region once valued by the Romans for its iron- and gold-rich earth. Asturias is bordered to the southeast by the imposing Picos de Europa, which are best accessed via the scenic coastal towns of Llanes or Ribadesella.

LUARCA

105 km (65 miles) east of Luarca, 92 km (57 miles) northeast of Oviedo.

The village of Luarca is tucked into a cove at the end of a final twist of the Río Negro, with a fishing port and, to the west, a sparkling bay. The town is a maze of cobblestone streets, stone stairways, and whitewashed houses, with a harborside decorated with painted flowerpots.

GETTING HERE AND AROUND
To get to Oviedo, Gijón, and other destinations to the east, you can take a FEVE train or an ALSA bus; it's about a two-hour trip. By car, take the A8 west along the coast from Oviedo and Gijón or east up through Luarca from A Coruña.

ESSENTIALS
Visitor Information Luarca ✉ *Pl. de Alfonso X El Sabio s/n* ☎ *985/640083* ⊕ *www.turismoluarca.com.*

WHERE TO EAT AND STAY

$$$$
SPANISH
✕ **Casa Consuelo.** One of the most popular spots on Spain's northern coast, this restaurant first opened in 1935 and is famed for *merluza* (hake) served with the northern Spanish delicacy of *angulas* (baby eels); this comes to about €55 for two, depending on market prices. This dish is one among many highlights of the busy restaurant, whose name means "house of comfort"; portions are generous and there are some 12,000 bottles of wine to choose from in the bodega. Otur is also known for its great beach. 💲 *Average main: €25* ✉ *CN634, Km 511, Otur, 6 km (4 miles) west of Luarca* ☎ *985/641809* ⊕ *www.casaconsuelo.com* ⌂ *Reservations essential* 🕒 *Closed Mon.*

$
SEAFOOD
✕ **El Barómetro.** Decorated with an ornate barometer to gauge the famously unpredictable local weather, this small, family-run seafood

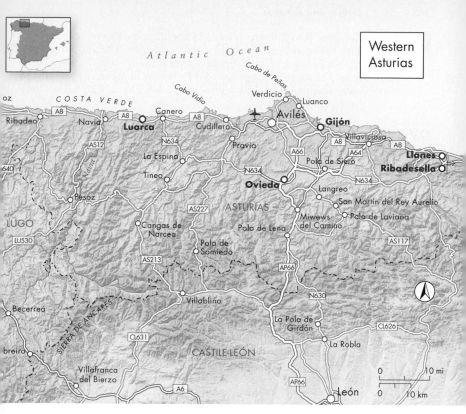

eatery is in a 19th-century building in the middle of the harborfront. In addition to an inexpensive menu of the day, there's also a good choice of local fresh fish, including *calamares* (squid) and *espárragos rellenos de erizo de mar* (asparagus stuffed with sea urchins). For a bit more money, you can dig into *bogavante*, a large-claw lobster. For dessert, the fig ice cream is delicious. $ *Average main: €12* ⊠ *Paseo del Muelle 4* ☎ *985/470662* ☾ *Closed Wed., Oct. 1–15, mid-May–mid-June.*

$$

SPANISH

✕ **Sport.** This friendly, family-run restaurant has been going since the 1950s. Here you will find large windows overlooking river views, walls adorned with artwork, and a kitchen adept at fabada. Sport specializes in seafood: locally caught fish or pulpo a la gallega are two of the tempting choices here. $ *Average main: €17* ⊠ *Calle Rivero 9* ☎ *985/641078* ☾ *Closed Jan. 6–Feb. No dinner Wed. and Sun.*

$$

B&B/INN

🏠 **Villa La Argentina.** Built in 1899 by a wealthy *indiano* (a Spaniard who made his fortune in South America), this charming Asturian mansion, on the hill above Luarca, offers modern apartments in the garden or Belle Époque suites in the main building. **Pros:** friendly staff; lovely gardens; peace and quiet. **Cons:** a short uphill walk from town. $ *Rooms from: €98* ⊠ *Urbanización Villar s/n* ☎ *985/640102* ⊕ *www. villalaargentina.com* 🛏 *9 rooms, 3 suites* ☾ *Closed early Jan.–mid-Mar.* ⦿ *No meals.*

EN ROUTE

Cudillero. The coastal road leads 35 km (22 miles) east of Luarca to this little fishing village, clustered around its tiny port. The emerald green of the surrounding hills, the bright blue of the water, and the white of the houses make this village one of the prettiest in Asturias. Seafood and cider restaurants line the central street, which turns into a boat ramp at the bottom of town.

OVIEDO

92 km (57 miles) southeast of Luarca, 50 km (31 miles) southeast of Cudillero, 30 km (19 miles) south of Gijón.

Inland, the Asturian countryside starts to look more prosperous. Wooden, tile-roofed horreos strung with golden bundles of drying corn replace the stark granite sheds of Galicia. A drive through the hills and valleys brings you to the capital city, Oviedo. Though primarily industrial, Oviedo has three of the most famous pre-Romanesque churches in Spain and a large university, giving it both ancient charm and youthful zest. Start your explorations with the two exquisite 9th-century chapels outside the city, on the slopes of Monte Naranco.

GETTING HERE AND AROUND

Oviedo is served by the A66 tollway, which links to Gijón and Avilés, where you can get on the A8 west to A Coruña or east toward Santander. Madrid is reached on the N630 south.

There are several buses per day to Gijón (30 minutes) and to Santiago and A Coruña (5 hours). Madrid is 5½ hours away by rail from Oviedo's RENFE station, situated on Calle Uría. The FEVE service operates across the north coast, with Gijón easily reached in half an hour and Bilbao just under eight hours away.

Local buses operate along the main arteries of Oviedo, between the train station and shopping areas, but skirt around the rim of the historical center, where Oviedo's oldest buildings are clustered in the labyrinth of streets around the Plaza Alfonso. Considering the short distances, walking is the best option, though taxis are inexpensive.

ESSENTIALS

Bus Station Oviedo ⊠ *Calle Pepe Cosmen.*

Train Station Oviedo ⊠ *C. Uría s/n* ☎ *902/240505.*

Visitor Information Oviedo ⊠ *Pl. de la Constitución 4* ☎ *985/213385* ⊕ *www.turismoviedo.es.*

EXPLORING

Cathedral. Oviedo's Gothic cathedral was built between the 14th and the 16th centuries around the city's most cherished monument, the **Cámara Santa** (Holy Chamber). King Ramiro's predecessor, Alfonso the Chaste (792–842), built it to hide the treasures of Christian Spain during the struggle with the Moors. Damaged during the Spanish Civil War, it has since been rebuilt. Inside is the gold-leaf **Cross of the Angels,** commissioned by Alfonso in 808 and encrusted with pearls and jewels. On the left is the more elegant **Victory Cross,** actually a jeweled sheath crafted in 908 to cover the oak cross used by Pelayo in the battle of Covadonga.

✉ *Pl. Alfonso II El Casto* ☎ *985/203117* ⊕ *www.catedraldeoviedo.es* 🎟 *Free; €5 combined ticket for Cámara Santa, cloister, and museum* ⊙ *Weekdays 10–2 and 4–7, Sat. 10–2 and 4–6.*

Museo Arqueológico de Asturias. Housed in the splendid Monastery of San Vicente (behind the cathedral), this museum contains fragments of pre-Romanesque buildings. ✉ *C. San Vicente 3–5* ☎ *985/208977* ⊕ *www.museoarqueologicodeasturias.com* 🎟 *Free* ⊙ *Wed.–Fri. 9:30–8, Sat. 9:30–2 and 5–8, Sun. and holidays 9:30–3.*

San Julián de los Prados (Santullano). Older than its more famous pre-Romanesque counterparts on Monte Naranco, the 9th-century church of Santullano has surprisingly well-preserved frescoes inside. Geometric patterns, rather than representations of humans or animals, cover almost every surface, along with a cross containing Greek letters. ✉ *C. Selgas 1* ☎ *607/353999* 🎟 *€1.20 (free Mon., without guide)* ⊙ *May–Sept., weekdays 10–12:30, Sat. 9:30–noon; Oct.–Apr., Mon. 10–12:30, Tues.–Sat. 9:30–11:30.*

Santa María del Naranco and San Miguel de Lillo. These two churches—the first with superb views and its plainer sister 300 yards uphill—are the jewels of an early architectural style called Asturian pre-Romanesque, a more primitive, hulking, defensive line that preceded Romanesque architecture by nearly three centuries. Commissioned as part of a summer palace by King Ramiro I when Oviedo was the capital of Christian Spain, these masterpieces have survived for more than 1,000 years. Tickets for both sites are available in the church of Santa María del Naranco. ✉ *Ctra. de los Monumentos, 2 km (1 mile) north of Oviedo* ☎ *638/260163* ⊕ *www.santamariadelnaranco.blogspot.com.es* 🎟 *€3, includes guided tour (free Mon., without guide)* ⊙ *Apr.–Sept., Tues.–Sat. 9:30–1 and 3:30–7, Sun. and Mon. 9:30–1; Oct.–Mar., Tues.–Sat. 10–2:30, Sun. and Mon. 10–12:30.*

WHERE TO EAT AND STAY

$$$$
SPANISH

✕**Casa Fermín.** Skylights, plants, and an air of modernity belie the age of this sophisticated restaurant, which opened in 1924 and is now in its fourth generation. The creative menu changes seasonally and might include *cigala en tocino ibérico con su caldo* (langoustines served in broth with ibérico ham), *lubina asada con salsa de su jugo y boletus* (roasted sea bass with a wild mushroom sauce), and wild game in season. There is also a tasting menu. 💲 *Average main: €24* ✉ *C. San Francisco 8* ☎ *985/216452* ⊕ *www.casafermin.com* ⊙ *Closed Sun.*

$$
SPANISH

✕**La Máquina de Lugones.** For the best fabada in Asturias, head 6 km (4 miles) outside Oviedo toward Avilés and stop at the farmhouse with the miniature train out front. The creamy fava beans of the signature dish are heaped with delicious hunks of morcilla sausage, chorizo, and bacon. To leave without trying the *arroz con leche* (rice pudding), though, would be a mistake. The simple, whitewashed dining room has attracted diners from across Spain for decades, some of whom think nothing of making a weekend trip just to eat here. 💲 *Average main: €15* ✉ *Av. Conde de Santa Bárbara 59, Lugones* ☎ *985/263636* ⊕ *www. lamaquinadelugones.es* ⊙ *Closed Sun. and Jun. 21–Jul. 20. No dinner.*

$ | **Barceló Oviedo Cervantes.** A playful revamp of this town house in the
HOTEL | city center added a neo-Moorish portico to the original latticed facade
and indulgent amenities like entertainment systems in some of the bathrooms. **Pros:** fun art and design features; central location close to train station. **Cons:** uninteresting views; confusing light switches. $ *Rooms from: €90* ⊠ *C. Cervantes 13* ☎ *985/255000* ⊕ *www.barcelo.com* ⇨ *72 rooms* ❍❘ *No meals.*

$$$ | **Hotel de la Reconquista.** Occupying an 18th-century hospice that's
HOTEL | emblazoned with a huge stone coat of arms, the luxurious Reconquista
Fodor's Choice | is by far the most distinguished hotel in Oviedo. **Pros:** spacious rooms;
★ | good breakfast. **Cons:** some rooms have uninteresting views; poorly lit rooms. $ *Rooms from: €135* ⊠ *C. Gil de Jaz 16* ☎ *985/241100* ⊕ *www.hoteldelareconquista.com* ⇨ *131 rooms, 11 suites* ❍❘ *No meals.*

NIGHTLIFE AND PERFORMING ARTS

Calle de Mon. Oviedo gets a little rowdy after dark on weekends, and there's plenty in the way of loud live music. Most of the bars are concentrated on Calle de Mon and its continuation, Calle Oscura. Calle Canóniga, off Calle de Mon, is another street with a number of bars. Calle Gascona is the place to try local Asturian cider in one of the popular *sidrerías* (cider bars) that line the street. Poured from a great height into the glass by the bartender, they impressively hit the mark each time—which also aerates the naturally still cider.

SHOPPING

Shops throughout the city carry **azabache jewelry** made of jet.

Casa Veneranda. Vacuum-packed fava beans are sold here. ⊠ *C. Melquíades Álvarez 23* ☎ *985/212454.*

SPORTS AND THE OUTDOORS

GOLF

Campo Municipal de Golf Las Caldas. This moderately difficult 18-hole course is surrounded by the rolling green hills of the Asturian countryside, just a few kilometers outside of Oviedo. ⊠ *La Premaña s/n, Las Caldas* ☎ *985/798132* ⊕ *www.golflascaldas.com.*

Real Club de Golf La Barganiza. These 18 holes have quite a backdrop: against the Picos de Europa mountain range. The course is 12 km (7 miles) outside of Oviedo. ⊠ *La Barganiza s/n, Siero* ☎ *985/742468* ⊕ *www.labarganiza.com.*

SKIING

San Isidro. In the Cantabrian Mountains, San Isidro has four chairlifts, eight drag lifts, and more than 22 km (14 miles) of slopes. ⊠ *Oficinas Sector Salencias, Puerto de San Isidro s/n, Puebla de Lillo, León, 69 km (43 miles) south of Oviedo* ☎ *987/731115* ⊕ *www.san-isidro.net.*

Valgrande Pajares. This resort has two chairlifts, eight slopes, and cross-country trails. ⊠ *Estación Invernal y de Montaña Valgrande-Pajares, Brañillín, Pajares, 60 km (37 miles) south of Oviedo* ☎ *985/957123, 985/957117* ⊕ *www.valgrande-pajares.com.*

GIJÓN

30 km (19 miles) north of Oviedo.

The Campo Valdés baths, dating back to the 1st century AD, and other reminders of Gijón's time as an ancient Roman port remain visible downtown. Gijón was almost destroyed in a 14th-century struggle over the Castilian throne, but by the 19th century it was a thriving port and industrial city. The modern-day city is part fishing port, part summer resort, and part university town, packed with cafés, restaurants, and sidrerías.

GETTING HERE AND AROUND

Oviedo is only 30 minutes away by ALSA bus or FEVE train, both of which run every half hour throughout the day. The A8 coastal highway runs east from Gijón to Santander, and west to Luarca, and eventually A Coruña.

ESSENTIALS

Bus Station Gijón ⊠ *C. Magnus Blikstad 1* ☎ *902/422242.*

Train Station Gijón ⊠ *C. Sanz Crespo s/n* ☎ *902/240505.*

Visitor Information Gijón ⊠ *C. Rodríguez San Pedro s/n* ☎ *985/341771* ⊕ *www.gijon.info.*

EXPLORING

Cimadevilla. This steep peninsula, the old fishermen's quarter, is now the hub of Gijón's nightlife. From the park at the highest point on the headland, beside Basque artist Eduardo Chillida's massive sculpture *Elogio del Horizonte* (In Praise of the Horizon), there's a panoramic view of the coast and city.

Muséu del Pueblu d'Asturies (*Museum of the People of Asturias*). Across the river on the eastern edge of town, past Parque Isabel la Católica, this rustic museum contains traditional Asturian houses, cider presses, a mill, and an exquisitely painted granary. Also here is the Museo de la Gaita (Bagpipe Museum). This collection of wind instruments explains their evolution both around the world and within Asturias. ⊠ *Paseo del Doctor Fleming 877, La Güelga s/n* ☎ *985/182960* ᠋ *€2.50 (free Sun.)* ⊘ *Oct.–Mar., Tues.–Fri. 9:30–6:30, weekends and public holidays 10–6:30; Apr.–Sept., Tues.–Fri. 10–7, weekends 10:30–7.*

Termas Romanas (*Roman baths*). Dating back to the time of Augustus, Gijón's baths are under the plaza at the end of the beach. ⊠ *Campo Valdés s/n* ☎ *985/185151* ᠋ *€2.50 (free Sun.)* ⊘ *Tues.–Fri. 9:30–2 and 5–7:30, weekends 10–2 and 5–7:30. Closed Jan. 1 and 6, Aug. 15, Christmas wk.*

BEACHES

The capital of the Costa Verde, Gijón, overlooks two attractive sandy beaches that are large enough to avoid overcrowding in summer.

Playa de Poniente. Tucked into the city's harbor, Playa de Poniente (Sunset Beach) is a horseshoe-shape curve of fine artificial sand and calm waters that's wonderful for a stroll as the evening draws in. **Amenities:**

lifeguards; showers; toilets. **Best for:** sunset; swimming; walking. ⊠ *C. Rodriguez San Pedro.*

Playa de San Lorenzo. Gijón's second popular beach, on the other side of the headland from Playa de Poniente, is a large stretch of golden sand backed by a promenade that extends from one end of town to the other. Across the narrow peninsula and the Plaza Mayor is the harbor, where the fishing fleet comes in with the day's catch. As long as the tide is out, you can sunbathe. The waves are generally moderate, although the weather and sea currents can be unpredictable along the northern coast. **Amenities:** food and drink; lifeguards; showers; toilets; water sports. **Best for:** sunset; swimming; walking. ⊠ *Av. Rufo García Rendueles.*

WHERE TO EAT AND STAY

$$$ ✕ **La Pondala.** This friendly, folksy, and romantic chalet was founded
SPANISH in 1891. When the weather cooperates, the terrace is a perfect spot for roast beef, rice with clams, or fabada asturiana. The restaurant is 3 km (2 miles) east of town. Ⓢ *Average main: €20* ⊠ *Av. de Dionisio Cifuentes 58* ☎ *985/369346* ⊕ *www.lapondala.com* ☾ *Closed Thurs. No dinner Sun.*

$$$ ⛉ **Parador de Gijón.** This is one of the simplest and friendliest paradores
HOTEL in Spain, and most of the rooms in the new wing have wonderful views over the lake or the park. **Pros:** park views; welcoming, down-to-earth staff; great food. **Cons:** austere guest rooms; fairly expensive; difficult to find; some distance from the old town. Ⓢ *Rooms from: €171* ⊠ *Av. Torcuato Fernández Miranda 15* ☎ *985/370511* ⊕ *www.parador.es* ⇌ *40 rooms* �🍴 *No meals.*

SPORTS AND THE OUTDOORS
BALLOONING
Globoastur. Stable weather conditions and outstanding mountain landscapes make the Picos de Europa ideal for year-round ballooning. ☎ *985/355818* ⊕ *www.globoastur.com* ⛁ *€139 per person for 1-hr flight (min. group of 6).*

GOLF
Campo Municipal de Golf La Llorea. Just outside Gijon, coastal Campo Municipal de Golf La Llorea presents wide fairways, which are punctuated by oak, hazelnut, and chestnut trees. ⊠ *N632, Km 62, no. 6779, La Llorea* ☎ *985/181030* ⊕ *www.golflallorea.com.*

Real Club de Golf de Castiello. A straightforward 18-hole course that runs through wooded and mountainous landscape. The club also has a swimming pool for adults and children. ⊠ *C. Camino del Golf 696, Bernueces* ☎ *985/366313* ⊕ *www.castiello.com.*

RIBADESELLA

67 km (40 miles) east of Gijón, 84 km (50 miles) northeast of Oviedo.

The N632 twists around green hills dappled with eucalyptus groves, allowing glimpses of the sea and sandy beaches below and the snow-capped Picos de Europa looming inland. This fishing village and beach resort is famous for its seafood, its cave, and the canoe races held on the Sella River the first Saturday of August.

GETTING HERE AND AROUND

FEVE and ALSA connect Ribadesella to Gijón and Oviedo by train and bus, a journey of 1½ to 2 hours. By car, you can take the A8 from Gijón and Oviedo past Villaviciosa to Ribadesella.

ESSENTIALS

Visitor Information Ribadesella ✉ *Paseo Princesa Letizia s/n* ☎ *985/860038.*

EXPLORING

Centro de Arte Rupestre Tito Bustillo. Discovered in 1968, the cave here has 20,000-year-old paintings on a par with those in Lascaux, France, and Altamira. Giant horses and deer prance about the walls. To protect the paintings, no more than 375 visitors are allowed inside each day, so reservations are essential. The guided tour is in Spanish. There's also a **museum** of Asturian cave finds, open year-round. ✉ *Av. de Tito Bustillo s/n* ☎ *902/306600* 🌐 *www.centrotitobustillo.com* 🎫 *€7.10, includes museum; €5.20 museum only* 🕒 *Cave: Apr.–Nov., Wed.–Sun. 10:15–5. Museum: July–mid-Sept., Wed.–Sun. 10–7; mid-Sept.–Dec. and Feb.–June, Wed.–Fri. 10–2:30 and 3:30–6, weekends 10–2:30 and 4–7.*

BEACHES

Playa Santa Marina. To the west of the Sella River's estuary, which divides the town, this gentle curve of golden sand is one of the prettiest beaches in Asturias, tucked neatly beneath the town's seafront promenade, which is lined with elegant 20th-century mansions. Moderate waves provide safe swimming conditions, although, as with all of Spain's Atlantic-facing beaches, currents and weather can be unpredictable. In high season (particularly in August), the beach can get very busy. This part of the coast is not called the "dinosaur coast" for nothing—over by the Punta'l Pozu Viewpoint, you can see footprints embedded in the rocks and cliff faces where dinosaurs left their mark millions of years ago. The amenities listed are only open between June and September. **Amenities:** food and drink; lifeguards; showers; toilets. **Best for:** sunbathing; surfing; swimming. ✉ *Paseo Agustin de Argüelles Marina.*

WHERE TO STAY

$$ B&B/INN 🏨 **Hotel Ribadesella Playa.** Spending a night in this quirky, restored, turn-of-the-20th-century mansion on the beach is unusually pleasant and peaceful: it's family run, and has a timeless, stately charm that may remind you of black-and-white European art films. **Pros:** proximity to the Tito Bustillo cave and the beach; lovely views of the Cantabrian sea. **Cons:** limited availability in high season. [$] *Rooms from: €125* ✉ *C. Ricardo Cangas 3* ☎ *985/860715* 🌐 *www.hotelribadesellaplaya.com* 🛏 *17 rooms* 🕒 *Closed Nov.–Mar.* 🍴 *Breakfast.*

LLANES

40 km (25 miles) east of Ribadesella.

This beach town is on a pristine stretch of the Costa Verde. The shores in both directions outside town have vistas of cliffs looming over white-sand beaches and isolated caves. A long canal connected to a small harbor cuts through the heart of Llanes, and along its banks rise colorful houses with glass galleries against a backdrop of the Picos de Europa. At the daily port-side fish market, usually held around 1 pm, vendors display heaping mounds of freshly caught seafood.

GETTING HERE AND AROUND

The scenic A8 coastal route from Gijón continues past Villaviciosa and Ribadesella and then winds through Llanes before heading east towards Santander. FEVE trains and ALSA buses make the trip in 2 to 3½ hours.

ESSENTIALS

Visitor Information Llanes ⊠ *Casa de Cultura, C. Posada Herrera 15* ☎ *985/400164.*

EXPLORING

Basílica de Santa María del Conceyu. This 13th-century church, which rises over the square here, is an excellent example of Romantic Gothic architecture. ⊠ *Pl. de Christo Rey.*

Mirador Panorámico La Boriza. Dotting the Asturian coast east and west of Llanes are *bufones* (blowholes), cavelike cavities that expel water when waves are sucked in. Active blowholes shoot streams of water as high as 100 feet into the air; although it's hard to predict when this will happen, as it depends on the tide and the size of the surf. They are clearly marked so you can find them, and there are barriers to protect you when they expel water. There's a blowhole east of Playa Ballota; try to watch it in action from this mirador east of Llanes, between the villages of Cué and Andrin, near to the entrance of the Campo de Golf Municipal de Llanes. If you miss it, the view is still worth a stop—on a clear day you can see the coastline all the way east to Santander.

Plaza Cristo Rey. Peaceful and well-conserved, this plaza marks the center of the old town, which is partially surrounded by the remains of its medieval walls.

BEACHES

Playa Ballota. Just 1 km (½ mile) east of Llanes is one of the area's most secluded beaches, the pristine Playa Ballota, with private coves and one of the few stretches of nudist sand in Asturias. **Amenities:** none. **Best for:** solitude; nudists; swimming; walking. ⊠ *Camino Ballota.*

Playa del Sablón. Steps from the old town is the protected Playa del Sablón (whose name derives from the Asturian word for "sand"), a little swath of beach that gets crowded on weekends. **Amenities:** food and drink; lifeguards; showers; toilets. **Best for:** swimming ⊠ *C. Sablón.*

Playa Torimbia. Farther west of Llanes is the partially nudist Playa de Torimbia, a wild, virgin beach as yet untouched by development. This one you can reach only via a footpath—roughly a 15-minute walk. A secluded crescent of fine, white sand and crystal-clear waters, backed by Asturias' green hills tumbling down upon it, makes this one of the region's most picturesque beaches. Winds can be strong, and there is no real infrastructure. **Amenities:** none. **Best for:** solitude; nudists; swimming; walking. ⊠ *Off C. Niembru, 8 km (5 miles) west of Llanes.*

Playa Toró. On the eastern edge of town is the Playa de Toró, where fine white sands are peppered with unique rock formations. This pristine beach is ideal for sunbathing and families. **Amenities:** lifeguards; showers; toilets. **Best for:** swimming. ✉ *Av. de Toró.*

WHERE TO EAT AND STAY

$ SEAFOOD 🍴 **La Casa del Mar.** Llanes has prettier, cleaner, and less noisy places to enjoy seafood, but if you feel like rubbing shoulders with Asturian fishermen and eating their catch cooked just the way they like it, then this spot by the port, guarded by a parrot named Paco, is for you. The glassed-in terrace has a view of the small harbor bobbing with boats, and the menu offers such local classics as baby squid in ink, spider crab, seafood meatballs, and razor clams, all with a minimum of fuss but maximum value. [$] *Average main: €10* ✉ *Calle El Muelle 4, C. Marinero* ☎ *985/401215.*

$$ B&B/INN 🏨 **La Posada de Babel.** This family-run inn just outside Llanes stands among oak, chestnut, and birch trees on the edge of the Sierra de Cuera. **Pros:** extremely amiable staff; comfy base for hiking. **Cons:** slippery stairs to certain rooms; closed in winter. [$] *Rooms from: €124* ✉ *La Pereda s/n, 4 km (2½ miles) southwest of Llanes* ☎ *985/402525* 🌐 *www.laposadadebabel.com* 🛏 *10 rooms, 2 suites* 🕒 *Closed Dec.–Mar.* 🍽 *No meals.*

SPORTS AND THE OUTDOORS

GOLF

Club de Golf La Cuesta. This picturesque 18-hole course lies between the Picos de Europa and Cantabrian Sea; its location, 325 feet above sea level, comes with excellent views. ✉ *C. Las Barqueras s/n* ✥ *3 km (2 miles) east of Llanes, between Cue and Andrin* ☎ *985/403319* 🌐 *www.golflacuesta.com.*

THE PICOS DE EUROPA

With craggy peaks soaring up to the 8,688-foot Torre Cerredo, the northern skyline of the Picos de Europa has helped seafarers and fishermen navigate the Bay of Biscay for ages. To the south, pilgrims on their way to Santiago enjoy distant but inspiring views of the snowcapped range from the plains of Castile between Burgos and León. Over the years, rain and snow have created canyons plunging 3,000 feet, natural arches, caves, and sinkholes (one of which is 5,213 feet deep).

The Picos de Europa National Park, covering 646.6 square km (250 square miles), is perfect for climbers and trekkers: you can explore the main trails, hang glide, ride horses, cycle, or canoe. There are two adventure-sports centers in Cangas de Onís, near the Roman Bridge.

CANGAS DE ONÍS

25 km (16 miles) south of Ribadesella, 70 km (43 miles) east of Oviedo.

The first capital of Christian Spain, Cangas de Onís is also the unofficial capital of the Picos de Europa National Park. Partly in the narrow valley carved by the Sella River, it has the feel of a mountain village.

ESSENTIALS

Visitor Information Cangas de Onís ✉ *Av. de Covadonga 1* ☎ *985/846135.*

Hiking in the Picos de Europa

EXPLORING

Medieval Bridge. A high, humpback medieval bridge (also known as the Puente Romano, or Roman Bridge, because of its style) spans the Sella River gorge with a reproduction of Pelayo's Victory Cross, or La Cruz de la Victoria, dangling underneath.

Picos de Europa Visitor Center. To help plan your rambles, consult the scale model of the park outside the visitor center, while staff inside can advise you on suitable routes. There are various stores on the same street that sell maps and guidebooks, a few in English. ✉ *Casa Dago, Av. Covadonga 33* ☎ *985/848614.*

WHERE TO EAT AND STAY

$$$

SPANISH

✕ **Restaurante Los Arcos.** This busy tavern on one of the town's main squares has lots of polished wood and serves local cider, fine Spanish wines, and sizzling T-bone steaks. The mouth-watering dishes include *revuelto de morcilla* (scrambled eggs with blood sausage), which is served on *torto de maíz* (a corn pastry base), and *pulpo de pedreu sobre crema fina de patata, oricios y germinados ecologicos* (octopus with creamed potato, sea urchins, and bean sprouts). Their well-priced lunchtime menu is a real draw. $ *Average main: €20* ✉ *Pl. del Ayuntamiento 3* ☎ *985/849277* ⊕ *www.restaurantelosarcos.es.*

$

B&B/INN

🏨 **Hotel Posada del Valle.** British couple Nigel and Joanne Burch converted a rustic, 19th-century, stone-wall farmhouse into an idyllic guesthouse; built near the side of a hill, it faces out over spectacular panoramas of the Picos. **Pros:** surrounded by nature; views of the Picos; wealth of local knowledge at your fingertips. **Cons:** remote and difficult to find; breakfast costs extra. $ *Rooms from: €79* ✉ *Collía, Arriondas*

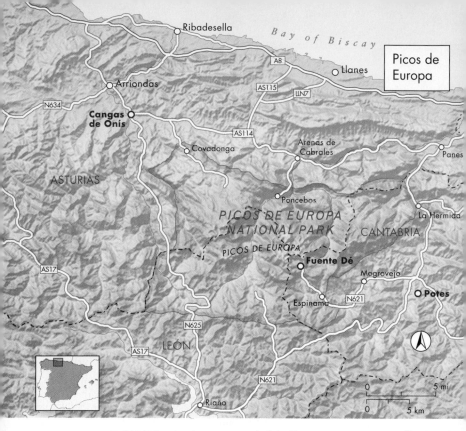

Picos de Europa

☎ *985/841157* ⊕ *www.posadadelvalle.com* ⇋ *12 rooms* ⊙ *Closed Nov.–Mar.* ⏀ *No meals.*

$$ ⌂ **Parador de Cangas de Onís.** On the banks of the Sella River just
HOTEL west of Cangas, this friendly parador is made up of an 8th-century
Benedictine monastery and a modern wing: the older building has 11
period-style rooms. **Pros:** helpful staff; gorgeous riverside location with
mountain views; oodles of history. **Cons:** limited menu; chilly corridors.
$ *Rooms from: €111* ⊠ *Monasterio de San Pedro de Villanueva, Vil-
lanueva s/n, Ctra. N625* ⊕ *From N634 take a right turn for Villanueva*
☎ *985/849402* ⊕ *www.parador.es* ⇋ *64 rooms* ⏀ *Breakfast.*

SPORTS AND THE OUTDOORS

The tourist office in Cangas de Onís can help you organize a Picos de
Europa trek. The Picos visitor center in Cangas has general information,
route maps, and a useful scale model of the range.

HIKING

AsturSellaAdventure. Part of the Hotel Montevedro, AsturSellaAdven-
ture can organize canoeing, canyon rappelling, spelunking, horseback
riding, and Jeep trips. ⊠ *Ramón Prada Vicente 5, Cangas de Onís*
☎ *985/848079* ⊕ *www.astursellaaventura.com.*

POTES

51 km (31 miles) southwest of San Vicente de la Barquera, 115 km (69 miles) southwest of Santander, 173 km (104 miles) north of Palencia, 81 km (50 miles) southeast of Cangas de Onís.

Known for its fine cheeses, the region of La Liébana is a highland domain also worth exploring for other reasons. Potes, the area's main city, is named for its ancient bridges and surrounded by the stunning 9th-century **monasteries** of Santo Toribio de Liébana, Lebeña, and Piasca. The gorges of the Desfiladero de la Hermida pass are 13 km (8 miles) north, and the rustic town of Mogrovejo is on the way to the vertiginous cable car at Fuente Dé, 10 km (6 miles) west of Potes.

GETTING HERE AND AROUND

Potes is just over 2 hours from Gijón and Oviedo via the A8, and 1½ hours from Santander via the A8 and N621.

ESSENTIALS

Visitor Information Potes ⊠ *Pl. de la Serna s/n* ☎ *942/730787.*

EXPLORING

El Mirador del Cable. As you approach the parador of Fuente Dé, at the head of the valley northwest of the hamlet of Espinama. you'll see a wall of gray rock rising 6,560 feet straight into the air. Visible at the top is the tiniest of huts: El Mirador del Cable (the cable-car lookout point). Get there via a 2,625-foot funicular (€16 round-trip). At the top, you can hike along the Ávila Mountain pasturelands, rich in wildlife, between the central and eastern massifs of the Picos. There's an official entrance to Picos de Europa National Park here. ☎ *942/736610* ⊕ *www.cantur. com* ⊙ *Daily 10–6; hrs vary Jan. 10–Feb. 10.*

WHERE TO EAT AND STAY

$$
SPANISH
✕ **El Bodegón.** A simple, friendly, and cozy space awaits behind the ancient stone facade of this restaurant, 200 meters from the main plaza. Part of the house is original, but much has been renovated, providing an attractive combination of traditional mountain design and modern construction. The menu focuses on standard highland comfort food, such as a delicious *cocido montañes* (mountain stew of sausage, garbanzo beans, and vegetables) at good prices. The lunch menu is one of the best values for miles around. $ *Average main: €15* ⊠ *C. San Roque 4* ☎ *942/730247* ⊙ *Closed Wed.*

$
B&B/INN
Hotel Valdecoro. In this family-run mountain house, which faces the main road through town, an efficient staff and guest rooms with modern appointments make for a pleasant stay. **Pros:** cozy, mountain feel; fine rustic restaurant. **Cons:** on the main road; rooms are efficient but lackluster. $ *Rooms from: €75* ⊠ *C. Roscabao 5* ☎ *942/730025* ⊕ *www. hotelvaldecoro.com* ⤳ *41 rooms* ⊙| *Breakfast.*

$$
B&B/INN
Parador de Fuente Dé. Although it has a good restaurant, this modern parador is somewhat spartan. It's still a fine no-frills base for serious climbers and walkers. **Pros:** mountainside location; next to cable car. **Cons:** simply furnished; limited access in winter snow. $ *Rooms from: €110* ⊠ *Crta. de Fuente Dé s/n, 23 km (14 miles) west of Potes*

🕾 *942/736651* ⊕ *www.parador.es* 🗪 *77 rooms* ☉ *Closed Dec.–Mar.*
¶◎¶ *No meals.*

CANTABRIA

Historically part of Old Castile, the province of Cantabria was called Santander until 1984, when it became an autonomous community. The most scenic route from Madrid via Burgos to Santander is the slow but spectacular N62, past the Ebro reservoir. Faster and safer is the N627 from Burgos to Aguilar de Campóo connecting to the A67 freeway down to Santander.

SANTANDER

390 km (242 miles) north of Madrid, 154 km (96 miles) north of Burgos, 116 km (72 miles) west of Bilbao, 194 km (120 miles) northeast of Oviedo.

One of the great ports on the Bay of Biscay, Santander is surrounded by beaches that can often be busy, but it still manages to avoid the package-tour feel of so many Mediterranean resorts. A fire destroyed most of the old town in 1941, so the rebuilt city looks relatively modern. The town gets especially fun and busy in summer, when its summer-university community and music-and-dance festival fill the city with students and performers.

From the 1st to the 4th century, under the Romans, Santander—then called Portus Victoriae—was a major port. Commercial life accelerated between the 13th and 16th century, but the waning of Spain's naval power and a series of plagues during the reign of Felipe II caused Santander's fortunes to plummet in the late 16th century. Its economy revived after 1778, when Seville's monopoly on trade with the Americas was revoked and Santander entered fully into commerce with the New World. In 1910 the Palacio de la Magdalena was built by popular subscription as a gift to Alfonso XIII and his queen, Victoria Eugenia, lending Santander prestige as one of Spain's royal watering holes.

Modern-day Santander benefits from several promenades and gardens, most of which face the bay. Walk east along the Paseo de Pereda, the main boulevard, to the Puerto Chico, a small yacht harbor. Then follow Avenida Reina Victoria to find the tree-lined park paths above the first of the city's beaches, Playa de la Magdalena. Walk onto the Península de la Magdalena to the Palacio de la Magdalena, today the summer seat of the University of Menéndez y Pelayo. Beyond the Magdalena Peninsula, wealthy locals have built mansions facing the long stretch of shoreline known as El Sardinero, Santander's best beach.

GETTING HERE AND AROUND

Santander itself is easily navigated on foot, but if you're looking to get to El Sardinero beach, take the bus from the central urban transport hub at Jardines de Pereda.

ESSENTIALS

Bus Station Santander ✉ *C. Navas de Tolosa s/n* ☎ *942/211995.*

Train Station Santander ✉ *Pl. de las Estaciones s/n* ☎ *902/240505.*

Visitor Information Santander ✉ *Mercado del Este, Hernán Cortés 4* ☎ *942/310708.*

EXPLORING

Catedral de Santander. The blocky cathedral marks the transition between Romanesque and Gothic. Though largely rebuilt in the neo-Gothic style after serious damage in the town's 1941 fire, the cathedral retained its 12th-century crypt. The chief attraction here is the tomb of Marcelino Menéndez y Pelayo (1856–1912), Santander's most famous literary figure. The cathedral is across Avenida de Calvo Sotelo from the Plaza Porticada. ✉ *Calle de Somorrostro s/n* ☎ *942/226024* 🖙 *Free* ⊙ *Daily 10–1 and 4:30–7:30 (except during services).*

Museo de Arte Moderno y Contemporáneo de Santander y Cantabria (*MAS*). The former Museo de Bellas Artes is now a bright and modern art space with a constantly rotating collection of sculptures, photography, paintings, and installations from up-and-coming artists, many of them local. ✉ *Calle Rubio 6* ☎ *942/203120* ⊕ *www.museosdesantander. com* 🖙 *Free* ⊙ *Mid-June–mid-Sept., Tues.–Sat. 10:30–1 and 6–9, Sun. 11–1:30; mid-Sept.–mid-June, Tues.–Sat. 10–1:30 and 5:30–9, Sun. 11–1:30.*

Biblioteca Menéndez y Pelayo. Next door to the Museo de Arte Moderno y Contemporáneo this library, with some 50,000 volumes, also holds the study of the scholarly writer Marcelino Menéndez y Pelayo (1856–1912), whose life is celebrated in an adjoining museum. ✉ *Calle Rubio 6* ☎ *942/234493 for museum, 942/234534 for library* 🖙 *Free* ⊙ *Library weekdays 9–1:30. Museum: June–Sept., weekdays 10:30–1 and 6:30–8, Sat. 10:30–1; Oct.–May, weekdays 10:30–1 and 5:30–8, Sat. 10:30–1.*

Plaza Porticada. In the old city, the center of life is this unassuming little square, officially called the Plaza Velarde. In August it's the venue for Santander's star event, the outdoor International Festival of Music and Dance.

BEACHES

Playa El Sardinero. Gently curving round the bay from the Magdalena Peninsula, Santander's longest and most popular beach has a full range of amenities and fine, golden sands. Although this northeast-facing stretch is exposed, moderate waves in summer make it generally fine for bathing, but its location on the Cantabrian coast keeps the water very cold. In winter months it is a favorite with surfers, particularly the part of the beach in front of Hotel Cuiqui. Be sure to arrive at the beach via the sun-dappled Piquío Gardens, where terraces filled with flowers and trees lead the way down to the beach. **Amenities:** food and drink; lifeguards; showers; toilets; water sports. **Best for:** sunbathing; surfing; swimming; walking.

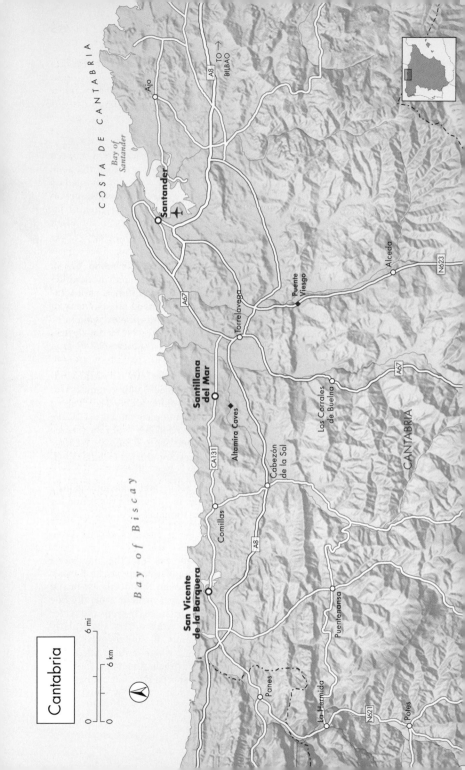

Cantabria

COSTA DE CANTABRIA

Bay of Biscay

Bay of Santander

Ajo

Santander

TO BILBAO →

A8

A67

Alceda

N623

Puente Viesgo

Torrelavega

Santillana del Mar

A67

Altamira Caves

Los Corrales de Buelna

CA131

Cabezón de la Sal

CANTABRIA

Comillas

A8

San Vicente de la Barquera

Puentenansa

Panes

La Hermida

Potes

N62

0   6 mi
0   6 km

WHERE TO EAT AND STAY

$$ SPANISH 🍴 **Bodega del Riojano.** The paintings on wine-barrel ends that decorate this classic restaurant have given it the nickname Museo Redondo (Round Museum). The building dates back to the 16th century, when it was a wine cellar, which you can see in the heavy wooden beams overhead and the rough and rustic tables. With culinary specialties from La Rioja and fresh seafood from the Bay of Biscay, there is much to choose from. The menu changes daily and seasonally, but the fish of the day is a sure bet. [$] *Average main: €17* ✉ *C. Río de la Pila 5* ☎ *942/216750* 🕓 *No dinner Sun.*

$$$$ SPANISH 🍴 **El Serbal.** Five blocks from Santander's marina, this elegant dining room maintains an impressive attention to detail: order the tasting menu, for instance, and you'll be served no fewer than five varieties of olive oil to accompany a delicious assortment of breads. Only the freshest ingredients are used, and the chef makes tasty use of Santander's famed seafood. The menu may feature cod *al pil pil* (a Biscayan sauce of olive oil and garlic) or suckling pig roasted with orange and flambéed with peach. The tasting menu is expensive, but worth it for the quality of the food and the experience. [$] *Average main: €24* ✉ *C. Andrés del Rio 7* ☎ *942/222515* 🌐 *www.restaurantesdesantander.es* ✍ *Reservations essential* 🕓 *Closed Mon. (except in Aug.). No dinner Sun.*

$$$ HOTEL 🏨 **Abba Santander.** Occupying the building of the historic Hotel México, Abba Santander has gradually been transformed from a family-run inn into a chain hotel with contemporary interiors and modern conveniences. **Pros:** cheerful service; central location. **Cons:** slippery bathroom floors; busy part of town. [$] *Rooms from: €130* ✉ *C. Calderón de la Barca 3* ☎ *942/212450, 902/153163* 🌐 *www.abbasantanderhotel.com* 🛏 *37 rooms* 🍽 *No meals.*

$$$ HOTEL 🏨 **Bahía.** Classical style combined with state-of-the-art technology and contemporary furnishings make this Santander's finest hotel—a grand and comfortable perch overlooking the water. **Pros:** in the center of town; great for watching maritime traffic. **Cons:** nearby cathedral bells can be noisy if you're not on the sea side of the hotel; not right on the beach. [$] *Rooms from: €177* ✉ *Av. Alfonso XIII 6* ☎ *942/205000* 🌐 *www.hotelbahiasantander.com* 🛏 *188 rooms* 🍽 *No meals.*

$$ B&B/INN 🏨 **Las Brisas.** Jesús García runs his family's century-old mansion as an upscale, cottage-style hotel by the sea. **Pros:** close to the shore; fresh and briny Atlantic air; friendly and helpful staff. **Cons:** mildly disorganized; some rooms are a bit cramped. [$] *Rooms from: €120* ✉ *C. la Braña 14, El Sardinero* ☎ *942/275011* 🌐 *www.hotellasbrisas.net* 🛏 *13 rooms* 🕓 *Closed Dec. 15–Feb. 15.* 🍽 *Breakfast.*

NIGHTLIFE

Most people start their evening drinking in the bars and taverns in Plaza de Cañadío, on Calle Hernán Cortés and the surrounding streets, while grazing on tapas that can be plucked straight from the top of the bar. Night owls can head to Calle del Sol and Calle de Santa Lucía, which have cozy spots for late-night drinking, some with live music.

Cañadio. An after-work favorite, Cañadio draws a lively evening crowd for tempting tapas and chilled beer on tap. ✉ *Calle de Gómez Oreña, 15* ☎ *942/314149* 🌐 *www.restaurantecanadio.com.*

The Altamira Museum's replica of a Paleolithic cave displays paintings of bison.

SHOPPING

For most items head to the center: the streets around the ayuntamiento are good for clothing, shoes, and sportswear. At the bustling Mercado de la Esperanza, just behind the ayuntamiento, you can find fish and shellfish that have been freshly plucked from the sea of Cantabria, and locally produced cheeses and meat. Open-air fruit and vegetable stalls mark the entrance.

Azul–Looky. A great shoe store. ⊠ *C. Santa Clara 2* ☎ *942/227769.*

Del Rosa al Amarillo. For fashions in a designer setting, this boutique carries a full range of hot items. ⊠ *C. Hernán Cortés 37* ☎ *942/313917* ⊕ *www.delrosaalamarillo.es.*

Mantequerías Cántabras. Fine foods, including the Santanderino specialty *dulces pasiegos* (light and sugary cakes), can be sampled and bought here. ⊠ *Pl. de Italia s/n* ☎ *942/272899.*

SANTILLANA DEL MAR

29 km (18 miles) west of Santander.

Fodor'sChoice
★ Santillana del Mar has developed a thriving tourism industry based on the famed cave art discovered 2 km (1 mile) north of town—and the town itself is worth a visit of at least a day. Just as the Altamira Caves have captured the essence of prehistoric life, the streets, plazas, taverns, and manor houses of Santillana del Mar paint a vivid portrait of medieval and Renaissance village life in northern Spain. Its stunning ensemble of 15th- to 17th-century stone houses is one of Spain's greatest architectural collections.

ESSENTIALS

Visitor Information Santillana del Mar ✉ *C. Jesús Otero 20* ☎ *942/818812.*

EXPLORING

Altamira Caves. These world-famous caves, 3 km (2 miles) southwest of Santillana del Mar, have been called the Sistine Chapel of prehistoric art for the beauty of their drawings, believed to be some 20,000 years old. First uncovered in 1875, the caves are a testament to early mankind's admiration of beauty and surprising technical skill in representing it, especially in the use of rock forms to accentuate perspective. The caves are closed to visitors, but the reproduction in the **museum** is open to all. ✉ *Museo de Altamira, Av. Marcelino Sanz de Sautuola s/n* ☎ *942/818005* 🌐 *museodealtamira.mcu.es* 🎟 *€3 (free Sat. afternoon and Sun.)* ⏲ *May–Oct., Tues.–Sat. 9:30–8, Sun. 9:30–3; Nov.–Apr., Tues.–Sat. 9:30–6, Sun. 9:30–3.*

Colegiata de Santa Juliana. Santillana del Mar is built around the Colegiata, Cantabria's finest Romanesque structure. Highlights include the 12th-century cloister, famed for its sculpted capitals, a 16th-century altarpiece, and the tomb of Santa Juliana, who is the town's patron saint and namesake. ✉ *Pl. Abad Francisco Navarro s/n* ☎ *639/830520* 🎟 *€3* ⏲ *Nov.–Mar., Tues.–Sun. 10–2 and 4–7; Apr.–Oct., Tues.–Sun. 10–2 and 4–8.*

Museo Diocesano. Inside the 16th-century Regina Coeli convent is a museum devoted to liturgical art, which includes wooden figures of saints, oil paintings of biblical scenes, altarpieces, and a collection of sacred treasures from the colonial New World. ✉ *C. El Cruce s/n* ☎ *942/840317* 🌐 *www.santillanamuseodiocesano.com* 🎟 *€3* ⏲ *Oct.–May, Tues.–Sun. 10–1:30 and 4–6:30; June–Sept., Tues.–Sun. 10–1:30 and 4–7:30.*

WHERE TO STAY

$$ B&B/INN

🏨 **Casa del Organista.** A typical *casona montañesa* (noble mountain manor) with painstakingly crafted stone and wood details, this intimate hideaway makes a slightly rustic, elegant base for exploring one of Spain's finest Renaissance towns. **Pros:** personal and friendly service; warm interior design; lovely views of tiled roofs and rolling hills. **Cons:** limited availability and difficult to book in high season; some rooms are very small. [$] *Rooms from: €93* ✉ *C. Los Hornos 4* ☎ *942/840352* 🌐 *www.casadelorganista.com* 🛏 *14 rooms* ⏲ *Closed Dec. 22–Jan. 15* 🍴 *No meals.*

$$$$ HOTEL Fodor's Choice ★

🏨 **Parador de Santillana Gil Blas.** Built in the 16th century, this lovely stone palace comes with baronial rooms, with heavy wood beams overhead and splendid antique furnishings. **Pros:** storybook surroundings; elegant and attentive service. **Cons:** expensive; a little breezy and chilly in winter. [$] *Rooms from: €188* ✉ *Pl. Ramón Pelayo 11* ☎ *942/028028* 🌐 *www.parador.es* 🛏 *27 rooms, 1 suite* 🍴 *No meals.*

OFF THE BEATEN PATH

Puente Viesgo. In 1903, in this 16th-century hamlet in the Pas Valley, four caves were discovered under the 1,150-foot peak of Monte del Castillo, two of which—Cueva del Castillo and Cueva de las Monedas—are open to the public. Bison, deer, bulls, and humanoid stick figures are depicted within the caves; the oldest designs are thought to be 35,000 years old.

Most arresting are the paintings of 44 hands (35 of them left, curiously), reaching out through time. The painters are thought to have blown red pigment around their hands through a hollow bone, leaving the negative image. Reservations are essential. ⊠ *Mt. del Castillo, Puente Viesgo* ☎ *942/598425* ⊕ *cuevas.culturadecantabria.com* ⊠ *€3 per cave* ⊙ *Nov.–Mar., Wed.–Fri. 9:30–3:30, weekends, 9:30–2:30 and 3:30–5:30; Apr.–mid-June and mid-Sept.–Oct., Wed.–Sun. 9:30–2:30 and 3:30–6:30; mid-June–mid-Sept., Tues.–Sun. 9:30–2:30 and 3:30–7:30.*

COMILLAS

49 km (30 miles) west of Santander.

This astounding pocket of Catalan Art Nouveau architecture in the green hills of Cantabria will make you rub your eyes in disbelief. The Marqués de Comillas, a Catalan named Antonio López y López (1817–83), whose daughter Isabel married Antoni Gaudí's patron Eusebi Güell, was the wealthiest and most influential shipping magnate of his time and a fervent patron of the arts. He encouraged the great Moderniste architects to use his native village as a laboratory. Gaudí's 1883–89 green-and-yellow-tile villa, El Capricho (a cousin of his Casa Vicens in Barcelona), is the town's main Moderniste attraction. The town cemetery is filled with Art Nouveau markers and monuments, most notably an immense angel by eminent Catalan sculptor Josep Llimona.

GETTING HERE AND AROUND
Comillas is 45 minutes from downtown Santander on the A67 and A8 motorways. From Gijón and Oviedo, the trip along the A8 takes just under two hours.

ESSENTIALS
Visitor Information Comillas ⊠ *Pl. Joaquín del Piélago 1* ☎ *942/722591.*

EXPLORING
Palacio Sobrellano. Built in the late 19th century by Catalan architect Joan Martorell for the Marqués de Comillas, Palacio Sobrellano is an exuberant neo-Gothic mansion. It now holds surprising collections of sculpture and paintings as well as archaeological and ethnographical material. The chapel has benches and kneeling stalls that were designed by Gaudí. ⊠ *Barrio el Parque* ⊠ *€3* ⊙ *Nov.–Feb., Tues.–Sun. 9:30–3:30; Mar.–Oct., Tues.–Sun. 9:30–2:30 and 3:30–6:30 (until 7:30 mid-June–mid-Sept.).*

SAN VICENTE DE LA BARQUERA

64 km (40 miles) west of Santander, 15 km (9 miles) west of Comillas.

This is one of the oldest and most beautiful maritime settlements in northern Spain; it was an important Roman port long before many other shipping centers (such as Santander) had gotten firmly established. The 28 arches of the ancient bridge **Puente de la Maza,** which spans the ría, welcome you to town.

GETTING HERE AND AROUND

To get to San Vicente de la Barquera, take an ALSA bus from Santander or drive down the A67 before turning on to the A8.

ESSENTIALS

Visitor Information San Vicente de la Barquera ⊠ *Av. del Generalísimo 20* ☎ *942/710797.*

EXPLORING

Nuestra Señora de los Ángeles (*Our Lady of the Angels*). The Romanesque portals of this 15th-century church are extremely striking. ⊠ *C. Alta 12.*

Plaza Mayor. Make sure you check out the arcaded porticoes here and the view over the town from the Unquera road (N634) just inland.

5

BILBAO AND THE BASQUE COUNTRY

with Navarra and La Rioja

Visit Fodors.com for advice, updates, and bookings

WELCOME TO BILBAO AND THE BASQUE COUNTRY

TOP REASONS TO GO

★ **Explore the Basque coast:** From colorful fishing villages to tawny beaches, the Basque Coast always delights the eye.

★ **Eat tapas in San Sebastián:** Nothing matches San Sebastián's old quarter, with the booming laughter of tavern-hoppers who graze at counters heaped with colorful morsels.

★ **Appreciate Bilbao's art and architecture:** The gleaming titanium Guggenheim and the Museo de Bellas Artes (Fine Arts Museum) shimmer where steel mills and shipyards once stood, while verdant pastures loom above and beyond.

★ **Run with the bulls in Pamplona:** Running with a pack of wild animals (and people) will certainly get the adrenaline pumping, but you might prefer to be a spectator.

★ **Drink in La Rioja wine country:** Spain's premier wine region is filled with wine-tasting opportunities and fine cuisine.

1 Bilbao and the Basque Coast to Getaria. The contrast between Bilbao and the rest of the Basque Country makes each half of the equation better: a city famous for steel and shipbuilding turned into a shimmering art and architecture hub, surrounded by sylvan hillsides, tiny fishing ports, and beautiful beaches.

2 San Sebastián to Hondarribia. San Sebastián lures travelers with its sophistication and a wide beach. Nearby Hondarribia is a fishing port on the Bidasoa river estuary border with France.

3 **Navarra and Pamplona.**
This region offers much
beyond Pamplona's running-
with-the-bulls blowout party.
The green Pyrenean hills to
the north contrast with the
lunar Bárdenas Reales to
the southeast, and the wine
country south of Pamplona
leads to lovely Camino de
Santiago way stations like
Estella. Medieval Vitoria is
the capital of Alava and the
whole Basque Country, and
is relatively undiscovered by
tourists.

GETTING ORIENTED

Bordering the coastline of the
Bay of Biscay, the Basque
Country and, farther inland,
Navarra and La Rioja are
a Spain apart—a land of
moist green foothills, lush
vineyards, and rolling
meadowlands. A fertile
slot between the Picos de
Europa and the Pyrenees
mountain ranges that stretch
from the Mediterranean
Cap de Creus all the way
to Fisterra ("World's End")
on the Atlantic in northwestern Galicia, this northern
Arcadia is an often rainy
but frequently comforting
reprieve from the bright, hot
Spanish *meseta* (high plain
or tableland) to the south.

Hondarribia
FRANCE
Lesaka

P Y R E N E E S

Pamplona

Puente
la Reina

3

Tafalla
Sangüesa
NAVARRA   **ARAGON**
Carcastillo
Caparroso

BÁRDENAS
REALES

Tudela

0   20 mi
0   20 km

4 **La Rioja.** Spain's wine
country is dedicated to
tastes of all kinds. The Sierra
de la Demanda mountain
range offers culinary destinations such as Ezcaray's
Echaurren or Viniegra de
Abajo's Venta de Goyo,
while the towns of Logroño,
Haro, and Laguardia are well
endowed with superb architecture and gastronomy.

EATING AND DRINKING WELL IN THE BASQUE COUNTRY

Basque cuisine, Spain's most prestigious regional gastronomy, derives from the refined French culinary sensibility combined with a rough-and-tumble passion for the camaraderie of the table and for perfectly prepared seafood, meat, and vegetables.

(top left) A nueva cocina interpretation of the classic *bacalao al pil pil* (top right) A colorful bowl of *marmitako* stew (bottom left) An expensive plate of *angulas*

The so-called *nueva cocina vasca* (new Basque cooking) is now about 30 years old, but it was originally inspired by the nouvelle cuisine of neighboring France, and meant the invention of streamlined versions of classic Basque dishes such as *marmitako* (tuna and potato stew). This region has the greatest concentration of Michelin-starred restaurants anywhere in the world.

Though experts have often defined Basque cooking as simply "the art of preparing fish," there is no dearth of lamb, beef, goat, or pork in the Basque diet or on menus. Cooking both beef and fish over coals is a popular favorite as are—new Basque cooking notwithstanding—bracing stews combining legumes such as lentils and garbanzos with sausage.

CIDER

Don't miss a chance to go to a *sidrería*, a cider house where the cider is poured from overhead and quaffed in a single gulp. *Chuletas de buey* (garlicky beefsteak grilled over coals) and *tortilla de bacalao* (cod omelet) provide ballast for hard apple cider *al txotx*. The cider-cod combination is linked to the Basque fishermen and whalers who carried the longer-lasting cider rather than wine in their galleys.

BABY EELS

Angulas, known as elvers in English, are a Basque delicacy that has become an expensive treat, with prices reaching €1,000 a kilogram (about 2.2 pounds). The 3- to 4-inch-long eels look like spaghetti, but with tiny black eyes, and are typically served in a small earthenware dish sizzling with olive oil, garlic, and a single slice of chili. A special wooden fork is used to eat them, to avoid any metallic taste, and because the wood works better with the slippery eels. Don't be misled by the plethora of "gulas" sold in lower-end tapas bars and groceries across Spain. They look just like angulas, but they're fake—synthetic eels made from reconstituted fish stock.

BACALAO

Codfish, a Basque favorite since the Stone Age, comes in various guises. Bacalao *al pil pil* is a classic Bilbao specialty simmered—rather than fried—with garlic and olive oil in its own juices. The "pil pil" refers to the sound of the emulsion of cod and olive oil bubbling up from the bottom of the pan. Served with a red chili pepper, this is a beloved Basque delicacy.

BESUGO A LA DONOSTIARRA

Besugo (sea bream) cooked San Sebastián style is baked in the oven, covered with flakes of garlic that look like scales (but taste better), with a last-minute splash of vinegar and parsley

on top. The flesh of the sea bream is flaky and firm.

OX

Oxen in the Basque Country have traditionally been work animals, fed and maintained with great reverence and care. When sacrificed for meat at the age of 12 or 13, their flesh is tender and marbled with streaks of fat rich with grassy aromas and tastes. Many of today's ox steaks/chops (*txuleta de buey,* also translated as "beef chop") may not be from authentic work oxen, but the meat, tender and fragrant, cooked over coals with garlic and a few flakes of sea salt, is dark and delicious.

TUNA AND POTATO STEW

Using the dark-maroon-color meat of the *Thunnus albacares* (yellowfin tuna), *marmitako,* a stick-to-your-ribs potato, tuna, and red pepper stew is the classic Basque fishermen's concoction made for the restoration of weather-beaten seafarers. Taken from the French name of the cooking pot (*marmite*), there are marmitako competitions held annually.

WINE

Basque *txakolítxakolí,* a young white wine made from tart green grapes, is refreshing with either seafood or meat. But those who prefer a Basque red with their Basque cuisine could choose a Rioja Alavesa, from the part of the Rioja wine country north of the Ebro.

Updated
by Suzanne
Wales

Northern Spain is a misty land of green hills, low russet rooflines, and colorful fishing villages; it's also home to the formerly industrial city of Bilbao, reborn as a center of art and architecture. The semiautonomous Basque Country—with its steady drizzle (onomatopoetically called the *siri-miri*), verdant landscape, and rugged coastline—is a distinct national and cultural entity.

Navarra is considered Basque in the Pyrenees and Navarran in its southern reaches, along the Ebro River. La Rioja, tucked between the Sierra de la Demanda (a mountain range that separates La Rioja from the central Castilian steppe) and the Ebro River, is Spain's premier wine country.

Called the País Vasco in Castilian Spanish and Euskadi in the linguistically mysterious, non-Indo-European Basque language Euskera, the Basque region is more a country within a country, or a nation within a state (the semantics are much debated). The Basques are known to love competition—it has been said that they will bet on anything that has numbers on it and moves (horses, dogs, runners). Such traditional rural sports as chopping mammoth tree trunks and lifting boulders reflect the Basques' attachment to the land as well as an enthusiasm for feats of endurance. Even poetry and gastronomy become contests in Euskadi, as *bertsolaris* (amateur poets) improvise duels of sharp-witted verse, and gastronomic societies compete in cooking contests to see who can make the best *sopa de ajo* (garlic soup) or marmitako.

The much-reported-on Basque separatist movement is made up of a small but radical sector of the political spectrum. The terrorist organization known as ETA, or Euskadi Ta Askatasuna (Basque Homeland and Liberty), has killed nearly 900 people in almost four decades of violence. Conflict has waxed and waned over the years, though it has never affected travelers. When ETA declared a permanent cease-fire in April 2006, hope flared for an end to Basque terrorism until a late-December bomb at Madrid's Barajas airport brought progress to a halt. In 2009 Basque *lehendakari* (president) Juan José Ibarretxe and the PNV (Basque Nationalist Party) lost, albeit narrowly, the Basque presidency in favor of Patxi López of the PSOE (Spanish Socialist Party) in coalition with the PP (the right-wing Partido Popular), reflecting voter weariness with the nationalist cause. In October 2011, ETA declared a permanent renunciation of violence, received by the Spanish government with some skepticism, and two years later the Strasbourg's European Court of Human Rights ordered the release of many long-term ETA prisoners, much to the dissatisfaction of the Spanish government and victim's rights associations. But overall there is hope that Spain's greatest post-Franco tragedy is nearing an end.

PLANNING

WHEN TO GO
Mid-April through June, September, and October are the best times to enjoy the temperate climate and both the coastal and upland landscapes of this wet and grassy corner of Spain—though any time of year except August, when Europeans are on vacation, is nearly as good.

Pamplona in July is bedlam, though for hard-core party animals it's heaven.

The Basque Country is rainy in winter, but the wet Atlantic weather is always invigorating and, as if anyone needed it in this culinary paradise, appetite-enhancing. Much of the classically powerful Basque cuisine evolved with the northern maritime climate in mind.

The September film festival in San Sebastián coincides with the spectacular whaleboat regattas, while the beaches are still ideal and largely uncrowded.

When you're looking for a place to stay, note that the largely industrial and well-to-do north is an expensive part of Spain, which is reflected in room rates. San Sebastián is particularly pricey, and Pamplona rates triple during San Fermín in July. Reserve ahead for nearly everywhere in summer, especially Bilbao, where the Guggenheim is filling hotels.

PLANNING YOUR TIME
A road trip through the Basque Country, Navarra, and La Rioja would require at least a week, but a glimpse, however brief, of Bilbao and its Guggenheim, can be done in two days. San Sebastián and its beach, La Concha, the Baztán Valley, Pamplona, Laguardia, and La Rioja's capital Logroño are the top must-see stops.

If you have more time, visit Mundaka and the coast of Vizcaya west of Bilbao; Getaria, Pasajes de San Juan, and Hondarribia near San Sebastián; and the wineries of Haro in La Rioja.

La Rioja's Sierra de la Demanda also has some of the finest landscapes in Spain, not to mention culinary pilgrimages to Echaurren in Ezcaray or Venta de Goyo in Viniegra de Abajo.

FESTIVALS
There's much more to this region's festival scene than the world-famous **San Fermín** and its running of the bulls in Pamplona, though this remains a massive draw. There are all kinds of events that could color your

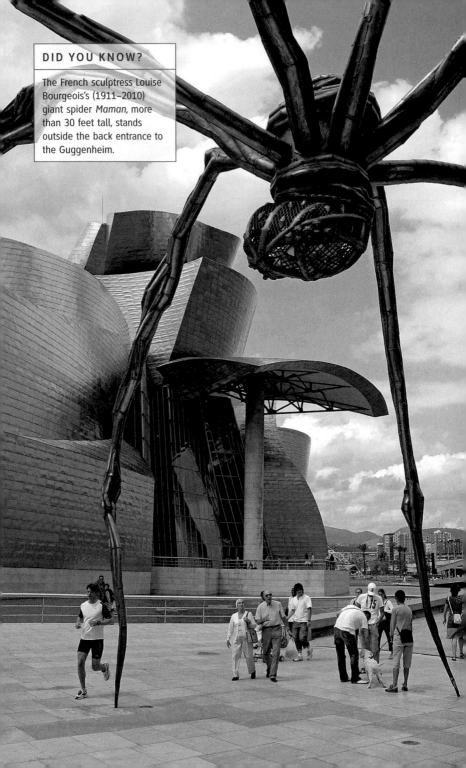

decision on when to travel, including music, dance, processions, and locals generally letting their hair down. For a few events, particularly San Fermín, you will have to take into consideration the higher cost of accommodations, but, for a once-in-a-lifetime experience, it could well be worth the expense.

Fiesta de la Virgen Blanca (*Festival of the White Virgin*). This weeklong festival (August 4–9) celebrate's Vitoria's patron saint with bullfights and more. ⊠ *Vitoria*.

Getaria festival. Every four years—the next in 2017—the little village of Getaria, near San Sebastián, celebrates Juan Sebastián Elcano's completion of Ferdinand Magellan's voyage around the world. Magellan is usually credited with this achievement but he died en route, and Elcano was actually the first man to circumnavigate the globe. Events include a solemn procession of weather-beaten, starving "survivors" trudging up from the port along with more lighthearted dances and street parties. ⊠ *Getaria*.

La Tamborrada. For the city's saint's day, this two-day event on January 19–20 has 100-plus platoons of chefs and Napoleonic soldiers parading hilariously through the streets of San Sebastián. ⊠ *San Sebastián*.

San Sebastián Film Festival. Glitterati descend on the city for its international film fest in the second half of September—exact dates vary, so check the website for details. ⊠ *San Sebastián* ⊕ *www.sansebastianfestival.com*.

San Sebastián Jazz Festival. Drawing many of the world's top performers, this late-July festival also attracts an international crowd of jazz devotees to the city. ⊠ *San Sebastián* ⊕ *www.heinekenjazzaldia.com*.

San Fermín. Pamplona's main event, made famous by Ernest Hemingway in his 1926 novel, *The Sun Also Rises,* remains best known for its running of the bulls, but also includes processions, bullfights, and fireworks. Held each year on July 6–14, every day begins at 8 am with a herd of fighting bulls being let loose to run through the narrow streets to the bullring, accompanied by daredevil—some say reckless—individuals testing their speed and agility in the hope of avoiding injury or death. Most, but not all, do. The atmosphere is electric and hotel rooms overlooking the course come at a price. ⇨ *See also Pamplona and the Close Up feature, "Running with the Bulls."* ⊠ *Pamplona* ⊕ *sanfermin.pamplona.es*.

Semana Grande. The "Big Week" is celebrated in Bilbao in mid-August with a fine series of street concerts and bullfights, notorious for featuring the largest bulls of the season. ⊠ *Bilbao*.

GETTING HERE AND AROUND

AIR TRAVEL

Bilbao's airport serves much of this area, and there are smaller airports at Hondarribia (serving San Sebastián), Logroño, and Pamplona, which are generally only used by domestic carriers in high season.

Airports Aeropuerto de Bilbao ⊕ *www.aeropuertodebilbao.net*.

CAR TRAVEL

Even the remotest points are an easy one-day drive from Madrid, and northern Spain is superbly covered by freeways.

The drive from Madrid to Bilbao is 397 km (247 miles)—about five hours; follow the A1 past Burgos to Miranda del Ebro, where you pick up the AP68. Car rentals are available in the major cities: Bilbao, Pamplona, San Sebastián, and Vitoria. Cars can also be rented at Hondarribia (Fuenterrabía) and the San Sebastián (Donostia) airport.

TAXI TRAVEL

Taxis normally can be hailed on the street, though from more remote spots, such as Pedro Subijana's Akelaŕe restaurant on Igueldo above San Sebastián, you'll need to call a taxi.

TRAIN TRAVEL

Direct RENFE trains from Madrid run to Bilbao (at 8 am and 4:05 pm), San Sebastián (at 8 and 4:05), Pamplona (7:30, 9:40, 3:05, 3:30, and 7:30), Vitoria (8, 8:48, 12:22, and 4:05), and Logroño (7:30, 12:30, 3:30, and 7:30). A car is the most convenient way to get around here, but if this isn't an option, many cities are connected by RENFE trains, and the regional company FEVE runs a delightful narrow-gauge train that winds through stunning landscapes. From San Sebastián, lines west to Bilbao (the Ueskotren) and east to Hendaye depart from Estación de Amara; most long-distance trains use RENFE's Estación del Norte. ⇨ *See the Travel Smart chapter for more information about train travel.*

RESTAURANTS

Though top restaurants are expensive in Bilbao, some of what is undoubtedly Europe's finest cuisine is served here in settings that range from the traditional hewn beams and stone walls to sleekly contemporary international restaurants all the way up to the Guggenheim itself, where superstar chef Martín Berasategui runs a dining room as superb as its habitat.

HOTELS

Ever since the Guggenheim reinvented Bilbao as a design darling, the city's hotel fleet has expanded and reflected (in the case of the Gran Hotel Domine, literally) the glitter and panache of Gehry's museum. Boutique hotels, high-design hotels, and high-rise mammoths have made the older hotels look small and quaint by comparison. Despite new developments, the López de Haro remains one of the city's best lodging options, and many longtime Bilbao visitors prefer the storied halls of the Hotel Carlton to the glass and steel labyrinths overlooking Abandoibarra and the Nervión estuary. *Hotel reviews have been shortened. For full information, visit Fodors.com.*

WHAT IT COSTS IN EUROS				
	$	$$	$$$	$$$$
Restaurants	under €13	€13–€17	€18–€22	over €22
Hotels	under €91	€91–€125	€126–€180	over €180

Prices are per person for a main course, or a combination of small plates, at dinner, and for two people in a standard double room in high season, excluding tax.

BILBAO AND THE BASQUE COAST TO GETARIA (GUETARIA)

Starring Frank Gehry's titanium brainchild—the Museo Guggenheim Bilbao—Bilbao has established itself as one of Spain's 21st-century magnets. The area around the coast of Vizcaya and east into neighboring Guipúzcoa province to Getaria and San Sebastián is a succession of colorful ports, ocher beaches, and green hills.

BILBAO

34 km (21 miles) southeast of Castro-Urdiales, 116 km (72 miles) east of Santander, 397 km (247 miles) north of Madrid.

Time in Bilbao (Bilbo, in Euskera) may be recorded as BG or AG (Before Guggenheim or After Guggenheim). Never has a single monument of art and architecture so radically changed a city. Frank Gehry's stunning museum, Norman Foster's sleek subway system, the Santiago Calatrava glass footbridge and airport, the leafy César Pelli Abandoibarra park and commercial complex next to the Guggenheim, and the Philippe Starck Alhóndiga Bilbao cultural center have contributed to an unprecedented cultural revolution in what was once the industry capital of the Basque Country.

Greater Bilbao encompasses almost 1 million inhabitants, nearly half the total population of the Basque Country. Founded in 1300 by Vizcayan noble Diego López de Haro, Bilbao became an industrial center in the mid-19th century, largely because of the abundance of minerals in the surrounding hills. An affluent industrial class grew up here, as did the working-class suburbs that line the Margen Izquierda (Left Bank) of the Nervión estuary.

Bilbao's new attractions get more press, but the city's old treasures still quietly line the banks of the rust-color Nervión River. The **Casco Viejo** (Old Quarter)—also known as Siete Calles (Seven Streets)—is a charming jumble of shops, bars, and restaurants on the river's Right Bank, near the Puente del Arenal bridge. This elegant proto-Bilbao nucleus was carefully restored after devastating floods in 1983. Throughout the Old Quarter are ancient mansions emblazoned with family coats of arms, wooden doors, and fine ironwork balconies. The most interesting square is the 64-arch Plaza Nueva, where an outdoor market is pitched every Sunday morning.

Walking the banks of the Nervión is a satisfying jaunt. After all, this was how—while out on a morning jog—Guggenheim director Thomas Krens first discovered the perfect spot for his project, nearly opposite the right bank's Deusto University. From the Palacio de Euskalduna upstream to the colossal Mercado de la Ribera, parks and green zones line the river. César Pelli's Abandoibarra project fills in the half mile between the Guggenheim and the Euskalduna bridge with a series of parks, the Deusto University library, the Meliá Bilbao Hotel, and a major shopping center.

On the left bank, the wide, late-19th-century boulevards of the **Ensanche** neighborhood, such as Gran Vía (the main shopping artery) and Alameda de Mazarredo, are the city's more formal face. Bilbao's cultural institutions include, along with the Guggenheim, a major museum of fine arts (the Museo de Bellas Artes) and an opera society (ABAO: Asociación Bilbaína de Amigos de la Ópera) with 7,000 members from Spain and southern France. In addition, epicureans have long ranked Bilbao's culinary offerings among the best in Spain. Don't miss a chance to ride the trolley line, the Euskotram, for a trip along the river from Atxuri Station to Basurto's San Mamés soccer stadium, reverently dubbed "la Catedral del Fútbol" (the Cathedral of Football).

GETTING HERE AND AROUND

Bilbao's Euskotram, running up and down the Ría de Bilbao (aka River Nervión) past the Guggenheim to the Mercado de la Ribera, is an attraction in its own right: silent, swift, and panoramic as it glides up and down its grassy runway. The EuskoTren leaving from Atxuri Station north of the Mercado de la Ribera runs along a spectacular route through Gernika and the Urdaibai Nature Preserve to Mundaka, probably the best way short of a boat to see this lovely wetlands preserve.

The BilbaoCard is good for tram, metro, and bus travel and is available in values of €6, €10, and €12, though the €6 ticket should suffice for the few subway hops you might need to get around town. BilbaoCards can be purchased at the main tourist office and at some newspaper stands and metro stations. Pass your ticket through the machine as you get on and off metros, tramways, or buses, and it is charged according to the length of your trip. Transfers cost extra. A single in-town (Zone 1) ride costs about €1.50 and can be purchased from a driver; with a BilbaoCard the cost is reduced to about €1.10.

Bilbobus provides bus service from 6:15 am to 10:55 pm. Plaza Circular and Plaza Moyúa are the principal hubs for all lines. Once the metro and normal bus routes stop service, take a night bus, known as a Gautxori (Night bird). Six lines run every 30 minutes between Plaza Circular and Plaza Moyúa and the city limits from 11:30 pm to 2 am Friday and until 7 am on Saturday.

Metro Bilbao is linear, running down the Nervión estuary from Basauri, above, or east of, the Casco Viejo, all the way to the mouth of the Nervión at Getxo, before continuing to the beach town of Plentzia. There is no main hub, but the Moyúa station is the most central stop and lies in the middle of Bilbao's Ensanche, or modern (post-1860) part. The second subway line runs down the left bank of the Nervión to Santurtzi. The fare is €1.70.

TOURS

Bilbao's tourist office, Bilbao Turismo, conducts weekend guided tours in English and Spanish. The Casco Viejo tour starts at 10 am at the tourist office on the ground floor of the main office on the Plaza Circular. The Ensanche and Abandoibarra tour begins at noon at the tourist office to the left of the Guggenheim entrance. The tours last 90 minutes and cost €4.50.

Bilbao Paso a Paso arranges custom-designed visits and tours of Bilbao throughout the week.

Stop Bilbao leads visits and tours of Bilbao and the province of Vizcaya.

Tour Information Bilbao Paso a Paso ✉ *Egaña 17, 5th fl., Casco Viejo* ☎ *944/153892* ⊕ *www.bilbaopasoapaso.com.* **Bilbao Turísmo** ✉ *Alameda de Mazarredo 66 (next to Guggenheim Museum), Ensanche* ☎ *944/795760* ⊕ *www. bilbao.net* ⊗ *Mon.–Sat. 10–7, Sun. 10–3 (till 7 July and Aug.).* **Stop Bilbao** ✉ *Portuondo Auzoa 4, Mundaka* ☎ *944/424689* ⊕ *www.stop.es.*

ESSENTIALS
Bus and Subway Informaton Bilbobus ☎ *944/790981* ⊕ *www.bilbobus.com.* **Metro Bilbao.** Customer services offices are in or near four stations: Areeta, San Inazio, Casco Viejo, and Ansio. Hours are weekdays 8:30–7:30, with the San Inazio location also open Saturday 8:30–3. ✉ *C. Navarra 2, Casco Viejo* ☎ *944/254025* ⊕ *www.metrobilbao.net.*

Bus Station Termibus Bilbao ✉ *Gurtubay 1, San Mamés* ☎ *944/395077* ⊕ *www.termibus.es.*

Train Station Bilbao Turismo ✉ *Edificio Terminus, Pl. Circular 2, El Ensanche* ☎ *94/479–5760* ⊕ *www.bilbaoturismo.net* ⊗ *Daily 9–9.* **EuskoTren** ✉ *C. Atxuri 8, Casco Viejo* ☎ *902/543210* ⊕ *www.euskotren.es.*

EXPLORING
TOP ATTRACTIONS
AlhóndigaBilbao. In the early 20th century this was a municipal wine-storage facility used by Bilbao's Rioja wine barons. Now, this city-block-size, Philippe Starck–designed civic center is filled with shops, cafés, restaurants, movie theaters, swimming pools, fitness centers, and nightlife opportunities at the very heart of the city. Conceived as a hub for entertainment, culture, wellness, and civic coexistence, it added another star to Bilbao's cosmos of architectural and cultural offerings when it opened in 2010. The complex regularly hosts film festivals and art exhibitions, and it's a cozy place to take refuge on a rainy afternoon. Locals lovingly call it "the meatball," because its name is one letter off from the Spanish word for meatballs, *albóndigas.* ✉ *Pl. Arriquibar 4, El Ensanche* ☎ *94/401–4014* ⊕ *www.alhondigabilbao.com* Ⓜ *Moyúa.*

OFF THE BEATEN PATH

Funicular de Artxanda. The panorama from the hillsides of Artxanda is the most comprehensive view of Bilbao, and the various typical *asadores* (roasters) here serve delicious beef or fish cooked over coals. ✉ *Pl. de Funicular s/n, Matiko* ☎ *94/445–4966* 🎫 *€0.92* ⊗ *Weekdays 7:15 am–10 pm, weekends 8:15 am–10 pm (till 11 June–Sept.)* Ⓜ *Casco Viejo.*

Fodor'sChoice ★

Mercado de la Ribera. This triple-decker ocean liner with its prow headed down the estuary toward the open sea is one of the best markets of its kind in Europe, as well as one of the biggest, with more than 400 retail stands covering 37,950 square feet. Like the architects of the Guggenheim and the Palacio de Euskalduna nearly 75 years later, the architect here was playful with this well-anchored, oceangoing grocery store in the river. From the stained-glass entryway over Calle de la Ribera to the tiny catwalks over the river or the diminutive restaurant on the second

The Guggenheim may be the most famous art museum in Bilbao these days, but the Museum of Fine Arts is also a very worthwhile destination.

floor, the market is an inviting place. Look for the farmers' market on the top floor, and down on the bottom floor ask how fresh a fish is some morning and you might hear, "Oh, that one's not too fresh: caught last night." ⊠ *C. de la Ribera 20, Casco Viejo* ☎ 946/023791 ⊕ *www.mercadodelaribera.net* ⊙ *Mon.–Thurs. 9:30–1 and 3:30–6, Fri.–Sat. 9–3* Ⓜ *Casco Viejo.*

Fodor's Choice **Museo de Bellas Artes** (*Museum of Fine Arts*). Considered one of the top
★ five museums in a country that has a staggering number of museums and great paintings, the Museo de Bellas Artes is like a mini-Prado, with representatives from every Spanish school and movement from the 12th through the 20th century. The museum's fine collection of Flemish, French, Italian, and Spanish paintings includes works by El Greco, Francisco de Goya y Lucientes, Diego Velázquez, Zurbarán, José Ribera, Paul Gauguin, and Antoni Tàpies. One large and excellent section traces developments in 20th-century Spanish and Basque art alongside works by better-known European contemporaries, such as Fernand Léger and Francis Bacon. Look especially for Zuloaga's famous portrait of La Condesa Mathieu de Moailles and Joaquín Sorolla's portrait of Basque philosopher Miguel de Unamuno. A statue of Zuloaga outside greets visitors to this sparkling collection at the edge of Doña Casilda Park and on the left bank end of the Deusto bridge, five minutes from the Guggenheim. Three hours might be barely enough to appreciate this international and pan-chronological painting course. The museum's excellent Arbolagaña restaurant offers a stellar lunch to break up the visit. ⊠ *Parque de Doña Casilda de Iturrizar, Museo Pl. 2D, El Ensanche* ☎ 94/439–6060 ⊕ *www.museobilbao.com* ⌛ €6 (free

Wed.), €13.50 Bono Artean combined ticket with Guggenheim (valid 1 yr) ☉ *Tues.–Sun. 10–8* Ⓜ *Moyúa.*

Fodor's Choice
★ **Museo Guggenheim Bilbao.** Described by the late Spanish novelist Manuel Vázquez Montalbán as a "meteorite," the Guggenheim, with its eruption of light in the ruins of Bilbao's shipyards and steelworks, has dramatically reanimated this onetime industrial city. How Bilbao and the Guggenheim met is in itself a saga: Guggenheim director Thomas Krens was looking for a venue for a major European museum, having found nothing acceptable in Paris, Madrid, or elsewhere, and glumly accepted an invitation to Bilbao. Krens was out for a morning jog when he found it—the empty riverside lot once occupied by the Altos Hornos de Vizcaya steel mills. The site, at the heart of Bilbao's steel and shipping port, was the perfect place for a metaphor for Bilbao's macro-reconversion from steel to titanium, from heavy industry to art, as well as a nexus between the early-14th-century Casco Viejo and the new 19th-century Ensanche and between the wealthy right bank and working-class left bank of the Nervión River.

Frank Gehry's gleaming brainchild, opened in 1997 and hailed as "the greatest building of our time" by architect Philip Johnson and "a miracle" by Herbert Muschamp of the *New York Times,* has sparked an economic renaissance in the Basque Country after more than a half century of troubles. In its first year, the Guggenheim attracted 1.4 million visitors.

At once suggestive of a silver-scaled fish and a mechanical heart, Gehry's sculpture in titanium, limestone, and glass is the perfect habitat for the contemporary and postmodern artworks it contains. The smoothly rounded jumble of surfaces and cylindrical shapes recalls Bilbao's shipbuilding and steel-manufacturing past, whereas the transparent and reflective materials create a shimmering, futuristic luminosity. With the final section of the La Salve bridge over the Nervión folded into the structure, the Guggenheim is both a doorway to Bilbao and an urban forum: the atrium looks up into the center of town and across the river to the Old Quarter and the tranquil green hillsides of Artxanda where livestock graze. Gehry's intent to build something as moving as a Gothic cathedral in which "you can feel your soul rise up," and to make it as playful and perfect as a fish—per the composer Franz Schubert's ichthyological homage in his famous "Trout Quintet"—is patent: "I wanted it to be more than just a dumb building; I wanted it to have a plastic sense of movement!"

Covered with 30,000 sheets of titanium, the Guggenheim became Bilbao's main attraction overnight. The enormous atrium, more than 150 feet high, connects to the 19 galleries by a system of suspended metal walkways and glass elevators. Vertical windows reveal the undulating titanium flukes and contours of this beached whale. The free Audio Guía explains everything you always wanted to know about contemporary art and the Guggenheim. Frank Gehry talks of his love of fish and how his creative process works, while the pieces in the collection are presented one by one.

The collection, described by Krens as "a daring history of the art of the 20th century," consists of more than 250 works, most from the New York Guggenheim and the rest acquired by the Basque government. The second and third floors reprise the original Guggenheim collection of abstract expressionist, cubist, surrealist, and geometrical works. Artists whose names are synonymous with the art of the 20th century (Wassily Kandinsky, Pablo Picasso, Max Ernst, Georges Braque, Joan Miró, Jackson Pollock, Alexander Calder, Kazimir Malevich) and European artists of the 1950s and 1960s (Eduardo Chillida, Tàpies, Jose Maria Iglesias, Francesco Clemente, and Anselm Kiefer) are joined by contemporary figures (Bruce Nauman, Juan Muñoz, Julian Schnabel, Txomin Badiola, Miquel Barceló, Jean-Michel Basquiat). The ground floor is dedicated to large-format and installation work, some of which—like Richard Serra's *Serpent*—was created specifically for the space. Claes Oldenburg's *Knife Ship,* Robert Morris's walk-in *Labyrinth,* and pieces by Joseph Beuys, Christian Boltanski, Richard Long, Jenny Holzer, and others round out the heavyweight division in one of the largest galleries in the world.

On holidays and weekends lines may develop, though no one seems too impatient. The longest lines tend to occur late morning through early afternoon, although you can buy tickets in advance online. The museum has no parking of its own, but underground lots throughout the area provide alternatives; check the website for information. ⊠ *Abandoibarra Etorbidea 2, El Ensanche* ☎ *944/359080* ⊕ *www.guggenheimbilbao.es* ⟁€11, *includes audio guide, €13.50 Bono Artean combined ticket with Museo de Bellas Artes* ⊙ *July and Aug., daily 10–8; Sept.– June, Tues.–Sun. 10–8. Ticket office closes at 7:30* Ⓜ *Moyúa.*

FAMILY **Museo Marítimo Ría de Bilbao** (*Maritime Museum of Bilbao*). This carefully researched nautical museum on the left bank of the Ría de Bilbao reconstructs the history of the Bilbao waterfront and shipbuilding industry beginning from medieval times. Temporary exhibits range from visits by extraordinary seacraft such as tall ships or traditional fishing vessels to thematic displays on 17th- and 18th-century clipper ships or the sinking of the *Titanic.* ⊠ *Muelle Ramón de la Sota 1, San Mamés* ☎ *94/608–5500* ⊕ *www.museomaritimobilbao.org* ⟁€6 *(free Tues. Sept.–June)* ⊙ *May 16–Sept. 14, Tues.–Sun. 10–8; Sept. 15–May 15, Tues.–Fri. 10–6, weekends 10–8* Ⓜ *San Mamés.*

Fodor'sChoice **Museo Vasco (Euskal Museoa Bilbao)** (*Basque Museum of Bilbao*). One
★ of the not-to-miss visits in Bilbao, this museum occupies an austerely elegant 16th-century convent. The collection centers on Basque ethnography, Bilbao history, and comprehensive displays from the lives of Basque shepherds, fishermen, and farmers—everything you ever wanted to know about this little-known culture. Highlights include *El Mikeldi* in the cloister, a pre-Christian, Iron Age, stone, animal representation that may be 4,000 years old; the Mar de los Vascos (Sea of the Basques) exhibit featuring whaling, fishing, and maritime activities; the second-floor prehistoric exhibit featuring a wooden harpoon recovered in the Santimamiñe caves at Kortezubi that dates from the 10th century BC. ⊠ *Pl. Unamuno 4, Casco Viejo* ☎ *94/415–5423* ⊕ *www.euskal-museoa. org* ⟁€3 *(free Thurs.)* ⊙ *Tues.–Sat. 11–5, Sun. 11–2* Ⓜ *Casco Viejo.*

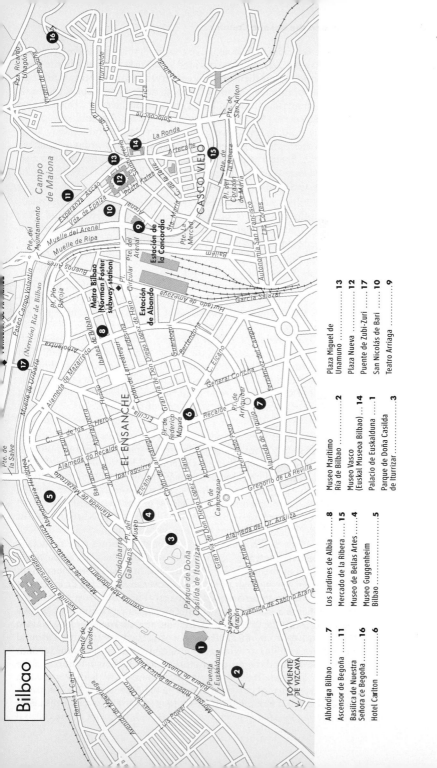

Bilbao

Alhóndiga Bilbao **7**
Ascensor de Begoña **11**
Basílica de Nuestra
Señora de Begoña **16**
Hotel Carlton **6**

Los Jardines de Albia **8**
Mercado de la Ribera **15**
Museo de Bellas Artes **4**
Museo Guggenheim
Bilbao **5**

Museo Marítimo
Ría de Bilbao **2**
Museo Vasco
(Euskal Museoa Bilbao) ... **14**
Palacio de Euskalduna **1**
Parque de Doña Casilda
de Iturrizar **3**

Plaza Miguel de
Unamuno **13**
Plaza Nueva **12**
Puente de Zubi-Zuri **17**
San Nicolás de Bari **10**
Teatro Arriaga **9**

Palacio de Euskalduna. In homage to the *astilleros Euskalduna* (Basque Country shipbuilders) who operated shipyards here beside the Euskalduna bridge into the late 20th century, this music venue and convention hall resembles a rusting ship, a stark counterpoint to Frank Gehry's shimmering titanium fantasy just up the Nervión. Designed by architects Federico Soriano and Dolores Palacios, Euskalduna opened in 1999 and is Bilbao's main opera venue and home of the Bilbao Symphony Orchestra. Free, guided tours are offered on Saturday at noon on a first-come, first-served basis. Weekday tours (€4 per person) can also be booked ahead. ⊠ *Av. Abandoibarra 4, El Ensanche* ☎ *94/403–5000* ⊕ *www.euskalduna.net* Ⓜ *San Mamés.*

Parque de Doña Casilda de Iturrizar. Bilbao's main park is a lush collection of exotic trees, ducks and geese, fountains, falling water, and great expanses of lawns usually dotted with lovers. It's a sanctuary from the hard-edged Ensanche, Bilbao's modern, post-1876 expansion. ⊠ *El Ensanche* Ⓜ *San Mamés.*

Plaza Miguel de Unamuno. Named for Bilbao's all-time greatest intellectual, this bright and open space at the upper edge of the Casco Viejo honors Miguel de Unamuno (1864–1936)—a philosopher, novelist, and professor. De Unamuno wrote some of Spain's most seminal works, including *Del sentimiento trágico de la vida en los hombres y los pueblos* (*The Tragic Sense of Life in Men and Nations*); his *Niebla* (*Mist*) has been generally accepted as the first existentialist novel, published in 1914 when Jean-Paul Sartre was but nine years old. Remembrances to Unamuno in the Casco Viejo include the philosopher's bust here, his birthplace at Calle de la Cruz 7, and the nearby Filatelia Unamuno, a rare stamp emporium that is a favorite of collectors. ⊠ *Casco Viejo* Ⓜ *Casco Viejo.*

Plaza Nueva. This 64-arch neoclassical plaza seems to be typical of every Spanish city from San Sebastián to Salamanca to Seville. With its Sunday-morning flea market, its December 21 natural-produce Santo Tomás market, and its permanent tapas and restaurant offerings, Plaza Nueva is an easy place in which to spend a lot of time. It was finished in 1851 as part of an ambitious housing project designed to ease the pressure on limited mid-19th-century Bilbao space. Note the size of the houses' balconies: it was the measure—the bigger, the better—of the social clout of their inhabitants. The tiny windows near the top of the facades were servants' quarters. The building behind the powerful coat of arms at the head of the square was originally the Diputación, or provincial government office, but is now the **Academia de la Lengua Vasca** (Academy of the Basque Language). The coat of arms shows the tree of Guernica (the Basque spelling is Gernika), symbolic of Basque autonomy, with the two wolves representing Don Diego López de Haro (López derives from *lupus,* meaning wolf). The bars and shops around the arcades include two **Victor Montes** establishments, one for tapas at Plaza Nueva 8 and the other for more serious sit-down dining at Plaza Nueva 2. The **Café Bar Bilbao,** at Plaza Nueva 6, also known as Casa Pedro, has photos of early Bilbao, while the **Argoitia,** at No. 15 across the square, has a nice angle on the midday sun and a coat of arms inside with the *zatzpiakbat* ("seven-one" in Basque), referring to the cultural

The exterior of the Bilbao Guggenheim is immediately recognized by many, but the interior is known for its large spaces, all the better for appreciating the stunning works of art.

unity of the three French and four Spanish Basque provinces. ⊠ *Casco Viejo* Ⓜ *Casco Viejo.*

Puente de Zubi-Zuri. Santiago Calatrava's signature span (the name means "white bridge" in Euskera) connects Campo Volantín on the right bank with the Ensanche on the left. Just a few minutes east of the Guggenheim, the playful seagull-shape bridge swoops brightly over the dark Nervión. The Plexiglas walkway suggests walking on water, though wear-and-tear has reduced the surface from transparent to merely translucent. The airport just west of Bilbao at Loiu, also designed by Calatrava, resembles a massive, white Concorde plane and has been dubbed La Paloma (The Dove), despite more closely resembling a snow goose poised for takeoff. Calatrava's third Vizcaya creation, the bridge at Ondarroa, completes this troika of gleaming white structures exploring the theme of flight. ⊠ *El Ensanche* Ⓜ *Moyúa.*

San Nicolás de Bari. Honoring the patron saint of mariners, San Nicolás de Bari, the city's early waterfront church was built over an earlier eponymous hermitage and opened in 1756. With a powerful facade over the Arenal, originally a sandy beach, San Nicolás was much abused by French and Carlist troops throughout the 19th century. Sculptures by Juan Pascual de Mena adorn the inside of the church. Look for the oval plaque to the left of the door marking the high-water mark of the flood of 1983. ⊠ *Pl. de San Nicolás 1, Casco Viejo* ☎ 94/416–3424 ☜ *Free* ⊙ *Mon.–Sat. 10:30–1 and 5:30–8, Sun. 11:30–2* Ⓜ *Casco Viejo.*

Teatro Arriaga. About a century ago, this 1,500-seat theater was as exciting a source of Bilbao pride as the Guggenheim is today. Built between 1886 and 1890, when Bilbao's population was a mere 35,000, the

Teatro Arriaga represented a gigantic per-capita cultural investment. Always a symbol of Bilbao's industrial might and cultural vibrancy, the original "Nuevo Teatro" (New Theater) de Bilbao was a lavish Belle Époque, neo-baroque spectacular modeled after the Paris Opéra by architect Joaquín Rucoba (1844–1909). The theater was renamed in 1902 for the Bilbao musician thought of as "the Spanish Mozart," Juan Crisóstomo de Arriaga (1806–26).

After a 1914 fire, the new version of the theater opened in 1919. Following years of splendor, the Teatro Arriaga (along with Bilbao's economy) gradually lost vigor; it closed down in 1978 for restoration work that was finally concluded in 1986. Now largely eclipsed by the splendid and more spacious Palacio de Euskalduna, the Arriaga stages opera, theater, concerts, and dance events September through June. Walk around the building to see the stained glass on its rear facade and the exuberant caryatids holding up the arches facing the river. ⊠ *Pl. Arriaga 1, Casco Viejo* ☎ *944/792036* ⊕ *www.teatroarriaga.com* ☉ *Ticket office: Aug.–June, Sat.–Tues. 11:30–2 and 5–7, Wed.–Fri. 11:30–2 and 5–8:30; July, Mon.–Sat. 11:30–2* Ⓜ *Casco Viejo.*

WORTH NOTING

Basílica de Nuestra Señora de Begoña. Bilbao's most cherished religious sanctuary, dedicated to the patron saint of Vizcaya, can be reached by the 313 stairs from Plaza de Unamuno or by the gigantic elevator (the **Ascensor de Begoña**) looming over Calle Esperanza 6 behind the San Nicolás church. The church's Gothic nave was begun in 1519 on the site of an early hermitage, where the Virgin Mary was alleged to have appeared long before. Finished in 1620, the basilica was completed with the economic support of the shipbuilders and merchants of Bilbao, many of whose businesses are commemorated on the inner walls of the church. The high ground the basilica occupies was strategically important during the Carlist Wars of 1836 and 1873, and as a result La Begoña suffered significant damage that was not restored until the beginning of the 20th century. Comparable in importance (if not in geographical impact) to Barcelona's Virgen de Montserrat, the Basílica de la Begoña is where the Athletic Bilbao soccer team makes its pilgrimage, some of the players often barefoot, in gratitude for triumphs. ⊠ *C. Virgen de Begoña 38, Begoña* ☎ *94/412–7091* ⊕ *www.basilicadebegona. com* ☜ *Free* ☉ *Mon.–Sat. 10:30–1:30 and 5:30–8:30, Sun. for Mass only* Ⓜ *Casco Viejo.*

Hotel Carlton. Bilbao's grande-dame favorite *(⇨ see also Where to Stay)* has hosted top-tier celebrities over the last century, from Orson Welles and Ernest Hemingway to Ava Gardner, casting giant Gretchen Rennell, and music czar John Court, not to mention Francis Ford Coppola. Opened in 1926, Architect Manuel María de Smith based this project on the London hotel of the same name, although the stained glass in the oval reception area is a reduced version of the one in Nice's Hotel Negresco. During the Spanish Civil War, this building was the seat of the Republican Basque government; later it housed a number of Nationalist generals. The hotel's bar, the Grill, has a clubby English feel to it, with murals painted by client Martinez Ortiz in 1947. The murals, representing an equestrian scene and some 10 bourgeois figures, are remarkable for the detailed painting of every hand and finger. ✉ *Pl. Federico Moyúa 2, El Ensanche* ☎ *94/416–2200* 🌐 *www.hotelcarlton.es* [M] *Moyúa.*

Los Jardines de Albia. One of the two or three places all bilbainos will insist you see is this welcoming green space in the concrete-and-asphalt surfaces of this part of town. Overlooking the square is the lovely Basque Gothic **Iglesia de San Vicente Mártir,** its Renaissance facade facing its own Plaza San Vicente. The amply robed sculpture of the Virgin on the main facade, as the story goes, had to be sculpted a second time after the original version was deemed too scantily clad. The Jardines de Albia are centered on the bronze effigy of writer Antonio de Trueba by the famous Spanish sculptor Mariano Benlliure (1866–1947), creator of monuments to the greatest national figures of the epoch. ✉ *Calle Colón de Larreátegui s/n, El Ensanche* [M] *Abando.*

NEED A BREAK?

Café La Granja. Founded in 1926, this café, near the Puente del Arenal, is a Bilbao classic, offering excellent coffee, cold beer, tortillas de patata, a good lunch menu—and free Wi-Fi. Hours are long (weekdays 7:30 am–12:30 am, Saturday 10:30 am–1:30 am), but it's closed Sunday. ✉ *Pl. Circular 3, Casco Viejo* ☎ *94/423–0813* 🌐 *www.grupoiruña.net* [M] *Abando.*

OFF THE BEATEN PATH

Puente de Vizcaya. Commonly called the **Puente Colgante** (Hanging Bridge), this has been one of Bilbao's most extraordinary sights ever since it was built in 1893. The bridge, a transporter hung from cables, ferries cars and passengers across the Nervión, uniting two distinct worlds: exclusive, bourgeois Las Arenas and Portugalete, a much older, working-class town. (Dolores Ibarruri, the famous Republican orator of the Spanish Civil War, known as "*La Pasionaria*" for her ardor, was born here.) Portugalete is a 15-minute walk from Santurce, where the quayside Hogar del Pescador serves simple fish specialties. Besugo is the traditional choice, but the grilled sardines are hard to surpass. To reach the bridge, take the subway to Areeta, or drive across the Puente de Deusto, turn left on Avenida Lehendakari Aguirre, and follow signs for Las Arenas; it's a 10- or 15-minute drive from downtown. ✉ *Barria 3, Las Arenas* ☎ *94/480–1012* 🌐 *www.puente-colgante.com* 🎫 *Pedestrians €0.35, car €1.35 (5 am–10 pm; price increases after 10); tour with audio guide €9; observation deck €7* [M] *Areeta.*

WHERE TO EAT

$$$$ SPANISH

🍴 **Aizian.** Euskera for "in the wind," the hotel restaurant for the Meliá Bilbao, under the direction of chef José Miguel Olazabalaga, has become one of the city's most respected dining establishments. Typical bilbaino culinary classicism doesn't keep Olazabalaga from creating surprising reductions and contemporary interpretations of traditional dishes such as *rape con espuma de patata y trufa e infusión de champiñones* (monkfish with potato and truffle cream and infusion of wild mushrooms) and *falda de buey Wagyu en láminas, con ajos en texturas y zanahoria* (Wagyu beef with "textured" garlic and carrots) in escabeche. The clean-lined contemporary dining room and the streamlined, polished cuisine are a perfect match. [$] *Average main: €40* ✉ *C. Lehendakari Leizaola 29, El Ensanche* ☎ *94/428–0039* 🌐 *www.restaurante-aizian.com* 🕒 *Closed Sun.* [M] *San Mamés.*

The streets of Bilbao's old town offer many welcoming shops, cafés, and restaurants.

$$$$ CONTEMPORARY Fodor's Choice ★ 🍴 **Arbolagaña.** On the top floor of the Museo de Bellas Artes, this elegant space has bay windows overlooking the lush Parque de Doña Casilda. A devotee of the 'slow food' movement, chef Aitor Basabe's modern cuisine offers innovative versions of Basque classics such as codfish on toast, venison with wild mushrooms, or rice with truffles and shallots. The €45 *menú de degustación* (tasting menu) is a superb affordable luxury, while the abbreviated *menú de trabajo* (work menu) provides a perfect light lunch. [$] *Average main: €30* ✉ *Museo de Bellas Artes, Alameda Conde Arteche s/n, El Ensanche* ☎ *94/442–4657* 🌐 *www.arbolagana.com* ✍ *Reservations essential* ⏲ *Closed Mon. No dinner Tues., Wed., and Sun.* [M] *Moyúa.*

$$$$ BASQUE 🍴 **Arriaga.** The cider-house experience is a must in the Basque Country, and Arriaga is a local institution, on the ground floor of an ancient tower where locals sing to the Virgin of Begoña on religious festival days. Cider *al txotx* (shot straight from the barrel), sausage stewed in apple cider, codfish omelets, *txuletón de buey* (beefsteaks), and Idiazabal cheese with quince jelly are the classic fare. Reserving a table is a good idea, especially on weekends. [$] *Average main: €30* ✉ *C. Santa Maria 13, Casco Viejo* ☎ *94/416–5670* 🌐 *www.asadorarriaga.com* ⏲ *No dinner Sun.* [M] *Casco Viejo.*

$$ BASQUE 🍴 **Berton.** Dinner is served until midnight in this sleek, contemporary but casual bistro in the Casco Viejo. Fresh wood tables with a green-tint polyethylene finish and exposed ventilation pipes give the dining room an industrial design look, while the classic cuisine ranges from Iberian ham to smoked salmon, foie gras, cod, beef, and lamb. [$] *Average main: €15* ✉ *C. Jardines 8, Casco Viejo* ☎ *94/416–7035* [M] *Casco Viejo.*

$$$$ SPANISH 🍴 **Bistro Guggenheim Bilbao.** Complementing the Guggenheim's visual feast with more sensorial elements, this spot overseen by Martín Berasategui is on everyone's short list of Bilbao restaurants. Try the *lomo de bacalao asado en aceite de ajo con txangurro a la donostiarra i pil pil* (cod flanks in garlic oil with crab San Sebastián–style and emulsified juices), a postmodern culinary pun on Bilbao's traditional codfish addiction. A lobster salad with lettuce-heart shavings and tomatoes at a table overlooking the Nervión, the University of Deusto, and the heights of Artxanda qualifies as a perfect 21st-century Bilbao moment. If you don't feel like splurging on the full menu, there's also a cafeteria and bar that serve tapas versions of some of the most popular dishes, with the same views and at a quarter of the price. [$] *Average main: €32* ✉ *Av. Abandoibarra 2, El Ensanche* ☎ *94/423–9333* 🌐 *www.restauranteguggenheim.com* ✍ *Reservations essential* 🕒 *Closed Mon. No dinner Tues., Wed., and Sun.* [M] *Moyúa.*

5

$$ CAFÉ Fodor's Choice ★ 🍴 **Café Iruña.** This is an essential Bilbao haunt on the Ensanche's most popular garden and square, Los Jardines de Albia. Famous for its interior design and boisterous ambience, the neo-Mudejar dining room overlooking the square is the place to be. (If they try to stuff you in the back dining room, resist or come back another time). The bar has two distinct sections: the elegant side near the dining room, and the older, more bare-bones Spanish side on the Calle Berástegui, with its plain marble counters and *pinchos morunos de carne de cordero* (lamb brochettes) as the house specialty. [$] *Average main: €17* ✉ *C. Berástegui 4, El Ensanche* ☎ *94/424–9059* 🌐 *www.grupoiruña.net* [M] *Moyúa.*

$$ BASQUE Fodor's Choice ★ 🍴 **Casa Rufo.** More than 100 years old, this place is a Bilbao institution that's actually a series of nooks and crannies tucked into a fine food, wine, olive oil, cheese, and ham emporium. It has become famous for its txuleta de buey. Let the affable owners bring on what you crave. The house wine is an excellent *crianza* (two years in oak, one in bottle) from La Rioja, but the 1,000-strong wine list offers a good selection from Ribera del Duero, Somontano, and Priorat as well. [$] *Average main: €18* ✉ *C. Hurtado de Amézaga 5, El Ensanche* ☎ *94/443–2172* 🌐 *www.casarufo.com* ✍ *Reservations essential* 🕒 *Closed Sun.* [M] *Abando.*

$$$$ BASQUE Fodor's Choice ★ 🍴 **El Perro Chico.** The global glitterati who adopted post-Guggenheim Bilbao favor this spot across the Puente de la Ribera footbridge below the market. Frank Gehry discovered the color "Bilbao blue"—the azure of the skies over Bilbao—on the walls here and used it for the Guggenheim's office building. Despite celebrity sightings, the restaurant retains its quaint style, with tiled floors and walls and authentic menu. Noteworthy are the *alcachofas a la plancha* (grilled artichokes) and the *bacalao con berenjena* (cod with eggplant). [$] *Average main: €30* ✉ *C. Arctxaga 2, El Ensanche* ☎ *94/415–0519* ✍ *Reservations essential* 🕒 *Closed Sun. and Mon.* [M] *Casco Viejo.*

$$$$ BASQUE 🍴 **Etxanobe.** This luminous top corner of the Euskalduna palace overlooks the Nervión River, the hills of Artxanda, and Bilbao. Fernando Canales creates homegrown, contemporary cuisine using traditional ingredients. Standouts are the five codfish recipes, the duckling with Pedro Ximenez sherry, poached eggs with lamb kidneys and foie gras, and the braised scallops with shallot vinaigrette. [$] *Average main:*

€70 ⊠ *Palacio de Euskalduna, Av. de Abandoibarra 4, El Ensanche* ☎ *94/442–1071* ⊕ *www.etxanobe.com* ☾ *Closed Sun.* Ⓜ *San Mamés.*

$$$$ ✕ **Guetaria.** With a wood paneled dining room decorated with antiques,
BASQUE   this family operation is a local favorite for fresh fish and meats cooked
Fodor's Choice   over coals. Named for the fishing village west of San Sebastián known
★   as *la cocina de Guipúzcoa* (the kitchen of Guipúzcoa province), Bilbao's Guetaria does its namesake justice. The kitchen, open to the clientele, cooks lubina, besugo, dorada, txuletas de buey, and *txuletas de cordero* (lamb chops) to perfection in a classic asador setting. $ *Average main: €50* ⊠ *Colón de Larreátegui 12, El Ensanche* ☎ *94/424–3923, 94/423–2527* ⊕ *www.guetaria.com* ⌂ *Reservations essential* ☾ *Closed Easter wk* Ⓜ *Moyúa.*

$$$$ ✕ **Guria.** The late Genaro Pildain, founder of the restaurant, learned
BASQUE   cooking from his mother in the tiny village of Arakaldo and always
Fodor's Choice   focused more on potato soup than truffles or caviar. Don Genaro's influ-
★   ence is still felt here in the restaurant's streamlined traditional Basque cooking that dazzles with its simplicity. Every ingredient and preparation is perfect, from *alubias "con sus sacramentos"* (fava beans, chorizo, and blood sausage) to *crema de puerros y patatas* (cream of potato and leek soup) to lobster salad with, in season, *perretxikos de Orduña* (wild mushrooms). $ *Average main: €50* ⊠ *Gran Vía 66, El Ensanche* ☎ *944/415780* ⊕ *www.restauranteguria.com* ⌂ *Reservations essential* ☾ *No dinner Sun.* Ⓜ *Indautxu.*

$$$$ ✕ **Kiskia.** A modern take on the traditional cider house, this rambling
BASQUE   tavern near the San Mamés soccer stadium serves the classic *sidrería*
Fodor's Choice   menu of chorizo sausage cooked in cider, codfish omelet, txuleta de
★   buey, Idiazabal with quince jelly and nuts, and as much cider as you can drink. Actors, sculptors, writers, soccer stars, and Spain's who's who frequent this boisterous marvel. $ *Average main: €25* ⊠ *C. Pérez Galdós 51, San Mamés* ☎ *94/442–0032* ⊕ *www.sidreria-kiskia-bilbao. com* ☾ *No dinner Sun.–Tues.* Ⓜ *San Mamés.*

$ ✕ **La Deliciosa.** For carefully prepared food at friendly prices, this simply
TAPAS   designed, intimate space is one of the best values in the Casco Viejo. The *crema de puerros* (cream of leeks) is as good as any in town, and the *dorada al horno* (roast gilthead bream) is fresh from the nearby La Ribera market. $ *Average main: €12* ⊠ *C. Jardines 1, Casco Viejo* ☎ *94/415–0944* Ⓜ *Casco Viejo.*

$ ✕ **La Taberna de los Mundos.** Sandwich-maker Ander Calvo is famous
BASQUE   throughout Spain, and his masterpiece is a sandwich on ciabatta of melted goat cheese with garlic, wild mushrooms, organic tomatoes, and sweet red piquillo peppers on a bed of acorn-fed wild Iberian ham. Calvo's two restaurants in Bilbao and one in Vitoria include creative interpretations of the sandwich along with photography, art exhibits, travel lectures, and a global interest reflected in his obsession with early maps and navigational techniques. The tapas bar is open longer hours than the dining room. $ *Average main: €12* ⊠ *C. Lutxana 1, El Ensanche* ☎ *94/416–8181, 94/441–3523* ⊕ *www.delosmundos.com* Ⓜ *Moyúa.*

$$$$ ✕ **Public Lounge.** For designer cuisine in a designer setting, this Guggen-
CONTEMPORARY   heim-inspired lounge creates sleek, postmodern fare in an exciting environment. The VIP table serves diners on Versace crockery and Baccarat

crystal, and the cooking is no less exquisite. The menu changes frequently, but expect up-to-the-minute tricks such as meat or fish cooked at low temperatures (45°C), salads with contrasting textures and temperatures, and some of the best risottos in Bilbao. [$] *Average main: €35* ✉ *C. Henao 54, El Ensanche* ☎ *94/405–2824* 🌐 *www.public-bilbao.com* 🕒 *Closed Sun. No dinner Mon.–Thurs.* [M] *Moyúa.*

$$$$ BASQUE 🍴 **Txakolí de Artxanda.** The funicular from the end of Calle Múgica y Butrón up to the mountain of Artxanda deposits you next to this excellent spot for a roast of one kind or another after a hike around the heights. Whether ordering lamb, beef, or the traditional Basque besugo, you would have a hard time going wrong at this picturesque spot with unbeatable panoramas over Bilbao. For weekend lunches, especially in springtime, it's best to call ahead or make a reservation—this is a popular spot for weddings. [$] *Average main: €30* ✉ *Ctra. Artxanda-Santo Domingo 19, El Arenal* ☎ *94/445–5015* 🌐 *www.eltxakoli.net* [M] *Abando.*

$$ TAPAS 🍴 **Victor Montes.** On the ground floor, there's a deli and tapas bar where the well-stocked counter might offer anything from wild mushrooms to *txistorra* (spicy sausages), Idiazabal, or, for the adventurous, *huevas de merluza* (hake roe)—all taken with splashes of Rioja, *txakolí* (a young, white wine made from tart green grapes), or cider. There's a sprawling terrace and a dining room upstairs, but the bar is most popular. [$] *Average main: €20* ✉ *Pl. Nueva 8, Casco Viejo* ☎ *94/415–7067* 🌐 *www.victormontesbilbao.com* ✍ *Reservations essential* 🕒 *Closed Aug. 1–15. No dinner Sun.* [M] *Casco Viejo.*

$ TAPAS 🍴 **Xukela.** Amid bright lighting and a vivid palette of green and crimson morsels of ham and bell peppers lining his bar, chef Santiago Ruíz Bombin creates some of the tastiest and most interesting and varied pintxos in all of tapas-dom. Among the specialties are grilled mushrooms, stuffed with smoked cod and topped with apple cream, or other varieties topped with cured duck or salmon and liver. [$] *Average main: €12* ✉ *C. El Perro 2, Casco Viejo* ☎ *94/415–9772* 🌐 *www.xukela.com* [M] *Casco Viejo.*

$$$$ SPANISH 🍴 **Yandiola.** Within the Philippe Starck–designed Alhóndiga Bilbao complex in the Ensanche, Yandiola serves chic designer cuisine. The atmosphere is cool and casual, especially on the terrace, and the market cooking is creative but soundly based on quality products. The *croquetas caseras de hongos* (homemade wild mushroom croquettes) are not to be missed, while the *fideuà cremosa de coliflor y langostas al ajillo* (vermicelli noodle paella with cauliflower and garlicky prawns) is a delicious nod to Spain's east coast culinary canon. [$] *Average main: €59* ✉ *Edificio Alhóndiga Bilbao, Pl. Arriquibar 4, El Ensanche* ☎ *94/413–3636* 🌐 *www.yandiola.com* ✍ *Reservations essential* 🕒 *Closed Mon. No dinner Sun.* [M] *Moyúa.*

$$$$ SPANISH 🍴 **Zortziko.** An ultramodern kitchen housed in an ultrahistoric building, this fine dining restaurant is run by chef Daniel García, one of the Basque Country's culinary stars—with a Michelin star to prove it. García also offers a cooking exhibition for groups of 10 or more at a special table where diners can watch him in action. Reserve your table online. [$] *Average main: €60* ✉ *C. Alameda Mazarredo 17, El Ensanche*

☎ 94/423–9743 ⊕ *www.zortziko.es* ▵ *Reservations essential* ✆ *Closed Sun. and Mon.* Ⓜ *Moyúa.*

WHERE TO STAY

$
B&B/INN
FAMILY
⊞ **Artetxe.** With rooms overlooking Bilbao from the heights of Artxanda, this Basque farmhouse with wood trimmings and eager young owners offers excellent value and tranquility. **Pros:** a peaceful, grassy place from which to enjoy Bilbao and the Basque countryside; great service; plenty of space for children to play **Cons:** far from the center, the museums, and the action. $ *Rooms from: €65* ✉ *C. de Berriz 112, off Ctra. Enékuri–Artxanda, Km 7, Artxanda* ☎ 94/474–7780 ⊕ *www.hotelartetxe.com* ⮐ *12 rooms* ⛌ *Breakfast.*

$$$$
HOTEL
Fodor'sChoice
★
⊞ **Castillo de Arteaga.** Built in the mid-19th century for Empress Eugenia de Montijo, wife of Napoleon III, this Neo-gothic limestone castle with rooms in the watchtowers and defensive walls is one of the most extraordinary lodging options in or around Bilbao. **Pros:** excellent wine and local food product tastings; views over the wetlands. **Cons:** somewhat isolated from village life and a half-hour drive to Bilbao. $ *Rooms from: €190* ✉ *Calle Gaztelubide 7, 40 km (24 miles) northwest of Bilbao, Gautegiz de Arteaga* ☎ 94/627–0440 ⊕ *www.castillodearteaga.com* ⮐ *7 rooms, 6 suites* ✆ *Closed late Dec.–early Jan.* ⛌ *Multiple meal plans.*

$
HOTEL
⊞ **Ercilla.** The taurine crowd fills this modern, hotel during Bilbao's Semana Grande in early August, partly because it's near the bullring and partly because it has taken over from the Carlton as the place to see and be seen. **Pros:** a Bilbao nerve center for journalists, politicians, and businesspeople. **Cons:** this might not be the place to stay if you're looking for a quiet getaway. $ *Rooms from: €89* ✉ *C. Ercilla 37* ☎ 94/470–5700 ⊕ *www.ercillahoteles.com* ⮐ *325 rooms* ⛌ *Multiple meal plans* Ⓜ *Moyúa.*

$$$
HOTEL
Fodor'sChoice
★
⊞ **Gran Hotel Domine Bilbao.** As much modern design celebration as hotel, this Silken chain establishment directly across the street from the Guggenheim showcases the conceptual wit of Javier Mariscal, creator of Barcelona's 1992 Olympic mascot Cobi, and the structural know-how of Bilbao architect Iñaki Aurrekoetxea. **Pros:** at the very epicenter and, indeed, part of Bilbao's art and architecture excitement; the place to cross paths with Catherine Zeta-Jones or Antonio Banderas. **Cons:** hard on the wallet and a little full of its own glamour. $ *Rooms from: €150* ✉ *Alameda de Mazarredo 61, El Ensanche* ☎ 94/425–3300, 94/425–3301 ⊕ *www.granhoteldominebilbao.com* ⮐ *139 rooms, 6 suites* ⛌ *Multiple meal plans* Ⓜ *Moyúa.*

$$$$
HOTEL
Fodor'sChoice
★
⊞ **Hotel Carlton.** This illustrious hotel exudes old-world grace and charm along with a sense of history—which it has aplenty (⇨ *see also Exploring*). **Pros:** historic, old-world surroundings that remind you that Bilbao has an illustrious past. **Cons:** surrounded by plenty of concrete and urban frenzy. $ *Rooms from: €320* ✉ *Pl. Federico Moyúa 2, El Ensanche* ☎ 94/416–2200 ⊕ *www.hotelcarlton.es* ⮐ *136 rooms, 6 suites* ⛌ *Breakfast* Ⓜ *Moyúa.*

$
HOTEL
⊞ **Hotel Sirimiri.** A small, attentively run hotel near the Atxuri station, this modest spot has modern rooms with views over some of Bilbao's oldest architecture. **Pros:** handy to the Mercado de la Ribera, Casco Viejo, and the Atxuri train station; excellent buffet-style breakfast. **Cons:** tight

quarters; lacking character of surrounding buildings. Ⓢ *Rooms from: €60* ✉ *Pl. de la Encarnación 3, Casco Viejo* ☎ *94/433–0759* ⊕ *www. hotelsirimiri.es* ➴ *28 rooms* ⦿⃝ *Breakfast* Ⓜ *Casco Viejo.*

$ **Iturrienea Ostatua.** Extraordinarily beautiful, with charm to spare,
B&B/INN this hotel is in a traditional Basque town house one flight above the
Fodor'sChoice street in Bilbao's Old Quarter. **Pros:** budget-friendly; all no-smoking;
★ exquisite rustic style; free Wi-Fi. **Cons:** nocturnal noise on the front side, especially on summer weekend nights—try for an interior room or bring earplugs. Ⓢ *Rooms from: €70* ✉ *Santa María 14, Casco Viejo* ☎ *94/416–1500* ⊕ *www.iturrieneaostatua.com* ➴ *19 rooms* ⦿⃝ *No meals* Ⓜ *Casco Viejo.*

$$ **López de Haro.** This luxury hotel five minutes from the Guggenheim
HOTEL is under the same ownership as the Ercilla and, like its sister hotel, it's becoming quite a scene now that the city is a bona fide contemporary art destination. **Pros:** state-of-the-art comfort, service, and cuisine; traditional and aristocratic setting. **Cons:** a less than relaxing, slightly hushed and stuffy scene; not for the shorts-and-tank-top set. Ⓢ *Rooms from: €100* ✉ *Obispo Orueta 2–4, El Ensanche* ☎ *94/423–5500* ⊕ *www. hotellopezdeharo.com* ➴ *49 rooms, 4 suites* ⦿⃝ *Breakfast* Ⓜ *Moyúa.*

$$ **Meliá Bilbao Hotel.** Designed by architect Ricardo Legorreta and
HOTEL inspired by the work of Basque sculptor Eduardo Chillida (1920–2002), this high-rise hotel was built over what was once the nerve center of Bilbao's shipbuilding industry, and it feels appropriately like a futuristic ocean liner. **Pros:** great views over the whole shebang if you can get a room facing the Guggenheim. **Cons:** a high-rise colossus that might be more at home in Miami or Malibu. Ⓢ *Rooms from: €105* ✉ *C. Lehendakari Leizaola 29, El Ensanche* ☎ *94/428–0000* ⊕ *www.melia.com* ➴ *199 rooms, 12 suites* ⦿⃝ *No meals* Ⓜ *San Mamés.*

$$ **Miró Hotel.** Perfectly placed between the Guggenheim and Bilbao's
HOTEL excellent Museo de Bellas Artes, this boutique hotel refurbished by Barcelona fashion designer Toni Miró competes with the reflecting facade of Javier Mariscal's Domine Bilbao just up the street. **Pros:** a design refuge that places you in the eye of Bilbao's art and architecture fiesta. **Cons:** not unpretentious; a hint of preciosity pervades these halls. Ⓢ *Rooms from: €110* ✉ *Alameda de Mazarredo 77, El Ensanche* ☎ *94/661–1880* ⊕ *www.mirohotelbilbao.com* ➴ *50 rooms* ⦿⃝ *No meals* Ⓜ *Moyúa.*

$ **Petit Palace Arana.** Across from the Teatro Arriaga in the Casco Viejo,
HOTEL this design hotel has a blended style of contemporary and antique. **Pros:** in the heart of traditional Bilbao. **Cons:** can be noisy at night on the street side of the building. Ⓢ *Rooms from: €83* ✉ *Bidebarrieta 2, Casco Viejo* ☎ *94/415–6411* ⊕ *www.hthoteles.com* ➴ *64 rooms* ⦿⃝ *Multiple meal plans* Ⓜ *Casco Viejo.*

$ **Pensión Méndez I & II.** This may be the best value in town, with small
HOTEL but impeccable and well-appointed rooms, some of which (nos. 1 and 2) overlook the facade of the Palacio Yohn. **Pros:** excellent value; location in the middle of the Casco Viejo. **Cons:** no a/c; rooms with best views are noisy at night. Ⓢ *Rooms from: €50* ✉ *Santa María 13, 1st and 4th fl., Casco Viejo* ☎ *94/416–0364* ⊕ *www.pensionmendez.com* ➴ *24 rooms* ⦿⃝ *No meals* Ⓜ *Casco Viejo.*

5

$$ ⊞ **Urgoiti Hotel Palacio.** This extraordinary hotel, occupying a recon-
HOTEL structed 17th-century country palace out toward the airport, is a great
FAMILY retreat for active travelers or families, with a nine-hole pitch-and-putt
in the hotel gardens and other activities nearby. **Pros:** handy train ser-
vice into Bilbao; nearly walking distance from the airport; elegant and
peaceful environment; golf and water sports nearby. **Cons:** Bilbao and
the Guggenheim a short excursion away; a particular flight path into the
airport can be teeth-rattling. $ *Rooms from: €115* ⊠ *Arritugane Kalea
s/n, 13 km (8 miles) west of Bilbao, 2 km (1.2 miles) from the airport,
Mungia* 🕾 *94/674–6868* ⊕ *www.palaciourgoiti.com* ⇆ *42 rooms, 1
suite* |◎| *Breakfast.*

SPORTS AND THE OUTDOORS
BULLFIGHTS
Bilbao's *Semana Grande* (Grand Week), in mid-August, is famous for
scheduling Spain's largest bullfights of the season, an example of the
Basque Country's tendency to favor contests of strength and character
over art. (Note that in Barcelona, bullfights are no longer allowed under
local legislation.)

Plaza de Toros Vista Alegre. Prices and times of the bullfights held here
vary by event; check the website for listings. ⊠ *Martín Agüero 1, San
Mamés* 🕾 *94/444–8698* ⊕ *www.plazatorosbilbao.com* Ⓜ *San Mamés.*

SHOPPING
The main stores for clothing are found around Plaza Moyúa in the
Ensanche, along streets such as Calle Iparraguirre and Calle Rodríguez
Arias. The Casco Viejo has dozens of smaller shops, many of them
handsomely restored early houses with gorgeous wooden beams and
ancient stones, specializing in an endless variety of products from crafts
to antiques. Wool items, foodstuffs, and wood carvings from around the
Basque Country can be found throughout Bilbao. *Txapelas* (berets, or
Basque *boinas*) are famous worldwide and make fine gifts.

The city is home to international fashion names from Coco Chanel to
Calvin Klein. The ubiquitous department store El Corte Inglés is an easy
one-stop shop, if a bit routine.

MUNDAKA

37 km (22 miles) northeast of Bilbao.

Tiny Mundaka, famous among surfers all over the world for its left-
breaking roller at the mouth of the Ría de Gernika, has much to offer
nonsurfers as well. The town's elegant summer homes and stately
houses bearing family coats of arms compete for pride of place with
the hermitage on the Santa Catalina peninsula and the parish church's
Renaissance doorway.

ESSENTIALS
Visitor Information Mundaka ⊠ *Josepa Deuna kalea s/n* 🕾 *94/617–7201*
⊕ *www.mundakaturismo.com.*

BEACHES

Mundaka Beach. Famous for its waves, rolling in and breaking on the left side of the mouth of the River Laidatxu, this beach is said to have the longest surf break in Europe and among the best in the world. This attracts summertime surfers from everywhere, but means that in summer and fall this beach is off limits for families who just want to splash around. Land around the river mouth is part of the Urdibai Natural Preserve, a UNESCO-designated biosphere. **Amenities:** lifeguards, water sports. **Best for:** surfing. ⊠ *Matadero Kalea.*

WHERE TO EAT AND STAY

$$$$
BASQUE

✕ **Baserri Maitea.** In the village of Forua, about 11 km (7 miles) south of Mundaka and 1 km (½ mile) northwest of Guernica, this restaurant is in a stunning 18th-century *caserío* (Basque farmhouse). Strings of red peppers and garlic hang from wooden beams in the cathedral-like interior, and the kitchen is famous for its hearty fish and meat dishes prepared over a wood-fired grill. $ *Average main: €25* ⊠ *BI635 to Bermeo, Km 2* ☎ *94/625–3408* ⊕ *www.baserrimaitea.com* ⊗ *No dinner Sun. July and Aug.; no dinner Sun.–Thurs. Sept.–June.*

$$$$
SEAFOOD
Fodor's Choice
★

✕ **Casino de Mundaka.** Built in 1818 as a fish auction house for the local fishermen's guild, this building in the center of town, with wonderful views of Mundaka's beach, is now a fine restaurant and a well-known and respected eating club. The public is welcome, and it's a favorite place for lunches and sunset dinners in summer, when you can sit in the glassed-in, upper-floor porch. Don't be confused by the name—there's no gambling here ("casino" means something like a gentleman's club in Castilian). $ *Average main: €25* ⊠ *Kepa Deunaren 1* ☎ *94/687–6005.*

$$$$
BASQUE

✕ **Portuondo.** Spectacular terraces outside a traditional caserío overlooking the Laida beach, the aromas of beef and fish cooking over coals, a comfortable country dining room upstairs, and an easy 15-minute walk outside Mundaka all make this a good stop for lunch or dinner (in summer—it's a good idea to book ahead). Offerings are balanced between meat and seafood, and the wine list covers an interesting selection of wines from all over Spain. The tapas area downstairs crackles with life on weekends and during the summer. $ *Average main: €50* ⊠ *Portuondo Auzoa 1, Ctra. Gernika–Bermeo (BI2235), Km 47* ☎ *94/687–6050* ⊕ *www.restauranteportuondo.com* ⊗ *Closed Mon.*

$$
HOTEL

🛏 **Atalaya.** Tastefully converted from a private house, this 1911 landmark has become a big favorite for quick rail-getaway overnights from Bilbao—the 37-km (22-mile) train ride out is spectacular. **Pros:** intimate retreat from Bilbao's sprawl and bustle; friendly family service; weekend specials. **Cons:** tight quarters in some rooms. $ *Rooms from: €110* ⊠ *Itxaropen Kalea 1* ☎ *94/687–6899* ⊕ *www.atalayahotel.es* ↪ *13 rooms* ⊗ *Multiple meal plans.*

$
HOTEL

🛏 **Boliña.** Just a few steps from the Plaza de los Fueros in downtown Guernica, the Boliña is a pleasant and modern base camp for exploring the Vizcayan coast. **Pros:** comfortable and efficient; central location; good value. **Cons:** small rooms; restaurant seats 100 and is a local favorite for wedding receptions and gatherings. $ *Rooms from: €35* ⊠ *Barrenkale 3* ☎ *94/625–0300* ⊕ *www.hotelbolina.es* ↪ *16 rooms* ⊗ *Multiple meal plans.*

5

$ 🏨 **Kurutziaga Jauregia.** Basque for Palacio de la Cruz, this elegant 18th-
HOTEL century town house is a perfect alternative to the Atalaya for an overnight getaway from Bilbao. **Pros:** cozy retreat in downtown Mundaka.
Cons: small rooms; tight streets; parking can be difficult. $ *Rooms from:*
€70 ✉ *Kurtzio Kalea 1* ☎ *94/687–6925* ⊕ *www.kurutziagajauregia.com*
↩ *23 rooms* ⏸ *Multiple meal plans.*

OFF THE
BEATEN
PATH

Bosque de Oma. On the road to Kortezubi, 5 km (3 miles) from Guernica, stop off at the Urdaibai Natural Reserve for a stroll through the
Bosque de Oma, also known simply as Bosque Pintado (Painted Forest)
because of the rows of trees vividly painted by Basque artist Agustín
Ibarrola. It's a striking and successful marriage of art and nature. The
nearby **Cuevas de Santimamiñe** have important prehistoric cave paintings that can be accessed virtually at a visitor center. ✉ *Barrio Basondo,
Kortezubi* ☎ *94/465–1657.*

AXPE

47 km (28 miles) east of Bilbao, 42 km (26 miles) south of Elantxobe.

The village of Axpe, in the valley of Atxondo, nestles under the limestone heights of 4,777-foot Amboto—one of the highest peaks in the
Basque Country outside the Pyrenees. Home of the legendary Basque
mother of nature—Mari Urrika or Mari Anbotokodama (María, Our
Lady of Amboto)—Amboto, with its spectral gray rock face, is a sharp
contrast to the soft green meadows running up to the very foot of the
mountain. According to Basque scholar and ethnologist José María de
Barandiarán in his *Mitología Vasca* (*Basque Mythology*), Mari was
"a beautiful woman, well constructed in all ways except for one foot,
which was like that of a goat."

GETTING HERE AND AROUND

To reach Axpe from Bilbao, drive east on the A8/E70 freeway toward
San Sebastián. Get off at the Durango exit 40 km (24 miles) from Bilbao
and take the BI632 toward Elorrio. At Apatamonasterio turn right onto
the BI3313 and continue to Axpe.

WHERE TO EAT AND STAY

$$$$ ✗ **Etxebarri.** Victor Arguinzoniz and his development of innovative tech-
SEAFOOD   niques for cooking over coals have been hot news around the Iberian
Fodor's Choice Peninsula for a decade now, with woods and coals tailored to differ-
★   ent ingredients and new equipment such as a pan to char-grill angulas
or caviar. Everything from clams and fish to meats and even the rice
with langoustines is healthy, flavorful, and exciting as prepared and
served in this blocky stone house in the center of a tiny mountain
town. $ *Average main: €40* ✉ *Pl. San Juan 1* ☎ *94/658–3042* ⊕ *www.
asadoretxebarri.com* ⚄ *Reservations essential* ⊗ *Closed Mon. and Aug.
No dinner Tues.–Fri.*

$ 🏨 **Mendigoikoa.** This handsome group of hillside farmhouses is among
HOTEL   the province of Vizcaya's most exquisite hideaways. **Pros:** gorgeous set-
Fodor's Choice ting; smart and attentive service. **Cons:** need a car to get here. $ *Rooms
★   from: €80* ✉ *Barrio San Juan 33* ☎ *94/682–0833* ⊕ *www.mendigoikoa.
com* ↩ *11 rooms* ⊗ *Closed Nov.–Easter* ⏸ *Breakfast.*

Continued on page 337

BASQUE CULTURE

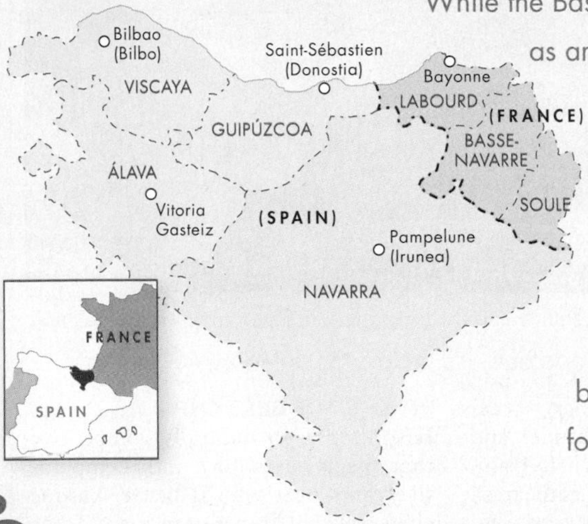
Bilbao
(Bilbo)
Saint-Sébastien
(Donostia)
Bayonne
VISCAYA
LABOURD
(FRANCE)
GUIPÚZCOA
BASSE-
NAVARRE
ÁLAVA
Vitoria
Gasteiz
(SPAIN)
SOULE
Pampelune
(Irunea)
NAVARRA
FRANCE
SPAIN

While the Basque Country's future as an independent nation-state has yet to be determined, the quirky, fascinating culture of the Basque people is not restricted by any borders. Experience it for yourself in the food, history, and sport.

The cultural footprints of this tiny corner of Europe, which straddles the Atlantic end of the border between France and Spain, have already touched down all over the globe. The sport of jai alai has come to America, international magazines give an ecstatic thumbs-up to Basque cooking, historians are pointing to Basque fishermen as the true discoverers of North America, and bestsellers, not without irony, proclaim *The Basque History of the World*. As in the ancient 4 + 3 = 1 graffiti equation, the three French (Labourd, Basse Navarre, and Soule) and the four Spanish (Guipúzcoa, Vizcaya, Álava, and Navarra) Basque provinces add up to a single people with a shared history. Although nationless, Basques have been Basques since Paleolithic times.

Stretching across the Pyrenees from Bayonne in France to Bilbao in Spain, the New Hampshire–sized Basque region retains a distinct culture, neither expressly French nor Spanish, fiercely guarded by its three million inhabitants. Fables stubbornly connect them with Adam and Eve, Noah's Ark, and the lost city of Atlantis, but a leading genealogical theory points to common bloodlines with the Celts. The most tenable theory is that the Basques are descended from aboriginal Iberian peoples who successfully defended their unique cultural identity from the influences of Roman and Moorish domination.

It was only in 1876 that Sabino Arana—a virulent anti-Spanish fanatic—proposed the ideal of a "pure" Basque independent state. That dream was crushed by Franco's dictatorial reign (1939–75, during which many Spanish Basques emigrated to France) and was immortalized in Pablo Picasso's *Guernica*. This famous painting, which depicts the catastrophic Nazi bombing of the Basque town of Gernika stands not only as a searing indictment of all wars but as a reminder of history's brutal assault upon Basque identity.

"THE BEST FOOD YOU'VE NEVER HEARD OF"

(left) Zurrukutuna, garlic soup with codfish. (right) Preparing canapes.

So says *Food & Wine* magazine. It's time to get filled in.

An old saying has it that every soccer team needs a Basque goaltender and every restaurant a Basque chef. Traditional Basque cuisine combines the fresh fish of the Atlantic and upland vegetables, beef, and lamb with a love of sauces that is rare south of the Pyrenees. Today, the *nueva cocina vasca* (new Basque cooking) movement has made Basque food less rustic and more nouvelle. And now that pintxos (the Basque equivalent of tapas) have become the rage from Barcelona to New York City, Basque cuisine is being championed by foodies everywhere. Even superchef Michel Guérard up in Eugénie-les-Bains has, though not himself a Basque, influenced and been influenced by the master cookery of the Pays Basque.

WHO'S THE BEST CHEF?

Basques are so naturally competitive that meals often turn into comparative rants over who is better: Basque chefs based in France or in Spain. Some vote for Bayonne's Jean-Claude Tellechea (his L'Auberge du Cheval Blanc is famed for groundbreaking surf-and-turf dishes like hake roasted in onions with essence of poultry) or St-Jean-Pied-de-Port's Firmin Arrambide (based at his elegant Les Pyrenees inn). Others prefer the postmodern lobster salads found over the border in San Sebastián and Bilbao, created by master chefs Juan Mark Arzak, Pedro Subijana, and Martin Berasategui, with wunderkind Andoni Aduriz and the Arbelaitz family nipping at their culinary heels.

SIX GREAT DISHES

Angulas. Baby eels, cooked in olive oil and garlic with a few slices of guindilla pepper.

Bacalao al pil-pil. Cod cooked at a low temperature in an emulsion of olive oil and fish juices, which makes a unique pinging sound as it sizzles.

Besugo. Sea bream, or besugo, is so revered that it is a traditional Christmas dish. Enjoy it with sagardo, the signature Basque apple cider.

Marmitako. This tuna stew with potatoes and pimientos is a satisfying winter favorite.

Ttoro. Typical of Labourd fishing villages such as St-Jean-de-Luz, this peppery Basque bouillabaisse is known as *sopa de pescado* (fish soup) south of the French border.

Txuleta de buey. The signature Basque meat is ox steaks marinated in parsley and garlic and cooked over coals.

BASQUE SPORTS: JAI-ALAI TO OXCART-LIFTING

Sports are at the core of Basque society, and few are immune to the Basque passion for competing, betting, and playing.

Over the centuries, the rugged physical environment of the Basque hills and the rough Cantabrian sea traditionally made physical prowess and bravery valued attributes. Since Basque mythology often involved feats of strength, it's easy to see why today's Basques are such rabid sports fans.

PELOTA

A Basque village without a *frontón* (pelota court) is as unimaginable as an American town without a baseball diamond. "The fastest game in the world," pelota is called *jai alai* in Basque (and translated officially as "merry festival"). With rubber balls flung from hooked wicker gloves at speeds up to 150 mph—the impact of the ball is like a machine-gun bullet—jai alai is mesmerizing. It is played on a three-walled court 175 feet long and 56 feet wide with 40-foot side walls.

Whether singles or doubles, the object is to angle the ball along or off of the side wall so that it cannot be returned. Betting is very much part of pelota and courtside wagers are brokered by bet makers as play proceeds. While pelota is the word for "ball," it also refers to the game. There was even a recent movie in Spain entitled *La Pelota Vasca*, used metaphorically to refer to the greater "ball game" of life and death.

HERRIKIROLAK

Herrikirolak (rural sports) are based on farming and seafaring. Stone lifters (*harrijasotzaileak* in Euskera) heft weights up to 700 pounds. *Aizkolari* (axe men) chop wood in various contests, *Gizon proba* (man trial) pits three-man teams moving weighted sleds; while *estropadak* are whaleboat rowers who compete in spectacular regattas (culminating in the September competition off La Concha beach in San Sebastián). *Sokatira* is tug of war, and *segalariak* is a scything competition. Other events include oxcart-lifting, milk-can carrying, and ram fights.

SOCCER

When it comes to soccer, Basque goaltenders have developed special fame in Spain, where Bilbao's Athletic Club and San Sebastian's Real Sociedad have won national championships with budgets far inferior to those of Real Madrid or FC Barcelona. Across the border, Bayonne's rugby team is a force in the French national competition; the French Basque capital is also home to the annual French pelota championship.

HABLA EUSKERA?

Although the Basque people speak French north of the border and Spanish south of the border, they consider Euskera their first language and identify themselves as the *Euskaldunak* (the "Basque speakers"). Euskera remains a great enigma to linguistic scholarship. Theories connect it with everything from Sanskrit to Japanese to Finnish.

What is certain is where Euskera did not come from, namely the Indo-European family of languages that includes the Germanic, Italic, and Hellenic language groups.

Currently used by about a million people in northern Spain and southwestern France, Euskera sounds like a consonant-ridden version of Spanish, with its five pure vowels, rolled "r," and palatal "n" and "l." Basque has survived two millennia of cultural and political pressure and is the only remaining language of those spoken in southwestern Europe before the Roman conquest.

The Euskaldunak celebrate their heritage during a Basque folk dancing festival.

A BASQUE GLOSSARY

Aurresku: The high-kicking *espata danza* or sword dance typically performed on the day of Corpus Christi in the Spanish Basque Country.

Akelarre: A gathering of witches that provoked witch trials in the Pyrénées. Even today it is believed that *jenti-lak* (magic elves) inhabit the woods and the Olentzaro (the evil Basque Santa Claus) comes down chimneys to wreak havoc—a fire is kept burning to keep him out.

Boina: The Basque beret or *txapela,* thought to have developed as the perfect protection from the siri-miri, the perennial "Scotch mist" that soaks the moist Basque Country.

Eguzki: The sun worship was at the center of the pagan religion that, in the Basque Country, gave way only slowly to

Christianity. The Basque solar cross is typically carved into the east-facing facades of ancient *caserios* or farmhouses.

Espadrilles: Rope-soled canvas Basque shoes, also claimed by the Catalans, developed in the Pyrénées and traditionally attached by laces or ribbons wrapped up the ankle.

Etxekoandre: The woman who commands all matters spiritual, culinary, and practical in a traditional Basque farmhouse. Basque matriarchal inheritance laws remain key.

Fueros: Special Basque rights and laws (including exemption from serving in the army except to defend the Basque Country) originally conceded by the ancient Romans and abolished at the end of the Carlist Wars in 1876 after cen-

turies of Castilian kings had sworn to protect Basque rights at the Tree of Gernika.

Ikurriña: The Basque flag, designed by the founder of Basque nationalism, Sabino Arana, composed of green and white crosses over a red background and said to have been based on the British Union Jack.

Lauburu: Resembling a four-leaf clover, lau (four) buru (head) is the Basque symbol.

Twenty: Basques favor counting in units of twenty (*veinte duros*—20 nickels—is a common way of saying a hundred pesetas, for example).

Txakolí: A slightly fizzy young wine made from grapes grown around the Bay of Biscay, this fresh, acidic brew happily accompanies tapas and fish.

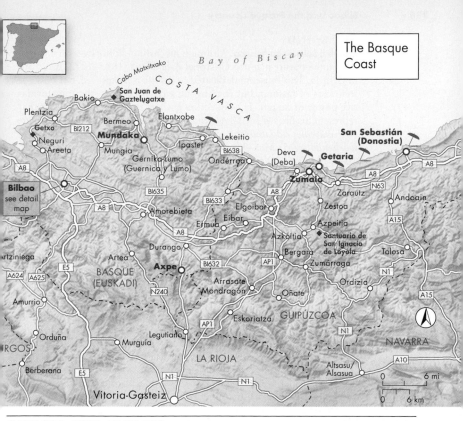

Bay of Biscay

Cabo Matxitxako

COSTA VASCA

GETARIA AND ZUMAIA

80 km (50 miles) east of Bilbao, 22 km (14 miles) west of San Sebastián.

Getaria (Guetaria in Spanish) is known as *la cocina de Guipúzcoa* (the kitchen of Guipúzcoa province) for its many restaurants and taverns. It was also the birthplace of Juan Sebastián Elcano (1487–1526), the first circumnavigator of the globe and Spain's most emblematic naval hero. Elcano took over and completed Magellan's voyage after Magellan was killed in the Philippines in 1521. The town's galleonlike church has sloping wooden floors resembling a ship's deck. Zarautz, the next town over, has a wide beach and many taverns and cafés.

Zumaia is a snug little port and summer resort with the estuary of the Urola River flowing—back and forth, according to the tide—through town. Zumaia and Getaria are connected along the coast road and by several good footpaths.

ESSENTIALS

Visitor Information Getaria ✉ *Parque Aldamar 2* ☎ *94/314-0957* ⊕ *www.getaria.net.* **Zumaia** ✉ *Pl. de Kantauri 13* ☎ *94/314-3396* ⊕ *zumaia.net.*

EXPLORING

Cristóbal Balenciaga Museoa. Although his fashion house lives on in Paris, the haute-couture maestro Cristóbel Balenciaga (1895–1972) was born in Getaria. This museum dedicated to his life is a must see, not only for followers of fashion, but for anyone who believes in the transformative power of design. The collection gathers together 1,200 pieces that represent his life's work. ✉ *Aldamar Parkea 6* ☎ *94/300–8840* 🌐 *www.cristobalbalenciagamuseoa.com* 🎟 *€10* 🕓 *Nov.–Feb., Tues.–Fri. 10–3, weekends 10–5; Mar.–May and Oct., Tues.–Fri. and Sun. 10–5, Sat. 10–7; June and Sept., Tues.–Sun. 10–7; July and Aug., daily 10–7.*

Museo Zuloaga. On the N634 at the eastern edge of town, this museum has an extraordinary collection of paintings by Goya, El Greco, Zurbarán, and others, in addition to works by the Basque impressionist Ignacio Zuloaga. The collection is housed in an ancient stone convent surrounded by gardens. With limited hours, the office phone often goes unanswered, so it's best to email with any requests. ✉ *Casa Santiago-Etxea 4* ☎ *67/707–8445* 🌐 *www.espaciozuloaga.com* 🎟 *€5* 🕓 *Mid-Apr.–mid-Sept., Fri.–Sun. 4–8*

WHERE TO EAT AND STAY

$$ BASQUE 🍴 **Bedua.** Zumaia natives like to access this rustic hideaway by boat when the tide is right, though you can also walk or drive. A specialist in *tortilla de patatas con pimientos verdes de la huerta* (potato omelet with homegrown green peppers), Bedua is also known for tortilla de bacalao, txuleta de buey, and fish of all kinds, especially the classic besugo cooked *a la donostiarra* (roasted and covered with a sauce of garlic and vinegar) and fresh baby eels, in season. [$] *Average main: €15* ✉ *Cestona, Barrio Bedua, up Urola, 3 km (2 miles) from Zumaia* ☎ *94/386–0551* 🌐 *www.bedua.es.*

$$ SEAFOOD 🍴 **Kaia Kaipe.** Suspended over Getaria's colorful and busy fishing port and with panoramas looking up the coast past Zarautz and San Sebastián all the way to Biarritz, this spectacular place puts together exquisite fish soups and serves fresh fish right off the boats—you can watch it being unloaded below. The town is the home of Txomin Etxaniz, the premier txakolí, and this is the ideal place to drink it. [$] *Average main: €15* ✉ *General Arnao 4* ☎ *94/314–0500* 🌐 *www.kaia-kaipe.com* 🕓 *Closed Mon. Oct.–June.*

$ B&B/INN FAMILY 🏨 **Landarte.** For a taste of life in a Basque caserío, spend a night or two in this lovely, restored, 16th-century, country manor house 1 km (½ mile) from Zumaia and an hour's walk from Getaria. **Pros:** warm, family-friendly atmosphere; traditional cuisine on request. **Cons:** some top-floor rooms under the low roof eaves could be tricky for taller guests; breakfast costs €6 extra per person. [$] *Rooms from: €88* ✉ *C. Artadi Anzoa 1, Zumaia* ☎ *94/386–5358* 🌐 *www.landarte.net* 🛏 *6 rooms* 🕓 *Closed mid-Dec.–Feb.* 🍽 *No meals.*

$$ HOTEL Fodor's Choice ★ 🏨 **Saiaz Getaria.** For panoramic views over the Bay of Biscay, this 15th-century house on Getaria's uppermost street is a perfect choice. **Pros:** opportunity to stay in a noble house in a unique fishing village; free Wi-Fi; discounts at nearby spa and gym. **Cons:** rooms on the seaside are small and undistinguished except for the views. [$] *Rooms from: €109*

✉ *Roke Deuna 25* ☎ *94/314–0143* ⊕ *www.saiazgetaria.com* ⇆ *17 rooms* ⊗ *Closed Dec. 20–Jan. 6* ⏸️*No meals.*

OFF THE BEATEN PATH **Pello Urdapilleta.** For a look at an authentic Basque caserío where the Urdapilleta family farms pigs, sheep, cattle, goats, chickens, and ducks, take a detour up to the village of Bidegoian, on the Azpeitia–Tolosa road. Pello Urdapilleta (which means "pile of pigs" in Euskera) sells artisanal cheeses and sausages, depending on what's available on the day. ✉ *Elola Azpikoa Baserria, Bidegoian* ☎ *605/701204* ⊕ *www. urdapilleta.eu.*

SAN SEBASTIÁN TO HONDARRIBIA

Graceful, chic San Sebastián invites you to slow down: stroll the beach, or wander the streets. East of the city is Pasajes, from which the Marquis de Lafayette set off to help the rebelling forces in the American Revolution and where Victor Hugo spent a winter writing. Just shy of the French border is Hondarribia, a brightly painted, flower-festooned port town.

SAN SEBASTIÁN

100 km (62 miles) northeast of Bilbao.

Fodor's Choice ★ San Sebastián (Donostia in Euskera) is a sophisticated city arched around one of the finest urban beaches in the world, **La Concha** (The Shell), so named for its resemblance to the shape of a scallop shell, with Ondarreta and Zurriola beaches at the southwestern and northeastern ends. The promontories of Monte Urgull and Monte Igueldo serve as bookends for La Concha, while Zurriola has Monte Ulía rising over its far end. The best way to see San Sebastián is to walk around: promenades and pathways lead up the hills that surround the city. The first records of San Sebastián date from the 11th century. A backwater for centuries, the city had the good fortune in 1845 to attract Queen Isabella II, who was seeking relief from a skin ailment in the icy Atlantic waters. Isabella was followed by much of the aristocracy of the time, and San Sebastián became a favored summer retreat for Madrid's well-to-do.

San Sebastián is divided by the **Urumea River,** which is crossed by three bridges inspired by late-19th-century French architecture. At the mouth of the Urumea, the incoming surf smashes the rocks with such force that white foam erupts, and the noise is wild and Wagnerian. The city is laid out with wide streets on a grid pattern, thanks mainly to the 12 different times it has been all but destroyed by fire. The last conflagration came after the French were expelled in 1813; English and Portuguese forces occupied the city, abused the population, and torched the place. Today, San Sebastián is a seaside resort on par with Nice and Monte Carlo. It becomes one of Spain's most expensive cities in the summer, when French vacationers descend in droves. It is also, like Bilbao, a center of Basque nationalism.

San Sebastián's neighborhoods include La Parte Vieja, tucked under Monte Urgull north of the mouth of the Urumea River; Gros (so named for a corpulent Napoleonic general), across the Urumea to the north; Centro, the main city nucleus around the cathedral; Amara, farther east toward the Anoeta sports complex; La Concha, at stage center around the beach; and El Antiguo, at the western end of La Concha. Igueldo is the high promontory over the city at the southwestern side of the bay. Alto de Miracruz is the high ground to the northeast toward France; Errenteria is inland east of Pasajes; Oiartzun is a village farther north; Astigarraga is in apple-cider country to the east of Anoeta.

GETTING HERE AND AROUND

San Sebastián is a very walkable city, though local buses (€1.65) are also convenient. Buses for Pasajes (Pasaia), Errenteria, Astigarraga, and Oiartzun originate in Calle Okendo, one block west of the Urumea River behind the Hotel Maria Cristina. Bus A-1 goes to Astigarraga; A-2 is the bus to Pasajes.

The EuskoTren, the city train, is popularly known as "El Topo" (The Mole) for the amount of time it spends underground. It originates at the Amara Viejo station in Paseo Easo and tunnels its way to Hendaye, France, every 30 minutes (€4.60; 45 minutes). EuskoTren also serves Bilbao (€5.60; 2 hours, 40 minutes) hourly and Zarautz (€3; 40 minutes) every half hour.

For the funicular up to Monte Igueldo (☎ *943/213525* ⊕ *www.monteigueldo.es* ✉ *€3.10*) the station is just behind Ondarreta beach at the western end of La Concha.

ESSENTIALS

Bus Information Bus station (Estación de autobuses) ✉ *C. de Fernando Sasiaín 7* ☎ *94/346–9074* ⊕ *www.dbus.es.*

Car Rental Europcar ✉ *Aeropuerto de San Sebastián (Hondarribia [Fuenterrabía]), C. Gabarrari 22* ☎ *94/366–8530* ⊕ *www.europcar.com.*

Train Information EuskoTren ☎ *90/254–3210* ⊕ *www.euskotren.es.* **San Sebastián train station** ✉ *Estación de Amara, Pl. Easo 9* ☎ *90/254–3210* ⊕ *www.euskotren.es* ✉ *Estación del Norte (RENFE), Paseo de Francia 22* ☎ *90/224–3402* ⊕ *www.renfe.es.*

Visitor Information San Sebastián–Donostia ✉ *Erregina Erregentearen 3, Blvd. 8* ☎ *94/348–1166* ⊕ *www.sansebastianturismo.com.*

EXPLORING

Every corner of Spain champions its culinary identity, but San Sebastián's refined fare is in a league of its own. Many of the city's restaurants and tapas spots are in the **Parte Vieja** (Old Quarter), on the east end of the bay beyond the elegant **Casa Consistorial** (City Hall) and formal **Alderdi Eder** gardens. The building that now houses city hall began as a casino in 1887; after gambling was outlawed early in the 20th century, the town council moved here from the Plaza de la Constitución, the Old Quarter's main square.

FAMILY **Aquarium Donostia–San Sebastián.** For a stroll through and under some 6,000 fish—ranging from tiger sharks to sea turtles, with one participative pool where kids are encouraged to touch and try to pick up fish—this is a great resource on one of San Sebastián's many rainy days. The illustrated history of Basque whaling and boatbuilding is also fascinating. ⊠ *Pl. Carlos Blasco de Imaz 1* ☎ *94/344–0099* ⊕ *www.aquariumss.com* ⊠ *€13* ⊘ *July and Aug., daily 10–9; Easter–June and Sept., weekdays 10–8, weekends 10–9; Oct.–Easter, weekdays 10–7, weekends 10–8.*

Catedral Buen Pastor (*Cathedral of the Good Shepherd*). Looking directly south from the front of Santa María, you can see the facade and of this 19th-century cathedral across town. With the tallest church spire in the province, the Cathedral of the Good Shepherd was constructed in the neo-Gothic style. It's worth a glimpse inside at beautiful stained-glass windows. ⊠ *Urdaneta Kalea 4, Pl. del Buen Pastor* ☎ *94/346–4516* ⊠ *Free* ⊘ *Weekdays 8:30–noon and 5–8, weekends for Mass only.*

Isla de Santa Clara. The tiny Isla de Santa Clara, right in the entrance to the bay, protects the city from Bay of Biscay storms, making La Concha one of the calmest beaches on Spain's entire northern coast. High promontories, Monte Urgull on the right and Monte Igueldo on the left, dominate the entrance to the bay. June through September, ferries run from the mainland every 30 minutes, and are packed on summer weekends. There's a small bar at the ferry dock, and lifeguard service at a beach that reveals itself only at low tide. Bring sandals, as the coastline is rocky.

Kursaal. Designed by renowned Spanish architect Rafael Moneo and located at the mouth of the Urumea River, the Kursaal is San Sebastián's postmodern concert hall, film society, and convention center. The gleaming cubes of glass that make up this bright complex were conceived as a perpetuation of the site's natural geography, an attempt to underline the harmony between the natural and the artificial and to create a visual stepping-stone between the heights of Monte Urgull and Monte Ulía. It has two auditoriums, a gargantuan banquet hall, meeting rooms, exhibition space, a set of terraces overlooking the estuary and the Ni Neu restaurant (⇨ *see Where to Eat*). For guided tours of the building, make arrangements in advance. ⊠ *Av. de Zurriola 1, Gros* ☎ *94/300–3000* ⊕ *www.kursaal.org.*

Monte Igueldo. On the western side of the bay, this promontory is a must-visit. You can walk or drive up or take the funicular (€3.10 roundtrip), with departures every 15 minutes. ☎ *94/321–3525 for funicular* ⊕ *www.monteigueldo.es* ⊘ *Funicular: Apr.–June, weekdays 11–8, weekends 10–9; July and Sept., daily 11–8; Oct.–Mar., Mon., Tues., Thurs., and Fri. 11–6, weekends 11–7; Aug., daily 10–10.*

Museo de San Telmo. In a 16th-century monastery behind the Parte Vieja, to the right (northeast) of the church of Santa María, the former chapel, now a lecture hall, was painted by José María Sert (1876–1945). The museum displays Basque ethnographic items, such as prehistoric steles once used as grave markers, and paintings by Zuloaga, Ribera, and El Greco. ⊠ *Pl. de Ignacio Zuloaga 1, Parte Vieja* ☎ *94/348–1581* ⊕ *www.museosantelmo.com* ⊠ *€5* ⊘ *Tues.–Sun. and holiday Mon. 10–8.*

Santa María. Just in from the harbor, in the shadow of Monte Urgull, is this baroque church, with a stunning carved facade of an arrow-riddled St. Sebastian flanked by two towers. The interior is strikingly restful; note the ship above the saint, high on the altar. ⊠ *C. 31 de Agosto 46 at C. Mayor* ☎ *94/342–3124* ⊠ *Free* ⊘ *Daily 10:15–1:15 and 4:45–7:45.*

BEACHES

FAMILY **La Concha.** San Sebastián's shell-shaped main beach is one of the most famous urban beaches in the world. Night and day, rain or shine, it's filled with locals and tourists alike, strolling and taking in the city's skyline and the uninhabited Santa Clara Island just offshore. Several hotels line its curved expanse, including the famed **Hotel de Londres y de Inglaterra** (⇨ *See Where to Stay).* The beach has clean, pale sand and few rocks or seaweed but only a bit of shade, near the promenade wall. Lounge chairs are available for rent. La Concha is safe night and day. **Amenities:** lifeguards, showers, toilets. **Best for:** sunrise, sunset, walking. ✉ *C. de la Concha Ibilbidea.*

Zurriola. Just across the Urumea River from San Sebastián's main La Concha beach lies this smaller, more tranquil beach. It offers the same views of Santa Clara Island but with fewer vendors and tourists. Summertime waves can make it too dangerous for children to swim, but they attract surfers—for blocks you'll see them, barefoot, wearing wet suits, and toting their surfboards beachward, particularly in summer and autumn when waves are biggest. **Amenities:** lifeguards, water sports. **Best for:** surfing. ✉ *Zurriola Ibilbidea.*

WHERE TO EAT

$$$$ ✕ **Akelare.** On the far side of Monte Igueldo (and the far side of culi-
CONTEMPORARY nary tradition, as well) presides chef Pedro Subijana, one of the most respected and creative chefs in the Basque Country. Prepare for tastes of all kinds, from Pop Rocks in blood sausage to mustard ice cream on tangerine peels. At the same time, Subijana's classical, dishes are monuments to traditional cookery: try the venison with apple and smoked chestnuts. Subijana also offers cooking classes; reserve online. $ *Average main: €155* ✉ *Paseo del Padre Orkolaga 56, Igueldo* ☎ *94/331–1209* ⊕ *www.akelarre.net* ⌂ *Reservations essential* ⊗ *Closed Mon. (and Tues. Jan.–June), Feb., and Oct. 1–15. No dinner Sun.*

$$$$ ✕ **Arzak.** Renowned chef Juan Mari Arzak's little house at the crest of
BASQUE Alto de Miracruz on the eastern outskirts of San Sebastián is interna-
Fodor'sChoice tionally famous, so reserve well in advance. Here, traditional Basque
★ products and preparations are enhanced to bring out the best in the natural ingredients. The ongoing culinary dialogue between Juan Mari

San Sebastián's famed, curving La Concha beach

and his daughter Elena, who share the kitchen, is one of the most endearing attractions here. The sauces are perfect, and every dish looks beautiful, but the prices (even of appetizers) are astronomical. $ *Average main: €189* ⊠ *Av. Alcalde Jose Elosegui 273, Alto de Miracruz* ☎ *94/327–8465, 94/328–5593* ⊕ *www.arzak.es* ⚮ *Reservations essential* ⊘ *Closed Sun. and Mon., June 15–July 2, and 3 wks in early Nov.*

$$
BASQUE ✗ **Astelena.** In what was once a banana warehouse, chef Ander González has transformed narrow stone rooms into one of the finest spots for modern Basque dining at a very good price. The €24 daily menu and the €36 weekend tasting menu list changing seasonal specials like *taco de bacalao sobre verduritas asadas* (salt-cod taco with grilled vegetables) and *magret de pato* (duck breast) or *alcachofas rellenas de rabo* (artichokes stuffed with bull's tail). The restaurant is conveniently located in the old quarter, near the Victoría Eugenia theater and Kursaal. $ *Average main: €15* ⊠ *Euskal Herria 3, Parte Vieja* ☎ *94/342–5867* ⊕ *www. restauranteastelena.com* ⊘ *Closed Mon. No dinner Sun.–Wed.*

$ ✗ **Bar Ganbara.** This busy favorite near Plaza de la Constitución is now
TAPAS run by the third generation of the same family. Specialty morsels range from shrimp and asparagus to Ibérico acorn-fed ham on croissants to anchovies, sea urchins, and wild mushrooms in season. $ *Average main: €10* ⊠ *C. San Jerónimo 21, Parte Vieja* ☎ *94/342–2575* ⊕ *www. ganbarajatetxea.com* ⊘ *Closed Mon. No dinner Sun.*

$ ✗ **Bar Gorriti.** Next to open-air La Brecha Market, this traditional little
TAPAS pintxos bar is a classic, filled with good cheer and delicious tapas. $ *Average main: €10* ⊠ *C. San Juan 3, Parte Vieja* ☎ *94/342–8353* ⊘ *Closed Sun.*

$ 🍴 **Bar San Marcial.** Nearly a secret, downstairs in the center of town, this
TAPAS is a very Basque spot with big wooden tables and a monumental bar filled with *cazuelitas* (small earthenware dishes) and tapas of all kinds. [$] *Average main: €10* ✉ *C. San Marcial 50, Centro* ☎ *94/343–1720* ⏲ *Closed Tues.*

$$$ 🍴 **Bergara Bar.** Winner of many a miniature cuisine award, this rustic
TAPAS tavern on the corner of Arteche and Bermingham offers a stylish take on traditional tapas and pintxos, and also serves meal-size roasts. [$] *Average main: €20* ✉ *General Arteche 8, Gros* ☎ *94/327–5026* 🌐 *www.pinchosbergara.es.*

$ 🍴 **Bernardo Etxea.** This hangout for locals during the week and everyone
TAPAS else on weekends serves excellent morsels: fried peppers, octopus, salmon with salsa, and especially fine pimientos with anchovies. There's a dining room for sit-down meals in the back, but the bar is most popular with the tapas crowd. [$] *Average main: €12* ✉ *C. Puerto 7, Parte Vieja* ☎ *94/342–2055* 🌐 *www.bernardoetxea.com* ⏲ *Closed Thurs. No dinner Wed.*

$$ 🍴 **Casa Vallés.** Beloved by locals, the bar combines great value with
TAPAS excellent food. Freshly prepared tapas creations go up on the bar at midday and again in the early evening, but it's open throughout the day for meals or snacks. There's a wood-paneled formal dining room out back, and tables on the sidewalk terrace out front. [$] *Average main: €15* ✉ *C. Reyes Católicos 10, Amara* ☎ *94/345–2210* 🌐 *www.barvalles.com* ⏲ *Closed Wed. No dinner Tues.*

$$ 🍴 **Casa Vergara.** This cozy bar, in front of the Santa María del Coro
TAPAS church, is always filled with reverent tapas devotees—and the counter is always piled high with delicious morsels. [$] *Average main: €15* ✉ *C. Mayor/Nagusia 21, Parte Vieja* ☎ *94/343–1073* 🌐 *www.casavergara.com* ⏲ *Closed Wed.*

$ 🍴 **Goiz Argi.** The specialty of this tiny bar—and the reason locals flock
TAPAS here on weekends—is the crisp yet juicy prawn brochette. [$] *Average main: €8* ✉ *Fermín Calbetón 4, Parte Vieja* ☎ *94/342–5204.*

$$$$ 🍴 **La Cepa.** This boisterous tavern has been around virtually forever (it
TAPAS opened in 1948). The ceiling of the wood-beamed bar is lined with dangling jamónes, the walls covered with old photos of San Sebastian and the room probably packed with locals. Everything from the Ibérico ham to the little olive, pepper, and anchovy combos called "penalties" will whet your appetite. [$] *Average main: €25* ✉ *C. 31 de Agosto 7, Parte Vieja* ☎ *94/342–6394* 🌐 *www.barlacepa.com* ⏲ *Closed Tues. and 2nd half of Nov.*

$$$$ 🍴 **Martín Berasategui.** One of the top restaurants in San Sebastián, sure
CONTEMPORARY bets here include the *lubina asada con jugo de habas, vainas, cebolletas*
Fodor's Choice *y tallarines de chipirón* (roast sea bass with juice of fava beans, green
★ beans, baby onions, and cuttlefish shavings), and the *salmón salvaje con pepino líquido y cebolleta a los fruitos rojos y rábanos* (wild salmon with liquid cucumber and spring onion, red fruits and radish), but go with whatever Martín suggests. [$] *Average main: €55* ✉ *C. Loidi 4, Lasarte, 8 km (5 miles) south of town* ☎ *94/336–6471, 94/336–1599* 🌐 *www.martinberasategui.com* ✍ *Reservations essential* ⏲ *Closed Mon., Tues., and mid-Dec.–mid-Jan. No dinner Sun.*

$$$$ SPANISH Fodor's Choice ★ 🍴 **Mugaritz.** This farmhouse in the hills above Errenteria, 8 km (5 miles) northeast of San Sebastián, is surrounded by spices and herbs tended by chef Andoni Aduriz and his crew. In a contemporary rustic setting with a bright and open feeling, Aduriz works to preserve and enhance natural flavors using avant-garde techniques such as *sous-vide* (cooking vacuum-packed foods slowly in low-temperature water) with pristine products from field, forest, and sea. The tasting menu is the only option here. [$] *Average main: €170* ✉ *Aldura Aldea 20, Otzazulueta Baserria, Errenteria* ☎ *94/352–2455, 94/351–8343* 🌐 *www.mugaritz.com* ✍ *Reservations essential* ⏲ *Closed Mon. and mid-Dec.–mid-Apr. No lunch Tues.; no dinner Sun.*

$$$$ CONTEMPORARY 🍴 **Ni Neu.** Chef Mikel Gallo's Ni Neu ("Me, Myself" in Euskera) occupies a bright corner of Rafael Moneo's dazzling Kursaal complex at the mouth of the Urumea River. The new formula here has been christened *bistronómico,* a term coined by French chef Sebastián Demorand to describe a less formal, family-bistro environment with more affordable and creative cuisine. Eggs fried at a low temperature with potatoes and codfish broth and pork ribs cooked for 40 hours and accompanied by creamy chicory and vanilla rice are two examples of comfort food with creative touches. The tapas-bar section of the restaurant is an excellent value. [$] *Average main: €25* ✉ *Avenida Zurriola 1, Gros* ☎ *94/300–3162* 🌐 *www.restaurantenineu.com* ⏲ *Closed Mon. No dinner Tues., Wed., and Sun.*

$$$$ BASQUE 🍴 **Sidrería Petritegui.** For hearty dining and a certain amount of splashing around in hard cider, make this short excursion southeast of San Sebastián to the town of Astigarraga. Gigantic wooden barrels line the walls, and *sidra al txotx* (cider drawn straight from the barrel) is classically accompanied by cider-house specialties such as tortilla de bacalao, txuleta de buey, the smoky local sheep's-milk cheese from the town of Idiazabal, and, for dessert, walnuts and *membrillo* (quince jelly). You can also buy cider in bulk, and take a tour of the factory. [$] *Average main: €30* ✉ *Ctra. San Sebastián–Hernani, Km 7, Astigarraga* ☎ *94/345–7188, 94/347–2208* 🌐 *www.petritegi.com* 💳 *No credit cards* ⏲ *Closed mid-Dec.–mid-Jan. No lunch Mon. and Tues.–Thurs. late Sept.–late June.*

$ TAPAS 🍴 **Zeruko.** It may look like just another tapas bar, but the pintxos served here are among the most advanced and beautiful concoctions in town. Don't miss the bacalao *al pil pil* that cooks itself on your plate. [$] *Average main: €10* ✉ *Pescadería 10, Parte Vieja* ☎ *94/342–3451* 🌐 *www.barzeruko.com* ⏲ *Closed Mon. No dinner Sun.*

$$$$ BASQUE Fodor's Choice ★ 🍴 **Zuberoa.** Working in a 15th-century Basque farmhouse 9.5 km (6 miles) northeast of San Sebastián outside the village of Oiartzun, Hilario Arbelaitz has long been one of San Sebastián's most celebrated chefs due to his original yet simple management of prime raw materials such as tiny spring cuttlefish, baby octopi, or woodcock. The *lenguado con verduritas y chipirones* (sole with baby vegetables and cuttlefish) is a tour de force. The atmosphere is unpretentious: just a few friends sitting down to dine simply—but very, very well. [$] *Average main: €40* ✉ *Araneder Bidea, Barrio Iturriotz, Oiartzun* ☎ *94/349–1228* 🌐 *www.*

5

zuberoa.com ⊘ *Closed Wed., and Sun. June–Oct. No dinner Sun., and Tues. Nov.–May.*

WHERE TO STAY

$

B&B/INN

FAMILY

⊞ **Aristondo.** A 15-minute drive above San Sebastián on Monte Igueldo, this comfortable and rustic farmhouse hideaway is a scenic and economical place to stay. **Pros:** good value; great views; bucolic peace and quiet. **Cons:** far from the action; requires a lot of walking, riding the funicular, or driving up and down Monte Igueldo. $ *Rooms from: €58* ⊠ *Camino de Pilotegui 70, Igueldo* ☎ *94/321–5558, 615/780682* ⊕ *www.aristondo.com* ⇔ *16 rooms* ❑ *No meals.*

$$$

HOTEL

Fodor's Choice

★

⊞ **Hotel de Londres y de Inglaterra.** On the main beachfront promenade overlooking La Concha, this stately hotel has a regal, old-world feel and Belle Époque aesthetic that starts in the elegant marble lobby, with its shimmering chandeliers, and continues throughout the hotel. **Pros:** sunsets from rooms on the Concha side are stunning; great location over the beach. **Cons:** street side can be noisy on weekends. $ *Rooms from: €129* ⊠ *Zubieta 2, La Concha* ☎ *94/344–0770* ⊕ *www.hlondres. com* ⇔ *139 rooms, 9 suites* ❑ *No meals.*

$$$$

HOTEL

⊞ **Hotel María Cristina.** The graceful beauty of the Belle Époque is embodied here, in San Sebastián's most luxurious hotel, which sits on the elegant west bank of the Urumea River. **Pros:** polished service; supreme elegance; *the* place to stay. **Cons:** staffers occasionally can be stiff. $ *Rooms from: €250* ⊠ *Paseo República Argentina 4, Centro* ☎ *94/343–7600* ⊕ *www.hotel-mariacristina.com* ⇔ *108 rooms, 28 suites* ❑ *Some meals.*

$$$

HOTEL

⊞ **Hotel Parma.** Overlooking the Kursaal concert hall and the Zurriola beach at the mouth of the Urumea River, this small but bright new hotel is also at the edge of the Parte Vieja, San Sebastián's prime grazing area for tapas and vinos. **Pros:** prime location; views; the crashing of the waves; free Wi-Fi. **Cons:** rooms are a bit cramped and cluttered; room style is efficient but drab. $ *Rooms from: €157* ⊠ *Paseo de Salamanca 10, Parte Vieja* ☎ *94/342–8893* ⊕ *www.hotelparma.com* ⇔ *27 rooms* ❑ *No meals.*

NIGHTLIFE AND PERFORMING ARTS

NIGHTLIFE

Bataplan. San Sebastián's top disco is near the western end of La Concha. Guest DJs and events determine the vibe, although you can count on high-energy dance music and enthusiastic drinking. ⊠ *Paseo de la Concha s/n, Centro* ☎ *94/347–3601* ⊕ *www.bataplandisco.com* ⊘ *Thurs.– Sat. midnight–7 am.*

Bebop. This publike bar, on the edge of the Urumea River, has regular live Latin and jazz music. Hours vary; check the website for listings. ⊠ *Paseo de Salamanca 3, Parte Vieja* ☎ *94/342–9869* ⊕ *www.barbebop.com.*

La Rotonda. Across the street from Bataplan and below Miraconcha, this is a top nightspot. ⊠ *Paseo de la Concha 6, Centro* ☎ *94/342–9095, 639/146268* ⊕ *www.rotondadisco.com.*

PERFORMING ARTS

Kursaal. Home of the Orquesta Sinfónica (Symphony Orchestra) de Euskadi, this venue is also a favorite for ballet, opera, theater, and jazz. ⊠ *Av. de la Zurriola, Gros* ☎ *94/300–3000* ⊕ *www.kursaal.com.*

Teatro Victoria Eugenia. In a stunning 19th century building, this elegant venue offers varied programs of theater, dance and more. ⊠ *Paseo de la República Argentina, 2, Centro* ☎ *94/348–1155, 94/348–1160* ⊕ *www.victoriaeugenia.com.*

SHOPPING

San Sebastián is a busy designer-shopping town. Wander Calle San Martín and the surrounding pedestrian-only streets to see what's in the windows.

Elkar. Previously known as Bilintx, this shop is one of the city's best bookstores—it's now part of the Basque bookstore chain Elkar. There's a decent selection of English-language books, as well as CDs, games, and stationary. ⊠ *Fermin Calbeton Kalea 21, Parte Vieja* ☎ *902/115210* ⊕ *www.elkar.com.*

Maitiena. Stop by this stylish shop for a fabulous selection of chocolates, hot chocolate, teas, and other fixes for sweet-tooths. ⊠ *Peña Florida 6, Centro* ☎ *94/342–4721* ⊕ *www.maitiana.com.*

Ponsol. The best place to buy Basque berets—the Leclerq family has been hatting (and clothing) the local male population for four generations, since 1838. It's closed between 1 and 4 pm, and all day Sunday. ⊠ *C. Narrica 4, at C. Sarriegui 3, Parte Vieja* ☎ *94/342–0876* ⊕ *www.casaponsol.com.*

PASAJES DE SAN JUAN

7 km (4 miles) east of San Sebastián.

Generally marked as Pasai Donibane, in Euskera, there are actually three towns around the commercial port of Rentería: **Pasajes Ancho,** an industrial port; **Pasajes de San Pedro,** a large fishing harbor; and historic **Pasajes de San Juan,** a colorful cluster of 16th- and 17th-century buildings along the shipping channel between the industrial port of Rentería and the sea. Best and most colorfully reached by driving into Pasai de San Pedro, on the San Sebastián side of the strait, and catching a launch across the mouth of the harbor (about €1, depending on the time of day), this is too sweet a side trip to pass up.

In 1777, at the age of 20, General Lafayette set out from Pasajes de San Juan to aid the American Revolution. Victor Hugo spent the summer of 1843 here writing his *Voyage aux Pyrénées.* The **Victor Hugo House** is the home of the tourist office and has an exhibit of traditional village dress. **Ondartxo,** a center of maritime culture, is directed by Xavier Agote, who taught boatbuilding in Rockland, Maine. Pasajes de San Juan can be reached via Pasajes de San Pedro from San Sebastián by cab or bus. Or, if you prefer to go on foot, follow the red-and-white-blazed GR trail that begins at the east end of the Zurriola beach—you're in for a spectacular three-hour hike along the rocky coast. By car, take N1 toward France and, after passing Juan Mari Arzak's landmark

Continued on page 352

MINIATURE FOOD, MAXIMUM FLAVOR

An Introduction to TAPAS

On the way home from work, colleagues in Spain rarely fail to hit a tapas bar for a *caña* (a 4- to 6-oz beer), invariably accompanied by tapas in one form or another. The ready availability of delicacies ranging from the lowly (but delicious) potato omelet to the relatively expensive (but *really* delicious) Ibérico ham is a uniquely Spanish phenomenon;

Itinerant, make-it-up-as-you-go grazing is one of Spain's many art forms. The variety of the tapas, the splash of beer or wine or sherry or txakoli to accompany the food, and the new faces and old friends in each tavern are quintessentially Spanish.

5

THE HISTORY OF SHRINKING PORTIONS

The origin of tapas is the stuff of heated tapas-bar debates. Various reports cloud the history of when and how it started. Some credit Alfonso X's diet and his delicate stomach. However, the most commonly accepted explanation is that a flat object (be it a slice of bread or a flat card with some nuts or sunflower seeds) was used to cover the rim of wine glasses to keep dive-bombing fruit flies out. (To cover something up is "tapar" in Spanish.)

it's a rambling, open cocktail party to which everyone is invited. Whether snagging *pinchos* (individual morsels on toothpicks) or sharing a *ración* (small plate) among two or three friends, this free-wheeling and spontaneous approach to food and socializing is at the heart of the Spanish experience. Eating tapas is such a way of life that a verb had to be created for it: *tapear* (to eat tapas) or *ir a tapeo* (to go eat tapas).

TAPAS ACROSS SPAIN

MADRID

It is often difficult to qualify what is authentically from Madrid and what has been gastronomically cribbed from other regions, thanks to Madrid's melting-pot status for people and customs all over Spain. While *croquetas, tortilla de patata* (also known as *tortilla española*, potato omelet), and even *paella* can be served as tapas, *patatas bravas* and *calamares* can be found in almost any restaurant in Madrid. The popular *patatas* are a very simple mixture of fried or roasted potatoes with a "Brava" sauce that is slightly spicy—surprising, given a country-wide aversion for dishes with the slightest kick. The *calamares*, fried in olive oil, can be served alone or with alioli sauce, mayonnaise, or—and you're reading correctly—in a sandwich. A slice of lemon usually accompanies your serving.

Tortilla de patata

Calamares

ANDALUSIA

Known for the warmth of its climate and its people, Andalusian bars tend to be very generous with their tapas—maybe in spite of the fact that they aren't exactly celebrated for their culinary inventiveness. But tapas here are traditional and among the best. Many times ordering a drink will bring you a sandwich large enough to make a meal, or a bowl of gazpacho that you could swim in. Seafood is also extremely popular in Andalusia, and you will find tapas ranging from sizzling prawns to small anchovies soaked in vinegar or olive oil.

Pescado frito or *boquerones* (fried fish) and *albóndigas* (meatballs) are two common tapas in the region, and it's worth grazing multiple bars to try the different preparations. The fish usually includes squid, anchovies, and other tiny fish, deep fried and served as is. Since the bones are very small, they are not removed and considered fine for digestion. If this idea bothers you, sip some more wine. The saffron-almond sauce (*salsa de almendras y azafrán*) that accompanies the meatballs might very well make your eyes roll with pleasure. And since saffron is not as expensive in Spain as it is in the United States, the meatballs are liberally drenched in it.

Boquerones

Not incidentally, Spain's biggest export, olives, grows in Andalusia, so you can expect many varieties among the tapas served with your drinks.

Albondigas

BASQUE COUNTRY

More than any other community in Spain, the Basque Country is known for its culinary originality. The tapas, like the region itself, tend to be more expensive and inventive. And since the Basques insist on doing things their way, they call their unbelievable bites *pintxos* (or *pinchos* in Spanish) rather than tapas. *Gildas*, probably the most ordered *pintxo* in the Basque Country, is a simple toothpick skewer composed of a special green pepper (called *guindilla vasca*), an anchovy, and a pitted olive. All the ingredients must be of the highest quality, especially the anchovy, which should be marinated in the best olive oil and not be too salty. *Pimientos rellenos de bacalao* (roasted red peppers stuffed with cod) are also popular, given the Basque Country's proximity to the ocean. The festive color of the red peppers and the savoriness of the fish make it a bite-sized Basque delicacy.

Red and green pepper *tapas*

A spread of tapas

GET YOUR TAPAS ON

Madrid
El Bocaíto. The best *pescaíto* (fried whitebait) and *tostas* (toast with toppings). ⊠ *Libertad 6, Chueca* ☎ *91/532–1219.*

Estay. Delicious *tortilla española* and excellent *rabas* (fried calamari strips). ⊠ *Hermosilla 46, Salamanca* ☎ *91/578–0470.*

Barcelona
Cal Pep. The best tapas counter in Barcelona, worth a twenty-minute wait. ⊠ *Plaça de les Olles 8, Born-Ribera* ☎ *93/310–7961*

El Vaso de Oro. Always busy for a good reason: excellent fare and a great vibe. ⊠ *Balboa 6, Barceloneta* ☎ *93/319–3098*

Andalusia
El Rinconcillo. Seville's oldest tavern, with everything from venison stew to gazpacho. ⊠ *C. Gerona 40, La Macarena, Seville* ☎ *95/422–3183*

Taberna San Miguel-Casa El Pisto. *Moriles, pinchos,* and *raciones* in a rustic tavern. ⊠ *Plaza San Miguel 1, Centro. Córdoba* ☎ *957/470166*

The Basque Country
La Cepa. One of the most spectacular tapas displays in San Sebastián. ⊠ *C. 31 de Agosto 7, Parte Vieja, San Sebastián* ☎ *943/426–394*

Xukela. Inventive *pinchos* in an atmospheric tavern. ⊠ *C. El Perro 2, Bilbao, Casco Viejo* ☎ *94/415–9772.*

Bite-size food and drink

Wine and tapas

TAPAS MENU DECODER

This cheat sheet will help you order tapas throughout Spain.

Tapas Terms

pincho, pintxo, tapa: snack-sized portion

ración: large portion of tapas, usually to share

media-ración: half-size portion of tapas

montadito: small open-faced sandwich/tapa mounted on small baguette slice

Method of Cooking/Preparation

a la plancha: grilled

a la parilla: barbecued

a leña: cooked slowly over wood fire

al horno: baked

brochette: on a stick (shish kebab)

en vinagre: marinated in vinegar brine (usually uncooked)

frito: fried (usually in olive oil, breaded)

surtido de . . . : an assortment

sandwich: smaller sandwich on sliced white bread

Asking for Help

What would you recommend? *¿Qué recomienda?*

What's in that dish? *¿Qué lleva ese plato?*

I don't eat meat. *No como carne.*

I'm allergic to . . . *Tengo alérgia a* . . .

Typical Tapas

aceitunas: olives

albóndigas: meatballs

almendras: almonds, usually fried or roasted

banderilla: small kebab of vegetables

boquerones: small fish, usually sardines or anchovies, in vinegar or fried

caracoles: small snails

champiñones, setas: mushrooms; wild mushrooms

chipirones: baby squid

croquetas: breaded, fried croquettes with béchamel and jamón or fish stuffing

embutidos: cured meats

empanadas, empanadillas: pastry stuffed with meat, fish, or vegetables; smaller version

ensalada Rusa: cold potato salad with mayonnaise, peas, and carrots

gambas al ajillo: shrimp sautéed with garlic

judias: beans

morcilla: blood sausage

morros: pig snout

patatas bravas: fried potatoes with spicy red sauce

patatas alioli: fried potatoes with garlic sauce

patatas mixta: fried potatoes with half red spicy sauce, half garlic sauce

pimientos de Padrón: fried and salted green peppers from Padrón, usually sweet but sometimes hot

pincho de tortilla: slice of potato and onion omelet

rabo de toro: stew made from bull's tail (usually fresh from the bull ring)

restaurant, Arzak, at Alto de Miracruz, look for a marked left turn into Pasaia or Pasajes de San Pedro.

EXPLORING

FAMILY **Barco Museo Mater** (*Mater Ship Museum*). A former Basque fishing boat now offers tours of the port, visits to a rowing club, and to the Victor Hugo house in Pasai Donibane, as well as a treasure hunt for young and old alike. You can join a one-hour trip or rent the ship out for the whole day (for groups of 10 or more). Book ahead, online or by phone. ✉ *Muelle Pesquero, Pasai San Pedro* ☎ *619/814225* 🌐 *www.itsasgela.org* 🎟 *€5 for 1-hr trip* 🕒 *Tues.–Thurs. at 5 and 6, weekends at noon and 1.*

WHERE TO EAT

$$$$ | SEAFOOD | Fodor's Choice ★ 🍴 **Casa Cámara.** Four generations ago, Pablo Cámara turned this 19th century fishing wharf on the Rentería narrows into a first-class seafood restaurant with classic fare. The dining room has lovely views over the shipping lane, and a central "live" tank that rises and falls with the tide and from which lobsters and crayfish can be hauled up for your inspection. A steaming *sopa de pescado* (fish soup) on a wet Atlantic day is a memorable event. Try *cangrejo del mar* (spider crab with vegetable sauce) or the superb *merluza con salsa verde* (hake in green sauce). [$] *Average main: €37* ✉ *C. San Juan 79, Pasai Donibane* ☎ *94/352–3699* 🌐 *www.casacamara.com* ✍ *Reservations essential* 🕒 *Closed Mon., and Wed. Nov.–Easter wk. No dinner Sun.*

5

HONDARRIBIA

18 km (11 miles) east of Pasajes.

Hondarribia (Fuenterrabía in Spanish) is the last fishing port before the French border. Lined with fishermen's homes and small fishing boats, the harbor is a beautiful but touristy spot. If you have a taste for history, follow signs up the hill to the medieval bastion and onetime castle of Carlos V, now a parador.

ESSENTIALS

Visitor Information Hondarribia ✉ *Pl. de Armas 9* ☎ *94/364–3677* 🌐 *www.bidasoaturismo.com.*

WHERE TO EAT AND STAY

$$$$ | BASQUE 🍴 **Alameda.** The three Txapartegi brothers—Mikel, Kepa and Gorka—are the star chefs behind this restaurant, which opened in 1997 after the brothers' apprenticeship with, among others, Lasarte's master chef Martín Berasategui. The elegantly restored house in upper Hondarribia is a delight, as are the seasonally rotated combinations of carefully chosen ingredients, from fish to duck to vegetables. Both surf and turf selections are well served here, from Ibérico ham to fresh tuna just in from the Atlantic. [$] *Average main: €50* ✉ *Minasoroeta 1* ☎ *94/364–2789* 🌐 *www.restaurantealameda.net* 🕒 *No dinner Sun., and Mon. and Tues. late Dec.–early Feb.*

$ | B&B/INN | FAMILY 🏨 **Casa Artzu.** Better hosts than this warm, friendly clan are hard to find, and their family house and barn—here in one form or another for some 800 years—offers modernized accommodations overlooking the Bidasoa estuary and the Atlantic. **Pros:** good value; friendly family. **Cons:** free parking; breakfast costs €3 extra. $\boxed{\$}$ *Rooms from: €47* ⊠ *Barrio Montaña* ☎ *94/364–0530* ⊕ *www.euskalnet.net/casartzu* ↩ *6 rooms* ⦾ *No meals.*

$$$$
HOTEL
FAMILY
Fodor's Choice
★

⊞ **Parador de Hondarribia.** You can live like a medieval lord in this 10th-century bastion, home in the 16th century of Spain's founding emperor, Carlos V—hence it's alternative name: Parador El Emperador. **Pros:** great sea views; impeccably comfortable. **Cons:** no restaurant. $\boxed{\$}$ *Rooms from: €220* ⊠ *Pl. de Armas 14* ☎ *94/364–5500* ⊕ *www.parador.es* ↩ *36 rooms* ⦾ *No meals.*

NAVARRA AND PAMPLONA

Bordering the French Pyrenees and populated largely by Basques, Navarra grows progressively less Basque toward its southern and eastern edges. Pamplona, the ancient Navarran capital, draws crowds with its annual feast of San Fermín, but medieval Vitoria, the Basque capital city in the province of Alava, is largely undiscovered by tourists. Olite, south of Pamplona, has a storybook castle, and the towns of Puente la Reina and Estella are visually indelible stops on the Camino de Santiago.

PAMPLONA

79 km (47 miles) southeast of San Sebastián.

Pamplona (Iruña in Euskera) is known worldwide for its running of the bulls, made famous by Ernest Hemingway in his 1926 novel *The Sun Also Rises*. The occasion is the festival of San Fermín, July 6–14, when Pamplona's population triples (along with hotel rates), so reserve rooms months in advance. Every morning at 8 sharp a rocket is shot off, and the bulls kept overnight in the corrals at the edge of town are run through a series of closed-off streets leading to the bullring, a 924-yard dash. Running before them are Spaniards and foreigners feeling festive enough to risk goring. The degree of peril in the running (or *encierro*, meaning "enclosing") is difficult to gauge. Serious injuries occur nearly every day during the festival; deaths are rare but always a possibility. What's certain is the sense of danger, the mob hysteria, and the exhilaration. Access to the running is free, but tickets to the bullfights (*corridas*) can be difficult to get.

Founded by the Roman emperor Pompey as Pompaelo, or Pampeiopolis, Pamplona was successively taken by the Franks, the Goths, and the Moors. In 750, the Pamplonians put themselves under the protection of Charlemagne and managed to expel the Arabs temporarily. But the foreign commander took advantage of this trust to destroy the city walls; when he was driven out once more by the Moors, the Navarrese took their revenge, ambushing and slaughtering the retreating Frankish army as it fled over the Pyrenees through the mountain pass of Roncesvalles in 778. This is the episode depicted in the 11th-century *Song of Roland*, although the anonymous French cast the aggressors as Moors. For centuries after that, Pamplona remained three argumentative towns until they were forcibly incorporated into one city by Carlos III (the Noble, 1387–1425) of Navarra.

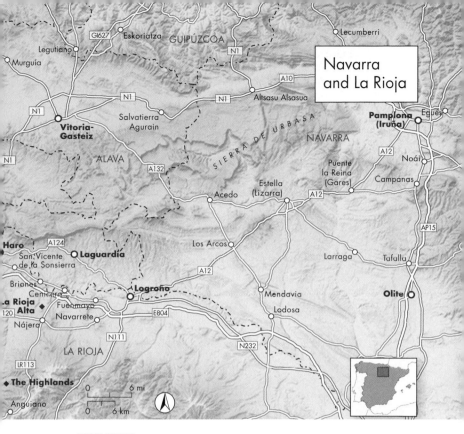

Navarra
and La Rioja

ESSENTIALS

Bus Station Pamplona ✉ *C. Yanguas y Miranda 2* 📞 *90/202–3651* 🌐 *www. estaciondeautobusesdepamplona.com.*

Car Rentals Europcar ✉ *Blanca de Navarra Hotel, Av. Pio XII 43* 📞 *94/817–2523* 🌐 *www.europcar.com* ✉ *Aeropuerto de Pamplona (Noain), Carretera Bellaterra s/n* 📞 *94/831–2798* 🌐 *www.europcar.com.*

Train Information Pamplona ✉ *Estación de Pamplona, Pl. de la Estación s/n* 📞 *90/232–0320, 90/243–2343* 🌐 *www.adif.es.*

Visitor Information Pamplona. In addition to Pamplona's main tourist office, there's a tourist information kiosk in Plaza Consistorial from Easter to September, open 10–8 daily. ✉ *Av. Roncesvalles 4* 📞 *84/842–0420* 🌐 *www.turismo depamplona.es.*

EXPLORING

Archivo Real y General de Navarra. This Rafael Moneo–designed structure of glass and stone, ingeniously contained within a Romanesque palace, is Pamplona's architectural treasure. Containing papers and parchments going back to the 9th century, the archive holds more than 25,000 linear yards of documents and has room for more than 18,500 yards more. The library and reading rooms are lined with cherrywood and topped with a gilded ceiling. ✉ *C. Dos de Mayo s/n* ☎ 84/842–4667, 84/842–4623 ⊕ *www.cfnavarra.es/agn* ✉ *Free* ☉ *Weekdays 8:30–2:30.*

Ayuntamiento (*Town hall*). Pamplona's most remarkable civic building is the ornate town hall on the Plaza Consistorial, with its rich ocher facade setting off brightly gilded balconies. The interior is a lavish wood-and-marble display of wealth, reinforcing Navarra's historic status as a wealthy kingdom in its own right. The present building was erected between 1753 and 1759. You can appreciate it from the outside and even step inside the lobby, but the building is not otherwise open to visitors. ✉ *Pl. Consistorial s/n.*

Café Iruña. Pamplona's gentry has been flocking to this ornate, French-style café since 1888, but Ernest Hemingway made it part of world literary lore in *The Sun Also Rises* in 1926. You can still have a drink with a bronze version of the author at his favorite perch at the far end of the bar, or enjoy views of the plaza from an outdoor table on the terrace. It's closed on Saturday afternoon. ✉ *Pl. del Castillo 44* ☎ *94/822–2064* ⊕ *www.cafeiruna.com.*

Cathedral. Near the portion of the ancient walls rebuilt in the 17th century, this is one of the most important religious buildings in northern Spain, thanks to the fragile grace and gabled Gothic arches of its cloister. Inside are the tombs of Carlos III and his wife, marked by an alabaster sculpture. The **Museo Catedralicio Diocesano** (Diocesan Museum) houses religious art from the Middle Ages and the Renaissance. Call in advance for guided tours in English. ✉ *C. Dormitaleria 3–5* ☎ *94/821–2594* ⊕ *www.catedraldepamplona.com* ✉ *€5* ☉ *Cathedral Mon.–Sat. 9–10:30 and 7–8:30, Sun. 10–2; museum Mon.–Sat. 10:30–5.*

Edificio Baluarte. The Palacio de Congresos y Auditorio de Navarra, built in 2003 by local architectural star Patxi Mangado, is a sleek assemblage of black Zimbabwean granite. It contains a concert hall of exquisite acoustical perfection, utilizing beechwood from upper Navarra's famed Irati *haya* (beech) forest. Performances and concerts, from opera to ballet, are held in this modern venue, built on the remains of one of the five bastions of Pamplona's 16th-century Ciudadela. ✉ *Plaza del Baluarte* ☎ *94/806–6066* ⊕ *www.baluarte.com.*

Plaza del Castillo. One of Pamplona's greatest charms is the warren of small streets near the Plaza del Castillo (especially Calle San Nicolás), which are filled with restaurants, taverns, and bars. Pamplonicas are hardy, rough-and-tumble sorts, well known for their eagerness and capacity to eat and drink.

Fundación–Museo Jorge Oteiza. Just 8 km (5 miles) east of Pamplona on the road toward France, this museum dedicated to the father of modern Basque art is a must-visit. Jorge Oteiza (1908–2003), in his seminal treatise, *Quosque Tandem,* called for Basque artists to find an aesthetic of their own instead of attempting to become part of the Spanish canon. Oteiza created a school of artists of which the sculptor Eduardo Chillida (1924–2002) was the most famous. The building itself is a large cube of earth-colored concrete designed by Oteiza's longtime friend, Pamplona architect Francisco Javier Sáenz de Oiza. The sculptor's living quarters, his studio, and the workshop used for teaching divide the museum into three sections. ✉ *C. de la Cuesta 7, Alzuza, 8 km from Pamplona on N150* ☎ *94/833–2074* 🌐 *www.museooteiza.org* 🎟 *€4 (free Fri.)* 🕒 *July and Aug., Tues.–Sat. 11–7, Sun. 11–3; Sept.–June, guided tours by reservation only, Tues. and Sat. at 11 and 1.*

WHERE TO EAT AND STAY

$$$ SPANISH 🍴 **Europa Restaurante.** Generally considered Pamplona's best restaurant, the Europa, in the hotel of the same name, offers a decidedly epicurean take on traditional Navarran cooking, with a Michelin star to show for it. The small and light first-floor dining room offers the perfect backdrop to dishes like slow-cooked lamb and pork, or the best bacalao al pil pil you may try on your trip. À la carte dining is reasonably priced, and there are excellent tasting menus available for €41, €48, and €60. [$] *Average main: €20* ✉ *C. Espoz y Mina 11* ☎ *94/822–1800* 🌐 *www.hreuropa.com* 🕒 *Closed Sun.*

$ TAPAS 🍴 **Gaucho.** A legendary address for *tapeo* (tapas grazing) and *txikiteo* (wine tippling), this small tavern serves some of the best tapas in Pamplona. Just off Plaza del Castillo, in the eye of the hurricane during San Fermín, there is a surprising sense of peace and quiet here, even as the fiesta spins out of control outside. Tapas range from the classical *chistorra* (spicy sausage) to contemporary creations such as the deconstructed *vieira* (scallop), an apt metaphor for Pamplona's blend of old and new. [$] *Average main: €7* ✉ *C. Espoz y Mina 7* ☎ *94/822–5073* 🌐 *www.cafebargaucho.com.*

$$$ HOTEL Fodor's Choice ★ 🏨 **Gran Hotel La Perla.** The oldest hotel in Pamplona, after several years of refurbishing, has reinvented itself as a luxury lodging option. **Pros:** read your worn copy of *The Sun Also Rises* in the place where the book was first conceived; impeccable comfort. **Cons:** round-the-clock mayhem during San Fermín. [$] *Rooms from: €155* ✉ *Pl. del Castillo 1* ☎ *94/822–3000* 🌐 *www.granhotellaperla.com* 🛏 *44 rooms* 🍽 *Breakfast.*

$ HOTEL Fodor's Choice ★ 🏨 **Hotel Europa.** More famous for its world-class Michelin-starred restaurant on the ground floor, this modest hotel is one of Pamplona's best-kept secrets, just a block and half from the bullring and within shouting distance of party-central Plaza del Castillo. **Pros:** central location; good value; special restaurant offers for hotel guests. **Cons:** noisy during the fiesta unless you score an interior room; rooms on the small side. As with all Pamplona properties, prices can double during the San Fermín festival. [$] *Rooms from: €88* ✉ *C. Espoz y Mina 11* ☎ *94/822–1800* 🌐 *www.hoteleuropapamplona.com* 🛏 *25 rooms* 🍽 *Breakfast.*

$ HOTEL FAMILY 🏨 **Hotel Maisonnave.** Renovated in early 2013 and reclassified as four-star, this modern hotel has a nearly perfect location, tucked away on a relatively quiet pedestrian street, just steps from all the action on Plaza del Castillo and Calle Estafeta. **Pros:** friendly, multilingual staff; great location; lively bar and restaurant. **Cons:** modern interior design lacks local character. [$] *Rooms from: €80* ✉ *C. Nueva 20* ☎ *948/222600* 🌐 *www.hotelmaisonnave.es* 🛏 *138 rooms* 🍽 *No meals.*

$$$ HOTEL 🏨 **Palacio Guendulain.** This 18th-century palace in the center of town has been restored to the original architecture and aristocratic style, including the wooden ceilings and the grand staircase. **Pros:** opportunity

CLOSE UP

Running with the Bulls

In *The Sun Also Rises*, Hemingway describes the Pamplona s (bull running) in anything but romantic terms. Jake Barnes hears the rocket, steps out onto his balcony, and watches the crowd run by: men in white with red sashes and neckerchiefs, those behind running faster than the bulls. "One man fell, rolled to the gutter, and lay quiet." It's a textbook move—an experienced runner who falls remains motionless (bulls respond to movement)—and first-rate observation and reporting. In the next encierro in the novel, a man is gored and dies. The waiter at Café Iruña mutters, "You hear? Muerto. Dead. He's dead. With a horn through him. All for morning fun."

Despite this, generations of young Americans and other internationals have turned this barnyard bull-management maneuver into one of the Western world's most famous rites of passage. The idea is simple: At daybreak, six fighting bulls are guided through the streets by 8 to 10 *cabestros,* or steers (also known as *mansos,* meaning "tame"), to the holding pens at the bullring, from which they will emerge to fight that afternoon. The course covers 902 yards. The Cuesta de Santo Domingo down to the corrals is the most dangerous part of the run, high in terror and short in distance. The walls are sheer, and the bulls pass quickly. The fear here is of a bull hooking along the wall of the Military Hospital on his way up the hill, forcing runners out in front of the speeding pack in a classic hammer-and-anvil movement. Mercaderes is next, cutting left for about 100 yards by the town hall, then right up Calle Estafeta. The outside of each turn and the

centrifugal force of 22,000 pounds of bulls and steers are to be avoided here. Calle Estafeta is the bread and butter of the run, the longest (about 400 yards), straightest, and least complicated part of the course.

The classic run, a perfect blend of form and function, is to remain ahead of the horns for as long as possible, fading to the side when overtaken. The long gallop up Calle Estafeta is the place to try to do it. The trickiest part of running with the bulls is splitting your vision so that with one eye you keep track of the bulls behind you and with the other you avoid falling over runners ahead of you.

At the end of Estafeta the course descends left through the *callejón,* the narrow tunnel, into the bullring. The bulls move more slowly here, uncertain of their weak forelegs, allowing runners to stay close and even to touch them as they glide down into the tunnel. The only uncertainty is whether there will be a pileup in the tunnel. The most dramatic photographs of the encierro have been taken here, as the galloping pack slams through what occasionally turns into a solid wall of humanity. If all goes well—no bulls separated from the pack, no mayhem—the bulls will have arrived in the ring in less than three minutes.

It is illegal, punishable by hefty fines, to attempt to attract a bull, thus removing him from the pack and creating a deadly danger. It's also illegal to participate while intoxicated or take photos.

to stay in a historical monument; central location; outstanding service. **Cons:** provides little refuge from the mayhem during San Fermín; noise from the street is a problem on weekends; extra charge for parking. [$] *Rooms from: €143* ✉ *Zapatería 53* ☎ *94/822–5522* 🌐 *www.palacioguendulain.com* 🛏 *23 rooms, 2 suites* 🍴 *Multiple meal plans.*

NIGHTLIFE

The city has a thumping student life year-round, especially along the length of Calle San Nicolas. Calle Estafeta is another hot spot.

Marengo. Dress up or you might flunk the bouncer's inspection at this barnlike rager, filled until dawn with young singles and couples. Cover charge depends on visiting DJs and events. ✉ *Av. Bayona 2* ☎ *94/826–5542* 🌐 *www.discotecamarengo.com* 🕒 *Thurs.–Sat. 1:30 am–6 am.*

SHOPPING

Botas are the wineskins from which Basques typically drink at bullfights or during fiestas. The art lies in drinking a stream of wine from a bota held at arm's length without spilling a drop, if you want to maintain your mojo (not to mention your clean shirt).

Casa Torrens. Navarran favorites such as piquillo peppers and chistorra sausages are sold here. It's closed on Saturday afternoon and Sunday. ✉ *C. San Miguel 12* ☎ *94/822–4286* 🌐 *www.torrensalimentacion.com.*

Manterola. Here you can buy some toffee called "La Cafetera," a café con leche sweet known all over Spain. The shop also sells Navarran wine and other delicacies. ✉ *C. Tudela 5* ☎ *94/822–3174* 🌐 *www.casamanterola.es.*

OFF THE BEATEN PATH

Olite. An unforgettable glimpse into the Spain of the Middle Ages is the reward for journeying to this town. The 11th-century church of San Pedro is revered for its finely worked Romanesque cloisters and portal, but it's the town's castle—restored by Carlos III in the French style and brimming with ramparts, crenellated battlements, and watchtowers—that captures the imagination most. You can walk the ramparts, and should you get tired or hungry, part of the castle has been converted into a parador, making a fine place to catch a bite or a few Z's. ✉ *Olite, 41 km (25 miles) south of Pamplona* ☎ *94/874–0000.*

VITORIA-GASTEIZ

70 km (44 miles) northwest of Estella, 100 km (62 miles) west of Pamplona, 93 km (56 miles) north of Logroño, 101 km (62 miles) southwest of San Sebastián, 64 km (40 miles) southeast of Bilbao.

Vitoria-Gasteiz was chosen as the European Green Capital in 2012 because of its abundance of green space, including its six parks, all within the city center.

The capital of the Basque Country, and its second-largest city after Bilbao, Vitoria-Gasteiz is nevertheless in many ways Euskadi's least Basque city. Neither a maritime city nor a mountain enclave, Vitoria occupies the steppelike *meseta de Alava* (Alava plain) and functions as a modern industrial center with a surprisingly medieval Casco Medieval (Medieval Quarter), which serves as a striking example of the successful integration of early and contemporary architecture. Founded by Sancho el Sabio (the Wise) in 1181, the city was built largely of granite, so Vitoria's oldest streets and squares seem especially weathered and ancient.

GETTING AROUND

Vitoria is a big city, but the area you'll spend your time in is small, only about 1 km (½ mile) square, and easily walked.

ESSENTIALS

Bus Station Vitoria ✉ *Pl. España 1* ☎ *94/516–1598* ⊕ *www.vitoria-gasteiz.org* ⊙ *Oct.–June, Mon.–Sat. 10–9, Sun. 11–2; July–Sept., daily 10–8.*

Visitor Information Vitoria-Gasteiz ✉ *Pl. España 1* ☎ *94/516–1598* ⊕ *www. vitoria-gasteiz.org.*

EXPLORING

Artium. Officially titled Centro-Museo Vasco de Arte Contemporáneo, this former bus station was opened in 2002 by King Juan Carlos, who called it "the third leg of the Basque art triangle, along with the Bilbao Guggenheim and San Sebastián's [now closed] Chillida Leku." The museum's permanent collection—including 20th- and 21st-century paintings and sculptures by Jorge Oteiza, Chillida, Agustín Ibarrola, and Nestor Basterretxea, among many others—makes it one of Spain's finest treasuries of contemporary art. ✉ *C. Francia 24* ☎ *94/520–9020* ⊕ *www.artium.org* 🎫 *€6 (suggested donation Wed. and weekends following exhibit openings)* ⊙ *Tues.–Fri. 11–2 and 5–8, weekends 11–9.*

Bibat. The 1525 Palacio de Bendaña and the adjoining bronze-plated building are home to one of Vitoria's main attractions, the Bibat, which combines the Museo Fournier de Naipes (Playing-Card Museum) with the Museo de la Arqueología. The project, by Navarran architect Patxi Mangado, is a daring combination of old and new architecture, though it was dubbed "the chest" because of its dark facade. The palacio houses the playing-card collection of Don Heraclio Fournier, who, in 1868, founded a playing-card factory and eventually found himself with 15,000 sets. As you survey rooms of hand-painted cards, the distinction between artwork and game piece is scrambled. The oldest sets date from the 12th century, and the story parallels the history of printing. The Archeology Museum, in the newest building, has Roman art and artifacts and the famous stele of the horseback rider, an early Basque tombstone. ✉ *C. Cuchillería 54* ☎ *94/520–3707* 🎫 *€3 (free 1st Sat. of every month)* ⊙ *Tues.–Fri. 10–2 and 4–6:30, Sat. 10–2, Sun. 11–2.*

Catedral de Santa María. Dating back to the 14th century, the cathedral is currently being restored but is still open for visitors—in fact, that's part of the fun. Tour guides hand out hardhats, and show you around the site. A prominent and active supporter of the project is British novelist Ken Follett, whose novel *World Without End* is about the construction of the cathedral. A statue of the author has been placed on one side of the cathedral. ✉ *C. Cuchillería 95* ☎ *94/512–2160, 94/525–5135* ⊕ *www.catedralvitoria.com* 🎫 *€8.50, €10.50 including tower* ⊙ *Daily 10–2 and 4–7.*

Museo de Bellas Artes (*Museum of Fine Arts*). Paintings by Ribera, Picasso, and the Basque painter Zuloaga are among the collection here.

The Plaza de la Virgen Blanca is surrounded by impressive buildings.

✉ *Paseo Fray Francisco de Vitoria 8* ☎ *94/518–1918* 💶 *€3* 🕐 *Tues.–Fri.*
10–2 and 4–6:30, Sat. 10–2 and 5–8, Sun. 10–2.

Museo Provincial de Armería (*Provincial Arms Museum*). Just south of the
park, this museum has prehistoric hatchets, 20th-century pistols, and
a reproduction of the 1813 battle between the Duke of Wellington's
troops and the French. ✉ *Paseo Fray Francisco de Vitoria 3* ☎ *94/518–*
1925 💶 *€3* 🕐 *Tues.–Fri. 10–2 and 4–6:30, Sat. 10–2, Sun. 11–2.*

Palacio de los Alava Esquivel. One of Vitoria's most splendid buildings,
this palace was erected in 1488 and reformed in 1535 and 1865. It's
reached from the Plaza de la Virgen Blanca along Calle de Herrería.
✉ *C. de la Soledad s/n.*

Palacio Villasuso. Don't miss this austere palace, built in 1538 across
from the church of San Miguel. ✉ *Pl. del Machete 1* ☎ *94/516–1260*
🕐 *Weekdays 8:30 am–9 pm (8:30–1:30 in summer).*

Plaza de la Virgen Blanca. In the southwest corner of old Vitoria, this
plaza is ringed by noble houses with covered arches and white-trim
glass galleries. The monument in the center commemorates the Duke
of Wellington's victory over Napoléon's army here in 1813.

Plaza del Machete. Overlooking Plaza de España, this plaza is named for
the sword used by medieval nobility to swear allegiance to the local
fueros (special Basque rights and privileges).

San Miguel Arcángel. A jasper niche in the lateral facade of this Gothic
church contains the Virgen Blanca (White Virgin), Vitoria's patron saint.
✉ *Pl. Virgen Blanca s/n* ☎ *94/516–1598.*

Torre de Doña Otxanda. This 15th-century tower houses Vitoria's **Museo de Ciencias Naturales**, which contains botanical, zoological, and geological collections along with amber from the nearby archaeological site at Peñacerrada-Urizaharra. ✉ *C. Siervas de Jesús 24* ☎ *94/518–1924* 🌐 *€3* 🕒 *Tues.–Fri. 10–2 and 4–6:30, Sat. 10–2, Sun. 11–2.*

WHERE TO EAT AND STAY

$$$ SPANISH Fodor's Choice ★ 🍴 **El Portalón.** With dark, creaky wood floors and staircases, bare brick walls, and ancient beams, pillars, and coats of arms, this rough and rustic 15th-century inn turns out classical Castilian and Basque specialties that reflect Vitoria's geography and social history. Try the *cochinillo lechal asado* (grilled suckling pig) or any of the *rape* (anglerfish) preparations. The wine cellar is a gold mine. Call 48 hours ahead to reserve any of the special tasting menus, a good value ranging between €35 and €61. Once a month the restaurant organizes a theater night (€65), where performers surround your table. [$] *Average main: €22* ✉ *C. Correría 147* ☎ *94/514–2755* 🌐 *www.restauranteelportalon.com* 🕒 *No dinner Sun.*

$$$$ CONTEMPORARY 🍴 **Zaldiarán.** Vitoria's most recent culinary star serves contemporary interpretations of classics and daring combinations of prime ingredients from black truffles to to lobster in a sleek environment. The tasting menu (€55) changes seven times a year. [$] *Average main: €55* ✉ *Av. Gasteiz 21* ☎ *94/513–4822* 🌐 *www.restaurantezaldiaran.com* 🕒 *Mon. and Thurs.–Sat. 1–3:30 and 9–11:30, Wed. and Sun. 1–3:30.*

$$ HOTEL 🏨 **NH Canciller Ayala.** This modern hotel is handy for in-town comfort, two minutes from the old quarter next to the lush Parque de la Florida. **Pros:** clean comfort; reliable chain brand. **Cons:** lacking any historical character. [$] *Rooms from: €110* ✉ *C. Ramón y Cajal 5* ☎ *94/513–0000, 90/257–0368* 🌐 *www.nh-hotels.com* 🛏 *184 rooms, 1 suite* 🍽 *No meals.*

$$ HOTEL 🏨 **Parador de Argómaniz.** This 17th-century palace has panoramic views of the Alava plains and retains a sense of romance with long halls peppered with antiques. **Pros:** contemporary rooms and comforts; gorgeous details and surroundings. **Cons:** isolated, about a 15-minute drive from Vitoria. [$] *Rooms from: €120* ✉ *N1, Km 363, east of Vitoria off N104 toward Pamplona, Argómaniz* ☎ *94/529–3200* 🌐 *www.parador.es* 🛏 *53 rooms* 🍽 *No meals.*

LAGUARDIA

66 km (40 miles) south of Vitoria, 17 km (10 miles) northwest of Logroño.

Founded in 908 to stand guard—as its name suggests—over Navarra's southwestern flank, Laguardia is on a promontory overlooking the Ebro River and the vineyards of the Rioja Alavesa wine country north of the Ebro in the Basque province of Alava. Flanked by the Sierra de Cantabria, the town rises shiplike, its prow headed north, over the sea of surrounding vineyards.

ESSENTIALS

Visitor Information Laguardia ✉ *C. Mayor 52* ☎ *94/560–0845* 🌐 *www.laguardia-alava.com.*

5

EXPLORING

Starting from the 15th-century Puerta de Carnicerías, or Puerta Nueva, the central portal off the parking area on the east side of town, the first landmark is the 16th-century **Ayuntamiento**, with its imperial shield of Carlos V. Farther into the square is the current town hall, built in the 19th century. A right turn down Calle Santa Engracia takes you past impressive facades—the floor inside the portal at No. 25 is a lovely stone mosaic, and a walk behind the triple-emblazoned 17th-century facade of No. 19 reveals a stagecoach, floor mosaics, wood beams, and an inner porch. The Puerta de Santa Engracia, with an image of the saint in an overhead niche, opens out to the right, and on the left, at the entrance to Calle Víctor Tapia, No. 17 bears a coat of arms with the Latin phrase "Laus Tibi" ("Praise Be to Thee").

Fodor's Choice ★ **Herederos de Marqués de Riscal.** The village of Elciego, 6 km (4 miles) southeast of Laguardia, is the site of the historic Marqués de Riscal winery. Tours of the vineyards as well as the cellars are conducted in many languages, including English. Reservations are required. The estate also includes the stunning Frank Gehry-designed **Hotel Marqués de Riscal** (⇨ *see Where to Eat and Stay*), crafted out of waves of metal reminiscent of his Guggenheim Bilbao. ✉ *C. Torrea 1, Elciego* ☎ *94/560–6000* 🌐 *www.marquesderiscal.com* 🎟 *€10.25 includes tour and tasting of 2 wines* 🕒 *Tours daily, but hrs vary; book ahead.*

Santa María de los Reyes. Laguardia's architectural crown jewel is Spain's only Gothic polychrome portal, on this church. Protected by a posterior Renaissance facade, the door centers on a lifelike effigy of La Virgen de los Reyes (Virgin of the Kings), sculpted in the 14th century and painted in the 17th by Ribera. To see it, ask at the tourist office. ✉ *C. Mayor s/n.*

WHERE TO EAT AND STAY

$$$$ BASQUE 🍴 **Marixa.** Aficionados travel great distances to dine in this restaurant, known for its excellent roasts, views, and value, in the Marixa hotel. The heavy, wooden interior is ancient, and the cuisine is Vasco-Riojano, combining the best of both worlds. House specialties are Navarran vegetable dishes and meat roasted over coals. There are also 10 guest rooms, which offer good-value half- or full-board terms, with meals taken in the restaurant. [$] *Average main: €30* ✉ *C. Sancho Abarca 8* ☎ *94/560–0165* 🌐 *www.hotelmarixa.com.*

$$$$ HOTEL Fodor's Choice ★ 🏨 **Hotel Marqués de Riscal.** Frank Gehry's post-Guggenheim Iberian eruption of genius looks as if a colony from outer space had taken up residence (or crashed) in the middle of La Rioja's oldest vineyards (⇨ *see Exploring*). **Pros:** dazzling architecture; 5-star environment; superb dining. **Cons:** expensive. [$] *Rooms from: €300* ✉ *C. Torrea 1, 6 km (4 miles) southwest of Laguardia, Elciego* ☎ *94/518–0880* 🌐 *www.hotel-marquesderiscal.com* 🛏 *43 rooms* 🍽 *Breakfast.*

$$ HOTEL Fodor's Choice ★ 🏨 **Posada Mayor de Migueloa.** This 17th-century palace is a beauty, with stone entryway floors and guest rooms that have original, rough-hewn ceiling beams. **Pros:** beautiful rooms; off-season specials. **Cons:** in a pedestrianized area a long way from your car; rooms on the front side exposed to boisterous racket on weekends. [$] *Rooms from: €92* ✉ *C. Mayor de Migueloa 20* ☎ *647/212947* 🌐 *www.mayordemigueloa.com* 🛏 *8 rooms* 🕒 *Closed Jan. 8–Feb. 8* 🍽 *Breakfast.*

LA RIOJA

A natural compendium of highlands, plains, and vineyards drained by the Ebro River, La Rioja (named for the River Oja) has historically produced Spain's finest wines. Most inhabitants live along the Ebro, in the cities of Logroño and Haro, though the mountains and upper river valleys hold many treasures. A mix of Atlantic and Mediterranean climates and cultures with Basque overtones and the meseta's arid influence, La Rioja is composed of the Rioja Alta (Upper Rioja), the moist and mountainous western end, and the Rioja Baja (Lower Rioja), the lower, dryer eastern extremity, more Mediterranean in climate. Logroño, the capital, lies between the two.

LOGROÑO

85 km (53 miles) southwest of Pamplona.

A busy industrial city of 153,000, Logroño has a lovely old quarter bordered by the Ebro and medieval walls, with **Breton de los Herreros** and **Muro Francisco de la Mata** the most characteristic streets.

Near Logroño, the Roman bridge and the *mirador* (lookout) at **Viguera** are the main sights in the lower Iregua Valley. According to legend, Santiago (St. James) helped the Christians defeat the Moors at the **Castillo de Clavijo,** another panoramic spot. The **Leza (Cañon) del Río Leza** is La Rioja's most dramatic canyon.

Logroño's dominant landmarks are the finest sacred structures in Rioja.

ESSENTIALS

Bus Station Logroño ⊠ *Av. España 1* ☎ *94/123–5983.*

Train Station Logroño ⊠ *Estación de Logroño, Av. de Colón 83* ☎ *90/243– 2343, 90/232–0320* ⊕ *www.adif.es.*

Visitor Information Logroño ⊠ *Portales 50* ☎ *94/129–1260* ⊕ *www. logroturismo.org.*

EXPLORING

Catedral de Santa María de La Redonda. Noted for its twin baroque towers, the present-day cathedral was rebuilt in the 16th century in a Gothic style, on top of the ruins of a 12th-century Roman church. ⊠ *C. Portales 14* ☎ *94/125–7611* ⊕ *www.laredonda.org* ☉ *Daily 8:30–1 and 6–9.*

Puente de Piedra (*Stone Bridge*). Many of Logroño's monuments, such as this elegant bridge, were built as part of the Camino de Santiago pilgrimage route.

San Bartolomé. The oldest still-standing church in Logroño, most of San Bartolomé was built between the 13th and 14th-centuries in a French Gothic style. Highlights include the 11th-century Mudejar tower and an elaborate 14th-century Gothic doorway. Some carvings on the stone facade depict scenes from the Bible. This is also a landmark on the Camino de Santiago pilgrimage path. ⊠ *Pl. San Bartolomé 2.*

Santa María del Palacio. This 11th-century church is known as La Aguja (the Needle) for its pyramid-shape, 45-yard Romanesque-Gothic tower. ✉ *C. del Marqués de San Nicolás 30.*

Santiago el Real (*Royal St. James's Church*). Reconstructed in the 16th century, this church is noted for its equestrian statue of the saint (also known as Santiago Matamoros, or St. James the Moorslayer), which presides over the main door. ✉ *C. Barriocepo 6* ☎ *94/120–9501.*

WHERE TO EAT AND STAY

For tapas, **Calle and Travesía del Laurel** or *el sendero de los elefantes* (the path of the elephants)—an allusion to *trompas* (trunks), Spanish for a snootful—offers bars with signature specialties: Bar Soriano for "*champis*" (*champiñones,* or mushrooms), Blanco y Negro for "*matrimonio*" (a green pepper–and–anchovy sandwich), and La Travesía for potato omelet. If you're ordering wine, a crianza brings out the crystal, a young cosecha comes in small glasses, and reserva (selected grapes aged three years in oak and bottle) elicits snifters for proper swirling, smelling, and tasting.

$$$ SPANISH 🍴 **Asador Emilio.** The Castilian rustic interior here includes a coffered wood ceiling that merits a long look. Roast lamb cooked over wood coals is the specialty, but *alubias* (kidney beans) and *migas de pastor* (literally, "shepherd's bread crumbs," cooked with garlic and sausage) are hard to resist. The wine list, not surprisingly, is stocked with most of La Rioja's top finds, from Roda I to Barón de Chirel Reserva. [$] *Average main: €20* ✉ *C. República Argentina 8* ☎ *94/125–8844* 🌐 *www.asadoremilio.com* 🕒 *Closed Aug. No dinner Sun.*

$$$$ SPANISH 🍴 **El Cachetero.** Local fare based on roast lamb, goat, and vegetables is the rule at this local favorite in the middle of Logroño's main food and wine preserve. Coming in from Calle del Laurel is something like stepping through the looking glass: from street pandemonium to the peaceful hush of this culinary sanctuary. Though the dining room is classical and elegant, with antique furnishings and a serious look, the cuisine is homespun, based on seasonally changing raw materials. *Patatas a la riojana* (potatoes stewed with chorizo) is a classic dish here. [$] *Average main: €25* ✉ *C. Laurel 3* ☎ *94/122–8463* 🌐 *www.cachetero.com* 🕒 *Closed Tues. and 1st 2 wks in Aug. No dinner Sun.*

$$ SPANISH Fodor's Choice ★ 🍴 **Tondeluna.** Francis Paniego's "gastro-bar," with David Gonzalez as chef de cuisine, strives to bring haute cuisine to everyone, and everyone into the kitchen. There are only six tables, and all have views into the kitchen. Gonzalez makes an excellent croqueta de jamón from Echaurren or La Zapatilla, a grilled open ham canapé. [$] *Average main: €15* ✉ *C. Muro de la Mata 9* ☎ *94/123–6425* 🌐 *www.tondeluna.com.*

$ HOTEL 🏨 **Marqués de Vallejo.** Close to the food- and wine-tasting frenzy of nearby Calle del Laurel, this small but trendy hotel within view of the cathedral is nearly dead center amid the most important historic sites and best architecture that Logroño has to offer. **Pros:** central location; traditional Logroño architecture with very modern, renovated interior. **Cons:** streetside rooms can be noisy in summer when windows are open. [$] *Rooms from: €80* ✉ *Marqués de Vallejo 8* ☎ *94/124–8333* 🌐 *www.hotelmarquesdevallejo.com* 🛏 *50 rooms* 🍽 *No meals.*

The fertile soil and fields of the Ebro River Valley make some of Spain's most colorful landscapes.

LA RIOJA ALTA

The Upper Rioja, the most prosperous part of La Rioja's wine country, extends from the Ebro River to the Sierra de la Demanda. La Rioja Alta has the most fertile soil, the best vineyards and agriculture, the most impressive castles and monasteries, a ski resort at Ezcaray, and the historic economic advantage of being on the Camino de Santiago.

Ezcaray. Enter the Sierra de la Demanda by heading south from Santo Domingo de la Calzada on LR111. Your first stop is the town of Ezcaray, with its aristocratic houses emblazoned with family crests, of which the **Palacio del Conde de Torremúzquiz** (Palace of the Count of Torremúzquiz) is the most distinguished. Excursions from here are the Valdezcaray ski station; the source of the River Oja at Llano de la Casa; La Rioja's highest point, the 7,494-foot Pico de San Lorenzo; and the Romanesque church of Tres Fuentes, at Valgañón. The hamlet is famous for its wild-mushroom-gathering residents—and the resulting tapas too.

Nájera. This town, 15 km (9 miles) west of Navarrete, was site of the court of the kings of Navarra and capital of Navarra and La Rioja until 1076, when La Rioja became part of Castile and the residence of the Castilian royal family. The monastery of **Santa María la Real** (☎ *941/363650* ⊕ *www.santamarialareal.net* ✉ *€3* ⊘ *Tues.–Sat. 10–1 and 4–5:30 [till 7 in summer], Sun. and holidays 10–1 and 4–7*), the "pantheon of kings," is distinguished by its 16th-century Claustro de los Caballeros (Cavaliers' Cloister), a flamboyant Gothic structure with 24 lacy, plateresque Renaissance arches overlooking a patio. The sculpted 12th-century tomb of Doña Blanca de Navarra is the monastery's best-known sarcophagus, while the 67 Gothic choir stalls dating from 1495 are among Spain's best.

Navarrete. From Logroño, drive 14 km (8 miles) west on the A12 to Navarrete to see its noble houses and 16th-century Santa María de la Asunción church.

Fodor's Choice ★ **San Millán de la Cogolla.** This town, southeast of Santo Domingo de la Calzada, has two monasteries on the UNESCO World Heritage sites list. Take LR205 southeast through Berceo to the **Monasterio de Yuso** (☎ *941/373049* 🌐 *www.monasteriodeyuso.org* 🎟 *€6* 🕒 *Easter–Sept., Tues.–Sun. 10–1:30 and 4–6:30 [also Mon. in Aug.]; Oct.–Easter, Tues.–Sat. 10–1 and 3:30–5:30, Sun. 10–1*), where a 10th-century manuscript on St. Augustine's *Glosas Emilianenses* contains handwritten notes in what is considered the earliest example of the Spanish language, the vernacular Latin dialect known as Roman Paladino. The nearby Visigothic **Monasterio de Suso** (☎ *941/373082* 🌐 *www.monasteriodesanmillan.com/suso* 🎟 *€3* 🕒 *Tues.–Sun. 9:55–1:25 and 3:55–5:25; obtain required reservation at Yuso ticket office*) is where Gonzalo de Berceo, recognized as the first Castilian poet, wrote his 13th-century verse in the Castilian tongue, now the language of more than 300 million people around the world.

Santo Domingo de la Calzada. This town has always been a key stop on the Camino. Santo Domingo was an 11th-century saint who built roads and bridges for pilgrims and founded the hospital that is now the town's parador. The **cathedral** (✉ *Pl. del Santo 4* ☎ *941/340033*) is a Romanesque-Gothic pile containing the saint's tomb, choir murals, and an altarpiece carved by Damià Forment in 1541. The live hen and rooster in a stone chicken coop commemorate a legendary local miracle in which a pair of roasted fowl came back to life to protest the innocence of a pilgrim hanged for theft. Stroll through the town's beautifully preserved medieval quarter. ✉ *20 km (12 miles) west of Nájera on the N120.*

WHERE TO STAY

$$$ HOTEL Fodor's Choice ★ 🏨 **Echaurren.** This rambling roadhouse, 7 km (4 miles) below Valdezcaray, La Rioja's best ski resort, is famous for its restaurants, El Portal, showcasing fine traditional cuisine engineered by Marisa Sánchez, and her son Francis Paniego's Bistrot Comilón. **Pros:** traditional building (though modernized inside); comfortable beds; family service. **Cons:** the bells from the church across the way. [$] *Rooms from: €140* ✉ *Padre José García 19, Ezcaray* ☎ *94/135–4047* 🌐 *www.echaurren.com* 🛏 *25 rooms* 🍴 *Some meals.*

$$ HOTEL 🏨 **Hospedería del Monasterio de San Millán.** Declared a World Heritage Site by UNESCO, this magnificent inn occupies a wing of the historic Monasterio de Yuso, famous as the birthplace of the Spanish language. **Pros:** historic site; graceful building. **Cons:** somewhat isolated; monastic interiors. [$] *Rooms from: €120* ✉ *Monasterio de Yuso, San Millán de la Cogolla* ☎ *94/137–3277* 🌐 *www.sanmillan.com* 🛏 *22 rooms, 3 suites* 🍴 *Breakfast.*

HARO

49 km (29 miles) west of Logroño.

Haro is the wine capital of La Rioja. Its Casco Viejo (Old Quarter) and best taverns are concentrated along the loop known as La Herradura (the Horseshoe), with the Santo Tomás church at the apex of its curve and Calle San Martín and Calle Santo Tomás leading down to the upper left-hand (northeast) corner of Plaza de la Paz. Up the left side of the horseshoe, Bar La Esquina is the first of many tapas bars. Bar Los Caños, behind a stone archway at San Martín 5, is built into the vaults and arches of the former church of San Martín and serves excellent local crianzas and reservas and a memorable pintxo of quail egg, anchovy, hot pepper, and olive.

ESSENTIALS

Visitor Information Haro ✉ *Pl. de la Paz* ☎ *94/130–3580* 🌐 *www.haroturismo.org.*

EXPLORING

Bodegas (*wineries*). Haro's century-old bodegas have been headquartered in the *barrio de la estación* (train-station district) ever since the railroad opened in 1863. Guided tours and tastings, some in English, can be arranged at the facilities themselves or through the tourist office.

Santo Tomás. The architectural highlight of Haro is the church of Santo Tomás, a single-naved Renaissance and late Gothic church completed in 1564, with an intricately sculpted plateresque portal on the south side and a baroque organ facade towering over the choir loft. ✉ *C. Santo Tomás 5.*

WHERE TO EAT AND STAY

$$$ SPANISH 🍴 **Terete.** A local favorite, this rustic spot has been roasting lamb in wood ovens since 1877 and serves a hearty *menestra de verduras* (vegetables stewed with ham) that is revered as a regional institution. With wooden tables distributed around dark stone, the medieval stagecoach-inn environment matches the traditional roasts. The wine cellar is a virtual museum stocked with some of the Rioja's best reservas and crianzas. [$] *Average main: €20* ✉ *C. Lucrecia Arana 17* ☎ *94/131–0023* 🌐 *www.terete.es* ⏲ *Closed Mon., 1st 2 wks in July, and last 2 wks in Nov. No dinner Sun.*

$ HOTEL 🏨 **Los Agustinos.** Across the street from the tourist office, Haro's best hotel is built into a 14th-century monastery with a cloister (now a beautiful covered patio) that's considered one of the best in La Rioja. **Pros:** gorgeous public rooms; convivial hotel bar; close to town center but in a quiet corner; free Wi-Fi. **Cons:** unexciting room interiors; staff not very helpful. [$] *Rooms from: €87* ✉ *San Agustín 2* ☎ *94/131–1308* 🌐 *www.hotellosagustinos.com* 🛏 *60 rooms, 2 suites* 🍽 *Some meals.*

THE HIGHLANDS

The rivers forming the seven main valleys of the Ebro basin originate in the Sierra de la Demanda, Sierra de Cameros, and Sierra de Alcarama. **Ezcaray** is La Rioja's skiing capital in the **valley of the Rio Oja,** just below Valdezcaray in the Sierra de la Demanda. The upper **Najerilla Valley** is La Rioja's mountain sanctuary, an excellent hunting and fishing preserve. The Najerilla River, a rich chalk stream, is one of Spain's best trout rivers. Look for the Puente de Hiedra (Ivy Bridge), its heavy curtain of ivy falling to the surface of the Najerilla. The **Monasterio de Valvanera,** off C113 near Anguiano, is the sanctuary of La Rioja's patron saint, the Virgen de Valvanera, a 12th-century Romanesque wood carving of the Virgin and Child. **Anguiano** is renowned for its Danza de los Zancos (Dance of the Stilts), held July 22, when dancers on wooden stilts plummet down through the steep streets of the town into the arms of the crowd at the bottom. At the valley's highest point are the Mansilla reservoir and the Romanesque Ermita de San Cristóbal (Hermitage of St. Christopher).

The upper **Iregua Valley,** off N111, has the prehistoric Gruta de la Paz caves at Ortigosa. The artisans of **Villoslada del Cameros** make the region's famous patchwork quilts, called *almazuelas.* Climb to **Pico Cebollera** for a superb view of the valley. Work back toward the Ebro along the River Leza, through Laguna de Cameros and San Román de Cameros (known for its basket weavers), to complete a tour of the Sierra del Cameros. The upper **Cidacos Valley** leads to the **Parque Jurásico** (Jurassic Park) at Enciso, famous for its dinosaur tracks. The main village in the upper **Alhama Valley** is **Cervera del Rio Alhama,** a center for handmade *alpargatas* (espadrilles).

WHERE TO EAT AND STAY

$$ SPANISH

🍴 **La Herradura.** High over the ancient bridge of Anguiano, this is an excellent place to try the local specialty, *caparrones colorados de Anguiano con sus sacramentos* (small, red kidney beans stewed with sausage and fatback) made with the much-prized hometown bean. Family-run La Herradura ("horseshoe") is a local favorite, usually filled with trout fishermen taking a break from the river. [$] *Average main: €15* ✉ *Ctra. de Lerma, Km 14, Anguiano* ☎ *94/137–7151.*

$ B&B/INN Fodor's Choice ★

🏨 **Venta de Goyo.** A favorite with anglers and hunters in season, this cheery spot across from the mouth of the Urbión River has wood-trim bedrooms with red-check bedspreads and an excellent restaurant specializing in venison, wild boar, and game of all kinds. **Pros:** excellent game and mountain cooking; charming rustic bar; unforgettable homemade jams. **Cons:** next to road; hot in summer. [$] *Rooms from: €42* ✉ *Puente Rio Neila 2, Ctra. LR113, Km 24.6, Viniegra de Abajo* ☎ *941/378007* 🌐 *www.ventadegoyo.es* 🛏 *22 rooms* 🍽 *Some meals.*

6

THE PYRENEES

WELCOME TO THE PYRENEES

TOP REASONS TO GO

★ **Appreciate the Romanesque:** Stop at Taüll and see the exquisite Romanesque churches and mural paintings of the Noguera de Tor Valley.

★ **Explore Spain's Grand Canyon:** The Parque Nacional de Ordesa y Monte Perdido has stunning scenery, along with marmots and mountain goats.

★ **Hike the highlands:** Explore the verdant Basque highlands of the Baztán Valley and follow the Bidasoa River down to colorful Hondarribia and the Bay of Biscay.

★ **Venture off the highway:** Discover the enchanting medieval town of Alquézar, where the impressive citadel, dating back to the 9th century, keeps watch over the Sierra y Cañones de Guara Natural Park and its prehistoric cave paintings.

★ **Ride the cogwheel train at Ribes de Freser, near Ripoll:** Ascend the gorge to the sanctuary and ski station at Vall de Núria, then hike to the remote highland valley and refuge of Coma de Vaca.

1 The Eastern Catalan Pyrenees. Start from Cap de Creus in the Empordà to get the full experience of the Pyrenean cordillera's rise from the sea; then move west through Camprodón, Setcases, the Ter Valley, and Ripoll.

2 La Cerdanya. The widest and sunniest valley in the Pyrenees, La Cerdanya is an east–west expanse that straddles the French border between two forks of the Pyrenean cordillera. The Segre River flows down the center of the valley, while snowcapped peaks rise to the north and south.

3 Western Catalan Pyrenees. West of La Seu d'Urgell, the western Catalan Pyrenees include the Vall d'Aran, the Parc Nacional d'Aigüestortes i Estany de Sant Maurici, and the Noguera de Tor Valley with its Romanesque treasures.

4 Aragón and the Central Pyrenees. Benasque is the jumping-off point for Aneto, the highest peak in the Pyrenees. Parque Nacional de Ordesa y Monte Perdido is an unforgettable daylong or two-day trek. Jaca, and the Hecho and Ansó valleys, are Upper Aragón at its purest, while Huesca and Zaragoza are good lowland alternatives in case bad weather blows you out of the mountains.

GETTING ORIENTED

The Pyrenean valleys, isolated from each other and the world below for many centuries, retain a rugged mountain character, mixing distinct traditions with a common highland spirit of magic and mystery. Here, at Spain's natural border with France, medieval people took refuge and exchanged culture and learning. A haven from the 8th-century Moorish invasion, the Pyrenees became an unlikely repository of Romanesque art and architecture as well as a natural preserve of wildlife and terrain.

6

5 The Navarran and Basque Pyrenees. Beginning in the Roncal Valley, the language you hear may be Euskera, the pre-Indo-European tonque of the Basques. The highlands of Navarra, from Roncesvalles and Burguete down through the Baztán Valley to Hondarribia, are a magical realm of rolling hillsides and emerald pastures.

EATING AND DRINKING WELL IN THE PYRENEES

Pyrenean cuisine is hearty mountain fare characterized by thick soups, stews, roasts, and local game. Ingredients are prepared with slightly different techniques and recipes in each valley, village, and kitchen.

(top left) Some typical dishes: grilled T-bone steak, chorizo and longaniza sausages with grilled peppers (top right) Wild black trumpet mushrooms (bottom left) Spring duckling with potatoes

The three main culinary schools across the Pyrenees match the three main cultural identities of the area—from east to west, they are Catalan, Aragonese, and Basque. Within these three principal groups there are further subdivisions corresponding to the valleys or regions of La Garrotxa, La Cerdanya, Ribagorça, Vall d'Aran, Benasque, Alto Aragón, Roncal, and Baztán. Game is common throughout. Trout, mountain goat, deer, boar, partridge, rabbit, duck, and quail are roasted over coals or cooked in aromatic stews called *civets* in Catalonia and *estofadas* in Aragón and the Basque Pyrenees. Fish and meat are often seared on slabs of slate (*a la llosa* in Catalan, *a la piedra* in Castilian Spanish). Sheep, goat, and cow cheeses vary from valley to valley, along with types of sausages and charcuterie.

WILD MUSHROOMS

Valued for their aromatic contribution to the taste process, wild mushrooms come into season in the autumn. They go well with meat or egg dishes. Favorites are *rovellons* (*Lactarius deliciosus* or saffron milk cap) sautéed with parsley, olive oil, and garlic, or *camagrocs* (*Cantharellus lutescens*, a type of chanterelle) scrambled with eggs.

HIGHLAND SOUPS

As with all mountain soups, *sopa pirenaica* combines restorative animal protein with vegetables and the high-altitude need for liquids. The Spanish version of the French *garbure,* the classic mountain soup from the north side of the Pyrenees, mixes legumes, vegetables, potatoes, pork, chicken, and sometimes lamb or wild boar into a tasty and energizing meal that will help hikers recover energy and be ready to go again the next morning. *Olha aranesa* (Aranese soup) is another Pyrenean power soup, with vegetables, legumes, pork, chicken, and beef in a long-cooked and slowly simmered unctuous stew. Similar to the ubiquitous Catalan *escudella,* another Pyrenean favorite, the olha aranesa combines chickpeas and pasta with a variety of meats and vegetables and is served, like the *cocido madrileño,* in various stages: soup, legumes, vegetables, and meats.

PYRENEAN STEWS

Wild boar stew is known by different names in the various languages of the Pyrenees—*civet de porc senglar* in Catalan, *estofado de jabalí* in Spanish. A dark and gamy treat in cold weather, wild boar is prepared in many ways between Catalonia, Aragón, and the Basque Country, but most recipes include onions, carrots, mushrooms, laurel, oranges, leeks, peppers, dry sherry, brown sugar, and sweet paprika.

Civet d'isard (mountain goat stew), known as *estofado de ixarso* in the Pyrenees of Aragón, is another favorite, prepared in much the same way but with a more delicate taste.

TRINXAT

The Catalan verb *trinxar* means to chop or shred, and *trinchat* is winter cabbage, previously softened by frost, chopped fine, and mixed with mashed potato and fatback or bacon. A quintessential high-altitude comfort food, *trinxat* plays the acidity of the cabbage against the saltiness of the pork, with the potato as the unifying element.

DUCK WITH TURNIPS

The traditional dish, *tiró amb naps,* goes back, as do nearly all European recipes that make use of turnips, to pre-Columbian times, before the potato's arrival from the New World. The frequent use of duck (*pato* in Spanish, *anec* in Catalan, *tiró* in La Cerdanya) in the half-France, half-Spain, all-Catalan Cerdanya Valley two hours north of Barcelona is a taste acquired from French Catalunya, just over the Pyrenees.

Updated by Elizabeth Prosser

Separating the Iberian Peninsula from the rest of the European continent, the snowcapped Pyrenees have always been a special realm, a source of legend and superstition. To explore the Pyrenees fully—the flora and fauna, the local cuisine, the remote glacial lakes and streams, the Romanesque art in a thousand hermitages—could take a lifetime.

Each Pyrenean mountain system is drained by one or more rivers, forming some three dozen valleys between the Mediterranean and the Atlantic; these valleys were all but completely isolated until around the 10th century. Local languages still abound, with Castilian Spanish and Euskera (Basque) in upper Navarra; Grausín, Belsetán, Chistavino, Ansotano, Cheso, and Patués (Benasqués) in Aragón; Aranés, a dialect of Gascon French, in the Vall d'Aran; and Catalan at the eastern end of the chain from Ribagorça to the Mediterranean.

Throughout history, the Pyrenees were a strategic barrier and stronghold to be reckoned with. The Romans never completely subdued Los Vascones (as Greek historian Strabo [63–21 BC] called the Basques) in the western Pyrenean highlands. Charlemagne lost Roland and his rear guard at Roncesvalles in 778, and his Frankish heirs lost all of Catalonia in 988. Napoléon Bonaparte never completed his conquest of the peninsula, largely because of communications and supply problems posed by the Pyrenees, and Adolf Hitler, whether for geographical or political reasons, decided not to use post–Civil War Spain to launch his African campaign in 1941. A D-Day option to make a landing on the beaches of northern Spain was scrapped because the Pyrenees looked too easily defendable (you can still see the south-facing German bunkers on the southern flanks of the western Pyrenean foothills). Meanwhile, the mountainous barrier provided a path to freedom for downed pilots, Jewish refugees, and POWs fleeing the Nazis, just as it later meant freedom for political refugees running north from the Franco regime.

PLANNING

WHEN TO GO

If you're a hiker, stick to the summer (June to September, especially July), when the weather is better and there's less chance of a serious snowfall—not to mention blizzards or lightning storms at high altitudes.

October, with comfortable daytime temperatures and chillier evenings, is ideal for enjoying the still-green Pyrenean meadows and valleys and hillside hunts for wild mushrooms. November brings colorful leaves, the last mushrooms, and the first frosts.

For skiing, come between December and April. The green springtime thaw, from mid-March to mid-April, is spectacular for skiing on the snowcaps and trout fishing or golfing on the verdant valley floors.

August is the only crowded month, when all of Europe is on summer vacation and the cooler highland air is at its best.

PLANNING YOUR TIME

You could walk all the way from the Atlantic to the Mediterranean in 43 days, but not many have that kind of vacation time. With 10 to 14 days you can drive from sea to sea: from a wade in the Mediterranean at Cap de Creus to Hondarribia and the Cabo Higuer lighthouse on the Bay of Biscay. A week is ideal for a single area—La Cerdanya and the Eastern Catalan Pyrenees, best accessed from Barcelona; the Western Catalan Pyrenees and Vall d'Aran; Jaca and the central Pyrenees, north of Zaragoza; or the Basque Pyrenees north of Pamplona.

A day's drive up through Figueres (in Catalonia) and Olot will bring you to **Camprodón. Beget, Sant Joan de les Abadesses,** and **Ripoll** are important stops, especially for the famous Sant Maria de Ripoll portal. La Cerdanya's **Puigcerdà, Llívia,** and **Bellver de Cerdanya** are must-visits, too.

To the west is **La Seu d'Urgell,** on the way to **Parc Nacional d'Aigüestortes i Estany de Sant Maurici,** the **Vall d'Aran,** and the winter-sports center Baqueira-Beret. Stop at **Taüll** and the **Noguera de Tor Valley's** Romanesque churches. Farther west, **Benasque** is the jumping-off point for Aneto, the highest peak in the Pyrenees.

Parque Nacional de Ordesa y Monte Perdido is Spain's most majestic canyon—reminiscent of North America's Grand Canyon. **Alquézar** and **Ainsa** are upper Aragon's best-preserved medieval towns, while **Jaca** is the central Pyrenees' most important city.

GETTING HERE AND AROUND

AIR TRAVEL

Barcelona's international airport, El Prat de Llobregat *(⇨ Barcelona)*, is the largest gateway to the Catalan Pyrenees. Farther west, the Pyrenees can be reached by international flights going through Madrid Barajas airport, or Toulouse Blagnac and Biarritz Airport in France. Smaller airports at Zaragoza, Pamplona, and San Sebastián's Hondarribia (Fuenterrabía) are useful for domestic flights.

DID YOU KNOW?

Trekking in the Pyrenees can be a very serious endeavor—it's possible to walk the entire way from the Atlantic Coast to the Mediterranean in about six weeks, but just as stunning are shorter, one- or two-day hikes.

BUS TRAVEL

Bus travel in the Pyrenees is the only way to cross from east to west (or vice versa), other than hiking or driving, but requires some zigzagging up and down. In most cases, four buses daily connect the main pre-Pyrenean cities (Barcelona, Zaragoza, Huesca, and Pamplona) and the main highland distributors (Puigcerdà, La Seu d'Urgell, Vielha, Benasque, and Jaca). The time lost waiting for buses makes this option a last resort.

Bus Lines Alosa ⊠ *Estación Central de Delicias, Avda. Navarra, Zaragoza* ☎ *902/490690* ⊕ *alosa.avanzabus.com.* **ALSA** ⊠ *Estación de Autobuses, Carrer Saracibar 2, Lleida* ☎ *902/422242* ⊕ *www.alsa.es* ⊠ *Estación de Autobuses, Barcelona Nord, Carrer d'Alí Bei 80, Barcelona* ☎ *902/422242* ⊕ *www.alsa. es.* **Conda** ⊠ *Estación de Autobuses, Carrer Yanguas y Miranda s/n, Pamplona* ☎ *902/422242* ⊕ *www.conda.es.*

CAR TRAVEL

The easiest way (and in many cases, the *only* way) to tour the Pyrenees is by car—and it comes with the best scenery. The Eje Pirenaico (Pyrenean Axis), or N260, is a carefully engineered, safe, cross-Pyrenean route that connects Cap de Creus, the Iberian Peninsula's easternmost point on the Mediterranean Costa Brava (east of Girona and Cadaqués), with Cabo de Higuer, the lighthouse west of Hondarribia at the edge of the Atlantic Bay of Biscay.

The Collada de Toses (Tosses Pass) to Puigcerdà is the most difficult route into the Cerdanya Valley, but it's toll-free, has spectacular scenery, and you get to include Camprodón, Olot, and Ripoll in your itinerary. Safer and faster but more expensive (tolls total more than €22 from Barcelona to Bellver de Cerdanya) is the E9 through the Tuñel del Cadí. Once you're there, most of the Cerdanya Valley's two-lane roads are wide and well paved. As you go west, roads can be more difficult to navigate, winding dramatically through mountain passes.

TRAIN TRAVEL

There are three small train stations deep in the Pyrenees: Ribes de Freser in the eastern Catalan Pyrenees, Puigcerdà, in the Cerdanya Valley; and La Pobla de Segur, in the Noguera Pallaresa Valley. The larger gateways are Zaragoza, Huesca, and Lleida. From Madrid, connect through Barcelona for the eastern Pyrenees, Zaragoza and Huesca for the central Pyrenees, and Pamplona or San Sebastián for the Navarran and Basque Pyrenees. For information on timetables and routes, consult ⊕ *www.renfe.com.*

HIKING THE PYRENEES

There are many reasons to visit the Pyrenees—skiing, food, art, and architecture—but hiking is one of the best ways to drink in the stunning landscape. No matter how spectacular the mountains seem from paved roads, they are exponentially more dazzling from upper hiking trails that are accessible only on foot. Day hikes or overnight two-day treks to mountain huts (*refugios,* or *refugis* in Catalan) in the Ordesa or Aigüestortes national parks, in the Alberes range, or on the hike from Col de Núria to Ulldeter reveal the full natural splendor of the Pyrenees.

Local tourist offices can provide maps and recommend day hikes, while specialized bookshops such as Barcelona's Libreria Quera (⊠ *Carrer*

Petritxol 2) have complete Pyrenean maps as well as books with detailed hiking instructions for the entire mountain range from the Atlantic to the Mediterranean. *Haute Randonnée Pyrénéenne* by Georges Véron (the 2007 edition is coauthored by Jérôme Bonneaux) is the classic guide across the Pyrenean crest. Other books to look for include *The Pyrenees* by Kev Reynolds (Cicerone Press), with practical information, maps, and photos by one of the United Kingdom's most widely used publishers of guidebooks for the outdoors, and *Trekking in the Pyrenees* (Trailblazer Publications). Also check out ⊕ *www.rural-pyrenees-guide. com* for trails and information about the areas.

Hiking in the Pyrenees should always be undertaken carefully: proper footwear, headwear, water supply, and weather-forecast awareness are essential. Even in the middle of summer, a sudden snowstorm can turn a day hike to tragedy. *See the "Hiking in the Pyrenees" box in this chapter for more details.*

RESTAURANTS

In the Alta Pyrenees, the cozy stone-wall inns, with their hearty cuisine and comfortable interiors, are a welcome sight after a day's hiking or sightseeing. Often family run and relaxed, they rarely have any kind of dress code and, often, a nourishing meal is brought to a close with a complimentary local *chupito* (shot) of liqueur, finishing the night off with a satisfying thump. Back down in the main cities, restaurants take inspiration from these traditional methods, but offer a more contemporary style and setting.

HOTELS

Most hotels in the Pyrenees are informal and outdoorsy, with a large fireplace in one of the public rooms. They are usually built of wood, glass, and stone, with steep slate roofs that blend in with the surrounding mountains. Most hotel establishments are family operations passed down from generation to generation. *Hotel reviews have been shortened. For full information, visit Fodors.com.*

WHAT IT COSTS IN EUROS				
	$	$$	$$$	$$$$
Restaurants	under €13	€13–€17	€18–€22	over €22
Hotels	under €91	€91–€125	€126–€180	over €180

Restaurant prices are the average cost of a main course or equivalent combination of smaller dishes at dinner. Hotel prices are the lowest cost of a standard double room in high season.

TOURS

Trekking, horseback riding, adventure sports such as canyoning and ballooning, and more contemplative outings like bird-watching and botanical tours are just a few of the specialties available in any of the main Pyrenean resorts.

Well populated with trout, the Pyrenees' cold streams provide excellent angling from mid-March to the end of August. Notable places to cast a line are the Segre, Aragón, Gállego, Noguera Pallaresa, Arga, Esera, and Esca rivers. Pyrenean ponds and lakes also tend to be rich in trout.

Tour Information Danica. Chema Ramón and his company, which is located just south of Benasque, can take you fly-fishing anywhere in the world by horse or helicopter, but the Pyrenees is their home turf. You'll be whisked to high Pyrenean lakes and ponds, streams and rivers, armed with equipment and expertise. Danica also offers wild-mushroom and botanical tours. ☎ 974/553493 ⊕ www.danicaguias.com ✉ From €120–€200 a day (depending on equipment). **Pyrenean Experience.** The British expat Georgina Howard, with her established company Pyrenean Experiences, specializes in showcasing Basque-Navarran culture, walking, and gastronomy. ☎ 01217/113428 in the U.K., 650/713759 ⊕ www.pyreneanexperience.com ✉ From £725 for a one-week walking tour, lodging included.

EASTERN CATALAN PYRENEES

Catalonia's easternmost Pyrenean valley, the Vall de Camprodón, is still hard enough to reach that, despite pockets of Barcelona summer colonies, it has retained much of its farm culture and mountain wildness. It has several exquisite towns and churches and, above all, mountains, such as the Sierra de Catllar. Vallter 2000, La Molina, and Núria are ski resorts at either end of the Pyrenean heights on the north side of the valley, but the lowlands in the middle and main body of the valley have remained pasture for sheep, cattle, and horses.

GETTING HERE AND AROUND

To reach the Vall de Camprodón from Barcelona, you can take the N152 through Vic and Ripoll. From Barcelona or the Costa Brava you can also go by way of either Figueres or Girona, through Besalú and Olot on route N260, and then through the C26 Capsacosta tunnel to Camprodón. From France, drive southwest from Céret on the D115 through the Col (Pass) d'Ares, which becomes C38 as it enters the Camprodón Valley after passing through Prats-de-Molló-La Preste.

CAMPRODÓN

127 km (80 miles) northwest of Barcelona, 80 km (48 miles) west of Girona.

Camprodón, the capital of its *comarca* (county), lies at the junction of the Ter and Ritort rivers—both excellent trout streams. The rivers flow by, through, and under much of the town, giving it a highland waterfront character (as well as a long history of flooding). Its best-known symbol is the elegant 12th-century stone bridge that broadly spans the Ter River in the center of town. The town owes much of its opulence to the summer residents from Barcelona who built mansions along **Passeig Maristany,** the leafy promenade at its northern edge.

GETTING HERE AND AROUND

The C38 runs into the center of town from both north (France) and south (Barcelona, Vic, or Ripoll) directions. If coming from France, the southbound D115 changes into the C38 once over the Spanish border.

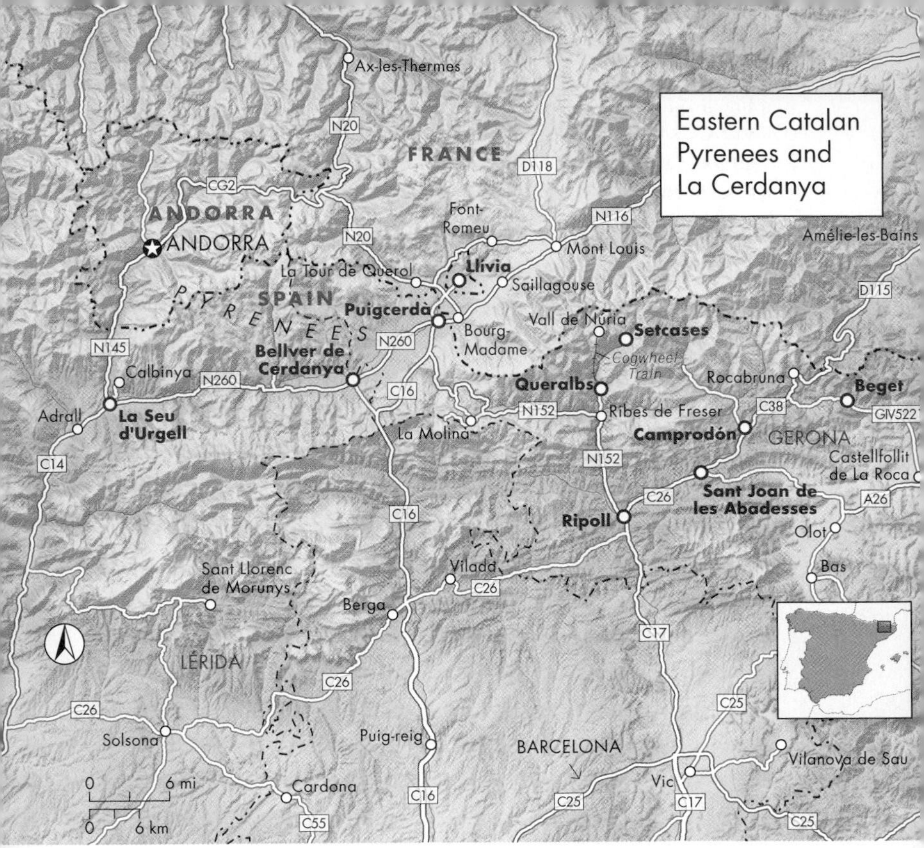

From either direction, the C38 heads straight toward the center of town. The best way to explore is on foot as the streets are narrow and can be complicated to navigate by car.

ESSENTIALS

Visitor Information Camprodón ✉ *Pl. Espanya 1* ☎ *972/740010.*

WHERE TO STAY

$$ B&B/INN FAMILY 🏨 **Fonda Rigà.** A highland inn with comfortable modern rooms and spectacular views that reach the sea, this mountain perch is an excellent base for hiking, horseback riding, and viewing Pyrenean flora and fauna. **Pros:** the views and the peace and quiet; well-maintained rooms and facilities. **Cons:** a serious 5 km (3 mile) drive above the valley floor; remote from Camprodón. [$] *Rooms from: €122* ✉ *Final de la ctra. de Tregurà, Ctra. de Tregurà de Dalt, Km 4.8, 10 km (6 miles) up the Ter Valley from Camprodón* ☎ *972/136000* 🌐 *www.fondariga.com* 🛏 *16 rooms* 🕒 *Closed 2 wks in June* 🍴 *Some meals.*

$$$ B&B/INN 🏨 **Hotel Maristany.** An elegant chalet on Camprodon's grandest promenade, this small but well-appointed hotel offers a chance to live like the 19th- and 20th-century Barcelona aristocracy that spent summers in this mountain retreat. **Pros:** outside of town center and quiet at night; excellent restaurant. **Cons:** rooms and baths are somewhat cramped; no children under 10 years allowed. [$] *Rooms from: €132* ✉ *Av. Maristany*

20 ☎ *972/130078* 🌐 *www.hotelmaristany.com* 🛏 *10 rooms* 🕒 *Closed Dec. 10–Mar. 1* 🍴 *Breakfast.*

$ HOTEL 🏨 **L'Hotel de Camprodón.** A perfect base for getting a sense of this stylish little mountain hub, this elegant Moderniste building has rooms over the bustling Plaça Dr. **Pros:** central location; charming Art Nouveau style and preserved features throughout; wonderful views over the river. **Cons:** no parking; rooms on the square can be noisy in summer; no Wi-Fi in rooms. [$] *Rooms from: €85* ✉ *Pl. del Dr. Robert 3* ☎ *972/740013* 🌐 *www.hotelcamprodon.com* 🛏 *50 rooms* 🍴 *No meals.*

SHOPPING

Cal Xec. This legendary sausage and cheese store also sells the much-prized, vanilla-flavored Birbas cookies. It's at the end of the Camprodón Bridge. ✉ *C. Isaac Albéniz 1* ☎ *972/740084.*

Mercat Setmanal. Held every Sunday from 9 am to 2 pm, this market sells all manner of artisanal food products, crafts, clothing, antiques, and bric-a-brac. ✉ *Pl. del Dr. Robert.*

EN ROUTE

Rocabruna. From Camprodón, take C38 north toward Molló and the French border. After 3 km (2 miles) turn east toward Rocabruna, a village of crisp, clean, Pyrenean stone houses at the source of the clear Beget River. The village is famous for the excellent Can Po restaurant (⇨ *Beget, below*), which makes a good stop for those on the way to Beget.

6

BEGET

17 km (10 miles) east of Camprodón.

Fodor's Choice ★

The village of Beget, considered Catalonia's *més bufó* (cutest), was completely cut off from motorized vehicles until the mid-1960s, when a *pista forestal* (Jeep track) was laid down; in 1980 Beget was finally fully connected to the rest of the world by an asphalt roadway, which can be hazardous when mist descends, as it often does. The GIV5223 road to Castellfollit de la Roca, 12 km (7 miles) away, is a spectacular drive through former volcanic peaks of the Alta Garrotxa. Beget's 30 houses are eccentric stone structures with heavy wooden doors and a golden color peculiar to the Vall de Camprodón. Archaic stone bridges span the stream where protected trout swim in clear mountain water.

GETTING HERE AND AROUND

Drive northeast out of Camprodón on Carrer Molló (C38) for 2 km (1 mile) before turning right onto the Carretera de Camprodón a Beget (GIV5223) for 14 km (9 miles) to Beget. Cars are not allowed to enter the village but there is parking just outside. When leaving, take the direction towards Oix, which leads to Castellfollit de la Roca and the N260, to avoid having to retrace your steps back up the mountain.

EXPLORING

Sant Cristòfol. The 12th-century Romanesque church of Sant Cristòfol (St. Christopher) has a diminutive bell tower and a rare 6-foot Majestat—a polychrome wood carving of the risen and reigning Christ in head-to-foot robes, dating from the 12th century. The church is usually closed, but ask in the bar-restaurant behind the church, or in El Forn de Beget and they will direct you to the keeper of the key. A €1 charge is used for church upkeep. ⊠ *Pl. Major s/n.*

WHERE TO EAT AND STAY

$ **✕ Can Po.** This ancient, ivy-covered, Pyrenean stone–and–mortar farm-
CATALAN house perched over a deep gully in nearby Rocabruna is famed for carefully prepared local dishes like *vedella amb crema de ceps* (veal in wild mushroom sauce) and the Catalan classic *oca amb peres* (goose stewed with pears). Try the *civet de porc senglar* (stewed wild boar) in season (winter) or any of the many varieties of wild mushrooms that find their way into the kitchen at this rustic mountain retreat. $ *Average main: €11* ⊠ *Ctra. de Beget s/n, Rocabruna* ☎ *972/741045* ⊘ *Closed mid-Feb.–Mar. 1, and Mon.–Thurs. Oct.–Jul. (except public holidays); call ahead to check in low season.*

$$ ⊡ **El Forn de Beget.** Tucked above the Trull River in the upper part of
B&B/INN the village, this little stone restaurant and hotel has panoramic views over Alta Garrotxa. **Pros:** a true hideaway lost in the Pyrenees. **Cons:** rooms are small and close together. $ *Rooms from: €119* ⊠ *Carrer Josep Duñach "En Feliça" 9* ☎ *972/741230* ⊕ *www.elforndebeget.com* ⊷ *4 rooms* ⦿ *Some meals.*

SETCASES

11 km (7 miles) northwest of Camprodón.

Although Setcases ("seven houses") is somewhat larger than its name would imply, this tiny village nestled at the head of the valley has a distinct mountain spirit.

GETTING HERE AND AROUND

From Camprodón, take the road 2 km (1 mile) northwest to Llanars. From Llanars, follow the Carretera Setcases for 9 km (6 miles). The town is small and easily explored on foot unless you are travelling on to the ski resort Vallter 2000.

ESSENTIALS

Visitor Information Setcases ⊠ *Pl. Major 1* ☎ *972/136089.*

EXPLORING

Llanars. On the road back down the valley from Setcases, Llanars, just short of Camprodón, has a 12th-century Romanesque church, **Sant Esteve de Llanars,** which has weathered to a rich shade of ocher. The wood-and-iron portal depicts the martyrdom of St. Stephen.

WHERE TO EAT

$$$ **✕ Can Tomàs.** On the immediate left when you enter town, this unusual
CATALAN place is covered with lovingly rendered portraits of wild mushrooms; it specializes in aromatic upland fungi used in original ways. The house favorites are *arròs de bolets* (a paella with wild mushrooms) and the *patatas Can Tomàs* (fried potatoes with mushrooms and egg), but the *encenalls de foie i tòfona* (shavings of duck liver with black truffles) and the cuttlefish with meatballs and *rossinyols* (chanterelles) are representative of the creativity and sophistication of this little gem. $ *Average main: €20* ⊠ *Carrer de Jesús 10* ☎ *972/136004* ⊕ *www.cantomas.com* ⊘ *Closed Wed. No dinner Tues.*

SPORTS AND THE OUTDOORS

Vallter 2000 ski area. Built into a glacial cirque (mountain basin) reaching a height of 8,216 feet, this ski area above Setcases has a dozen lifts and, on very clear days at the top, views east all the way to the Bay of Roses on the Costa Brava. ☎ 972/136057 ⊕ www.vallter2000.com.

SANT JOAN DE LES ABADESSES

21 km (13 miles) southeast of Setcases, 14 km (9 miles) south of Camprodón.

The site of an important church, Sant Joan de les Abadesses is named for the 9th-century abbess Emma and her successors. Emma was the daughter of Guifré el Pilós (Wilfred the Hairy), the hero of the Christian Reconquest of Ripoll and the founder of Catalonia. The town's arcaded Plaça Major offers a glimpse of the town's medieval past, as does the broad, elegant, 12th-century bridge over the Ter.

GETTING HERE AND AROUND

Exit southwest of Camprodón, on the Carrer Molló (C38) for 9 km (6 miles), passing through Sant Pau de Segúries. At the traffic circle, take the first exit onto the N260 for 4 km (2½ miles) to Sant Joan de les Abadesses. If you're coming from Ripoll, take the northbound N260 for 10 km (6 miles). Once here, it's an easy stroll.

ESSENTIALS

Visitor Information Sant Joan de les Abadesses ⊠ *Pl. de la Abadía 9* ☎ *972/720599.*

EXPLORING

Sant Joan. In the 12th-century Romanesque church of Sant Joan, the altarpiece—a 13th-century polychrome wood sculpture of the Descent from the Cross—is one of the most expressive and human of that epoch. ⊠ *Pl. de la Abadía s/n* ☎ *972/722353* 💶 *€3* ◷ *July and Aug., daily 10–7; Sept.–June, daily 10–2 and 4–6.*

RIPOLL

10 km (6 miles) southwest of Sant Joan de les Abadesses, 105 km (65 miles) north of Barcelona.

One of Catalonia's first Christian strongholds of the Reconquest and a center of religious erudition during the Middle Ages, Ripoll is known as the *bressol* (cradle) of Catalonia's liberation from Moorish domination and the spiritual home of Guifré el Pilós (Wilfred the Hairy), the Count of Barcelona, who is widely considered founder of the nation in the late 9th century. A dark, mysterious country town built around a 9th-century Benedictine monastery, Ripoll was a focal point of culture throughout French Catalonia and the Pyrenees, from the monastery's 879 founding until the mid-1800s, when Barcelona began to eclipse it.

GETTING HERE AND AROUND

The C17 northbound from Vic heads into Ripoll for the center. From Camprodón and Sant Joan de les Abadesses, head southwest on the C38, which turns into the N260 for the center of Ripoll. There are direct trains from Barcelona (⊕ *www.renfe.com*), but buses connections must be made through Girona. It's a 10-minute walk from the station to the center, and the small town is easy to explore on foot.

ESSENTIALS
Visitor Information Ripoll ⊠ *Pl. de l'Abat Oliva s/n* ☏ *972/702351.*

EXPLORING
Camino dels Enginyers. From the ski area of Núria, at an altitude of 6,562 feet, the dramatic, occasionally heart-stopping "engineers' path" is best done in the summer months. The three-hour trek, aided at one point by a cable handrail, leads to the remote highland valley of Coma de Vaca, where a cozy refuge and hearty replenishment await. Phone ahead to make sure there's space. In the morning you can descend along the riverside Gorges de Freser trail, another three-hour walk, to Queralbs, where there are connecting trains to Ribes de Freser. ⊠ *Refugi de Coma de Vaca, Termino Municipal de Queralbs dentro del Espacio protegido Ter Freser, Queralbs* ☏ *649/229012* ⊕ *www.comadevaca.com* ⊘ *Refuge closed Nov.–Apr. and weekdays Oct. and May (but open for groups by reservation).*

FAMILY **Cogwheel train.** The train ride from the town of Ribes de Freser up
Fodor'sChoice to Núria provides one of Catalonia's most unusual excursions—in
★ few other places in Spain does a train make such a precipitous ascent. Known as the *cremallera* (zipper), the line was completed in 1931 to connect Ribes with the Santuari de la Mare de Déu de Núria (Mother of God of Núria) and with mountain hiking and skiing. The ride takes 45 minutes and costs €22.30 round-trip. ⊠ *14 km (9 miles) north of Ripoll, Ribes de Freser* ☏ *972/732020* ⊕ *www.valldenuria.cat* ⊘ *Closed Nov. Subject to change—check website.*

Santa Maria. Decorated with a pageant of biblical figures, the 12th-century doorway to the church is one of Catalonia's great works of Romanesque art, crafted as a triumphal arch by stone masons and sculptors of the Roussillon school, which was centered around French Catalonia and the Pyrenees. You can pick up a guide to the figures surrounding the portal in the nearby Centro de Interpretación del Monasterio, in Placa de l'Abat. The center has an interactive exhibition that explains the historical, cultural, and religious relevence of this cradle of Catalonia. It also provides information about guided tours. ⊠ *Pl. Monasterio s/n* ☏ *972/704203* ▱ *Cloister and door €3, museum €4, Centro de Interpretación del Monasterio (exhibition) €2* ⊘ *Cloister daily 10–1 and 3–6 (until 7 Mar.–Sept.); museum Tues.–Sat. 10–1:30 and 4–6, Sun. 10–2; Centro de Interpretación del Monasterio Tues.–Sun. 9:30–1:30 and 4–6 (until 7 Mar.–Sept).*

Santuari de la Mare de Déu de Núria. The legend of the Santuari de la Mare de Déu de Núria, a Marian religious retreat, is based on the story of Sant Gil of Nîmes, who did penance in the Núria Valley during the 7th century. The saint left behind a wooden statue of the Virgin Mary, a bell he used to summon shepherds to prayer, and a cooking pot; 300 years later, a pilgrim found these treasures in this sanctuary. The bell and the pot came to have special importance to barren women, who, according to local beliefs, were blessed with as many children as they wished after placing their heads in the pot and ringing the bell. ✉ *26 km (16 miles) north of Ripoll, Núria* 🎫 *Free* ⏲ *Daily, except during Mass. Closed Nov.*

WHERE TO STAY

$$$$ HOTEL 🏨 **Hotel Vall de Núria.** A mountain refuge and hotel run by the government of Catalonia, this family-oriented base camp with double, triple, and quadruple rooms offers comfortable lodging and dining at 6,500 feet above sea level. **Pros:** perfect location in the heart of the Pyrenees; pristine mountain air; simplicity. **Cons:** hotel feels slightly institutional, with quasi-monastic austerity; minimum 2-night stay in high season; high rates. [$] *Rooms from: €181* ✉ *Estación de Montaña Vall de Núria, Queralbs* ☎ *972/732020* 🌐 *www.valldenuria.com* 🛏 *65 rooms, 12 apartments* ⏲ *Closed Nov.* 🍴 *Some meals.*

QUERALBS

21 km (13 miles) north of Ripoll.

The three-hour walk down the mountain from Vall de Núria to the sleepy village of Queralbs follows the course of the cogwheel train on a rather precipitous but fairly easy route, as long as it's not done during the snow season. The path overlooks gorges and waterfalls, overshadowed by sheer peaks, before exiting into the surprisingly charming and tiny village of Queralbs, where houses made of stone and wood cling to the side of the mountain. There is a well-preserved **Romanesque church,** notable for its six-arch portico, marble columns, single nave, and pointed vault.

Queralbs is a picturesque and relaxed alternative to staying up in the more functional and busier Vall de Núria hotel. However, note that outside of weekends and vacation periods, the village restaurant and bars have limited service and the Hostal Les Roquetes does not serve dinner. The town of Ribes de Freser, a few minutes farther down the mountain either by car or on the cogwheel train, has more restaurants and hotels.

WHERE TO STAY

$ B&B/INN 🏨 **Hostal Les Roquetes.** A short walk from the cogwheel train station and the center of the village, this *hostal* has cheerful rooms and some spectacular views. **Pros:** fantastic setting and views; friendly service; good base for walks in the area. **Cons:** limited food options outside of weekends; only accessible by local road or cogwheel train, and those times are limited. [$] *Rooms from: €66* ✉ *Crta. de Ribes 5* ☎ *972/727369* 🛏 *8 rooms* ⏲ *Closed Nov.* 🍴 *No meals.*

LA CERDANYA

The widest, sunniest valley in the Pyrenees is said to be in the shape of the handprint of God. High pastureland bordered north and south by snow-covered peaks, La Cerdanya starts in France, at Col de la Perche (near Mont Louis), and ends in the Spanish province of Lleida, at Martinet. Split between two countries and subdivided into two more provinces on each side, the valley has an identity all of its own. Residents

6

Climbing in La Cerdanya

on both sides of the border speak Catalan, a Romance language derived from early Provençal French, and regard the valley's political border with undisguised hilarity. Unlike any other valley in the upper Pyrenees, this one runs east–west and thus has a record annual number of sunlight hours.

PUIGCERDÀ

170 km (105 miles) northwest of Barcelona, 65 km (40 miles) northwest of Ripoll.

Puigcerdà is the largest town in the valley; in Catalan, *puig* means "hill," and *cerdà* derives from "Cerdanya." From the promontory upon which it stands, the views down across the meadows of the valley floor and up into the craggy peaks of the surrounding Pyrenees are dramatic. The 12th-century **Romanesque bell tower**—all that remains of the town church of Santa Maria, destroyed in 1936 at the outset of the Spanish Civil War—and the sunny sidewalk cafés facing it are among Puigcerdà's prettiest spots, as is the Gothic church of **Sant Domènec.** Serving primarily as a base for skiers and hikers from both sides of the border, Puigcerdà has lively restaurants and a bustling shopping promenade. On Sunday, markets sell clothes, cheeses, fruits, vegetables, and wild mushrooms to shoppers.

GETTING HERE AND AROUND

From Ripoll take the northwest-bound N260 for 63 km (39 miles) toward Ribes de Freser. Several trains a day (they are less frequent on weekends) run from Barcelona Sants to Puigcerdà (⊕ *www.renfe.com*).

Buses go from Barcelona Estación del Nord (🌐 *www.barcelonanord.com*). Once you reach the center, there is ample parking, and the easiest way to get around town is on foot.

ESSENTIALS

Visitor Information Puigcerdà ✉ *Carrer Querol 1* ☎ *972/880542.*

EXPLORING

FAMILY **Le petit train jaune.** The "little yellow train" has service from Bourg-Madame and from La Tour de Querol, both easy hikes into France from Puigcerdà. The border at La Tour, a pretty one-hour hike, is marked only by a stone painted with the Spanish and French flags. It can also be picked up in Villefranche. The *carrilet* (narrow-gauge railway) is the last in the Pyrenees and is used for tours as well as transportation; it winds through the Cerdanya to the walled town of Villefranche de Conflent. The 63-km (39-mile) tour can take most of the day, especially if you stop to browse in Mont Louis or Villefranche. Be aware that in low season the trains are infrequent. Timetables are available at the stations or on the website. ✉ *Puigcerdà, France* 🌐 *www.ter-sncf.com.*

Plaça Cabrinetty. Along with its porticoes and covered walks, this square also has a sunny northeastern corner where farmers gather for the Sunday morning market. It's protected from the wind and ringed by two- and three-story houses of various pastel colors, some with decorative sgraffito designs and all with balconies.

WHERE TO EAT AND STAY

$$ CATALAN 🍴 **Tap de Suró.** Named for the classic bottle stopper (*tap*) made of cork oak bark (*suró*), this wine store, delicatessen, restaurant, and tapas emporium is tucked into the western edge of the town ramparts; it's the perfect place for sunsets, with views down the length of the Cerdanya Valley to the walls of the Sierra del Cadí. Cheeses, duck and goose liver, Ibérico hams, and oysters are the kinds of delicacies best represented on the varied menu here, with a frequently changing selection of wines—new and old—from all over Spain and southern France. [$] *Average main: €17* ✉ *Carrer Querol 21* ☎ *678/655928* 🕒 *Closed Mon.*

$$$ HOTEL 🏨 **Hotel del Lago.** A comfortable old favorite near Puigcerdà's emblematic lake, this spa hotel has a graceful series of buildings around a central garden. **Pros:** picturesque and central location on the iconic lake at the edge of town; family treatment and service. **Cons:** rooms can be hot on summer days. [$] *Rooms from: €135* ✉ *Av. Dr. Piguillem 7* ☎ *972/881000* 🌐 *www.hotellago.com* 🛏 *24 rooms* 🍽 *No meals.*

$$$$ HOTEL Fodor's Choice ★ 🏨 **La Torre del Remei.** Brilliantly restored by José María and Loles Boix, owners of the legendary Boix restaurant in Martinet, this 1910 Moderniste tower provides luxurious accommodations about 3 km (2 miles) west of Puigcerdà. **Pros:** perfect comfort and sublime cuisine; surrounded by a hiking, skiing, and golfing paradise. **Cons:** the price; the slightly hushed stiffness. [$] *Rooms from: €305* ✉ *Camí del Remei 3, Bolvir de Cerdanya* ☎ *972/140182* 🌐 *www.torredelremei.com* 🛏 *4 rooms, 7 suites* 🍽 *Breakfast.*

$$$ HOTEL 🏨 **Villa Paulita.** This stately town-house complex at the edge of Puigcerdà's famous lake has some of the best rooms and food in the Cerdanya Valley. **Pros:** renowned restaurant on site; near the

center of the town's markets, restaurants, and general action but tucked into a quiet and scenic corner. **Cons:** some of the rooms are cramped and noisy (avoid the ones on the ground floor); small pool. [$] *Rooms from: €180* ✉ *Av. Pons i Gasch 15* ☎ *972/884622* 🌐 *www.hotelvillapaulita.com* 🛏 *38 rooms* 🍴 *Breakfast.*

> **TIP**
>
> If you're planning a long-distance hiking trip, local bus connections will get you to your starting point and retrieve you from the finish line.

SHOPPING

Puigcerdà is one big shopping mall—one that's long been a center for contraband clothes, cigarettes, and other items smuggled across the French border.

Carrer Major. This is an uninterrupted row of stores selling books, jewelry, fashion, sports equipment, and lots more. Check out **Agau Joier,** at Ramón Cosp 12, just off the main street, for jewelry designed by Andrés Santana. ✉ *Carrer Major.*

Pasteleria Cosp. For the best *margaritas* in town—no, not those; these are crunchy-edged madeleines made with almonds—head for the oldest commercial establishment in Catalonia, founded in 1806. ✉ *Carrer Major 20* ☎ *972/880103.*

Sunday market. On Sunday morning (9–2), head for this weekly market, which, like those in most Cerdanya towns, is a great place to look for local crafts and specialties such as herbs, goat cheese, wild mushrooms, honey, and baskets. ✉ *Paseo 10 de Abril.*

LLÍVIA

6 km (4 miles) northeast of Puigcerdà.

A Spanish enclave in French territory, Llívia was marooned by the 1659 Peace of the Pyrenees treaty, which ceded 33 villages to France. Incorporated as a *vila* (town) by royal decree of Carlos V—who spent a night here in 1528 and was impressed by the town's beauty and hospitality—Llívia managed to remain Spanish.

GETTING HERE AND AROUND

From Puigcerdà you could walk to Llívia, as it is only 6 km (4 miles) northbound through the border of France, but there is a bus, which departs from Puigcerdà train station. By car, follow the Camí Vell de Llívia onto the N154, which goes directly to Llívia.

ESSENTIALS

Visitor Information Llívia ✉ *Carrer dels Forns 10* ☎ *972/896313.*

EXPLORING

Mare de Déu dels Àngels. At the upper edge of town, this fortified church has wonderful acoustics; check to see if any classical music events are on—especially in August, when it hosts an annual classical music festival. Information about the festival's concerts is released in June. ✉ *Carrer dels Forns 13* ☎ *972/896301.*

Mosaic. In the middle of town, look for the mosaic commemorating Lampègia, *princesa de la pau i de l'amor* (princess of peace and of love), erected in memory of the red-haired daughter of the Duke of Aquitania and lover of Munuza, a Moorish warlord who governed the Cerdanya in the 8th century during the Arab domination.

Museu de la Farmacia. Across from the Mare de Déu dels Àngels church, this ancient pharmacy was founded in 1415 and has been certified as the oldest in Europe. ✉ *Carrer dels Forns 10* ☎ *972/896011* 🎫 *€3* ⏲ *Mid-June–mid-Sept., Tues.–Sat. 10–8, Sun. 10–2; mid-Sept.–mid-June, Tues.–Fri. 10–6, Sat. 10–8, Sun. 10–2.*

WHERE TO EAT

$$ SPANISH

🍴 **Can Ventura.** Inside a flower-festooned 17th-century town house made of ancient stones, this is one of the Cerdanya's best addresses for both fine cuisine and good value. Beef *a la llosa* (seared on slabs of slate) and duck with orange and spices are house specialties, and the wide selection of *entretenimientos* (hors d'oeuvres or tapas) is the perfect way to begin. Ask the owner, Jordi Pous, who's a food and wine savant, about wine selections, game, and wild mushrooms in season. [$] *Average main: €17* ✉ *Pl. Major 1* ☎ *972/896178* 🌐 *www.canventura.com* ✍ *Reservations essential* ⏲ *Closed Mon. and Tues.*

$$$ SPANISH
Fodor's Choice ★

🍴 **La Formatgeria de Llívia.** Set on Llívia's eastern edge (en route to Saillagousse, France), this restaurant is in a former cheese factory, and the proprietors continue the tradition by producing fresh homemade cheese on the premises while you watch; there are tasting tables in the bar for cheese-sampling sessions. Juanjo Meya and his wife, master chef Marta Pous, have had great success offering fine local cuisine, which comes with panoramic views looking south toward Puigmal and across the valley, and general charm and good cheer. There's also an innovative tasting menu. [$] *Average main: €20* ✉ *Pl. de Ro s/n, Gorguja* ☎ *972/146279* 🌐 *www.laformatgeria.com* ✍ *Reservations essential* ⏲ *Closed Tues. and Wed., and 1st 2 wks in July.*

BELLVER DE CERDANYA

31 km (19 miles) southwest of Llívia, 18 km (11 miles) southwest of Puigcerdà.

Fodor's Choice ★

Bellver de Cerdanya has preserved its slate-roof-and-fieldstone Pyrenean architecture more successfully than many of the Cerdanya's larger towns. Perched on a promontory over the **Río Segre,** which winds around much of the town, Bellver is a mountain version of a fishing village—trout fishing, to be exact. The town's Gothic church of **Sant Jaume** and the arcaded **Plaça Major,** in the upper part of town, are lovely examples of traditional Pyrenean mountain-village design.

GETTING HERE AND AROUND

Take the southwest-bound N260 from Puigcerdà; once here, it's easily explored on foot.

ESSENTIALS

Visitor Information Bellver de Cerdanya ✉ *Pl. de Sant Roc 9* ☎ *973/510229.*

WHERE TO STAY

$$ B&B/INN [🏨] **Aparthotel Bellver.** The warmth of the terra-cotta tiles, the great views, and traditional fireplaces in some of the rooms add to the charm of this mountain lodge and apartment block within the winding streets of central Bellver. **Pros:** centrally located; open year-round. **Cons:** two-night minimum stay in July and August. [$] *Rooms from: €110* ✉ *Carrer de la Batllia 61–63* ☎ *973/510627* 🌐 *www.aparthotelbellver.com* 🛏 *12 rooms* 🍴 *No meals.*

> **SAY HELLO IN THE PYRENEES**
>
> In Spanish: "Buenos días"
>
> In Catalan: "Bon dia"
>
> In Euskera (Basque): "Egun on"
>
> In Fabla Aragonesa: "Buen Diya"

LA SEU D'URGELL

20 km (12 miles) south of Andorra la Vella (in Andorra), 45 km (28 miles) west of Puigcerdà, 200 km (120 miles) northwest of Barcelona.

Fodor's Choice ★ La Seu d'Urgell is an ancient town facing the snowy rock wall of the Sierra del Cadí. As the seat (*seu*) of the regional archbishopric since the 6th century, it has a rich legacy of art and architecture. The Pyrenean feel of the streets, with their dark balconies and porticoes, overhanging galleries, and colonnaded porches—particularly **Carrer dels Canonges**—makes Seu mysterious and memorable. Look for the medieval **grain measures** at the corner of Carrer Major and Carrer Capdevila. The tiny food shops on the arcaded Carrer Major are good places to assemble lunch for a hike.

GETTING HERE AND AROUND

Take the N260 southwest from Puigcerdà via Bellver de Cerdanya for 45 km (28 miles). From the direction of Lleida, head north on the C13 for 63 km (39 miles), then take the C26 after Balaguer, before joining the C14 for 32 km (20 miles) and then the N260 into the center. There are buses daily from Barcelona. The town is compact and can be explored on foot.

ESSENTIALS

Bus Contacts ALSA ✉ *Estación de Autobuses, Bisbe Benlloch 1* ☎ *902/422242* 🌐 *www.alsa.es.*

Visitor Information La Seu d'Urgell ✉ *Calle Mayor 8* ☎ *973/351511* 🌐 *www.turismeseu.com.*

EXPLORING

Fodor's Choice ★ **Catedral de Santa Maria.** This 12th-century cathedral is the finest in the Pyrenees, and the sunlight casting the rich reds and blues of Santa Maria's southeastern rose window into the deep gloom of the transept is a moving sight. The 13th-century cloister is famous for the individually carved, often whimsical capitals on its 50 columns, crafted by the same Roussillon school of masons who carved the doorway on the church of Santa Maria in Ripoll. Don't miss the haunting, 11th-century chapel of **Sant Miquel** or the **Diocesan Museum,** which has a collection of striking medieval murals from various Pyrenean churches and a colorfully illuminated 10th-century Mozarabic manuscript of the monk Beatus de Liébana's commentary on the apocalypse. ✉ *Pl. dels Oms* ☎ *973/353242* 🌐 *www.museudiocesaurgell.org* 🎟 *Cathedral, cloister, and museum €3* 🕒 *Nov.–Mar., daily 10–1; Apr.–mid-June and mid-Sept.–Oct., daily 10–1 and 4–6; mid-June–mid-Sept., daily 10–1 and 4–7.*

WHERE TO STAY

$ B&B/INN Fodor's Choice ★ 🏨 **Cal Serni.** Ten minutes north of La Seu d'Urgell in the Pyrenean village of Calbinyà, this enchanting 15th-century farmhouse and inn exudes rustic charm and provides inexpensive meals against a backdrop of panoramic views. **Pros:** mountain authenticity just minutes from La Seu; good value. **Cons:** small rooms, tight public spaces. [$] *Rooms from: €75* ✉ *Ctra. de Calbinyà s/n, Valls de Valira, Calbinyà* ☎ *973/352809* 🌐 *www.calserni.com* 🛏 *6 rooms* 🍴 *Breakfast.*

$$$$ HOTEL 🏨 **El Castell de Ciutat.** Just outside town, this wood-and-slate structure beneath La Seu's castle is one of the finest places to stay in the Pyrenees—rooms on the second floor have balconies overlooking the river, those on the third have slanted ceilings and dormer windows, and suites include a salon. **Pros:** best restaurant for many miles; supremely comfortable rooms. **Cons:** right next to a busy highway; misses out on the feel of the town. [$] *Rooms from: €225* ✉ *Ctra. de Lleida (N260), Km 229* ☎ *973/350000* 🌐 *www.hotelelcastell.com* 🛏 *33 rooms, 5 suites* 🍴 *Breakfast.*

$$$ HOTEL 🏨 **Parador de la Seu d'Urgell.** These comfortable quarters right in the center of town are built into the 14th-century convent of Sant Domènec. **Pros:** next to the Santa Maria Cathedral; handy for wandering through the town. **Cons:** some may feel that the minimalist lines and contemporary interior design clash with the medieval feel of the town. [$] *Rooms from: €171* ✉ *Calle Sant Domènec 6* ☎ *973/352000* 🌐 *www.parador.es* 🛏 *79 rooms* 🕒 *Closed Jan. 6–Feb. 14* 🍴 *No meals.*

WESTERN CATALAN PYRENEES

"The farther from Barcelona, the wilder" is the rule of thumb, and this is true of the rugged countryside and fauna in the western part of Catalonia. Three of the greatest destinations in the Pyrenees are here: the harmonious, Atlantic-influenced Vall d'Aran; the Noguera de Tor Valley (aka Vall de Boí), with its matching set of gemlike Romanesque churches; and Parc Nacional d'Aigüestortes i Estany de Sant Maurici, which has a network of pristine lakes and streams. The main geographical units in this section are the valley of the Noguera Pallaresa River, the Vall d'Aran headwaters of the Atlantic-bound Garonne, and the Noguera Ribagorçana River Valley, Catalonia's western limit.

SORT

59 km (37 miles) west of La Seu d'Urgell, 136 km (84 miles) north of Lleida, 259 km (160 miles) northwest of Barcelona.

The capital of the Pallars Sobirà (Upper Pallars Valley) is the area's epicenter for skiing, fishing, and white-water kayaking. The word *sort*

6

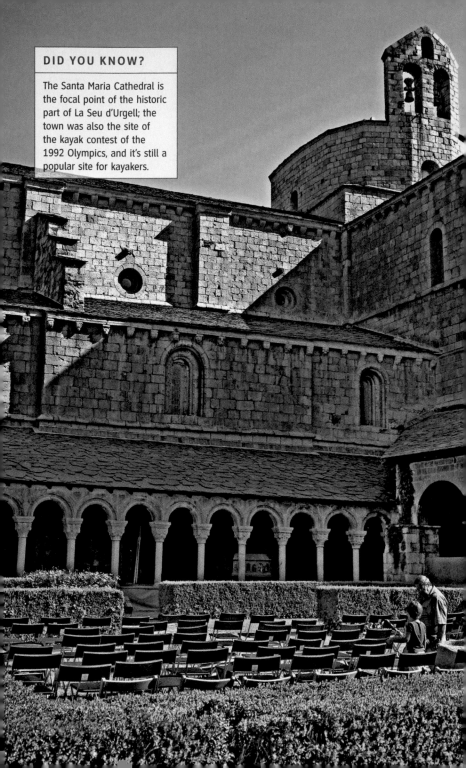

is Catalan for "luck," and its local lottery shop, La Bruixa d'Or (The Gold Witch), became a tourist attraction by living up to the town's name and selling more than an average number of winning tickets. Don't be fooled by the town you see from the main road: one block back, Sort is honeycombed with tiny streets and protected corners built to stave off harsh winter weather.

GETTING HERE AND AROUND

Heading westward from La Seu d'Urgell, take the N260 toward Lleida, head west again at Adrall, staying on the N260, and drive 53 km (33 miles) over the Cantó Pass to Sort.

ESSENTIALS

Visitor Information Pallars Sobirà ✉ *Camí de la Cabanera s/n* ☎ *973/621002* 🌐 *www.turisme.pallarssobira.cat.*

WHERE TO EAT

$$$$ SPANISH Fodor's Choice ★ 🍴 **Fogony.** If you hit Sort at lunchtime, then this restaurant makes an excellent reason to stop: it's one of the best of its kind in the Pyrenees. Come here for contemporary creations by its acclaimed chef, Zaraida Cotonat: *pollo (pota blava ecológico) a la cocotte con trufa* (organic bluefoot chicken with truffle), *solomillo de ternera de los Pirineos con ligero escabeche de verduras y setas* (filet of Pyrenean veal with marinated vegetables and mushrooms), or the *colmenillas con salsa de foie de pato macerado con Armagnac y Oporto* (wild mushrooms with sauce of duck liver macerated in Armagnac and port wine). An economical fixed-price menu is also available, which is more traditional and uses organic produce. [$] *Average main: €25* ✉ *Av. Generalitat 45* ☎ *973/621225* 🌐 *www.fogony.com* ⏲ *Closed Mon. and Tues. (except Christmas wk, Easter wk, and Aug.) and 2 wks in Jan. No dinner Sun.*

PARC NACIONAL D'AIGÜESTORTES I ESTANY DE SANT MAURICI

33 km (20 miles) north of Sort, 168 km (104 miles) north of Lleida, 292 km (175 miles) northwest of Barcelona.

Catalonia's only national park is a dramatic and unspoiled landscape that was shaped through 2 million years of glacial activity. Hikers can reach the park from the Noguera Pallaresa and Ribagorçana valleys, from the villages of Espot to the east, and Taüll and Boí to the west.

GETTING HERE AND AROUND

The C13 road north up the Noguera Pallaresa Valley covers 14 km (8 miles) from Sort to Llavorsí. The road up to Espot and into the park forks west 4 km (2½ miles) after Escaló, which is 8 km (5 miles) northwest of Llavorsí.

Fodor's Choice ★ **Parc Nacional d'Aigüestortes i Estany de Sant Maurici.** The breathtaking scenery of this national park is formed by jagged peaks, steep rock walls, and an abundance of high mountain terrain, all of which lie in the shadow of the twin peaks of Els Encantats. More than 300 glacial lakes and lagoons trickle through forests and meadows of wildflowers to the meandering Noguera River watercourses: the Pallaresa to the east and the Ribagorçana to the west. The land range sweeps from soft

6

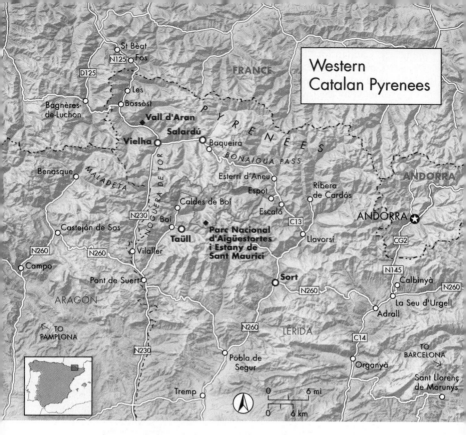

lower meadows below 5,000 feet to the highest crags at nearly double that height. The twin Encantats measure more than 9,000 feet, and the surrounding peaks of Beciberri, Peguera, Montarto, and Amitges hover between 8,700 feet and a little under 10,000 feet.

The nine mountain refuges here range from the 18-bed Besiberri—the highest bivouac in the Pyrenees at 9,174 feet—to the 70-bed Ventosa i Calvell, at 7,326 feet at the foot of Punta Alta. Between June and September these mountain accommodations fill with tired and hungry hikers sharing trail tips and lore and it is essential to make a reservation.

The park has strict rules: no camping, no fires, no swimming, no vehicles beyond certain points, and no unleashed pets. ■ TIP→ **Though driving inside the park is not allowed, it is possible to organize a taxi in Boí or Espot.** For information and refuge reservations, contact the park's administration office, Casa del Parque de Boí. ⊠ *Calle de les Graieres, 2, Ca de Simamet, Boí* ☎ *973/696189* ⊕ *reddeparquesnacionales.mma. es/en/parques/aiguestortes/index.htm* ⊠ *Free.*

WHERE TO STAY

There are no hotels in the park, but the nine refuges have staff who provide beds and dinner for hikers from June to October and during shorter periods at Christmas and Easter. When these are not open or staffed, shelter is still available in parts of the park, and fireplaces can be used for cooking, but hikers must supply the food and the utensils. A charming alternative is to stay in the pretty village of Taüll, on the western side of the park, where there are hotel and restaurant options.

$ B&B/INN **Refugi d'Amitges.** This refuge is near the Amitges lakes, at 7,920 feet. [$] *Rooms from: €43* ✉ *Espot* ☎ *973/250109, 973/641681* 🌐 *www.amitges.com* 🛏 *74 beds* 🕒 *Closed Oct.–June, except Easter wk* 🍴 *Some meals.*

$ B&B/INN **Refugi Ernest Mallafré.** At the foot of Els Encantats, this refuge is near Lake Sant Maurici. [$] *Rooms from: €39* ✉ *Espot* ☎ *973/250118, 933/720283* 🌐 *www.refugiosonline.com* 🛏 *34 beds* 🕒 *Closed Oct.–June, except Easter wk.* 🍴 *Some meals.*

$ B&B/INN **Refugi Josep Maria Blanc.** At 10,892 feet, this refuge is at the base of a peninsula reaching out into the Tort de Peguera Lake. [$] *Rooms from: €43* ✉ *Espot* ☎ *973/250108, 973/641681* 🌐 *www.jmblanc.com* 🛏 *60 beds* 🕒 *Closed Oct.–June, except Easter wk* 🍴 *Some meals.*

TAÜLL

58 km (36 miles) south of Vielha.

Taüll is a town of narrow streets and tight mountain design—wooden balconies and steep, slate roofs—that makes an attractive base for exploring the Parque Nacional de Aigüestortes. The high-sided valley also has one of the greatest concentrations of Romanesque architecture in Europe, and the famous Taüll churches of **Sant Climent** and **Santa María** are among the best examples of Romanesque architecture in the Pyrenees. Other important churches near Taüll include Sant Feliu, at Barruera; Sant Joan Baptista, at Boí; Santa Maria, at Cardet; Santa Maria, at Col; Santa Eulàlia, at Erill la Vall; La Nativitat de la Mare de Deu and Sant Quirze, at Durro.

GETTING HERE AND AROUND

Take the N230 northbound from Lleida for 138 km (86 miles), passing through El Pont de Suert. At Erill la Vall, go east for 4 km (2 ½ miles) toward Boí and Taüll. Taüll is small enough to walk around unless you are headed to the ski resort, in which case a car is needed. Four-wheel-drive taxis into the Parc Nacional d'Aigüestortes can be organized from Boí (☎ *973/694000 for tourist office*).

ESSENTIALS

Visitor Information Centre del Romànic de la Vall de Boí. For the secrets of the valley's eight Romanesque churches and one hermitage, which UNESCO designated part of the Patrimony of Humanity, take a guided tour led by the Romanesque Center. English-language tours require a reservation in advance. Erill-la-Vall is west of Taüll, 2 km (1 mile) beyond Boí. ✉ *Carrer del Batalló 5, Erill-la-Vall* ☎ *973/696715* 🌐 *www.centreromanic.com* 🎟 *One church €2, three churches €7, all churches €10* 🕒 *Mid-Apr.–mid-Oct., daily 9–2 and 5–7.* **Taüll** ✉ *Passeig de St. Feliu 43, Barruera, Vall de Boí* ☎ *973/694000* 🌐 *www.vallboi.com.*

EXPLORING

Boí Taüll. Taüll's ski resort is at the head of the Sant Nicolau Valley. It is also open in summer for hiking. ☎ *902/406640* 🌐 *www.boitaullresort.com.*

Fodor's Choice ★ **Sant Climent.** At the edge of town, this exquisite three-nave Romanesque church was built in 1123. The six-story belfry has perfect proportions, Pyrenean stone that changes hues with the light, and a sense of intimacy and balance. In 1922 Barcelona's Museu Nacional d'Art de Catalunya removed the murals for safekeeping, including the famous *Pantocrator,* the work of the "Master of Taüll." The murals presently in the church are reproductions. ✉ *Ctra. de Taüll s/n* 🌐 *www.centreromanic.com* 🎫 *€5* 🕒 *Daily 10–2 and 4–7.*

WHERE TO EAT AND STAY

$$$$ SPANISH 🍴 **La Cabana.** Lamb and goat cooked over coals are the specialties of this simple, up-country restaurant, which also serves a fine *escudella* (sausage, vegetable, bean, noodle and potato stew) and an excellent *crema de carredetes* (cream of meadow mushroom) soup. [$] *Average main: €28* ✉ *Ctra. de Taüll 16–21, 2.5 km (1.6 miles) from Taüll (direction Boí)* ☎ *973/696316* 🌐 *www.lacabanadeboi.com* 🕒 *Closed Mon. Call ahead for hours in low season.*

$$ B&B/INN Fodor's Choice ★ 🏨 **Hotel Santa María.** Lovingly restored, this 200-year-old stone house has a quiet central courtyard and stone arches, antique furnishings, and a knowledgeable owner who speaks some English. **Pros:** authentic cottage experience; atmospheric; interesting antique features. **Cons:** creaky floorboards; entrance hall and dining area feel somber. [$] *Rooms from: €94* ✉ *Pl. Cap del Riu 3* ☎ *973/696170, 609/316233* 🌐 *www.taull.com* 🛏 *6 rooms* 🍽 *Breakfast.*

VALL D'ARAN AND ENVIRONS

58 km (35 miles) northwest of Espot, 79 km (49 miles) northwest of Sort, 160 km (96 miles) north of Lleida, 297 km (178 miles) northwest of Barcelona.

The Vall d'Aran is at the western edge of the Catalan Pyrenees and the northwestern corner of Catalonia. North of the main Pyrenean axis, it's the Catalan Pyrenees' only Atlantic valley, opening north into the plains of Aquitania and drained by the Garonne, which flows into the Atlantic Ocean above Bordeaux. The 48-km (30-mile) drive from Bonaigua Pass to the Pont del Rei border with France follows the riverbed.

The valley's Atlantic personality is evidenced by its climate—wet and cold—and its language: the 6,000 inhabitants speak Aranés, a dialect of Gascon French derived from the Occitan language group. (Spanish and Catalan are also universally spoken.) Originally part of the Aquitanian county of Comminges, the Vall d'Aran maintained feudal ties to the Pyrenees of Spanish Aragón and became part of Catalonia–Aragón in the 12th century. In 1389 the valley was assigned to Catalonia.

Neither as wide as the Cerdanya nor as oppressively narrow and vertical as Andorra, the Vall d'Aran has a sense of well-being and order, an architectural harmony unique in Catalonia. The clusters of iron-gray slate roofs, the lush vegetation, and the dormer windows (a sign of French influence) all make the Vall d'Aran a distinct geographic and cultural pocket that happens to have washed up on the Spanish side of the border.

GETTING HERE AND AROUND
The C13 road continues north 6 km (4 miles) from the Espot turnoff to Esterri d'Aneu, and then becomes C28 and runs west over the Bonaigua Pass 32 km (19 miles) to Baqueira. From Baqueira the C28 continues 14 km (8½ miles) west to Vielha.

VIELHA

79 km (49 miles) northwest of Sort, 297 km (185 miles) northwest of Barcelona, 160 km (99 miles) north of Lleida.

Vielha (Viella in Spanish), capital of the Vall d'Aran, is a lively crossroads vitally involved in the Aranese movement to defend and reconstruct the valley's architectural, institutional, and linguistic heritage. At first glance, the town looks like a typical ski-resort base, but the compact and bustling old quarter has a Romanesque church and narrow streets filled with a good selection of restaurants and a couple of late-night bars. Hiking and climbing are popular around Vielha; guides are available year-round and can be arranged through the tourist office.

GETTING HERE AND AROUND
From the direction of Taüll, head south on the L500 for 15 km (9 miles) toward El Pont de Suerte. At Campament de Tor turn right onto the Carretera Lleida–Vielha (N230) northbound to Vielha. Vielha's town center is fairly compact and everything can be reached on foot, but you'll need a car to get to Salardú, Arties, and the ski station of Baqueira-Beret.

ESSENTIALS
Visitor Information Vielha ⊠ *Carrer Sarriulera 10* ☎ *973/640110* ⊕ *www.visitvaldaran.com.*

EXPLORING

EN ROUTE

The village of Arties makes a very good stop; it's here you'll find the famous Casa Irene restaurant and a historic parador (⇨ *See Where to Eat and Stay*).

Sant Miquel. Vielha's octagonal, 14th-century bell tower on the Romanesque parish church of Sant Miquel is one of the town's trademarks, as is its 15th-century Gothic altar. The partly damaged 12th-century wood carving *Cristo de Mig Aran,* displayed under glass, evokes a sense of mortality and humanity with a power unusual in medieval sculpture. ⊠ *Pl. de la Iglesia* ⊙ *Daily 10–7.*

WHERE TO EAT AND STAY

$$ ✕ **Era Mola** (*Restaurante Gustavo y María José*). This rustic former
SPANISH stable with whitewashed walls serves Aranese dishes with a modern, often French twist. Duck, either stewed with apples or served with *carreretes* (wild mushrooms from the valley), and roast kid and lamb are favorites, as are *espuma de patata con foie a la plancha* (potato foam with grilled foie gras). The wine list is particularly strong on Rioja, Ribera del Duero, and Somontano reds, as well as full-bodied whites, such as Albariño from Rías Baixas and Rueda from Valladolid. $ *Average main: €17* ⊠ *Carrer Marrec 14* ☎ *973/642419* ⊱ *Reservations*

6

Hiking in the Pyrenees

Walking the Pyrenees, with one foot in France and the other in Spain, is an exhilarating experience.

In fall and winter, the Alberes Mountains between Cap de Creus, the Iberian Peninsula's easternmost point, and the border with France at Le Perthus are a grassy runway between the Côte Vermeille's curving beaches to the north and the green patchwork of the Empordá to the south. The well-marked GR (Gran Recorrido) 11 is a favorite two-day spring or autumn hike, with an overnight stay at the Refugi de la Tanyareda, just below and east of Puig Neulós, the highest point in the Alberes.

The eight-hour walk from Coll de Núria to Ulldeter over the Sierra Catllar, above Setcases, is another grassy corridor in good weather from April to October. The luminous Cerdanya Valley is a hiker's paradise year-round, while the summertime round-Andorra hike is a memorably scenic 360-degree tour of the tiny country.

The Parc Nacional d'Aigüestortes i Estany de Sant Maurici is superb for trekking from spring through fall. The ascent of the highest peak in the Pyrenees, the 11,168-foot Aneto peak above Benasque, is a long day's round trip best approached in summer and only by fit and experienced hikers. Much of the hike is over the Maladeta

Glacier, from the base camp at the Refugio de La Renclusa.

In Parque Nacional de Ordesa y Monte Perdido you can take day trips up to the Cola de Caballo waterfall and back around the southern rim of the canyon or, for true mountain goats, longer hikes via the Refugio de Góriz to La Brèche de Roland and Gavarnie or to Monte Perdido, the parador at La Pineta, and the village of Bielsa. Another prized walk has bed and dinner in the base-camp town of Torla or a night up at the Refugio de Goriz at the head of the valley.

The section of the Camino de Santiago walk from Saint-Jean-Pied-de-Port to Roncesvalles is a marvelous 8- to 10-hour trek any time of year, though weather reports should be checked carefully from October to June.

Local *excursionista* (outing) clubs can help you get started; local tourist offices may also have brochures and rudimentary trail maps. Note that the higher reaches are safely navigable only in summer.

Some useful contacts for hiking are **Cercle d'Aventura** (☎ 972/881017 ⊕ www.cercleaventura.com), **Giroguies** (☎ 636/490830 ⊕ www.giroguies.com), **Guies de Meranges** (☎ 616/855535 ⊕ www.guiesmeranges.com), and **Guies de Muntanya** (☎ 629/591516 ⊕ www.guiesdemuntanya.com).

---

essential ⊘ Closed May, June, and Oct. No lunch weekdays Dec.–Apr. (except during Christmas and Easter).

$$
TAPAS
✕ **Eth Paer.** The early evening (open from 3 pm) draws a drinks-and-tapas crowd to Eth Paer: they huddle around barrels outside by the door, comparing stories of the day's skiing or walking. Later on it becomes a laid-back wine bar that's also good for a casual meal. The creative salads are deliciously fresh, with ingredients such as tuna belly

and warm duck, and there is a good selection of tapas, including *carpaccio de ciervo* (venison carpaccio) and *tostada de emmental, panceta, y ceps confitados* (toast with Swiss cheese, pancetta, and mushroom confit). There is also a choice of *embutidos* (cold cuts), pâtés, and cheeses. The staff are happy to recommend a decent wine from the many lined up against each wall, and the shop here is great place to pick up a culinary souvenir, such as locally made savory and sweet preserves. [$] *Average main: €17* ✉ *Carrer Major 1* ⏲ *Closed Mon.–Wed. in Oct. and Nov. No lunch.*

$$ TAPAS 🍴 **Tauèrnes Urtau.** The area's most happening tapas chain is friendly, fun, and always busy. Customers can help themselves at the bar to an assortment of 40 mouthwatering *pinchos* (pieces of bread on sticks with a variety of creative toppings) such as a minihamburger, king prawn with mushrooms, or ravioli with foie gras. There is also a tapas menu and table service. It's a good pick-me-up for weary limbs following the Romanesque trails. Another branch is in Arties at Plaza de Ortau 12. [$] *Average main: €16* ✉ *Av. Pas d'Arrò 4* ☎ *973/642671* 🌐 *www.urtau.com* ⏲ *Closed 2 wks in Oct. or Nov.*

$$$$ B&B/INN 🏨 **Casa Irene.** A rustic haven, this inn is known for fine mountain cuisine with a French flair, and the personal style and spacious and elegant rooms make this a highly recommended address for a stay as well as a meal. **Pros:** small and personalized; aesthetically impeccable. **Cons:** streetside rooms can be noisy on summer nights; restaurant is closed on Monday; fairly expansive. [$] *Rooms from: €250* ✉ *Carrer Major 22, Arties, 6 km (4 miles) east of Vielha* ☎ *973/644364* 🌐 *www.hotelcasairene.com* ✍ *Reservations essential* 🛏 *22 rooms* ⏲ *Closed May., Jun., Oct., and Nov.* 🍽 *Breakfast.*

$ B&B/INN 🏨 **Hotel El Ciervo.** In Vielha's old quarter, and next to one of the town's most attractive pedestrian-only streets, this family-run inn resembles an idyllic winter cottage, and the personal service includes a breakfast, available for a small additional charge, that former guests have touted it as the best in Spain. **Pros:** quirky and inviting; excellent breakfast; pleasant furnishings. **Cons:** rooms are a little cramped; the somewhat feminine style may not appeal to everyone; breakfast costs a bit extra. [$] *Rooms from: €85* ✉ *Pl. de San Orencio 3* ☎ *973/640165* 🌐 *www.hotelelciervo.net* 🛏 *20 rooms* ⏲ *Closed June and Nov.* 🍽 *No meals.*

$$$ HOTEL 🏨 **Parador de Arties.** Built around the Casa de Don Gaspar de Portolà, once home to the founder of the colony of California, this modern parador with friendly staff has views of the Pyrenees and is handy for exploring the Romanesque sights in nearby villages. **Pros:** marvelous panoramas; quiet and personal for a parador. **Cons:** neither at the foot of the slopes nor in the thick of the Vielha après-ski vibe; requires driving; feels old-fashioned. [$] *Rooms from: €163* ✉ *Calle San Juan 1, Arties* ☎ *973/640801* 🌐 *www.parador.es* 🛏 *54 rooms, 3 suites* ⏲ *Closed after Easter wk.–end of May.* 🍽 *No meals.*

NIGHTLIFE

Bar La Lluna. Inside a typical Aranese house, this local favorite has live performances on Wednesday. ✉ *Pl. de Ortau 7, Arties.*

Eth Clòt. This hot *bar musicale* is popular on weekends, when it hosts a variety of live music and DJs. ✉ *Pl. Corralets 7, Arties.*

Eth Saxo. This is the most popular late-night bar for all ages in downtown Vielha. ✉ *Carrer Marrec 6.*

SPORTS AND THE OUTDOORS

Skiing, white-water rafting, hiking, climbing, horseback riding, and fly fishing are just some of the sports available throughout the Vall d'Aran.

Baqueira-Beret Estación de Esquí (*Baqueira-Beret Ski Station*). This ski center offers Catalonia's most varied and reliable skiing. Its 87 km (57 miles) of *pistas* (slopes), spread over 53 runs, range from the gentle Beret slopes to the vertical chutes of Baqueira. The Bonaigua area is a mixture of steep and gently undulating trails, with some of the longest, most varied runs in the Pyrenees. A dozen restaurants and four children's areas are scattered about the facilities, and the thermal baths at Tredós are 4 km (2½ miles) away. ✉ *C. Baqueira Beret* ☎ *973/639025* 🌐 *www.baqueira.es.*

SALARDÚ

9 km (6 miles) east of Vielha.

Salardú is a pivotal point in the Vall d'Aran, convenient to Baqueira-Beret, the Montarto peak, the lakes and Circ de Colomers, Aigüestortes National Park, and the villages of Tredós, Unha, and Montgarri. The town itself, with a little more than 700 inhabitants, is known for its steep streets and its octagonal fortified bell tower.

GETTING HERE AND AROUND

The C28 east out of Vielha goes straight to Salardú and Tredós in 9 km (6 miles) and onto Baqueira-Beret in 13 km (8 miles).

OFF THE BEATEN PATH

Santa Maria de Montgarri. Partly in ruins, this 11th-century chapel was once an important way station on the route into the Vall d'Aran from France. The beveled, hexagonal bell tower and the rounded stones, which look as if they came from a brook bottom, give the structure a stippled appearance that's a bit like a Pyrenean trout. The Romería de Nuestra Señora de Montgarri (Feast of Our Lady of Montgarri), on July 2, is a country fair with feasting, games, music, and dance. The sanctuary can be reached by following the C142 road until Beret and then walking 6 km (4 miles) along a dirt track that can also be accessed by off-road vehicles. It is difficult to get there during the winter snow season.

WHERE TO EAT AND STAY

$$$ SPANISH

🍴 **Casa Rufus.** Fresh pine on the walls and the floor, red-and-white checked curtains, and snowy white tablecloths cozily furnish this restaurant that's in the tiny, gray-stone village of Gessa, between Vielha and Salardú. Try the *conejo relleno de ternera y cerdo* (rabbit stuffed with veal and pork). *Civets* (stews) of mountain goat or venison, although not on the menu, can be requested in advance. If you're making a special trip to eat here, it's a good idea to call ahead to confirm its hours. [$] *Average main: €18* ✉ *Sant Jaume 8, Gessa* ☎ *973/645246* 🕒 *Closed May and June, weekdays Oct. and Nov., and Sun. Oct.–Apr.*

$$$$ HOTEL **Val de Ruda.** For rustic surroundings—light on luxury but long on comfort—that are only a two-minute walk from the lift, this modern-traditional construction of glass, wood, and stone is a good choice. **Pros:** pleasant and outdoorsy; warm and welcoming after a day in the mountains; friendly family service. **Cons:** some of the dormer rooms are cozy but tiny; hotel is only open during ski season; not inexpensive. [$] *Rooms from: €220* ✉ *Ctra. Baqueira-Beret Cota 1500* ☎ *973/645258* 🌐 *www.hotelvalderudabaqueira.com* 🛏 *35 rooms* 🕓 *Closed end of Easter wk–Dec.* 🍴 *Breakfast.*

ARAGÓN AND CENTRAL PYRENEES

The highest, wildest, and most spectacular range of the Pyrenees is the middle section, farthest from sea level. From Benasque on Aragón's eastern side to Jaca at the western edge are the great heights and most dramatic landscapes of Alto Aragón (Upper Aragón), including the Maladeta (11,165 feet), Posets (11,070 feet), and Monte Perdido (11,004 feet) peaks, the three highest points in the Pyrenean chain.

Communications between the high valleys of the Pyrenees were all but nonexistent until the 19th century: four-fifths of the region had never seen a motor vehicle of any kind until well into the 20th century, and the 150-km (93-mile) border with France between Portalet de Aneu and Vall d'Aran had never had an international crossing. This combination of high peaks, deep defiles (mountain passages), and isolation has produced some of the Iberian Peninsula's best-preserved towns and valleys. Delightful examples of these are the atmospheric old towns of Aínsa and Alquézar, worth discovering off the main track. Today, numerous ethnological museums bear witness to a way of life that has nearly disappeared since the 1950s. Residents of Upper Aragón speak neither Basque nor Catalan, but local dialects such as Grausín, Chistavino, Belsetán, and Benasqués (collectively known as *fabla aragonesa*), which have more in common with each other and with Occitan or Langue d'Oc (the southwestern French language descended from Provençal) than with modern Spanish and French. Furthermore, each valley has its own variations on everything from the typical Aragonese folk dance, the *jota,* to cuisine and traditional costume.

The often-bypassed cities of Huesca and Zaragoza are both useful Pyrenean gateways and historic destinations in themselves. With its Mudejar (Moorish-influenced) churches such as the dazzling La Seo, its own Alhambra-like Aljafería fortress, and the immense basilica of La Pilarica, Zaragoza is much more than just a drive-by between Barcelona and Bilbao; and Huesca has a memorable old quarter. Both cities retain an authentic provincial character that is refreshing in today's cosmopolitan Spain.

The Aragüés, Hecho, and Ansó valleys, drained by the Estarrún, Osia, Veral, and Aragón Subordán rivers, are the westernmost valleys in Aragón and rank among the wildest and most unspoiled reaches of the Pyrenees. Today these sleepy hollows are struggling to generate an economy that will save this endangered species of Pyrenean life. With

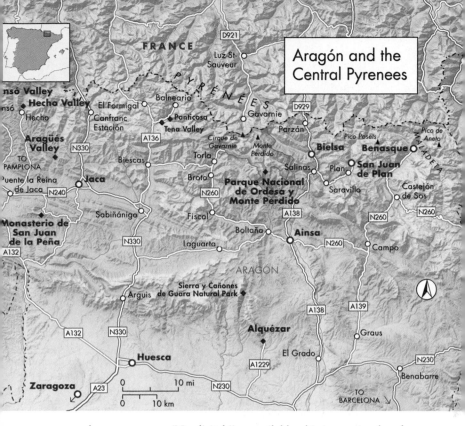

only cross-country (Nordic) skiing available, this is a region less frequented by tourists.

ZARAGOZA

138 km (86 miles) west of Lleida, 307 km (184 miles) northwest of Barcelona, 164 km (98 miles) southeast of Pamplona, 322 km (193 miles) northeast of Madrid.

Despite its hefty size (population 680,000), this sprawling provincial capital midway between Barcelona, Madrid, Bilbao, and Valencia is a detour from the tourist track connected by the AVE, Spain's high-speed railroad, with both Madrid and Barcelona only 90 minutes away. The first decade of this century were major boom years here, and it's been rated one of Spain's most desirable places to live because of its air quality, low cost of living, and low population density.

Straddling Spain's greatest river, the Ebro, Zaragoza was originally named Caesaraugusta, for the Roman emperor Augustus, and established as a thriving river port by 25 BC. Its legacy contains everything from Roman ruins and Jewish baths to Moorish, Romanesque, Gothic-Mudejar, Renaissance, baroque, neoclassical, and Art Nouveau architecture. Parts of the **Roman walls** are visible near the city's landmark

Mountain trekking in the Huesca province

Basílica de Nuestra Señora del Pilar. Nearby, the medieval **Puente de Piedra** (Stone Bridge) spans the Ebro. Checking out the **Lonja** (Stock Exchange), La Seo cathedral, the Moorish **Aljafería** (Fortified Palace and Jewel Treasury), the **Mercado de Lanuza** (Produce Market), and the many **Mudejar churches** in the old town is a good way to navigate Zaragoza's jumble of backstreets.

Excursions from Zaragoza include Francisco José de Goya y Lucientes's birthplace at **Fuendetodos,** 44 km (26 miles) to the southeast, and **Belchite,** another 20 km (12 miles) east of Fuendetodos, site of the ruins of a town destroyed in one of the fiercest battles of the Spanish Civil War and left untouched since as a war memorial.

GETTING HERE AND AROUND

There are several trains per day between Zaragoza and Barcelona, Lleida, and Huesca (⊕ *www.renfe.com*). The bus company Alosa runs buses between Zaragoza, Huesca, and Jaca. By car, travel west from Barcelona on the E90 motorway. All of Zaragoza's main sights are accessible on foot as the center is compact and much of it is traffic-free.

ESSENTIALS

Bus Station Zaragoza ⊠ *Estación Central de Autobuses, Calle Miguel Roca i Junyent* ☎ *976/700599* ⊕ *www.estacion-zaragoza.es.*

Visitor Information Zaragoza ⊠ *Central Square, Pl. de Nuestra Señora del Pilar* ☎ *976/201200* ⊕ *www.zaragozaturismo.es.*

EXPLORING

Fodor's Choice   **Basílica de Nuestra Señora del Pilar** (*Basilica of Our Lady of the Pillar*).
★   Hulking on the banks of the Ebro, the basilica, often known simply
as "La Pilarica," or "El Pilar," is Zaragoza's symbol and pride. An
immense baroque structure with no fewer than 11 tile cupolas, La Pilarica is the home of the Virgen del Pilar, the patron saint not only of
peninsular Spain but of the entire Hispanic world. The fiestas honoring
this most Spanish of saints, held the week of October 12, are events of
extraordinary pride and Spanish fervor, with processions, street concerts, bullfights, and traditional *jota* dancing. The cathedral was built
in the 18th century to commemorate the appearance of the Virgin on
a pillar (*pilar*), or pedestal, to St. James, Spain's other patron saint,
during his legendary appearance as Santiago Matamoros (St. James
the Moorslayer) in the 9th century. La Pilarica herself resides in a side
chapel that dates from 1754. Among the basilica's treasures are two
frescoes by Goya, one of them, *El Coreto de la Vírgen,* painted when he
was young and the other, the famous *Regina Martirum,* after his studies
in Italy. The bombs displayed to the right of the altar of La Pilarica chapel fell through the roof of the church in 1936 and miraculously failed
to explode. You can still see both of the holes, one in the corner of the
earlier Goya fresco and the other by the top of the column overhead to
the left. Behind La Pilarica's altar is the tiny opening where the devout
line up to kiss the rough marble pillar where La Pilarica is believed
to have been discovered. There is an elevator in one of the towers for
easy access to great views of the city. ⊠ *Pl. del Pilar s/n* ☎ *Basilica free,
tower €3* ⊙ *Basilica Mon.–Sat. 6:45 am–8:30 pm, Sun. 6:45 am–9:30
pm; tower daily 10–1:30 and 4–5:30.*

Iglesia de San Pablo. After the basilica and La Seo, this church, with
examples of Mudejar architecture in its brickwork, is considered
by zaragozanos to be the "third cathedral." ⊠ *Carrer San Pablo 42*
☎ *976/2012200 for tourist office* ⊙ *For services only.*

La Seo (*Catedral de San Salvador*). Zaragoza's cathedral, at the eastern
end of the Plaza del Pilar, is the city's bishopric, or diocesan *seo* (seat).
An amalgam of architectural styles ranging from the Mudéjar brick-
and-tile exterior to the Gothic altarpiece to exuberant Churrigueresque
doorways, the Seo nonetheless has an 18th-century baroque facade
that seems to echo those of La Pilarica. The **Museo de Tapices** within
contains medieval tapestries. The nearby medieval **Casa y Arco del
Deán** form one of the city's favorite corners. ⊠ *Pl. de la Seo 2* ☎ *Cathedral and museum €4* ⊙ *Cathedral and museum: weekdays 10–2 and
4–6:30, Sat. 10–12:30 and 4–6:30, Sun. and public holidays 10–noon
and 4–6:30.*

Museo Camón Aznar. A fine collection of Goya's works, particularly
engravings, are on view here. ⊠ *Carrer Espoz y Mina 23* ☎ *976/397387*
⊕ *www.museo.ibercaja.es* ☎ *Free* ⊙ *Tues.–Sat. 10–1.45 and 5–8:45,
Sun. 10–1:45.*

Museo de Zaragoza. This museum contains a rich treasury of works
by Zaragoza's emblematic painter, Goya, including his portraits of
Fernando VII and his best graphic works: *Desastres de la guerra,*

Overlooking the Ebro River and Zaragoza's Basílica de Nuestra Señora del Pilar

Caprichos, and *La tauromaquia.* ⊠ *Pl. de los Sitios 5* ☎ *976/222181* 🎟 *Free* ⊙ *Tues.–Sat. 10–2 and 5–8, Sun. 10–2.*

Museo del Foro. Remains of the Roman forum and the Roman sewage system can be seen here. Two more Roman sites, the **thermal baths** at Calle de San Juan y San Pedro and the **river port** at Plaza San Bruno, are also open to the public. You can organize in advance to see the presentation videos in English through the Museo del Teatro Romano (☎ 976/726075), and English-language audio guides are also available. ⊠ *Pl. de la Seo s/n* ☎ *976/399752* 🎟 *€3* ⊙ *Tues.–Sat. 10–2 and 5–9, Sun. 10–2:30.*

Museo del Teatro Romano. In addition to the restored Roman amphitheater here, you can also see objects recovered during the excavation process, including theatrical masks, platters, and even Roman hairpins. ⊠ *Calle San Jorge 12* ☎ *976/726075* 🎟 *€4* ⊙ *Tues.–Sat. 10–2 and 5–9, Sun. 10–2:30.*

Museo Diocesano. Portraits of archbishops (one by Goya), Flemish tapestries, Renaissance and medieval paintings, and the remains of the Romanesque door of Zaragoza's church of Santiago form parts of this museum's collection. ⊠ *Pl. de la Seo 5* ☎ *976/399488* ⊕ *www.mudiz. net* 🎟 *€5* ⊙ *Tues.–Sat. 10–1:30 and 5–8:30, Sun. 10–1:30.*

Museo Pablo Gargallo. This is one of Zaragoza's most treasured and admired gems, both for the palace in which it is housed and for its collection—Gargallo, born near Zaragoza in 1881, was one of Spain's greatest modern sculptors. ⊠ *Pl. de San Felipe 3* ☎ *976/724922* 🎟 *€4* ⊙ *Tues.–Sat. 10–2 and 5–9, Sun. and public holidays 10–2:30.*

Museo Pablo Serrano. A collection of works by the famous 20th-century sculptor Pablo Serrano (1908–85) and his wife, Juana Francés, are housed in this museum. ✉ *Paseo María Agustín 20* ☎ *976/280659* 🌐 *www.iaacc.es* 🎟 *Free* 🕒 *Tues.–Sat. 10–2 and 5–9, Sun. 10–2.*

Palacio de La Aljafería. One of Spain's three greatest Moorish palaces. If Córdoba's Mezquita shows the energy of the 10th-century Caliphate and Granada's Alhambra is the crowning 14th-century glory of Al-Andalus (the 789-year Moorish empire on the Iberian Peninsula), then the late-11th-century Aljafería can be seen as the intermediate step. Originally a fortress and royal residence, and later a seat of the Spanish Inquisition, the Aljafería is now the home of the Cortes (Parliament) de Aragón. The 9th-century Torre del Trovador (Tower of the Troubadour) appears in Giuseppe Verdi's opera *Il Trovatore.* ✉ *Diputados s/n* ☎ *976/289683* 🌐 *www.cortesaragon.es* 🎟 *€5* 🕒 *Apr.–Oct., daily 10–2 and 4:30–8; Nov.–Mar., daily 10–2 and 4:30–6:30.*

OFF THE BEATEN PATH

Monasterio de Piedra. An hour's drive southwest of Zaragoza brings you to the Cistercian Monasterio de Piedra, a lush oasis on the arid Aragonese *meseta* (plain). Founded in 1195 by Alfonso II of Aragón and named for the nearby Río Piedra (Stone River, named for the calcified limestone deposits along its banks), the monastery has a 16th-century Renaissance section that is now a private hotel (62 rooms at €98 to €136), with rooms that are still somewhat monastic and austere. Even if you don't stay for the night, come to visit the 12th-century cloister, wine museum, and park—the caves, waterfalls, and walkways suspended over the riverbed are spectacular. ✉ *Rte. C202, 113 km (70 miles) southwest of Zaragoza via A2, Nuévalos* ☎ *902/196052* 🌐 *www.monasteriopiedra.com* 🎟 *€15, includes park, monastery, and exhibitions* 🕒 *Monastery and exhibitions: Mar.–Oct., daily 10–1 and 3–6; Nov.–Feb., daily 11:15–1:15 and 3:15–5:15. Park: Apr.–Oct., daily 9–8; Nov.–Mar., daily 9–6.*

6

WHERE TO EAT

$$ TAPAS

🍴 **Bodegas Almau.** The walls of this popular bodega are crammed with enticing bottles of wine and cava, while the bar is loaded with superlative anchovies, croquettes, and potato omelets. It's mainly standing room only here, so join the jostling crowds, shout out your drinks order, and grab whatever takes your fancy off the top of the bar. Popular choices include *vermut con anchoas* (a small plate of anchovies and a serving of house vermouth). There is also a pretty terrace overlooking the Mudéjar San Gil church. [$] *Average main: €15* ✉ *Calle de los Estébanes 10* ☎ *976/299834* 🕒 *Closed Sun. evening.*

$$$ SPANISH

🍴 **Gran Taberna Tragantua.** This rollicking place serves surprisingly great food, including *solomillicos con salsa de trufa* (little beef filets with truffle sauce) and *albóndigas de solomillicos* (meatballs of beef filet). The beer is fresh and cold, and the house wines, usually from Upper Aragón's own Somontano D.O., are of top value and quality. Carlos Ayora, the owner and chief waiter, seems to thrive on ensuring that his guests enjoy themselves. [$] *Average main: €19* ✉ *Plaza Santa Marta s/n* ☎ *976/299174* 🌐 *www.grupoloscabezudos.es* 🕒 *Closed 2nd wk in June.*

$ TAPAS

🍴 **La Cueva en Aragón.** Although it may not be much to look at from the outside, this tiny establishment is worth popping into for its freshly stacked mushrooms grilled with garlic and olive oil and topped with a prawn—the only dish it serves. Piled high on skewers with a slice of bread beneath to soak up the garlic-infused oil and served on wooden boards, they can be washed down with a chilled artisan beer from the tap. $ *Average main: €10* ✉ *Libertad 16* ☎ *976/204645.*

$
TAPAS
✕ **La Miguería.** It's functional rather than charming, but this is *the* place in town to stop and try *migas*—bread crumbs, accompanied by garlic, olive oil, chorizo, and, in some cases, topped with a fried egg and a bemusing scattering of grapes. This bustling locale also makes varieties on a theme, including *migas con bacalao* (with cod), *migas con jamon* (with ham), and *migas con setas* (with wild mushrooms). $ *Average main: €12* ✉ *Calle Estébanes 4* ☎ *976/200736* ⊕ *www.lamigueria.es* ⊘ *Closed Sun. (except public holidays).*

$$
TAPAS
✕ **Los Victorinos.** Victorinos are a much-feared and respected breed of fighting bulls, and this rustic tavern, located behind the Seo, is heavily adorned with bullfight-related paraphernalia. It offers an elaborate and inventive selection of pinchos and original tapas of all kinds. *Jamón ibérico de bellota* (acorn-fed Iberian ham), Spain's best-known luxury food, is always a natural choice, though quail eggs or the classic *gilda*—olives, green peppers, and anchovies on a toothpick—are also on the bar and hard to resist. It opens at 7:30 pm. $ *Average main: €15* ✉ *Calle José de la Hera 6* ☎ *976/394213* ⊘ *No dinner Sun. Closed 2 wks in May.*

$$$$
TAPAS
✕ **Palomeque.** For upscale tapas, larger portions, and a sit-down restaurant atmosphere, Palomeque makes a great choice. Using fresh market produce, dishes are based on traditional recipes and finished off with a clean, modern look. There is a seemingly endless selection of tapas and wines, with advice on which would provide the best pairings. Highlights on the menu include *virutas de foie de pato* (duck foie gras shavings on bread) and *tacos de solomillo de ternera al ajillo* (tender sirloin steak with garlic). If it's too hard to choose, make it easy by opting for the *surtido de tapas* (selection of mixed tapas). $ *Average main: €25* ✉ *Calle Agustín Palomeque 11* ☎ *976/214082* ⊕ *www.restaurantepalomeque.es* ⊘ *Closed Sun.*

WHERE TO STAY

$
HOTEL
🛏 **Catalonia El Pilar.** Overlooking the lovely Plaza Justicia and the baroque Santa Isabel church, this early-20th-century Art Nouveau building is a tourist sight in its own right, housing an original Moderniste wooden elevator and a facade with wrought-iron decorations. **Pros:** quiet location on one of the city's prettiest squares; five-minute walk from the Basílica de Nuestra Señora del Pilar; spotless and efficient. **Cons:** rooms are immaculate but somewhat characterless. $ *Rooms from: €90* ✉ *Manifestación 16* ☎ *976/205858* ⊕ *www.hoteles-catalonia.com* ⤳ *66 rooms* ❍| *Breakfast.*

$
HOTEL
🛏 **Hotel Zenit Don Yo.** Ideally located for exploring Zaragoza's sights, this is an in-and-out type of hotel—somewhere to lay your head. **Pros:** central and convenient; good sized rooms for a city hotel; valet parking; good value. **Cons:** lacks personality and feels a bit stuck in the past. $ *Rooms from: €75* ✉ *Calle Bruil 4–6* ☎ *976/226741* ⊕ *www.zenithoteles.com* ⤳ *146 rooms* ❍| *Breakfast.*

$$ HOTEL [🏨] **Palafox.** One of Zaragoza's top hotels, Palafox combines contemporary design with traditional urban service and elegance. **Pros:** top comfort and service; bright reception area; good restaurant. **Cons:** modern and somewhat antiseptic. [$] *Rooms from: €113* ✉ *Calle Marqués Casa Jiménez s/n* ☎ *976/237700* 🌐 *www.palafoxhoteles.com* 🛏 *179 rooms* 🍴 *Breakfast.*

HUESCA

68 km (42 miles) northeast of Zaragoza, 123 km (74 miles) northwest of Lleida.

Once a Roman colony, Huesca would later become the capital of Aragón, until the royal court moved to Zaragoza in 1118. The town's university was founded in 1354 and now specializes in Aragonese studies.

GETTING HERE AND AROUND

From Zaragoza there are several trains a day (🌐 *www.renfe.com*). Alosa runs buses between Huesca and Zaragoza, Lleida and Jaca. By car from Zaragoza, head northwest toward Huesca on the A23 for 68 km (42 miles). The center is quite small and it's easier to go on foot to the sights, because the traffic and one-way system can be tricky.

ESSENTIALS

Visitor Information Huesca ✉ *Pl. López Allué s/n* ☎ *974/292170* 🌐 *www.huescaturismo.com.*

EXPLORING

Cathedral. An intricately carved gallery tops the eroded facade of Huesca's 13th-century Gothic cathedral. Damián Forment, a protégé of the 15th-century Italian master sculptor Donatello, created the alabaster altarpiece, which has scenes from the Crucifixion. ✉ *Pl. de la Catedral s/n* ☎ *974/231099* 🎟 *€4, includes tower and museum* ⏲ *Cathedral: weekdays 10:30–2 and 4–7, Sat. 10:30–2 and 4:30–6:30, Sun. 9–1 and 4:30–6:30. Tower and museum: weekdays 10:30–2 and 4–7, Sat. 10:30–2.*

Museo Arqueológico Provincial. An octagonal patio here is ringed by eight chambers, including the **Sala de la Campana** (Hall of the Bell), where the beheadings of 12th-century nobles took place. The museum occupies parts of the former royal palace of the kings of Aragón and holds paintings by Aragonese primitives, including *La Virgen del Rosario* by Miguel Jiménez, and several works by the 16th-century Maestro de Sigena. ✉ *Pl. de la Universidad* ☎ *974/220586* 🎟 *Free* ⏲ *Tues.–Sat. 10–2 and 5–8, Sun. 10–2.*

San Pedro el Viejo. This church has an 11th-century cloister. Ramiro II and his father, Alfonso I, the only Aragonese kings not entombed at San Juan de la Peña, rest in a side chapel. ✉ *Pl. de San Pedro s/n* 🎟 *€2.50* ⏲ *Oct.–May, Mon.–Sat. 10–1:30 and 4–6, Sun. 11–12:15 and 1–2; June–Sept., Mon.–Sat. 10–1:30 and 4–7:30, Sun. 11–12:15 and 1–2.*

OFF THE BEATEN PATH

Castillo de Loarre. This massively walled 11th-century monastery, 36 km (22 miles) west of Huesca off Route A132 on A1206, is nearly indistinguishable from the rock outcroppings that surround it. Inside the walls are a church, a tower, a dungeon, and even a medieval toilet with views of the almond and olive orchards in the Ebro basin. ✉ C.

Fuente 2, Loarre ☎ *974/342161* ⊕ *www.castillodeloarre.es* 🎫 *€3.90* 🕙 *Nov.–Feb., Tues.–Sun. 11–5:30; Mar.–mid-June and mid-Sept.– Oct., daily 10–7; mid-June–mid-Sept., daily 10–8.*

WHERE TO EAT AND STAY

$$$$

SPANISH

✕ **Las Torres.** Huesca's top restaurant makes inventive use of first-rate local ingredients, including wild mushrooms, wild boar, venison, and lamb. The glass-walled kitchen is as original as the cooking that emerges from it, and the wine list is strong in Somontano, Huesca's own Denomination of Origin. Look for *lomo de ternasco cocinado a baja temperatura con embutidos de Graos* (veal cooked at low temperature with Graos sausage) or *paticas de cordero deshuesados* (boned lamb's trotters) for a taste of pure upper Aragón. $ *Average main: €23* ✉ *Calle María Auxiliadora 3* ☎ *974/228213* ⊕ *www.lastorres-restaurante.com* 🕙 *Closed Sun. and Aug. 15–31.*

$

HOTEL

🏨 **Hotel Abba Huesca.** The most stylish hotel in Huesca has modern and comfortable rooms and a buzzing contemporary bar where guests and locals mingle. **Pros:** excellent value for money; upscale feel. **Cons:** slightly outside the center of town. $ *Rooms from: €80* ✉ *Calle de Tarbes 14* ☎ *974/292900* ⊕ *www.abbahuescahotel.com* 🛏 *84 rooms* 🍽 *No meals.*

A PAMPLONA ALTERNATIVE

For an unspoiled Pamplona-like fiesta in another pre-Pyrenean capital, with bullfights, *encierros* (running of the bulls through the streets), and all-night revelry, try Huesca's San Lorenzo celebration August 9–15. Spain's top bullfighters are the main attraction, along with concerts, street dances, and liberal tastings of the excellent Somontano wines of upper Huesca. *Albahaca* (basil) is the official symbol of Huesca, and the ubiquitous green sashes and bandanas will remind you that this is Huesca, not Pamplona (where red is the trimming).

ALQUÉZAR

51 km (32 miles) northeast of Huesca, 123 km (76 miles) northeast of Zaragoza.

Fodor's Choice

★

Almost as though carved from the rock itself, Alquézar overlooks the Sierra y Cañones de Guara Natural Park and is one of Aragón's most attractive old towns. A labyrinth of cobbled, winding streets and low archways coil around the town's central square, and many of the buildings' facades bear coat-of-arms motifs dating back to the 16th century. The uniquely shaped town square, formed with no cohesive plan or architectural style, has a porched area that was built to provide shelter from the sun and rain.

GETTING HERE AND AROUND

From Huesca, travel eastward on the A22 or N240 for 29 km (18 miles) before joining the A1229 toward Alquézar. Cars cannot enter the old quarter, so the only way to see the town is on foot.

ESSENTIALS

Visitor Information Alquézar ✉ *Calle Arrabal s/n* ☎ *974/318940* ⊕ *www.alquezar.es.*

EXPLORING

Colegiata de Santa María. Keeping watch over the Sierra de Guara, the Colegiata, originally a 9th-century Moorish citadel, was conquered by the Christians in 1067. An interesting mix of Gothic, Mudejar, and Renaissance details are found in the shaded cloister, and there are biblical murals that date back to the Romanesque era. The church, built in the 16th century, contains an almost life-size Romanesque figure of Christ, but restoration has taken away some of its charm—its interior brickwork is now only a painted representation. ✉ *Diseminado Afueras, off Calle la Iglesia* 🕒 *Apr.–Oct., daily 11–1:30 and 4:30–7:30; Nov.–early Jan., daily 11–1:30 and 4–6; early Jan.–Feb., weekends 11–1:30 and 4–6.*

River Vero Cultural Park. Declared a UNESCO world heritage site in 1998, this park within the Sierra de Guara contains more than 60 limestone caves with prehistoric cave paintings. Some date back to around 22,000 BC, although the majority are between 12,000 BC and 4000 BC. Information and guided tours are available through the interpretation center in Colungo. Opening hours can change, so call ahead. ✉ *Calle Las Braules 2, Colunga, 9½ km (6 miles) east of Alquézar* ☎ *974/318185, 974/306006* 🕒 *Mar. and Sept.–Dec., weekends 10–2; Apr., May, and June, weekends 10–2 and 4–7; July and Aug., Tues.–Sun. 10–2 and 4:30–7:30.*

6

WHERE TO EAT AND STAY

$$$$ SPANISH 🍴 **Casa Pardina.** Elegant, romantic dining at a reasonable price is the draw here, with a choice of two fixed menus. Locally sourced ingredients come together to create a traditional Araganese menu, adapted for contemporary tastes, and the wine is from the nearby Somontano region. Every meal starts with a tasting of local olive oils. Tucked away downstairs, the small inviting dining room and traditional arched stone walls makes it a cozy choice for winter, but the highlight is the leafy summer dining terrace with a stunning backdrop of the Sierra de Guara and San Miguel church. [$] *Average main: €27* ✉ *Calle Medio s/n* ☎ *974/318425* 🌐 *www.casapardina.com* 🕒 *Closed Tues. No lunch weekdays Oct.–Easter.*

$ B&B/INN 🏨 **Hotel Santa María de Alquézar.** Just outside the old town walls, this hotel has the best views in town—overlooking the River Vero canyon and the Colegiata de Santa María. **Pros:** breathtaking views; bright rooms; relaxed ambience. **Cons:** guests can be heard in other rooms; street-facing rooms can be noisy; in high season parking is difficult to find. [$] *Rooms from: €89* ✉ *Paseo San Hipolito s/n* ☎ *974/318436* 🌐 *www.hotel-santamaria.com* 🛏 *21 rooms* 🕒 *Closed Jan. and Feb. (except last two weekends in Feb.)* 🍽 *Breakfast.*

SPORTS AND THE OUTDOORS

The Sierra de Guara is one of Europe's best places for canyoning (descending mountain gorges, usually in or near streams and other water sources).

Avalancha. There are several agencies in Alquézar that specialize in guided private or group trips for all levels and ages. Avalancha is one of the best for canyoning equipment, including wet suits and helmets. ✉ *Paseo San Hipolito s/n* ☎ *974/318299* 🌐 *www.avalancha.org.*

BENASQUE

113 km (70 miles) northeast of Alquézar, 140 km (87 miles) northeast of Huesca, 148 km (89 miles) north of Lleida, 221 km (133 miles) northeast of Zaragoza.

Benasque, Aragón's easternmost town, has always been an important link between Catalonia and Aragón. This elegant mountain hub, with a population of just over 2,200, harbors a number of notable buildings, including the 13th-century Romanesque church of **Santa Maria Mayor** and the ancient, dignified manor houses of the town's old families, such as the **palace of the counts of Ribagorça,** on Calle Mayor, and the **Torre Juste.** Take a walk around and peer into the entryways and patios of these palatial facades, left open for this purpose.

GETTING HERE AND AROUND

Take the A22 eastward from Huesca for 112 km (70 miles) before exiting onto the N240 towards Barbastro. At Barbastro join the N123 towards Graus for 27 km (17 miles). At Campo take the N260 toward Benasque for 32 km (20 miles). The town itself is small and easily explored on foot.

For the ski resort and village of Anciles, the best way to go is by car. The short 2-km (1-mile) detour south of Benasque means you'll be able to see its beautiful collection of 16th-century houses, and sample some well-prepared Aragonese dishes at the Restaurante Ansils.

ESSENTIALS

Visitor Information Benasque ✉ *Calle San Sebastián 5* ☎ *974/551289* 🌐 *www.benasque.com.*

EXPLORING

OFF THE BEATEN PATH

Pico De Aneto. Benasque is the traditional base camp for excursions to Aneto, which, at 11,168 feet, is the highest peak in the Pyrenees. You can rent crampons and a *piolet* (ice ax) for the two- to three-hour crossing of the Aneto glacier at any sports store in town or at the Refugio de la Renclusa, a way station for mountaineers that's an hour's walk above the parking area, which is 15 km (9 miles) north of Benasque, off A139. The trek to the summit and back is not difficult, just long—some 20 km (12 miles) round-trip, with a 4,500-foot vertical ascent. Allow a full 12 hours.

WHERE TO EAT AND STAY

$$$ SPANISH

🍴 **Asador Ixarso.** Roast goat or lamb cooked over a raised fireplace in the corner of the dining room is why this place is a fine refuge in chilly weather. The *revuelto de setas* (eggs scrambled with wild mushrooms) is a classic highland specialty, while the salads are varied and refreshing, especially after a morning or afternoon of skiing, hiking, or climbing. The mixed grill is a house favorite, and the opportunity to try whatever game—venison, wild boar, or partridge—is on the menu should not be missed. [$] *Average main: €20* ✉ *Calle San Pedro 12* ☎ *974/552057* ⏲ *Closed mid-Sept.–Nov. and Apr.–mid-June.*

$$ SPANISH

🍴 **Restaurante Ansils.** This rustic spot in Anciles is ingeniously designed in glass, wood, and stone and specializes in local Benasqué and Aragonese dishes, such as *civet de jabalí* (wild boar stew) and *perdiz guisada con setas de temporada* (partridge stew with wild mushrooms), which is a

The city of Benasque, nestled in the valley

perennial house favorite: the meat is cooked to perfection. The restaurant is sometimes closed unexpectedly on weekdays and out of season, so check before you go. Memorable and exuberant holiday meals are served on Christmas and Easter; reserve well in advance. [$] *Average main: €15* ✉ *Calle General Ferraz 6, Anciles* ☎ *974/551150* ⏲ *Closed weekdays in Oct., Nov., May, and June.*

$ HOTEL 🏨 **Hospital de Benasque.** Constructed and furnished in stone and wood, this mountain retreat is an ideal base camp for hiking and cross-country skiing. **Pros:** lovely location in a wide meadow surrounded by peaks; literally a breath of fresh air. **Cons:** rooms are spartan; can get hot on summer days. [$] *Rooms from: €86* ✉ *Camino Real de Francia s/n, about 13 km (8 miles) north of Benasque off A139* ☎ *974/552012* 🌐 *www.llanosdelhospital.com* 🛏 *52 rooms* 🍴 *Breakfast.*

$$ HOTEL FAMILY 🏨 **Hotel Aneto.** The only four-star hotel in the area, the Aneto is handy for central Benasque and just a few minutes by car to mountain trails and skiing. **Pros:** clean and spacious; best option for children in the area; close to local attractions and amenities. **Cons:** modern design lacks charm. [$] *Rooms from: €115* ✉ *Ctra. de Francia 4* ☎ *974/551061* 🛏 *75 rooms* ⏲ *Closed Sept.–Dec. Closed wk after Easter–mid-June* 🍴 *No meals.*

$$ B&B/INN Fodor's Choice ★ 🏨 **Hotel Selba d'Ansils.** Attention to detail, impeccable service, and absolute peace and tranquility are the hallmarks of this mountain cottage—by far the best option in the area, whether for a romantic getaway or a family vacation. **Pros:** perfect for escaping city madness; peaceful; personal service from friendly and professional staff. **Cons:** not for those who value the anonymity of a hotel; a car is necessary. [$] *Rooms from: €110* ✉ *Ctra. Anciles, Km 1.5* ☎ *974/552054, 636/876241* 🌐 *www.hotelselbadansils.com* 🛏 *10 rooms* 🍴 *Breakfast.*

SPORTS AND THE OUTDOORS

Cerler ski area. Built on a shelf over the valley, at an altitude of 5,051 feet, Cerler (6 km [4 miles] east of Benasque) has 67 ski runs and 19 lifts on the slopes of the Gallinero peak (8,629 feet). ☎ *974/551012* 🌐 *www.cerler.com.*

Danica Guías de Pesca. This outfitter can show you the top spots and techniques for Pyrenean fly fishing. ✉ *Ctra. Benasque s/n* ☎ *974/553493* 🌐 *www.danicaguias.com* 🎟 *€190 per person with guide at the river, €225 at higher mountain lakes.*

AÍNSA

66 km (41 miles) southwest of Benasque, 120 km (72 miles) northeast of Huesca, 214 km (128 miles) northeast of Zaragoza.

Persevere through the uninspiring outskirts of Aínsa's new town, until the road turns sharply upward toward one of Aragón's most impressive walled medieval towns, where houses are jammed together along narrow cobbled streets. Declared a UNESCO artistic and historic monument, it perches above the new town and offers sweeping views of the surrounding mountains and Odesa National Park.

GETTING HERE AND AROUND

Head north out of Huesca on the E7/N330 for 39 km (24 miles) and then turn right onto the N260 for 10 km (6 miles). Aínsa can only be explored on foot once you're through the old city walls.

ESSENTIALS

Visitor Information Aínsa ✉ *Av. Pirenaica 1* ☎ *974/500767* 🌐 *www.villadeainsa.com.*

EXPLORING

Citadel. The citadel and castle, originally built by the Muslims in the 11th century, was conquered by the Christians and reconstructed in the 16th century. ✉ *Old Quarter.*

Santa María. This 12th-century Romanesque church, with its quadruple-vaulted door and 13th-century cloister, is in the corner of the attractive porticoed Plaza Mayor. ✉ *C. Santa Cruz, Old Quarter* 🎟 *Free* 🕒 *Daily 10–2 and 4–8.*

WHERE TO EAT AND STAY

$$$ SPANISH 🍴 **Bodegas del Sobrarbe.** Lamb and suckling pig or kid roasted in a wood oven are among the specialties at this excellent restaurant, which had been built into an 11th-century wine cellar. After the welcoming bar at the entrance, a succession of small dining rooms under arches gives a sense of privacy. The tables are decorated with handcrafted ceramic tiles from Teruel, and the setting is rustic and medieval, with vaulted ceilings of heavy wood and stone. [$] *Average main: €18* ✉ *Pl. Mayor 2* ☎ *974/500237* 🌐 *www.bodegasdelsobrarbe.com.*

$$ B&B/INN 🏨 **Hotel Los Arcos.** Next door to Hotel Siete Reyes, Los Arcos provides the same level of service and is welcoming and helpful toward all of its guests. **Pros:** excellent service; comfortable furnishings. **Cons:** noise from the square; cramped breakfast room. [$] *Rooms from: €100* ✉ *Pl.*

Mayor 23 ☎ *974/500016* 🌐 *www.hotellosarcosainsa.com* 🛏 *6 rooms* 🍴 *Breakfast.*

$$$ B&B/INN **Hotel Los Siete Reyes.** One of two boutique hotels in Ainsa's Plaza Mayor, Los Siete Reyes occupies a handsome restored historic house with good-size and artistically decorated bedrooms overlooking the square. **Pros:** charming and atmospheric; central location. **Cons:** noise from the square; interior design makes rooms dark. [$] *Rooms from: €129* ✉ *Pl. Mayor s/n* ☎ *974/500681* 🌐 *www.lossietereyes.com* 🛏 *6 rooms* 🍴 *Breakfast.*

BIELSA

34 km (21 miles) northeast of Aínsa, 154 km (92 miles) northeast of Huesca, 221 km (133 miles) northeast of Zaragoza.

Bielsa, at the confluence of the Cinca and Barrosa rivers, is a busy summer resort with some lovely mountain architecture and an ancient, porticoed town hall. Northwest of Bielsa the **Monte Perdido glacier** and the icy **Marboré Lake** drain into the **Pineta Valley** and the Pineta Reservoir. You can take three- or four-hour walks from the parador up to Larri, Munia, or Marboré Lake among remote peaks.

6

GETTING HERE AND AROUND

Continue north out of Aínsa on the A138 for 34 km (21 miles). The town itself is small and can be explored on foot. For the Parador de Bielsa and the Parque Nacional de Ordesa y Monte Perdido, a car is required.

ESSENTIALS

Visitor Information Bielsa ✉ *Pl. Mayor s/n* ☎ *974/501127 (seasonal), 974/501000 for town hall.*

WHERE TO STAY

$ B&B/INN **Hotel Valle de Pineta.** This corner castle overlooking the river junction is the most spectacular nest and refuge in town—try for the top corner room, which looks across both the Barrosa and Cinca valleys. **Pros:** central location in the village; family service. **Cons:** upper rooms are cozy but tiny; it gets hot if the wind dies down during the hottest part of summer. [$] *Rooms from: €56* ✉ *Calle Baja s/n* ☎ *974/501010* 🌐 *www.hotelvalledepineta.com* 🛏 *26 rooms* 🕒 *Closed weekdays in Nov., Jan., and Feb.* 🍴 *Breakfast.*

$$$ HOTEL **Parador Bielsa.** Glass, steel, and stone define this remote modern structure overlooking the national park, the peak of Monte Perdido, and the source of the Cinca River. **Pros:** surrounded by nature in complete comfort; views of the highest peaks in the Pyrenees; country cooking. **Cons:** indifferent service typical of paradors; a little chilly at 4,455 feet above sea level; a 20-minute drive from Bielsa. [$] *Rooms from: €173* ✉ *Valle de Pineta s/n* ☎ *974/501011* 🌐 *www.parador.es* 🛏 *39 rooms* 🕒 *Closed Dec.–Mar.* 🍴 *No meals.*

EN ROUTE **Valle de Pineta.** You can explore the Valle from the source of the Cinca River, at the head of the valley above Bielsa. From Bielsa, drive back down to Aínsa on the A138, and turn west on N260 for Broto, Torla, and the Parque Nacional de Ordesa.

PARQUE NACIONAL DE ORDESA Y MONTE PERDIDO

79 km (47 miles) west of Bielsa, 45 km (27 miles) west of Aínsa, 92 km (55 miles) north of Huesca.

This great but often overlooked park is was founded by royal decree in 1918 to protect the natural integrity of the central Pyrenees. It has expanded from 4,940 to 56,810 acres as provincial and national authorities have added the Monte Perdido massif, the head of the Pineta Valley, and the Escuain and Añisclo canyons.

ESSENTIALS

Visitor Information Torla ✉ *Calle Fatás s/n, Torla* ☎ *974/486378.*

EXPLORING

Fodor's Choice **Ordesa and Monte Perdido National Park.** The entrance to this natural
★ wonder is under the vertical walls of Monte Mondarruego, the source of the Ara River and its tributary, the Arazas, which forms the famous Ordesa Valley. Defined by the Ara and Arazas rivers, the Ordesa Valley is endowed with pine, fir, larch, beech, and poplar forests; lakes, waterfalls, and high mountain meadows. Protected wildlife includes trout, boar, chamois, and the sarrio or isard (*Rupicapra pyrenaica*) mountain goat.

Well-marked mountain trails lead to waterfalls, caves, and spectacular observation points. The standard tour, a full day's hike (eight hours), runs from the parking area in the Pradera de Ordesa, 8 km (5 miles) northeast of Torla, up the Arazas River, past the *gradas de Soaso* (Soaso risers—a natural stairway of waterfalls) to the *cola de caballo* (horse's tail), a lovely fan of falling water at the head of the Cirque de Cotatuero, a sort of natural amphitheater. There is one refuge, Refugio Gorez, north of the cola de caballo. A return walk on the south side of the valley, past the Cabaña de los Cazadores (hunters' hut), offers a breathtaking view followed by a two-hour descent back to the parking area. A few spots, although not technically difficult, may seem precarious. Information and guidebooks are available at the booth on your way into the park at Pradera de Ordesa. The best time to come is May to mid-November, but check conditions with the tourist office, Centro de Visitantes de Torla, before risking driving into a blizzard in May or missing out on *el veranillo de San Martín* ("Indian summer") in fall. ✉ *Av. Ordesa s/n, Torla* ☎ *974/486472 for Centro de Visitantes de Torla* ⊕ *www.ordesa.net* ⊠ *Free.*

EN ROUTE **Broto** is a prototypical Aragonese mountain town with an excellent 16th-century Gothic church. Nearby villages, such as **Oto,** have stately manor houses with classic local features: baronial entryways, conical chimneys, and wooden galleries. **Torla** is the park's main entry point, with regular buses that go up to the park entrance during summer, and is a popular base camp for hikers.

WHERE TO EAT AND STAY

$$ ✕ **El Rebeco.** In this graceful, rustic building in the upper part of town,
SPANISH   the dining rooms are lined with historic photographs of Torla during the 19th and 20th centuries. The black marble-and-stone floor and the *cadiera*—a traditional open fireplace room with an overhead smoke

DID YOU KNOW?

The Ordesa and Monte
Perdido National Park is
sometimes called a junior
version of the Grand Canyon.
The region was designated
a national park partly to
protect the Pyrenean ibex,
which nevertheless became
extinct in 2000.

vent—are extraordinary original elements of Pyrenean architecture. In late fall and winter, *civets* (stews) of deer, boar, and mountain goat are the order of the day. In summer, lighter fare and hearty mountain soups restore hikers between treks. $ *Average main: €14* ⊠ *Calle Fatás 55* ☎ *974/486068* ☾ *Closed Nov.–Easter.*

$ **⌂ Villa de Torla.** This classic mountain refuge, with sundecks, terraces, **B&B/INN** and a private dining room, has rooms of various shapes and sizes. **Pros:** in the middle of a postcard-perfect Pyrenean village; helpful staff. **Cons:** streetside rooms can be noisy on weekends and summer nights. $ *Rooms from: €70* ⊠ *Pl. Aragón 1* ☎ *974/486156* ⊕ *www.hotelvilladetorla.com* ⤳ *38 rooms* ☾ *Closed early Jan.–mid-Mar.* ⦿ *No meals.*

EN ROUTE Follow N260 (sometimes marked C140) west over the Cotefablo Pass from Torla to Biescas. This route winds interminably through the pine forest leading up to and down from the pass; expect it to take five times longer than it looks like it should on a map.

JACA

24 km (15 miles) southwest of Biescas, 164 km (98 miles) north of Zaragoza.

Jaca, the most important municipal center in Alto Aragón, is anything but sleepy. Bursting with ambition and endowed with the natural resources, jacetanos are determined to make their city the site of a Winter Olympics someday. Founded in 1035 as the kingdom of Jacetania, Jaca was an important stronghold during the Christian Reconquest of the Iberian Peninsula and proudly claims never to have bowed to the Moorish invaders. Indeed, on the first Friday of May the town still commemorates the decisive battle in which the appearance of a battalion of women, their hair and jewelry flashing in the sun, so intimidated the Moorish cavalry that they beat a headlong retreat.

GETTING HERE AND AROUND

Alosa runs daily buses between Jaca and Zaragoza. There is also the option of taking the train between Jaca and Huesca or Zaragoza (⊕ *www.renfe.com*). By car take the E7/N330 northbound from Huesca via Sabiñánigo for 73 km (45 miles). The town sights are easily accessible on foot.

ESSENTIALS

Visitor Information Jaca ⊠ *Pl. San Pedro 11–13* ☎ *974/360098.*

EXPLORING

Ayuntamiento (*Town Hall*). The door to Jaca's town hall has a notable Renaissance design. ⊠ *Calle Mayor 24* ☎ *974/355758.*

Canfranc. In July and August a guided train tour departs from the Jaca RENFE station, covering the valley and Canfranc's magnificent Belle Époque train station, now abandoned. Surely the largest and most ornate building in the Pyrenees, the station has a bewitching history, and was used as a location in the 1965 film *Doctor Zhivago.* Ask the tourist office for schedules and train prices—it's a good idea to book ahead of time. In addition, a nontourist train runs year-round between

Jaca and Canfranc. ✉ *Canfranc Estación* 🌐 *www.elcanfranero.com, www.renfe.com.*

Catedral de San Pedro. An important stop on the pilgrimage to Santiago de Compostela, Jaca's 11th-century Romanesque cathedral has lovely carved capitals and was the first French-Romanesque Cathedral in Spain, paving the way for later Spanish-Romanesque architecture. ✉ *Pl. de San Pedro 1* 🕑 *Daily 9–1:30 and 4–8 (except during services).*

Museo Diocesano. Inside the cathedral and near the cloisters, the museum is filled with an excellent collection of Romanesque and Gothic frescoes and artifacts. ✉ *Pl. de la Catedral* ☎ *974/362185 for museo* 🌐 *www.diocesisdejaca.org* 🎫 *€6* 🕑 *Weekdays 10–1:30 and 4–7, Sat. 10–1:30 and 4–8, Sun. 10–1:30.*

Ciudadela. The massive pentagon-shaped Ciudadela is an impressive example of 17th-century military architecture. It has a display of more than 35,000 military miniatures, arranged to represent different periods of history. Check the website to confirm hours. ✉ *Avda. del Primer Viernes de Mayo s/n* ☎ *974/361124, 974/357157* 🌐 *www.ciudadeladejaca.es* 🎫 *Citadel €6, museum €6, combined ticket €10* 🕑 *Tues.–Sun. 10:30–1:30 and 4:30–7:30.*

6

WHERE TO EAT AND STAY

$$$ SPANISH 🍴 **La Cocina Aragonesa.** This Jaca mainstay is an elegant, rustic space decorated with local farming and mountaineering objects and centered on a mammoth fireplace. Its Aragonese-Basque cuisine is justly famous around town and beyond for constantly changing, fresh, and innovative creations, especially game in season: venison, wild boar, partridge, and duck. Try the *perdiz roja estofada con foie* (redleg partridge stuffed with foie gras) or the *cebollitas glaseadas y trufa negra* (glazed baby onions with black truffles). [$] *Average main: €20* ✉ *Hotel Conde Aznar, Calle Cervantes 5* ☎ *974/361050* 🌐 *www.condeaznar.com* 🕑 *Closed Mon. and 10 days in June and Nov. No dinner Sun.*

$$$ TAPAS 🍴 **La Tasca de Ana.** For a taste of Spanish tapas in the Pyrenees, this cozy and fun tavern is one of Jaca's finest. With only a handful of tables and standing room by the bar, it's not the setting for a quiet romantic dinner, but it is recommended for anyone spending an evening in Jaca, whether simply to kick-start the evening with a glass of local wine and a tapas appetizer, such as their signature *rodolfito* (langoustine in sauce), or for something more substantial. Staff are friendly and efficient with the constant stream of orders. [$] *Average main: €20* ✉ *Calle Ramiro I 3* ☎ *974/363621* 🌐 *www.latascadeana.com* 🕑 *Closed 2 wks in May and 2 wks in Sept. No lunch weekdays in winter.*

$ HOTEL 🏨 **Gran Hotel.** This rambling hotel—Jaca's traditional official clubhouse—is central to life, sports, and tourism in this Pyrenean hub. **Pros:** quiet location just west of the town center; professional and polished service. **Cons:** modern and functional construction with no special charm or Pyrenean features; neo–motel room style. [$] *Rooms from: €79* ✉ *Paseo de la Constitución 1* ☎ *974/360900* 🌐 *www.granhoteljaca.com* 🛏 *165 rooms* 🍽 *No meals.*

$$ B&B/INN 🏨 **Hotal Rural El Mirador de los Pirineos.** On the way to the Monasterio de San Juan de la Peña, this peaceful spot is more of a small retreat

than a place to simply rest for the night, with its own spa and outdoor pool—not to mention stunning views. **Pros:** a peaceful and charming alternative to urban Jaca; beautiful setting; spa retreat. **Cons:** only two restaurants nearby; staff not always on hand; not for those looking for complete hotel service. [$] *Rooms from: €99* ✉ *Calle Ordana 8, Santa Cruz de la Serós, 10 km (6 miles) from Jaca* ☎ *974/355593* 🌐 *www.elmiradordelospirineos.com* 🛏 *7 rooms* 🕓 *Closed Apr.–May. (dates depend on Easter, so call ahead) and 2 wks in Nov.* 🍴 *Breakfast.*

$$$ B&B/INN Fodor's Choice ★ 🏨 **Hotel Barosse.** In a small village on the outskirts of Jaca, this intimate bed-and-breakfast is worth sacrificing a central location to gain the sweeping mountain views and helpful, personalized service. **Pros:** attractive rural setting; boutique-style accommodations; friendly service. **Cons:** a car is necessary; not in the center of Jaca. [$] *Rooms from: €130* ✉ *Calle de Estirás 4, Barós* ☎ *974/360582, 638/845992* 🌐 *www.barosse.com* 🛏 *5 rooms* 🕓 *Closed 1st wk in Sept.* 🍴 *Breakfast.*

NIGHTLIFE

Jaca's music bars are concentrated in the old town, on Calle Ramiro I and along Calle Gil Bergés and Calle Bellido. Santa Locura, La Trampa, El Pintakoda, and La Dama Blanca are among the most popular.

MONASTERIO DE SAN JUAN DE LA PEÑA

21 km (13 miles) southwest of Jaca, 185 km (111 miles) north of Zaragoza, 90 km (54 miles) east of Pamplona.

South of the Aragonese valleys of Hecho and Ansó, and 23 km (14 miles) southwest of Jaca, is the Monastery of San Juan de la Peña, a site connected to the legend of the Holy Grail and one of the centers of Christian resistance during the 700-year Moorish occupation of Spain.

Fodor's Choice ★ **Monasterio de San Juan de la Peña.** The origins of this arresting religious sanctuary can be traced to the 9th century, when a hermit monk named Juan settled here on the *peña* (cliff). A monastery was founded on the spot in 920, and in 1071 Sancho Ramirez, son of King Ramiro I, made use of this structure, which was built into the mountain's rock wall, to found this Benedictine monastery. The **cloister,** tucked under the cliff, dates from the 12th century and contains intricately carved capitals depicting biblical scenes. The church of the New Monastery contains the **Kingdom of Aragon Interpretation Centre,** with a 45-minute audiovisual show (in Spanish, except for pre-booked groups). ✉ *Off N240* ✣ *From Jaca, drive 11 km (7 miles) west on N240 toward Pamplona to a left turn clearly signposted for San Juan de la Peña. From there it's another 11 km (7 miles) to the monastery* ☎ *974/355119* 🌐 *www.monasteriosanjuan.com* 🎟 *€12* 🕓 *June–Aug., daily 10–2 and 3–8; Mar.–May, Sept., and Oct., daily 10–2 and 3:30–7; Nov.–Feb., Sun.–Fri. 10–2, Sat. 10–5.*

The San Juan de la Peña monastery near Jaca

HECHO AND ANSÓ VALLEYS

The Hecho Valley is 49 km (30 miles) northwest of Jaca. The Ansó Valley is 25 km (15 miles) west of Hecho, 118 km (71 miles) east of Pamplona.

The Valle de Ansó is Aragón's western limit. Rich in fauna (mountain goats, wild boar, and even a bear or two), it follows the Veral River up to Zuriza. Towering over the head of the valley is Navarra's highest point, the 7,989-foot **Mesa de los Tres Reyes** (Plateau of the Three Kings), named not for the Magi but for the kings of Aragón, Navarra, and Castile, whose 11th-century kingdoms bordered here, allowing them to meet without leaving their respective realms. The **Selva de Oza** (Oza Forest), at the head of the Hecho Valley, is above the **Boca del Infierno** (Mouth of Hell), a tight draw that road and river barely squeeze through.

It's worth stopping at the pretty village of **Ansó,** where a preserved collection of stone houses are tightly bunched together along narrow cobbled streets dominated by the oversize Gothic **church of San Pedro** overlooking the valley. Try to be there on the last Sunday in August, when residents dress in their traditional medieval costumes and perform ancestral dances of great grace and dignity. If heading to this area from Jaca, keep your eye out for the town of **Aragüés del Puerto** if you wish to explore the adjacent Hecho and Ansó valleys.

GETTING HERE AND AROUND

You can reach the Valle de Hecho from Jaca by heading west on the N240 and then north on the A176.

ESSENTIALS

Visitor Information Hecho ✉ *Pallar d'Agustín, Hecho* ☎ *974/375505.*

EXPLORING

Monasterio de San Pedro de Siresa. The area's most important monument is a 9th-century retreat above the town of Hecho. Although now only the 11th-century church remains, it is a marvelous example of Romanesque architecture. Cheso, a medieval Aragonese dialect descended from the Latin spoken by the Siresa monks, is thought to be the closest to Latin of all Romance languages and dialects. It has been kept alive in the Hecho Valley, especially in the works of the poet Veremundo Méndez Coarasa. ✉ *Calle San Pedro, Siresa* 🎫 *€2* 🕒 *July–Sept., daily 11–1 and 5–8; Oct.–June, daily 11–1 and 3–5. If closed call Juana (628/212764) for the key.*

WHERE TO STAY

$ B&B/INN 🏨 **Gaby-Casa Blasquico.** This cozy inn is a typical mountain chalet with flowered balconies and a plethora of memorabilia inside. **Pros:** two cute dormered rooms; fine mountain cuisine. **Cons:** rooms lack space; public rooms cluttered. [$] *Rooms from: €53* ✉ *Pl. la Fuente 1, Hecho* ☎ *974/375007* 🌐 *www.casablasquico.es* 🛏 *6 rooms* 🕒 *Closed weekdays Nov. 5–Mar. 19* 🍴 *No meals.*

$ B&B/INN 🏨 **Posada Magoría.** All the rooms in this carefully restored Art Nouveau house, now an eco-friendly B&B, have a splendid view and are furnished with original furniture and knickknacks from the 1920s, as well as pristine bedding and modern comforts. **Pros:** feel-at-home, relaxed atmosphere; cozy retreat in beautiful surroundings. **Cons:** noise can sometimes be heard from other parts of the house—choose a room on a higher floor. [$] *Rooms from: €60* ✉ *Calle Milagro 32A, Ansó* ☎ *974/370049* 🌐 *www.posadamagoria.com* 🛏 *7 rooms* 🍴 *No meals.*

$ B&B/INN 🏨 **Usón.** For an eco-friendly, totally solar-powered base for exploring the upper Hecho Valley or the Oza Forest, look no farther. **Pros:** friendly service; great value; stunning views into the mountains. **Cons:** no elevator; remote setting. [$] *Rooms from: €58* ✉ *Ctra. Selva de Oza, HU2131, Km 7, Usón* ☎ *608/729369* 🌐 *www.hoteluson.com* 🛏 *8 rooms, 4 apartments* 🕒 *Closed Nov. 5–Mar. 15* 🍴 *No meals.*

EN ROUTE From Ansó, head west to Roncal on the narrow and winding but panoramic 17-km (11-mile) road through the Sierra de San Miguel. To enjoy this route fully, count on taking a good 45 minutes to reach the Esca River and the Valle de Roncal.

THE NAVARRAN AND BASQUE PYRENEES

Moving west into the Roncal Valley and the Basque Country, you will note smoother, rolling hills and softer meadows as the rocky central Pyrenees of Aragón begin to descend toward the Bay of Biscay. These wet and fertile uplands and verdant beech forests are a melting pot of Basque-Navarran folklore, culture, tradition, and cuisine. The Basque highlands of Navarra from Roncal through the Irati Forest to Roncesvalles and along the Bidasoa River seem like an Arcadian paradise as the jagged Pyrenean peaks give way to sheep-filled pasturelands, 15th-century caseríos, and sleepy watermills.

RONCAL VALLEY

17 km (11 miles) west of Ansó Valley, 72 km (43 miles) west of Jaca, 86 km (52 miles) northeast of Pamplona.

The Roncal Valley, the eastern edge of the Basque Pyrenees, is notable for the sheep's-milk cheese of the same name and as the birthplace of Julián Gayarre (1844–90), the leading tenor of his time. The 34-km (21-mile) drive through the towns of **Burgui** and **Roncal** to **Isaba** winds through green hillsides past caseríos, classical Basque farmhouses covered by long, sloping roofs that were designed to house animals on the ground floor and the family up above to take advantage of the body heat of the livestock. Burgui's red-tile roofs backed by rolling pastures contrast with the vertical rock and steep slate roofs of the Aragonese and Catalan Pyrenees; Isaba's wide-arched bridge across the Esca is a graceful reminder of Roman aesthetics and engineering.

GETTING HERE AND AROUND

To get to the valley from Jaca, take N240 west along the Aragón River; a right turn north on A137 follows the Esca River from the head of the Yesa Reservoir up the Roncal Valley.

ESSENTIALS

Visitor Information Roncal ✉ *Barrio Iriartea s/n, Roncal* ☎ *948/475256* ⊕ *www.turismo.navarra.es.*

EXPLORING

El Tributo de las Tres Vacas (*The Tribute of the Three Cows*). Try to be in the Roncal Valley for this event, which has been celebrated every July 13 since 1375. The mayors of the valley's villages, dressed in traditional gowns, gather near the summit of San Martín to receive the symbolic payment of three cows from their French counterparts, in memory of the settlement of ancient border disputes. Feasting and celebrating follow.

RONCESVALLES (ORREAGA)

64 km (40 miles) northwest of Isaba in the Roncal Valley, 48 km (30 miles) north of Pamplona.

Roncesvalles (often listed as Orreaga, its name in Euskera) is a small village and site of the Battle of Roncesvalles (or Battle of Roncevaux Pass) when Charlemagne's army, under the command of Roland, was attacked and overcome by Basque soldiers in AD 778. This battle became the inspiration for one of France's most revered literary poems, Le Chanson de Roland (The Song of Roland), written in the 11th century.

The village's strategic position, 23 km (14 miles) from the original starting line of St-Jean-de-Port in France, has made it the first stop-off point for pilgrims on the Camino de Santiago since the 10th century. Its Gothic Colegiata—built in the style of the Nôtre Dame Cathedral in Paris—hospital, and 12th-century chapel have provided shelter since

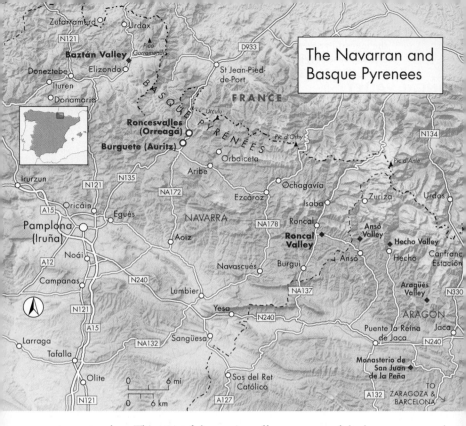

then. This part of the camino offers up some of the best scenery, and many modern-day pilgrims start in Roncesvalles.

GETTING HERE AND AROUND
The N135 northbound out of Pamplona goes straight to Roncesvalles.

ESSENTIALS
Visitor Information Orreaga-Roncesvalles ⊠ *Antiguo Molino, Calle de Nuestra Señora de Roncesvalles* ☎ *948/760301.*

EXPLORING
Colegiata. Built on the orders of King Sancho VII el Fuerte (the Strong), the Collegiate Church houses the king's tomb, which measures more than 7 feet long. ⊠ *Calle de Nuestra Señora de Roncesvalles* ⊕ *www. roncesvalles.es.*

Ibañeta Pass. This 3,468-foot pass, above Roncesvalles, is a gorgeous route into France. A *menhir* (monolith) marks the traditional site of the legendary battle in *The Song of Roland,* during which Roland fell after calling for help on his ivory battle horn. The well-marked eight-hour walk to or from St-Jean-Pied-de-Port (which does *not* follow the road) is one of the most beautiful and dramatic sections of the Santiago pilgrimage.

WHERE TO STAY

$ **Casa de Beneficiados.** Whether or not you are embarking on the
HOTEL pilgrimage, this hotel, in a restored 18th-century building adjoining
the Colegiata, provides warm, atmospheric shelter for the night, with
low-lit, stone-wall common areas and modern, comfortable rooms.
Pros: historic building; friendly service; at the center of the pilgrim
action. **Cons:** rooms lack the charm of the common areas. $\boxed{S}$ *Rooms
from: €90* ✉ *Calle Nuestra Señora de Roncesvalles s/n* ☎ *948/760105,
639/754449* ⊕ *www.casadebeneficiados.com* ⟿ *16 rooms* ☉ *Dec.–mid-
Mar.* �’⏣❘ *No meals.*

BURGUETE (AURITZ)

2 km (1 mile) south of Roncesvalles.

Burguete (Auritz, in Euskera) lies between two mountain streams forming the headwaters of the Urobi River and is surrounded by meadows
and forests. The town was immortalized in Ernest Hemingway's *The
Sun Also Rises,* with its evocative description of trout fishing in an ice-
cold stream above a Navarran village. Hemingway himself spent time
here doing just that, and he stayed at the Hostal Burguete.

GETTING HERE AND AROUND

The N135 northbound out of Pamplona goes to Burguete in 44 km (27
miles). From Roncesvalles, it's just 2 km south on the N135.

WHERE TO STAY

$ **Hotel Loizu.** An inn for pilgrims since the 18th century, the Loizu is
B&B/INN now a country-style hotel that makes an excellent base for exploring the
Selva de Irati. **Pros:** family-run; friendly service; comfortable and good-
sized rooms. **Cons:** bathrooms, although adequate, are small and fairly
cramped. $\boxed{S}$ *Rooms from: €85* ✉ *Calle San Nicolás 13* ☎ *948/760008*
⊕ *www.loizu.com* ⟿ *27 rooms* ☉ *Closed mid-Dec.–mid-Mar.* ❘⏣❘ *No
meals.*

**EN
ROUTE** To skip Pamplona and stay on the trans-Pyrenean route, continue
21 km (13 miles) southwest of Burguete on NA135 until you reach
NA138, just before Zubiri. A right turn takes you to Urtasun, where
the small NA252 leads left to the town of Iragui and over the pass at
Col d'Egozkue (from which there are superb views over the Arga and
Ultzana River valleys) to Olagüe, where it connects with NA121 some
20 km (12 miles) north of Pamplona. Turn right onto N121A and
climb over the Puerto de Velate (Velate Pass)—or, in bad weather (or in
a hurry), through the tunnel—to the turn for Elizondo and the Baztán
Valley, N121B. (Take a good map if you're setting off into the hills.)

BAZTÁN VALLEY

*62 km (38 miles) northwest of Roncesvalles, 80 km (50 miles) north
of Pamplona.*

Fodor's Choice Tucked neatly above the headwaters of the Bidasoa River, beneath the
★ peak of the 3,545-foot Gorramendi Mountain that looms over the border with France, is the Valle de Baztán. These rounded green hills are
a scenic halfway stop-off point between the central Pyrenees and the

Atlantic. Here the roads of this enchanted Navarran valley meander through picture-perfect villages of geranium-covered, whitewashed, stone-and-mortar houses with red-tile roofs grouped around a central *frontón* (handball court).

This once-isolated pocket of the Basque-Navarran Pyrenees is peppered with smugglers' trails and is the site of the Camino de Baztanas, the oldest stretch of the Camino de Santiago. You can follow in the ancient footsteps of pilgrims from the main starting point in the historic village of Urdax. Nearby, close to the village of Zugarramurdi, you can visit a collection of limestone caves, otherwise known as *las cuevas de las brujas* (witches' caves), where so-called witches held covens and pagan rituals before their eventual and brutal persecution in the 1600s.

Try to be in the village of Ituren in late September for its Carnival—The Day of the Joaldunak—which has been recognized as one of the oldest celebrations in Europe. Here you can see striking costumes hung with clanging cowbells as participants parade from farm to farm and house to house paying homage to their ancestors; some anthropologists argue that the rituals go back to pagan times. Check the exact dates with the tourist office as each year's schedule depends on the phases of the moon.

ESSENTIALS

Visitor Information Bidasoa and Baztan Valleys ✉ *Centro de Turismo Rural de Bértiz, Bertiz Natural Park, Oieregi* ☎ *948/592323* ⊕ *www.consorciobertiz.org.*

WHERE TO EAT

$$$$ ✕ **Donamariako Benta.** This family-run restaurant is notable for its high
BASQUE   quality and refined level of service. Created from a former 19th-cen-
FAMILY   tury residence and stables, the restaurant is cozy in winter, with its
Fodor's Choice   crackling fire, and a treat in summer, when you can be seated in the
★   peaceful garden filled with willow trees overlooking the river and old salmon leap. Prix-fixe menus change seasonally and are based on traditional recipes, such as *secreto de cerdo ibérico con crema de hongas* (grilled tender pork steak with a wild mushroom sauce) or *txangurro a la Donostiarra* (baked crab), all sublimely executed. It is advisable to make a reservation if you're coming in August or around public holidays. $ *Average main: €30* ✉ *Barrio de Las Ventas 4, Donamaria* ☎ *948/450708* ⊕ *www.donamariako.com* ⊗ *Closed Mon. and Dec. 10–Jan. 5. No dinner Sun.*

7

BARCELONA

WELCOME TO BARCELONA

TOP REASONS TO GO

★ **Explore La Boqueria:** Barcelona's produce market may be the most exciting cornucopia in the world.

★ **Visit Santa Maria del Mar:** The early Mediterranean Gothic elegance, rhythmic columns, and unbroken spaces make this church peerless.

★ **See La Sagrada Família:** Gaudí's unfinished masterpiece is the city's most iconic treasure.

★ **Experience El Palau de la Música Catalana:** This Art Nouveau tour de force is alive with music.

★ **Shop for fashion and design:** How could a city famous for its architecture not offer an abundance of innovative clothing, furniture, and design shops as well?

★ **Watch castellers and sardanas:** Human castles and Catalonia's national dance are two fun ways to appreciate Catalan culture.

1 The Rambla and the Raval. *Ciutat Vella* (the Old City) is bisected by the Rambla, the city's all-purpose runway and home of the Boqueria market, the city's heart, soul, and stomach. The Raval is a funky multicultural sprawl, spread out around the MACBA contemporary art museum and the medieval Hospital de la Santa Creu.

2 Barri Gòtic and Born-Ribera. Northeast of the Rambla, Ciutat Vella's Gothic Quarter surrounds the cathedral and a jumble of ancient (mostly pedestrianized) streets filled with shops, cafés, and Gothic architecture. Born-Ribera is across Via Laietana, around Santa Maria del Mar.

3 Barceloneta, Ciutadella, and Port Olímpic. Barceloneta is a charmingly Naples-like fisherman's village, filled with seafood restaurants and lined with sandy beaches. Port Olímpic, built for the 1992 Olympic

Map labels:

TO PEDRALBES
TO SARRIA
5
Travessera de les Corts
Pl. de Francesc Macià
Travessera de Gràcia
Avda. Diagonal
C. de Berlín
C. de Numància
Avda. de Josep Tarradellas
C. de París
C. de Còrsega
C. del Rosselló
C. de Provença
Avda. de Roma
Estació Sants
Pl. Països Catalans
4 EIXAMPLE
C. de València
C. d'Aragó
C. de la Diputació
C. del Comte d'Urgell
C. de Villarroel
C. de Casanova
C. de Muntaner
C. d'Aribau
C. de Balmes
Plaça Universitat
Gran Via de les Corts Catalanes
C. de Sepúlveda
C. de Floridablanca
C. de Tamarit
C. de Manso
Avda. de Mistral
Avda. del Paral·lel
Avda. de Sant Pau
MACBA
Rda. de Sant Antoni
Hospital de la Santa Creu
Santa Creu
La Boqueria Market
C. de Sant Pau
C. Nou de la Rambla
C. de la Unió
Plaça d'Espanya
C. de la Creu Coberta
C. de Tarragona
Avda. Reina M. Cristina
Mies van der Rohe Pavilion
Pl. de les Cascades
MNAC
Jardins de Joan Maragall
6
MONTJUÏC
Fundació Joan Miró
Avda. de Miramar
Estadi Olímpic
Camí dels Tres Pins
Parc de Montjuïc
Castell de Montjuïc
Jardins de Miramar
Moll de Sant Bertran
Pg. de Montjuïc
Plaça Portal de la Pau

GETTING ORIENTED

The baseball-diamond-shape jumble at the bottom of the map of Barcelona is Ciutat Vella (Old City). This is the heart of the city and a sensory feast, from the Rambla's human parade and the Boqueria's fish, fruit, and vegetables to the steamy corners of the Born. The wide checkerboard grid above Ciutat Vella is the post-1860 Eixample (Expansion), rich in Modernista architecture and shops. The outlying villages of Gràcia and Sarrià each have their own personalities: Gràcia a cauldron of youthful energy, trendy bars and boutiques; Sarrià is more rustic and leafy. The Montjuïc promontory hovering over the port is a repository of paintings, from the Miró Foundation to the MNAC and CaixaFòrum, while Tibidabo, the other high point, offers panoramic views on clear days.

Games, is a sprawling succession of restaurants and discos. Ciutadella, just inland, was originally a fortress but is now a park with the city zoo.

4 The Eixample. The post-1860 Eixample spreads out above Plaça de Catalunya and contains most of the city's Art Nouveau (in Catalan, Modernista) architecture, including Gaudí's

iconic Sagrada Família church, along with hundreds of shops and places to eat.

5 Upper Barcelona. The village of Gràcia nestles above the Diagonal, with Gaudí's Park Güell at its upper edge. Sarrià and Pedralbes spread out farther west, with two Gaudí buildings, a stunning monastery and cloister, and a rustic village surrounded

by upscale residential development.

6 Montjuïc. The promontory over the south side of the city lacks street vibe but the artistic treasure massed here is not to be missed: Miró, the MNAC, Mies van der Rohe, and CaixaFòrum.

EATING AND DRINKING WELL IN BARCELONA

Barcelona cuisine draws from Catalonia's rustic country cooking and uses ingredients from the Mediterranean, the Pyrenees, and inland farmlands. Historically linked to France and Italy, cosmopolitan influences and experimental contemporary innovation have combined to make Barcelona an important food destination.

(top left) A stew of broad beans and black and white botifarra sausage (top right) *Esqueixada*, raw codfish salad (bottom left) A dessert of *mel i mató* (honey with fresh cheese)

The Mediterranean diet of seafood, vegetables, olive oil, and red wine comes naturally to Barcelona. A dish you'll see on many menus is *pa amb tomaquet*: bread rubbed with ripe tomato (garlic optional), then drizzled with olive oil. Fish of all kinds, shrimp, shellfish, and rice dishes combining them are common, as are salads of seafood and Mediterranean vegetables. Vegetable and legume combinations are standard. Seafood and upland combinations, the classic *mar i muntanya* (surf and turf) recipes, join rabbit and prawns or cuttlefish and meatballs, while salty and sweet tastes—a Moorish legacy—are found in recipes such as duck with pears or goose with figs.

CAVA

Order Champagne in Barcelona and you'll get anything from French bubbly to dirty looks. Ask, instead, for *cava*, sparkling wine from the Penedès region just southwest of the city. The first cava was produced in 1872 after the phylloxera plague wiped out most of Europe's vineyards. Cava (from the "cave" or wine cellar where it ferments) has a drier, earthier taste than Champagne, and slightly larger bubbles.

SALADS

Esqueixada is a cold salad consisting of strips of raw, shredded, salt-cured cod marinated in oil and vinegar with onions, tomatoes, olives, and red and green bell peppers. Chunks of dried tuna can also be included and chickpeas, roast onions, and potatoes can be added, too. *Escalibada* is another classic Catalan salad of red and green bell peppers and eggplant that have been roasted over coals, cut into strips, and served with onions, garlic, and olive oil.

LEGUMES

Botifarra amb mongetes (sausage with white beans) is the classic Catalan sausage made of pork and seasoned with salt and pepper, grilled and served with stewed white beans and *allioli* (an olive oil and garlic emulsion); botifarra can also be made with truffles, apples, eggs, wild mushrooms, and even chocolate. *Mongetes de Santa Pau amb calamarsets* (tiny white beans from Santa Pau with baby squid) is a favorite mar i muntanya.

VEGETABLES

Espinaques a la catalana (spinach with pine nuts, raisins, and garlic) owes a debt to the Moorish sweet-salt counterpoint and to the rich vegetable-growing littoral along the Mediterranean coast north and south of Barcelona. Bits of bacon, fatback, or *jamón ibérico* may be added; some recipes use fine almond

flakes as well. *Albergínies* (eggplant or aubergine) are a favorite throughout Catalunya, whether roasted, stuffed, or stewed, while *carxofes* (artichokes) fried to a crisp or stewed with rabbit is another staple.

FISH

Llobarro a la sal (sea bass cooked in salt) is baked in a shell of rock salt that hardens and requires a tap from a hammer or heavy knife to break and serve. The salt shell keeps the juices inside the fish and the flesh flakes off in firm chunks, while the skin of the fish prevents excessive saltiness from permeating the meat. *Suquet* is favorite fish stew, with scorpion fish, monkfish, sea bass, or any combination thereof stewed with potatoes, onions, and tomatoes.

DESSERTS

Crema catalana (Catalan cream) is the most popular dessert in Catalonia, a version of the French crème brûlée, custard dusted with cinnamon and confectioner's sugar and burned with a blowtorch (traditionally, a branding iron was used) before serving. The branding results in a hardened skim of caramelized sugar on the surface. The less sweet and palate-cleansing *mel i mató* (honey and fresh cheese) is a close second in popularity.

7

BARCELONA'S BEST BEACHES

Over the last decade, Barcelona's *platjas* (beaches) have been improved, now stretching some 4 km (2½ miles) from Barceloneta's Platja de Sant Sebastià at the southwestern end, northward via the Platjas de Sant Miquel, Barceloneta, Passeig Marítim, Port Olímpic, Nova Icària, Bogatell, Mar Bella (the last bit of which is a nudist enclave), and La Nova Mar Bella to Llevant. The Barceloneta beach is the most popular stretch, easily accessible by several bus lines, notably the No. 64, and from the L4 metro stop at Barceloneta or at Ciutadella–Vila Olímpica. The best surfing is at the northeastern end of the Barceloneta beach, while the boardwalk offers miles of runway for walkers, cyclers, and joggers. Topless bathing is common on all beaches in and around Barcelona.

WORD OF MOUTH

"The beaches between Port Olimpic and Barceloneta [are] a bit more popular because you have small supermarketsa stone's throw away from the beach in case you need some food or drinks. Or [you can try] the beachfront restaurants and bars . . . take the metro to Barceloneta station and walk down Pg J. Borbo on the nice promenade along the old harbor. Several bus lines go down to the beach from many parts of the city. I'd try to avoid Sundays, because it gets really busy, and the beach bars (almost) double their prices." —Cowboy 1968

PLATJA DE LA BARCELONETA

Just to the left at the end of Passeig Joan de Borbó, this is the easiest beach to get to, hence the most crowded and the most fun from a people-watching standpoint. Along with swimming, there are windsurfing and kitesurfing rentals to be found just up behind the beach at the edge of La Barceloneta. Rebecca Horn's sculpture *L'Estel Ferit*, a rusting stack of cubes, expresses nostalgia for the beach-shack restaurants that lined the beach here until 1992. Surfers trying to catch a wave wait just off the breakwater in front of the excellent beachfront Agua restaurant.

PLATJA DE LA MAR BELLA

Closest to the Poblenou metro stop near the eastern end of the beaches, this is a thriving gay enclave and the unofficial nudist beach of Barcelona (but clothed bathers are welcome, too). The watersports center Base Nàutica de la Mar Bella rents equipment for sailing, surfing, and windsurfing. Outfitted with showers, safe drinking fountains, and a children's play area, La Mar Bella also has lifeguards who warn against swimming near the breakwater. The excellent Els Pescadors restaurant is just inland on Plaça Prim.

PLATJA DE LA NOVA ICÀRIA

One of Barcelona's most popular beaches, this strand is just east of the Olympic Port with the full range of entertainment, restaurant, and refreshment venues close at hand. (Mango and El Chiringuito de Moncho are two of the most popular restaurants.) The beach is directly across from the area developed as the residential Vila Olímpica for the 1992 Games, an interesting housing project that has now become a popular residential neighborhood.

PLATJA DE SANT SEBASTIÀ

The landmark of Barceloneta's most southwestern beach (at the end of Passeig Joan de Borbó) now is the ultramodern W Barcelona Hotel, but Sant Sebastià is in fact the oldest of the city beaches, where 19th-century Barcelonins cavorted in bloomers and bathing costumes. On the west end is the Club Natació de Barcelona, and there is a semiprivate feel that the beaches farther east seem to lack.

PLATJA DE GAVÀ-CASTELLDEFELS

A 15-minute train ride south of Barcelona (from the Estació de Sants) to Gavà brings you to the broad swath of clean golden sand at Gavà Mar, a popular outing for Barcelona families and beach party aficionados. Gavà Mar extends some 4 km (2½ miles) south to join the busier beach at Castelldefels; returning to Barcelona from Castelldefels allows for a hike down the beach to a variety of seaside shacks and restaurants serving local favorites like calçots and paella.

7

Updated by
Jared Lubar-
sky, Steve
Tallantyre,
and Suzanne
Wales

The infinite variety of street life, the nooks and crannies of the medieval Barri Gòtic, the ceramic tile and stained glass of Art Nouveau facades, the art and music, the throb of street life, the food (ah, the food!)—one way or another, Barcelona will find a way to get your full attention.

The Catalonian capital greets the new millennium with a cultural and industrial rebirth comparable only to the late-19th-century Renaix-ença (Renaissance) that filled the city with its flamboyant Moderniste (Art Nouveau) buildings. An exuberant sense of style—from hip new fashions to cutting-edge interior design, to the extravagant visions of star-status postmodern architects—gives Barcelona a vibe like no other in the world. Barcelona is Spain's most-visited city, and it's no wonder: it's a 2,000-year-old master of the art of perpetual novelty.

Barcelona's present boom began on October 17, 1987, when Juan Antonio Samaranch, president of the International Olympic Commit-tee, announced that his native city had been chosen to host the 1992 Olympics. This single masterstroke allowed Spain's so-called second city to throw off the shadow of Madrid and its 40-year "internal exile" under Franco, and resume its rightful place as one of Europe's most dynamic destinations. The Catalan administration lavished millions in subsidies from the Spanish government for the Olympics, then used the Games as a platform to broadcast the news about Catalonia's cultural and national identity from one end of the planet to the other. More Mediterranean than Spanish, historically closer and more akin to Mar-seille or Milan than to Madrid, Barcelona has always been ambitious, decidedly modern (even in the 2nd century), and quick to accept the most recent innovations. (The city's electric light system, public gas system, and telephone exchange were among the first in the world.) Its democratic form of government is rooted in the so-called Usatges Laws instituted by Ramon Berenguer I in the 11th century, which amounted to a constitution. This code of privileges represented one of the earli-est known examples of democratic rule; Barcelona's Consell de Cent (Council of 100), constituted in 1274, was Europe's first parliament and one of the cradles of Western democracy. The center of an important seafaring commercial empire with colonies spread around the Mediterranean as far away as Athens, when Madrid was still a Moorish outpost on the arid Castilian steppe—it was Barcelona that absorbed new ideas and styles first. It borrowed navigation techniques from the Moors. It embraced the ideals of the French Revolution. It nurtured artists like Picasso and Miró, who blossomed in the city's air of freedom and individualism. Barcelona, in short, has always been ahead of the curve.

PLANNING

PLANNING YOUR TIME

The best way to get around Barcelona is on foot; the occasional resort to subway, taxi, or tram will help you make the most of your visit. The comfortable FGC (Ferrocarril de la Generalitat de Catalunya) trains that run up the center of the city from Plaça de Catalunya to Sarrià put you within 20- to 30-minute walks of nearly everything. (The metro and the FGC close just short of midnight Monday through Thursday and Sunday, and at 2 am on Friday; on Saturday, the metro runs all night. The main attractions you need a taxi or the metro to reach are Montjuïc (Miró Foundation, MNAC, Mies van der Rohe Pavilion, CaixaFòrum, and Poble Espanyol), most easily accessed from Plaça Espanya; Park Güell above Plaça Lesseps; and the Auditori at Plaça de les Glòries. You can reach Gaudí's Sagrada Família by two metro lines (2 and 5), but you may prefer the walk from the FGC's Provença stop, as it's an enjoyable half-hour jaunt that passes by three major Moderniste buildings: Palau Baró de Quadras, Casa Terrades (les Punxes), and Casa Macaia.

Sarrià and Pedralbes are easily explored on foot. The Torre Bellesguard and the Col.legi de les Teresianes are uphill treks; you might want to take a cab. It's a pleasant stroll from Sarrià down through the Jardins de la Vil.la Cecilia and Vil.la Amèlia to the Cátedra Gaudí (the pavilions of the Finca Güell, with Gaudí's amazing wrought-iron dragon gate); from there, you can get to the Futbol Club Barcelona through the Jardins del Palau Reial de Pedralbes and the university campus, or catch a two-minute taxi.

All of Ciutat Vella (Barri Gòtic, La Rambla, El Raval, Born-Ribera, and Barceloneta) is best explored on foot. If you stay in Barceloneta for dinner (usually not more than €12), have the restaurant call you a taxi to get back to your hotel.

The city bus system is also a viable option—you get a better look at the city as you go—but the metro is faster and more comfortable. The tramway offers a quiet ride from Plaça Francesc Macià out Diagonal to the Futbol Club Barcelona, or from behind the Ciutadella Park out to Glòries and the Fòrum at the east end of Diagonal.

WHEN TO GO

For optimal weather and marginally fewer tourists, the best times to visit Barcelona, Catalonia, and Bilbao are April through June and mid-September through mid-December. Catalans and Basques vacation in August, causing epic traffic jams at both ends of the month.

7

BARCELONA

JAN.	FEB.	MAR.	APR.	MAY	JUNE
55°F/13°C	57°F/14°C	61°F/16°C	64°F/18°C	70°F/21°C	77°F/25°C

JULY	AUG.	SEPT.	OCT.	NOV.	DEC.
82°F/28°C	82°F/28°C	77°F/25°C	70°F/21°C	61°F/16°C	55°F/13°C

DISCOUNTS AND DEALS

The very worthwhile **Barcelona Card** (⊕ *www.barcelona-card.com*) comes in two-, three-, four-, and five-day versions: for €33.30, €42.30, €50.40, and €55.80. You get unlimited travel on public transport and free entrance at numerous museums, and discounts on restaurants, leisure sights, and stores. You can get the card in Turisme de Barcelona offices in Plaça de Catalunya and Plaça Sant Jaume and in the Sants Estació del Nord train stations, and El Prat airport, among other sites.

GETTING HERE AND AROUND

AIR TRAVEL

Most flights arriving in Spain from the United States and Canada pass through Madrid's Barajas (MAD), but the major gateway to Catalonia and other regions in this book is Spain's second-largest airport, Barcelona's spectacular glass, steel, and marble El Prat del Llobregat (BCN). The T1 terminal, which opened in 2009, is a sleek ultramodern facility that uses solar panels for sustainable energy and offers a spa, a fitness center, restaurants and cafés, and more VIP lounges. This airport is served by numerous international carriers, but Catalonia also has two other airports that handle passenger traffic, including charter flights. One is just south of Girona, 90 km (56 miles) north of Barcelona and convenient to the resort towns of the Costa Brava. Bus and train connections from Girona to Barcelona work well and cheaply, provided you have the time. The other Catalonia airport is at Reus, 110 km (68 miles) south of Barcelona and a gateway to Tarragona and the beaches of the Costa Daurada. Flights to and from the major cities in Europe and Spain also fly into and out of Bilbao's Loiu (BIL) airport. For information about airports in Spain, consult ⊕ *www.aena.es*.

Airport Information Aeroport de Girona-Costa Brava (*GRO*). ⊠ *Girona* ☎ 913/211000, 972/186600. **Aeropuerto de Reus** (*REU*). ⊠ *Autovia Tarragona–Reus, Reus* ☎ 902/404704, 913/211000. **Aeropuerto Internacional de Bilbao** (*BIL*). ⊠ *Carretera Aeropuerto, Loiu* ☎ 902/404704, 913/211000. **Barajas Aeropuerto de Madrid** (*MAD*). ⊠ *Av. de la Hispanidad s/n, Madrid* ☎ 902/404704, 913/211000. **El Prat de Llobregat** (*BCN*). ☎ 91/3211000, 902/404704.

GROUND TRANSPORTATION

Check first to see if your hotel in Barcelona provides airport-shuttle service. Few do: visitors normally get into town by train, bus, taxi, or rental car.

The Aerobus leaves the airport for Plaça de Catalunya every 10 minutes between 6 am and 1 am. From Plaça de Catalunya the bus leaves for the airport every 10 or 20 minutes between 5:30 am and 12:30 am. The fare is €5.90 one-way and €10.20 round-trip. Aerobuses for terminals 1 and 2 pick up and drop off passengers at the same stops en route, so if you're outward bound make sure that you board the right one. The A1 Aerobus for Terminal 1 is two-tone light and dark blue; the A2 Aerobus for Terminal 2 is dark blue and yellow.

Cab fare from the airport into town is €30–€35, depending on traffic, the part of town you're heading to, and the amount of baggage you have (there's a €1 surcharge for each suitcase that goes in the trunk). If you're driving your own car, follow signs to the Centre Ciutat, from which you can enter the city along Gran Vía. For the port area, follow signs for the Ronda Litoral. The journey to the center of town can take 25–45 minutes, depending on traffic.

CITY BUS, SUBWAY, AND TRAM TRAVEL
City buses run daily 5:30 am–11:30 pm. Barcelona's 17 night buses generally run until about 5 am. Route maps are displayed at bus stops. Schedules are available at bus and metro stations or at ⊕ *www.bcn.es/ guia/welcomea.htm.*

Barcelona's new tramway system is divided into two subsectors: Trambaix serves the western end of the Diagonal, and Trambesòs serves the eastern end.

In Barcelona the underground metro, or subway, is the fastest, cheapest, and easiest way to get around. Metro lines run Monday through Thursday and Sunday 5 am to midnight, Friday to 2 am Saturday, and holiday evenings all night. The FGC trains run 5 am to just after midnight on weekdays and to 1:52 on weekends and the eves of holidays. Sunday trains run on weekday schedules.

TICKET/PASS	PRICE
Single Fare	€2
10-Ride Pass	€9.80

Subway Info Transports Metropolitans de Barcelona (*TMB*). ☎ *93/2987000* ⊕ *www.tmb.net.*

TAXI TRAVEL
In Barcelona taxis are black and yellow and show a green rooftop light on the front right corner when available for hire. The meter currently starts at €2.05 and rises in increments of €0.98 every kilometer. These rates apply 6 am to 10 pm weekdays. At hours outside of these, the rates rise 20%. There are official supplements of €1 per bag for luggage.

Trips to or from a train station, or the quay where the cruise ships put in, entail a supplemental charge of €2.10; airport runs add a supplemental charge of €4.20, as do trips to or from a football match. There are cabstands (*parades,* in Catalan) all over town, and you can also hail cabs on the street, though if you are too close to an official stand they may not stop. You can call for a cab by phone 24 hours a day. Drivers do not expect a tip, but rounding up the fare is standard.

Taxi Companies Barna Taxi ☎ *93/3222222* ⊕ *www.barnataxi.com.*
Cooperativa Radio-Taxi Metropolitana Barcelona ☎ *93/225000.* **Radio**

Taxi ☎ *93/2250000*. Taxi Class Rent ☎ *93/3070707*. Teocar Mercedes
☎ *93/3083434*.

TRAIN TRAVEL

International overnight trains to Barcelona arrive from many European
cities, including Paris, Grenoble, Geneva, Zurich, and Milan; the route
from Paris takes 11½ hours. Almost all long-distance trains arrive at
and depart from Estació de Sants, though many make a stop at Passeig de Gràcia that comes in handy for hotels in the Eixample or in
the Ciutat Vella. Estació de França, near the port, handles only a few
regional trains within Catalonia. Train service connects Barcelona with
most other major cities in Spain; in addition a high-speed Euromed
route connects Barcelona to Tarragona and Valencia.

A twice-daily high-speed train, linking Barcelona and Paris in just six
and a half hours, went into service in December 2013. Only the 200-km
(124-mile) section of track between Perpignan and Nîmes is still unable
to handle the TGV speed.

Information on the local/commuter lines (*rodalies* in Catalan, *cercanias*
in Castilian) can be found at ⊕ *www.renfe.es/cercanias*. Rodalies go, for
example, to Sitges from Barcelona, whereas you would take a regular
RENFE train to, say, Tarragona. It's important to know whether you
are traveling on RENFE or on rodalies (the latter distinguished by a
stylized C), so you don't end up in the wrong line.

General Information Estació de França ✉ *Av. Marquès de l'Argentera 1, Born-
Ribera* ☎ *902/240202, 902/320320* ⊕ *www.renfe.es.* **Estació de Passeig de
Gràcia** ✉ *Passeig de Gràcia/Carrer Aragó, Eixample* ☎ *902/240202.* **Estació
de Sants** ✉ *Pl. dels Països Catalans s/n, Eixample* ☎ *902/240202, 902/432343.*
Ferrocarrils de la Generalitat de Catalunya (FGC) ☎ *93/2051515* ⊕ *www.fgc.
es.* **RENFE** ☎ *902/240202* ⊕ *www.renfe.es.*

Information and Passes Eurail. ⊕ *www.eurail.com.* **Rail Europe** ✉ *44 S.
Broadway, White Plains, New York* ☎ *800/6228600* ⊕ *www.raileurope.com*
☎ *905/6024195 in Canada, 800/3617245* ⊕ *www.raileurope.ca.*

TOURS
ART TOURS

The Ruta del Modernisme (Moderniste Route), a self-guided tour,
provides an excellent guidebook (available in English) that interprets
116 Moderniste sites from the Sagrada Família and the Palau de la
Música Catalana to Art Nouveau building facades, lampposts, and
paving stones. The €12 Guide, sold at the Plaça de Catalunya Tourist
Office, Pavellons Güell, and Hospital de Sant Pau, comes with a book
of vouchers good for discounts up to 50% on admission to most of the
Moderniste buildings and sites in the Guide in Barcelona and 13 other
towns and cities in Catalonia, as well as free guided tours in English at
Pavellons Güell (daily 10:15 and 12:15) and the Hospital de Sant Pau
(daily at 10, 11, noon and 1).

**Contacts Centre del Modernisme, Centre d'Informació de Turisme de
Barcelona** ✉ *Pl. Catalunya, 17, soterrani, Eixample* ☎ *93/2853834* ⊕ *www.
rutadelmodernisme.com.* **Centre del Modernisme, Hospital de la Santa Creu
i Sant Pau** ✉ *C. Sant Antoni Maria Claret 167, Eixample* ☎ *93/2682444* ⊕ *www.*

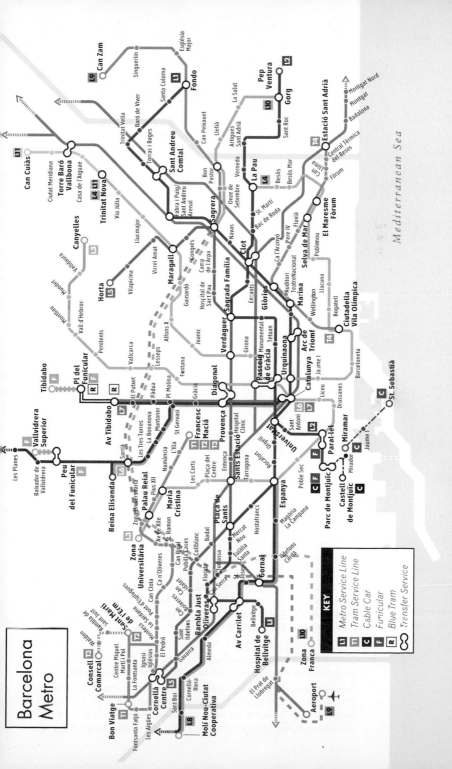

Barcelona Metro

rutadelmodernisme.com Ⓜ *Sant Pau/Dos de Maig.* **Centre del Modernisme, Pavellons Güell** ✉ *Av. de Pedralbes 7, Pedralbes* ☎ *93/3177652, 93/2562504* ⊕ *www.rutadelmodernisme.com* Ⓜ *Palau Real.* **Urbancultours** ✉ *info@urbancultours.com* ⊕ *www.urbancultours.com.*

Contacts Aula Gastronómica ✉ *Sagristans 5, Barri Gòtic* ☎ *93/3011944* ⊕ *www.aulagastronomica.com.* **Epicureanways** ✉ *1208 Wellford St., Charlottesville, Virginia* ☎ *434/7382293 in the U.S., 93/8022688 in Spain* ✉ *info@epicureanways.com* ⊕ *www.epicureanways.com.* **Spanish Journeys** ✉ *805 Long Pond Rd., Wellfleet, Massachusetts* ☎ *508/3499769* ⊕ *www.spanishjourneys.com.*

DAY TOURS AND GUIDES

BOAT TOURS

Golondrina harbor boats make short trips from the Portal de la Pau, near the Columbus monument. The fare is €7 for a 40-minute "Barcelona Port" tour of the harbor and €14.80 for the "Barcelona Sea" 90-minute ride out past the beaches and up the coast to the Fòrum at the eastern end of Diagonal. Departures are spring and summer (Easter week through September), daily 11:15 to 5:15 for the Port tour, 12:30 and 3:30 for the Sea tour; fall and winter, weekends and holidays only, 11 to 5. It's closed mid-December through early January.

Fees and Schedules Las Golondrinas and Trimar y Ómnibus ✉ *Pl. Portal de la Pau s/n, Rambla* ☎ *93/4423106* ⊕ *www.lasgolondrinas.com* Ⓜ *Drassanes.*

BUS TOURS

The Bus Turístic (9 or 9:30 am to 7 or 8 pm every 5–25 minutes, depending on the season), sponsored by the tourist office, runs on three circuits that pass all the important sights. The blue route covers upper Barcelona; the red route tours lower Barcelona; and the green route runs from the Port Olímpic along Barcelona's beaches to the Fòrum at the eastern end of Diagonal (April through September only). A one-day ticket, which you can buy online (with a 10% discount) for €23.40 (a two-day ticket is €30.60), or on the bus for €26 (€34 for two days), also covers the fare for the Tramvía Blau, funicular, and Montjuïc cable car across the port. You receive a booklet with discount vouchers for various attractions. The blue and red bus routes start at Plaça de Catalunya near Café Zurich. The green route starts at Port Olímpic next to the Hotel Arts. Passengers can jump off and catch a later bus at any stop along the way; some stops are "hubs" where you can switch to a bus on one of the other routes.

Contacts Bus Turístic ✉ *Pl. de Catalunya 3* ☎ *93/2853832* ⊕ *www. barcelonabusturistic.cat.* **Julià Tours** ✉ *Ronda Universitat 5, Eixample* ☎ *93/4026951* ⊕ *www.juliatravel.com/en/tours-barcelona.html.* **Pullmantur** ✉ *Gran Vía 645, Eixample* ☎ *902/240070* ⊕ *www.pullmantur.es.*

PRIVATE GUIDES

Guides from the organizations listed below are generally competent, though the quality of language skills and general showmanship may vary.

Contacts Associació Professional d'Informadors Turístics. Book half-day or full-day tours with an English-speaking guide, for Moderniste Barcelona, the Gothic Quarter, and/or the major museums. ☎ *93/319–8416* ⊕ *www. informadoresturisticos.com/index.html.* **Barcelona Guide Bureau.** Book here for five-hour coach tours (from €59) of the major sites in Barcelona, offered daily, and get fast-track entrance to museums and popular venues like the Sagrada Família. ✉ *Via Laietana 54* ☎ *93/268–2422, 93/315–2261* ⊕ *www. barcelonaguidebureau.com.*

WALKING TOURS

Turisme de Barcelona offers weekend walking tours of the Barri Gòtic, the Waterfront, Picasso's Barcelona, Modernisme, a shopping circuit, and Gourmet Barcelona in English (at 10:30 am). Prices range from €15 to €21, with 10% discounts for purchases online. The Picasso tour, which includes the entry fee for the Picasso Museum, is a real bargain. Tours depart from the Plaça de Catalunya tourist office. For private tours, Julià Tours and Pullmantur *(⇨ Bus Tours)* both lead walks around Barcelona. Tours leave from their offices, but you may be able to arrange a pick-up at your hotel. Prices per person are €35 for half a day and €90 for a full day, including lunch.

Contact Turisme de Barcelona ✉ *Pl. de Catalunya 17, soterrani, Eixample* ☎ *93/2853834* ⊕ *www.barcelonaturisme.com.*

VISITOR INFORMATION

Turisme de Barcelona ✉ *Pl. de Catalunya 17, soterrani, Eixample* ☎ *93/2853834* ⊕ *www.barcelonaturisme.com.*

EXPLORING BARCELONA

7

Barcelona has several main areas to explore. Between Plaça de Catalunya and the port lies the Old City, or Ciutat Vella, including El Barri Gòtic (the Gothic Quarter); the shop-, bar-, and tapas-rich Ribera (the waterfront, also known as Born-Ribera); the populous central promenade of the Rambla; and the Raval, the former slums or outskirts southwest of the Rambla. Above Plaça de Catalunya is the grid-pattern expansion known as the Eixample (literally, the "Expansion") built after the city's third series of defensive walls were torn down in 1860; this area contains most of Barcelona's Moderniste architecture. Farther north and west, Upper Barcelona includes the former outlying towns of Gràcia and Sarrià, Pedralbes, and, rising up behind the city, Tibidabo and the green hills of the Collserola nature preserve.

Though built in the mid-18th century, Barceloneta is generally considered part of Ciutat Vella. The Port Olímpic, a series of vast terrace restaurants and discos, is just beyond the Frank Gehry goldfish and the Hotel Arts. The Ciutadella park, once a fortress built not to protect but to dominate Barcelona, is just inland.

A final area, less important from a visitor's standpoint, is Diagonal Mar, from Torre Agbar and Plaça de les Glòries, east to the mouth of the Besòs River. This is the new Barcelona built for the 2004 Fòrum de les Cultures.

CIUTAT VELLA: THE RAMBLA AND THE RAVAL

The promenade in the heart of premodern Barcelona was originally a watercourse, dry for most of the year, that separated the walled Ciutat Vella from the outlying Raval. In the 14th century, the city walls were extended and the arroyo was filled in, so it gradually became a thoroughfare where peddlers, farmers, and tradesmen hawked their wares. (The watercourse is still there, under the pavement. From time to time a torrential rain will fill it, and the water rises up through the drains.) The poet-playwright Federico García Lorca called this the only street in the world he wished would never end—and in a sense, it doesn't.

TOP ATTRACTIONS

Fodor's Choice ★ **Antic Hospital de la Santa Creu i Sant Pau.** Founded in the 10th century, this is one of Europe's earliest medical complexes, and contains some of Barcelona's most impressive Gothic architecture. The buildings that survive today date mainly to the 15th and 16th centuries; the first stone for the hospital was laid by King Martí el Humà (Martin the Humane) in 1401. From the entrance on Carrer del Carme, the first building on the left is the 18th-century **Reial Acadèmia de Cirurgia i Medecina** (Royal Academy of Surgery and Medicine); the amphitheater is kept just as it was in the days when students learned by observing dissections. (One assumes that the paupers' hospital next door was always ready to oblige with cadavers.) The Academy is open to the public on Wednesday from 10 am to 1 pm. (For guided tours by appointment call ☎93/3171686.) Across the way on the right is the gateway into the patio of the **Casa de la Convalescència**, where patients who survived their treatment in the hospital were moved for recuperation; it now houses the Institute for Catalan Studies. The walls of the forecourt are covered with brightly decorated scenes of the life of St. Paul in blue-and-yellow ceramic tiles; the story begins with the image to the left of the door to the inner courtyard, recounting the moment of the saint's conversion: "*Savle, Savle, quid me persegueris?*" ("Saul, Saul, why do you persecute me?"). The ceramicist, Llorenç Passolas, also designed the late 17th-century tiles around the inner patio. The image of St. Paul in the center of the pillared courtyard, over what was once a well, pays homage to the building's first benefactor, Pau Ferran. Look for the horseshoes, two of them around the keyholes, on the double wooden doors in the entryway: tokens of good luck for the afflicted who came here to recover—again, in reference to benefactor Ferran, from *ferro* (iron), as in *ferradura* (horseshoe).

Through a gate to the left of the Casa de Convalescència is the garden-courtyard of the hospital complex, the **Jardins de Rubió i Lluc,** centered on a baroque cross and lined with orange trees. On the right is the **Biblioteca de Catalunya** (✉ *Carrer de l'Hospital 56* ☎ *93/270–2300* ⊕ *www.bnc.cat* ⊙ *Weekdays 9–8, Sat. 9–2*), Catalonia's national library and—with some 2 million volumes in its collection—second only to Madrid's Biblioteca Nacional. The stairway under the arch, leading up to the library, was built in the 16th century; the Gothic well to the left of the arch is from the 15th century, as is the little Romeo-and-Juliet balcony in the corner to the left of the doors to the Escola Massana

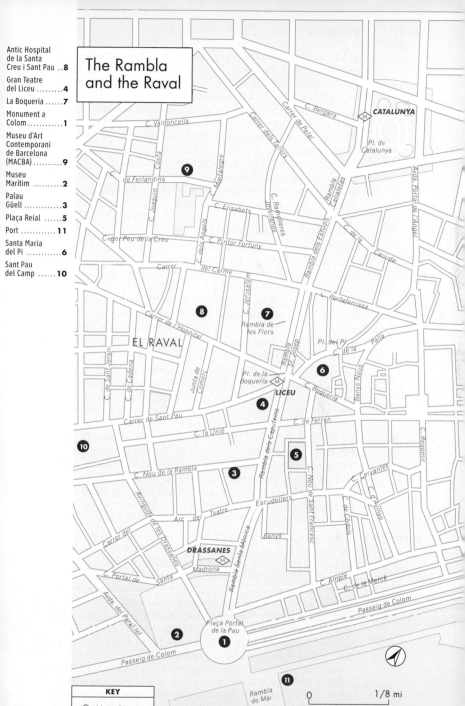

The Rambla and the Raval

C. Valdoncella

C. de Ferlandina

C. Joaquin

C. Costa

C. Montalegre

C. Elisabets

C. del Peu de la Creu

C. Pintor Fortuny

C. dels Àngels

Carrer   del Carme

Carrer de l'Hospital

EL RAVAL

C. de Sant Jeroni

C. de Cadena

Junta de Comerç

Carrer de Sant Pau

C. la Unió

C. Nou de la Rambla

Arc   de   Teatre

Carrer de

Avinguda de les Drassanes

C. Portal de   Santa

Avda. del Paral.lel

Passeig de Colom

Madrona

DRASSANES Ⓜ

Plaça Portal
de la Pau

Passeig de Colom

Rambla Santa Mònica

Escudellers

Banys

Rambla
de Mar

Rambla dels Caputxins

C. Jerusalem

Rambla dels Estudis

Rambla St. Josep

Rambla de
les Flors

Pl. de la
Boqueria

LICEU Ⓜ

C. de Ferran

C. Boqueria

Pl. del Pi

C. de la   Palla

Pl. del Pi

C. de la

Banys Nous

C. Nou de Sant Francesc

C. Cervantes

C. d'Avinyó

C. de Còdols

C. Ample

C. de la Mercé

C. Regomir

Carrer de Pelai

C. Bergara

Ⓜ **CATALUNYA**

Pl. de
Catalunya

Carrer dels Tallers

C. Ramalleres
Joveriianos

Rambla
Canaletas

C. de la   Canuda

Avda. Portal de l'Angel

C. Portaferrissa

❶ ❷ ❸ ❹ ❺ ❻ ❼ ❽ ❾ ❿ ⓫

academy of design. The library itself is spectacular: two parallel halls—once the core of the hospital—70 meters (230 feet) long, with towering Gothic arches and vaulted ceilings, designed in the 15th century by the architect of the church of Santa Maria del Pi, Guillem Abiell. This was the hospital where Antoni Gaudí was taken, unrecognized and assumed to be a pauper, after he was struck by a trolley on June 7, 1926. Among the library's collections are archives recording Gaudí's admittance and photographs of the infirmary and the private room where he died. The staggering antiquarian resources here go back to the earliest history of printing, and range from silver medieval book covers to illuminated manuscripts from the *Llibre Vermell* (*Red Book*) of medieval Catalonian liturgical music, to rare editions of Cervantes. (For free guided tours by appointment, contact Sr. Sergi Font at ☎ *93/270–2300, ext. 2123* or by email at ✉ *sfont@bcn.cat.*)

Leave the complex through the heavy wooden doors to Carrer Hospital, and turn left, towards La Rambla. The next set of doors leads to the **Capella** (Chapel) of the Hospital, an interesting art space well worth a visit. Built in the early 15th century, on the site of what had been the old Hospital de Colom (founded in 1219), it is now a showcase for promising young artists, chosen by a jury of prominent museum directors and given this impressive space, with its Romanesque tunnel vault and medieval arches, to exhibit their work (⊕ *www.bnc.cat/lacapella* ☉ *Tues.–Sat. 12–2 and 4–8, Sun. 11–2*).

In 1587 King Felip II granted the Hospital de Santa Creu i Sant Pau the privilege of mounting theatrical performances, the proceeds to be used to support its charitable work. In the early 17th century the Hospital built its own theater for this purpose (variously called the Casa de Comèdias or the Teatre de la Santa Creu); it was the city's sole venue for itinerant theater and opera companies until it burned down in 1787. Rebuilt, it kept its royal monopoly on entertainment in Barcelona until 1844, when Queen Isable II gave the Societat del Liceu permission to build a bigger, grander opera house on La Rambla. The Teatre de la Santa Creu became the Teatre Principal, and remained a rival to the Licea until it, too, burned down in 1915. ⊠ *Carrer Hospital 56 (or Carrer del Carme 45), El Raval* ☎ *93/270–2300* Ⓜ *Liceu.*

Fodor's Choice ★ **La Boqueria.** Barcelona's most spectacular food market, also known as the Mercat de Sant Josep, is an explosion of life and color graced with wonderful little tapas bar-restaurants (with counter seating only). Stall after stall of fruit, herbs, wild mushrooms, vegetables, nuts, candied preserves, cheese, ham, fish, poultry, and provender of every imaginable genus and strain greet you as you turn in from La Rambla and wade through the throng of shoppers and casual visitors. Under a Moderniste hangar of wrought-iron girders and stained glass, the market occupies a neoclassical square built in 1840 by architect Francesc Daniel Molina. The ionic columns visible around the edges of the market were part of the mid-19th-century neoclassical square constructed here after the original Sant Josep convent was torn down, uncovered in 2001 after more than a century of neglect. Highlights include the sunny greengrocer's market outside (to the right if you've come in from La Rambla), along with **Pinotxo** (Pinocchio), just inside to the right, where owner

Domènech i Montaner's Hospital de Sant Pau is the world's only Art Nouveau hospital.

Juanito Bayén and his family serve some of the best food in Barcelona. (The secret? "Fresh, fast, hot, salty, and garlicky.") Pinotxo—marked with a ceramic portrait of the wooden-nosed prevaricator himself—is typically overbooked. But take heart; the **Kiosko Universal,** over toward the port side of the market, or **Quim de la Boqueria** both offer delicious alternatives. Don't miss the herb- and wild-mushroom stand at the back of La Boqueria, with its display of *fruits del bosc* (fruits of the forest): wild mushrooms, herbs, nuts, and berries. ⊠ *La Rambla 91, Rambla* ⊕ *www.boqueria.info* ⊘ *Mon.–Sat. 8–8* Ⓜ *Liceu.*

Fodor's Choice
★
Museu d'Art Contemporani de Barcelona (*Barcelona Museum of Contemporary Art, MACBA*). Designed by American architect Richard Meier in 1992, this gleaming explosion of light and geometry in the darkest corner of El Raval houses a permanent collection of contemporary art, and regularly mounts special thematic exhibitions of works on loan. Meier gives a nod to Gaudí (with the Pedrera-like wave on one end of the main facade), but his minimalist building otherwise looks a bit like the scaffolding hadn't been taken down yet. That said, the MACBA is unarguably an important addition to the cultural capital of this once-shabby neighborhood. ⊠ *Pl. dels Àngels s/n, El Raval* ☎ *93/412–0810* ⊕ *www.macba.es* ☎ *€9* ⊘ *Mon. and Wed.–Fri. 11–7:30, Sat. 10–9, Sun. 10–3; free guided tours daily at 4 (Mon. at 4 and 6)* Ⓜ *Catalunya.*

FAMILY
Fodor's Choice
★
Museu Marítim. The superb Maritime Museum, which is currently under renovation, is housed in the 13th-century **Drassanes Reials** (Royal Ship-yards), at the foot of La Rambla adjacent to the harbor front. This vast covered complex launched the ships of Catalonia's powerful Mediterranean fleet directly from its yards into the port (the water once reached

the level of the eastern facade of the building). Today these are the world's largest and best-preserved medieval shipyards; centuries ago, at a time when Greece was a province of the House of Aragón (1377–88), they were of crucial importance to the sea power of Catalonia (then the heavyweight in an alliance with Aragón). On the Avinguda del Paral. lel side of Drassanes is a completely intact section of the 14th- to 15th-century walls—Barcelona's third and final ramparts—that encircled El Raval along the Paral.lel and the Rondas de Sant Pau, Sant Antoni, and Universitat. (*Ronda,* the term used for the "rounds" or patrols soldiers made atop the defensive walls, became the name for the avenues that replaced them.) The earliest part of Drassanes is the section farthest from the sea along Carrer de Portal de Santa Madrona. Subsequent naves were added in the 17th and 18th centuries.

Though the shipyards seem more like a cathedral than a naval construction site, the Maritime Museum is filled with vessels, including a spectacular collection of ship models. The life-size reconstruction of the galley of Juan de Austria, commander of the Spanish fleet in the Battle of Lepanto, is perhaps the most impressive display in the museum. ✉ *Av. de les Drassanes s/n, Rambla* ☎ *93/342–9920* ⊕ *www.mmb.cat* 🖃 *€3.50 (free Sun.)* ☻ *Daily 10–8* Ⓜ *Drassanes.*

Fodor'sChoice   **Palau Güell.** Gaudí built this mansion in 1886–89 for textile baron Count
★   Eusebi de Güell Bacigalupi, his most important patron. (The prominent four bars of the *senyera,* the banner of Catalunya, on the facade between the parabolic arches of the entrance attest to the nationalist fervor the two men shared.) Gaudí's principal obsession in this project was to find a way to illuminate this seven-story house, hemmed in as it is by other buildings in the cramped quarters of El Raval. The dark facade is a dramatic foil for the brilliance of the inside, where spear-shaped Art Nouveau columns frame the windows, rising to support a series of detailed and elaborately carved wood ceilings.

The basement stables are famous for the "fungiform" (mushroom-like) columns carrying the weight of the whole building. Note Gaudí's signature parabolic arches between the columns and the way the arches meet overhead, forming a canopy of palm fronds. (The beauty of the construction was probably little consolation to the political prisoners held here during the 1936–39 Civil War.) The patio where the horses were groomed receives light through a skylight, one of many devices Gaudí used to brighten the space. Don't miss the figures of the faithful hounds, with the rings in their mouths for hitching horses, or the wooden bricks laid down in lieu of cobblestones in the entryway upstairs and on the ramp down to the basement grooming area, to deaden the sound of horses' hooves. The chutes on the Carrer Nou de la Rambla side of the basement were for loading feed straight in from street level overhead; the catwalk and spiral staircase were for the servants to use, en route to their duties.

The dining room is dominated by a beautiful mahogany banquet table seating ten, an Art Nouveau fireplace in the shape of a deeply curving horseshoe arch, and walls with floral and animal motifs. Note the Star of David in the woodwork over the window and the Asian religious themes in the vases on the mantelpiece. From the outside rear terrace, the polished Garraf marble of the main part of the house is exposed; the brick servants' quarters are on the left. The passageway built toward La Rambla was all that came of a plan to buy an intervening property and connect three houses into one grand structure, a scheme that never materialized.

Gaudí is most himself on the roof, where his playful, polychrome ceramic chimneys seem like preludes to later works like the Park Güell and La Pedrera. Look for the flying-bat weather vane over the main chimney, a reference to the Catalan king Jaume I, who brought the house of Aragón to its 13th-century imperial apogee in the Mediterranean. Jaume I's affinity for bats is said to have stemmed from his Mallorca campaign, when, according to one version, he was awakened by a fluttering *rat penat* (literally, "condemned mouse") in time to stave off a Moorish night attack. Another version attributes the presence of the bat in Jaume I's coat of arms to his gratitude to the Sufi sect that helped him to successfully invade Mallorca, using the bat as a signal indicating when and where to attack. See if you can find the hologram of COBI, Javier Mariscal's 1992 Olympic mascot, on a restored ceramic chimney (hint: the all-white one at the Rambla end of the roof terrace). ⊠ *Nou de la Rambla 3–5, Rambla* ☎ *93/472–5775* ⊕ *palauguell.cat/come-palace* ⊠ *€12* ⊙ *Apr.–Oct., Tues.–Sun. 10–8; Nov.–Mar., Tues.–Sun. 10–5:30* Ⓜ *Drassanes, Liceu.*

Plaça Reial. Nobel Prize–winning novelist Gabriel García Márquez, architect and urban planner Oriol Bohigas, and Pasqual Maragall, former president of the Catalonian Generalitat, are among the many famous people said to have acquired apartments overlooking this elegant square, a chiaroscuro masterpiece in which neoclassical symmetry clashes with big-city street funk. Plaça Reial is bordered by stately ocher facades with balconies overlooking the wrought-iron **Fountain of the Three Graces,** and an array of lampposts designed by Gaudí in 1879. Cafés and restaurants—several of them excellent—line the square. Plaça Reial is most colorful on Sunday morning, when collectors gather to trade stamps and coins; after dark it's a center of downtown nightlife for the jazz-minded, the young, and the adventurous (it's best to be streetwise touring this area in the late hours). Bar Glaciar, on the uphill corner toward La Rambla, is a booming beer station for young international travelers. Tarantos has top flamenco performances, and Jamboree offers world-class jazz. ⊠ *Rambla* Ⓜ *Liceu.*

Fodor's Choice
★ **Sant Pau del Camp.** Barcelona's oldest church was originally outside the city walls (*del camp* means "in the fields") and was a Roman cemetery as far back as the 2nd century, according to archaeological evidence. A Visigothic belt buckle found in the 20th century confirmed that Visigoths used the site as a cemetery between the 2nd and 7th centuries. What you see now was built in 1127 and is the earliest Romanesque structure in Barcelona. Elements of the church—the classical marble capitals atop the columns in the main entry—are thought to be from the 6th and 7th centuries. Sant Pau is bulky and solid, featureless (except for what may be the smallest stained-glass window in Europe, high on the facade facing Carrer Sant Pau), with stone walls three feet thick

and more; medieval Catalan churches and monasteries were built to be refuges for the body as well as the soul, bulwarks of last resort against Moorish invasions—or mauraders of any persuasion. Check local events listings carefully for musical performances here; the church is an acoustical gem. (Rebecca Ryan's Mercyhurst Madrigal Singers sang American composer Horatio Parker's "Lord We Beseech Thee" here in 2009.) ⊠ *Sant Pau 99, El Raval* ☎ *93/441–0001* 🖼 *Cloister €3* 🕙 *Cloister: Mon.–Sat. 10–1:30 and 4–7, Sun. Mass at 10:30, 12:30, and 8* Ⓜ *Paral.lel.*

Santa Maria del Pi (*St. Mary of the Pine*). Sister church to Santa Maria del Mar and to Santa Maria de Pedralbes, this early Catalan Gothic structure is perhaps the most fortresslike of all three: hulking, dark, and massive, and perforated only by the main entryway and the mammoth rose window, said to be the world's largest. Try to see the window from inside in the late afternoon to get the best view of the colors. The church was named for the lone *pi* (pine tree) that stood in what was a marshy lowland outside the 4th-century Roman walls. An early church dating back to the 10th century preceded the present Santa Maria del Pi, which was begun in 1322 and finally consecrated in 1453. The interior compares poorly with the clean and lofty lightness of Santa Maria del Mar, but there are two interesting things to see: the original wooden choir loft, and the Ramón Amadeu painting *La Mare de Deu dels Desamparats* (*Our Lady of the Helpless*), in which the artist reportedly used his wife and children as models for the Virgin and children.

The adjoining squares, **Plaça del Pi** and **Plaça de Sant Josep Oriol,** are two of the liveliest and most appealing spaces in the Old Quarter, filled with much-frequented outdoor cafés and used as a venue for markets selling natural products or paintings, or as an impromptu concert hall for musicians. The handsome entryway and courtyard at Plaça de Sant Josep Oriol 4 across from the lateral facade of Santa Maria del Pi is the **Palau Fivaller,** now seat of the Agricultural Institute, an interesting patio to have a look through. ⊠ *Pl. del Pi 7, Rambla* ☎ *93/318–4743* 🖼 *€3 (visits to the basilica only are free 9:30–11 am and 6–8:30 pm)* 🕙 *Museum and basilica weekdays 11–6, Sat. 11–3, Sun. 4–8* Ⓜ *Liceu.*

WORTH NOTING

Fodor's Choice ★ **Gran Teatre del Liceu.** Barcelona's opera house has long been considered one of the most beautiful in Europe, a rival to Milan's La Scala. First built in 1848, this cherished cultural landmark was torched in 1861, later bombed by anarchists in 1893, and once again gutted by an accidental fire in early 1994. During that most recent fire, Barcelona's soprano Montserrat Caballé stood on La Rambla in tears as her beloved venue was consumed. Five years later, a restored Liceu, equipped for modern productions, opened anew. Even if you don't see an opera, don't miss a tour of the building; some of the Liceu's most spectacular halls and rooms, including the glittering foyer known as the Saló dels Miralls (Room of Mirrors), were untouched by the fire of 1994, as were those of Spain's oldest social club, El Círculo del Liceu. ⊠ *La Rambla 51–59, Rambla* ☎ *93/485–9914, 93/485–9900 for backstage tour reservations* ✎ *visites@liceubarcelona.cat* ⊕ *www.liceubarcelona. cat* 🖼 *Guided tours weekdays €11.50, Sat. and Sun. €10.50, 20-min.*

express tour €5.50 ☉ *Tours daily at 10 am in Spanish and English; guided express tours daily at 11:30, noon, 12:30, and 1 pm. Backstage tours in Spanish at 9 am, including wardrobe and dressing rooms (€12.50), by reservation only* Ⓜ *Liceu.*

Monument a Colom (*Columbus Monument*). This Barcelona landmark to Christopher Columbus sits grandly at the foot of La Rambla along the wide harbor-front promenade of Passeig de Colom, not far from the very shipyards (**Drassanes Reials**) that constructed two of the ships of his tiny but immortal fleet. Standing atop the 150-foot-high iron column—the base of which is aswirl with gesticulating angels—Columbus seems to be looking out at "that far-distant shore" he discovered; in fact he's pointing, with his 18-inch-long finger, in the general direction of Sicily. The monument was erected for the 1888 Universal Exposition to commemorate the commissioning of Columbus's voyage, in Barcelona, by the monarchs Ferdinand and Isabella, in 1491. Since the royal court was at that time (and, until 1561, remained) itinerant, Barcelona's role in the discovery of the New World is, at best, circumstantial. In fact, Barcelona was consequently excluded from trade with the Americas by Isabella, so Catalonia and Columbus have never really seen eye to eye. ✉ *Portal de la Pau s/n, Rambla* ☎ *93/285–3832* 💲 *€4* ☉ *Mar.–Oct., daily 8:30–8:30; Nov.–Feb., daily 8:30–7:30* Ⓜ *Drassanes.*

Port. Beyond the Columbus monument—behind the ornate Duana (now the Barcelona Port Authority headquarters)—is **Rambla de Mar,** a boardwalk with a drawbridge designed to allow boats into and out of the inner harbor. Rambla de Mar extends out to the **Moll d'Espanya,** with its Maremagnum shopping center, IMAX theater, and the excellent **Aquarium.** Next to the Duana you can board a Golondrina boat for a tour of the port and the waterfront or, from the Moll de Barcelona on the right, take a cable car to Montjuïc or Barceloneta. Trasmediterránea and the fleeter Buquebus passenger ferries leave for Italy and the Balearic Islands from the Moll de Barcelona; at the end of the quay is Barcelona's World Trade Center and the Eurostars Grand Marina Hotel. Ⓜ *Drassanes.*

CIUTAT VELLA: BARRI GÒTIC AND BORN-RIBERA

No city in Europe has an ancient quarter to rival Barcelona's Barri Gòtic in its historic atmosphere and the sheer density of its monumental buildings. It's a stroller's delight, where you can expect to hear the strains of a flute or a classical guitar from around the next corner. The Barri Gòtic comprises the area around the Catedral de la Seu and rests squarely atop the first Roman settlement. This high ground the Romans called Mons Taber coincides almost exactly with the early 1st- to 4th-century fortified town of Barcino. Sights to see here include the Plaça del Rei, the remains of Roman Barcino underground beneath the Museum of the History of the City, the Plaça Sant Jaume and the area around the onetime Roman Forum, the medieval Jewish Quarter, and the ancient Plaça Sant Just.

Across Via Laietana is the Barri de la Ribera, or Born-Ribera, once the waterfront district around the basilica of Santa Maria del Mar.

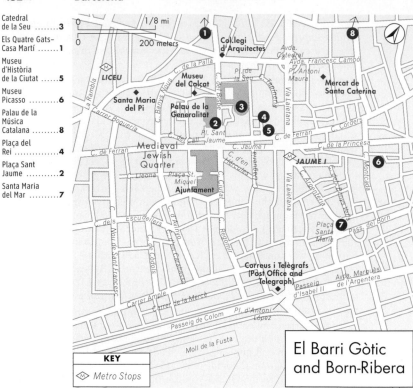

El Barri Gòtic
and Born-Ribera

KEY

Metro Stops

The Born-Ribera includes Carrer Montcada, lined with 14th- to 18th-century Renaissance palaces; Passeig del Born, where medieval jousts were held; Carrer Flassaders and the area around the early mint; the shop- and restaurant-rich Carrer Banys Vells; Plaça de les Olles; and Pla del Palau, where La Llotja, Barcelona's early maritime exchange, housed the fine-arts school where Picasso, Gaudí, and Domènech i Montaner all studied, as did many more of Barcelona's most important artists and architects.

Long a depressed neighborhood, La Ribera began to experience a revival in the 1980s; liberally endowed now with intimate bars, cafés, and trendy boutiques, it continues to enjoy the blessings of gentrification. An open excavation in the center of El Born, the onetime market restored as a multipurpose cultural center, offers a fascinating view of pre-1714 Barcelona, dismantled by the victorious troops of Felipe V at the end of the War of the Spanish Succession. The Passeig del Born, La Rambla of medieval Barcelona, is once again a pleasant leafy promenade.

TOP ATTRACTIONS

Fodor's Choice **Museu d'Història de la Ciutat** (*Museum of the History of the City*). This
★ fascinating museum (MUHBA for short) just off Plaça del Rei traces Barcelona's evolution from its first Iberian settlement through its

Roman and Visigothic ages and beyond. Antiquity is the focus here: the Romans took the city during the Punic Wars, and the striking underground remains of their Colonia Favencia Julia Augusta Paterna Barcino (Favored Colony of the Father Julius Augustus Barcino), through which you can roam on metal walkways, are the museum's main treasure. Archaeological finds include the walls of houses, mosaics and fluted columns, and workshops (for pressing olive oil and salted fish paste), marble busts, and funerary urns. Especially fascinating is to see how the Visgoths and their descendents built the early medieval walls on top of these ruins, recycling whatever came to hand: chunks of Roman stone and concrete, bits of columns—even headstones. The price of admission to the museum includes entry to the other treasures of the **Plaça del Rei,** including the **Palau Reial Major,** the splendid **Saló del Tinell,** and the chapel of **Santa Àgata.** ⊠ *Palau Padellàs, Carrer del Veguer 2, Barri Gòtic* ☎ *93/256–2122* ⊕ *www.museuhistoria. bcn.cat* ⊠ *€7, includes admission to Monestir de Pedralbes, Centre d'Interpretació del Park Güell, Centre d'Interpretació del Call, Centre d'Interpretació Històrica, Refugi 307, and Museu-Casa Verdaguer (free with the Barcelona Card, and Sun. after 3)* ☉ *Tues.–Sat. 10–7, Sun. 10–8* Ⓜ *Catalunya, Liceu, Jaume I.*

Fodor's Choice **Museu Picasso** (*Picasso Museum*). This museum focused on the works
★ of famous Spanish artist Pablo Picasso is housed in five adjoining palaces on Carrer Montcada, a street known for Barcelona's most elegant medieval palaces. Picasso spent his key formative years in Barcelona (1895–1904), and this collection, while it does not include a significant number of his best paintings, is particularly strong on his early work. The museum was begun in 1962 on the suggestion of Picasso's crony Jaume Sabartés, and the initial donation was from the Sabartés collection. Later Picasso donated his early works, and in 1981 his widow, Jaqueline Roque, added 141 pieces.

Displays include childhood sketches, works from the artist's Rose and Blue periods, and the famous 1950s Cubist variations on Velázquez's *Las Meninas* (in Rooms 22–26). The lower-floor sketches, oils, and schoolboy caricatures and drawings from Picasso's early years in La Coruña are perhaps the most fascinating part of the whole museum, showing the facility the artist seemed to possess almost from the cradle. His *La Primera Communión* (*First Communion*), painted at the age of 16, gives an idea of his early accomplishment. On the second floor you see the beginnings of the mature Picasso and his Blue Period in Paris, a time of loneliness, cold, and hunger for the artist. ⊠ *Carrer Montcada 15–19, Born-Ribera* ☎ *93/319–6310* ⊕ *www.museupicasso. bcn.cat* ⊠ *€11 (free 1st Sun. of month, free Sun. 3–8)* ☉ *Tues.–Sun. 10–8* Ⓜ *Jaume I.*

QUICK
BITES
Mercat de Santa Caterina. This marketplace, a splendid carnival of colors with a roller-coaster rooftop, was restored by the late Enric Miralles, whose widow Benedetta Tagliabue finished the project in 2005. Undulating wood and colored-ceramic mosaic ceilings redolent of both Gaudí and Miró cover a bustling and dramatically illuminated market with an

excellent restaurant, Cuines de Santa Caterina (☎ *93/268–9918*), and several good bars and cafés. The archeological section of the building is at the eastern end, showing Visigothic remains and sections of the 13th-century church and convent that stood here until the early 18th century. ⊠ *Av. Francesc Cambó s/n, Born-Ribera* ⊕ *www. mercatsantacaterina.com* Ⓜ *Jaume I, Urquinaona.*

> **WATCH YOUR STUFF**
>
> While muggings are practically unheard of in Barcelona, petty thievery is common. Handbags, backpacks, camera cases, and wallets are favorite targets, so tuck those away. Should you carry a purse, use one with a short strap that tucks tightly under your arm.

Fodor's Choice ★ **Palau de la Música Catalana.** On Carrer Amadeus Vives, just off Via Laietana, a 10-minute walk from Plaça de Catalunya, is one of the world's most extraordinary music halls. From its polychrome ceramic tile ticket windows on Carrer de Sant Pere Més Alt side to the row overhead of busts of (from left to right) Palestrina, Bach, Beethoven, and—around the corner on Carrer Amadeus Vives—Wagner, the Palau is a flamboyant tour de force, a riot of color and form designed in 1908 by Lluís Domènech i Montaner. It was meant by its sponsors, the Orfeó Català musical society, to celebrate the importance of music in Catalan culture and the life of its ordinary people (as opposed to the Liceu opera house, with its Castilian-speaking, monarchist upper-class patrons, and its music from elsewhere), but the Palau turned out to be anything but commonplace; it and the Liceu were for many decades opposing crosstown forces in Barcelona's musical as well as philosophical discourse. If you can't fit a performance into your itinerary, you owe it to yourself to at least take a tour of this amazing building.

The exterior is remarkable. The Miquel Blay sculptural group over the corner of Amadeu Vives and Sant Pere Més Alt is a hymn in stone to Catalonia's popular traditions, with hardly a note left unsung: St. George the dragon slayer (at the top), women and children at play and work, fishermen with oars over their shoulders—a panoply of everyday life. (The glass facade over the present ticket-window entrance is one of the city's best examples of nonintrusive modern construction wedded to heritage from the past.) Inside, the decor of the Palau assaults your senses before the first note of music is ever heard. Wagner's Valkyrie burst from the right side of the stage over a heavy-browed bust of Beethoven; Catalonia's popular music is represented by the graceful maidens of Lluís Millet's song "Flors de Maig" ("Flowers of May") on the left. Overhead, an inverted stained-glass cupola seems to channel the divine gift of music straight from heaven; painted rosettes and giant peacock feathers adorn the walls and columns; across the entire back wall of the stage is a relief of muselike Art Nouveau musicians in costume. ⊠ *Carrer Sant Pere Més Alt 4–6, Sant Pere* ☎ *93/295–7200* ⊕ *www.palaumusica.org* 🎫 *Tour €17* ☉ *Sept.–June, tours (every 30 mins) daily 10–3:30; July and Aug., tours daily 10–7* Ⓜ *Urquinaona.*

Fodor's Choice
★
Plaça del Rei. This little square is as compact a nexus of history as anything the Gothic Quarter has to offer. Long held to be the scene of Columbus's triumphal return from his first voyage to the New World—the precise spot where Ferdinand and Isabella received him is purportedly on the stairs fanning out from the corner of the square (though evidence indicates that the Catholic monarchs were at a summer residence in the Empordá)—the **Palau Reial Major** was the official royal residence in Barcelona. The main room is the **Saló del Tinell,** a magnificent banquet hall built in 1362. To the left is the **Palau del Lloctinent** (Lieutenant's Palace); towering overhead in the corner is the dark 15th-century **Torre Mirador del Rei Martí** (King Martin's Watchtower). The 14th-century **Capilla Reial de Santa Àgueda** (Royal Chapel of St. Agatha) is on the right side of the stairway, and behind and to the right as you face the stairs is the **Palau Clariana-Padellàs,** moved to this spot stone by stone from Carrer Mercaders in the early 20th century and now the entrance to the **Museu d'Història de la Ciutat.** ⊠ *Barri Gòtic* Ⓜ *Liceu, Jaume I.*

Plaça Sant Jaume. Facing each other across this oldest epicenter of Barcelona (and often politically on opposite sides as well) are the seat of Catalonia's regional government, the Generalitat de Catalunya, in the **Palau de La Generalitat,** and the City Hall, the Ayuntamiento de Barcelona, in the **Casa de la Ciutat.** Just east of the Cathedral, this square was the site of the Roman forum 2,000 years ago, though subsequent construction filled the space with buildings. The square was cleared in the 1840s; the two imposing government buildings facing each other across it are much older: the Ayuntamiento dates to the 14th century; the Generalitat was built between the 15th and mid-17th centuries. ⊠ *Pl. Sant Jaume, Barri Gòtic* ⊕ *www.bcn.es* ☉ *Guided tours of the Ayuntamiento (in English) weekends at 11 am; tours of the Generalitat, 2nd and 4th weekends every month 10:30 am–1 pm, by reservation only.* Ⓜ *Jaume I.*

Fodor's Choice
★
Santa Maria del Mar. The most beautiful example of early Catalan Gothic architecture, Santa Maria del Mar is extraordinary for its unbroken lines and elegance. The lightness of the interior is especially surprising considering the blocky exterior. The site, originally outside the 1st- to 4th-century Roman walls at what was then the water's edge, was home to a Christian cult from the late 3rd century. Built by stonemasons who chose, fitted, and carved each stone hauled down from the same Montjuïc quarry that provided the sandstone for the 4th-century Roman walls, Santa Maria del Mar is breathtakingly and nearly hypnotically symmetrical.

Ironically, the church owes its present form to the anticlerical fury of anarchists who, on July 18, 1936, burned nearly all of Barcelona's churches as a reprisal against the alliance of army, church, and oligarchy during the military rebellion. The basilica, filled with ornate side chapels and choir stalls, burned for 11 days, and nearly crumbled as a result of the heat. Restored after the end of the Civil War by a series of Bauhaus-trained architects, Santa Maria del Mar has become one of the city's most universally admired architectural gems.

The paintings in the keystones overhead represent, from the front, the Coronation of the Virgin, the Nativity, the Annunciation, the equestrian figure of the father of Pedro IV, King Alfons, and the Barcelona coat of arms. The 34 lateral chapels are dedicated to different saints and images. The first chapel to the left of the altar (No. 20) is the Capella del Santo Cristo (Chapel of the Holy Christ), its stained-glass window an allegory of Barcelona's 1992 Olympic Games, complete with names of medalists and key personalities of the day in tiny letters. An engraved stone riser to the left of the side door onto Carrer Sombrerers commemorates the spot where San Ignacio de Loyola, founder of the Jesuit Order, begged for alms in 1524 and 1525.

Set aside at least a half hour to see Santa Maria del Mar. *La Catedral del Mar* (*The Cathedral of the Sea*) by Ildefonso Falcons chronicles the construction of the basilica and 14th-century life in Barcelona. Check the leisure announcements in the weekly magazines for concerts in the basilica; the setting and the acoustics here make the performance of the Mozart Requiem, for example, an unforgettable experience. ⊠ *Pl. de Santa Maria, Born-Ribera* ☎ *93/3102390* ☉ *Mon.–Sat. 9–1:30 and 4:30–8, Sun. 10:30–1:30 and 4:30–8* Ⓜ *Jaume I.*

WORTH NOTING

Fodor's Choice
★

Catedral de la Seu. Barcelona's cathedral is a repository of centuries of the city's history and legend—although as a work of architecture visitors might find it a bit of a disappointment, compared to the Mediterranean Gothic Santa Maria del Mar and Gaudí's Moderniste Sagrada Família. It was built between 1298 and 1450; work on the spire and neo-Gothic facade began in 1892 and was not completed until 1913. Historians are not sure about the identity of the architect: one name often proposed is Jaume Fabre, a native of Mallorca. The plan of the church is cruciform, with transepts standing in as bases for the great tower—a design also seen in England's Exeter Cathedral. The building is perhaps most impresssive at night, floodlit with the stained-glass windows illuminated from inside; book a room with a balcony at the Hotel Colon, facing the Cathedral square, and make the most of it.

This is reputedly the darkest of all the world's great cathedrals—even at high noon the nave is enveloped in shadows, which give it magically much larger dimensions than it actually has—so it takes a while for your eyes to adjust to the rich, velvety pitch of the interior. Don't miss the beautifully carved choir stalls of the Knights of the Golden Fleece; the intricately and elaborately sculpted organ loft over the door out to Plaça Sant Iu (with its celebrated *Saracen's Head* sculpture); the series of 60-odd wood sculptures of evangelical figures along the exterior lateral walls of the choir; the cloister with its fountain and geese in the pond; and, in the crypt, the tomb of Santa Eulàlia.

St. Eulàlia, originally interred at Santa Maria del Mar—then known as Santa Maria de les Arenes (St. Mary of the Sands)—was moved to the cathedral in 1339, and venerated here as its patron and protector. *Eulalistas* (St. Eulàlia devotees, rivals of a sort to the followers of La Mercé, or Our Lady of Mercy) celebrate the fiesta of La Laia (the nickname for Eulàlia) February 9–15, and would like to see the cathedral named for her, but for the moment it is known simply as La Catedral, or in Catalan *La Seu* (the See, or seat of the bishopric).

Enter from the front portal (there are also entrances through the cloister and from Carrer Comtes down the left side of the apse), and the first thing you see are the high-relief sculptures of the **story of St. Eulàlia,** on the near side of the choir stalls. The first scene, on the left, shows St. Eulàlia in front of Roman Consul Decius with her left hand on her heart and her outstretched right hand pointing at a cross in the distance. In the next, she is tied to a column and being whipped by the Consol's thugs. To the right of the door into the choir the unconscious Eulàlia is being hauled away, and in the final scene on the right she is being lashed to the X-shaped cross upon which she was crucified in mid-February in the year 303. To the right of this high relief is a sculpture of the martyred heroine, resurrected as a living saint.

Among the two-dozen ornate and gilded chapels in the basilica, pay due attention to the **Capilla de Lepanto,** dedicated to Santo Cristo de Lepanto, in the far right corner as you enter through the front door. According to legend, the 15th-century polychrome wood sculpture of a battle-scarred, dark-skinned Christ, visible on the altar of this 100-seat chapel behind a black-clad Mare de Deu dels Dolors (Our Lady of the Sorrows), was the bowsprit of the flagship Spanish galley at the battle fought between Christian and Ottoman fleets on October 7, 1571. (A plaque next to the alms box of the chapel notes that, though John of Austria was the commander in chief, the captain who led the fleet into battle was Lluís de Requesens, a Catalan aristocrat and prominent Spanish general during the reign of Felipe II.

Outside the main nave of the cathedral to the right, you'll find the leafy, palm tree–shaded **cloister** surrounding a tropical garden, and a pool populated by 13 snow-white geese, one for each of the tortures inflicted upon St. Eulàlia in an effort to break her faith. Legend has it that they are descendants of the flock of geese from Rome's Capitoline Hill, whose honking alarms roused the city to repel invaders during the days of the Roman Republic. Don't miss the fountain with the bronze sculpture of an equestrian St. George, hacking away at his perennial foe, the dragon, on the eastern corner of the cloister. On the day of Corpus Christi, this fountain is one of the more spectacular displays of the traditional *ou com balla* ("dancing egg"). The intimate **Santa Llúcia chapel** is at the front right corner of the block (reached by a separate entrance or from the cloister). Another Decius victim, St. Llúcia allegedly plucked out her own eyes to dampen the Roman consul's ardor, whereupon she miraculously generated new ones. Patron saint of seamstresses, of the blind, and of the light of human understanding, St. Llúcia is portrayed over the altar in the act of presenting her plucked-out eyes, sunny-side up on a plate, to an impassive Decius.

In front of the cathedral is the grand square of **Plaça de la Seu,** where on Saturday from 6 pm to 8 pm, Sunday morning, and occasional evenings, barcelonins gather to dance the *sardana,* the circular folk dance performed for centuries as a symbol-in-motion of Catalan identity and the solidarity of the Catalan people. ⊠ *Pl. de la Seu s/n, Barri*

Gòtic ☎ *93/315–1554* ⊕ *www.catedralbcn.org* ☜ *Free 8–12:45 and 5:15–7:30, €6 1–5 pm* ☉ *Daily 8 am–7:30 pm* Ⓜ *Jaume I.*

Els Quatre Gats–Casa Martí. Built by Josep Puig i Cadafalch for the Martí family, this Art Nouveau house, a three-minute walk from the cathedral, was the fountainhead of Bohemianism in Barcelona. It was here in 1897 that four friends, notable dandies all—Ramon Casas, Pere Romeu, Santiago Russinyol and Miguel Utrillo—started a café-restaurant called the Quatre Gats (Four Cats), meaning to make it *the* place for artists and art lovers to gather and shoot the breeze, in the best Left Bank tradition. (One of their wisest decisions was to mount a show, in February 1900, for an up-and-coming young painter named Pablo Picasso, who had done the illustration for the cover of the menu.) The exterior was decorated with figures by sculptor Eusebi Arnau (1864–1934), a darling of the Moderniste movement—notice the wrought-iron St. George and the dragon, that no Puig i Cadafalch project ever failed to include, over the door. Inside, the Four Cats hasn't changed an iota: the tile and stained glass are as they were; the bar is at it was; the walls are hung with copies of work by the original owners and their circle. (Pride of place goes to the Casas self-portait, smoking his pipe, comedically teamed up on a tandem bicycle with Romeu.) Drop in for a break: Who knows? You might be taking your café au lait in Picasso's chair. ⊠ *Carrer Montsió 3 bis, Barri Gòtic* ☎ *93/302–4140* ⊕ *www.4gats.com* ☉ *Daily 10 am–1 am* Ⓜ *Catalunya.*

BARCELONETA AND LA CIUTADELLA

Barceloneta and La Ciutadella make a historical fit. In the early 18th century, some 1,000 houses in the Barrio de la Ribera, then the waterfront neighborhood around Plaça del Born, were ordered torn down, to create fields of fire for the cannon of La Ciutadella, the newly built fortress that kept watch over the rebellious Catalans. Barceloneta, then a wetland, was developed almost four decades later, in 1753, to house families who had lost homes in La Ribera.

Open water in Roman times and gradually silted in only after the 15th-century construction of the port, it became Barcelona's fishermen's and stevedores' quarter. With its tiny original apartment blocks, and its history of seafarers, Barceloneta even now maintains its carefree flavor.

TOP ATTRACTIONS

Barceloneta. Once Barcelona's pungent fishing port, Barceloneta retains much of its salty maritime flavor, even as it undergoes a long-overdue gentrification. Stop in Plaça de la Barceloneta to see the baroque church of **Sant Miquel del Port,** with its oversize sculpture of the winged archangel. Look for the splendidly remodeled Barceloneta market and its upstairs and downstairs restaurants, Lluçanès and Els Fogons de la Barceloneta. The original two-story houses and the restaurant Can Solé on Carrer Sant Carles are historic landmarks. Barceloneta's surprisingly clean and sandy **beach,** though overcrowded in midsummer, offers swimming, surfing, and a lively social scene late May through September.

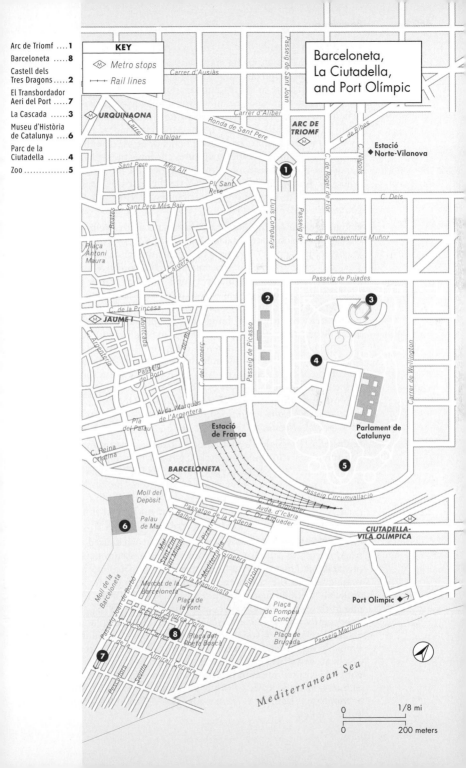

KEY

◈ Metro stops

←——→ Rail lines

Barceloneta, La Ciutadella, and Port Olímpic

Passeig de Sant Joan

Carrer d'Ausiàs

Carrer d'Alibei

Ronda de Sant Pere

◈ URQUINAONA

Carrer de Trafalgar

ARC DE TRIOMF Ⓜ

C. de Bribes

C. de Nàpols

Estació ◆ Norte-Vilanova

Sant Pere Més Alt

Pl. Sant Pere

C. de Roger de Flor

❶

C. Dels

Fusina

C. Sant Pere Més Baix

Lluis Companys

Passeig de

C. de Buenaventura Muñoz

Plaça Antoni Maura

Carders

C. de la Princesa

Passeig de Pujades

◈ JAUME I

Montcada

C. Argenteria

❷

❸

Passeig de Picasso

❹

Carrer de Wellington

Passeig del Born

C. del Comerç

Avda. Marquès de l'Argentera

Pla del Palau

Estació de França

Parlament de Catalunya

C. Reina Cristina

BARCELONETA

❺

Ⓜ

Passeig Circumvallacio

Moll del Depòsit

C. Dr. Aiguader

Avda. d'Icària

C. Dr. Aiguader

Palau de Mar

❻

C. Balboa

Passatge de la Cadena

CIUTADELLA-VILA OLÍMPICA

Ⓜ

Mar

Sant Elm

Sant Miquel

C. de Ginebra

Moll de la Barceloneta

Passeig Joan de Borbó

Mercat de la Barceloneta

C. de la Maquinista

Pinzon

Port Olímpic ◆ →

Plaça de la Font

C. Andrea Doria

Plaça de Pompeu Gener

Passeig Marítim

Plaça del Poeta Boscà

❽

Plaça de Brugada

Escuder

❼

Almirall Cervera

Mediterranean Sea

⊕

0 ——— 1/8 mi

0 ——— 200 meters

WORTH NOTING

Arc de Triomf. This imposing, exposed-redbrick arch was built by Josep Vilaseca as the grand entrance for the 1888 Universal Exhibition. Similar in size and sense to the traditional triumphal arches of ancient Rome, this one refers to no specific military triumph anyone can recall. In fact, Catalunya's last military triumph of note may have been Jaume I el Conqueridor's 1229 conquest of the Moors in Mallorca—as suggested by the bats (always part of Jaume I's coat of arms) on either side of the arch itself. The Josep Reynés sculptures adorning the structure represent Barcelona hosting visitors to the exhibition on the west (front) side, while the Josep Llimona sculptures on the east side depict the prizes being given to its outstanding contributors. ✉ *Passeig de Sant Joan, La Ciutadella* Ⓜ *Arc de Triomf.*

El Transbordador Aeri del Port (*cable car*). This hair-raising cable-car ride over the Barcelona harbor from Barceloneta to Montjuïc (with a midway stop in the port) is spectacular—an adrenaline rush with a view. The rush comes from being packed in with 18 other people, standing-room only, in a tiny gondola swaying a hundred feet or so above the Mediterranean. The cable car leaves from the tower at the end of Passeig Joan de Borbó and connects the Torre de San Sebastián on the Moll de Barceloneta, the tower of Jaume I in the port boat terminal, and the Torre de Miramar on Montjuïc. Critics maintain, not without reason, that the ride is expensive, not very cool, and actually pretty scary. On the positive side, this is undoubtedly the slickest way to connect Barceloneta and Montjuïc, and the Torre de Altamar restaurant in the tower at the Barceloneta end serves excellent food and wine. ✉ *Passeig Joan de Borbó s/n, Barceloneta* ☎ *93/225–2718, 93/430–4716* 💶 *€16.50 round-trip, €11 one-way* ☉ *Sep.–June, daily 11–7; Jul. and Aug., daily 11–8* Ⓜ *Barceloneta.*

La Cascada. The sights and sounds of Barcelona seem far away when you stand near this monumental, slightly overdramatized creation by Josep Fontseré, presented as part of the 1888 Universal Exhibition. The waterfall's somewhat overwrought rocks were the work of a young architecture student named Antoni Gaudí—his first public work, appropriately natural and organic, and certainly a hint of things to come. ✉ *Parc de la Ciutadella, Ciutadella* Ⓜ *Arc de Triomf.*

Museu d'Història de Catalunya. Established in what used to be a port warehouse, this state-of-the-art interactive museum makes you part of Catalonian history from prehistoric times through more than 3,000 years and into the contemporary democratic era. After centuries of "official" Catalan history dictated from Madrid (from 1714 until the mid-19th century Renaixença, and from 1939 to 1975), this offers an opportunity to revisit Catalonia's autobiography. Explanations of the exhibits appear in Catalan, Castilian, and English. Guided tours are available on Sunday at noon and 1 pm. The rooftop restaurant has excellent views over the harbor and is open to the public (whether or not you visit the museum itself) during museum hours. ✉ *Pl. Pau Vila 3, Barceloneta* ☎ *93/2254700* ⊕ *www.mhcat.net* 💶 *€4 (free 1st Sun. of month)* ☉ *Tues. and Thurs.–Sat. 10–7, Wed. 10–8, Sun. 10–2:30* Ⓜ *Barceloneta.*

FAMILY **Parc de la Ciutadella** (*Citadel Park*). Once a fortress designed to consolidate Madrid's military occupation of Barcelona, the Ciutadella is now the city's main downtown park. The clearing dates from shortly after the War of the Spanish Succession in the early 18th century, when Felipe V demolished some 1,000 houses in what was then the Barri de la Ribera to build a fortress and barracks for his soldiers and a *glacis,* or open space, between rebellious Barcelona and his artillery positions. The fortress walls were pulled down in 1868 and replaced by gardens laid out by Josep Fontseré. In 1888 the park was the site of the Universal Exposition that put Barcelona on the map as a truly European city; today it is home to the Castell dels Tres Dragons, built by architect Lluís Domènech i Montaner as the café and restaurant for the exposition (the only building to survive that project, now a botanical research center), the Catalan parliament, and the city zoo. ⊠ *Ciutadella* Ⓜ *Barceloneta, Arc de Triomf, Ciutadella–Vila Olímpica.*

FAMILY **Zoo.** Barcelona's excellent zoo occupies the whole eastern end of the Parc de la Ciutadella. There's a superb reptile house and a full assortment of African animals. The dolphin show usually plays to a packed house. ⊠ *Parc de la Ciutadella, Ciutadella* ☎ *93/2256780* ⊕ *www. zoobarcelona.cat* ⊠ *€19.60* ☉ *Winter, daily 10–5:30; summer, daily 10–8* Ⓜ *Ciutadella–Vila Olímpica, Barceloneta.*

EIXAMPLE

7

Barcelona's most famous neighborhood, this late 19th-century urban development is known for its dazzling Art Nouveau architecture. Called the "Expansion" in Catalan, the Eixample (ay-*shom*-pla) is an open-air Modernist museum. Designed as a grid, in the best Cartesian tradition, the Eixample is oddly difficult to find your way around in; the builders neglected to number the buildings or alphabetize the streets, and even Barcelona residents can get lost in it. The grid was the work of engineer Ildefons Cerdà, and much of the construction was done in the peak years of the Moderniste movement by a who's who of Art Nouveau architects, starring Gaudí, Domènech i Montaner, and Puig i Cadafalch; rising above it all is Gaudí's Sagrada Família church.

TOP ATTRACTIONS

Fodor's Choice
★

Casa Milà. Usually referred to as **La Pedrera** (The Stone Quarry), this building, with its wavy, curving stone facade undulating around the corner of the block, is one of Gaudí's most celebrated yet initially reviled designs. Topped by chimneys so eerie they were nicknamed *espanta-bruxes* (witch scarers), the Casa Milà was unveiled in 1910 to the horror of local residents. The sudden appearance of this strange facade on the city's most fashionable street led to the immediate coining of unflattering descriptions; newspapers called it the "Rock Pile," and made unflattering references to the gypsy cave dwellings in Granada's Sacromonte. The exterior has no straight lines; the curlicues and wrought-iron foliage of the balconies, sculpted by Josep Maria Jujol, and the rippling, undressed stone, made you feel, as one critic put it, "as though you are on board a ship in an angry sea."

Rebecca Horn's sculpture on Barceloneta's beach is reminiscent of the little shack restaurants that once crowded this sandy spot.

The building was originally meant to be dedicated to the Mother of God and crowned with a sculpture of the Virgin Mary. The initial design was altered by owner Pere Milà i Camps, who, after the anticlerical violence of the Setmana Tràgica (Tragic Week) of 1909, decided that the religious theme would be an invitation to a new outbreak of mayhem. Gaudí's rooftop chimney park, alternately interpreted as veiled Saharan women or helmeted warriors, is as spectacular as anything in Barcelona, especially in late afternoon, when the sunlight slants over the city into the Mediterranean. Inside, the handsome **Espai Gaudí** (Gaudí Space) in the attic has excellent critical displays of Gaudí's works from all over Spain, as well as explanations of theories and techniques, including an upside-down model (a reproduction of the original in the Sagrada Família museum) of the Güell family crypt at Santa Coloma, made of weighted hanging strings. This hanging model is based on the theory of the reversion of the catenary, which says that a chain suspended from two points will spontaneously hang in the exact shape of the inverted arch required to convert the stress to compression, thus providing structural support. The **Pis de la Pedrera** apartment is an interesting look into the life of a family that lived in La Pedrera in the early 20th century. Everything from the bathroom to the kitchen is filled with reminders of how comprehensively life has changed in the last century. People still live in the other apartments.

In the summer high season the lines of visitors waiting to see the Pedrera can stretch a block or more; if you can, sign up for Pedrera Secreta (Secret Pedrera), a private guided tour of the building by night, offered with or without dinner, daily March–October between 8:15 pm and midnight, November–February Wednesday–Saturday from 7:15 to 11. Bookings are essential: call ☎ *902/202138* or reserve online at ✉ *reserves@lapedreracom*. There are also guided tours in various languages, weekdays at 6 pm, weekends at 11 am; call ☎ *902/202138* or email ✉ *grupslapedrera@oscatalunyacaixa.com* for bookings and information. On *Nits d'Estiu* (Summer Nights; Thursday, Friday, and Saturday, June 20–September 7) the Espai Gaudí and the roof terrace are open for drinks and jazz concerts; the doors open at 9:45 and concerts begin at 10:30. Admission is €27. ✉ *Passeig de Gràcia 92, Eixample* ☎ *902/202138* 🎫 *€16.50; Pedrera Secreta tours €30/€49* ⊘ *Nov.–Feb., daily 9–6:30; Mar.–Oct., daily 9–8* Ⓜ *Diagonal, Provença.*

Fodor's Choice
★

Manzana de la Discòrdia. The name is a pun on the Spanish word *manzana*, which means both "apple" and "city block," alluding to the three-way architectural counterpoint on this street and to the classical myth of the Apple of Discord (which played a part in that legendary tale about the Judgment of Paris and the subsequent Trojan War). The houses here are spectacular and encompass three monuments of Modernisme—Casa Lleó Morera, Casa Amatller, and Casa Batlló. Of the three contrasting buildings (four if you count Sagnier i Villavecchia's comparatively tame 1910 Casa Mulleras at No. 37), Casa Batlló is clearly the star attraction and the only one of the three offering visits to the interior. ✉ *Passeig de Gràcia 35–43, Eixample.*

Casa Amatller. The neo-Gothic Casa Amatller was built by Josep Puig i Cadafalch in 1900, when the architect was 33 years old. Eighteen years younger than Domènech i Montaner and 15 years younger than Gaudí, Puig i Cadafalch was one of the leading statesmen of his generation, mayor of Barcelona and, in 1917, president of Catalonia's first home-rule government since 1714, the Mancomunitat de Catalunya. Puig i Cadafalch's architectural historicism sought to recover Catalonia's proud past, in combination with eclectic elements from Flemish and Dutch architectural motifs. Note the Eusebi Arnau sculptures—especially his St. George and the dragon, and the figures of a drummer with his dancing bear. The flowing-haired "Princesa" is thought to be Amatller's daughter; the animals above the motif are depicted pouring chocolate, a reference to the source of the Amatller family fortune. The upper floors are generally closed to the public, although the Fundació Institut Amatller d'Art Hispànic holds occasional cultural events upstairs. The small gallery on the first floor, which mounts various exhibitions related to Modernisme, is open to the public free of charge; a quick visit will give you a sense of what the rest of the building is like—and a chance to buy some chocolate *de la casa* at the boutique. ✉ *Passeig de Gràcia 41, Eixample* ☎ *93/487–7217* ⊕ *www.amatller. org* Ⓜ *Passeig de Gràcia.*

Casa Batlló. Gaudí at his most spectacular, the Casa Batlló is actually a makeover: it was originally built in 1877 by Emili Sala Cortés, one of Gaudí's teachers, and acquired by the Batlló family in 1900. Batlló wanted to tear down the undistinguished Sala building and start over, but let Gaudí persuade him to remodel the facade and the interior instead. The result is astonishing: the facade, with its rainbow of colored glass and *trencadís* polychromatic tile fragments, and the toothy

The Eixample

Carrer de la Independència

Carrer del dos de Maig

Carrer de Cartagena

Carrer de Castillejos

Carrer de Padilla

Carrer de Lepant

Carrer de Marina

Carrer Sardenya

Carrer Sicília

Carrer de Nápols

Carrer de Roger de Flor

Passeig de Sant Joan

Carrer de Bailèn

Carrer de Girona

Carrer del Bruc

Carrer de Roger de Llúria

Carrer de Pau Claris

Passeig de Gràcia

Rambla de Catalunya

Carrer de Balmes

Carrer d'Enric Granados

Carrer d'Aribau

Carrer de Muntaner

Carrer de Casanova

Carrer de Villarroel

Carrer del Comte D'Urgell

Carrer de Provença

Carrer de Mallorca

Carrer de València

Carrer d'Aragó

Carrer del Consell de Cent

Carrer de la Diputació

Gran Via de las Corts Catalanes

Carrer dels Enamorats

Avinguda Meridiana

C-31

Pl. de las Glòries Catalanes

HOSPITAL DE SANT PAU

Carrer de la Indústria

Carrer de Còrsega

C. de Sardenya

Travessera de Gràcia

C. de Sant Antoni Maria Claret

Carrer de la Indústria

Carrer de Còrsega

Carrer del Rosselló

Carrer de Provença

Carrer de Mallorca

SAGRADA FAMÍLIA

Casa Macaia

Diagonal

Pl. de Tetuan

VERDAGUER

Avda.

Carrer de Bailèn

C. de Girona

Carrer de l'Herria

C. de Penti

Carrer de Còrsega

Carrer Torrent de l'Olla

C. de Progrés

C. de Bonavista

Casa Àsia—Palau Baró de Quadras

PASSEIG DE GRÀCIA

Carrer del Consell de Cent

Carrer de la Diputació

Gran Via de las Corts Catalanes

Plaça de Catalunya

C. de Joan Carles I

Plaça de Joan Carles I

DIAGONAL

C. Gran de Gràcia

C. de la Riera de St. Miquel

Via Augusta

Avinguda Diagonal

Carrer de Provença

Carrer de Mallorca

Carrer de València

Carrer d'Aragó

Carrer del Consell de Cent

Gran Via de las Corts Catalanes

HOSPITAL CLÍNIC

0   1/4 mi

0   400 meters

KEY

◇ Metro Stops

Casa Milà **3**

Casa Montaner i
Simó—Fundació Tàpies **2**

Casa de les Punxes **4**

Manzana de la Discòrdia
(Casa Lleó Morera,
Casa Amatller,
Casa Batlló) **1**

Recinte Modernista de
Sant Pau **6**

Temple Expiatori
de la Sagrada
Família **5**

masks of the wrought-iron balconies projecting outward toward the street, is an irresistible photo op. Nationalist symbolism is at work here: the scaly roof line represents the Dragon of Evil impaled on St. George's cross, and the skulls and bones on the balconies are the dragon's victims—allusions to medieval Catalonia's code of chivalry and religious piety. Gaudí is said to have directed the composition of the facade from the middle of Passeig de Gràcia, calling instructions to workmen on the scaffolding, about how to place the trencadís. Inside, the translucent windows on the landings of the central staircase light up the maritime motif and the details of the building, all whorls and spirals and curves: here, as everywhere in his oeuvre, Gaudí opted for natural shapes and rejected straight lines. ⊠ *Passeig de Gràcia 43, Eixample* ☎ *93/216–0306* ⊕ *www.casabatllo.es* 🎫 *€20.35* ☉ *Daily 9–9 (hrs subject to change)* Ⓜ *Passeig de Gràcia.*

Casa Lleó Morera. The ornate Casa Lleó Morera was extensively rebuilt from 1902 to 1906 by Palau de la Música Catalana architect Domènech i Montaner and is a treasure house of Catalan Modernisme. The facade is covered with ornamentation and sculptures depicting female figures using the modern inventions of the age: the telephone, the telegraph, the camera, and the Victrola. The inside, presently closed to the public, is even more astounding, another anthology of Art Nouveau techniques assembled by the same team of glaziers, sculptors, and mosaicists Domènech i Montaner directed in the construction of the Palau de la Música Catalana. The Eusebi Arnau sculptures around the top of the walls on the main floor are based on the Catalan lullaby "La Dida de l'Infant del Rei" (The Nurse of the King's Baby); while the stained-glass scenes in the old dining room, of Lleó Morera family picnics, resemble Moderniste versions of impressionist paintings. (Though Casa Lleó Morera is not open to the public at this writing, check the current status with the Modernisme Centre (☎ 93/317–7652) and ask how to arrange a visit.) ⊠ *Passeig de Gracia 35, Eixample* Ⓜ *Passeig de Gracia.*

Fodor's Choice **Temple Expiatori de la Sagrada Família.** Barcelona's most emblematic archi-
★ tectural icon, Antoni Gaudí's Sagrada Família, is still under construction 130 years after it was begun. This striking and surreal creation was conceived as nothing short of a Bible in stone, a gigantic representation of the entire history of Christianity, and it continues to cause responses from surprise to consternation to wonder. No building in Barcelona and few in the world are more deserving of the investment of a few hours to the better part of a day in getting to know well. In fact, a quick visit can be more tiring than an extended one, as there are too many things to take in at once. However long your visit, it's a good idea to bring binoculars.

Looming over Barcelona like some magical midcity *massif* of needles and peaks, left by eons of wind erosion and exuberant growth, the Sagrada Família can at first seem like piles of caves and grottoes heaped on a labyrinth of stalactites, stalagmites, and flora and fauna of every stripe and sort. The sheer immensity of the site and the energy flowing from it are staggering. The scale alone is daunting: the current lateral facades will one day be dwarfed by the main Glory facade and central spire—the **Torre del Salvador** (Tower of the Savior), which will be crowned by an illuminated polychrome ceramic cross and soar to a final height 1 yard shorter than the Montjuïc mountain (564 feet) guarding the entrance to the port (Gaudí felt it improper for the work of man to surpass that of God). Today, for a €4.50 additional charge (cash only), you can take an elevator skyward to the top of the **bell towers** for some spectacular views. Back on the ground, visit the **museum,** which displays Gaudí's scale models, photographs showing the progress of construction, and images of the vast outpouring at Gaudí's funeral; the architect is buried under the basilica, to the left of the altar in the **crypt.**

Soaring spikily skyward in intricately twisting levels of carvings and sculptures, part of the Nativity facade is made of stone from Montserrat, Barcelona's cherished mountain sanctuary and home of Catalonia's patron saint, La Moreneta, the Black Virgin of Montserrat. Gaudí himself was fond of comparing the Sagrada Família to the shapes of the sawtooth massif 50 km (30 miles) west of the city; a plaque in one of Montserrat's caverns reads, *"Lloc d'inspiració de gaudí"* ("Place of inspiration of Gaudí").

History of Construction and Design. "My client is not in a hurry," Gaudí was fond of replying to anyone curious about the timetable for the completion of his mammoth project—and it's a lucky thing, because the Sagrada Família was begun in 1882 under architect Francesc Villar, passed on in 1891 to Gaudí (who worked on the project until his death in 1926), and is still thought to be 15 or 20 years from completion, despite the ever-increasing velocity of today's computerized construction techniques. After the church's neo-Gothic beginnings, Gaudí added Art Nouveau touches to the crypt (the floral capitals) and in 1893 went on to begin the Nativity facade of a new and vastly ambitious project. Conceived as a symbolic construct encompassing the complete story and scope of the Christian faith, the Sagrada Família was intended by Gaudí to impress the viewer with the full sweep and force of the Gospel. At the time of his death in 1926, however, only one tower of the Nativity facade had been completed.

Gaudí's plans called for three immense facades, the Nativity and Passion facades on the northeast and southwest sides of the church, and the even larger Glory facade designed as the building's main entry, facing east over Carrer de Mallorca. The four bell towers over each facade would represent the 12 apostles, a reference to the celestial Jerusalem of the Book of Revelation. The four larger towers around the central Tower of the Savior will represent the evangelists Mark, Matthew, John, and Luke. Between the central tower and the reredos at the northwestern end of the nave will rise the 18th and second-highest tower, crowned with a star, in honor of the Virgin Mary. The naves are not supported by buttresses but by treelike helicoidal (spiraling) columns. The first bell tower, in honor of Barnabas—the only one Gaudí lived to see—was completed in 1921. Presently there are eight towers standing: Barnabas, Simon, Judas, and Matthias (from left to right) over the Nativity facade and James, Bartholomew, Thomas, and Phillip over the Passion facade.

Meaning and Iconography. Reading the existing facades is a challenging course in Bible studies. The three doors on the **Nativity facade** are named for Charity in the center, Faith on the right, and Hope on the left. As explained by Joan Serra, onetime vicar of the parish of the Sagrada Família and devoted Gaudí scholar, the architect often described the symbology of his work to visitors although he never wrote any of it down. Thus, much of this has come directly from Gaudí via the oral tradition. In the Nativity facade Gaudí addresses nothing less than the fundamental mystery of Christianity: Why does God the Creator become, through Jesus Christ, a mortal creature? The answer, as Gaudí explained it in stone, is that God did this to free man from the slavery of selfishness, symbolized by the iron fence around the serpent of evil at the base of the central column of the **Portal of Charity**. The column is covered with the genealogy of Christ going back to Abraham.

Above the central column is a portrayal of the birth of Christ; above that, the Annunciation is flanked by a grotto-like arch of water. Overhead are the constellations in the Christmas sky at Bethlehem: if you look carefully you'll see two babies, representing the Gemini, and the horns of a bull, for Taurus.

To the right, the **Portal of Faith** chronicles scenes of Christ's youth: Jesus preaching at the age of 13 and Zacharias prophetically writing the name of John. Higher up are grapes and wheat, symbols of the Eucharist, and a sculpture of a hand and an eye, symbols of divine providence.

The left-hand **Portal of Hope** begins at the bottom with flora and fauna from the Nile; the slaughter of the innocents; the flight of the Holy Family into Egypt; Joseph, surrounded by his carpenter's tools, contemplating his son; the marriage of Joseph and Mary. Above this is a sculpted boat with an anchor, representing the Church, piloted by St. Joseph assisted by the Holy Spirit in the form of a dove. Overhead is a typical peak or spire from the Montserrat massif.

Gaudí planned these slender towers to house a system of tubular bells (still to be created and installed) capable of playing more complete and complex music than standard bell-ringing changes had previously been able to perform. At a height of one-third of the bell tower are the seated figures of the apostles. The peaks of the towers represent the apostles' successors, each in the form of a mitre, the official headdress of a bishop of the Western Church.

The **Passion facade** on the Sagrada Família's southwestern side, over Carrer Sardenya and the Plaça de la Sagrada Família, is a dramatic contrast to the Nativity facade. In 1986, sculptor Josep Maria Subirachs was chosen by project director Jordi Bonet to finish the Passion facade. Subirachs was picked for his starkly realistic, almost geometrical, sculptural style, which many visitors and devotees of Gaudí find gratingly off the mark. Subirachs pays double homage to the great Moderniste master in the Passion facade: Gaudí himself appears over the left side of the main entry, making notes or drawings, the evangelist in stone, while the Roman soldiers farther out and above are modeled on Gaudí's helmeted warriors from the roof of La Pedrera. Art critic Robert Hughes calls the homage "sincere in the way that only the worst art can be: which is to say, utterly so."

Framed by leaning tibia-like columns, the bones of the dead, and following an S-shaped path across the Passion facade, the scenes represented begin at the lower left with the Last Supper. The faces of the disciples are contorted in confusion and dismay, especially that of Judas, clutching his bag of money behind his back over the figure of a reclining hound, symbol of fidelity in contrast with the disciple's perfidy. The next sculptural group to the right represents the prayer in the Garden of Gethsemane and Peter awakening, followed by the kiss of Judas.

In the center, Jesus is lashed to a pillar during his flagellation, a tear track carved into his expressive countenance. Note the column's top stone is out of kilter, reminder of the stone soon to be removed from Christ's sepulchre. To the right of the door are a rooster and Peter, who is lamenting his third denial of Christ "ere the cock crows." Farther to the right are Pilate and Jesus with the crown of thorns, while just above, starting back to the left, Simon of Cyrene helps Jesus with the cross after his first fall.

Over the center is the representation of Jesus consoling the women of Jerusalem and a faceless (because her story is considered legendary, not historical fact) St. Veronica with the veil she gave Christ to wipe his face with on the way to Calvary. To the left is the likeness of Gaudí taking notes, and farther to the left is the equestrian figure of a centurion piercing the side of the church with his spear, the church representing the body of Christ. Above are the soldiers rolling dice for Christ's clothing and the naked, crucified Christ at the center. The moon to the right of the crucifixion refers to the darkness at the moment of Christ's death and to the full moon of Easter; to the right are Peter and Mary at the sepulchre. At Christ's feet is a figure with a furrowed brow, perhaps suggesting the agnostic's anguished search for certainty. It is thought to be a self-portrait of Subirachs, characterized by the sculptor's giant hand and an *S* on his right arm.

Over the door will be the church's 16 prophets and patriarchs under the cross of salvation. Apostles James, Bartholomew, Thomas, and Phillip appear at a height of 148 feet on their respective bell towers. Thomas, the apostle who demanded proof of Christ's resurrection (thus the expression "doubting Thomas"), is visible pointing to the palm of his hand, asking to inspect Christ's wounds. Bartholomew, on the left, is turning his face upward toward the culminating element in the Passion facade, the 26-foot-tall gold metallic representation of the resurrected Christ on a bridge between the four bell towers at a height of 198 feet.

Future of the project. The apse of the basilica, consecrated by Pope Benedict XVI in November 2010, has space for 15,000 people and a choir loft for 1,500 and occupies an area large enough to encompass the entire church of Santa Maria del Mar. The towers still to be completed over the apse include those dedicated to the four evangelists—Matthew, Mark, Luke, and John—the Virgin Mary, and the highest of all, dedicated to Christ the Savior. By 2022, the 170th anniversary of the birth of Gaudí, the great central tower and dome, resting on four immense columns of Iranian porphyry, considered the hardest of all stones, will soar to a height of 564 feet, making the Sagrada Família Barcelona's tallest building. By 2026, the 100th anniversary of Gaudí's death, after 144 years of construction in the tradition of the great medieval and Renaissance cathedrals of Europe, the Sagrada Família may well be complete enough to be called finished. ⊠ *Pl. de la Sagrada Família s/n, Eixample* ☎ *93/2073031* ⊕ *www.sagradafamilia.org* ✉ *€14.80 (€18 with audio guide), bell-tower elevator €4.50* ⊙ *Oct.–Mar., daily 9–6; Apr.–Sept., daily 9–8* Ⓜ *Sagrada Família.*

WORTH NOTING

Casa de les Punxes (*House of the Spikes*). Also known as Casa Terrades for the family that owned the house and commissioned Puig i Cadafalch to build it, this extraordinary cluster of six conical towers ending in impossibly sharp needles is another of Puig i Cadafalch's northern European inspirations, this one rooted in the Gothic architecture of Nordic countries. One of the few freestanding Eixample buildings, visible from 360 degrees, this ersatz Bavarian or Danish castle in downtown Barcelona is composed entirely of private apartments. Some of them are built into the conical towers themselves and consist of three circular levels connected by spiral stairways, about right for a couple or a very small family. Interestingly, Puig i Cadafalch also designed the Terrades family mausoleum, albeit in a much more sober and respectful style. ⊠ *Av. Diagonal 416–420, Eixample* Ⓜ *Diagonal.*

Casa Montaner i Simó–Fundació Tàpies. This former publishing house—and the city's first building to incorporate iron supports, built in 1880—has been handsomely converted to hold the work of preeminent contemporary Catalan painter Antoni Tàpies, as well as temporary exhibits. Tàpies, who died in 2012, was an abstract painter, although influenced by surrealism, which may account for the sculpture atop the structure—a tangle of metal entitled *Núvol i cadira* (*Cloud and Chair*). The modern, airy split-level gallery also has a bookstore that's strong on Tàpies, Asian art, and Barcelona art and architecture. ⊠ *Carrer Aragó 255, Eixample* ☎ *93/4870315* ⊕ *www.fundaciotapies.org* ✉ *€7* ⊙ *Tues.–Sun. 10–8* Ⓜ *Passeig de Gràcia.*

Fodor's Choice ★ **Recinte Modernista de Sant Pau.** Among the more recent tourist attractions in Barcelona, the Recinte Modernista (Modernist Complex) is set in what was surely one of the most beautiful public projects in the world: the Hospital de Sant Pau. A World Heritage site, the complex is extraordinary in its setting and style, and in the idea that inspired it. Architect Lluís Domènech i Montaner believed that trees and flowers and fresh air were likely to help people recover from what ailed them more than anything doctors could do in emotionally sterile surroundings. The hospital wards were set among gardens, their brick facades topped with polychrome ceramic tile roofs in extravagant shapes and details. Domènech also believed in the therapeutic properties of form and color, and decorated the hospital with Pau Gargallo sculptures and colorful mosaics, replete with motifs of hope and healing and healthy growth. Begun in 1900, this monumental production won Domènech i Montaner his third Barcelona "Best Building" award in 1912. (His previous two prizes were for the Palau de la Música Catalana and Casa Lleó Morera.)

No longer a functioning hospital (the new Sant Pau—comparatively soulless but fully functional and state-of-the-art—is uphill from the complex), many of the buildings have been taken over for other purposes. The Sant Manuel Pavillion, for example, now houses the **Casa Àsia,** a comprehensive resource for cultural and business-related research on all the countries of Asia, with library holdings of books, films, and music from each of them. Tours of the Complex are offered in English daily at 10, 11, noon and 1 pm. ⊠ *Carrer Sant Antoni Maria Claret 167, Eixample* ☎ *93/553–7801, 93/269–2444* ⊕ *www.santpaubarcelona.org* 🎫 *Tour €10* Ⓜ *Hospital de Sant Pau.*

UPPER BARCELONA: SARRIÀ AND PEDRALBES

Sarrià was originally a country village, overlooking Barcelona from the foothills of the Collserola. Eventually absorbed by the westward-expanding city, the village, 15 minutes by FGC commuter train from Plaça de Catalunya, has become a unique neighborhood with at least four distinct populations: the old-timers, who speak only Catalan among themselves, and talk of "going down to Barcelona" to shop; writers, artists and designers, and people in publishing and advertising, drawn here in the 1970s and 1980s by the creative vibe; yuppie starter families, who largely support Sarriá's gourmet shops and upscale restaurants; and a cadre of expats, who prize the neighborhood for its proximity to the international schools.

Did we mention gourmet shops? J. V. Foix, the famous Catalan poet, was a native son of Sarrià; his father founded what is arguably the best patisserie in Barcelona, and his descendants still run the quintessential Sarrià family business. On Sundays, barcelonins come to the village from all over town; Sunday just wouldn't be Sunday without a cake from Foix. Cross Avinguda Foix from Sarriá and you're in Pedralbes—the wealthiest residential neighborhood in the city. (Fútbol superstar Leo Messi has his multimillion-euro home here; the exclusive Real Club de Tenis de Barcelona is not far off.) The centerpiece of this district is the 14th-century Monestir (Monastery) de Pedralbes; other points of interest include Gaudí's Pavellons de la Finca Güell on Avinguda de Pedralbes, and the gardens of the Palau Reial de Pedralbes, a 20-minute walk downhill from the monastery. The Futbol Club Barcelona's 98,000-seat Camp Nou stadium and museum are another 20 minutes' walk, down below the Diagonal.

TOP ATTRACTIONS

Camp Nou. If you're in Barcelona between September and June, a chance to witness the celebrated FC Barcelona play soccer (preferably against Real Madrid, if you can get in) at Barcelona's gigantic stadium is a seminal Barcelona experience. Just the walk down to the field from the Diagonal with another hundred thousand fans walking fast and hushed in electric anticipation is unforgettable. Games are played Saturday night at 9 or Sunday afternoon at 5, though there may be international Champions League games on Tuesday or Wednesday evenings as well. A worthwhile alternative to seeing a game is the guided tour of the FC Barcelona museum—the city's most visited tourist attraction—and

Continued on page 480

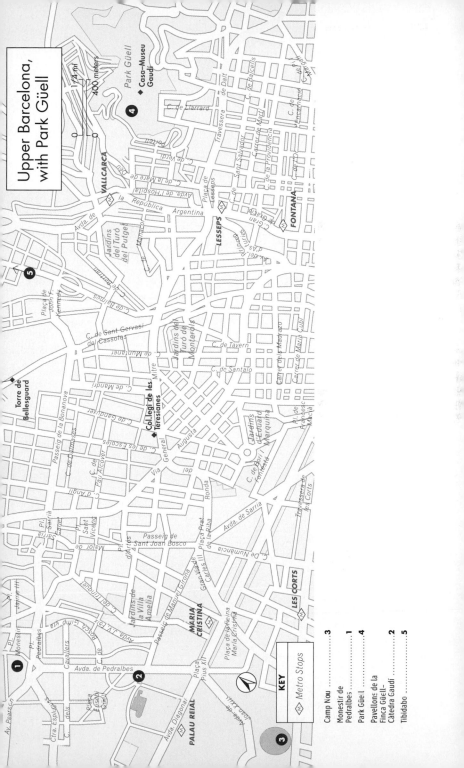

Upper Barcelona, with Park Güell

Park Güell
● Casa-Museu Gaudí

VALLCARCA

LESSEPS

FONTANA

Torre de
Bellesguard

Col.legi de les
Teresianes

MARIA
CRISTINA

PALAU REIAL

LES CORTS

Camp Nou 3

Monestir de
Pedralbes 1

Park Güel l 4

Pavellons de la
Finca Güell–
Càtedra Gaudí 2

Tibidabo 5

GAUDÍ

ARCHITECTURE
THROUGH
THE LOOKING
GLASS

(left) The undulating rooftop of Casa Batlló. (top) Right angles are notably absent in the Casa Milà façade.

Before his 75th birthday in 1926, Antoni Gaudí was hit by a trolley car while on his way to Mass. The great architect—initially unidentified—was taken to the medieval Hospital de la Santa Creu in Barcelona's Raval and left in a pauper's ward, where he died two days later without regaining consciousness. It was a dramatic and tragic end for a man whose entire life seemed to court the extraordinary and the exceptional.

Gaudí's singularity made him hard to define. Indeed, eulogists at the time, and decades later, wondered how history would treat him. Was he a religious mystic, a rebel, a bohemian artist, a Moderniste genius? Was he, perhaps, all of these? He certainly had a rebellious streak, as his architecture stridently broke with tradition. Yet the same sensibility that created the avant-garde benchmarks Park Güell and La Pedrera also created one of Spain's greatest shrines to Catholicism, the *Temple Expiatori de la Sagrada Família* (Expiatory Temple of the Holy Family), which architects agree is one of the world's most enigmatic structures; work on the cathedral continues to this day. And while Gaudí's works suggest a futurist aesthetic, he also reveled in the use of ornamentation, which 20th century architecture largely eschewed.

What is no longer in doubt is Gaudí's place among the great architects in history. Eyed with suspicion by traditionalists in the 1920s and 30s, vilified during the Franco regime, and ultimately redeemed as a Barcelona icon after Spain's democratic transition in the late 70s, Gaudí has finally gained universal admiration.

THE MAKING OF A GENIUS

Gaudí was born in 1852 the son of a boilermaker and coppersmith in Reus, an hour south of Barcelona. As a child, he helped his father forge boilers and cauldrons in the family foundry, which is where Gaudí's fascination with three-dimensional and organic forms began. Afflicted from an early age with reoccuring rheumatic fever, the young architect devoted his energies to studying and drawing flora and fauna in the natural world. In school Gaudí was erratic: brilliant in the subjects that interested him, absent and disinterested in the others. As a seventeen-year-old architecture student in Barcelona, his academic results were mediocre. Still, his mentors agreed that he was brilliant.

Unfortunately being brilliant didn't mean instant success. By the late 1870s, when Gaudí was well into his twenties, he'd only completed a handful of projects, including the Plaça Reial lampposts, a flower stall, and the factory and part of a planned workers' community in Mataró. Gaudí's career got the boost it needed when, in 1878, he met Eusebi Güell, heir to a textiles fortune and a man who, like

Gaudí, had a refined sensibility. (The two bonded over a mutual admiration for the visionary Catalan poet Jacint Verdaguer.) In 1883 Gaudí became Güell's architect and for the next three decades, until Güell's death in 1918, the two collaborated on Gaudí's most important architectural achievements, from high-profile endeavors like Palau Güell, Park Güell, and Pabellones Güell to smaller projects for the Güell family.

(top) Interior of Casa Batlló. (bottom) Chimneys on rooftop of Casa Milà recall helmeted warriors or veiled women.

GAUDÍ TIMELINE

1883-1884

Gaudí builds a summer palace, *El Capricho* in Comillas, Santander for the brother-in-law of his benefactor, Eusebi Güell. Another gig comes his way during this same period when Barcelona ceramics tile mogul Manuel Vicens hires him to build his town house, *Casa Vicens*, in the Gràcia neighborhood.

El Capricho

1884-1900

Gaudí whips up the Pabellones Güell, Palau Güell, the Palacio Episcopal of Astorga, Barcelona's Teresianas school, the Casa de los Botines in León, Casa Calvet, and Bellesguard. These have his classic look of this time, featuring interpretation of Mudéjar (Moorish motifs), Gothic, and Baroque styles.

Palacio Episcopal

BREAKING OUT OF THE T-SQUARE PRISON

If Eusebi Güell had not believed in Gaudí's unusual approach to Modernisme, his creations might not have seen the light of day. Güell recognized that Gaudí was imbued with a vision that separated him from the crowd. That vision was his fascination with the organic. Gaudí had observed early in his career that buildings were being composed of shapes that could only be drawn by the compass and the T-square: circles, triangles, squares, and rectangles—shapes that in three dimensions became prisms, pyramids, cylinders and spheres. He saw that in nature these shapes are unknown. Admiring the structural efficiency of trees, mammals, and the human form, Gaudí noted ". . . neither are trees prismatic, nor bones cylindrical, nor leaves triangular." The study of natural forms revealed that bones, branches, muscles, and tendons are all supported by internal fibers. Thus, though a surface curves, it is supported from within by a fibrous network that Gaudí translated into what he called "ruled geometry," a system of inner reinforcement he used to make hyperboloids, conoids, helicoids, or parabolic hyperboloids.

These tongue-tying words are simple forms and familiar shapes: the femur is hyperboloid; the way shoots grow off a

Hyperboloid

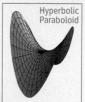

Hyperbolic Paraboloid

The top of the gatehouse in Park Güell at the main entrance; note the mushroom-like form.

branch is helicoidal; the web between your fingers is a hyperbolic paraboloid. To varying degrees, these ideas find expression in all of Gaudí's work, but nowhere are they more clearly stated than in the two masterpieces La Pedrera and Park Güell.

IN FOCUS 7 GAUDÍ: ARCHITECTURE THROUGH THE LOOKING GLASS

1900–1917

Gaudí's Golden Years—his most creative, personal, and innovative period. Topping each success with another, he tackles Park Güell, the reform of Casa Batlló, the Güell Colony church, Casa Milà (La Pedrera), and the Sagrada Família school.

Casa Batlló's complex chimneys

1918–1926

A crushing blow: Gaudí suffers the death of his assistant, Francesc Berenguer. Grieving and rudderless, he devotes himself fully to his great unfinished opus, la Sagrada Família—to the point of obsession. On June 10th, 1926, he's hit by a trolley car. He dies two days later.

La Sagrada Família

Pabellones Güell. A mosaic dragon greets visitors on Park Güell's central staircase.

La Sagrada Família. Tubular bell towers over the Nativity façade were designed by Gaudí for an innovative carillon musical system.

Palau Güell. The rooftop chimneys display organic form. Using colorful broken tiles, each of a unique structure almost like a topiary garden.

Casa Calvet. The vestibule, elevator, and stairwell are beginning to warp and heave into organic suggestions.

Casa Milà (La Pedrera). The undulating stone façade seems to reflect the Mediterranean's rolling surface.

HOW TO SEE GAUDÍ IN BARCELONA

Few architects have left their stamp on a major city as thoroughly as Gaudí did in Barcelona. Paris may have the Eiffel Tower, but Barcelona has Gaudí's still unfinished masterpiece, the **Temple Expiatori de la Sagrada Família,** the city's most emblematic structure. Dozens of other buildings, parks, gateways and even paving stones around town bear Gaudí's personal Art Nouveau signature, but the continuing progress on his last and most ambitious project makes his creative energy an ongoing part of everyday Barcelona life in a unique and almost spectral fashion.

(top) The serpentine ceramic bench at Park Güell, designed by Gaudí collaborator Josep Maria Jujol, curves sinuously around the edge of the open square. (bottom) Sculptures by Josep María Subirachs grace the temple of the Sagrada Família.

In Barcelona, nearly all of Gaudí's work can be visited on foot or, at most, with a couple of metro or taxi rides. A walk from **Palau Güell** near the Mediterranean end of the Rambla, up past **Casa Calvet** just above Plaça Catalunya, and on to **Casa Batlló** and **Casa Milà** is an hour's stroll, which, of course, could take a full day with thorough visits to the sites. **Casa Vicens** is a half hour's walk up into Gràcia from **Casa Milà. Park Güell** is another thirty- to forty-minute walk up from that. **La Sagrada Família,** on the other hand, is a good hour's hike from the next nearest Gaudí point and is best reached by taxi or metro. The **Teresianas** school, the **Bellesguard Tower,** and **Pabel-lones Güell** are within an hour's walk of each other, but to get out to Sarrià you will need to take the comfortable Generalitat (FGC) train.

facilities. ⊠ *Arístides Maillol 12–18, Les Corts* ☎ *93/496–3600 for museum, 902/189900 for club office* ⊕ *www.fcbarcelona.cat* 🖃 *Museum €23, includes tour of museum, field, and sports complex* ⊙ *Museum Mon.–Sat. 10–6:30 (until 8 Apr.–Oct.), Sun. 10–2:30. On match days, the museum closes 3 hrs early, and stadium tours are not available.* Ⓜ *Collblanc, Palau Reial.*

Fodor's Choice ★ **Monestir de Pedralbes.** This marvel of a monastery, named for its original white stones (*pedres albes*), is really a convent, founded in 1326 for the Franciscan order of Poor Clares by Reina (Queen) Elisenda. The three-story Gothic cloister, one of the finest in Europe, surrounds a lush garden. The day cells, where the nuns spend their mornings praying, sewing, and studying, circle the arcaded courtyard. The queen's own cell, the Capella de Sant Miquel, just to the right of the entrance, has murals painted in 1346 by Catalan master Ferrer Bassa. Look for the letters spelling out *"Joan no m'oblides"* ("John, do not forget me.") scratched between the figures of St. Francis and St. Clare (with book and quill), written by a brokenhearted novice. Farther along, inscriptions over the tombs of nuns who died here can be seen through the paving grates. The nuns' upstairs dormitory contains the convent's treasures: paintings, liturgical objects, and seven centuries of artistic and cultural patrimony. Temporary exhibits are displayed in this space. The refectory where the Poor Clares dined in silence has a pulpit used for readings, while wall inscriptions exhort *"Silentium"* ("Silence"), *"Audi tacens"* ("Listening makes you wise."), and *"Considera morientem"* ("Consider, we are dying."). Notice the fading mural in the corner, and the paving tiles broken by heavy cannon positioned here during the 1809 Napoleonic occupation. Your ticket also includes admission to Museu d'Història de la Ciutat, Centre d'Interpretació del Park Güell, Centre d'Interpretació del Call, Centre d'Interpretació Històrica, Refugi 307, and Museu-Casa Verdaguer. ⊠ *Baixada Monestir 9, Pedralbes* ☎ *93/2563434* ⊕ *www.bcn.cat/monestirpedralbes* 🖃 *€7 (free Sun. after 3)* ⊙ *Oct.–Mar., Tues.–Fri. 10–2, weekends 10–5; Apr.–Sept., Tues.–Fri. 10–5, Sat. 10–7, Sun. 10–8* Ⓜ *Reina Elisenda.*

Pavellons de la Finca Güell–Càtedra Gaudí. Work on the Finca began in 1883 as an extension of the Count Eusabi Güell's family estate. Gaudí, the count's architect of choice, was commissioned to do the gardens and the two entrance pavilions (1884-87); the rest of the project was never finished. The pavilions now belong to the University of Barcelona; the one on the right houses the Càtedra Gaudí, a Gaudí library and study center. The fierce wrought-iron dragon gate is Gaudí's reference to the Garden of the Hesperides, as described by national poet Jacint Verdaguer's epic poem *L'Atlàntida*—the *Iliad* of Catalunya's historic/mythic origins—published in 1877. The property is open for guided tours in English on Saturday and Sunday at 10:15 and 12:15. Admission is limited to 25 visitors: call ahead, or book on the Ruta del Modernisme website. (The Ruta is a walking tour covering 115 masterworks of the Moderniste period, including Gaudí, Domenech i Muntaner, and Puig i Catafalch. Pick up a guide—which includes a map and discounts for admission to many of the sites—here at the Pavellons or at the **Turisme de Barcelona** office in the Plaça de Catalunya.) ✉ *Av. Pedralbes 7, Pedralbes* ☎ *93/3177652* ⊕ *www.rutadelmodernisme.com* Ⓜ *Palau Reial.*

Sarrià. The village of Sarrià was originally a cluster of farms and country houses overlooking Barcelona from the hills. The 10th-century Romanesque **Church of Sant Vicenç** dominates the square; the bell tower, illuminated on weekend nights, is truly impressive. Across Passeig de la Reina Elisenda from the church (50 yards to the left) is the 100-year-old Moderniste **Mercat de Sarriá.**

From the square, cut through the Placeta del Roser to the left of the church to the elegant **Town Hall** (1896) in the Plaça de la Vila; note the buxom bronze sculpture of **Pomona,** goddess of fruit, by famed Sarrià sculptor Josep Clarà (1878–1958). Follow the tiny Carrer dels Paletes, to the left of the Town Hall (the saint enshrined in the niche is Sant Antoni, patron saint of *paletes,* or bricklayers), and right on Major de Sarrià, the High Street of the village. ■ **TIP→** Lunch time? Try Casa Raphael, on the right as you walk down—in business (and virtually unchanged) since 1873. Further on, turn left into **Carrer Canet.** The two-story row houses on the right were first built for workers on the village estates; these, and the houses opposite at Nos. 15, 21, and 23, are among the few remaining original village homes in Sarrià. Turn right at the first corner on Carrer Cornet i Mas and walk two blocks down to Carrer Jaume Piquet.

On the left is No. 30, Barcelona's most perfect small-format **Moderniste house,** thought to be the work of architect Domènech i Montaner, complete with faux-medieval upper windows, wrought-iron grillwork, floral and fruited ornamentation, and organically curved and carved wooden doors either by or inspired by Gaudí himself. The next stop down Cornet i Mas is Sarrià's prettiest square, **Plaça Sant Vicens,** a leafy space ringed by old Sarrià houses and centered on a statue of Sarrià's patron, St. Vicenç, portrayed, as always, beside the millstone used to sink him to the bottom of the Mediterranean after he was martyred in Valencia in 302. **Can Pau,** the café on the lower corner with Carrer Mañé i Flaquer, is the local hangout, a good place for coffee and once a haven for authors Gabriel García Marquez and Mario Vargas Llosa, who lived in Sarrià in the late 1960s and early 1970s.

Other Sarrià landmarks to look for include the two **Foix** pastry stores, one at Plaça Sarrià 9–10 and the other at Major de Sarrià 57, above Bar Tomás. The late J. V. Foix (1893–1987), son of the store's founders, was one of the great Catalan poets of the 20th century, a key player in keeping the Catalan language alive during the 40-year Franco regime. The shop on Major de Sarrià has a bronze plaque identifying the house as the poet's birthplace and inscribed with one of his most memorable verses, translated as, "Every love is latent in the other love/ every language is the juice of a common tongue/every country touches the fatherland of all/every faith will be the lifeblood of a higher faith." ✉ *Pl. Sarrià, Sarrià* Ⓜ *Sarrià, Reina Elisenda (FGC Line L6).*

Torre Bellesguard. For a Gaudí experience to the last drop, climb up above Plaça de la Bonanova to this private residence built between 1900 and 1909 over the ruins of the summer palace of the last of the sovereign count-kings of the Catalan-Aragonese realm, Martí I l'Humà (Martin I the Humane), whose reign ended in 1410. In homage to this medieval history, Gaudí endowed the house with a tower, gargoyles, and crenellated battlements; the rest—the catenary arches, the *trencadis* (broken bits of polychromatic ceramic tile) of the facade, the stained-glass windows—are pure Art Nouveau. Look for the red and gold Catalan *senyera* (banner) on the tower, topped by the four-armed Greek cross Gaudí often used. Over the front door is the inscription *sens pecat fou concebuda* (without sin was she conceived) referring to the Immaculate Conception of the Virgin Mary; on either side of the front door are benches with trencadís mosaics of playful fish bearing the crimson *quatre barres* (four bars) of the Catalan flag as well as the Corona d'Aragó (Crown of Aragón).

Still a private home and long closed to visitors, the Torre Bellesguard is now accessible to small groups. ■TIP➔ Sign up (✉ reserva@belles-guardgaudi.com) for a guided tour: this is a treat not to be missed. ✉ *Bellesguard 16–20, Sant Gervasi* ☎ *93/250–4093, 646/800127* ⊕ *www.bellesguardgaudi.com* 🖾 *€16 full tour (reservations required), €7 grounds only (with audio guide)* ⊗ *Guided 1-hr tours of house and grounds in English (max. 15 persons) weekdays at 11 am; open visits to grounds Nov.–Mar., weekdays 10–3; Apr.–Oct., weekdays 10–7:30* Ⓜ *Sarrià.*

Park Güell. This park is one of Gaudí's, and Barcelona's, most visited attractions. Named for and commissioned by Gaudí's steadfast patron, Count Eusebi Güell, it was originally intended as a gated residential community based on the English Garden City model, centered on a public square, where impromptu dances and plays could be performed, built over a covered marketplace. Only two of the houses were ever built (one of which, designed by Gaudí's assistant Francesc Berenguer, became Gaudí's home from 1906 to 1926 and now houses the **Casa-Museu Gaudí** museum of memorabilia). Ultimately, as Barcelona's bourgeoisie seemed happier living closer to "town," the Güell family turned the area over to the city as a public park—which it still is, for local residents; as of September 2013, visitors are assessed an entrance fee.

An Art Nouveau extravaganza with gingerbread gatehouses, Park Güell is a perfect place to visit on a sunny afternoon, when the blue of the Mediterranean is best illuminated by the western sun. The gatehouse on the right, topped with a rendition in ceramic tile of the hallucinogenic red-and-white fly ammanite wild mushroom (rumored to have been a Gaudí favorite) houses the Center for the Interpretation and Welcome to Park Güell. The center has plans, scale models, photos, and suggested routes analyzing the park in detail. Atop the gatehouse on the left sits the *phallus impudicus* (no translation necessary). Other Gaudí highlights include the Room of a Hundred Columns—a covered market supported by tilted Doric-style columns and mosaic medallions; the double set of stairs; and the iconic lizard guarding the fountain between them. There's also the fabulous serpentine, polychrome bench enclosing the square. The bench is one of Gaudí assistant Josep Maria Jujol's most memorable creations, and one of Barcelona's best examples of the trencadís technique of making colorful mosaics with broken bits

DID YOU KNOW?

Park Güell was originally designed as an exclusive gated garden community, but failed to attract enough would-be residents. One of the only two houses built here became Gaudí's residence from 1906 to 1926.

of tile. From the metro at Plaça de Lesseps, or the Bus Turistic stop on Travessera de Dalt, take Bus No. 24 to the park entrance, or make the steep 10-minute climb uphill on Carrer de Lallard. ⊠ *Carrer d'Olot s/n, Gràcia* ⊕ *www.parkguell.es* ☎ *€8 (€7 online)* ⊙ *Jan.–Oct., daily 8–9:30; Nov. and Dec., daily 8:30–6* Ⓜ *Lesseps.*

WORTH NOTING

FAMILY **Tibidabo.** One of Barcelona's two promontories, this hill bears a distinctive name, generally translated as "To Thee I Will Give"—referring to the Catalan legend that this was the spot from which Satan tempted Christ with all the riches of the earth below (namely, Barcelona). On a clear day, the views from this 1,789-foot peak are legendary. Tibidabo's skyline is marked by a neo-Gothic church, the work of Enric Sagnier in 1902, and—off to one side, near the village of Vallvidrera—the 854-foot communications tower, the **Torre de Collserola,** designed by Sir Norman Foster. Do you have youngsters in tow? Take the cute little San Francisco–style Tramvía Blau (Blue Trolley) cable car from Plaça Kennedy to the overlook at the top, and transfer to the funicular to the 100-year-old **Amusement Park** at the summit. ⊠ *Pl. Tibidabo 3–4, Tibidabo* ☎ *93/211–7942* ⊕ *www.tibidabo.cat* ⊡ *Amusement Park €28.50* ⊙ *Noon–7* Ⓜ *Tibidabo.*

Mirablau. This bar overlooks the city lights and is a popular late-night hangout. ⊠ *Pl. Doctor Andreu s/n* ☎ *93/4185879.*

El Mirador de la Venta. You may come here for the great views, but El Mirador de la Venta has good contemporary cuisine to accompany them. ⊠ *Pl. Doctor Andreu s/n* ☎ *93/212–6455.*

MONTJUÏC

This hill overlooking the south side of the port is said to have originally been named Mont Juif for the Jewish cemetery once on its slopes. Montjuïc is now Barcelona's largest and lushest public space, a vast complex of museums and exhibition halls, gardens and picnic grounds, sports facilities—and even a Greek-style amphitheater.

A bit remote from the bustle of Barcelona street life, Montjuïc more than justifies a day or two of exploring. The Miró Foundation, the Museu Nacional d'Art de Catalunya, the minimalist Mies van der Rohe Pavilion, the lush Jardins de Mossèn Cinto Verdaguer, and the gallery and auditorium of the CaixaFòrum (the former Casaramona textile factory) are all among Barcelona's must-see sights. There are buses within Montjuïc that visitors can take from sight to sight.

Fodor's Choice **Fundació Miró.** The Miró Foundation, a gift from the artist Joan Miró ★ to his native city, is one of Barcelona's most exciting showcases of contemporary art. The airy, white building, with panoramic views north over Barcelona, was designed by the artist's close friend and collaborator Josep Lluís Sert and opened in 1975; an extension was added by Sert's pupil Jaume Freixa in 1988. Miró's playful and colorful style, filled with Mediterranean light and humor, seems a perfect match for its surroundings, and the exhibits and retrospectives that open here tend to be progressive and provocative. Look for Alexander

Architect Arata Isozaki designed the futuristic Palau Sant Jordi Sports Palace.

Calder's fountain of moving mercury. Miró himself rests in the cemetery on Montjuïc's southern slopes. During the Franco regime, which he strongly opposed, Miró first lived in self-imposed exile in Paris, then moved to Mallorca in 1956. When he died in 1983, the Catalans gave him a send-off amounting to a state funeral. ⊠ *Av. Miramar 71, Montjuïc* ☎ *93/4439470* ⊕ *www.fundaciomiro-bcn.org* 🖾 *€11* ☉ *Tues., Wed., Fri., and Sat. 10–7, Thurs. 10–9:30, Sun. 10–2:30.*

Mies van der Rohe Pavilion. One of the masterpieces of the Bauhaus School, the legendary Pavelló Mies van der Rohe—the German contribution to the 1929 International Exhibition, reassembled between 1983 and 1986—remains a stunning "less is more" study in interlocking planes of white marble, green onyx, and glass. In effect, it is Barcelona's aesthetic antonym (possibly in company with Richard Meier's Museu d'Art Contemporani and Rafael Moneo's Auditori) to the flamboyant Art Nouveau—the city's signature Modernisme—of Gaudí and his contemporaries. Don't fail to note the mirror play of the black carpet inside the pavilion with the reflecting pool outside, or the iconic Barcelona chair designed by Mies van der Rohe (1886–1969); reproductions of the chair have graced modern interiors around the world for decades. A free guided tour in English is offered on Saturday at 10 am. ⊠ *Av. Francesc Ferrer i Guàrdia 7, Montjuïc* ☎ *93/4234016* ⊕ *www.miesbcn. com* 🖾 *€5* ☉ *Daily 10–8; guided tours Sat. at 10.* Ⓜ *Espanya.*

Fodor's Choice **Museu Nacional d'Art de Catalunya** (*Catalonian National Museum of Art, MNAC*). Housed in the imposingly domed, towered, frescoed, and columned **Palau Nacional**, built in 1929 as the centerpiece of the International Exposition, this superb museum was renovated in 1995 by Gae

Aulenti, architect of the Musée d'Orsay in Paris. In 2004 the museum's three holdings—Romanesque, Gothic, and the Cambó Collection—an eclectic trove, including a Goya, donated by Francesc Cambó—were joined by the 19th- and 20th-century collection of Catalan impressionist and Moderniste painters. Also now on display is the Thyssen-Bornemisza collection of early masters, with works by Zurbarán, Rubens, Tintoretto, Velázquez, and others. With this influx of artistic treasure, the MNAC (Museu Nacional d'Art de Catalunya) becomes Catalonia's grand central museum. Pride of place goes to the Romanesque exhibition, the world's finest collection of Romanesque frescoes, altarpieces, and wood carvings, most of them rescued from chapels in the Pyrenees during the 1920s to save them from deterioration, theft, and art dealers. Many, such as the famous fresco *Cristo de Taüll* (from the church of Sant Climent de Taüll in Taüll), have been painstakingly removed from crumbling walls of abandoned sites and remounted on ingenious frames that exactly reproduce the contours of their original settings. The central hall of the museum, with its enormous pillared and frescoed cupola, is stunning. ⊠ *Palau Nacional, Montjuïc* ☎ *93/6220376* ⊕ *www.mnac. cat* ⊠ *€12, valid for day of purchase and one other day in same month (free Sat. 3–6 and 1st Sun. of the month)* ⊙ *Jun.–Sept., Tues.–Sat. 10–8, Sun. 10–3; Oct.–May, Tues.–Sat. 10–6, Sun. 10–3* Ⓜ *Espanya.*

WHERE TO EAT

Barcelona's restaurant scene is an ongoing adventure. Between avant-garde culinary innovation and the more rustic dishes of traditional Catalan fare, there is a fleet of brilliant classical chefs producing some of Europe's finest Mediterranean cuisine.

Catalans are legendary lovers of fish, vegetables, rabbit, duck, lamb, game, and natural ingredients from the Pyrenees or the Mediterranean. The *mar i muntanya* (literally "sea and mountain," or "surf and turf") is a standard. Combining salty and sweet tastes—a Moorish legacy—is another common theme.

The Mediterranean diet—based on olive oil, seafood, fibrous vegetables, onions, garlic, and red wine—is at home in Barcelona, embellished by Catalonia's four basic sauces: *allioli* (whipped garlic and olive oil), *romesco* (almonds, nyora peppers, hazelnuts, tomato, garlic, and olive oil), *sofregit* (fried onion, tomato, and garlic), and *samfaina* (a ratatouille-like vegetable mixture).

Use the coordinate (✥ B2) at the end of each listing to locate a site on the corresponding map.

MEALTIMES

Barcelona dines late. Lunch is served 1:30–4 and dinner 9–11.

RESERVATIONS

Nearly all of Barcelona's best restaurants require reservations.

PRICES

Whereas low-end fixed-price lunch menus can be found for as little as €10, most good restaurants cost closer to €30 to €40 ordering à la carte. For serious evening dining, plan on spending €55–€80 per person. *Prices in the restaurant reviews are the average cost of a main course at dinner or, if dinner is not served, at lunch; for tapas bars, the price reflects the cost of a light meal of 4–5 selections.*

TIPPING AND TAXES

Tipping is not required as gratuity is included. If you do tip, 5% to 10% is acceptable.

WHAT IT COSTS IN EUROS				
	$	$$	$$$	$$$$
Restaurants	under €16	€16–€22	€23–€29	over €29

Prices are per person for a main course at dinner.

CIUTAT VELLA: BARRI GÒTIC, BORN-RIBERA, LA RAMBLA, AND EL RAVAL

Chic new restaurants come and go, but the top places in the Old City endure.

BARRI GÒTIC

$$ ✕ **Agut.** Wainscoting and 1950s' canvases are the background for the
CATALAN mostly Catalan crowd in this homey restaurant in the lower reaches of the Gothic Quarter. Agut was founded in 1924, and its popularity has never waned—after all, hearty Catalan fare at a fantastic value is always in demand. In season (September–May), try the *pato silvestre agridulce* (sweet-and-sour wild duck). There's a good selection of wine, but no frills such as coffee or liqueur. $ *Average main: €16* ✉ *Gignàs 16, Barri Gòtic* ☎ *93/315–1709* ⊕ *www.restaurantagut.com* ☽ *Closed Mon., and 2 wks in Aug. No dinner Sun.* Ⓜ *Jaume I* ✛ *D5.*

$$ ✕ **Café de l'Acadèmia.** With wicker chairs, stone walls, and classi-
CATALAN cal music playing, this place is sophisticated-rustic, and the excellent contemporary Mediterranean cuisine specialties such as *timbal d'escalibada amb formatge de cabra* (roast vegetable salad with goat cheese) or *crema de pastanaga amb gambes i virutes de parmesá* (cream of carrot soup with shrimp and Parmesan cheese shavings) make it more than a mere café. Politicians and functionaries from the nearby Generalitat frequent this dining room, which is always boiling with life. Be sure to reserve at lunchtime. $ *Average main: €18* ✉ *Lledó 1, Barri Gòtic* ☎ *93/319–8253* ☽ *Closed weekends and 2 wks in Aug.* Ⓜ *Jaume I* ✛ *D5.*

$$ ✕ **Cometacinc.** In an increasingly chic neighborhood of artisans and anti-
CATALAN quers, this stylish place in the Barri Gòtic is a fine example of Barcelona's new-over-old architecture and interior-design panache. Although the 30-foot, floor-to-ceiling, wooden shutters are already a visual feast, the carefully prepared interpretations of old standards such as the *xai al forn* (roast lamb) or the more surprising *raviolis de vieiras* (scallop

BEST BETS FOR BARCELONA DINING

Fodor'sChoice★

Ca l'Isidre, $$$$, p. 494

Casa Leopoldo, $$$$, p. 495

Cinc Sentits, $$$$, p. 498

El Vaso de Oro, $, p. 496

Embat, $$, p. 499

Enoteca, $$$$, p. 496

Gelonch, $$$, p. 499

Gresca, $$, p. 499

La Mar Salada, $$, p. 497

La Taverna Del Clinic, $$$, p. 500

Manairó, $$, p. 500

Quimet i Quimet, $, p. 495

Roca Moo, $$$, p. 501

Silvestre, $$, p. 503

Tram-Tram, $$$, p. 504

Via Veneto, $$$$, p. 504

By Price

$

Bambarol, p. 503

Ca l'Estevet, p. 494

Cera 23, p. 495

El Vaso de Oro, p. 496

Irati Taverna Basca, p. 489

Vivanda, p. 504

$$

Café de l'Acadèmia, p. 487

Cometacinc, p. 487

Embat, p. 499

Gresca, p. 499

La Mar Salada, p. 497

Manairó, p. 500

Silvestre, p. 503

$$$

Espai Sucre, p. 488

Gelonch, p. 499

Ipar-Txoko, p. 502

La Taverna Del Clinic, p. 500

Roca Moo, p. 501

Tram-Tram, p. 504

$$$$

Ca l'Isidre, p. 494

Casa Leopoldo, p. 495

Cinc Sentits, p. 498

Enoteca, p. 496

Via Veneto, p. 504

raviolis) awaken the palate brilliantly. The separate dining room, for a dozen to two-dozen diners, is a perfect place for a private party. $ *Average main: €17 ⌧ Carrer Cometa 5, Barri Gòtic ☎ 93/310–1558 ⊕ www. cometacinc.com ⦿ No lunch ⓂJaume I ⊹ D5.*

$$$
ECLECTIC
✕ **Cuines Santa Caterina.** A lovingly restored market designed by the late Enric Miralles and completed by his widow Benedetta Tagliabue provides a spectacular setting for one of the city's most original dining operations. Under the undulating wooden superstructure of the market, the breakfast and tapas bar, open from dawn to midnight, offers a variety of culinary specialties cross-referenced by different cuisines (Mediterranean, Asian, vegetarian) and products (pasta, rice, fish, meat), all served on sleek counters and long wooden tables. $ *Average main: €22 ⌧ Av. Francesc Cambó 16, Barri Gòtic ☎ 93/268–9918 ⊕ www. cuinessantacaterina.com Ⓜ Urquinaona, Jaume I ⊹ E4.*

$$
CATALAN
✕ **El Bitxo.** An original wine list and an ever-rotating selection of interesting cavas accompany creative tapas and small dishes from foie (duck or goose liver) to ibérico hams and cheeses, all in a rustic wooden setting 50 yards from the Palau de la Música, close enough for intermissions. $ *Average main: €10 ⌧ Carrer Verdaguer i Callis, 9, Sant Pere ☎ 93/268–1708 ⦿ Tues.–Sat. 1–1, Mon. 7 pm–1 am Ⓜ Urquinaona ⊹ E4.*

$$$
ECLECTIC
✕ **Espai Sucre.** The world's first dessert-only restaurant sounds like one of those terrible ideas that receives ridicule on reality TV shows, but Espai Sucre has been making a success of this distinctive concept since 2000. Attached to a creative and pioneering patisserie school that Willy

Wonka would be proud of, this 30-seat restaurant serves multicourse tasting menus based around sweet-and-savory "desserts" that never fail to astonish and somehow never feel overwhelming. Consider "goat-cheesecake" with raspberries, red pepper, and ginger; or squid rice with saffron custard and passion fruit. The innovation-for-innovation's-sake has been scaled back in recent years, but this is still a long way from a conventional dining experience—expect the unexpected. $ *Average main: €28* ✉ *Princesa 53, Born-Ribera* ☎ *93/268–1630* ⊕ *www.espaisucre.com* ⚲ *Reservations essential* ⊘ *Closed Sun. and Mon. No lunch* Ⓜ *Arc de Triomf* ✛ *E5.*

$ ✕ **Irati Taverna Basca.** There's only one drawback to this lively Basque
TAPAS bar between Plaça del Pi and the Rambla: it's narrow at the street end and harder to squeeze into than the Barcelona metro at rush hour. Try coming on the early side, at 1 pm or 7:30 pm. The tapas—skip the ones on the bar and opt for the plates brought out piping-hot from the kitchen—should be accompanied by a freezing and refreshing *txakolí,* the young Basque white wine with a spritzer. The dozen tables in the back are surprisingly relaxed and crowd-free, and serve excellent Basque cuisine. $ *Average main: €7* ✉ *Cardenal Casañas 17, Barri Gòtic* ☎ *902/520522* ⊕ *www.iratitavernabasca.com* ⊘ *10 am–midnight* Ⓜ *Liceu* ✛ *D4.*

$$ ✕ **Pla.** Filled with young couples night after night, this combination
CATALAN music, drinking, and dining place is candlelit and sleekly designed in glass over ancient stone, brick, and wood. The cuisine is light and contemporary, featuring inventive salads and fresh seafood. Open until 3 am (kitchen until 12:30 am) on Friday and Saturday, Pla is a good postconcert option. $ *Average main: €18* ✉ *Carrer Bellafila 5, Barri Gòtic* ☎ *93/412–6552* ⊕ *www.elpla.cat* ⊘ *No lunch* Ⓜ *Jaume I* ✛ *D5.*

$$$$ ✕ **Saüc.** Saüc's location in the Hotel Ohla two steps from the Palau de
CATALAN la Música Catalana has catapulted chef Xavi Franco's inventive culinary offerings to increased acclaim. Named for the curative elderberry plant, Saüc's elegantly modern decor—wide wood-plank floors and softly draped tablecloths—sets the mood, and the avant-garde tabletop centerpiece is the first hint that the fare here is far from standard. This postmodern *cuina d'autor* (original cuisine) uses fine ingredients and combines them in flavorful surprises such as scallops with cod tripe and black sausage or monkfish with snails. The tasting menu is an unbroken series of unusual combinations of standard products, none of which fail to please. Try the *coulant de chocolate y maracuyá* (chocolate pudding with passion fruit) for dessert. $ *Average main: €34* ✉ *Via Laietana 49, Barri Gòtic* ☎ *93/321–0189* ⊕ *www.ohlahotel.com* ⚲ *Reservations essential* ⊘ *Daily 1:30–4 and 8:30–11* Ⓜ *Urquinaona* ✛ *D4.*

$ ✕ **Taberna Les Tapes.** Proprietors and chefs Barbara and Santi offer a
TAPAS special 10-selection tapas anthology at this narrow, cozy, cheery place, just behind the town hall and just seaward of Plaça Sant Jaume. Barbara, originally from Worcestershire, England, takes especially good care of visitors from abroad. The 10-tapa medley for two (€12.75) with croquettes, squash omelet, wild mushrooms, patatas bravas, chistorra, pimientos de Padrón, and four more according to market and season is a popular choice here. $ *Average main: €15* ✉ *Pl. Regomir*

7

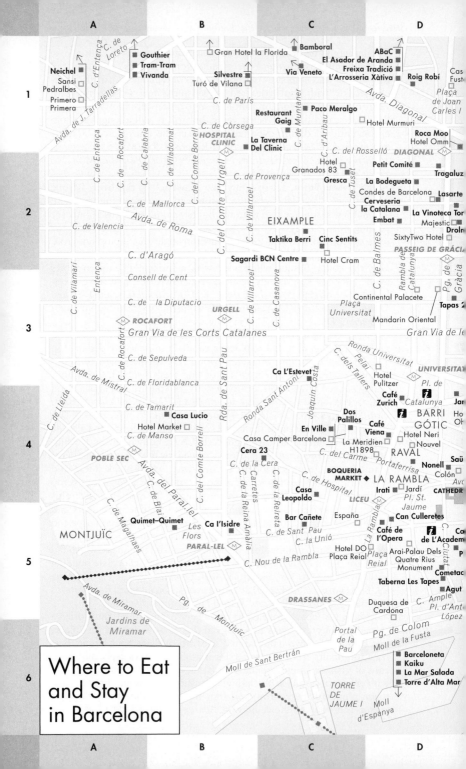

A   **B**   **C**   **D**

1

Neichel ■
Sansi
Pedralbes ■
Primero
Primera □

C. d'Enteça
C. de Loreto

↑ Gouthier ■
Tram-Tram ■
Vivanda ■

Silvestre ■
Turó de Vilana □

□ Gran Hotel la Florida

■ Bamboral

Via Veneto ■

ABaC ■
El Asador de Aranda ■
Freixa Tradició ■
L'Arrosseria Xàtiva ■   Roig Robí ■

Cas
Fust

Avda. Diagonal

Plaça
de Joan
Carles I

C. de París

Avda. de J. Tarradellas

C. de Córsega

**HOSPITAL
CLINIC** Ⓜ

Restaurant
Gaig ■

La Taverna
Del Clinic ■

■ Paco Meralgo

□ Hotel Murmuri

Roca Moo ■
Hotel Omm

DIAGONAL Ⓜ

C. de Enteça

C. de Rocafort

C. de Calabria

C. de Viladomat

C. del Comte Borrell

C. de Provença

Hotel
Granados 83 □

Gresca ■

C. del Rosselló

Petit Comité ■

La Bodegueta ■

Condes de Barcelona ■
Cerveseria
la Catalana ■   La Vinoteca Tor

Tragaluz ■

Lasarte ■

C. d'Aribau

C. de Muntaner

C. de Tuset

2

C. de Mallorca

Avda. de Roma

C. de Valencia

C. de Valencia

EIXAMPLE

Taktika Berri ■

Sagardi BCN Centre ■

Cinc Sentits ■

Hotel Cram □

Embat ■

SixtyTwo Hotel □

PASSEIG DE GRÁCIA Ⓜ

Majestic □

Drol

C. del Comte d'Urgell

C. de Villarroel

C. de Balmes

Rambla de
Catalunya

Pg. de
Gràcia

3

C. de Vilamarí

Enteça

C. d'Aragó

Consell de Cent

C. de la Diputacio

URGELL Ⓜ

Ⓜ **ROCAFORT** Ⓜ

Gran Via de les Corts Catalanes

C. de Rocafort

C. de Villarroel

C. de Casanova

Plaça
Universitat

Continental Palacete ■

Mandarin Oriental ■

Tapas 2

Gran Via de le

4

Avda. de Mistral

C. de Lleida

C. de Sepulveda

C. de Floridablanca

C. de Tamarit

Casa Lucio ■

Hotel Market □

C. de Manso

POBLE SEC

Avda. del Paral·lel

Rda. de Sant Pau

Ronda Sant Antoni

Ca L'Estevet ■

Casa Camper Barcelona □

Cera 23 ■

C. de la Cera

Ronda Universitat

Pelai

C. dels Tallers

Joaquin Costa

Dos
Palillos ■

En Ville ■

Café
Viena ■

La Meridien □

C. del Carme

Hotel
Pulitzer □

Café
Zurich ■

Catalunya

🛈

Pl. de

UNIVERSITAT Ⓜ

**BARRI
GÒTIC**

Jar

Ho
Oh

Hotel Neri □
Nouvel

5

MONTJUÏC

C. de Magalhaes

Avda. del Paral·lel

Avda. de Blai

C. del Comte Borrell

Les
Flors

Quimet–Quimet ■

Ca l'Isidre ■

PARAL·LEL Ⓜ

C. Nou de la Rambla

C. de la Cera

Carretes

C. de la Reina Amàlia

C. de la Retreta

C. de Hospital

**BOQUERIA
MARKET** ◆

Casa
Leopoldo ■

Bar Cañete ■

España ■

C. de Sant Pau

C. la Unió

Hotel DO □
Plaça Reial

LA RAMBLA

Irati ■

LICEU Ⓜ

Café de
l'Opera ■

Arai-Palau Dels
Quatre Rius ■

Jardí □
Pl. St.
Jaume

Can Culleretes ■

🛈
de L'Academ

RAVAL

Portaferrisa

Nonell ■

Colón ■

CATHEDR

Jardí □

La Rambla

C. d'Ciutat

Saü

Avd

Co

P

Monument

Cometac

Taberna Les Tapes ■

Agut ■

Duquesa de
Cardona ■

C. Ample

Pl. d'Ant
López

DRASSANES Ⓜ

Portal
de la
Pau

Pg. de Colom

Moll de la Fusta

Barceloneta ■
Kaiku ■
La Mar Salada ■
Torre d'Alta Mar ■

6

Avda. de Miramar

Pg. de Montjuïc

Jardins de
Miramar

Moll de Sant Bertrán

**TORRE
DE
JAUME I**   Moll
d'Espanya

Where to Eat
and Stay
in Barcelona

A   **B**   **C**   **D**

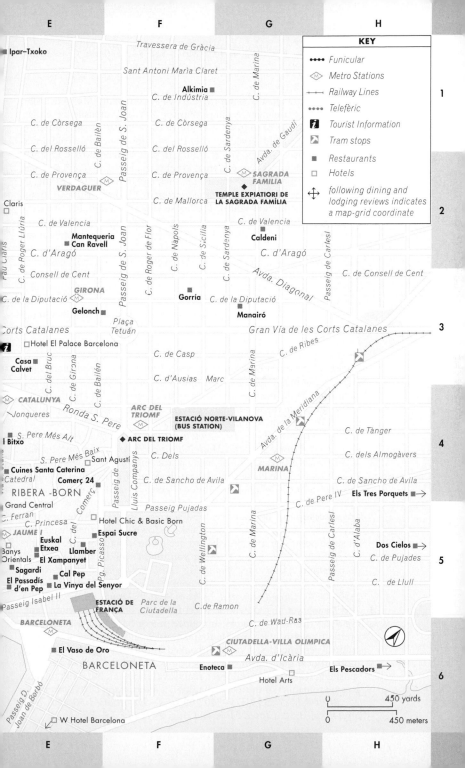

4, Barri Gòtic ☏ *93/302–4840* ⊙ *Mon.–Sat. 5–11:30 pm. Closed Aug.* Ⓜ *Jaume I* ✛ *D5.*

BORN-RIBERA

$$
TAPAS

✕ **Cal Pep.** Cal Pep, a two-minute walk east from Santa Maria del Mar, has been in a permanent feeding frenzy for 30 years, intensified even further by the hordes of tourists who now flock here. Pep serves a selection of tapas, cooked and served hot over the counter. Generally avoid ordering the fish dishes (unless you're willing to part with an extra €35–€50), and stick with green peppers, fried artichokes, garbanzos and spinach, baby shrimp, the "trifasic" (mixed tiny-fish fry), the nonpareil tortilla de patatas, and *botifarra trufada en reducción de Oporto* (truffled sausage in Port-wine reduction sauce). The house wines are good, but the Torre la Moreira Albariño perfectly complements Pep's offerings. Be prepared to wait for 20 minutes for a place at the counter. Reservations for the tables in the tiny back room are accepted, but reserve well in advance and know that you'll miss out on the lively counter scene. Ⓢ *Average main: €18* ✉ *Pl. de les Olles 8, Born-Ribera* ☏ *93/310–7961* ⊕ *www. calpep.com* ⊙ *Closed Sun. and 3 wks in Aug. No lunch Mon.; no dinner Sat.* Ⓜ *Jaume I, Barceloneta* ✛ *E5.*

$$$$
CATALAN

✕ **Comerç 24.** Artist, aesthete, and chef Carles Abellán playfully reinterprets traditional Catalan favorites and creates new ones at this artfully decorated dining spot on Carrer Comerç. Try the *arroz d'ànec amb foie* (rice with duck and foie gras). For dessert, don't miss the postmodern version of the traditional Spanish after-school snack of chocolate, olive oil, salt, and bread. Abellán trained under superstar Ferran Adrià and is as original as the master; the best way to experience his creativity is to throw budget to the winds and order one of the two tasting menus (€92 and €116, without wine). Ⓢ *Average main: €32* ✉ *Carrer Comerç 24, Born-Ribera* ☏ *93/319–2102* ⊕ *www.projectes24.com* ⚲ *Reservations essential* ⊙ *Closed Sun. and Mon. No lunch* Ⓜ *Arc de Triomf* ✛ *E4.*

$$$$
SEAFOOD

✕ **El Passadís d'en Pep.** Hidden away at the end of a narrow unmarked passageway off the Pla del Palau, near the Santa Maria del Mar church, this restaurant is a favorite with local politicos and fat cats from the nearby stock exchange. Sit down, and waiters begin to serve a rapid-fire succession of delicious seafood starters, whatever's freshest that day in the market. Don't bother asking for a menu: there isn't one. At some point you may be asked to decide on a main course; if you're already full, feel free to pass—but you might well be missing a *pièce de résistance.* Ⓢ *Average main: €38* ✉ *Pl. del Palau 2, Born-Ribera* ☏ *93/310–1021* ⊕ *www.passadis.com* ⊙ *Mon.–Sat. 12:30–3:30 and 8:30–11:30. Closed Sun. and 3 wks in Aug.* Ⓜ *Jaume I* ✛ *E5.*

$
TAPAS

✕ **El Xampanyet.** Just down the street from the Picasso Museum, hanging *botas* (leather wineskins) announce one of Barcelona's liveliest and prettiest taverns, with marble-topped tables and walls decorated with colorful ceramic tiles; it's usually packed to the rafters with a rollicking mob of local and out-of-town celebrants. Avoid the oversweet house sparkling wine (go for draft beer, real Cava, or wine), but don't miss the pa amb tomaquet or the ibérico ham. Ⓢ *Average main: €10* ✉ *Montcada 22, Born-Ribera* ☏ *93/319–7003* ⊙ *Tues.–Sat. noon–3:30 and 7–11, Sun. noon–3:30. Closed Mon. and Aug.* Ⓜ *Jaume I* ✛ *E5.*

$$ ✕ **Euskal Etxea.** An elbow-shaped, pine-panel space, this spot (one of
BASQUE the Sagardi group of Basque restaurants) is one of the better grazing
destinations in the Gothic Quarter, with a colorful array of tapas and
canapés on the bar ranging from the olive-pepper-anchovy on a tooth-
pick to chunks of tortilla or *pimientos de piquillo* (red piquillo peppers)
stuffed with codfish paste. An excellent and usually completely booked
restaurant (don't miss the Euskal Txerria confit and crispy suckling
pig with thistle and walnuts) and a Basque cultural circle and art gal-
lery round out this social and gastronomical oasis. $ *Average main:
€18* ⊠ *Placeta de Montcada 1–3, Born-Ribera* ☏ *902/520522* ⊕ *www.
euskaletxeataberna.com* ⊙ *Daily 11 am–midnight* Ⓜ *Jaume I* ✢ *E5.*

$ ✕ **Llamber.** Although it may look like one of the many stylish, tourist-
TAPAS trap tapas restaurants that have sprung up here in recent years, Lla-
FAMILY mber's culinary pedigree sets it apart from the competition. Chef
Francisco Heras learned his chops in Spain's top restaurants before
opening his own establishments in his home region of Asturias and
then Llamber in Barcelona. Efficient and friendly, this dapper space
attracts a mixed crowd of couples and families with its excellent wine
list and well-crafted tapas based on classic Spanish and Catalan recipies.
Consider the splendidly light eggplant with honey, and potatoes stuffed
with *cabrales* cheese and hazelnut praline. Year-round late-night hours
make it a handy option. $ *Average main: €11* ⊠ *Carrer de la Fusina 5,
Born-Ribera* ☏ *93/319–6250* ⊕ *www.llamberbarcelona.com* ⊙ *Daily
12:30 pm–1:30 am* Ⓜ *Jaume 1* ✢ *E5.*

$$ ✕ **Sagardi.** An attractive wood-and-stone cider-house replica, Sagardi
BASQUE piles the counter with a dazzling variety of cold tapas; even better are
the hot offerings straight from the kitchen. The restaurant in back serves
Basque delicacies like veal sweetbreads with artichokes and *txuletas
de buey* (beef steaks) grilled over coals. The other Sagardi branches at
Carrer Muntaner 70–72 and Avinguda Diagonal 3 (in Diagonal Mar)
are equally good. $ *Average main: €22* ⊠ *Carrer Argenteria 62, Born-
Ribera* ☏ *93/319–9993* ⊕ *www.sagardi.com* ⊙ *Daily 1:30–3:30 and
8–midnight* Ⓜ *Jaume I* ✢ *E5.*

LA RAMBLA

$ ✕ **Café de l'Opera.** Directly across from the Liceu opera house, this high-
CAFÉ ceiling Art Nouveau–interior café has welcomed operagoers and performers for more than 100 years. It's a central point on the Rambla
traffic pattern and a good place to run into unexpected friends and ex-
lovers. But don't expect to fill up here, just catch a drink and take in
the scene. $ *Average main: €7* ⊠ *Rambla 74, Rambla* ☏ *93/317–7585*
⊕ *www.cafeoperabcn.com* ⊙ *Daily 8 am–2:30 am* Ⓜ *Liceu* ✢ *D5.*

$ ✕ **Café Viena.** There are more than 40 Viena cafés in Catalonia, but this
CAFÉ particular branch is always packed with international travelers trying
what Mark Bittman of the *New York Times* once consecrated as "the
best sandwich in the world." One wonders if it was the only one he'd
ever eaten: the *flautas de jamón ibérico* (thin bread "flutes" of ibérico
ham anointed with tomato squeezings) here are perfectly adequate
but no better than those served in any typical Spanish bar and, at €9,
are considerably more expensive. Viena is a pleasant enough place to
have a snack, especially when the pianist is playing on the balcony,

but it doesn't live up to the hype. Ⓢ *Average main: €8* ⊠ *La Rambla 115, Rambla* ☎ *93/317–1492* ⊕ *www.viena.es* ⊘ *Daily 8 am–1:30 am* Ⓜ *Catalunya* ⊹ *D4.*

$ ✕ **Café Zurich.** This traditional café at the top of La Rambla and directly
CAFÉ astride the main metro and transport hub remains the city's prime meeting point. Prices are reasonable, considering the location, but the sandwiches and snacks could most charitably be described as ordinary. Forget the food and enjoy a beer or coffee at a table on the terrace, perhaps the best spot in the city to observe street life. Pickpockets are rife here, so watch your belongings as closely as you watch the passersby. Ⓢ *Average main: €5* ⊠ *Pl. Catalunya 1, Rambla* ☎ *93/317–9153* ▬ *No credit cards* ⊘ *Weekdays 8 am–11 pm, weekends 9 am–midnight* Ⓜ *Catalunya* ⊹ *D4.*

$ ✕ **Can Culleretes.** Just off La Rambla in the Gothic Quarter, this family-
CATALAN run restaurant founded in 1786 displays tradition in both decor and culinary offerings. Generations of the Manubens and Agut families have kept this unpretentious spot—Barcelona's oldest restaurant (listed in the *Guinness Book of Records*)—popular for more than two centuries. Wooden beams overhead and bright paintings of sea- and landscapes on the walls surround a jumble of tables. The cooking is solid rather than sophisticated, but traditional Catalan specialties such as spinach cannelloni with cod, wild boar stew, and white beans with botifarra sausage are competently presented. Ⓢ *Average main: €13* ⊠ *Calle Quintana 5, Rambla* ☎ *93/317–3022* ⊕ *www.culleretes.com* ⊘ *Closed Mon. and July. No dinner Sun.* Ⓜ *Liceu* ⊹ *D5.*

EL RAVAL

$ ✕ **Ca l'Estevet.** Journalists, students, and artists haunt this romantic little
CATALAN spot near the MACBA (contemporary art museum), across the street from Barcelona's journalism school, and around the block from the former offices of Barcelona's *La Vanguardia* daily newspaper. Estevet and family are charming, and the carefully elaborated Catalan cuisine sings, especially at these prices. Try the asparagus cooked over coals, the *chopitos gaditanos* (deep-fried baby octopus), or the *magret de pato* (duck breast). The house wine is inexpensive, light, and perfectly drinkable. Ⓢ *Average main: €14* ⊠ *Valldonzella 46, El Raval* ☎ *93/302–4186* ⊕ *www.restaurantestevet.com* ⊘ *No dinner Sun.* Ⓜ *Universitat* ⊹ *C3.*

$$$$ ✕ **Ca l'Isidre.** A throwback to an age before foams and food science took
CATALAN over the gastronomic world, this restaurant has elevated simplicity to
Fodor's Choice the level of the spectacular since the early 1970s. Isidre and Montserrat
★ share their encyclopedic knowledge of local cuisine with guests while their daughter, Núria, cooks traditional Catalan dishes to an extraordinarily high standard using fresh produce from the nearby Boqueria market. Ignore the menu—just follow their recommendations and order whatever's in season. The restaurant is decorated with original works by a slew of luminaries, including Miró and Dalí, both former patrons. Spain's King Juan Carlos celebrated his wedding anniversary here. Ⓢ *Average main: €38* ⊠ *Les Flors 12, El Raval* ☎ *93/441–1139* ⊕ *www.calisidre.com* ⊰ *Reservations essential* ⊘ *Closed Sun., Easter wk, and 1st 2 wks of Aug.* Ⓜ *Paral.lel* ⊹ *B5.*

$$$$ CATALAN Fodor's Choice ★ 🍴 **Casa Leopoldo.** In a hard-to-find pocket of the Raval, west of the Rambla, this family-run restaurant serves fine seafood and Catalan fare. To get here, approach along Carrer Hospital, take a left through the Passatge Bernardí Martorell, and go 50 feet right on Sant Rafael to the front door. Try the *revuelto de ajos tiernos y gambas* (eggs scrambled with young garlic and shrimp) or the famous *cap-i-pota* (stewed head and hoof of pork). Albariños and Priorats are among owner Rosa Gil's favorite wines. [$] *Average main: €38* ✉ *Sant Rafael 24, El Raval* ☎ *93/441–3014* 🌐 *www.casaleopoldo.com* ⏲ *Closed Mon. and late July–late Aug. No dinner Sun.* [M] *Liceu* ✥ *C4.*

$ SPANISH 🍴 **Cera 23.** The pick of a crop of new restaurants putting the razzle back into the run-down Raval, Cera 23 offers a winning combination of great service and robust cooking in a fun, friendly setting. Stand at the bar and enjoy a blackberry mojito cocktail while you wait for your table. The open kitchen is in the dining area, so guests can watch the cooks creating contemporary presentations of traditional dishes. Try the Volcano of Black Rice, with seafood "rocks" and saffron-flavored "lava," and the homemade duck foie gras *mi-cuit* (cooked partly through). The reasonably priced restaurant is usually packed until late, but the surrounding area can be intimidating at night; get a taxi to the end of the street. [$] *Average main: €14* ✉ *Carrer de la Cera 23, El Raval* ☎ *93/442–0808* 🌐 *www.cera23.com* ⏲ *No lunch* [M] *Sant Antoni* ✥ *B4.*

$$ BISTRO 🍴 **En Ville.** With French-Mediterranean cuisine and reasonable prices, this attractive bistro 100 yards west of the Rambla in the MACBA section of the Raval is a keeper. The lunch menu for under €10 would be reason enough to try their *risotto de setas y esparragos trigueros* (wild mushroom risotto with wild asparagus), while à la carte choices are tempting and economical. [$] *Average main: €16* ✉ *Dr. Dou 14, El Raval* ☎ *93/302–8467* 🌐 *www.envillebarcelona.es* ✍ *Reservations essential* ⏲ *Closed Mon. No dinner Sun.* [M] *Catalunya, Liceu, Universitat* ✥ *C4.*

POBLENOU

$$ TAPAS 🍴 **Els Tres Porquets.** Somewhat off the beaten path (though handy to the Auditori and the Teatre Nacional de Catalunya and not that far from the Sagrada Familia), Els Tres Porquets (The Three Little Pigs) packs in foodies and bon vivants. A wide range of morsels, tapas, and small plates are the way to go here, with everything from ibérico ham to *torta del Casar* cheeses and regional specialties from all around the Iberian Peninsula. [$] *Average main: €16* ✉ *Rambla del 165, Poblenou* ☎ *93/300–8750* 🌐 *www.elstresporquets.es* ✍ *Reservations essential* ⏲ *Mon.–Sat. 10–4 and 8:30–11.* [M] *Glòries, Clot* ✥ *H4.*

POBLE SEC

$ TAPAS Fodor's Choice ★ 🍴 **Quimet i Quimet.** A foodie haunt, this tiny place is hugely popular with locals and in-the-know visitors alike. If you come too late, you might not be able to get in. Come before 1:30 pm and 7:30 pm, and you will generally find a stand-up table. Fourth-generation chef-owner Quim and his family improvise ingenious canapés. All you have to do is orient them toward cheese, anchovies, or whatever it is you might crave, and they masterfully do the rest *and* recommend the wine to go with it. [$] *Average main: €15* ✉ *Poeta Cabanyes 25, Poble Sec* ☎ *93/442–3142*

🕐 *Weekdays noon–4 and 7–10:30, Sat. noon–4* 🕐 *Closed Aug.* Ⓜ *Paral. lel* ✛ *B5.*

BARCELONETA AND THE PORT OLÍMPIC

Barceloneta and the Port Olímpic (Olympic Port) have little in common beyond their seaside location: the former is a traditional fishermen's quarter; the latter is a crazed disco strip with thousand-seat restaurants.

$$$
SEAFOOD

✕ **Barceloneta.** This restaurant, in an enormous riverboat-like building at the end of the yacht marina in Barceloneta, is definitely geared up for high-volume business. But the food is delicious, the service impeccable, and the hundreds of fellow diners make the place feel like a cheerful New Year's Eve celebration. Rice and fish dishes are the house specialty, and the salads are excellent. $ *Average main: €24* ✉ *L'Escar 22, Barceloneta* ☎ *93/221–2111* ⊕ *www.restaurantbarceloneta.com* Ⓜ *Barceloneta* ✛ *D6.*

$$$
SEAFOOD
FAMILY

✕ **Els Pescadors.** A kilometer northeast of the Olympic Port in the interesting Sant Martí neighborhood, this handsome late-19th-century bistro-style dining room has a lovely terrace on a little square shaded by immense ficus trees. Kids can play safely in the traffic-free square while their parents concentrate on well-prepared seafood specialties such as paella, fresh fish, or *fideuá* (paella made with noodles). $ *Average main: €26* ✉ *Pl. de Prim 1, Sant Martí* ☎ *93/225–2018* ⊕ *www.elspescadors. com* Ⓜ *Poblenou* ✛ *H6.*

$
TAPAS
Fodor'sChoice
★

✕ **El Vaso de Oro.** A favorite with gourmands from Barcelona and beyond, this often overcrowded little counter serves some of the best beer and tapas in town. The artisanal draught beer, specially brewed for this classic bar, is drawn and served with loving care, with just the right amount of foam and always at the correct temperature. The high rate of consumption ensures you will never encounter a stale keg. To eat, the *solomillo con foie y cebolla* (beef filet mignon with duck liver and onions) is an overwhelming favorite, but the fresh fish prepared *a la plancha* (on the grill) is also excellent. $ *Average main: €10* ✉ *Balboa 6, Barceloneta* ☎ *93/319–3098* ⊕ *www.vasodeoro.com* Ⓜ *Barceloneta* ✛ *E6.*

$$$$
CATALAN
Fodor'sChoice
★

✕ **Enoteca.** Located in the Hotel Arts, Enoteca has established a reputation for creative and surprising cooking using peerless Mediterranean and Pyrenean products, from the finest wild-caught turbot to black trumpet wild mushrooms in season to spring lambs from Burgos. The gorgeous white-on-white dining room captures a fresh modern look. White rectangular shelving echos the wall of windows that keeps things light. A 550-bottle wine list and the bottle theme in the decoration remind diners that this is, after all, an enoteca or wine library. $ *Average main: €40* ✉ *Hotel Arts, Marina 19, Port Olímpic* ☎ *93/483–8108* ⊕ *www.hotelartsbarcelona.com* 🕐 *Closed Sun.* Ⓜ *Ciutadella–Vila Olímpica* ✛ *G6.*

$$
SEAFOOD
FAMILY

✕ **Kaiku.** You could easily pass by this undistinguished-looking little dining room on the edge of the beach at the end of Passeig Joan de Borbó. But seeking it out is worth your while; the seafood here is excellent and the value is ironclad. Rice dishes, mussels, sea anemones, fish soup are all hearty. Try the *arròs del xef*, a smoky rice with calamari, asparagus, and wild mushrooms. The wine list has some surprising choices at reasonable prices. $ *Average main: €16* ⌧ *Pl. del Mar 1, Barceloneta* ☎ *93/221–9082* ⊕ *www.restauranTKaiku.cat* ⌦ *Reservations essential* ✆ *Closed Tues. No dinner mid-Sept.–mid-May* Ⓜ *Barceloneta* ✛ *D6.*

$$ ✕ **La Mar Salada.** This restaurant stands out along a street of seafood
SEAFOOD specialists by offering creative twists on classic dishes at rock-bottom
Fodor's Choice prices. Traditional favorites such as paella, black rice, fideuá, and simple
★ fresh fish are invigorated by the cooking of Chef Marc Sengla—also consider the delicious creations of dessert chef Albert Enrich. The fixed-price lunch menu changes weekly and offers a budget-friendly way to try what's in season. Freshness is assured, as the main ingredients come directly from the *lonja* fish quay across the street, a lively auction where Barcelona's small fishing fleet sells its wares. You can't do much better for value and quality in Barceloneta. $ *Average main: €18* ⌧ *Passeig Joan de Borbó 58, Barceloneta* ☎ *93/221–2127* ⊕ *www.lamarsalada. cat* ✆ *Closed Tues.* Ⓜ *Barceloneta* ✛ *D6.*

$$$$ ✕ **Torre d'Alta Mar.** Location, location, location: at a height of 250 feet
MEDITERRANEAN over the Barcelona waterfront in the Eiffel-tower-like Sant Sebastià cable-car station over the far side of the port, this restaurant has spectacular 360-degree views of Barcelona as well as far out into the Mediterranean. Seafood of every stripe, spot, fin, and carapace emanates from the kitchen here, but the mar i muntanya combination of pork and prawns adds a meaty twist for carnivores. $ *Average main: €33* ⌧ *Torre de San Sebastián, Passeig Joan de Borbó 88, Barceloneta* ☎ *93/221–0007* ⊕ *www.torredealtamar.com* ⌦ *Reservations essential* ✆ *Closed Mon. No lunch Sun.* Ⓜ *Barceloneta* ✛ *D6.*

EIXAMPLE

Eixample dining, invariably upscale and elegant, ranges from traditional cuisine to designer fare in sleek minimalist spaces.

$$$$ ✕ **Alkimia.** Chef Jordi Vilà is making news here with his inventive cre-
CATALAN ations and tasting menus at €68 and €94 that still manage to pass for a bargain at the top end of Barcelona culinary culture even in the current economy. The €39 price tag on the midday menu is daunting, but well worth the outlay. Vilà's deconstructed pa amb tomaquet served in a shot glass is just a culinary wink before things get deadly serious with raw tuna strips, baby squid, or turbot. Venison or beef brings the taste progression to a close before dessert provides a sweet ending. $ *Average main: €30* ⌧ *Indústria 79, Eixample* ☎ *93/207–6115* ⊕ *alkimia. cat* ⌦ *Reservations essential* ✆ *Closed weekends* Ⓜ *Sagrada Família, Joanic* ✛ *G1.*

$$$ ✕ **Caldeni.** This clean, simple place par excellence is the perfect antidote
CATALAN to the sensory overload of Gaudí's nearby Sagrada Família. A past winner of the Chef of the Year award in the annual Fòrum Gastronòmic de Girona, Dani Lechuga produces streamlined cuisine that is invariably long on taste and short on cost, especially if you take advantage of the bargain lunch prix-fixe menu. A specialist in beef of all kinds (Wagyu, Kobe, Angus, Girona, Asturian oxen), Caldeni also does tapas, soups, and an assortment of tastings, making any stop here a gastronomical

event. $ *Average main: €26* ✉ *València 452, Eixample* ☎ *93/232–5811* ⊕ *www.caldeni.com* ⊙ *Closed Sun., Mon., and 3 wks in Aug.* Ⓜ *Sagrada Família* ✛ *G2.*

$$$ ✕ **Casa Calvet.** It's hard to pass up the opportunity to break bread in a
MEDITERRANEAN Gaudí-designed building. Completed in 1900, the Art Nouveau Casa Calvet includes a graceful dining room decorated in Moderniste ornamentation, from looping parabolic door handles to polychrome stained glass, etched glass, and wood carved in floral and organic motifs. Popular with local business people who want to entertain guests in style, the restaurant exudes velvet-and-mahogany charm and also attracts couples seeking an intimate meal for two. Chef Miguel Ajita's Catalan and Mediterranean fare is contemporary, seasonal and market-inspired. $ *Average main: €28* ✉ *Casp 48, Eixample* ☎ *93/412–4012* ⊕ *www.casacalvet.es* ⊙ *Closed Sun.* Ⓜ *Urquinaona* ✛ *E3.*

$$$ ✕ **Casa Lucio.** With preserved and fresh ingredients and original dishes
TAPAS flowing from the kitchen, this miniaturesque and handsome (though not inexpensive) dazzler two blocks south of the Mercat de Sant Antoni is well worth tracking down. Lucio's wife, chef Maribel, is relentlessly inventive. Try the *tastum albarole* (cured sheep cheese from Umbria) or the *pochas negras con morcilla* (black beans with black sausage). $ *Average main: €24* ✉ *Viladomat 59, Eixample* ☎ *93/424–4401* ⊙ *Mon.–Sat. 1–4 and 8–11* Ⓜ *Sant Antoni* ✛ *B4.*

$$ ✕ **Cerveseria la Catalana.** A bright and booming bar with a few tables on
TAPAS the sidewalk, this spot is always packed for a reason: excellent food at fair prices. Try the small *solomillos* (filets mignons), minimorsels that will take the edge off your carnivorous appetite without undue damage to your wallet, or the jumbo shrimp brochettes. $ *Average main: €15* ✉ *Mallorca 236, Eixample* ☎ *93/216–0368* Ⓜ *Diagonal, Passeig de Gracia* ✛ *D2.*

$$$$ ✕ **Cinc Sentits.** The engaging Artal clan—led by master chef Jordi—is
CATALAN a Catalan-Canadian family offering something unique in Barcelona:
Fodor's Choice cutting-edge, contemporary cooking explained eloquently in English.
★ There's no à la carte option, only tasting menus: *Essèncias* is the simplest and *Sensacions* is more creative, while the lunchtime-only *Gastronomic* is top-of-the-line, foodie nirvana. The wine pairings, like the food, are obsessively local and scrupulously selected. Expect to spend from €59 to a budget-busting €109, not including drinks, depending on the menu. $ *Average main: €36* ✉ *Aribau 58, Eixample* ☎ *93/323–9490* ⊕ *cincsentits.com* ✍ *Reservations essential* ⊙ *Closed Sun. and Mon.* Ⓜ *Provença* ✛ *C2.*

$$$$ ✕ **Dos Cielos.** Twins Javier and Sergio Torres have leaped to the top of
MEDITERRANEAN Barcelona's culinary charts as well as to the top tower of the Hotel ME. It only seems fitting that their restaurant be named Dos Cielos, *cielo* being Spanish for heaven. A panoramic dining room around a vast open kitchen offers dazzling 360-degree views of the city. The cuisine, combining Brazilian, French, and Valencian touches reflecting the twins' accumulated culinary experiences around the world, is no less brilliant: pasta with black olives and sun-dried tomatoes, steamed organic vegetables, and *crema de mandioquinha con caviar de sagú* (cream of Brazilian white carrot with pearls of sago palm). $ *Average main: €42*

⌗ *Pere IV 272–286, Eixample* ☎ *93/367–2070* ⊕ *www.doscielos.com* ⌕ *Reservations essential* ☾ *Closed Sun. and Mon.* Ⓜ *Poble Nou* ✛ *H5.*

$$$
ECLECTIC
✕ **Dos Palillos.** After 10 years as the chief cook and favored disciple of the pioneering chef Ferran Adrià, Albert Raurich opened this Asian fusion restaurant with a Spanish-Mediterranean touch—and he's garnered a Michelin star for it. Past the typical Spanish bar in the front room, the dining room inside is a canvas of rich black surfaces bordered with red chairs around the kitchen, where an international staff of Japanese, Chinese, Colombian, and Scottish cooks do cooking performances of Raurich's eclectic assortment of tastes and textures. Nippon burgers (beef, ginger, cucumber, and shiso on steamed bun), dumplings, dim sum, and tataki of 150-day-aged Galician beef vie for space on the €75 and €90 tasting menus. Ⓢ *Average main: €28* ⌗ *Elisabets 9, Eixample* ☎ *93/304–0513* ⊕ *www.dospalillos.com* ⌕ *Reservations essential* ☾ *Closed Sun. and Mon. No lunch Tues. and Wed.* Ⓜ *Catalunya, Universitat* ✛ *C4.*

$$
CATALAN
Fodor'sChoice
★
✕ **Embat.** An *embat* is a puff of wind in Catalan, and this little "bistronomic" is a breath of fresh air in the swashbuckling Eixample. The highly affordable market cuisine is always impeccably fresh and freshly conceived, starring thoughtful combinations such as the *cazuelita de alcachofas con huevo poché y papada* (casserole of artichokes and poached egg with pork dewlap) or the *pichón con bizcocho de cacao y cebolla confitada* (wood pigeon with cacao biscuit and onion confit). Ⓢ *Average main: €18* ⌗ *Mallorca 304, Eixample* ☎ *93/458–0885* ⊕ *www.restaurantembat.es* ⌕ *Reservations essential* ☾ *Closed Sun. and Mon. No dinner Tues. and Wed.* Ⓜ *Verdaguer* ✛ *D2.*

$$$
CATALAN
Fodor'sChoice
★
✕ **Gelonch.** This gem of a restaurant is something of a secret sensation in Barcelona. Listed in few guides, it caters mainly to clued-in locals who have fallen in love with chef-owner Robert Gelonch's relentless creativity and pursuit of perfection. It's worth making the effort to join them—the restaurant is off the beaten tourist track but still near the center of the neighborhood. Once there, depending on how hungry you are, expect to be astonished by a procession of small dishes from the short (€56) or long (€74) tasting menu. Ⓢ *Average main: €25* ⌗ *Bailen 56, Eixample* ☎ *93/265–8298* ⊕ *www.gelonch.es* ⌕ *Reservations essential* ☾ *Closed Sun., Mon., and last wk in Aug.–1st wk Sept. No lunch* Ⓜ *Tetuan, Girona* ✛ *F3.*

$$
BASQUE
✕ **Gorría.** Named for founder Fermín Gorría, this is quite simply the best straightforward Basque-Navarran cooking in Barcelona. Everything from the stewed *pochas* (white beans) to the heroic *chuletón* (steak) is as clear and pure in flavor as the Navarran Pyrenees. The Castillo de Sajazarra reserva, a semisecret brick-red Rioja, provides the perfect accompaniment. Ⓢ *Average main: €22* ⌗ *Diputació 421, Eixample* ☎ *93/245 1164* ⊕ *www.restaurantegorria.com* ☾ *Closed Sun., Easter wk, and Aug. No dinner Mon.* Ⓜ *Monumental* ✛ *F3.*

$$
CATALAN
Fodor'sChoice
★
✕ **Gresca.** Spearhead of the so-called "bistronomic" movement in Barcelona, head chef and owner Rafa Peña aims to put the creativity and skill he learned in the world's most celebrated kitchens within the reach of those on less astronomical budgets. In his small, minimalist restaurant, he cranks out inventive dishes based on humble ingredients to a fervently loyal customer base of local foodies. Expect limited choice,

7

a well-chosen but shallow wine list, and some of the most delightful dishes you can find in Barcelona. The tasting menu is the best way to sample what's on offer. [$] *Average main: €20* ✉ *Provença 230, Eixample* ☎ *93/451–6193* 🌐 *www.gresca.net* ✍ *Reservations essential* ⏲ *Closed Sun. and last wk Aug.–1st wk Sept. No lunch Sat.* [M] *Diagonal* ✥ *C2.*

$$$$ BASQUE 🍴 **Lasarte.** Martin Berasategui, one of San Sebastián's fleet of master chefs, opened his Barcelona restaurant in early 2006 and triumphed from day one. Berasategui has placed his kitchen in the capable hands of Alex Garés, who trained with the best and serves an eclectic selection of Basque, Mediterranean, market, and personal interpretations and creations. Expect whimsical aperitifs and dishes with serious flavor such as foie and smoked eel or simple wood pigeon cooked to perfection. [$] *Average main: €40* ✉ *Mallorca 259, Eixample* ☎ *93/445–3242* 🌐 *www.restaurantlasarte.com* ✍ *Reservations essential* 👔 *Jacket required* ⏲ *Closed Sun., Mon., and 2 wks in Aug.* [M] *Diagonal* ✥ *D2.*

$$$ TAPAS Fodor's Choice ★ 🍴 **La Taverna Del Clinic.** The Simoes brothers have earned a solid reputation with discerning locals for serving creative and contemporary tapas based on traditional Catalan and Galician flavors. Chef Antonio left his family's restaurant to study under masters, including the late Santi Santamaria, before launching La Taverna with his brother, Manuel, a sommelier. Their cramped bar spills out onto a sunny street terrace where customers can enjoy truffle canelones, oyster tartare, and an award-winning variation on patatas bravas, paired with selections from the excellent wine list. [$] *Average main: €25* ✉ *Carrer Roselló 155, Eixample* 🌐 *www.latavernadelclinic.com* ⏲ *Closed Sun.* [M] *Hospital Clinic* ✥ *B1.*

$$ CATALAN Fodor's Choice ★ 🍴 **Manairó.** A *manairó* is a mysterious Pyrenean elf and Jordi Herrera may be the culinary version. A demon with meat cooked *al clavo ardiente* (à la burning nail)—fillets warmed from within by red-hot spikes producing meat both rare and warm and never undercooked—Jordi also serves an unforgettable version of squid with blowtorch-fried eggs (*calamari de huevo frito*) and a palate-cleansing gin and tonic with liquid nitrogen, gin, and lime. The intimate and edgy design of the dining room is a perfect reflection of the cuisine. [$] *Average main: €20* ✉ *Diputació 424, Eixample* ☎ *93/231–0057* 🌐 *www.manairo.com* ✍ *Reservations essential* ⏲ *Closed Sun. and 1st wk of Jan.* [M] *Sagrada Família* ✥ *G3.*

$ TAPAS 🍴 **Mantequeria Can Ravell.** Lovers of exquisite wines, hams, cheeses, oils, whiskies, cigars, caviars, baby eels, anchovies, and any other delicacy you can think of—this is your spot. The backroom table open from midmorning to early evening is first come, first served; complete strangers share tales, tastes, and textures at this foodie forum. [$] *Average main: €15* ✉ *Carrer Aragó 313, Eixample* ☎ *93/457–5114* 🌐 *www.ravell.com* ⏲ *Tues.–Sat. 10–9, Sun. 10–3* [M] *Girona* ✥ *E2.*

$ TAPAS 🍴 **Paco Meralgo.** The name, a pun on *para comer algo* ("to eat something" with an Andalusian accent), may be only marginally amusing, but the tapas here are no joke at all, from the classical *calamares fritos* (fried cuttlefish rings) to the *pimientos de Padrón* (green peppers, some fiery, from the Galician town of Padrón.) Whether à table, at the counter, or in the private dining room upstairs, this modern space always rocks. [$] *Average main: €12* ✉ *Carrer Muntaner 171, Eixample* ☎ *93/430–9027* 🌐 *www.pacomeralgo.com* ⏲ *Mon.–Sat. 1–4 and 8–12:30* [M] *Hospital Clinic* ✥ *C1.*

$$ CATALAN 🍴 **Restaurant Gaig.** A rustic interpretation of the traditional cuisine that has made the Gaig family culinary stars, this cozy split-level restaurant has made a name for itself in Barcelona's ever-changing dining scene. As passions cooled for molecular gastronomy, Carles Gaig and a growing number of top chefs have returned to simpler and more affordable models. Look for standards such as *botifarra amb mongetes de ganxet* (sausage with white beans) or *perdiu amb vinagreta calenta* (partridge withe warm vinagrette) or *tartar de llobarro i gamba* (sea bass and shrimp tartare). The ample dining room is, in contrast to the cuisine, stylishly contemporary, with comfortable armchairs à table. [$] *Average main: €18* ✉ *Còrsega 200, Eixample* ☎ *93/453–2020, 93/429–1017* 🌐 *www.restaurantgaig.com* ✍ *Reservations essential* ⏲ *Closed Mon. and 2 wks in Aug. No dinner Sun.* [M] *Hospital Clínic* ✥ *C1.*

$$$ CATALAN Fodor's Choice ★ 🍴 **Roca Moo.** In any space as spectacular as Roca Moo, located in the Hotel Omm, there's a real risk of the food playing second fiddle to the surroundings. Fortunately, head chef Felip Llufriu keeps the spotlight firmly on the menu designed by the world-renowned El Cellar de Can Roca team. From behind the counter of an open kitchen he cooks with a zenlike precision that suits the restaurant's Tokyo vibe. The dishes, like the space, are stylish and creative but draw on deep wells of Spanish culinary traditions, elevating humble barroom snacks like Russian salad and pig-trotter carpaccio with prawns to dazzling heights. The Menu Joan Roca is the chef's favorite, a tour-de-force balancing act of gutsy flavors and contemporary techniques matched with impressive wine selections. [$] *Average main: €28* ✉ *Roselló 265, Eixample* ☎ *93/445–4000* 🌐 *www.hotelomm.es/en/roca-moo* ⏲ *Closed Sun., Mon., and Jan. 6–15* [M] *Diagonal* ✥ *D1.*

$ TAPAS 🍴 **Tapas 24.** Celebrity chef Carles Abellán's irrepressibly creative Comerç 24 has been a hit for years, and his tapas emporium has followed suit. Here Abellán shows us how much he admires traditional Catalan and Spanish bar food, from patatas bravas to *croquetas de jamón ibérico* (croquettes made of Iberian ham). The counter can get crowded, but you can always take refuge on the terrace. [$] *Average main: €14* ✉ *Carrer Diputació 269, Eixample* ☎ *93/488–0977* 🌐 *www.carlesabellan.es/restaurantes-tapas-24* ⏲ *Mon.–Sat. 8 am–midnight* [M] *Passeig de Gràcia* ✥ *D3.*

$$ BASQUE 🍴 **Taktika Berri.** Specializing in San Sebastián's favorite dishes, this Basque restaurant has only one drawback—a table is hard to score unless you call weeks in advance (an idea to consider before you travel). Your backup plan? The tapas served over the first-come, first-served bar: They're of such a high quality, you can barely do better à table. And the charming family that owns and runs this gem is the very definition of hospitality. [$] *Average main: €20* ✉ *Valencia 169, Eixample* ☎ *93/453–4759* ✍ *Reservations essential* ⏲ *Closed Sun. No dinner Sat.* [M] *Hospital Clinic* ✥ *C2.*

$$$ MEDITERRANEAN 🍴 **Tragaluz.** *Tragaluz* means skylight and this is an excellent choice if you're still on a design high from shopping at Vinçon or visiting Gaudí's

7

Pedrera. The sliding roof opens to the stars in good weather, while the chairs, lamps, and fittings by Javier Mariscal (creator of 1992 Olympic mascot Cobi) reflect Barcelona's ongoing passion for playful design. The Mediterranean cuisine is traditional yet light and innovative. Luis de Buen's TragaFishh (an outpost from his restaurant Fishhh!) is the downstairs oyster bar. The redesigned main dining room upstairs is reached via the kitchen, and the top floor is an informal space for coffee or an after-dinner drink. $ *Average main: €28* ⊠ *Passatge de la Concepció 5, Eixample* ☎ *93/487–0621* ⊕ *www.grupotragaluz.com* ⌂ *Reservations essential* ⊙ *Daily 1:30–4 and 8:30–11:30* Ⓜ *Diagonal* ✣ *D2.*

GRÀCIA

This exciting yet intimate neighborhood has everything from the most sophisticated cuisine in town to lively Basque taverns.

$$$
BASQUE
✕ **Ipar-Txoko.** This excellent little Basque enclave has managed to stay largely under the radar, and for that reason, among others (the cuisine is authentic, the prices are fair, and the service is personal and warm), it's a fantastic choice. A balanced menu offers San Sebastián specialties such as *txuleta de buey* (ox steak) or *besugo a la donostiarra* (sea bream covered with scales of crispy garlic and a vinegar sauce), flawlessly prepared, while the wine list presents classic Riojas and freezing Txomin Etxaniz txakolí straight from Getaria. $ *Average main: €24* ⊠ *Carrer Mozart 22, Gràcia* ☎ *93/218–1954* ⊕ *www.ipar-txoko.com* ⌂ *Reservations essential* ⊙ *Closed Sun. and Aug. No dinner Mon.* Ⓜ *Gràcia, Diagonal* ✣ *E1.*

$$$
SPANISH
✕ **L'Arrosseria Xàtiva.** This rustic dining room in Gràcia, a spinoff from the original in Les Corts, evokes the rice paddies and lowlands of Valencia and eastern Spain. Low lighting imparts a warm glow over exposed brick walls, beamed ceilings, and bentwood chairs. It's a great spot to savor some of Barcelona's finest paellas and rice dishes. Fish, seafood, and meats cooked over coals round out a complete menu prepared with loving care and using top ingredients. $ *Average main: €24* ⊠ *Torrent d'en Vidalet 26, Gràcia* ☎ *93/284–8502* ⊕ *www.arrosseriaxativa.com* Ⓜ *Joanic* ✣ *D1.*

$$$$
CATALAN
✕ **Roig Robí.** Rattan chairs and a garden terrace characterize this simple-yet-polished dining spot in the bottom corner of Gràcia just above the Diagonal (near Via Augusta). Rustic and relaxed, Roig Robí (ruby red in Catalan, as in the color of certain wines) maintains a high level of culinary excellence, serving traditional Catalan market cuisine with original touches directed by chef Mercé Navarro. A good example? The *arròs amb espardenyes i carxofes* (rice with sea cucumbers and artichokes). $ *Average main: €32* ⊠ *Seneca 20, Gràcia* ☎ *93/218–9222* ⊕ *www.roigrobi.com* ⌂ *Reservations essential* ⊙ *Closed Sun. and Aug. No lunch Sat.* Ⓜ *Diagonal* ✣ *D1.*

SARRIÀ, PEDRALBES, AND SANT GERVASI

An excursion to the upper reaches of town offers an excellent selection of restaurants, little-known Gaudí sites, shops, cool evening breezes, and a sense of village life in Sarrià.

$ CATALAN

🍴 **Bambarol.** The unpretentious nature of this new restaurant isn't what you might expect when looking at the galaxy of stars that chef-owners Ferran Maicas and Albert Ferrer have helped earn for some of Spain's most famous kitchens. The décor is simple, the names of dishes straightforward, and the cooking style entirely absent of palate-twisting molecular gastronomy. Despite—or perhaps because of—this, it's booked solid every night, with a growing waiting list of locals and in-the-know tourists. Friendly service and honest cooking executed to a very high standard for modest prices provides a winning combination. The menu is a mix of Catalan and Asian tapas—try the wonderful scallops with pork and wild mushrooms. [$] *Average main: €13* ✉ *Carrer Santaló 21, Tres Torres* ☎ *93/250–7074* 🌐 *www.bambarol.cat* ✍ *Reservations essential* 🕒 *Closed Sun. No lunch Tues.–Fri.* [M] *Gràcia* ✥ *C1.*

$$$ CATALAN

🍴 **Freixa Tradició.** When wunderkind molecular gastronomist Ramón Freixa turned the family restaurant back over to his father, Josep Maria Freixa, there was some speculation about the menu's headlong rush into the past. Now that the results are in, Barcelona food cognoscenti are coming in droves for the authentic Catalan fare that made El Racó d'en Freixa great before experimental cuisine took over the culinary landscape. Creamy rice with cuttlefish, monkfish with fried garlic, pig trotters with prunes and pine nuts and robust selection of local specialties are making the new-old Freixa better than ever. The dining room is all white-tablecloth elegance, but a witty installation of copper pots on the wall gives a wink to its traditional roots. [$] *Average main: €21* ✉ *San Elies 22, Sant Gervasi* ☎ *93/209–7559* 🌐 *www.freixatradicio.com* 🕒 *Closed Mon., Easter wk, and Aug. No dinner Sun.* [M] *Sant Gervasi* ✥ *D1.*

$$$ MEDITERRANEAN

🍴 **Neichel.** Originally from Alsace, chef Jean-Louis Neichel skillfully manages a vast variety of exquisite ingredients such as foie gras, truffles, wild mushrooms, herbs, and the best seasonal vegetables. With his son Mario now at the burners, and his identical triplet daughters taking turns serving tables, Neichel is fully a family operation. His flawless Mediterranean delicacies include *ensalada de gambas de Palamós al sésamo con puerros* (shrimp from Palamós with sesame-seed and leeks) and *espardenyes amb salicornia* (sea cucumbers with saltwort) on sun-dried tomato paste. The dining room is classically elegant with bold red accent walls and contrasting crisp white tablecloths. [$] *Average main: €27* ✉ *Carrer Bertran i Rózpide 1, Pedralbes* ☎ *93/203–8408* 🌐 *www.neichel.es* ✍ *Reservations essential* 🕒 *Closed Sun., Mon., and Aug.* [M] *Maria Cristina* ✥ *A1.*

$$ MEDITERRANEAN
Fodor's Choice ★

🍴 **Silvestre.** A graceful and easygoing mainstay in Barcelona's culinary galaxy, this restaurant serves modern cuisine to some of the city's most discerning and distinguished diners. Located just below Via Augusta, Silvestre's series of intimate dining rooms and cozy corners are carefully tended by chef Guillermo Casañé and his charming wife Marta Cabot, a fluent English–speaking maître d' and partner. Look for fresh market produce lovingly prepared in dishes such as tuna tartare, noodles and shrimp, or wood pigeon with duck liver. Willy's semisecret list of house wines is always surprising for its quality and value. [$] *Average main: €20* ✉ *Santaló 101, Sant Gervasi* ☎ *93/241–4031* 🌐 *www.*

restaurante-silvestre.com ⏲ *Closed Sun., 3 wks in Aug., and Easter wk. No lunch Sat.* [M] *Muntaner* ✣ *B1.*

$$$ CATALAN Fodor's Choice ★ 🍴 **Tram-Tram.** At the end of the old tram line above the village of Sarrià, this restaurant offers one of Barcelona's finest culinary stops, with Isidre Soler and his wife Reyes at the helm. Try the menú de degustació and you might be lucky enough to get marinated tuna salad, cod medallions, and venison filet mignon, among other tasty creations. Perfectly sized portions and a streamlined, airy white space within this traditional Sarrià house add to the experience. In nice weather, request a table in the garden out back. [$] *Average main: €22* ✉ *Major de Sarrià 121, Sarrià* ☎ *93/204–8518* 🌐 *www.tram-tram.com* ✍ *Reservations essential* ⏲ *Closed Sun., Mon., Easter wk, and 2 wks in Aug.* [M] *Reina Elisenda* ✣ *A1.*

$$$$ CATALAN Fodor's Choice ★ 🍴 **Via Veneto.** Open since 1967, this family-owned temple of fine Catalan dining offers a contemporary menu punctuated by old-school classics. Elegant and stylish, the restaurant was a favorite of Salvador Dalí and now attracts local sports stars and politicians. Service is impeccable, and diners can safely place themselves in the hands of the expert staff to guide them through modern variations of regional specialties and a daunting 10,000-bottle wine list. The starter of tagliolini pasta with free-range eggs cooked at a low temperature and served with Alba (Piedmont) white truffle threatens to be a showstopper, but the theatrical presentation of roast baby duck, deboned and pressed at the table, provides a memorable second act. [$] *Average main: €38* ✉ *Ganduxer 10, Sarrià* ☎ *93/200–7244* 🌐 *www.viavenetorestaurant.com* ⏲ *Closed Sun. and Aug. 1–20. No lunch Sat.* [M] *Hospital Clínic* ✣ *C1.*

$ MEDITERRANEAN 🍴 **Vivanda.** Just above Plaça de Sarrià, Vivanda produces traditional Catalan miniatures, *para picar* (small morsels), *platillos* (little dishes), and half rations of meat and fish listed as *platillos de pescado* and *platillos de carne*, thanks to a redesigned menu by Alkimia's Jordi Vilà. The *coca de pa de vidre con tomate* (a delicate shell of bread with tomato and olive oil) and the venison-like *presa de ibérico* (filet of ibérico pig) are both exquisite. Weather permitting, book a table in the lush back garden for lunch. [$] *Average main: €12* ✉ *Major de Sarrià 134, Sarrià* ☎ *93/203–1918* ⏲ *No dinner Sun.* [M] *Reina Elisenda* ✣ *A1.*

TIBIDABO

$$$$ CATALAN 🍴 **ABaC.** Chef Jordi Cruz, the youngest chef ever to win a Michelin star and author of two books on his culinary philosophy and techniques, is known for his devotion to impeccable raw materials and his talent for combining creativity and tradition. The tasting menu is the only reasonable choice here: trust this chef to give you the best he has (and any attempt at economy is roughly analagous to quibbling about deck chairs on the Titanic). The hypercreative sampling has ranged from tartare of oysters with green-apple vinegar, fennel, and seawort to veal royal with concentrate of Pedro Ximénez sherry and textures of apples in cider. Connected to an exquisite five-star boutique hotel of the same name, the dining room, awash in beige and white linens with dark wooden floors in wide planks, delivers a suitably elegant backdrop. [$] *Average main: €48* ✉ *Av. del Tibidabo 1–7, Tibidabo* ☎ *93/319–6600* 🌐 *www.*

abacbarcelona.com ⧉ *Reservations essential* ⊘ *Closed Sun. and Mon. No lunch.* Ⓜ *Tibidabo* ✛ *D1.*

$$$$ ✕ **El Asador de Aranda.** It's a hike to this immense palace a few-min-
SPANISH utes walk above the Avenida Tibidabo metro station—but worth it if you're in upper Barcelona. The kitchen specializes in Castilian cook-ing, with *cordero lechal* (roast suckling lamb), *morcilla* (black sau-sage), and *pimientos de piquillo* (sweet red peppers) as star players. The Art Nouveau details here—carved-wood trim, stained-glass partitions, engraved glass, Moorish archways, and terra-cotta floors—belie the fact that this extravagantly beautiful building was originally a nun-nery, funded by wealthy members of the Catalan industrial bourgeoisie as a place to stash their errant daughters. Ⓢ *Average main: €46* ⊠ *Av. del Tibidabo 31, Tibidabo* ☎ *93/417–0115* ⊕ *www.asadordearanda. com* ⧉ *Reservations essential* ⊘ *No dinner Sun.* Ⓜ *Penitents, Vallcarca, Tibidabo* ✛ *D1.*

WHERE TO STAY

Barcelona's hotel trade may be centuries removed from Miguel de Cer-vantes's 17th-century description of it as a "repository of courtesy, travelers' shelter," but in the 400 years or so since *Don Quijote* the city has never lost its talent for pampering visitors.

Barcelona's pre-Olympics hotel surge in the early 1990s was matched only by its post-Olympics hotel surge in the early 2000s. Barcelona is the premier tourist destination in Spain and the major cruise port in the Mediterranean. Starchitects like Ricardo Bofill and Rafael Moneo have changed the skyline with skyscraper hotels of eye-popping luxury; the Grand Hyatt group is about to add another, acquiring Jean Nou-vel's emblematic Torre Agbar for the latest in it its collection. The real heroes of this story, however, are the architect-designer teams that take one after another of the city's historic properties and restore them with an astonishing tour de force of taste. Hotel restaurants, too—from the Arts's Enoteca to the Mandarin's Moments—are among the superstar attractions in the city's gastronomic scene.

Use the coordinate (✛ B2) at the end of each listing to locate a site on the corresponding map.

Hotel reviews have been shortened. For full information, visit Fodors. com.

WHAT IT COSTS IN EUROS			
$	$$	$$$	$$$$
Hotels	under €125	€125–€174	€175–€225	over €225

Prices are for two people in a standard double room in high season, excluding tax.

BEST BETS FOR BARCELONA LODGING

Fodor's Choice★	Majestic Hotel & Spa, $$$, p. 511	Hotel Murmuri, p. 511
Arai-Palau Dels Quatre Rius Monument, $$$, p. 506	Primero Primera, $$$, p. 512	**$$$**
Casa Fuster, $$$$, p. 512	Turó de Vilana, $, p. 512	Arai-Palau Dels Quatre Rius Monument, p. 506
Claris, $$$$, p. 510	W Barcelona, $$$$, p. 510	Hotel España, p. 509
Condes de Barcelona, $$, p. 510	**By Price**	Majestic Hotel & Spa, p. 511
Continental Palacete, $$, p. 510	**$**	Hotel Neri, p. 507
H1898, $$$$, p. 508	Banys Orientals, p. 508	Hotel Ohla, p. 507
Hotel Arts, $$$$, p. 510	Jardí, p. 508	Primero Primera, p. 512
Hotel España, $$$, p. 509	Turó de Vilana, p. 512	**$$$$**
Hotel Granados 83, $$, p. 511	**$$**	Casa Fuster, p. 512
Hotel Murmuri, $$, p. 511	Colón, p. 506	Claris, p. 510
Hotel Neri, $$$, p. 507	Condes de Barcelona, p. 510	H1898, p. 508
Hotel Omm, $$$$, p. 511	Continental Palacete, p. 510	Hotel Arts, p. 510
Jardí, $, p. 508	Duquesa de Cardona, p. 508	Hotel DO Plaça Reial, p. 508
Le Méridien Barcelona, $$$$, p. 509	Hotel Granados 83, p. 511	Hotel Omm, p. 511
		Mandarin Oriental, p. 511
		W Barcelona, p. 510

CIUTAT VELLA

The Ciutat Vella includes the Rambla, Barri Gòtic, Born-Ribera, and Raval districts between Plaça de Catalunya and the port.

BARRI GÒTIC

$$$ HOTEL FAMILY Fodor's Choice ★ Arai-Palau Dels Quatre Rius Monument. You couldn't ask for a better location from which to explore Barcelona's Gothic Quarter—or for a bivouac more elegant—than one of the aparthotel suites in this stunning restoration. **Pros:** warm, attentive service; double shower heads in the bath; top-tier amenities; strategic location; superb soundproofing. **Cons:** pool on the rooftop terrace is tiny; no spa; no room service; rooms on the top floor lack some of the historic charm below. $ *Rooms from: €200* ⊠ *Avinyó 30, Barri Gòtic* ☎ *93/320–3950* ⊕ *www.hotelarai.com/#!en/home* ⌨ *30 rooms* ❖*No meals* ✛ *D5.*

$$ HOTEL Colón. The Colón opened in 1951, and feels like it's been around forever: quiet, conservative, correct. **Pros:** walking distance from all of central Barcelona; pet-friendly; attentive staff. **Cons:** can feel a bid stodgy; pricey breakfast; undistinguished dining. $ *Rooms from: €150* ⊠ *Av. Catedral 7, Barri Gòtic* ☎ *93/301–1404* ⊕ *www.hotelcolon.es* ⌨ *15 singles, 121 doubles, 5 suites* ❖*No meals* Ⓜ *Catalunya* ✛ *D4.*

WHERE TO STAY?

	Neighborhood Vibe	Pros	Cons
Ciutat Vella	Busy. The Rambla never sleeps, the Raval is exciting and exotic, the Barri Gòtic is quiet and medieval, and Born-Ribera hums with restaurants and taverns.	The pulse of the metropolis beats strongest here; the Boqueria, Santa Caterina, and Barceloneta markets throng with shoppers, while must-see sites are only steps away.	The incessant crush of humanity along the Rambla can be overwhelming, though the Barri Gòtic and Born-Ribera are quieter. The Raval is rough and seedy.
Eixample	Some of Gaudí's best buildings take pride of place here, and many of the city's finest hotels and restaurants are right around the corner. And then there's the shopping . . .	The Eixample remains the world's only Art Nouveau neighborhood, constantly rewarding to the eye. Gaudí's unfinished masterpiece La Sagrada Família is within walking distance.	A bewildering grid without numbers or alphabetization, the Eixample can seem hard-edged compared to the older, quirkier, parts of Barcelona.
Barceloneta and Port Olímpic	The onetime fisherman's quarter, Barceloneta retains its informal and working-class ambience, with laundry flapping over the streets and sidewalk restaurants lining Passeig Joan de Borbó.	Near the beach, this part of town has a laid-back feel. The Port Olímpic is a world apart, but Barceloneta is brimming with the best seafood dining spots in town.	Barceloneta offers few hotel opportunities, while the Port Olímpic's principal offering, the monolithic Hotel Arts, can feel like a tourist colony away from the rest of town.
Pedralbes, Sarrià, and Upper Barcelona	Upper Barcelona is leafy and residential, and the air is always a few degrees cooler. Pedralbes holds Barcelona's finest mansions; Sarrià is a rustic village suspended in the urban sprawl.	Getting above the fray and into better air has distinct advantages, and the upper reaches of Barcelona offers them. A 15-minute train ride connects Sarrià with the Rambla.	The only drawback to staying in Upper Barcelona is the 15-minute commute to the most important monuments and attractions. After midnight on weeknights this will require a taxi.

7

$$$
HOTEL
Fodor's Choice
★

Hotel Neri. Built into an 18th-century palace just steps from the Cathedral, this elegant upscale boutique hotel marries ancient and avant-garde design. **Pros:** central location; hip design; roof terrace for cocktails and breakfast. **Cons:** noise from adjacent Plaça Sant Filip Neri can be a problem on summer nights (and winter-morning school days); impractical hanging bed lights. $ *Rooms from: €200* ⊠ *Sant Sever 5, Barri Gòtic* ☏ *93/304–0655* ⊕ *www.hotelneri.com* 📞 *14 doubles, 8 suites* ⭕*No meals* Ⓜ *Liceu, Catalunya* ✛ *D4.*

$$$
HOTEL

Hotel Ohla. One of Barcelona's top new design hotels, the Ohla's neoclassical exterior (not counting the goofy eyeballs stuck to the facade) belies its avant-garde interior, full of witty, design-conscious touches. **Pros:** strategic location, a two-minute walk from the Palau de la Música Catalana; attentive, professional staff. **Cons:** layout in some rooms sacrifices privacy to design; Via Laietana, just outside, is a nonstop noisy traffic artery. $ *Rooms from: €215* ⊠ *Via Laietana 49, Barri Gòtic* ☏ *93/341–5050* ⊕ *www.ohlahotel.com* 📞 *73 rooms, 1 suite* ⭕*No meals* Ⓜ *Urquinaona* ✛ *D4.*

$ HOTEL Fodor's Choice ★ **Jardí.** Facing charming Plaça del Pi and Plaça Sant Josep Oriol, this family-friendly little budget hotel couldn't be better situated for exploring La Rambla and the Barri Gòtic. **Pros:** central location; good value for price; impeccable bathrooms. **Cons:** no pets; no room service. [$] *Rooms from: €95* ✉ *Pl. Sant Josep Oriol 1, Barri Gòtic* ☎ *93/301–5900* 🌐 *www.eljardi-barcelona.com* 🛏 *40 rooms* 🍴 *No meals* [M] *Liceu, Catalunya* ✥ *D4.*

BORN-RIBERA

$ HOTEL **Banys Orientals.** Despite its name, the "Oriental Baths" has, for the moment, no spa, but what it does have is chic, high-contrast design, with dark stained wood and crisp white bedding, and strategic location at a reasonable price. **Pros:** central location; tasteful design; good value. **Cons:** no pets; no parking; no laundry service; communal fridge on each floor, but no room minibars. [$] *Rooms from: €115* ✉ *Argenteria 37, Born-Ribera* ☎ *93/268–8460* 🌐 *www.hotelbanysorientals.com* 🛏 *43 rooms, 14 suites* 🍴 *No meals* [M] *Jaume I* ✥ *E5.*

$$ HOTEL **Hotel Chic & Basic Born.** A revolutionary concept best illustrated by the middle-of-your-room glass shower stalls, the Chic & Basic chain is a hit with young hipsters looking for the combo package of splashy design with affordable prices. **Pros:** perfectly situated for Barcelona's hot Born-Ribera scene; clean-lined sleek design. **Cons:** tumultuous nightlife around the hotel requires closed windows on weekends; rooms and spaces are small. [$] *Rooms from: €150* ✉ *Carrer Princesa 50, Born-Ribera* ☎ *93/295–4652* 🌐 *www.chicandbasic.com/hotel-barcelona-born/en* 🛏 *31 rooms* 🍴 *No meals* [M] *Jaume I* ✥ *E5.*

LA RAMBLA

$$$$ HOTEL Fodor's Choice ★ **H1898.** Overlooking La Rambla, this imposing mansion, once the headquarters of the Compañiá General de Tabacos de Filipinas, couldn't be better located—especially with the Liceu just around the corner, for opera fans. **Pros:** impeccable service; equally ideal for families and romantic couples. **Cons:** subway rumble discernible in lower rooms on the Rambla side. [$] *Rooms from: €255* ✉ *La Rambla 109, Rambla* ☎ *93/552–9552* 🌐 *www.hotel1898.com* 🛏 *166 rooms, 3 suites* 🍴 *No meals* [M] *Catalunya, Liceu* ✥ *D4.*

$$ HOTEL **Duquesa de Cardona.** A refurbished 16th-century town house, this hotel on the port is a 10-minute walk from everything in the Barri Gòtic and Barceloneta, and no more than a 30-minute walk from the main Eixample attractions. **Pros:** great combination of traditional and contemporary; key spot near the port; ample roof terrace. **Cons:** rooms on the small side; no gym or spa; Passeig de Colom is a busy, noisy artery. [$] *Rooms from: €150* ✉ *Passeig de Colom 12, Port* ☎ *93/268–9090* 🌐 *www.hduquesadecardona.com* 🛏 *35 rooms, 5 junior suites* 🍴 *No meals* [M] *Drassanes* ✥ *D5.*

$$$$ HOTEL **Hotel DO Plaça Reial.** Just at the entrance to the Neoclassic Plaça Reial, this 2012 addition to Barcelona's growing collection of boutique hotels—with its with two restaurants, La Terraza (under the arcades on the square) and La Cuina (downstairs under graceful brick vaulting)—is a find for foodies and lovers of tasteful design. **Pros:** walking distance from everything you will want to see in the old city center; perfect

soundproofing; helpful multilingual staff. **Cons:** hard on the wallet; neighborhood can be rowdy at night. ⓢ *Rooms from: €280 ⊠ Plaça Reial 1, Rambla* ☎ *93/481–3666* ⊕ *www.hoteldoreial.com* ⟳ *18 rooms* ⎟⊚⎟ *Breakfast* Ⓜ *Liceu* ✛ *D5.*

$$$$ ⊡ **Le Méridien Barcelona.** There's no dearth of hotels along La Rambla,
HOTEL in the heart of the city, but few rival the upscale Méridien. **Pros:** cen-
Fodor's Choice tral location; spot-on professional service; gym open 24 hours. **Cons:**
★ no pool; rooms just a tad small for the price; €55/day surcharge for
pets. ⓢ *Rooms from: €250 ⊠ La Rambla 111, Rambla* ☎ *93/318–6200*
⊕ *www.lemeridien.com/barcelona* ⟳ *190 rooms, 40 suites* ⎟⊚⎟ *No meals*
Ⓜ *Catalunya* ✛ *D4.*

EL RAVAL

$$$ ⊡ **Casa Camper Barcelona.** A marriage between the Camper footwear
HOTEL empire and the Vinçon design store produced this brainchild, a 21st-
century hotel halfway between La Rambla and the MACBA (Museum
of Contemporary Art). **Pros:** handy location in mid-Raval; just steps
from MACBA and the Boqueria; hip, friendly staff. **Cons:** no pets;
no way to get a car close to the hotel door; a bit pricey for what you
get. ⓢ *Rooms from: €195 ⊠ C. Elisabets 11, El Raval* ☎ *93/342–6280*
⊕ *www.casacamper.com* ⟳ *20 rooms, 5 suites* ⎟⊚⎟ *Breakfast* Ⓜ *Catalu-
nya* ✛ *C4.*

$$$ ⊡ **Hotel España.** This recently renovated Art Nouveau gem is among
HOTEL the oldest and best of Barcelona's smaller hotels. **Pros:** strategic loca-
Fodor's Choice tion; steeped in artistic history; friendly staff; excellent restaurant ($$).
★ **Cons:** the lower rooms on Carrer Sant Pau get some street noise despite
the double-glazing; rooftop pool, spa, and gym only open April 23
through mid-October. ⓢ *Rooms from: €180 ⊠ Sant Pau 9–11, El Raval*
☎ *93/550–0000* ⊕ *www.hotelespanya.com* ⟳ *81 rooms, 1 suite* ⎟⊚⎟ *No
meals* Ⓜ *Liceu* ✛ *C5.*

$ ⊡ **Hotel Market.** Wallet-friendly and design-conscious, this boutique
HOTEL hotel is named for the Mercat de Sant Antoni a block away. **Pros:**
well equipped, designed, and positioned for a low-cost Barcelona visit;
young and friendly staff. **Cons:** rooms are a little cramped. ⓢ *Rooms
from: €69 ⊠ Carrer Comte Borrell 68, entrance on Passatge Sant
Antoni Abat 10, El Raval* ☎ *93/325–1205* ⊕ *www.markethotel.com.
es* ⟳ *59 rooms* ⎟⊚⎟ *No meals* Ⓜ *Sant Antoni* ✛ *B4.*

$$ ⊡ **Sant Agustí.** In a leafy square just off La Rambla, the Sant Agustí
HOTEL bills itself as the oldest billet in Barcelona—built in 1720 as a convent
and reborn as a hotel in 1840. **Pros:** central location near the Boqueria
market, La Rambla and the Liceu opera house; traditional design with
modern comfort; good value for price; family-friendly. **Cons:** Plaça Sant
Agusti can be a homeless hangout; soundproofing less than best; so-so
breakfast; service is hit-or-miss. ⓢ *Rooms from: €135 ⊠ Pl. Sant Agustí
3, El Raval* ☎ *93/318–1658* ⊕ *www.hotelsa.com* ⟳ *72 rooms, 8 suites*
⎟⊚⎟ *Breakfast* Ⓜ *Liceu* ✛ *E4.*

7

BARCELONETA, PORT OLÍMPIC, AND FÒRUM

$$$$
HOTEL
Fodor'sChoice
★
🏨 **Hotel Arts.** This luxurious Ritz-Carlton-owned, 44-story skyscraper overlooks Barcelona from Port Olímpic, providing stunning views of the Mediterranean, the city, the Sagrada Família, and the mountains beyond. **Pros:** excellent views over Barcelona; impeccable service; fine restaurants; minutes from the beach; family-friendly. **Cons:** a 20-minute hike, at least, from central Barcelona; hard on the budget. $ *Rooms from: €535* ⊠ *Calle de la Marina 19–21, Port Olímpic* ☎ *93/221–1000* ⊕ *www.hotelartsbarcelona.com* ⏎ *365 rooms, 44 suites, 28 apartments* ⫩⊙⫨ *No meals* Ⓜ *Ciutadella–Vila Olímpica* ⌖ *G6.*

$$$$
HOTEL
Fodor'sChoice
★
🏨 **W Barcelona.** This towering sail-shape monolith dominates the skyline on the Barcelona waterfront. **Pros:** unrivaled views and general design excitement and glamour; excellent restaurants; rooms are bright, clean-lined, with nonpareil views in all directions. **Cons:** the high-rise icon could seem garish to some; a good hike from the Barri Gòtic or the nearest public transportation. $ *Rooms from: €310* ⊠ *Pl. de la Rosa del Vents 1, Moll de Llevant, Barceloneta* ☎ *93/295–2800* ⊕ *www.w-barcelona.com* ⏎ *406 rooms, 65 suites* ⫩⊙⫨ *No meals* Ⓜ *Barceloneta* ⌖ *E6.*

EIXAMPLE

$$$$
HOTEL
Fodor'sChoice
★
🏨 **Claris.** Acclaimed as one of Barcelona's best hotels, the Claris is an artful icon of design and tradition, as is evident from the building itself: the glass-and-steel upper floors seem to have sprouted from the 19th-century town house below. **Pros:** elegant service and furnishings; central location for shopping and Moderniste sightseeing; spot-on friendly service. **Cons:** bathrooms are designer chic but a bit cramped; no spa. $ *Rooms from: €245* ⊠ *Carrer Pau Claris 150, Eixample* ☎ *93/487–6262* ⊕ *www.hotelclaris.com* ⏎ *82 rooms, 42 suites* ⫩⊙⫨ *No meals* Ⓜ *Passeig de Gràcia* ⌖ *E2.*

$$
HOTEL
Fodor'sChoice
★
🏨 **Condes de Barcelona.** One of Barcelona's most popular hotels, the Condes de Barcelona is perfectly placed for exploring the sights (and shops) of the city's most fashionable quarter, and—for the priveleged location—offers exception value. **Pros:** elegant Moderniste building with subdued contemporary furnishings; prime spot in the middle of the Eixample. **Cons:** no spa; substantial surcharge (€45) for pets; restaurant Lasarte difficult to book. $ *Rooms from: €165* ⊠ *Passeig de Gràcia 73-75, Eixample* ☎ *93/4674780* ⊕ *www.condesdebarcelona.com* ⏎ *125 rooms, 1 suite* ⫩⊙⫨ *No meals* Ⓜ *Passeig de Gràcia* ⌖ *D2.*

$$
HOTEL
Fodor'sChoice
★
🏨 **Continental Palacete.** This former palatial family home, or *palacete*, provides a splendid drawing room, a location nearly dead center for Barcelona's main attractions, views over leafy Rambla de Catalunya, and a 24-hour free buffet. **Pros:** family-friendly; attentive staff; ideal location; microwaves in all the rooms; good value. **Cons:** room decor is relentlessly pink and over-draped; bathrooms are a bit cramped and lack amenities. $ *Rooms from: €143* ⊠ *Rambla de Calatunya 30, at Diputació, Eixample* ☎ *93/445–7657* ⊕ *www.hotelcontinental.com* ⏎ *20 rooms, 2 suites* ⫩⊙⫨ *Breakfast* Ⓜ *Passeig de Gràcia* ⌖ *D3.*

$$$$
HOTEL
🏨 **Hotel El Palace Barcelona.** Founded in 1919 by Caesar Ritz, this is the original Ritz, the grande dame of Barcelona hotels, renamed in

2005. **Pros:** equidistant from Barri Gòtic and central Eixample; excellent service; old-world elegance throughout. **Cons:** no pool; painfully pricey. $ *Rooms from: €575* ✉ *Gran Via de les Corts Catalanes 668, Eixample* ☎ *93/510–1130* ⊕ *www.hotelpalacebarcelona.com* ⤴ *119 rooms, 6 suites* |◎| *No meals* Ⓜ *Passeig de Gràcia* ✚ *E3.*

$$$$ 🖵 **Hotel Cram.** A short walk from La Rambla, this Eixample design
HOTEL hotel offers impeccable midcity accommodations with cheerful avant-garde décor and luxurious details. **Pros:** dazzlingly designed; strategic location; smart and friendly staff. **Cons:** Aribau is a major uptown artery, noisy at all hours; rooms are a bit small for the price; no gym or spa; no pets. $ *Rooms from: €228* ✉ *Carrer Aribau 54, Eixample* ☎ *93/216–7700* ⊕ *www.hotelcram.com* ⤴ *65 rooms, 2 suites* |◎| *No meals* Ⓜ *Universitat, Provença (FGC)* ✚ *C2.*

$$ 🖵 **Hotel Granados 83.** Designed in the style of a New York City loft
HOTEL on a tree-shaded street in the heart of the Eixample, this hotel blends
Fodor'sChoice exposed brick, steel, and glass with Greek and Italian marble and Indo-
★ nesian tamarind wood to achieve a downtown cool. **Pros:** quiet strategic location; polished professional service; wide variety of good casual restaurants nearby; excellent value. **Cons:** rooms a bit small; pricey buffet breakfast. $ *Rooms from: €170* ✉ *Carrer Enric Granados 83, Eixample* ☎ *93/492–9670* ⊕ *www.hotelgranados83.com* ⤴ *70 rooms, 7 suites* |◎| *No meals* Ⓜ *Provença* ✚ *C2.*

$$ 🖵 **Hotel Murmuri.** British designer Kelly Hoppen took this 19th-century
HOTEL townhouse on Rambla de Catalunya and transformed it in 2008 into a
FAMILY chic, intimate urban retreat. **Pros:** warm, professional service; strategic
Fodor'sChoice Eixample location; child-friendly; excellent value for price. **Cons:** no
★ pool, gym or spa (though guest privileges at the nearby affiliated Hotel Majestic); no pets. $ *Rooms from: €169* ✉ *Rambla de Catalunya 104, Eixample* ☎ *93/550–0600* ⊕ *www.murmuri.com* ⤴ *51 rooms, 2 suites, 5 apartments* |◎| *No meals* Ⓜ *Diagonal, Provença (FGC)* ✚ *C1.*

$$$$ 🖵 **Hotel Omm.** The lobby of this postmodern architectural stunner tells
HOTEL you what to expect throughout: perfect comfort, cutting-edge design,
FAMILY and meticulous attention to every detail. **Pros:** perfect location for the
Fodor'sChoice upper Eixample; spot-on, attentive service; oyster bar in the lobby;
★ superb spa; family-friendly. **Cons:** small plunge pools; restaurant pricey and a little precious; parking is expensive; no pets. $ *Rooms from: €330* ✉ *Roselló 265, Eixample* ☎ *93/445–4000* ⊕ *www.hotelomm.es* ⤴ *83 rooms, 8 suites* |◎| *No meals* Ⓜ *Diagonal, Provença (FGC)* ✚ *D2.*

$$$ 🖵 **Majestic Hotel & Spa.** With an unbeatable location on Barcelona's most
HOTEL stylish boulevard, steps from Gaudí's La Pedrera and a stone's throw
Fodor'sChoice to the boulevard's swankiest shops, this hotel is a near-perfect place to
★ stay. **Pros:** very professional service; rooftop terrace with views of the ocean, Montjuïc and the Sagrada Família; 24-hour room service; good value. **Cons:** classic furniture a little dated; no pets; parking fees are a bit steep. $ *Rooms from: €189* ✉ *Passeig de Gràcia 68, Eixample* ☎ *93/488–1717* ⊕ *www.hotelmajestic.es* ⤴ *271 rooms, 32 suites* |◎| *No meals* Ⓜ *Passeig de Gràcia* ✚ *D2.*

$$$$ 🖵 **Mandarin Oriental Barcelona.** A carpeted ramp leading from the ele-
HOTEL gant Passeig de Gràcia (flanked by Tiffany and Brioni boutiques) lends
FAMILY this hotel the air of a privileged—and pricey—inner sanctum. **Pros:**

central location; babysitters and/or parties for the kids, on demand. **Cons:** rooms fairly small for a 5-star accommodation; wardrobes lack drawer space; lighting a bit dim; very pricey breakfast. $ *Rooms from: €440* ⊠ *Passeig de Gràcia 38–40, Eixample* ☎ *93/151–8888* ⊕ *www. mandarinoriental.com* ⟿ *120 rooms* ⦿ *No meals* Ⓜ *Passeig de Gràcia, Diagonal, Provença (FGC)* ✛ *D3.*

GRÀCIA

$$$$
HOTEL
Fodor'sChoice
★

Ⓣ **Casa Fuster.** This hotel offers one of two chances (the other is the Hotel España) to stay in an Art Nouveau building designed by Lluís Domènech i Montaner, architect of the sumptuous Palau de la Música Catalana. **Pros:** well placed for exploring both Gràcia and the Eixample; ample-size rooms; polished, professional service. **Cons:** rooms facing Passeig de Gràcia could use better soundproofing; no pets; hard on the budget, for what you get. $ *Rooms from: €500* ⊠ *Passeig de Gràcia 132, Gràcia* ☎ *93/255–3000* ⊕ *www.hotelescenter.com/casafuster* ⟿ *86 rooms, 19 suites* ⦿ *No meals* Ⓜ *Diagonal* ✛ *D1.*

SARRIÀ, SANT GERVASI, AND PEDRALBES

$$$
HOTEL
Fodor'sChoice
★

Ⓣ **Primero Primera.** The Perez family converted their apartment building on a leafy sidestreet in the quiet upscale residential neighborhood of Tres Torres and opened it as an exquisitely designed, homey, boutique hotel in 2011. **Pros:** warm, professional service; family-friendly (babysitter service available); great value. **Cons:** bit of a distance from the action downtown. $ *Rooms from: €190* ⊠ *Doctor Carulla 25–29, Sant Gervasi* ☎ *93/417–5600* ⊕ *www.primeroprimera.com* ⟿ *22 rooms, 8 suites* ⦿ *Breakfast* ✛ *A1.*

$
HOTEL
Fodor'sChoice
★

Ⓣ **Turó de Vilana.** In an upscale residential neighborhood above Passeig de la Bonanova, this boutique accommodation can make you forget you've come to a prime tourist destination in Spain. **Pros:** quiet surroundings; very good value. **Cons:** something of a trip (30 minutes in all) to the center of town; no pool or spa. $ *Rooms from: €115* ⊠ *Vilana 7, Sant Gervasi* ☎ *93/434–0363* ⊕ *www.turodevilana.com* ⟿ *22 rooms* ⦿ *Breakfast* Ⓜ *Sarrià* ✛ *B1.*

TIBIDABO

$$$
HOTEL
FAMILY

Ⓣ **Gran Hotel la Florida.** Two qualities set this luxurious mountaintop retreat apart: its peace and privacy, and its stunning panoramic view. **Pros:** first-rate spa and fully equipped gym; Club Luna is the hotel's own jazz night spot; friendly and attentive front staff. **Cons:** old building with occasional maintenance problems; pricey food and beverage add-ons; pets accepted with an €80 surcharge; décor in the "Design Suites" a bit over-the-top. $ *Rooms from: €220* ⊠ *Ctra. Vallvidrera al Tibidabo 83–93, Tibidabo* ☎ *93/259–3000* ⊕ *www.hotellaflorida.com* ⟿ *62 rooms, 8 suites* ⦿ *No meals* Ⓜ *Tibidabo* ✛ *B1.*

NIGHTLIFE AND PERFORMING ARTS

Barcelona's art and nightlife scenes start early and never quite stop. To find out what's on, check *"agenda"* listings in Barcelona's leading daily newspapers *El País, La Vanguardia,* and *El Periódico de Catalunya*. The weekly *Guía Del Ocio (Leisure Guide)*, published on Thursday, has a section in English and is available at newsstands all over town. Weekly online magazine *Le Cool* (⊕ *barcelona.lecool.com*) preselects noteworthy events and activities. Look also for the free monthly English-language *Barcelona Metropolitan* magazine in English-language bookstores and hotel lobbies. Barcelona city hall's website (⊕ *barcelonacultura.bcn.cat*) also publishes complete listings and highlights, and has an English edition. *Activitats*, available at the Palau de la Virreina (⊠ *La Rambla* 99) or the Centre Santa Monica (⊠ *La Rambla* 7), lists cultural events.

FESTIVALS

Fodor'sChoice **El Grec** (*Festival del Grec*). Barcelona's annual summer arts festival runs ★ from late June to the end of July. Many of the concerts and theater and dance performances take place outdoors in such historic places as Plaça del Rei and the Teatre Grec on Montjuic, as well as in the Mercat de les Flors. ☎ *93/301–7775* ⊕ *www.bcn.es/grec*.

Festival Ciutat Flamenco. This festival, organized by the Taller de Músics (Musicians' Workshop) and held in the Mercat de les Flors in May, offers a chance to hear the real thing and skip the often disappointing tourist fare available at most of the formal flamenco dinner-and-show venues around town. ☎ *93/443–4346* ⊕ *www.ciutataflmenco.com*.

Primavera Sound. From its modest beginnings in the Poble Espanyol, this event has evolved into one of the biggest and most exciting music festivals in Spain, attracting more than 100,000 visitors a year from all over Europe. Concerts are organized in small venues around the city during the weeks leading up to the event, but the main stint takes place for five days in late May or early June at the Parc del Fòrum. Everybody who's anybody, from Blur to Nick Cave, have played here, and you can rest assured that whoever is doing the big festival circuit this summer will pass through Primavera Sound. Full-festival tickets can be bought online. ⊠ *Parc del Fòrum, Poblenou* ⊕ *www.primaverasound.com* Ⓜ *El Maresme Fòrum*.

PERFORMING ARTS

CASTELLERS AND SARDANAS

The Sunday-morning papers carry announcements for local neighborhood celebrations, flea markets and produce fairs, puppet shows, storytelling sessions for children, sardana folk dancing, bell-ringing concerts, and, best of all, castellers (⊕ *www.bcn.es* has listings in English). The *castellers,* complex human pyramids sometimes reaching as high as 10 stories, are a quintessentially Catalan phenomenon that originated in the 17th century, in the Penedés region west of Barcelona. Castellers perform regularly at neighborhood fiestas and key holidays: in Plaça Sant Jaume during the Festes de la Mercé on Sunday in late September, in Sarrià during the Festes de Sarrià in early October, in Plaça Sant Jaume during the Festes de Santa Eulàlia in February, and during other big feast days during the year.

Sardanas are performed in front of the cathedral at 1 pm every Saturday and Sunday.

CONCERTS

The basilica of Santa Maria del Mar, the church of Santa Maria del Pi, the Monestir de Pedralbes, Drassanes Reials, and the Saló del Tinell, among other ancient and intimate spaces, hold concerts.

BARRI GÒTIC

Fodor'sChoice **Palau de la Música Catalana.** Barcelona's most spectacular concert hall
★ is a Moderniste masterpiece, largely regarded as Domènech i Montaner's best work, just off the bustling Via Laietana. Performances run year-round. While the focus is generally on classical (the Palau de la Música Catalana is the historic home of the Orfeó Català, or Catalan Choir), major music festivals—such as Barcelona's Jazz Festival and even Sónar—generally have a date or two on the Palau's magnificently ornate stage. A sensitive extension to the original building by local architect Oscar Tusquets accommodates the Petit Palau, a smaller venue for recitals and shows for children. Tickets for most classical and family concerts can be bought at the box office, where you can also book a guided tour of the building. ⊠ *Carrera Sant Pere Més Alt 4–6, Urquinaona* ☎ *902/442882* ⊕ *www.palaumusica.cat* ☉ *Box Office daily 9:30–3:30* Ⓜ *Urquinaona.*

EIXAMPLE

L'Auditori de Barcelona. Functional, sleek, and minimalist, the Rafael Moneo-designed Auditori schedules a full program of classical music—with regular forays into jazz, flamenco, and pop—near Plaça de les Glòries. Orchestras that perform here include the Orquestra Simfònica de Barcelona i Nacional de Catalunya (OBC) and the Orquestra Nacional de Cambra de Andorra. The excellent Museu de la Música is situated on the first floor. ⊠ *Lepant 150, Eixample* ☎ *93/247–9300* ⊕ *www. auditori.cat* Ⓜ *Marina, Monumental.*

DANCE

Ballet troupes, both local and from abroad, perform at the Liceu Opera House with some regularity; contemporary dance troupes perform in a variety of theaters around town. The Mercat de les Flors theater is the city's main dance center.

EIXAMPLE

El Mercat de les Flors. An old flower market converted into a modern performance space, theater, and dance school, the Mercat de Les Flors is the home of the Institut de Teatre and is set on lovely, expansive grounds at the foot of verdant Montjuïc. Modern dance is the mercat's raison d' être, but theater is also performed here as well, particularly during the summer Grec festival. Sunday is kids' day, with theater or musical concerts starting at midday. A great on-site café and plenty of wide, open space outside make it an excellent morning out for the family. ⊠ *Lleida 59, Eixample* ☎ *93/426–1875* ⊕ *www.mercatflors.cat* Ⓜ *Espanya.*

FILM

Though many foreign films are dubbed, Barcelona has a full complement of original-language cinema; look for listings marked *"v.o."* (*versión original*).

EIXAMPLE

Renoir Floridablanca. A five-minute walk from the Plaça de la Universitat, this cinema is a good choice for recently released English-language features of all kinds, primarily of the indie ilk. ✉ *Floridablanca 135, Eixample* ☎ *91/542–2702* ⊕ *www.cinesrenoir.com* Ⓜ *Universitat.*

GRÀCIA

Cines Verdi. Gràcia's movie center—and a great favorite for the pre- and postshow action in the bars and restaurants in the immediate vicinity—unfailingly screens recent releases (with a preference for serious-minded cinema) in their original-language versions. The sister cinema Verdi Park is just around the corner, and also shows films in *v.o.* ✉ *Verdi 32, Gràcia* ☎ *93/238–7990* ⊕ *www.cines-verdi.com* Ⓜ *Gràcia, Fontana.*

PORT OLÍMPIC

Icaria Yelmo. In a barren shopping mall, the Icaria Yelmo offers a solid mix of blockbusters and the latest releases in *v.o.*, with many screenings in 3-D as well. ✉ *Salvador Espriu 61, Port Olímpic* ☎ *93/221–7585* ⊕ *www.yelmocines.es* Ⓜ *Ciutadella–Vila Olímpica.*

FLAMENCO

In Catalunya, flamenco, like bullfighting, is regarded as an import from Andalusia. However, unlike bullfighting, there is a strong interest in and market for flamenco in Barcelona.

BARRI GÒTIC

Los Tarantos. This small, basement boîte spotlights some of Andalusia's best flamenco in 30-minute shows of dance, percussion, and song. Think of them as flamenco "tapas" as opposed to a full-course meal of dance. At only €10 a pop, they're a good intro to the art and feel much less touristy than most standard flamenco fare. ✉ *Pl. Reial 17, Barri Gòtic* ☎ *93/304–1210* ⊕ *www.masimas.com/en/tarantos* ☾ *Performances nightly at 8:30, 9:30, and 10:30* Ⓜ *Liceu.*

MONTJUÏC

El Tablao de Carmen. Large tour groups come to this venerable flamenco dinner-theater venue in the Poble Espanyol named after, and dedicated to, the legendary dancer Carmen Amaya. Die-hard flamenco aficionados might dismiss the ensembles that perform here as a tad touristy, but the dancers, singers, and guitarists are technically excellent and put on a good show. Visitors can enjoy one of the two nightly performances over a drink or over their choice of a full-course, prix-fixe meal. Reservations are recommended. ✉ *Poble Espanyol, Avda. Francesc Ferrer i Guàrdia 13, Montjuïc* ☎ *93/325–6895* ⊕ *www.tablaodecarmen.com* ☾ *Shows Tues.–Sun. at 7 and 9:30* Ⓜ *Espanya.*

OPERA
LA RAMBLA

Fodor's Choice **Gran Teatre del Liceu.** Barcelona's famous opera house on La Rambla—in
★ all its gilt, stained-glass, and red plush glory—runs a full season September through June, combining the Liceu's own chorus and orchestra with first-tier, invited soloists. In addition, touring dance companies—ballet, flamenco, and modern dance—appear here. The downstairs foyer often holds early-evening recitals, while the Petit Liceu program sees child-friendly opera adaptations (though not always held in the Liceu itself). The Espai Liceu in the opera house annex includes an excellent café and a gift shop for music-related DVDs, CDs, books, instruments, and knickknacks. A tiny 50-seat theater projecting fragments of operas and a video of the history of the Liceu can be viewed as part of a tour of the building (tickets available online or in the Espai Liceu). Seats for performances can be expensive and hard to get; reserve well in advance. ⊠ *La Rambla 51–59, La Rambla* ☎ *93/485–9900* ⊕ *www. liceubarcelona.cat* ۞ *Tours daily at 10 am (subject to performances and rehearsals). Espai Liceu weekdays 11–8. Box office weekdays 1:30–8 and 1 hr before performances on weekends* Ⓜ *Liceu.*

THEATER
POBLE SEC
El Molino. For most of the 20th century, this venue was the most legendary of all the cabaret theaters on Avinguda Paral.lel. Modeled after Paris's Moulin Rouge, it closed in the late 1990s as the buidling was becoming dangerously run-down. After an ambitious refurbishment, El Molino opened again in 2010 as one of the most stunning state-of-the-art cabaret theaters in Europe. The building now has five, instead of the original two, stories, with a bar and terrace on the third; the interior has been decked out with complex lighting systems that adapt to every change on the small stage. What has remained the same, however, is its essence—a contemporary version of burlesque, but bump-and-grind all the same. You can purchase tickets at the box office before performances, which start at 6:30 and 9:30. ⊠ *Vilà i Vilà 99, Poble Sec* ☎ *93/205–5111* ⊕ *www.elmolinobcn.com* Ⓜ *Paral.lel.*

EIXAMPLE
Teatre Nacional de Catalunya. Near Plaça de les Glòries, at the eastern end of the Diagonal, this grandiose glass-enclosed classical temple was designed by Ricardo Bofill, architect of Barcelona's airport. Programs cover everything from Shakespeare to avant-garde theater. Most productions, as the name suggests, are in Catalan. ⊠ *Carrer l'Art 1, Eixample* ☎ *93/306–5700* ⊕ *www.tnc.cat* Ⓜ *Glòries.*

NIGHTLIFE

BARRI GÒTIC
MUSIC CLUBS: JAZZ AND BLUES
Harlem Jazz Club. This small but exciting live music venue is a five-minute walk from Plaça Reial. The name is a bit deceiving; everything from Senegalese song to gypsy soul can be heard here, too (check website for details). Most concerts start at 10 and finish around 1 am, with musos

and aficionados hanging around after ten until closing. ✉ *Comtessa de Sobradiel 8, Barri Gòtic* ☎ *93/310–0755* ⊕ *www.harlemjazzclub.es* ☉ *Tues.–Sun. 8 pm–3 am* Ⓜ *Jaume I, Liceu.*

BARS

La Vinya del Senyor. Ambitiously named "The Lord's Vineyard," this excellent wine bar directly across from the entrance to the lovely church of Santa Maria del Mar is etched into the ground floor of an ancient building. The best table is up a rickety ladder on the pint-sized mezzanine, or head outside on the terrace for people-watching. ✉ *Pl. de Santa Maria 5, Born-Ribera* ☎ *93/310–3379* ⊕ *www.lavinyadelsenyor. com* ☉ *Tues.–Thurs. noon–1 am, Fri. and Sat. noon–2 am, Sun. noon–midnight* Ⓜ *Jaume I* ✛ *E5.*

LA RAMBLA

BARS

Bar Pastis. In a tiny street off the bottom of La Rambla, this tiny hole-in-the-wall is a city treasure. Since 1947 Bar Pastis has provided a little slice of Paris deep in the Barrio Chino—the nicotine-stained walls, dusty shelves filled with ancient bottles, and bohemian patrons are all genuine. It holds acoustic gigs most nights of the week (generally starting around 10 pm) of tango, cançon, soft jazz, or anything that fits with the bar's speakeasy groove. ✉ *Santa Mònica 4, Rambla* ☎ *634/938422* ⊕ *www. barpastis.com* ☉ *Daily 7:30 pm–2:30 am* Ⓜ *Drassanes.*

Jamboree-Jazz and Dance-Club. This pivotal nightspot, another happy fiefdom of the imperial Mas siblings, is a center for jazz and blues and turns into a wild hip-hop and R&B dance club after performances. Local jazz greats Randy Greer, Jordi Rossy, Billy McHenry, Gorka Benítez, and Llibert Fortuny all perform here regularly, while on Monday night the popular WTF jam sessions hold sway. ✉ *Pl. Reial 17, Rambla* ☎ *93/301–7564* ⊕ *www.masimas.com/jamboree* ☉ *Mon.–Sun. 8 pm–5 am. Concerts at 8 pm and 10 pm, club starts at midnight* Ⓜ *Liceu.*

EL RAVAL

BARS

Casa Almirall. The twisted wooden fronds framing the bar's mirror and Art Nouveau touches from curvy door handles to organic-shape table lamps to floral chair design make this one of the most authentic bars in Barcelona, and also the second-oldest, dating from 1860. (The oldest is the Marsella, another Raval favorite.) It's a good spot for evening drinks after hitting the nearby the MACBA (Museu d'Art Contemporani de Barcelona) or a prelunch *vermut* on weekends. ✉ *Joaquín Costa 33, El Raval* ☎ *93/318–9917* ☉ *Mon.–Thurs. 6 pm–2 am, Fri. 6 pm–3 am, Sat. noon–3 am, Sun. noon–1 am* Ⓜ *Universitat.*

L'Ovella Negra. With heavy wooden tables, stone floors, and some cozy nooks and crannies to drink in, "the Black Sheep" is the city's top student tavern, especially for the barely legal. Aromas of brews gone by never completely abandon the air in this cavernous hangout; the raucous crowd is usually a good match for the surroundings, though even they often get drowned out by the volume of the TV when a major-league match is on. ✉ *Sitges 5, El Raval* ☎ *93/317–1037* ⊕ *www.ovellanegra. com* ☉ *Weekdays 9 pm–3 am, weekends 5 pm–3 am* Ⓜ *Catalunya.*

London Bar. The trapeze (often in use) suspended above the bar adds even more flair to this Art Nouveau circus haunt in the Barrio Chino. Stop in at least for a look, as this is one of the Raval's old standards, which has entertained generations of Barcelona visitors and locals with nightly gigs of jazz, blues, and occassionaly a hairy head-banger outfit. Concerts start at 10:30. ⊠ *Nou de la Rambla 34, El Raval* ☎ *93/318–5261* ☉ *Weekdays 10 pm–3 am, weekends 6 pm–3:30 am* Ⓜ *Liceu, Drassanes.*

MUSIC CLUBS: JAZZ AND BLUES

Jazz Sí Club. Run by the Barcelona contemporary music school next door, this workshop and (during the day) café is a forum for musicians, teachers, and fans to listen and debate their art. There is jazz on Monday; pop, blues, and rock jam sessions on Tuesday; jazzmen jamming on Wednesday; Cuban salsa on Thursday; flamenco on Friday; and rock and pop on weekends. The small cover charge (€5–€9, depending on which night you visit) includes a drink; no cover charge Wednesday. Gigs start between 7:30 and 8:45 pm. ⊠ *Requesens 2, El Raval* ☎ *93/329–0020* ⊕ *www.tallerdemusics.com* ☉ *Daily 7 pm–11 pm* Ⓜ *Sant Antoni.*

BARCELONETA AND PORT OLÍMPIC

BARS

Fodor's Choice
★ **Eclipse Bar.** On the 26th floor of the seaside W Hotel, Eclipse is undoubtedly the bar with the best view in all of Barcelona. Owned by a London hospitality group experienced in satisfying a demanding clientele, its slick interior design and roster of international DJs attract scores of beautiful people, Euro nighthawks, and local VIPs. Dress rules (i.e., your best glad rags) apply. ⊠ *Pl. de la Rosa dels Vents 1, Barcelona* ☎ *93/295–2800* ⊕ *www.w-barcelona.es* ☉ *Mon. and Wed. 7 pm–2 am, Tues. and Thurs. 7 pm–3 am, Fri.–Sun. 7 pm–4 am.*

CASINOS

Gran Casino de Barcelona. Situated on the shore underneath the Hotel Arts, Barcelona's modern casino has everything from slot machines to roulette, plus restaurants, a bar, and a dance club. The casino regularly plays host to Texas Hold 'em poker tournaments, which add an air of Vegas-style excitement. ⊠ *Marina 19–21, Port Olímpic* ☎ *93/225–7878* ⊕ *www.casino-barcelona.com* ☉ *Mon.–Sun. 9 am–5 am* Ⓜ *Ciutadella–Vila Olímpica.*

DANCE CLUBS

Shôko. The hottest of the glitzerati spots below the Hotel Arts and the Frank Gehry fish, this is the place to see and be seen in Barcelona these days. The excellent restaurant morphs into a disco around midnight and continues until the wee hours of the morning, with all manner of local and international celebrities perfectly liable to make an appearance at one time or another. ⊠ *Passeig Marítim de la Barceloneta 36, Port Olímpic-Barceloneta* ☎ *93/225–9200* ⊕ *www.shoko.biz* ☉ *Restaurant daily noon–midnight. Lounge club daily midnight–3 am* Ⓜ *Ciutadella–Vila Olímpica.*

EIXAMPLE
BARS
Dry Martini Bar. The namesake drink of this stately and discreet establishment is the best in town, though there's not much the adept barmen can't shake up. This is a popular hangout for mature romantics: husbands and wives (though not necessarily each other's) in an environment of genteel wickedness. ⊠ *Aribau 162, Eixample* ☎ *93/217–5072* ⊕ *www.drymartinibcn.com* ☉ *Mon.–Thurs. 1 pm–2:30 am, Fri. 1 pm–3 am, Sat. 6:30 pm–3 am, Sun. 6:30 pm–2:30 am* Ⓜ *Provença.*

Milano. Just off Plaça Catalunya, this basement bar is an unexpected gem in an area dominated by student bars and tourist traps. Indeed, there's something naughty and exciting about stepping into Milano, as if by crossing the doorstep you were transported back to a Prohibition-era speakeasy of the more glamorous type: the large room with wooden floorboards and red velvet sofas, the waiters in white livery, and the large variety of whiskeys behind the bar. Live jazz and be-bop most nights (generally starting at 8:30 pm) keeps the genial vibes flowing. ⊠ *Ronda Universitat 35, Eixample* ☎ *93/112–7150* ⊕ *www.camparimilano.com* ☉ *Daily noon–3 am* Ⓜ *Catalunya.*

La Vinoteca Torres. Miguel Torres of the Torres wine dynasty has finally given Passeig de Gràcia a respectable address for tapas and wine, with more than 50 selections from Torres wineries around the world. The menu runs from selected Spanish olives to Ramón Peña seafood from the Rías de Galicia to stick-to-your-ribs *lentejas estofadas* (stewed lentils) or diced chunks of Galician beef with peppers from Gernika. ⊠ *Passeig de Gràcia 78, Eixample* ☎ *93/272–6625* ⊕ *www.lavinotecatorres.com* ☉ *Daily noon–4 and 7–1* Ⓜ *Passeig de Gràcia* ✛ *D2.*

Fodor's Choice ★ **Monvínic.** "Wineworld" in Catalan, Monvínic offers 3,500 wines ranging in price from €10 to a mind-popping €5,000, ordered up from their wine cellar via a tablet or explained by the exceptionally friendly staff in a sleekly designed space, concevied by veteran local desinger Alfons Tost. Small plates of perfect *jamón* and creative riffs on classical Catalan cuisine complement the vino, and full meals are available at the restaurant in back. ⊠ *Diputació 249, Eixample* ☎ *93/272–6187* ⊕ *www.monvinic.com* ☉ *Weekdays 1 pm–11 pm* Ⓜ *Passeig de Gràcia.*

DANCE CLUBS
Antilla BCN Latin Club. This exuberantly Caribbean spot sizzles with salsa, son cubano, and merengue from the moment you step in the door. From 10 to 11 each night, enthusiastic dance instructors "teach you the secrets of the hips" for free. After that, the dancing begins and rarely stops to draw breath. This self-proclaimed "Caribbean cultural center" cranks out every variation of salsa ever invented. Thursday, see live concerts while on Friday and Saturday, the mike gives way to animated Latin DJs. ⊠ *Aragó 141, Eixample* ☎ *93/451–2151* ⊕ *www.antillasalsa.com* ☉ *Wed. 10 pm–5 am, Thurs. 11 pm–5 am., Fri.–Sat. 11 pm–5 am, Sun. 7 pm–5 am* Ⓜ *Urgell, Hospital Clinic.*

Bikini Barcelona. This sleek megaclub, which was reborn as part of L'Illa shopping center, boasts the best sound system in Barcelona. A smaller sala puts on concerts of emerging and cult artists—the Nigerian singer-songwriter Asa, local soulsters The Pepper Pots, and Gil Scott-Heron in one of his final performances are just some of the more memorable Bikini performances of recent years. When the gigs finish around midnight the walls roll back, and the space ingeniously turns into a sweaty nightclub for the postgrad crowd. ⊠ *Diagonal 547, Eixample* ☎ *93/322–0800* ⊕ *www.bikinibcn.com* ⊙ *Club Thurs.–Sat. midnight–6 am; concert times vary* Ⓜ *Les Corts.*

Costa Breve. Open Thursday through Saturday, midnight to dawn, this hip and happening disco just above the Diagonal has DJs that spin pop, funk, and dance music until 5 am. Though popular with the young college crowd (particularly on Thursday for University Lifestyle night), postgraduates still manage to find some dance-floor turf. ⊠ *Aribau 230, Eixample* ☎ *93/414–7195* ⊕ *www.grupocostabreve.com* ⊙ *Thurs.–Sat. midnight–5 am* Ⓜ *Provença.*

Luz de Gas. This always-wired, faux–music hall hub of musical and general nightlife activity has something going on every night, from live performances to wild late-night dancing. Though the weekly schedule varies with the arrival of international names and special events, you can generally plan for world music and Latin sounds in the live sets, while the club music is focused on soul and standards. ⊠ *Muntaner 246, Eixample* ☎ *93/209–7711* ⊕ *www.luzdegas.com* ⊙ *Club: Tues.–Sun. midnight–5 am. Live performance times vary, but shows generally start around 9 pm* Ⓜ *Muntaner, Provença.*

Nick Havanna. One of the original *bars diseny* (designer bars) that proliferated the city in the late '80s and early '90s, sadly little of Nick Havanna's ground-breaking postmodern decor—which included a giant pendulum swaying over the dance floor—remains. The clientele has modified, too, with a young, postgrad crowd instead of the former creative class. Regulars throng to this mid-Eixample bar from Thursday onward, kicking up their end-of-week heels to thumping feel-good standards and Latino hits. ⊠ *Rosselló 208, Eixample* ☎ *639/471679* ⊕ *www.nickhavannabcn.com* ⊙ *Thurs.–Sat. midnight–6 am, Sun. midnight–5:30 am* Ⓜ *Provença.*

Otto Zutz. Just off Via Augusta, above Diagonal, this nightclub and disco is a perennial Barcelona favorite that keeps attracting a glitzy mix of Barcelona movers and shakers, models, ex-models, wannabe models, and the hoping-to-get-lucky mob that predictably follows this sort of pulchritude. Hip-hop, house, and Latino make up the standard soundtrack on the dance floor, with mellower notes upstairs and in the coveted Altos Club Privé (or VIP section, to you and me). ⊠ *Lincoln 15, Eixample* ☎ *93/238–0722* ⊕ *www.ottozutz.com* ⊙ *Wed.–Sat. midnight–6 am* Ⓜ *Sant Gervasi, Plaça Molina.*

GRÀCIA
BARS
Bonobo. The only item or furniture recalling the times when this Gràcia bar was a traditional bodega is the large wooden fridge behind the bar. As for the rest, the Catalan chansons have been replaced by funk and soul music and the occassional football match on the TV, the elderly men at the bar by cheerful thirtysomethings, the cheap wine

by elaborate gin-tonics. What remains, however, is a distinctly local and honest atmosphere, rejecting all pretense of "see-and-be-seen" and inviting everyone, regardless of age or nationality, to come in and have a good time. ⊠ *Santa Rosa 14, Gràcia* ☎ *93/218–8796* ⊗ *Mon.–Sat. 4 pm–3 am* Ⓜ *Fontana.*

Fodor's Choice ★ **Viblioteca.** Viblioteca is the latest project of the owners of the bohemian Gràcia cocktail bar La Baignore, and here they've moved things up a notch. Dazzling white interiors, a large assortment of cured meats, cheeses, and salads, a few choice liquors—plus a selection of exquisite wines, each in limited supply, personally sourced and served together with the story behind it. Come for a quick glass at the bar or have a bottle or two at your table. It is best to reserve in advance since the small space fills up quickly. ⊠ *Vallfogona 12, Gràcia* ☎ *93/284–4202* ⊕ *www.viblioteca.com* ⊗ *Weekdays 6 pm–1 am, Sat. 1–4 pm and 6 pm–1 am, Sun. 1–4 pm and 7–midnight* Ⓜ *Fontana.*

POBLENOU
MUSIC CLUBS

Sala Razzmatazz. Razzmatazz stages weeknight concerts featuring international draws from James Taylor to Moriarty The small-format environment is extraordinarily intimate and beats out sports stadiums or the immense Palau Sant Jordi as a top venue for concerts. It shares its Friday and Saturday club madness with neighboring sister venture the Loft, around the corner, and has four other smaller *salas* where anything could happen, from an indie film shoot to Jarvis Cocker spinning discs at a private party. ⊠ *Almogavers 122, Poblenou* ☎ *93/320–8200* ⊕ *www.salarazzmatazz.com* ⊗ *Concert times vary (but shows generally start around 10 pm)* Ⓜ *Marina, Bogatell.*

SPORTS AND THE OUTDOORS

BICYCLING

Bike Tours Barcelona. This company offers a three-hour bike tour (in English) for €22, with a drink included. Just look for the guide with a bike and a red flag at the northeast corner of the Town Hall in Plaça Sant Jaume, outside the Tourist Information Office. Tours depart at 11 am and 4:30 pm, daily from April 1 to September 15. The company will also organize private guided tours through the Barri Gòtic, parks, Port Olímpic and Barceloneta, the Moderniste Route and other itineraries on request. ⊠ *Carrer Esparteria 3, Barri Gòtic* ☎ *93/2682105* ⊕ *www. biketoursbarcelona.com* Ⓜ *Jaume I.*

Classic Bikes. Just off pivotal Plaça Catalunya, bicycles are available for rent here every day of the week from 9:30 am to 8 pm. The 24-hour rate is €15; take a bike in the morning and return it by closing time for €12; or ride for two hours for €6. ⊠ *Tallers 45, El Raval* ☎ *93/317–1970* ⊕ *www.classicbikes.es* Ⓜ *Pl. Catalunya.*

SOCCER

Camp Nou. If you're in Barcelona between September and June, a chance to witness the celebrated FC Barcelona play soccer (preferably against Real Madrid, if you can get in) at Barcelona's gigantic stadium is a seminal Barcelona experience. Just the walk down to the field from the Diagonal with another hundred thousand fans walking fast and hushed in electric anticipation is unforgettable. Games are played Saturday night at 9 or Sunday afternoon at 5, though there may be international Champions League games on Tuesday or Wednesday evenings as well. A worthwhile alternative to seeing a game is the guided tour of the FC Barcelona museum—the city's most visited tourist attraction—and facilities. ⊠ *Arístides Maillol 12–18, Les Corts* ☎ *93/496–3600 for museum, 902/189900 for club office* ⊕ *www.fcbarcelona.cat* ⊠ *Museum €23, combined ticket including tour of museum, field, and sports complex* ☉ *Museum Mon.–Sat. 10 am–6:30 pm (until 8 Apr.–Oct.), Sun. 10–2:30. On match days, the museum closes 3 hrs early, and stadium tours are not available.* Ⓜ *Collblanc, Palau Reial.*

Futbol Club Barcelona. Founded in 1899, the Futbol Club Barcelona attained its greatest glory in May 2009, when its victory over Manchester United in Rome sealed the club's third European Championship and Spain's first-ever *triplete* (triple), taking home all of the silverware: League, Cup, and European titles. Even more impressive, to friend and foe alike, was the way they did it, playing a wide-open razzle-dazzle style of soccer rarely seen in the age of cynical defensive lockdowns and muscular British-style play. Barça, as the club is affectionately known, is Real Madrid's perennial nemesis (and vice-versa) as well as a sociological and historical phenomenon of deep significance in Catalonia. Ticket windows at Access 14 to the stadium are open Monday though Saturday and game-day Sunday 10–2 and 5–8; you can also buy tickets at Servicaixa ATMs at Caixa de Catalunya banks, through ticket agencies, and directly online. ⊠ *Camp Nou, Aristides Maillol 12, Les Corts* ☎ *93/496–3600, 902/189900* ⊕ *www.fcbarcelona.com* Ⓜ *Collblanc.*

Spain Ticket Bureau. This company can score seats for Barça home games, as well as other sporting events, concerts, and musicals, in Barcelona and elsewhere in Spain. Booking ahead online is a good idea, especially for headliner events, but expect to pay a healthy premium. ⊠ *Rambla de Catalunya 89, Entl. A, Eixample* ☎ *93/4882266, 902/903912* ⊕ *www. spainticketbureau.com* Ⓜ *Passeig de Gràcia, Catalunya.*

SHOPPING

Between the surging fashion scene, a host of young clothing designers, clever home furnishings, rare and delicious foodstuffs, and art and antiques, Barcelona might just be the best place in Spain to unload extra ballast from your wallet.

SHOPPING DISTRICTS

Barcelona's prime shopping districts are the Passeig de Gràcia, Rambla de Catalunya, Plaça de Catalunya, Porta de l'Àngel, and Avinguda Diagonal up to Carrer Ganduxer.

For high fashion, browse along **Passeig de Gràcia** and **Rambla Catalunya** and along the **Diagonal** between Plaça Joan Carles I and Plaça Francesc Macià. **Bulevard Rosa** is a fashion and shopping mall off Passeig de Gràcia. For old-fashioned Spanish shops, prowl the Gothic Quarter, especially **Carrer Ferran.** The area surrounding **Plaça del Pi,** from the Boqueria to Carrer Portaferrissa and Carrer de la Canuda, is thick with boutiques, jewelers, and design shops. The **Barri de la Ribera,** around Santa Maria del Mar, especially the Born area, has a cluster of design, fashion, and food shops. Design, jewelry, and knickknacks shops cluster on Carrer Banys Vells and Carrer Flassaders, near Carrer Montcada. The place to go for antiques is the Gothic Quarter, where **Carrer de la Palla** and **Carrer Banys Nous** are lined with shops full of prints, maps, books, paintings, and furniture. An antiques market is held in front of the Catedral de la Seu every Thursday 10–8. **Carrer Tuset,** north of the Diagonal, has lots of small boutiques. The **Maremagnum** mall, in Port Vell, is convenient to downtown. **Diagonal Mar,** at the eastern end of the diagonal, and the **Fòrum** complex offer many shopping options in a mega-shopping-mall environment. **Les Arenes,** the former bullring at Plaça Espanya, has reopened as a shopping mall with FNAC, Mango, Desigual, and Sephora among other stores, as well as 12 movie theaters, restaurants, and the Museu del Rock. **Carrer Lledó,** just off Plaça Sant Just, in the Barri Gòtic behind Plaça Sant Jaume, is a lovely little street lined with shops selling clothes, gifts, and design items. For art, browse the cluster of galleries on Carrer Consell de Cent between Passeig de Gràcia and Carrer Balmes and around the corner on Rambla de Catalunya. The Born–Santa Maria del Mar quarter is another art destination, along Carrer Montcada and the parallel Carrer Banys Vells.

Not to be overlooked are Barcelona's many street markets and fairs. On Thursday, a natural-produce market (honey, cheese) fills Plaça del Pi with interesting tastes and aromas. On Sunday morning, Plaça Reial hosts a stamp and coin market, Plaça Sant Josep Oriol holds a painter's market, and there is a general crafts and flea market near the Columbus Monument at the port end of the Rambla. Sarrià holds a farmers' market with excellent cheeses, sausages, cavas, and vegetables from the Catalonian hinterlands in Plaça de Sarrià on the second and fourth Sunday of every month.

BARRI GÒTIC

ANTIQUES

Antigüedades Fernández. Bric-a-brac is piled high in this workshop near the middle of this slender artery in the medieval Jewish Quarter. This master craftsman restores and sells antique furniture of all kinds. Stop by and stick your head in for the fragrance of the shellacs and wood shavings and a look at one of the last simple carpentry and woodworking shops you'll encounter in contemporary, design-mad, early-21st-century Barcelona. ⊠ *Carrer Sant Domènec del Call 9, Barri Gòtic* ☎ *93/301–0045* ⊙ *Mon.–Sat. 10–2 and 5–8* Ⓜ *Liceu, Jaume I.*

ART GALLERIES

Sala Parès. The dean of Barcelona's art galleries, this place opened in 1840 as an art-supplies shop; as a gallery, it dates to 1877, and has shown every Barcelona artist of note since then. Picasso and Miró showed here, as did Casas and Rossinyol before them. Nowadays, Catalan artists like Perico Pastor and Miquel Macaya get pride of place. ⊠ *Petritxol 5, Barri Gòtic* ☎ *93/318–7020* ⊕ *www.salapares.com* ⊙ *Mon. 4–8, Tues.–Fri. 10:30–2 and 4–8, Sat. 10:30–2 and 4:30–8:30, Sun. (June–Oct. only) 11:30–2* Ⓜ *Liceu, Catalunya.*

BOOKS AND STATIONERY

Papirum. Exquisite hand-printed papers, marbleized blank books, and writing implements await you and your muse at this tiny, medieval-tone shop. ⊠ *Baixada de la Llibreteria 2, Barri Gòtic* ☎ *93/310–5242* ⊕ *www.papirum-bcn.com* ⊙ *Weekdays 10–8:30, Sat. 10–2 and 5–8:30* Ⓜ *Jaume I.*

CERAMICS

Art Escudellers. Ceramic pieces from all over Spain are on display at this large store across the street from restaurant Los Caracoles; more than 140 different artisans are represented, with maps showing what part of Spain the work is from. Wine, cheese, and ham tastings are held downstairs, and you can even throw a pot yourself in the workshop. ⊠ *Carrer Escudellers 23–25, Barri Gòtic* ☎ *93/412–6801* ⊕ *www.escudellers-art.com* ⊙ *Daily 11–11* Ⓜ *Liceu, Drassanes.*

CLOTHING

Decathlon. Whether you're planning a trek through the Pyrenees or a beach yoga session, this mega–sports emporium should be your first port of call. From waterproof clothing to footballs to bike repairs, it caters to every conceivable sport and active hobby. Affordable and always busy, Decathlon is the best place to pick up practical travel clothing, such as that forgotten fleece jacket for a sudden cold snap. ⊠ *Canuda 20, Barri Gòtic* ☎ *93/342–6161* ⊕ *www.decathlon.es* ⊙ *Mon.–Sat. 9:30–9:30* Ⓜ *Catalunya.*

L'Arca de L'Àvia. As the name of the place ("grandmother's trunk") suggests, this is a miscellaneous potpourri of ancient goods of all kinds, especially period clothing, from shoes to gloves to hats and hairpins. Despite the found-object attitude and ambience of the place, they're not giving away these vintage baubles, so don't be surprised at the hefty price tags. ⊠ *Banys Nous 20, Barri Gòtic* ☎ *93/302–1598* ⊕ *www.larcadelavia.com* ⊙ *Weekdays 11–2 and 5–8, Sat. 11–2 and 5–8:30* Ⓜ *Liceu.*

Fodor'sChoice ★ **The Outpost.** A shop dedicated exclusively to men's accessories of the finest kind, the Outpost was created by a former Prada buyer who considers it his mission to bring stylishness to Barcelona men with this little island of avant-garde. The constantly changing window displays are little works of art, providing a first taste of what's to be found inside: Christian Peau shoes, Albert Thurston suspenders, Roland Pineau belts, Yves Andrieux hats, Balenciaga ties. ⊠ *Rosselló 281, bis, Eixample*

🕿 *93/457–7137* ⊕ *www.theoutpostbcn.com* ⊗ *Mon.–Sat. 10:30–2:30 and 4:30–8:30* Ⓜ *Diagonal.*

Sita Murt. The local Catalan designer Sita Murt produces smart, grown-up women's wear under her own label in this minimalist space near Plaça Sant Jaume. Colorful chiffon dresses and light, gauzy tops and knits characterize this line of clothing popular with professional women and weddinggoers. ✉ *Mallorca 242, Eixample* 🕿 *93/215–2231* ⊕ *www. sitamurt.com* ⊗ *Mon.–Sat. 10–8:30* Ⓜ *Passeig de Gràcia.*

FOOD

Caelum. At the corner of Carrer de la Palla and Banys Nous, this tea-room and coffee shop sells crafts and foods such as honey and preserves made in convents and monasteries all over Spain. The café and tearoom section extends neatly out into the intersection of Carrer Banys Nous (which means "new baths") and Carrer de la Palla, directly over the site of the medieval Jewish baths. ✉ *Carrer de la Palla 8, Barri Gòtic* 🕿 *93/302–6993* ⊕ *www.caelumbarcelona.com* ⊗ *Mon.–Thurs. 10:30–8:30, Fri.–Sat. 10:30 am–11 pm, Sun. 10:30–9* Ⓜ *Jaume I.*

MARKETS

Mercat Gòtic. A browser's bonanza, this interesting if somewhat pricey Thursday market for antique clothing, jewelry, and art objects occupies the plaza in front of the cathedral. ✉ *Pl. de la Seu s/n, Barri Gòtic* ⊕ *www.mercatgotic.com* Ⓜ *Jaume I, Urquinaona.*

SHOES

Fodor'sChoice ★ **La Manual Alpargatera.** If you appreciate old-school craftsmanship in footwear, visit this boutique just off Carrer Ferran. Handmade rope-sole sandals and espadrilles are the specialty, and this shop has sold them to everyone—including the Pope. The flat, beribboned espadrille model used for dancing the sardana is available, as are newly fashionable wedge heels with peep toes and comfy slippers. ✉ *Avinyó 7, Barri Gòtic* 🕿 *93/301–0172* ⊕ *www.lamanual.net* ⊗ *Mon.–Sat. 9:30–1:30 and 4:30–8* Ⓜ *Liceu, Jaume I.*

BORN-RIBERA

CLOTHING AND JEWELRY

Coquette. Coquette specializes in the kind of understated, feminine beauty that Parisian women know to do so well. The now three shops (two in the Born, one uptown) present a small, careful selection of mainly French designers, like Isabel Marant, Vanessa Bruno, Laurence Doligé, and Chloé. Whether it's a romantic or a seductive look you're after, Coquette makes sure you'll feel both comfortable and irresistible. ✉ *Rec 65, Born-Ribera* 🕿 *93/319–2976* ⊕ *www.coquettebcn.com* ⊗ *Weekdays 11–3 and 5–9, Sat 11:30–8:30* Ⓜ *Jaume I.*

Fodor'sChoice ★ **Cortana.** A sleek and breezy Balearic Islands–look for women is what this designer from Mallorca brings to the fashion scene of urban Barcelona in a whitewashed shop reminiscent of an art gallery. Her dresses transmit a casual, minimalistic elegance and have graced many a red carpet in Madrid. ✉ *Flassaders 41, Born-Ribera* 🕿 *93/310–1255* ⊕ *www.cortana.es* ⊗ *Mon. 3–8, Tues.–Sat. 11–2 and 3–8* Ⓜ *Jaume I.*

7

Custo Barcelona. Ever since Custido Dalmau and his brother David returned from a round-the-world motorcycle tour with visions of California surfing styles dancing in their heads, Custo Barcelona has been a runaway success doling out clingy cotton tops in bright and cheery hues. Now scattered all over Barcelona and the globe, Custo is scoring even more acclaim by expanding into coats, dresses, and kidswear. ⊠ *Pl. de les Olles 7, Born-Ribera* ☎ *93/268–7893* ⊕ *www.custo-barcelona. com* ⊗ *Daily 10–9* Ⓜ *Jaume I.*

FOOD

Fodor'sChoice
★ **Casa Gispert.** On the inland side of Santa Maria del Mar, this shop is one of the most aromatic and picturesque in Barcelona, bursting with teas, coffees, spices, saffron, chocolates, and nuts. The star element in this olfactory and aesthetic feast is an almond-roasting stove in the back of the store—purportedly the oldest in Europe, dating from 1851, like the store itself. But don't miss the acid engravings on the office windows or the ancient wooden back door before picking up a bag of freshly roasted nuts to take with you. ⊠ *Sombrerers 23, Born-Ribera* ☎ *93/319–7547* ⊕ *www.casagispert.com* ⊗ *Tues.–Sat. 9:30–2 and 4–8:30, Sat. 10–2 and 5–8:30 (also Mon. late Oct.–Dec.)* Ⓜ *Jaume I.*

El Magnífico. This coffee emporium just up the street from Santa Maria del Mar is famous for its sacks of coffee beans from all over the globe. Coffee to go is also available—enjoy it on the little bench outside. ⊠ *Carrer Argenteria 64, Born-Ribera* ☎ *93/319–3975* ⊕ *www. cafeselmagnifico.com* ⊗ *Mon.–Sat. 10–8* Ⓜ *Jaume I.*

Pastelería Hofmann. Mey Hofmann, a constellation in Barcelona's gourmet galaxy for the last three decades through her restaurant and cooking courses, has a sideline dedicated exclusively to pastry. Everything from the lightest, flakiest croissants to the cakes, tarts, and ice creams are about as good they get in this sweets emporium just off the Passeig del Born. ⊠ *Flassaders 44, Born-Ribera* ☎ *93/268–8221* ⊕ *www. hofmann-bcn.com* ⊗ *Mon.–Wed 9–2 and 3:30–8, Thurs.–Sat. 9–2 and 3:30–8:30, Sun. 9–2:30* Ⓜ *Jaume I.*

La Botifarreria de Santa Maria. This busy emporium next to the church of Santa Maria del Mar stocks excellent cheeses, hams, pâtés, and homemade sobrasadas. *Botifarra*, Catalan for sausage, is the main item here, with a wide range of varieties, including egg sausage for meatless Lent and sausage stuffed with spinach, asparagus, cider, cinnamon, and Cabrales cheese. ⊠ *Santa Maria 4, Born-Ribera* ☎ *93/319–9123* ⊕ *www.labotifarreria.com* ⊗ *Weekdays 8:30–2:30 and 5–8:30, Sat. 8:30–3* Ⓜ *Jaume I.*

Fodor'sChoice
★ **Vila Viniteca.** Near Santa Maria del Mar, this is perhaps the best wine treasury in Barcelona, with tastings, courses, and events meriting further investigation, including a hugely popular street party to welcome in new-harvest wines (usually late October or early November). The tiny family grocery store next door offers exquisite artisanal cheeses ranging from French goat cheese to Extremadura's famous Torta del Casar. ⊠ *Carrer Agullers 7, Born-Ribera* ☎ *93/777–7017* ⊕ *www.vilaviniteca. es* ⊗ *Mon.–Sat 8:30–8:30* Ⓜ *Jaume I.*

LA RAMBLA

MARKETS

Mercat de La Boqueria. The oldest of its kind in Europe, Barcelona's most colorful and bustling food market is a must-see for anybody interested in food, and especially Catalan cuisine. Predictably, the front stalls cater more to tourists with juices to go, bags of candy, and the like. Make your way to the center to the remarkable sea-creature stalls, bloody-offal sellers, and many stand-up bars where famous chefs on their daily sourcing missions sit cheek-by-jowl with banana vendors taking a break. Standout stalls include Petràs, the wild mushroom guru at the back of the market on Plaça de la Gardunya, and Juanito Bayen of the world-famous collection of bar stools known as Pinotxo. ⊠ *Rambla 91, Rambla* ☎ *93/318–2017* ⊕ *www.boqueria.info* ⊗ *Mon.–Sat. 8–8* Ⓜ *Liceu, Catalunya.*

EL RAVAL

BOOKS

La Central del Raval. This luscious bookstore in the former chapel of the Casa de la Misericòrdia sells books amid stunning architecture and holds regular cultural events. ⊠ *Elisabets 6, El Raval* ☎ *902/884–990* ⊕ *www.lacentral.com* ⊗ *Weekdays 9:30–9, Sat. 10–9* Ⓜ *Catalunya.*

EIXAMPLE

ANTIQUES

Bulevard dels Antiquaris. Look carefully for the stairway leading one flight up to this 73-store mother ship of all antiques arcades off Passeig de Gràcia. You never know what you might find here in this eclectic serendipity: dolls, icons, Roman or Visigothic objects, paintings, furniture, cricket kits, fly rods, or toys from a century ago. Haggle? Of course— but Catalan antiques dealers are tough nuts to crack. ⊠ *Passeig de Gràcia 55, Eixample* ☎ *93/215–4499* ⊕ *www.bulevarddelsantiquaris. com* ⊗ *Daily 10–2 and 4–8* Ⓜ *Passeig de Gràcia.*

ART GALLERIES

Galeria Joan Prats. "La Prats" has been one of the city's top galleries since the 1920s, showing international painters and sculptors from Henry Moore to Antoni Tàpies. Barcelona painter Joan Miró was a prime force in the founding of the gallery when he became friends with Joan Prats. The motifs of bonnets and derbies on the gallery's facade attest to the trade of Prats's father. José Maria Sicilia and Juan Ugalde have shown here, while Erick Beltrán, Hannah Collins, and Eulàlia Valldosera are among the regulars. ⊠ *Rambla de Catalunya 54, Eixample* ☎ *93/216–0920* ⊕ *www.galeriajoanprats.com* ⊗ *Tues.–Sat. 11–8* Ⓜ *Passeig de Gràcia.*

Joan Gaspar. One of Barcelona's most prestigious galleries, Joan Gaspart and his father before him brought Picasso and Miró back to Catalunya during the '50s and '60s, along with other artists considered politically taboo during the Franco regime. These days you'll find leading

7

contemporary lights such as Joan Pere Viladecans, Rafols Casamada, or Susana Solano here. ⊠ *Pl. Dr. Letamendi 1, Eixample* ☎ *93/323–0748* ⊕ *www.galeriajoangaspar.com* ☉ *Mon.–Sat. 10:30–1:30 and 4:30–8* Ⓜ *Universitat.*

Sala Dalmau. An old timer in the established Consell de Cent gallery scene, Sala Dalmau shows an interesting and heterodox range of Catalan and international artists. ⊠ *Consell de Cent 349, Eixample* ☎ *93/215–4592* ⊕ *www.saladalmau.com* ☉ *Mon.–Sat. 11–1:30 and 5–8:30. Closed Sat. in July and Aug.* Ⓜ *Passeig de Gràcia.*

BOOKS

BCN Books. This midtown Eixample bookstore is a prime address for books in English. ⊠ *Roger de Llúria 118, Eixample* ☎ *93/457–7692* ⊕ *www.bcnbooks.com* ☉ *Weekdays 10–8, Sat. 10–2* Ⓜ *Verdaguer, Diagonal.*

Casa del Llibre. On Barcelona's most important shopping street, Casa del Llibre is a major book feast with a wide variety of English titles. ⊠ *Passeig de Gràcia 62, Eixample* ☎ *902/026–407* ⊕ *www.casadellibro. com* ☉ *Mon.–Sat. 9:30–9:30* Ⓜ *Passeig de Gràcia.*

CERAMICS

Fodor's Choice ★ **Lladró.** This Valencia company is famed worldwide for the beauty and quality of its figures. Barcelona's only Lladró factory store, this location has exclusive pieces of work, custom-designed luxury items of gold and porcelain, and classic and original works. Watch for the cheeky figurines by Jaime Hayon, a young Spanish designer put in charge of injecting the 60-year old company with some colorful postmodernism. ⊠ *Passeig de Gràcia 101, Eixample* ☎ *93/270–1253* ⊕ *www.lladro.com* ☉ *Mon.–Sat. 10–8:30* Ⓜ *Diagonal.*

CLOTHING

Adolfo Domínguez. One of Barcelona's longtime fashion giants, this is one of Spain's leading clothes designers, with many locations around town. Famed as the creator of the Iberia Airlines uniforms, Adolfo Domínguez has been in the not-too-radical mainstream and at the forefront of Spanish clothes design for the last quarter century. ⊠ *Passeig de Gràcia 32, Eixample* ☎ *619/660–277* ⊕ *www.adolfodominguez.com* ☉ *Mon.–Sat. 10-8:30* Ⓜ *Passeig De Grácia.*

Loewe. Occupying the ground floor of Lluís Domènech i Montaner's Casa Lleó Morera, Loewe is Spain's answer to Hermès, a classical clothing and leather emporium for men's and women's fashions and luxurious handbags that whisper status. Farther north along the Passeig de Grácia at No. 91, the Galería Loewe holds stylish, sporadic shows on fashion and costume. ⊠ *Passeig de Gràcia 35, Eixample* ☎ *93/216–0400* ⊕ *www.loewe.es* ☉ *Mon.–Sat. 10–8:30* Ⓜ *Passeig de Gràcia.*

Purificación García. Known as a gifted fabric expert whose creations are invariably based on the qualities and characteristics of her raw materials, Galicia-born Purificación García enjoys solid prestige in Barcelona. Understated hues and subtle combinations of colors and shapes place this contemporary designer squarely in the camp of the less-is-more school, and although her women's range is larger and more diverse, she is one female designer who understands men's tailoring. ⊠ *Provença 292, Eixample* ☎ *93/496–1336* ⊕ *www.purificaciongarcia. com* ⊗ *Mon.–Sat. 10–8:30* Ⓜ *Diagonal.* ⊠ *Av. Pau Casals 4, Eixample* ☎ *93/200–6089* ⊕ *www.purificaciongarcia.com* ⊗ *Mon.–Sat. 10:30– 8:30* Ⓜ *Muntaner*

DEPARTMENT STORES

El Corte Inglés. This iconic and ubiquitous Spanish department store has its main Barcelona branch on Plaça Catalunya, with an annex 100 yards away in Porta de l'Àngel. You can find just about anything here— clothing, shoes, perfumes, electrical gadgets—and there is a wonderful supermarket on the lower-ground floor. ⊠ *Pl. de Catalunya 14, Eixample* ☎ *93/306–3800* ⊕ *www.elcorteingles.es* ⊗ *Mon.–Sat. 9:30–9:30* Ⓜ *Catalunya* ⊠ *Av. Diagonal 617, Diagonal/Les Corts* ☎ *93/419–2828* Ⓜ *Maria Cristina* ⊠ *Pl. Francesc Macià, Av. Diagonal 471, Eixample* ☎ *93/419–2020* Ⓜ *La Bonanova* ⊠ *Portal de l'Àngel 19–21, Barri Gòtic* ☎ *93/306–3800* Ⓜ *Catalunya.*

FOOD

Fodor's Choice **Mantequeria Can Ravell.** Can Ravell is one of Barcelona's best, and cer-
★ tainly most charming, fine-food and wine emporiums. Open for the good part of a century, it is a cult favorite with local and visiting gour- mands and has a superb selection of everything you ever might want to savor, from the finest anchovies from La Scala to the best cheese from Idiazabal. Through the kitchen and up the tiny spiral staircase, the dining room offers a memorable, if pricey, lunch, while the tasting table downstairs operates on a first-come, first-served basis. ⊠ *Aragó 313, Eixample* ☎ *93/457–5114* ⊕ *www.ravell.com* ⊗ *Tues.–Sat. 10–9, Sun. 10–3* Ⓜ *Girona.*

GIFTS AND SOUVENIRS

Jaime Beriestain Concept Store. The concept store of one of the city's hot- test interior designers provides mere mortals the chance to appreciate the Beriestain groove. Reflecting his projects for hotels and restaurants, the shop offers an exciting mixture of midcentury-modern classics and new design pieces, peppered with freshly cut flowers (also for sale), French candles, handmade stationery, and the latest international design and architecture magazines to dress up your coffee table. The in-store café is worth a visit. ⊠ *Pau Claris 167, Eixample* ☎ *93/515–0779* ⊕ *www.beriestain.com* ⊗ *Mon.–Sat. 10–9* Ⓜ *Diagonal.*

Fodor's Choice **Vinçon.** A design giant some 70 years old, Vinçon steadily expanded
★ its stylish premises through a rambling Moderniste house that was once the home and studio of the Art Nouveau artist Ramón Casas. It stocks everything from letter openers to Eames furniture, and has an interesting front-of-house section for chic, locally made knickknacks. If you can tear your eyes away from all the design, seek out the spec- tacular Moderniste fireplace on the first floor (in reality the furniture department), designed in wild Art Nouveau exuberance with a gigantic hearth in the form of a stylized face. ⊠ *Passeig de Gràcia 96, Eixample* ☎ *93/215–6050* ⊕ *www.vincon.com* ⊗ *Mon.–Sat. 10–8:30* Ⓜ *Diagonal.*

7

MARKETS

Els Encants Vells. One of Europe's oldest flea markets, Els Encants has recently been gifted with a new home—a stunning, glittering metal canapy that protects the rag-and-bone merchants (and their keen customers) from the elements. Stalls, and a handful of standup bars, have become a bit more upmarket, too, although you'll still find plenty of oddities to barter over in the central plaza. ⊠ *Plaça de Les Glóries Catalans s/n, Eixample* ☎ *93/246–3030* ⊕ *www.encantsbcn.com* ۞ *Mon., Wed., and Fri.–Sat. 9–8* Ⓜ *Glòries.*

POBLENOU

HOUSEHOLD ITEMS AND FURNITURE

bd (*Barcelona Design*). This spare, cutting-edge home-furnishings store has just moved into a former industrial building near the sea. Cofounder Oscar Tusquets, master designer and architect, gives contemporary design star Javier Mariscal plenty of space here, while past giants such as Gaudí with his Casa Calvet chair, or Salvador Dalí and his Gala love seat, are also available—if your pockets are deep enough. ⊠ *Ramón Turró 126, Poblenou* ☎ *93/457–0052* ⊕ *www.bdbarcelona. com* ۞ *Weekdays 9–6* Ⓜ *Llacuna, Bogatell.*

8

CATALONIA, VALENCIA, AND THE COSTA BLANCA

8

WELCOME TO CATALONIA, VALENCIA, AND THE COSTA BLANCA

TOP REASONS TO GO

★ **Pax Girona:** Explore a city where the monuments of Christian, Jewish, and Islamic cultures that coexisted for centuries are only steps apart.

★ **Valencia Reborn:** The past 20 years has seen a transformation of the Turia River into a treasure trove of museums, concert halls, parks, and architectural wonders.

★ **Great Restaurants:** Foodies argue that the fountainhead of creative gastronomy has moved from France to Spain—and in particular to the great restaurants of the Empordà and Costa Brava.

★ **Dalí's Home and Museum:** Surreal doesn't begin to describe the Dalí Museum in Figueres or the wild coast of the artist's home at Cap de Creus.

★ **Las Fallas Festival:** Valencia's Las Fallas, in mid-March, a week of fireworks and solemn processions and a finale of spectacular bonfires, is one of the best festivals in Europe.

Montblan

Santa Maria de Poblet ◆

Valls

TARRAGONA

Reus

Gandesa   Tarragona

La Ametlla
De Mar

Tortosa

Morella   San Carlos
                            de la Rapita

Vinaroz

CASTELLON Peniscola
DE LA PLANA

COSTA DEL AZAHAR

Torreblanca

Alcora   Borriol

Jerica   Castello de la Plana

Segorbe   Burriana

Vall De Uxo   COSTA

El Puerto

Burjasot

3 Valencia

Montserrat   Albufera Nature Park

VALENCIA

Cullera

Tabernes De Valldigna

Gandia

Almansa

Denia

Onteniente   Cabo De La Nao

Yecla   Villena   Alcoy   Callosa D'En Sarriá
        ALICANTE   Benidorm

Elda   **4**

Pinoso   BLANCA

Elche   Alicante

              COSTA

Orihuela

Torrevieja

San Javier

0		20 mi
0		20 km

GETTING ORIENTED

Year-round, Catalonia is the most visited of Spain's autonomous communities. The Pyrenees that separate it from France provide some of the country's best skiing, and the rugged Costa Brava in the north and the Costa Dorada to the south are havens for sunseekers. The interior is full of surprises, too: an expanding rural tourism industry and the region's growing international reputation for food and wine give Catalonia a broad-based appeal. Excellent rail, air, and highway connections link Catalonia to the beach resorts of Valencia, its neighbor to the south.

1 Northern Catalonia. Inland and westward from the towns of Girona and Figueres is perhaps the most dramatic and beautiful part of old Catalonia; it's a land of medieval villages and hilltop monasteries, volcanic landscapes, and lush green valleys. The ancient city of Girona, often ignored by people bound for the Costa Brava, is an easy and interesting day trip from Barcelona. The upland towns of Besalú and Ripoll are Catalonia at its most authentic.

2 Costa Brava. Native son Salvador Dalí put his mark on the northeasternmost corner of Catalonia, where the Costa Brava (literally "rugged coast") begins, especially in the fishing village of Cadaqués and the coast of Cap de Creus. From here, south and west toward Barcelona, lie the beaches, historical settlements, and picturesque towns like Sant Feliu de Guixols that draw millions of summer visitors to the region.

3 Southern Catalonia and Around Valencia. Spain's third-largest city, with a rich history and tradition, Valencia is now a cultural magnet for its modern-art museum and its space-age City of Arts and Sciences complex. The Albufera Nature Park, just to the south, is an important wetland and wildlife sanctuary. North of Valencia, the monastery of Montserrat is a popular pilgrimage, Sitges has a lovely beach, and Santes Creus and Poblet are beautiful Cistercian monasteries. Roman remains, chief among them the Circus Maximus, are the reason to go to Tarragona, and to this the Middle Ages added wonderful city walls and citadels.

4 Costa Blanca. Culturally and geographically diverse, the Costa Blanca's most populated coastal resorts stretch north from the provincial capital of Alicante to Dénia. Alicante's historic center and vibrant night-owl scene occupy the hub of a rich agricultural area punctuated by towns like Elche, a UNESCO World Heritage site. Dénia, capital of the Marina Alta region and a port for ferries to the Balearic Islands, is a charming destination.

8

EATING AND DRINKING WELL IN CATALONIA, VALENCIA, AND THE COSTA BLANCA

Catalonia and Valencia share the classic Mediterranean diet, and Catalans feel right at home with paella valenciana. Fish preparations are similar along the coast, though inland favorites vary from place to place.

Top left: Paella valenciana in a classic paella pan. Top right: Fresh calçots. Bottom left: Suquet of fish, potatoes, onions, and tomatoes.

The grassy inland meadows of Catalonia's northern Alt Empordà region put quality beef on local tables; from the Costa Brava comes fine seafood, such as anchovies from L'Estartit and *gambas* (jumbo shrimp) from Palamós, both deservedly famous. *Romescu*—a blend of almonds, peppers, garlic, and olive oil—is used as a fish and seafood sauce in Tarragona, especially during the *calçotadas* (spring onion feasts) in February. *Allioli*, garlicky mayonnaise, is another popular topping. The Ebro Delta is renowned for fresh fish and eels, as well as *rossejat* (fried rice in a fish broth). Valencia and the Mediterranean coast are the homeland of *paella valenciana*. *Arròs a banda* is a variant in which the fish and rice are cooked separately.

CALÇOTS

The winter calçotada is a beloved event in Catalonia. The *calçot* is a sweet spring onion developed by a 19th-century farmer who discovered how to extend the edible portion by packing soil around the base. On the last weekend of January, the town of Valls holds a calçotada where upward of 30,000 people gather for meals of onions, sausage, lamb chops, and red wine.

RICE

Paella valenciana (Valencian paella) is one of Spain's most famous gastronomic contributions. A simple country dish dating from the early 18th century, "paella" refers to the wide frying pan with short, sturdy handles that's used to cook the rice. Anything fresh from the fields that day, along with rice and olive oil, traditionally went into the pan but paella valenciana has particular ingredients: short-grain rice, chicken, rabbit, *garrofó* (a local legume), tomatoes, green beans, sweet peppers, olive oil, and saffron. Artichokes and peas are also included in season. *Paella marinera* (seafood paella) is a different story: rice, cuttlefish, squid, mussels, shrimp, prawns, lobster, clams, garlic, olive oil, sweet paprika, and saffron, all stewed in fish broth. Many other paella variations are possible, including paella *negra,* a black rice dish made with squid ink; *arròs a banda* made with peeled seafood; and *fideuá,* paella made with noodles in place of rice.

SEAFOOD STEWS

Sèpia amb pèsols is a vegetable and seafood *mar i muntanya* (surf and turf) beloved on the Costa Brava: cuttlefish and peas are stewed with potatoes, garlic, onions, tomatoes, and a splash of wine. The *picadillo*—the finishing touches of flavors and textures—includes parsley, black pepper, fried bread, pine nuts, olive oil, and salt. *Es niu* ("the nest") of

game fowl, cod, tripe, cuttlefish, pork, and rabbit is another Costa Brava favorite. Stewed for a good five hours until the darkness of the onions and the ink of the cuttlefish have combined to impart a rich chocolate color to the stew, this is a much-celebrated wintertime classic. You'll also find *suquet de peix,* the Catalan fish stew, at restaurants along the Costa Brava.

FRUITS AND VEGETABLES

Valencia and the eastern Levante region have long been famous as Spain's *huerta,* or garden. The alluvial soil of the littoral produces an abundance of everything from tomatoes to asparagus, peppers, chard, spinach, onions, artichokes, cucumbers, and the whole range of Mediterranean bounty. Catalonia's Maresme and Empordà regions are also fruit and vegetable bowls, making this coastline a true cornucopia of fresh produce.

WINES

The Penedès wine region west of Barcelona has been joined by new wine Denominations of Origin from all over Catalonia. Alt Camp, Tarragona, Priorat, Montsant, Costers del Segre, Pla de Bages, Alella, and the Empordà all produce excellent reds and whites to join Catalonia's sparkling Cava on local wine lists; the rich, full-bodied reds of Montsant and the Priorat, especially, are among the best in Spain.

8

Updated by
Jared Lubarsky The long curve of the Mediterranean from the French border to Cabo Cervera, below Alicante, encompasses the two autonomous communities of Catalonia and Valencia, with the country's second- and third-largest cities (Barcelona and Valencia, respectively). Rivals in many respects, the two communities share a language, history, and culture that set them clearly apart from the rest of Spain.

Girona is the gateway to Northern Catalonia and its attractions—the Pyrenees, the volcanic region of La Garrotxa, and the beaches of the rugged Costa Brava. Northern Catalonia is memorable for the soft, green hills of the Empordàn farm country and the Alberes mountain range at the eastern end of the Pyrenees. Sprinkled across the landscape are *masías* (farmhouses) with austere, staggered-stone roofs and square towers that make them look like fortresses. Even the tiniest village has its church, arcaded square, and *rambla*, where villagers take their evening *paseo* (stroll).

Artist Salvador Dalí's deep connection to the Costa Brava is literally enshrined in the Teatre-Museu Dalí, in Figueres: he's buried in the crypt beneath it. His former home, a castle in Púbol, is where his wife, Gala, is buried. His summer home in Port Lligat Bay, north of Cadaqués, is now a museum of the Surrealist's life and work.

The province of Valencia was incorporated into the Kingdom of Aragón, Catalonia's medieval Mediterranean empire, when it was conquered by Jaume I in the 13th century. Along with Catalonia, Valencia became part of the united Spanish state in the 15th century, but defenders of its separate cultural and linguistic identity still resent the centuries of Catalan domination. The Catalan language prevails in Tarragona, a city and province of Catalonia, but Valenciano—a dialect of Catalan—is spoken and used on street signs in the Valencian provinces.

The *huerta* (a fertile, irrigated coastal plain) is devoted mainly to citrus and vegetable farming, which lends color to the landscape and fragrance to the air. Arid mountains form a stark backdrop to the lush coast. Over the years these shores have entertained Phoenician, Greek, Carthaginian, and Roman visitors; the Romans stayed several centuries and left archaeological remains all the way down the coast, particularly in Tarragona, the capital of Rome's Spanish empire by 218 BC. Rome's dominion did not go uncontested, however; the most serious challenge came from the Carthaginians of North Africa. The three Punic Wars, fought over this territory between 264 and 146 BC, established the reputation of the Carthaginian general Hannibal.

The coastal farmland and beaches that attracted the ancients now call to modern-day tourists, though a chain of ugly developments has marred much of the shore. Inland, however, local culture survives intact. The rugged and beautiful territory is dotted with small fortified towns, several of which bear the name of Spain's 11th-century national hero, El Cid, commemorating the battles he fought here against the Moors some 900 years ago.

PLANNING

WHEN TO GO
Come for the beaches in the hot summer months, but expect crowds and serious heat—in some places up to 40°C (104°F). The Mediterranean coast is more comfortable in May and September.

February and March are the peak months for skiing in the Pyrenees. Winter traveling in the region has other advantages: Valencia still has plenty of sunshine, and if you're visiting villages and wineries in the countryside you might find you've got the run of the place! A word of warning: many restaurants outside the major towns may close on weekdays in winter, so call ahead. Museums and centers of interest tend to have shorter winter hours, many closing at 6 pm.

The Costa Blanca beach area gets hot and crowded in summer, and accommodations are at a premium. In contrast, spring is mild and an excellent time to tour the region, particularly the rural areas, where blossoms infuse the air with pleasant fragrances and wildflowers dazzle the landscape.

PLANNING YOUR TIME
Not far from Barcelona, the beautiful towns of Vic, Ripoll, Girona, and Cadaqués are easily reachable from the city by bus or train in a couple of hours. Figueres is a must if you want to see the Dalí Museum. Girona makes an excellent base from which to explore La Garrotxa; for that, you'll need to rent a car. Tarragona and its environs are definitely worth a few days; it's easily reached from Barcelona via RENFE, or allow 1½ hours to drive, especially on weekends and in summer. If you're driving, a visit to the wineries in the Penedès region en route is well worth the detour. Most of Spain's cava comes from here. Tarragona's important Roman wonders are best seen on foot at a leisurely pace, broken up with a meal at any of the fine seafood restaurants in the Serallo fishing quarter.

Valencia is three hours by express train from Barcelona; if you have a flexible schedule, you might think about stopping in Tarragona on your way. From Tarragona, it's a comfortable one-hour train ride to Valencia; by car, you have the option of stopping for a meal and a walkabout in one of the coastal towns like Peñiscola or Castellon. Historic Valencia and the Santiago Calatrava-designed City of Arts and Sciences complex can be covered in two days, but you might well want one more to indulge in the city's food and explore the nightlife in the Barrio del Carmen.

A day trip to the nature reserve at Delta de l'Ebre, outside Valencia, is also highly recommended.

Travel agencies in Alicante can arrange tours of the city and bus and train tours to Guadalest, the Algar waterfalls, the Peñón de Ifach (Calpe) on the Costa Blanca, to the nearby island of Tabarca, and inland to Elche.

FESTIVALS
In Valencia, the **Las Fallas** fiestas begin March 1 and reach a climax between March 15 and El Día de San José (St. Joseph's Day) on March 19, which is Father's Day in Spain. Las Fallas originated from St. Joseph's role as patron saint of carpenters; in medieval times, carpenters' guilds celebrated the arrival of spring by cleaning out their shops and making bonfires with scraps of wood. These days it's a 19-day celebration ending with fireworks, floats, carnival processions, and bullfights. On March 19, huge wood and papier-mâché effigies, typically of political figures and other personalities, the result of a year's work by local community groups, are torched to end the fiestas.

GETTING HERE AND AROUND
AIR TRAVEL
El Prat de Llobregat in Barcelona is the main international airport for the Costa Brava; Girona is the closest airport to the region, with bus connections directly into the city and to Barcelona. Valencia has an international airport with direct flights to London, Paris, Brussels, Lisbon, Zurich, and Milan as well as regional flights from Barcelona, Madrid, Málaga, and other cities in Spain. There is a regional airport in Alicante serving the Valencian region and Murcia.

BOAT AND FERRY TRAVEL
Many short-cruise lines along the coast offer the chance to view the Costa Brava from the sea. Visit the port areas in the main towns *listed below* and you'll quickly spot several tourist cruise lines. Plan to spend around €15–€27, depending on the length of the cruise. Many longer cruises include a stop en route for a swim. The glass-keeled Nautilus boats for observation of the Islas Medes underwater park cost €19 and run daily between April and October and weekends between November and March.

The shortest ferry connections to the Balearic Islands originate in Dénia. Balearia sails from there to Ibiza, Formentera, and Mallorca.

Boat and Ferry Information Balearia ☎ *902/160180* ⊕ *www.balearia.com.* **Creuers Badia de Roses** ✉ *Carrer Gravina 4, Roses* ☎ *608/431762.* **Iscomar** ☎ *902/119128* ⊕ *www.iscomar.com.* **Nautilus** ✉ *Passeig Marítim 23, Toroella, L'Estartit* ☎ *972/751489* ⊕ *www.nautilus.es.* **Roses Serveis Marítims.** Two departures are scheduled daily, for diving excursions (€36 with equipment rental) to the Cap de Creus Natural Park. ⊠ *Carrer Eugeni D'ors 15, Roses* ☎ *609/893389* ⊕ *www.rosesub.com.* **Viajes Marítimos** ⊠ *Carrer de Sant Pere 5, Lloret de Mar* ☎ *972/369095.*

BUS TRAVEL

Bus travel is generally inexpensive and comfortable. Private companies run buses down the coast and from Madrid to Valencia, and to Alicante. Alsa is the main bus line in this region; local tourist offices can help with timetables. Sarfa operate buses from Barcelona to Blanes, Lloret, Sant Feliu de Guixols, Platja d'Aro, Palamos, Begur, Roses, and Cadaqués.

Contacts Alsa ☎ *902/422242* ⊕ *www.alsa.es.* **Barcelonabus** ☎ *902/130014, 93/593–1300* ⊕ *www.barcelonabus.com.* **Sagalés** ⊠ *Passeig Sant Joan 52, Barcelona* ☎ *902/130014* ⊕ *www.sagales.com.* **Sarfa.** Sarfa buses connect the towns along the Costa Brava and the Empordà with Barcelona. ⊠ *Estació del Nord, Alí Bei 80, Barcelona* ☎ *972/301293, 902/302025* ⊕ *www.sarfa.com* Ⓜ *Arc de Triomf.*

CAR TRAVEL

A car is a practical necessity for explorations inland, where much of the driving is smooth, uncrowded, and scenic. Catalonia and Valencia have excellent roads; the only drawbacks are the high cost of fuel and the high tolls on the *autopistas* (highways, usually designed with the letters AP). The coastal N340 can get clogged, however, so you're often better off on toll roads if your time is limited.

TRAIN TRAVEL

Most of the Costa Brava is *not* served directly by railroad. A local line runs up the coast from Barcelona but takes you only to Blanes; from there it turns inland and connects at Maçanet-Massanes with the main line up to France. Direct trains stop only at major connections, such as Girona, Flaçà, and Figueres. To visit one of the smaller towns in between, you can take a fast direct train from Barcelona to Girona, for instance, then get off and wait for a local to come by. The stop on the main line for the middle section of the Costa Brava is Flaçà, where you can take a bus or taxi to your final destination. Girona and Figueres are two other towns with major bus stations that feed out to the towns of the Costa Brava. The train serves the last three towns on the north end of the Costa Brava: Llançà, Colera, and Portbou.

Express intercity trains reach Valencia from all over Spain, arriving at the new Joaquin Sorolla station; from there, a shuttle bus takes you to the Estación del Norte, the terminus in the center of town, for local connections. From Barcelona there are 15 trains a day, including the fast train TALGO, which takes 3½ hours. There are 22 daily trains to Valencia from Madrid; the high-speed train takes about 1 hour 40 minutes.

For the Costa Blanca, the rail hub is Alicante; for southern Catalonia, make direct train connections to Tarragona from either Barcelona or Valencia.

TOURS

Bus tours from Barcelona to Girona and Figueres (including the Dalí Museum) are run by Julià Travel. Buses leave Barcelona Tuesday through Sunday at 8:30 and return around 6. The price is €71 per person. Pullmantur runs tours to several points on the Costa Brava.

Hiking, cycling, and walking tours around Valencia and the Costa Blanca are an alternative to relaxing at the beach. The Sierra Mariola and Sierra Aitana regions are both easily accessible from the Costa Blanca resorts, and many companies—including Ciclo Costa Blanca and Mountain Walks—plan itineraries with hotels included.

There are also riding schools in a number of towns in the region, which provide classes as well as trekking opportunities. Pick up brochures at the local tourist offices.

Water sports are widely available, and you can learn to sail in most of the major resorts. Kite surfing is becoming increasingly popular; the necessary gear is available for rent at many of the beaches, including Santa Pola, and the same applies to windsurfing. A wide range of companies offer scuba-diving excursions, and in the smaller coastal towns it's possible to dive in the protected waters of offshore nature reserves if you book ahead.

If pedal power is more your thing, several companies offer a range of cycling holidays: Ciclo Costa Blanca is a good place to start.

Contacts Abdet ⊕ www.abdet.com. **Ciclo Costa Blanca** ⊠ Comercio Enara 2, Camino Viejo de Altea 24, Alfaz del Pi, Alicante ☎ 699/045475 ⊕ www.ciclocostablanca.com. **Julià Travel** ⊠ Ronda Universidad 5, Barcelona ☎ 93/317–6454, 902/024443 ⊕ www.juliatravel.com. **Mountain Walks** ☎ 965/511044 ⊕ www.mountainwalks.com.

FARMHOUSE STAYS IN CATALONIA

Dotted throughout Catalonia are farmhouses (*casas rurales* in Spanish, and *cases de pagès* or *masíes* in Catalan), where you can spend a weekend or longer. Accommodations vary from small, rustic homes to spacious, luxurious farmhouses with fireplaces and pools. Sometimes you stay in a guest room, as at a bed-and-breakfast; in other places you rent the entire house and do your own cooking. Most tourist offices, including the main Catalonia Tourist Office in Barcelona, have info and listings for the *cases de pagès* of the region. Several organizations in Spain have detailed listings and descriptions of Catalonia's farmhouses, and it's best to book through one of these.

Contacts Confederació del Turisme Rural i l'Agroturisme de Catalunya ⊕ www.catalunyarural.info. **Federació del Turisme Rural d'Unió de Pagesos de Catalunya** ⊕ www.agroturisme.org.

RESTAURANTS

Catalonia's eateries are deservedly famous. Girona's El Celler de Can Roca was voted the best restaurant in the world in 2013 in the annual critics' poll conducted by British magazine *Restaurant,* and a host of other first-rate establishments continue to offer inspiring fine dining in Catalonia, which began in the hinterlands at the legendary Hotel Empordà. You needn't go to an internationally acclaimed restaurant, however, to dine well. Superstar chef Ferran Adrià of the former foodie paradise elBulli dines regularly at dives in Roses, where straight-up fresh fish is the day-in, day-out attraction. Northern Catalonia's Empordà region is known not only for seafood, but also for a rich assortment of inland and upland products. Beef from Girona's verdant pastureland is prized throughout Catalonia, while wild mushrooms from the Pyrenees and game from the Alberes range offer seasonal depth and breadth to menus across the region. From a simple beachside paella or *llobarro* (sea bass) at a *chiringuito* (shack) with tables on the sand, to the splendor of a meal at Celler de Can Roca, playing culinary hopscotch through Catalonia is a good way to organize a tour.

HOTELS

Lodgings on the Costa Brava range from the finest hotels to spartan *pensions*. The better accommodations are usually well situated and have splendid views of the seascape. Many simple hotels provide a perfectly adequate stopover. If you plan to visit during the high season (July and August), be sure to book reservations well in advance at almost any hotel in this area, especially the Costa Brava, which remains one of the most popular summer resort areas in Spain. Many Costa Brava hotels close down in the winter season, between November and March. *Hotel reviews have been shortened. For full information visit Fodors.com.*

WHAT IT COSTS IN EUROS				
	$	$$	$$$	$$$$
Restaurants	under €13	€13–€17	€18–€22	over €22
Hotels	under €91	€91–€125	€126–€180	over €180

Prices are per person for a main course, or a combination of small plates, at dinner, and for two people in a standard double room in high season, excluding tax.

8

NORTHERN CATALONIA

Northern Catalonia is for many *the* reason to visit Spain. The historic center of Girona, its principal city, is a labyrinth of climbing cobblestone streets and staircases, with remarkable Gothic and Romanesque buildings at every turn. El Call—the Jewish Quarter here—is one of the best preserved in Europe, and the Gothic cathedral is an architectural masterpiece. Streets in the modern part of the city are lined with smart shops and boutiques, and the overall quality of life in Girona is considered among the best in Spain.

The nearby towns of Besalú and Figueres couldn't be more different from each other. Figueres is an unexceptional town made exceptional by the Dalí Museum. Besalú is a picture-perfect Romanesque village on a bluff overlooking the River Fluvià, with at least one of the most prestigious restaurants in Catalonia. Less well known are the medieval towns in and around La Garrotxa: Ripoll, Rupit, and Olot boast arguably the best produce in the region.

GIRONA

97 km (60 miles) northeast of Barcelona.

At the confluence of four rivers, Girona (population: 96,000) keeps intact the magic of its historic past—with its brooding hilltop castle, soaring cathedral, and dreamy riverside setting, it resembles a vision from the Middle Ages. Today, as a university center, Girona combines past and vibrant present: art galleries, chic cafés, and trendy boutiques have set up shop in many of the restored buildings of the Old Quarter, known as the Força Vella (Old Fortress), which is on the east side of the River Onya. Built on the side of the mountain, it presents a tightly packed labyrinth of medieval buildings and monuments on narrow cobblestone streets with connecting stairways. You can still see vestiges of the Iberian and Roman walls in the cathedral square and in the patio of the old university. In the centermost quarter is El Call, one of Europe's best-preserved ancient (12th- to 15th-century) Jewish communities and an important center of cabalistic studies.

The main street of the Old Quarter is Carrer de la Força, which follows the old Via Augusta, the Roman road that connected Rome with its provinces.

The best way to get to know Girona is on foot. As you wander through the Força Vella you will be repeatedly surprised by new discoveries. One of Girona's treasures is its setting, high above where the Onyar merges with the Ter; the latter flows from a mountain waterfall that can be glimpsed in a gorge above the town. Regardless of your approach, walk first along the west bank of the Onyar, between the train trestle and the Plaça de la Independència, to admire the classic view of the Old Town, with its pastel yellow, pink, and orange waterfront facades. Many of the windows and balconies—always draped with colorful drying laundry—are adorned with fretwork grilles of embossed wood or delicate iron tracery. Cross Pont de Sant Agustí over to the Old Quarter from under the arcades in the corner of Plaça de la Independència and find your way to the Punt de Benvinguda tourist office, to the right at Rambla Llibertat 1. Then work your way up through the labyrinth of steep streets, using the cathedral's huge baroque facade as a guide.

GETTING HERE AND AROUND

There are more than 20 daily trains from Barcelona to Girona (continuing on to the French border). Bus service to the city center is limited, but there are frequent Barcelonabus buses to Girona airport that take an average of 75 minutes and cost €16 one-way, €25 round-trip. Getting around the city is easiest on foot or by taxi; several bridges connect the historic old quarter with the more modern town across the river.

DISCOUNTS AND DEALS

The GironaMuseus card is good for discount admission to all the city's museums. ■TIP➔ **Some are free on the first Sunday of every month.** Check with the tourist office or at the Punt de Benvinguda welcome center, which can also arrange guided tours.

Punt de Benvinguda. Look for this visitor information center—where you can also get help with hotel bookings—at the entrance to Girona from

Northern Catalonia
and the Costa Brava

the town's main parking area on the right bank of the Onyar River. ⊠ *Carrer Berenguer Carnisser 5* ☎ *972/211678.*

ESSENTIALS

Bus Information Barcelona Bus ⊠ *Passeig de Sant Joan 52, Barcelona* ☎ *902/130014* ⊕ *www.barcelonabus.com.*

Visitor Information Girona Office of Tourism ⊠ *Carrer Joan Maragall 1* ☎ *972/975975* ⊕ *www.girona.cat/turisme* ⊠ *Rambla de la Llibertat 1* ☎ *972/226575.*

EXPLORING
TOP ATTRACTIONS

Fodor's Choice
★

Cathedral. At the heart of the Old City, the cathedral looms above 90 steps and is famous for its nave—at 75 feet, the widest in the world and the epitome of the spatial ideal of Catalan Gothic architects. Since Charlemagne founded the original church in the 8th century, it has been through many fires, changes, and renovations, so you are greeted by a Rococo-era facade, "eloquent as organ music" and impressively set off by a spectacular flight of 17th-century stairs, which rises from its own plaça. Inside, three smaller naves were compressed into one gigantic hall by the famed architect Guillermo Bofill in 1416. The change was typical of Catalan Gothic "hall" churches, and it was done to facilitate

There's more to Girona's cathedral than the 90 steps to get to it; inside there's much to see, including the Treasury.

preaching to crowds. Note the famous silver canopy, or *baldaquí* (baldachin). The oldest part of the cathedral is the 11th-century Romanesque **Torre de Carlemany** (Charlemagne Tower).

The cathedral's 12th-century cloister has an obvious affinity with the cloisters in the Roussillon area of France. Inside the Treasury are a 10th-century copy of Beatus's manuscript *Commentary on the Apocalypse* (illuminated in the dramatically primitive Mozarabic style), the Bible of Emperor Charles V, and the celebrated Tapís de la Creació (Tapestry of the Creation), considered by most experts to be the finest tapestry surviving from the Romanesque era. It depicts the seven days of Creation as told in Genesis in the primitive but powerful fashion of early Romanesque art. Made of wool, with predominant colors of green, brown, and ocher, the tapestry once hung behind the main altar as a pictorial Bible lesson. The four seasons, stars, winds, months of the year and days of the week, plants, animals, and elements of nature circle around a central figure, likening paradise to the eternal cosmos presided over by Christ. In addition to its intrinsic beauty, the bottom band (which appears to have been added at a later date) contains two *iudeis,* or Jews, dressed in the round cloaks they were compelled to wear to set them apart from Christians. This scene is thought to be the earliest portrayal of a Jew (other than biblical figures) in Christian art. ✉ *Pl. de la Catedral s/n* 🕾 *972/427189, 972/215814* ⊕ *www.catedraldegirona.org* 🕾 *€7 (free Sun.)* ⊗ *Apr.–Oct., daily 10–7:30; Nov.–Mar., daily 10–6:30.*

El Call. Girona is especially noted for its 13th-century Jewish Quarter, El Call, which can be found branching off Carrer de la Força, south of the Plaça Catedral. The word *call* (pronounced "kyle" in Catalan) may come from an old Catalan word meaning "narrow way" or "passage," derived from the Latin word *callum* or *callis*. Others suggest that it comes from the Hebrew word *qahal*, meaning "assembly" or "meeting of the community." Owing allegiance to the Spanish king (who exacted tribute for this distinction) and not to the city government, this once-prosperous Jewish community—one of the most flourishing in Europe during the Middle Ages—was, at its height, a center of learning. An important school of the Kabala was centered here. The most famous teacher of the Kabala from Girona was Rabbi Mossé ben Nahman (also known as Nahmànides), who wrote an important religious work based on meditation and the reinterpretation of the Bible and the Talmud.

The earliest presence of Jews in Girona is uncertain, but the first historical mention dates from 982, when a group of 25 Jewish families moved to Girona from nearby Juïgues. Today the layout of El Call bears no resemblance to what this area looked like in the 15th century, when Jews last lived here. Space was at a premium inside the city walls in Girona, and houses were destroyed and built higgledy-piggledy one atop the other.

WORTH NOTING

Banys Arabs (*Arab Baths*). A misnomer, the Banys Arabs were actually built by Morisco craftsmen (workers of Moorish descent) in the late 12th century, long after Girona's Islamic occupation (714–797) had ended. Following the old Roman model that had disappeared in the West, the custom of bathing publicly may have been brought back from the Holy Land with the Crusaders. These baths are sectioned off into three rooms in descending order: a *frigidarium*, or cold bath, a square room with a central octagonal pool and a skylight with cupola held up by two stories of eight fine columns; a *tepidarium*, or warm bath; and a *caldarium*, or steam room, beneath which is a chamber where a fire was kept burning. Here the inhabitants of the old Girona came to relax, exchange gossip, or do business. ⊠ *Carrer Ferran el Catòlic s/n* ☎ *972/190797* ⊕ *www.banysarabs.cat* 🗺 *€2* ⏰ *Apr.–Sept., Mon.–Sat. 10–7, Sun. 10–2; Oct.–Mar., daily 10–2.*

Centre Bonastruc ça Porta. Housed in a former synagogue and dedicated to the preservation of Girona's Jewish heritage, this center organizes conferences, exhibitions, and seminars. The **Museu de Història dels Jueus** (Museum of Jewish History) contains 21 stone tablets, one of the finest collections in the world of medieval Jewish funerary slabs. These came from the old Jewish cemetery of Montjuïc, revealed when the railroad between Barcelona and France was laid out in the 19th century. Its exact location, about 1½ km (1 mile) north of Girona on the road to La Bisbal and known as La Tribana, is being excavated. The center also holds the **Institut d'Estudis Nahmànides,** with an extensive library of Judaica. ⊠ *Carrer de la Força 8* ☎ *972/216761* ⊕ *www.girona.cat/ call/eng/museu.php* 🗺 *€4* ⏰ *Sept.–June, Tues.–Sat. 10–6, Sun. and Mon. 10–2; July and Aug., Mon.–Sat. 10–8, Sun. 10–2.*

Museu d'Art. The Episcopal Palace near the cathedral contains the wide-ranging collections of Girona's main art museum. You'll see everything from superb Romanesque *majestats* (carved wood figures of Christ) to reliquaries from Sant Pere de Rodes, illuminated 12th-century manuscripts, and works of the 20th-century Olot school of landscape painting. ⊠ *Pujada de la Catedral 12* ☏ *972/203834* ⊕ *www.museuart.com* ⬚ *€2* ⊙ *May–Sept., Tues.–Sat. 10–7, Sun. 10–2; Oct.–Apr., Tues.–Sat. 10–6, Sun. 10–2.*

QUICK BITES

La Vienesa. Fortify yourself for sightseeing with some superb tea and plump pastries at La Vienesa. One of the town's best-loved gathering points for conversation, this cozy spot is good place to regroup and reorient.
⊠ *Carrer La Pujada del Pont de Pedra 1* ☏ *972/486046.*

FAMILY **Museu del Cinema.** An interactive museum, this spot has artifacts and movie-related paraphernalia starting from Chinese shadows, the first rudimentary moving pictures, to Lyon's Lumière brothers. The Cine Nic toy filmmaking machines, originally developed in 1931 by the Nicolau brothers of Barcelona and now being relaunched commercially, allow even novices to put together their own movies. ⊠ *Carrer de la Sèquia 1* ☏ *972/412777* ⊕ *www.museudelcinema.cat* ⬚ *€5 (free 1st Sun. of month)* ⊙ *May, June, and Sept., Tues.–Sat. 10–8, Sun. 11–3; July and Aug., Tues.–Sun. 10–8; Oct.–Apr., Tues.–Fri. 10–6, Sat. 10–8, Sun. 11–3.*

Museu d'Història de la Ciutat. On Carrer de la Força, this fascinating museum is filled with artifacts from Girona's long and embattled past. From pre-Roman objects to paintings and drawings from the notorious siege at the hands of Napoleonic troops, to the early municipal lighting system and the medieval printing press, there is plenty to see here. You will definitely come away with a clearer idea of Girona's past. ⊠ *Carrer de la Força 27* ☏ *972/222229* ⊕ *www.girona.cat/museuciutat* ⬚ *€4 (free 1st Sun. of month)* ⊙ *Tues.–Sat. 10:30–5:30 (until 6:30 May–Sept.), Sun. 10:30–1:30.*

Passeig Arqueològic. The landscaped gardens of this stepped archaeological walk are below the restored walls of the Old Quarter (which you can walk, in parts) and have good views from belvederes and watchtowers. From there, climb through the Jardins de la Francesa to the highest ramparts for a view of the cathedral's 11th-century Charlemagne Tower.

Placeta del Institut Vell. In this small square on Carrer de la Força you can study a tar-blackened 3-inch-long, half-inch-deep groove carved shoulder-high into the stone of the right-hand doorpost as you enter the square. It indicates the location of a *mezuzah*, a small case or tube of metal or wood containing a piece of parchment with verses from the Torah (declaring the essence of Jewish belief in one God). Anyone passing through the doorway touched the mezuah as a sign of devotion. Evidence of the labyrinthine layout of a few street ruts in the Old Quarter may still be seen inside the antiques store Antiguitats la Canonja Vella at Carrer de la Força 33.

Sant Feliu. The vast bulk of this structure is landmarked by one of Girona's most distinctive belfries, topped by eight pinnacles. One of Girona's most beloved churches, it was repeatedly rebuilt and altered over four centuries and stands today as an amalgam of Romanesque columns, Gothic nave, and Baroque facade. It was founded over the tomb of St. Felix of Africa, a martyr under the Roman emperor Diocletian.

✉ *Pujada de Sant Feliu 29* ☎ *972/201407* 🎟 *Included with €7 Cathedral admission* ☉ *Mon.–Sat. 10–5:30, Sun. 1–5:30.*

Torre de Gironella. A five-minute walk uphill behind the cathedral leads to a park and this four-story tower (no entry permitted) dating from the year 1190; the tower marks the highest point in the Jewish Quarter. Girona's Jewish community took refuge here in early August 1391, emerging 17 weeks later to find their houses in ruins. Even though Spain's official expulsion decree did not go into effect until 1492, this attack effectively ended the Girona Jewish community. Destroyed in 1404, reconstructed in 1411, and destroyed anew by retreating Napoleonic troops in 1814, the Torre de Gironella was the site of the celebration of the first Hanukkah ceremony in Girona in 607 years, held on December 20, 1998, with Jerusalem's chief Sephardic rabbi Rishon Letzion presiding. ✉ *Ctra. Sant Gregori 91.*

WHERE TO EAT

$$

TAPAS

✕ **Bubbles Gastro Bar.** Excellent Catalan cuisine with Mediterrean-fusion touches is served here in an elegant setting just across the river from the Old City. Try the innovative tapas, or choose from two dinner tasting menus for €25 or €45. 💲 *Average main: €15* ✉ *Passeig José Canalejas 6* ☎ *972/226002* ⊕ *www.gastrobubbles.com* ☉ *Closed Sun. and Mon.*

$$$$

CONTEMPORARY

Fodor'sChoice

★

✕ **Celler de Can Roca.** Annointed in 2013 by an international panel of food critics and chefs as the best restaurant in the world, Celler de Can Roca is a life-changing experience for anybody persistent enough to get a reservation. The Roca brothers, Joan, Josep, and Jordi, showcase their masterful creations in two tasting menus, at €155 and €190; consider your visit blessed if yours includes signature dishes like lobster *parmentier* with black trumpet mushrooms, or Iberian suckling pig with pepper sauce and garlic and quince terrine, or Dublin Bay prawns with curry smoke (the Rocas pioneered the technique of roasting in the aromas of spices during the cooking process). For dessert, try any of maître confectioner Jordi's spectacular innovations. Don't be embarrassed to ask Josep, the sommelier, for guidance through the encyclopedic wine list. 💲 *Average main: €38* ✉ *Can Sunyer 48* ☎ *972/222157* ⌔ *Reservations essential* ☉ *Closed Sun., Mon., and Aug.*

WHERE TO STAY

$$$$

RENTAL

FAMILY

Fodor'sChoice

★

🏠 **Alemanys 5.** Award-winning architect Anna Noguera and partner Juan-Manuel Ribera transformed a 16th-century house steps from the cathedral into two extraordinary apartments: one for up to five people, the other for six. **Pros:** perfect for families or small groups; ideal location. **Cons:** difficult to reach by car; minimum stay required. 💲 *Rooms from: €250* ✉ *Carrer Alemanys 5* ☎ *649/885136* ⊕ *www.alemanys5. com* ⤳ *2 apartments* 🍽 *No meals.*

$$

HOTEL

Fodor'sChoice

★

🏠 **Hotel Històric y Apartaments Històric Girona.** Perfectly placed for exploring the Jewish Quarter, this boutique hotel occupies a 9th-century house, with remnants of a 3rd-century Roman wall and a Roman aqueduct on the ground floor and in one of the apartments. **Pros:** good location; historical features; top amenities and comforts. **Cons:** rooms and apartments are a little cramped; difficult to get a car in; no pets.

8

With its picturesque rivers, Girona is often called the Spanish Venice.

$ *Rooms from: €114* ✉ *Carrer Bellmirall 4A* ☎ *972/223583* ⊕ *www.* *hotelhistoric.com* ⤴ *6 rooms, 7 apartments, 2 suites* ⦿⎮ *No meals.*

NIGHTLIFE AND PERFORMING ARTS

Girona is a university town, so the night scene is especially lively during the school year.

Platea. This nightspot, popular with students and visitors alike, has both disco and live bands in concert, depending on the day of the week. ✉ *Carrer Jeroni Real de Fontclara 4* ☎ *972/227288, 972/411902* ⊙ *Wed.–Sat. 10 pm–5:30 am.*

SHOPPING

Boutique Carlos Falcó. Men will find fine plumage here, from suits to accessories. ✉ *Carrer Josep Maluquer Salvador 16* ☎ *972/207156.*

Despiral. Young people stock up on threads at Despiral. ✉ *Carrer Santa Clara 43* ☎ *972/221448.*

Dolors Turró. Painter and sculptor Dolors Turró knows her angels: making them—in all shapes, sizes and styles—is what she does best. Drop in to her quirky atelier in the old city. ✉ *Carrer de les Ballesteries 19* ☎ *972/410193.*

Gluki. This chocolatier and confectioner has been in business since 1880. ✉ *Carrer Santa Clara 44* ☎ *972/201989.*

Llibreria 22. Girona's best bookstore has travel guidebooks and a selection of English fiction. ✉ *Carrer Hortes 22* ☎ *972/212395* ⊕ *www.* *llibreria22.net.*

Peacock. For shoes, go to one of Peacock's four Girona locations—the others are at Carrer Migdia 18, Plaça de Vi 4, and Carrer Pare Claret 29. ⊠ *Carrer Nou 15* ☎ *972/226848* ⊕ *www.peacock.cat.*

Rocambolesc. Couldn't get a table at El Celler de Can Roca? Keep trying, but in the meantime there's Rocambolesc, the latest of the Roca family culinary undertakings: an ice-cream parlor in the heart of the city that serves up master confectioner Jordi Roca's exquisite *helados* and takeaway desserts. Expect long lines. ⊠ *Carrer Santa Clara 50* ☎ *972/416667.*

FIGUERES

37 km (23 miles) north of Girona on the A7.

Figueres is the capital of the *comarca* (county) of the Alt Empordà, the bustling county seat of this predominantly agricultural region. Local people come from the surrounding area to shop at its many stores and stock up on farm equipment and supplies. Thursday is market day, and farmers gather at the top of La Rambla to do business and gossip, taking refreshments at cafés and discreetly pulling out and pocketing large rolls of bills, the result of their morning transactions. What brings the tourists to Figueres in droves, however, has little to do with agriculture—unless, of course, you use a broader definition of fertilizer: the jaw-dropping Dalí Museum, one of the most visited museums in Spain.

Artist Salvador Dalí is Figueres's most famous son. With a painterly technique that rivaled that of Jan van Eyck, a flair for publicity so aggressive it would have put P. T. Barnum in the shade, and a penchant for shocking (he loved telling people Barcelona's historic Barri Gòtic should be knocked down), Dalí enters art history as one of the foremost proponents of Surrealism, the movement launched in the 1920s by André Breton. His most lasting image may be the melting watches in his iconic 1931 painting *The Persistence of Memory*. The artist, who was born in Figueres and died there in 1989, decided to create a museum-monument to himself during the last two decades of his life. Dalí often frequented the Cafeteria Astòria at the top of La Rambla (still the center of social life in Figueres), signing autographs for tourists or just being Dalí: he once walked down the street with a French omelet in his breast pocket instead of a handkerchief.

GETTING HERE AND AROUND

Figueres is one of the stops on the regular train service from Barcelona to the French border. Local buses are also frequent, especially from nearby Cadaqués, with more than eight services daily. The town is sufficiently small to explore on foot.

ESSENTIALS

Visitor Information Figueres ⊠ *Pl. del Sol s/n* ☎ *972/503155* ⊕ *en.visitfigueres.cat.*

EXPLORING

Castell de Sant Ferran. Just a minute's drive northwest of Figueres is this imposing 18th-century fortified castle, one of the largest in Europe. Only when you start exploring can you appreciate how immense it is.

Catalonia's National Dance

The *sardana*, Catalonia's national dance, is often perceived as a solemn and measured affair performed by older folks in front of the Barcelona Cathedral at midday on weekends. Look for an athletic young *colla* (troupe), though, and you'll see the grace and fluidity the sardana can create. The mathematical precision of the dance, consisting of 76 steps in sets of four, each dancer needing to know exactly where he or she is at all times, demands intense concentration. Said to be a representation of the passing of time, a choreography of the orbits and revolutions of the moon and stars, the circular sardana is recorded in Greek chronicles dating back 2,000 years. Performed in circles of all sizes and by dancers of all ages, the sardana is accompanied by an ensemble called the *cobla*: five wind instruments, five brass, and a director who plays a three-holed flute called the *flabiol* and a small drum, the *tabal*, which he wears attached to his flute arm (normally the right).

The parade grounds extend for acres, and the arcaded stables can hold more than 500 horses; the perimeter is roughly 4 km (2½ miles around). This castle was the site of the last official meeting of the Republican parliament (on February 1, 1939) before it surrendered to Franco's forces. Ironically, it was here that Lieutenant Colonel Antonio Tejero was imprisoned after his failed 1981 coup d'état in Madrid. ■TIP➡ Call a day ahead and arrange for the "Catedral de l'Aiguas" 2-hour guided tour in English (€15), including a trip through the castle's subterranean water system by zodiac pontoon boat. ⊠ *Pujada del Castell s/n* ☎ *972/506094, 972/514585* ⊕ *www.lesfortalesescatalanes.info* ☞ *€3* ⊙ *Apr.–June and mid-Sept.–Oct., daily 10–6; July–mid-Sept., daily 10–8; Nov.–Mar., daily 10–3. Last admission 1 hr before closing.*

FAMILY **Museu del Joguet de Catalunya.** Hundreds of antique dolls and toys are on display here—including collections owned by, among others, Salvador Dalí, Federico García Lorca, and Joan Miró. It also hosts Catalonia's only *caganer* exhibit, from mid-December to mid-January in odd-numbered years. These playful little figures answering nature's call have long had a special spot in the Catalan *pessebre* (Nativity scene). Farmers are the most traditional figures, squatting discreetly behind the animals, but these days you'll find Barça soccer players and politicians, too. Check with the museum for exact dates. ⊠ *Hotel Paris, Carrer de Sant Pere 1* ☎ *972/504585* ⊕ *www.mjc.cat* ☞ *€6* ⊙ *June–Sept., Mon.–Sat. 10–7, Sun. 11–6; Oct.–May, Tues.–Sat. 10–6, Sun. 11–2.*

Fodor'sChoice **Teatre-Museu Dalí.** "Museum" was not a big enough word for Dalí, so
★ he christened his monument a "Theater." And, in fact, the building was once the Old Town theater, reduced to a ruin in the Spanish Civil War. Now topped with a glass geodesic dome and studded with Dalí's iconic egg shapes, the multilevel museum pays homage to his fertile imagination and artistic creativity. It includes gardens, ramps, and a spectacular dropcloth Dalí painted for Les Ballets de Monte Carlo. Don't look for his greatest paintings here, although there are some

The Dalí Museum in Figueres is itself a work of art. Note the eggs on the exterior: they're a common image in his work.

memorable images, including *Gala at the Mediterranean,* which takes the body of Gala (Dalí's wife) and morphs it into the image of Abraham Lincoln once you look through coin-operated viewfinders. The sideshow theme continues with other coin-operated pieces, including *Taxi Plujós* (Rainy Taxi), in which water gushes over the snail-covered occupants sitting in a Cadillac once owned by Al Capone, or *Sala de Mae West,* a trompe-l'oeil vision in which a pink sofa, two fireplaces, and two paintings morph into the face of the onetime Hollywood sex symbol. Fittingly, another "exhibit" on view is Dalí's own crypt. When his friends considered what flag to lay over his coffin, they decided to cover it with an embroidered heirloom tablecloth instead. Dalí would have liked this unconventional touch, if not the actual site: he wanted to be buried at his castle of Púbol next to his wife, but the then-mayor of Figueres took matters into his own hands. All in all, the museum is a piece of Dalí dynamite. ⊠ *Pl. Gala-Salvador Dalí 5* ☎ 972/677500 ⊕ *www.salvador-dali.org* ⊠ *€12* ☉ *July–Sept., daily 9–7:15 (with night visits late July–late Aug., 10–12:15); Mar.–June and Oct., Tues.–Sun. 9:30–5:15; Nov.–Feb., Tues.–Sun. 10:30–5:15.*

OFF THE BEATEN PATH

Casa-Museu Gala Dalí. The third point of the Dalí triangle is the medieval castle of Púbol, where the artist's wife, Gala, is buried in the crypt. During the 1970s this was Gala's residence, though Dalí also lived here in the early 1980s. It contains paintings and drawings, Gala's haute-couture dresses, elephant sculptures in the garden, furniture, and other objects chosen by the couple. Púbol, roughly between Girona and Figueres, is near the C255, and is not easy to find. If you are traveling by train, get off at the Flaçà station on RENFE's Barcelona–Portbou line;

walk or take a taxi 4 km (2½ miles) to Púbol. By bus, the Sarfa bus company has a stop in Flaçà and on the C255 road, some 2 km (1¼ miles) from Púbol. ✉ *Pl. Gala-Dalí s/n, Púbol* ☎ *972/488655* 🌐 *www.salvador-dali.org* 🎟 *€8* 🕒 *Mid-Mar.–mid-June and mid-Sept.–Oct., Tues.–Sun. 10–6; mid-June–mid-Sept., daily 10–8; Nov.–Dec., Tues.–Sun. 10–5. Last admission 45 mins before closing.*

WHERE TO STAY

$ HOTEL 🏨 **Hotel Duràn.** Dalí had his own private dining room in this former stagecoach relay station, and you can take a meal amid pictures of the great Surrealist. **Pros:** good central location; family-friendly. **Cons:** rooms lack character; parking inconvenient; no pets. [$] *Rooms from: €80* ✉ *Carrer Lasauca 5* ☎ *972/501250* 🌐 *www.hotelduran.com* 🛏 *65 rooms* 🍴 *No meals.*

$ HOTEL Fodor's Choice ★ 🏨 **Hotel Empordà.** Just a mile north of town, this hotel houses the elegant restaurant run by Jaume Subirós that's been hailed as the birthplace of modern Catalan cuisine and has become a beacon for gourmands. **Pros:** historic culinary destination; convenient to the Teatre-Museu Dalí. **Cons:** on an unprepossessing roadside lot beside the busy N11 highway. [$] *Rooms from: €80* ✉ *Av. Salvador Dalí i Domènech 170, 1.5 km (1 mile) north of town* ☎ *972/500562* 🌐 *www.hotelemporda.com* 🛏 *39 rooms, 3 suites* 🍴 *No meals.*

BESALÚ

34 km (21 miles) north of Girona, 25 km (15 miles) west of Figueres.

Besalú, the capital of a feudal county until power was transferred to Barcelona at the beginning of the 12th century, remains one of the best-preserved medieval towns in Catalonia. Among its main sights are the 12th-century Romanesque fortified bridge over the Fluvià river; two churches, Sant Vicenç (set on an attractive, café-lined plaza) and Sant Pere; and the ruins of the convent of Santa Maria on the hill above town.

GETTING HERE AND AROUND

With a population of just over 2,400, the village is easily small enough to stroll through, with all the restaurants and sights within easy distances of each other. There is bus service to Besalú from Figueres and the surrounding Costa Brava resorts.

ESSENTIALS

Visitor Information Besalú ✉ *Carrer del Pont Vell 1* ☎ *972/591240* 🌐 *www.besalu.cat.*

Guided tours. Guided tours of Besalú, offered by the visitor information center (daily at 1 pm in English, setting out from Carrer Major), cover the churches of Sant Pere and Sant Vincenç, archaeological sites, the Jewish Quarter, and the bridge. A nighttime Medieval Tour (July and August, Wednesday at 10 pm), is led by a knight on horseback and a retinue of various characters in costume. Phone reservations are recommended. ■ **TIP→ At the Church of Sant Pere, which has a 13th-century ambulatory, you may hear Gregorian chant.** ☎ *972/591240* 🎟 *Day tours €2.20 (30 mins) and €4.50 (1 hr), night tours €15.*

Besalú contains astonishingly well-preserved medieval buildings.

EXPLORING

Església de Sant Vicenç. Founded in 977, this pre-Romanesque gem contains the relics of St. Vincent as well as the tomb of its benefactor, Pere de Rovira. La Capella de la Veracreu (Chapel of the True Cross) displays a reproduction of an alleged fragment of the True Cross brought from Rome by Bernat Tallafer in 977 and stolen in 1899. ✉ *Carrer de Sant Vicenç s/n.*

Pont Fortificat. The town's most emblematic feature is this Romanesque 11th-century fortified bridge with crenellated battlements spanning the Fluvià River.

WHERE TO EAT

$$$$ CATALAN Fodor's Choice ★ 🍴 **Els Fogons de Can Llaudes.** A faithfully restored 10th-century Romanesque chapel holds proprietor Jaume Soler's outstanding restaurant, one of Catalonia's best. A typical main dish is *confitat de bou i raïm glacejat amb el seu suc* (beef confit au jus with glacé grapes). There is no à la carte menu; call at least one day in advance to reserve the €60 *menú de degustació* (tasting menu). [$] *Average main: €25* ✉ *Prat de Sant Pere 6* ☎ *972/590858, 629/782388* ✍ *Reservations essential* ⏲ *Closed Tues. and last 2 wks of Nov.*

OLOT

21 km (13 miles) west of Besalú, 55 km (34 miles) northwest of Girona.

Capital of the *comarca* (administrative region) of Garrotxa, Olot is famous for its 19th-century school of landscape painters and has several excellent Art Nouveau buildings, including the Casa Solà-Morales, which has a facade by Lluís Domènech i Montaner, architect of Barcelona's Palau de la Música. The Sant Esteve church at the southeastern end of Passeig d'en Blay is famous for its El Greco painting *Christ Carrying the Cross* (1605).

WHERE TO EAT AND STAY

$$$$
CATALAN

X **Ca l'Enric.** Chefs Jordi and Isabel Juncà have become legends in the town of La Vall de Bianya just north of Olot, where symposia on culinary matters such as woodcock preparation have inspired prizewinning books. Cuisine firmly rooted in local products, starring game of all sorts, is taken to another level here. What's on offer varies with the season; order the tasting menu (€90), and sample a full range of the Juncàs's virtuosity. $ *Average main: €30* ⊠ *N260, Km 91, La Vall de Bianya* ☎ *972/290015* ⊕ *www.calenric.net* ⚘ *Reservations essential* ⊘ *Closed Mon., Jan.1–17, and 1st 2 wks in July. No dinner Sun.–Wed.*

$$$$
CATALAN

X **Les Cols.** Off the road east to Figueres, Fina Puigdevall has made this ancient *masía* (Catalan farmhouse) a design triumph. The sprawling 18th-century rustic structure is filled with glassed-in halls, intimate gardens, and wrought-iron and steel details. The cuisine is seasonal and based on locally grown products, from wild mushrooms to the extraordinarily flavorful legumes and vegetables produced by the rich, volcanic soil of La Garrotxa. There are five rooms for overnight stays. $ *Average main: €85* ⊠ *Mas les Cols, Ctra. de la Canya s/n* ☎ *972/269209* ⊕ *www.lescols.com* ⚘ *Reservations essential* ⊘ *Closed 1st 3 wks in Jan.*

RIPOLL

34 km (21 miles) west of Olot, 91 km (56 miles) north of Girona.

From Olot, it's an easy drive farther west on Route N260 to Ripoll—the wellspring, in a sense, of Catalonia's earliest history. The town's principal attraction is the Benedictine **Monastery of Santa Maria**, established in the late 9th century by Wilfred II—then Count of Barcelona—who wrested the independence of the province from the control of the Frankish Empire. Founder of the first dynastic line of Catalan kings, he rejoiced in the historical nickname Guifré el Pelós: Wilfred the Hairy.

GETTING HERE AND AROUND

RENFE has 16 commuter trains daily from Sants Station in Barcelona—the trip takes about 2 hours. By car, it's quicker—you can drive to Ripoll from Barcelona on the C17/C33 highways in about 90 minutes, traffic permitting.

EXPLORING

Monastery of Santa Maria de Ripoll. Earthquakes, local wars, and neglect have taken their toll on the monastery; it was largely rebuilt in the 19th century, but the sculptured portico is original—a Romanesque masterpiece—and the cloisters are a haven of peace. The family mausoleum of the counts of Barcelona, the building houses the tombs of Wilfred ("the Hairy") and his descendants in the dynastic line of Ramón Berenguer I. In medieval times, the monastery was the spiritual center of Catalonia; the better-known and grander Benedictine Abbey of Monserrat, where the Black Virgin is enshrined, was ancillary to it until 1409. ⊠ *Pl. de l'Abat Oliba s/n.*

THE COSTA BRAVA

The Costa Brava (Wild Coast) is a nearly unbroken series of sheer rock cliffs dropping down to clear blue-green waters, punctuated with innumerable coves and tiny beaches on narrow inlets, called *calas*. It basically begins at Blanes and continues north along 135 km (84 miles) of coastline to the French border at Portbou. Although the area does have spots of real-estate excess, the rocky terrain of many pockets (Tossa, Cap de Begur, and Cadaqués) has discouraged overbuilding. On a good day here, the luminous blue of the sea contrasts with red-brown headlands and cliffs, and the distant lights of fishing boats reflect on wine-color waters at dusk. Small stands of umbrella pine veil the footpaths to many of the secluded coves and little patches of white sand—often, the only access is by boat.

GETTING HERE AND AROUND

From Barcelona, the fastest way to the Costa Brava by car is to start up the inland AP7 tollway toward Girona, then take *Sortida* (Exit) 10 for Blanes, Lloret de Mar, Tossa de Mar, Sant Feliu de Guíxols, S'Agaró, Platja d'Aro, Palamós, Calella de Palafrugell, and Palafrugell. From Palafrugell, you can head inland for La Bisbal and from there on to Girona, in the heart of Northern Catalonia. To head to the middle section of the Costa Brava, get off at Sortida 6, the first exit after Girona; this will point you directly to the Iberian ruins of Ullastret. To reach the northern part of the Costa Brava, get off the AP7 before Figueres at Sortida 4 for L'Estartit, L'Escala, Empúries, Castelló d'Empúries, Aïguamolls de l'Empordà, Roses, Cadaqués, Sant Pere de Rodes, and Portbou. Sortida 4 will also take you directly to Figueres, Peralada, and the Alberes mountains. The old national route, N11, is slow, heavily traveled, and more dangerous, especially in summer.

COSTA BRAVA BEACHES AND SITES

BLANES

60 km (37 miles) northeast of Barcelona, 45 km (28 miles) south of Girona.

The beaches closest to Barcelona are at Blanes (60 km [37 miles] northeast of Barcelona; 45 km [28 miles] south of Girona). The Costa Brava begins here with five different beaches, running from Punta Santa Anna on the far side of the port—a tiny cove with a pebbly beach at the bottom of a chasm encircled by towering cliffs, fragrant pines, and deep blue-green waters—to the 2½-km-long (1½-mile-long) S'Abanell beach, which draws the crowds. Small boats can take you from the harbor to Cala de Sant Francesc or the double beach at Santa Cristina between May and September.

The town's castle of Sant Joan, on a mountain overlooking the town, goes back to the 11th century. The watchtower on the coast was built in the 16th century to protect against Barbary pirates. Most travelers skip the working port of Blanes.

TOSSA DE MAR

80 km (50 miles) northeast of Barcelona, 41 km (25 miles) south of Girona.

The next stop north from Blanes on the coast road—by way of the mass-market resort of Lloret de Mar—is Tossa de Mar (80 km [50 miles] northeast of Barcelona, 41 km [25 miles] south of Girona), christened "Blue Paradise" by painter Marc Chagall, who summered here for four decades. Tossa's walled medieval town and pristine beaches are among Catalonia's best.

Set around a blue buckle of a bay, Tossa de Mar is a symphony in two parts: the Vila Vella, or Old Town—a knotted warren of steep, narrow, cobblestone streets with many restored buildings (some dating back to the 14th century)—and the Vila Nova, or New Town. The former is encased in medieval walls and towers, but the New Town is open to the sea and is itself a lovely district threaded by 18th-century lanes. Girdling the Old Town, on the Cap de Tossa promontory that juts out into the sea, the 12th-century walls and towers at water's edge are a local pride and joy, the only example of a fortified medieval town on the entire Catalan coast.

Ava Gardner filmed the 1951 British drama *Pandora and the Flying Dutchman* here (a statue dedicated to her stands on a terrace on the medieval walls). Things may have changed since those days, but this beautiful village retains much of the unspoiled magic of its past. The primary beach at Tossa de Mar is the Platja Gran (Big Beach) in front of the town beneath the walls, and just next to it is Mar Menuda (Little Sea), where the small, colorfully painted fishing boats—maybe the same ones that caught your dinner—pull up onto the beach.

The main bus station (the local tourist office is here) is on Plaça de les Nacions Sense Estat. Take Avinguda Ferran and Avinguda Costa Brava to head down the slope to the waterfront and the Old Town, which you enter via the Torre de les Hores, and head to the Vila Vella's heart—the Gothic church of Sant Vicenç—for a journey back in time to the Middle Ages.

WHERE TO EAT AND STAY

$$$ CATALAN 🍴 **La Cuina de Can Simon.** Elegantly rustic, this restaurant right beside Tossa del Mar's medieval walls serves a combination of classical Catalan cuisine with up-to-date innovative touches. The menu changes with the season; two tasting menus (€68 and €98) provide more than enough to sample. The service is top-shelf, from the welcoming tapa with a glass of cava to the little pastries accompanying coffee. [$] *Average main: €20* ✉ *Carrer del Portal 24* ☎ *972/341269* 🕒 *Closed Mon. and Tues., Nov. 7–26, last 2 wks of Jan., and Oct.–May. No dinner Sun.*

$ HOTEL 🏨 **Hotel Capri.** The hotel is on the beach, in hailing distance of the old quarter in the medieval fortress, and proprietor Maria-Eugènia Serrat, a native Tossan, lavishes warm personal attention on every guest. **Pros:** family-friendly; perfect location; good value. **Cons:** rooms a little small; minimal amenities; no private parking. [$] *Rooms from: €93* ✉ *Passeig del Mar 17* ☎ *972/340358* 🌐 *www.hotelcapritossa.com* 🛏 *22 rooms* 🕒 *Closed Nov.–Mar.* 🍽 *Breakfast.*

DID YOU KNOW?

The artist Marc Chagall loved to vacation in Tossa de Mar and felt inspired by its vivid-blue ocean seascape.

$$ HOTEL Fodor's Choice ★ 🏨 **Hotel Diana.** Built in 1906 by architect Antoni Falguera, this Art Nouveau gem sits on the square in the heart of the old town, steps from the beach. **Pros:** attentive service; ideal location. **Cons:** minimal amenities; room rates unpredictable. [$] *Rooms from: €165* ✉ *Pl. de Espanya 6* ☎ *972/341886* 🌐 *www.hotelesdante.com* 🛏 *20 rooms, 1 suite* 🕒 *Closed Nov.–Mar.* 🍴 *Breakfast.*

SANT FELIU DE GUIXOLS

23 km (15 miles) north of Tossa de Mar.

The little fishing port of Sant Feliu de Guixols, 23 km (15 miles) north of Tossa de Mar, is set in a small bay; handsome Moderniste mansions line the seafront promenade, recalling a time when the cork industry made this one of the wealthier towns on the coast. In front of them, a long crescent beach of fine white sand leads around to the fishing harbor at its north end. Behind the promenade, a well-preserved old quarter of narrow streets and squares leads to a 10th-century gateway with horseshoe arches (all that remains of a pre-Romanesque monastery); nearby, a church still stands that combines Romanesque, Gothic, and baroque styles. To get here, take the C65 highway from Tossa del Mar—though adventurous souls might prefer the harrowing hairpin curves of the G1682 coastal corniche.

WHERE TO EAT AND STAY

$ CATALAN ✕ **Can Segura.** Half a block in from the beach at Sant Feliu de Guixols, this restaurant serves home-cooked seafood and upland specialties; the *pimientos de piquillos rellenos de brandada* (sweet red peppers stuffed with codfish mousse) are first-rate, as are the rice dishes and the *escudella*. The dining room is always full, with customers waiting their turn in the street, but the staff is good at finding spots at the jovially long communal tables. Lunch menus at €11, €14, and €16 are a bargain. There are very basic rooms (doubles at €80, without breakfast) available for overnight sojourns. [$] *Average main: €11* ✉ *Carrer de Sant Pere 11, Sant Feliu de Guixols* ☎ *972/321009* 🕒 *Closed Nov.–June (except New Year's Eve weekend)* 🍴 *No meals.*

$$$ CATALAN Fodor's Choice ★ ✕ **El Dorado.** Lluis Cruañes, who once owned superb Catalan restaurants in Barcelona and New York, returns to his roots in Sant Feliu. With his daughter Suita running the dining room and Iván Álvarez as chef, this smartly designed restaurant with contemporary lines, a block back from the beach, serves tasty dishes from *llom de tonyina a la plancha amb tomàquets agridolços, cebas i chíps d'escarchofa* (grilled tuna with pickled tomato, baby onions, and artichoke chips) to *llobarro rostít amb emulsió de cítrics i espàrrecs trigueros* (roast sea bass with a citric emulsion and wild asparagus), all cooked to perfection. Try the *patates braves* (new potatoes in allioli and hot sauce). [$] *Average main: €20* ✉ *Rambla Vidal 19, Sant Feliu de Guixols* ☎ *972/821414* 🕒 *Closed Tues. No lunch Oct.–Easter.*

$$$$ CATALAN ✕ **Villa Mas.** This Moderniste villa on the coast road from Sant Feliu to S'Agaró, with a lovely turn-of-the-20th-century zinc bar, serves up typical Catalan and seasonal Mediterranean dishes like *arròs a la cassola* (deep-dish rice) with shrimp brought fresh off the boats in Palamos, just up the coast. The terrace is a popular and shady spot just across

the road from the beach. [$] *Average main: €25* ✉ *Passeig de Sant Pol 95* ☎ *972/822526* ⏲ *Closed Mon. and mid-Dec.–mid-Jan. No dinner Tues.–Thurs. and Sun. Oct.–Mar.*

$$ HOTEL 🏨 **Hostal del Sol.** Once the summer home of a wealthy family, this Moderniste hotel has a grand stone stairway and medieval-style tower, as well as a garden and a lawn where you can take your ease by the pool. **Pros:** family-friendly; good value. **Cons:** bathrooms a bit claustrophobic; far from the beach; on a busy road. [$] *Rooms from: €98* ✉ *Ctra. a Palamós 194, Sant Feliu de Guixols* ☎ *972/320193* 🌐 *www.hostaldelsol.cat/en* 🛏 *41 rooms* 🍴 *Breakfast.*

S'AGARÓ

3 km (2 miles) north of Sant Feliu.

An elegant gated community on a rocky point at the north end of the cove, S'Agaró is 3 km (2 miles) north of Sant Feliu. The 30-minute walk along the **sea wall** from Hostal de La Gavina to Sa Conca Beach is a delight. Likewise, the one-hour hike from Sant Pol Beach over to Sant Feliu de Guixols for lunch and back offers a superb view of the Costa Brava at its best.

WHERE TO STAY

$$$$ HOTEL Fodor's Choice ★ 🏨 **L'Hostal de la Gavina.** Orson Welles, who used to spend weeks at a time here, called this the finest resort hotel in Spain. **Pros:** in a gated community; impeccable service and amenities; sea views. **Cons:** hard on the budget *and* habit-forming. [$] *Rooms from: €410* ✉ *Pl. de la Rosaleda s/n, S'Agar* ☎ *972/321100* 🌐 *www.lagavina.com* 🛏 *51 rooms, 23 suites* ⏲ *Closed Nov.–Easter* 🍴 *Breakfast.*

CALELLA DE PALAFRUGELL AND AROUND

Up the coast from S'Agaró, the C31 brings you to Palafrugell and Begur; to the east are some of the prettiest, least developed inlets of the Costa Brava. One road leads to **Llafranc,** a small port with waterfront hotels and restaurants, and forks right to the fishing village of **Calella de Palafrugell,** known for its July habaneras festival. (The *habanera* is a form of Cuban dance music brought to Europe by Catalan sailors in the late 19th century; it still enjoys a nostalgic cachet here.) Just south is the panoramic promontory of **Cap Roig,** with views of the barren Formigues Isles.

North along the coast lie **Tamariu, Aiguablava, Fornell, Platja Fonda,** and (around the point at Cap de Begur) **Sa Tuna** and **Aiguafreda.** There's not much to do in any of these hideaways (only Llafranc has a long enough stretch of seafront to accommodate a sandy beach), but you can luxuriate in the wonderful views and the soothing quiet.

WHERE TO EAT AND STAY

$$$ CATALAN Fodor's Choice ★ 🍴 **Pa i Raïm.** "Bread and Grapes" in Catalan, this excellent restaurant in Josep Pla's ancestral family home in Palafrugell has one rustic dining room as well as another in a glassed-in winter garden. In summer the leafy terrace is the place to be. The menu ranges from traditional country cuisine to more streamlined contemporary fare such as strawberry gazpacho. The *canelón crujiente de verduritas y setas* (crisped cannelloni with young vegetables and wild mushrooms) and the prawn

tempura with soy sauce emulsion are two standouts. $ *Average main:* *€18* ⊠ *Torres i Jonama 56, Palafrugell* ☎ *972/304572* ⊕ *www.pairaim.com* ⊙ *Closed Mon. and mid-Dec.–early Jan. No dinner Sun.; no lunch Mon. and Tues. July and Aug.*

$$$$
B&B/INN
FAMILY
El Far Hotel-Restaurant. Rooms in this 17th-century hermitage attached to a 15th-century watchtower have original vaulted ceilings, hardwood floors, and interiors accented with floral prints. **Pros:** friendly service; graceful architecture; spectacular views. **Cons:** longish drive from the beach; a bit pricy for the amenities. $ *Rooms from: €255* ⊠ *Muntanya de San Sebastia, Carrer Uruguai s/n, Llafranc–Palafrugell* ☎ *972/301639* ⊕ *www.elfar.net* ➵ *8 rooms, 1 suite* ⊙ *Closed Jan.* ⦿ *Breakfast.*

BEGUR AND AROUND

From Begur, you can go east through the calas or take the inland route past the rose-color stone houses and ramparts of the restored medieval town of **Pals.** Nearby **Peratallada** is another medieval fortified town with a castle, tower, palace, and well-preserved walls. North of Pals there are signs for **Ullastret,** an Iberian village dating from the 5th century BC.

EXPLORING
Empúries. The Greco-Roman ruins here are Catalonia's most important archaeological site. This port is one of the most monumental ancient engineering feats on the Iberian Peninsula. As the Greeks' original point of arrival in Spain, Empúries was also where the Olympic Flame entered Spain for Barcelona's 1992 Olympic Games.

WHERE TO EAT AND STAY
$$$
CATALAN
✕ **Restaurant Ibèric.** This excellent pocket of authentic Costa Brava tastes and aromas serves everything from snails to woodcock in season. Wild mushrooms scrambled with eggs or stewed with hare are specialties, as are complex and earthy red wines made by enologist Jordi Oliver of the Oliver Conti vineyard in the Alt Empordà's village of Capmany. The terrace is ideal for leisurely dining. $ *Average main: €19* ⊠ *Carrer Valls 11, Ullastret* ☎ *972/757108* ⊙ *Closed Mon., and Tues.–Wed. Nov.–Mar. No dinner Sun. Nov.–Mar.*

$$$$
HOTEL
El Convent Hotel and Restaurant. Built in 1730, this elegant former convent is a 10-minute walk to the beach at the Cala Sa Riera—the quietest and prettiest inlet north of Begur. **Pros:** outstanding architecture; quiet and private. **Cons:** minimum stay required in summer. $ *Rooms from: €235* ⊠ *Ctra. de la Platja del Racó 2, Begur* ☎ *972/623091* ⊕ *www.conventbegur.com* ➵ *24 rooms, 1 suite* ⦿ *Breakfast.*

$$$$
HOTEL
FAMILY
Fodor's Choice
★
Hotel Aigua Blava. What began as a small hostal in the 1920s is now a sprawling luxury hotel, run by the fourth generation of the same family. **Pros:** impeccable service; gardens and pleasant patios at every turn; private playground. **Cons:** lots of stairs to negotiate; no beach in the inlet. $ *Rooms from: €209* ⊠ *Platja de Fornells s/n, Begur* ☎ *972/624562* ⊕ *www.aiguablava.com* ➵ *66 rooms, 19 suites* ⦿ *Breakfast.*

$$$$
HOTEL
Parador de Aiguablava. The vista from this modern white parador, 9 km (6 miles) north of Calella de Palafrugell, is the classic postcard Costa Brava: the rounded Cala d'Aiguablava wraps around the shimmering

blue Mediterranean. **Pros:** magnificent views; good-size rooms. **Cons:** building itself lacks character; minimum stays required in summer; service can be perfunctory. $\boxed{\$}$ *Rooms from: €188* ✉ *Playa d'Aiguablava s/n, Begur* ☎ *972/622162* ⊕ *www.parador.es* ➾ *68 rooms, 10 suites* ⊗ *Closed Jan. 6–Feb. 20* ⏁ *No meals.*

CADAQUÈS AND AROUND

Spain's easternmost town, Cadaqués, still has the whitewashed charm that transformed this fishing village into an international artists' haunt in the early 20th century. The Marítim bar is the central hangout both day and night; after dark, you might also enjoy the Jardí, across the square. Salvador Dalí's house, now a museum, is at Port Lligat, a 15-minute walk north of town.

EXPLORING

Cap de Creus. North of Cadaqués, Spain's easternmost point is a fundamental pilgrimage, if only for the symbolic geographical rush. The hike out to the lighthouse—through rosemary, thyme, and the salt air of the Mediterranean—is unforgettable. The Pyrenees officially end (or rise) here. New Year's Day finds mobs of revelers awaiting the first emergence of the "new" sun from the Mediterranean. Gaze down at heart-pounding views of the craggy coast and crashing waves with a warm mug of coffee in hand or fine fare on the table at **Bar Restaurant Cap de Creus,** which sits on a rocky crag above the Cap de Creus.

Casa Museu Salvador Dalí. This was Dalí's summerhouse and a site long associated with the artist's notorious frolics with everyone from poets Federico García Lorca and Paul Eluard to filmmaker Luis Buñuel. Filled with bits of the Surrealist's daily life, it's an important point in the "Dalí triangle," completed by the castle at Púbol and the Teatre-Museu Dalí in Figueres. You can get here by a 3-km (2-mile) walk north along the beach from Cadaqués. Only small groups of visitors are admitted at any given time; reservations are required. ✉ *Port Lligat s/n* ☎ *972/251015* ⊕ *www.salvador-dali.org* 💳*€11* ⊗ *Mid-June–mid-Sept., daily 9:30–9; early Feb.–mid-June and mid-Sept.–early Jan., Tues.–Sun. 10:30–6.*

Castillo Púbol. Dalí's former home is now the resting place of Gala, his perennial model and mate. It's a chance to wander through another Dalí-esque landscape: lush gardens, fountains decorated with masks of Richard Wagner (the couple's favorite composer), and distinctive elephants with giraffe's legs and claw feet. Two lions and a giraffe stand guard near Gala's tomb. ✉ *Pl. Gala Dalí s/n, on Rte. 255, about 15 km (9 miles) east of A7 toward La Bisbal, Púbol-la Pera* ☎ *972/488655* 💳*€8* ⊗ *Mid-June–mid-Sept., daily 10–8; mid-Mar.–mid-June and mid-Sept.–early Nov., Tues.–Sun. 10–6; early Nov.–Dec., Tues.–Sun. 10–5.*

Fodor'sChoice ★ **Sant Pere de Rodes.** The monastery of Sant Pere de Rodes, 7 km (4½ miles) by car (plus a 20-minute walk) above the pretty fishing village El Port de la Selva, is one of the most spectacular sites on the Costa Brava. Built in the 10th and 11th centuries by Benedictine monks—and sacked and plundered repeatedly since—this Romanesque monolith, recently restored, commands a breathtaking panorama of the Pyrenees, the Empordà plain, the sweeping curve of the Bay of Roses, and Cap de Creus. (Topping off the grand trek across the Pyrenees, Cap de Creus

The popular harbor of Cadaqués

is a spectacular six-hour walk from here on the well-marked GR11 trail.) One-hour guided visits to the monastery in English are available (€2.95). **■ TIP→ In July and August, the monastery is the setting for the annual Festival Sant Pere (🌐 www.festivalsantpere.com ☎ 972/194233, 610/310073), drawing top-tier classical musicians from all over the world.** The website publishes the calendar of events (in Spanish); phone for reservations—and to book a postconcert dinner in the monastery's refectory-style restaurant. ✉ *Camí del Monestir s/n, El Porte de la Selva* ☎ *972/387559* 🌐 *www.mhcat.cat* 🎟 *€4.50* ⏲ *June–Sept., Tues.–Sun. 10–8; Oct.–May, Tues.–Sun. 10–5:30.*

WHERE TO EAT AND STAY

$$$$ SEAFOOD Fodor's Choice ★ 🍴 **Casa Anita.** Simple, fresh, and generous dishes are the draw at this informal little eatery—an institution in Cadaqués for nearly half a century. Tables are shared, and there is no menu; the staff recites the offerings of the day, which might include wonderful local prawns and sardines a la plancha, mussels, and sea bass. There's also a fine selection of inexpensive regional wines. The walls are plastered with pictures of the celebrities who have made the pilgrimage here, including Dalí himself. Call for reservations, or come early and wait for a table. [$] *Average main: €25* ✉ *Carrer Miquel Rosset 16* ☎ *972/258471* ✍ *Reservations essential* ⏲ *Closed mid-Oct.–Nov. and Mon. Sept.–May. No lunch Mon. in summer.*

$$$ HOTEL 🏨 **Hotel Playa Sol.** Open for more than 50 years, this hotel sits in the cove of Es Pianc, just a five-minute walk from the village center. **Pros:** attentive, friendly service; family-friendly; great views. **Cons:** redecorated rooms in relentless white could use a splash of color; best rooms,

with balcony and sea views, are hard to book. [$] *Rooms from: €178* ✉ *Riba Es Pianc 3* ☎ *972/258100* 🌐 *www.playasol.com* 🛏 *48 rooms* 🕓 *Closed mid-Nov.–mid-Feb.* 🍴 *Breakfast.*

SOUTHERN CATALONIA AND AROUND VALENCIA

South of the Costa Brava, the time machine takes you back some 20 centuries. Tarragona, the principal town of southern Catalonia, was in Roman times one of the finest and most important outposts of the empire. Its wine was already famous and its population was the first *gens togata* (literally, the toga-clad people) in Spain, which conferred on them equality with the citizens of Rome. Roman remains, chief among them the Circus Maximus, bear witness to Tarragona's grandeur, and to this the Middle Ages added wonderful city walls and citadels.

Farther south lies Valencia, Spain's third-largest city and the capital of its region and province, equidistant from Barcelona and Madrid. If you have time for a day trip (or you decide to stay in the beach town of El Saler), make your way to the Albufera, a scenic coastal wetland teeming with native wildlife, especially migratory birds.

TARRAGONA

98 km (61 miles) southwest of Barcelona, 251 km (155 miles) northeast of Valencia.

With its vast Roman remains, walls, and fortifications and its medieval Christian monuments, Tarragona has been designated a World Heritage Site. The city today is a vibrant center of culture and arts, a busy fishing and shipping port, and a natural jumping-off point for the towns and pristine beaches of the Costa Daurada, 216 km (134 miles) of coastline north of the Costa del Azahar.

Though modern Tarragona is very much an industrial and commercial city, it has preserved its heritage superbly. Stroll along the town's cliff-side perimeter and you'll see why the Romans set up shop here: Tarragona is strategically positioned at the center of a broad, open bay, with an unobstructed view of the sea. As capital of the Roman province of Hispania Tarraconensis (from 218 BC), Tarraco, as it was then called, formed the empire's principal stronghold in Spain. St. Paul preached here in AD 58, and Tarragona became the seat of the Christian church in Spain until it was superseded by Toledo in the 11th century.

Entering the city from Barcelona, you'll pass the **Triumphal Arch of Berà,** dating from the 3rd century BC, 19 km (12 miles) north of Tarragona; and from the Lleida (Lérida) autopista, you can see the 1st-century **Roman aqueduct** that helped carry fresh water 32 km (19 miles) from the Gaià River. Tarragona is divided clearly into old and new by Rambla Vella; the Old Town and most of the Roman remains are to the north, while modern Tarragona spreads out to the south. You could start your visit at acacia-lined Rambla Nova, at the end of which is a balcony overlooking the sea, the **Balcó del Mediterràni.** Then walk uphill along Passeig de les Palmeres; below it is the ancient amphitheater, the curve of which is echoed in the modern, semicircular Imperial Tarraco hotel on the promenade.

GETTING HERE AND AROUND

Tarragona is well connected by train: there are half-hourly express trains from Barcelona (1 hour and 20 minutes; €7.50) and regular train service from other major cities, including Madrid.

The bus trip from Barcelona to Tarragona is easy; 7 to 10 buses leave Barcelona's Estación Vilanova-Norte every day. Connections between Tarragona and Valencia are frequent. There are also bus connections with the main Andalusian cities, plus Alicante, Madrid, and Valencia.

The €18 Tarragona Card, valid for two days, gives free entry to all the city's museums and historical sites, free rides on municipal buses, and discounts at more than 100 shops, restaurants, and bars. It's sold at the main tourist office and at most hotels.

Tours of the cathedral and archaeological sites are conducted by the tourist office, located just below the cathedral.

ESSENTIALS

Visitor Information Tarragona ✉ *Carrer Major 39* ☎ *977/250795* ⊕ *www.tarragonaturisme.cat/en.*

EXPLORING
TOP ATTRACTIONS

Amphitheater. Tarragona—the Emperor Augustus's favorite winter resort—had arguably the finest amphitheater in Roman Iberia. The remains of the amphitheater, built in the 2nd century AD for gladiatorial and other contests, have a spectacular view of the sea. You're free to wander through the access tunnels and along the tiers of seats. In the center of the theater are the remains of two superimposed churches, the earlier of which was a Visigothic basilica built to mark the bloody martyrdom of St. Fructuós and his deacons in AD 259. ∎ TIP➜ **€11.05 buys a combination ticket valid for all Tarragona archeological museums and sites.** ✉ *Parc de l'Amphiteatre Roma s/n* ☎ *977/242579, 977/242220* 🖪 *€3.30* ☉ *Tues.–Sat. 10–7 (until 9 June–Sept.), Sun. 10–3.*

Catedral. Built between the 12th and 14th centuries on the site of a Roman temple and a mosque, this cathedral shows the transition from Romanesque to Gothic style. The initial rounded placidity of the Romanesque apse gave way to the spiky restlessness of the Gothic; the result is somewhat confusing. If no mass is in progress, enter the cathedral through the cloister, which houses the cathedral's collection of artistic and religious treasures. The main attraction here is the 15th-century Gothic alabaster altarpiece of St. Tecla by Pere Joan, a richly detailed depiction of the life of Tarragona's patron saint. Converted by St. Paul and subsequently persecuted by local pagans, St. Tecla was repeatedly saved from demise through divine intervention. ✉ *Pl. de la Seu s/n* ☎ *977/226935, 977/238685* 🖪 *€5* ☉ *Weekdays 10–8, Sat. 10–7 (until 7:30 Apr.–Oct.), Sun. for Mass only.*

Circus Maximus. Students have excavated the vaults of the 1st-century-AD Roman arena, near the amphitheater. The plans just inside the gate

Tarragona's cathedral is a mix of Romanesque and Gothic styles.

show that the vaults now visible formed only a small corner of a vast space (350 yards long), where 23,000 spectators gathered to watch chariot races. As medieval Tarragona grew, the city gradually engulfed the circus. ⊠ *Pl. del Rei, Rambla Vella s/n* ☎ *977/251515* 🖷 *€3.30, €11.05 combination ticket with Casa Castellarnau and Praetorium* ☉ *Apr.–Sept., Mon.–Sat. 10–9, Sun. 9–3; Oct.–Mar., Tues.–Sat. 10–7, Sun. 10–3.*

WORTH NOTING

Casa Castellarnau. Now an art and historical museum, this Gothic *palauet* (town house) built by Tarragona nobility in the 18th century includes stunning furnishings from the 18th and 19th centuries. The last member of the Castellarnau family vacated the house in 1954. ⊠ *Carrer dels Cavallers 14* ☎ *977/242220* 🖷 *€3.30, €11.05 combination ticket with Circus Maximus and Praetorium* ☉ *Tues.–Sun. 10–3.*

El Serrallo. The always entertaining fishing quarter and harbor are below the city near the bus station and the mouth of the Francolí River. Attending the afternoon fish auction is a golden opportunity to see how choice seafood starts its journey toward your table in Barcelona or Tarragona. Restaurants in the port, like Manolo (⊠ *Carrer Gravina 61* ☎ *977/223484*), are excellent choices for no-frills fresh fish in a rollicking environment.

Gaudí Centre. In this small museum showcasing the life and work of the city's most illustrious son, there are copies of the models Gaudí made for his major works and a replica of his studio. His original notebook—with English translations—is filled with his thoughts on structure and ornamentation, complaints about clients, and calculations of cost-and-return on his projects. A pleasant café on the third floor overlooks the main square of the old city and the bell tower of the Church of Sant Pere. The Centre also houses the **Tourist Office**; pick up information here about visits to two of Domènech's most important buildings: the Casa Navàs (by appointment) and the Institut Pere Mata (€5). ⊠ *Pl. del Mercadal 3, Reus* 🕾 *977/010670* ⊕ *www.gaudicentre.cat/ en* 🎟 *€7* ⊙ *Early Jan.–mid-June and mid-Sept.–Dec., Mon.–Sat. 10–2 and 4–7, Sun. 11–2; mid-June–mid-Sept., Mon.–Sat. 10–8, Sun. 11–2.*

Museu Nacional Arqueològic de Tarragona. A 1960s neoclassical building contains this museum housing the most significant collection of Roman artifacts in Catalonia. Among the items are Roman statuary and domestic fittings such as keys, bells, and belt buckles. The beautiful mosaics include a head of Medusa, famous for its piercing stare. Don't miss the video on Tarragona's history. ⊠ *Pl. del Rei 5* 🕾 *977/236209* 🎟 *€2.40 combined ticket with the Necrópolis i Museu Paleocristìa* ⊙ *June–Sept., Tues.–Sat. 9:30–8:30, Sun. 10–2; Oct.–May, Tues.–Sat. 9:30–6, Sun. 10–2.*

Museu Pau Casals. The family house of renowned cellist Pau Casals (1876–1973) is on the beach at Sant Salvador, just east of the town of El Vendrell. Casals, who left Spain in self-imposed exile after Franco seized power in 1939, left a museum of his possessions here, including several of his cellos, original music manuscripts, paintings and sculptures. Other exhibits describe the Casals campaign for world peace (Pau, in Catalan, is both the name Paul and the word for peace), his speech and performance at the inauguration of the United Nations in 1958 (at the age of 82), and his haunting interpretation of *El Cant dels Ocells* (*The Song of the Birds*), his homage to his native Catalonia. Across the street, the Auditori Pau Casals holds frequent concerts and, in July and August, a classical music festival. ⊠ *Av. Palfuriana 67* 🕾 *977/684276* ⊕ *www.paucasals.org* 🎟 *€6* ⊙ *Mid-June–mid-Sept., Tues.–Sat. 10–2 and 5–9, Sun. 10–2; mid-Sept.–mid-June, Tues.–Fri. 10–2 and 4–6, Sat. 10–2 and 4–7, Sun. 10–2.*

Passeig Arqueològic. A 1.5-km (1-mile) circular path skirting the surviving section of the 3rd-century-BC Ibero-Roman ramparts, this walkway was built on even earlier walls of giant rocks. On the other side of the path is a glacis, a fortification added by English military engineers in 1707 during the War of the Spanish Succession. Look for the rusted bronze of Romulus and Remus. ⊠ *Access from Via de l'Imperi Romà.*

Praetorium. This towering building was Augustus's town house, and is reputed to be the birthplace of Pontius Pilate. Its Gothic appearance is the result of extensive alterations in the Middle Ages, when it housed the kings of Catalonia and Aragón during their visits to Tarragona. The Praetorium is now the city's **Museu d'Història** (History Museum), with plans showing the evolution of the city. The museum's highlight is the **Hippolytus Sarcophagus,** which bears a bas-relief depicting the legend of Hippolytus and Fraeda. You can access the remains of the Circus Maximus from the Praetorium. ⊠ *Pl. del Rei* 🕾 *977/221736, 977/242220* 🎟 *€3.30, €11.05 combination ticket with*

CLOSE UP

Reus: Birthplace of Modernisme

No city matches Barcelona for the sheer density of its Modernisme, but it all began in **Reus** (13 km [8 miles] northwest of Tarragona), where Antoni Gaudí was born and where his contemporary, Lluís Domènech i Montaner—lesser known but in some ways the more important architect—lived and worked for much of his early career. The oldest part of the city—defined by a ring of streets called *ravals,* where the medieval walls once stood—has narrow streets and promenades with many of Reus's smartest shops, boutiques, and coffeehouses. Inside the ring, and along the nearby Carrer de Sant Joan, are some 20 of the stately homes by Domènech, Pere Caselles, and Joan Rubió that make Reus a must for fans of the Moderniste movement.

Getting Here An express bus service operates some 30 daily buses between Tarragona (main bus station) and Reus (Avenida Jaume I); the trip takes about 30 minutes each way. There are five buses daily between Barcelona and Reus (only two on Saturday, one on Sunday), and regular train service connects Reus with Tarragona and other Catalonian and Andalusian destinations.

Casa Castellarnau and Circus Maximus 🕐 *May.–Sept., Tues.–Sat. 10–9, Sun. 10–3; Oct.–Apr., Tues.–Sat. 10–7, Sun. 10–3.*

WHERE TO EAT AND STAY

$$$$ CATALAN 🍴 **Les Coques.** If you have time for only one meal in the city, take it at this elegant little restaurant in the heart of historic Tarragona. The menu is bursting with both mountain and Mediterranean fare. Start off with the *canelons d'auberginia amb ànec* (eggplant and duck cannelloni); seafood fans should try the *tronc de lluç al forn amb patates* (oven-baked hake with potatoes). The prix-fixe lunch at €18 is a bargain. [$] *Average main: €24* ✉ *Carrer Sant Llorenç 15* ☎ *977/228300* 🕐 *Closed Sun.*

$ CATALAN Fodor's Choice ★ 🍴 **Les Voltes.** Built into the vaults of the Roman Circus Maximus, this out-of-the-way spot serves a hearty cuisine. You'll find Tarragona specialties, mainly fish dishes, as well as international recipes, with *calçots* (spring onions, grilled over a charcoal fire) in winter. (For the *calçotadas,* you need to reserve a day—preferably two—in advance.) [$] *Average main: €11* ✉ *Carrer Trinquet Vell 12* ☎ *977/230651* 🌐 *www.restaurantlesvoltes.cat* 🕐 *No dinner Sun.; no lunch Mon. Oct.–Mar.*

$ HOTEL 🏨 **Imperial Tarraco.** Large and white, this half-moon-shape hotel has a superb position overlooking the Mediterranean. **Pros:** facing the Mediterrranean and overlooking the fishing port and the Roman amphitheater. **Cons:** on a very busy intersection with heavy traffic. [$] *Rooms from: €85* ✉ *Passeig Palmeres s/n* ☎ *977/233040* 🌐 *www.hotelhusaimperialtarraco.com* 🛏 *151 rooms, 19 suites* 🍽 *No meals.*

$ HOTEL 🏨 **Plaça de la Font.** The central location and the cute rooms at this budget choice just off the Rambla Vella in the Plaça de la Font make for a comfortable base in downtown Tarragona. **Pros:** easy on the budget; comfortable, charming rooms. **Cons:** rooms are on the small side; rooms with balconies can be noisy on weekends. [$] *Rooms from: €55* ✉ *Pl.*

8

de la Font 26 ☎ *977/240822* ⊕ *www.hotelpdelafont.com* ⤴ *20 rooms* ⦾ *No meals.*

NIGHTLIFE AND PERFORMING ARTS

Nightlife in Tarragona takes two forms: older and quieter in the upper city, younger and more raucous down below. There are some lovely rustic bars in the Casc Antic, the upper section of Old Tarragona. Port Esportiu, a pleasure-boat harbor separate from the working port, has another row of dining and dancing establishments; young people flock here on weekends and summer nights.

Café L'Antiquari. For a dose of culture with your cocktail, this laid-back bar hosts readings, art exhibits, and occasional screenings of classic or contemporary movies. ⊠ *Carrer Santa Anna 3* ☎ *977/241843.*

Teatre Metropol. This is Tarragona's center for music, dance, theater, and cultural events ranging from *castellers* (human-castle formations, usually performed in August and September) to folk dances. ⊠ *Rambla Nova 46* ☎ *977/244795.*

SHOPPING

Carrer Major. You have to haggle for bargains, but Carrer Major has some exciting antiques stores. They're worth a thorough rummage, as the gems tend to be hidden. ⊠ *Carrer Major.*

MONTSERRAT

50 km (31 miles) west of Barcelona.

GETTING HERE AND AROUND

If you're driving, follow the A2/A7 autopista on the upper ring road (Ronda de Dalt), or from the western end of the Diagonal as far as Salida 25 to Martorell. Bypass this industrial center and follow signs to Montserrat. Alternatively, you can take the FGC train from the Plaça d'Espanya metro station (hourly 7:36 am–5:41 pm, connecting with the funicular leaving every 15 minutes), or go on a guided tour with Pullmantur or Julià *(⇨ Tours in Barcelona Planning).*

EXPLORING

Fodor'sChoice ★ **La Moreneta.** A favorite side trip from Barcelona is a visit to the shrine of La Moreneta (the Black Virgin of Montserrat), Catalonia's patron saint, in a Benedictine monastery high in the Serra de Montserrat, west of town. These dramatic, sawtooth peaks have given rise to countless legends: here St. Peter left a statue of the Virgin Mary, carved by St. Luke; Parsifal found the Holy Grail; and Wagner sought musical inspiration. Montserrat is as memorable for its strange topography as it is for its religious treasures, so be sure to explore the area. The monastic complex is dwarfed by the grandeur of the jagged peaks, and the crests above bristle with chapels and hermitages. The hermitage of Sant Joan can be reached by funicular. The views over the mountains to the Mediterranean and, on a clear day, to the Pyrenees are breathtaking; the rugged, boulder-strewn terrain makes for dramatic walks and hikes. Although a monastery has stood on the same site in Montserrat since the early Middle Ages, the present 19th-century building replaced the rubble left by Napoléon's troops in 1812. The shrine is world famous

Valencia and
the Costa Blanca

and one of Catalonia's spiritual sanctuaries—honeymooning couples flock here by the thousands seeking La Moreneta's blessing on their marriages, and twice a year, on April 27 and September 8, the diminutive statue of Montserrat's Black Virgin becomes the object of one of Spain's greatest pilgrimages. Only the basilica and museum are regularly open to the public. The basilica is dark and ornate, its blackness pierced by the glow of hundreds of votive lamps. Above the high altar stands the famous polychrome statue of the Virgin and Child, to which the faithful can pay their respects by way of a separate door. ■TIP→ The famous Escolania de Montserrat boys' choir sing the Salve and Virulai from the liturgy Monday–Saturday at 1 pm and Sunday at noon. ⊠ Montserrat ☉ Daily 7–10:30 and noon–6:30.

SITGES, SANTES CREUS, AND SANTA MARIA DE POBLET

This trio of attractions south and west of Barcelona can be seen in a day. Sitges is the prettiest and most popular resort in Barcelona's immediate environs, with an excellent beach and a whitewashed and flowery old quarter. It's also one of Europe's premier gay resorts. Monolithic Romanesque architecture and beautiful cloisters characterize the Cistercian monasteries west of here, at Santes Creus and Poblet.

GETTING HERE AND AROUND

By car, head southwest along Gran Via or Passeig Colom to the freeway that passes the airport on its way to Castelldefels. From here, the freeway and tunnels will get you to Sitges in 20 to 30 minutes. From Sitges, drive inland toward Vilafranca del Penedès and the A7 freeway. The A2 (Lleida) leads to the monasteries. Regular trains leave Sants and Passeig de Gràcia for Sitges; the ride takes a half hour. To get to Santes Creus or Poblet from Sitges, take a Lleida-line train to L'Espluga de Francolí, 4 km (2½ miles) from Poblet; there's one direct train in the morning at 7:37 and four more during the day with transfers at Sant Vicenç de Calders. From L'Espluga, take a cab to the monastery.

SITGES

43 km (27 miles) southwest of Barcelona.

The pristine, fine white sand of the Sitges beach is elbow-to-elbow with sun-worshippers April through September. The eastern end of the strand is dominated by an alabaster statue of the 16th-century painter El Greco, usually associated with Toledo, where he spent most of his professional career. The artist Santiago Rusiñol is to blame for this surprise; he was such an El Greco fan that he not only installed two El Greco paintings in his Museu Cau Ferrat but also had this sculpture planted on the beach.

EXPLORING

Cau Ferrat. This is the most interesting museum in Sitges, established by the Bohemian artist and co-founder of the Els Quatre Gats café in Barcelona, Santiago Rusiñol (1861–1931), and containing some of his own paintings together with two El Grecos. Connoisseurs of wrought iron will love the beautiful collection of *cruces terminales,* crosses that once marked town boundaries. Next door is the **Museu Maricel de Mar,** with more artistic treasures; **Casa Llopis,** a romantic villa offering a tour of the house and tasting of local wine, is a short walk across town, at Carrer Sant Gaudeni 1. ⊠ *Carrer Fonollar s/n* ☎ *93/894–0364* ⊕ *www. museusdesitges.cat* ☎ *€3.50, €6.40 ticket valid for all 3 museums (free 1st Wed. of the month)* ☉ *June 14–Sept., Tues.–Sat. 10–2 and 3:30–7, Sun. 11–3; Oct.–June 13, Tues.–Sat. 11–8, Sun. 11–3.*

WHERE TO EAT

$$$ ✕ **Vivero.** Perched on a rocky point above the bay, Vivero specializes
SEAFOOD in paellas and seafood; try their *mariscada,* a meal-in-itself ensemble of lobster, mussels, and prawns. Inside, the dining areas are geared up for banquets and large groups, but weather permitting, the best seats in the house are on the terraces, with their wonderful views of the water—especially on the night of August 23rd, when the *fiesta major* of Sitges is ushered out with a spectacular display of fireworks. $ *Average main: €22* ⊠ *Passeig Balmins s/n, Playa San Sebastián* ☎ *93/894–2149, 608/942474* ⊕ *www.elviverositges.com* ☉ *Closed Mon. No dinner Sun. Dec. 20–May.*

■ **EN ROUTE** **Bodegas Miguel Torres.** After leaving Sitges, make straight for the A2 autopista by way of Vilafranca del Penedès. Wine buffs may want to stop here to taste some excellent Penedès wines; you can tour and sip at the Bodegas Miguel Torres (Finca Mas la Plana). ⊠ *Ctra. St. Martí*

Whitewashed buildings dominate the landscape in Sitges.

Sarroca, *Finca El Maset s/n, Pacs del Penedès* ☎ *93/817–7568, 93/817–7330* ⊕ *www.torres.es* ✉ *€6.60 includes standard tour and a single wine tasting.*

Vinseum (*Museu de les Cultures del Vi de Catalunya*). This interesting wine museum in the Royal Palace has exhibits describing wine-making history in Catalonia. ⊠ *Pl. Jaume I 5, Vilafranca* ☎ *93/890–0582* ⊕ *www.vinseum.cat* ✉ *€10, includes tastings and audioguide* ☉ *Mon.–Sat. 10–2 and 4–7, Sun. 10–2.*

SANTES CREUS
95 km (59 miles) west of Barcelona.

Sitges, with its summer festivals of dance and music, film and fireworks, is anything but solemn. Head inland, however, some 45 minutes' drive west, and you discover how much the art and architecture—the very tone of Catalan culture—owes to its medieval religious heritage.

EXPLORING
Montblanc. The ancient gates are too narrow for cars, and a walk through its tiny streets reveals Gothic churches with stained-glass windows, a 16th-century hospital, and medieval mansions. ⊠ *Off A2 at Exit 9.*

Santes Creus. Founded in 1157, Santes Creus is the first of the monasteries you'll come upon as A2 branches west toward Lleida; take Exit 11 off the highway. Three austere aisles and an unusual 14th-century apse combine with the newly restored cloisters and the courtyard of the royal palace. ⊠ *Pl. Jaume el Just s/n, Aguamúrcia* ☎ *977/638329* ✉ *€4.50* ☉ *Tues.–Sun. 10–6:30 (until 7 June–Sept.).*

8

SANTA MARIA DE POBLET

8 km (5 miles) west of Santes Creus.

Fodor's Choice **Santa Maria de Poblet.** This splendid Cistercian foundation at the foot
★ of the Prades Mountains is one of the great masterpieces of Spanish
monastic architecture. The cloister is a stunning combination of lightness and size, and on sunny days the shadows on the yellow sandstone
are extraordinary. Founded in 1150 by Ramón Berenguer IV in gratitude for the Christian Reconquest, the monastery first housed a dozen
Cistercians from Narbonne. Later, the Crown of Aragón used Santa
Maria de Poblet for religious retreats and burials. The building was
damaged in an 1836 anticlerical revolt, and monks of the reformed
Cistercian Order have managed the difficult task of restoration since
1940. Today, monks and novices again pray before the splendid retable
over the tombs of Aragonese rulers, restored to their former glory by
sculptor Frederic Marès; they also sleep in the cold, barren dormitory
and eat frugal meals in the stark refectory. ⊠ *Off A2* ☎ *977/870254*
⊕ *www.poblet.cat* 🖾 *€7, €10 with guide* ☉ *Guided tours available by
reservation daily 10–12:30 and 3–5:30.*

Valls. This town, famous for its early spring calçotada held on the last
Sunday of January, is 10 km (6 miles) from Santes Creus and 15 km
(9 miles) from Poblet. Even if you miss the big day, calçots are served
from November to April at rustic and rambling farmhouses such as **Cal
Ganxo** in nearby Masmolets (⊠ *Carrer Església 13* ☎ *977/605960*); and
also the **Xiquets de Valls,** Catalonia's most famous castellers, might be
putting up a living skyscraper.

VALENCIA

*351 km (210 miles) southwest of Barcelona, 357 km (214 miles) south-
east of Madrid.*

Valencia is a proud city. During the Civil War, it was the last seat of the
Republican Loyalist government (1935–36), holding out against Franco's National forces until the country fell to 40 years of dictatorship.
Today it represents the essence of contemporary Spain—daring design
and architecture along with experimental cuisine—but remains deeply
conservative and proud of its traditions. Though it faces the Mediterranean, Valencia's history and geography have been defined most significantly by the River Turia and the fertile huerta that surrounds it.

The city has been fiercely contested ever since it was founded by the
Greeks. El Cid captured Valencia from the Moors in 1094 and won his
strangest victory here in 1099: he died in the battle, but his corpse was
strapped into his saddle and so frightened the besieging Moors that it
caused their complete defeat. In 1102 his widow, Jimena, was forced
to return the city to Moorish rule; Jaume I finally drove them out in
1238. Modern Valencia was best known for its frequent disastrous
floods until the River Turia was diverted to the south in the late 1950s.
Since then the city has been on a steady course of urban beautification.
The lovely bridges that once spanned the Turia look equally graceful
spanning a wandering municipal park, and the spectacularly futuristic
Ciutat de les Arts i les Ciències (City of Arts and Sciences), most of

it designed by Valencia-born architect Santiago Calatrava, has at last created an exciting architectural link between this river town and the Mediterranean. If you're in Valencia, an excursion to Albufera Nature Park is a worthwhile day trip.

GETTING HERE AND AROUND

By car, Valencia is about 3½ hours from Madrid via the A3 motorway, and about the same from Barcelona on the AP7 toll road. Valencia is well connected by bus and train, with regular service to and from cities throughout the country, including nine daily AVE high-speed express trains from Madrid, making the trip in 1 hour 40 minutes, and six Euromed express trains daily from Barcelona, taking about three-and-a-half hours. Valencia's bus station is across the river from the old town; take Bus No. 8 from the Plaza del Ayuntamiento. Frequent buses make the four-hour trip from Madrid and the five-hour trip from Barcelona. Dozens of airlines, large and small, serve Valencia airport, connecting the city with dozens of cities throughout Spain and the rest of Europe.

Once you're here, the city has an efficient network of buses, trams, and metro. For timetables and more information, stop by the local tourist office. The double-decker Valencia Bus Turístic runs daily 9:45–7:45 (until 9:15 in summer) and departs every 20 to 30 minutes from the Plaza de la Reina. It travels through the city, stopping at most of the main sights: 24- and 48-hour tickets (€17 and €19 respectively) let you get on and off at eight main boarding points, including the Institut Valencià d'Art Modern, Museo de Bellas Artes, and the Ciutat de les Arts i les Ciències. The same company also offers a two-hour guided trip (€16) to Albufera Nature Park, including an excursion by boat through the wetlands, departing from the Plaza de la Reina. In summer (and sometimes during the rest of the year) Valencia's tourist office organizes tours of Albufera. You see the port area before continuing south to the lagoon itself, where you can visit a traditional *barraca* (thatch-roofed farmhouse).

ESSENTIALS

Bus Station Valencia ⊠ *Av. Menendez Pidal 3* ☎ *963/466266.* **Valencia– Estación del Norte** ⊠ *Xativa 24* ☎ *902/240505, 902/240202.*

Visitor Information Valencia ⊠ *Pl. de la Reina 19* ☎ *963/153931* ⊕ *www. visitvalencia.com* ⊠ *Pl. del Ayuntamiento s/n* ☎ *963/524908* ⊕ *www. turisvalencia.es.*

Tours Valencia Bus Turístic ⊠ *Pl. de la Reina 8* ☎ *963/414400, 699/982514* ⊕ *www.valenciabusturistico.com.*

EXPLORING

TOP ATTRACTIONS

Fodor's Choice **Cathedral.** Valencia's 13th- to 15th-century cathedral is the heart of the
★ city. The building has three portals—Romanesque, Gothic, and Rococo. Inside, Renaissance and Baroque marble was removed to restore the original Gothic style, as is now the trend in Spanish churches. The Capilla del Santo Cáliz (Chapel of the Holy Chalice) displays a purple agate vessel purported to be the Holy Grail (Christ's cup at the Last Supper) and thought to have been brought to Spain in the 4th century.

Behind the altar you can see the left arm of **St. Vincent,** who was martyred in Valencia in 304. Stars of the cathedral **museum** are Goya's two famous paintings of St. Francis de Borja, Duke of Gandia. To the left of the cathedral entrance is the octagonal tower **El Miguelete,** which you can climb (207 steps) to the top: the roofs of the old town create a kaleidoscope of orange and brown terra-cotta, with the sea in the background. It's said that you can see 300 belfries from here, many with bright-blue cupolas made of ceramic tiles from nearby Manises. The tower was built in 1381 and the final spire added in 1736. ■**TIP→** The Portal de los Apostoles, on the west side of the Cathedral, every Thursday at noon is the scene of the 1,000-year-old ceremony of the Water Tribunal. The judges of this ancient court assemble here, in traditional costume, to hand down their decisions on local irrigation-rights disputes. ⊠ *Pl. de la Reina s/n, Ciutat Vella* ☎ *963/918127* ⊕ *www.catedraldevalencia.es* ☒ *Cathedral and museum €4.50, tower €2* ☉ *Mon.–Sat. 10–6:30, Sun. 2–6:30.*

FAMILY
Fodor'sChoice
★
Ciutat de les Arts i les Ciències. Designed mainly by native son Santiago Calatrava, this sprawling futuristic complex is the home of Valencia's **Museu de les Ciències Príncipe Felipe** (Prince Philip Science Museum), **L'Hemisfèric** (Hemispheric Planetarium), **L'Oceanogràfic** (Oceanographic Park), and **Palau de les Arts** (Palace of the Arts). With resplendent buildings resembling combs and crustaceans, the Ciutat is a favorite of architecture buffs and curious kids. The Science Museum has soaring platforms filled with lasers, holograms, simulators, hands-on experiments, and a swell "zero gravity" exhibition on space exploration. The eye-shaped planetarium projects 3-D virtual voyages on its huge IMAX screen. At l'Oceanogràfic (the work of architect Felix Candela), the largest marine park in Europe, you can take a submarine ride through a coastal marine habitat. Recent additions include an amphitheater, an indoor theater, and a chamber-music hall. ⊠ *Av. Autovía del Saler 7* ☎ *902/100031* ⊕ *www.cac.es* ☒ *€8 Museu de les Ciències, €27.90 L'Oceanogràfic, €8.80 L'Hemisfèric, €36.25 combination ticket* ☉ *Museu de les Ciències: early Jan.–mid-Apr., Mon.–Thurs. 10–6, Fri.–Sun. 10–7; mid-Apr.–June and early Sept.–Dec., daily 10–7; July–early Sept., daily 10–9. L'Oceanogràfic: early Jan.–mid-June and Oct.–Dec., Sun.–Fri. 10–6, Sat. 10–7; mid- to late June and mid- to late Sept., Sun.–Fri. 10–7, Sat. 10–8; early to mid-July and mid- to late Sept., daily 10–8; mid-July–Aug., daily 10–midnight. L'Hemisfèric: Sun.–Thurs. 10–8, Fri.–Sat. 10–9, with shows hourly from 11.*

Lonja de la Seda (*Silk Exchange*). On the Plaza del Mercado, this 15th-century building is a product of Valencia's golden age, when the city's prosperity as one of the capitals of the Corona de Aragón made it a leading European commercial and artistic center. The Lonja was constructed as an expression of this splendor. Widely regarded as one of Spain's finest civil Gothic buildings, its facade is decorated with ghoulish gargoyles, complemented inside by high vaulting and slender helicoidal (twisted) columns. Opposite the Lonja stands the **Iglesia de los Santos Juanes** (Church of the St. Johns), gutted during the 1936–39 Spanish Civil War, and, next door, the Moderniste **Mercado Central** (Central Market), with its wrought-iron girders and stained-glass windows.

Valencia

0 — 1/8 mi

0 — 200 meters

Valencia's L'Oceanografi (City of Arts and Sciences) has amazing exhibits, as well as an underwater restaurant.

The bustling food market (at 8,160 square meters, one of the largest in Europe) is open Monday through Saturday 8 to 2; locals and visitors alike queue up at the 1,247 colorful stalls to shop for fruit, vegetables, meat, fish, and confections. ⊠ *Pl. del Mercado s/n, Ciutat Vella* ☎ *963/525478, 926/085143* ⊕ *www.lonjadevalencia.com* ⊠ *€2* ☉ *Tues.–Sat. 10–2 and 4:30–8:30, Sun. 10–3.*

Fodor's Choice ★ **Museo de Bellas Artes** (*Museum of Fine Arts*). Valencia was a thriving center of artistic activity in the 15th century—one reason that the city's Museum of Fine Arts, with its lovely palm-shaded cloister, is among the best in Spain. To get here, cross the old riverbed by the Puente de la Trinidad (Trinity Bridge) to the north bank; the museum is at the edge of the **Jardines del Real** (Royal Gardens; open daily 8–dusk), with its fountains, rose gardens, tree-lined avenues, and small zoo. The permanent collection of the museum includes many of the finest paintings by Jacomart and Juan Reixach, members of the group known as the Valencian Primitives, as well as work by Hieronymus Bosch—or El Bosco, as they call him here. The ground floor has a number of the brooding, 17th-century Tenebrist masterpieces by Francisco Ribalta and his pupil José Ribera, a Diego Velázquez self-portrait, and a room devoted to Goya. Upstairs, look for Joaquín Sorolla (Gallery 66), the Valencian painter of everyday Spanish life in the 19th century. ⊠ *Calle San Pío V 9, Trinitat* ☎ *963/870300* ⊕ *www.museobellasartesvalencia.gva.es* ⊠ *Free* ☉ *Tues.–Sun. 10–7, Mon. 11–5.*

Palacio del Marqués de Dos Aguas (*Ceramics Museum*). This building near Plaza Patriarca has gone through many changes over the years and now has elements of several architectural styles, including a fascinating baroque alabaster facade. Embellished with carvings of fruits and vegetables, the facade was designed in 1740 by Ignacio Vergara. It centers on the two voluptuous male figures representing the Dos Aguas (Two Waters), a reference to Valencia's two main rivers and the origin of the noble title of the Marqués de Dos Aguas. Since 1954, the palace has housed the **Museo Nacional de Cerámica**, with a magnificent collection of local and artisanal ceramics. Look for the Valencian kitchen on the second floor. ⊠ *Calle Poeta Querol 2* ☎ *963/516392* ⊕ *www. mceramica.mcu.es* 🎫 *Palace and museum €3 (free Sat. 4–8 and Sun.)* ⊙ *Tues.–Sat. 10–2 and 4–8, Sun. 10–2. Night visits July–Aug., Sat. 10–midnight.*

WORTH NOTING

Casa Museo José Benlliure. The modern Valencian painter and sculptor José Benlliure is known for his intimate portraits and massive historical and religious paintings, many of which hang in Valencia's Museo de Bellas Artes (Museum of Fine Arts). Here in his elegant house and studio are 50 of his works, including paintings, ceramics, sculptures, and drawings. On display are also works by his son, Pepino, who painted in the small, flower-filled garden in the back of the house, and iconographic sculptures by Benlliure's brother, the well-known sculptor Mariano Benlliure. ⊠ *Calle Blanquerías 23* ☎ *963/911662* 🎫 *€2 (free Sun.)* ⊙ *Mid-Mar.–mid-Oct., Tues.–Sat. 10–2 and 3–7, Sun. 10–3; mid-Oct.–mid-Mar., Tues.–Sat. 10–2 and 3–6, Sun. 10–3.*

Estación del Norte. Designed by Demetrio Ribes Mano in 1917, the train station—declared a National Historical-Artistic monement in 1983—is a splendid Moderniste structure decorated with motifs of Valencia oranges. The tops of the two towers seem to sprout like palm trees. ⊠ *Calle Xátiva 24* ☎ *902/240202.*

Institut Valèncià d'Art Modern (IVAM). Dedicated to modern and contemporary art, this blocky, uninspired building on the edge of the old city—where the riverbed makes a loop—houses a permanent collection of 20th-century avant-garde painting, European Informalism (including the Spanish artists Antonio Saura, Antoni Tàpies, and Eduardo Chillida), pop art, and photography. ⊠ *Carrer de Guillem de Castro 118, Ciutat Vella* ☎ *963/863000* ⊕ *www.ivam.es* 🎫 *€2 (free Sun.)* ⊙ *Tues.–Sun. 10–7; Closed Mon.*

Palau de la Generalitat. On the left side of the Plaza de la Virgen, fronted by orange trees and box hedges, is this elegant facade. The Gothic building was once the home of the Cortes Valencianas (Valencian Parliament), until it was suppressed by Felipe V for supporting the losing side during the 1700–14 War of the Spanish Succession. The two *salones* (reception rooms) in the older of the two towers have superb woodwork on the ceilings. Don't miss the Salon de los Reyes, a long corridor lined with portraits of Valencia's kings through the ages. Call in advance for permission to enter. ⊠ *Calle Caballeros 2* ☎ *963/863461* ⊙ *Weekdays 9–2.*

Palau de la Música (*Music Palace*). On one of the nicest stretches of the Turia riverbed is this huge glass vault, Valencia's main concert venue. Supported by 10 arcaded pillars, the dome gives the illusion of

8

a greenhouse, both from the street and from within its sun-filled, tree-landscaped interior. Home of the Orquesta de Valencia, the main hall also hosts touring performers from around the world, including chamber and youth orchestras, opera, and an excellent concert series featuring early, baroque, and classical music. For concert schedules, pick up a Turia guide or one of the local newspapers at any newsstand. To see the building without concert tickets, pop into the **art gallery,** which hosts free changing exhibits. ⊠ *Paseo de la Alameda 30* ☎ *963/375020* ⊕ *www.palauvalencia.com* ⊘ *Gallery daily 10–1:30 and 5–9:30.*

Plaza del Ayuntamiento. With the massive baroque facades of the Ayuntamiento and the *Correos* (central Post Office) facing each other across the park, this plaza is the hub of city life. City Hall itself houses the municipal tourist office and a museum of paleontology. ■**TIP→** Pop in just for a moment to marvel at the Post Office, with its magnificent stained-glass cupola and ring of classical columns. They don't build 'em like that any more. ⊠ *Pl. del Ayuntamiento 1* ☎ *963/525478* ⊘ *Ayuntamiento weekdays 8:30–2:30.*

Plaza de Toros. Adjacent to the train station, this bullring is one of the oldest in Spain. The best bullfighters are featured during Las Fallas in March, particularly on March 18 and 19. ⊠ *Calle Xátiva 28, Ciutat Vella* ☎ *963/519315*

  Museo Taurino *(Bullfighting Museum).* This museum has bullfighting memorabilia, including bull heads and matador swords. ⊠ *Pasaje Dr. Serra 10, Ciutat Vella* ☎ *963/883738* ⊡ *€2* ⊘ *Tues.–Sat. 10–6, Sun. and Mon. 10–2.*

Real Colegio del Corpus Christi *(Iglesia del Patriarca).* This seminary, with its church, cloister, and library, is the crown jewel of Valencia's Renaissance architecture and one of the city's finest sites. Founded by San Juan de Ribera in the 16th century, it has a lovely Renaissance patio and an ornate church, and its museum holds works by Juan de Juanes, Francisco Ribalta, and El Greco. ⊠ *Calle de la Nave 3* ☎ *963/514176* ⊡ *€1.20* ⊘ *Daily 11–1:30.*

San Nicolás. A small plaza contains Valencia's oldest church, once the parish of the Borgia Pope Calixtus III. The first portal you come to, with a tacked-on, Rococo bas-relief of the Virgin Mary with cherubs, hints at what's inside: every inch of the originally Gothic church is covered with exuberant ornamentation. ⊠ *Calle Caballeros 35* ☎ *963/913317* ⊡ *Free* ⊘ *Mon. 7:30 am–8 pm, Tues.–Sat. 9:30–11 and 6:30–8, Sun. 10–1.*

BEACHES

Playa las Arenas. When it gets hot in Valencia—and it gets *hot*—it can often seem like half the population has taken itself to this grandest of municipal beaches. Unusually wide (nearly 450 feet), it stretches north from the port and the America's Cup marina more than a kilometer (½ mile), before it gives way to the even busier and livelier Platja de Malvarossa. The Paseo Marìtimo promenade runs the length of the beach and is lined with restaurants and small hotels, including the **Neptuno** (⇨ *see Where to Stay*). Las Arenas is a baking beach: there's no shade anywhere, but the fine golden sand is kept pristine, the water is fairly calm and shallow, and the bottom is clean and smooth. There are three lifeguard posts and three first-aid stations. Brisk offshore winds can make this ideal for wind surfing and small-craft sailing; there's a sailing school on the beach to meet the demand. **Amenities:** food and drink; lifeguards; showers; toilets; water sports. **Best for:** sunset; swimming; walking; windsurfing. ⊠ *Las Arenas, 10 mins west of the city center by car, bus, or tram.*

WHERE TO EAT

$$$
SEAFOOD
✕ **El Timonel.** Decorated—nay, festooned—with nautical motifs, this restaurant two blocks east of the bullring serves outstanding shellfish. The cooking is simple but makes use of the freshest ingredients; try the grilled *lenguado* (sole) or *lubina* (sea bass). Also top-notch are the eight different kinds of rice dishes, including paella with lobster and arroz a banda, with peeled shrimp, prawns, mussels, and clams. For a sweet finale, try the house special *naranjas a la reina,* oranges spiced with rum and topped with *salsa de fresa* (strawberry sauce). Lunch attracts businesspeople, and dinner brings in a crowd of locals and visitors. ⓢ *Average main: €18* ⊠ *Carrer Félix Pizcueta 13, L'Eixample* ☎ *963/526300* ⊕ *www.eltimonel.com.*

$$
SPANISH
✕ **La Pepica.** Locals regard this bustling informal restaurant, on the promenade at the El Cabanyal beach, as the best in town for seafood paella. Founded in 1898, the walls of the establishment are covered with signed pictures of appreciative visitors, from Ernest Hemingway to King Juan Carlos and the royal family. Try the *arroz marinero* (seafood paella) topped with shrimp and mussels or hearty platters of *calamares* (squid) and *langostinos* (prawns). Save room for the delectable tarts made with fruit in season. ⓢ *Average main: €15* ⊠ *Paseo Neptuno 6* ☎ *963/710366* ⊕ *www.lapepica.com* ⊗ *Closed last 2 wks Nov. No dinner Sun., and Mon.–Thurs. Sept.–May.*

$$
SPANISH
✕ **La Riuà.** A favorite with Valencia's well connected and well-to-do since 1982, this family-run restaurant a few steps from the Plaza de la Reina specializes in seafood dishes like *anguilas* (eels) prepared with *all i pebre* (garlic and pepper), *pulpitos guisados* (stewed baby octopus), and traditional paellas. Lunch begins at 2 and not a moment before. The walls are covered with decorative ceramics and the gastronomic awards the restaurant has won over the years. ⓢ *Average main: €13* ⊠ *Carrer del Mar 27, bajo* ☎ *963/914571* ⊕ *www.lariua.com* ⚲ *Reservations essential* ⊗ *Closed Sun., Easter wk, and last 2 wks Aug. No dinner Mon.*

$$$$
MEDITERRANEAN
✕ **La Sucursal.** This thoroughly modern but comfortable restaurant in the Institut Valencià d'Art Modern is likely to put a serious dent in your budget, but it's unlikely you'll sample venison carpaccio anywhere else or partake of an *arroz caldoso de bogavante* (soupy rice with lobster) any better. All dinner menus are prix fixe, costing €45, €55, or €65. A great choice for lunch is the informal downstairs eatery, on the terrace of the museum, where the €12 prix-fixe lunch gets you a three-course feast. ⓢ *Average main: €45* ⊠ *Carrer Guillem de Castro 118, El Carmen* ☎ *963/746665* ⊕ *www.restaurantelasucursal.com* ⚲ *Reservations essential.*

8

WHERE TO STAY

$ **Antigua Morellana.** Run by four convivial sisters, this 18th-century
B&B/INN   town house provides the ultimate no-frills accommodations in the
Fodor's Choice   heart of the old city. **Pros:** friendly service; excellent location; com-
★   plimentary tea in the lounge. **Cons:** no parking; soundproofing leaves
much to be desired. $ *Rooms from: €50 ☒ C. En Bou 2, Ciutat Vella*
☎ *963/915773 ⊕ www.hostalam.com ⇌ 18 rooms* ⦿ *No meals.*

$$$ **Caro Hotel.** A triumph of design, opened in 2012, this elegant mod-
HOTEL   ern hotel is seamlessly wedded to an important historical property:
Fodor's Choice   a 14th-century Gothic palace, built on the 12th-century Arabic wall
★   and over the Roman circus, fragments of which, discovered during the
renovation, are on display. **Pros:** good location, a few minutes' walk
from the cathedral; spot-on, attentive service; oasis of quiet. **Cons:** the
two top-floor rooms have low, slanted ceilings; valet parking is rather
pricy; decidedly not family-friendly. $ *Rooms from: €150 ☒ C. Almi-
rante 14* ☎ *963/059000 ⊕ www.carohotel.com ⇌ 24 rooms, 2 suites*
⦿ *No meals.*

$ **Hotel Husa Reina Victoria.** Valencia's grande dame is an excellent choice
HOTEL   for traditional atmosphere and good location, just steps from the Plaza
del Ayuntamiento. **Pros:** ideal location; walking distance to train station
and major sights. **Cons:** soundproofing not up to par; not especially
family-oriented. $ *Rooms from: €81 ☒ Carrer Barcas 4* ☎ *963/520487*
⊕ *www.husareinavictoria.com ⇌ 96 rooms* ⦿ *No meals.*

$$$$ **Westin Valencia.** Built in 1921 as a cotton mill, with successive recy-
HOTEL   clings as a fire station and a stable for the mounted National Police
Corps, this classic property was transformed in 2006 into the odds-on
premier luxury hotel in Valencia. **Pros:** attentive, professional, multi-
lingual staff; location steps from the metro that connects directly to
the airport; pet-friendly. **Cons:** rates are high—and climb to astro-
nomical levels during special events like Las Fallas and the Formula
One races. $ *Rooms from: €207 ☒ Av. Amadeo de Saboya 16, Pl. del
Reial* ☎ *963/625900 ⊕ www.westinvalencia ⇌ 124 rooms, 11 suites*
⦿ *Breakfast.*

NIGHTLIFE AND PERFORMING ARTS

Valencianos have perfected the art of doing without sleep. The city's
nocturnal way of life survives even in summer, when locals disappear
on vacation and vie with the hordes of visitors for space on the beach.
Nightlife in the old town centers on Barrio del Carmen, a lively web of
streets that unfolds north of Plaza del Mercado. Popular bars and pubs
dot Calle Caballeros, leading off Plaza de la Virgen; the Plaza del Tossal
also has some popular cafés, as does Calle Alta, off Plaza San Jaime.

Some of the funkier, newer places are to be found in and around Plaza
del Carmen. Across the river in the new town, look for appealing hang-
outs along Avenida Blasco Ibáñez and on Plaza de Cánovas del Castillo.
Out by the sea, Paseo Neptuno and Calle de Eugenia Viñes are lined
with loud clubs and bars most active during the summer. The monthly
English-language nightlife and culture magazine *2/7 Valencia* is free at
tourist offices and various bars and clubs around the city; leisure guides
in Spanish include *Hello Valencia* and *La Guía Go.*

Café de la Seu. For quiet after-dinner drinks, try this jazzy, lighthearted bar, with contemporary art and animal-print chairs, open daily from 6. ⊠ *Carrer Santo Cáliz 7, Ciutat Vella* ☎ *963/915715* ⊕ *www. cafedelaseu.com.*

Café del Duende. For a taste of *el ambiente andaluz* (Andalusian atmosphere), tuck into tapas and cocktails at this flamenco club in the heart of the Barrio del Carmen. It's open Wednesday to Saturday from 10 pm, with live performances on Thursday and Friday nights. ⊠ C. *Túria 62, El Carmen* ☎ *630/455289.*

Café Tertulia 1900. A *tertulia* is a social gathering or a group discussion; lots of Valencianos out to make a night of it start here, to plan the rest of the evening over a mojito or two or maybe one of the café's 18 different gin-and-tonics. ⊠ C. *Alta 4, El Carmen* ☎ *963/922068.*

Calcutta. Need tangible proof that Valencia never sleeps? Find it at this Barrio del Carmen disco (Friday and Saturday only, from midnight), where a young-to-thirtysomething crowd grooves to house and techno music in a restored 17th-century palacio. Drop in at 6 am, if you want: Calcutta will still be open. ⊠ C. *Reloj Viejo 6, La Seu* ☎ *637/488505.*

Feria de Julio. Valencia's monthlong festival, in July, celebrates theater, film, dance, and music. ⊕ *www.feriadejulio.com.*

Jimmy Glass Jazz Bar. Aficionados of modern jazz gather at this bar, open daily 8 pm to 3 am, which books an impressive range of local and international combos and soloists. Cover charge usually runs €10 to €20. ⊠ C. *Baja 28, El Carmen* ⊕ *www.jimmyglassjazz.net.*

Fodor's Choice **Las Fallas.** If you want nonstop nightlife at its frenzied best, come during
★ the climactic days of this festival, March 15–19, when revelers throng the streets and last call at many of the bars and clubs isn't until the wee hours, if at all. ⊕ *www.fallas.com.*

Radio City. The airy, perennially popular, bar–club–performance space Radio City offers eclectic nightly shows featuring music from flamenco to Afro-jazz fusion. ⊠ *Carrer Santa Teresa 19, Ciutat Vella* ☎ *963/914151.*

SHOPPING

A few steps from the Cathedral, off the upper end of Calle San Vicente Mártir, the newly restored **Plaza Redonda** (literally "Round Square") is lined with stalls selling all sorts of souvenirs and traditional crafts. Browse here for **ceramics,** and especially for embroidered table linens and children's clothing designed in the intricate Valencian style.

Lladró. The world-famous porcelain figurines of Lladró originated and are still made not far from Valencia. If you can't spare time in your itinerary for a (free) tour of the factory and museum in Tavernes Blanques (⊠ *Ctra. de Alboraya s/n* ☎ *963/187008* ☉ *Weekdays 9:30–5, Sat. 9:30–1*), then at least make a visit to the flagship salesroom in the old town. ⊠ C. *Poeta Querol 9, Ciutat Vella* ☎ *963/511625.*

Nela. Browse here, in the heart of the old city, for *abanicos* (traditional silk folding fans), hand-embroidered *mantillas* (shawls), and parasols. ⊠ C. *San Vicente Màrtir 2, Ciutat Vella* ☎ *963/923023.*

ALBUFERA NATURE PARK

11 km (7 miles) south of Valencia.

GETTING HERE AND AROUND

From Valencia, buses depart from the corner of Sueca and Gran Vía de Germanías every hour (every half hour in summer) daily 7 am to 9 pm.

EXPLORING

Albufera Nature Park. This beautiful freshwater lagoon was named by Moorish poets—*albufera* means "the sun's mirror." Dappled with rice paddies, the park is a nesting site for more than 250 bird species, including herons, terns, egrets, ducks, and gulls. Admission is free, and there are miles of lovely walking and cycling trails. Bird-watching companies offer boat rides all along the Albufera. For maps, guides, and tour arrangements, start your visit at the Park's information center, the Centre d'Interpretació Raco del'Olla in El Palmar. ✉ *Ctra. de El Palmar s/n* ☎ *961/627345* 🌐 *www.albufera.com* 🕒 *Tues.–Sun. 9–2.*

El Palmar. This is the major village in the area, with restaurants specializing in various types of paella. The most traditional kind is made with rabbit or game birds, though seafood is also popular in this region because it's so fresh.

WHERE TO EAT

$$ SPANISH 🍴 **La Matandeta.** With its white garden walls and rustic interior, this restaurant is a culinary island in the rice paddies. Valencian families come here on Sunday, when many of the city's restaurants are closed. Host-owners Maria Dolores Baixauli and Rafael Gálvez preside over evening meals on the terrace, even as the next generation (Rubén Ruiz Vilanova in the kitchen and Helena Gálvez Baixauli as maître d') begin to contribute new energy. Fish fresh off the boats is grilled over an open fire, and the traditional main dish is the *paella de pato, pollo, y conejo* (rice with duck, chicken, and rabbit). Choose from 50 types of olive oil on the sideboard for your bread or salad. [$] *Average main: €16* ✉ *Ctra. Alfafar–El Saler (CV1045), Km 4* ☎ *962/112184* 🌐 *www.lamatandeta.es* 🕒 *Closed Mon.*

8

THE COSTA BLANCA

The stretch of coastline known as the Costa Blanca (White Coast) begins at Dénia, south of Valencia, and stretches down roughly to Torrevieja, below Alicante. It's best known for its magical vacation combo of sand, sea, and sun, and there are some excellent albeit crowded beaches here, as well as more secluded coves and stretches of sand. Alicante itself—with two long beaches, a charming Old Quarter, and mild and sunny weather most of the year—is a favorite destination for visitors from northern Europe.

DÉNIA

Dénia is the port of departure on the Coast Blanca for the ferries to Ibiza, Formentera, and Mallorca—but if you're on your way to or from the islands, you would do well to stay at least a night in the lovely little town in the shadow of a dramatic clifftop fortress. At the very least, spend a few hours wandering in the Baix la Mar, the old fishermen's quarter with its brightly painted houses, and exploring the historic town center.

ESSENTIALS

Visitor Information Dénia ✉ *Calle Jorge Juan 7* ☎ *966/422367* 🌐 *www.denia.net.*

EXPLORING

Castillo de Dénia. Dénia's most interesting architectural attraction is the castle overlooking the town, and the **Palau del Governador** (Governor's Palace) inside. On the site of an 11th-century Moorish fortress, the Renaissance-era palace was built in the 17th century and was later demolished. A major restoration project is underway. The fortress has an interesting archaeological museum as well as the remains of a Renaissance bastion and a Moorish portal with a lovely horseshoe arch. ✉ *Calle San Francisco s/n* ☎ *966/420656* 🎟 *€3* 🕒 *Apr. and May, daily 10–1:30 and 3:30–7; June, daily 10–1:30 and 4–7:30; July and Aug., daily 10–1:30 and 5–8:30; Sept., daily 10–1:30 and 4–8; Oct., daily 10–1 and 3–6:30; Nov.–Mar., daily 10–1 and 3–6.*

FAMILY **Cueva de las Calaveras** (*Cave of the Skulls*). Inland from Dénia, this 400-yard-long cave was named for the 12 Moorish skulls found here when it was discovered in 1768. The cave of stalactites and stalagmites has a dome rising to more than 60 feet and leads to an underground lake. ✉ *Ctra. Benidoleig–Pedreguera, Km 1.5, Benidoleig* ☎ *966/404235* 🌐 *www.cuevadelascalaveras.com* 🎟 *€3.50* 🕒 *June–Oct., daily 9–8; Nov.–May, daily 9–6.*

WHERE TO EAT

$ SEAFOOD 🍴 **El Port.** In the old fishermen's quarter just across from the port, this classic dining spot features all kinds of fish fresh off the boats. There are also shellfish dishes and a full range of rice specialties, from *arros negre* (black rice) to a classic *paella marinera* (seafood and rice). The tapas here are ample and excellent. El Port is a favorite with locals, resident expats, and tour groups alike; in summer high season it gets hectic, which can sometimes put a strain on service and consistency. [$] *Average main: €10* ✉ *Esplanada Bellavista 12* ☎ *965/784973* 🕒 *Closed Thurs.*

$$ SEAFOOD 🍴 **El Raset.** Across the harbor, this Valencian favorite has been serving traditional cuisine with a modern twist for about 25 years. From a terrace with views of the water you can choose from an array of excellent seafood dishes. House specialties include *arroz en caldero* (rice with monkfish, lobster, or prawns) and *gambas rojas* (local red prawns). À la carte dining can be expensive; set menus are easier on your wallet. The same owners run a very comfortable and modern hotel three houses down on the same street *(⇨ see Where to Stay).* [$] *Average main: €16* ✉ *C. Bellavista 7* ☎ *965/785040* 🌐 *www.grupoelraset.com.*

$$$ SPANISH Fodor's Choice ★ 🍴 **La Seu.** Under co-owners Fede and Diana Cervera and chef Xicu Ramón, this distinguished restaurant in the center of town continues to reinvent and deconstruct traditional Valencian cuisine. The setting is an architectural tour de force: a 16th-century town house transformed into a sunlit modern space with an open kitchen and a three-story-high

wall sculpted to resemble a billowing white curtain. The tasting menus, available for lunch or dinner, include a selection of creative tapas—minicourses, really, that might include a soup and/or a salad—and one rice dish or other main course, giving you a good idea of the chef's repertoire at an unbeatable price. $ *Average main: €20* ✉ *Calle Loreto 59* ☎ *966/424478* ⊕ *www.laseu.es* ⊗ *Closed Mon. No dinner Sun.*

WHERE TO STAY

$
B&B/INN

☷ **Art Boutique Hotel Chamarel.** Ask the staff and they'll tell you that *chamarel* means a "mixture of colors," and this hotel, built as a grand family home in 1840, is certainly a genial blend of styles, cultures, periods, and personalities. **Pros:** friendly staff; individual attention; petfriendly. **Cons:** no pool; not on the beach. $ *Rooms from: €85* ✉ *Calle Cavallers 13* ☎ *966/435007* ⊕ *www.hotelchamarel.com* ⮡ *10 rooms, 5 suites* ❙⊙❙ *Breakfast.*

$$$
B&B/INN
Fodor's Choice
★

☷ **El Raset.** Just across the esplanade from the port, where the Balearia ferries depart for Mallorca and Ibiza, this upscale boutique hotel has amenities that few lodgings in Dénia offer. **Pros:** staff is friendly, attentive, and multilingual; good location. **Cons:** no pool; overhead lighting in rooms a bit dim; private parking is pricey. $ *Rooms from: €141* ✉ *C. Bellavista 1, Port* ☎ *965/786564* ⊕ *www.hotelelraset.com* ⮡ *20 rooms* ❙⊙❙ *Breakfast.*

$
HOTEL
Fodor's Choice
★

☷ **Hostal Loreto.** Travelers on tight budgets will appreciate this impeccable lodging, on a central pedestrian street in the historic quarter just steps from the Town Hall. **Pros:** great location; good value; broad comfy roof terrace. **Cons:** no elevator; no amenities. $ *Rooms from: €70* ✉ *Calle Loreto 12, Dénia* ☎ *966/435419* ⊕ *www.hostalloreto.com* ⮡ *43 rooms* ❙⊙❙ *No meals.*

$$$
HOTEL

☷ **La Posada del Mar.** A few steps across from the harbor, this hotel in the 13th-century customs house has an inviting rooftop terrace and rooms with views. **Pros:** serene environment; close to center of town. **Cons:** pricey parking; no pool. $ *Rooms from: €180* ✉ *Pl. de les Drassanes 2, Dénia* ☎ *966/432966* ⊕ *www.laposadadelmar.com* ⮡ *20 rooms, 11 suites* ❙⊙❙ *Breakfast.*

EN
ROUTE

The Playa del Arenal, a tiny bay cut into the larger one, is worth a visit in summer. You can reach it via the coastal road, CV736, between Dénia and Jávea.

8

CALPE (CALP)

35 km (22 miles) south of Dénia.

Calpe has an ancient history, as it was chosen by the Phoenicians, Greeks, Romans, and Moors as a strategic point from which to plant their Iberian settlements. The real-estate developers were the latest to descend upon it: much of Calpe today is overbuilt with high-rise resorts and urbanizaciónes. But the Old Town is a delightful maze of narrow streets and small squares, archways and cul-de-sacs, houses painted in Mediterranean blue, red, ocher, and sandstone: wherever there's a broad expanse of building wall, you'll likely discover a mural. Calpe is, in short, a delightful place to wander.

Dénia's massive fort overlooks the harbor and provides a dramatic element to the skyline, with the Montgü mountains in the background.

ESSENTIALS

Visitor Information Calpe ⊠ *Pl. del Mosquit s/n* ☎ *965/838532* ⊕ *www.calpe.es.*

EXPLORING

Fish Market. The fishing industry is still very important in Calpe, and every evening the fishing boats return to port with their catch. The subsequent auction at the Fish Market can be watched from the walkway of La Lonja de Calpe. ⊠ *Port* ☽ *Weekdays 4:30–8 pm.*

Mundo Marino. Choose here from a wide range of sailing trips, including cruises up and down the coast. Some of the vessels have glass bottoms, the better to observe the abundant marine life. ⊠ *Esplanade Maritime s/n* ☎ *966/423066* ⊕ *www.mundomarino.es.*

Peñón d'Ifach. The landscape of Calpe is dominated by this huge rock more than 1,100 yards long, 1,090 feet high, and joined to the mainland by a narrow isthmus. The area has more than 300 species of plants and 80 species of land and marine birds. A visit to the top is not for the fainthearted; wear shoes with traction for the hike, which includes a trip through a tunnel to the summit. The views reach to Ibiza on a clear day. Check with the local visitor information center (⊠ *Centro de Interpretación, C. Isla de Formentera s/n* ☎ *679/195912*) about guided tours for groups.

WHERE TO EAT

$$
MEDITERRANEAN

✗**Patio de la Fuente.** In an intimate little space with wicker chairs and pale mauve walls, this restaurant in the old town serves a bargain three-course, prix-fixe dinner, wine included. Try the pears baked in blue cheese sauce or the crispy confit of duck with ginger and plum sauce.

In summer, dine on the comfortable patio in back. $ *Average main:* €13 ✉ *Carrer del Dos de Maig 16* ☎ *965/831695* ⊘ *Closed Sun. and Mon. No lunch.*

ALTEA

11 km (7 miles) southwest of Calpe.

Overbuilt along the beachfront, like much of the Costa Blanca during its orgiastic days of development, Altea is still well preserved on the heights above a truly lovely little old quarter, with narrow cobblestone streets and stairways, and gleaming white houses. At the center is the striking church of Nuestra Señora del Consuelo, with its blue ceramic-tile dome, and the Plaza de la Iglesia in front.

ESSENTIALS

Visitor Information Altea ✉ *Pl. José Maria Planella 7* ☎ *965/844114* ⊕ *www. altea.es.*

WHERE TO EAT

$$$
SPANISH
✕ **El Torreón de Paula.** This pleasant little restaurant specializes in the cuisine of Castile–Léon, especially lamb and suckling pig roasted on a spit in the *asador* (wood-fired oven), and sports a very Spanish interior to match, with stone arches and terra-cotta floors. Swords and antique farming tools adorn the walls—and there's even a cannon. For the roast lamb, you have to order a day ahead. Well worth the effort, especially when your meal is served to you on the terrace overlooking the ocean and the magnificent Peñon d'Ifach peninsula. $ *Average main:* €18 ✉ *Carrer Sant Josep 1, Casco Antiguo* ☎ *966/888098, 609/645149* ⚑ *Reservations essential* ⊘ *No lunch July and Aug., or Mon.–Thurs. Sept.–June.*

$$$
CATALAN
✕ **La Costera.** This popular restaurant focuses on fine French and Catalan fare, with such specialties as house-made foie gras, roasted *lubina* (sea bass), and fondue bourguignonne. There's also a variety of game in season, including venison and partridge. Book a table on the small and leafy terrace for a particularly romantic dinner. $ *Average main:* €18 ✉ *Costera del Mestre la Música 8* ☎ *965/840230* ⊕ *www. lacosteradealtea.com* ⊘ *Closed Mon.*

$$
EUROPEAN
✕ **Oustau de Altea.** In one of the prettiest corners of Altea's old town, this eatery was formerly a cloister and a school. Today the dining room and terrace combine contemporary design gracefully juxtaposed with a rustic setting. Named for the Provençal word for inn or hostelry, Oustau serves polished international cuisine with a French flair. Dishes are named for classic films, such as *Love Story* (beef and strawberry coulis), and film stars, like the "Sophia Loren" tomato and mozarella salad. Contemporary artists display work here, so the art changes regularly. $ *Average main:* €12 ✉ *Calle Mayor 5, Casco Antiguo* ☎ *965/842078* ⊕ *www.oustau.com* ⚑ *Reservations essential* ⊘ *Closed Mon. and Feb. No lunch Oct.–June.*

8

ALICANTE (ALACANT)

82 km (51 miles) northeast of Murcia, 183 km (113 miles) south of Valencia, 52km (31 miles) south of Alctea.

The Greeks called it Akra Leuka (White Summit) and the Romans named it Lucentum (City of Light). A crossroads for inland and coastal routes since ancient times, Alicante has always been known for its luminous skies. The city is dominated by the Castillo de Santa Bárbara but also memorable is its grand **Esplanada,** lined with date palms. Directly under the castle is the city beach, the Playa del Postiguet, but the city's pride is the long, curved Playa de San Juan, which runs north from the Cap de l'Horta to El Campello.

GETTING HERE AND AROUND

Alicante has two train stations: the main Estación de Madrid and the local Estación de la Marina, from which the local FGV line runs along the Costa Blanca from Alicante to Dénia. The Estación de la Marina is at the far end of Playa Postiguet and can be reached by buses C1 and C2 from downtown.

The narrow-gauge TRAM train goes from the city center on the beach to El Campello. From the same open-air station in Alicante, the Line 1 train departs to Benidorm, with connections on to Altea, Calpe, and Dénia.

ESSENTIALS

Tours Tortuga Tours. Rent a bicycle by the hour (€3) or by the day (€12) from this company, which also organizes guided walking and jitney tours of the old town, as well as day trips to Calpe, Elche, and other Costa Blanca destinations. ⊠ *C. Major 45* ☎ *656/606676* ⊙ *Daily 9–2 and 4–9.*

Tram Contact TRAM ☎ *965/262233* ⊕ *www.tramalicante.es.*

Visitor Information Alicante ⊠ *Explanada de España 1* ☎ *965/147038* ⊕ *www.alicanteturismo.com.*

EXPLORING

OLD TOWN

Ayuntamiento. Constructed between 1696 and 1780, the town hall is a beautiful example of Baroque civic architecture. Inside, a gold sculpture by Salvador Dalí of San Juan Bautista holding the famous cross and shell rises to the second floor in the stairwell. Ask gate officials for permission to explore the ornate halls and Rococo chapel on the first floor. ⊠ *Pl. de Ayuntamiento* ☎ *965/149100.*

Basílica de Santa María. Constructed in a Gothic style over the city's main mosque between the 14th and 16th centuries, this is Alicante's oldest house of worship. The main door is flanked by beautiful Baroque stonework by Juan Bautista Borja, and the interior highlights are the golden Rococo high altar, a Gothic image in stone of St. Mary, and a sculpture of Sts. Juanes by Rodrigo de Osona. ⊠ *Pl. de Santa María s/n* ☎ *965/216026* ⊙ *Tues.–Sun. 4–8:30.*

Concatedral of San Nicolás de Bari. Built between 1616 and 1662 on the site of a former mosque, this church (called a *concatedral* because it shares the seat of the bishopric with the Concatedral de Orihuela) has an austere facade designed by Agustín Bernardino, a disciple of the

8

Alicante's Esplanada de España, lined with date palms, is the perfect place for a stroll. The municipal brass band offers concerts on the bandstand of the Esplanada on Sunday evenings in July and August.

great Spanish architect Juan de Herrera. Inside, it's dominated by a dome nearly 150 feet high, a pretty cloister, and a lavish Baroque side chapel, the Santísima Sacramento, with an elaborate sculptured stone dome of its own. Its name comes from the day that Alicante was reconquered—December 6, 1248—which is the feast day of St. Nicolás. ⊠ *Pl. Abad Penalva 1* ☎ *965/212662* ⊙ *Daily 11:30–12:30 and 5:30–6:30.*

Museo de Bellas Artes Gravina. Inside the beautiful 18th-century Palacio del Conde de Lumiares, MUBAG, as it's best known, has some 500 works of art ranging from the 16th to the early 20th century. ⊠ *Calle de Gravina 13–15* ☎ *965/146780* ⊕ *www.mubag.org* 🎫 *Free* ⊙ *July and Aug., Tues.–Sat. 11–9, Sun. 11–3; Sept.–June, Tues.–Sat. 10–8, Sun. 10–2.*

EXPLORING
OUTSIDE OLD TOWN

Fodor'sChoice ★ **Castillo de Santa Bárbara** (*Saint Barbara's Castle*). One of the largest existing medieval fortresses in Europe, Castillo de Santa Bárbara sits atop 545-foot-tall Mt. Benacantil. From this strategic position you can gaze out over the city, the sea, and the whole Alicante plain for many miles. Remains from civilizations dating from the Bronze Age onward have been found here; the oldest parts, at the highest level, are from the 9th to 13th century. The castle is most easily reached by first walking through a 200-yard tunnel entered from Avenida Jovellanos 1 along Postiguet Beach by the pedestrian bridge, then taking the elevator up 472 feet to the entrance. Guided tours (€3) are offered Monday–Saturday at 11, 12:30 and 5, and a "theatrical tour" (€5), with performers in costume interpreting the history of the castle take place on Sunday at noon from

March 17 to June 16—alas! only in Spanish. ✉ *Monte Benacantil s/n* ☎ *965/263131* ⊕ *www.castillodesantabarbara.com* 🎫 *Free, elevator €2.50* ⊘ *Apr.–Sept., daily 10–8; Oct.–Mar., daily 9–7. Last elevator up at 7:30.*

Museo Arqueológico Provincial. Inside the old hospital of San Juan de Dios, this museum has a collection of artifacts from the Alicante region dating from the Paleolithic era to modern times, with a particular emphasis on Iberian art. The MARQ, as it is known, has won recognition as the European Museum Forum's European Museum of the Year. ✉ *Pl. Dr. Gómez Ulla s/n* ☎ *965/149000* ⊕ *www.marqalicante.com* 🎫 *€3* ⊘ *July and Aug., Tues.–Sat. 11–2 and 6–midnight, Sun. 11–2; Sept.–June, Tues.–Sat. 10–7, Sun. 10–2.*

Museo Taurino. In the Plaza de Toros, the Bullfighting Museum is a must for taurine aficionados, with fine examples of matador costumes (the "suits of lights"), bull heads, posters, capes, and sculptures. ✉ *Pl. de España 7* ☎ *965/219930, 965/217678* 🎫 *Free* ⊘ *July–Sept., Tues.–Sat. 10:30–1:30 and 6–9; Oct.–June, Tues.–Sat. 10:30–1:30 and 5–8.*

WHERE TO EAT AND STAY

$$
TAPAS

✕ **Cervecería Sento.** The bar and the grill behind it are the center of attention at this historic eatery just off the Rambla, serving up what many claim are the town's best tapas and montaditos. Try the melt-in-your-mouth *solomillo con foie* (sirloin with foie gras) or the sandwich made with marinated pork, mushrooms, and red peppers, accompanied by a glass of red from the excellent wine cellar. $ *Average main: €15* ✉ *Calle Teniente Coronel Chapuli s/n* ☎ *966/373655.*

$$$
TAPAS
Fodor'sChoice
★

✕ **La Taberna del Gourmet.** This comfortable restaurant and wine bar in the heart of the casco antiguo earns high marks from locals and international visitors alike. Two dining rooms in back are furnished with thick butcher-block tables and dark brown leather chairs, and the subdued lighting adds to the quietly and casually elegant dining experience. The bar in front offers a selection of fresh seafood tapas—oysters, mussels, razor clams—to complement a well-chosen list of wines from La Rioja, Ribera del Duero, and the Priorat. Try the codfish with rucula and sun-dried tomatoes or the baby lamb chops, and order half portions to sample more of the menu. $ *Average main: €18* ✉ *C. San Francisco 10* ☎ *965/204233* ⊕ *www.latabernadelgourmet.com.*

$$
HOTEL
Fodor'sChoice
★

🛏 **Eurostars Mediterránea Plaza.** You'll find this elegant hotel tucked under the arches in the central plaza. **Pros:** spacious bedrooms; double-glazed French windows; gym and sauna; good value. **Cons:** no lobby space to speak of; private parking a bit steep; no pets. $ *Rooms from: €99* ✉ *Pl. del Ayuntamiento 6* ☎ *965/210188* ⊕ *www.eurostarshotels.com* ⟳ *50 rooms* ⫪ *No meals.*

$
HOTEL

🛏 **Hostal Les Monges Palace.** In a restored 1912 building, this family-run hostal is in Alicante's central old quarter. **Pros:** personalized service; ideal location; plenty of character. **Cons:** all services cost extra (breakfast is €6); must book well in advance. $ *Rooms from: €54* ✉ *Calle San Agustín 4* ☎ *965/215046* ⊕ *www.lesmonges.es* ⟳ *22 rooms, 2 suites* ⫪ *No meals.*

8

592 <   Catalonia, Valencia, and the Costa Blanca

NIGHTLIFE

El Barrio, the old quarter west of Rambla de Méndez Núñez, is the prime nightlife area of Alicante, with music bars and discos every couple of steps. In summer, or after 3 am, the liveliest places are along the water, on Ruta del Puerto and Ruta de la Madera.

Ananda. The hottest club in the casco antiguo area, this place rocks the otherwise tranquil Plaza Portal de Elche with house and pop music on Thursday to Saturday night, from 11:30 pm till the sun comes up. ⊠ *C. Bailen 2* ☎ *965/143893.*

El Coscorrón. It's an Alicante tradition to start an evening out here, with El Coscorrón's generous mojitos. ⊠ *Calle Tarifa 3* ☎ *609/550749.*

SHOPPING

Moran Berrutti. Look for distinctive one-off versions of traditional blue-and-white Alicantean ceramics at the potter's own studio-gallery in the old town. ⊠ *C. Toledo 27* ☎ *645/501718.*

IBIZA AND THE
BALEARIC ISLANDS

Visit Fodors.com for advice, updates, and bookings

WELCOME TO IBIZA AND THE BALEARIC ISLANDS

TOP REASONS TO GO

★ **Pamper yourself:** Luxurious boutique hotels on restored and redesigned rural estates are *the* hip places to stay in the Balearics. Many have their own holistic spas: restore and redesign yourself at one of them.

★ **Enjoy seafood delicacies:** Seafood specialties come straight from the boat to portside restaurants all over the islands.

★ **Party hard:** Ibiza's summer club scene is the biggest, wildest, and glitziest in the world.

★ **Take in the gorgeous views:** The *miradores* (lookouts) of Mallorca's Tramuntana, along the road from Valldemossa to Sóller, highlight the most spectacular seacoast in the Mediterranean.

★ **Discover Palma:** Capital of the Balearics, Palma is one of the unsung great cities of the Mediterranean—a showcase of medieval and modern architecture, a venue for art and music, a mecca for sailors, and a killer place to shop for shoes.

1 Ibiza. Sleepy from November to May, the island is Party Central in midsummer for retro hippies and nonstop clubbers. Dalt Vila, the medieval quarter of Eivissa, the capital, on the hill overlooking the town, is a UNESCO World Heritage site.

2 Formentera. Day-trippers from Ibiza chill out on this (comparatively) quiet little island with long stretches of protected beach.

3 Mallorca. Palma, the island's capital, is a trove of art and architectural gems. The Tramuntana, in the northwest, is a region of forested peaks and steep sea cliffs that few landscapes in the world can match.

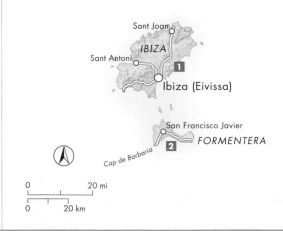

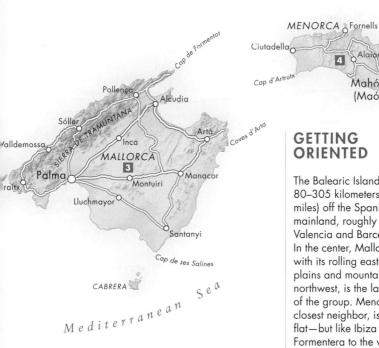

MENORCA ⌒ Fornells

Ciutadella⌒

Cap d'Artrutx

4

Alaior⌒

Mahón
(Maó)

Cap de Formentor

Pollença⌒   Alcudia⌒

Sóller⌒

SIERRA DE TRAMUNTANA   Artà⌒

Valldemossa⌒   Inca⌒   *Coves d'Arta*

MALLORCA   **3**

Palma⌒   Manacor⌒

raitx⌒   Montuiri⌒

Lluchmayor⌒

Santanyi⌒

Cap de ses Salines

CABRERA

M e d i t e r r a n e a n   S e a

GETTING ORIENTED

The Balearic Islands lie 80–305 kilometers (50–190 miles) off the Spanish mainland, roughly between Valencia and Barcelona. In the center, Mallorca, with its rolling eastern plains and mountainous northwest, is the largest of the group. Menorca, its closest neighbor, is virtually flat—but like Ibiza and tiny Formentera to the west, it has a rugged coastline of small inlets and sandy beaches.

9

4 Menorca. Mahón, the capital city, commands the largest and deepest harbor in the Mediterranean. Many of the houses above the port date to the 18th-century occupation by the British Navy.

EATING AND DRINKING WELL IN THE BALEARIC ISLANDS

Mediterranean islands should guarantee great seafood—and the Balearics deliver, with superb products from the crystalline waters surrounding the archipelago. Inland farms supply free-range beef, lamb, goat, and cheese.

(top left) Tumbet is a traditional vegetable dish, served in a clay pot. (top right) Clams are one of the many seafood options you'll find in the Balearics. (bottom left) Local cheese from Menorca

Ibiza's fishermen head out into the tiny inlets for sea bass and bream, which are served in beach shacks celebrated for *bullit de peix* (fish casserole), *guisat* (fish and shellfish stew), and *burrida de ratjada* (ray with almonds). Beyond the great seafood, there are traditional farm dishes that include *sofrit pagès* (lamb or chicken with potatoes and red peppers), *botifarro* (sausage), and *rostit* (oven-roasted pork). Mallorcans love their *sopas de peix* (fish soup) and their *panades de peix* (fish-filled pastries), while Menorca's harbor restaurants are famous for *llagosta* (spiny lobster), grilled or served as part of a *caldereta*—a soupy stew. Interestingly, mayonnaise is widely believed to have been invented by the French in Mahón, Menorca, after they took the port from the British in 1756.

BALEARIC ALMONDS

Almonds are omnipresent in the Balearics, used in sweets as well as seafood recipes. Typically used in the *picada*—the ground nuts, spices, and herbs on the surface of a dish—almonds are essential to the Balearic economy. After a 19th-century phylloxera plague decimated Balearic vineyards, almond trees replaced vines and the almond crop became a staple.

VEGETABLES

The *tumbet mallorquin* is a classic Balearic dish made of layers of fried zucchini, bell peppers, potatoes, and eggplant with tomato sauce between each layer. It's served piping hot in individual earthenware casseroles.

SEAFOOD

There are several seafood dishes to look out for in the Balearics. *Burrida de rat-jada* (ray with almonds) is boiled ray baked between layers of potato. The *picada* covering the ray during the baking includes almonds, garlic, egg, a slice of fried bread, parsley, salt, pepper, and olive oil. *Caldereta de llagosta* (spiny lobster soup) is a quintessential menorcan staple sometimes said to be authentic only if the menorcan spiny lobster is used. *Guisat de marisc* (shellfish stew) is an Ibiza stew of fish and shellfish cooked with a base of onions, potatoes, peppers, and olive oil. Nearly any seafood from the waters around Ibiza may well end up in this staple.

PORK

Rostit (roast pork) is baked in the oven with liver, eggs, bread, apples, and plums. *Sobrasada* (finely ground pork seasoned with sweet red paprika and stuffed in a sausage skin) is one of Mallorca's two most iconic food products (the other is the *ensaimada,* a sweet spiral pastry made with *saïm,* or lard). Sobrasada originated in Italy but

became popular in Mallorca during the 16th century.

MENORCAN CHEESE

Mahón cheese is a Balearic trademark, and Menorca has a Denominación de Origen (D.O.), one of the 12 officially designated cheese-producing regions in Spain. The *curado* (fully cured) cheese is the tastiest.

WINE

With just 2,500 acres of vineyards (down from 75,000 in 1891), Mallorca's two D.O. wine regions—Binissalem, near Palma, and Pla i Llevant on the eastern side of the island—will likely remain under the radar to the rest of the world. While you're here, though, treat yourself to a Torre des Canonge white, a fresh, full, fruity wine, or a red Ribas de Cabrera from the oldest vineyard on the island, Hereus de Ribas in Binissalem, founded in 1711. Viticulture on Menorca went virtually extinct with the reversion of the island to Spain after its 18th-century British occupation, but since the last half of the 20th century, a handful of ambitious, serious winemakers—mainly in the area of Sant Lluís—have emerged to put the local product back on the map.

9

BEST BEACHES OF THE BALEARICS

When it comes to oceanfront property, the Balearic Islands have vast and varied resources: everything from long sweeps of beach on sheltered bays to tiny crescents of sand in rocky inlets and coves called *calas*—some so isolated you can reach them only by boat.

(top left) Ibiza is Party Island and its beaches get crowded. (top right) The benefits of the popular beaches are their ample amenities. (bottom left) For peace and quiet, head to Macarella on Mallorca.

Not a few of the Balearic beaches, like their counterparts on the mainland coasts, have become destinations for communities of holiday chalets and retirement homes, usually called *urbanizaciónes,* their waterfronts lined with the inevitable shopping centers and pizza joints—skip these and head to the simpler and smaller beaches in or adjoining the Balearics' admirable number of nature reserves. Granted you'll find few or no services, and be warned that smaller beaches mean crowds in July and August, but these are the Balearics' best destinations for sun and sand. The local authorities protect these areas more rigorously, as a rule, than they do those on the mainland, and the beaches are gems. *Some of our favorites are on the following page.*

BEACH AMENITIES

Be prepared: services at many of the smaller Balearic beaches are minimal or nonexistent. If you want a deck chair or something to eat or drink, bring it with you or make sure to ask around to see if your chosen secluded inlet has at least a *chiringuito*: a waterfront shack where the food is likely to feature what the fisherman pulled in that morning.

SES SALINES, IBIZA

Easy to reach from Eivissa, Ibiza's capital, this is one of the most popular beaches on the island, but the setting—in a protected natural park area—has been spared overdevelopment. The beach is relatively narrow, but the fine golden sand stretches more than a kilometer (nearly a mile) along the curve of Ibiza's southernmost bay. Two other great choices, on the east coast, are Cala Mastella, a tiny cove tucked away in a pine woods where a kiosk on the wharf serves the fresh catch of the day, and Cala Llenya, a family-friendly beach in a protected bay with shallow water.

PLATJES DE SES ILLETES, FORMENTERA

The closest beach to the port at La Savina, where the ferries come in from Ibiza, Ses Illetes is Formentera's preeminent party scene: some 3 km (2 miles) of fine, white sand with beach bars and snack shacks, and Jet Skis and windsurfing gear for rent.

ES TRENC, MALLORCA

One of the few long beaches on the island that's been spared the development of resort hotels, this pristine 3-km (2-mile) stretch of soft, white sand southeast of Palma, near Colònia Sant Jordi, is a favorite with nude bathers—who stay mainly at the west end—and day-trippers who arrive by boat. The water is crystal-clear blue and shallow for some distance out. The 10-km (6-mile) walk along the beach from Colònia Sant Jordi to the Cap Salines lighthouse is one of Mallorca's treasures.

PLATJA DE MAGALUF, MALLORCA

At the western end of the Bay of Palma, about 16 km (10 miles) from the city, this long, sandy beach with a promenade makes Magaluf Mallorca's liveliest resort destination in July and August. The town is chock-a-block with hotels, holiday apartments, cafés, and clubs, and there are also two water parks in Magaluf—Aqualand and the Western Waterpark—in case the kids tire of windsurfing or kite surfing.

CALA MACARELLA/CALA MACARETTA, MENORCA

This pair of beautiful, secluded coves edged with pines is about a 20-minute walk through the woods from the more developed beach at Santa Galdana, on Menorca's south coast. Macarella is the larger and busier of the two; Macaretta, a few minutes farther west along the path, is popular with nude bathers and boating parties. Cala Pregonda, on the north coast of Menorca, is a splendid and secluded beach with walk-in access only: it's a lovely crescent cove with pine and tamarisk trees behind and dramatic rock formations at both ends, though it's more difficult to get to.

9

Updated by
Jared Lubarsky

Could anything go wrong in a destination that gets, on average, 300 days of sunshine a year? True, the water is only warm enough for a dip May through October, but the climate does seem to give the residents of the Balearics a sunny disposition year-round. They are a remarkably hospitable people, not merely because tourism accounts for such a large chunk of their economy, but because history and geography have combined to put them in the crossroads of so much Mediterranean trade and traffic.

The Balearic Islands were outposts, successively, of the Phoenician, Carthaginian, and Roman empires before the Moors invaded in 902 and took possession for some 300 years. In 1235, Jaume I of Aragón ousted the Moors, and the islands became part of the independent kingdom of Mallorca until 1343, when they returned to the Crown of Aragón under Pedro IV. With the marriage of Isabella of Castile to Ferdinand of Aragón in 1469, the Balearics were joined to a united Spain. Great Britain occupied Menorca in 1704, during the War of the Spanish Succession, to secure the superb natural harbor of Mahón as a naval base, but returned it to Spain in 1802 under the Treaty of Amiens.

During the Spanish Civil War, Menorca remained loyal to Spain's democratically elected Republican government, while Mallorca and Ibiza sided with Francisco Franco's insurgents. Mallorca then became a base for Italian air strikes against the Republican holdouts in Barcelona. This topic is still broached delicately on the islands; they remain fiercely independent of one another in many ways. Even Mahón and Ciutadella, at opposite ends of Menorca—all of 44 km (27 miles) apart—remain estranged over differences dating from the war.

The tourist boom, which began during Franco's regime (1939–75), turned great stretches of Mallorca's and Ibiza's coastlines into strips of high-rise hotels, fast-food restaurants, and discos.

PLANNING

WHEN TO GO

July and August are peak season in the Balearics; it's hot, and even the most secluded beaches are crowded. Weatherwise, May and October are ideal, with June and September just behind. Winter is quiet; it's too cold for the beach but fine for hiking, golfing, and exploring—though on Menorca the winter winds are notoriously fierce. The clubbing season on Ibiza begins in June.

Note: Between November and March or April many hotels and restaurants are closed for their own vacations or seasonal repairs.

PLANNING YOUR TIME

Most European visitors to the Balearics pick one island and stick with it, but you could easily see all three. Start in Mallorca with **Palma.** Begin early at the cathedral and explore the Llotja, the Almudaina Palace, and the Plaça Major. The churches of Santa Eulàlia and Sant Francesc and the Arab Baths are a must. Staying overnight in Palma means you can sample the nightlife and have time to visit the museums.

Take the old train to **Sóller** and rent a car for a trip over the Sierra de Tramuntana to **Deiq, Son Marroig,** and **Valldemossa.** The roads are twisty, so give yourself a full day. Spend the night in Sóller, and you can drive from there in less than an hour via **Lluc** and **Pollenéa** to the Roman and Moorish ruins at **Alcúdia.**

By fast ferry it's just over three hours from Port d'Alcúdia to **Ciutadella,** on Menorca; the port, the **cathedral,** and the narrow streets of the old city can be explored in half a day. Make your way across the island to **Mahón,** and devote an afternoon to the highlights there. From Mahón, you can take a 30-minute interisland flight to **Eivissa.** On Ibiza, plan a full day for the World Heritage site of **Dalt Vila** and the shops of **Sa Penya,** and the better part of another for **Santa Gertrudis** and the north coast. If you've come to Ibiza to party, of course, time has no meaning.

FESTIVALS

In addition to the major public holidays, towns and villages on each of the islands celebrate a panoply of patron saints' days, fairs, and festivals of all their own. Highlights include the following:

Eivissa Medieval. Held in Ibiza's capital on the second weekend in May (Thursday to Sunday evening), this event celebrates the designation of the Dalt Vila as a UNESCO World Heritage site. ⊠ *Eivissa, Ibiza.*

Festa de Nostra Sanyora de la Victoria. On the second Sunday in May in Sóller, mock battles are staged to commemorate an attack by Turkish pirates in 1561. ⊠ *Sóller, Mallorca.*

Festa de Sant Antoni d'Abat. Celebrated on Ibiza and Mallorca, this festival, held on January 16 and 17, includes bonfires, costume parades, and a ceremonial blessing of the animals.

Festa de Sant Bartolomé. Spectacular fireworks mark this festival, which takes place in Sant Antoni on August 24. ⊠ *Sant Antoni, Ibiza.*

Festa del Mar. Honoring Our Lady of Carmen, this festival is celebrated on July 16 in the Ibizan towns of Eivissa, Santa Eulària, Sant Antoni, and Sant Josep, and also on Formentera.

Festa des Vermar. The grape harvest festival, complete with processional floats and concerts, is held in Binissalem on the last Sunday in September. ⊠ *Binissalem, Mallorca.*

Festa Major de Sant Joan (*Feast of St. John the Baptist*). Held on June 23 and 24, this festival is celebrated throughout the island of Ibiza. ⊠ *Ibiza.*

Festes de Sant Joan. At this event on June 23 and 24, riders in costume parade through the streets of Ciutadella on horseback, urging the horses up to dance on their hind legs while spectators pass dangerously under their hooves. ⊠ *Ciutadella, Menorca.*

Festes de Santa Eulàlia. Ibiza's boisterous winter carnival, held on February 12, includes folk dancing and music. ⊠ *Ibiza.*

Fiestas de Gràcia. Held from September 7–9 in Mahón, this celebration is Menorca's final blowout of the season. ⊠ *Mahón, Menorca.*

Processo dels Tres Tocs (*Procession of the Three Knocks*). Held in Ciutadella on January 17, this festival celebrates the 1287 victory of King Alfonso III over the Moors. ⊠ *Ciutadella, Menorca.*

Romería de Sant Marçal (*Pilgrimage of St. Mark*). On June 30 in Sa Cabaneta, a procession of costumed townspeople heads to the church of their patron saint, to draw water from a consecrated cistern that's thought to give health and strength of heart. ⊠ *Sa Cabaneta, Menorca.*

Sant Ciriac. On August 8, this festival celebrates the Reconquest of Ibiza from the Moors; it's capped with a watermelon fight beneath the walls of Eivissa's old city and a fireworks display. ⊠ *Eivissa, Ibiza.*

Sant Josep. This festival on March 19 is known for folk dancing, which you can also see in Sant Joan every Thursday evening. ⊠ *Ibiza.*

Sant Lluís. Celebrations of this saint's day, which are held at the end of August in Menorca, center on equestrian activities. ⊠ *Menorca.*

Virgen del Carmen. The patron saint of sailors (Our Lady of Mount Carmel) is honored on July 15 and 16 in Formentera with a blessing of the boats in the harbor. The holiday is also celebrated on Ibiza. ⊠ *Formentera.*

GETTING HERE AND AROUND
AIR TRAVEL
Each of the islands is served by an international airport, all of them within 15 or 20 minutes by car or bus from the capital city. There are daily domestic connections to each from Barcelona (about 50 minutes), Madrid, and Valencia: no-frills and charter operators fly to Eivissa, Palma, and Mahón from many European cities, especially during the summer. There are also flights between the islands. In high season, book early.

BIKE TRAVEL
The Balearic Islands—especially Ibiza and Formentera—are ideal for exploration by bicycle. Ibiza is relatively flat and easy to negotiate, though side roads can be in poor repair. Formentera is level, too, with

bicycle lanes on all connecting roads. Parts of Mallorca are quite mountainous, with challenging climbs through spectacular scenery; along some country roads, there are designated bike lanes. Bicycles are easy to rent, and tourist offices have details on recommended routes. Menorca is relatively flat, with lots of roads that wander through pastureland and olive groves to small coves and inlets.

BOAT AND FERRY TRAVEL

From Barcelona: The Acciona Trasmediterránea and Balearia car ferries serve Ibiza and Menorca from Barcelona; Iscomar ferries ply between Ibiza and neighboring Formentera. The most romantic way to get to the Balearic Islands is by overnight ferry from Barcelona to Palma, sailing (depending on the line and the season) between 11 and 11:30 pm; you can watch the lights of Barcelona sinking into the horizon for hours—and when you arrive in Palma, around 7 am, see the spires of the cathedral bathed in the morning sun. Overnight ferries have lounges and private cabins. Round-trip fares vary with the line, the season, and points of departure and destination but from Barcelona are around €110 for lounge seats or €259 per person for a double cabin (tax included).

Fast ferries and catamarans, also operated by Acciona Trasmediterránea and Balearia, with passenger lounges only, speed from Barcelona to Eivissa (Ibiza), to Palma and Alcúdia (Mallorca), and to Mahón (Menorca). Depending on the destination, the trip takes between three and five hours.

From Valencia: Acciona Trasmediterránea ferries leave Valencia late at night for Ibiza, arriving early in the morning. Balearia fast ferries (no vehicles) leave Valencia for Sant Antoni on Ibiza in the late afternoon, making the crossing in about two-and-a-half hours. There are also ferries from Valencia to Menorca. Acciona Trasmediterránea and Balearia both have services from Valencia to Mallorca, leaving midmorning for Palma, arriving early evening, and to Mahón (Menorca). Departure days and times vary with the season, with service more frequent in summer.

From Denia: Balearia runs a daily three-hour fast ferry service for passengers and cars between Denia and Eivissa, another between Denia and Formentera, and a similar eight-hour service between Denia and Palma on weekends. Iscomar runs a car-and-truck ferry service between Denia and Sant Antoni, Ibiza.

Interisland: Daily fast ferries connect Ibiza and Palma; one-way fares range from €43 to €121, depending on the type of accommodations. The Pitiusa and Transmapi lines offer frequent fast ferry and hydrofoil service between Ibiza and Formentera. Daily ferries connect Alcúdia (Mallorca) and Ciutadella (Menorca) in three to four hours, depending on the weather; a hydrofoil makes the journey in about an hour.

Boat and Ferry Information Acciona Trasmediterránea ☎ *902/454645* ⊕ *www.trasmediterranea.es.* **Balearia** ⊕ *www.balearia.com.* **Formentera port** ✉ *Formentera* ☎ *971/322057.* **Iscomar** ⊕ *www.iscomar.ferries.org.* **Mediterránea Pitiusa**. Fares for the shuttle ferry from Eivissa port to La Savina on Formentera are €26.80 (Jet Line) and €23.80 (Express Line) one-way, €46 and

€43 round-trip. ✉ *Eivissa, Ibiza* ☎ *670/771297, 650/694743* ⊕ *www.medpitiusa. net/en.* **Trasmapi** ☎ *902/314433* ⊕ *www.trasmapi.com.*

BUS TRAVEL

There is bus service on all the islands, though it's not extensive, especially on Formentera. *Check each island's Getting Here and Around information for details.*

CAR TRAVEL

Ibiza is best explored by car or motor scooter: many of the beaches lie at the end of rough, unpaved roads. Tiny Formentera can almost be covered on foot, but renting a car or a scooter at La Sabina is a time saver. A car is essential if you want to beach-hop on Mallorca or Menorca.

TAXI TRAVEL

On Ibiza, taxis are available at the airport and in Eivissa, Figueretas, Santa Eulàlia, and Sant Antoni. On Formentera, there are taxis in La Sabina and Es Pujols. Legal taxis on Ibiza and Formentera are metered, but it's a good idea to get a rough estimate of the fare from the driver before you climb aboard. Taxis in Palma are metered. For trips beyond the city, charges are posted at the taxi stands. On Menorca, you can pick up a taxi at the airport or in Mahón or Ciutadella.

TRAIN TRAVEL

The public *Ferrocarriles de Mallorca* railroad track connects Palma and Inca, with stops at about half a dozen villages en route.

A journey on the privately owned Palma–Sóller railroad is a must: completed in 1912, it still uses the carriages from that era. The train trundles across the plain to Bunyola, then winds through tremendous mountain scenery to emerge high above Sóller. An ancient tram connects the Sóller terminus to Port de Sóller, leaving every hour on the hour, 8 to 7; the Palma terminal is near the corner of the Plaça d'Espanya, on Calle Eusebio Estada next to the Inca train station.

RESTAURANTS

On the Balearic Islands many restaurants tend to have short business seasons. This is less true of Mallorca, but on Menorca, Ibiza, and especially on Formentera, it might be May (or later) before the shutters are removed from that great seafood shack you've heard so much about. Really fine dining experiences are in short supply on the islands; in the popular beach resorts, the promenades can seem overrun with paella and pizza joints. Away from the water, however, there are exceptional meals to be had—and the seafood couldn't be any fresher.

HOTELS

Many hotels on the islands include a continental or full buffet breakfast in the room rate.

IBIZA

Ibiza's high-rise resort hotels and holiday flats are mainly in Sant Antoni, Talamanca, Ses Figueretes, and Playa d'en Bossa. Overbuilt Sant Antoni has little but its beach to recommend it. Playa d'en Bossa, close to Eivissa, is prettier but lies under a flight path. To get off the beaten track and into the island's largely pristine interior, look for *agroturismo* lodgings in Els Amunts (The Uplands) and in villages such as Santa Gertrudis or Sant Miquel de Balanzat.

FORMENTERA

If July and August are the only months you can visit, reserve well in advance. Accommodations on Formentera, the best of them on the south Platja de Mitjorn coast, tend to be small private properties converted to studio apartment complexes, rather than megahotels.

MALLORCA

Mallorca's large-scale resorts—more than 1,500 of them—are concentrated mainly on the southern coast and primarily serve the package-tour industry. Perhaps the best accommodations on the island are the number of grand, old, country estates and townhouses that have been converted into boutique hotels, ranging from simple and relatively inexpensive agroturismos to stunning outposts of luxury.

MENORCA

Apart from a few hotels and hostals in Mahón and Ciutadella, almost all of Menorca's tourist lodgings are in beach resorts. As on the other islands, many of these are fully reserved by travel operators in the high season and often require a week's minimum stay, so it's generally most economical to book a package that combines airfare and accommodations. Alternatively, inquire at the tourist office about boutique and country hotels, especially in and around Sant Lluís.

Hotel reviews have been shortened. For full information, visit Fodors. com.

WHAT IT COSTS IN EUROS				
	$	$$	$$$	$$$$
Restaurants	under €13	€13–€17	€18–€22	over €22
Hotels	under €91	€91–€125	€126–€180	over €180

Prices in the reviews are the average cost of a main course or equivalent combination of smaller dishes at dinner. Hotel prices are the lowest cost of a standard double room in high season.

TOURS

Ibiza resorts run trips to neighboring beaches and to smaller islands. Trips from Ibiza to Formentera include an escorted bus tour. In Sant Antoni, there are a number of tour organizers to choose from.

Most Mallorca hotels and resorts offer guided tours. Typical itineraries are the Caves of Artà or Drac, on the east coast, including the nearby Auto Safari Park and an artificial-pearl factory in Manacor; the Chopin museum in the old monastery at Valldemossa, returning through the writers' and artists' village of Deià; the port of Sóller and the Arab gardens at Alfàbia; the Thursday market and leather factories in Inca; Port de Pollença; Cape Formentor; and the northern beaches.

The resorts also run excursions to neighboring beaches and coves—many inaccessible by road—and to the islands of Cabrera and Dragonera. Boats generally depart from Colònia Sant Jordi, 47 km (29 miles) southeast of Palma, six times daily from 9 am. Tickets for the 2½-hour trip are €40, which you can buy on the dock at Carrer Babriel Roca. Visitors to Cabrera can take a self-guided tour of the island's underwater ecosystem—using a mask and snorkel with their own sound system; the recording explains the main points of interest as you swim. Contact Excursions a Cabrera or the National Park Office in Palma.

On Menorca, sightseeing trips on glass-bottom catamarans leave Mahón's harbor from the quayside near the Xoriguer gin factory; adult fares are €12. Departure times vary; check with the tourist information office on the Moll de Ponent, at the foot of the winding stairs from the old city to the harbor.

Contacts Excursions a Cabrera ☎ *971/649034, 627/881885* ⊕ *www. excursionsacabrera.es.* **Mahón Port** ✉ *Moll de Llevant 2, Mahón, Menorca* ☎ *971/355952, 902/929015* ✉ *Pl. Explanada s/n, Mahón, Menorca* ☎ *971/363790, 902/929015.* **Parque Nacional del Archipiélago de Cabrera.** For guided tours of the Illa de Cabrera, and diving excursions offshore, inquire first at the Visitor Center (Centro de Vistantes Ses Salines) in Colònia Sant Jordi. Three companies in the Colònia are authorized to take groups of visitors to this protected area: **Excursions a Cabrera** (☎ *971/649034*), **Transports Gregal** (☎ *971/657012*), and **Marcabrera** (☎ *622/574806 or 971/656403*)—this last one operates every day, year-round. If you have a self-charter, and want to lay over off the island, you will need to apply for permission to dock and scuba dive at the Oficina Administrativa del Parque Nacional Maritimo in Palma. ✉ *Visitor Center, Carrer Gabriel Roca s/n, corner of Pl. Es Dolç, Colònia Sant Jordi, Mallorca* ☎ *971/656282 for Visitor Center, 971/177641 for Administration Office, Palma.*

IBIZA

Settled by the Carthaginians in the 5th century BC, Ibiza has seen successive waves of invasion and occupation—the latest of which began in the 1960s, when it became a tourist destination. With a full-time population of barely 140,000, it now gets some 2 million visitors a year. It's blessed with beaches—56 of them, by one count—and also has the world's largest nightclub. About a quarter of the people who live on Ibiza year-round are expats.

October through April, the pace of life here is decidedly slow, and many of the island's hotels and restaurants are closed. In the 1960s and early 1970s, Ibiza was discovered by sun-seeking hippies and eventually emerged as an icon of counterculture chic. Ibizans were—and still are—friendly and tolerant of their eccentric visitors. In the late 1980s and 1990s, club culture took over. Young ravers flocked here from all over the world to dance all night and pack the sands of built-up beach resorts like Sant Antoni. That party-hearty Ibiza is still alive and well, but a new wave of luxury rural hotels, offering oases of peace and privacy, with spas and high-end restaurants, marks the most recent transformation of the island into a venue for more upscale tourism.

GETTING HERE AND AROUND

Ibiza is a 55-minute flight or a nine-hour ferry ride from Barcelona.

Ibizabus serves the island. Buses run to Sant Antoni every 15–30 minutes from 7:30 am to midnight, June through October (until 10:30 pm November through May) from the bus station on Avenida d'Isidor Macabich in Eivissa, and to Santa Eulàlia every half hour from 6:50 am to 11:30 pm Monday to Saturday (until 10:30 November to April), with late buses on Saturday in the summer party season at midnight, 1, and 2 am; Sunday service is hourly from 7:30 am to 11:30 pm (until 10:30 pm November to April). Buses to other parts of the island are less frequent, as is the cross-island bus between Sant Antoni and Santa Eulàlia.

On Ibiza, a six-lane divided highway connects the capital with the airport and Sant Antoni. Traffic circles and one-way streets make it a bit confusing to get in and out of Eivissa, but out in the countryside driving is easy and in any case is the only feasible way of getting to some of the island's smaller coves and beaches.

ESSENTIALS

Bus Contact Ibizabus ⊕ *www.ibizabus.com.*

Taxi Contacts Cooperativa Limitada de Taxis de Sant Antoni ⊠ *Sant Antoni* ☎ *971/343764, 971/340074.* **Radio-Taxi** ⊠ *Carrer Galicia 9, local 26, Eivissa* ☎ *971/398483.*

Visitor Information Aeropuerto de Ibiza ⊠ *Eivissa* ☎ *971/809118, 971/809132.* **Sant Antoni** ⊠ *Passeig de Ses Fonts s/n, Sant Antoni* ☎ *971/343363.* **Santa Eulària des Riu** ⊠ *Carrer Mariano Riquer Wallis 4, Santa Eulària des Riu* ☎ *971/330728.*

EIVISSA (IBIZA TOWN)

Hedonistic and historic, Eivissa (Ibiza, in Castilian) is a city jam-packed with cafés, nightspots, and trendy shops; looming over it are the massive stone walls of **Dalt Vila**—the medieval city declared a UNESCO World Heritage site in 1999—and its Gothic cathedral. Squeezed between the north walls of the old city and the harbor is **Sa Penya**, a long labyrinth of stone-paved streets with some of the city's best offbeat shopping, snacking, and exploring.

ESSENTIALS

Visitor Information Eivissa ⊠ *Paseig de Vara de Rey 1* ☎ *971/301900, 971/301740* ⊙ *Mon.–Sat. 9–3.*

Tours Dalt Vila tours. On nearly every Saturday evening, a one-hour dramatized tour of Dalt Vila departs from the old market, at the foot of the walls. Three performers in period costume enact a legendary 15th-century love story as they move through the medieval scenes. Reservations are essential. ⊠ *Es Mercat Vell, Pl. de la Constitució* ☎ *971/399232* ✐ *informacioturistica@eivissa. es* ☜ *€10, audio guide in English €6* ⊙ *Mid-May–Aug., Sat. 9 pm; Sept. and Apr., Sat. 8 pm; Oct. and Mar., Sat. 7 pm; Nov.–Feb., Sat. 6 pm.*

EXPLORING

Bastió de Sant Bernat (*Bastion of St. Bernard*). From here, behind the cathedral, a promenade with sea views runs west to the bastions of Sant Jordi and Sant Jaume, past the **Castell**—a fortress formerly used as an army barracks. In 2007 work began to transform it into a luxury

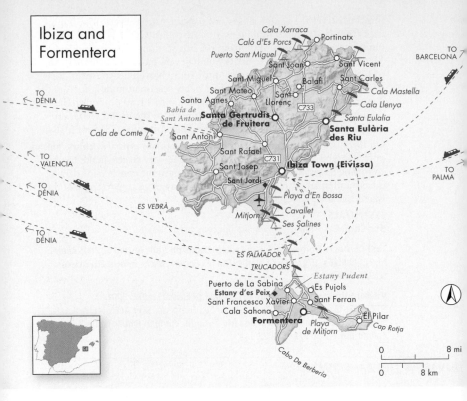

Ibiza and Formentera

parador, but archaeological discoveries under the work site have delayed the reconstruction indefinitely. The promenade ends at the steps to the **Portal Nou** (New Gate). ⊠ *Eivissa, Ibiza.*

Catedral. Ibiza's cathedral has a Gothic tower and a baroque nave, and a small museum of religious art and artifacts. It was built in the 13th and 14th centuries and renovated in the 18th century. The site has been used for temples and other religious buildings since the time of the Phoenicians. ⊠ *Pl. de la Catedral s/n, Dalt Vila* ☎ 971/312774 📷 *Museum €1* 🕙 *Apr.–Oct., Tues.–Sat. 10–1:30 and 5–8; Nov.–Mar., Tues.–Sat. 10–1:30.*

Centre d'Interpretació Madina Yabisa. A few steps from the cathedral, this center has a fascinating collection of audiovisual materials and exhibits on the period when the Moors ruled the island. ⊠ *Carrer Major 2, Dalt Vila* ☎ 971/399232 ⊕ *www.madinayabisa.eivissa.es* 📷 *€1.50* 🕙 *Apr.–June and Sept., Tues.–Fri. 10–2 and 5–8, weekends 10–2; July and Aug., Tues.–Fri. 10–2 and 6–9, weekends 10–2; Oct.–Mar., Tues.–Fri. 10–4:30, weekends 10–2.*

Museu d'Art Contemporani. Just inside the old city portal arch, this museum houses a collection of paintings, sculpture, and photography from 1959 to the present. The scope of the collection is international, but the emphasis is on artists who were born or lived in Ibiza during their careers. There isn't much explanatory material in English, however. ✉ *Ronda Pintor Narcis Putget s/n, Dalt Vila* ☎ *971/302723* 🎟 *Free* 🕒 *Apr.–June and Sept., Tues.–Fri. 10–1:30 and 5–8, weekends 10–2; July and Aug., Tues.–Fri. 10–2 and 6–9, weekends 10–2; Oct.–Mar., Tues.–Fri. 10–4:30, weekends 10–2.*

Sant Domingo. The roof of this 16th-century church is an irregular landscape of tile domes. The nearby *ajuntament* (town hall) is housed in the church's former monastery. ✉ *Carrer de Balanzat s/n.*

BEACHES

Ses Salines. Very much a place to see and be seen, the beach at Ses Salines is a mile-long narrow crescent of golden sand about 10 minutes' drive from Eivissa, in a Wildlife Conservation area. Trendy restaurants and bars, like the Jockey Club and Malibu, bring drinks to you on the sand and have DJs for the season, keeping the beat in the air all day long. The beach has different areas: glitterati in one zone, naturists in another, gay couples in another. There are no nearby shops, but the commercial vacuum is filled by vendors of bags, sunglasses, fruit drinks, and so on, who can be irritating. The sea is shallow, with a gradual drop-off, but on a windy day breakers are good enough to surf. **Amenities:** food and drink; lifeguards; parking (fee); showers; restrooms; water sports. **Best for:** partiers; nudists; windsurfing; swimming. ✉ *Eivissa, Ibiza* ✣ *10 km (6 miles) west on the E20 ring road from Eivassa toward the airport, then south on local road PM802 to the beach.*

WHERE TO EAT AND STAY

$$$ SPANISH 🍴 **El Portalón.** A bit of a climb from the main gate into Dalt Vila, this intimate restaurant has two dining rooms—one medieval, with heavy beams, antiques, and coats of arms; the other modern, with dark-orange walls and sleek black furniture. There's also a terrace for alfresco dining. The spaces are perfect metaphors for the traditional cuisine with contemporary touches served here. Excellent offerings include *pato con salsa de moras* (duck with mulberry sauce), *rape* (anglerfish), and baked *dorada* (sea bream). [$] *Average main: €18* ✉ *Pl. Desamparados 1–2* ☎ *971/303901* 🕒 *Closed Sun. Nov.–Easter. No dinner Sun. Easter–Oct.; no lunch Mon.–Sat.*

$$$$ BASQUE 🍴 **S'Oficina.** Some of the best Basque cuisine on Ibiza is served at this restaurant, just 2 km (1 mile) outside town in Sant Jordi. Marine prints hang on the white walls and ships' lanterns from the ceiling; the bar is adorned with ships' wheels. *Lomo de merluza con almejas* (hake with clams) and *kokotxas* (cod cheeks) are among the specialties. [$] *Average main: €23* ✉ *Carrer de les Begonies 17, Playa d'en Bossa, Ibiza* ✣ *From Eivissa, take the highway toward the airport and turn off for Playa d'en Bossa; S'Oficina is on the left in the first block past the roundabout on the road to the beach.* ☎ *971/390081* 🌐 *www.restaurantesoficina.com* 🕒 *No dinner Sun.–Tues. Oct.–Mar.*

$$$ HOTEL 🏨 **Hotel Montesol.** The island's first hotel, the Montesol, opened in 1934 and retains its grand exterior—fashion photographers love the balconies facing the promenade. **Pros:** value for price; convenient; good for meeting people. **Cons:** noisy; small rooms; minimal amenities; no pets.

9

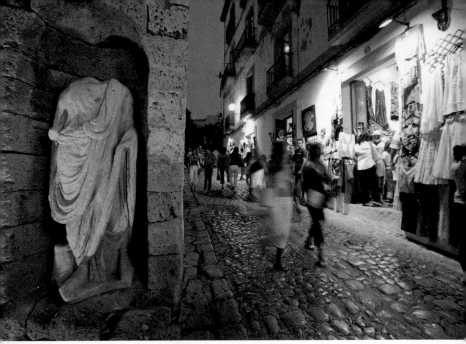

An evening stroll among the shops in Eivissa

$ *Rooms from: €127* ✉ *Paseo Vara de Rey 2* ☎ *971/931493* ⊕ *www.hotelmontesol.com* ⮌ *55 rooms* ⦿ *No meals.*

$$$
B&B/INN
🏨 **La Ventana.** Inside the medieval walls, this intimate hillside hotel has fine views of the old town and the harbor from some of the rooms. **Pros:** historic setting; good value. **Cons:** rooms are small; lots of stairs to climb, especially if you want a room with a view; surroundings can be noisy until the wee hours. $ *Rooms from: €165* ✉ *Sa Carrossa 13* ☎ *971/390857* ⊕ *www.laventanaibiza.com* ⮌ *12 rooms, 2 suites* ⦿ *No meals.*

NIGHTLIFE

Fodor'sChoice
★
Ibiza's discos are famous throughout Europe. Keep your eyes open during the day for free invitations handed out on the street—these can save you expensive entry fees. Between June and September, an all-night "Discobus" service (☎ *971/313447* ⊕ *www.discobus.es*) runs between Eivissa, Sant Antoni, Santa Eulàlia/Es Canar, Playa d'En Bossa, and the major party venues. The cost is €3 for one ride, €12 for a five-trip ticket.

Amnesia. This popular club in San Rafael opened in 1980 and it's still going strong, with several ample dance floors that throb to house and funk. ✉ *Ctra. Eivissa-Sant Antoni, Km 5, San Rafael, Ibiza* ☎ *971/198041* ⊘ *June–Sept.*

Carrer de la Verge. Gay nightlife converges on this street in Sa Penya.

Casino de Ibiza. This is a small gaming club with roulette tables, blackjack, slots, and poker. You need your passport or other picture ID/proof of age to enter. There are Texas Hold'em tournaments every Friday, from 9 pm. ✉ *Paseo de Juan Carlos I 17, Ibiza Nueva* ☎ *971/806806* ⊕ *www.casinoibiza.com* 🎫 *€5* ⊘ *July–Sept., daily 6 pm–6 am; May,*

June, and Oct., daily 8 pm–5 am; Nov.–Apr., Tues.–Thurs. 8 pm–4 am, Fri.–Sat. 8 pm–5 am.

Keeper. Clubbers start the evening here, where there's no cover and the action starts at 11 pm. The indoor space at Keeper can get a bit cramped, but out on the terrace freedom reigns. ⊠ *Paseo Marítimo s/n, Ibiza Nueva* ☎ *971/310509* ⊕ *www.keeperibiza.com.*

Pacha. A young, international crowd gathers after 2 am at the flagship club of this empire, where each of the five rooms offers a diffent style, including techno, house music, R&B, and hip-hop. ⊠ *Av. 8 de Agosto s/n* ☎ *971/313612* ⊕ *www.pacha.com.*

Privilege. Billing itself as the largest club in the world, the long-running center of Ibiza's nightlife has a giant dance floor, a swimming pool, and more than a dozen bars. ⊠ *Ctra. Eivissa–Sant Antoni, Km 7, San Rafael, Ibiza* ☎ *971/198160.*

Space. Space is the word for it: the main room here would make a comfortable fit for an airplane hangar or two. The opening and closing parties of the season here are legendary. ⊠ *Playa d'en Bossa s/n* ☎ *971/396793* ⊕ *www.space-ibiza.es.*

Teatre Pereyra. The stylish lobby bar here opens for breakfast at 9 am Monday to Saturday and just keeps on going, morphing from bar to live music club—when the prices of drinks go up—to the wee hours of the morning. Teatre Pereyra is open year-round. ⊠ *Carrer del Conde de Roselló 3* ☎ *971/304432* ⊕ *www.teatropereyra.com.*

SPORTS AND THE OUTDOORS
MULTI-SPORT OUTFITTERS
Ibiza Mundo Activo. This company can organize many kinds of outdoor activities, including walking and hiking tours, rock climbing, cycling, snorkeling and kayaking. ⊠ *Carrer Arquebisbe Cardona Riera 19* ☎ *676/075704* ⊕ *www.ibizamundoactivo.blogspot.es.*

BOATING
Coral Yachting. You can charter all sorts of seaworthy craft with this company. ⊠ *Marina Botafoc, Local 323–324* ☎ *971/313926* ⊕ *www. coralyachting.com.*

Ibiza Azul. Rent motorboats and Jet Skis here, as well as a 40-foot live-aboard sailboat for weekend or weeklong charters. ⊠ *Ctra. Eivissa–Portinatx, Km 16.5, Sant Joan, Ibiza* ☎ *971/325264, 607/907456* ⊕ *www. ibizazul.com.*

CYCLING
Extra Rent. You can rent mountain bikes, cars, and scooters here. ⊠ *Avda. Santa Eulária des Riu 17* ☎ *971/191717, 900/506013.*

GOLF
Club de Golf Ibiza. Ibiza's only golf club combines the 9 holes at the Club Roca Llisa resort complex with a more challenging 18-hole course nearby. ⊠ *Ctra. Jesús–Cala Llonga s/n, Santa Eulària, Ibiza* ☎ *971/196118* ⊕ *www.golfibiza.com* ⌘ *18-hole course: 6000 meters (6564 yards). Par 72. Greens fees €90/day. 9-hole course: 2865 meters (3134 yards). Par 36 in/35 out.* ☞ *Driving range, putting green, golf carts, pull carts, rental clubs, lessons, restaurant, bar.*

HORSEBACK RIDING

Can Mayans. Hire horses here for rides along the coast and inland. Can Mayans has a riding school, and has a gentle touch with beginners. ⊠ *Ctra. Santa Gertrudis–Sant Lorenç, Km 3, Santa Gertrudis, Ibiza* ☎ *971/187388, 626/222127* ☉ *Summer, Tues.–Sun. 10–1 and 6–9; winter, Tues.–Sun. 10–1 and 4–6.*

SCUBA DIVING

Active Dive. Instruction and guided dives, as well as kayaking, parasailing, and boat rentals are available here. ⊠ *Carrer S'Embarcador s/n, San Antoni, Ibiza* ☎ *971/341344, 670/364914* ⊕ *www.active-dive.com.*

Ibiza Diving College. Book lessons and dives here, from beginner level to advanced, with PADI-trained instructors and guides. ⊠ *Carrer Santa Rosalia 30, Sant Antoni, Ibiza* ☎ *680/394619, 971/347436* ⊕ *www. ibiza-diving-college.com.*

Policlínica de Nuestra Señora del Rosario. A team with a decompression chamber is on standby throughout the year at this hospital. ⊠ *Via Romana s/n* ☎ *971/301916.*

Sea Horse Sub-Aqua Centre. A short distance from Sant Antoni, this aquatic center offers basic scuba training as well as excursions to nearby dive sites. ⊠ *Edificio Yais 5, Playa Port des Torrent s/n, Sant Josep, Ibiza* ☎ *629/349499, 678/717211* ⊕ *www.seahorsedivingibiza.com.*

Subfari. This is one of the best places to come for diving in Sant Joan. ⊠ *Cala Portinatx, San Joan, Ibiza* ☎ *971/337558, 677/466040* ⊕ *www. subfari.es.*

TENNIS

Ibiza Club de Campo. With six clay and two composition courts, this is the most extensive tennis club on the island. Nonmembers can play here for €6 per hour. ⊠ *Ctra. Sant Josep, Km 0.4* ☎ *971/300088* ⊕ *www. ibiza-spotlight.com/clubdecampo.*

SHOPPING

Although the Sa Penya area of Eivissa still has a few designer boutiques, much of the area is now given over to the so-called hippie market, with stalls selling clothing and crafts of all sorts between May and October. Try Avenida Bartolomeu Rosselló for casual clothes and accessories.

Enotecum. This store has a good range of wines, including labels produced in the Balearics, and spirits. ⊠ *Avda. d'Isidoro Macabich 43* ☎ *971/399167* ⊕ *www.enotecum.es.*

Ibiza Republic. This shop sells trendy casual gear, sandals, belts, and bags. ⊠ *Carrer Antoni Mar 15* ☎ *971/314175.*

SANTA EULÀRIA DES RIU

15 km (9 miles) northeast of Eivissa.

At the edge of this town on the island's eastern coast, to the right below the road, a Roman bridge crosses what some claim is the only permanent river in the Balearics (hence *des Riu,* or "of the river"). The town itself follows the curve of a long sandy beach, a few blocks deep with restaurants, shops, and holiday apartments. From here it's a 10-minute drive to Sant Carles and the open-air hippie market held there every Saturday morning.

GETTING HERE AND AROUND

By car, take the C733 from Eivissa. From May to October, buses run from Eivissa every half hour Monday to Saturday, every hour on Sunday. Service is less frequent the rest of the year.

WHERE TO EAT AND STAY

$$$ ITALIAN 🍴 **Mezzanotte.** This charming little portside restaurant has just 12 tables, softly lit with candles and track lighting. In summer, the seating expands to an interior patio and tables on the sidewalk—and the service can get a bit ragged. The kitchen prides itself on hard-to-find fresh ingredients flown in from Italy. The linguine with jumbo shrimp, saffron, and zucchini or with *bottarga* (dried and salted mullet roe from Sardinia) is wonderful. The prix-fixe menu, served at dinner in summer and lunch in winter, is a bargain. [$] *Average main: €18* ✉ *Paseo de s'Alamera 22, Santa Eulària* ☎ *971/319498* 🕒 *Closed Jan., Feb., and Sun. No lunch June and Aug.*

$$$$ B&B/INN 🏨 **Can Curreu.** The traditional architecture here, reminiscent of a Greek Island village, features a cluster of low buildings with thick whitewashed walls, the edges and corners gently rounded off—and each room has one of these buildings to itself, with a private patio artfully separated from its neighbors. **Pros:** superbly designed; friendly, efficient staff; riding stables. **Cons:** pricey; bit of a drive to the nearest beaches; no pets. [$] *Rooms from: €275* ✉ *Ctra. de Sant Carles, Km 12, Santa Eulària* ☎ *971/335280* 🌐 *www.cancurreu.com* 🛏 *3 rooms, 15 suites* 🍽 *Breakfast.*

$$$$ B&B/INN Fodor's Choice ★ 🏨 **Can Gall.** Santi Marí Ferrer remade his family's *finca* (farmhouse), with its massive stone walls and native *savina*-wood beams, into one of the island's friendliest and most comfortable country inns. **Pros:** family-friendly; espresso maker in room; fluffy terry robes. **Cons:** 15-minute drive to beaches; no pets. [$] *Rooms from: €220* ✉ *Crta. Sant Joan, Km 17.2, Sant Llorenç* ☎ *971/337031, 670/876054* 🌐 *www.agrocangall.com* 🛏 *2 rooms, 7 suites* 🕒 *Closed Oct.–Apr.* 🍽 *Breakfast.*

$ HOTEL 🏨 **Hostal Yebisah.** The longtime residents and civic boosters Toni and Tanya Molio, who are credited with the idea of dredging sand from the bay to create the beach at Santa Eulària, run this simple lodging on the little promenade in the heart of town. **Pros:** friendly service; ideal location; good value. **Cons:** bathrooms a bit cramped; minimal amenities. [$] *Rooms from: €80* ✉ *Paseo S'Alamera 13* ☎ *971/330160, 650/100120* 🌐 *www.hostalyebisah.com* 🛏 *26 rooms* 🍽 *No meals.*

SPORTS AND THE OUTDOORS

CYCLING

Kandani ✉ *Carrer César Puget Riquer 27* ☎ *971/339264* 🌐 *www.kandani.es.*

SANTA GERTRUDIS DE FRUITERA

15 km (9 miles) north of Eivissa.

Blink and you miss it: that's true of most of the small towns in the island's interior and especially so of Santa Gertrudis, not much more than a bend in the road. But Santa Gertrudis is worth a look. The brick-paved town square is closed to vehicle traffic—perfect for the sidewalk cafés. From here, you are only a few minutes' drive from some of the island's flat-out best resort hotels and spas and the most beautiful secluded northern coves and beaches: **S'Illa des Bosc, Benirrás** (where they have drum circles to salute the setting sun), **S'Illot des Renclí, Portinatx,** and **Caló d'En Serra**. Artists and expats like it here: they've given the town an appeal that now makes for listings of half a million dollars or more for a modest two-bedroom house.

GETTING HERE AND AROUND

By car, take the C733 from Ibiza Town. From May to October, buses run from Eivissa every 90 minutes on weekdays, less frequently on weekends and the rest of the year.

WHERE TO EAT AND STAY

$$ ✕ **Can Caus.** Ibiza might pride itself on its seafood, but there comes a
SPANISH time for meat and potatoes. When that time comes, take the 20-minute drive to the outskirts of Santa Gertrudis to this family-style roadside restaurant. Feast on skewers of barbecued sobrasada, goat chops, lamb kebabs, or grilled sweetbreads with red peppers, onions, and eggplant—most of the ingredients are from the restaurant's own farms. Most people eat at the long wooden tables on the terrace. $ *Average main: €16 ✉ Ctra. Sant Miquel, Km 3.5 ☎ 971/197516 ⊕ www.cancaus-ibiza.com ⊘ Closed Mon. Sept.–June.*

$$$ ✕ **Sa Cornucopia** (*Chez Paul*). Dine by candlelight in one of this lovely
MEDITERRANEAN little restaurant's four intimate rooms. On a chilly, late-spring evening,
Fodor's Choice there may be a fire in the fireplace; in the summer, book a table on
★ the terrace, which has jasmine and grapevines hanging overhead. Chef Oscar Bueno's dishes, a mix of Ibizan, North African, and Provençal, are served in heroic portions; try the couscous with lamb and black sausage or the country-style roast chicken, and choose from a small but distinguished list of wines from La Rioja and Ribera del Duero. Sa Cornucopia has been a fixture in Sana Gertrudis for decades and just keeps getting better. $ *Average main: €21 ✉ Venda de Sa Picasa ☎ 971/197274 ⊕ www.sacornucopia.com ✍ Reservations essential ⊘ Closed Sun. No lunch.*

$$$$ ☷ **Cas Gasí.** A countryside setting makes this a quiet escape in a lively
B&B/INN destination, with photo-ready views of Ibiza's only mountain (1,567-
Fodor's Choice foot Sa Talaiassa), set in a lovely late-19th-century manor house on
★ a hillside overlooking a valley. **Pros:** countryside setting; great views; attentive personal service; peace and quiet; on-site organic garden used for menus; free yoga classes in the morning. **Cons:** minimum stay required in July and August; not geared to families; very expensive. $ *Rooms from: €395 ✉ Cami Vell a Sant Mateu s/n ☎ 971/197700 ⊕ www.casgasi.com ⤹ 9 rooms, 1 suite ⼝ Breakfast.*

Bar Costa. This is just the right place to sit out under the awning with a coffee and croissant or a *bocadillo* (sandwich) and contemplate your next move. Inclement weather? The back room has a fireplace, and the walls are covered with funny, irreverent modern art from the owner's collection. ⊠ *Pl. de la Iglesia s/n* ☎ *971/197021.*

SHOPPING
te Cuero. This store specializes in hand-tooled leather bags and belts with great designer buckles. November through February the store tends to keep irregular hours, so call ahead. ⊠ *Pl. de la Iglesia s/n* ☎ *971/197100* ⊙ *Closed Sun.*

FORMENTERA

Environmental protection laws shield much of Formentera, making it a calm respite from neighboring Ibiza's dance-until-you-drop madness. Though it does get crowded in the summer, the island's long white-sand beaches are among the finest in the Mediterranean; inland, you can explore quiet country roads by bicycle in relative solitude.

From the port at La Sabina, it's only 3 km (2 miles) to Formentera's capital, **Sant Franēesc Xavier,** a few yards off the main road. There's an active hippie market in the small plaza in front of the church. At the main road, turn right toward Sant Ferran, 2 km (1 mile) away. Beyond Sant Ferran the road travels 7 km (4 miles) along a narrow isthmus, staying slightly closer to the rougher northern side, where the waves and rocks keep yachts—and thus much of the tourist trade—away.

The plateau on the island's east side ends at the lighthouse **Faro de la Mola.** Nearby is a **monument to Jules Verne,** who set part of his 1877 novel *Hector Servadac* (published in English as *Journey on a Comet*), in Formentera. The rocks around the lighthouse are carpeted with purple thyme and sea holly in spring and fall.

Back on the main road, turn right at Sant Ferran toward Es Pujols. The few hotels here are the closest Formentera comes to beach resorts, even if the beach is not the best. Beyond Es Pujols the road skirts **Estany Pudent,** one of two lagoons that almost enclose La Sabina. Salt was once extracted from Pudent, hence its name, which means "stinking pond," although the pond now smells fine. At the northern tip of Pudent, a road to the right leads to a footpath that runs the length of **Trucadors,** a narrow sand spit. The long, windswept beaches here are excellent.

GETTING HERE AND AROUND
Formentera is a one-hour ferry ride from Ibiza or 25 minutes on the jet ferry. Both Balearia and Iscomar operate ferry services to Formentera from Ibiza and Denia, the nearest landfall on the Spanish mainland.

On Ibiza, you can also take ferries from Santa Eulària and Sant Antoni to Formentera's La Sabina (1 hour, €23) as well as numerous ferries to the coves and calas on the east and west coasts of Ibiza. Day-trippers can travel to Formentera for a few hours in the sun before heading back to Ibiza to plug into the nightlife.

A very limited bus service connects Formentera's villages, shrinking to one bus each way between San Francisco and Pilar on Saturday and disappearing altogether on Sunday and holidays.

ESSENTIALS

Ferry Contacts Balearia 🌐 *www.balearia.com.* **Iscomar** 🌐 *www.iscomar.com.*

Taxi Information Parada de Taxis La Sabina ✉ *La Sabina* ☎ *971/322002.*

Visitor Information Formentera ✉ *Poligon de la Marina s/n, Port de La Sabina* ☎ *971/322057.*

BEACHES

Platjas de Ses Illetes. The closest beach to the port at La Savina is an exquisitely beautiful string of dunes stretching to the tip of the Trucador Peninsula at Es Pau. Collectively called Ses Illetes, they form part of a national park. Ibiza clubbers like to take the fast ferry over from Eivissa after a long night and chill out here, tapping the sun for the energy to party again; this sort of photosynthesis is especially popular with young Italian tourists. The water is fairly shallow and the meadows of seagrass in it shelter colorful varieties of small fish; the fairly constant breezes are good for windsurfing. Nude and topless sunbathing raises no eyebrows anywhere along the dunes. Be warned: there's no shade here at all, and rented umbrellas fetch premium prices. **Amenities:** food and drink; lifeguards; showers; toilets; water sports. **Best for:** nudists; snorkeling; swimming; windsurfing. ✉ *4 km (2½ miles) north of La Savina.*

WHERE TO EAT AND STAY

$$$$ B&B/INN

🏨 **Can Aisha.** With only five apartments, this converted stone farmhouse can feel like a family compound, especially when everyone is gathered on the sundeck or around the communal barbecue. **Pros:** all apartments have private terraces; shops and restaurants nearby; kitchenettes with basic equipment. **Cons:** no kids and no pets; short season. [$] *Rooms from: €280* ✉ *Venda de Sa Punta 3205, Es Pujols* ☎ *616/654982* 🌐 *www.canaisha.com* 🛏 *5 apartments* 🕒 *Closed roughly Oct.–May* 🍴 *Breakfast.*

SHOPPING

El Pilar is the chief crafts village here. Stores and workshops sell handmade items, including ceramics, jewelry, and leather goods. El Pilar's crafts market draws shoppers on Sunday afternoon May through September, and also Wednesday June through August. May through September, crafts are sold in the morning at the San Françesc Xavier market and in the evening in Es Pujols.

SPORTS AND THE OUTDOORS

CYCLING

Moto Rent Mitjorn. This company rents bicycles and motorcycles. ⊠ *Puerto de la Savina s/n* ☎ *971/323201, 971/321111* ⊕ *www.motorent migjorn.com.*

DIVING

Vell Marí. You can take diving courses from Monday to Saturday here. ⊠ *Puerto Deportivo, Local 14–16, Marina de Formentera, La Sabina* ☎ *971/322105.*

MALLORCA

Saddle-shaped Mallorca is more than five times the size of Menorca or Ibiza. The Sierra de Tramuntana, a dramatic mountain range soaring to nearly 5,000 feet, runs the length of its northwest coast, and a ridge of hills borders the southeast shores; between the two lies a flat plain that in early spring becomes a sea of almond blossoms, the so-called snow of Mallorca. The island draws more than 10 million visitors a year, many of them bound for summer vacation packages in the coastal resorts. The beaches are beautiful, but save time for the charms of the northwest and the interior: caves, bird sanctuaries, monasteries and medieval towns, local museums, outdoor cafés, and village markets.

GETTING HERE AND AROUND

From Barcelona, Palma de Mallorca is a 50-minute flight, an 8-hour overnight ferry, or a 4½-hour catamaran journey.

If you're traveling by car, Mallorca's main roads are well surfaced, and a four-lane, 25-km (15-mile) motorway penetrates deep into the island between Palma and Inca. The Vía Cintura, an efficient beltway, rings Palma. For destinations in the north and west, follow the "Andratx" and "Oeste" signs on the beltway; for the south and east, follow "Este" signs. Driving in the mountains that parallel the northwest coast and descend to a corniche (a cliffside road) is a different matter; you'll be slowed not only by the winding roads but also by tremendous views and tourist traffic.

ESSENTIALS

Visitor Information Oficina de Turismo de Mallorca ⊠ *Aeropuerto de Palma, Palma* ☎ *971/789556* ⊕ *www.illesbalears.es.*

PALMA DE MALLORCA

If you look north of the cathedral (La Seu, or the seat of the bishopric, to Mallorcans) on a map of the city of Palma, you can see around the Plaça Santa Eulàlia a jumble of tiny streets that made up the earliest settlement. Farther out, a ring of wide boulevards traces the fortifications built by the Moors to defend the larger city that emerged by the 12th century. The zigzags mark the bastions that jutted out at regular intervals. By the end of the 19th century, most of the walls had been demolished; the only place where you can still see the massive defenses is at Ses Voltes, along the seafront west of the cathedral.

A *torrent* (streambed) used to run through the middle of the old city, dry for most of the year but often a raging flood in the rainy season. In the 17th century it was diverted to the east, along the moat that ran outside the city walls. Two of Palma's main arteries, La Rambla and the Passeig d'es Born, now follow the stream's natural course. The traditional evening *paseo* (promenade) takes place on the Born.

If you come to Palma by car, park in the garage beneath the Parc de la Mar (the ramp is just off the highway from the airport, as you reach the cathedral) and stroll along the park. Beside it run the huge bastions guarding the Almudaina Palace; the cathedral, golden and massive, rises beyond. Where you exit the garage, there's a **ceramic mural** by the late Catalan artist and Mallorca resident Joan Miró, facing the cathedral across the pool that runs the length of the park.

If you begin early enough, a walk along the ramparts at Ses Voltes from the mirador beside the cathedral is spectacular. The first rays of the sun turn the upper pinnacles of La Seu bright gold and begin to work their way down the sandstone walls. From the Parc de la Mar, follow Avinguda Antoni Maura past the steps to the palace. Just below the Plaça de la Reina, where the **Passeig d'es Born** begins, turn left on Carrer de la Boteria into the Plaça de la Llotja (if the Llotja itself is open, don't miss a chance to visit—it's the Mediterranean's finest Gothic-style civic building). From there stroll through the Plaça Drassana to the **Museu d'Es Baluard,** at the end of Carrer Sant Pere. Retrace your steps to Avinguda Antoni Maura. Walk up the Passeig d'es Born to Plaça Joan Carles I, then right on Avenida de La Unió.

GETTING HERE AND AROUND

You can hire a horse-drawn carriage with driver at the bottom of the Born, and also on Avinguda Antonio Maura, in the nearby cathedral square, and on the Plaça d'Espanya, at the side farthest from the train station. A tour of the city costs €30 for a half hour, €50 for an hour. ■ TIP➜ Haggle firmly, and the driver might come down a bit off the posted fare.

Boats from Palma to neighboring beach resorts leave from the jetty opposite the Auditorium, on the Passeig Marítim. The tourist office has a schedule.

ESSENTIALS

Bus Information Empresa Municipal de Transports. Palma's Empresa Municipal de Transports (EMT) runs 65 bus lines and a tourist train in and around the Mallorcan capital. Most buses leave from the Intermodal station, next to the Inca railroad terminus on the Plaça d'Espanya; city buses leave from the ground floor, while intercity buses leave from the underground level. The tourist office on the Plaça d'Espanya has schedules. Bus No. 1 connects the airport with the city center and the port. Bus No. 2 circumnavigates the historic city center. Bus nos. 3 and 20 connect the city center with Porto Pi; No. 46 goes to the Fundació Pilar i Joan Miró. The No. 21 connects S'Arenal with the airport. Fare for a single local ride is €1.50; to the airport it's €3. ⊠ *Estacio Intermodal, Pl. d'Espanya* ⊕ *www.emtpalma.es.*

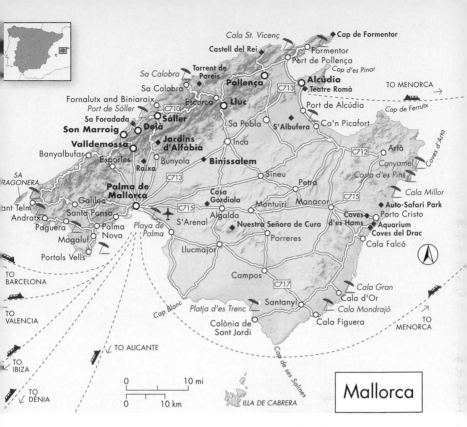

Mallorca

Bus Station Palma de Mallorca ⊠ *Plaça d'Espanya* ☎ 971/177777.

Taxi Information Associación Servicios Fono-Taxi ⊠ *Passeig Santa Catalina de Sena 2* ☎ 971/728081. **Radio-Taxi** ⊠ *Francesc Sancho 7* ☎ 971/201212.

Tour Bus Information City Sightseeing. The open-top City Sightseeing bus leaves every 20–25 minutes starting at 9:30 am and makes 16 stops throughout the town, including Plaça de la Reina, the Passeig Marítim, and the Castell de Bellver. Tickets are valid for 24 hours, and you can get on and off as many times as you wish. All Palma tourist offices have information and details. ⊠ *Av. Antoni Maura 24, behind the Palau de la Almudaina* ☎ 902/101081 ⊕ *www. city-sightseeing.com* 💳 €17.

Train Station Palma Train Station ⊠ *Ferrocarriles de Mallorca, Pl. d'Espanya* ☎ 971/752224.

Visitor Information Palma ⊠ *Pl. de la Reina 2* ☎ 971/173990 ⊕ *www. palmademallorca.es.* ⊠ *Parc de Ses Estacions s/n, across from Pl. d'Espanya* ☎ 902/102365

Cathedral of Palma de Mallorca

EXPLORING
TOP ATTRACTIONS

Banys Arabs (*Arab Baths*). One of Palma's oldest monuments, the 10th-century public bathhouse has a wonderful walled garden of palms and lemon trees. In its day, it was not merely a place to bathe but a social institution where you could soak, relax, and gossip with your neighbors. ⊠ *Carrer Can Serra 7* ☎ *637/046534* 🖭 *€2.50* 🕙 *Apr.–Nov., daily 9:30–7; Dec.–Mar., daily 9:30–5:30.*

Castell de Bellver (*Bellver Castle*). Overlooking the city and the bay from a hillside, the castle was built at the beginning of the 14th century, in Gothic style but with a circular design—the only one of its kind in Spain. It houses an archaeological museum of the history of Mallorca, and a small collection of classical sculpture. The Bus Turistic and the EMT municipal bus nos. 3, 4, 20, 21 and 22 all stop near the entrance. ⊠ *Camilo José Cela s/n* ☎ *971/730657, 971/735065* 🖭 *€4 (free Sun.)* 🕙 *Apr.–Sept., Mon. 8:30–1, Tues.–Sat. 8:30–8, Sun. 10–5; Oct.–Mar., Mon. 8:30–1, Tues.–Sat. 8:30–6, Sun. 10–5.*

Fodor's Choice ★ **Catedral de Mallorca.** Palma's cathedral is an architectural wonder that took almost 400 years to build. Begun in 1230, the wide expanse of the nave is supported by 14 70-foot-tall columns that fan out at the top like palm trees. The nave is dominated by an immense rose window, 40 feet in diameter, from 1370. Over the main altar (consecrated in 1346) is the surrealistic **baldoquí** (baldachin) by Antoni Gaudí, completed in 1912. This enormous canopy, with lamps suspended from it like elements of a mobile, rises to a Crucifixion scene at the top. To the right, in the Chapel of the Santísimo, is an equally remarkable 2007 work by the sculptor Miquel Barceló: a painted ceramic tableau covering the walls like a skin. Based on the New Testament account of the miracle of the loaves and fishes, it's a bizarre composition of rolling waves, gaping cracks, protruding fish heads, and human skulls. The **bell tower** above the cathedral's Plaça Almoina door holds nine bells, the largest of which is called N'Eloi, meaning "Praise." The 5-ton N'Eloi, cast in 1389, requires six men to ring it and has shattered stained-glass windows with its sound. ■TIP➔ February through November, there's an organ concert here on the first Tuesday of the month, starting at noon. ⊠ *Pl. Almoina s/n* ☎ *971/723130, 902/022445* ⊕ *www.catedraldemallorca.org* ⊠ *€6* ⊙ *Apr., May, and Oct., weekdays 10–5:15, Sat. 10–2:15; June–Sept., weekdays 10–6:15, Sat. 10–2:15; Nov.–Mar., weekdays 10–3:15, Sat. 10–2:15. Sun. Mass year-round 8:30–1:45 and 6:30–7:45.*

Fodor'sChoice
★ **Museu d'Es Baluard** (*Museum of Modern and Contemporary Art of Palma*). West of the city center, this museum rises on a long-neglected archaeological site, parts of which date back to the 12th century. The building itself is an outstanding convergence of old and new: the exhibition space uses the surviving 16th-century perimeter walls of the fortified city, including a stone courtyard facing the sea and a promenade along the ramparts. There are three floors of galleries, and the collection includes work by Miró, Picasso, Henri Magritte, Antoni Tàpies, Alexander Calder, and other major artists. The courtyard café-terrace Restaurant del Museu affords a fine view of the marina. To get here, take the narrow Carrer de Sant Pere through the old fishermen's quarter, from Plaça de la Drassana. ⊠ *Pl. Porta de Santa Catalina 10* ☎ *971/908200* ⊕ *www.esbaluard.org* ⊠ *€6 Wed.–Sun., €4.50 Tues.* ⊙ *Tues.–Sat. 10–8, Sun. 10–3.*

Museu Fundació Pilar y Joan Miró (*Pilar and Joan Miró Foundation Museum*). The permanent collection here includes a great many drawings and studies by the Catalan artist, who spent his last years on Mallorca, but it exhibits far fewer finished paintings and sculptures than the Fundació Miró in Barcelona. Don't miss the adjacent studio, built for Miró by his friend the architect Josep Lluis Sert. The artist did most of his work here from 1957 on. ⊠ *Carrer Joan de Saridakis 29, Cala Major* ☎ *971/701420* ⊕ *miro.palmademallorca.es* ⊠ *€6 (free Sat.)* ⊙ *May 16–Sept. 15, Tues.–Sat. 10–7; Sept. 16–May 15, Tues.–Sat. 10–6, Sun. 10–3.*

Museu Fundación Juan March. A few steps from the north archway of the Plaça Major is the Museu Fundación Juan March. This fine little museum was established to display what had been a private collection of modern Spanish art. The building itself was a sumptuous private home built in the 18th century. The second and third floors were redesigned to accommodate a series of small galleries, with one or two works at most—by Pablo Picasso, Joan Miró, Juan Gris, Salvador Dalí, Antoni Tàpies, and Miquel Barceló, among others—on each wall. ⊠ *Carrer Sant Miguel 11* ☎ *971/713515* ⊕ *www.march.es/museupalma* ⊠ *Free* ⊙ *Weekdays 10–6:30, Sat. 10:30–2.*

Plaça Major. A crafts market fills this elegant neoclassical space from 10 to 2 on Friday and Saturday (Monday to Saturday in July and August).

Until 1823, this was the local headquarters of the Inquisition. A flight of steps on the east side of the Plaça Major leads down to **Las Ramblas,** a pleasant promenade lined with flower stalls.

Sant Francesc. The 13th-century monastery church of Sant Francesc was established by Jaume II when his eldest son took monastic orders and gave up rights to the throne. Fra Junípero Serra, the missionary who founded San Francisco, California, was later educated here; his statue stands to the left of the main entrance. The basilica houses the tomb of the eminent 13th-century scholar Ramón Llull. The cloisters (enter via the side door, on the right) are especially beautiful and peaceful. ⊠ *Pl. Sant Francesc 7* 🕾 *971/712695* 🕾 *€1.50* ⊙ *Mon.–Sat. 9:30–1 and 3:30–6, Sun. 9:30–1.*

Santa Eulalia. Carrer de la Cadena leads to this imposing Gothic church, where, in 1435, 200 Jews were forced to convert to Christianity after their rabbis were threatened with being burned at the stake. ⊠ *Pl. Santa Eulàlia 2* 🕾 *971/714625.*

WORTH NOTING

Ajuntament (*Town Hall*). Along Carrer Colom is the 17th-century Ajuntament. Stop in to see the collection of *gigantes,* the huge painted and costumed mannequins paraded through the streets during festivals, which are on display in the lobby. The olive tree on the right side of the square is one of Mallorca's so-called *olivos milenarios*—purported to be more than 1,000 years old. The adjacent building is the Palau del Consell, the headquarters of the island's government, a late 19th-century building on the site of a medieval prison. The Palau has its own collection of gigantes, and an impressive stained-glass window over the ornate stone staircase; visits inside can be arranged by appointment (✑ *visites@conselldemallorca.net*). ⊠ *Pl. Cort 1* 🕾 *971/225900.*

Can Corbella. On the corner of Carrer de Jaume II is this gem of Palma's early Moderniste architecture, designed in the 1890s by Nicolás Lliteras. ⊠ *Pl. Cort 3.*

Can Forteza Rei. Designed by Luis Forteza Rei in 1909, this Art Nouveau delight has twisted wrought-iron railings and surfaces inlaid with bits of polychrome tile which are signature touches of Antoni Gaudí and his contemporaries. A wonderful carved stone face in a painful grimace, flanked by dragons, ironically frames the stained-glass windows of a third-floor dental clinic. There's a chocolate shop on the ground floor. ⊠ *Pl. Marqués Palmer 1.*

QUICK BITES

Ca'n Joan de S'aigo. This café, on a side street behind the church of Sant Francesc, is one of Palma's venerable institutions, in business since 1700. Drop in for coffee or hot chocolate with an *ensaimada crema*—a spiral-shape Mallorcan pastry with a rich cream-cheese filling. With its green-glass chandeliers, cane-back chairs, and marble tabletops, the setting is a treat in itself. ⊠ *Carrer de Ca'n Sanç 10* 🕾 *971/710759.*

Casas Casasayas. The ornate facades of these buildings, on opposite corners of Costa de Can Santacilia, were designed by the Moderniste architect Francesc Roca Simó in 1908. ⊠ *Pl. del Mercat 13–14.*

Caixa Forum (*Grand Hotel*). Built between 1901 and 1903 by Luis Domènech i Montaner, originator of Barcelona's Palau de la Música Catalana, this former hotel has an alabaster facade sculpted like a wedding cake, with floral motifs, angelic heads, and coats of arms. The original interiors are gone, however. The building is owned and used by the Fundació La Caixa, a cultural and social organization funded by the region's largest bank. Don't miss the permanent exhibit of paintings by the Mallorcan Impressionist Hermenegildo Anglada Camarasa. ⊠ *Pl. Weyler 3* ☎ *971/178500, 971/178512* ⊕ *www.lacaixa.es/obrasocial/ caixaforum.palma* 🔊 *€4* ⊙ *Mon.–Sat. 10–9, Sun. 10–2.*

Llotja (*Exchange*). On the seafront west of the Plaça de la Reina, the 16th-century Llotja connects via an interior courtyard to the **Consolat de Mar** (Maritime Consulate). With its decorative turrets, pointed battlements, fluted pillars, and Gothic stained-glass windows—part fortress, part church—it attests to the wealth Mallorca achieved in its heyday as a Mediterranean trading power. The interior (the Merchants' Chamber) and patio are only open to the public during special exhibitions organized by the local government; dates and hours are unpredictable. The adjacent garden and chapel are open only on March 1, the Dia de les Illes Balears (National Day of the Balearic Islands). ⊠ *Pl. Llotja 5* ☎ *971/711705.*

Palau Reial de l'Almudaina (*Almudaina Palace*). Opposite Palma's cathedral, this palace was originally an Arab citadel, then became the residence of the ruling house during the Middle Ages. It's now a military headquarters and the king's official residence when he is in Mallorca. Guided tours generally depart hourly during open hours. If you want to explore on your own, audio guides are available. ■ **TIP→ Try to catch the changing of the Honor Guard ceremony, which takes place in front of the Palace at noon on the last Saturday of the month.** ⊠ *Carrer Palau Reial s/n* ☎ *971/214134* 🔊 *€9, €15 with guided tour; €2 audio guide (free Wed. and Thurs. after 5 and for EU passport holders)* ⊙ *Apr.– Sept., Tues.–Sun. 10–7; Oct.–Mar., Tues.–Sun. 10–5.*

San Nicolau. On Plaça del Mercat, this 14th-century church has a hexagonal bell tower. ⊠ *Carrer Orfila 1.*

Teatre Principal. Take time to appreciate the neoclassical symmetry of this theater, Palma's chief venue for classical music; there are guided tours of the building (€5) on Saturdays at noon. The opera season here is April and May. Near the steps on the right is the **Forn des Teatre** bakery, famed for its pastries. ⊠ *Carrer de la Riera 2A* ☎ *971/219691* ⊕ *www.teatreprincipal.com.*

BEACHES

Es Trenc. Even though it's nearly an hour's drive from Palma, this pristine 2-km (2¼-mile) stretch of fine white sand on Mallorca's southern coast, much longer than it is wide, is one of the most popular beaches on the island—arrive late on a Saturday or Sunday in summer, and you'll be hard-pressed to find a space to stretch out. At times the water can be a bit choppy, and there are occasional patches of seaweed—but otherwise the clear, clean water slopes off gently from the shore for some 30 feet, making it ideal for families with younger kids. Es Trenc

DID YOU KNOW?

The beach at Cala Pi is named for the surrounding pine trees.

is in a protected natural area free of hotels and other developments, which makes for good bird-watching. Naturists lay their claim to part of the beach's eastern end. **Amenities:** food and drink; lifeguards; parking (fee); toilets. **Best for:** partiers; nudists; swimming; walking. ✉ *MA6040 s/n, 10 km (6 miles) south of Campos, 6½ km (4 miles) east of Colònia Sant Jordi.*

WORD OF MOUTH

"Palma and the little towns in the north have lots of foreign residents, but they're still very Spanish. The weather is great, and the people are very friendly."
—Fiona

Platja de Magaluf. Magaluf is Mallorca's Party Central and the site of one of the island's best beaches—a 1.5-km-long (1-mile-long) gentle curve of fine white sand that rates a Blue Flag designation for cleanliness and safety. The water is calm and clear, without strong currents or sudden drop-offs. A promenade of shops, bars, and restaurants runs the length of the beach, which is at the west end of the Bay of Palma, 15 km (9 miles) from the city. A favorite with young British and Scandinavian tourists, the beach is also first-rate for families—especially in the mornings, before the clubbers roll out of bed—but the town itself is pretty rowdy most of the time. The little knob of Black Lizard Island, about 440 yards offshore, is a challenging swim. **Amenities:** food and drink; lifeguards; parking (fee); showers; toilets; water sports. **Best for:** swimming; walking. ✉ *7 km (4 miles) south of Calvia, Magaluf.*

WHERE TO EAT

$ TAPAS 🍴 **Café la Lonja** (*Sa Llotja*). A great spot for hot chocolate or a unique tea or coffee, this classic establishment in the old fishermen's neighborhood has a young vibe that goes well with the style of the place. Both the sunny terrace in front of the Llotja and the bar inside are excellent places for drinks and sandwiches. The seasonal menu (served two doors down, at the Orient Express) might include a salad of tomato, avocado, and Cabrales cheese; fluffy quiche; and tapas of squid or mushrooms. It's a good rendezvous point and watering hole. [$] *Average main: €9* ✉ *Carrer Sa Lonja del Mar 2* ☎ *971/722799* 🕒 *Closed Dec. 10–Jan. 17.*

$ TAPAS 🍴 **La Bóveda.** Within hailing distance of the Llotja, this popular restaurant serves tapas and inexpensive platters such as chicken or ham croquettes, grilled cod, garlic shrimp, and *revueltos de ajos con morcilla* (scrambled eggs with garlic and black sausage). The tables in the back are always at a premium (they're cooler on summer days), but there's additional seating at the counter or on stools around upended wine barrels. The huge portions of traditional tapas are nothing fancy but they are very good. [$] *Average main: €12* ✉ *Carrer de la Botería 3* ☎ *971/714863* 🕒 *Closed Sun.*

$$$ CONTEMPORARY 🍴 **Simply Fosh.** While Palma suffers no dearth of rough-and-ready eateries, Simply Fosh has little or no competition in the fine-dining category. The renowned chef Marc Fosh may only offer a few menu choices, but he executes them superbly. Surprising twists transform the best local seasonal produce into dishes such as a duck and foie gras terrine with orange blossom, quince, and chocolate salt, and slow-cooked rump of lamb in a saffron crust, with red pepper and a black olive sauce. The

9

restaurant occupies the glorious medieval former refectory of the Mission of San Vicente de Paul, with high vaulted ceilings, a 210-foot gallery with stone arches, and an interior courtyard. White walls display contemporary art, and the smaller dining room has palm trees growing through the ceiling. There is a tasting menu at €75 (plus €40 with matching wines), and a seasonal prix fixe at €50. [$] *Average main: €22* ⌂ *Carrer de la Missió 7A* ☎ *971/720114* ⊕ *www.simplyfosh.com/en* ⌕ *Reservations essential* ⊙ *Closed Sun.*

WHERE TO STAY

$$
HOTEL
Fodor'sChoice
★
 Born. Romanesque arches and a giant palm tree spectacularly cover the central courtyard and reception area of this hotel, which occupies the former mansion of a noble Mallorcan family. **Pros:** convenient for sightseeing; romantic courtyard floodlit at night; good value. **Cons:** small rooms on the street side; poor soundproofing; no elevator. [$] *Rooms from: €115* ⌂ *Carrer Sant Jaume 3* ☎ *971/712942* ⊕ *www. hotelborn.com* ⌿ *30 rooms* ¦○¦ *Breakfast.*

$$$$
HOTEL
Fodor'sChoice
★
 Cap Rocat. What was once a 19th-century military fortress on the southern flank of the bay of Palma has been converted into one of Mallorca's—and arguably Europe's—most distinctive hotels. **Pros:** stunning backdrop; superb cuisine; impeccable service. **Cons:** isolated from the bustle—and nightlife; lacks a sandy beach; sky-high prices. [$] *Rooms from: €650* ⌂ *Ctra. de Enderrocat s/n, Cala Blava* ☎ *971/747878* ⊕ *www.caprocat.com* ⌿ *25 suites* ⊙ *Closed Nov.–Feb.* ¦○¦ *Breakfast.*

$$
B&B/INN
 Dalt Murada. In an ideal location in the old part of Palma, a minute's walk to the cathedral, this townhouse, dating back to the 15th century, was the Sancho Moragues home until 2001, when the family opened it as a hotel. **Pros:** helpful service; homey. **Cons:** thin walls; no parking; no pets. [$] *Rooms from: €110* ⌂ *Carrer Almudaina 6A* ☎ *971/425300* ⊕ *www.daltmurada.com* ⌿ *23 rooms, 2 suites* ⊙ *Closed Nov.–Apr.* ¦○¦ *No meals.*

$
HOTEL
 Hostal Apuntadores. A favorite among budget travelers, this lodging in the heart of the old town, within strolling distance of the bustling Passeig d'es Born, has a rooftop terrace with what is arguably the city's best view—overlooking the cathedral and the sea. **Pros:** good value; good place to meet people. **Cons:** can be noisy; the cheapest rooms share bathrooms. [$] *Rooms from: €65* ⌂ *Carrer Apuntadores 8* ☎ *971/713491* ⊕ *www.palmahostal.com* ⌿ *27 rooms (18 with bath)* ¦○¦ *No meals.*

$$$
HOTEL
 Hotel Almudaina. Business travelers from the mainland favor this comfortable, central hotel and it's an excellent choice for vacationers as well. **Pros:** steps from Palma's upscale shopping; courteous, efficient service. **Cons:** public spaces are small and not for socializing. [$] *Rooms from: €140* ⌂ *Avda. Jaume III, 9* ☎ *971/727340* ⊕ *www.hotelalmudaina.com* ⌿ *78 rooms* ¦○¦ *Breakfast.*

$$
B&B/INN
 Misión de San Miguel. Conveniently between the transportation hub at Plaza Espanya and the Plaça Major, this boutique hotel has rooms that are simply but stylishly furnished. **Pros:** close to major city attractions; friendly, multilingual staff. **Cons:** not especially child-friendly; no elevator; can be noisy at night. [$] *Rooms from: €119* ⌂ *Can Maçanet 1a, Carrer de Can Perpinyà* ☎ *971/214848* ⎙ *971/214545* ⊕ *www.*

urhotels.com/en/hotel-ur-mision-san-miguel-majorca.html *26 rooms, 6 suites* 🍴 *No meals.*

$$$ B&B/INN **Palau Sa Font.** Warm Mediterranean tones and crisp, clean lines give this boutique hotel in the center of the shopping district an atmosphere very different from anything else in the city. **Pros:** buffet breakfast until 11; helpful English-speaking staff; chic design; family-friendly. **Cons:** pool is small; surroundings can be noisy in summer. [$] *Rooms from: €165* ✉ *Carrer Apuntadores 38* ☎ *971/712277* 📠 *971/712618* 🌐 *www.palausafont.com* *4 singles, 12 doubles, 3 suites* 🍴 *Breakfast.*

NIGHTLIFE

Mallorca's nightlife is never hard to find. Many of the hot spots are concentrated 6 km (4 miles) west of Palma at **Punta Portals,** in Portals Nous, where King Juan Carlos I often moors his yacht when he's in Mallorca in early August for the Copa del Rey international regatta. Another major area is on **Avinguda Gabriel Roca.** This section of the Passeig Marítim holds many taverns, pubs, and clubs.

BCM Planet Dance. June through September, head to the nearby suburb of Magaluf and dance the night away at this gargantuan disco. ✉ *Av. S'Olivera s/n, Magaluf* ☎ *675/746729, 971/132715* 🌐 *www.bcmplanetdance.com/en.*

Bluesville Bar. This fun little venue for live blues (with occasional forays into reggae and rock) is on a hard-to-find alleyway between Carrer d'Estanc and Carrer d'Apuntadores. Bands hit their stride around midnight, and keep going till 4 am. ✉ *Carrer Ma del Morro 3* ☎ *634/537202.*

Carrer Apuntadores. On the west side of Passeig d'es Born in the old town, this street is lined with casual bars and cafés that appeal to night owls in their twenties and thirties. On the weekend, you can often come across impromptu live rock and pop acts performing on small stages.

Gran Casino de Mallorca. Palma's casino is a short distance from the harbor. You can get a free first-visit pass from the Casino's website, but you'll need your passport, driver's license, or other official photo ID to enter. Dress is informal, but T-shirts, shorts, and sandals are frowned on. No-limit poker tables and Texas Hold-'em tournaments are the big attraction here. It's open daily, except between 5 and 10 am. ✉ *Gabriel Roca 54, Porto Pi Centro Comercial* ☎ *971/130000* 🌐 *www.casinodemallorca.com.*

Jazz Voyeur Club. Some of Palma's best jazz combos—and the occasional rock group—play this small, smoky club in the old portside neighborhood. ✉ *Carrera Apuntadores 5* ☎ *971/720780* ⏲ *Weekdays and Sun. 8:30 pm–1 am, Sat. 8:30–3.*

Plaça de la Llotja. This square, along with the surrounding streets, is the place to go for *copas* (drinking, tapas sampling, and general carousing).

Bar Abaco. Giving a touch of elegance to what's otherwise a fairly funky neighborhood, this bar sits you down amid bouquets of flowers, plants and bowls of fruit, soothes you with mostly baroque music, and plies you with tasty cocktails. Open from 8 pm (except Sunday), you can languish here until midnight (until 3 am on Friday and Saturday). ✉ *Carrer de Sant Joan 1* ☎ *971/714939* 🌐 *www.barabaco.com.*

Tito's. Outdoor elevators transport you from the street to the dance floor at the sleek and futuristic Tito's. ⊠ *Passeig Marítim s/n* ☎ *971/730017* ⊕ *www.titosmallorca.com.*

SPORTS AND THE OUTDOORS

BALLOONING

Mallorca Balloons. For spectacular views of the island, float up in a hot-air balloon, which lift off daily from March to October, weather permitting, at sunrise and sunset. Call for a reservation: the office is open from 10 to 1, and 5 to 8. ⊠ *Autovia Palma–Manacor NA15, Exit 44, Manacor* ☎ *971/596969, 639/818109 (cell phone)* ⊕ *www.mallorcaballoons. com* ⛄ *1-hr flight €160.*

BIRD-WATCHING

Mallorca has two notable nature reserves.

S'Albufera de Mallorca. This is the largest wetlands zone in Mallorca. ⊠ *Ctra. Port d'Alcúdia–Ca'n Picafort, Alcúdia* ☎ *971/892250* ⊕ *www. mallorcaweb.net/salbufera* ⊗ *Daily 9–5 (until 6 Apr.–Sept.).*

Sa Dragonera. This island and its large colony of sea falcons are accessible by boat from Sant Elm, at the western tip of Mallorca. The boats, run by the operator Cruceros Margarita, leave from in front of the restaurant El Pescador at the port of Sant Elm daily every 30 minutes. No boats run November through March. ⊠ *Sa Dragonera* ☎ *971/180632 for Sa Dragonera, 639/617545 for Cruceros Margarita* ⊕ *www. crucerosmargarita.com* ⛄ *€12* ⊗ *Departures Feb. and Mar., Mon.– Sat. 10:15–1:15; Apr.–Sept., daily 9:45–3:45; Oct., daily 10:15–1:15.*

CYCLING

With long flat stretches and heart-pounding climbs, Mallorca's 675 km (420 miles) of rural roads adapted for cycling make the sport the most popular on the island; many European professional teams train here. Tourist-board offices have excellent leaflets on bike routes with maps, details about the terrain, sights, and distances. The companies below can rent you bikes for exploring Palma itself.

Embat Ciclos. Some 10 km from the city center, on the beach in Platja de Palma, Embat has both standard touring and electric bikes for rent, and will happily assist with organizing tours of the island. ⊠ *Bartolomé Riutort 27, Can Pastilla* ☎ *971/492358* ⊕ *www.embatciclos.com.*

Palma on Bike. This bike-rental shop, just below the Plaça de la Reina in Palma, is open seven days a week, 9:30–2 and 4–8. ⊠ *Avda. Antoni Maura 10* ☎ *610/355570, 971/718062.*

GOLF

Federación Balear de Golf (*Balearic Golf Federation*). Mallorca has more than 20 18-hole golf courses, among them PGA championship venues of fiendish difficulty. The federation can provide more information. ⊠ *Cami de Son Vida 110* ☎ *971/722753* ⊕ *www.fbgolf.com.*

Canyamel Golf. This club, some 64 km (40 miles) from Palma, at the far eastern tip of the island, has wonderful views of the sea. ⊠ *Av. d'Es Cap Vermell s/n, Capdepera* ☎ *971/841313* ⊕ *www.canyamelgolf.com* ⛳ *18 holes, 6196 meters (6778 yds). Par 73. Greens fee €76–€97 for*

18 holes, €53–€63 for 9 holes, depending on the season. ☞ *Driving range, putting green, pull carts, buggies, rental clubs, restaurant, bar.*

Golf Alcanada. This 18-hole course, designed by Robert Trent Jones Jr. and Sr., is widely regarded as the best club on the island, with spectacular views of the bay and lighthouse. Fees for nonmembers are €130 for 18 holes and €66 for 9 holes. ⊠ *Ctra. del Faro s/n, Alcúdia* ☎ *971/545944* ⊕ *www.golf-alcanada.com/en* 🏌 *18 holes, 6499 m. (7110 yds), par 72* ☞ *Driving range, golf carts, pull carts, rental clubs, putting green, pitching area, lessons, restaurant, bar.*

HANG GLIDING

Club Vol Lliure Mallorca. Weekend and intensive hang-gliding courses are conducted here. ⊠ *C. Bellavista s/n, Petra* ☎ *655/766443, 871/950859.*

Escuela de Parapente Alfàbia. Paragliding courses and tandem flights are available here year-round, weather permitting. ⊠ *Camino del Puig s/n, Sineu, Alcúdia* ☎ *687/626536, 971/891366* ⊕ *www.parapentealfabia. com.*

Escuela de Ultraligeros El Cruce (*Club de Vuelo ULM Es Cruce*). For memorable views of the island, glide above it on an ultralight hang glider. ⊠ *Ctra. Palma-Manacor s/n, Vilafranca de Bonany* ☎ *629/392776, 971/832073.*

HIKING

Mallorca is excellent for hiking. In the Sierra de Tramuntana, you can easily arrange to trek one way and take a boat, bus, or train back. Ask the tourist office for the free booklet *20 Hiking Excursions on the Island of Mallorca,* with detailed maps and itineraries.

Grup Excursionista de Mallorca (*Mallorcan Hiking Association*). This associaton can provide hiking information. ⊠ *Carrer dels Horts 1* ☎ *971/718823* ⊕ *www.gemweb.org.*

SAILING

Club de Mar. Famous among yachties, this club has its own hotel, bar, disco, and restaurant. ⊠ *Av. Gabriel Roca s/n, Muelle de Pelaires* ☎ *971/403611* ⊕ *www.clubdemar-mallorca.com.*

Cruesa Mallorca Yacht Charter. A wide range of sailing craft and motor boats are available for rent here, by the day or the week. ⊠ *Carrer Contramuelle Mollet 12* ☎ *971/282821, 663/947005* ⊕ *www.cruesa.com.*

Federación Balear de Vela (*Balearic Sailing Federation*). For information on sailing, contact the federation. ⊠ *Av. Joan Miró 327, San Agustin* ☎ *971/402412* ⊕ *www.federacionbalearvela.org.*

SCUBA DIVING

Big Blue. This dive center, next to the Hotel Hawaii on the beach boardwalk in Palmanova, offers PADI certified courses for beginners (€269), including two dives with full equipment: tanks, wetsuits, regulators, masks and fins. ⊠ *Carrer Martin Ros Garcia 6, Palmanova* ☎ *971/681686* ⊕ *www.bigbluediving.net.*

TENNIS

Federació de Tennis de les Illes Balears (*Balearic Tennis Federation*). Tennis is very popular here—the more so for world champion Rafael Nadal being a Mallorcan. There are courts at many hotels and private clubs,

Mallorca is a popular place for cyclists, and many European professionals train here.

and tennis schools as well. The federation can provide information about playing in the area. ⊠ *Carrer Uruguai s/n* ☎ *971/720956* ⊕ *www. ftib.net.*

SHOPPING

Mallorca's specialties are shoes and leather clothing, utensils carved from olive wood, porcelain and handblown glass, and artificial pearls. Look for designer fashions on the **Passeig des Born** and for antiques on **Costa de la Pols,** a narrow little street near the Plaça Riera. The **Plaēa Major** has a modest crafts market Friday and Saturday 10–2 (in summer the market is also open on weekdays). Another crafts market is held May 15–October 15, 8 pm–midnight in **Plaēa de les Meravelles.**

Many of Palma's best shoe shops are on Avenida Rei Jaime III, between the Plaça Juan Carles I and the Passeig Mallorca.

Alpargatería La Concepción. Mallorca's most popular footwear is the simple, comfortable slip-on espadrille (usually with a leather front over the first half of the foot and a strap across the back of the ankle). Look for a pair here. ⊠ *Carrer de la Concepción 17* ☎ *971/710709.*

Camper. This company has an internationally popular line of sport shoes. ⊠ *Av. de Jaime III 16* ☎ *971/714635.*

Carmina. This is the place for top-quality handcrafted men's dress shoes and boots, which can cost more than €500. ⊠ *Carrer de la Unió 4* ☎ *971/229047.*

Colmado Santo Domingo. This is a wonderful little shop for the artisanal food specialties of Mallorca: sobrasada of black pork, sausages of all sorts, cheeses, jams, and honeys and preserves. It's closed on

Sunday. ⊠ *Carrer Santo Domingo 1* ☎ *971/714887* ⊕ *www.colmado santodomingo.com.*

Forn des Teatre. Near the steps leading up to the right of the Teatre Principal, this bakery is known for its *ensaimadas* (a typically Spanish fluffy pastry) and *cocas* (meat pies). ⊠ *Pl. Weyler 8* ☎ *971/727383.*

Gordiola. Glassmakers since 1719, Gordiola has a factory-showroom in Alguida, on the Palma–Manacor road, where you can watch the glass being blown and even try your hand at making a piece. ⊠ *Ctra. Palma-Manacor, Km 16, Algaida* ☎ *971/665046.*

Jaime Mascaró. This store is known for its original high-fashion designer shoes for women. ⊠ *Av. Rei Jaime III, 10* ☎ *971/729842.*

Lotusse. Shop here for high-end shoes, leather coats, and accessories. ⊠ *Av. Jaume III 5* ☎ *971/710203.*

SHOE HEAVEN

For shoe shopping, go to Inca, 27 km (17 miles) from Palma. **Camper** (⊠ *Poligon Industrial s/n* ☎ *971/888361*), **Barrats 1890** (⊠ *Av. General Luque 480* ☎ *971/504207*), and **Munper** (⊠ *Carrer Jocs 170* ☎ *971/881000*) have factory showrooms here, and there are dozens of smaller boutiques all over town specializing in footwear and leather apparel. Inca's Thursday market is the largest on Mallorca, though it has the same stuff you'll find at other markets. If you're here, stop at Celler C'an Amer for lunch.

VALLDEMOSSA

18 km (11 miles) north of Palma.

The jumping-off point for a drive up the spectacular coast of the Tramuntana, this little town north of Palma has but one claim to fame, but the claim is compelling: the vast complex of the Royal Carthusian Monastery.

GETTING HERE AND AROUND

Valldemossa is a 20-minute drive from Palma on the MA1130. Regular bus service from the Plaça d'Espanya in Palma gets you to Valldemossa in about a half hour.

ESSENTIALS

Visitor Information Valldemossa ⊠ *Av. de Palma 7* ☎ *971/612019.*

EXPLORING

Fodor's Choice

★ **Reial Cartuja** (*Royal Carthusian Monastery*). The monastery was founded in 1339, but after the monks were expelled in 1835, it acquired a new lease on life by offering apartments for travelers. The most famous lodgers were Frédéric Chopin and his lover, the Baroness Amandine Dupin—the French novelist better known by her pseudonym, George Sand. The two spent three difficult months here in the cold, damp winter of 1838–39.

In the **church,** note the frescoes above the nave—the monk who painted them was Goya's brother-in-law. The **pharmacy,** made by the monks in 1723, is almost completely preserved. A long corridor leads to the apartments, furnished in period style, occupied by Chopin and Sand. The piano is original. Nearby, another set of apartments houses the local **museum,** with mementos of Archduke Luis Salvador and a collection of old printing blocks. From here you return to the ornately furnished **King Sancho's palace,** a group of rooms originally built by King Jaume II for his son. The tourist office, in Valldemossa's main plaza, sells a ticket good for all of the monastery's attractions. ✉ *Pl. de la Cartuja 11* ☎ *971/612106, 971/612986* 🌐 *www.cartujadevalldemossa.com* 🎫 *€8.50* 🕒 *Dec. and Jan., Mon.–Sat. 9:30–3, Sun. 10–1; Feb., Mar., Oct., and Nov., Mon.–Sat. 9:30–5, Sun. 10–1; Apr.–Sept., Mon.–Sat. 9:30–6:30, Sun. 10–1.*

WHERE TO EAT AND STAY

$$ SPANISH

🍴 **Celler C'an Amer.** A *celler* is a uniquely Mallorcan combination of wine cellar and restaurant, and Inca has no fewer than six. This is the best, with heavy oak beams and huge wine vats lining the walls behind the tables and banquettes. Antonia, the dynamic chef-owner, serves heroic portions of the island's best *lechona* (suckling pig) and *tumbet* (vegetables baked in layers). Winter specialties include a superb oxtail soup prepared with red wine and seasonal mushrooms. After lunching here, enjoy your coffee around the corner in the pleasant square of Plaça de Santa Maria la Major. [$] *Average main: €17* ✉ *Carrer Pau 39* ☎ *971/501261* 🕒 *Closed weekends.*

$$$$ HOTEL Fodor's Choice ★

🏨 **Gran Hotel Son Net.** About equidistant from Palma and Valldemossa, this restored estate house—parts of which date back to 1672—is one of Mallorca's most luxurious hotels. **Pros:** attentive staff; family-friendly; convenient to Palma; no minimum booking. **Cons:** a bit far from the beaches; no pets; all this luxury comes at a high price. [$] *Rooms from: €385* ✉ *Carrer Castillo de Son Net s/n, Puigpunyent* ☎ *971/147000* 🌐 *www.sonnet.es* 🛏 *31 rooms, 7 suites* 🍽 *Breakfast.*

$$$$ B&B/INN Fodor's Choice ★

🏨 **Mirabó de Valldemossa.** At the far end of a winding dirt road in the hills overlooking the Reial Cartuja, across the valley of Valldemossa, this luxurious little agroturismo is a romantic hideaway that's hard to reach and even harder to tear yourself away from. **Pros:** friendly, personal service; peace and quiet. **Cons:** no restaurants nearby; no gym or spa; those low stone doorways can be hard on the head. [$] *Rooms from: €260* ✉ *Ctra. Valldemossa, Km 16* ☎ *661/285215* 🛏 *8 rooms, 1 suite* 🍽 *Breakfast.*

$$$$ B&B/INN

🏨 **Valldemossa Hotel.** Once part of a monastery, this beautifully restored boutique hotel sits on a hill amid acres of olive trees; the breathtaking views of the Tramuntana mountains alone are worth a stay. **Pros:** private; peaceful surroundings. **Cons:** restaurant needs more variety; not especially child-friendly; lots of stairs to navigate; no pets. [$] *Rooms from: €380* ✉ *Carrer Cami Antic a Palma s/n* ☎ *971/612626* 🌐 *www.valldemossahotel.com* 🛏 *4 rooms, 8 suites* 🕒 *Closed mid-Nov.–Feb.* 🍽 *Breakfast.*

DEIÀ

9 km (5½ miles) southwest of Sóller.

Deià is perhaps best known as the adopted home of the English poet and writer Robert Graves, who lived here off and on from 1929 until his death in 1985. The village is still a favorite haunt of writers and artists, including Graves's son Tomás, author of *Pa amb Oli (Bread and Olive Oil),* a guide to Mallorcan cooking, and British painter David Templeton. Ava Gardner lived here for a time; so, briefly, did Picasso. The setting is unbeatable—all around Deià rise the steep cliffs of the Sierra de Tramuntana. There's live jazz on summer evenings, and on warm afternoons literati gather at the beach bar in the rocky cove at Cala de Deià, 2 km (1 mile) downhill from the village. Walk up the narrow street to the village church; the small **cemetery** behind it affords views of mountains terraced with olive trees and of the coves below. It's a fitting spot for Graves's final resting place, in a quiet corner.

About 4 km (2½ miles) west of Deià is **Son Marroig,** one of the estates of Austrian archduke Luis Salvador (1847–1915), who arrived in Mallorca as a young man and fell in love with the place. The archduke acquired huge tracts of land along the northwest coast, where he built miradores at the most spectacular points but otherwise left the pristine beauty of the land intact. If you're driving, the best way to reach Son Marroig is the twisty MA10.

GETTING HERE AND AROUND

The Palma–Port de Sóller bus (€4.35) passes through Deià six times daily in each direction Monday through Saturday, five times on Sunday. Taxis to Deià from Palma cost €45 by day, €50 at night; from the airport the fares are €50/€55, and from Sóller €22/€24. Intrepid hikers can walk from Deià through the mountains to Sóller, on a trail of moderate difficulty, in about 2½ hours.

EXPLORING

Ca N'Alluny (*La Casa de Robert Graves*). The Fundació Robert Graves opened this museum dedicated to Deià's most famous resident in the house he built in 1932. The seaside house is something of a shrine: Graves's furniture and books, personal effects, and the press he used to print many of his works are all preserved. ⊠ *Ctra. Deià–Sóller s/n* ☎ *971/636185* ⊕ *www.lacasaderobertgraves.com* 🖙 *€7* ♡ *Apr.–Oct., weekdays 10–5, Sat. 9–3; Nov.–Mar., Tues. and Fri. 10:30–1:30. Last visit 40 mins before closing.*

Monestir de Miramar. Located on the road south from Deià to Valldemossa, this monastery was founded in 1276 by Ramón Llull, who established a school of Asian languages here. It was bought in 1872 by the Archduke Luis Salvador and restored as a mirador. Explore the garden and the tiny cloister, then walk below through the olive groves to a spectacular lookout. ⊠ *MA10. Deià–Valldemossa, Km 67* ☎ *971/616073* 🖙 *€4* ♡ *Apr.–Oct., Mon.–Sat. 9–5; Nov.–Mar., Mon.–Sat. 9–4:45.*

Son Marroig. This estate belonged to Austrian archduke Luis Salvador (1847–1915), who arrived here as a young man and fell in love with the place. He acquired huge tracts of land along the northwestern coast, building miradores at the most spectacular points but otherwise leaving the pristine beauty intact. Below the mirador, you can see **Sa Foradada,** a rock peninsula pierced by a huge archway, where the archduke moored his yacht. Now a museum, the estate house contains the archduke's collections of Mediterranean pottery and ceramics, Mallorcan furniture, and paintings. The garden is especially fine. From April through early October, the Deià International Festival holds classical concerts here. ✉ *MA10 Deià–Valldemossa, Km 65* ☎ *971/639158, 649/913832* 🌐 *www.sonmarroig.com* 🎫 *€4* 🕓 *June–Aug., Mon.–Sat. 10–7:30; Sept.–May, Mon.–Sat. 10–6:30.*

WHERE TO STAY

$$$$ HOTEL Fodor's Choice ★ 🏨 **Es Molí.** A converted 17th-century manor house in the hills above the valley of Deià, this peaceful hotel is known for its traditional sense of luxury. **Pros:** attentive service; heated pool with spacious terrace; chamber-music concerts twice a week during the summer; great value for price. **Cons:** steep climb to annex rooms; no pets; short season; three-night minimum for some stays in high season. [$] *Rooms from: €280* ✉ *Ctra. Valldemossa-Deià s/n* ☎ *971/639000* 🌐 *www.esmoli.com* 🛏 *84 rooms, 3 suites* 🕓 *Closed Nov.–Apr.* 🍴 *Breakfast.*

$$$$ HOTEL Fodor's Choice ★ 🏨 **Belmond La Residencia.** Two 16th- and 17th-century manor houses, on a hill facing the village of Deià, have been artfully combined to make this exceptional hotel, superbly furnished with Mallorcan antiques, modern canvases, and canopied four-poster beds. **Pros:** impeccable service; view from the terrace; organized activities for kids; tennis coach, pro shop, and clinic. **Cons:** very expensive; only gnomes can negotiate the stairs to the Tower Suite. [$] *Rooms from: €660* ✉ *Son Canals s/n* ☎ *971/639011* 🌐 *www.laresidencia.com* 🛏 *36 rooms, 31 suites, 1 villa* 🍴 *Breakfast.*

$$$ B&B/INN 🏨 **s'Hotel D'es Puig.** This family-run "hotel on the hill" has a back terrace with a lemon-tree garden and a wonderful view of the mountains. **Pros:** peaceful setting; friendly service. **Cons:** pool is small; beds could be more comfortable; parking difficult; no pets. [$] *Rooms from: €160* ✉ *Es Puig 4* ☎ *971/639409, 637/820805* 🌐 *www.hoteldespuig.com* 🛏 *8 rooms, 1 suite* 🕓 *Closed Dec. and Jan.* 🍴 *Breakfast.*

JARDINS D'ALFÀBIA

17 km (10½ miles) north of Palma, 13 km (8½ miles) south of Sóller.

The springs and hidden irrigation systems that make up these gardens were created by the Moorish viceroy of the island, sometime in the 12th century. It's a remarkable oasis.

Jardins d'Alfàbia. Here's a sound you don't often hear in the interior of Mallorca: the rush of falling water. The irrigation system in these gardens nourish around 40 varieties of trees, climbers, and flowering shrubs. A 17th-century manor house, furnished with antiques and painted panels, has a collection of original documents that chronicles the history of the estate. ✉ *Ctra. Palma–Sóller, Km 17, Bunyola* ☎ *971/613123* 🌐 *www.jardinesdealfabia.com* 🎫 *€6.50* 🕓 *Mon.–Sat. 9:30–6:30.*

SÓLLER

13 km (8½ miles) north of Jardins d'Alfàbia, 30 km (19 miles) north of Palma.

All but the briefest visits to Mallorca should include at least an overnight stay in Sóller, one of the most beautiful towns on the island, with palatial homes built in the 19th and early 20th centuries by the landowners and merchants who thrived on the export of the region's oranges, lemons, and almonds. Many of the buildings here, like the **Church of Sant Bartomeu** and the **Bank of Sóller,** on the Plaça Constitució, and the nearby **Can Prunera,** are gems of the Moderniste style, designed by contemporaries of Antoni Gaudí. The tourist information office in the **town hall,** next to Sant Bartomeu, has a walking tour map of the important sites.

GETTING HERE AND AROUND

The mountain road between Sóller and Palma is spectacular—lemon and olive trees on stone-walled terraces, farmhouses perched on the edges of forested cliffs—but demanding. ■**TIP→** If you're driving to Sóller, take the tunnel (🚗 €5.05) at Alfabia instead. Save your strength for even better mountain roads ahead.

ESSENTIALS

Trolley Contacts Tren de Sóller. You can travel in retro style from Palma to Sóller on one of the six daily trains from Plaça d'Espanya—a string of wooden rail cars with leather-covered seats dating from 1912. The train trundles along for about an hour, making six stops along the 27-km (16-mile) route; the scenery gets lovely—especially at Bunyola and the Mirador Pujol—as you approach the peaks of the Tramuntana. ⊠ *Pl. d'Espanya 6, Palma* ☎ *971/752051, 902/364711* ⊕ *www.trendesoller.com* 🚗 *€19.50 round-trip.*

Tranvia de Sóller. Sóller's charming old trolley car, called the Tranvia de Sóller, threads its way from the train station down through town to the Port de Sóller. The fare is €5 each way. You can also buy a combination round-trip ticket for the train and the tram for €28. ⊠ *Pl. d'Espanya 6* ⊕ *www.trendesoller.com/en.*

Visitor Information Port de Sóller ⊠ *Canonge Oliver 10, Port de Sóller* ☎ *971/633042* **Sóller** ⊠ *Pl. Constitució 1* ☎ *971/638008.*

EXPLORING

Can Prunera. A minute's walk or so from the Plaça de la Constitució, along Sóller's main shopping arcade, brings you to this charming museum, where Moderniste style comes to life. In the lovingly restored family rooms on the first floor of this imposing town house you can see how Sóller's well-to-do embraced the art-deco style: the ornate furniture and furnishings, the stained glass and ceramic tile, and the carved and painted ceilings all helped announce their status in turn-of-the-century Mallorcan society. Upstairs, Can Prunera also houses a small collection of paintings by early modern masters, among them Man Ray, Santiago Rusiñol, Paul Klee, and Joan Miró; the garden is an open-air museum in its own right, with sculptures by José Siguiri, Josep Sirvent, and other Mallorcan artists. ⊠ *Carrer de la Lluna 86–90* ☎ *971/638973*

9

⊕ *www.canprunera.com* ≣€5 ☉ *Apr.–Oct., daily 10:30–6:30; Nov.–Mar., Tues.–Sun. 10:30–6:30.*

Station Building Galleries. Maintained by the Fundació Tren de l'Art, these galleries have two small but remarkable collections—one of engravings by Miró, the other of ceramics by Picasso. ⊠ *Pl. de Espanya 6* ☎ *971/630301* ≣ *Free* ☉ *Daily 10:30–6:30.*

WHERE TO EAT AND STAY

$$ | ✕ **Sa Cova.** On Sóller's busy central square, this friendly and informal restaurant specializes in traditional local cooking, with a nod to touristic expectations. Skip the inevitable paella, and opt instead for the *sopas mallorquines,* a thick vegetable soup served over thin slices of bread, or the Mallorcan pork loin, stuffed with nuts and raisins. Sa Cova has great people-watching: the tram to Port de Sóller passes right in front of its outside tables. $ *Average main: €16* ⊠ *Pl. Constitució 7* ☎ *971/633222.*

CATALAN

$$$ | ⌷ **Ca'n Abril.** A minute's walk or so from the main square, this family-friendly boutique hotel, opened in a restored town house in 2010, is an oasis of quiet in summer, when Sóller gets most of its tourist traffic. **Pros:** friendly service; honesty bar; good value. **Cons:** no elevator; no pets; limited parking (€10 per day). $ *Rooms from: €158* ⊠ *Carrer Pastor 26* ☎ *971/633579, 672/360507* ⊕ *www.hotel-can-abril-soller.com* ↝ *6 rooms, 4 suites* ☉ *Closed Nov.–Feb.* ❙❍❙ *Breakfast.*

B&B/INN

$$$ | ⌷ **Can Isabel.** Just across the tram tracks from the railway station, this former home still feels much like a family hideaway. **Pros:** convenient location; good value for price. **Cons:** no pool; no elevator; no private parking. $ *Rooms from: €130* ⊠ *Carrer Isabel II 13* ☎ *971/638097* ⊕ *www.canisabel.com* ↝ *6 rooms* ☉ *Closed Dec.–Feb.* ❙❍❙ *Breakfast.*

B&B/INN

$$$$ | ⌷ **Gran Hotel Sóller.** A former private estate with an imposing Moderniste facade, this is the biggest hotel in town. **Pros:** friendly and efficient service in at least five languages; short walk from town center. **Cons:** pricey. $ *Rooms from: €245* ⊠ *Carrer Romaguera 18* ☎ *971/638686* ⊕ *www.granhotelsoller.com* ↝ *35 rooms, 5 suites* ❙❍❙ *Breakfast.*

HOTEL

$$$ | ⌷ **La Vila.** Owner Toni Oliver obviously put a lot of work into this lovingly restored town house on Sóller's central square. **Pros:** friendly service; good location. **Cons:** rooms on the square can be noisy; no elevator; no pets. $ *Rooms from: €130* ⊠ *Pl. Constitució 14* ☎ *971/634641* ⊕ *www.lavilahotel.com* ↝ *8 rooms* ❙❍❙ *Breakfast.*

B&B/INN

SHOPPING

Ben Calçat. Shop here for hand-stitched shoes and traditional Mallorcan slip-ons, made on the premises. ⊠ *Carrer Sa Lluna 74* ☎ *971/632874* ⊕ *www.bencalcat.es.*

Eugenio. For three generations, the craftsmen of the Eugenio family—originally sculptors and furniture makers—have been making bowls, cutting boards, and all sorts of kitchen utensils by hand, from old olive wood. The wood can only be cut between September and April; it's soaked in water for five weeks and then cured for a year before the carver turns his hand to it, and the resulting shapes and textures are lovely. The shop, across the street from the tram station, is always

Mallorca's Tramuntana Mountains provide excellent views for hikers.

packed. Eugenio is happy to ship purchases abroad. ✉ *Carrer Jerónimo Estades 11* ☎ *971/630984.*

SPORTS AND THE OUTDOORS

Ten minutes or so from the center of Sóller on the tram, the beachfront at Port de Sóller offers all sorts of water-based fun

Escola d'Esports Nàutics. On the northwest coast at Port de Sóller, this place has canoes, windsurfers, dinghies, motor launches, and water-skiing gear available for rent from May to October. ✉ *Platja de Can Generós s/n, Port de Sóller* ☎ *609/354132* ⊕ *www.nauticsoller.com.*

ALCÚDIA

54 km (34 miles) northeast of Palma.

The first city to be located here was a Roman settlement, in 123 BC. The Moors reestablished a town, and after the Reconquest it became a feudal possession of the Knights Templar; the first ring of city walls dates to the early 14th century. Begin your visit at the **Church of Sant Jaume** and walk through the maze of narrow streets inside to the **Porta de Xara,** with its twin crenellated towers.

GETTING HERE AND AROUND

Porta de Alcúdia, where the ferry arrives from Ciutadella, is a 3-km (2-mile) taxi ride from the center of Alcúdia. There is also direct bus service from Palma.

ESSENTIALS

Visitor Information Alcúdia ✉ *Carrer Major 7* ☎ *971/549022.*

EXPLORING

Museu Monogràfic de Pollentia. The museum has a small collection of statuary and artifacts from the nearby excavations, whose finds date from when Alcúdia was the Roman capital of the island. ⊠ *Carrer Sant Jaume 30* ☎ *971/547004, 971/897102* ☎ *€3 ticket for museum and archaeological site* ☉ *Mid-June–Sept., Tues.–Sun. 9:30–8:30; Oct.–mid-June, Tues.–Fri. 10–3:30, weekends 10:30–1:30.*

POLLENÇA

8 km (5 miles) from Alcúdia, 50 km (31 miles) from Palma.

The history of this pretty little town goes back at least as far as the Roman occupation of the island; the only trace of that period is the stone **Roman Bridge** at the edge of town. In the 13th century, Pollença and much of the land around it was owned by the Knights Templar— who built the imposing church of **Nuestra Senyora de Los Ángeles** on the west side of the present-day Plaça Major. The church looks east to the 1,082-foot peak of the Puig de Maria, with the 15th-century sanctuary at the top. The **Calvari** of Pollença is a flight of 365 stone steps to a tiny chapel, and a panoramic view as far as Cap de Formentor. There's a colorful weekly market at the foot of the steps on Sunday mornings.

GETTING HERE AND AROUND

Pollença is a fairly easy drive from Palma on the MA013. A few buses each day connect Pollença with Palma and Alcúdia.

ESSENTIALS

Visitor Information Pollença ⊠ *Carrer Sant Domingo s/n* ☎ *971/535077.*

EXPLORING

**OFF THE
BEATEN
PATH**

Cap de Formentor. The winding road north from Port de Pollença to the tip of the island is spectacular. Stop at the Mirador de la Cruete, where the rocks form deep narrow inlets of multishaded blue. A stone tower called the Talaia d'Albercuix marks the highest point on the peninsula.

WHERE TO STAY

**$$
B&B/INN**

Hotel Juma. This little hotel, which opened in 1907, is on Pollença's main square, making it a good choice for a weekend stay because of the Sunday market that takes place there. **Pros:** great location; tasty breakfast in the bar downstairs; good value. **Cons:** parking can be a problem. $ *Rooms from: €120* ⊠ *Pl. Major 9* ☎ *971/535002* ⊕ *www.pollensahotels.com* ➘ *7 rooms* ⦿ *Breakfast.*

**$$$
B&B/INN
Fodor'sChoice
★**

Hotel Son Sant Jordi. A favorite way station for groups of cyclists touring the island, the Son Sant Jordi is a small family-friendly gem of a boutique hotel, formerly the convent of the adjacent Church of Sant Jordi. **Pros:** cheerful, helpful service; sauna; live jazz on the front terrace every Friday night. **Cons:** a tad pricey; June through September, the minimum stay is three nights. $ *Rooms from: €200* ⊠ *Carrer Sant Jordi 29* ☎ *971/530389, 629/307473* ⊕ *www.hotelsonsantjordi.com/en* ➘ *9 rooms, 3 suites* ⦿ *Breakfast.*

$$$$
RESORT
Fodor's Choice
★

🗷 **Son Brull.** "Oasis" is what springs to mind when driving up through the family vineyards to this brilliantly restored medieval monastery, reborn in 2003 as a deluxe resort hotel. **Pros:** spot-on, friendly, multilingual service; peace and quiet; strategic location for exploring Pollença, Alcúdia, and the S'Albufereta wildlife reserve. **Cons:** pricey; minimum booking for some arrivals in high season; no pets. $ *Rooms from: €450* ⊠ *Crta. Palma–Pollença, Km 50* 🕾 *971/535353, 610/772242* ⊕ *www.sonbrull.com* ⥲ *16 rooms, 7 suites* ⊙ *Closed Dec. and Jan.* †⊙† *Breakfast.*

PERFORMING ARTS

Festival Pollença. An acclaimed international music event, this festival is held each July and August. Started in 1961, it has attracted such performers as Mstislav Rostropovic, Jessye Norman, the St. Petersburg Philharmonic, the Camerata Köln, and the Alban Berg Quartet. Concerts are held in the cloister of the Convent of Sant Domingo. 🕾 *971/534011* ⊕ *www.festivalpollenca.org.*

LLUC

20 km (12 miles) southwest of Pollença.

The Santuari de Lluc, which holds the Black Virgin and is a major pilgrimage site, is widely considered Mallorca's spiritual heart.

GETTING HERE AND AROUND

The Santuari is about midway between Sóller and Pollença on the hairpin route over the mountains called MA10. Two buses daily connect these towns, stopping in Lluc. Taxi fare from either town is about €35.

EXPLORING

Santuari de Lluc. La Moreneta, also known as La Virgen Negra de Lluc (the Black Virgin of Lluc), is a votary statue of the Virgin Mary that's held in a 17th-century **church,** the center of this sanctuary complex. The **museum** has an eclectic collection of prehistoric and Roman artifacts, ceramics, paintings, textiles, folk costumes, votive offerings, Nativity scenes, and work by local artists. Between September and June, a children's choir sings psalms in the chapel at 1:15 pm, Monday to Saturday, and at 11 am for Sunday Mass. The Christmas Eve performance of "Cant de la Sibila" ("Song of the Sybil") is an annual choral highlight. ⊠ *Pl. dels Peregrins 1* 🕾 *971/871525* 🗷 *Monastery free, museum €4* ⊙ *Museum weekdays and Sun. 10–2, monastery daily 10–5.*

MENORCA

Menorca, the northernmost of the Balearics, is a knobby, cliffbound plateau with some 193 km (120 miles) of coastline and a central hill called El Toro, from whose 1,100-foot summit you can see the whole island. Prehistoric monuments—*taulas* (huge stone T-shapes), *talayots* (spiral stone cones), and *navetes* (stone structures shaped like overturned boats)—left by the first Neolithic settlers are all over the island.

Tourism came late to Menorca, which aligned with the Republic in the Spanish Civil War; Franco punished the island by discouraging the investment in infrastructure that fueled the Balearic boom on Mallorca and Ibiza. Menorca has avoided many of the problems of overdevelopment: there are still very few high-rise hotels, and the herringbone road system, with a single central highway, means that each resort is small and separate. There's less to see and do on Menorca, and more unspoiled countryside than on the other Balearics. The island, home to some 220 species of birds and more than 1,000 species of plants, was designated a Biosphere Reserve in 1993. Menorca is where Spaniards and Catalans tend to take their families on vacation.

GETTING HERE AND AROUND
To get to Menorca from Barcelona take the overnight ferry, fast hydrofoil (about 3 hours), or a 40-minute flight. It's a six-hour ferry ride from Palma.

Several buses a day run the length of Menorca between Mahón and Ciutadella, stopping en route at Alaior, Mercadal, and Ferreries. The bus line Autos Fornells serves the northeast; Transportes Menorca connects Mahón with Ciutadella and with the major beaches and calas around the island. From smaller towns there are daily buses to Mahón and connections to Ciutadella. In summer, regular buses shuttle beachgoers from the west end of Ciutadella's Plaça Explanada to the resorts to the south and west; from Mahón, excursions to Menorca's most remote beaches leave daily from the jetty next to the Nuevo Muelle Comercial.

If you want to beach-hop in Menorca, it's best to have your own transportation, but most of the island's historic sights are in Mahón or Ciutadella, and once you're in town everything is within walking distance. You can see the island's archaeological remains in a day's drive, so you may want to rent a car for just that part of your visit.

ESSENTIALS
Bus Contacts Autos Fornells. Schedules and fares of all IB08 bus connections can be found on the website. ⊕ *www.autosfornells.com.* **Autocares Torres** ☎ *902/075066* ⊕ *www.bus.e-torres.net/en.* **Transportes Menorca** ☎ *971/360475* ⊕ *www.tmsa.es.*

9

MAHÓN (MAÓ)

Established as the island's capital in 1722, when the British began their nearly 80-year occupation, Mahón still bears the stamp of its former rulers. The streets nearest the port are lined with four-story Georgian townhouses; the Mahónese drink gin and admire Chippendale furniture; English is widely spoken. The city is quiet for much of the year, but between June and September the waterfront pubs and restaurants swell with foreigners.

GETTING HERE AND AROUND
There's ferry service here from Mallorca, but it's much less frequent than to Ciutadella. Within Mahón, Torres Alles Autocares has three bus lines around the city and to the airport.

ESSENTIALS
Bus Contact Autocares Torres ☎ *902/075066* ⊕ *www.bus.e-torres.net/en.*

Menorca

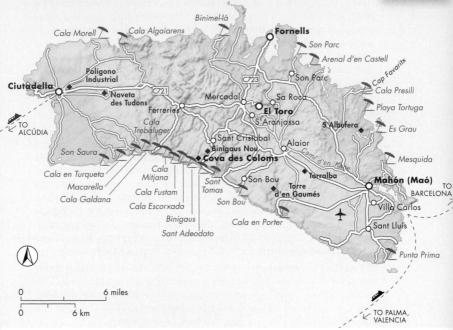

```
0                    6 miles
0          6 km
```

TO PALMA,
VALENCIA

Bus Station Estació Autobuses ⊠ *Carrer Josep Anselm Clavé s/n*
☎ *971/360475.*

Taxi Contact Radio-Taxi ☎ *971/367111.*

Visitor Information Aeropuerto de Menorca ⊠ *Arrivals Terminal*
☎ *971/157115.* **Mahón** ⊠ *Moll de Llevant 2* ☎ *971/355952.*

EXPLORING

Carrer Isabel II. This street is lined with many Georgian homes. To get
here, walk up Carrer Alfons III and turn right at the Ajuntament. ⊠ *Pl.
de la Constitució* ☎ *971/369800.*

La Verge del Carme. This church has a fine painted and gilded altarpiece.
Adjoining the church are the cloisters, now a **market,** with stalls selling
fresh produce and a variety of local cheeses and sausages. The central
courtyard is a venue for a number of cultural events throughout the
year. ⊠ *Pl. del Carme* ☎ *971/362402.*

Plaça de la Conquesta. Behind the church of Santa María, this plaza
has a statue of Alfons III of Aragón, who wrested the island from the
Moors in 1287.

Puerta de San Roque. At the end of Carrer Rector Mort, this massive
gate is the only surviving portion of the 14th-century city walls. They

were rebuilt in 1587 to protect the city from the pirate Barbarossa (Redbeard).

Santa María. Dating from the 13th century, this church was rebuilt in the 18th century, during the British occupation, and then restored again after being sacked during Spain's Civil War. The church's pride is its baroque, 3,006-pipe organ, imported from Austria in 1810. Organ concerts are given here at 7:30 on Saturday evenings, and at 11 am and 7 pm on Sundays. The altar, and the half-dome chapels on either side, have exceptional frescos. ⊠ *Pl. de la Constitució* ☎ *971/363949.*

Teatre Principal. Opera companies from Italy en route to Spain made the Teatre Principal in Mahón their first port of call; if the Mahónese gave a production a poor reception, it was cut from the repertoire. Built in 1824, it has five tiers of boxes, red plush seats, and gilded woodwork: a La Scala in miniature. Lovingly restored, it still hosts a brief opera season. If you're visiting in the first week of December or June, buy tickets well in advance. ⊠ *Carrer Costa Deià 40* ☎ *971/355603* ⊕ *www. teatremao.com.*

Torralba. Puzzle over Menorca's prehistoric past at this megalithic site with a number of stone constructions, including a massive taula. Behind it, from the top of a stone wall, you can see, in a nearby field, the monolith **Fus de Sa Geganta.** To get here from Mahón, drive west and turn south at Alaior on the road to Cala en Porter; it's 2 km (1 mile) ahead at a bend in the road, marked by an information kiosk on the left.

Torre d'en Gaumés. This is a complex set of stone constructions—fortifications, monuments, deep pits of ruined dwellings, huge vertical slabs, and taulas. To reach it, turn south toward Son Bou on the west side of Alaior. After about 1 km (½ mile), the first fork left will lead you to the ruins. ⊠ *Alaior.*

BEACHES

Cala Galdana. A smallish horseshoe curve of fine white sand, framed by almost vertical pine-covered cliffs, is where Menorca's only river, the Agendar, reaches the sea through a long limestone gorge. The surrounding area is under environmental protection—the handful of resort hotels and chalets above the beach (usually booked solid June to September by package tour operators) were grandfathered in. Cala Galdana is family-friendly in the extreme, with calm shallow waters, and a nearby waterpark/playground for the kids. A favorite with Menorcans and visitors alike, it gets really crowded in high season, but a 20-minute walk through the pine forest leads to the otherwise inaccessible little coves of Macarella and Macaretta, remote beaches popular with naturists and boating parties. **Amenities:** food and drink, lifeguards, showers, water sports. **Best for:** swimming, walking. ⊹ *35 km (21 miles) from Mahón, via the ME1 hwy. to Ferreries and south from there on the local road.*

WHERE TO EAT

$$$$
SEAFOOD
✕ **El Jàgaro.** This simple waterfront restaurant, at the east end of the harbor promenade, is a local favorite. The lunchtime crowd comes for the platter of lightly fried mixed fish with potatoes; knowledgeable clients home in on local specialties like *cap-roig* (scorpion fish) with garlic and wine sauce, or paella *bogavante* (clawed lobster). The menu takes

a major leap in price for the €67 spiny lobster, a delicacy prepared in a variety of ways. The prix-fixe lunch, a good value, is €15. [$] *Average main: €24* ✉ *Moll de Llevant 334–35* ☎ *971/362390, 659/462467* 🕒 *Closed Mon. No dinner Sun. Nov.–Mar.*

$$$$ SPANISH Fodor's Choice ★ 🍴 **Es Moli de Foc.** Originally a flour mill—*de foc* means "of fire," signifying that the mill was powered by internal combustion—this is the oldest building in the village of Sant Climent. The interior, with paintings by local artists on the mellow yellow walls, is inviting, but the food is exceptional. Prawn carpaccio with cured Mahón cheese and artichoke oil, black paella with monkfish and squid, and *carrilleras de ternera* (boiled beef cheeks) with potato purée are standouts, or ask for the separate menu of *arroces* (rice dishes)—the best on the island and arguably some of the best in Spain. End with some local-cheese ice cream and figs. In summer, book a table on the terrace. With a brewery on the premises, visible behind glass, you'll know what to drink. [$] *Average main: €24* ✉ *Carrer Sant Llorenç 65, Sant Climent, 4 km (2½ miles) southwest of town* ☎ *971/153222* 🌐 *www.esmolidefoc.es* 🕒 *Closed Jan. and Mon. Oct.–May. No dinner Sun.; no lunch Mon. July and Aug.*

$$$$ CONTEMPORARY Fodor's Choice ★ 🍴 **Marivent.** This trendy waterfront restaurant in Mahón, reopened in 2013, has two levels: an informal first-floor open terrace for tapas; and a more classical dining room upstairs, where traditional Menorcan ingredients and recipes emerge in creations like *caldereta* (spiny lobster stew), *arroz negro* (rice in squid ink) with cuttlefish and red prawns, and croquettes of prawn and monkfish. Starter portions are especially generous—just right for sharing around the table. Don't miss the homemade carrot cake. The wine list is excellent. [$] *Average main: €24* ✉ *Moll de Llevant 314* ☎ *971/363594, 666/865407* 🕒 *Closed Nov.–Apr. No lunch weekends; no dinner weekdays.*

WHERE TO STAY

$$$$ B&B/INN Fodor's Choice ★ 🏨 **Biniarroca Boutique Hotel.** Antique embroidered bed linens, shelves with knickknacks, and comfy chairs—this is an English vision of a peaceful and secluded rural retreat, and its glory is the garden of irises, lavender, and flowering trees. **Pros:** friendly personal service; some suites have private terraces. **Cons:** bit of a drive to the beach; some low ceilings; not child-friendly. [$] *Rooms from: €210* ✉ *Cami Vell 57, Sant Lluís* ☎ *971/150059, 619/460942* 🌐 *www.biniarroca.com* 🛏 *17 rooms, 1 suite* 🕒 *Closed Nov.–Mar.* 🍽 *Breakfast.*

$$$ B&B/INN 🏨 **Casa Albertí.** In a perfect location for exploring Mahón, this historic property has a new lease on life as a friendly, comfortable boutique hotel. **Pros:** good-natured, anything-to-help hospitality; walking distance to the port. **Cons:** no parking; bathrooms could use some modernization; no elevator. [$] *Rooms from: €160* ✉ *Carrer Isabel II 9* ☎ *686/393569* 🌐 *www.casalberti.com* 🛏 *5 rooms, 2 suites* 🕒 *Closed Oct.–Apr.* 🍽 *Breakfast.*

$$$$ HOTEL 🏨 **Hotel Port Mahón.** Renovated in 2012, this standby may not win many prizes for imaginative design, but it's a solid choice, with rooms with hardwood floors, generic but comfortable furniture, and plenty of closet space. **Pros:** decent value for price; friendly service; good buffet breakfast; easy to park nearby. **Cons:** pool and garden front on a busy street;

no pets. $ *Rooms from: €200* ✉ *Av. Fort de l'Eau s/n* ☎ *971/362600* ⊕ *www.sethotels.com/en/hotel-port-mahon-menorca.php* ⌁ *74 rooms, 8 suites* ☉ *Breakfast.*

$$$$
B&B/INN
Fodor's Choice
★
🏠 Jardi de Ses Bruixes. Built in 1811 by a Spanish ship captain, this *casa señorial* (town house) in the heart of Mahón was lovingly restored by its architect and co-owner Fernando Pons and opened in 2014 as a boutique hotel. **Pros:** amiable, eager-to-please staff; strategic location; at-home atmosphere. **Cons:** difficult to reach by car, or to park; bathtubs in the bedrooms sacrifice privacy to design. $ *Rooms from: €230* ✉ *Calle de San Fernando 6* ☎ *620/226912, 971/363166* ⊕ *www. hotelsesbruixes.com* ⌁ *8 rooms* ☉ *Breakfast.*

$$$$
B&B/INN
🏠 Sant Joan de Binissaida. An avenue lined with chinaberry and fig trees leads to this lovely restored farmhouse with environmental qualities, including some solar power and organic produce from the farm. **Pros:** vistas clear to the port of Mahón, about 15 km (10 miles) away; huge pool; child-friendly. **Cons:** bit of a drive to the nearest beach; rooms in the annex lack privacy; short season, with minimum booking three nights in summer. $ *Rooms from: €266* ✉ *Camí de Toraixa a Binissaida 108, Es Castell* ☎ *971/355598* ⊕ *www.binissaida.com* ⌁ *9 rooms, 3 suites* ☉ *Closed Jan.–Apr.* ☉ *No meals.*

NIGHTLIFE

Akelarre Jazz & Dance Club. This stylish bar near the port has a café-terrace downstairs and live jazz and blues on Thursday and Friday nights. It's open year-round from 10:30 am to 4 am, and serves tapas and snacks to share in the evening. ✉ *Moll de Ponent 41–43* ☎ *971/368520.*

Club El Padrino. This lively spot on the waterfront is open all year, with live music and stage shows, from 8 pm to 4 am. ✉ *Carrer Andana de Llevant 66* ☎ *971/365367.*

Cova d'en Xoroi. The hottest spot in Menorca is a 20-minute drive from Mahón in the beach resort of Cala en Porter. This dance-until-dawn disco is in a series of caves in a cliff high above the sea that, according to local legend, was once the refuge of a castaway Moorish pirate. ✉ *Carrer Cova s/n, Cala d'en Porter* ☎ *971/377236* ⊕ *www.covadenxoroi. com* 🎫 *Afternoon/evening chill-out sessions with live music from €12, night sessions from €20.*

Es Cau. Dug like a cave into the bluff of the little cove of Cala Corb, this is where locals gather (Thursday through Saturday night, from 10 pm to 3 am) to sing and play guitar—*habañeras,* love songs, songs of exile and return; everyone knows the songs and they all join in. It's hard to find, but anybody in Es Castell can point the way. ✉ *Cala Corb s/n, Es Castell.*

SPORTS AND THE OUTDOORS
CYCLING

Asociación Cicloturista de Menorca. Ask here about organized bike tours of the island. ✉ *Moll de Llevant 173* ☎ *971/364816, 610/464816* ⊕ *www. menorcacicloturista.com/en.*

Bike Menorca ✉ *Av. Francesc Femenias 44* ☎ *971/353798.*

9

DIVING

The clear Mediterranean waters here are ideal for diving. Equipment and lessons are available at Cala En Bosc, Son Parc, Fornells, Ciutadella, and Cala Tirant, among others.

GOLF

Golf Son Parc. Menorca's sole golf course, designed by Dave Thomas, is 9 km (6 miles) east of Mercadal, about a 20-minute drive from Mahon in the Son Parc urbanización. Rocky bunkers, and the occasional stray peacock on the fairways, make this an interesting and challenging course. The club, open year-round, also has two composition tennis courts. ⊠ *Urbinización Son Parc s/n, Es Mercadal* ☎ *971/188875, 971/359059* ⊕ *www.golfsonparc.com* ⚓ *18 holes, par 69, 5655 yds. Greens fee: €40–€69 for 18 holes, €20–€45 for 9 holes* ☞ *Facilities: driving range, putting green, pitching area, pull carts, buggies, rental clubs, lessons, restaurant, bar.*

WALKING

In the south, each cove is approached by a *barranca* (ravine or gully), often from several miles inland. The head of **Barranca Algendar** is down a small, unmarked road immediately on the right of the Ferreries–Cala Galdana Road; the barranca ends at the local beach resort, and from there you have a lovely walk north along the sea to an unspoiled half moon of sand at **Cala Macarella**. Extend your walk north, if time allows, through the forest along the riding trail to **Cala Turqueta,** where you'll find some of the island's most impressive grottoes.

SHOPPING

Menorca is known for shoes and leather goods, as well as cheese, gin, and wine. Wine was an important part of the menorcan economy as long back as the 18th century: the British, who knew a good place to grow grapes when they saw one, planted the island thick with vines. Viticulture was abandoned when Menorca returned to the embrace of Spain, and it has reemerged only in the past few years.

Boba's. Duck into the little alley between Carrer Nou and Carrer de l'Angel, and discover the atelier where Llorenç Pons makes his *espardenyes d'autor*: traditional rope-soled sandals in original and surprising designs. ⊠ *Pont de l'Angel 4* ☎ *647/587456.*

Bodegas Binifadet. This is the most promising of the handful of the local wineries, with robust young reds and whites on the shelves all over Menorca. The owners have expanded their product line into sparkling Chardonnay (sold only on the premises), olive oil, jams and conserves, and wine-based soaps and cosmetics. It's all well worth a visit, not merely for tastings, but (weather permitting) for a meal on the terrace, open from 9 am to 1 am, June through October. Binifadet's young Italian-Argentine chef serves up light breakfasts, lunches, and dinners— the Menorcan red prawns in sea salt (€17) are great. In midsummer reservations are a must. ⊠ *Ses Barraques s/n, Sant Lluís* ☎ *971/150715* ⊕ *www.binifadet.com.*

Pons Quintana. This showroom has a full-length window overlooking the factory where its very chic women's shoes are made. It's closed weekends. ✉ *Carrer Sant Antoni 120, Alaior* ✛ *13 km (8 miles) northeast of Mahón* ☎ *971/379320* ⊕ *www.ponsquintana.com/en.*

Xoriguer. One gastronomic legacy of the British occupation was gin. Visit this distillery on Mahón's quayside near the ferry terminal, where you can take a guided tour, sample various types of gin, and buy some to take home. ✉ *Anden de Poniente 91* ☎ *971/362197.*

CIUTADELLA

44 km (27 miles) west of Mahón.

Ciutadella was Menorca's capital before the British settled in Mahón, and its history is richer. Settled successively by the Phoenicians, Greeks, Carthaginians, and Romans, Ciutadella fell to the Moors in 903 and became a part of the Caliphate of Córdoba until 1287, when Alfonso III of Aragón reconquered it. He gave estates in Ciutadella to nobles who aided him in the battle, and to this day the old historic center of town has a distinctively aristocratic tone. In 1558 a Turkish armada laid siege to Ciutadella, burning the city and enslaving its inhabitants. It was later rebuilt, but never quite regained its former stature.

As you arrive via the ME1, the main artery across the island from Mahón, turn left at the second traffic circle and follow the ring road to the Passeig Marítim; at the end, near the **Castell de Sant Nicolau** is a **monument to David Glasgow Farragut,** the first admiral of the U.S. Navy, whose father emigrated from Ciutadella to the United States. From here, take Passeig de Sant Nicolau to the **Plaēa de s'Esplanada** and park near the Plaça d'es Born.

GETTING HERE AND AROUND
Autocares Torres has a single bus line running between Ciutadella and the beaches and calas near the city.

ESSENTIALS
Bus Contact Autocares Torres ⊕ *www.bus.e-torres.net/en.*

Bus Station Ciutadella ✉ *Pl. de S'Esplanada s/n.*

Taxi Contact Parada de Taxis de Ciutadella ☎ *971/482222.*

Visitor Information Ciutadella ✉ *Pl. des Born, Edifici Ajuntament* ☎ *971/484155.*

EXPLORING
Catedral. Carrer Major leads to this Gothic edifice, which has some beautifully carved choir stalls. The side chapel has round Moorish arches, remnants of the mosque that once stood on this site; the bell tower is a converted minaret. ✉ *Pl. de la Catedral at Pl. Píus XII* ☎ *971/380343* ☉ *Daily 8–1:30 and 5:30–8.*

Convento de Santa Clara. Carrer del Seminari is lined on the west side with some of the city's most impressive historic buildings. Among them is this 17th-century convent, which hosts Ciutadella's summer festival of classical music but is otherwise not open to the public. ✉ *Carrer del Seminari at Carrer Obispo Vila.*

9

Ciutadella's harbor, just below the main square and lined with restaurants, is perfect for a summer evening stroll.

Mirador d'es Port. From a passage on the left side of Ciutadella's columned and crenellated Ajuntament on the west side of the Born, steps lead up to this lookout. From here you can survey the harbor. ✉ *Pl. d'Es Born.*

Museu Municipal. The museum houses artifacts of Menorca's prehistoric, Roman, and medieval past, including records of land grants made by Alfonso III to the local nobility after defeating the Moors. It occupies an ancient defense tower, the Bastió de Sa Font (Bastion of the Fountain), at the east end of the harbor. ✉ *Pl. de sa Font s/n* ☎ *971/380297* ⊕ *www.ciutadella.org/museu* 🖾 *€2.46 (free Wed.)* 🕙 *Tues–Sat. 10–2.*

Palau Salort. This is the only noble house in Ciutadella that's open to the public, albeit at unpredictable times. The coats of arms on the ceiling are those of the families Salort (*sal* and *ort*, a salt pit and a garden) and Martorell (a marten). ✉ *Carrer Major des Born* 🖾 *€2* 🕙 *May–Oct., Mon.–Sat. 10–2 (hrs vary).*

Palau Torresaura. The blocklong 19th-century Palau Torresaura was built by the Baron of Torresaura, one of the noble families from Aragón and Catalonia that moved to Menorca after it was captured from the Moors in the 13th century. The interesting facade faces the plaza, though the entrance is on the side street. It is not open to the public. ✉ *Carrer Major del Born 8.*

Port. Ciutadella's port is accessible from steps that lead down from Carrer Sant Sebastià. The waterfront here is lined with seafood restaurants, some of which burrow into caverns far under the Born.

BEACHES

Cala Macarella and Cala Macaralleta. What just might be the two most beautiful of Menorca's small beaches, Cala Macarella and Cala Macaralleta, are reachable three ways: by boat, by car from the ME1 Mahón–Ciutadella highway, or on foot, from the little resort town of Cala Galdana (for the robust and ambitious, this last option is definitely the best way). Best among the hotels and chalets in Cala Galdana itself is probably the Artiem Audex Spa & Wellness Center, for its privileged place on the outlook at the end of the beach; just across the road you pick up the Cami de Cavalls riding trail, a 30-minute-or-so walk through the pine forest, around the point of the cove, to Cala Macarella. It's worth the effort: the water off this little crescent of white-sand beach on the southwest coast is breathtakingly turquoise and blue, calm and shallow, and sheltered by rocks on both sides. Remote as it is, Cala Macarella is popular with locals as well as vacationers; a 10-minute walk along the cliffs brings you to the even smaller and more tranquil Cala Macaralleta, where there are no facilities and fewer sunseekers. **Amenities:** food and drink; lifeguard; parking; toilets. **Best for:** swimming; walking. ✉ *Urbinización Serpentona, 4 km (2½ miles) west of Cala Galdana, via Costa Mirador.*

WHERE TO EAT AND STAY

$$$ SEAFOOD 🍴 **Cafe Balear.** Seafood doesn't get much fresher than here, as the owners' boat docks nearby every day except Sunday. The relaxed atmosphere welcomes either a quick bite or a full dining experience. The house special, *arroz caldoso de langosta* (lobster and rice stew), is very impressive, as is the *carpaccio d'emperador* (thin slices of swordfish marinated in lemon, salt, and olive oil), *cigalas* (crayfish), lobster with onion, and grilled *navajas* (razor clams). [$] *Average main: €19* ✉ *Paseo San Juan 15* ☎ *971/380005* 🕒 *Closed Nov., Mon. July–Sept., and Sun. Dec.–June.*

$$$$ SEAFOOD 🍴 **S'Amarador.** Located at the foot of the stairs that lead down to the port, this recent addition to the Ciutadella restaurant scene has a café-terrace out front that's perfect for people-watching, drinks, and tapas—and a pleasant umbrella-shaded patio inside. Fresh seafood in any form is a sure bet here: try the John Dory, baked, grilled, or fried with garlic (€25)—or spring for the caldereta (€65), spiny lobster stew. The wine list at S'Amarador is impressive, with local labels and rich reds from Priorat, Montsant, La Rioja, and Ribera del Duero. [$] *Average main: €23* ✉ *Port de Ciutadella s/n* ☎ *971/383524* 🕒 *Closed Feb., and Mon. Nov.–Mar.*

$$$$ B&B/INN FAMILY 🏨 **Hotel Rural Sant Ignasi.** About 10 minutes by car from the central square, this comfortable manor house dates to 1777 and is a favorite with young Spanish families. **Pros:** good value for price; friendly staff. **Cons:** kids in the pool all day; short season; minimum 3-day stay in summer. [$] *Rooms from: €245* ✉ *Ronda Norte s/n* ✣ *Take the Ronda Norte to the second roundabout at the Poligon Industrial; just past the roundabout turn left on Son Juaneda and follow the signs* ☎ *971/385575* 🌐 *www.santignasi.com* 🛏 *16 rooms, 9 suites* 🕒 *Closed Oct. 28–Apr. 25* 🍽 *Breakfast.*

9

$$$$ B&B/INN Fodor's Choice ★ [H] **Hotel Tres Sants.** This chic boutique hotel is in the heart of Ciutadella, on a narrow cobblestone street behind the cathedral, and has killer views from the rooftop terrace, extending over the old city and (in good weather) across the ocean as far as Mallorca. **Pros:** suites for families; ideal location for exploring the city. **Cons:** no parking; no elevator; no pets; communal breakfasts don't suit everyone. [$] *Rooms from: €190* ✉ *C. Sant Cristofol 2* ☎ *971/482208, 626/053536* 🌐 *www.hoteltressants.com* 🛏 *6 rooms, 2 suites* 🍴 *Breakfast.*

SPORTS AND THE OUTDOORS

HORSEBACK RIDING

Horseback riding, breeding, and dressage have been traditions on the island for hundreds of years, and the magnificent black Menorcan horses play an important role, not only as work animals and for sport, but also in shows and colorful local festivals. There are 17 riding clubs on the island, a number of which offer excursions on the rural lanes of the unspoiled countryside. The Camí de Cavalls is a riding route in 20 stages that completely circumnavigates the island. Cavalls Son Angel in Ciutadella, Centre Equestre Equimar in Es Castell, and Menorca a Cavall in Ferreries organize excursions for adults and children. Son Martorellet, on the road to the beach at Cala Galdana, is a ranch where you can visit the stables and watch dressage training exhibitions every Wednesday and Thursday afternoon at 3:30; there's an equestrian show in traditional costume every Saturday at 4:30, from February to November.

Cavalls Son Àngel. This equestrian center specializes in excursions along the Cami de Cavalls, the horseback route that circumnavigates the island, with rides that range from 1–3 hours for beginners to 5-day trips with lunches en route. ✉ *Camí d'Algaiarens s/n* ☎ *609/833902, 649/488098* 🌐 *www.cavallssonangel.com.*

FAMILY **Centre Ecuestre Equimar.** One-hour beginner classes here are €20; excursions on horseback to the beach or countryside are from €20 to €72, depending on the length of the ride and the destination; there are also 30-minute pony rides for €10. ✉ *Calle Verdi, Km 1, Es Castell* ☎ *685/532637, 669/255487* 🌐 *www.menorcahorseriding.com.*

Menorca a Cavall ✉ *Finca Es Calafat, Ctra. Ferreries–Cala Galdana (ME22), Km 4.3, Ferreries* ☎ *971/374637, 626/593737* 🌐 *www.menorcaacavall.com.*

Son Martorellet ✉ *Ctra. Ferreries–Cala Galdana, Km 1.7, Ferreries* ☎ *971/373406, 639/156851* 🌐 *www.sonmartorellet.com.*

SHOPPING

The industrial complex (*polígono industrial*) on the right as you enter Ciutadella has a number of shoe factories, each with a shop. Prices may be the same as in stores, but the selection is wider. In Plaça d'es Born, a market is held on Friday and Saturday.

For the best shopping, try the Ses Voltes area, the Es Rodol zone near Plaça Artrutx and Ses Voltes, and along the Camí de Maó between Plaça Palmeras and Plaça d'es Born.

ARTEME (*Associació d'Empreses d'Artesania de Menorca*). The town's only *alferería* (pottery workshop) can be found here. ⊠ *Carrer Comerciants Botiguer 9, Polígono Industrial* ☎ 971/381550 ⊕ *www. artesansdemenorca.org.*

Hort Sant Patrici. This is a good place to buy the tangy, Parmesanlike Mahón cheese. There's a shop, beautiful grounds with a small vineyard and botanical garden, and a display of traditional cheese-making techniques and tools. On Monday, Tuesday, Thursday, and Saturday from 9–11 am you can watch the cheese being made. Hort Sant Patrici has its own vineyards and olive trees, and nestled among them is a new B&B, the **Canaxini** (⊕ *www.canaxini.com/home_en*), with eight rooms done in dazzling minimalist white. ⊠ *Camí Sant Patrici s/n, Ferreries* ✛ *18 km (11 miles) east of the ME1 at the second roundabout after Ferreries, on to Camí Sant Patrici* ☎ 971/373702 ⊕ *www. santpatrici.com* ☉ *Winter, weekdays 9–1 and 4–6, Sat. 9–1; summer, Mon.–Sat. 9–1:30 and 4:30–8.*

Jaime Mascaró. The showroom here, on the main highway from Alaior to Cuitadella, features not only shoes and bags but fine leather coats and belts for men and women. ⊠ *Polígono Industrial s/n, Ferreries, 18 km (11 miles) east of Ciutadella* ☎ 971/373837, 971/374539 ⊕ *www. mascaro.com.*

Maria Juanico. Maria Juanico makes her interesting plated and anodized silver jewelry and accessories at a workshop in the back of her store. It's closed on Saturday afternoon and Sunday. ⊠ *Carrer Seminari 38, Ciutadella* ☎ 971/480879 ⊕ *www.mariajuanico.com/en/tienda.*

Nadia Rabosio. This inventive designer has created an original selection of jewelry and hand-painted silks. ⊠ *Carrer Santissim 4* ☎ 971/384080.

EL TORO

9

24 km (15 miles) northwest of Mahón.

The peak of El Toro is Menorca's highest point, at all of 1,555 feet. From the monastery on top you can see the whole island and across the sea to Mallorca.

GETTING HERE

Follow signs in Es Mercadal, the crossroads at the island's center.

WHERE TO EAT

$$$ ✕ **Molí d'es Reco.** A great place to stop for a lunch of typical local cuisine, CATALAN this restaurant is in an old windmill at the west end of Es Mercadal, on the ME1 highway, about halfway between Mahón and Ciutadella and about 4 km (2½ miles) from El Toro. It has fortress-thick whitewashed stone walls and low vaulted ceilings, and a constant air of cheerful bustle. On warm summer days there are tables on the terrace. Menorcan specialties here include squid stuffed with anglerfish and shrimp, and chicken with *centollo* (spider crab). The thick vegetable soup, called *sopas menorquinas,* is excellent. $ *Average main: €19* ⊠ *Carrer Major 53, Mercadal* ☎ 971/375392.

FORNELLS

35 km (21 miles) northwest of Mahón.

A little village (full-time population: 500) of whitewashed houses with red-tile roofs, Fornells comes alive in the summer high season, when Spanish and Catalan families arrive in droves to open their holiday chalets at the edge of town and in the nearby beach resorts. The bay—Menorca's second largest and deepest—is good for windsurfing, sailing, and scuba diving. The first fortifications built here to defend the Bay of Fornells from pirates date to 1625.

GETTING HERE AND AROUND

Buses leave the Estació Autobusos on Calle José Anselmo Clavé in Mahón for the 50-minute 40-km (24-mile) trip to Fornells at 10:30, 12:30, 3, 5 and 7. By car, it's an easy half-hour drive north on route PM710.

WHERE TO EAT

$$$ ✕ **Es Pla.** The modest wooden exterior of this harborside restaurant is
SEAFOOD misleading—Es Pla has hosted royalty. King Juan Carlos made detours here during his sailing holidays in the Balearics, to sample its justly famous caldereta de langosta. This single costly dish skews an otherwise reasonably priced menu, but a prix-fixe caldereta menu, with steamed mussels or scallops in their shell for starters, along with dessert and coffee, is a bargain. Other excellent seafood dishes include grilled scorpion fish, scallops drizzled with olive oil, and anglerfish with *marisco* (seafood) sauce. $ *Average main: €22* ✉ *Pasaje Es Pla s/n, Puerto de Fornells* ☎ *971/376655.*

SPORTS AND OUTDOORS
SAILING

Several miles long and a mile wide but with a narrow entrance to the sea and virtually no waves, the Bay of Fornells gives the beginner a feeling of security and the expert plenty of excitement.

Wind Fornells. Here, on the beach just off Carrer del Rosari, you can rent windsurfing boards and dinghies, and take lessons, individually or in groups. It's open May through October. ✉ *Ctra. Es Mercadal–Fornells s/n, Es Mercadal* ☎ *664/335801* ⊕ *www.windfornells.com.*

COVA DES COLOMS

40 km (24 miles) west of Mahón.

There are caverns and grottoes all over the Balearics, some of them justly famous because of their size, spectacular formations, and subterranean pools. This one is well worth a visit.

Cova des Coloms (*Cave of Pigeons*). This massive cave is the most spectacular on Menorca, with eerie rock formations rising up to a 77-foot-high ceiling. To reach the cave, drive along the road from Ferreries to St. Adeodato, then head down to the beach and walk west on the footpath about 10 minutes to the beach at Binigaus. Signs direct you from there to the gully, where you descend to the cave.

ANDALUSIA

WELCOME TO ANDALUSIA

TOP REASONS TO GO

★ **Appreciate exquisite architecture:** Granada's Alhambra and Córdoba's Mezquita are two of Spain's—if not the world's—most impressive sites.

★ **Dance the flamenco:** "Olé" deep into the night at a heel-clicking flamenco performance in Jerez de la Frontera, the "cradle of flamenco."

★ **Admire priceless paintings:** Bask in the golden age of Spanish art at Seville's Museo de Bellas Artes.

★ **Explore ancient glory:** Cádiz, believed to be the oldest port in Europe, is resplendent with its sumptuous architecture and a magnificent cathedral.

★ **Visit the white villages:** Enjoy the simple beauty of a bygone age by exploring the gleaming *pueblos blancos*.

BADAJOZ
PORTUGAL
CÓRDOBA
4
Aracena
Cortegana
Santa Olalla
Del Cala
Córdoba
Posadas
Valverde
del Camino
Palma Del Río
SEVILLE
1
Carmona
HUELVA 2
Itálica
Seville
Gibraleón
La Palma
Écija
Lucena
Marchena
San Juan del Puerto
Estepa
Huelva
El Arahal
Gulf of Cádiz
Utrera
Doñana
National Park
Antequera
Sanlucar
de Barrameda
Algodonales
MÁLAGA
Grazalema
Ronda
Jerez de
la Frontera
3
Marbella
Cádiz
CÁDIZ
Fuengirola
COSTA DE LA LUZ
Estepona
Conil
Algeciras
GIBRALTAR (U.K.)
Tarifa
STRAIT OF GIBRALTAR
CEUTA (Spain)
Tánger
MOROCCO

1 Seville. Long Spain's chief riverine port, the captivating city of Seville sits astride the Guadalquivir River, which launched Christopher Columbus to the New World and Ferdinand Magellan around the globe. South of the capital is fertile farmland; in the north are highland villages. Don't miss stunning, mountaintop Ronda (an hour's drive away), which has plenty of atmosphere and memorable sights.

2 Huelva. Famed as live oak–forested grazing grounds for the treasured *cerdo ibérico* (Iberian pig), Huelva's Sierra de Aracena is a fresh and leafy mountain getaway on the border of Portugal. The province's Doñana National Park is one of Spain's greatest national treasures.

3 Cádiz Province and Jerez de la Frontera. Almost completely surrounded by water, the

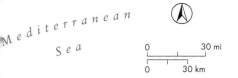

GETTING ORIENTED

Andalusia is infinitely varied and diverse within its apparent unity. Seville and Granada are like feuding sisters, one vivaciously flirting, the other darkly brooding; Córdoba and Cádiz are estranged cousins, one landlocked, the other virtually under sail; Huelva is a verdant Atlantic Arcadia; and Jaén is an upland country bumpkin—albeit one with Renaissance palaces—compared with the steamy cosmopolitan seaport of Málaga which, along with the southern Andalusian cities and towns of Marbella and Tarifa, is covered in the Costas chapter.

10

city of Cádiz is Western Europe's oldest continually inhabited city, a dazzling bastion at the edge of the Atlantic. Jerez de la Frontera is known for its sherry, flamenco, and equestrian culture.

4 Córdoba. A center of world science and philosophy in the 9th and 10th centuries, Córdoba is a living monument to its past glory. Its prized building is the Mezquita (mosque). In

the countryside, acorns and olives thrive.

5 Jaén. Andalusia's northeasternmost province is a striking contrast of olive groves, pristine wilderness, and Renaissance towns with elegant palaces and churches.

6 Granada. Christian and Moorish cultures are dramatically counterposed in Granada, especially in the graceful enclave of the Alhambra.

EATING AND DRINKING WELL IN ANDALUSIA

Andalusian cuisine, as diverse as the geography of seacoast, farmland, and mountains, is held together by its Moorish aromas. Cumin seed and other Arabian spices, along with sweet-salty combinations, are ubiquitous.

(top left) A cool bowl of gazpacho, with accompaniments to be added as desired (top right) Crispy fried fish are an Andalusian delicacy. (bottom left) Fried calamari with lemon

The eight Andalusian provinces cover a wide geographical and culinary spectrum. Superb seafood is at center stage in Cádiz, Puerto de Santa María, and Sanlúcar de Barrameda. *Jamon ibérico de bellota* (Iberian acorn-fed ham) and other Iberico pork products rule from the Sierra de Aracena in Huelva to the Pedroches Mountains north of Córdoba. In Seville look for products from the Guadalquivir estuary, the Sierra, and the rich Campiña farmland all prepared with great creativity. In Córdoba try *salmorejo cordobés* (a thick gazpacho), *rabo de toro* (oxtail stew), or representatives of the salty-sweet legacy from Córdoba's Moorish heritage such as *cordero con miel* (lamb with honey). Spicy *crema de almendras* (almond soup) is a Granada favorite along with *habas con jamón* (broad beans with ham) from the Alpujarran village of Trevélez.

SHERRY

Dry sherry from Jerez de la Frontera (*fino*) and from Sanlúcar de Barrameda (*manzanilla*), share honors as favorite tapas accompaniments. Manzanilla, the more popular choice, is fresher and more delicate, with a slight marine tang. Both are the preferred drinks at Andalusian *ferias* (fairs), particularly in Seville in April and Jerez de la Frontera in May.

COLD VEGETABLE SOUPS

Spain's most popular contribution to world gastronomy after paella may well be *gazpacho*, a simple peasant soup served cold and filled with scraps and garden ingredients. Tomatoes, cucumber, garlic, oil, bread, and chopped peppers are the ingredients, and side plates of chopped onion, peppers, garlic, tomatoes, and croutons accompany, to be added to taste. *Salmorejo cordobés*, a thicker cold vegetable soup with the same ingredients but a different consistency, is used to accompany tapas.

MOORISH FLAVORS

Andalusia's 781-year sojourn at the heart of Al-Andalus, the Moorish empire on the Iberian Peninsula, left as many tastes and aromas as mosques and fortresses. Cumin-laced *boquerones en adobo* (marinated anchovies) or the salty-sweet *cordero a la miel* (lamb with honey) are two examples, along with coriander-spiked *espinacas con garbanzos* (spinach with garbanzo beans) and *perdiz con dátiles y almendras* (partridge stewed with dates and almonds). Desserts especially reflect the Moorish legacy in morsels such as *pestiños*, cylinders or twists of fried dough in anise-honey syrup.

FRIED FISH

Andalusia is famous for its fried fish, from *pescaito frito* (fried whitebait) to *calamares fritos* (fried squid rings).

Andalusians are masters of deep-frying techniques using very hot olive and vegetable oils that produce peerlessly crisp, dry *frituras* (fried seafood); much of Andalusia's finest tapas repertory is known for being served up piping hot and crunchy. Look for *tortilla de camarones*, a delicate lacework of tiny fried shrimp.

STEWS

Guisos are combinations of vegetables, with or without meat, cooked slowly over low heat. *Rabo de toro* is a favorite throughout Andalusia, though Córdoba claims the origin of this dark and delicious stew made from the tail of a fighting bull. The segments of tail are cleaned, browned, and set aside before leeks, onions, carrots, garlic, and bay leaves are stewed in the same pan. Cloves, salt, pepper, a liter of wine, and a half liter of beef broth are added to the stew with the meat, and they're all simmered for two to three hours until the meat is falling off the bone and thoroughly tenderized. *Alboronía*, also known as *pisto andaluz,* is a traditional stew of eggplant, bell peppers, and zucchini, a recipe traced back to 9th-century Baghdad and brought to Córdoba by the Umayyad dynasty.

10

ANDALUSIA'S WHITE VILLAGES

Looking a bit like sugar cubes spilled onto a green tablecloth, Andalusia's *pueblos blancos* (white villages) are usually found nestled on densely wooded hills, clinging to the edges of deep gorges, or perched precariously on hilltops.

(top left) The white houses, with their red-tile roofs, are quintessential Andalusia. (top right) The winding streets of Frigiliana can be confusing. (bottom left) Gaucín is an easy trip from Ronda.

The picturesque locations of the pueblos blancos usually have more to do with defense than anything else, and many have crumbling walls and fortifications that show their use as defensive structures along the frontier between the Christian and Moorish realms. In a few, the remains of magnificent Moorish castles can be spied. The suffix *de la frontera*, literally meaning "on the frontier," tacked onto a town's name relates to this historical border position. A visit to the white villages gives a glimpse into a simpler time when the economy was based on agriculture, architecture was built to withstand the climate, and life moved at more of a donkey-plod pace. Little wonder that many foreign residents have moved to these rural communities in a bid to discover a more tranquil life, far from the crowds and clamor of the coast.

PICASSO'S CUBES

It's been suggested that Picasso, who was born in Málaga, was inspired to create Cubism by the pueblos blancos of his youth. The story may be apocryphal, but it's nonetheless easy to imagine—there *is* something wondrous and inspiring about Andalusia's whitewashed villages, with their houses that seem to tumble down the mountain slopes like giant dice.

VEJER DE LA FRONTERA

This dazzling white town is perched high on a hill, perfectly positioned to protect its citizens from the threat of marauding pirates. Today it is one of the most charming pueblos blancos on the Cádiz coast, known for its meandering cobbled lanes, narrow arches, and large number of atmospheric bars and restaurants. More recently, Vejer has been popular with an artsy crowd that has brought contemporary art galleries, crafts shops, and low-key music venues.

FRIGILIANA

This impossibly pretty whitewashed village is 7 km (4½ miles) north of the well-known resort of Nerja. Despite the encroachment of modern apartment buildings, the old center has remained relatively unchanged. Pots of crimson geraniums decorate the narrow streets, while the bars proudly serve the local sweet wine. Frigiliana is a good place for seeking out ceramics made by the town's craftspeople. Hikers can enjoy the 3-km (2-mile) hike from the old town to the hilltop El Fuerte, site of a 1569 skirmish between the Moors and the Christians (⇨ Chapter 11).

GAUCÍN

The countryside surrounding Ronda is stunning, especially in the spring when the ground is carpeted with wildflowers, including exquisite purple orchids. Not surprisingly, the Serranía de Ronda

(as this area is known) is famous for its superb walking. Gaucín is a lovely village crowned by a ruined Moorish castle. It is popular with artists who open their studios to the public each year (see ⊕ *www.artgaucin.com* for dates). The town also has several excellent restaurants and a couple of sophisticated boutique hotels.

PITRES AND LA TAHA

Granada's Alpujarras Mountains are home to some of Andalusia's most unspoiled white villages. Two of the best known are Bubión and Capileira, while Pitres and La Taha villages of Mecina, Mecinilla, Fondales, Ferreirola, and Atalbéitar are lovely hamlets separated by rough tracks that wind through orchards and woodland, set in a valley that attracts few visitors.

GRAZALEMA

About a half hour from Ronda, Grazalema is the prettiest—and the whitest—of the white towns. It's a lovely, small town, worth some time wandering, and well situated for a visit to the mountains of the Sierra de Grazalema Natural Park.

10

Updated by
Joanna Styles

Gypsies, flamenco, horses, bulls—Andalusia is the Spain of story and song, simultaneously the least and most surprising part of the country: least surprising because it lives up to the hype and stereotype that long confused all of Spain with the Andalusian version, and most surprising because it is, at the same time, so much more.

To begin with, five of the eight Andalusian provinces are maritime, with colorful fishing fleets and a wealth of seafood usually associated with the north. Second, there are snowcapped mountains and ski resorts in Andalusia, the kind of high sierra resources normally associated with the Alps, or even the Pyrenees, yet the Sierra Nevada, with Granada at the foothills, is within sight of North Africa. Third, there are wildlife-filled wetlands and highland pine and oak forests rich with game and trout streams, not to mention free-range Iberian pigs. And last, there are cities like Seville that somehow manage to combine all of this with the creativity and cosmopolitanism of London or Barcelona.

Andalusia—for 781 years (711–1492) a Moorish empire and named for Al-Andalus (Arabic for "Land of the West")—is where the authentic history and character of the Iberian Peninsula and Spanish culture are most palpably, visibly, audibly, and aromatically apparent.

An exploration of Andalusia must begin with the cities of Seville, Córdoba, and Granada as the fundamental triangle of interest and identity. All the romantic images of Andalusia, and Spain in general, spring vividly to life in Seville: Spain's fourth-largest city is a cliché of matadors, flamenco, tapas bars, Gypsies, geraniums, and strolling guitarists, but there's so much more than these urban treasures. A more thorough Andalusian experience includes such unforgettable natural settings as Huelva's Sierra de Aracena and Doñana wetlands, Jaén's Parque Natural de Cazorla, Cádiz's pueblos blancos, and Granada's Alpujarras mountains.

PLANNING

WHEN TO GO

The best months to go to Andalusia are October and November and April and May. It's blisteringly hot in the summer, so, if that's your only chance to come, plan time in the Pedroches of northern Córdoba province, Granada's Sierra Nevada and Alpujarras highlands, or the Sierra de Cazorla in Jaén to beat the heat. Autumn catches the cities going about their business, the temperatures are moderate, and you will rarely see a line form.

December through March tends to be cool, uncrowded, and quiet, but come spring, it's fiesta time, with Seville's Semana Santa (Holy Week, between Palm Sunday and Easter) the most moving and multitudinous. April showcases whitewashed Andalusia at its floral best, every patio and facade covered with flowers from bougainvillea to honeysuckle.

PLANNING YOUR TIME

A week in Andalusia should include visits to Córdoba, Seville, and Granada to see, respectively, the Mezquita, the cathedral and its Giralda minaret, and the Alhambra. Two days in each city nearly fills the week, though the extra day would be best spent in Seville, Andalusia's most vibrant concentration of art, architecture, culture, and excitement.

Indeed, a week or more in Seville alone would be ideal, especially during the Semana Santa celebration, when the city becomes a giant street party. With more time on your hands, Cádiz, Jerez de la Frontera, and Sanlúcar de Barrameda form a three- or four-day jaunt through flamenco, sherry, Andalusian equestrian culture, and tapas emporiums.

A three-day trip through the Sierra de Aracena will introduce you to a lovely Atlantic upland, filled with Mediterranean black pigs deliciously fattened on acorns, while the Alpujarras, the mountain range east of Granada, is famed for its pueblos blancos. In this region you can find anywhere from three days to a week of hiking and trekking opportunities in some of the highest and wildest reaches in Spain. For nature enthusiasts, the highland Cazorla National Park and the wetland Doñana National Park are Andalusia's highest and lowest outdoor treasures.

10

FESTIVALS

Andalusia has some of Spain's most important and most colorful festivals, and highlights include **Carnival,** on the days leading up to Ash Wednesday, and **Semana Santa** (Holy Week, between Palm Sunday and Easter). Both are big celebrations, especially in Cádiz, Córdoba, and Seville. Other events range from international music festivals to more localized celebrations, such as the early August horse races on the beaches of Sanlúcar de Barrameda and the mid-October olive harvest in Jaén.

Concurso Nacional de Flamenco (*National Flamenco Competition*). Devotees of Spain's unique style of music and dance flock to the city for this event, held every third year—the next is in 2016—in November. ✉ *Córdoba.*

Cruces de Mayo (*Festival of Crosses*). Celebrated throughout the Spanish-speaking world, this ancient festival is a highlight of Córdoba's calendar of events, with lots of flower-decked crosses and other floral displays, processions, and music. ⊠ *Córdoba*.

Encuentro Flamenco. Some of the country's best performers are featured in this early-December event in Granada. ⊠ *Granada*.

Feria de Abril (*April Fair*). Held two weeks after Easter, this secular celebration focuses on horses and bullfights. ⊠ *Seville*.

Ferio de Mayo. The city's foremost street party is held during the last week of May. ⊠ *Córdoba*.

Feria del Caballo (*Horse Fair*). In early May, carriages and riders fill the streets of Jerez and purebreds from the School of Equestrian Art compete in races and dressage displays. ⊠ *Jerez de la Frontera*.

Festival de los Patios (*Patio Festival*). This celebration is held during the second week of May, a fun time to be in the city, when owners throw open their flower-decked patios to visitors (and to judges, who nominate the best), and the city celebrates with food, drink, and flamenco. ⊠ *Córdoba*.

Festival Internacional de Jazz de Granada. Established in 1980, this November festival attracts big names from the world of jazz. Oscar Peterson, Dizzy Gillespie, Miles Davis, and Herbie Hancock, among many others, have delighted fans. ⊠ *Granada* ⊕ *www.jazzgranada.net*.

Festival Internacional de Música y Danza de Granada. With some events in the Alhambra itself, this international music and dance festival runs from mid-June to mid-July. Tickets go on sale in mid-April. ⊠ *Granada* ⊕ *www.granadafestival.org*.

Fiesta de Otoño (*Autumn Festival*). In September, this festival in Jerez celebrates the grape harvest and includes a procession, the blessing of the harvest on the steps of the cathedral, and traditional-style grape treading. ⊠ *Jerez de la Frontera*.

International Guitar Festival. During the first two weeks of July, an array of major international artists perform at this celebration of guitar music, including classical, jazz, rock, folk, and—of course—flamenco. In addition to a full schedule of concerts, there are exhibitions, workshops, and conferences. ⊠ *Córdoba* ⊕ *www.guitarracordoba.org*.

La Bienal de Flamencol. Celebrating flamenco, this festival is held in Seville every two years, the next being in 2016. ⊠ *Seville* ⊕ *www.labienal.com*.

Romería del Rocío. Early June in Huelva means this gypsy favorite—a pilgrimage on horseback and by carriage to the hermitage of La Virgen del Rocío (Our Lady of the Dew). ⊠ *Huelva*.

GETTING HERE AND AROUND
AIR TRAVEL
Andalusia's regional airports can be reached via Spain's domestic flights or from major European hubs. Málaga Airport (⇨ *Costa del Sol and Costa de Almería*) is one of Spain's major hubs and a good access point for exploring this part of Andalusia.

The region's second-largest airport, after Málaga, is in Seville. The smaller Aeropuerto de Jerez is 7 km (4 miles) northeast of Jerez on the road to Seville. Buses run from the airport to Jerez and Cádiz. Flying into Granada's airport is also a good option if you want to start your trip in Andalusia. It's easy to get into Granada from the airport.

BUS TRAVEL

The best way to get around Andalusia, if you're not driving, is by bus. Buses serve most small towns and villages and are faster and more frequent than trains. ALSA is the major bus company; tickets can be booked online.

Bus Line ALSA ☎ *902/422242* ⊕ *www.alsa.es.*

CAR TRAVEL

If you're planning to explore beyond Seville, Granada, and Córdoba, a car makes travel convenient.

The main road from Madrid is the A4 through Córdoba to Seville, a four-lane *autovía* (highway). From Granada or Málaga, head for Antequera, then take A92 autovía by way of Osuna to Seville. Road trips from Seville to the Costa del Sol (by way of Ronda) are slow but scenic. Driving in western Andalusia is easy—the terrain is mostly flat land or slightly hilly, and the roads are straight and in good condition. From Seville to Jerez and Cádiz, the A4 toll road gets you to Cádiz in under an hour. The only way to access Doñana National Park by road is to take the A49 Seville–Huelva highway, exit for Almonte/Bollullos Par del Condado, then follow the signs for El Rocío and Matalascañas. The A49 west of Seville will also lead you to the freeway to Portugal and the Algarve. There are some beautiful scenic drives here, about which the respective tourist offices can advise you. The A369, heading southwest from Ronda to Gaucín, passes through stunning whitewashed villages.

With the exception of parts of the Alpujarras, most roads in this region are smooth, and touring by car is one of the most enjoyable ways to see the countryside. Local tourist offices can advise about scenic drives. One good route heads northwest from Seville on the A66 passing through stunning scenery; turn northeast on the A461 to Santa Olalla de Cala to the village of Zufre, dramatically set at the edge of a gorge. Backtrack and continue on to Aracena. Return via the Minas de Riotinto (signposted from Aracena), which will bring you back to the A66 heading east to Seville.

Rental contact Autopro ✉ *Málaga* ☎ *952/176545* ⊕ *www.autopro.es.*

FERRY TRAVEL

From Cádiz, Trasmediterránea operates ferry services to the Canary Islands with stops at Las Palmas de Gran Canaria (39 hours) and connecting ferries on to La Palma (19 hours) and Santa Cruz de Tenerife (4 hours). There are no direct ferries from Seville.

Contact Acciona Trasmediterránea ✉ *Estación Marítima, Cádiz* ☎ *902/454645* ⊕ *www.trasmediterranea.es.*

10

TAXI TRAVEL

Taxis are plentiful throughout Andalusia and may be hailed on the street or from specified taxi stands. Fares are reasonable, and meters are strictly used; the minimum fare is about €4. You are not required to tip taxi drivers, although rounding off the amount is appreciated.

In Seville or Granada, expect to pay around €20–€25 for cab fare from the airport to the city center.

TRAIN TRAVEL

From Madrid, the best approach to Andalusia is via the high-speed AVE. In just 2½ hours, the spectacular ride winds through olive groves and rolling fields of Castile to Córdoba and on to Seville.

Seville, Córdoba, Jerez, and Cádiz all lie on the main rail line from Madrid to southern Spain. Trains leave Madrid for Seville (via Córdoba); two of the non-AVE trains continue to Jerez and Cádiz. Travel time from Seville to Cádiz is 1¾ hours. Trains also depart regularly for Barcelona (3 daily, 5½ hours), and Huelva (3 daily, 1½ hours). From Granada, Málaga, Ronda, and Algeciras, trains go to Seville via Bobadilla.

RESTAURANTS

Eating out is an intrinsic part of the Andalusian lifestyle. Whether it's sharing some tapas with friends over a prelunch drink or a three-course à la carte meal, many Andalusians eat out at some point during the day. Unsurprisingly, there are literally thousands of bars and restaurants throughout the region catering to all budgets and tastes.

At lunchtime, check out the daily menus (*menús del día*) offered by many restaurants, usually three courses and excellent value (expect to pay between €8 and €15, depending on the type of restaurant and location). Roadside restaurants, known as *ventas,* usually provide good food in generous portions and at reasonable prices. Be aware that many restaurants add a service charge (*cubierto*), which can be as much as €3 per person, and some restaurant prices don't include value-added tax (*impuesto sobre el valor añadido/I.V.A.*) at 10%.

Andalusians tend to eat later than their fellow Spaniards—lunch is between 2 and 4 pm, and dinner starts at 9 pm (10 pm in the summer). In cities, many restaurants are closed Sunday night (fish restaurants tend to close on Monday) and in inland towns and cities, some close for all of August.

HOTELS

Seville has grand old hotels, such as the Alfonso XIII, and a number of former palaces converted into sumptuous hostelries.

The Parador de Granada, next to the Alhambra, is a magnificent way to enjoy Granada. Hotels on the Alhambra hill, especially the parador, must be reserved far in advance. Lodging establishments in Granada's city center, around the Puerta Real and Acera del Darro, can be unbelievably noisy, so if you're staying there, ask for a room toward the back. Though Granada has plenty of hotels, it can be difficult to find lodging during peak tourist season (Easter to late October).

In Córdoba, several pleasant hotels occupy houses in the old quarter, close to the mosque. Other than during Holy Week and the May Patio Festival, it's easy to find a room in Córdoba, even without a reservation.

Not all hotel prices include value-added tax (I.V.A.) and the 10% tax may be added to your final bill. Check when you book. *Hotel reviews have been shortened. For full information, visit Fodors.com.*

WHAT IT COSTS IN EUROS				
	$	$$	$$$	$$$$
Restaurants	under €13	€13–€17	€18–€22	over €22
Hotels	under €91	€91–€125	€126–€180	over €180

Restaurant prices are the average cost of a main course or equivalent combination of smaller dishes at dinner. Hotel prices are the lowest cost of a standard double room in high season

TOURS

Alúa. For help with planning and getting the equipment for hiking, rock climbing, mountain biking, caving, and other active sports throughout Andalusia, this is a good place to start. ⊠ *Calle Concejal Francisco Ruiz Librero, Bormujos, Seville* ☎ *955/984182* ⊕ *www.alua.es* ✆ *From €15.*

Cabalgar Rutas Alternativas. This is an established Alpujarras equestrian agency that organizes horseback riding in the Sierra Nevada. ⊠ *C. Ermita, Bubión* ☎ *958/763135* ⊕ *www.ridingandalucia.com* ✆ *From €25.*

Dallas Love. Trail rides in the Alpujarras, lasting up to a week, can be organized through this company. The price includes airport transfers, overnight stays, and most meals. ⊠ *Ctra. de la Sierra, Bubión* ☎ *608/453802* ⊕ *www.spain-horse-riding.com* ✆ *From €550.*

Excursiones Bujarkay. Guided hikes, horseback riding, and four-wheel-drive tours in the Sierra de Cazorla are offered. They can also help with rural accommodations. ⊠ *Calle Martínez Falero 28, Cazorla* ☎ *953/721111* ⊕ *www.bujarkay.com* ✆ *From €30.*

Faro del Sur. Activities such as trekking, cycling, sailing, and kayaking in western Andalusia are available, and tours include kayaking along the Guadalquivir River and sailing along the Huelva coastline. ⊠ *Puerto Deportivo L-1, Isla Cristina, Huelva* ☎ *959/344490* ⊕ *www.farodelsur.com* ✆ *From €500.*

Glovento Sur. Up to five people at a time are taken in balloon trips above Granada, Ronda, Sevilla, Córdoba, or other parts of the region. ⊠ *Placeta Nevot 4, 1A, Granada* ☎ *958/290316* ⊕ *www.gloventosur.com* ✆ *From €150 per person.*

Nevadensis. Based in the Alpujarras, Nevadensis leads guided hiking, climbing, and skiing tours of the Sierra Nevada. ⊠ *Pl. de la Libertad, Pampaneira* ☎ *958/763127* ⊕ *www.nevadensis.com* ✆ *From €150.*

SierraeXtreme. Choose from a wide range of adventure sports such as walking, climbing, caving, and canyoning in the Andalusian

10

mountains with this company. ☎ *637/727365* ⊕ *www.sierraextreme. net* ✉ *From €15.*

SEVILLE

550 km (340 miles) southwest of Madrid.

Seville's whitewashed houses bright with bougainvillea, ocher-color palaces, and baroque facades have long enchanted both *sevillanos* and travelers. It's a city for the senses—the fragrance of orange blossom (orange trees line many streets) intoxicates the air in spring, the sound of flamenco echoes through the alleyways in Triana and Santa Cruz, and views of the great Guadalquivir River accompany you at every turn. This is also a fine city in its architecture and people—stroll down the swankier pedestrian shopping streets and you can't fail to notice just how good-looking everyone is. Aside from being blessed with even features and flashing dark eyes, sevillanos exude a cool sophistication that seems more Catalan than Andalusian.

This bustling city of more than 700,000 does have some downsides: traffic-choked streets, high unemployment, a notorious petty-crime rate, and at times the kind of impersonal treatment you won't find in the smaller cities of Granada and Córdoba.

The layout of the historic center of Seville makes exploring easy. The central zone—**Centro**—around the cathedral, the Alcázar, Calle Sierpes, and Plaza Nueva is splendid and monumental, but it's not where you'll find Seville's greatest charm. **El Arenal,** home of the Maestranza bullring, the Teatro de la Maestranza concert hall, and a concentration of picturesque taverns, still buzzes the way it must have when stevedores loaded and unloaded ships from the New World. Just southeast of Centro, the medieval Jewish quarter, **Barrio de Santa Cruz,** is a lovely, whitewashed tangle of alleys. The **Barrio de la Macarena** to the northeast is rich in sights and authentic Seville atmosphere. The fifth and final neighborhood to explore, on the far side of the Guadalquivir River, is in many ways, the best of all—**Triana,** the traditional habitat for sailors, bullfighters, and flamenco artists, as well as the main workshop for Seville's renowned ceramicists.

GETTING HERE AND AROUND

AIR TRAVEL

Seville's airport is about 7 km (4½ miles) east of the city. There's a bus from the airport to the center of town every half hour daily (5:20 am–1:15 am; €4 one way). Taxi fare from the airport to the city center is around €22 during the day, and €25 at night and on Sunday. A number of private companies operate private airport-shuttle services.

BIKE TRAVEL

As an almost completely flat city, Seville is perfect for bike travel, and there are several bike rental companies within the city, including Bici4City *(see Essentials, below).*

BUS TRAVEL   Seville has two intercity bus stations: Estación Plaza de Armas, the main one, with buses serving Córdoba, Granada, Huelva, and Málaga in Andalusia, plus Madrid and Portugal, and other international destinations; and the smaller Estación del Prado de San Sebastián, serving Cádiz and nearby towns and villages.

Seville's urban bus service is efficient and covers the greater city area. Buses C1, C2, C3, and C4 run circular routes linking the main transportation terminals with the city center. The C1 goes east in a clockwise direction from the Santa Justa train station via Avenida de Carlos V, Avenida de María Luisa, Triana, the Isla de la Cartuja, and Calle de Resolana. The C2 follows the same route in reverse. The C3 runs from the Avenida Menéndez Pelayo to the Puerta de Jerez, Triana, Plaza de Armas, and Calle de Recaredo. The C4 does that route counterclockwise. The tram (called Metro Centro) runs between the San Bernardo station and Plaza Nueva. Buses do not run within the Barrio de Santa Cruz because the streets are too narrow, though they amply serve convenient access points around the periphery of this popular tourist area.

City buses operate limited night service between midnight and 2 am, with no service between 2 and 4 am. Single rides cost €1.40, but if you're going to be busing a lot, it's more economical to buy a rechargeable multitravel pass, which ends up being €0.69 per ride. Special tourist passes (*Tarjeta Turística*) valid for one or three days of unlimited bus travel cost (respectively) €5 and €10. Tickets are sold at newsstands and at the main bus station, Prado de San Sebastián.

CAR TRAVEL
Getting in and out of Seville by car isn't difficult, thanks to the SE30 ring road, but getting around in the city by car is problematic. We advise leaving your car at your hotel or in a lot while you're here.

TRAIN TRAVEL
Train connections include the high-speed AVE service from Madrid, with a journey time of less than 2½ hours.

TOURS
In Seville, the **Asociación Provincial de Informadores Turísticos, Guidetour,** and **ITA** can hook you up with a qualified English-speaking guide. The tourist office (⇨ *Visitor Information)* has information on various organized tours.

10

History and Tapas Tour. Glean local, historical, and culinary knowledge on a variety of tours around sights and tapas bars. ⊕ *sevilleconcierge. com* ☜ *From €50.*

Sevilla Bike Tour. Guided tours, leaving from the Makinline Shop on Calle Arjona at 10:30 am, take in the major sights of the city and offer interesting stories and insider information along the way. You'll cover about 10 km (6 miles) in the three hours. Reservations are required on weekends and recommended on weekdays. ⊠ *Calle Arjona 8, Centro* ☎ *954/562625* ⊕ *www.sevillabiketour.com* ☜ *€25.*

Sevilla Walking Tours. A choice of three walking tours are conducted in English: the Walking Tour, leaving Plaza Nueva from the statue of San Fernando; the Alcázar Tour, leaving Plaza del Triunfo from the central statue; and the Cathedral Tour, also leaving from the Plaza del Triunfo central statue. ☎ *902/158226, 616/501100* ⊕ *www.sevillawalkingtours.*

Seville's grand Alcázar is a UNESCO World Heritage site and an absolute must-see.

com ✉ €7–€15 ⊙ *Walking Tour Mon.–Sat. 10:30 (Mon., Wed., and Sat. only in Jan. and Aug.); Alcázar Tour Tues., Thurs., and Sat. at 1; Cathedral Tour Mon., Wed., and Fri. at 1.*

SevillaTour. Open-top buses leave every half hour (every 20 mins in summer) from the Torre del Oro, with stops at Parque María Luisa and Isla Mágica theme park. You can hop on and off at any stop. The complete tour lasts about an hour. ✉ *C. Jaén 2* ⊕ *www.city-sightseeing. com* ✉ *€15.50.*

Seville Tapas Tours. Local food and wine expert Shawn Hennessey leads guided tours round Seville's best tapas bars (traditional and gourmet). Choose from several different tours, lunch or evening. ⊕ *www.azahar-sevilla.com* ✉ *From €60.*

ESSENTIALS

Bike Contacts Bici4City ✉ *Calle Peral 6* ☎ *954/389383* ⊕ *www.bici4city.com.*

Bus Stations Estación del Prado de San Sebastián ✉ *Calle Vázquez Sagastizábal, El Arenal* ☎ *954/417118.* **Estación Plaza de Armas** ✉ *Puente Cristo de la Expiración, Centro* ☎ *955/038665* ⊕ *www.autobusesplazadearmas.es.*

Taxi Contact Radio Taxi Giralda ☎ *954/998070.*

Train Station Estación Santa Justa ✉ *Av. Kansas City, El Arenal* ☎ *902/320320.*

Visitor Information Ciy & Province of Seville ✉ *Pl. de Triunfo 1, by cathedral, Barrio de Santa Cruz* ☎ *954/210005* ⊕ *www.turismosevilla.org.*

EXPLORING

CENTRO

TOP ATTRACTIONS

Fodor'sChoice
★ **Alcázar.** The Plaza del Triunfo forms the entrance to the Mudejar palace, the official residence of the king and queen when they're in town, built by Pedro I (1350–69) on the site of Seville's former Moorish *alcázar* (fortress). Don't mistake the Alcázar for a genuine Moorish palace like Granada's Alhambra. It may look like one, and it was designed and built by Moorish workers brought in from Granada, but it was commissioned and paid for by a Christian king more than 100 years after the reconquest of Seville.

Entering the Alcázar through the Puerta del León (Lion's Gate) and the high, fortified walls, you'll first find yourself in a garden courtyard, the **Patio del León** (Courtyard of the Lion). Off to the left are the oldest parts of the building, the 14th-century **Sala de Justicia** (Hall of Justice) and, next to it, the intimate **Patio del Yeso** (Courtyard of Plaster), the only part of the original 12th-century Almohad Alcázar. Cross the **Patio de la Montería** (Courtyard of the Hunt) to Pedro's Mudejar palace, arranged around the beautiful **Patio de las Doncellas** (Court of the Damsels), resplendent with delicately carved stucco. Opening off this patio, the **Salón de Embajadores** (Hall of the Ambassadors), with its cedar cupola of green, red, and gold, is the most sumptuous hall in the palace.

Other royal rooms include the three baths of Pedro's powerful and influential mistress, María de Padilla. María's hold on her royal lover—and his courtiers—was so great that legend says they all lined up to drink her bathwater. The **Patio de las Muñecas** (Court of the Dolls) takes its name from two tiny faces carved on the inside of one of its arches, no doubt as a joke on the part of its Moorish creators. Here Pedro reputedly had his half brother, Don Fadrique, slain in 1358; and here, too, he murdered guest Abu Said of Granada for his jewels—one of which, a huge ruby, is now among England's crown jewels. (Pedro gave it to the Black Prince, Edward, Prince of Wales [1330–76], for helping during the revolt of his illegitimate brother in 1367.)

The Renaissance **Palacio de Carlos V** (Palace of Carlos V) is endowed with a rich collection of Flemish tapestries depicting Carlos's victories at Tunis. Look for the map of Spain: it shows the Iberian Peninsula upside down, as was the custom in Arab mapmaking. There are more goodies—rare clocks, antique furniture, paintings, and tapestries—on the upper floor, in the **Estancias Reales** (Royal Chambers).

In the **gardens**, inhale the fragrances of jasmine and myrtle, wander among terraces and baths, and peer into the well-stocked goldfish pond. From here, a passageway leads to the **Patio de las Banderas** (Court of the Flags), which has a classic view of the Giralda.

Allow at least two hours for your visit. ■TIP→ Buy tickets online to avoid waiting in line. ✉ *Pl. del Triunfo, Santa Cruz* ☎ *954/502.32.3* ⊕ *www.alcazarsevilla.org* ⌚ *€9.50 (free Apr.–Sept., Mon. 6–7; Oct.– Mar., Mon. 5–6)* ☉ *Apr.–Sept., daily 9:30–7; Oct. Mar., daily 9:30–5.*

10

Fodor'sChoice **Cathedral.** Seville's cathedral can be
★ described only in superlatives: it's
the largest and highest cathedral
in Spain, the largest Gothic building in the world, and the world's
third-largest church, after St. Peter's
in Rome and St. Paul's in London.
After Ferdinand III captured Seville
from the Moors in 1248, the great
mosque begun by Yusuf II in 1171
was reconsecrated to the Virgin
Mary and used as a Christian cathedral. In 1401 the people of Seville
decided to erect a new cathedral,
one that would equal the glory of

> **WHERE'S COLUMBUS?**
>
> Christopher Columbus knew both
> triumph and disgrace, yet he
> found no repose—he died, bitterly
> disillusioned, in Valladolid in 1506.
> No one knows for certain where
> he's buried; he was reportedly
> laid to rest for the first time in
> the Dominican Republic and then
> moved over the years to other
> locations. A portion of his remains
> can be found in Seville's cathedral.

their great city. They pulled down the old mosque, leaving only its
minaret and outer courtyard, and built the existing building in just over
a century—a remarkable feat for the time.

The cathedral's dimly illuminated interior, aside from the well-lighted
high altar, can be disappointing: Gothic purity has been largely sub-
merged in ornate baroque decoration. In the central nave rises the
Capilla Mayor (Main Chapel). Its magnificent *retablo* (altarpiece) is
the largest in Christendom (65 feet by 43 feet). It depicts some 36 scenes
from the life of Christ, with pillars carved with more than 200 figures.
Restoration of the altarpiece was completed in 2014.

On the south side of the cathedral is the **monument to Christopher
Columbus**: his coffin is borne aloft by the four kings representing the
medieval kingdoms of Spain: Castile, León, Aragón, and Navarra.
Columbus's son Fernando Colón (1488–1539) is also interred here;
his tombstone is inscribed with the words *"A Castilla y a León,
mundo nuevo dio Colón"* ("To Castile and León, Columbus gave a
new world").

On the opposite north side, don't miss the **Altar de Plata** (Silver Altar),
an 18th century masterpiece of intricate silversmithery.

In the **Sacristía de los Cálices** (Sacristy of the Chalices) look for Juan
Martínez Montañés's wood carving *Crucifixion, Merciful Christ*; Juan
de Valdés Leal's *St. Peter Freed by an Angel*; Francisco de Zurbarán's
Virgin and Child; and Francisco José de Goya y Lucientes's *St. Justa and
St. Rufina*. The **Sacristía Mayor** (Main Sacristy) holds the keys to the
city, which Seville's Moors and Jews presented to their conqueror, Ferdinand III. Finally, in the dome of the **Sala Capitular** (Chapter House),
in the cathedral's southeastern corner, is Bartolomé Estéban Murillo's
Immaculate Conception, painted in 1668.

One of the cathedral's highlights, the **Capilla Real** (Royal Chapel), is
concealed behind a ponderous curtain, but you can duck in if you're
quick, quiet, and properly dressed (no shorts or sleeveless tops): enter
from the Puerta de los Palos, on Plaza Virgen de los Reyes (signposted
"Entrada para Culto"—entrance for worship). Along the sides of the
chapel are the tombs of the Beatrix of Swabia, wife of the 13th century's

Ferdinand III, and their son Alfonso X ("the Wise"); in a silver urn before the high altar rest the relics of Ferdinand III himself, Seville's liberator. Canonized in 1671, he was said to have died from excessive fasting.

Don't forget the **Patio de los Naranjos** (Courtyard of Orange Trees), on the church's northern side, where the fountain in the center was used for ablutions before people entered the original mosque. Near the Puerta del Lagarto (Lizard's Gate), in the corner near the Giralda, try to find the wooden crocodile—thought to have been a gift from the emir of Egypt in 1260 as he sought the hand of the daughter of Alfonso the Wise—and the elephant tusk, found in the ruins of Itálica.

The Christians could not bring themselves to destroy the tower when they tore down the mosque, so they incorporated it into their new cathedral. In 1565–68 they added a lantern and belfry to the old minaret and installed 24 bells, one for each of Seville's 24 parishes and the 24 Christian knights who fought with Ferdinand III in the reconquest. They also added the bronze statue of Faith, which turned as a weather vane— *el giraldillo,* or "something that turns," thus the whole tower became known as the **Giralda.** With its baroque additions, the slender Giralda rises 322 feet. Inside, instead of steps, 35 sloping ramps—wide enough for two horsemen to pass abreast—climb to a viewing platform 230 feet up. It is said that Ferdinand III rode his horse to the top to admire the city he had conquered. Admission also includes the visit to the Iglesia del Salvador. ⊠ *Pl. Virgen de los Reyes, Centro* ☎ *954/214971* 🖳 *€8 (free Mon. from 4:30 if you prebook)* ⊗ *Sept.–June, Mon. 11–3:30, Tues.–Sat. 11–5, Sun. 2:30–6; July and Aug., Mon. 9:30–2:30, Tues.– Sat. 9:30–4, Sun. 2:30–6.*

Fodor's Choice
★ **Palacio de la Condesa de Lebrija.** This lovely palace has three ornate patios, including a spectacular courtyard graced by a Roman mosaic taken from the ruins in Itálica, surrounded by Moorish arches and fine azulejos. The side rooms house a collection of archaeological items. The second floor contains the family apartments and visits are by guided tour only. ■TIP➔ It's well worth paying the extra for the second floor tour, which gives an interesting insight into the collections and the family. ⊠ *Calle Cuna 8, Centro* ☎ *954/227802* 🖳 *€5 1st fl. only; €8 with 2nd-fl. tour (free Mon. 6–7)* ⊗ *Weekdays 10:30–7:30, Sat. 10–2 and 4–6, Sun. 10–2.*

WORTH NOTING

Ayuntamiento (*City Hall*). This Diego de Riaño original, built between 1527 and 1564, is in the heart of Seville's commercial center. A 19th-century plateresque facade overlooks the Plaza Nueva. The other side, on the Plaza de San Francisco, is Riaño's work. Visits must be pre-booked via ⊕ *www.visitasevilla.es.* ⊠ *Pl. Nueva 1, Centro* ☎ *954/470243* 🖳 *€4 (free Sat.)* ⊗ *Tours Sept.–June, Mon.–Thurs. at 4:30 and 7:30, Sat. at 10.*

Iglesia del Salvador. Built between 1671 and 1712, the Church of the Savior stands on the site of Seville's first great mosque, of which remains can be seen in its Courtyard of the Orange Trees. Also of note are the sculptures *Jesús de la Pasión* and *St. Christopher* by Martínez Montañés. In 2003 archeologists discovered an 18th-century burial site here;

10

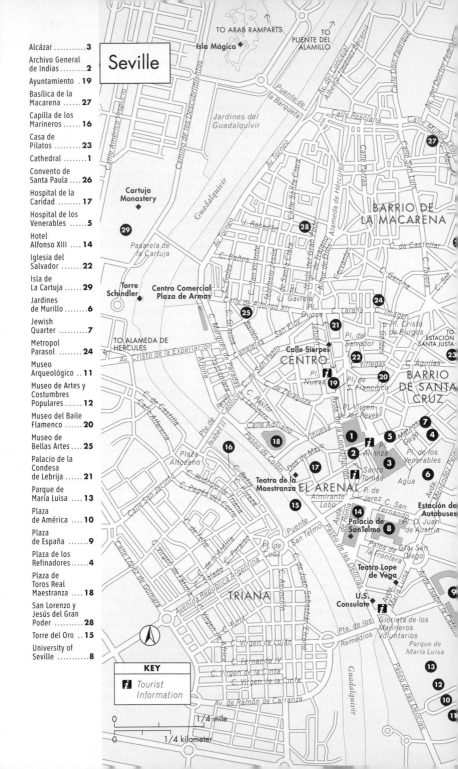

Seville

walkways have been installed to facilitate visits. ✉ *Pl. del Salvador, Centro* ☎ *954/211679* 🖸 *€3 with guide, €8 combined ticket with Cathedral* ⊗ *Mon.–Sat. 11–5:30, Sun. 3–7.*

Metropol Parasol. This huge square, at the west end of Calle Cuna, is home to the world's largest wooden structure, 492 feet long by 230 feet wide. The design represents giant trees, reminiscent of Gaudí, and walkways run through the "tree tops" affording great views of the city, especially at sunset. At ground level, there are interesting archaeological remains (mostly Roman) and a large indoor food market. ✉ *Pl. de la Encarnación, Centro* 🖸 *€3* ⊗ *10:30 am–midnight (until 1 am Fri. and Sat.).*

BARRIO DE SANTA CRUZ

TOP ATTRACTIONS

Fodor'sChoice **Casa de Pilatos.** With its fine patio and superb azulejo decorations, this
★ palace is a beautiful blend of Spanish Mudejar and Renaissance architecture, and is considered a prototype of an Andalusian mansion. It was built in the first half of the 16th century by the dukes of Tarifa, ancestors of the present owner, the Duke of Medinaceli. It's known as Pilate's House because Don Fadrique, first marquis of Tarifa, allegedly modeled it on Pontius Pilate's house in Jerusalem, where he had gone on a pilgrimage in 1518. The upstairs apartments, which you can see on a guided tour, have frescoes, paintings, and antique furniture. Admission prices include an audio guide in English. ✉ *Pl. de Pilatos 1, Barrio de Santa Cruz* ☎ *954/225298* 🖸 *€6 1st fl. only, €8 with 2nd-fl. tour* ⊗ *Daily 9–6 (until 7 Apr.–Oct.).*

Fodor'sChoice **Jewish Quarter.** The twisting alleyways and traditional whitewashed
★ houses add to the tourist charm of this *barrio.* On some streets, bars alternate with antiques and souvenir shops, but most of the quarter is quiet and residential. On the Plaza Alianza, pause to enjoy the antiques shops and outdoor cafés. In the Plaza de Doña Elvira, with its fountain and azulejo benches, young sevillanos gather to play guitars. Just around the corner from the hospital, at Callejón del Agua and Jope de Rueda, Gioacchino Rossini's Figaro serenaded Rosina on her Plaza Alfaro balcony. Adjoining the Plaza Alfaro, in the Plaza Santa Cruz, flowers and orange trees surround a 17th-century filigree iron cross, which marks the site of the erstwhile church of Santa Cruz, destroyed by Napoléon's General Jean-de-Dieu Soult. ✉ *Barrio de Santa Cruz.*

Fodor'sChoice **Museo del Baile Flamenco.** This private museum in the heart of Santa
★ Cruz (follow the signs) was opened in 2007 by the legendary flamenco dancer Cristina Hoyos and includes audiovisual and multimedia displays explaining the history, culture, and soul of Spanish flamenco. There are also regular classes and shows. ✉ *Calle Manuel Rojas Marcos 3, Barrio de Santa Cruz* ☎ *954/340311* ⊕ *www.museoflamenco.com* 🖸 *€10* ⊗ *Daily 10–7.*

WORTH NOTING

Archivo General de Indias (*Archives of the Indies*). Opened in 1785 in the former Lonja (Merchants' Exchange), this dignified Renaissance building stores a valuable archive of more than 40,000 documents, including drawings, trade documents, plans of South American towns, and even

10

the autographs of Columbus, Magellan, and Cortés. Temporary exhibitions showcase different archives. ⊠ *Av. de la Constitución 3, Barrio de Santa Cruz* ☎ *954/500528* ☞ *Free* ⊙ *Mon.–Sat. 9:30–4:45, Sun. 10–2.*

Hospital de los Venerables. Once a retirement home for priests, this baroque building has a splendid azulejo patio with an interesting sunken fountain (designed to cope with low water pressure) and an upstairs gallery, but the highlight is the chapel, featuring frescoes by Valdés Leal and sculptures by Pedro Roldán. The building now houses a cultural foundation that organizes on-site art exhibitions. ⊠ *Pl. de los Venerables 8, Barrio de Santa Cruz* ☎ *954/562696* ☞ *€5.50, includes audio guide (free Sun. 4–8)* ⊙ *Daily 10–1:30 and 4–8.*

Jardines de Murillo (*Murillo Gardens*). From the Plaza Santa Cruz you can stroll through these shady gardens, where you'll find a statue of Christopher Columbus and some welcome shade in the summer. ⊠ *Pl. Santa Cruz, Barrio de Santa Cruz.*

Plaza de los Refinadores. This shady square filled with palms and orange trees is separated from the Murillo Gardens by an iron grillwork and ringed with stately glass balconies. At its center is a monument to Don Juan Tenorio, the famous Don Juan known for his amorous conquests. ⊠ *Barrio de Santa Cruz.*

EL ARENAL AND PARQUE MARÍA LUISA

Parque María Luisa is part shady, midcity forestland and part monumental esplanade. El Arenal, named for its sandy riverbank soil, was originally a neighborhood of shipbuilders, stevedores, and warehouses. The heart of El Arenal lies between the Puente de San Telmo, just upstream from the Torre de Oro, and the Puente de Isabel II (Puente de Triana). El Arenal extends as far north as Avenida Alfonso XII to include the Museo de Bellas Artes. Between the park and El Arenal is the university.

TOP ATTRACTIONS

Fodor'sChoice
★
Museo de Bellas Artes (*Museum of Fine Arts*). This museum—one of Spain's finest for Spanish art—is in the former convent of La Merced Calzada, most of which dates from the 17th century. The collection includes works by Murillo and the 17th-century Seville school, as well as by Zurbarán, Diego Velázquez, Alonso Cano, Valdés Leal, and El Greco. You will also see outstanding examples of Sevillian Gothic art and baroque religious sculptures in wood (a quintessentially Andalusian art form). In the rooms dedicated to Sevillian art of the 19th and 20th centuries, look for Gonzalo Bilbao's *Las Cigarreras*, a group portrait of Seville's famous cigar makers. ⊠ *Pl. del Museo 9, El Arenal* ☎ *954/786491* ⊕ *www.museosdeandalucia.es* ☞ *€1.50* ⊙ *Sept. 16–May 31, Tues.–Sat. 10–8:30, Sun. 10–5:30; June 1–Sept. 15 Tues.–Sat. 9:15–3:30, Sun. 10–5.*

Fodor'sChoice
★
Parque de María Luisa. Formerly the garden of the Palacio de San Telmo, this park blends formal design and wild vegetation. In the burst of development that gripped Seville in the 1920s, it was redesigned for the 1929 World's Fair, and the impressive villas you see now are the fair's remaining pavilions, many of them consulates or schools; the old Casino holds the Teatro Lope de Vega, which puts on mainly musicals.

Seville's cathedral is the largest and highest cathedral in Spain, the largest Gothic building in the world, and the third-largest church in the world, after St. Peter's in Rome and St. Paul's in London.

Note the Anna Huntington **statue of El Cid** (Rodrigo Díaz de Vivar, 1043–99), who fought both for and against the Muslim rulers during the Reconquest. The statue was presented to Seville by the Massachusetts-born sculptor for the 1929 World's Fair. ✉ *Main entrance: Glorieta San Diego, Parque Maria Luisa.*

FAMILY **Plaza de España.** This grandiose half-moon of buildings on the eastern edge of the Parque de María Luisa was Spain's centerpiece pavilion at the 1929 World's Fair. The brightly colored azulejo pictures represent the provinces of Spain, while the four bridges symbolize the medieval kingdoms of the Iberian Peninsula. In summer you can rent small boats to row along the arc-shaped canal. ✉ *Parque Maria Luisa.*

Plaza de Toros Real Maestranza (*Royal Maestranza Bullring*). Sevillanos have spent many a thrilling evening in this bullring, one of the oldest and loveliest *plazas de toros* in Spain, built between 1760 and 1763. The 20-minute tour (in English) takes in the empty arena, a museum with elaborate costumes and prints, and the chapel where matadors pray before the fight. Bullfights take place in the evening Thursday through Sunday, April through July and in September. Tickets can be booked online or by phone. ✉ *Paseo de Colón 12, El Arenal* ☎ *954/210315 for visits, 954/501382 for bullfights* ⊕ *www.realmaestranza.es* 🎟 *Tours €7 (free Mon. 3–7)* ⊙ *Tours daily 9:30–7; on bullfight days call to check.*

WORTH NOTING

Hospital de la Caridad. Behind the Maestranza Theater is this almshouse for the sick and elderly, where six paintings by Murillo (1617–82) and two gruesome works by Valdés Leal (1622–90), depicting the Triumph of Death, are displayed. The baroque hospital was founded in 1674 by

Seville's original Don Juan, Miguel de Mañara (1626–79). A nobleman of licentious character, Mañara was returning one night from a riotous orgy when he had a vision of a funeral procession in which the partly decomposed corpse in the coffin was his own. Accepting the apparition as a sign from God, Mañara devoted his fortune to building this hospital and is buried before the high altar in the chapel. Admission includes an audio guide (available in English). ⊠ *Calle Temprado 3, El Arenal* ☎ *954/223232* ⊠ *€5* ⊘ *Mon.–Sat. 9:30–1 and 3:30–7, Sun. 9–12:30.*

Hotel Alfonso XIII. Seville's most emblematic hotel (⇨ *See also Where to Stay*), this grand, Mudejar-style building next to the university was built and named for the king when he visited for the 1929 World's Fair. Extensive renovations were completed in 2012. Even if you are not staying here you can admire the gracious Moorish-style courtyard, best appreciated while sipping an ice-cold fino from the adjacent bar. ⊠ *Calle San Fernando 2, El Arenal* ☎ *954/917000* ⊕ *www.hotel-alfonsoxiii.es.*

Museo Arqueológico (*Museum of Archaeology*). This fine Renaissance-style building has artifacts from Phoenician, Tartessian, Greek, Carthaginian, Iberian, Roman, and medieval times. Displays include marble statues and mosaics from the Roman excavations at Itálica and a faithful replica of the fabulous Carambolo treasure found on a hillside outside Seville in 1958: 21 pieces of jewelry, all 24-karat gold, dating from the 7th and 6th centuries BC. ⊠ *Pl. de América, El Arenal* ☎ *954/120632* ⊠ *€1.50* ⊘ *Sept. 16–May 31, Tues.–Sat. 10–8:30, Sun. 10–5; June 1–Sept. 15, Tues.–Sat. 9–3:30, Sun. 10–5.*

FAMILY **Museo de Artes y Costumbres Populares** (*Museum of Arts and Traditions*). Among the fascinating items of mainly 19th- and 20th-century Spanish folklore in this museum, in the Mudejar pavilion opposite the Museum of Archaeology, is an impressive Díaz Velázquez collection of lace and embroidery—one of the finest in Europe. There's a reconstruction of a typical late-19th-century Sevillian house on the first floor, while upstairs, exhibits include 18th- and 19th-century court dress, stunning regional folk costumes, religious objects, and musical instruments. In the basement, you can see ceramics, pottery, furniture, and household items from bygone ages. ⊠ *Pl. de América 3, El Arenal* ☎ *954/712391* ⊕ *www.museosdeandalucia.es* ⊠ *€1.50* ⊘ *Sept. 16–June 15, Tues.–Sat. 10–8:30, Sun. 10–5; June 16–Sept. 15, Tues.–Sun 10–5.*

FAMILY **Plaza de América.** Walk to the south end of the Parque de María Luisa, past the Isla de los Patos (Island of Ducks), to find this plaza designed by Aníbal González and typically carpeted with a congregation of white doves (children can buy grain from a kiosk here to feed them). It's a blaze of color, with flowers, shrubs, ornamental stairways, and fountains tiled in yellow, blue, and ocher. The three impressive buildings surrounding the square—in neo-Mudejar, Gothic, and Renaissance styles—were built by González for the 1929 World's Fair. Two of them now house Seville's museums of archaeology and arts and traditions. ⊠ *Parque Maria Luisa.*

Torre del Oro (*Tower of Gold*). Built by the Moors in 1220 to complete the city's ramparts, this 12-sided tower on the banks of the Guadalquivir served to close off the harbor when a chain was stretched across the river from its base to a tower on the opposite bank. In 1248, Admiral Ramón de Bonifaz broke through the barrier, and Ferdinand III captured Seville. The tower houses a small naval museum. ⊠ *Paseo Alcalde Marqués de Contadero s/n, El Arenal* ☎ *954/222419* 💰 *€3 (free Mon.)* ⊙ *Weekdays 9:30–6:45, weekends 10:30–6:45.*

University of Seville. Fans of Bizet's opera *Carmen* will want to come here, to see where the famous heroine reputedly rolled cigars on her thighs. At the far end of the Jardines de Murillo, opposite Calle San Fernando, stands what used to be the **Real Fábrica de Tabacos** (Royal Tobacco Factory). Built in the mid-1700s, the factory employed some 3,000 *cigarreras* (female cigar makers) less than a century later. Free, guided tours in English are available Monday to Thursday at 11. ⊠ *Calle San Fernando 4, Parque Maria Luisa* ☎ *954/551052* 💰 *Free* ⊙ *Weekdays 9 am–9:30 pm.*

BARRIO DE LA MACARENA

This immense neighborhood covers the entire northern half of historic Seville and deserves to be walked many times. Most of the best churches, convents, markets, and squares are concentrated around the center in an area delimited by the Arab ramparts to the north, the Alameda de Hercules to the west, the Santa Catalina church to the south, and the Convento de Santa Paula to the east. The area between the Alameda de Hercules and the Guadalquivir is known to locals as the Barrio de San Lorenzo, a section that's ideal for an evening of tapas grazing.

Basílica de la Macarena. This church holds Seville's most revered image, the Virgin of Hope—better known as La Macarena. Bedecked with candles and carnations, her cheeks streaming with glass tears, the Macarena steals the show at the procession on Holy Thursday, the highlight of Seville's Holy Week pageant. The patron of gypsies and the protector of the matador, her charms are so great that young Sevillian bullfighter Joselito spent half his personal fortune buying her emeralds. When he was killed in the ring in 1920, the Macarena was dressed in widow's weeds for a month. The adjacent museum tells the history of Holy Week traditions through processional and liturgical artifacts amassed by the Brotherhood of La Macarena over four centuries. ⊠ *Calle Bécquer 1, La Macarena* ☎ *954/901800* 💰 *Basilica free, museum €5* ⊙ *Daily 9–2 and 5–9.*

Fodor's Choice **Convento de Santa Paula.** This 15th-century Gothic convent has a fine
★ facade and portico, with ceramic decoration by Nicolaso Pisano. The chapel has some beautiful azulejos and sculptures by Martínez Montañés. It also contains a small museum and a shop selling delicious cakes and jams made by the nuns. ⊠ *Calle Santa Paula 11, La Macarena* ☎ *954/536330* 💰 *€3* ⊙ *Tues.–Sun. 10–1.*

San Lorenzo y Jesús del Gran Poder. This 17th-century church has many fine works by such artists as Martínez Montañés and Francisco Pacheco, but its outstanding piece is Juan de Mesa y Velasco's *Jesús del Gran Poder* (Christ Omnipotent). ⊠ *Pl. San Lorenzo 13, La Macarena* ☎ *954/915672* 💰 *Free* ⊙ *Sept. 16–June 19, Mon.–Thurs. 9–1:30 and 6–9, Fri. 7:30 am–10 pm, weekends 8–1:30 and 6–9; June 20–Sept.*

10

15, Mon.–Thurs. 8–1:30 and 6–9, Fri. 7:30–2 and 5–10, weekends 8–2 and 6–9.

TRIANA

Triana used to be Seville's Gypsy quarter. Today, it has a tranquil, neighborly feel by day and a distinctly flamenco feel at night. Cross over to Triana via the **Puente de Isabel II**, an iron bridge built in 1852 and the first to connect the city's two sections. Start your walk in the **Plaza del Altozano**, the center of the Triana district and traditionally the meeting point for travelers from the south crossing the river to Seville. Admire the facade of the Murillo pharmacy here before walking up **Calle Jacinto.** Look out for the fine **Casa de los Mensaque** (now the dis-

trict's administrative office and usually open on weekday mornings), home to some of Triana's finest potters and housing some stunning examples of Seville ceramics. Turn right into **Calle Alfarería** (Pottery Street) and visit some of the ceramic shops. Return via Calle Betis along the riverside. To reach attractions in La Cartuja, take the C1 bus.

Capilla de los Marineros. This seamen's chapel is one of Triana's most important monuments and home to the Brotherhood of Triana, whose Holy Week processions are among the most revered in the city. ⊠ *Calle Pureza 2, Triana* ☎ *954/332645* 🎟 *Free* ⊙ *Mon.–Sat. 10–1:30 and 5:30–9, Sun. 10–2 and 5:30–8:30.*

Isla de La Cartuja. Named after its 14th-century Carthusian monastery, this island in the Guadalquivir River across from northern Seville was the site of the decennial Universal Exposition (Expo) in 1992. The island has the Teatro Central, used for concerts and plays; Parque del Alamillo, Seville's largest, least known park; and the Estadio Olímpico, a 60,000-seat covered stadium. The best way to get to La Cartuja is by walking across one or both (one each way) of the superb Santiago Calatrava bridges spanning the river. The Puente de la Barqueta crosses to La Cartuja, and downstream the Puente del Alamillo connects the island with Seville. Buses C1 and C2 also serve La Cartuja. ⊠ *Triana.*

Monasterio de Santa María de las Cuevas (*Monasterio de La Cartuja*). The 14th-century monastery was regularly visited by Christopher Columbus, who was also buried here for a few years. Part of the building houses the **Centro Andaluz de Arte Contemporáneo**, which has an absorbing collection of contemporary art. ⊠ *Av. Américo Vespucio, La Cartuja* ☎ *955/037070* 🎟 *€3 (free Tues.–Fri. 7–9)* ⊙ *Tues.–Sat. 11–9, Sun. 11–3.*

Isla Mágica. The eastern shore of Isla de la Cartuja holds this theme park with more than 20 attractions, including the hair-raising Jaguar

The half moon of Plaza de España

roller coaster. ⊠ *Isla de la Cartuja, Av. de los Descubrimiento, s/n, Triana* ☎ *902/161716* ⊕ *www.islamagica.es* 🎫 *€30* ⊙ *Apr.–June, weekends 11–10; July–Sept. 7, daily 11–11; Sept. 7–Nov. 2, weekends 11–9.*

WHERE TO EAT

Use the coordinate (✛ B2) at the end of each listing to locate a site on the corresponding map.

CENTRO

$
TAPAS
✕ **Casa Morales.** Down a side street off the Avenida de la Constitución, this atmospheric bar takes you back to 19th-century Seville with its wooden shelving stacked with wine bottles, beamed ceiling, and tiled walls. It was established in 1850 as a wine store and is still run by the same family. There are two bar areas—the largest fronts the store and looks out onto the street, and the other is home to huge ceramic wine barrels. Locals pack the place at lunchtime, when popular dishes include *menudo con garbanzos* (tripe with chickpeas) and *albóndigas de choco* (cuttlefish croquettes). The wine list is, as you would expect, extensive. $ *Average main: €8* ⊠ *Calle García de Vinuesa 11, Centro* ☎ *954/221242* ⊙ *Closed Sun. July–Sept. 15. No dinner Sun. Sept. 16–June* ✛ *B3.*

$
TAPAS
Fodor'sChoice
★
✕ **Espacio Eslava.** The crowds gathered outside this local favorite off the Alameda de Hercules may be off-putting at first, but the creative, inexpensive tapas (from €2.50) are well worth the wait. Try delicacies like the *cigarro para Bécquer* (seaweed mousse with squid and cuttlefish, and garlic sauce) or *solomillo al eneldo* or *con cabrales* (sirloin with dill or Cabrales cheese) or *huevo sobre bizcocho boletus y vino dulce*

10

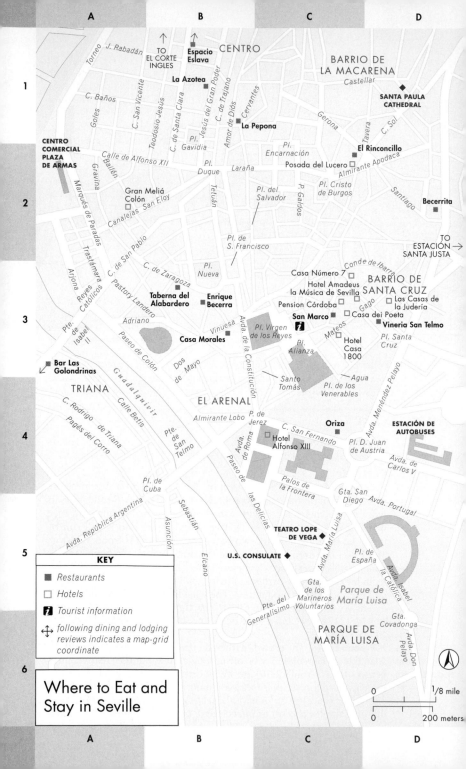

Where to Eat and Stay in Seville

A B C D

↑
TO
EL CORTE
INGLES

Espacio
Eslava

CENTRO

BARRIO DE
LA MACARENA

Castellar

SANTA PAULA
CATHEDRAL

J. Rabadán
Torneo

La Azotea

C. San Vicente
C. Baños
Goles
C. de Santa Clara
Teodosio Jesús
Jesús del Gran Poder
C. de Trajano
Cervantes
Amor de Diós

La Pepona

Gerona

C. Sol
Tavera

1

CENTRO
COMERCIAL
PLAZA
DE ARMAS

Calle de Alfonso XII
Caballón
Gravina
Marqués de Paradas

Gran Meliá
Colón

Canalejas San Eloy
C. de San Pablo

Pl.
Gavidia

Pl.
Duque

Tetuán
Laraña

Pl.
Encarnación

Pl. del
Salvador

P. Galdos
Pl. Cristo
de Burgos

Pl.
Encarnación

El Rinconcillo

Posada del Lucero
Almirante Apodaca

Santiago

Becerrita

2

Trastámara
Ariona
Reyes
Católicos
Pte.
de
Isabel
II

C. de Zaragoza
C. de Pastory Landero
Adriano
Vinuesa

Taberna del
Alabardero

Enrique
Becerra

Casa Morales

Pl.
Nueva

Pl. de
S. Francisco

Pl. Virgen
de los Reyes

Avda. de la Constitución

Conde de Ibarra

Casa Número 7
Hotel Amadeus
la Música de Sevilla
Pension Córdoba
San Marco
Gago
Mateos

BARRIO DE
SANTA CRUZ

Las Casas de
la Judería
Casa dei Poeta

Vineria San Telmo

Pl. Santa
Cruz

Hotel
Casa
1800

TO
ESTACIÓN →
SANTA JUSTA

3

Bar Las
Golondrinas
↙

TRIANA

C. Rodrigo de Triana
Pagés del Corro

Paseo de Colón
Guadalquivir
Calle Betis
Dos
de
Mayo

EL ARENAL

Almirante Lobo
Pte.
de
San
Telmo

Santo
Tomás

Pl. de los
Venerables

Agua

Avda. Menéndez Pelayo

4

Pl. de
Cuba

Avda. República Argentina

Sebastián
Asunción

Elcano

P. de
Jerez
Avda. de Roma

Hotel
Alfonso XIII

C. San Fernando

Oriza

Palos de
la Frontera

Paseo de las Delicias
Pte. del Generalísimo

Gta. San
Diego

Pl. D. Juan
de Austria

ESTACIÓN DE
AUTOBUSES

Avda. de
Carlos V

Avda. Portugal

Avda. María Luisa

Pl. de
España

Avda. Isabel la Católica

5

KEY

■ *Restaurants*

□ *Hotels*

🛈 *Tourist information*

✛ *following dining and lodging
reviews indicates a map-grid
coordinate*

TEATRO LOPE
DE VEGA ◆

U.S. CONSULATE ◆

Gta. de los
Marineros
Voluntarios

Parque de
María Luisa

Gta.
Covadonga

PARQUE DE
MARÍA LUISA

Avda. Don
Pelayo

0   1/8 mile

0   200 meters

6

A B C D

caramelizado (egg on mushroom pie with caramelized sweet wine). The house specialty, however, is the Basque dessert *sokoa,* so be sure to leave some room. Tables at the tapas bar can't be booked (a call will get you a reservation at the next-door Eslava restaurant), so arrive early to avoid a wait. [$] *Average main: €10* ✉ *Calle Eslava 3, Centro* ☎ *954/906568* ✍ *Reservations not accepted* ⏲ *Closed Mon. No dinner Sun.* ✥ *B1.*

$$ SPANISH 🍴 **La Azotea.** With a young vibe and a vast and inventive menu, this tiny restaurant offers a welcome change from Seville's typical fried fare. The owners' haute-cuisine ambitions are reflected in excellent service and lovingly prepared food, but not in the prices. The menu changes according to the season, but typical dishes include salmon tartare, baby squid with cream of goat's cheese and orange, and Iberian pork in red wine *au gratin.* Reservations are available for weekday lunches only; at any other time, put your name on the waiting list and pop round to the Azotea bar just round the corner for a drink and generous tapa (€4) while you wait. [$] *Average main: €14* ✉ *Calle Jesus del Gran Poder 31, Centro* ☎ *955/116748* ⏲ *Closed Sun., Mon., and 2 wks in Aug. (phone to check)* ✥ *B1.*

$ TAPAS 🍴 **La Pepona.** Establishing itself as a serious contender on the Seville tapas scene, this bar, opposite Calle Cuna and just around the corner from Metropol Parasol, has a sleek modern interior that's welcoming and cozy. Tapas focus on innovative recipes, all made with fresh, locally produced ingredients. Highlights on the 20-tapa menu include *sardinas marinadas sobre pan de sésamo* (marinated sardines on sesame bread) and *gambones a la plancha sobre trigo negro* (grilled king prawns on black buckwheat). Wash your tapas (€3–€5) down with wine from the lengthy list, all available by the glass. [$] *Average main: €12* ✉ *Calle Orfila 2, Centro* ☎ *954/215026* ⏲ *Closed Sun.* ✥ *B1.*

BARRIO DE SANTA CRUZ

$$$ SPANISH Fodor's Choice ★ 🍴 **Becerrita.** The affable Jesús Becerra runs this cozy establishment, where several small dining rooms are decorated with traditional columns, tiles, and colorful paintings of Seville by local artists. Diligent service and tasty modern treatments of such classic Spanish dishes as *bacalao gratinado con Idiazábal sobre una salsa de piquillos* (Basque-cheese grilled cod with pepper sauce) and *brazuelo de cordero lechal asado al tomillo* (roast suckling lamb with thyme) have won the favor of sevillanos, as have the signature oxtail croquettes. Smaller appetites can try such tasty tapas as stuffed calamari and garlic-spiked prawns. The restaurant has parking for customers. [$] *Average main: €22* ✉ *Calle Recaredo 9, Santa Cruz* ☎ *954/412057* 🌐 *www.becerrita.com* ✍ *Reservations essential* ⏲ *No dinner Sun.* ✥ *D2.*

$$$$ SPANISH 🍴 **Oriza.** Basque chef Eneko Galarraga took over from José Mari Egaña in early 2014 and has maintained the high culinary standards. On the edge of the Murillo Gardens opposite the university, Oriza has an atrium-style dining room with high ceilings and wall-to-wall stained-glass windows. In warm weather, you can eat on the terrace under the orange trees. The menu emphasizes the chef's Basque origins and includes *merluza en salsa verde con ajetes tiernos* (cod in green sauce with tender garlic shoots) and *solomillo de ternera con foie a la plancha* (grilled filet steak with foie gras). The adjoining Bar España serves

tapas (€3.50), including mushroom tart and mustard pork chop. Private dining rooms are also available. $ *Average main: €30* ✉ *Calle San Fernando 41, Santa Cruz* ☎ *954/227211* ☉ *Closed Sun.* ✚ *C4.*

$ ✕ **San Marco.** In the heart of Santa Cruz is one of Seville's surprises—an
ITALIAN   Italian restaurant in a 12th-century Arab bath house where original features blend with modern design. At this venue, you might be dining under authentic bath vaults studded with star shapes or sitting surrounded by starkly modern oil paintings in the area where bathers once received massages. Fountains provide a soothing backdrop, blending with live classical guitar music every evening. Specialties include creamy cheese ravioli al pesto and leg of lamb with honey and prunes, and there's an extensive choice of homemade desserts. Service, led by owner Angelo Ramacciotti, is excellent and many clients are regulars. It's wise to reserve for the evening. $ *Average main: €12* ✉ *Calle Mesón del Moro 6, Santa Cruz* ☎ *954/214390* ✚ *C3.*

$ ✕ **Vineria San Telmo.** Whether you eat in the dimly lit dining room or on
SPANISH   the street-level terrace, prepare to spend some time perusing a menu that
Fodor'sChoice   is full of surprises. All dishes are superb and sophisticated, especially
★   the eggplant stew with tomato, goat's cheese and smoked salmon, the Iberian pork with curried pumpkin and rocket, and the oxtail in filo pastry. Dishes come as tapas, half portions, or full portions—ideal for sharing—and the Argentine-owned restaurant's vast glass-front wine cellar includes an extensive choice of Spanish vino. It's near the touristy Alcazar and its popularity sometimes works to its detriment—it can get very crowded and noisy at times, when it would not be the ideal place for a romantic meal for two. $ *Average main: €12* ✉ *Paseo Catalina de Ribera 4, Santa Cruz* ☎ *954/410600* ✚ *D3.*

EL ARENAL AND PARQUE MARÍA LUISA

$$$ ✕ **Enrique Becerra.** Excellent tapas (€3.50—try the lamb kebab with
SPANISH   dates and couscous), a lively bar, and an extensive wine list await at
Fodor'sChoice   this restaurant run by the fifth generation of a family of celebrated res-
★   taurateurs (Enrique's brother Jesús owns Becerrita). The menu focuses on traditional, home-cooked Andalusian dishes, such as *pez espada al amontillado* (swordfish cooked in dark sherry) and *albóndigas de cordero a la hierbabuena* (lamb meatballs with mint). Don't miss the fried eggplant stuffed with prawns. If you want a quiet meal, call to reserve a table in one of the small upstairs rooms. $ *Average main: €21* ✉ *Calle Gamazo 2, El Arenal* ☎ *954/213049* ☉ *Closed Aug. (call for dates). No dinner Sun.* ✚ *B3.*

$$$$ ✕ **Taberna de Alabardero.** In a magnificent manor house with a stunning
SPANISH   patio, this restaurant's upstairs dining rooms are set around a central arcade, with tables arranged under the tinkling crystal of chandeliers. Exquisite paintings and a pale green and yellow color scheme add to the charm. The cuisine is innovative and sophisticated, with dishes like sole with baby eel, squid and macadamia nuts, and steak in bloody mary sauce with salmon tartare. The ground-level bistro offers a good-value lunchtime *menú del día* (daily specials are €12.90 weekdays, €17.50 weekends). $ *Average main: €24* ✉ *Calle Zaragoza 20, El Arenal* ☎ *954/502721* ☉ *Closed Aug.* ✚ *B3.*

BARRIO DE LA MACARENA

$ SPANISH 🍴 **El Rinconcillo.** Founded in 1670, this lovely spot serves a classic selection of dishes, such as the *pavía de bacalao* (fried breaded cod), a superb salmorejo, and espinacas con garbanzos, all in generous portions. Tapas are keenly priced at from €2. The views of the Iglesia de Santa Catalina out the front window upstairs are unbeatable, and your bill is chalked up on the wooden counters as you go. This is a big favorite with locals so be prepared for crowds. [$] *Average main: €10* ✉ *Calle Gerona 40, La Macarena* ☎ *954/223183* ✣ *C2.*

TRIANA

$ SPANISH 🍴 **Bar Las Golondrinas.** Run by the same family for more than 50 years and lavishly decorated in the colorful tiles that pay tribute to the neighborhood's potters, Las Golondrinas is a fixture of Triana life. The staff never changes, and neither does the menu: the recipes for the *punta de solomillo* (sliced sirloin), *chipirones* (fried baby squid) and *caballito de jamón* (ham on bread) have been honed to perfection, and they're served in tapas (€2) or large portions that keep everyone happy. [$] *Average main: €12* ✉ *Calle Antillano Campos 26, Triana* ☎ *954/331626* ✣ *A3.*

WHERE TO STAY

Use the coordinate (✣ B2) at the end of each listing to locate a site on the corresponding map.

CENTRO

$$ HOTEL 🏨 **Posada del Lucero.** The country's only 16th-century building being used as a posada has architecture that combines Mudejar-style flourishes with cutting-edge modern design. **Pros:** lots of historic atmosphere; excellent central position. **Cons:** no soundproofing; rooms lack storage space. [$] *Rooms from: €120* ✉ *Calle Almirante Apodaca 7, Centro* ☎ *954/502480* 🌐 *www.hotelposadadellucero.com* 🛏 *37 rooms, 1 suite* 🍽 *No meals* ✣ *C2.*

BARRIO DE SANTA CRUZ

$$$ HOTEL 🏨 **Casa del Poeta.** Up a narrow alleyway, behind an ordinary facade, a 17th-century palace has become one of Seville's newest boutique hotels—a cool oasis of calm just a heartbeat from some bustling Santa Cruz streets. **Pros:** peaceful, central location; authentic palatial atmosphere. **Cons:** difficult to reach by car (call shortly before arrival for staff to meet you); no restaurant on site. [$] *Rooms from: €167* ✉ *Calle Don Carlos Alonso Chaparro 3, Santa Cruz* ☎ *954/213868* 🌐 *www.casadelpoeta.es* 🛏 *14 rooms, 4 suites* 🍽 *No meals* ✣ *C3.*

$$$$ B&B/INN Fodor's Choice ★ 🏨 **Casa Número 7.** Dating from 1850, this converted townhouse retains an elegant but lived-in feel, with family photographs, original oil paintings, and plush furnishings throughout. **Pros:** the personal touch of a B&B; delightfully different; great location. **Cons:** uninteresting breakfast. [$] *Rooms from: €200* ✉ *Calle Virgenes 7, Santa Cruz* ☎ *954/221581* 🌐 *www.casanumero7.com* 🛏 *6 rooms* 🍽 *Breakfast* ✣ *C3.*

$$ HOTEL Fodor's Choice ★ **Hotel Amadeus La Música de Sevilla.** With pianos in some of the soundproof rooms, other instruments for guests to use, a music room off the central patio, and regular classical concerts, this acoustic oasis is ideal for touring professional musicians and music fans in general. **Pros:** small but charming rooms; roof terrace. **Cons:** certain rooms are noisy and lack privacy; ground-floor rooms can be dark. [$] *Rooms from: €112* ✉ *Calle Farnesio 6, Santa Cruz* ☎ *954/501443* 🌐 *www.hotelamadeussevilla.com* 🛏 *30 rooms* 🍴 *No meals* ✥ *C3.*

$$$ B&B/INN Fodor's Choice ★ **Hotel Casa 1800.** This classy boutique hotel, in a refurbished 19th-century mansion, is an oasis in bustling Santa Cruz. **Pros:** top-notch amenities; great service. **Cons:** the rooms facing the patio can be noisy; no restaurant; prices rocket for a three-week period around Easter. [$] *Rooms from: €150* ✉ *C. Rodrigo Caro 6, Santa Cruz* ☎ *954/561800* 🌐 *www.hotelcasa1800sevilla.com* 🛏 *23 rooms, 1 suite* 🍴 *No meals* ✥ *C3.*

$$$$ HOTEL **Las Casas de la Judería.** This labyrinthine hotel occupies 24 houses and three of Santa Cruz's old palaces, each arranged around an inner courtyard with fountains, traditional tile work, and plenty of greenery, giving the impression of a self-contained village in the city center. **Pros:** lovely buildings; unique experience. **Cons:** communal areas and some rooms look very tired; difficult to find your way round the hotel. [$] *Rooms from: €240* ✉ *Calle Santa María la Blanca 5, Santa Cruz* ☎ *954/415150* 🌐 *www.casasypalacios.com* 🛏 *166 rooms, 12 suites* 🍴 *No meals* ✥ *D3.*

$ HOTEL **Pensión Córdoba.** Just a few blocks from the cathedral, nestled in the heart of Santa Cruz, this small, family-run inn is an excellent value. **Pros:** quiet, central location; friendly staff. **Cons:** no entry after 3 am; no breakfast. [$] *Rooms from: €65* ✉ *Calle Farnesio 12, Santa Cruz* ☎ *954/227498* 🌐 *www.pensioncordoba.com* 🛏 *12 rooms* 🍴 *No meals* ✥ *C3.*

EL ARENAL AND PARQUE MARÍA LUISA

$$$$ HOTEL **Gran Meliá Colón.** Originally opened for 1929's Ibero-American Exposition and renovated in 2009, this classic hotel retains many original features, including a marble staircase leading up to a central lobby crowned by a magnificent stained-glass dome and crystal chandelier. **Pros:** good central location; excellent restaurant; some great views. **Cons:** some rooms overlook airshaft; on a busy and noisy street. [$] *Rooms from: €310* ✉ *Calle Canalejas 1, El Arenal* ☎ *954/505599* 🌐 *www.granmeliacolon.com* 🛏 *159 rooms, 30 suites* 🍴 *Breakfast* ✥ *A2.*

$$$$ HOTEL Fodor's Choice ★ **Hotel Alfonso XIII.** Inaugurated by King Alfonso XIII in 1929 and restored in 2011, this grand hotel *(⇨ see also Exploring)* is a splendid, historic, Mudejar-style palace, built around a central patio and surrounded by ornate brick arches. **Pros:** both stately and hip; impeccable service. **Cons:** a tourist colony; expensive. [$] *Rooms from: €390* ✉ *Calle San Fernando 2, El Arenal* ☎ *954/917000* 🌐 *www.luxurycollection.com/alfonsoxiii* 🛏 *132 rooms, 19 suites* 🍴 *Breakfast* ✥ *C4.*

PERFORMING ARTS

Seville has a lively nightlife and plenty of cultural activity. The free monthly magazine *El Giraldillo* (🌐 *www.elgiraldillo.es*) lists classical and jazz concerts, plays, dance performances, art exhibits, and films in

Outdoor restaurants in Seville's Santa Cruz quarter

Seville and all major Andalusian cities. (For American films in English, look for the designation *v.o.*, or *versión original*.)

FLAMENCO CLUBS

Seville has a handful of commercial *tablaos* (flamenco clubs), patronized more by tourists than locals. They generally offer somewhat mechanical flamenco at high prices, with mediocre cuisine. Check local listings and ask at your hotel for performances by top artists. Spontaneous flamenco is often found for free in *peñas flamencas* (flamenco clubs) and flamenco bars in Triana.

BARRIO DE SANTA CRUZ

Fodor's Choice
★

Casa de la Memoria de Al-Andalus. Set in an 18th-century palace, this flamenco club has a nightly show plus dance classes for the intrepid. It's a small venue so book to be sure of a seat. ⊠ *Calle Cuna 6, Santa Cruz* ☎ *954/560670* ⊕ *www.casadelamemoria.es* ⊠ *€16* ⊙ *Shows nightly at 7:30 and 9.*

La Carbonería. This rambling former coal yard is now a bar, open most evenings when you can watch spontaneous flamenco. ⊠ *Calle Levíes 18, Santa Cruz* ☎ *954/229945* ⊠ *Free, but you have to buy a drink.*

Los Gallos. This intimate club in the heart of Santa Cruz attracts mainly tourists. Performances are entertaining and reasonably authentic. ⊠ *Pl. Santa Cruz 11, Santa Cruz* ☎ *954/216981* ⊕ *www.tablaolosgallos.com* ⊠ *€35, includes one drink* ⊙ *Shows nightly at 8:15 and 10:30.*

10

Continued on page 691

FLAMENCO
THE HEARTBEAT OF SPAIN

Palmas, the staccato clapping of flamenco.

Rule one about flamenco: You don't see it. You feel it. There's no soap-opera emoting here. The pain and yearning on the dancers' faces and the eerie voices —typically communicating grief over a lost love or family member—are real. If the dancers manage to summon the supernatural *duende* and allow this inner demon to overcome them, then they have done their jobs well.

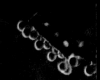

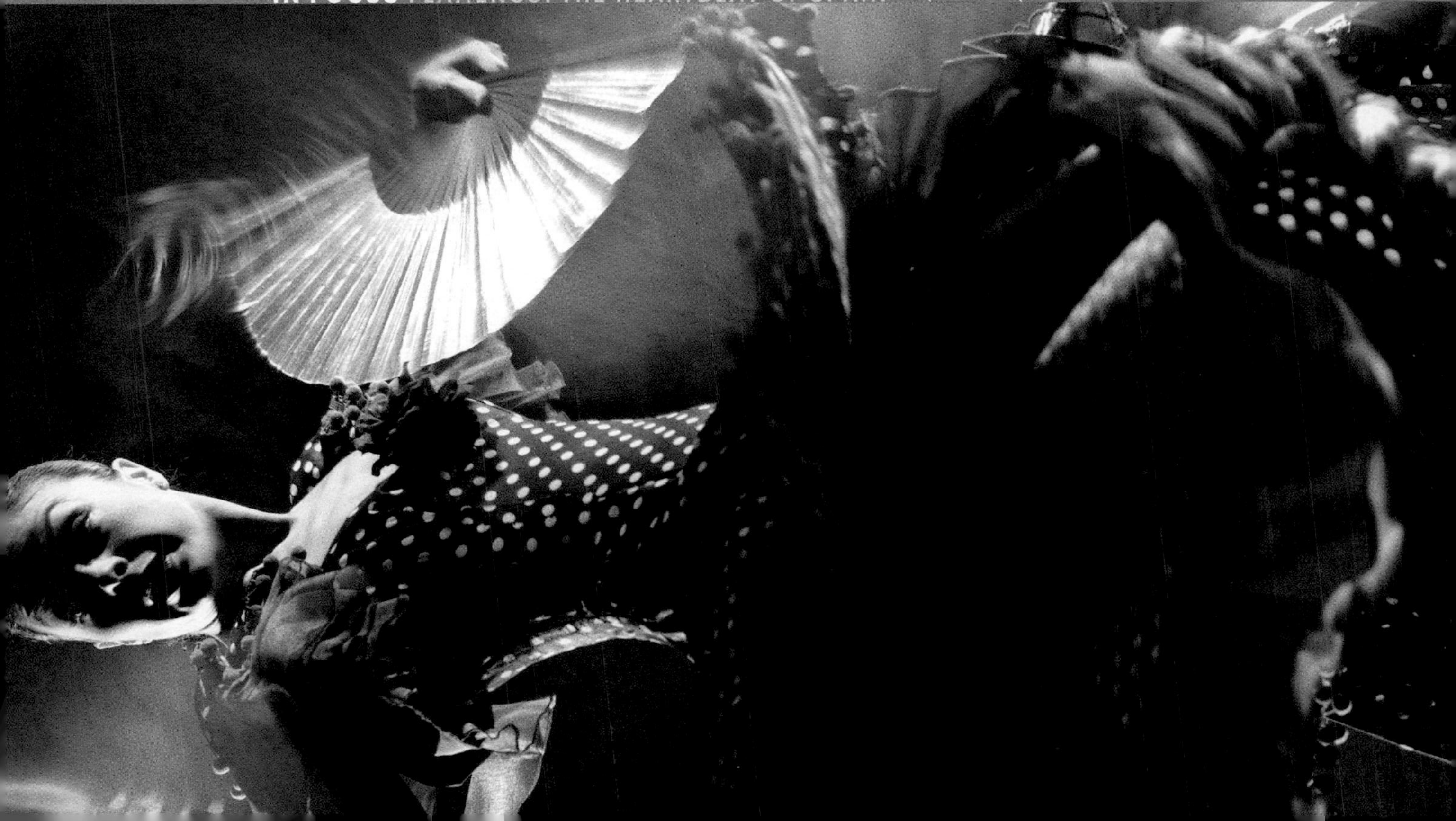

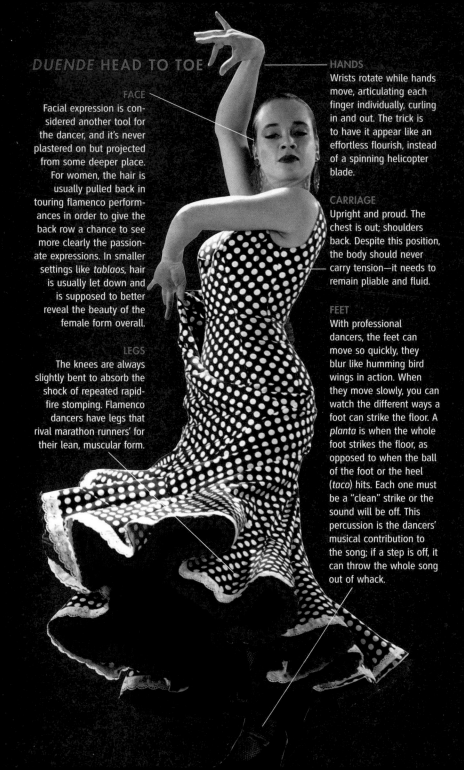

DUENDE HEAD TO TOE

FACE

Facial expression is con-
sidered another tool for
the dancer, and it's never
plastered on but projected
from some deeper place.
For women, the hair is
usually pulled back in
touring flamenco perform-
ances in order to give the
back row a chance to see
more clearly the passion-
ate expressions. In smaller
settings like *tablaos*, hair
is usually let down and
is supposed to better
reveal the beauty of the
female form overall.

LEGS

The knees are always
slightly bent to absorb the
shock of repeated rapid-
fire stomping. Flamenco
dancers have legs that
rival marathon runners' for
their lean, muscular form.

HANDS

Wrists rotate while hands
move, articulating each
finger individually, curling
in and out. The trick is
to have it appear like an
effortless flourish, instead
of a spinning helicopter
blade.

CARRIAGE

Upright and proud. The
chest is out; shoulders
back. Despite this position,
the body should never
carry tension—it needs to
remain pliable and fluid.

FEET

With professional
dancers, the feet can
move so quickly, they
blur like humming bird
wings in action. When
they move slowly, you can
watch the different ways a
foot can strike the floor. A
planta is when the whole
foot strikes the floor, as
opposed to when the ball
of the foot or the heel
(*taco*) hits. Each one must
be a "clean" strike or the
sound will be off. This
percussion is the dancers'
musical contribution to
the song; if a step is off, it
can throw the whole song
out of whack.

FLAMENCO 101

All the elements of flamenco working in harmony.

ORIGINS

The music is largely Arabic in its beginnings, but you'll detect echoes of Greek dirges and Jewish chants, with healthy doses of Flemish and traditional Castillian thrown in. Hindu sways, Roman mimes, and other movement informs the dance, but we may never know the specific origins of flamenco.

The dance, along with the nomadic Gypsies, spread throughout Andalusia and within a few centuries had developed into many variations and styles, some of them named after the city where they were born (such as Malagueñas, Sevillanas) and others taking on the names after people, emotions, or bands. In all, there are over 50 different styles (or *palos*) of flamenco, four of which are the stylistic pillars others branch off from—differing mainly in rhythm and mood: *Toná*, *Soleá*, *Fandango*, and *Seguidilla*.

CLAPPING AND CASTANETS

The sum of its parts are awe-inspiring, but if you boil it down, flamenco is a combination of music, singing, and dance. Staccato hand-clapping almost sneaks in as a fourth part—the sounds made from all the participants' palms, or *palmas* is part of the *duende*—but this element remains more of a

continued on following page

10

THE FLAMENCO HOOK-UP

When *duende* leads to love.

That cheek-to-cheek chemistry that exists between dance partners isn't missing in flamenco—it's simply repositioned between the dancer and the musicians. In fact, when you watch flamenco, you may feel what seems like an electric wire connecting the dancer to the musicians. In each *palo* (style) of music there are certain *letras* (lyrics) inherent within the song that tip off dancers and spark a change in rhythm. If the cues are off, the dancer may falter or simply come off flat. At its best, the dancer and the guitarist are like an old married couple that can musically finish each other's sentences. This interconnectedness has been known to lead into the bedroom, and it's not unusual for dancers and musicians to hook up offstage. Two famous couples include dancer Eva La Yerbabuena with guitarist Paco Jarano and dancer Manuela Carrasco with guitarist Joaquín Amador.

connector that all in the performance take part in when their hands are free.

Hand-clapping was likely flamenco's original key instrument before the guitar, *cajón* (wooden box used for percussion), and other instruments arrived on the scene. Perhaps the simplest way to augment the clapping is to add a uniquely designed six-string guitar, in which case you've got yourself a *tablao*, or people seated around a singer and clapping. Dance undoubtedly augments the experience, but isn't necessary for a *tablao*. These exist all throughout Andalusia and are usually private affairs with people who love flamenco. One needn't be a Gypsy in order to take part in it. But it doesn't hurt.

Castanets (or *palillos*) were absorbed by the Phoenician culture and adopted by the Spanish, now part of their own folklore. They accompany other traditional folk dances in Spain and are used pervasively throughout flamenco (though not always present in some forms of dance). Castanets can be secured in any number of ways. The most important thing is that they are securely fastened to the hand (by thumb or any combination of fingers) so that the wrist can snap it quickly and make the sound.

FLAMENCO NOW

Flamenco's enormous international resurgence has been building for the past few decades. Much of this revival can be attributed to pioneers like legendary singer Camarón de la Isla, guitarist Paco de Lucía, or even outsiders like Miles Davis fusing flamenco with other genres like jazz and rock. This melding brought forth flamenco pop—which flourished in the '80s and continues today—as well as disparate fusions with almost every genre imaginable, including heavy metal and hiphop. Today the most popular flamenco fusion artists include Ojos de Brujo and Chambao—all of which have found an audience outside of Spain.

IT'S A MAN'S WORLD

Joaquín Cortés

In the U.S., our image of a flamenco dancer is usually a woman in a red dress. So you may be surprised to learn that male dancers dominate flamenco and always have. In its beginnings, men did all the footwork and only since the '40s and '50s have women started to match men step-for-step and star in performances. And in the tabloids, men usually get the sex symbol status more than women (as seen through Farruquito and Cortés). Suits are the traditional garb for male dancers, and recent trends have seen female dancers wearing them as well—presumably rebelling against the staid gender roles that continue to rule Spain. Today, male dancers tend to wear a simple pair of black trousers and a white button-down shirt. The sex appeal comes from unbuttoning the shirt to flash a little chest and having the pants tailor-made to a tightness that can't be found in any store. In traditional *tablaos*, male dancers perform without accessories, but in touring performances—upping the razzle dazzle—anything goes: canes, hats, tuxedos, or even shirtless (much to the delight of female fans).

EL ARENAL AND PARQUE MARÍA LUISA

Teatro de la Maestranza. Long prominent in the opera world, Seville is proud of its opera house. Tickets go quickly, so book well in advance (online is best). ⊠ *Paseo de Colón 22, El Arenal* ☎ *954/223344 for info, 954/226573 for tickets* ⊕ *www.teatrodelamaestranza.es.*

Teatro Lope de Vega. Classical music, ballet, and musicals are performed here. ⊠ *Av. María Luisa s/n, Parque Maria Luisa* ☎ *954/472828 for info, 955/472822 for tickets* ⊕ *www.teatrolopedevega.org.*

TRIANA

Casa Anselma. In the heart of Triana, this is an unmarked bar on the corner of Antillano Campos where Anselma and her friends sing and dance for the pure joy and catharsis that are at the heart of flamenco. Admission is free, but you have to buy a drink. ⊠ *Calle Pagés del Corro 49, Triana* ☎ *Free* ☉ *Shows Mon.–Sat. at midnight.*

Teatro Central. This modern venue on the Isla de la Cartuja stages theater, dance, and classical and contemporary music. Tickets can be bought via ⊕ *www.ticketmaster.es* or at Caixa ATMs. ⊠ *Calle José de Gálvez 6, Triana* ☎ *955/037200 for info, 902/150025 for tickets.*

BULLFIGHTING

Bullfighting season is Easter through Columbus Day (no bullfights in August); most *corridas* (bullfights) are held on Sunday. The highlight is the April Fair, with Spain's leading toreros; other key dates are Corpus Christi (about seven weeks after Easter), Assumption (August 15), and the last weekend in September.

Despacho de Entradas. Tickets are expensive; buy them in advance alongside the bullring from this official ticket office. Unofficial *despachos* sell tickets on Calle Sierpes but charge a 20% commission. ⊠ *Calle Adriano 37, El Arenal* ☎ *954/501382.*

Maestranza Bullring. This is the site for Seville's bullfights. ⊠ *Paseo de Colón 12, El Arenal* ☎ *954/224577* ⊕ *www.realmaestranza.es.*

SHOPPING

Seville is the region's main shopping area and the place for archetypal Andalusian souvenirs, most of which are sold in the Barrio de Santa Cruz and around the cathedral and Giralda, especially on Calle Alemanes. The shopping street for locals is Calle Sierpes, along with neighboring Cuna, Tetuan, Velázquez, Plaza Magdalena, and Plaza Duque—boutiques abound here. For antiques, try Mateos Gago, opposite the Giralda, and in the Barrio de Santa Cruz on Jamerdana and Rodrigo Caro, off Plaza Alianza. For ceramics in the Barrio de Santa Cruz, browse along Mateos Gago; on Romero Murube, between Plaza Triunfo and Plaza Alianza, on the edge of the barrio; and between Plaza Doña Elvira and Plaza de los Venerables. Flamenco wear can be expensive; local women will gladly spend the equivalent of a month's grocery money, or more, on their frills, with dresses ranging from €100 to €400 and up.

10

CENTRO

Calle Sierpes. This is Seville's classy main shopping street. Near the southern end, at No. 85, a plaque marks the spot where the Cárcel Real (Royal Prison) once stood. Miguel de Cervantes began writing *Don Quixote* in one of its cells. ⊠ *Centro.*

El Corte Inglés. The main branch of this pan-Spanish department store chain has everything from high fashion to local wine. It does not close for siesta. ⊠ *Pl. Duque de la Victoria 8, Centro* ☎ *954/597000.*

La Campana. Under the gilt-edged ceiling at Seville's most celebrated pastry outlet (founded in 1885), you can enjoy the flanlike *tocino de cielo,* or "heavenly bacon." ⊠ *Calle Sierpes 1, Centro* ☎ *954/223570.*

Lola Azahares. For flamenco wear, this is one of Seville's most highly regarded stores. ⊠ *Calle Cuna 31, Centro* ☎ *954/222912.*

Martian Ceramics. In central Seville, Martian has high-quality dishes, especially the finely painted flowers-on-white patterns native to Seville. ⊠ *Calle Sierpes 74, Centro* ☎ *954/213413.*

Molina. Flamenco dresses and traditional foot-tapping shoes are sold here. ⊠ *Calle Sierpes 11, Centro* ☎ *954/229254.*

Plaza del Duque. A few blocks north of Plaza Nueva, Plaza del Duque has a crafts market on Thursday, Friday, and Saturday. ⊠ *Centro.*

Taller de Diseño. Come here for privately fitted and custom-made flamenco dresses. ⊠ *Calle Luchana 6, Centro* ☎ *954/227186.*

BARRIO DE SANTA CRUZ

Artesanía Textil. You can find blankets, shawls, and embroidered table-cloths woven by local artisans at the two shops of Artesanía Textil. ⊠ *Calle García de Vinuesa 33, El Arenal* ☎ *954/215088* ⊠ *Calle Sierpes 70, Santa Cruz* ☎ *954/220125.*

El Torno. Andalusia's convents are known for their homemade pastries, and you can sample sweets from several convents at El Torno, named after the revolving tray the nuns use to display their wares. ⊠ *Pl. del Cabildo, Santa Cruz* ☎ *954/219190.*

Extraverde. Taste a selection of olive oils at this restaurant-shop in the heart of Santa Cruz. ⊠ *Pl. Doña Elvira 8, Santa Cruz* ☎ *954/218417* ⊕ *www.extraverde.es.*

Librería Vértice. A large assortment of books in English, Spanish, French, and Italian can be found at this American-owned store near the cathedral. ⊠ *Calle San Fernando 33–35, Santa Cruz* ☎ *954/211654.*

EL ARENAL AND PARQUE MARÍA LUISA

El Postigo. This permanent arts-and-crafts market opposite El Corte Inglés is open every day except Sunday. ⊠ *Pl. de la Concordia, El Arenal.*

BARRIO DE LA MACARENA

El Jueves. This antiques and flea market is held in the Barrio de la Macarena on Thursday morning. ⊠ *Calle Feria, La Macarena.*

TRIANA

Mercado de Triana. Since 2005, the Triana market, which began as an improvised fish market on the banks of the Guadalquivir in the 1830s, has been housed in a shiny new building and given the stamp

"Traditional Shopping Center." The vendors, however, continue to sell the same colorful mix of food, flowers, cheap fashion, and costume jewelry as before. It closes at 3 pm and is not open on Sunday. ⊠ *Pl. del Alzotano, Triana* 🖃 *No credit cards.*

Potters' district. Look for traditional azulejo tiles and other ceramics in the Triana potters' district, on Calle Alfarería and Calle Antillano Campos. ⊠ *Triana.*

AROUND SEVILLE

CARMONA

32 km (20 miles) east of Seville off A4.

Wander the ancient, narrow streets here and you'll feel as if you've been transported back in time. Claiming to be one of the oldest inhabited places in Spain (both Phoenicians and Carthaginians had settlements here), Carmona, on a steep, fortified hill, became an important town under the Romans and the Moors. There are many Mudejar and Renaissance churches and convents (several open weekend mornings only), medieval gateways, and simple whitewashed houses of clear Moorish influence, punctuated here and there by a baroque palace. Local fiestas are held in mid-September.

ESSENTIALS

Visitor Information Carmona ⊠ *Alcázar de la Puerta de Sevilla* ☎ *954/190955* ⊕ *www.turismo.carmona.org.*

EXPLORING
TOP ATTRACTIONS

Alcázar del Rey Don Pedro (*King Pedro's Fortress*). The Moorish Alcázar was built on Roman foundations and converted by King Pedro the Cruel into a Mudejar palace. Pedro's summer residence was destroyed by a 1504 earthquake, and all that remains are ruins that can be viewed but not visited. However, the parador within the complex (⇨ *see Where to Stay*) has a breathtaking view, and the café and restaurant are lovely spots to have a refreshment or meal. ⊠ *Calle Los Alcázares s/n.*

FAMILY **Museo de la Ciudad.** Reopened in 2014 following restoration work, this museum behind Santa María has exhibits on Carmona's history. There's plenty for children, and the interactive exhibits are labeled in English and Spanish. ⊠ *Calle San Ildefonso 1* ☎ *954/140128* 💰 *€3* ⊙ *Sept. 16–June 16, Mon. 11–2, Tues.–Sun. 11–7; June 16–Sept. 15, Mon. 10–2, Tues.–Fri. 10–2 and 6:30–8:30, weekends 9:30–2.*

Roman Necropolis. At the western edge of town 900 tombs were placed in underground chambers between the 2nd and 4th centuries BC. The necropolis walls, decorated with leaf and bird motifs, have niches for burial urns and tombs such as the **Elephant Vault** and the **Servilia Tomb**, a complete Roman villa with colonnaded arches and vaulted side galleries. ⊠ *Calle Enmedio* ☎ *600/143632* 💰 *€1.50* ⊙ *Tues.–Sat. 10–6:30, Sun. 10–5.*

10

Santa María. This Gothic church was built between 1424 and 1518 on the site of Carmona's former Great Mosque and retains its beautiful Moorish courtyard, studded with orange trees. ✉ *Calle Martín* 🎫 *€3* 🕒 *Weekdays 9–2 and 5–7, Sat. 9–2, Sun. 9–11:30.*

WORTH NOTING

Alcázar de la Puerta de Sevilla. Park your car near the Puerta de Sevilla in the imposing Alcázar, a Moorish fortification built on Roman foundations. Maps are available at the tourist office, in the tower beside the gate. ✉ *Pl. de Blas Infante* 🎫 *€2 (free Mon.)* 🕒 *Sept.–June, Mon.–Sat. 10–6, Sun. 10–3; July and Aug., weekdays 10:30–3 and 4:30–6, weekends 10–3.*

Plaza San Fernando. Up Calle Prim, this plaza in the heart of the old town is bordered by 17th-century houses with Moorish overtones.

Puerta de Córdoba (*Córdoba Gate*). Stroll down to this old gateway on the eastern edge of town. It was first built by the Romans around AD 175, then altered by Moorish and Renaissance additions. Viewing of the interior is on weekends (12:30–1:30) by appointment only. You can book by phone or at the tourist office. ✉ *Calle Dolores Quintanilla* ☎ *615/540505* 🎫 *€2.*

San Bartolomé. Just up the street from the Puerta de Sevilla is the church of San Bartolomé, a 15th-century building with a baroque interior, including a fine 18th-century altarpiece. ✉ *Calle Prim 29* 🎫 *Free* 🕒 *Fri.–Wed. 11–1:45.*

WHERE TO STAY

$$$ HOTEL 🏨 **Parador Alcázar del Rey Don Pedro.** This parador has superb views from its hilltop position among the ruins of Pedro the Cruel's summer palace. **Pros:** unbeatable views over the fields; great sense of history. **Cons:** feels slightly lifeless after Seville. [$] *Rooms from: €135* ✉ *Calle del Alcázar* ☎ *954/141010* 🌐 *www.parador.es* 🛏 *63 rooms* 🍴 *No meals.*

ITÁLICA

12 km (7 miles) north of Seville, 1 km (½ mile) beyond Santiponce.

Neighboring the small town of Santiponce, Itálica is Spain's oldest Roman site and one of its greatest, and is well worth a visit when you're in Seville. If you're here during June or July, try to get tickets for the International Dance Festival held in the ruins (🌐 *www.festivalitalica.es*).

GETTING HERE AND AROUND

The C1 bus route runs frequently (daily from 7 am to 11 pm) between the Plaza de Armas bus station in Seville and Itálica. Journey time is 30 minutes. If you have a rental car, you could include a visit to the ruins on your way to Huelva. Allow at least three hours for your visit.

EXPLORING

Fodor's Choice ★ **Itálica.** One of Roman Iberia's most important cities in the 2nd century, with a population of more than 10,000, Itálica today is a monument of Roman ruins. Founded by Scipio Africanus in 205 BC as a home for veteran soldiers, Itálica gave the Roman world two great emperors: Trajan (AD 52–117) and Hadrian (AD 76–138). You can find traces of city streets, cisterns, and the floor plans of several villas, some with mosaic floors, though all the best mosaics and statues have been removed to Seville's Museum of Archaeology. Itálica was abandoned and plundered as a quarry by the Visigoths, who preferred Seville. It fell into decay around AD 700. The remains include the huge, elliptical **amphitheater**, which held 40,000 spectators, a **Roman theater**, and **Roman baths**. The small visitor center offers information on daily life in the city. ⊠ *Av. Extremadura 2, Santiponce* ☎ *955/123847* ⊕ *www.juntadeandalucia. es/cultura/italica* ⊠ *€1.50* ☉ *Sept. 16–Mar. 31, Tues.–Sat. 10–6:30, Sun. 10–5; Apr.–June 15, Tues.–Sat. 10–8:30, Sun. 10–5; June 16–Sept. 15, Tues.–Sun. 10–5.*

RONDA

147 km (91 miles) southeast of Seville, 61 km (38 miles) northwest of Marbella.

Fodor's Choice
★
Ronda, one of the oldest towns in Spain, is known for its spectacular position and views. Secure in its mountain fastness on a rock high over the Río Guadalevín, the town was a stronghold for the legendary Andalusian bandits who held court here from the 18th to the early 20th century. Ronda's most dramatic element is its ravine (360 feet deep and 210 feet across)—known as **El Tajo**—which divides La Ciudad, the old Moorish town, from El Mercadillo, the "new town," which sprang up after the Christian Reconquest of 1485. Tour buses roll in daily with sightseers from the coast 49 km (30 miles) away, and on weekends affluent *sevillanos* flock to their second homes here. Stay overnight midweek to see this noble town's true colors.

In the lowest part of town, known as El Barrio, you can see parts of the old walls, including the 13th-century Puerta de Almocobar and the 16th-century Puerta de Carlos V gates. From here, the main road climbs past the Iglesia del Espíritu Santo (Church of the Holy Spirit) and up into the heart of town.

GETTING HERE AND AROUND
By road, the most attractive approach is from the south. The winding but well-maintained A376 from San Pedro de Alcántara travels north up through the mountains of the Serranía de Ronda. At least four daily buses run here from Marbella, nine from Málaga, and three from Seville. The Ronda tourist office publishes an updated list (available online).

EXPLORING
TOP ATTRACTIONS
Juan Peña El Lebrijano. Immediately south of the Plaza de España, this is Ronda's most famous bridge (also known as the Puente Nuevo, or New Bridge), an architectural marvel built between 1755 and 1793. The bridge's lantern-lit parapet offers dizzying views of the awesome gorge. Just how many people have met their ends here nobody knows, but the architect of the Puente Nuevo fell to his death while inspecting work on the bridge. During the civil war, hundreds of victims were hurled from it.

10

La Ciudad. Cross the Puente Nuevo to enter the old Moorish town, with twisting streets and white houses with birdcage balconies.

Palacio de Mondragón (*Palace of Mondragón*). This stone palace with twin Mudejar towers was probably the residence of Ronda's Moorish kings. Ferdinand and Isabella appropriated it after their victory in 1485. Today, it's the museum of Ronda and you can wander through the patios, with their brick arches and delicate Mudejar-stucco tracery, and admire the mosaics and *artesonado* (coffered) ceiling. The second floor holds a small museum with archaeological items found near Ronda, plus the reproduction of a dolmen, a prehistoric stone monument. ✉ *Pl. Mondragón* ☎ *952/870818* 🎫 *€3 (free Wed.)* ⊙ *Weekdays 10–6 (until 7 in summer), weekends 10–3.*

Plaza de Toros. The main sight in Ronda's commercial center, El Mercadillo, is the bullring. Pedro Romero (1754–1839), the father of modern bullfighting and Ronda's most famous native son, is said to have killed 5,600 bulls here during his long career. In the museum beneath the plaza you can see posters for Ronda's very first bullfights, held here in 1785. The plaza was once owned by the late bullfighter Antonio Ordóñez, on whose nearby ranch Orson Welles's ashes were scattered (as directed in his will)—indeed, the ring has become a favorite of filmmakers. Every September, the bullring is the scene of Ronda's *corridas goyescas,* named after Francisco Goya, whose bullfight sketches (*tauromaquias*) were inspired by Romero's skill and art. The participants and the dignitaries in the audience don the costumes of Goya's time for the occasion. Seats for these fights cost a small fortune and are booked far in advance. Other than that, the plaza is rarely used for fights except during Ronda's May festival. ✉ *Calle Virgen de la Paz* ☎ *952/874132* ⊕ *www.rmcr.org* 🎫 *€6.50* ⊙ *Daily 10–6 (until 7 May–Sept.).*

WORTH NOTING

Baños Arabes (*Arab Baths*). The excavated remains of the Arab Baths date from Ronda's tenure as capital of a Moorish *taifa* (kingdom). The star-shape vents in the roof are an inferior imitation of the ceiling of the beautiful bathhouse in Granada's Alhambra. The baths are beneath the Puente Árabe (Arab Bridge) in a ravine below the Palacio del Marqués de Salvatierra. ✉ *Calle San Miguel* 🎫 *€3 (free Mon.)* ⊙ *Weekdays 10–6 (until 7 Apr.–Oct.), weekends 10–3.*

Santa María la Mayor. This collegiate church, which serves as Ronda's cathedral, has roots in Moorish times: originally the Great Mosque of Ronda, the tower and adjacent galleries, built for viewing festivities in the square, retain their Islamic design. After the mosque was destroyed (when the Moors were overthrown), it was rebuilt as a church and dedicated to the Virgen de la Encarnación after the Reconquest. The naves are late Gothic, and the main altar is heavy with baroque gold leaf. The church is around the corner from the remains of a mosque, Minarete Arabe (Moorish Minaret) at the end of the Marqués de Salvatierra. ✉ *Pl. Duquesa de Parcent* 🎫 *€4* ⊙ *Mon.–Sat. 10–6, Sun. 10–12:30 and 2–6.*

Alameda del Tajo. Beyond the bullring in El Mercadillo, you can relax in these shady gardens, one of the loveliest spots in Ronda. At the end of

OFF THE BEATEN PATH

The stunningly perched hilltop town of Ronda

the gardens, a balcony protrudes from the face of the cliff, offering a vertigo-inducing view of the valley below. Stroll along the clifftop walk to the Reina Victoria hotel, built by British settlers from Gibraltar at the turn of the 20th century as a fashionable rest stop on the Algeciras–Bobadilla rail line. ⊠ *Paseo Hemingway.*

WHERE TO EAT

$$ ✕ **Almocábar.** Tucked agreeably away from the main tourist hub on
SPANISH the south side of town, this unpretentious tapas bar and restaurant on a lovely plaza offers a refined and inventive cuisine. Dishes include unusual and tasty starters, like goat-cheese salad with mango sauce, and mains based on local fare such as roast suckling lamb flavored with mountain herbs. Get here early if you want to sample the tapas (€1.50–€4), as the narrow bar gets packed with the local crowd on their *tapear* (bar crawl). The delicious *patatas alioli* (cooked potatoes in a creamily pungent garlic sauce) are great for sharing. $ *Average main: €15* ⊠ *Calle Ruedo Alameda 5* 🕾 *952/875977* ⊘ *Closed Tues. and Sept. 1–20.*

$ ✕ **Entre Vinos.** Just off the main road opposite the Hotel Colón, this small
TAPAS and cozy bar has established itself as one of Ronda's best for tapas and wine. Inside, the wood-paneled barrel ceiling and wine bottles lining the walls add to the *bodega* (wine cellar) atmosphere. Local Ronda wines are a specialty here—in fact, they're the only ones available, although with over 60 on the wine list, you'll be spoiled for choice; ask the waiter for recommendations. Tapas (from €1) include *fideos negros con chipirones y alioli* (black noodles with baby squid and garlic sauce) and a mini–beef burger with foie gras. This place is popular and fills up

quickly so arrive early (1:30 pm or 8 pm) to be sure of a place. Service is excellent. [$] *Average main: €5* ✉ *Calle Pozo 2* ⏲ *Closed during the Ronda Fair. No dinner Sun.; no lunch Mon.*

$$$ SPANISH 🍴 **Pedro Romero.** Named for the father of modern bullfighting, this restaurant opposite the bullring is packed with bullfight paraphernalia. Mounted bulls' heads peer down at you as you tuck into *choricitos al vino blanco de Ronda* (small sausages in Ronda white wine) or *rabo de toro Pedro Romero* (slow-cooked oxtail stew with herbs) and, for dessert, *tarat de queso con frutillos rojos* (cheesecake with red berries). Previous diners include Ernest Hemingway and Orson Welles, whose photos are displayed. [$] *Average main: €18* ✉ *Calle Virgen de la Paz 18* ☎ *952/871110.*

WHERE TO STAY

$$ B&B/INN 🏨 **Alavera de los Baños.** Fittingly, given its location next to the Moorish baths, there's an Arab-influenced theme throughout this small, German-run hotel (which was used as a backdrop for the film classic *Carmen*). **Pros:** very atmospheric and historic; owners speak several languages. **Cons:** rooms vary in size; steep climb into town. [$] *Rooms from: €97* ✉ *Calle San Miguel s/n* ☎ *952/879143* 🌐 *www.alaveradelosbanos.com* 🛏 *9 rooms, 2 suites* ⏲ *Closed Jan.* 🍽 *Breakfast.*

$$ B&B/INN FAMILY 🏨 **El Molino del Santo.** In a converted olive mill next to a rushing stream near Benaoján, 16 km (10 miles) west of Ronda, this British-run establishment appeals for its "green" credentials and proximity to great mountain walks. **Pros:** superb for hikers; friendly owners. **Cons:** you won't hear much Spanish spoken (most guests are British); a car is essential if you want to explore farther afield. [$] *Rooms from: €119* ✉ *Estación de Benaoján, Benaoján* ☎ *952/167151* 🌐 *www.molinodelsanto.com* 🛏 *15 rooms, 3 suites* ⏲ *Closed Nov.–end Feb.* 🍽 *Breakfast.*

$ B&B/INN 🏨 **Finca la Guzmana.** This traditional Andalusian *cortijo* (farmhouse), 4 km (2½ miles) east of Ronda, has been lovingly restored with bright, fresh color schemes to complement the original beams, wood-burning stoves, and sublime setting. **Pros:** surrounded by beautiful countryside; very peaceful. **Cons:** it's a hike to Ronda and the stores; no restaurant. [$] *Rooms from: €75* ✉ *Off A366, on El Burgo road* ☎ *600/006305* 🌐 *www.laguzmana.com* 🛏 *6 rooms* 🍽 *Breakfast.*

$$ B&B/INN 🏨 **Montelirio.** The 18th-century mansion of the Count of Montelirio, perched over the deep plunge to the Tajo, has been carefully refurbished, maintaining some original features, but the highlight is the breathtaking view over the valley. **Pros:** great views; friendly staff. **Cons:** some rooms have windows to the street. [$] *Rooms from: €120* ✉ *Calle Tenorio 8* ☎ *952/873855* 🌐 *www.hotelmontelirio.com* 🛏 *12 rooms, 3 suites* 🍽 *No meals.*

$ B&B/INN Fodor's Choice ★ 🏨 **San Gabriel.** In the oldest part of Ronda, this hotel is run by a family who converted their 18th-century home into an enchanting, informal hotel. **Pros:** traditional Andalusian house; excellent service. **Cons:** some rooms are rather dark; no panoramic views. [$] *Rooms from: €88* ✉ *Calle Marqués de Moctezuma 19* ☎ *952/190392* 🌐 *www.hotelsangabriel.com* 🛏 *21 rooms, 1 suite* 🍽 *No meals.*

AROUND RONDA: CAVES, ROMANS, AND PUEBLOS BLANCOS

This area of spectacular gorges, remote mountain villages, and ancient caves is fascinating to explore and a dramatic contrast to the clamor and crowds of the coast.

Acinipo. Old Ronda, 20 km (12 miles) north of Ronda, is the site of this old Roman settlement, a thriving town in the 1st century AD that was abandoned for reasons that still baffle historians. Today it's a windswept hillside with piles of stones, the foundations of a few Roman houses, and what remains of a theater. Views across the Ronda plains and to the surrounding mountains are spectacular. The site is often closed because excavations are under way. Call to check before visiting. ⊠ *Ronda la Vieja* ✛ *Take A376 toward Algodonales; turnoff for the ruins is 9 km (5 miles) from Ronda on MA449* ☎ *951/041452 1* ⧉ *Free* ☉ *Hrs vary depending on staff availability; call to check.*

Cueva de la Pileta (*Pileta Cave*). At this prehistoric site, 20 km (12 miles) west of Ronda, a Spanish guide (who speaks some English) will hand you a paraffin lamp and lead you on a roughly 60-minute walk that reveals prehistoric wall paintings of bison, deer, and horses outlined in black, red, and ocher. One highlight is the Cámara del Pescado (Chamber of the Fish), whose drawing of a huge fish is thought to be 15,000 years old. Tours take place whenever 25 people have accumulated. ⊠ *Benaoján* ✛ *Drive west from Ronda on A374 and take the left exit for the village of Benaoján from where the caves are well signposted* ☎ *952/167343* ⧉ *€8* ☉ *Daily 10–1 and 4–5 (until 6 May–Oct.).*

Olvera. Here, 13 km (8 miles) north of Setenil, two imposing silhouettes dominate the crest of the hill: the 11th-century castle Vallehermoso, a legacy of the Moors, and the neoclassical church of La Encarnación, reconstructed in the 19th century on the foundations of the old mosque.

Setenil de las Bodegas. This small city, in a cleft in the rock cut by the Guadalporcín River, is 8 km (5 miles) north of Acinipois. The streets resemble long, narrow caves, and on many houses the roof is formed by a projecting ledge of heavy rock.

Zahara de la Sierra. A solitary watchtower dominates a crag above this village, its outline visible for miles around. The tower is all that remains of a Moorish castle where King Alfonso X once fought the emir of Morocco; the building remained a Moorish stronghold until it fell to the Christians in 1470. Along the streets you can see doorknockers fashioned like the hand of Fatima: the fingers represent the five laws of the Koran and are meant to ward off evil. ✛ *From Olvera, drive 21 km (13 miles) southwest to the village of Algodonales then south on A376 for 5 km (3 miles).*

10

GRAZALEMA AND THE SIERRA DE GRAZALEMA

Grazalema: 28 km (17 miles) northwest of Ronda.

The village of Grazalema is the prettiest of the pueblos blancos. Its cobblestone streets of houses with pink-and-ocher roofs wind up the hillside, red geraniums splash white walls, and black wrought-iron lanterns and grilles cling to the housefronts.

The Sierra de Grazalema Natural Park encompasses a series of mountain ranges known as the Sierra de Grazalema, which straddle the provinces of Málaga and Cádiz. These mountains trap the rain clouds that roll in from the Atlantic, and the area has the distinction of being the wettest place in Spain, with an average annual rainfall of 88 inches. Because of the park's altitude and prevailing humidity, it's one of the last habitats for the rare fir tree *Abies pinsapo*; it's also home to ibex, vultures, and birds of prey. Parts of the park are restricted, accessible only on foot and when accompanied by an official guide.

GETTING HERE AND AROUND
The village of Grazalema itself is quite small and is best reached by private car as there's little public transport.

ESSENTIALS
Visitor Information Grazalema. At the time of writing, the visitor center was about to relocate and the new location was unknown. Call first, or inquire locally. ☎ 956/132225.

EXPLORING
El Bosque. Another excursion from Grazalema takes you through the heart of this protected reserve, home to a trout stream and information center. Follow the A344 west through dramatic mountain scenery, past Benamahoma.

Ubrique. From Grazalema, the A374 takes you to this town on the slopes of the Saltadero Mountains, known for its leather tanning and embossing industry. Look for the **Convento de los Capuchinos** (Capuchin Convent), the church of **San Pedro**, and, 4 km (2½ miles) away, the ruins of the Moorish castle **El Castillo de Fátima.**

WHERE TO STAY
$
B&B/INN
Fodor's Choice
★

La Mejorana. An ideal base for exploring the area, this is the spot to find rural simplicity and stunning mountain views. **Pros:** in the center of the village; tastefully furnished; excellent service. **Cons:** no TV in rooms. $ *Rooms from: €58* ⊠ *Calle Santa Clara 6* ☎ *956/132327* ⊕ *www.lamejorana.net* ↝ *6 rooms* ❍ *Breakfast.*

HUELVA

When you've had enough of Seville's urban bustle, nature awaits in Huelva. From the Parque Nacional de Doñana to the oak forests of the Sierra de Aracena, nothing is much more than an hour's drive from Seville. If you prefer history, hop on the miners' train at Riotinto or visit Aracena's spectacular caves. Columbus's voyage to the New World was sparked near here, at the monastery of La Rábida and in Palos de la Frontera. The visitor center at La Rocina has Doñana information.

Once a thriving Roman port, the city of Huelva, an hour east of Faro, Portugal, was largely destroyed by the 1755 Lisbon earthquake. As a result, it claims the dubious honor of being the least distinguished city in

Andalusia. If you do end up here, **Taberna el Condado** or El Chiringuito de Antonio are the places to go for shellfish tapas and rice.

GETTING HERE AND AROUND
Huelva has good bus connections from Seville, but traveling to the main sights in the province is difficult by public transportation so you're better off renting a car.

ESSENTIALS
Bus Station Huelva ✉ *Av. Alemania s/n, Huelva* ☎ *959/256900.*

Taxi Contact Tele Taxi ☎ *959/250022.*

Train Station Huelva ✉ *Av. de Italia, Huelva* ☎ *902/320320.*

DOÑANA NATIONAL PARK

100 km (62 miles) southwest of Seville.

The jewel in Spain's crown when it comes to national parks, and one of Europe's most important wetlands, Doñana is a paradise for wildlife in their natural habitat. Most of the park is heavily protected and closed to visitors, although you can visit with one of the authorized tour companies who organize visits by jeep, foot, or horseback.

GETTING HERE AND AROUND
To explore Doñana and its surroundings you need your own transportation, particularly to get to the different visitor centers, all some distance apart.

ESSENTIALS
In addition to the centers listed here, there is a visitor center for the park at Sanlúcar de Barrameda.

Visitor Information El Acebuche Two kilometers (1 mile) before Matalascañas, this is Doñana National Park's main interpretation center and the departure point for jeep tours. ✉ *Matalascañas* ☎ *959/439569* ☉ *Daily 8–3 and 4–7 (until 9 June–Sept.).* **La Rocina Visitor Center** At this visitor center, less than 2 km (1 mile) from the center of El Rocío, you can peer at the park's many bird species from a 3½-km (2-mile) footpath. ☎ *959/439569* ☉ *Daily 9–3 and 4–7.* **Palacio de Acebrón** Five kilometers (3 miles) away from La Rocina Visitor Center, an exhibit at the Palacio de Acebrón explains the park's ecosystems. ✉ *Ctra. de la Rocina* ☎ *959/506162* ☉ *Daily 9–3 and 4–7; last admission 1 hr before closing.*

10

EXPLORING

FAMILY
Fodor'sChoice
★

Doñana National Park. One of Europe's most important swaths of unspoiled wilderness, these wetlands spread out along the west side of the Guadalquivir estuary. The site was named for Doña Ana, wife of a 16th-century duke, who, prone to bouts of depression, one day crossed the river and wandered into the wetlands, never to be seen alive again. The 188,000-acre park sits on the migratory route from Africa to Europe and is the winter home and breeding ground for as many as 150 rare species of birds. Habitats range from beaches and shifting sand dunes to marshes, dense brushwood, and sandy hillsides of pine and cork oak. Two of Europe's most endangered species, the imperial

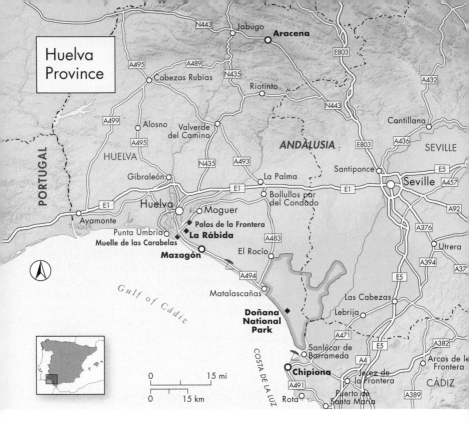

eagle and the lynx, make their homes here, and kestrels, kites, buzzards, egrets, storks, and spoonbills breed among the cork oaks.

WHERE TO STAY

$ **Toruño.** Despite its location behind the famous Rocío shrine, the
HOTEL   theme at this simple, friendly hotel is nature—it's run by the same cooperative that leads official park tours, and has become a favorite of birders. **Pros:** views over the wetlands; bird-watching opportunities. **Cons:** floors and hallways resonant; beds only moderately comfortable; best for a brief stay. **$** *Rooms from: €74 ✉ Pl. del Acebuchal 22, El Rocío-Huelva ☏ 959/442323 ⊕ www.toruno.es ⤳ 30 rooms ⧉ Breakfast.*

MAZAGÓN

19 km (12 miles) south of Huelva.

There isn't much to see or do in this coastal town, but the parador makes a good base for touring La Rábida, Palos de la Frontera, and Moguer. Mazagón's sweeping sandy beach, sheltered by steep cliffs, is among the region's nicest.

ESSENTIALS

Visitor Information Mazagón ✉ *Av. de los Conquistadores* ☏ *959/376246.*

BEACHES

Playa de Mazagón. The 5-km (3-mile) stretch of fine golden sand running from Mazagón to the frontier of the Doñana National Park forms one of the last unspoiled beaches in Andalusia. Dunes flank most of the beach, along with attractive sandstone cliffs; the Parador de Mazagón perches here. At the western end, the beach is popular with locals and visitors, beach bars are plentiful, and towel space at a premium in August. Walk in an easterly direction, however, and the beach becomes a much quieter affair. Bathing is generally safe, but watch for rip currents when it's windy. **Amenities:** (June 15–September 15 only) food and drink; lifeguards; showers; toilets; water sports. **Best for:** sunset; swimming; walking.

WHERE TO STAY

$$$$
HOTEL

Parador de Mazagón. This peaceful modern parador stands on a cliff surrounded by pine groves, overlooking a sandy beach 3 km (2 miles) southeast of Mazagón. **Pros:** nice views; good base for birding and biking through the wetlands. **Cons:** mediocre breakfast; long flight of steps to get to (and back up from) the beach. $ *Rooms from: €195* ⊠ *Pl. de Mazagón* ☎ *959/536300* ⊕ *www.parador.es* ⤳ *63 rooms* ⦿ *No meals.*

LA RÁBIDA

8 km (5 miles) northwest of Mazagón.

La Rábida's monastery is worth a stop if you're a history buff: it's nicknamed "the birthplace of America" because in 1485 Columbus came from Portugal with his son Diego to stay in the Mudejar-style Franciscan monastery, where he discussed his theories with friars Antonio de Marchena and Juan Pérez. They interceded on his behalf with Queen Isabella, who had originally rejected his planned expedition.

EXPLORING

Muelle de las Carabelas (*Caravel's Wharf*). Two kilometers (1 mile) from La Rábida's monastery, on the seashore, this is a reproduction of a 15th-century port. The star exhibits here are the full-size models of Columbus's flotilla, the *Niña, Pinta,* and *Santa María,* built using the same techniques as in Columbus's day. You can go aboard each and learn more about the discovery of the New World in the adjoining museum. ⊠ *Paraje de la Rábida* ☎ *959/530597* 🎫 *€3.55* ⊙ *Sept. 16–June 14, Tues.–Sun. 9:30–8; June 15–Sept. 15, Tues.–Sun. 10:30–10.*

Santa María de La Rábida. The Mudejar-style Franciscan monastery of this church has a much-venerated 14th-century statue of the **Virgen de los Milagros** (Virgin of Miracles). There are relics from the discovery of America displayed in the museum and the **frescoes** in the gatehouse were painted by Daniel Vázquez Díaz in 1930. ⊠ *Camino del Monasterio, Ctra. de Huelva* ☎ *959/350411* ⊕ *www.monasteriodelarabida. com* 🎫 *€3* ⊙ *Apr.–July and Sept.–Oct., Tues.–Sat. 10–1 and 4–7, Sun. 10:45–1 and 4–7; Nov.–Mar., Tues.–Sat. 10–1 and 4–6:15, Sun. 10:45–1 and 4–6:15; Aug., Mon.–Sat. 10–1 and 4:45–8, Sun. 10:45–1 and 4:45–8.*

10

ARACENA

105 km (65 miles) northeast of Huelva, 100 km (62 miles) northwest of Seville.

Stretching north of the provinces of Huelva and Seville is the 460,000-acre Sierra de Aracena nature park, an expanse of hills cloaked in cork and holm oak. This region is known for its cured ibérico hams, which come from the prized free-ranging Iberian pigs that gorge on acorns in the autumn months before slaughter; the hams are buried in salt and then hung in cellars to dry-cure for at least two years. The best ibérico hams have traditionally come from the village of **Jabugo**.

COLUMBUS SETS SAIL

On August 2, 1492, the *Niña*, the *Pinta*, and the *Santa María* set sail from the town of Palos de la Frontera. At the door of the church of **San Jorge** (1473), the royal letter ordering the levy of the ships' crew and equipment was read aloud, and the voyagers took their water supplies from the fountain known as La Fontanilla at the town's entrance.

ESSENTIALS

Visitor Information Aracena ✉ *Calle Pozo de la Nieve, at cave entrance* ☎ *663/937877.*

EXPLORING

FAMILY **Gruta de las Maravillas** (*Cave of Marvels*). In the town of Aracena, the capital of the region, the main attraction is this spectacular cave. Its 12 caverns contain long corridors, stalactites and stalagmites arranged in wonderful patterns, and stunning underground lagoons. Visitor numbers are limited to 1000 per day, so go early if visiting in high season. ✉ *Calle Pozo de la Nieve, Pedraza de la Sierra* ☎ *663/937876* 🎟 *€8.50* ⏲ *Hourly guided tours, if sufficient numbers, daily 10–1:30 and 3:30–6.*

WHERE TO EAT AND STAY

$$ SPANISH 🍴 **Montecruz.** The downstairs bar here serves simple tapas, but it's the upstairs restaurant that makes it worth a visit. The rustic dining room is decorated with wall paintings and hunting trophies, and the kitchen serves only regional produce and dishes. Try the *gurumelos salteados con jamón y gambas* (a type of mushroom stir-fried with ham and prawns), *lomo de jabalí* (boar tenderloin), or the outstanding ham; chestnut stew is the standout for dessert. Vegetarian and organic menus are available. [$] *Average main: €15* ✉ *Pl. de San Pedro* ☎ *959/126013* ⏲ *Closed Wed.*

$$$ B&B/INN Fodor's Choice ★ 🏨 **Finca Buenvino.** This lovely country house, 6 km (4 miles) from Aracena, is nestled in 150 acres of woods and is run by a charming British couple, Sam and Jeannie Chesterton, who include big breakfasts in the room price and offer dinner for a small fee. **Pros:** intimate and personal; friendly hosts. **Cons:** somewhat removed from village life. [$] *Rooms from: €140* ✉ *N433, Km 95, Los Marines* ☎ *959/124034* 🌐 *www.fincabuenvino.com* 🛏 *4 rooms, 3 cottages* 🍽 *Breakfast.*

$$$$ B&B/INN 🏨 **La Casa Noble.** In this lovingly restored town house, built in 1914 as one of the town's finest buildings, you'll find luxury, relaxation, and friendly service from an engaging owner. **Pros:** luxury surroundings and

Wild Andalusian horses near the village of El Rocío, in Donana National Park

amenities; central location. **Cons:** breakfast is delicious but has limited choices; no children under 16. $ *Rooms from: €195* ✉ *Calle Campito 35* ☎ *959/127778* ⊕ *www.lacasanoble.net* ⇆ *6 suites* ✆ *Closed Dec. 15–Jan. 15* ⦿ *Breakfast.*

CÁDIZ PROVINCE AND JEREZ DE LA FRONTERA

A trip through this province is a journey into the past. Winding roads take you through scenes ranging from flat and barren plains to seemingly endless vineyards, and the rolling countryside is carpeted with blindingly white soil known as *albariza*—unique to this area and the secret to the grapes used in sherry. In Jerez de La Frontera, you can savor the town's internationally known sherry and delight in the skills and forms of purebred Carthusian horses.

Throughout the province, the pueblos blancos provide striking contrasts with the terrain, especially at Arcos de la Frontera, where the village sits dramatically on a crag overlooking the gorge of the Guadalete River. In the city of Cádiz you can absorb about 3,000 years of history in what is generally considered the oldest continuously inhabited city in the Western world.

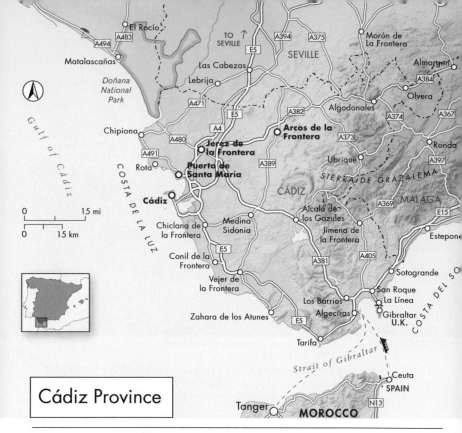

Cádiz Province

JEREZ DE LA FRONTERA

97 km (60 miles) south of Seville.

Jerez, world headquarters for sherry—the city was European Wine City in 2014—is surrounded by vineyards of chalky soil, producing Palomino grapes that have funded a host of churches and noble mansions. Names such as González Byass, Domecq, Harvey, and Sandeman are inextricably linked with Jerez. The word "sherry," first used in Great Britain in 1608, is an English corruption of the town's old Moorish name, Xeres. Both sherry and horses are the domain of Jerez's Anglo-Spanish aristocracy, whose Catholic ancestors came here from England centuries ago. At any given time, more than half a million barrels of sherry are maturing in Jerez's vast aboveground cellars.

GETTING HERE AND AROUND

Jerez is a short way from Seville with frequent daily trains (journey time is around an hour) and buses (1 hour 15 minutes), fewer on weekends. If you're traveling to the city by car, park in one of the city-center lots or at your hotel as street parking is difficult.

ESSENTIALS

Bus Station Jerez de la Frontera ⊠ *Pl. de la Estación* ☎ *956/149990.*

Taxi Contact Tele Taxi ☎ *956/344860.*

Train Station Jerez de la Frontera ⊠ *Pl. de la Estación s/n, off Calle Diego Fernández Herrera* ☎ *902/320320.*

Visitor Information Jerez de la Frontera ⊠ *Edificio Los Arcos, Pl. del Arenal* ☎ *956/338874* ⊕ *www.turismojerez.com.*

EXPLORING
TOP ATTRACTIONS

Alcázar. Once the residence of the caliph of Seville, the 12th-century Alcázar and its small, octagonal **mosque** and **baths** were built for the Moorish governor's private use. The baths have three sections: the *sala fría* (cold room), the larger *sala templada* (warm room), and the *sala caliente* (hot room) for steam baths. In the midst of it all is the 17th-century **Palacio de Villavicencio**, built on the site of the original Moorish palace. A camera obscura, a lens-and-mirrors device that projects the outdoors onto a large indoor screen, offers a 360-degree view of Jerez. ⊠ *Calle Alameda Vieja* ☎ *956/149955* 🎟 *€5, €7 including camera obscura* ⊙ *Mar.–Oct., weekdays 9:30–6 (until 8 July–mid-Sept.), weekends 9:30–3; Nov.–Feb., daily 9:30–3.*

Catedral de Jerez. Across from the Alcázar and around the corner from the González Byass winery, the cathedral has an octagonal cupola and a separate bell tower, as well as Zurbarán's canvas *La Virgen Niña* (The Virgin as a Young Girl). ⊠ *Pl. de la Encarnación* ☎ *956/169059* 🎟 *€5* ⊙ *Mon.–Sat. 10–6:30.*

Fodor's Choice ★ **Plaza de la Asunción.** Here on one of Jerez's most intimate squares you can find the Mudejar church of **San Dionisio** and the ornate **cabildo municipal** (city hall), with a lovely plateresque facade dating from 1575. ⊠ *Jerez de la Frontera, Cádiz.*

FAMILY
Fodor's Choice ★ **Real Escuela Andaluza del Arte Ecuestre** (*Royal Andalusian School of Equestrian Art*). This prestigious school operates on the grounds of the Recreo de las Cadenas, a 19th-century palace. The school was masterminded by Alvaro Domecq in the 1970s, and every Thursday (and at various other times throughout the year) the Cartujana horses—a cross between the native Andalusian workhorse and the Arabian—and skilled riders in 18th-century riding costume demonstrate intricate dressage techniques and jumping in the spectacular show "Cómo Bailan los Caballos Andaluces" (roughly, "The Dancing Horses of Andalusia"). Reservations are essential. Admission price depends on how close to the arena you sit; the first two rows are the priciest. At certain other times you can visit the stables and tack room, and watch the horses being schooled. ⊠ *Av. Duque de Abrantes* ☎ *956/319635 for info* ⊕ *www.realescuela.org* 🎟 *Shows €21–€27, stables tour and training sessions €11* ⊙ *Times for shows, tours, and training sessions vary throughout the year; check website for up-to-date details.*

WORTH NOTING

Domecq. This is Jerez's oldest bodega, founded in 1730. Aside from sherry, Domecq makes the world's best-selling brandy, Fundador. Harveys Bristol Cream is also part of the Domecq group. ⊠ *Calle San Ildefonso 3* ☎ *956/151552* ⊕ *www.bodegasfundadorpedrodomecq.com*

10

WINERY TOURS IN JEREZ

On a *bodega* (winery) visit, you'll learn about the *solera* method of blending old wine with new, and the importance of the *flor* (yeast that forms on the wine as it ages) in determining the kind of sherry.

Phone ahead for an appointment to make sure you join a group that speaks your language. Admission fees start at €7 (more for extra wine tasting or tapas) and tours, which last between 60 and 90 minutes, go through the aging cellars, with their endless rows of casks. (You won't see the actual fermenting and bottling, which take place in more modern, less romantic plants outside town.) Finally, you'll be invited to sample generous amounts of pale, dry *fino*, nutty *amontillado*, or rich, deep *oloroso*, and, of course, to purchase a few robustly priced bottles in the winery shop.

⊙ *Tours Mar.–Oct., weekdays at 10, noon, 1, 2, 3 and 4, Sat. at noon, 1 and 2; Jan., Feb., Nov., and Dec., Mon.–Sat. at noon, 1, and 2.*

González Byass. If you have time for only one bodega, make it this one—home of the famous Tío Pepe. The tour is well organized and includes La Concha, an open-air aging cellar designed by Gustave Eiffel. Tours in English daily at noon, 1, 2 and 5 (no afternoon tour on Sunday). ⊠ *Calle Manuel María González* ☎ *956/357016* ⊕ *www.bodegastiopepe.com* ⊙ *Tours Mon.–Sat. at noon, 1, 2, and 5, Sun. at noon.*

Jerez Plaza de Toros. Jerez's bullring is northeast of the city center. Tickets are sold at the official ticket office on Calle Porvera, but only about five bullfights are held each year, in May and October. ⊠ *Calle Circo.*

Museo Arqueológico. Diving into the maze of streets that form the scruffy San Mateo neighborhood east of the town center, you come to one of Andalusia's best archaeological museums, which were extensively restored prior to 2012. The collection is strongest on the pre-Roman period and the star item, found near Jerez, is a Greek helmet dating from the 7th century BC. ⊠ *Pl. del Mercado s/n* ☎ *956/149561* 🏛 *€5* ⊙ *Tues.–Fri. 10–2 and 4–7, weekends 10–2.*

Museo Taurino. Six blocks from the bullring is this bullfighting museum, where admission includes a drink. ⊠ *Calle Pozo del Olivar 6* ☎ *956/319000* 🏛 *€2.50* ⊙ *Mon.–Sat. 10–2.*

FAMILY **Parque Zoológico.** Just west of the town center, the Jerez zoo is set in lush botanical gardens where you can usually spy up to 33 storks' nests. Primarily a place for the rehabilitation of injured or endangered animals native to the region, the zoo also houses white tigers, elephants, a giant red panda, and the endangered Iberian lynx (the only place where you can see the lynx in captivity). ⊠ *Calle Madreselva* ☎ *956/149785* ⊕ *www.zoobotanicojerez.com* 🏛 *€9.30* ⊙ *May–mid-June., Tues.–Sun. 10–7; mid-June–mid-Sept., daily 10–7; Oct.–Apr., Tues.–Sun. 10–6.*

San Miguel. One block from the Plaza del Arenal, near the Alcázar, stands the church of San Miguel. Built over the 15th and 16th centuries, it's interior illustrates the evolution of Gothic architecture, with various

Riders fill the streets during Jerez's Feria del Caballo (Horse Fair), in early May.

styles mixed into the design. ⊠ *Pl. de San Miguel* ☎ *956/343347* 🎫 *Free* 🕓 *Weekdays 9:30–1:30 and 4:30–6:30, by appointment.*

Sandeman. This brand of sherry is known for its dashing man-in-a-cape logo. ⊠ *Calle Pizarro 10* ☎ *675/647177* ⊕ *www.sandeman.eu.*

Yeguada de la Cartuja. This farm just outside Jerez de la Frontera specializes in Carthusian horses. In the 15th century, a Carthusian monastery on this site started the breed for which Jerez and the rest of Spain are now famous. Visits include a full tour of the stables and training areas, and a show. Book ahead. ⊠ *Finca Fuente El Suero, Ctra. Medina–El Portal, Km 6.5* ☎ *956/162809* ⊕ *www.yeguadacartuja.com* 🎫 *€15.50–€21.50* 🕓 *Tour and show Sat. at 11 am.*

WHERE TO EAT

$$ — SPANISH — ✕ **Albores.** Opposite the city hall, this restaurant, with pleasant outdoor seating under orange trees and a sleek interior with low lighting, serves modern dishes with a traditional base. The menu is extensive and changes often, although must-try staples include *barriga de atún con salsa cremosa de soja y mermelada de tomate* (tuna belly with cream of soy sauce and tomato jam) and *lomo de ciervo con boniato y salsa de mostaza* (venison filet with sweet potato and mustard sauce). Portions are generous and sharing is encouraged, but half portions are also available if you want something for yourself. This is a busy venue (book on weekends), but service is always efficient and reasonably swift. Ⓢ *Average main: €13* ⊠ *Calle Consistorio 12* ☎ *956/320266.*

$$$ — SPANISH — ✕ **El Bosque.** In an early-20th-century villa with contemporary paintings of bullfights, this is one of the most stylish dining spots in town, and the smaller of the two dining rooms has picture windows overlooking

a park. The food is contemporary Spanish: *Sopa de galeras* (shrimp soup) is a rich appetizer; follow up with the local favorite *arroz con langostinos* (rice with jumbo shrimps) or *rabo de toro al estilo El Bosque* (oxtail in sherry). Desserts are less exciting but include a delicious *tocino de cielo* (egg-yolk pudding). Service is excellent. $ *Average main: €22* ⊠ *Av. Alcalde Alvaro Domecq 26* ☎ *956/307030* ⊙ *Closed Sun. and Mon.*

$$
SPANISH
Fodor'sChoice
★

✕ **La Carboná.** In a former bodega, this eatery has a rustic atmosphere with arches, beams, and a fireplace for winter nights, and in summer you can often enjoy live music and sometimes flamenco dancing while you dine. The chef has worked at several top restaurants, and his menu includes traditional grilled meats as well as innovative twists on classic dishes, such as foie gras terrine with strawberry coulis, and cod with artichoke and fino cream. Try the sherry *menú de degustación* (€32)— five courses, each accompanied by a different type of sherry. Both the tapas menu and the wine list are excellent. $ *Average main: €14* ⊠ *Calle San Francisco de Paula 2* ☎ *956/347475* ⊙ *Closed Tues.*

$
SPANISH

✕ **Mesón del Asador.** Just off the Plaza del Arenal, this rustic meat restaurant is always packed with young locals who crowd around the bar for cheap and generous tapas (from €2.50). Oxtail stew, fried chorizo, black pudding, and pig's-cheek stew come in huge portions, resulting in an incredibly inexpensive meal. Choose table service to try the excellent oxtail sirloin or other type of meat, barbecued or grilled on hot stones. $ *Average main: €12* ⊠ *Calle Remedios 2–4* ☎ *952/322658* ⌳ *Reservations not accepted.*

$$
SPANISH
Fodor'sChoice
★

✕ **Sabores.** The walled garden at this eatery, widely regarded as the best restaurant in town, is a cool spot on a warm night. The staff's enthusiasm and culinary knowledge will help guide your choice. Consider kickstarting your meal with the creative tapas, such as roast pork, tomato and Manchego cheese on toast, and fried hake with lemon sauce. Innovative main dishes include fish of the day with sauteed eggplant and asparagus, and slow-cooked oxtail in sherry, carrot and ginger. $ *Average main: €16* ⊠ *Chancilleria Hotel, Calle Chancilleria 21* ☎ *956/329835* ⌳ *Reservations essential* ⊙ *No lunch Mon.*

$
SEAFOOD

✕ **Venta Antonio.** Crowds come to this roadside inn for superb, fresh seafood cooked in top-quality olive oil. You enter through the busy bar, where lobsters await their fate in a tank. Try the specialties of the Bay of Cádiz, such as *sopa de mariscos* (shellfish soup) followed by succulent *bogavantes de Sanlúcar* (local lobster). Be prepared for large, noisy Spanish families dining here on the weekends, particularly during the winter months. $ *Average main: €12* ⊠ *Ctra. de Jerez–Sanlúcar, Km 5* ☎ *956/140535* ⊙ *Closed Mon.*

WHERE TO STAY

$
B&B/INN
Fodor'sChoice
★

⌃ **Hotel Palacio Garvey.** Dating from 1850, this luxurious boutique hotel was once the home of the prestigious Garvey family, and the original neoclassical architecture and interior decoration has been exquisitely restored. **Pros:** in the center of town; fashionable and contemporary feel. **Cons:** breakfast offers few choices; inadequate parking. $ *Rooms from: €85* ⊠ *Calle Tornería 24* ☎ *956/326700* ⊕ *www.hotelpalaciogarvey. com* ⌔ *7 rooms, 9 suites* ⏲ *Breakfast.*

$ HOTEL **Hotel San Andrés.** This low-rise hotel on a quiet side street off the center has an inviting traditional entrance patio and rooms set around a courtyard filled with plants, local tile work, and graceful arches. **Pros:** friendly owners; easy on-street parking. **Cons:** small rooms; accommodation only. [$] *Rooms from: €40* ✉ *Calle Morenos 12* ☎ *956/340983* 🌐 *www.hotel-sanandres.com* 🛏 *30 rooms* 🍴 *No meals.*

$$ B&B/INN **Hotel Villa Jerez.** Tastefully furnished, this hacienda-style hotel offers luxury on the outskirts of town. **Pros:** elegant surroundings; noble architecture. **Cons:** outside of town center; small pool. [$] *Rooms from: €100* ✉ *Av. de la Cruz Roja 7* ☎ *956/153100* 🌐 *www.hace.es/hotelvillajerez* 🛏 *14 rooms, 4 suites* 🍴 *No meals.*

$ HOTEL **La Fonda Barranco.** A block away from the cathedral and behind the police station, this typical Jerez townhouse has been restored to its full bourgeois glory, preserving original tiled floors, beamed ceilings, and a light central patio. **Pros:** personalized attention; central location; good value. **Cons:** some rooms are dark; no elevator. [$] *Rooms from: €75* ✉ *Calle Barranco 12* ☎ *956/332141* 🌐 *www.lafondabarranco.com* 🛏 *8 rooms, 2 apartments* 🍴 *No meals.*

$ HOTEL **Las Palomas.** This inexpensive hotel also happens to be one of the oldest in town, and the restored rooftop terrace, with its sweeping views, is the perfect spot to relax with a drink. **Pros:** simple and homey rooms; friendly English-speaking owners. **Cons:** rooms facing the patio are noisy. [$] *Rooms from: €36* ✉ *Calle Higueras 17* ☎ *956/343773* 🌐 *www.pension-las-palomas.es* 🛏 *35 rooms* 🍴 *No meals.*

SPORTS AND THE OUTDOORS

Circuito Permanente de Velocidad. Formula One Grand Prix races—including the Spanish motorcycle Grand Prix on the first weekend in May—are held at Jerez's racetrack. ✉ *Ctra. Arcos, Km 10* ☎ *956/151100* 🌐 *www.circuitodejerez.com.*

SHOPPING

Calle Corredera and **Calle Bodegas** are the places to go if you want to browse for wicker and ceramics.

ARCOS DE LA FRONTERA

31 km (19 miles) east of Jerez.

Fodor's Choice ★ Its narrow and steep cobblestone streets, whitewashed houses, and finely crafted wrought-iron window grilles make Arcos the quintessential Andalusian pueblo blanco. Make your way to the main square, the Plaza de España, the highest point in the village; one side of the square is open, and a balcony at the edge of the cliff offers views of the Guadalete Valley. On the opposite end is the church of **Santa María de la Asunción**, a fascinating blend of architectural styles—Romanesque, Gothic, and Mudejar—with a plateresque doorway, a Renaissance *retablo* (altarpiece), and a 17th-century baroque choir. The Ayuntamiento stands at the foot of the old castle walls on the northern side of the square; across is the Casa del Corregidor, onetime residence of the governor and now a parador. Arcos is the westernmost of the 19 pueblos blancos dotted around the Sierra de Cádiz.

Just about the whole city turns out for Jerez's Feria del Caballo, and traditional Andalusian costumes are a common sight.

GETTING HERE AND AROUND

Arcos is best reached by private car, but there are frequent bus services here from Cádiz, Jerez, and Seville on weekdays. Weekend services are less frequent.

ESSENTIALS

Visitor Information Arcos de la Frontera ✉ *Cuesta de Belén 5* ☎ *956/702264* 🌐 *www.turismoarcos.es.*

WHERE TO EAT

$ TAPAS 🍴 **El Paquetito.** At the bottom of the climb up to the old town, this small restaurant serves—according to many—the best tapas (from €2.50) in Arcos. Signature tapas are *paquetitos* (little parcels) of filo pastry with seven different fillings; the most requested are the goat cheese with spinach and pine nuts, and the salmon with herbed cheese. Tapas change on the weekend. *Berenjenas con miel* (fried eggplant with honey) and the filet steak with Pedro Ximénez sherry are other house specialties. The interior is cheap and cheerful, with plastic tables on the pleasant outside terrace and wooden ones inside. [$] *Average main: €8* ✉ *Av. Miguel Mancheño 1* ☎ *956/704937* 🕓 *Closed Wed. mid-Sept.–June. No lunch weekends July–mid-Sept.*

$ SPANISH 🍴 **Mesón del Corregidor.** The old town has only one real restaurant—this one within the parador hotel—and it boasts perhaps the best views ever from a table. Wherever you choose to sit (bar, terrace, or restaurant), you'll dine looking over the clifftop to the miles of green countryside beyond. Parador fare is justly famed in Spain and the food on offer here is no exception. Try the *corvina a la roteña* (sea bass Rota style, steamed with vegetables) or the *carrillera de cerdo en salsa de* *almendra* (pig's cheek in almond sauce). Finish with *delicias del cielo* ("heavenly delights"—cream of coconut). $ *Average main: €12* ✉ *Parador Casa del Corregidor, Pl. del Cabildo* ☎ *956/700500.*

> **NOTABLE RESIDENTS**
>
> Christopher Columbus and author Washington Irving once lived in the small fishing village of Puerto de Santa María.

WHERE TO STAY

$ 🏨 **El Convento.** Perched atop the cliff behind the town parador, this tiny hotel in a former 17th-century convent shares the amazing view of another hotel in town, its swish neighbor (La Casa Grande). **Pros:** location; intimacy. **Cons:** small spaces; lots of stairs. $ *Rooms from: €82* ✉ *Calle Maldonado 2* ☎ *956/702333* ⊕ *www.hotelelconvento.es* ⇄ *13 rooms* ⊙ *Closed Nov.–Feb.* ☉ *No meals.*

B&B/INN
Fodor'sChoice
★

$ 🏨 **La Casa Grande.** Built in 1729, this extraordinary 18th-century mansion encircles a central patio with lush vegetation and is perched on the edge of the 400-foot cliff to which Arcos de la Frontera clings. **Pros:** attentive owner; impeccable aesthetics. **Cons:** inconvenient parking; long climb to the top floor. $ *Rooms from: €90* ✉ *Calle Maldonado 10* ☎ *956/703930* ⊕ *www.lacasagrande.net* ⇄ *7 rooms* ☉ *No meals.*

B&B/INN
Fodor'sChoice
★

$$$ 🏨 **Parador Casa del Corregidor.** Expect a spectacular view from the terrace, as this parador clings to the cliffside, overlooking the rolling valley of the Guadalete River. **Pros:** gorgeous views from certain rooms; elegant interiors. **Cons:** public areas a little tired; expensive bar and cafeteria. $ *Rooms from: €171* ✉ *Pl. del Cabildo* ☎ *956/700500* ⊕ *www.parador.es* ⇄ *24 rooms* ☉ *No meals.*

HOTEL

PUERTO DE SANTA MARÍA

12 km (7 miles) southwest of Jerez, 17 km (11 miles) north of C diz.

This attractive if somewhat dilapidated little fishing port on the northern shores of the Bay of Cádiz, with lovely beaches nearby, has white houses with peeling facades and vast green grilles covering the doors and windows. The town is dominated by the Terry and Osborne sherry and brandy bodegas. Columbus once lived in a house on the square that bears his name (Cristobal Colón), and Washington Irving spent the autumn of 1828 at Calle Palacios 57. The marisco bars along the Ribera del Marisco (Seafood Way) are Puerto de Santa María's main claim to fame. La Dorada, Romerijo La Guachi, and Casa Paco Ceballos are among the most popular, along with El Betis, at Misericordia 7. The tourist office organizes several tours round the port and some include visits to the more than 70 tapas bars in the town!

ESSENTIALS

Visitor Information Puerto de Santa María ✉ *Pl. del Castillo* ☎ *956/483715* ⊕ *www.turismoelpuerto.com.*

EXPLORING

Castillo de San Marcos. This castle was built in the 13th century on the site of a mosque. Created by Alfonso X, it was later home to the Duke of Medinaceli. Among the guests were Christopher Columbus—who

10

Puerto de Santa María is a wonderful tapas and sherry-tasting destination.

tried unsuccessfully to persuade the duke to finance his voyage west—and Juan de la Cosa, who, within these walls, drew up the first map ever to include the Americas. The red lettering on the walls is a 19th-century addition. Visits are by tour only (in English at 1) and include the bodega next door. ✉ *Pl. de Alfonso X* ☎ *956/851751* 🎫 *€6* ⏲ *Tues. 11:30–1:30, Wed. and Sat. 10–2.*

Plaza de Toros. The stunning neo-Mudejar bullring was built in 1880 thanks to a donation from the winemaker Thomas Osborne. It originally had seating for exactly 12,816 people, the entire population of Puerto at that time. ✉ *Los Moros* 🎫 *Free* ⏲ *Tues.–Fri., 11–1. Closed to visitors on bullfight days plus days before and after.*

WHERE TO EAT AND STAY

$$$$ SPANISH Fodor's Choice ★

🍴 **Aponiente.** Deemed one of the world's top ten chefs by the New York Times in 2014 and worthy of a Michelin star in 2013, Ángel León showcases his creative seafood dishes in this elegant restaurant where edgy interior design combines lime green with crisp white lighting and table linen. Aponiente serves two *menús de degustación* (€80 for 14 dishes or €115 for 22), or you can mix and match food and wine for €45. Expect plenty of gastronomic inventions such as marine cheese, cuttlefish with potatoes, and rice with plankton and sea cucumber. León avoids species of fish that have become scarce, championing more abundant species such as sardines, shrimp, and cuttlefish. [$] *Average main: €75* ✉ *Calle Puerto Escondido 6* ☎ *856/151186* 🌐 *www.aponiente.com* ✍ *Reservations essential* ⏲ *Closed Sun. and Mon. Nov.–mid-Mar. (phone for exact dates).*

$$$ SPANISH 🍴 **El Faro del Puerto.** In a villa outside town, the "Lighthouse in the Port" is run by the same family that established the classic El Faro in Cádiz. Like its predecessor, it serves excellent seafood, most of which is freshly caught locally. The chef places the emphasis on seasonal fare, which is reflected in the daily specials, and the restaurant has its own vegetable garden. The impressive wine list runs to over 400 choices. Dining alfresco on the outside terrace is particularly pleasant. Cheaper but just as tasty dishes are available at the bar. [$] *Average main: €20* ✉ *Ctra. Fuentebravia–Rota, Km 0.5* ☎ *956/870952* 🌐 *www.elfarodelpuerto.com* 🕓 *No dinner Sun., except in Aug.*

$ HOTEL Fodor's Choice ★ 🏨 **Monasterio San Miguel.** Dating from 1733, this former monastery is a few blocks from the harbor; there's nothing spartan about the former cells, which are now plush suites with all the trappings. **Pros:** supremely elegant; efficient service. **Cons:** some furnishings worn out; breakfast has little variety. [$] *Rooms from: €90* ✉ *Calle Virgen de los Milagros 27* ☎ *956/540440* 🌐 *www.sanmiguelhotelmonasterio.com* 🛏 *141 rooms, 24 suites* 🍽 *Breakfast.*

CÁDIZ

32 km (20 miles) southwest of Jerez, 149 km (93 miles) southwest of Seville.

Fodor's Choice ★ With the Atlantic Ocean on three sides, Cádiz is a bustling town that's been shaped by a variety of cultures, and has the varied architecture to prove it. Founded as Gadir by Phoenician traders in 1100 BC, Cádiz claims to be the oldest continuously inhabited city in the Western world. Hannibal lived in Cádiz for a time, Julius Caesar first held public office here, and Columbus set out from here on his second voyage, after which the city became the home base of the Spanish fleet. In the 18th century, when the Guadalquivir silted up, Cádiz monopolized New World trade and became the wealthiest port in Western Europe. Most of its buildings—including the cathedral, built in part with wealth generated by gold and silver from the New World—date from this period. The old city is African in appearance and immensely intriguing—a cluster of narrow streets opening onto charming small squares. The golden cupola of the cathedral looms above low white houses, and the whole place has a slightly dilapidated air. Spaniards flock here in February to revel in the carnival celebrations, but in general it's not very touristy.

GETTING HERE AND AROUND

Every day, around 15 local trains connect Cádiz with Seville, Puerto de Santa María, and Jerez. The city has two bus stations. The main one, run by Comes, serves most destinations in Andalusia and farther afield; the other, run by Socibus, serves Córdoba and Madrid. There are buses to and from Sanlúcar de Barrameda (12 on weekdays), Arcos de la Frontera (4 daily), and the Costa del Sol (4 daily). Cádiz is easy to get to and navigate by car. Once there, the old city is easily explored by foot.

ESSENTIALS

Bus Station Cádiz–Estación de Autobuses Comes ✉ *Pl. de Sevilla* ☎ *902/199208.* **Cádiz-Estación de Autobuses Socibus** ✉ *Av. León de Carranza 20* ☎ *902/229292.*

Taxi Contact Radiotaxi ☎ *956/212121.*

Train Station Cádiz ✉ *Pl. de Sevilla s/n* ☎ *902/320320.*

Visitor Information Local Tourist Office ✉ *Paseo de Canalejas*
☎ *956/241001* ⊕ *www.turismo.cadiz.es* ✉ *Av. Caballerizas Reales s/n, Judería,*
Córdoba ☎ *902/201774.* **Provincial Tourist Office** ✉ *Pl. de San Antonio 3,*
2nd fl. ☎ *956/807061.* **Regional Tourist Office** ✉ *Av. Ramón de Carranza s/n*
☎ *956/203191* ⊕ *www.cadizturismo.com.*

EXPLORING
Begin your explorations in the Plaza de Mina, a large, leafy square with palm trees and plenty of benches.

TOP ATTRACTIONS
Cádiz Cathedral. Five blocks southeast of the Torre Tavira are the gold dome and baroque facade of Cádiz's cathedral, begun in 1722, when the city was at the height of its power. The Cádiz-born composer Manuel de Falla, who died in 1946 at the age of 70, is buried in the **crypt.** The cathedral **museum,** on Calle Acero, displays gold, silver, and jewels from the New World, as well as Enrique de Arfe's processional cross, which is carried in the annual Corpus Christi parades. The cathedral is known as the New Cathedral because it supplanted the original 13th-century structure next door, which was destroyed by the British in 1592, rebuilt, and rechristened the church of **Santa Cruz** when the New Cathedral came along. ✉ *Pl. Catedral* ☎ *956/286154* 💳 *€5, includes crypt, museum, and church of Santa Cruz* ⊙ *Museum, crypt, and Santa Cruz: Mon.–Sat. 10–6:30, Sun. 1:30–6:30; Cathedral: Mass Sun. at noon.*

Museo de Cádiz (*Provincial Museum*). On the east side of the Plaza de Mina is Cadiz's provincial museum. Notable pieces include works by Murillo and Alonso Cano as well as the *Four Evangelists* and a set of saints by Zurbarán. The archaeological section contains Phoenician sarcophagi from the time of this ancient city's birth. ✉ *Pl. de Mina* ☎ *956/203368* 💳 *€1.50* ⊙ *June–Sept., Tues.–Sat. 9–3, Sun. 10–5; Oct.–May, Tues.–Sat. 10–8:30, Sun. 10–5.*

Oratorio de San Felipe Neri. A walk up Calle San José from the Plaza de la Mina will bring you to this church, where Spain's first liberal constitution (known affectionately as *La Pepa*) was declared in 1812. It was here, too, that the Cortes (Parliament) of Cádiz met when the rest of Spain was subjected to the rule of Napoléon's brother, Joseph Bonaparte (more popularly known as Pepe Botella, for his love of the bottle). On the main altar is an *Immaculate Conception* by Murillo, the great Sevillian artist who in 1682 fell to his death from a scaffold while working on his *Mystic Marriage of St. Catherine* in Cádiz's Chapel of Santa Catalina. ✉ *Calle Santa Inés 38* ☎ *956/229120* 💳 *€3 (free Sun.)* ⊙ *Tues.–Fri. 10–1:45 and 5–7:45, Sat. 10–1:45, Sun. 11–1:45.*

FAMILY
Fodor's Choice
★

Torre Tavira. At 150 feet, this is the highest point in the old city. More than a hundred such watchtowers were used by Cádiz ship owners to spot their arriving fleets. A camera obscura gives a good overview of the city and its monuments; the last show is a half hour before closing time. ✉ *Calle Marqués del Real Tesoro 10* ☎ *956/212910* 💳 *€5* ⊙ *Daily 10–6 (until 8 May–Sept.).*

Cádiz's majestic cathedral, as seen from the Plaza de la Catedral

WORTH NOTING

Ayuntamiento (*City hall*). This impressive building overlooks the Plaza San Juan de Diós, one of Cádiz's liveliest hubs. It's attractively illuminated at night and open to visits on Saturday mornings. Just ring the bell next to the door. ⊠ *Pl. de San Juan de Dios* ⊙ *Sat. 11–12:45.*

Gran Teatro Manuel de Falla. Four blocks west of Santa Inés is the Plaza Manuel de Falla, overlooked by this amazing neo-Mudejar redbrick building. The classic interior is impressive as well; try to attend a performance. ⊠ *Pl. Manuel de Falla* ☎ *956/220828.*

Museo de las Cortes. Next door to the Oratorio de San Felipe Neri, this small but pleasant museum has a 19th-century mural depicting the establishment of the Constitution of 1812. Its real showpiece, however, is a 1779 ivory-and-mahogany model of Cádiz, with all of the city's streets and buildings in minute detail, looking much as they do now. ⊠ *Calle Santa Inés 9* ☎ *956/221788* ⊠ *Free* ⊙ *Tues.–Fri. 9–6, weekends 9–2.*

Oratorio de la Santa Cueva. A few blocks east of the Plaza de Mina, next door to the Iglesia del Rosario, this oval 18th-century chapel has three frescoes by Goya. ⊠ *Calle Rosario 10* ☎ *956/222262* ⊠*€3* ⊙ *Apr.–Oct., Tues.–Fri. 11–2 and 5:30–8:30, weekends 11–2; Nov.–Mar., Tues.–Fri. 10–1 and 4:30–7:30, weekends 10–1.*

Plaza San Francisco. Near the Ayuntamiento is this pretty square surrounded by white-and-yellow houses and filled with orange trees and elegant streetlamps. It's especially lively during the evening *paseo* (promenade). ⊠ *Cádiz, Cádiz.*

10

WHERE TO EAT AND STAY

$ SPANISH Fodor's Choice ★ 🍴 **Casa Manteca.** Cádiz's most quintessentially Andalusian tavern is in the neighborhood of La Viña, named for the vineyard that once grew here. *Chacina* (Iberian ham or sausage) and *chicharrones de Cádiz* (cold pork) served on waxed paper and washed down with manzanilla are standard fare at the low wooden counter that has served bullfighters and flamenco singers, as well as dignitaries from around the world, since 1953. The walls are covered with colorful posters and other memorabilia from the annual carnival, flamenco shows, and ferias. No hot dishes are available. [$] *Average main: €8* ✉ *Corralón de los Carros 66* ☎ *956/213603* ⏲ *No dinner Sun. and Mon.*

$$$ SPANISH Fodor's Choice ★ 🍴 **El Faro.** This famous fishing-quarter restaurant near Playa de la Caleta is deservedly known as one of the best in the province. From the outside, it's one of many whitewashed houses with ocher details and shiny black lanterns; inside it's warm and inviting, with half-tile walls, glass lanterns, oil paintings, and photos of old Cádiz. Fish dishes dominate the menu, of course, but meat and vegetarian options are always available. If you don't want to go for the full splurge (either gastronomically or financially), there's an excellent tapas bar. [$] *Average main: €20* ✉ *Calle San Felix 15* ☎ *956/211068.*

$$$ SPANISH 🍴 **El Ventorrillo del Chato.** Standing on its own on the sandy isthmus between the Atlantic and the Bay of Cádiz, this former inn was founded in 1780 by a man ironically nicknamed "El Chato" ("the small-nosed") for his prominent proboscis. Run by a scion of El Faro's Gonzalo Córdoba, the restaurant serves tasty regional specialties in charming Andalusian surroundings. Seafood is a favorite, but meat, stews, and rice dishes are also well represented on the menu, and the wine list is very good. [$] *Average main: €18* ✉ *Vía Augusta Julia* ☎ *956/250025* 🌐 *www.ventorrillodelchato.com* ⏲ *No dinner Sun. except in Aug.*

$$ B&B/INN 🏨 **Argantonia.** This small, family-run hotel in the historic center of town combines traditional style and modern amenities with impressive results. **Pros:** friendly and helpful staff; great location. **Cons:** some rooms on the small side. [$] *Rooms from: €119* ✉ *Calle Argantonio 3* ☎ *956/211640* 🌐 *www.hotelargantonio.com* 🛏 *16 rooms, 1 suite* 🍽 *Breakfast.*

$$$ HOTEL 🏨 **Las Cortes de Cádiz.** This colonial-style lodging, clustered around a delightful light-filled atrium, has an attractive and stylish appeal and a rooftop terrace with sweeping views. **Pros:** tastefully renovated building; excellent service. **Cons:** few staffers speak English; interior rooms rather dark, with no external windows. [$] *Rooms from: €135* ✉ *Calle San Francisco 9* ☎ *956/220489* 🌐 *www.hotellascortes.com* 🛏 *36 rooms* 🍽 *No meals.*

$$$$ HOTEL 🏨 **Parador de Cádiz.** Totally reformed in 2013, this parador has a privileged position overlooking the bay. **Pros:** great views of the bay; central location; bright and cheerful. **Cons:** could be too modern for some. [$] *Rooms from: €185* ✉ *Av. Duque de Nájera 9* ☎ *956/226905* 🌐 *www.parador.es* 🛏 *106 rooms, 18 suites* 🍽 *No meals.*

CÓRDOBA'S HISTORY

The Romans invaded Córdoba in 206 BC, later making it the capital of Rome's section of Spain. Nearly 800 years later, the Visigoth king Leovigildus took control, but the tribe was soon supplanted by the Moors, whose emirs and caliphs held court here from the 8th to the early 11th century. At that point Córdoba was one of the greatest centers of art, culture, and learning in the Western world; one of its libraries had a staggering 400,000 volumes. Moors, Christians, and Jews lived together in harmony within Córdoba's walls. In that era, it was considered second in importance only to Constantinople; but in 1009, Prince Muhammad II and Omeyan led a rebellion that broke up the caliphate, leading to power flowing to separate Moorish kingdoms.

Córdoba remained in Moorish hands until it was conquered by King Ferdinand in 1236 and repopulated from the north of Spain. Later, the Catholic Monarchs used the city as a base from which to plan the conquest of Granada. In Columbus's time, the Guadalquivir was navigable as far upstream as Córdoba, and great galleons sailed its waters. Today, the river's muddy water and marshy banks evoke little of Córdoba's glorious past, but an old Arab waterfall and the city's bridge—of Roman origin, though much restored by the Arabs and successive generations, the most recent in 2012—recall a far grander era.

CÓRDOBA

166 km (103 miles) northwest of Granada, 407 km (250 miles) southwest of Madrid, 239 km (143 miles) northeast of Cádiz, 143 km (86 miles) northeast of Seville.

Strategically located on the north bank of the Guadalquivir River, Córdoba was the Roman and Moorish capital of Spain, and its old quarter, clustered around its famous Mezquita, remains one of the country's grandest and yet most intimate examples of its Moorish heritage. Once a medieval city famed for the peaceful and prosperous coexistence of its three religious cultures—Islamic, Jewish, and Christian—Córdoba is also a perfect analogue for the cultural history of the Iberian Peninsula.

Córdoba today, with its modest population of a little more than 300,000, offers a cultural depth and intensity—a direct legacy from the great emirs, caliphs, philosophers, physicians, poets, and engineers of the days of the caliphate—that far outstrips the city's current commercial and political power. Its artistic and historical treasures begin with the Mezquita-Catedral (mosque-cathedral), as it is ever-more-frequently called, and continue through the winding, whitewashed streets of the Judería (the medieval Jewish quarter); the jasmine-, geranium-, and orange blossom–filled patios; the Renaissance palaces; and the two dozen churches, convents, and hermitages, built by Moorish artisans directly over former mosques.

10

GETTING HERE AND AROUND

BUS TRAVEL

Córdoba is easily reached by bus from Granada, Málaga and Seville. The city has an extensive public bus network with frequent service. Buses usually start running at 6:30 or 7 am and stop around midnight. You can buy 10-trip passes at newsstands and the bus office in Plaza de Colón. A single-trip fare is €1.20.

Córdoba has organized open-top bus tours of the city that can be booked via the tourist office.

CAR TRAVEL

The city's one-way system can be something of a nightmare to navigate, and it's best to park in one of the signposted lots outside the old quarter.

TRAIN TRAVEL

The city's modern train station is the hub for a comprehensive network of regional trains, with regular service to Seville, Málaga, Madrid, and Barcelona. Trains for Granada change at Bobadilla.

ESSENTIALS

Bike Travel Never designed to support cars, Córdoba's medieval layout is ideal for bicycles, and there's a good network of designated bicycle tracks. **Solo Bici.** You can rent bikes here at reasonable rates here: €6 for 3 hours or €15 for the day. ⊠ *Calle Maria Cristina 5, behind Ayuntamiento* ☎ *957/485766* ⊕ *www. solobici.net.*

Bus Station Córdoba ⊠ *Glorieta de las Tres Culturas* ☎ *957/404040* ⊕ *www. estacionautobusescordoba.es.*

Taxi Contact Radio Taxi ☎ *957/764444.*

Train Contacts Train Station ⊠ *Glorieta de las Tres Culturas* ☎ *902/320320.*

Visitor Information Tourist Office ⊠ *Pl. de las Tendillas 5, 3A, Centro* ☎ *902/201774* ⊕ *www.cordobaturismo.org.*

EXPLORING

Córdoba is an easily navigable city, with twisting alleyways that hold surprises around every corner. The main city subdivisions used in this book are the **Judería** (which includes the Mezquita); **Sector Sur,** around the **Torre de la Calahorra** across the river; the area around the **Plaza de la Corredera,** a historic gathering place for everything from horse races to bullfights; and the **Centro Comercial,** from the area around Plaza de las Tendillas to the Iglesia de Santa Marina and the Torre de la Malmuerta. Incidentally, the last neighborhood is much more than a succession of shops and stores. The town's real life, the everyday hustle and bustle, takes place here, and the general atmosphere is very different from that of the tourist center around the Mezquita, with its plethora of souvenir shops. Some of the city's finest Mudejar churches and best taverns, as well as the Palacio de los Marqueses de Viana, are in this pivotal part of town well back from the Guadalquivir waterfront.

Some of the most characteristic and rewarding places to explore in Córdoba are the parish churches and the taverns that inevitably accompany them, where you can taste *finos de Moriles,* a dry, sherrylike wine from the Montilla-Moriles district, and *tentempiés* (tapas; literally, "keep you on your feet"). The *iglesias fernandinas* (so called for their construction after Fernando III's conquest of Córdoba) are nearly always built over mosques with stunning horseshoe-arch doorways and Mudejar towers, and taverns tended to spring up around these populous hubs of city life. Examples are the Taberna de San Miguel (aka Casa el Pisto) next to the church of the same name, and the Bar Santa Marina (aka Casa Obispo) next to the Santa Marina Church.

■ **TIP→** Córdoba's officials frequently change the hours of the city's sights; before visiting an attraction, confirm hours with the tourist office or the sight itself.

TOP ATTRACTIONS

Alcázar de los Reyes Cristianos (*Fortress of the Christian Monarchs*). Built by Alfonso XI in 1328, the Alcázar is a Mudejar-style palace with splendid gardens. (The original Moorish Alcázar stood beside the Mezquita, on the site of the present Bishop's Palace.) This is where, in the 15th century, the Catholic Monarchs held court and launched their conquest of Granada. Boabdil was imprisoned here in 1483, and for nearly 300 years the Alcázar served as the Inquisition's base. The most important sights here are the Hall of the Mosaics and a Roman stone sarcophagus from the 2nd or 3rd century. ⊠ *Pl. Campo Santo de los Mártires, Judería* ☎ *957/420151* ✆ *€4.50* ⊘ *June 15–Sept. 15, Tues.–Sun. 8:30–3:30; Sept. 16–June 14, Tues.–Fri. 8:30 am–8:45 pm, weekends 8:30–4:30.*

Calleja de las Flores. You'd be hard pressed to find prettier patios than those along this tiny street, a few yards off the northeastern corner of the Mezquita. Patios, many with ceramics, foliage, and iron grilles, are key to Córdoba's architecture, at least in the old quarter, where life is lived behind sturdy white walls—a legacy of the Moors, who honored both the sanctity of the home and the need to shut out the fierce summer sun. Between the first and second week of May—right after the **Cruces de Mayo** (Crosses of May) competition, when neighborhoods compete at setting up elaborate crosses decorated with flowers and plants—Córdoba throws a **Patio Festival,** during which private patios are filled with flowers, opened to the public, and judged in a municipal competition. Córdoba's tourist office publishes an itinerary of the best patios in town (downloadable from ⊕ *www.turismodecordoba.org*)—note that most are open only in the late afternoon on weekdays, but all day on weekends. ⊠ *Córdoba.*

Fodor's Choice ★ **Madinat Al-Zahra** (*Medina Azahara*). Built in the foothills of the Sierra Morena by Abd ar-Rahman III for his favorite concubine, az-Zahra (the Flower), this once-splendid summer pleasure palace was begun in 936. Historians say it took 10,000 men, 2,600 mules, and 400 camels 25 years to erect this fantasy of 4,300 columns in dazzling pink, green, and white marble and jasper brought from Carthage. A palace, a mosque, luxurious baths, fragrant gardens, fish ponds, an aviary, and a zoo stood on three terraces here, and for around 70 years the Madinat was the de facto capital of al-Andalus, until, in 1013, it was sacked and destroyed by Berber mercenaries. In 1944 the Royal Apartments were

10

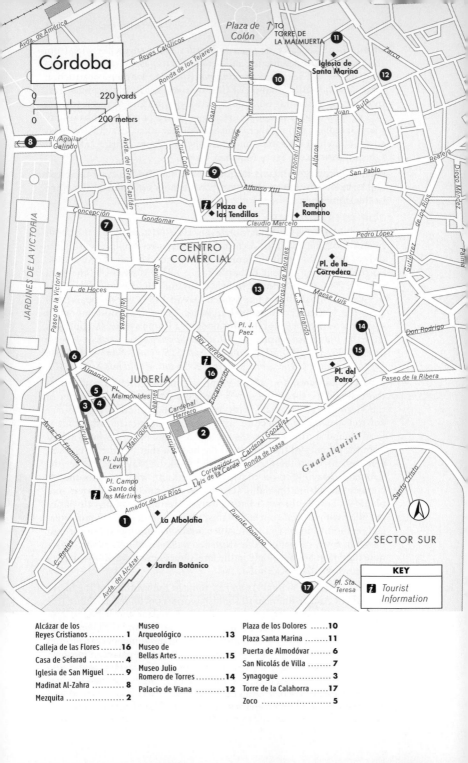

Córdoba

0 ___ 220 yards
0 ___ 200 meters

Plaza de Colón

TO TORRE DE LA MALMUERTA

Iglesia de Santa Marina

Pl. Aguilar Galindo

Plaza de las Tendillas

Templo Romano

CENTRO COMERCIAL

Pl. de la Corredera

Pl. J. Paez

JUDERÍA

Pl. del Potro

Pl. Maimónides

Cardenal Herrero

Pl. Juda Levi

Pl. Campo Santo de los Mártires

La Albolafia

Guadalquivir

SECTOR SUR

Jardín Botánico

Pl. Sta. Teresa

JARDINES DE LA VICTORIA

Streets and landmarks labeled on map

Avda. de América
C. Reyes Católicos
Ronda de los Tejares
José Cruz Conde
Avda. del Gran Capitán
Concepción
Paseo de la Victoria
L. de Hoces
Valladares
Sevilla
Gondomar
Alfonso XIII
Claudio Marcelo
Osario
Conde
Tortes
Cabrera
Cartonell y Morand
Alfaros
Juan Rufo
San Pablo
Pedro López
Ambrosio de Morales
C. S. Fernando
Maese Luis
Don Rodrigo
Paseo de la Ribera
Rey Heredia
Encarnación
Deanes
Manriquez
Almanzor
Cairuán
Buitres
Corregidor Luis de la Cerda
Cardenal González
Ronda de Isasa
Amador de los Ríos
Puente Romano
Santo Cristo
Zarco
Realejo
Diego Méndez
Gutiérrez de los Ríos
Palma
C. Reyes
Avda. del Alcázar
Avda. Dr. Fleming

KEY

i Tourist Information

rediscovered, and the throne room carefully reconstructed. The outline of the mosque has also been excavated. The only covered part of the site is the Salon de Abd ar-Rahman III (currently being restored); the rest is a sprawl of foundations and arches that hint at the splendor of the original city-palace. Visits begin at the nearby museum, which provides background information and a 3-D reconstruction of the city, and continue with a walk among the ruins, where you can only imagine the bustle and splendor of days gone by. There's no public transportation, but a tourist bus runs twice daily (three times on Saturday); the tourist office can provide details of stops and schedule. ⊠ *Ctra. de Palma del Río, Km 5.5, 8 km (5 miles) west of Córdoba on C431* ☎ *957/352860* ⊕ *www.museosdeandalucia.es* ✉ *€1.50* ⊙ *Tues.–Sat. 9–6:30 (until 8:30 Apr.–mid-Sept.), Sun. 10–5.*

Fodor'sChoice
★

Mezquita (*Mosque*). Built between the 8th and 10th centuries, Córdoba's mosque is one of the earliest and most transportingly beautiful examples of Spanish Islamic architecture. The plain, crenellated exterior walls do little to prepare you for the sublime beauty of the interior. As you enter through the **Puerta de las Palmas** (Door of the Palms), some 850 columns rise before you in a forest of jasper, marble, granite, and onyx. The pillars are topped by ornate capitals taken from the Visigothic church that was razed to make way for the mosque. Crowning these, red-and-white-stripe arches curve away into the dimness, and the ceiling is of delicately carved tinted cedar. The Mezquita has served as a cathedral since 1236, but its origins as a mosque are clear. Built in four stages, it was founded in 785 by Abd ar-Rahman I (756–88) on a site he bought from the Visigoth Christians. He pulled down their church and replaced it with a mosque, one-third the size of the present one, into which he incorporated marble pillars from earlier Roman and Visigothic shrines. Under Abd ar-Rahman II (822–52), the Mezquita held an original copy of the Koran and a bone from the arm of the prophet Mohammed and became a Muslim pilgrimage site second only in importance to Mecca.

Al Hakam II (961–76) built the beautiful **mihrab** (prayer niche), the Mezquita's greatest jewel. Make your way over to the **qiblah,** the south-facing wall in which this sacred prayer niche was hollowed out. (Muslim law decrees that a mihrab face east, toward Mecca, and that worshippers do likewise when they pray. Because of an error in calculation, this one faces more south than east. Al Hakam II spent hours agonizing over a means of correcting such a serious mistake, but he was persuaded to let it be.) In front of the mihrab is the **maksoureh,** a kind of anteroom for the caliph and his court; its mosaics and plasterwork make it a masterpiece of Islamic art. A last addition to the mosque as such, the maksoureh was completed around 987 by Al Mansur, who more than doubled its size.

After the Reconquest, the Christians left the Mezquita largely undisturbed, dedicating it to the Virgin Mary and using it as a place of Christian worship. The clerics did erect a wall closing off the mosque from its courtyard, which helped dim the interior and thus separate the house of worship from the world outside. In the 13th century, Christians had the **Capilla de Villaviciosa** built by Moorish craftsmen, its Mudejar architecture blending with the lines of the mosque. Not so the

10

heavy, incongruous baroque structure of the **cathedral,** sanctioned in the very heart of the mosque by Carlos V in the 1520s. To the emperor's credit, he was supposedly horrified when he came to inspect the new construction, exclaiming to the architects, "To build something ordinary, you have destroyed something that was unique in the world." (Not that this sentiment stopped him from tampering with the Alhambra to build his Palacio Carlos V). Rest up and reflect in the **Patio de los Naranjos** (Orange Court), perfumed in springtime by orange blossoms. The **Puerta del Perdón** (Gate of Forgiveness), so named because debtors were forgiven here on feast days, is on the north wall of the Orange Court and is the formal entrance to the mosque. The **Virgen de los Faroles** (Virgin of the Lanterns), a small statue in a niche on the outside wall of the mosque along the north side on Cardenal Herrero, is behind a lantern-hung grille, rather like a lady awaiting a serenade. The **Torre del Alminar,** the minaret once used to summon the Muslim faithful to prayer, has a baroque belfry. Allow a good hour for your visit. ⊠ *Calle de Torrijos, Judería* ☎ *957/470512* ⬛ *€8* ⊗ *Mon.–Sat. 10–6, Sun. 8:30–11:30 and 3–6 (Mass at 11 and 1).*

NEED A BREAK?

La Casa Andalusí. A few blocks from the Mezquita, this place is a beautiful spot for tea, with a courtyard, side rooms filled with cushions, and a shop selling Moroccan clothing. It's open daily from 10 am to 7 pm. ⊠ *Calle del Buen Pastor 13, Judería* ☎ *957/487984* ⬛ *€2.50.*

Fodor's Choice
★

Museo de Bellas Artes. Hard to miss because of its deep-pink facade, Córdoba's Museum of Fine Arts, in a courtyard just off the Plaza del Potro, belongs to a former Hospital de la Caridad (Charity Hospital). It was founded by Ferdinand and Isabella, who twice received Columbus here. The collection, which includes paintings by Murillo, Valdés Leal, Zurbarán, Goya, and Joaquín Sorolla y Bastida, concentrates on local artists. Highlights are altarpieces from the 14th and 15th centuries, and the large collection of prints and drawings including some by Fortuny, Goya, and Sorolla. ⊠ *Pl. del Potro 1, San Francisco* ☎ *957/103639* ⊕ *www.juntadeandalucia.es/cultura/museos/MBACO* ⬛ *€1.50* ⊗ *Tues.–Sun. 10–8:30.*

Palacio de Viana. This 17th-century palace is one of Córdoba's most splendid aristocratic homes. Also known as the **Museo de los Patios,** it contains 12 interior patios, each one different; the patios and gardens are planted with cypresses, orange trees, and myrtles. Inside the building are a carriage museum, a library, embossed leather wall hangings, filigree silver, and grand galleries and staircases. As you enter, note that the corner column of the first patio has been removed to allow the entrance of horse-drawn carriages. ⊠ *Pl. Don Gomé 2, Centro* ☎ *957/496741* ⬛ *Patios €5, patios and interior €8* ⊗ *Tues.–Fri. 10–7, weekends 10–3.*

Plaza de San Miguel. The square and café terraces around it, and its excellent tavern, Taberna San Miguel–Casa El Pisto, form one of the city's finest combinations of art, history, and gastronomy. The San Miguel church has an interesting facade with Romanesque doors built around Mudejar horseshoe arches. ⊠ *Centro.*

Torre de la Calahorra. The tower on the far side of the Puente Romano (Roman Bridge), which was restored in 2008, was built in 1369 to guard the entrance to Córdoba. It now houses the **Museo Vivo de Al-Andalus** (Al-Andalus is Arabic for "Land of the West"), with films and audiovisual guides (in English) on Córdoba's history. Climb the narrow staircase to the top of the tower for the view of the Roman bridge and city on the other side of the Guadalquivir. ⊠ *Av. de la Confederación, Sector Sur* ☎ *957/293929* ⊕ *www.torrecalahorra.com* ≅ *€4.50, includes audio guide; slide show €1.20 extra* ⊙ *Daily 10–6.*

WORTH NOTING

Casa de Sefarad. This private museum opposite the synagogue is dedicated to the culture of Sephardic Jews in the Mediterranean. Providing a very personal insight, the museum's director leads visitors through the five rooms of the 14th-century house, where displays cover Sephardic domestic life, music, festivities, the history of Córdoba's Jewish district, and finally a collection of contemporary paintings of the women of al-Andalus. ⊠ *Calle Judíos 17, Judería* ☎ *957/421404* ⊕ *www. casadesefarad.es* ≅ *€4* ⊙ *Mon.–Sat. 10–6, Sun. 11–2.*

QUICK BITES **Gaudí Juda Levi.** The lively Juda Levi plaza, surrounded by a maze of narrow streets and squares, lies at the heart of the Judería and makes a great spot for indulging in a little people-watching and a well-earned break. Sit outside here with a drink or, better still, an ice cream, sandwich, or snack. ⊠ *Pl. Juda Levi.*

Museo Arqueológico. In the heart of the old quarter, this museum has finds from Córdoba's varied cultural past. The ground floor has ancient Iberian statues and Roman statues, mosaics, and artifacts; the upper floor is devoted to Moorish art. By chance, the ruins of a Roman theater were discovered right next to the museum in 2000—have a look from the window just inside the entrance. The alleys and steps along Altos de Santa Ana make for great wandering. ⊠ *Pl. Jerónimo Paez, Judería* ☎ *957/355517* ⊕ *www.museosdeandalucia.es/culturayedeporte/museos* ≅ *€1.50* ⊙ *Tues.–Sat. 10–8:30, Sun. 10–5.*

Museo Julio Romero de Torres. Across the courtyard from the Museum of Fine Arts, this museum is devoted to the early-20th-century Córdoban artist Julio Romero de Torres (1874–1930), who specialized in mildly erotic portraits of demure, partially dressed Andalusian temptresses. Romero de Torres, who was also a flamenco *cantador* (singer), died at the age of 56 and is one of Córdoba's greatest folk heroes. Restoration of the 19th-century palace that houses the museum was completed in early 2012. ⊠ *Pl. del Potro 1–4, San Francisco* ☎ *957/470356* ⊕ *www. museojulioromero.cordoba.es* ≅ *€4.50* ⊙ *Tues.–Fri. 8:30 am–8:45 pm, Sat. 8:30–4:30, Sun. 8:30–2:30.*

Plaza de los Dolores. The 17th-century Convento de Capuchinos surrounds this small square north of Plaza San Miguel. The square is where you feel most deeply the city's languid pace. In its center, a statue of **Cristo de los Faroles** (Christ of the Lanterns) stands amid eight lanterns hanging from twisted wrought-iron brackets. ⊠ *Centro.*

10

Plaza Santa Marina. At the edge of the **Barrio de los Toreros,** a quarter where many of Córdoba's famous bullfighters were born and raised, stands a statue of the famous bullfighter Manolete (1917–47) opposite the lovely fernandina church of Santa Marina de Aguas Santas (St. Marina of Holy Waters). Not far from here, on the Plaza de la Lagunilla, is a bust of Manolete. ⊠ *Centro.*

Puerta de Almodóvar. Outside this old Moorish gate at the northern entrance of the Judería is a statue of **Seneca,** the Córdoba-born philosopher who rose to prominence in Nero's court in Rome and was forced to commit suicide at his emperor's command. The gate stands at the top of the narrow and colorful Calle San Felipe. ⊠ *Judería.*

San Nicolás de Villa. This classically dark Spanish church displays the Mudejar style of Islamic decoration and art forms. Córdoba's well-kept city park, the pleasant **Jardines de la Victoria,** with tile benches and manicured bushes, is a block west. ⊠ *Calle San Felipe, Centro.*

Synagogue. The only Jewish temple in Andalusia to survive the expulsion and inquisition of the Jews in 1492, Córdoba's synagogue is also one of only three ancient synagogues left in all of Spain (the other two are in Toledo). Though it no longer functions as a place of worship, it's a treasured symbol for Spain's modern Jewish communities. The outside is plain, but the inside, measuring 23 feet by 21 feet, contains some exquisite Mudejar stucco tracery. Look for the fine plant motifs and the Hebrew inscription saying that the synagogue was built in 1315. The women's gallery, not open for visits, still stands, and in the east wall is the ark where the sacred scrolls of the Torah were kept. ⊠ *Calle Judíos, Judería* ☎ *957/202928* 🎫 *Free* ☉ *Tues.–Sun. 9:30–2:45.*

Zoco. The Spanish word for the Arab souk (*zoco*) recalls the onetime function of this courtyard near the synagogue. It's now the site of a daily crafts market, where you can see artisans at work, and evening flamenco in summer. ⊠ *Calle Judíos 5, Judería* ☎ *957/204033* 🎫 *Free* ☉ *Craft stalls daily 10–8; workshops weekdays 10–2 and 5–8, weekends 11–2.*

NEED A BREAK?

Plaza de las Tendillas. Wander over to this plaza, which is halfway between the Mezquita and Plaza Colón, for a visit to the terraces of Café Boston or Café Siena, both enjoyable places to relax with a coffee when the weather is warm. ⊠ *Centro.*

WHERE TO EAT

$
INTERNATIONAL

✕ **Amaltea.** Satisfying both vegetarians and their meat-eating friends, this organic restaurant includes some meat and fish dishes on the menu. There's a healthy mix of Mexican, Asian, Spanish, and Italian-influenced dishes, including pasta with artichokes, chicken curry with mango and apricots, and several inventive dishes with *bacalao* (cod). The interior is warm and inviting, and diners are treated to a soothing musical backdrop of jazz, blues, and chill-out music. Tap water is served free in attractive bottles. 🟊 *Average main: €10* ⊠ *Ronda de Isasa 10, Centro* ☎ *957/491968* ☉ *No dinner Sun.; no lunch Aug.*

$ ✕ **Bar Santos.** This very small, quintessentially Spanish bar, with no
TAPAS seats and numerous photos of matadors and flamenco dancers, seems
out of place surrounded by the tourist shops and overshadowed by the
Mezquita, but its appearance—and its prices—are part of its charm.
Tapas (from €2) such as *morcilla ibérica* (black pudding) and *bocadillos*
(sandwiches that are literally "little mouthfuls") are excellent in quality
and value, while the *tortilla de patata* (potato omelet) is renowned and
celebrated both for its taste and its heroic thickness—so much so that
on weekends, they sell up to 60 a day. When it's busy, drinks and food
are served on plastic and you often have to eat outside on the street.
$ *Average main: €6* ✉ *Calle Magistral González Francés 3, Judería*
☎ *957/479360.*

$$ ✕ **Bodegas Campos.** A block east of the Plaza del Potro, this traditional
SPANISH old wine cellar is the epitome of all that's great about Andalusian cui-
Fodor'sChoice sine and high-quality service. The dining rooms are in barrel-heavy
★ rustic rooms and leafy traditional patios (take a look at some of the
signed barrels—you may recognize a name or two, such as the former
UK Prime Minister Tony Blair. Magnificent vintage flamenco posters
decorate the walls. Regional dishes include *solomillo del Valle de los
Pedroches dos salsas y patatas a lo pobre* (local pork with two sauces—
green and sherry—and creamy potatoes) and *dados de bacalao frito con
ali-oli* (fried dices of cod with garlic mayonnaise). Vegetables come from
the restaurant's own market garden. There's also an excellent tapas bar
(from €3). $ *Average main: €16* ✉ *Calle Los Lineros 32, San Pedro*
☎ *957/497500* ☽ *No dinner Sun.*

$$ ✕ **Casa Mazal.** In the heart of the Judería, this pretty little restaurant
ECLECTIC serves a modern interpretation of Sephardic cuisine, with organic dishes
that are more exotic than the usual Andalusian fare. The many vegetarian options include *berenjena timbal* (eggplant and tomato "pie"), and
the *cordero especiado* (spiced lamb) and *pollo a la miel* (chicken with
honey, dates, and raisins) are delicious. Try a bottle of kosher wine, and
for dessert consider the rose mousse or ginger ice cream. The romantic
atmosphere is compounded by two violinists playing Sephardic music
on the patio. $ *Average main: €17* ✉ *Calle Tomás Conde 3, Judería*
☎ *957/941888.*

$$$ ✕ **Casa Pepe de la Judería.** Geared toward a tourist clientele, this place
SPANISH is always packed, noisy, and fun. Antiques and some wonderful old oil
paintings fill this three-floor labyrinth of rooms just around the corner
from the mosque, near the Judería. There is live Spanish guitar music
most summer nights. A full selection of tapas and house specialties
includes *tostón de cochinillo con palmentier de patata* (crispy suck-
ling pig with herby roast potatoes) and the solidly traditional rabo de
toro. The cured-ham croquettes are reputedly the best in town. $ *Aver-
age main: €19* ✉ *Calle Romero 1, off Deanes, Judería* ☎ *957/200744*
⌖ *Reservations essential.*

$$$ ✕ **El Blasón.** One block west of Avenida Gran Capitán and down an
SPANISH unpromising side street, El Blasón has a Moorish-style entrance bar
leading onto a patio enclosed by ivy-covered walls where tapas are
served. Downstairs is a lounge with a red tile ceiling and old polished
clay plates on the walls. Upstairs are two elegant dining rooms where

10

blue walls, white silk curtains, and candelabras evoke early-19th-century luxury. The menu includes *lomos de merluza con ciruelas* (hake steaks with prunes) and *magret de pato al perfume de vinagre de frambuesa* (duck breast with aroma of raspberry wine vinegar). Innovative tapas (€4) are also available such as the *crujiente de trigueros con queso de rulo* (asparagus in filo pastry with goat's cheese). $ *Average main: €18* ⊠ *Calle José Zorrilla 11, Centro* ☎ *957/480625* ☉ *No dinner Sun.*

$$$ ✕ **El Caballo Rojo.** This is one of the most famous traditional restaurants
SPANISH   in Andalusia, frequented by royalty and society folk. The interior resem-
Fodor'sChoice   bles a cool, leafy Andalusian patio, and the dining room is furnished
★   with stained glass and dark wood; the upstairs terrace overlooks the Mezquita. The menu combines traditional specialties, such as *rabo de toro* and *salmorejo*, with more modern versions, such as *alcachofas a la Montillana* (artichoke in sweet Montilla wine) and *pez espada a la cordobesa con gambas* (swordfish Cordoba-style with prawns). A delicious selection of homemade tarts and flans are served from a trolley. $ *Average main: €18* ⊠ *Calle Cardenal Herrero 28, Judería* ☎ *957/475375* ⊕ *www.elcaballorojo.com* ⌕ *Reservations essential.*

$$ ✕ **El Choco.** The city's most exciting restaurant, which renewed its
SPANISH   Michelin star in 2013, El Choco has renowned chef Kisko Garcia at the
Fodor'sChoice   helm whipping up innovative dishes with a twist of traditional favorites
★   such as *cochinillo crujiente con crema de ajos y naranjas* (crispy suckling pig with cream of garlic and oranges) and *atún fresco de Almadraba que quiso ser cerdo ibérico* (traditionally caught fresh tuna "that wished it were an Iberian pig"—cooked in pork stock and roasted on an oak log fire). The *caldo blanco de Sierra Morena* (creamy stock with potatoes and ham) is a highly acclaimed starter. The restaurant has a minimalist interior, with charcoal-color walls and glossy parquet floors. El Choco is outside the city center to the east and not easy to find, so take a taxi. $ *Average main: €17* ⊠ *Compositor Serrano Lucena 14, Centro* ☎ *957/264863* ☉ *Closed Mon. and Aug. No dinner Sun.*

$$$ ✕ **El Churrasco.** The name suggests grilled meat, but this restaurant in the
SPANISH   heart of the Judería serves much more than that. In the colorful bar try tapas (from €3) such as the *berenjenas crujientes con salmorejo* (crispy fried eggplant slices with thick gazpacho). In the restaurant, the grilled fish is supremely fresh, and the steak is the best in town, particularly the namesake *churrasco* (grilled meat, served here in a spicy tomato-based sauce). On the inner patio, there's alfresco dining when it's warm outside, also the season to try another specialty: *gazpacho blanco de piñones con manzanas y pasas* (a white gazpacho made with pine nuts, apple and raisins). Save some room for the creamy fried ice cream. $ *Average main: €20* ⊠ *Calle Romero 16, Judería* ☎ *957/290819* ⊕ *www. elchurrasco.com* ☉ *Closed Aug.*

$ ✕ **Mesón San Basilio.** This unpretentious local eatery just outside the
SPANISH   tourist center serves excellent simple, hearty meat and fish dishes, all prepared in a large kitchen visible from the patio terrace and bar. The menu is dominated by *revueltos* (scrambled eggs with varying ingredients) and roast meat dishes like leg of lamb and suckling pig. Try the *mollejas* (grilled sweetbreads) accompanied by a mixed salad and a bottle of decent house red. At weekday lunchtime, a set menu offers great

A typical Córdoba patio, filled with flowers

value. This is a busy and noisy venue so not somewhere for a quiet meal. [$] *Average main: €9* ✉ *Calle San Basilio 19, Judería* ☎ *957/297007* 🕒 *No dinner Sun.*

$ TAPAS 🍴 **Taberna de San Miguel.** Just a few minutes' walk from the Plaza de las Tendillas and opposite the lovely San Miguel Church, this popular tapas spot—also known as the Casa el Pisto (House of Ratatouille)—was established in 1880. You can choose to squeeze in at the bar and dine on tapas (€2.10) or spread out a little more on the patio decked with ceramics and bullfighting memorabilia, where half and full portions are served. Legenadary toreador Manolete is particularly revered here. The menu is one long list of typical local dishes so expect to find oxtail, salmorejo and *flamenquín* (breaded pork filet with cheese). [$] *Average main: €11* ✉ *Pl. San Miguel 1, Centro* ☎ *957/470166* 🕒 *Closed Sun.*

10

$ TAPAS 🍴 **Taberna Sociedad de Plateros.** On a narrow side street just steps away from the Plaza del Potro, this delightful spot dates from the 17th century. One of the city's most historic inns, it has a large patio that adjoins a traditional marble bar where locals meet. Photographs of iconic local bullfighter Manolete line the walls, and the patio is decorated with giddily patterned tiles and bricks plus a giant flat-screen television. The food is solid home-style cooking, with choices including fried green peppers, Spanish potato omelet, and hearty oxtail stew. Choose from tapas (€2) or full portions. [$] *Average main: €7* ✉ *Calle San Francisco 6, Pl. de la Corredera* ☎ *957/470042* 🕒 *Closed Mon. Sept.–mid-May; closed Sun. mid-May–Aug.*

WHERE TO STAY

$ B&B/INN
🏨 **Casa de los Azulejos.** This 17th-century house still has original details like the majestic vaulted ceilings and, with the use of stunning azulejos—hence the name—it mixes Andalusian and Latin American influences. **Pros:** interesting architecture; friendly staff. **Cons:** hyper-busy interior design; limited privacy. [$] *Rooms from: €83* ✉ *Calle Fernando Colón 5, Centro* ☎ *957/470000* 🌐 *www.casadelosazulejos.com* 🛏 *7 rooms, 2 suites* 🍴 *Breakfast.*

$ HOTEL
🏨 **Gonzalez.** A few minutes from the Mezquita, the Gonzalez was originally built in the 16th-century as a palace for ancestors of the famous local artist Julio Romero de Torres. **Pros:** central location. **Cons:** public areas rather jaded; exterior rooms noisy. [$] *Rooms from: €79* ✉ *Calle Manrique 3, Judería* ☎ *957/479819* 🌐 *www.hotel-gonzalez.com* 🛏 *29 rooms* 🍴 *No meals.*

$$$ B&B/INN Fodor's Choice ★
🏨 **Hospederia de El Churrasco.** This small hotel, occupying a collection of houses just a stone's throw from the Mezquita, combines enchanting antique furnishings with modern amenities, but its greatest asset is its exceptionally helpful staff. **Pros:** beautiful interiors; rooms are equipped with computers. **Cons:** rooms facing street can be noisy. [$] *Rooms from: €178* ✉ *Calle Romero 38, Judería* ☎ *957/294808* 🛏 *9 rooms* 🍴 *Breakfast.*

$$$$ HOTEL Fodor's Choice ★
🏨 **Hospes Palacio del Bailío.** One of the city's top lodging options, this tastefully renovated 17th-century mansion is built over the ruins of a Roman house (visible beneath glass floors) in the historic center of town. **Pros:** dazzling interiors; impeccable comforts. **Cons:** not easy to access by car. [$] *Rooms from: €235* ✉ *Calle Ramírez de las Casas Deza 10–12, Plaza de la Corredera* ☎ *957/498993* 🌐 *www.hospes.es* 🛏 *49 rooms, 4 suites* 🍴 *No meals.*

$ HOTEL
🏨 **Hotel Maestre.** Around the corner from the Plaza del Potro, this is an affordable hotel in which Castilian-style furniture, gleaming marble, and high-quality oil paintings add elegance to excellent value. **Pros:** good location; great value. **Cons:** no elevator and lots of steps; ancient plumbing. [$] *Rooms from: €56* ✉ *Calle Romero Barros 4–6, San Pedro* ☎ *957/472410* 🌐 *www.hotelmaestre.com* 🛏 *26 rooms* 🍴 *No meals.*

$$$ HOTEL
🏨 **NH Amistad Córdoba.** Two 18th-century mansions overlooking Plaza de Maimónides in the heart of the Judería have been melded into a modern business hotel with a cobblestone Mudejar courtyard, carved-wood ceilings, and a plush lounge. **Pros:** pleasant and efficient service; great value. **Cons:** parking is difficult; access via steep steps with no ramp. [$] *Rooms from: €155* ✉ *Pl. de Maimónides 3, Judería* ☎ *957/420335* 🌐 *www.nh-hoteles.com* 🛏 *108 rooms* 🍴 *No meals.*

$$$ HOTEL
🏨 **Parador de Córdoba.** On the slopes of the Sierra de Córdoba, on the site of Abd ar-Rahman I's 8th-century summer palace, this modern parador has sunny rooms and nice views. **Pros:** wonderful views from south-facing rooms; sleek interiors; quality traditional cuisine. **Cons:** characterless modern building; far from main sights. [$] *Rooms from: €165* ✉ *Av. de la Arruzafa 39, El Brillante, 5 km (3 miles) north of Córdoba* ☎ *957/275900* 🌐 *www.parador.es* 🛏 *88 rooms, 6 suites* 🍴 *No meals.*

$$ | **Viento 10.** Tucked away to the east of the old quarter, but within
HOTEL | just 10 minutes' walk of the Mezquita is a quiet, romantic haven, once part of the 17th-century Sacred Martyrs Hospital. **Pros:** quiet but central location; personalized service. **Cons:** no car access to hotel entrance. [$] *Rooms from: €115* ⊠ *Calle Ronquillo Briceño 10* ⊕ *www. hotelviento10.es* ↪ *6 rooms* ⊙ *Closed Jan. and 2 wks in Aug. (phone for dates)* ⭫ *No meals.*

NIGHTLIFE AND PERFORMING ARTS

NIGHTLIFE

Córdoba locals hang out mostly in the areas of Ciudad Jardín (the old university area), Plaza de las Tendillas, and the Avenida Gran Capitán.

Bodega Guzman. For some traditional tipple, check out this atmospheric bodega, near the old synagogue. Its sherries are served straight from the barrel in a room that doubles as a bullfighting museum. ⊠ *Calle de los Judios 6, Judería.*

Café Málaga. A block from Plaza de las Tendillas, this is a laid-back hangout for jazz and blues aficionados. ⊠ *Calle Málaga 3, Centro.*

La Casa de los Azulejos. Live music (jazz, flamenco, and pop) is performed Friday from 9 pm in the patio area of this hotel. ⊠ *Calle Fernando Colón 5, Centro* ☏ *957/470000.*

FLAMENCO

Tablao Cardenal. Córdoba's most popular flamenco club is worth the trip just to see the courtyard of the 16th-century building, which was Córdoba's first hospital. Admission is €23 (including drink) and the 90-minute shows take place Monday to Saturday at 10:30 pm. ⊠ *Calle Torrijos 10, Judería* ☏ *957/483320.*

SHOPPING

Córdoba's main shopping district is around Avenida Gran Capitán, Ronda de los Tejares, and the streets leading away from Plaza Tendillas.

Meryan. This is one of Córdoba's best workshops for embossed leather. ⊠ *Calleja de las Flores 9* ☏ *957/475902* ⊕ *www.meryancor.com.*

Fodor'sChoice **Zoco.** Córdoba's artisans have workshops and sell their crafts in the
★ Zoco, open daily 10–8 (workshops closed weekdays 2–5, weekends 11–2). ⊠ *Calle Judíos, opposite Synagogue, Judería* ☏ *957/290575.*

SIDE TRIPS FROM CÓRDOBA

If you have time to go beyond Córdoba and have already seen the Medina Azahara palace ruins, head south to the wine country around Montilla, olive oil–rich Baena, and the Subbética mountain range, a cluster of small towns virtually unknown to travelers.

The entire Subbética region is protected as a natural park, and the mountains, canyons, and wooded valleys are stunning. You'll need a car to explore, though, and in some parts, the roads are rather rough. To reach these enticing towns in *la campiña* (the countryside), take the low road (A318) through Montilla, cutting north to Baena via Zuheros, or take the high road (A307) through Espejo and Baena, cutting south through Cabra.

For park information or hiking advice, contact the **Mancomunidad de la Subbética** (✉ *Ctra. Carcabuey–Zagrilla, Km 5.75, Carcabuey* ☎ *957/704106* ⊕ *www. turismodelasubbetica.es*).

You can also pick up information, including a pack of maps titled *Rutas Senderistas de la Subbética,* from any local tourist office. The handy cards detail 15 walks with sketched maps.

Southern Córdoba is also the province's main olive-producing region, with the town of **Lucena** at its center. If you follow the Ruta del Aceite (olive-oil route), you'll pass some of the province's most picturesque villages. In Lucena is the Torre del Moral, where Granada's last Nasrid ruler, Boabdil, was imprisoned in 1483 after launching an unsuccessful attack on the Christians; and the Parroquia de San Mateo, a small but remarkable Renaissance–Gothic cathedral. Furniture and brass and copper pots are made in the town. Southeast of Lucena, C334 crosses the **Embalse de Iznájar** (Iznájar Reservoir) amid spectacular scenery. On C334, halfway between Lucena and the reservoir, in **Rute,** you can sample the potent *anís* (anise) liqueur for which this small, whitewashed town is famous.

MONTILLA

46 km (28 miles) south of Córdoba.

Heading south from Córdoba toward Málaga, you'll pass through hills ablaze with sunflowers in early summer before you reach the vineyards of the Montilla–Moriles. Every fall, 47,000 acres' worth of Pedro Ximénez grapes are crushed here to produce the region's rich Montilla wines, which are similar to sherry. Montilla-Moriles has developed a young white wine similar to Portugal's Vinho Verde.

ESSENTIALS
Visitor Information Montilla ✉ *Calle Capitán Alonso de Vargas 3* ☎ *957/652462.*

EXPLORING
Bodegas Alvear. Founded in 1729, this bodega in the center of town is Montilla's oldest. Besides being informative, the fun tour and wine tasting gives you the chance to buy a bottle or two of Alvear's tasty version of the sweet Pedro Ximenez aged sherry. Sunday tours are available by appointment only. ✉ *Calle María Auxiliadora 1* ☎ *957/652939* ⊕ *www. alvear.es* 🎫 *€6* ☉ *Mon.–Sat. 12:30.*

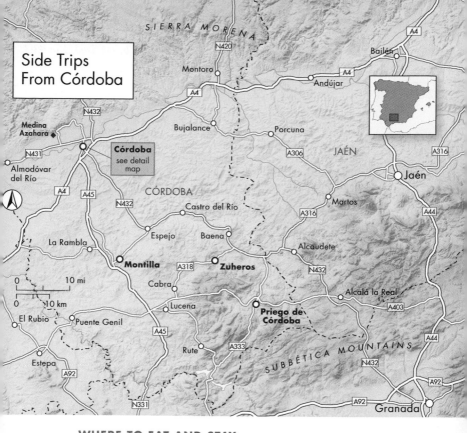

Side Trips From Córdoba

SIERRA MORENA

N420
Montoro
A4
Bailén
Andújar
A4
A4
Bujalance
Porcuna
JAÉN
A306
Jaén
A316
Medina
Azahara
Córdoba
see detail
map
N431
Almodóvar
del Río
A4
A45
CÓRDOBA
N432
Castro del Río
Martos
A44
A316
La Rambla
Espejo
Baena
Alcaudete
Montilla
A318
Zuheros
N432
Cabra
Alcalá la Real
Lucena
A403
El Rubio
Puente Genil
A45
Priego de
Córdoba
A44
Estepa
Rute
A333
SUBBÉTICA MOUNTAINS
N432
A92
A92
N331
A92
Granada

0   10 mi
0   10 km

WHERE TO EAT AND STAY

$ ✕ **Las Camachas.** The best-known restaurant in southern Córdoba Prov-
SPANISH ince is in an Andalusian-style hacienda outside Montilla—near the main
road toward Málaga. Start with tapas in the attractive bar, then move
on to one of the six dining rooms, where regional specialties include
alcachofas al Montilla (artichokes braised in Montilla wine), *salmorejo*
(a thick, garlicky gazpacho), *perdiz a la campiña* (country-style partridge), and *pierna de cordero lechal* (leg of suckling lamb). You
can also try local wines here; the *fino* is particularly good. $ *Average main:*
€12 ✉ *Av. Europa 3* ☎ *957/650004.*

$ ⌂ **Don Gonzalo.** Just south of town is one of Andalusia's better roadside
HOTEL hotels, with a highly regarded and elegant restaurant. **Pros:** easy to get
to; refreshing pool. **Cons:** some rooms in need of refurbishment; outside
of town. $ *Rooms from: €65* ✉ *Ctra. Córdoba–Málaga (N331), Km*
47, 3 km (2 miles) south ☎ *957/650658* ⊕ *www.hoteldongonzalo.com*
↪ *32 rooms, 2 suites* ⦿ *Breakfast.*

SHOPPING

On the outskirts of town, coopers' shops produce barrels of various
sizes, some small enough to serve as creative souvenirs.

Tonelería J. L. Rodríguez. On Montilla's main road, it is worth stopping
here not just to buy barrels and local wines, but also to pop in the back

and see the barrels being made. ✉ *Ctra. Córdoba–Málaga, Km 43.3* ☎ *957/650563* ⊕ *www.toneleriajlrodriguez.com.*

ZUHEROS

80 km (50 miles) southeast of C rdoba.

Zuheros, at the northern edge of the Subbética mountain range and at an altitude of 2,040 feet, is one of the most attractive villages in the province of Córdoba. From the road up, it's hidden behind a dominating rock face topped off by the dramatic ruins of a castle built by the Moors over a Roman castle. There's an expansive view back over the valley from here. Next to the castle is the Iglesia de Santa María, built over a mosque. The base of the minaret is the foundation for the bell tower.

EXPLORING

Cueva de los Murciélagos (*Cave of the Bats*). Some 4 km (2½ miles) above Zuheros along a winding road, the Cueva de los Murciélagos runs for about 2 km (1 mile), although only about half of that expanse is open to the public. The main attractions are the wall paintings dating from the Neolithic Age (6000–3000 BC) and Chalcolithic Age (3000–2000 BC), but excavations have indicated that the cave was inhabited as far back as 35,000 years ago. Items from the Copper and Bronze ages as well as from the Roman period and the Middle Ages have also been found here. Visits are by guided tour only and must be booked in advance, by phone or email (✎ *turismo@zuheros.es*) or at Calle Nueva 1 in the village. ✉ *CV-247, off Calle Santo* ☎ *957/694545 Tues.–Fri. 10–1:30* ✉ *€6* ☉ *Guided tours Tues.–Fri. at 12:30 and 4:30 (last tour at 5:30 in summer), weekends at 11, 12:30, 2, 4, and 5:30 (last two tours at 5 and 6:30 in summer).*

Museo de Costumbres y Artes Populares Juan Fernandez Cruz. Housed in an impressive square mansion from 1912, this museum is at the edge of the village. Exhibits detail local customs and traditions. ✉ *Calle Santo 29* ☎ *957/694690* ✉ *€3* ☉ *May–Sept., Tues.–Fri. noon–2 and 5:30–8:30, weekends 10:30–2:30 and 5:30–8:30; Oct.–Apr., Tues.–Fri. noon–2 and 4–7, weekends 10:30–2:30 and 4–7.*

Museo Histórico-Arqueológico Municipal. This museum displays archaeological remains found in local caves and elsewhere; some date back to the Middle Paleolithic period some 35,000 years ago. You can also visit the remains of the Renaissance rooms in the castle, across the road. Visits are by guided tour only. ✉ *Pl. de la Paz 2* ☎ *957/694545* ✉ *€2* ☉ *Guided tours on the hour 10–2 and 4–6 (also at 7 Apr.–Sept.).*

WHERE TO STAY

$

B&B/INN

Fodor's Choice

★

🏨 Hacienda Minerva. This stylish hotel was created out of a country estate dating from the late 19th century, and its original features, including the historic oil mill, have been preserved. **Pros:** tranquil surroundings; superb restaurant. **Cons:** outside of town. **$** *Rooms from: €80* ✉ *Crta. Zuheros, Doña Mencia* ☎ *957/090951* ⊕ *www.haciendaminerva.com* ➦ *25 rooms* ⦿ *Breakfast.*

$

B&B/INN

🏨 Zuhayra. This small hotel on a narrow street has comfortable rooms painted a sunny yellow with views over the village rooftops to the valley below. **Pros:** cozy public spaces; stunning vistas; good service. **Cons:** plain decoration. [$] *Rooms from: €70* ✉ *Calle Mirador 10* ☎ *957/694693* 🌐 *www.zercahoteles.com* 🛏 *18 rooms* 🍴 *Breakfast.*

PRIEGO DE CÓRDOBA

103 km (64 miles) southeast of Córdoba, 25 km (15 miles) southeast of Zuheros.

Fodor's Choice ★ The jewel of Córdoba's countryside is Priego de Córdoba, a town of 23,500 inhabitants at the foot of Mt. Tinosa. Wander down Calle del Río, opposite the town hall, to see 18th-century mansions, once the homes of silk merchants. At the end of the street is the Fuente del Rey (King's Fountain), with some 130 water jets, built in 1803. Don't miss the lavish baroque churches of La Asunción and La Aurora or the Barrio de la Villa, an old Moorish quarter with a maze of narrow streets of white-walled buildings.

GETTING HERE AND AROUND

Priego has a reasonable bus service from Córdoba (2½ hours) and Granada (1½ hours), although your best bet is to visit by car en route to either of these cities. Once there, it's perfect for pedestrian exploration.

ESSENTIALS

Visitor Information Priego de Córdoba ✉ *Pl. de la Constitución 3* ☎ *957/700625* 🌐 *www.turismodepriego.com.*

WHERE TO EAT AND STAY

$$ MEDITERRANEAN 🍴 **La Paloma.** About 30 km (18 miles) south of Priego de Córdoba, this restaurant overlooks the rolling hills of the Subbética. It's run by an Italian-Spanish couple; wife Elena hails from Tuscany and honed her culinary skills in one of Marbella's more exclusive restaurants before opting for the Córdoba countryside. The menu has plenty of Italian influence, including dishes like roast lamb filets with herbs and mustard and jumbo shrimp in creamy garlic sauce. Most of the vegetables are from the couple's organic garden. [$] *Average main: €13* ✉ *Crta. Salinas-Iznajar, Km 63, Villanueva de Tapia* ☎ *952/750409* ⏲ *Closed Mon., 1st wk in Feb., and 2 wks in Nov. (dates vary; call to check).*

$$$$ HOTEL FAMILY 🏨 **Barceló La Bobadilla.** On its own 1,000-acre estate amid olive and oak trees, 42 km (24 miles) west of Priego de Córdoba, this complex resembles a Moorish village of white-wall buildings with tile roofs and patios, and there are fountains and an artificial lake on the property. **Pros:** spacious, comfortable rooms; lovely setting; many activities. **Cons:** pricey; limited covered parking; rather isolated. [$] *Rooms from: €405* ✉ *Finca La Bobadilla, Apdo 144 E, Loja* ☎ *958/321861* 🌐 *www.barcelolabobadilla.com* 🛏 *60 rooms, 10 suites* ⏲ *Closed Nov.–Feb.* 🍴 *Breakfast.*

$ RESORT 🏨 **Villa Turística de Priego.** In the heart of the Subbética nature park, 6 km (4 miles) north of town, this complex of semidetached units is clustered to form a gleaming white Andalusian pueblo. **Pros:** family-friendly vibe; quiet retreat. **Cons:** far from town; some areas could do with refurbishment. [$] *Rooms from: €81* ✉ *Aldea de Zagrilla* ☎ *957/703503* 🌐 *www.*

10

Olive groves near Priego de Córdoba

villasdeandalucia.com ⤴ *52 apartments/villas* ⊙ *Closed for a month in winter (check website for dates)* ⧉ *No meals.*

JAÉN PROVINCE

Jaén is dominated by its Alcázar. To the northeast are the olive-producing towns of Baeza and Úbeda. Cazorla, the gateway to the Parque Natural Sierra de Cazorla Segura y Las Villas, lies beyond.

JAÉN

107 km (64 miles) southeast of Córdoba, 93 km (58 miles) north of Granada.

Nestled in the foothills of the Sierra de Jabalcuz, Jaén is surrounded by towering peaks and olive-clad hills. The modern part of town holds little interest for travelers these days, but the old town is an atmospheric jumble of narrow cobblestone streets hugging the mountainside. Jaén's grand parador, in the city's hilltop castle, is a great reason to stop here.

The Arabs called this land *Geen* (Route of the Caravans) because it formed a crossroad between Castile and Andalusia. Captured from the Moors by Ferdinand III in 1246, Jaén became a frontier province, the site of many a skirmish and battle over the following 200 years between the Moors of Granada and Christians from the north and west.

GETTING HERE AND AROUND

You can reach Jaén by bus from Granada, Madrid, and Málaga (ALSA ☎ 902/422242 ⊕ *www.alsa.es*), and also by train from Granada. Jaén is compact and all sights are easy to visit on foot, with the exception of the castle, 3 km (2 miles) from the center and a steep climb—if you can't face the ascent, take a taxi.

ESSENTIALS

Visitor Information Jaén ✉ *Calle Maestra 8* ☎ *953/190455* ⊕ *www.tur jaen.org.*

EXPLORING

Baños Árabes. Explore the narrow alleys of old Jaén as you walk from the cathedral to the Baños Árabes (Arab Baths), which once belonged to Ali, a Moorish king of Jaén, and probably date from the 11th century. In 1592, Fernando de Torres y Portugal, a viceroy of Peru, built himself a mansion, the **Palacio de Villardompardo**, right over the baths, so it took years of painstaking excavation to restore them to their original form. The palace contains a fascinating, albeit small, museum of folk crafts and a larger museum devoted to native art. The baths and museums were restored to great acclaim in 2012. ✉ *Palacio de Villardompardo, Pl. Luisa de Marillac* ☎ *953/248068* 💶 *Free* ⊙ *Tues.–Sat. 9–2:30 and 4–8:30, Sun. 9–2:30.*

Basílica Menor de San Ildefonso (*Smaller Basilica of Saint Ildefonso*). Set on the square and in the district of the same name, this large church is one of Jaén's treasures. Built mainly in the Gothic style with baroque details, the magnificent gilded altar is the highlight. ✉ *Pl. de San Ildefonso* ☎ *953/190346* 💶 *Free* ⊙ *Mon.–Thurs. 8:30–12:30 and 5–8, Fri. 8:30–10:30 and 5–8, weekends 9–1:30 and 5–8.*

Fodor's Choice ★ **Castillo de Santa Catalina.** This castle, perched on a rocky crag 400 yards above the center of town, is Jaén's star monument. It may have originated as a tower built by Hannibal, but whatever its start, the site was fortified continuously over the centuries. The Nasrid king Alhamar, builder of Granada's Alhambra, constructed an alcázar here, but Ferdinand III captured it from him in 1246 on the feast day of Santa Catalina (St. Catherine). Catalina consequently became Jaén's patron saint, so when the Christians built a castle and chapel here, they dedicated both to her. The castle is currently undergoing renovations, and is due to reopen in mid-2014. ✉ *Ctra. del Castillo de Santa Catalina* ☎ *953/120733* 💶 *Free* ⊙ *June–Sept., Tues.–Fri. 10–2, weekends 10–2 and 5–9; Oct.–May, Tues.–Fri. 10–2, weekends 10–2 and 3:30–7:30 (hrs are approximate; call to check).*

Jaén Cathedral. Looming above the modest buildings around it, the cathedral was begun in 1492 on the site of a former mosque and took almost 300 years to build. Its chief architect was Andrés de Vandelvira (1509–75)—many more of his buildings can be seen in Úbeda and Baeza. The ornate facade was sculpted by Pedro Roldán, and the figures on top of the columns include San Fernando (Ferdinand III) and the four evangelists. The cathedral's most treasured relic is the **Santo Rostro** (Holy Face), the cloth with which, according to tradition, St. Veronica cleansed Christ's face on the way to Calvary, leaving his image imprinted on the fabric. The rostro is displayed every Friday. In the underground **museum**, look for the paintings *San Lorenzo*, by Martínez Montañés; the *Immaculate Conception*, by Alonso Cano; and a Calvary scene by Jácobo Florentino. ✉ *Pl. Santa María* ☎ *953/241448* 🎟 *€5* 🕐 *July–Sept., weekdays 10–2 and 5–8, weekends 10–noon and 5–7; Oct.–June, weekdays 10–2 and 4–7, weekends 10–noon and 4–6.*

Museo de Jaén. This museum has one of the best collections of Iberian (pre-Roman) artifacts in Spain—the newest wing has 20 life-size Iberian sculptures discovered by chance near the village of Porcuna in 1975. The museum proper is in a 1547 mansion and has a patio with the facade of the erstwhile Church of San Miguel. The fine-arts section has a room full of Goya lithographs. ✉ *Paseo de la Estación 29* ☎ *953/313339* 🎟 *€1.50* 🕐 *Tues.–Sat. 10–8:30, Sun. 10–5.*

WHERE TO EAT AND STAY

$$$ SPANISH 🍴 **Casa Antonio.** Exquisite Andalusian food with a contemporary twist is served at this somber yet elegant restaurant with three small dining rooms, all with cherry-paneled walls and dramatic contemporary artwork. Try the *alcachofas de la tierra con salsa de almendras* (locally-grown artichokes in almond sauce) or *cochinillo lechal con cebolleta a la naranja y cardamomo* (suckling pig with orange- and cardamom-flavored spring onion). [$] *Average main: €19* ✉ *Calle Fermín Palma 3* ☎ *953/270262* 🕐 *Closed Mon. and Aug. No dinner Sun.*

$$ SPANISH 🍴 **Taberna El Zurito.** Locals and visitors rave about this tiny bar less than 10 minutes' walk north of the cathedral. It's one of the oldest bars in the city (established in 1912), has just two tables plus bar space, and is crammed with Jaén memorabilia, but the homemade dishes more than make up for the lack of elbow room. The free tapas that come with every drink are tasty and generous, and menu highlights include *rabo de toro dehuesado con jamón* (deboned oxtail with ham) and *ventresca de atún rojo* (red tuna belly). [$] *Average main: €15* ✉ *Calle Correa Weglison 6* ☎ *605/988016* 🕐 *Closed Sun.*

$$ HOTEL Fodor's Choice ★ 🏨 **Parador de Jaén.** Built amid the mountaintop towers of the Castillo de Santa Catalina, this 13th-century castle is one of the showpieces of the parador chain and a good reason to visit Jaén. **Pros:** architectural grandeur; panoramic views. **Cons:** outside Jaén. [$] *Rooms from: €125* ✉ *Calle Castillo de Santa Catalina* ☎ *953/230000* 🌐 *www.parador.es* 🛏 *45 rooms* 🍽 *No meals.*

BAEZA

Fodor's Choice ★ *48 km (30 miles) northeast of Jaén on N321.*

The historic town of Baeza, nestled between hills and olive groves, is one of the best-preserved old towns in Spain. Founded by the Romans, it later housed the Visigoths and became the capital of a Moorish *taifa*, one of some two dozen mini-kingdoms formed after the Ummayad Caliphate was subdivided in 1031. Ferdinand III captured Baeza in 1227, and for the next 200 years it stood on the frontier of the Moorish kingdom of Granada. In the 16th and 17th centuries, local nobles gave the city a wealth of Renaissance palaces.

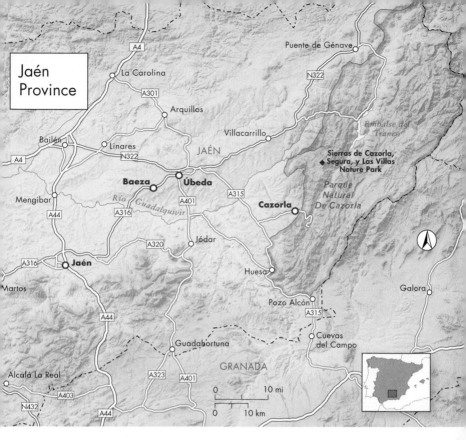

GETTING HERE AND AROUND

Frequent buses (15 weekdays, 10 weekends; ALSA ☎ 902/422242
⊕ *www.alsa.es*) connect Baeza with Jaén and Úbeda, although a private car is the best option given the remoteness of the town and that you may want to explore nearby Úbeda on the same day. Baeza is small and flat, and with its sights clustered round the very center it's very easy to explore on foot.

ESSENTIALS

Visitor Information Baeza ✉ *Pl. del Pópulo* ☎ *953/779982* ⊕ *www. ubedaybaezaturismo.com.*

Tours Semer Guided Tours. Two-hour guided tours around Baeza (in English, minimum two people) recount the history, culture, and traditions of the town. Tours of Úbeda are also available, with a discount for combined tours of both towns. ✉ *Portales Carbonería 15* ☎ *953/757916* ⊕ *www.semerturismo.com* 🎟 *€12* 🕐 *Mon.–Thurs. at 11, Fri. and Sat. at 11 and 5 (6 June–Sept.).*

EXPLORING

TOP ATTRACTIONS

Ayuntamiento (*Town hall*). Baeza's town hall was designed by cathedral master Andrés de Vandelvira. The facade is ornately decorated with a mix of religious and pagan imagery; look between the balconies for the coats of arms of Felipe II, the city of Baeza, and the magistrate Juan de Borja. Ask at the tourist office about visits to the *salón de plenos,* a meeting hall with painted, carved woodwork. ⊠ *Pl. Cardenal Benavides.*

Baeza Cathedral. Originally begun by Ferdinand III on the site of a former mosque, the cathedral was largely rebuilt by Andrés de Vandelvira, architect of Jaén's cathedral, between 1570 and 1593, though the west front has architectural influences from an earlier period. A fine 14th-century rose window crowns the 13th-century Puerta de la Luna (Moon Door). Don't miss the baroque silver monstrance (a vessel in which the consecrated Host is exposed for the adoration of the faithful), which is carried in Baeza's Corpus Christi processions—the piece is kept in a concealed niche behind a painting, but you can see it in all its splendor by putting a coin in a slot to reveal the hiding place. Next to the monstrance is the entrance to the clock tower, where a small donation and a narrow spiral staircase take you to one of the best views of Baeza. The remains of the original mosque are in the cathedral's Gothic cloisters. ⊠ *Pl. de Santa María* ☏ *953/742188* 🖵 *Cathedral free, cloister and museum €4* ⊙ *Weekdays 10–2 and 4–6, Sat. 10–6 (until 7 Apr.–Sept.), Sun. 10–5.*

Museo de Baeza. Tucked away behind the tourist office, the Baeza Museum is in itself a museum piece. Housed in a 15th-century noble palace, the facade and interiors are home to an interesting display of Baeza's history, from Roman remains to more recent religious paintings. ⊠ *Calle Casas Nuevas* ☏ *953/741582* 🖵 *€2* ⊙ *Tues.–Fri. 10–2 and 4:30–7:30, weekends 10–2.*

WORTH NOTING

Casa del Pópulo. In the central paseo—where the Plaza del Pópulo (or Plaza de los Leones) and Plaza de la Constitución (or Plaza del Mercado Viejo) merge to form a cobblestone square—this is a graceful town house built around 1530. The first Mass of the Reconquest was supposedly celebrated on its curved balcony; it now houses Baeza's tourist office. ⊠ *Pl. del Pópulo.*

Convento de San Francisco. This 16th-century convent is one of Vandelvira's religious architectural masterpieces. The building was spoiled by the French army and partially destroyed by a light earthquake in the early 1800s, but you can see its restored remains. ⊠ *Calle de San Francisco.*

Fuente de los Leones (*Fountain of the Lions*). In the center of the town square is an ancient Iberian-Roman statue thought to depict Imilce, wife of Hannibal; at the foot of her column is the Fuente de los Leones. ⊠ *Pl. del Pópulo.*

San Felipe Neri. The ancient student custom of inscribing names and graduation dates in bull's blood (as in Salamanca) is still evident on the walls of the seminary of San Felipe Neri, opposite the cathedral and built in 1660. ⊠ *Cuesta de San Felipe* 🖵 *Free* ⊙ *Weekdays 9–2.*

WHERE TO EAT AND STAY

$$

SPANISH

✗ **La Góndola.** Service comes with a smile at this rustic restaurant on Baeza's Plaza de la Constitución, and it's popularity with locals is a good endorsement. The interior is typically Andalusian, with agricultural implements adding a rustic touch, and there's a pleasant and shady outside terrace. Specialties include snails as well as hearty fare such as homemade partridge pâté, and suckling pig and lamb, and there are some local dishes to choose from—*patatas baezanas* (roast potatoes served with mushrooms), for instance. The daily three-course menú del día and the dish of the day (usually a stew) are a good value. $ *Average main: €15* ⊠ *Portales Carbonería 13* ☎ *953/742984.*

$ 🏨 **La Casona del Arco.** Housed in an old stone building just inside the
HOTEL   walls of the historic center, this comfortable hotel is an excellent base for excursions to the surrounding towns. **Pros:** central yet quiet; modern fixtures. **Cons:** unimaginative breakfast; no parking. $ *Rooms from: €56* ⊠ *Calle Sacramento 3* ☎ *953/747208* ⊕ *www.lacasonadelarco.com* 🛏 *18 rooms* ⃝ *No meals.*

ÚBEDA

9 km (5½ miles) northeast of Baeza on N321.

Fodor'sChoice   Úbeda's *casco antiguo* (old town) is one of the most outstanding
★   enclaves of 16th-century architecture in Spain. It's a stunning surprise in the heart of Jaén's olive groves, set in the shadow of the wild Sierra de Cazorla mountain range. For crafts enthusiasts, this is Andalusia's capital for many kinds of artisan goods. Follow signs to the Zona Monumental, where there are countless Renaissance palaces and stately mansions, though most are closed to the public.

GETTING HERE AND AROUND
Frequent buses (15 weekdays, 10 weekends; ALSA ☎ 902/422242 ⊕ *www.alsa.es*) connect Úbeda with Jaén and Baeza, although a private car is the best option given the remoteness of the town and that you may want to explore nearby Baeza in the same day. Úbeda's sights are all within easy reach of the center so exploring on foot is easy.

ESSENTIALS
Visitor Information Úbeda ⊠ *Palacio Marqués del Contadero, Calle Baja del Marqués 4* ☎ *953/779204* ⊕ *www.ubeda.com.*

Tours Semer Guided Tours. Two-hour guided tours around Úbeda (in English, minimum two people) recount the history, culture, and traditions of the town. Tours of Baeza are also available, with a discount on combined tours of both towns. ⊠ *Calle Juan Montilla 3* ☎ *953/757916* ⊕ *www.semerturismo.com* 💶 *€14, includes all entry fees* ⊙ *Tours Mon.–Thurs. at 11, Fri.–Sat. at 11 and 5 (6 June–Sept.).*

EXPLORING
TOP ATTRACTIONS
Ayuntamiento Antiguo (*Old Town Hall*). Begun in the early 16th century but restored as a beautiful arcaded baroque palace in 1680, the former town hall is now a conservatory of music. From the hall's upper balcony, the town council watched celebrations and *autos-da-fé* ("acts of faith"—executions of heretics sentenced by the Inquisition) in the square below. You can't enter the town hall, but on the north side you can visit the 13th-century church of San Pablo, with an Isabelline south portal. ⊠ *Pl. Primero de Mayo, off Calle María de Molina*

10

The picturesque city of Cazorla, in Jaén province

☎ 953/750637 ✉ *Church free* ⊘ *Church only: Tues. and Wed. 11–noon and 5–7:30, Thurs. and Fri. 11–1 and 5–7:30, Sat. 11–1, Sun. 12:15–1:30.*

Hospital de Santiago. Sometimes jokingly called the Escorial of Andalusia (in allusion to Felipe II's monolithic palace and monastery outside Madrid), this is a huge, angular building in the modern section of town, and yet another one of Vandelvira's masterpieces in Úbeda. The plain facade is adorned with ceramic medallions, and over the main entrance is a carving of Santiago Matamoros (St. James the Moorslayer) in his traditional horseback pose. Inside are an arcaded patio and a grand staircase. Now a cultural center, it holds some of the events at the International Spring Dance and Music Festival. ✉ *Av. Cristo Rey* ☎ *953/750842* ✉ *Free* ⊘ *Daily 10–2:30 and 5–9:30.*

Sacra Capilla de El Salvador. The Plaza Vázquez de Molina, in the heart of the old town, is the site of this building, which is photographed so often that it's become the city's unofficial symbol. It was built by Vandelvira, but he based his design on some 1536 plans by Diego de Siloé, architect of Granada's cathedral. Considered one of the masterpieces of Spanish Renaissance religious art, the chapel was sacked in the frenzy of church burnings at the outbreak of the civil war, but it retains its ornate western facade and altarpiece, which has a rare Berruguete sculpture. ✉ *Pl. Vázquez de Molina* ☎ *609/279905* ✉ *€5 (free Mon.–Sat. 9:30–10, Sun. 6–7)* ⊘ *Mon.–Sat. 9:30–2 and 4–6, Sun. 11:30–2 and 4–7.*

WORTH NOTING

Casa Museo Arte Andalusi. This interesting museum is in an attractive building with a traditional patio and displays a former private collection of period antiques, including Moorish, Mudejar, and Mozarabic pieces. ✉ *Calle Narvaez 11* ☎ *619/076132* 🎟 *€2* 🕐 *Daily 11–2 and 5–8.*

WHERE TO EAT

$$$ SPANISH 🍴 **Asador de Santiago.** At this adventurous restaurant just off the main street, the chef prepares both Spanish classics like white shrimp from Huelva or suckling pig from Segovia and innovative dishes like *ajoblanco de piñones con granizado de mango* (cream of garlic and almond soup with pine nuts and mango sorbet). There's a delicious menú de degustación. Vegetarian choices such as risotto can be prepared on request. The candle-filled interior is more traditional than the menu and has terra-cotta tiles, dark-wood furnishings, and crisp white linens. [$] *Average main: €18* ✉ *Av. Cristo Rey 4* ☎ *953/750463* ✍ *Reservations essential* 🕐 *No dinner Sun.*

$$ SPANISH 🍴 **La Imprenta.** Housed in a former printer's workshop in the historic center of town, this cozy restaurant and tapas bar offers a refreshing alternative to more traditional establishments. The short but well-balanced menu includes inventions like scorpion fish in a sea urchin cream and sea bass pastry with prawns in Barbadillo wine sauce, along with an excellent *solomillo con foie* (sirloin with foie gras) and unusual rice dishes. Portions are generous, the staff attentive, and the wine list will surprise even connoisseurs. [$] *Average main: €16* ✉ *Pl. Doctor Quesada 1* ☎ *953/755500.*

$$ SPANISH 🍴 **Mesón Gabino.** A stalwart defender of Úbeda's culinary traditions, this cavelike restaurant serves such standards as *andrajos de Úbeda* (fish, pasta, and vegetable stew) and the beef, lamb, and fish cooked over coals are always delicious. The wine list offers an ample range of Rioja and Ribera del Duero selections. You can have tapas at the bar and, for a more substantial repast, the good-value lunchtime menú del día offers appetizers, three courses including dessert, and one drink. It's on the edge of town near the Puerta del Losal, but it's well worth the walk from Plaza 1 de Mayo. [$] *Average main: €15* ✉ *Calle Fuente Seca s/n* ☎ *953/757553* 🕐 *No dinner Mon.*

WHERE TO STAY

$$ HOTEL 🏨 **Hotel Sercotel Rosaleda de Don Pedro.** This beautiful 16th-century mansion, in the city's Zona Monumental, blends the best of the old with many of the comforts a modern traveler would want, including king-size beds. **Pros:** easy parking; good value; has a pool. **Cons:** hard to find; basement reception and restaurant areas a little dingy. [$] *Rooms from: €119* ✉ *Calle Obispo Toral 2* ☎ *953/796111* 🌐 *www.hotelrosaledadonpedro.com* 🛏 *60 rooms* 🍽 *No meals.*

$$$ B&B/INN Fodor's Choice ★ 🏨 **Palacio de la Rambla.** In old Úbeda, this stunning 16th-century mansion has been in the same family since it was built—it still hosts the Marquesa de la Rambla when she's in town—and eight of the rooms are available for overnighters. **Pros:** central location; elegant style. **Cons:** little parking. [$] *Rooms from: €132* ✉ *Pl. del Marqués 1* ☎ *953/750196* 🌐 *www.palaciodelarambla.com* 🛏 *6 rooms, 2 suites* 🕐 *Closed 3 wks in Jan.* 🍽 *Breakfast.*

$$$
HOTEL
Fodor'sChoice
★

Parador de Úbeda. Designed by Andrés de Vandelvira, this splendid parador is in a 16th-century ducal palace in a prime location on the Plaza Vázquez de Molina, next to the Capilla del Salvador. **Pros:** elegant surroundings; perfect location. **Cons:** parking is difficult; church bells in the morning. $ *Rooms from: €165* ⊠ *Pl. Vázquez de Molina s/n* ☎ *953/750345* ⊕ *www.parador.es* ⊅ *35 rooms, 1 suite* ☉ *No meals.*

SHOPPING

Little Úbeda is the crafts capital of Andalusia, with workshops devoted to carpentry, basket weaving, stone carving, wrought iron, stained glass, and, above all, the city's distinctive green-glaze pottery. Calle Valencia is the traditional potters' row, running from the bottom of town to Úbeda's general crafts center, northwest of the old quarter (follow signs to Calle Valencia or Barrio de Alfareros).

Úbeda's most famous potter was Pablo Tito, whose craft is carried on at three different workshops run by two of his sons, Paco and Juan, and a son-in-law, Melchor, each of whom claims to be the sole true heir to the art.

Alfarería Góngora. All kinds of ceramics are sold here. ⊠ *Calle Cuesta de la Merced 32* ☎ *953/754605.*

Juan Tito. The extrovert Juan Tito can often be found at the potter's wheel in his rambling shop, which is packed with ceramics of every size and shape. You can also shop online. ⊠ *Pl. del Ayuntamiento 12* ☎ *953/751302* ⊕ *www.alfareriatito.com.*

Melchor Tito. You can see classic green-glazed items—the focus of Melchor Tito's work—being made in his workshops in Calle Valencia and Calle Fuenteseca 17, which are both also shops. ⊠ *Calle Valencia 44* ☎ *953/753692.*

Paco Tito. Clay sculptures of characters from *Don Quixote*, fired by Paco Tito in an old Moorish-style kiln, are the specialty of this studio and shop. There is also a museum (Monday–Saturday 8–2 and 4–8, Sunday 10–2) on the premises. ⊠ *Calle Valencia 22* ☎ *953/751496.*

CAZORLA

48 km (35 miles) southeast of Úbeda.

Unspoiled and remote, the village of Cazorla is at the east end of Jaén province. The pine-clad slopes and towering peaks of the Cazorla and Segura sierras rise above the village, and below it stretch endless miles of olive groves. In spring, purple jacaranda trees blossom in the plazas.

GETTING HERE AND AROUND

The remoteness and size of Cazorla Nature Park plus the lack of frequent public transportation make this somewhere to explore by car.

ESSENTIALS

Visitor Information Cazorla Tourist Office ⊠ *Paseo Santo Cristo 19* ☎ *953/710102* ⊕ *www.cazorla.es.*

EXPLORING

FAMILY **Parque Natural Sierra de Cazorla, Segura y Las Villas** (*Cazorla, Segura and Las Villas Nature Park*). For a break from man-made sights, drink in the scenery or watch for wildlife in this park, a carefully protected patch of mountain wilderness 80 km (50 miles) long and 30 km (19 miles) wide. Deer, wild boar, and mountain goats roam its slopes and hawks, eagles, and vultures soar over the 6,000-foot peaks. Within the park, at **Cañada de las Fuentes** (Fountains' Ravine), is the source of Andalusia's great river, the Guadalquivir. The road through the park follows the river to the shores of **Lago Tranco de Beas.** Alpine meadows, pine forests, springs, waterfalls, and gorges make Cazorla a perfect place to hike. Past Lago Tranco and the village of Hornos, a road goes to the **Sierra de Segura** mountain range, the park's least crowded area. At 3,600 feet, the spectacular village of **Segura de la Sierra,** on top of the mountain, is crowned by an almost perfect castle with impressive defense walls, a Moorish bath, and a nearly rectangular bullring. There's also a **hunting museum,** with random attractions such as the interlocked antlers of bucks who clashed in autumn rutting season, became helplessly trapped, and died of starvation. Nearby are a **botanical garden** and a **game reserve.**

Early spring is the ideal time to visit; try to avoid the summer and late-spring months, when the park teems with tourists and locals. It's often difficult, though by no means impossible, to find accommodations in fall, especially on weekends during hunting season (between September and February). Between June and October, the park maintains seven well-equipped campgrounds. For information on hiking, camping, canoeing, horseback riding, or guided excursions, contact the **Agencia de Medio Ambiente** (✉ *Tejares Altos* ☎ *953/711534*), or the park visitor center. For hunting or fishing permits, apply to the Jaén office well in advance.

Centro de Interpretación Torre del Vinagre. A short film shown in the interpretive center introduces the park's main sights. Displays explain the plants and geology, and the staff can advise about camping, fishing, and hiking trails. ✉ *Ctra. del Tranco (A319), Km 48, Torre del Vinagre* ☎ *953/713017* ⊕ *www.sierrasdecazorlaseguraylasvillas.es* ☉ *Sept.–June, daily 10–2 and 4–7; July and Aug., daily 10–2 and 5–8.*

Turisnat. Four-wheel-drive trips can be taken into restricted areas of the park to observe the flora and fauna and photograph the larger animals. ✉ *Paseo del Santo Cristo 19* ☎ *953/721351* ⊕ *www.turisnat.es.*

EN ROUTE
Guadalquivir River Gorge. Leave Cazorla Nature Park by an alternative route—drive along the spectacular gorge carved by the Guadalquivir River, a rushing torrent beloved by kayaking enthusiasts. At the El Tranco Dam, follow signs to Villanueva del Arzobispo, where N322 takes you back to Úbeda, Baeza, and Jaén.

WHERE TO EAT AND STAY

$ ✗ **Gastro Bar La Sarga.** Combining a cheerfully kitschy interior with spec-
SPANISH tacular views over the valley below, this gastro bar combines attentive service with good local food. Expect to find traditional cooked meat alongside more elaborate dishes like *setas en salsa de almendras* (oyster

mushrooms in an almond sauce) and *alcachofas en salsa de romero* (artichokes with rosemary). There's a daily *plato del día* and a tapas tasting menu (each tapa costs €2), all in generous portions. The kitchen opens at lunchtime and again at 8:30 for dinner (9 in summer). [$] *Average main: €10* ✉ *Pl. del Mercado* ☎ *953/721507.*

$$ HOTEL **Coto del Valle.** This delightful modern hotel in Cazorla's foothills—easily recognized by the huge fountain outside—is surrounded by pine trees and has been built using a traditional highland stone architectural style, with wooden beams and terra-cotta tiles. **Pros:** nature lover's paradise; great spa. **Cons:** indifferent service; 10-minute drive from town. [$] *Rooms from: €100* ✉ *Ctra. del Tranco, Km 34.3* ☎ *953/124067* 🌐 *www.hotelcotodelvalle.com* 🛏 *39 rooms, 1 suite* ⏲ *Closed 2 wks in Dec. and 2 wks in Jan (phone for dates)* 🍴 *No meals.*

$ RENTAL **Hotel Villa de Cazorla.** On a hill with superb views of the village of Cazorla, this leisure complex rents semidetached apartments that sleep two to four guests. **Pros:** self-catering option. **Cons:** noisy families; in need of refurbishment; some may find it too basic. [$] *Rooms from: €72* ✉ *Ladera de San Isicio s/n* ☎ *953/724090* 🌐 *www.villasdeandalucia.com* 🛏 *32 apartments* 🍴 *Breakfast.*

$$ HOTEL **Parador de Cazorla.** You'll find this modern parador isolated in a valley at the edge of the nature reserve, 26 km (16 miles) north of Cazorla, in a quiet place that's popular with hunters and anglers. **Pros:** lovely views from the pool; mountain cooking. **Cons:** not all rooms have views; access difficult. [$] *Rooms from: €95* ✉ *Sierra de Cazorla s/n* ☎ *953/727075* 🌐 *www.parador.es* 🛏 *32 rooms, 2 suites* ⏲ *Closed Nov.–Feb.* 🍴 *No meals.*

GRANADA

430 km (265 miles) south of Madrid, 261 km (162 miles) east of Seville, 160 km (100 miles) southeast of Córdoba.

The Alhambra and the tomb of the Catholic Monarchs are the pride of Granada. The city rises majestically from a plain onto three hills, dwarfed—on a clear day—by the Sierra Nevada. Atop one of these hills perches the reddish-gold Alhambra palace, whose stunning view takes in the sprawling medieval Moorish quarter, the caves of the Sacromonte, and, in the distance, the fertile *vega* (plain), rich in orchards, tobacco fields, and poplar groves. In 2013, Granada celebrated its 1,000th anniversary as a kingdom.

Split by internal squabbles, Granada's Moorish Nasrid dynasty gave Ferdinand of Aragón his opportunity in 1491. Spurred by Isabella's religious fanaticism, he laid siege to the city for seven months, and on January 2, 1492, Boabdil, the "Rey Chico" (Boy King), was forced to surrender the keys of the city. As Boabdil fled the Alhambra via the Puerta de los Siete Suelos (Gate of the Seven Floors), he asked that the gate be sealed forever.

GETTING HERE AND AROUND
AIR TRAVEL
Three daily flights connect Granada with Madrid and two with Barcelona.

BUS TRAVEL
Granada's main bus station is at Carretera de Jaén, 3 km (2 miles) northwest of the center of town beyond the end of Avenida de Madrid. Most buses operate from here, except for buses to nearby destinations such as Fuentevaqueros, Viznar, and some buses to Sierra Nevada, which leave from the city center's Plaza del Triunfo near the RENFE station. Luggage lockers (*la consigna*) are available at the main bus and train stations, and you can also leave your luggage at Pensión Atlántida (✉ *Gran Vía 57*).

Autocares Bonal operates buses between Granada and the Sierra Nevada. **ALSA** buses run to and from Las Alpujarras (9 times daily), Córdoba (8 times daily), Seville (9 times daily), Málaga (18 times daily), and Jaén, Baeza, Úbeda, Cazorla, Almería, Almuñecar, and Nerja (several times daily).

In Granada, **J. González** buses (€3) run between the center of town and the airport, leaving every hour between 5:20 am and 8 pm from the Palacio de Congresos and making a few other stops along the way to the airport. Times are listed at the bus stop.

Granada has an extensive public bus network within the city. You can buy 5-, 10- and 20-trip discount passes on the buses and at newsstands. The single-trip fare is €1.20. Granada Cards include bus trips plus guaranteed tickets for the Alhambra and other main monuments. The three-day card costs €33.50 and the five-day card €37.50, saving at least a third on regular prices. You can purchase the cards at the municipal tourist office, but it's best to buy them online via the tourist office website in advance of your visit (you can print them at the tourist office).

TRAIN TRAVEL
There are regular trains from Seville and Almería, but service from Málaga and Córdoba is less convenient, necessitating a change at Bobadilla. A new fast track is currently under construction, however, which will reduce journey times considerably. There are a couple of daily trains from Madrid, Valencia, and Barcelona.

ESSENTIALS
Airport Contact Aeropuerto de Granada (*Aeropurto Federico García Lorca*). ☎ *958/245200.*

Bus Station Granada ✉ *Ctra. Jaén, Granada* ☎ *902/422242.*

Taxi Contacts Radio Taxi ☎ *958/132323.* **Tele Radio Taxi** ☎ *958/280654.*

Train Contacts Station ✉ *Av. de los Andaluces* ☎ *902/320320.*

Visitor Information Municipal Tourist Office ✉ *Pl. del Carmen, Centro* ☎ *958/248286* ⊕ *www.granadatur.com.* **Provincial Tourist Office** ✉ *Pl. Mariana Pineda 10, Centro* ☎ *958/247128* ⊕ *www.turismodegranada.org.*

10

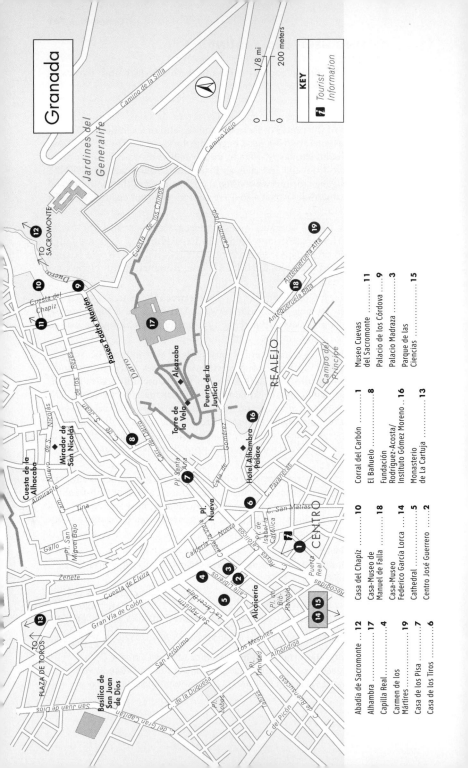

Granada

KEY

🇮 Tourist
Information

0   1/8 mi
0   200 meters

Jardines del Generalife

Camino de la Silla

Camino Viejo

Camino de la Silla

TO SACROMONTE

Cuesta de los Chinos

Cuesta del Chapiz

Paseo Padre Manjón

Darro

Mirador de San Nicolás

Cuesta de la Alhacaba

Almirante

Tinta

Gallo

Zenete

Cuesta de Elvira

Gran Vía de Colón

PLAZA DE TOROS

Basílica de San Juan de Dios

San Agustín

San Jerónimo

Los Mesones

Alhóndiga

Pl. de Bib-Rambla

Puerta Real

Reyes Católicos

CENTRO

C. San Matías

REALEJO

Campo del Príncipe

Antequeruela Alta

Antequeruela Baja

Alcazaba

Torre de la Vela

Puerta de la Justicia

Hotel Alhambra Palace

C. Pavaneras

Pl. Nueva

Pl. Santa Ana

Gomérez

Casa de las Chirimías

TO SACROMONTE

Abadía de Sacromonte ... **12**
Alhambra **17**
Capilla Real **4**
Carmen de los
Mártires **19**
Casa de los Pisa **7**
Casa de los Tiros **6**

Casa del Chapíz **10**
Casa-Museo de
Manuel de Falla **18**
Casa-Museo
Federico García Lorca ... **14**
Cathedral **5**
Centro José Guerrero ... **2**

Corral del Carbón **1**
El Bañuelo **8**
Fundación
Rodríguez-Acosta/
Instituto Gómez Moreno .. **16**
Monasterio
de La Cartuja **13**

Museo Cuevas
del Sacromonte **11**
Palacio de los Córdova ... **9**
Palacio Madraza **3**
Parque de las
Ciencias **15**

TOURS

Cycling Country. For information about cycling tours around Granada (and Andalusia), from one day to 10 days long, contact this company, run by husband-and-wife team Geoff Norris and Maggi Jones in a town about 55 km (33 miles) away. ✉ *Calle Salmerones 18, Alhama de Granada* ☎ *958/360655* ⊕ *www.cyclingcountry.com* ✉ *From €30.*

Granada Tour. Large open-top buses provide a hop-on, hop-off service, including informative commentary on the major sights. They take in the sights in the lower city and there's also a minibus service that winds up to the Alhambra and through the narrow streets of Albayzín. The price includes 48 hours unlimited travel. ⊕ *www.granadatour.com* ✉ *€18 (discount available online).*

EXPLORING

Granada can be characterized by its major neighborhoods: East of the Darro River and up the hill is **La Alhambra.** South of it and around a square and a popular hangout area, Campo del Príncipe, is **Realejo.** To the west of the Darro and going from north to south are the two popular neighborhoods, **Sacromonte** and **Albayzín** (also spelled Alba-icín). The latter is the young and trendy part of Granada, full of color, flavor, charming old architecture, and narrow, hilly streets. On either side of Gran Vía de Colón and the streets that border the cathedral (Reyes Católicos and Recogidas—the major shopping areas) is the area generally referred to as **Centro,** the city center. These days much of the Alhambra and Albayzín areas are closed to cars, but starting from the Plaza Nueva there are minibuses—nos. 30, 31, 34, and 35—that run frequently to these areas.

LA ALHAMBRA

Fodor's Choice ★ **Alhambra.** With more than 3 million visitors a year, the Alhambra is Spain's most popular attraction. The complex has three main parts: the Alcazaba, the Palacios Nazaríes (Nasrid Palaces), and the Generalife, the ancient summer palace. The Museo de la Alhambra is in the Alhambra building, too. ⇨ *See the Alhambra In Focus feature for more details.*

Carmen de los Mártires. Up the hill from the Hotel Alhambra Palace, this turn-of-the-20th-century *carmen* (private villa) and its gardens—the only area open to tourists—are like a Generalife in miniature. ✉ *Paseo de los Mártires, Alhambra* ☎ *958/227953* ✉ *Free* ☉ *Apr.–July and Sept.–Oct., weekdays 10–2 and 6–8, weekends 10–8; Nov.–Mar., week-days 10–2 and 4–6, weekends 10–6.*

Casa-Museo de Manuel de Falla. The composer Manuel de Falla (1876–1946) lived and worked for many years in this rustic house tucked into a charming hillside lane with lovely views of Las Alpujarras. In 1986 Granada paid homage to him by naming its new concert hall (down the street from the Carmen de los Mártires) the Auditorio Manuel de Falla—from this institution, fittingly, you have a view of his little white house. Note the bust in the small garden: It's placed where the com-poser once sat to enjoy the sweeping vista. ✉ *Calle Antequeruela Alta 11, Alhambra* ☎ *958/222189* ⊕ *www.museomanueldefalla.com* ✉ *€3* ☉ *Tues.–Fri. 9:30–6:30, weekends 9–2:30.*

10

REALEJO

Casa de los Tiros. This 16th-century palace, adorned with the coat of arms of the Grana Venegas family who owned it, was named House of the Shots for the musket barrels that protrude from its facade. The stairs to the upper-floor displays are flanked by portraits of miserable-looking Spanish royals, from Ferdinand and Isabella to Felipe IV. The highlight is the carved wooden ceiling in the Cuadra Dorada (Hall of Gold), adorned with gilded lettering and portraits of royals and knights. Old lithographs, engravings, and photographs show life in Granada in the 19th and early 20th centuries. ⊠ *Calle Pavaneras 19, Realejo* ☎ *958/221072* ⊕ *www.juntadeandalucia.es/cultura/museos/MCTGR* 🎫 *€1.50* ☉ *Tues.–Sat. 10–8:30, Sun. 10–5.*

Casa Sefardí (*Sephardic House*). This restored house, typical of the Realejo district, offers a fascinating insight into the life of the Sephardic Jews, an essential component of Granada's history, and their contributions to science and the arts. Visits are by guided tour. ⊠ *Pl. Berrocal 5, Realejo* ☎ *958/220578* ⊕ *www.museosefardidegranada.es/en* 🎫 *€5* ☉ *Apr.–Oct., daily 10–2 and 5–9; Nov.–Mar., daily 10–2 and 4–8.*

Fundación Rodríguez-Acosta/Instituto Gómez Moreno. A few yards from the impressive Alhambra Hotel, this nonprofit organization was founded at the bequest of the painter José Marí Rodríguez-Acosta. Inside a typical carmen, it houses works of art, archaeological findings, and a library collected by the Granada-born scholar Manuel Gómez-Moreno Martínez. Other exhibits include valuable and unique objects from Asian cultures and the prehistoric and classical eras. Call or email ahead, as advance reservations (minimum two days) are required. ⊠ *Callejón Niños del Rollo 8, Realejo* ☎ *958/227497* ✎ *info@fundacionrodriguezacosta.com* ⊕ *www.fundacionrodriguezacosta.com* 🎫 *€5* ☉ *Daily 10–6.*

SACROMONTE

The third of Granada's three hills, the Sacromonte rises behind the Albayzín. The hill is covered with prickly pear cacti and riddled with caverns. The Sacromonte has long been notorious as a domain of Granada's Gypsies and thus a den of thieves and scam artists, but its reputation is largely undeserved. The quarter is more like a quiet Andalusian *pueblo* (village) than a rough neighborhood. Many of the quarter's colorful *cuevas* (caves) have been restored as middle-class homes, and some of the old spirit lives on in a handful of *zambras* (flamenco performances in caves, which are garishly decorated with brass plates and cooking utensils). These shows differ from formal flamenco shows in that the performers mingle with you, usually dragging one or two onlookers onto the floor for an improvised dance lesson. Ask your hotel to book you a spot on a cueva tour, which usually includes a walk through the neighboring Albayzín and a drink at a tapas bar in addition to the zambra.

Abadía de Sacromonte. The caverns on Sacromonte are thought to have sheltered early Christians; 15th-century treasure hunters found bones inside and assumed they belonged to San Cecilio, the city's patron saint. Thus, the hill was sanctified—*sacro monte* (holy mountain)—and an abbey built on its summit, the Abadía de Sacromonte. ⊠ *C. del Sacromonte, Sacromonte* ☎ *958/221445* ⌛ *€4* ⌚ *Tues.–Sat. 10–12.50 and 4–6, Sun. 11–1 and 4–6; guided tours every 40 mins (Spanish only).*

Museo Cuevas del Sacromonte. The Museo Etnográfico shows how people lived here, and other areas in this interesting complex show the flora and fauna of the area as well as cultural activities. There are live flamenco concerts during the summer months. ⚠ **Even if you take the minibus no. 35 (from Plaza Nueva) or the city sightseeing bus to get here, you will still be left with a steep walk of more than 200 meters to reach the center.** ⊠ *Barranco de los Negros, Sacromonte* ☎ *958/215120* ⊕ *www.sacromontegranada.com* ⌛ *€5* ⌚ *Apr.–Oct., daily 10–8; Nov.–Mar., daily 10–6.*

> ### BICYCLING IN GRANADA
>
> At the foot of the Iberian Peninsula's tallest mountain—the 11,427-foot Mulhacén peak—Granada offers challenging mountain-biking opportunities, and spinning through the hairpin turns of the Alpujarras east of Granada is both scenic and hair-raising. For organized cycling tours, contact **Cycling Country** (⇨ *Tours*).

ALBAYZÍN

Fodor's Choice ★

Covering a hill of its own, across the Darro ravine from the Alhambra, this ancient Moorish neighborhood is a mix of dilapidated white houses and immaculate *carmenes* (private villas in gardens enclosed by high walls). It was founded in 1228 by Moors who had fled Baeza after Ferdinand III captured the city. Full of cobblestone alleyways and secret corners, the Albayzín guards its old Moorish roots jealously, though its 30 mosques were converted to baroque churches long ago. A stretch of the Moors' original city wall runs beside the ridge called the **Cuesta de la Alhacaba.** If you're walking—the best way to explore—you can enter the Albayzín from either the Cuesta de Elvira or the Plaza Nueva. Alternatively, on foot or by taxi (parking is impossible), begin in the Plaza Santa Ana and follow the Carrera del Darro, Paseo Padre Manjón, and Cuesta del Chapíz. One of the highest points in the quarter, the plaza in front of the church of San Nicolás—called the **Mirador de San Nicolás**—has one of the finest views in all of Granada: on the hill opposite, the turrets and towers of the Alhambra form a dramatic silhouette against the snowy peaks of the Sierra Nevada. The sight is most magical at dawn, dusk, and on nights when the Alhambra is floodlighted. Take note of the mosque just next to the church—views of the Alhambra from the mosque gardens are just as good as those from the Mirador de San Nicolás and a lot less crowded. Interestingly, given the area's Moorish history, the two sloping, narrow streets of Calderería Nueva and Calderería Vieja that meet at the top by the Iglesia San Gregorio have developed into something of a North African bazaar, full of shops and vendors selling clothes, bags, crafts, and trinkets. The numerous little teahouses and restaurants here have a decidedly Moroccan flavor. Be warned that there have been some thefts in the area, so keep your money and valuables out of sight.

Casa de los Pisa. Originally built in 1494 for the Pisa family, the claim to fame of this house is its relationship to San Juan de Dios, who came to Granada in 1538 and founded a charity hospital to take care of the poor. Befriended by the Pisa family, he was taken into their home when he fell ill in February 1550. A month later, he died there, at the age of 55. Since that time, devotees of the saint have traveled from around the world to this house with a stone Gothic facade, now run by the Hospital Order of St. John. Inside are numerous pieces of jewelry, furniture, priceless religious works of art, and an extensive collection of paintings and sculptures depicting St. John. ⊠ *Calle Convalecencia 1, Albayzín* ☎ *958/222144* ⊠ *€3* ⊙ *Mon.–Sat. 10–1:30.*

Casa del Chapíz. There's a delightful garden in this fine 16th-century Morisco house (built by Moorish craftsmen under Christian rule). It houses the School of Arabic Studies. ⊠ *Cuesta del Chapíz 22, Albayzín* ☎ *958/222290* ⊙ *Weekdays 9–6 (until 3 in July and Aug.).*

El Bañuelo (*Little Bath House*). These 11th-century Arab steam baths might be a little dark and dank now, but try to imagine them some 900 years ago, filled with Moorish beauties. Back then, the dull brick walls were backed by bright ceramic tiles, tapestries, and rugs. Light comes in through star-shape vents in the ceiling, à la the bathhouse in the Alhambra. ⊠ *C. del Darro 31, Albayzín* ☎ *958/229738* ⊠ *Free* ⊙ *Daily 10–6.*

QUICK
BITES

Paseo Padre Manjón. Along the Darro River, this *paseo* is also known as the Paseo de los Tristes (Promenade of the Sad Ones) because funeral processions once passed this way. The cafés and bars here are a good place for a coffee break. The park, dappled with wisteria-covered pergolas, fountains, and stone walkways, has a stunning view of the Alhambra's northern side. ⊠ *Albayzín.*

Palacio de los Córdova. At the end of the Paseo Padre Manjón, this 17th-century noble house today holds Granada's municipal archives and is used for municipal functions and art exhibits. You're free to wander about the large garden. ⊠ *Cuesta del Chapiz 4, Albayzín* ⊠ *Free* ⊙ *Nov.–Mar., weekdays 10–2 and 4–6, weekends 10–6; Apr.–Oct., weekdays 10–2 and 6–8, weekends 10–8.*

CENTRO

Capilla Real (*Royal Chapel*). Catholic Monarchs Isabella of Castile and Ferdinand of Aragón are buried at this shrine. The couple originally planned to be buried in Toledo's San Juan de los Reyes, but Isabella changed her mind when the pair conquered Granada in 1492. When she died in 1504, her body was first laid to rest in the Convent of San Francisco (now a parador), on the Alhambra hill. The architect Enrique Egas began work on the Royal Chapel in 1506 and completed it 15 years later, creating a masterpiece of the ornate Gothic style now known in Spain as Isabelline. In 1521 Isabella's body was transferred to a simple lead coffin in the Royal Chapel crypt, where it was joined by that of her husband, Ferdinand, and later her unfortunate daughter, Juana la Loca (Joanna the Mad), and son-in-law, Felipe el Hermoso (Philip the Handsome). Felipe died young, and Juana had his casket borne about the peninsula with her for years, opening the lid each night to kiss her embalmed spouse good night. A small coffin to the right contains the remains of Prince Felipe of Asturias, a grandson of

Continued on page 763

ALHAMBRA: PALACE-FORTRESS

Floating mirage-like on its promontory overlooking Granada, the mighty and mysterious Alhambra shimmers vermilion in the clear mountain air, with the white peaks of the Sierra Nevada rising behind it. This sprawling palace-fortress, named from the Arabic for "red citadel" *(al-Qal'ah al-Hamra)*, was the last bastion of the 800-year Moorish presence on the Iberian Peninsula. Composed of royal residential quarters, court chambers, baths, and gardens, surrounded by defense towers and massive walls, the Alhambra is an architectual gem where Moorish kings worked and played—and murdered their enemies.

LOOK UP

Among the stylistic elements you can see in the Alhambra are **Arabesque** geometrical designs, and elaborate **Mocárabe** arches.

Built of perishable materials, the Alhambra was meant to be forever replenished and replaced by succeeding generations. The Patio de los Leones' (above) has recently been restored to its original appearance.

INSIDE THE FORTRESS

More than 3 million annual visitors come to the Alhambra today, making it Spain's top attraction. Vistors revel in the palace's architectural wonders, most of which had to be restored after the alterations made after the Christian reconquest of southern Spain in 1492 and the damage from an 1821 earthquake. Incidentally, Napoléon's troops commandeered the site in 1812 with intent to level it but their attempts were foiled.

The courtyards, patios, and halls offer an ethereal maze of Moorish arches, columns, and domes containing intricate stucco carvings and patterned ceramic tiling. The intimate arcades, fountains, and light-reflecting pools throughout are identified in the ornamental inscriptions as physical renderings of paradise taken from the Koran and Islamic poetry. The contemporary visitor to this dreamlike space feels the fleeting embrace of a culture that brought its light to a world emerging from medieval darkness.

ARCHITECTURAL TERMS

Arabesque: An ornament or decorative style that employs flower, foliage, or fruit, and sometimes geometrical, animal, and figural outlines to produce an intricate pattern of interlaced lines.

Mocárabe: A decorative element of carved wood or plaster based on juxtaposed and hanging prisms resembling stalactites. Sometimes called *muquarna* (honeycomb vaulting), the impression is similar to a beehive and the "honey" has been described as light.

Mozárabe: Sometimes confused with Mocárabe, the term Mozárabe refers to Christians living in Moorish Spain. Thus, Christian artistic styles or recourses in Moorish architecture (such as the paintings in the Sala de los Reyes) are also identified as *mozárabe,* or, in English, mozarabic.

Mudéjar: This word refers to Moors living in Christian Spain. Moorish artistic elements in Christian architecture, such as horseshoe arches in a church, also are referred to as Mudéjar.

ALHAMBRA'S ARCHITECTURAL HIGHLIGHTS

The **columns** used in the construction of the Alhambra are unique, with extraordinarily slender cylindrical shafts, concave base moldings, and carved rings decorating the upper extremities. The capitals have simple cylindrical bases under prism-shaped heads decorated in a variety of vegetal motifs. Nearly all of these columns support false arches constructed purely for decorative purposes. The 124 columns surrounding the Patio de los Leones (Court of the Lions) are the best examples.

Court of the Lions

Cursive epigraphy is used to quote the Koran and Arabic poems. Considered the finest example of this are the Ibn-Zamrak verses that decorate the walls of the Sala de las Dos Hermanas.

Cursive epigraphy

Glazed ceramic tiles covered with geometrical patterns in primary colors cover the walls of the Alhambra with a profusion of styles and shapes. Red, blue, and yellow are the colors of magic in Sufi tradition, while green is the life-giving color of Islam.

Ceramic tiles

The **horseshoe arch**, widening before rounding off with lower ends extending around the circle until they begin to converge, was the quintessential Moorish architectural innovation, used not only for aesthetic and decorative purposes but because it allowed greater height than the classical, semicircular arch inherited from the Greeks and Romans. The horseshoe arch also had a mystical significance in recalling the shape of the *mihrab*, the prayer niche in the *qibla* wall of a mosque indicating the direction of prayer and suggesting a door to Mecca or to paradise. Horseshoe arches and arcades are found throughout the Alhambra.

Gate of Justice

The Koran describes paradise as "gardens underneath which rivers flow," and **water** is used as a practical and ornamental architectural element throughout the Alhambra. Whether used musically, as in the canals in the Patio de los Leones or visually, as in the reflecting pool of the Patio de los Arrayanes, water is used to enhance light, enlarge spaces, or provide musical background for a desert culture in love with the beauty and oasis-like properties of hydraulics in all its forms.

Alhambra fountains

The Alcazaba was built chiefly by Nasrid kings in the 1300s.

LAY OF THE LAND

The complex has three main parts: the Alcazaba, the Palacio Nazaríes (Nasrid Royal Palace), and the Generalife. Across from the main entrance is the original fortress, the Alcazaba. Here, the watchtower's great bell was once used to announce the opening and closing of the irrigation system on Granada's great plain.

A wisteria-covered walkway leads to the heart of the Alhambra, the Palacios Nazaríes. Here, delicate apartments, lazy fountains, and tranquil pools contrast vividly with the hulking fortifications outside. It is divided into three sections: the *mexuar,* where business, government, and palace administration were headquartered; the *serrallo,* a series of state rooms where the sultans held court and entertained their ambassadors; and the *harem,* which in its time was entered only by the sultan, his family, and their most trusted servants, most of them eunuchs. Nearby is the Renaissance Palacio de Carlos V (Palace of Charles V), featuring a perfectly square exterior but a circular interior courtyard. Designed by Pedro Machuca, a pupil of Michelangelo, it is where the sultan's private apartments once stood. Part of the building houses the free Museo de la Alhambra, devoted to Islamic art. Upstairs is the more modest Museo de Bellas Artes.

Over on Cerro del Sol (Hill of the Sun) is Generalife, the ancient summer palace of the Nasrid kings.

TIMELINE

1238 First Nasrid king, Ibn el-Ahmar, begins Alhambra.

1391 Nasrid Palaces is completed.

1492 Boabdil surrenders Granada to Ferdinand and Isabella, parents of King Henry VIII's first wife, Catherine of Aragon.

1524 Carlos V begins Renaissance Palace.

1812 Napoléonic troops arrive with plans to destroy Alhambra.

1814 The Duke of Wellington sojourns here to escape the pressures of the Peninsular War.

1829 Washington Irving lives on the premises and writes *Tales of the Alhambra,* reviving interest in the crumbling palace.

1862 Granada municipality begins Alhambra restoration that continues to this day.

IN FOCUS ALHAMBRA

10

ALHAMBRA'S PASSAGES OF TIME

From Columbus's commissioning to a bloody murder, historic events as well as everyday affairs happened between these walls.

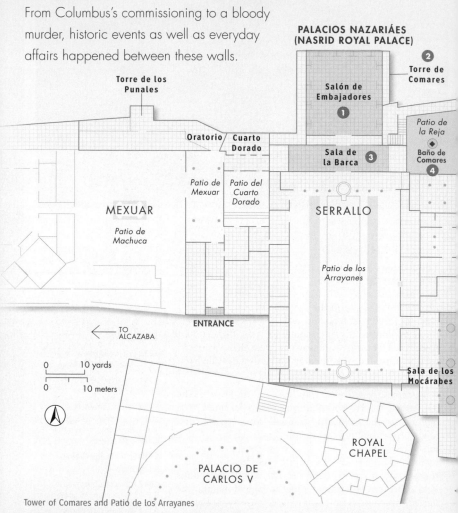

PALACIOS NAZARIÁES (NASRID ROYAL PALACE)

Torre de los Punales

Torre de Comares ❷

Salón de Embajadores ❶

Oratorio / Cuarto Dorado

Patio de la Reja

Sala de la Barca ❸

Baño de Comares ❹

Patio de Mexuar

Patio del Cuarto Dorado

MEXUAR

SERRALLO

Patio de Machuca

Patio de los Arrayanes

ENTRANCE

← TO ALCAZABA

0 — 10 yards
0 — 10 meters

Sala de los Mocárabes

ROYAL CHAPEL

PALACIO DE CARLOS V

Tower of Comares and Patio de los Arrayanes

❶ In El Salón de Embajadores, Boabdil drew up his terms of surrender, and Christopher Columbus secured royal support for his historic voyage in 1492. The carved wooden ceiling is a portrayal of the seven Islamic heavens, with six rows of stars topped by a seventh-heaven cupulino or micro-cupola.

❷ Torre de Comares, a lookout in the corner of this hall is where Carlos V uttered his famous line, "Ill-fated the man who lost all this."

❸ Mistakenly named from the Arabic word *baraka* (divine blessing), Sala de la Barca has a carved wooden ceiling often described as an inverted boat.

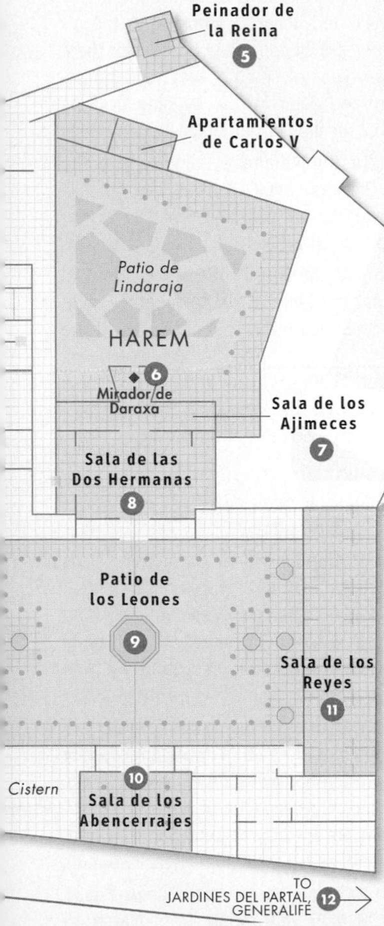
Peinador de la Reina
5
Apartamientos de Carlos V
Patio de Lindaraja
HAREM
6
Mirador de Daraxa
Sala de los Ajimeces
7
Sala de las Dos Hermanas
8
Patio de los Leones
9
Sala de los Reyes
11
10
Cistern
Sala de los Abencerrajes
TO JARDINES DEL PARTAL, GENERALIFE
12

4 The **Baño de Comares** is where the sultan's favorites luxuriated in brightly tiled pools beneath star-shape pinpoints of light from the ceiling above.

5 **El Peinador de la Reina**, a nine-foot-square room atop a small tower was the Sultana's boudoir. The perforated marble slab was used to infiltrate perfumes while the queen performed her toilette. Washington Irving wrote his *Tales of the Alhambra* in this romantic tree-house-like perch.

Sala de los Reyes

6 Sultana Zoraya often found refuge in this charming little balcony (**Mirador de Daraxa**) overlooking the Lindaraja garden.

7 Shhh, don't tell a secret here. In the **Sala de los Ajimeces**, a whisper in one corner can be clearly heard from the opposite corner.

8 In the **Sala de las Dos Hermanas**, twin slabs of marble embedded in the floor are the "sisters," though Washington Irving preferred the story of a pair of captive Moorish beauties.

9 In the **Patio de Los Leones** (Court of the Lions), a dozen crudely crafted lions (restored to their former glory in 2012) support the fountain at the center of this elegant courtyard, representing the signs of the zodiac sending water to the four corners.

10 In the **Sala de los Abencerrajes**, Muley Hacen (father of Boabdil) murdered the male members of the Abencerraje family in revenge for their chief's seduction of his daughter Zoraya. The rusty stains in the fountain are said to be bloodstains left by the pile of Abencerraje heads.

The star-shaped cupola, reflected in the pool, is considered the Alhambra's most beautiful example of stalactite or honeycomb vaulting.

The octagonal dome over the room is best viewed at sunset when the 16 small windows atop the dome admit sharp, low sunlight that refracts kaleidoscopically through the beehive-like prisms.

11 In the **Sala de los Reyes**, the ceiling painting depicts the first 10 Nasrid rulers. It was painted by a Christian artist since Islamic artists were not allowed to usurp divine power by creating human or animal figures.

The overhead painting of the knight rescuing his lady from a savage man portrays chivalry, a concept introduced to Europe by Arabic poets.

12 The terraces of **Generalife** grant incomparable views of the city.

Generalife gardens

PLANNING YOUR VISIT

The acoustics in the Palace of Charles V are ideal for the summer symphony concerts at the Alhambra.

GETTING HERE

Getting to the Alhambra on foot requires a 1-km uphill climb, so we recommend taking a taxi or bus from Plaza Nueva. Buses 30 and 32 make several stops in the Alhambra complex, including the ticket office (Entrance Pavilion). If you're driving, use the Alhambra parking lot or park underground on Calle San Agustín, just north of the cathedral, and take a taxi or the minibus from Plaza Nueva.

BEST ROUTES IN THE ALHAMBRA

There are three recommended options for visiting the Alhambra, and you can only see the Nasrid Palaces during the time slot on your ticket.

A: Alcazaba-Nasrid Palaces-Generalife

B: Nasrid Palaces-Alcazaba-Generalife

C: Generalife-Alcazaba-Nasrid Palaces

WHEN TO GO

Winter's low, slanting sunlight is best for seeing the Alhambra, and the temperatures are ideal for walking. Spring brings lush floral colors to the gardens. Fall is also sharp, cooler, and clear. July and August are crowded and hot.

The **Festival Internacional de Música y Danza de Granada** (☎ 34 958/221844 ⊕ www.granadafestival.org) held annually from mid-June to mid-July offers visitors an opportunity to hear a concert in the Alhambra or watch a ballet in the Generalife amphitheater.

GETTING TICKETS

Buy your tickets in advance to avoid the very long lines, and because entrance to the Alhambra is strictly controlled by quotas. There are three types of timed tickets: morning, afternoon, and evening (the evening ticket is valid only for the Nasrid Palaces).

Tickets for the Alhambra complex and the Nasrid Palaces cost €13. They can be purchased at ⊕ www.ticketmaster.es or at the Alhambra ticket offices.

You can visit the Palace of Charles V and its two museums (Museo de la Alhambra and Museo de Bellos Artes) independently of the Alhambra. They're open Oct. 15–March 14, Wed.–Sat. 8:30–6, Tues. and Sun. 8:30–2; March 15–Oct. 14, Wed.–Sat. 8:30–8, Tues. and Sun. 8:30–2. Free entrance.

TIMED VISITING HOURS

The Alhambra is open every day except December 25 and January 1.

October 15 through March 14, morning visits are daily from 8:30 to 2, with a maximum capacity of 3,300; afternoon visits are daily from 2 to 6, with a maximum capacity of 2,100; and evening visits are Friday and Saturday from 8 to 9:30, with a maximum capacity of 400.

March 15 to October 14, morning visits are daily from 8:30 to 2, with a maximum capacity of 3,300; afternoon visits are daily from 2 to 8, with a maximum capacity of 3,300; and evening visits are Tuesday through Saturday from 10 to 11:30, with a maximum capacity of 400.

Visits to the main gardens are allowed daily, from 8:30 to 6 year-round; from March 15 through October 14 access is until 8.

CONTACT INFORMATION

Patronato de la Alhambra ☎ 34 958/027–971 ⊕ www.alhambra-patronato.es.

the Catholic Monarchs and nephew of Juana la Loca who died in his infancy. The **crypt** containing the five lead coffins is quite simple, but it's topped by elaborate marble **tombs** showing Ferdinand and Isabella lying side by side (commissioned by their grandson Carlos V and sculpted by Domenico Fancelli).

The **altarpiece,** by Felipe Vigarini (1522), comprises 34 carved panels depicting religious and historical scenes; the bottom row shows Boabdil surrendering the keys of the city to its conquerors and the forced baptism of the defeated Moors.

The **sacristy** holds Ferdinand's sword, Isabella's crown and scepter, and a fine collection of Flemish paintings once owned by Isabella. ⊠ *Calle Oficios, Centro* ☎ *958/229239* ⊕ *www.capillarealgranada.com* ⬛*€4* ⊙ *Apr.–Oct., Mon.–Sat. 10:15–1:30 and 4–7:30, Sun. 11–1:30 and 4–7:30; Nov.–Mar., Mon.–Sat. 10:30–1:30 and 3:30–6:30, Sun. 10:30–1:30 and 3:30–6:30.*

Cathedral. Carlos V commissioned the cathedral in 1521 because he considered the Royal Chapel "too small for so much glory" and wanted to house his illustrious late grandparents someplace more worthy. Carlos undoubtedly had great intentions, as the cathedral was created by some of the finest architects of its time: Enrique Egas, Diego de Siloé, Alonso Cano, and sculptor Juan de Mena. Alas, his ambitions came to little, for the cathedral is a grand and gloomy monument, not completed until 1714 and never used as the crypt for his grandparents (or parents). Enter through a small door at the back, off the Gran Vía. Old hymnals are displayed throughout, and there's a museum, which includes a 14th-century gold-and-silver monstrance (used for communion) given to the city by Queen Isabella. Audio guides are available for an extra €3. ⊠ *Gran Vía, Centro* ☎ *958/222959* ⬛*€4* ⊙ *Nov.–Mar., Mon.–Sat. 10:45–1:30 and 4–6:45, Sun. 4–6:45; Apr.–Oct., Mon.–Sat. 10:45–1:30 and 4–7:45, Sun. 4–7:45.*

Centro José Guerrero. Just across a lane from the Cathedral and Capilla Real, this building houses colorful modern paintings by José Guerrero. Born in Granada in 1914, Guerrero traveled throughout Europe and lived in New York in the 1950s before returning to Spain. The center also runs excellent temporary contemporary art shows. ⊠ *Calle Oficios 8, Centro* ☎ *958/225185* ⊕ *www.centroguerrero.org* ⬛ *Free* ⊙ *Tues.–Sat. 10:30–2 and 4:30–9, Sun. 10:30–2.*

Corral del Carbón (*Coal House*). This building was used to store coal in the 19th century, but its history is much longer. Dating from the 14th century, it was used by Moorish merchants as a lodging house, and then by Christians as a theater. It's one of the oldest Moorish buildings in the city and the only Arab structure of its kind in Spain. ⊠ *Pl. Mariana Pineda, Centro* ⬛ *Free* ⊙ *Daily 10–8.*

Palacio Madraza. This building conceals the Islamic seminary built in 1349 by Yusuf I. The intriguing baroque facade is elaborate; inside, across from the entrance, an octagonal room is crowned by a Moorish dome. It hosts occasional free art and cultural exhibitions. ⊠ *Calle Zacatín, Centro* ☎ *958/241299* ⬛*€2* ⊙ *Daily 10–7:30.*

10

OUTSKIRTS OF TOWN

Casa-Museo Federico García Lorca. Granada's most famous native son, the poet Federico García Lorca, gets his due here, in the middle of a park devoted to him on the southern fringe of the city. Lorca's onetime summer home, **La Huerta de San Vicente,** is now a museum—run by his niece Laura García Lorca—with such artifacts as his beloved piano and changing exhibits on specific aspects of his life. ⊠ *Parque García Lorca, Virgen Blanca, Arabial* ☎ *958/258466* ⊕ *www.huertadesanvicente.com* 🖃 *€3 (free Wed.)* ⊙ *June 15–Sept. 15, Tues.–Sun. 9:15–2:15; Apr.– June 14 and Sept. 16–30, Tues.–Sun. 9:15–2:15 and 5–8; Oct.–Mar., Tues.–Sun. 9:15–2:15 and 4–7. Guided tours every 45 mins until 30 mins before closing.*

Monasterio de La Cartuja. This Carthusian monastery in northern Granada (2 km [1 mile] from the center of town and reached by Bus No. 8) was begun in 1506 and moved to its present site in 1516, though construction continued for the next 300 years. The exterior is sober and monolithic, but inside are twisted, multicolor marble columns; a profusion of gold, silver, tortoiseshell, and ivory; intricate stucco; and the extravagant sacristy—it's easy to see why it has been called the Christian answer to the Alhambra. Among its wonders are the trompe l'oeil spikes, shadows and all, in the Sanchez Cotan cross over the *Last Supper* painting at the west end of the refectory. If you're lucky you may see small birds attempting to land on these faux perches. ⊠ *C. de Alfacar, Cartuja* ☎ *958/161932* 🖃 *€4* ⊙ *Apr.–Oct., daily 10–1 and 4–8; Nov.–Mar., daily 10–1 and 3–6.*

FAMILY **Parque de las Ciencias** (*Science Park*). Across from Granada's convention center and easily reached on either Bus No. 1 or 5, this museum (the most visited in Andalusia) has a planetarium and interactive demonstrations of scientific experiments. The 165-foot observation tower has views to the south and west. ⊠ *Av. del Mediterráneo, Zaidín* ☎ *958/131900* ⊕ *www.parqueciencias.com* 🖃 *Park €6.50, planetarium €2.50* ⊙ *Tues.–Sat. 10–7, Sun. and holidays 10–3.*

WHERE TO EAT

One of the great things about Granada tapas bars is that you receive a free tapa (often very generous) with every drink. You can't choose your tapa, but you'll rarely be disappointed. Poke around the streets between the Carrera del Darro and the Mirador de San Nicolás, particularly around the bustling Plaza San Miguel Bajo, for Granada's most colorful twilight hangouts. Also try the bars and restaurants in the arches underneath the Plaza de Toros (Bullfighting Ring), on the west side of the city, a bit farther from the city center.

For a change, check out some Moroccan-style tea shops, known as *teterías*—these first emerged in Granada and are now also popular in Seville and Málaga, particularly among students. Tea at such places can be expensive, so be sure to check the price of your brew before you order. The highest concentration of teterías is in the Albayzín, particularly around Calle Calderería Nueva where, within a few doors from each other, you find El Oriental, Ali Baba, and El Jardín de los Sueños.

Part of the Holy Week procession in Granada

Tetería Ábaco, up the steep Cuesta del Perro Alto side street, is worth the climb for the Alhambra views from its roof terrace.

$$$ ✕ **Bodegas Castañeda.** A block from the cathedral across Gran Vía, this
SPANISH is a delightfully typical Granadino bodega with low ceilings and dark wood furniture. In addition to the wines, specialties here are plates of cheese, pâté, and *embutidos* (cold meats). The extensive list of tapas includes *queso viejo en aceite* (cured cheese in olive oil), bacon with Roquefort cheese, and *jamón de Trevélez* (ham from the village of Trevélez). If you like garlic, don't miss the Spanish tortilla with creamy alioli. $ *Average main: €18* ✉ *Calle Almireceros 1–3, Centro* ☎ *958/215464.*

$ ✕ **Café Botánico.** Southeast of Granada's cathedral, this is a modern hot
TAPAS spot, a world apart from Granada's usual traditional tapas bar. Here you'll find a bright orange and beige interior and an eclectic crowd of students, families, and business people. The diverse menu has a distinctly international feel to it with Mexican fajitas, Indonesian woks, and Indian tikka masala wraps all sitting side by side. The good value lunchtime menu offers three courses plus a drink for €11.90. Seating is outside on the pleasant sidewalk overlooking the Botanical Garden or inside in two sizeable dining areas. $ *Average main: €10* ✉ *Calle Málaga 3, Centro* ☎ *958/271598.*

$$ ✕ **Casa Juanillo.** Slightly off the beaten track, on the Sacromonte "path-
TAPAS way," this place has spectacular views over the Alhambra and Generalife from its terrace. Food is based around traditional local fare and includes tortillas (the Sacromonte tortilla is made with lamb brains), prawns, and lamb chops (roasted on an open fire and reputedly the best in this part of Granada). Diners may be treated to a occasional

10

spontaneous flamenco performance. $ *Average main: €13* ⊠ *C. del Sacromonte 81, Sacromonte* ☎ *958/223094.*

$$$
SPANISH

✕ **Cunini.** Around the corner from the cathedral, this is one of Granada's best fish restaurants. Catch-of-the-day fish and shellfish, fresh from the boats at Motril, are displayed in the window at the front of the tapas bar, adjacent to the cozy wood-paneled dining room. Both the *frito* (fried) and the *parrillada* (grilled) fish are good choices. If it's chilly, you can warm up with *caldereta de arroz, pescado y marisco* (rice, fish, and seafood stew). There are tables outdoors overlooking a busy plaza. $ *Average main: €20* ⊠ *Pl. Pescadería 14, Centro* ☎ *958/250777* ⊘ *Closed Mon. No dinner Sun.*

$$$
SPANISH
Fodor's Choice
★

✕ **Damasqueros.** The modern, wood-paneled dining room and warm light form the perfect setting for the creative Andalusian cuisine cooked here by local Lola Marín who learnt her trade with some of Spain's top chefs such as Martín Berasategui. The concise menu includes dishes like fresh tuna with pumpkin ravioli, pesto, and fried almonds, and Iberian pork with couscous, apricots, and yogurt. The wine list runs to more than 120 types, including several Granada wines. Thanks to its slightly hidden location in the Realejo, Damasqueros is not highly frequented by tourists. $ *Average main: €20* ⊠ *Calle Damasqueros 3, Realejo* ☎ *958/210550* ⊕ *www.damasqueros.com* ⊘ *Closed Mon. No dinner Sun.*

$
SPANISH

✕ **El Lagarto de Lorca.** In the choicest square in the Albayzín, which is covered with tables and chairs in the summer, this restaurant (named after a Lorca poem about a lizard, serves solidly traditional cuisine that includes rabo de toro, *habas con jamón* (ham with broad beans), and meat grilled over a log fire. The house specialties include *caracoles* (snails) and tapas (€1.50). There are three upstairs terraces whose views take in the Alhambra and Granada, and downstairs among the rustic interior design and Alhambra murals, the fireplace will warm your toes when there's snow on the Sierras. $ *Average main: €9* ⊠ *Pl. San Miguel Bajo 15, Albayzín* ☎ *958/563542.*

$$
SPANISH

✕ **El Pilar del Toro.** This bar and restaurant, just off Plaza Nueva, is in a 17th-century palace with a stunning patio (complete with original marble columns) and peaceful garden. A change of management in late 2013 has led to a menu emphasizing meat dishes such as *carrillada al vino tinto* (meat stew in red wine), *cordero lechal al aroma de romero* (suckling lamb with a hint of rosemary) and the house specialty, oxtail stew. The downstairs patio and bar serve tapas only with the elegant restaurant upstairs. $ *Average main: €15* ⊠ *Calle Hospital de Santa Ana 12, Albayzín* ☎ *958/225470.*

$
TAPAS
Fodor's Choice
★

✕ **La Brujidera.** Also known simply as "Casa de Vinos", this place, up a pedestrian street just behind Plaza Nueva, is a must for Spanish wine lovers. The cozy interior is reminiscent of a ship's cabin, with wood panelling lining the walls, along with bottles of more than 150 Spanish wines. A different wine is featured each week and vermouth and sherries are on tap in barrels behind the counter. Tapas specialize in cold meats, cheeses, and patés, served on 11 types and sizes of boards (€9–€22). The house board includes 3 cold meats, goat's cheese, and two pâtés.

[$] *Average main: €10* ✉ *Monjas del Carmen 2, Centro* ☎ *958/222595* 🕒 *Closed 1 wk in Feb. (call for dates).*

$$$$ SPANISH 🍴 **Las Estrellas de San Nicolás.** Near the Mirador San Nicolás, this elegant restaurant has panoramic views of the Alhambra from the elegant upstairs room and terrace. Renowned chef Enrique Martín from Córdoba has introduced such innovative dishes as black pudding crumble with caramelized mango and duck with pears, grapes, and apple puree but also offers a more traditional menu of oxtail stew, grilled sea bass, and creamy rice with lobster (the house specialty). Service is exemplary. [$] *Average main: €23* ✉ *Callejón Atarazana Vieja 1, Albayzín* ☎ *958/288739* 🕒 *No lunch Tues.*

$ TAPAS 🍴 **Los Diamantes.** This cheap and cheerful bar is a big favorite with locals and draws crowds whatever the time of year. Specialties include fried fish and seafood—try the *surtido de pescado* (assortment of fried fish) to sample the best—as well as *mollejas fritas* (fried lamb brains). No reservations are taken and there's no seating, so arrive early (1:30 pm or 8 pm) to be sure of some bar space or a tall table outside. Even when it's crowded, the service comes with a smile. [$] *Average main: €12* ✉ *Calle Navas 28, Centro* ☎ *958/222572.*

$$$ SPANISH 🍴 **Mirador de Morayma.** Buried in the Albayzín, this hard-to-find restaurant might appear to be closed, but ring the doorbell—once inside, you'll have unbeatable views across the gorge to the Alhambra, particularly from the wisteria-laden outdoor terrace. In colder weather you can enjoy the open fireplace and attractive dining space inside. The menu has some surprising sweet-savory mixes such as *bacalao gratinado con alioli de manzana* (grilled cod with apple-garlic mayonnaise), and *presa ibérica con salsa de higos, vino dulce, membrillo y puerros* (Iberian pork with fig and sweet-wine sauce, quince, and leeks). Service is sometimes a little on the slow side. The restaurant has several flights of steps. [$] *Average main: €19* ✉ *Calle Pianista García Carrillo 2, Albayzín* ☎ *958/228290* 🕒 *No dinner Sun.*

$$ SPANISH 🍴 **Oliver.** The interior may look a bit bare, but whatever this fish restaurant lacks in warmth it makes up for with the food. Less pricey than its neighbor Cunini, it serves simple but high-quality dishes like grilled mullet, dorado baked in salt, prawns with garlic, and monkfish in saffron sauce. The tapas bar, which is more popular with locals than the dining room, offers classic dishes (€1.50) like *migas* (fried bread crumbs), beans with serrano ham, and tortilla *del Sacromonte* (with lamb testicles and brains, as traditionally prepared by the Sacromonte's gypsies). Granada visitors on Fodor's website community highlight the good, friendly service here. [$] *Average main: €15* ✉ *Pl. Pescadería 12, Centro* ☎ *958/262200* 🕒 *Closed Sun.*

$$ VEGETARIAN 🍴 **Paprika.** Inside a pretty brick building and with an informal terrace sprawling over the wide steps of the Cuesta de Abarqueros, Paprika offer unpretentious vegetarian food for a mainly young clientele. Most ingredients and wines are organic, and dishes include salads, stir-fries, and curries, such as Thai curry with tofu, coconut, and green-curry sauce. There's a good choice of vegan and gluten-free dishes. [$] *Average main: €13* ✉ *Cuesta de Abarqueros 3* ☎ *958/804785* 🌐 *www.paprika-granada.com.*

$$$ SPANISH 🍴 **Puerta del Carmen.** This bustling bar and restaurant occupies an elegant townhouse and exudes a whiff of tradition with its dark-wood furnishings, lofty ceilings, and tasteful color scheme. Granada's Círculo Taurino (bullfighting society) used to meet here as can be seen in some of the wall decorations. A congenial staff and a reliably good menu add to the appeal. It's popular with the business community, and there are plenty of plates to share, including goat's cheese and mango pastry. Main courses include fresh fish of the day and steak tartare (the house specialty). The wine list is superb. A plus: the kitchen doesn't close between lunch and dinner. [$] *Average main: €18* ✉ *Pl. Carmen 1, Centro* ☎ *958/223737.*

$$$$ BASQUE 🍴 **Restaurante Arriaga.** Run by Basque chef Álvaro Arriaga, this restaurant sits on the top floor of the Museo de la Memoria de Andalucía just outside the city (take a taxi to get here) and enjoys panoramic views of Granada with Sierra Nevada behind. Choose from two tasting menus (€55), both with eight dishes, one based around the chef's Basque roots and the other, known as "Play," a succession of surprises. À la carte specialties include Basque cod and hake, and beef slow-cooked for 40 hours! Expect innovative desserts such as the *pastilla de jabón de leche de almendras con "champú" de lavanda* (almond milk "soap" with lavender "shampoo"). [$] *Average main: €25* ✉ *Av. de las Ciencias 2, Ctra. de la Armilla* ☎ *958/132619* ⏲ *No dinner Sun.*

$$ SPANISH 🍴 **Ruta del Azafrán.** A charming surprise nestled at the foot of the Albayzín by the Darro River—this sleek contemporary space in the shadow of the Alhambra offers a selection of specialties. The menu is interesting and diverse and includes dishes like chicken *pastela* (sweet-savory pie); lamb couscous; and several salads including one that features watercress, fried mushrooms, quince, and pine nuts. The three-course set menu (€12) sets high standards. Steel furniture and a black and red color scheme contribute to the air of sophistication. The kitchen is open from 1 to 11 pm (midnight in summer). [$] *Average main: €15* ✉ *Paseo de los Tristes 1, Albayzín* ☎ *958/226882.*

$$$ SPANISH 🍴 **Ruta del Veleta.** A short drive out of town on the way to Sierra Nevada, this established restaurant serves innovative twists on Spanish recipes using seasonal ingredients—many of the vegetables are grown in the restaurant's own garden. Innovative options include *librito del Valle Tropical de Granada* (a layered stack of salmon trout and caviar) and *picantón asado* (roast chicken with potato couscous and sheep's milk sauce). [$] *Average main: €22* ✉ *Ctra. de la Sierra 136, Cenes de la Vega* ☎ *958/486134.*

$ SPANISH 🍴 **Taberna Tofe.** One of an energetic stretch of similarly appealing traditional and contemporary bars and restaurants, this is a good choice for tapas or more substantial fare like roasted chicken. The *surtido de tapas* is a platter of tasty selections that includes *patatas bravas* (fried potatoes in a spicy chili-spiked tomato sauce), meatballs in an almond sauce, and wedges of tortilla. A jug of sangria makes a good accompaniment. The interior is an attractive (but slightly dark) space with pine furniture, and there is an outside terrace for alfresco dining. [$] *Average main: €8* ✉ *Campo del Principe 18, Centro* ☎ *958/226207* ⏲ *Closed Tues.*

WHERE TO STAY

Staying in the immediate vicinity of the Alhambra tends to be pricier than the city center. The latter is a good choice if you want to combine your Alhambra trip with visits to the vibrant commercial center with its excellent shops, restaurants, and magnificent cathedral. The Albayzín is also a good place to stay for sheer character: this historic Arab quarter still has a tangible Moorish feel with its pint-size plazas and winding pedestrian streets.

$$$
B&B/INN
Fodor's Choice
★
Carmen de la Alcubilla del Caracol. In a traditional Granadino villa on the slopes of the Alhambra, this privately run lodging is one of Granada's most stylish hotels. **Pros:** great views; personal service; impeccable taste. **Cons:** tough climb in hot weather; mediocre breakfast. **$** *Rooms from: €140* ⊠ *Calle Aire Alta 12, Alhambra* ☎ *958/215551* ⊕ *www.alcubilladelcaracol.com* ⤺ *7 rooms* ☽ *Closed Aug.* ❑ *No meals.*

$$$
B&B/INN
Fodor's Choice
★
Casa Morisca. The architect who owns this 15th-century building transformed it into a hotel so distinctive that he received Spain's National Restoration Award for his preservation of original architectural elements, including barrel-vaulted brickwork, wooden ceilings, and the original pool. **Pros:** historic location; award-winning design; easy parking; free Wi-Fi. **Cons:** stuffy interior rooms; no full restaurant on site. **$** *Rooms from: €127* ⊠ *Cuesta de la Victoria 9, Albayzín* ☎ *958/221100* ⊕ *www.hotelcasamorisca.com* ⤺ *12 rooms, 2 suites* ❑ *No meals.*

$$$$
HOTEL
Hospes Palacio de los Patos. This beautifully restored palace is unmissable, sitting proudly on its own in the middle of one of Granada's busiest shopping streets. **Pros:** central location; historic setting. **Cons:** expensive parking; indifferent service. **$** *Rooms from: €250* ⊠ *Calle Solarillo de Gracia 1, Centro* ☎ *958/535790* ⊕ *www.hospes.es* ⤺ *42 rooms* ❑ *No meals.*

$$$$
HOTEL
Hotel Alhambra Palace. Built by a local duke in 1910, this neo-Moorish hotel is on leafy grounds at the back of the Alhambra hill, and 2012 saw completion of the restoration of its very Arabian Nights interior (think orange-and-brown overtones, multicolor tiles, and Moorish-style arches and pillars). **Pros:** bird's-eye views; location near but not in the Alhambra. **Cons:** steep climb up from Granada; doubles as a popular convention center—there are five spacious meeting rooms—so often packed with business folk. **$** *Rooms from: €210* ⊠ *Pl. Arquitecto García de Paredes 1, Alhambra* ☎ *958/221468* ⊕ *www.h-alhambrapalace.es* ⤺ *115 rooms, 11 suites* ❑ *Breakfast.*

$$$$
HOTEL
Hotel Carmen. This hotel has a prized city-center location on a busy shopping street and rooms that are spacious with modern, minimalist interiors. **Pros:** downtown location; rooftop pool; website offers can reduce the cost dramatically. **Cons:** can be noisy; dark reception area. **$** *Rooms from: €200* ⊠ *Acera del Darro 62, Centro* ☎ *958/258300* ⊕ *www.hotelcarmen.com* ⤺ *222 rooms, 4 suites* ❑ *No meals.*

$$
HOTEL
Hotel Párraga Siete. This family-run hotel in the heart of the old quarter within easy walking distance of sights and restaurants offers excellent value and amenities superior to its two-star official rating. **Pros:** central quiet location; good service. **Cons:** difficult to access by car; interiors might be too sparse for some. **$** *Rooms from: €120* ⊠ *Calle*

10

Párraga 7, Centro ☎ *958/264227* 🌐 *www.hotelparragasiete.com* 🛏 *20 rooms* 🍴 *No meals.*

$$$ B&B/INN 🏨 **Palacio de los Navas.** In the center of the city, this palace was built by aristocrat Francisco Navas in the 16th century and it later became the Casa de Moneda (the Mint). **Pros:** great location; peaceful oasis. **Cons:** can be noisy at night; breakfast uninspiring. [$] *Rooms from: €137* ✉ *Calle Navas 1, Centro* ☎ *958/215760* 🌐 *www.palaciodelosnavas.com* 🛏 *19 rooms, 1 suite* 🍴 *Breakfast.*

$$$$ HOTEL Fodor's Choice ★ 🏨 **Parador de Granada.** This is Spain's most expensive and most popular parador, right within the walls of the Alhambra. **Pros:** good location; lovely interiors; garden restaurant. **Cons:** no views in some rooms; removed from city life. [$] *Rooms from: €336* ✉ *Calle Real de la Alhambra, Alhambra* ☎ *958/221440* 🌐 *www.parador.es* 🛏 *35 rooms, 5 suites* 🍴 *No meals.*

NIGHTLIFE AND PERFORMING ARTS

PERFORMING ARTS

FLAMENCO

Flamenco can be enjoyed throughout the city, especially in the Gypsy cuevas of the Albayzín and Sacromonte, where zambra shows—informal performances by Gypsies—take place almost daily year-round. The most popular cuevas are along the Camino de Sacromonte, the major street in the neighborhood of the same name. Be warned that this area has become very tourist oriented, and prepare to part with lots of money (€20–€25 is average) for any show. Some shows include the price of round-trip transportation to the venue from your hotel, usually cheaper than two taxi journeys. In July and August, an annual flamenco festival takes place in the delightful El Corral del Carbón square (🌐 *www.losveranosdelcorral.es*). A program of flamenco in the city is available on 🌐 *www.granadaesflamenco.com.*

El Templo del Flamenco. Slightly off the beaten track (take a taxi to get here) and less touristy because of it, this venue has shows, at 9 on Friday and Saturday. ✉ *Calle Parnaleros Alto 41, Albayzín* ☎ *958/963904.*

La Rocío. This is a good spot for authentic flamenco shows, staged nightly at 10 and 11. ✉ *C. del Sacromonte 70, Albayzín* ☎ *958/227129.*

Los Tarantos cave. The flamenco show here, every evening at 9:30 and 10:45, takes place among the spectators (there's no stage), who can number up to 150. ✉ *C. del Sacromonte 9, Sacromonte* ☎ *958/224525* 🌐 *www.cuevaslostarantos.com.*

María La Canastera. This is one of the cuevas on Camino de Sacromonte with zambra shows at 9:30 pm daily. ✉ *C. del Sacromonte 89, Sacromonte* ☎ *958/121183.*

Sala Albaicín. Various options are scheduled at the well-established Sala Albaicín, including shows (at 9:15 and 10:30 pm) and walks to the Mirador de San Nicolás combined with a subsequent show. ✉ *Mirador San Cristóbal, Ctra. Murcia, Albayzín* ☎ *958/804646* 🌐 *www.flamencoalbayzin.com.*

NIGHTLIFE

Granada's ample student population makes for a lively bar scene. Some of the trendiest bars are in converted houses in the Albayzín and Sacromonte and in the area between Plaza Nueva and Paseo de los Tristes. Calle Elvira, Calderería Vieja, and Calderería Nueva are crowded with laid-back coffee and pastry shops. In the modern part of town, Pedro Antonio de Alarcón and Martinez de la Rosa have larger but less glamorous offerings. Another nighttime gathering place is the Campo del Príncipe, a large plaza surrounded by typical Andalusian taverns.

Dar Ziryab. A selection of live music (flamenco, jazz, and African, among others) plays nightly in this typical tea shop in the Albayzín. ⊠ *Calle Calderería Nueva 11, Albayzín* ☎ *958/229429.*

El Eshavira. At this dimly lighted club you can hear sultry jazz (Wednesday and Thursday) and flamenco (Sunday) at 10 pm. Admission includes a drink. ⊠ *Calle Postigo de la Cuna 2, Albayzín* ☎ *958/290829.*

Granada 10. You'll mingle with an upscale crowd at this discothèque in a former theater. ⊠ *Calle Carcel Baja 10, Centro* ☎ *958/224001.*

SHOPPING

A Moorish aesthetic pervades Granada's ceramics, marquetry (especially the *taraceas,* wooden boxes with inlaid tiles on their lids), woven textiles, and silver-, brass-, and copper-ware. The main shopping streets, centering on the Puerta Real, are the Gran Vía de Colón, Reyes Católicos, Zacatín, Ángel Ganivet, and Recogidas. Most antiques shops are on Cuesta de Elvira and Alcaicería—off Reyes Católicos. Cuesta de Gómerez, on the way up to the Alhambra, also has several handicrafts shops and guitar workshops.

Capricho del Artesano. Typical Granada ceramics—blue-and-green patterns on white, with a pomegranate in the center—are sold at this shop near the cathedral, and it doesn't close at lunchtime. ⊠ *Pl. Pescadería 4, Centro* ☎ *958/288192.*

Espartería San José. For wicker baskets and esparto-grass mats and rugs, head to this shop off the Plaza Pescadería. ⊠ *Calle Jáudenes 22, Centro* ☎ *958/267415.*

10

SIDE TRIPS FROM GRANADA

The fabled province of Granada spans the Sierra Nevada, with the beautifully rugged Alpujarras and the highest peaks on mainland Spain— Mulhacén at 11,407 feet and Veleta at 11,125 feet. This is where you can find some of the prettiest, most ancient villages, and it's one of the foremost destinations for Andalusia's increasingly popular rural tourism. Granada's vega, covered with orchards, tobacco plantations, and poplar groves, stretches for miles around.

EN ROUTE Twelve kilometers (8 miles) south of Granada on A44, the road reaches a spot known as the **Suspiro del Moro** (Moor's Sigh). Pause here a moment and look back at the city, just as Granada's departing "Boy King," Boabdil, did 500 years ago. As he wept over the city he'd surrendered to the Catholic Monarchs, his scornful mother pronounced her now legendary rebuke: "You weep like a woman for the city you could not defend as a man."

FUENTEVAQUEROS

19½ km (12 miles) northwest of Granada.

Museo Casa Natal Federico García Lorca. Born in the village of Fuentevaqueros on June 5, 1898, the poet lived here until age six. His childhood home opened as a museum in 1986, when Spain commemorated the 50th anniversary of his assassination (he was shot without trial by Nationalists at the start of the civil war in August 1936) and celebrated his reinstatement as a national figure after 40 years of nonrecognition during the Francisco Franco regime. The house has been restored with original furnishings, and the former granary, barn, and stables have been converted into exhibition spaces, with temporary art shows and a permanent display of photographs, clippings, and other memorabilia. A two-minute video shows the only existing footage of Lorca. Visits are by guided tour only. ⊠ *C. del Poeta García Lorca 4* ☏ *958/516453* ⊕ *www.patronatogarcialorca.org* ✉ *€1.80* ☉ *Tours on the hr: July and Aug., Tues.–Sun 10–2; Apr.–June and Sept., Tues.–Sat. 10–1 and 5–6, Sun. 10–1; Oct.–Mar., Tues.–Sat. 10–1 and 4–5, Sun. 10–1.*

THE SIERRA NEVADA

The drive southeast from Granada to Pradollano along the A395— Europe's highest road, by way of Cenes de la Vega—takes about 45 minutes. It's wise to carry snow chains from mid-November to as late as April or even May. The mountains here make for an easy and worthwhile excursion, especially for those keen on trekking.

EXPLORING

Mulhacén. To the east of Granada, the mighty Mulhacén, the highest peak in mainland Spain, soars to 11,427 feet. Legend has it that it came by its name when Boabdil, the last Moorish king of Granada, deposed his father, Muly Abdul Hassan, and had the body buried at the summit of the mountain so that it couldn't be desecrated. For more information on trails to the two summits, call the National Park Service office (☏ *958/763127* ⊕ *www.nevadensis.com*) in Pampaneira.

Pico de Veleta. Peninsular Spain's second-highest mountain is 11,125 feet high. The view from its summit across Las Alpujarras to the sea at distant Motril is stunning, and on a very clear day you can see the coast of North Africa. When the snow melts (July and August) you can drive or take a minibus from the Albergue Universitario (Universitario mountain refuge) to within around 400 yards of the summit—a trail takes you to the top in around 45 minutes. ■TIP➔ It's cold up there, so take a warm jacket and scarf, even if Granada is sizzling hot.

SPORTS AND THE OUTDOORS

SKIING

FAMILY **Estación de Esquí Sierra Nevada.** Europe's southernmost ski resort is one of its best equipped. At the Pradollano and Borreguiles stations, there's good skiing December through April or May; each has a special snowboarding circuit, floodlighted night slopes, a children's ski school, and après-ski sun and swimming in the Mediterranean less than an hour away. In winter, buses (*Autocares Bonal* ☎ *958/465022*) to Pradollano leave Granada's bus station three times a day on weekdays and four times on weekends and holidays. Tickets are € 9 round-trip. As for Borreguiles, you can get there only on skis. There's an information center (☎ *902/708090* ⊕ *www.cetursa.es*) at Plaza de Andalucía 4.

THE ALPUJARRAS

Fodor'sChoice *Village of Lanjarón: 46 km (29 miles) south of Granada.*
★
A trip to the Alpujarras, on the southern slopes of the Sierra Nevada, takes you to one of Andalusia's highest, most remote, and most scenic areas, home for decades to painters, writers, and a considerable foreign population. The Alpujarras region was originally populated by Moors fleeing the Christian Reconquest (from Seville after its fall in 1248, then from Granada after 1492). It was also the final fiefdom of the unfortunate Boabdil, conceded to him by the Catholic Monarchs after he surrendered Granada. In 1568 rebellious Moors made their last stand against the Christian overlords, a revolt ruthlessly suppressed by Felipe II and followed by the forced conversion of all Moors to Christianity and their resettlement farther inland and up Spain's eastern coast. The villages were then repopulated with Christian soldiers from Galicia, who were granted land in return for their service. To this day, the Galicians' descendants continue the Moorish custom of weaving rugs and blankets in the traditional Alpujarran colors of red, green, black, and white, and they sell their crafts in many of the villages. Be on the lookout for handmade basketry and pottery as well.

Houses here are squat and square; they spill down the southern slopes of the Sierra Nevada, bearing a strong resemblance to the Berber homes in the Rif Mountains, just across the Mediterranean in Morocco. If you're driving, the road as far as Lanjarón and Orgiva is smooth sailing; after that come steep, twisting mountain roads with few gas stations. Beyond sightseeing, the area is a haven for outdoor activities such as hiking and horseback riding. Inquire at the **Information Point** at Plaza de la Libertad, at Pampaneira.

EN
ROUTE
Lanjarón and Nearby Villages. The western entrance to the Alpujarras is some 46 km (29 miles) from Granada at Lanjarón. This spa town is famous for its mineral water, collected from the melting snows of the Sierra Nevada and drunk throughout Spain. **Orgiva**, the next and largest town in the Alpujarras, has a 17th-century castle. Here you can leave A348 and follow signs for the villages of the Alpujarras Altas (High Alpujarras), including **Pampaneira, Capileira,** and especially **Trevélez,** which lies on the slopes of the Mulhacén at 4,840 feet above sea level. Reward yourself with a plate of locally produced *jamón serrano* (cured

10

ham). Trevélez has three levels, the Barrio Alto, Barrio Medio, and Barrio Bajo; the butchers are concentrated in the lowest section (Bajo). The higher levels have narrow cobblestone streets, whitewashed houses, and shops.

WHERE TO STAY

$
HOTEL
Fodor's Choice
★

🖫 **Alquería de Morayma.** Close to the banks of the Guadalfeo River, the buildings in this charming complex have been remodeled in the old alpujarreño style, including some rooms in an old chapel. **Pros:** tranquil location; lots of activities. **Cons:** need a car to get around; could be too quiet for some. Ⓢ *Rooms from: €70* ⊠ *Ctra. A348, Km 50, Cádiar* 🖀 *958/343303* ⊕ *www.alqueriamorayma.com* ⌦ *13 rooms, 10 apartments* ⑩ *No meals.*

$
HOTEL

🖫 **Las Terrazas de las Alpujarras.** Located in the pretty whitewashed village of Bubión, on the way to Trevélez and a short walk from Pitres, this family-run hostal offers rooms and apartments with south-facing terraces that have panoramic views of the mountains (and Africa on a clear day). **Pros:** amazing views; excellent value; good location for exploring. **Cons:** could be too basic for some. Ⓢ *Rooms from: €36* ⊠ *Pl. del Sol 7, Bubión* 🖀 *958/763034* ⊕ *www.terrazasalpujarra.com* ⌦ *17 rooms, 3 apartments* ⑩ *No meals.*

$
HOTEL
FAMILY

🖫 **Taray Botánico.** This hotel—a perfect base for exploring the Alpujarras, and with its own organic farm—occupies a low, typical Alpujarran building. **Pros:** fun for families; great organic food. **Cons:** somewhat isolated; livestock attract abundant flies. Ⓢ *Rooms from: €78* ⊠ *Ctra. Tablate–Albuñol, Km 18, Órgiva* 🖀 *958/784525* ⊕ *www.hoteltaray. com* ⌦ *15 bungalows* ⑩ *No meals.*

COSTA DEL SOL
AND COSTA
DE ALMERÍA

WELCOME TO THE COSTA DEL SOL AND COSTA DE ALMERÍA

TOP REASONS TO GO

★ **Enjoy the sun and sand:** Relax at any of the beaches; they're all free, though in summer there isn't much towel space.

★ **Soak up the atmosphere:** Spend a day in Málaga, Picasso's birthplace, visiting the museums, exploring the old town, and strolling along the Palm Walkway in the port.

★ **Check out Puerto Banús:** Wine, dine, and celebrity-watch at the Costa's most luxurious and sophisticated port.

★ **Visit Cabo de Gata:** This protected natural reserve is one of the wildest and most beautiful stretches of coast in Spain.

★ **Shop for souvenirs:** Check out the weekly market in one of the Costa resorts to pick up bargain-price souvenirs, including ceramics.

1 The Costa de Almería. This Costa region is hot and sunny virtually year-round and is notable for its spectacular beaches, unspoiled countryside, and (less appealingly) plastic greenhouse agriculture. Right on the coast is Almería, a handsome, under-rated city with a fascinating historic center with narrow pedestrian streets flanked by sunbaked ocher buildings and tapas bars.

2 The Costa Tropical. Less developed than the Costa del Sol, this stretch of coastline is distinctive for its attractive seaside towns, rocky coves, excellent water sports, and mountainous interior.

CÓRDOBA   Iznalle

SEVILLA   Santa Fe

Archidona   Loja   Granada

Antequera   SIERRA ALMIJARA   Durcal

MÁLAGA   Casabermeja   Sierra Tejeda   AXARQUIA

3   MONTES DE MÁLAGA

CÁDIZ   Ronda   Vélez-   Nerja   Salobre

Cártoma   Málaga   Málaga

Marbella   Torremolinos

Fuengirola

Puerto Banús   COSTA DEL SOL

Estepona

La Linea **4**   Mediterranean Sea

GIBRALTAR (U.K.)

11

3 Málaga Province.
Don't miss the capital of the province: this up-and-coming cruise port retains a traditional Andalusian feel; better known are the coastal resorts due west with their sweeping beaches and excellent tourist facilities.

GETTING ORIENTED

The towns and resorts along the southeastern Spanish coastline vary considerably according to whether they lie to the east or to the west of Málaga. To the east are the Costa de Almería and Costa Tropical, less developed stretches of coastline. Towns like Nerja act as a gateway to the dramatic mountainous region of La Axarquía. West from Málaga along the Costa del Sol proper, the strip between Torremolinos and Marbella is the most densely populated. Seamless though it may appear, as one resort merges into the next, each town has a distinctive character, with its own sights, charms, and activities.

```
0          30 mi
0       30 km
```

4 Gibraltar. The "Rock" is an extraordinary combination of Spain and Britain, with a fascinating history. There are also some fine restaurants here, as well as traditional Olde English pubs.

EATING AND DRINKING WELL ALONG SPAIN'S SOUTHERN COAST

Spain's southern coast is known for fresh fish and seafood, grilled or quickly fried in olive oil. Sardines roasted on spits are popular along the Málaga coast, while upland towns offer more robust mountain fare, especially in Almería.

(top left) Beachside dining on the Costa del Sol (top right) Sardines being roasted over glowing logs (bottom left) A classic potato-based stew

Chiringuitos, small shanty shacks along the beaches, are summer-only Costa del Sol restaurants that serve fish fresh off the boats. Málaga is known for seafood restaurants serving *fritura malagueña de pescaíto* (fried fish). In the mountain towns, you'll find superb *rabo de toro* (oxtail), goat and sheep cheeses, wild mushrooms, and game dishes. Almería shares Moorish aromas of cumin and cardamom with its Andalusian sisters to the west but also turns the corner toward its northern neighbor, Murcia, where delicacies such as *mojama* (salt-dried tuna) and *hueva de maruca* (ling roe) have been favorites since Phoenician times. Almería's wealth of vegetables and legumes combine with pork and game products for a rougher, more powerful culinary canon of thick stews and soups.

TO DRINK

Málaga has long been famous for the sweet muscatel wine that Russian empress Catherine the Great loved so much she imported it to Saint Petersburg duty-free in 1792. Muscatel was sold medicinally in pharmacies in the 18th century for its curative powers and is still widely produced and often served as accompaniment to dessert or tapas.

11

COLD ALMOND AND GARLIC SOUP

Ajoblanco, a summer staple in Andalusia, is a refreshing salty-sweet combination served cold. Exquisitely light and sharp, the almond and garlic soup has a surprisingly creamy and fresh taste. Almonds, garlic, hard white bread, olive oil, water, sherry vinegar, and a topping of muscat grapes are the standard ingredients.

FRIED FISH MÁLAGA-STYLE

A popular dish along the Costa del Sol and the Costa de Almería, *fritura malagueña de pescaíto* is basically any sort of very small fish—such as anchovies, cuttlefish, baby squid, whitebait, and red mullet—fried in oil so hot that the fish end up crisp and light as a feather. The fish are lightly dusted in white flour, crisped quickly, and drained briefly before arriving piping hot and bone-dry on your plate. For an additional Moorish aroma, fritura masters add powdered cumin to the flour.

ALMERÍA STEWS

Almería is known for heartier fare than neighboring Málaga. *Puchero de trigo* (wheat and pork stew) is a fortifying winter comfort stew of whole, boiled grains of wheat cooked with chickpeas, pork, black sausage, fatback, potatoes, saffron, cumin, and fennel. *Ajo colorao*, another popular stew that's also known as *atascaburras*, consists of potatoes, dried peppers, vegetables, and fish that

are simmered into a thick red-orange stew *de cuchara* (eaten with a spoon). Laced with cumin and garlic and served with thick country bread, it's a stick-to-your-ribs mariner's soup.

ROASTED SARDINES

Known as *moraga de sardinas*, or *espeto de sardinas*, this method of cooking sardines is popular in the summer along the Pedregalejo and La Carihuela beaches east and west of Málaga: the sardines are skewered and extended over logs at an angle so that the fish oils run back down the skewers instead of falling into the coals and igniting a conflagration. Fresh fish and cold white wine or beer make this a beautiful and relaxing sunset beach dinner.

A THOUSAND AND ONE EGGS

Something about the spontaneous nature of Spain's southern latitudes seems to lend itself to the widespread use of eggs to bind ingredients together. In Andalusia and especially along the Costa del Sol, *huevos a la flamenca* (eggs flamenco-style) is a time-tested dish combining peppers, potatoes, ham, and peas with an egg broken over the top and baked sizzling hot in the oven. *Revuelto de setas y gambas* (scrambled eggs with wild mushrooms and shrimp) is a tasty combination and a common entrée. And, of course, there is the universal Iberian potato omelet, the *tortilla de patatas*.

BEST BEACHES OF THE SOUTHERN COAST

Tourists have been coming to the Costa del Sol since the 1950s, attracted by its magical combination of brochure-blue sea, miles of beaches, and reliably sunny weather.

(top left) One of the many resorts in Torremolinos (top right) Tarifa is known for its wind: great for windsurfing, kiteboarding, and kite flying. (bottom left) Crashing waves at Cabo de Gata

The beaches here range from the gravel-like shingle in Almuñécar, Nerja, and Málaga to fine, gritty sand from Torremolinos westward. The best—and most crowded—beaches are east of Málaga and those flanking the most popular resorts of Nerja, Torremolinos, Fuengirola, and Marbella. For more secluded beaches, head west of Estepona and past Gibraltar to Tarifa and the Cádiz coast. The beaches change when you hit the Atlantic, becoming appealingly wide with fine golden sand. The winds are usually quite strong here, which means that although you can't read a newspaper while lying out, the conditions for windsurfing and kiteboarding are near perfect.

Beaches are free and busiest in July, August, and on Sunday from May to October when malagueño families arrive for a full day on the beach and lunch at a chiringuito.

OVER THE TOPLESS

In Spain, as in many parts of Europe, it is perfectly acceptable for women to go topless on the beach, although covering up is the norm at beach bars. There are several nude beaches on the Costas; look for the "*playa naturista*" sign. The most popular are in Maro (near Nerja), Benalmádena Costa, and near Tarifa.

BEST BEACHES

LA CARIHUELA, TORREMOLINOS
This former fishing district of Torremolinos has a wide stretch of beach. The chiringuitos here are some of the best on the Costa, and the promenade, which continues until Benalmádena port, with its striking Asian-inspired architecture and great choice of restaurants and bars, is delightful for strolling.

CARVAJAL, FUENGIROLA
Backed by low-rise buildings and greenery, the beach here is unspoiled and refreshingly low-key. East of Fuengirola center, the Carvajal beach bars have young crowds, with regular live music in summer. It's also an easily accessible beach on the Málaga–Fuengirola train, with a stop within walking distance of the sand.

PLAYA LOS LANCES, TARIFA
This white sandy beach is one of the least spoiled in Andalusia. Near lush vegetation, lagoons, and the occasional campsite and boho-chic hotel (⇨ *See listing for the Hurricane Hotel*), Tarifa's main beach is famed throughout Europe for its windsurfing and kiteboarding, so expect some real winds: *levante* from the east and *poniente* from the west.

CABO DE GATA, ALMERÍA
Backed by natural parkland, with volcanic rock formations creating dramatic cliffs and secluded bays,

Almería's stunning Cabo de Gata coastline includes superb beaches and coves within the protected UNESCO Biosphere Reserve. The fact that most of the beaches here are only accessible via marked footpaths adds to their off-the-beaten-track appeal.

PUERTO BANÚS, MARBELLA
Looking for action? Some great beach scenes flank the world-famous luxurious port. Pedro's Beach is known for its excellent, laid-back Caribbean seafood restaurants, good music, and hip, good-looking crowd. Another superb sandy choice is the Sala Beach, one of the so-called boutique beaches, with a club area and massages available, as well as an attractive beach and tempting shallow waters.

EL SALADILLO, ESTEPONA
Between Marbella and Estepona (take the Cancelada exit off the A7), this relaxed and inviting beach is not as well known as its glitzier neighbors. It's harder to find, so mainly locals in the know frequent it. There are two popular seafood restaurants here, including Pepe's Beach (dating from the 1970s), plus a volleyball net, showers, and sun beds and parasols for hire.

Updated by
Joanna Styles

With roughly 320 days of sunshine a year, the Costa del Sol well deserves the nickname "the Sunshine Coast." It's no wonder much of the coast has been built up with resorts and high-rises. Don't despair, though; you can still find some classic Spanish experiences, whether in the old city of Marbella or one of the smaller villages like Casares. And despite the hubbub of high season, visitors can always unwind here, basking or strolling on mile after mile of sandy beach.

Technically, the stretch of Andalusian shore known as the Costa del Sol runs west from the Costa Tropical, near Granada, to the tip of Tarifa, the southernmost point in Europe, just beyond Gibraltar. For most of the Europeans who have flocked here over the past 40 years, though, the Sunshine Coast has been largely restricted to the 70-km (43-mile) sprawl of hotels, vacation villas, golf courses, marinas, and nightclubs between Torremolinos, just west of Málaga, and Estepona, down toward Gibraltar. Since the late 1950s this area has mushroomed from a group of impoverished fishing villages into an overdeveloped seaside playground and retirement haven. The city of Almería and its coastline, the Costa de Almería, is southwest of Granada's Alpujarras region, and due east of the Costa Tropical (around 147 km [93 miles] from Almuñécar).

PLANNING

WHEN TO GO

May, June, and September are the best times to visit this coastal area, when there's plenty of sunshine but fewer tourists than in the hottest season of July and August. Winter can have bright sunny days, but you may feel the chill: many hotels in the lower price bracket have heat for only a few hours a day; you can also expect several days of rain. Holy Week, the week before Easter Sunday, is a fun time to visit.

PLANNING YOUR TIME

Travelers with their own wheels who want a real taste of the area in just a few days could start by exploring the relatively unspoiled villages of the Costa Tropical: wander around quaint Salobreña, then hit the larger coastal resort of Nerja and head inland for a look around pretty Frigiliana.

Move on to Málaga next; it has lots to offer, including museums, excellent restaurants, and some of the best tapas bars in the province. It's also easy to get to stunning, mountaintop Ronda *(⇨ Chapter 10)*, which is also on a bus route.

Hit the coast at Marbella, the Costa del Sol's swankiest resort, and then take a leisurely stroll around Puerto Banús. Next, head west to Gibraltar for a day of shopping and sightseeing before returning to the coast and Torremolinos for a night on the town.

Choose your base carefully, as the various areas here make for very different experiences. Málaga is a vibrant Spanish city, virtually untainted by tourism, while Torremolinos is a budget destination catering mostly to the mass market. Fuengirola is quieter, with a large population of middle-aged expatriates; farther west, the Marbella–San Pedro de Alcántara area is more exclusive and expensive.

FESTIVALS

It's worth timing your visit to coincide with one of the Costa del Sol's many traditional festivals. The annual **ferias** (more general and usually lengthier celebrations than fiestas) in Málaga (early August) and Fuengirola (early October) are among the best for sheer exuberance.

Feast of San Juan. Midnight bonfires light up beaches all along the coast on June 23, and the celebrations continue the next day.

San Isidro. This celebration on May 15 is marked by typically Andalusian ferias, with plenty of flamenco and *fino* (sherry), in Nerja and Estepona.

Semana Santa. Holy Week processions are particularly dramatic in Málaga.

Virgen del Carmen. The patron saint of fishermen is honored in coastal communities, particularly in Los Boliches (Fuengirola) and Velez-Málaga, on her feast day, July 16.

GETTING HERE AND AROUND
AIR TRAVEL

Delta Airlines runs direct flights from JFK (New York) to Málaga June through August and via Charles de Gaulle (Paris) for the rest of the year. All other flights from the United States connect in Madrid. British Airways flies once daily from London (City, Gatwick, and Heathrow) to Málaga, and numerous British budget airlines, such as easyJet and Monarch, also link the two cities. There are direct flights to Málaga from most other major European cities on Iberia or other airlines. Iberia has two flights daily from Madrid (flying time is 1 hour 20 minutes), four flights a day from Barcelona (1½ hours), and regular flights from other Spanish cities.

Málaga's Costa del Sol airport is 10 km (6 miles) west of town and is one of Spain's most modern. Trains from the airport into town run every 20 minutes (6:44 am–12:24 am, journey time 12 minutes, €1.75) and from the airport to Fuengirola every 20 minutes (6:06 am–11:42 pm, journey time 34 minutes, €2.65), stopping at several resorts en route, including Torremolinos and Benalmádena.

From the airport there's also bus service to Málaga every half hour from 7 am to midnight (€3). At least 10 daily buses (more from July–September) run between the airport and Marbella (journey time 45 minutes, €8). Taxi fares from the airport to Málaga, Torremolinos, and other resorts are posted inside the terminal: from the airport to Marbella is about €65, to Torremolinos €15, and to Fuengirola €35. Many of the better hotels and all tour companies will arrange for pickup at the airport.

BIKE TRAVEL

The Costa del Sol is famous for its sun and sand, but many people supplement their beach time with mountain-bike forays into the hilly interior, particularly around Ojén, near Marbella, and along the mountain roads around Ronda. A popular route, which affords sweeping vistas, is via the mountain road from Ojén west to Istán. The Costa del Sol's temperate climate is ideal for biking, though it's best not to exert yourself on the trails in July and August, when temperatures soar. There are numerous bike-rental shops in the area, particularly in Marbella, Ronda, and Ojén; many shops also arrange bike excursions. The cost to rent a mountain bike for the day is around €20. Guided bike excursions, which include bikes, support staff, and cars, generally start at about €50 a day.

Contact Marbella Rent a Bike. The roughly 100 bikes available from this company come with locks and third-party liability insurance. They can be delivered to locations throughout the Costa del Sol. ☎ 952/811062 ⊕ www.marbellarentabike.com.

BUS TRAVEL

Until the high-speed AVE train line opens between Antequera and Granada sometime around 2016, buses are the best way to reach the Costa del Sol from Granada, and, aside from the train service from Málaga to Fuengirola, the best way to get around once you're here. During holidays it's wise to reserve your seat in advance for long-distance travel.

On the Costa del Sol, bus services connect Málaga with Cádiz (4 daily), Córdoba (4 daily), Granada (17 daily), and Seville (6 daily). In Fuengirola you can catch buses for Mijas, Marbella, Estepona, and Algeciras. The Portillo-Avanzabus bus company (☎ 902/020052 ⊕ www.avanzabus.com) serves most of the Costa del Sol and Cádiz. ALSA (☎ 902/422242 ⊕ www.alsa.es) serves Granada, Córdoba, Seville, and Nerja. Los Amarillos (☎ 902/210317 ⊕ www.losamarillos.es) serves Jerez and Ronda.

11

CAR TRAVEL

A car allows you to explore Andalusia's mountain villages. Mountain driving can be hair-raising but is getting better as highways are improved.

Málaga is 536 km (335 miles) from Madrid, taking the A4 to Córdoba, then the A44 to Granada, the A92 to Antequera, and the A45; 162 km (101 miles) from Córdoba via Antequera; 220 km (138 miles) from Seville; and 131 km (82 miles) from Granada by the shortest route of A92 to Loja, then A45 to Málaga.

To take a car into Gibraltar you need, in theory, an insurance certificate and a logbook (a certificate of vehicle ownership). In practice, all you need is your passport. Head for the well-signposted multistory car park, as street parking on the Rock is scarce.

National Car-Rental Agencies Goldcar ☎ *902/119726* ⊕ *www.goldcar.es.*

TAXI TRAVEL

Taxis are plentiful throughout the Costa del Sol and may be hailed on the street or from specified taxi ranks marked "Taxi." Restaurants are usually happy to call a taxi for you, too. Fares are reasonable, and meters are strictly used. You are not required to tip taxi drivers, though rounding up the amount will be appreciated.

TRAIN TRAVEL

Málaga is the main rail terminus in the area, with 12 high-speed trains a day from Madrid (from 2 hours 25 minutes to 2 hours 50 minutes, depending on the train). Málaga is also linked by high-speed train with Barcelona (3 daily, 5 hours 45 minutes). Six daily trains also link Seville with Málaga in just under two hours.

From Granada to Málaga (3–3½ hours), you must change at Bobadilla, making buses more efficient from here (a high-speed AVE line is currently under construction from Granada to Antequera, due for completion in 2016). Málaga's train station is a 15-minute walk from the city center, across the river.

RENFE connects Málaga, Torremolinos, and Fuengirola, stopping at the airport and all resorts along the way. The train leaves Málaga every 20 minutes between 5:20 am and 11:30 pm and Fuengirola every half hour from 6:10 am to 11:50 pm. For the city center, get off at the last stop. A daily train connects Málaga and Ronda via the dramatic Chorro gorge. The travel time is 1 hour 45 minutes.

RESTAURANTS

Málaga is best for traditional Spanish cooking, with a wealth of bars and seafood restaurants serving fritura malagueña, the city's famous fried seafood. Torremolinos's Carihuela district is also a good destination for lovers of Spanish seafood. The area's resorts serve every conceivable foreign cuisine, from Thai to the Scandinavian smorgasbord. For delicious cheap eats, try the chiringuitos. Strung out along the beaches, these summer-only restaurants serve seafood fresh off the boats. Because there are so many foreigners here, meals on the coast are served earlier than elsewhere in Andalusia; most restaurants open at 1 or 1:30 for lunch and 7 or 8 for dinner.

HOTELS

Most hotels on the developed stretch between Torremolinos and Fuengirola offer large, functional rooms near the sea at competitive rates, but the area's popularity as a budget destination means that most such hotels are booked in high season by package-tour operators. Finding a room at Easter, in July and August, or over holiday weekends can be difficult if you haven't reserved in advance. In July and August many hotels require a stay of at least three days. Málaga is an increasingly attractive base for visitors to this corner of Andalusia and has some good hotels. Marbella, meanwhile, has more than its fair share of grand lodgings, including some of Spain's most expensive rooms. Gibraltar's handful of hotels tends to be more expensive than most comparable lodgings in Spain.

There are also apartments and villas for short- or long-term stays, ranging from traditional Andalusian farmhouses to luxury villas. An excellent source for apartment and villa rentals is **Spain Holiday** (☎ 952/204435 ⊕ *www.spain-holiday.com*). For Marbella, you can also try **Nordica Rentals** (☎ 952/811552 ⊕ *www.nordicarentals.com*), and, for high-end rentals, ⊕ *www.theluxuryvillacollection.com*. Our local writers vet every hotel to recommend the best overnights in each price category, from budget to expensive. Unless otherwise specified, you can expect a private bath, phone, and TV in your room. *Hotel reviews have been shortened. For full information, visit Fodors.com.*

WHAT IT COSTS IN EUROS				
	$	$$	$$$	$$$$
Restaurants	under €13	€13–€17	€18–€22	over €22
Hotels	under €91	€91–€125	€126–€180	over €180

Restaurant prices are the average cost of a main course or equivalent combination of smaller dishes at dinner. Hotel prices are the lowest cost of a standard double room in high season.

GOLF IN THE SUN

Nicknamed the "Costa del Golf," the Sun Coast has some 45 golf courses within putting distance of the Mediterranean. Most of the courses are between Rincón de la Victoria (east of Málaga) and Gibraltar, and the best time for golfing is October to June; greens fees are lower in high summer. Check out the comprehensive website ⊕ *www.golfinspain.com* for up-to-date information.

TOURS

Several companies run one- and two-day excursions from Costa del Sol resorts. You can book with local travel agents and hotels; excursions leave from Málaga, Torremolinos, Fuengirola, Marbella, and Estepona, with prices varying by departure point. Most tours last half a day, and in most cases you can be picked up at your hotel. Popular tours include Málaga, Gibraltar, the Cuevas de Nerja, Mijas, Tangier, and Ronda. The Costa del Sol's varied landscape is also wonderful for hiking and walking, and several companies offer walking or cycling tours.

Tour Operators Bicycling Holidays. A good range of rural and urban guided cycling tours to suit all levels. ☎ *952/471720* ⊕ *www.sierracycling.com* ✉ *From €480 a week.* **John Keo Walking Tours.** This company provides guided walks and hikes around eastern Costa del Sol, weekdays only. Reservations are essential. ☎ *647/273502* ⊕ *www.hikingwalkingspain.com* ✉ *From €15.* **Julia Travel.** One of the largest tour operators in Spain, with a good selection of excursions on the Costa del Sol. ☎ *917/690707* ⊕ *www.juliatravel.com* ✉ *From €4.50.* **Viajes Rusadir.** This local firm specializes in Costa del Sol excursions and private tours. ☎ *952/463458* ⊕ *www.viajesrusadir.com* ✉ *Prices vary.*

VISITOR INFORMATION

The official website for the Costa del Sol is ⊕ *www.visitacostadelsol. com*; it has good information on sightseeing and events, guides to towns and villages, as well as contact details for the regional and local tourist offices, which are listed under their respective towns and cities. Tourist offices are generally open Monday–Saturday 10–7 (until 8 in summer) and Sunday 10–2.

THE COSTA DE ALMERÍA

South of Spain's Murcia Coast lie the shores of Andalusia, beginning with the Costa de Almería. Several of the coastal towns here, including Agua Amarga, have a laid-back charm, with miles of sandy beaches and a refreshing lack of high-rise developments. The mineral riches of the surrounding mountains gave rise to Iberia's first true civilization, whose capital can still be glimpsed in the 4,700-year-old ruins of Los Millares, near the village of Santa Fe de Mondújar. The small towns of Níjar and Sorbas maintain an age-old tradition of pottery making and other crafts, and the western coast of Almería has tapped unexpected wealth from a parched land, thanks to modern techniques of growing produce in plastic greenhouses. In contrast to the inhospitable landscape of the mountain-fringed Andarax Valley, the area east of Granada's Alpujarras, near Alhama, has a cool climate and gentle landscape, both conducive to making fine wines.

THE CABO DE GATA NATURE RESERVE

40 km (25 miles) east of Almería, 86 km (53 miles) south of Mojácar.

The southeast corner of Spain is one of the country's last unspoiled wildernesses, and much of the coastline is part of a highly protected nature reserve. San José, the largest village, has a pleasant bay, though these days the village has rather outgrown itself and can be very busy in summer. Those preferring smaller, quieter destinations should look farther north, at places such as Agua Amarga and the often-deserted beaches nearby.

GETTING HERE AND AROUND

You need your own wheels to explore the nature reserve and surrounding villages, including San José. When it's time to hit the beach, Playa de los Genoveses and Playa Monsul, to the south of San José, are some of the best. A rough road follows the coast around the spectacular cape,

Costa de Almería and Costa Tropical

SIERRA DE LOS FILABRES

SIERRA NEVADA

SIERRA DE GADOR

SIERRA DE LA CONTRAVIESA

SIERRA DE ALMIJARA

ALMERIA

GRANADA

JAEN

CÓRDOBA

MÁLAGA

COSTA DE ALMERÍA

COSTA TROPICAL

Mediterranean Sea

Gulf of Almería

San José and Cabo de Gata Nature Reserve
Agua Amarga
San José
Faro de Cabo de Gata (lighthouse)
Cabo de Gata
El Cabo de Gata
Playa de los Muertos

Carboneras
Garrucha
Huércal-Overa
Almería
Roquetas de Mar
Almerimar
El Ejido
Adra
Berja
Guardias Viejas
Playa de Balerma
Benahadux
Gérgal
Serón
Baza
Olula del Río
Tabernas

Ugíjar
Cádiar
Órgiva
Lanjarón
Dúrcal
Padul
Mulhacén 3,482m
Pico Veleta 3,394m

Castell de Ferro
Calahonda
Cabo Sacratif
Motril
Salobreña
Almuñécar
Playa de Velilla
Nerja
Cuevas de Nerja
Frigiliana
Torrox
Torre del Mar
Vélez-Málaga
Rincón de la Victoria
The Axarquía
Playa de Burriana

Guadix
Granada
Santa Fe
Guadahortuna
Alcalá la Real
Montefrío
Alhama de Granada
Loja
Archidona
Antequera
Casabermeja
Málaga
Torremolinos
Alcaudete
Baena
Cabra

10 mi
10 km

A7
A334
A315
A92
A44
A401
A323
A308
A92
A92
A338
A4155
A400
A356
A45
A92
A333
A316
A333
N432
N432
A92
A347
A347
N340
N340
N340
A348
A337
A7
A7
A4050
A7

eventually linking up with the N332 to Almería. Alternatively, follow the signs north for the towns of Níjar (approximately 20 km [12½ miles] north) and Sorbas (32 km [20 miles] northeast of Níjar); both towns are famed for their distinctive green-glazed pottery, which you can buy directly from the workshops.

EXPLORING

Parque Natural Marítimo y Terrestre Cabo de Gata–Níjar. Birds are the main attraction at this nature reserve just south of San José; it's home to several species native to Africa, including the *camachuelo trompetero* (large-beaked bullfinch), which is not found anywhere else outside Africa. Check out the Centro Las Amoladeras visitor center at the park entrance, which has an exhibit and information on the region and organizes guided walks and tours of the area. ✉ *Road from Almería to Cabo de Gata, Km 6* ☎ *950/380299* 🌐 *www.cabodegata-nijar.com* 🕒 *Daily 10–2 and 5–8.*

BEACHES

El Playazo. *Playazo* literally means "one great beach," and this sandy cove is certainly one of the gems in the Cabo de Gata Nature Reserve. Just a few minutes' drive from the village of Rodalquilar (once home to Spain's only gold mine), the yellow-sand beach is surrounded by ocher-colored volcanic rock; an 18th-century fortress stands at one end. These are sheltered waters, so bathing is safe and warm, and the offshore rocks make for great snorkeling. This beach is deserted during most of the year, and its isolation and lack of amenities mean that even in the summer months you won't come across too many other beachgoers. Although nude bathing isn't officially allowed here, it is tolerated. **Amenities:** none. **Best for:** snorkeling; solitude; sunrise. ✉ *Rodalquilar* 💳 *No credit cards.*

Playa de los Genoveses. Named after the Genovese sailors who landed here in 1127 to aid King Alfonso VII, this beach is one of the area's best-known and most beautiful. The long, sandy expanse is backed by pines, eucalyptus trees, and low-rising dunes. The sea is shallow, warm, and crystal clear here—snorkeling is popular around the rocks at either end of the cove. Parking is available September through June; in July and August you must park in nearby San José and take a minibus to the beach. The beach can also be reached via an easy coastal walk from San José, a 7-km (4½-mile) round trip. The beach has no amenities to speak of, so take plenty of water if it's hot. **Amenities:** parking (seasonal). **Best for:** snorkeling; solitude; sunset; walking. 💳 *No credit cards.*

WHERE TO STAY

$ B&B/INN 🏨 **Hostal La Isleta.** This low-rise, white, blocky building with blue trim is nothing fancy—what you're paying for is the location, within a stone's throw of the beach on a charming bay, with superb, relaxing sea views. **Pros:** fabulous location. **Cons:** no frills; can be noisy with families in summer. [$] *Rooms from: €50* ✉ *C. Isleta del Moro* ☎ *950/389713* 🛏 *10 rooms* 🍴 *No meals.*

Dramatic views of the coastline from Cabo de Gata Natural Park

AGUA AMARGA

22 km (14 miles) north of San José, 55 km (30 miles) east of Almería.

Like other coastal hamlets, Agua Amarga started out in the 18th century as a tuna-fishing port. These days, as perhaps the most pleasant village on the Cabo de Gata coast, it attracts lots of visitors, although it remains much less developed than San José. One of the coast's best beaches is just to the north: the dramatically named **Playa de los Muertos** (Beach of the Dead), a long stretch of fine gravel bookended with volcanic outcrops.

GETTING HERE AND AROUND

If you're driving here from Almería, follow signs to the airport, then continue north on the A7; Agua Amarga is signposted just north of the Parque Natural Cabo de Gata. The village itself is small enough to explore on foot.

WHERE TO EAT AND STAY

$$$ MEDITERRANEAN

🍴 **La Villa.** Mediterranean and international dishes blend seamlessly at this intimate restaurant. Its three main rooms are all romantically, somewhat dimly lit, a theme carried through to the outside dining area around the pool. Diners come from far and wide for the Nebraska Angus burgers, marinated grilled octopus over aromatic tabbouleh, and foie-gras ravioli with a creamy wine sauce. Sit under the stars at the outside bar for a summer cocktail. [$] *Average main: €18* ✉ *Ctra. Carboneras 18, Agua Amarga* ☎ *950/138090* ✍ *Reservations essential* ⏲ *Closed mid-Jan.–mid-Mar. No lunch.*

$$$ HOTEL **MiKasa.** This complex includes a small and stylish hotel, with spa and wellness center, plus MiKasa La Joya (suites) and MiKasa Villas—the latter comprising seven smart town houses. **Pros:** wonderful breakfasts; heated pool; feels like a romantic hideaway. **Cons:** could be too quiet for some; not suitable for young children or late-night partying. [$] *Rooms from: €130* ✉ *Ctra. de Carboneras 16, Agua Amarga* ☎ *950/138073* 🌐 *www.mikasasuites.com* 🛏 *18 rooms, 12 suites, 7 townhouses* 🍴 *Breakfast.*

ALMERÍA

183 km (114 miles) east of Málaga.

Warmed by the sunniest climate in Andalusia, Almería is a youthful Mediterranean city, basking in sweeping views of the sea from its coastal perch and close to several beaches. It's also a capital of the grape industry, thanks to its wonderfully mild climate in spring and fall. Rimmed by tree-lined boulevards and some landscaped squares, the city's core is a maze of narrow, winding alleys formed by flat-roof, distinctly Mudejar houses. Now surrounded by modern apartment blocks, these dazzling-white older homes continue to give Almería an Andalusian flavor.

GETTING HERE AND AROUND

The No. 20 bus runs roughly every 70 minutes from Almería airport to the center of town (Calle del Doctor Gregorio Marañón).

The city center is compact, and most of the main sights are within easy strolling distance of each other.

ESSENTIALS

Visitor Information Almería Visitor Information ✉ *Pl. de la Constitución* ☎ *950/210538* 🌐 *www.almeria-turismo.org.*

EXPLORING

Alcazaba. Dominating the city is this fortress, built by Caliph Abd ar-Rahman I and given a bell tower by Carlos III. From here you have sweeping views of the port and city. Among the ruins of the fortress, which was damaged by earthquakes in 1522 and 1560, are landscaped gardens of rock flowers and cacti. ✉ *C. Almanzor* ☎ *950/801008* 🎫 *Free* 🕒 *June–Sept. 15, Mon.–Sat. 9–3:30 and 6:30–10, Sun. 10–5; Sept. 16–Mar., Tues.–Sat. 9–6:30, Sun. 10–5; Apr.and May, Tues.–Sun. 9–8, Sun. 10–5.*

Cathedral. Below the Alcazaba is the local cathedral, with buttressed towers that give it the appearance of a castle. It's in Gothic style, but with some classical touches around the doors. Guided tours are available, and admission includes a visit to the ecclesiastical museum. ✉ *Pl. de la Catedral* 🎫 *€5* 🕒 *Weekdays 10–1:30 and 4–5, Sat. 10–1:30.*

Refugios de la Guerra Civil (*Civil War Shelters*). Almería, the last bastion of the Republican government during the Spanish Civil War, was heavily bombed via air and sea by Nationalist forces. To protect civilians, 4½ km (2¾ miles) of tunnels were built under the city to provide shelter for over 34,000 people. About 1 km (½ mile) can now be visited on a tour that covers the food stores, sleeping quarters, and an operating theater for the wounded, with its original medical equipment. Visits, which are guided, must be booked by phone in advance. ✉ *Pl. Manuel Pérez García s/n* ☎ *950/268696* 🎫 *€3* 🕒 *June–Sept., Tues.–Thurs. and Sun. 10:30–1:30, Fri. and Sat. 10:30–1:30 and 6–9; Oct.–May, Tues.–Thurs. and Sun. 10–1, Fri. and Sat. 10–1 and 5–8.*

OFF THE BEATEN PATH

Los Millares. This important archaeological site is 2.3 km (1½ miles) southwest from the village of Santa Fe de Mondújar and 19 km (12 miles) from Almería. This collection of ruins scattered on a windswept hilltop was the birthplace of civilization in Spain nearly 5,000 years ago. Large, dome-shape tombs show that the community had an advanced society, and the existence of formidable defense walls indicates it had something to protect. A series of concentric fortifications shows that the settlement increased in size, eventually holding some 2,000 people. The town was inhabited from 2700 to 1800 BC and came to dominate the entire region. Guided tours are available; call in advance to book. Allow two hours for your visit. ✉ *Santa Fe de Mondújar* ☎ *677/903404* 🎫 *Free* 🕒 *Wed.–Sun. 10–2.*

WHERE TO EAT AND STAY

$$ SPANISH

🍴 **La Encina.** This justly popular restaurant is housed in an 1860s building that also incorporates an 11th-century Moorish well. Time may have stood still with the setting, but the cuisine reflects a modern twist on traditional dishes, including seafood mains like *merluza en papillote con almejas y gambas* (hake with clams and shrimp, cooked in parchment) or *carpaccio de champiñón a lo Idiazábal* (mushroom "carpaccio" with Idiazabal, a traditional Basque cheese). There's also a reasonably priced and generous tasting menu (€35), and the wine and gin lists are among the best in the city. The restaurant is fronted by a popular tapas bar (€2.50 including drink) that is generally filled with a boisterous business crowd. [$] *Average main: €17* ✉ *C. Marín 3* ☎ *950/273429* 🌐 *www.restaurantelaencina.es* 🕒 *Closed Mon.*

$$$ SPANISH

🍴 **Valentín.** This popular, central spot serves fine regional specialties, such as *cazuela de rape* (monkfish baked in a sauce of almonds and pine nuts), *arroz negro* (rice flavored with squid ink), and the deliciously simple *pescado en adobo* (dogfish baked in clay with garlic, oregano, and paprika). If you're open to serious credit-card overdrive, go for the lobster. The surroundings are rustic-yet-elegant Andalusian: whitewashed walls, dark wood, and exposed brick. Come on the early side (around 9) to get a table for dinner. [$] *Average main: €18* ✉ *Tenor Iribarne 10* ☎ *950/264475.*

$ HOTEL

🏨 **AC Almería.** Covered in creams, beiges, and browns, this hotel, part of the Marriott chain, is modern and corporate, and in a good location. **Pros:** good value; great for people-watching on the plaza. **Cons:** can be crowded with business and tour groups; parking not included in price. [$] *Rooms from: €70* ✉ *P. de las Flores, 5* ☎ *950/234999* 🌐 *www.marriott.com* 🛏 *97 rooms* 🍽 *No meals.*

$ HOTEL

🏨 **Nuevo Torreluz.** Value is the overriding attraction at this comfortable and elegant modern hotel, which has slick, bright rooms and the kind of amenities you'd expect to come at a higher price. **Pros:** great central location; large rooms; good value. **Cons:** no pool; breakfast served in hotel next door. [$] *Rooms from: €55* ⌷ *Pl. de las Flores 10* ☎ *950/234399* ⊕ *www.torreluz.com* ⮌ *98 rooms* ❏❘ *No meals.*

$$$
HOTEL

⌶ **Plaza Vieja Hotel & Lounge.** In the heart of the old quarter, early-19th-century architecture sits comfortably beside all comfortable and up-to-date amenities in this boutique hotel with strong design features. **Pros:** personal service; central location; designer look. **Cons:** the bathrooms are in view from the rest of the guest rooms; poor noise insulation in hotel. [$] *Rooms from: €129* ⌷ *Pl. de la Constitución 4* ☎ *950/282096* ⊕ *www.plazaviejahl.com* ⮌ *6 rooms, 4 suites* ❏❘ *No meals.*

NIGHTLIFE

In Almería, the action's on **Plaza Flores,** moving down to the beach in summer.

Peña El Taranto. This excellent venue is one of the main centres for flamenco in Andalusia (it celebrated its 50th anniversary in 2013), and foot-stomping live flamenco is performed every two weeks, from mid-October to May. Check ahead of time for the exact times and dates. ⌷ *C. Tenor Iribame 20* ☎ *950/235057* ⊕ *www.eltaranto.com.*

THE COSTA TROPICAL

East of Málaga and west of Almería lies the Costa Tropical. Housing developments resemble buildings in Andalusian villages rather than the bland high-rises elsewhere, and its tourist onslaught has been mild. A flourishing farming center, the area earns its keep from tropical fruit, including avocados, mangoes, and pawpaws (also known as custard apples). You may find packed beaches and traffic-choked roads at the height of the season, but for most of the year the Costa Tropical is relatively free of other tourists, if not also devoid of expatriates.

◸
EN
ROUTE

Salobreña. About 13 km (8 miles) east of Almuñécar, this unspoiled village of near-perpendicular streets and old white houses on a steep hill beneath a Moorish fortress is a true Andalusian pueblo, separated from the beachfront restaurants and bars in the newer part of town. It's great for a quick visit. You can reach Salobreña by descending through the mountains from Granada or by continuing west from Almería on A7.

ALMUÑÉCAR

85 km (53 miles) east of Málaga.

This small-time resort with a shingle beach is popular with Spanish and Northern European vacationers. It's been a fishing village since Phoenician times, 3,000 years ago, when it was called Sexi; later, the Moors built a castle here for the treasures of Granada's kings. The road west from Motril and Salobreña passes through what was the empire of the sugar barons, who brought prosperity to Málaga's province in the 19th century: the cane fields now give way to lychees, limes, mangoes, pawpaws, and olives.

The village is actually two, separated by the dramatic rocky headland of Punta de la Mona. To the east is Almuñécar proper, and to the west is **La Herradura,** a quiet fishing community. Between the two is the

A religious procession in Almuñécar

Marina del Este yacht harbor, which, along with La Herradura, is a popular diving center.

GETTING HERE AND AROUND
The A7 highway runs north of town. There is an efficient bus service to surrounding towns and cities, including Málaga, Granada, Nerja, and, closer afield, La Herradura. Almuñécar's town center is well laid out for strolling, and the local tourist office has information on bicycle and scooter rental.

ESSENTIALS
Visitor Information Almuñécar ✉ *Palacete de la Najarra, Av. de Europa* ☎ *958/631125.*

EXPLORING
Castillo de San Miguel (*St. Michael's Castle*). A Roman fortress once stood here, later enlarged by the Moors, but the castle's present aspect, crowning the city, owes more to 16th-century additions. The building was bombed during the Peninsular War in the 19th century, and what was left was used as a cemetery until the 1990s. You can wander the ramparts and peer into the dungeon; the skeleton at the bottom is a reproduction of human remains discovered on the spot. ✉ *C. San Miguel Bajo* 🖾 *€2.35, includes admission to Cueva de Siete Palacios* ⊙ *July–mid-Sept., Tues.–Sat. 10–1:30 and 6:30–9, Sun. 10–1; mid-Sept.–Oct. and Apr.–June, Tues.–Sat. 10–1:30 and 5–7:30, Sun. 10–1; Nov.–Mar., Tues.–Sat. 10–1:30 and 4–6:30, Sun. 10–1.*

Cueva de Siete Palacios (*Cave of Seven Palaces*). Beneath the Castillo de San Miguel is this large, vaulted, stone cellar of Roman origin, now Almuñécar's archaeological museum. The collection is small but interesting, with Phoenician, Roman, and Moorish artifacts. ✉ *C. San Miguel Bajo* 🎫 *€2.35, includes admission to Castillo de San Miguel* 🕒 *July–mid-Sept., Tues.–Sat. 10–1:30 and 6:30–9, Sun. 10–1; mid-Sept.–Oct. and Apr.–June, Tues.–Sat. 10–1:30 and 5–7:30, Sun. 10–1; Nov.–Mar., Tues.–Sat. 10–1:30 and 4–6:30, Sun. 10–1.*

WHERE TO EAT AND STAY

$ INTERNATIONAL Fodor's Choice ★ 🍴 **El Arbol Blanco.** Though slightly away from the center of town, it's worth the hike to dine at this superb restaurant run by the congenial brothers Jorge and Nacho Rodriguez; they provide excellent service. The light and airy dining room is elegantly decorated with sunny yellow tablecloths and colorful art on the walls, and there's a covered terrace as well. The dishes, all creatively presented, include traditional options like the oven-baked lamb, as well as more innovative choices like monkfish in a creamy leek sauce, which goes well with the excellent local white wine, Calvente blanco. The desserts are sublime, particularly the cheesecake. [$] *Average main: €12* ✉ *Av. de la Costa del Sol, Urbanización Costa Banana s/n* ☎ *958/631629* 🕒 *Closed Wed.*

$ HOTEL 🏨 **Casablanca.** This quaint, family-run hotel comes with a pink-and-white neo-Moorish facade, a choice location next to the beach and near the botanical park, and comfortable rooms that are all different. **Pros:** family-run; atmospheric. **Cons:** rooms vary, and some are small; parking can be difficult. [$] *Rooms from: €70* ✉ *Pl. San Cristóbal 4* ☎ *958/635575* 🌐 *www.hotelcasablancaalmunecar.com* 🛏 *39 rooms* 🍽 *No meals.*

NERJA

52 km (32 miles) east of Málaga, 22 km (14 miles) west of Almuñécar.

Nerja—the name comes from the Moorish word *narixa,* meaning "abundant springs"—has a large community of expats, who live mainly outside town in *urbanizaciones* ("village" developments). The old village is on a headland above small beaches and rocky coves, which offer reasonable swimming despite the gray, gritty sand. In July and August, Nerja is packed with tourists, but the rest of the year it's a pleasure to wander the old town's narrow streets.

GETTING HERE AND AROUND

Nerja is a speedy hour's drive east from Málaga on the A7. If you're driving, park in the underground lot just west of the Balcón de Europa (it's signposted) off Calle La Cruz. The town is small enough to explore on foot.

ESSENTIALS

Visitor Information Nerja ✉ *C. Carmen 1* ☎ *952/521531* 🌐 *www.nerja.org.*

EXPLORING

FAMILY Fodor's Choice ★ **Balcón de Europa.** The highlight of Nerja, this tree-lined promenade is on a promontory just off the central square, with magnificent views of the mountains and sea. You can gaze far off into the horizon using the strategically placed telescopes, or use this as a starting point for a horse and carriage clip-clop ride around town.

Cuevas de Nerja (*Nerja Caves*). Located between Almuñécar and Nerja, these caves are on a road surrounded by giant cliffs and dramatic seascapes. Signs point to the cave entrance above the village of Maro, 4 km (2½ miles) east of Nerja. Its spires and turrets, created by millennia of dripping water, are now floodlit for better views. One suspended pinnacle, 200 feet long, is the world's largest known stalactite. The cave painting of seals discovered here may be the oldest example of art in existence—and the only ones known to have been painted by Neanderthals. The awesome subterranean chambers create an evocative setting for concerts and ballets during the Nerja Festival of Music and Dance, held annually during the third week of July. There is also a bar-restaurant near the entrance with a spacious dining room that has superb views. ■ **TIP→ Visits take at 45 minutes so arrive at least an hour before closing time. Private tours in English are available (€15, info@cuevasdenerja.es).** ✉ *Maro* ☎ *952/529520* 🌐 *www.cuevadenerja.com* 🎟 *€9* 🕓 *July and Aug., daily 10–7; Sept.–June, daily 10–1:30 and 4–6:30.*

OFF THE BEATEN PATH

Frigiliana. On an inland mountain ridge overlooking the sea, this village has spectacular views and an old quarter of narrow, cobbled streets and dazzling white houses decorated with pots of geraniums. It was the site of one of the last battles between the Christians and the Moors. Frigiliana is a short drive from the highway to the village; if you don't have a car, you can take a bus here from Nerja, which is 8 km (5 miles) away.

BEACHES

Las Alberquillas. One of the string of coves on the coastline west of Nerja, this beach of gray sand mixed with shingle is backed by pine trees and scrub that perfume the air. Reachable only via a stony track down the cliffs, this protected beach is one of the few on the Costa del Sol to be almost completely untouched by tourism. Its moderate waves mean you need to take care when bathing. The snorkeling around the rocks at either end of the beach is among the best in the area. This spot's seclusion makes the beach a favorite with couples and nudists—it's quiet even at the height of summer. Limited parking is available off the N340 highway, but there are no amenities, so take plenty of water. **Amenities:** none. **Best for:** nudists; snorkeling; solitude. ✉ *N340, Km 299.*

WHERE TO EAT AND STAY

$ SPANISH

🍴 **El Mesón de Julio.** Check the blackboard outside this longstanding and reliably good restaurant for the day's specialties and the long list of tapas. There's comfortable seating outside on the terrace or in an attractive pine-clad interior with bare brick columns, wood beams, and an inviting bar (tapas €1.50). The menu includes familiar Andalusian standbys like steaks and lamb chops, along with fish dishes and more international options, including deep-fried Camembert with strawberry preserves and goat cheese, all in large portions. Julio's is popular with the local business community at midday, so get here early if you want a table for lunch. [$] *Average main: €12* ✉ *C. Cristo 7* ☎ *952/521190.*

$ B&B/INN Fodor's Choice ★

🏨 **Hotel Carabeo.** Down a side street near the center of town but still near the sea, this British-owned boutique hotel combines a great location and views with comfortable, pleasant rooms. **Pros:** friendly owners; great location. **Cons:** not open out of season. [$] *Rooms from: €85*

Views of the Mediterranean Sea, with the mountains in the background

✉ *C. Hernando de Carabeo 34* ☎ *952/525444* ⊕ *www.hotelcarabeo.com* 🛏 *7 rooms* ⊘ *Closed late Oct.–late Mar.* ⦿| *Breakfast.*

NIGHTLIFE AND PERFORMING ARTS
El Colono. Although the flamenco show is undeniably touristy, this club has an authentic *olé* atmosphere. The food is good, and local specialties, including paella, are served. Dinner shows (€38), with a three-course meal, begin at 9 pm on Wednesday from March until December. ✉ *C. Granada 6* ☎ *952/521826* ⊘ *Closed Jan. and Feb.*

THE AXARQUÍA

Vélez-Málaga: 36 km (22 miles) east of Málaga.

The Axarquía region stretches from Nerja to Málaga, and the area's charm lies in its mountainous interior, peppered with pueblos, vineyards, and tiny farms. Its coast consists of narrow, pebbly beaches and drab fishing villages on either side of the high-rise resort town of Torre del Mar.

GETTING HERE AND AROUND
Although the bus routes are fairly comprehensive throughout the Axarquía, reaching the smaller villages may involve long delays; renting a car is convenient and lets you get off the beaten track and experience some of the beautiful unspoiled hinterland in this little-known area. The four-lane A7 highway speeds across the region a few miles in from the coast; traffic on the old coastal road (N340) is slower.

ESSENTIALS
Visitor Information Cómpeta ✉ *Av. de la Constitucion* ☎ *952/553685.*

EXPLORING

Ruta del Sol y del Vino and the Ruta de la Pasa. The Axarquía has a number of tourist trails that take in the best of local scenery, history, and culture. Two of the best are the Ruta del Sol y del Vino (Sunshine and Wine Trail), through Algarrobo, Cómpeta (the main wine center), and Nerja; and the Ruta de la Pasa (Raisin Trail), which goes through Moclinejo, El Borge, and Comares. The trails are especially spectacular during the late-summer grape-harvest season or in late autumn, when the leaves of the vines turn gold. A visit to nearby Macharaviaya (7 km [4 miles] north of Rincón de la Victoria) might lead you to ponder this sleepy village's past glory: in 1776 one of its sons, Bernardo de Gálvez, became the Spanish governor of Louisiana and later fought in the American Revolution (Galveston, Texas, is named for him). Macharaviaya prospered under his heirs and for many years enjoyed a lucrative monopoly on the manufacture of playing cards for South America. 💳 *No credit cards.*

Vélez-Málaga. Vélez-Málaga is the capital of the Axarquía: it's a pleasant agricultural town of white houses, strawberry fields, and vineyards. Worth quick visits are the **Thursday market,** the ruins of a **Moorish castle,** and the church of **Santa María la Mayor,** built in the Mudejar style on the site of a mosque that was destroyed when the town fell to the Christians in 1487.

WHERE TO EAT AND STAY

$ SPANISH 🍴 **Museo del Vino.** There's no museum here—instead it's a rambling arts-and-crafts shop, a bodega lined with barrels and bottles of muscatel wine, and a restaurant. The latter is suitably rustic, with brick walls and a wood-beam ceiling. Start out the evening sampling the local wines (they're sold in plastic flagons), and tasty tapas, including pungent Manchego cheese, cured hams, and garlic-spiked olives. If you're still hungry, settle in for a full meal featuring grilled meats and baked suckling pig, the house specialty. [$] *Average main: €11* ✉ *Av. Constitución s/n, Cómpeta* ☎ *952/553314* 🌐 *www.museodelvinocompeta.com* 🕒 *Closed Mon.*

$ B&B/INN 🏨 **Hotel Rural Alberdini.** A couple of kilometers out of town, this rural inn has colorful mosaics, tiles, and other features, all put together in a Gaudí-esque style. **Pros:** very reasonably priced. **Cons:** long walk to village; hotels rooms can be noisy. [$] *Rooms from: €40* ✉ *Pago La Lornilla 85, Cómpeta* ☎ *952/516294* 🌐 *www.alberdini.com* 🛏 *7 rooms, 4 bungalows* 🍽 *Breakfast.*

MÁLAGA PROVINCE

The city of Málaga and the provincial towns of the upland hills and valleys to the north create the kind of contrast that makes travel in Spain so tantalizing. The region's Moorish legacy—tiny streets honeycombing the steamy depths of Málaga, the layout of the farms, and the crops themselves, including olives, grapes, oranges, and lemons—is a unifying visual theme. Ronda and the whitewashed villages of Andalusia behind the Costa del Sol make for one of Spain's most scenic and emblematic driving routes.

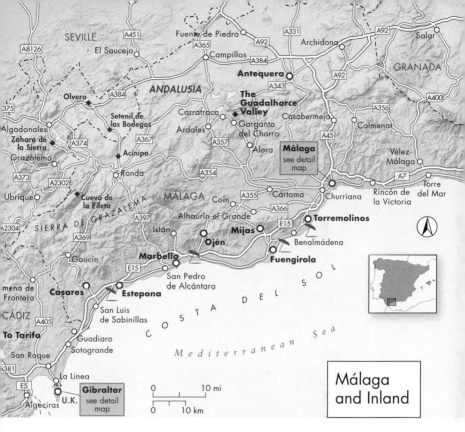

To the west of Málaga, along the coast, the sprawling outskirts of Torremolinos signal that you're entering the Costa del Sol, with its beaches, high-rise hotels, and serious number of tourists. On the far west, you can still discern Estepona's fishing village and Moorish old quarter amid its booming coastal development. Just inland, Casares piles whitewashed houses over the bright-blue Mediterranean below.

MÁLAGA

175 km (109 miles) southeast of Córdoba.

Málaga is one of southern Spain's most welcoming and happening cities, and it more than justifies a visit. Visitor figures have soared since the Picasso Museum opened a decade ago and a new cruise-ship terminal opened in 2011, and much of the city has had a well-earned face-lift. Many of its historic buildings have been restored or are undergoing restoration; the area between the river and the port is being spruced up and transformed into the Málaga Arte Urbano Soho (MAUS Art District); and some great shops, and lively bars and restaurants have sprung up all over the center.

True, the approach from the airport certainly isn't that pretty, and you'll be greeted by huge 1970s high-rises that march determinedly toward

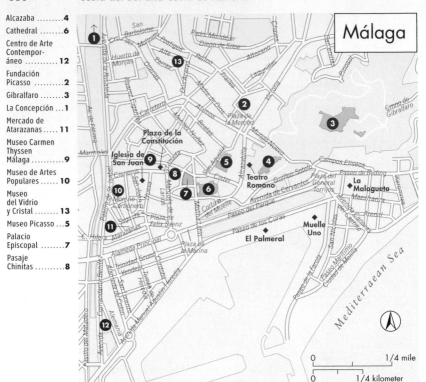

Torremolinos. But don't give up so soon: in its center and eastern suburbs, this city of about 550,000 people is a pleasant port, with ancient streets and lovely villas amid exotic foliage. Blessed with a subtropical climate, it's covered in lush vegetation and averages some 324 days of sunshine a year.

Central Málaga lies between the Guadalmedina River and the port, and the city's main attractions are all located here. The Centro de Arte Contemporáneo sits next to the river; to the east lies the MAUS district, slowly being hoisted from its former seedy red-light reputation to a vibrant art center with galleries and up-and-coming restaurants. Around La Alameda boulevard, with its giant weeping fig trees, is old-town Málaga: elegant squares, pedestrian shopping streets such as Calle Marqués de Larios, and the major monuments, which are often tucked away in labyrinthine alleys.

Eastern Málaga starts with the pleasant suburbs of El Palo and Pedregalejo, once traditional fishing villages. Here you can eat fresh fish in the numerous chiringuitos and stroll Pedregalejo's seafront promenade or the tree-lined streets of El Limonar. A few blocks inland is Málaga's bullring, **La Malagueta,** built in 1874, and continuing west, Muelle Uno (port-front commercial center). It's great for a drink and for soaking up views of the old quarter.

GETTING HERE AND AROUND

If you're staying at one of the coastal resorts between Málaga and Fuengirola, the easiest way to reach Málaga is via the train (every 20 minutes). If you're driving instead, there are several well-signposted underground parking lots, and it's not that daunting to negotiate by car. Note that the city is in the process of constructing the second section of a metro, the first of which is scheduled to open by 2015.

Málaga is mostly flat, so the best way to explore it is on foot or by bike via the good network of designated bike paths. To get an overview of the city in a day, hop on the Málaga Tour City Sightseeing Bus. There is a comprehensive bus network, too, and the tourist office can advise on routes and schedules.

Pick up a free audio guide to Málaga at the visitor information center in Plaza de la Marina. The guides talk you through the history and local anecdotes along five different walking routes. Guides are available for 48 hours' use, and you need to show your passport and a credit card.

ESSENTIALS

Airport Contact Aeropuerto Costa del Sol (AGP) (*Aeropuerto de Málaga*). ⊠ *Av. Comandante García Morato s/n* ☎ *952/048804* ⊕ *www.aena.es.*

Bike Rental Contact Málaga Bike Tours. A 4-hour guided bike tour round the city sights costs €25. Bikes are also available for rent. ⊠ *Calle Trinidad Grund 4* ☎ *606/978513* ⊕ *www.malagabiketours.eu.*

Bus Contact Málaga bus station ⊠ *Paseo de los Tilos* ☎ *952/350061* ⊕ *www. estabus.emtsam.es.*

Car Rental Contacts Europcar ⊠ *Málaga Costa del Sol Airport* ☎ *902/503010* ⊕ *www.europcar.es.* **Niza Cars** ⊠ *Málaga Costa del Sol Airport* ☎ *951/013520* ⊕ *www.nizacars.es.*

Taxi Company Unitaxi ☎ *952/320000* ⊕ *www.unitaxi.es.*

Tour Information Málaga Tour City Sightseeing Bus. This open-top, hop-on hop-off bus tour gives you an overview of Málaga's main sites in a day; it includes the Gibralfaro. Buy tickets online ahead of your trip or when you board the bus. ⊕ *www.city-sightseeing.com/tours/spain/malaga.htm* 🎫 *€16.50.* **Tapas in Málaga.** Eat your way around Málaga with a guided tour of some of its best tapas. Other tour options (from €55) cover the Picasso Museum and flamenco. ⊕ *www.tapasinmalaga.com.*

Train Information Málaga train station ⊠ *Explanada de la Estación* ☎ *902/320320* ⊕ *www.renfe.com.*

Visitor Information Málaga ⊠ *Pl. de la Marina, Paseo del Parque* ☎ *951/926620* ⊕ *www.malagaturismo.com.*

EXPLORING

TOP ATTRACTIONS

Alcazaba. Just beyond the ruins of a Roman theater on Calle Alcazabilla stands Málaga's greatest monument. This fortress was begun in the 8th century, when Málaga was the principal port of the Moorish kingdom, though most of the present structure dates from the 11th century. The inner palace was built between 1057 and 1063, when the Moorish emirs took up residence; Ferdinand and Isabella lived here for a while after conquering the city in 1487. The ruins are dappled with orange trees and bougainvillea and include a small museum; from the highest point you can see over the park and port. ⊠ *Entrance on C. Alcazabilla* ⌨ *€2.20, €3.55 combined entry with Gibralfaro* ⊘ *Nov.–Mar., Tues.– Sun. 9–6; Apr.–Oct., Tues.–Sun. 9:30–8.*

Málaga's Cathedral. Built between 1528 and 1782, the cathedral is a triumph, although a generally unappreciated one, having been left unfinished when funds ran out. Because it lacks one of its two towers, the building is nicknamed *La Manquita* (the One-Armed Lady). The enclosed choir, which miraculously survived the burnings of the civil war, is the work of 17th-century artist Pedro de Mena, who carved the wood wafer-thin in some places to express the fold of a robe or shape of a finger. The choir also has a pair of massive 18th-century pipe organs, one of which is still used for the occasional concert. Adjoining the cathedral is a small museum of religious art and artifacts. A walk around the cathedral on Calle Cister will take you to the magnificent Gothic Puerta del Sagrario. ⊠ *C. de Molina Larios* ☏ *952/215917* ⌨ *€5 (free on weekends)* ⊘ *Weekdays 10–6, Sat. 10–5, Sun. 2–6.*

Mercado de Atarazanas. From the Plaza Felix Saenz, at the southern end of Calle Nueva, turn onto Sagasta to reach the Mercado de Atarazanas. The typical, 19th-century, iron structure incorporates the original **Puerta de Atarazanas,** the exquisitely crafted 14th-century Moorish gate that once connected the city with the port. Don't miss the magnificent, stained-glass window depicting highlights of this historical port city as you stroll round the stalls, filled with local produce. ⊠ *C. de la Atarazanas* ⊘ *Mon.–Sat. 9–3.*

Fodor'sChoice   **Museo Picasso.** Part of the charm of this art gallery, one of the city's most ★   prestigious museums, is that its small collection is such a family affair. These are the works that Pablo Picasso kept for himself or gave to his family, including the heartfelt *Paulo con gorro blanco* (*Paulo with a White Cap*), a portrait of his firstborn son painted in the early 1920s; and *Olga Kokhlova con mantilla* (*Olga Kokhlova with Mantilla*), a 1917 portrait of his insane first wife. The holdings were largely donated by two family members—Christine and Bernard Ruiz-Picasso, the artist's daughter-in-law and her son. The works are displayed in chronological order according to the periods that marked Picasso's development as an artist, from Blue and Rose to Cubism and beyond. The museum is housed in a former palace where, during restoration work, Roman and Moorish remains were discovered. These are now on display, together with the permanent collection of Picassos and temporary exhibitions. Guided tours in English are available (book at least five days ahead). ⊠ *C. de San Agustín* ☏ *952/127600* ⊕ *www.museopicassomalaga.org* ⌨ *Permanent exhibition €7, combined permanent and temporary exhibition €9.50 (free Sun. 6–8)* ⊘ *Tues.–Thurs. and Sun. 10–8, Fri. and Sat. 10–9.*

WORTH NOTING

Centro de Arte Contemporáneo (*Contemporary Arts Center*). This museum includes photographic studies and paintings, some of them immense. The 7,900 square feet of bright exhibition hall are used to showcase

ultramodern artistic trends—the four exhibitions are used for a changing show from the permanent collection, two temporary shows, and one show dedicated to up-and-coming Spanish artists. The gallery attracts world-class modern artists like South African William Kentridge or the British duo Gilbert and George. Óleo, the riverside restaurant, is popular at lunchtime (closed Monday) and a favored summer evening venue for cocktails. Outside, don't miss the giant murals behind the museum painted by the street artists Shepard Fairey and Dean Stockton (aka D*Face). ✉ *Alemania s/n* ☎ *952/120055* ⊕ *www.cacmalaga.org* 🎫 *Free* ⊘ *Sept.–June, Tues.–Sun. 10–8; July and Aug., Tues.–Sun. 10–2 and 5–7.*

Fundación Picasso. Málaga's most famous native son, Pablo Picasso, was born here in 1881, in what's now the Fundación Picasso. The building has been painted and furnished in the style of the era and houses a permanent exhibition of the artist's early sketches and sculptures, as well as memorabilia, including his christening robe and family photos. ✉ *Pl. de la Merced 15* ☎ *951/926060* ⊕ *www.fundacionpicasso.es* 🎫 *€2* ⊘ *Daily 9:30–8.*

Gibralfaro (*fortress*). Surrounded by magnificent vistas and floodlit at night, these fortifications were built for Yusuf I in the 14th century; the Moors called them Jebelfaro, from the Arab word for "mount" and the Greek word for "lighthouse," after a beacon that stood here to guide ships into the harbor and warn of pirates. The lighthouse has been succeeded by a small parador (⇨ *see Where to Stay*). You can drive here by way of Calle Victoria or take a minibus that leaves 10 times a day, between 11 and 7, roughly every 45 minutes, from the bus stop in the park near the Plaza de la Marina. ✉ *Gibralfaro Mountain* 🎫 *€2.20, €3.55 combined entry with Alcazaba* ⊘ *Daily 9–6 (until 8 Apr.–Oct.).*

La Concepción. A 150-year-old botanical garden, La Concepción was created by the daughter of the British consul, who married a Spanish shipping magnate—the captains of the Spaniard's fleet had standing orders to bring back seedlings and cuttings from every "exotic" port of call. The garden is just off the exit road to Granada—too far to walk, but well worth the cab fare or the bus journey from the city center. Buses leave from La Alameda every hour, from 10 to 5. ✉ *Ctra. de las Pedrizas, Km 216* ☎ *952/250745* 🎫 *€5.20* ⊘ *Apr.–Sept., Tues.–Sun. 9:30–8:30; Oct.–Mar., Tues.–Sun. 9:30–5:30.*

▌**QUICK BITES**

Antigua Casa de Guardia. Around the corner from the Mercado de Atarazanas, this is Málaga's oldest bar, founded in 1840. Andalusian wines and finos (sherries) flow straight from the barrel, the walls are lined with sepia photos of old Málaga—including some of Picasso. The floor is ankle-deep in discarded shrimp shells. Closed Sunday. ✉ *C. Alameda 18* ☎ *952/214680.*

Museo Carmen Thyssen Málaga. Like Madrid, Málaga has its own branch of this museum, with over 200 works from Baroness Thyssen's private collection. Shown in a renovated 16th-century palace, the collection features mainly Spanish paintings from the 19th century, but does also have work from two great 20th-century artists, Joaquín Sorolla y Bastida and Romero de Torres. The museum also hosts regular exhibitions and talks and workshops on art. ✉ *C. Compañia 10* ☎ *902/303131* ⊕ *www.*

carmenthyssenmalaga.org 🎟 *€6 permanent exhibition, €4 temporary exhibition* 🕒 *Tues.–Sun. 10–8.*

FAMILY **Museo de Artes Populares** (*Arts and Crafts Museum*). In the old Mesón de la Victoria, a 17th-century inn, this museum displays horse-drawn carriages and carts, old agricultural implements, folk costumes, a forge, a bakery, an ancient grape press, and painted clay figures and ceramics. ✉ *Pasillo de Santa Isabel 10* ☎ *952/217137* 🌐 *www.museoartespopulares.com* 🎟 *€4* 🕒 *Weekdays 10–5, Sat. 10–2.*

SOMETHING SWEET

For coffee and cakes, malagueños favor Lepanto, the classy shop at Calle Marqués de Larios 7, where uniform-clad staff serve a variety of pastries, cakes, and other sweets. Just next door at Casa Mira is delicious homemade ice cream.

Museo del Vidrio y Cristal (*Museum of Glass and Crystal*). More than 3,000 pieces of glass and crystal, lovingly collected by the owner, are displayed throughout this 18th-century mansion, which is a museum piece in its own right. The pieces, whether ancient Egyptian or from Europe's Lalique and Whitefriars, give a unique insight into man's decorative use of glass. Visits are by guided tour only. ✉ *Plazuela Santísimo Cristo de la Sangre 2* ☎ *952/220271* 🌐 *www.museovidrioycristalmalaga.com* 🎟 *€5, includes guided tour* 🕒 *Sept.–July, Tues.–Sun. 11–7.*

Palacio Episcopal (*Bishop's Palace*). Facing the cathedral's main entrance, this is a fine 18th-century mansion with one of the most stunning facades in the city, as well as interesting interior details. The inside is only viewable when there are temporary exhibitions. ✉ *Pl. Obispo 6* ☎ *951/294051* 🎟 *Free* 🕒 *Tues. 2:30–8, Wed.–Sat. 10–8, Sun. 10–2.*

Pasaje Chinitas. The narrow streets and alleys on each side of Calle Marqués de Larios have charms of their own. The most famous is Pasaje Chinitas, off Plaza de la Constitución and named for the notorious Chinitas cabaret here. Peep into the dark, vaulted bodegas where old men down glasses of *seco añejo* or *Málaga Virgen,* local wines made from Málaga's muscatel grapes. Silversmiths and vendors of religious books and statues ply their trades in shops that have changed little since the early 1900s. Backtrack across Larios, and, in the streets leading to Calle Nueva, you can see shoeshine boys, lottery-ticket vendors, Gypsy guitarists, and tapas bars serving wine from huge barrels.

WHERE TO EAT

$$ MEDITERRANEAN 🍴 **El Palmeral.** Set among the Palm Walk near the cruise-ship terminal and with first-class views of the harbor, this restaurant quickly become a firm favorite with locals and visitors when it opened in 2012. Sit inside the modern glass cube for elegant dining or outside for a more informal meal (or just coffee). Try the homemade croquettes or octopus carpaccio for starters, and follow with one of the paellas—the highlight is the *arroz caldoso con bogavante* (creamy rice with lobster) or fresh fish. Make sure you leave plenty of room for the *canutillos de almendra con mousse de chocolate blanco* (almond snaps with white-chocolate mousse). Service is friendly and fast even when busy. [$] *Average main: €16* ✉ *Muelle 2* ☎ *648/675528* 🌐 *www.palmeralmalaga.com.*

$$ ✕ **El Trillo.** A longstanding favorite for traditional Andalusian cuisine, El
SPANISH   Trillo could fit in happily in Madrid with its hams over the bar, well-
worn tiles, and dark wood furniture. Alcoves add to the intimate feel,
and the outside tables overlook the smart shopping street Marques de
Larios. The menu includes Córdoba-style oxtail and house cod and hake
specialties, such as *suprema de bacalao a los cinco tomates* (cod fillets
in a creamy sauce with five different kinds of tomatoes). $ *Average
main: €14* ✉ *C. Don Juan Diaz 4* ☎ *952/603920* ⊕ *www.grupotrillo.es.*

$$ ✕ **La Plaza.** The pleasant terrace here, one of the few that gets the win-
SPANISH   ter afternoon sun in the city, overlooks the Plaza de la Merced and is a
couple of doors down from the Fundación Picasso, helping make it great
for people-watching. If you'd rather be inside, the tapas bar is cozy and
the dining room is elegant and airy. This all-day pit stop serves breakfast and tapas (the goat cheese with caramelized onion and beet is particularly good) as well as mains, which might include Moroccan lamb
couscous and a curry made with the rosada fish, with a mango cream
sauce. $ *Average main: €17* ✉ *Pl. de la Merced 18* ☎ *952/608491.*

$$ ✕ **Los Patios de Beatas.** Sandwiched between the Museo Picasso and Fun-
SPANISH   dación Picasso is one of Málaga's largest wine collections (there are over
Fodor'sChoice   500 on the list). The two historic mansions that make up this restaurant
★   include an original patio and 17th-century stone wine vats. Sit on bar
stools in the beamed tapas section, where the walls are lined with dozens
of wine bottles, or dine on the airy patio, which is covered with stained
glass. Each of the creative dishes here can be paired with its own wine
if you wish: marinated sardines with caramelized tomato and red tuna
tartare might come with manzanilla, for instance, and black cod with
purple potato and coconut sauce arrive with white Málaga wine. Wine
and olive-oil tasting sessions, led by the owner, are available on request,
or you can try three different wines at any time for €7.50. $ *Average
main: €14* ✉ *C. Beatas 43* ☎ *952/210350* ⊕ *www.lospatiosdebeatas.com.*

$$ ✕ **Tapadaki.** It isn't on the way to any of the main monuments, but a
ECLECTIC   visit to this tapas venue that fuses Mediterranean and Asian cuisine is
more than worth the slight detour. Inside, choose from bar seating or
more formal dining; there's also a pleasant outdoor terrace to enjoy
the unusual menu. Here, you'll find tapas (from €3) such as an octopus
kebab with smoked potato puree and peanut and lime sauce, an oxtail
spring roll, stewed lamb with kimchi sauce, and vegetable couscous as
well as an extensive sushi menu. Tapadaki is hugely popular with locals,
so book ahead to be sure of a seat. $ *Average main: €14* ✉ *Calle Car-
retería 69* ☎ *952/217966* ⊙ *Closed Mon. No dinner Sun.*

WHERE TO STAY

$ ⌂ **Castilla.** In 2013, this centrally located and gracious hotel underwent
HOTEL   a total refurbishment that brought it completely up-to-date. **Pros:** great
location between the city center and the port; parking. **Cons:** rooms are
small; no restaurant. $ *Rooms from: €58* ✉ *C. Córdoba 7* ☎ *952/218635*
⊕ *www.hotelcastillaguerrero.com* ⟿ *51 rooms* ⦿ *No meals.*

$$$ ⌂ **Parador de Málaga–Gibralfaro.** The attractive rooms at this cozy, gray-
HOTEL   stone parador are some of the best in Málaga, with spectacular views
Fodor'sChoice   of the city and the bay, so reserve well in advance. **Pros:** some of the
★   best views on the Costa; excellent service. **Cons:** some distance from

town; books up quickly. $\boxed{\$}$ *Rooms from: €145* ✉ *Monte de Gibralfaro s/n, Monte* ☎ *952/221902* ⊕ *www.parador.es* ↴ *38 rooms* ❧ *No meals.*

$ ❧ **Petit Palace Plaza Malaga.** The sumptuous historic exterior belies the
HOTEL modern interior and amenities in this sleek business-oriented hotel.
Pros: superb central location; great for business travel. **Cons:** may be too
corporate and modern for some; no bar. $\boxed{\$}$ *Rooms from: €80* ✉ *C. Nicasio 5* ☎ *952/222132* ⊕ *www.hthoteles.com* ↴ *66 rooms* ❧ *No meals.*

$$ ❧ **Room Mate Larios.** On the central Plaza de la Constitución, in the
HOTEL middle of a sophisticated shopping area, this elegantly restored 19th-
century building holds luxuriously furnished rooms. **Pros:** stylish; efficiently run. **Cons:** on busy shopping street that can be noisy in daytime;
interior rooms are dark. $\boxed{\$}$ *Rooms from: €100* ✉ *Marqués de Larios 2*
☎ *952/222200* ⊕ *www.room-matehotels.com* ↴ *41 rooms, 1 studio, 3
apartments* ❧ *No meals.*

NIGHTLIFE AND PERFORMING ARTS

Málaga's main nightlife districts are Maestranza, between the bullring and the Paseo Marítimo, and the beachfront in the suburb of
Pedregalejo. Central Málaga also has a lively bar scene around the Plaza
Uncibay and Plaza de la Merced.

Palacio Flamenco Kelipé. Flamenco shows are held here on Thursday,
Friday, and Saturday nights at 9 pm. The cost ranges from €20–€35.
✉ *C. Álamos 7* ☎ *692/829885* ⊕ *www.kelipe.net.*

ANTEQUERA

64 km (40 miles) north of Málaga, 87 km (52 miles) northeast of Ronda.

The town of Antequera holds a surprising number of magnificent
baroque monuments (including some 30 churches)—it provides a
unique snapshot of a historic Andalusian town, one a world away from
the resorts on the Costa del Sol. It became a stronghold of the Moors
after their defeat at Córdoba and Seville in the 13th century. Its fall
to the Christians in 1410 paved the way for the Reconquest of Granada;
the Moors' retreat left a fortress on the town heights.

Next to the town fortress is the former church of **Santa María la Mayor.**
Built of sandstone in the 16th century, it has a ribbed vault that is now
used as a concert hall. The church of **San Sebastián** has a brick baroque
Mudejar tower topped by a winged figure called the Angelote ("big
angel"), the symbol of Antequera. The church of **Nuestra Señora del Carmen** (Our Lady of Carmen) has an extraordinary baroque altarpiece that
towers to the ceiling. On Thursday, Friday, and Saturday evenings in the
summer, many monuments are floodlighted and open until midnight.

GETTING HERE AND AROUND

There are several daily buses from Málaga and Ronda to Antequera.
Drivers will arrive via the A367 and A384, and should head for the
underground parking lot on Calle Diego Ponce in the center of town,
which is well signposted.

ESSENTIALS

Visitor Information Antequera ✉ *Pl. de San Sebastian 7* ☎ *952/702505*
⊕ *turismo.antequera.es.*

EXPLORING

Archidona. About 8 km (5 miles) from Antequera's Lovers' Rock, the village of Archidona winds its way up a steep mountain slope beneath the ruins of a Moorish castle. This unspoiled village is worth a detour for its **Plaza Ochavada,** a magnificent 17th-century octagon resplendent with contrasting red and ocher stone. ⊠ *Along A45.*

Dolmens. These mysterious prehistoric megalithic burial chambers, just outside Antequera, were built some 4,000 years ago out of massive slabs of stone weighing more than 100 tons each. The best-preserved dolmen is La Menga. ⊠ *Signposted off Málaga exit rd.* ☎ *952/712206* ☞ *Free* ☉ *Tues.–Sat. 9–6:30, Sun. 10–5.*

Fuente de Piedra. Europe's major nesting area for the greater flamingo is a shallow saltwater lagoon. In February and March, these birds arrive from Africa by the thousands to breed, returning to Africa in August when the water dries up. The visitor center has information on wildlife. Bring binoculars if you have them. On weekends and public holidays in April and May, which is flamingo hatching time, the visitor center remains opens from 10 to 7. Guided tours are available in English (€6 per person, book ahead of time by phone). ⊠ *10 km (6 miles) northwest of Antequera, off A92 to Seville* ☎ *952/712554* ☞ *Free* ☉ *Apr.–Sept., daily 10–2 and 5–7; Oct.–Mar., daily 10–2 and 4–6.*

Museo de la Ciudad de Antequera. The town's pride and joy is *Efebo*, a beautiful bronze statue of a boy that dates back to Roman times. Standing almost 5 feet high, it's on display along with other ancient, medieval, and Renaissance artifacts and art in this impressive museum. ⊠ *Pl. Coso Viejo* ☎ *952/708300* ⊕ *turismo.antequera.es* ☞ *€3 (free Sun.)* ☉ *July and Aug., weekdays 9:30–2 and 7–9, Sat. 9:30–2 and 4–7, Sun. 10–2; Sept.–June, weekdays 9:30–2 and 4:30–6:30, Sat. 9:30–2 and 4–7, Sun. 10–2.*

Fodor'sChoice
★
Parque Natural del Torcal de Antequera (*El Torcal Nature Park*). Well-marked walking trails (stay on them) guide you at this park, where you can walk among eerie pillars of pink limestone sculpted by aeons of wind and rain. Guides can be arranged for longer hikes. The visitor center has a small museum. ⊠ *Centro de Visitantes, Ctra. C3310, 10 km (6 miles) south of Antequera* ☎ *952/243324* ☞ *Free* ☉ *Apr.–Sept., daily 10–7, Oct.–Mar., daily 10–5.*

Peña de los Enamorados. East of Antequera, along A45, is the dramatic silhouette of the Peña de los Enamorados (Lovers' Rock), an Andalusian landmark. Legend has it that a Moorish princess and a Christian shepherd boy eloped here one night and cast themselves to their deaths from the peak the next morning. The rock's outline is often likened to the profile of the Cordobés bullfighter Manolete.

WHERE TO EAT AND STAY

$
SPANISH
✕ **Caserío San Benito.** If it weren't for the cell-phone tower looming next to this country restaurant 11 km (7 miles) north of Antequera, you might think you'd stumbled into an 18th-century scene. Popular dishes include *porra antequerana* (a thick gazpacho topped with diced ham) and a giant *flamenquín* (a rolled and breaded filet of pork and ham). There are more innovative dishes here as well, like Moroccan-style

chicken and *arroz cremoso* (creamy rice) with pork loin and asparagus. The restaurant's a popular Sunday lunch spot for hungry malagueños in the winter months (in summer they head for the beach). While you're there visit the museum, filled with antiques and agricultural implements. $ *Average main: €10* ⊠ *Ctra. Málaga–Córdoba, Km 108* 🕾 *952/034000* ⊕ *www.caseriodesanbenito.com* ⊗ *No dinner Sun.–Thurs.*

$ **SPANISH** ✕ **El Mesón Ibérico Dehesa Las Hazuelas.** Down the road from the tourist office, this ordinary-looking restaurant serves excellent and abundant Spanish cooking for some of the best prices in the area. Inside, traditional wine barrels share space with modern leather stools, pine furniture, and a wide-screen television. There's also an outside terrace. Open all day from early to late, the Mesón serves breakfast, snacks, tapas, lunch and dinner—it's often bustling and more than a little loud. Specialties include *pulpo a la brasa* (grilled octopus), *solomillo al jerez con cabrales* (pork steak in a sherry and blue-cheese sauce) and *pluma ibérica al foie* (Iberian pork with foie gras). The service is friendly, although it can be slow when the restaurant's busy. Finish off with a liqueur or something from the impressive gin list. $ *Average main: €10* ⊠ *C. Encarnación 9* 🕾 *952/704582.*

$$$ **HOTEL** ⛻ **Parador de Antequera.** Within a few minutes' walk of the historic center, this parador provides a welcome oasis of calm for relaxing after sightseeing; panoramic vistas of the Peña de los Enamorados peak can be seen from the gardens, restaurant, and some rooms. **Pros:** very quiet; perfect setting for a romantic break. **Cons:** service in restaurant can be frosty; decor could be too impersonal for some. $ *Rooms from: €134* ⊠ *Pl. García del Olmo 2* 🕾 *952/840261* ⊕ *www.parador.es* ⤳ *58 rooms* ⍾ *No meals.*

THE GUADALHORCE VALLEY

About 5 km (3 miles) from Antequera.

Coming from Antequera, take the El Torcal exit, turning right onto A343, then from the village of Alora, follow the small road north to the awe-inspiring **Garganta del Chorro** (Gorge of the Stream), a deep limestone chasm where the Guadalhorce River churns and snakes its way some 600 feet below the road. The railroad track that worms in and out of tunnels in the cleft is, amazingly, the main line heading north from Málaga for Bobadilla junction and, eventually, Madrid. Clinging to the cliffside is the **Caminito del Rey** (King's Walk), a suspended catwalk built for a visit by King Alfonso XIII at the beginning of the 19th century. It has been closed since 1992, but the €9 million renovations, which finally started in early 2014, may be completed in 2015.

North of the gorge, the Guadalhorce has been dammed to form a series of scenic reservoirs surrounded by piney hills, which constitute the **Parque de Ardales** nature area. Informal, open-air restaurants overlook the lakes and a number of picnic spots. Driving along the southern shore of the lake, you reach Ardales and, turning onto A357, the old spa town of **Carratraca**. Once a favorite watering hole for both Spanish and foreign aristocracy, it has a Moorish-style *ayuntamiento* (town hall) and an unusual polygonal bullring. Today the 1830 guesthouse has been renovated into the luxury Villa Padierna spa hotel. The splendid Roman-style marble-and-tile bathhouse has benefited from extensive restoration.

TORREMOLINOS

11 km (7 miles) west of Málaga, 16 km (10 miles) northeast of Fuengirola, 43 km (27 miles) east of Marbella.

Torremolinos is all about fun in the sun. It may be more subdued than it was in the action-packed 1960s and 1970s, but it remains the gay capital of the Costa del Sol. Scantily attired Northern Europeans of all ages still jam the streets in season, shopping for bargains on Calle San Miguel, downing sangria in the bars of La Nogalera, and congregating in the bars and English pubs. By day, the sun seekers flock to El Bajondillo and La Carihuela beaches, where, in high summer, it's hard to find towel space on the sand.

Torremolinos has two sections. The first, Central Torremolinos, is built around the Plaza Costa del Sol; Calle San Miguel, the main shopping street; and the brash Nogalera Plaza, which is full of overpriced bars and restaurants. The Pueblo Blanco area, off Calle Casablanca, is more pleasant; and the Cuesta del Tajo, at the far end of Calle San Miguel, winds down a steep slope to Bajondillo Beach. Here, crumbling walls, bougainvillea-clad patios, and old cottages hint at the quiet fishing village of bygone years.

The second, much nicer, section of Torremolinos is La Carihuela. To get here, head west out of town on Avenida Carlota Alessandri and turn left following the signs. This more authentically Spanish area still has a few fishermen's cottages and excellent seafood restaurants. The traffic-free esplanade is pleasant for strolling, especially on a summer evening or Sunday at lunchtime, when it's packed with Spanish families. Just 10 minutes' walk north from the beach is the Parque de la Batería, a very pleasant park with fountains, ornamental gardens, and good views of the sea.

ESSENTIALS

Bus Contact Bus Station ⊠ *C. Hoyo* ☎ *No phone.*

Taxi Contact Radio Taxi Torremolinos ☎ *952/380600.*

Visitor Information La Carihuela ⊠ *Paseo Marítimo, next to Tropicana on the seafront* ☎ *952/372956* ⊘ *Closed weekends.* **Torremolinos** ⊠ *Pl. Comunidades Autónomas* ☎ *952/371909* ⊘ *Closed Mon.*

BEACHES

FAMILY **La Carihuela.** This 2-km (1½-mile) stretch of sand running from the Torremolinos headland to Puerto Marina in Benalmádena is a perennial favorite with Málaga residents as well as visitors. Several hotels, including the Tropicana (⇨ *see Where to Eat and Stay*), flank a beach promenade that's perfect for a stroll, and there are plenty of beach bars where you can rent a lounger and parasol—and also enjoy some of the best *pescaíto* (fried fish) on the coast. The gray sand is cleaned regularly, and the moderate waves make for safe bathing. Towel space (and street parking) is in short supply during the summer months, but outside high

Beach umbrellas at the edge of the surf in Torremolinos

season this is a perfect spot for soaking up some winter sunshine. **Amenities:** food and drink; lifeguards (mid-June–mid-September); showers; toilets; water sports. **Best for:** swimming; walking. ✉ *West end of town, between the center and Puerto Marina.*

WHERE TO EAT

$$ SEAFOOD 🍴 **Casa Juan.** Thanks to the *malagueño* families who flock here on weekends for the legendary fresh seafood, this restaurant has been steadily increasing its capacity. Now seating 170 inside and 150 outside, the complex is in an attractive square, one line back from the seafront. Try for a table overlooking the mermaid fountain. This is a good place to indulge in fritura malagueña or *arroz marinera* (seafood with rice), one of 11 different rice dishes prepared here; others include lobster rice, vegetable rice, and black rice flavored with squid ink. The generous set menus feature different types of seafood, fish or rice dishes. Service can be brisk and impersonal. [$] *Average main: €14* ✉ *Pl. San Gines, La Carihuela* ☎ *952/373512.*

$$$ SPANISH 🍴 **La Cónsula.** Just north of Torremolinos (toward Coín), this cooking school is well worth the detour. Surrounded by tropical gardens, the main building dates from 1856—in the 1850s an American family lived here, and Ernest Hemingway was a frequent visitor. Today, diners can enjoy excellent and innovative cuisine prepared by the students. The menu changes twice yearly, but expect to find dishes such as lobster with ginger and lemongrass, roast venison with polenta, mushrooms, and dill sauce, and desserts like the finger-licking cream of chestnuts with a raspberry filling. There's also an interesting tasting menu (€35).

[$] *Average main: €22* ✉ *Finca La Consula, Churriana* ☎ *952/436026* 🌐 *www.laconsula.com* ✍ *Reservations essential* ⏲ *Closed weekends. No dinner.*

$ SPANISH 🍴 **Yate El Cordobes.** Ask the locals which beachfront chiringuito they prefer and El Yate will almost always be the answer. Run and owned by an affable Cordobes family, the menu holds few surprises, but the seafood is freshly caught, and meat and vegetables are top quality. Have the classic Córdoba *salmorejo* soup (thick, garlicky gazpacho, topped with diced egg and ham) as a starter. Then you may be tempted by the barbecued sardines; or choose a freshly grilled fish like dorada or lubina. The back terrace with its sea and sand views fills up fast, but the dining room is pleasant too, given its large and light picture windows. Service is friendly and fast, although little or no English is spoken. Desserts are the usual limited choice of crème caramel, rice pudding, and similar, but at least they're locally made. [$] *Average main: €9* ✉ *Paseo Marítimo Playamar s/n* ☎ *952/384956* ⏲ *Closed mid-Dec.–mid-Feb.*

WHERE TO STAY

$$$$ HOTEL 🏨 **Hotel Amaragua.** Despite the concrete anonymity of this hotel's looming exterior, this is one of the classiest and most comfortable places to stay on this strip of coastline, with spacious rooms and grand sea views. **Pros:** close to beach and port; multilingual staff. **Cons:** parking costs extra; common areas are slightly dated; expensive for the area. [$] *Rooms from: €208* ✉ *C. Los Nidos 23* ☎ *952/384700* 🌐 *www.amaragua.com* 🛏 *263 rooms, 16 suites* 🍽 *Breakfast.*

$$ HOTEL 🏨 **Hotel La Luna Blanca.** A touch of Asia comes to Torremolinos at Spain's only Japanese hotel, tucked away at the western end of the resort and a few minutes walk from La Carihuela beach. **Pros:** peaceful; friendly staff; free parking. **Cons:** can be difficult to find; steep walk back from the beach. [$] *Rooms from: €98* ✉ *Pasaje del Cerrillo 2* ☎ *952/053711* 🌐 *www.hotellalunablanca.com* 🛏 *9 rooms, 2 suites* 🍽 *Breakfast.*

$$$ HOTEL 🏨 **Tropicana.** On the beach at the far end of the Carihuela, in one of the most pleasant parts of Torremolinos, this low-rise resort hotel has a loyal following for its friendly and homey style and comfortable, bright rooms. **Pros:** great for families; surrounded by bars and restaurants; has its own beach club. **Cons:** can be noisy; a half-hour walk to the center of Torremolinos. [$] *Rooms from: €140* ✉ *Trópico 6, La Carihuela* ☎ *952/386600* 🌐 *www.hoteltropicana.es* 🛏 *84 rooms* ⏲ *Closed Dec. and Jan. (call for exact dates)* 🍽 *No meals.*

NIGHTLIFE AND PERFORMING ARTS

Most nocturnal action is in the center of Torremolinos, and most of its gay bars are in or around the Plaza de la Nogalera, in the center, just off the Calle San Miguel.

Taberna Flamenca Pepe López. Many of the better hotels stage flamenco shows, but you may also want to check out this venue, which has shows throughout the year: November–February, Friday or Saturday (call to confirm); March, Thursday–Saturday; April–June, September and October, Monday–Saturday; July and August, Wednesday–Saturday. ✉ *Pl. de la Gamba Alegre* ☎ *952/381284.*

FUENGIROLA

16 km (10 miles) west of Torremolinos, 27 km (17 miles) east of Marbella.

Fuengirola is less frenetic than Torremolinos. Many of its waterfront high-rises are vacation apartments that cater to budget-minded sun seekers from Northern Europe and, in summer, a large contingent from Córdoba and other parts of Spain. The town is also a haven for British retirees (with plenty of English and Irish pubs to serve them) and a shopping and business center for the rest of the Costa del Sol. The Tuesday market here is the largest on the coast and a major tourist attraction.

GETTING HERE AND AROUND

Fuengirola is the last stop on the train line from Málaga. There are also regular buses that leave from Málaga's main bus station.

ESSENTIALS

Bike Rental Contact Marbella Rent a Bike. This company is based in Marbella but will deliver bikes to Fuengirola. Rental costs are from €15 a day. ⊠ *Poligono Nueva La Campana 63, Marbella* ☎ *952/811062* ⊕ *www.marbellarentabike.com.*

Bus Contact Bus Station ⊠ *Av. Alfonso X 111* ☎ *No phone.*

Taxi Contact Radio Taxi Fuengirola ☎ *952/471000.*

Visitor Information Fuengirola ⊠ *Av. Jesús Santos Rein 6* ☎ *952/467457* ⊕ *www.visitafuengirola.com.*

EXPLORING

FAMILY **Bioparc Fuengirola.** In this modern zoo, wildlife live in a cageless environment in habitats as close to their natural ones as possible. The Bioparc is involved in almost 50 international breeding programs for species in danger of extinction and also supports conservation projects in Africa and several prominent ecological initiatives. Four different habitats have been created, and chimpanzees, big cats, and crocodiles may be viewed, together with other mammals such as white tigers and pygmy hippos, as well as reptiles and birds. There are also daily shows and exhibitions, and various places to get refreshments. In July and August, the zoo stays open late to allow visitors to see the nocturnal animals. ⊠ *Av. José Cela 6* ☎ *952/666301* ⊕ *www.bioparcfuengirola.es* 🎟 *€17.90* ⏱ *Sept.–June, daily 10–dusk; July and Aug., 10–midnight.*

BEACHES

FAMILY **Carvajal.** Lined with low-rises and plenty of greenery, this typically urban beach is between Benalmádena and Fuengirola. One of the Costa del Sol's "blue flag" holders (awarded to the cleanest beaches with the best facilities), the 1¼ -km (¾-mile) beach has yellow sand and safe swimming conditions, which make it very popular with families. There's a choice of beach bars that rent lounge chairs and umbrellas, and regular live music in the summer. Like most beaches in the area, Playa Carvajal is packed throughout July and August, and most summer weekends, but at any other time this beach is quite quiet. The Benalmádena end has a seafront promenade and on-street parking, and the Carvajal train station (on the Fuengirola–Málaga line) is just a few yards from the beach. **Amenities:** food and drink; lifeguards (mid-June tó mid-September); parking; showers; toilets; water sports. **Best for:** sunrise; swimming. ⊠ *N340, Km 214–216.*

WHERE TO EAT AND STAY

$

INTERNATIONAL

✗ **Moochers Jazz Cafe.** Inside an old fisherman's cottage, this classic restaurant lies in the heart of Fuengirola's "Fish Alley," just off the seafront promenade. It's popular with expats as well as tourists—there's live music every evening, and tables are surrounded by jazz and other music memorabilia. Specialties include very spicy chili con carne as well as both sweet and savory pancakes, which come in very generous portions. There's also a piano bar for drinks and cocktails, and in summer, the rooftop terrace comes into its own for starlit dining. $ *Average main:* €12 ⊠ *C. de la Cruz* ☎ *952/477154* ⊘ *No lunch.*

$$

SPANISH

✗ **Restaurante La Solera.** Tucked into the elbow of a narrow street near the main church square, this Spanish restaurant serves up superb dishes, including *pimientos rellenos de bacalao con arroz* (peppers stuffed with cod and rice), and *alcachofas salteadas con almejas y langostinos* (stir-fried artichokes with clams and king shrimps). The three-course daily menu (€15) offers a wide range of choices. The interior is warm and rustic, with lots of dark wood and beamed ceilings. The tapas bar comes with a tempting display of light bites, and the wine selection is well conceived and extensive. $ *Average main:* €15 ⊠ *C. Capitán 13* ☎ *952/467708* ⊘ *Closed Tues.*

$

VEGETARIAN

Fodor'sChoice

★

✗ **Vegetalia.** This attractive, long-established restaurant has a large, pleasant dining space decorated with giant prints of (surprise, surprise) vegetables. It's best known for its excellent, and vast, lunchtime buffet, which includes salads and hot dishes like lentil burgers and soy "meatballs"; it's a popular place for expatriate "veggies." The dinner menu includes curries, vegetable lasagna, pasta dishes, and pancakes. Leave room for the house-made desserts, especially the blueberry pie, which is made by the Finnish owner Katja's mother. Biodynamic wines and beer are available, as are more mainstream Spanish varieties. $ *Average main:* €7 ⊠ *C. Santa Isabel 8, Los Boliches* ☎ *952/586031* ⊕ *www.restaurantevegetalia.com* ⊘ *Closed Sun. and July and Aug. No dinner Mon.–Thurs.*

$$$

HOTEL

🛏 **Florida Hotel & Spa.** This glossy spa hotel has a sophisticated edge on its high-rise neighbors, with light and airy rooms and private terraces overlooking the port and surrounding beach. **Pros:** great location; in-house spa. **Cons:** not all rooms have a sea view; can be an overload of business travelers; very small pool. $ *Rooms from:* €130 ⊠ *C. Galvez Ginachero* ☎ *952/922700* ⊕ *www.hotel-florida.es* ⇆ *184 rooms* ❑| *No meals.*

$

B&B/INN

🛏 **Hostal Italia.** Right off the main plaza and near the beach, this deservedly popular family-run hotel has bright and comfortable but small rooms; guests return year after year, particularly during the October feria. **Pros:** friendly owners; spotless rooms. **Cons:** not much English spoken; rooms are small. $ *Rooms from:* €57 ⊠ *C. de la Cruz 1* ☎ *952/474193* ⊕ *www.hostal-italia.com* ⇆ *40 rooms* ❑| *No meals.*

NIGHTLIFE AND PERFORMING ARTS

Palacio de la Paz. For theater and concerts—including classical, rock, and jazz—check out the modern Palacio de la Paz between Los Boliches and the town center. ⊠ *Av. Jesús Santo Rein, Recinto Ferial* ☎ *952/585836.*

Horsewomen in Fuengirola's El Real de la Feria

Salón de Variétés Theater. From October through June, amateur local troupes stage plays and musicals in English at the Salón de Variétés Theater. ✉ *Emancipación 30* ☎ *952/474542* ⊕ *www.salonvarietestheatre.com.*

MIJAS

8 km (5 miles) north of Fuengirola, 18 km (11 miles) west of Torremolinos.

Mijas is in the foothills of the sierra just north of the coast. Long ago foreign retirees discovered the pretty, whitewashed town, and though the large, touristy square may look like an extension of the Costa, beyond it are hilly residential streets with timeworn homes. Try to visit late in the afternoon, after the tour buses have left.

Mijas extends down to the coast, and the coastal strip between Fuengirola and Marbella is officially called **Mijas-Costa.** This area has several hotels, restaurants, and golf courses.

GETTING HERE AND AROUND

Buses leave Fuengirola every half hour for the 25-minute drive through hills peppered with large houses. If you have a car and don't mind a mildly hair-raising drive, take the more dramatic approach from Benalmádena-Pueblo, a winding mountain road with splendid views. You can park in the underground parking garage signposted on the approach to the village.

ESSENTIALS

Visitor Information Mijas ✉ *Avda. Virgen de la Peña* ☎ *952/589034.*

EXPLORING

Bullring. Bullfights take place from April to November, usually on Sunday at 4:30, at Mijas's tiny bullring, one of the few square ones in the country. During the the height of summer, they are frequently preceded by a flamenco show. The ring is off the Plaza Constitución—Mijas's old village square—and up the slope beside the Mirlo Blanco restaurant. ✉ *Pl. Constitución* ☎ *952/485248* 🎟 *Museum €3* 🕓 *May–Oct., daily 10–9; Nov.–Apr., daily 10–7.*

Iglesia Parroquial de la Inmaculada Concepción (*Immaculate Conception*). This delightful village church is worth a visit. It's impeccably decorated, especially at Easter, and the terrace and spacious gardens have a splendid panoramic view. The church is up the hill from the bullring. Opening hours are sporadic; ask at the tourist office. ✉ *Pl. Constitución.*

Museo Mijas. This charming museum occupies the former town hall. Its themed rooms, including an old-fashioned bakery and bodega, surround a patio, and regular art exhibitions are mounted in the upstairs gallery. ✉ *Pl. de la Libertad* ☎ *952/590380* 🎟 *€1* 🕓 *May–Oct., daily 10–3 and 5–10; Nov.–Apr., daily 9–7.*

QUICK BITES

Bar Porras. On Plaza de la Libertad (at the base of Calle San Sebastián—the most photographed street in the village), this bar attracts a regular crowd of locals with its well-priced, tasty tapas and strategically placed outside tables. ✉ ***Pl. de la Libertad.***

WHERE TO EAT AND STAY

$ SPANISH

🍴 **El Cañuelo.** A major appeal of this restaurant is that it is slightly off the well-trodden tourist route and has a strong local following, especially at tapas time (they start at €1). The intimate, rustic-style dining room provides a welcoming setting for enjoying a wide range of dishes, including surprisingly good pizzas as well as generous portions of heartwarming local specialties like braised oxtail, *bacalao al pisto* (cod with ratatouille), and prawns in a spicy chili sauce. Barbecued meat and fish are available in the summer. [$] *Average main: €8* ✉ *C. Málaga 38* ☎ *952/486581* 🕓 *Closed Mon. and Feb.*

$$$ SPANISH

🍴 **Mirlo Blanco.** In an old house on the pleasant Plaza de la Constitución, with a terrace for outdoor dining, this restaurant is run by a Basque family that's been in the Costa del Sol restaurant business for decades. The interior is welcoming and intimate, with original and noteworthy artwork interspersed among the arches, hanging plants, and traditional white paintwork. Good choices here are Basque specialties such as *txangurro* (spider crab) and *kokotxas de bacalau* (cod cheeks). And don't miss the sensational Grand Marnier soufflé for dessert. There's an outside terrace for alfresco summer dining and a permanent exhibition of paintings by local foreign artists. [$] *Average main: €18* ✉ *Cuesta de la Villa 13* ☎ *952/485700* 🌐 *www.mirlo-blanco.es* ✍ *Reservations essential* 🕓 *Closed Jan.*

$$ EUROPEAN

🍴 **Valparaíso.** Halfway up the road from Fuengirola on the way to Mijas, this sprawling house is in its own garden, complete with swimming pool. There's live music nightly, ranging from flamenco to opera and jazz. This is a favorite among local (mainly British) expatriates, some of whom come in full evening dress to celebrate birthdays or other events. In winter, logs burn in a cozy fireplace. The *pato a la naranja* (duck in orange sauce) is popular, but there's also an emphasis on Italian cuisine, with pasta choices that include fusilli with lamb meatballs and risotto with asparagus and scallops. $ *Average main: €17* ✉ *Ctra. de Mijas–Fuengirola, Km 4* 🕿 *952/485975* ⊕ *www.restaurantevalparaiso.net* ⊗ *No lunch Mon.–Sat. No lunch Sun. June–Oct., no dinner Sun. Nov.–May.*

$$$ 🏨 **Hotel IPV Beatriz Palace.** Right on the beach and in the shadow of
HOTEL Fuengirola Castle, this modern hotel is a great base for sightseeing on this side of the Costa del Sol. **Pros:** well-maintained; beachfront location. **Cons:** pool crowded in summer; long walk to the center of town. $ *Rooms from: €140* ✉ *A7, Km 207, Mijas-Costa* 🕿 *952/922000* ⊕ *www.beatrizhoteles.com* ⇗ *279 rooms, 6 suites* 🍽 *Breakfast.*

MARBELLA

27 km (17 miles) west of Fuengirola, 28 km (17 miles) east of Estepona, 50 km (31 miles) southeast of Ronda.

Fodor's Choice   Thanks to its year-round mild climate and a spectacular natural back-
★   drop, Marbella has been a playground for the rich and famous since the 1950s, when wealthy Europeans first put Marbella on the map as a high-end tourist destination. Grand hotels, luxury restaurants, and multimillion-euro mansions line the waterfront. Marbella itself is a mixture of a charming Casco Antiguo (Old Quarter), where visitors can get a taste of the real Andalusia; an ordinary, tree-lined main thoroughfare (Avenida Ricardo Soriano) flanked by high-rises; and a buzzing Paseo Marítimo (Seafront Promenade), which now stretches some 10 km (6 miles) to San Pedro in the west. The best beaches are to the east of the town between El Rosario and the Don Carlos Hotel. Puerto Banús, the place to see and be seen during the summer, is Spain's most luxurious marina, home to some of the most expensive yachts you will see anywhere. A bevy of restaurants, bars, and designer boutiques are nearby.

GETTING HERE AND AROUND
There are regular buses departing from the bus station to the surrounding resorts and towns, including Fuengirola, Estepona (both every 30 minutes), and Málaga (hourly).

ESSENTIALS
Bus Contact Bus Station ✉ *Av. Trapiche* 🕿 *no phone.*

Visitor Information Marbella. The Marbella tourist office can provide a map of the town and information on exhibits and events. ✉ *Pl. de los Naranjos 1* 🕿 *952/768707* ⊕ *www.marbellaexclusive.com.*

EXPLORING
Museo de Bonsai. In a modern building just east of Marbella's old quarter is this collection of miniature trees, including a 300-year-old olive tree from China. ✉ *Parque Arroyo de la Repesa, Av. Dr. Maiz Viñal* 🕿 *952/862926* 🎫 *€4* ⊗ *July and Aug., weekdays 10:30–1:30 and 5–8, weekends 10:30–7.30; Sept.–June, weekdays 10:30–1:30 and 4–6:30, weekends 10:30–6:30.*

Museo del Grabado Español Contemporáneo. The museum, in a restored 16th-century palace in the heart of the old town, shows some of the best in contemporary Spanish prints. Some of Spain's most famous 20th-century artists, including Picasso, Miró, and Tàpies, are on show. Temporary exhibitions are also mounted here. ✉ *Hospital Bazán* ☎ *952/765741* ⊕ *www.museodelgrabado.es* 💶 *€3* ⊙ *Sept. 22–June 20, Mon. and Sat. 10–2:30, Tues.–Fri. 10–2:30 and 5–9; July and Aug., Mon. and Sat. 10–2:30, Tues.–Fri. 10–2:30 and 6:30–10.*

> **TAKE A BOAT**
>
> A 30-minute ferry trip runs between Marbella and Puerto Banús (⊕ *www.fly-blue.com* 💶 *€8.50 one-way* ⊙ *Mar.–Nov.*), giving you the chance to admire the Marbella mountain backdrop and maybe catch a glimpse of the local dolphins. If you're feeling energetic, walk back the 7 km (4½ miles) along the beachfront promenade stopping at one of the many beach bars for a welcome refreshment or ice cream.

Plaza de los Naranjos. Marbella's appeal lies in the heart of its Old Town, which remains surprisingly intact. Here, a block or two back from the main highway, narrow alleys of whitewashed houses cluster around the central Plaza de los Naranjos (Orange Square), where colorful, albeit pricey, restaurants vie for space under the orange trees. Climb onto what remains of the old fortifications and stroll along the Calle Virgen de los Dolores to the Plaza de Santo Cristo.

QUICK BITES

La Taberna del Pintxo. Enjoy a glass of wine and a transplanted Basque delight at La Taberna del Pintxo. A *pintxo* is a little morsel served on a slice of bread. This restaurant serves platter after platter of creative examples, including shellfish, slices of omelet, mushrooms baked in garlic, and homemade burgers. Prices (€1.15–€1.95) are signaled by the length and size of the stick holding the pintxo together. The kitchen is open continuously from 12:30 pm. ✉ *Av. Miguel Cano 7* ☎ *952/829321.*

Puerto Banús. Marbella's wealth glitters most brightly along the Golden Mile, a tiara of star-studded clubs, restaurants, and hotels west of town and stretching from Marbella to Puerto Banús. A mosque, an Arab bank, and the former residence of Saudi Arabia's late King Fahd reveal the influence of middle-eastern oil money in this wealthy enclave. About 7 km (4½ miles) west of central Marbella (between Km 175 and Km 174), a sign indicates the turnoff leading down to Puerto Banús. Though now hemmed in by a belt of high-rises, Marbella's plush marina, with 915 berths, is a gem of ostentatious wealth, a Spanish answer to St. Tropez. Huge yachts, beautiful people, and countless expensive stores and restaurants make up the glittering parade that marches long into the night. The backdrop is an Andalusian pueblo—built in the 1960s to resemble the fishing villages that once lined this coast.

BEACHES

FAMILY **Marbella East Side Beaches.** Marbella's best beaches are to the east of town, between Los Monteros and Don Carlos hotels, and include Costa Bella and El Alicate beaches. The 6-km (3¾-mile) stretch of yellow sand is lined with residential complexes and sand dunes (some of the last remaining on the Costa del Sol). The sea remains shallow for some distance, so bathing is safe. Beach bars catering to all tastes and budgets dot the sands, as do several exclusive beach clubs (look for Nikki Beach, for instance, where luxury yachts are anchored offshore). Tourists and locals flock to these beaches in the summer, but take a short walk away from the beach bars and parking lots, and you'll find a less crowded spot for your towel. **Amenities:** food and drink; lifeguards (mid-June to mid-September); parking (fee in summer); showers; toilets; water sports. **Best for:** swimming; walking. ⊠ *A7, Km 187–193* ⊟ *No credit cards.*

Playas de Puerto Banús. These small sandy coves are packed almost to bursting in the summer, when they're crowded with young, bronzed, perfect bodies: topless sunbathing is almost de rigueur. The sea is shallow along the entire stretch, which is practically wave free and seems warmer than other beaches nearby. In the area are excellent Caribbean-style beach bars with good seafood and fish, as well as lots of options for sundown drinks. This is also home to the famous beach clubs Ocean Club and Sala Beach with their oversized sun beds, champagne, and nightlong parties. **Amenities:** food and drink; lifeguards (mid-June to mid-September); showers; toilets; water sports. **Best for:** partiers; sunset; swimming. ⊠ *Puerto Banús.*

WHERE TO EAT

$ ✕**Altamirano.** The modest, old-fashioned exterior of this local favorite is
SEAFOOD a bit deceiving: when you step inside you'll be greeted not with stodgy decoration but rather with three spacious dining rooms with Spanish soccer memorabilia, photos of famous patrons, and tanks of fish. Traditional blue tiles complete the look. Fish and seafood choices include fried or grilled squid, spider crab, lobster, sole, red snapper, and sea bass. If you're not a fish eater, though, you'll have to make do with little more than a roll and dessert. The latter includes homemade rice pudding and chocolate mousse. This is a popular venue with locals and tourists, so go early to be sure of a table—especially if you want to dine outside, on the lovely terrace in the plaza. $ *Average main: €12* ⊠ *Pl. Altamirano* 🕾 *952/824932* 🕐 *Closed Wed.*

$$ ✕**Amore e Fantasía.** Without knowing better, you might mistake this for
ITALIAN an antiques-and-housewares shop rather than a restaurant, what with the Buddha statues, gilt mirrors, Moorish lights, and Pompeii-theme frieze. It was one of the first restaurants to open in the port, back in the 1980s, and the menu is vast, with traditional and deliciously prepared Italian choices like *risotto al funghi porcini* (with porcini mushrooms), more sophisticated dishes including lasagne with spicy chicken, and a well-priced daily lunch menu (€15). Opt for the superbly moist dark-chocolate soufflé served with vanilla ice cream if it's available. One of the original partners is from Naples, a fact reflected in the superb crisp pizzas, prepared in a traditional wood-burning oven. The only major negative here are the inflated prices of drinks, especially mineral water—ask for a jug of *agua del grifo* (tap water) instead. $ *Average main: €17* ⊠ *Muelle Benabolá 5–6, Puerto Banús* 🕾 *952/813464* ⊕ *www.amorefantasia.com.*

$$$
INTERNATIONAL
Fodor's Choice
★

✕ **Cappuccino.** Just under the Don Pepe Hotel and right on the promenade, this place is the perfect spot to get some refreshment before/after you tackle a long stroll along the seafront. Done in navy and white with wicker chairs, this outdoor café-restaurant has a fitting nautical theme, and if the temperature drops, blankets and gas heaters are at the ready. Meals are available all day, starting with a range of breakfast options and continuing with brunch-style dishes such as Caesar salad with king prawns and cured-ham croquettes, or something a little more filling like minute steaks with fries. Drinks are on the expensive side (€2.80 for coffee), but the ocean-gazing venue is well worth it. $ *Average main: €18* ✉ *C. de José Meliá, on seafront near Don Pepe Hotel* ☎ *952/868790.*

$$$$
MEDITERRANEAN

✕ **Dani García Restaurante.** The avant-garde celebrity chef Dani Garcia has moved his Michelin-star culinary skills slightly west in Marbella, to the Puente Romano Hotel. Using food-science-inspired methods, he transforms traditional ingredients into innovatively textured, flavored, and visually stunning dishes. Liquid nitrogen, for instance, is used to maximize the flavors in dishes such as the "false tomato." Other signature offerings include carrot cupcake, foie gras yogurt with smoked eel topping, and tuna with *chilmole* (slightly spicy guacamole). The space manages to be zen minimalist, yet warm and intimate, and the entire kitchen performs before diners' eyes. Both à la carte and prix-fixe menus (€65 and €145) are available. For more conventional (and less expensive) dishes, pop into the informal Bibo bistro next door. $ *Average main: €35* ✉ *Puente Romano Hotel, Bulevar Hohenlohe s/n* ☎ *952/764252* ⊘ *Closed Sun. and Mon., and Jan.*

$$$$
MEDITERRANEAN

✕ **Messina.** Between the Old Quarter and the seafront, this innovative restaurant has an unpromising, plain exterior, but forge ahead; its interior's chocolate browns and deep reds make for cozy surroundings for a quiet dinner. The menu has an Italian slant, with more than a sprinkling of Spanish cuisine in its unusual fusion dishes. Try the parsnip-and-goat-cheese foam with quail egg, Iberian ham, and black pudding to start, followed by an Iberian ham filet with couscous, dates, and fresh tomato. Homemade pasta also features. Finish off with a truly international dessert—*torrija Thai* (Spanish-influenced French toast with a touch of Asian-inspired spice). $ *Average main: €24* ✉ *Av. Severo Ochoa 12* ☎ *952/864895* ⊕ *www.restaurantemessina.com* ⊘ *Closed Sun. No lunch.*

$$$$
MEDITERRANEAN
Fodor's Choice
★

✕ **Zozoi.** Tucked into the corner of one of the town's squares, this upbeat, Belgian-owned restaurant consistently receives rave reviews. The fashionably Mediterranean menu makes little distinction between starters and mains, as all the portions are generous; it shows imaginative use of ingredients in such dishes as reindeer carpaccio with sheep's cheese and herb oil, and roast monkfish wrapped in crispy potatoes and served with a red citrus butter. Innovative pizzas are also an option. For dessert, try the forest fruits Pavlova or the warm white soup with mandarin sorbet. The large courtyard terrace is cozy and traditional, with brightly tiled walls and a terra-cotta floor. $ *Average main: €24* ✉ *Pl. Altamirano 1* ☎ *952/858868* ⊕ *www.zozoi.com* ⌖ *Reservations essential* ⊘ *Closed Sun. No lunch.*

WHERE TO STAY

$$$$ HOTEL 🏨 **Claude.** This stylish boutique hotel is in a sumptuous 17th-century mansion in which all the original architectural features and finishes have been preserved. **Pros:** fabulous breakfast; extra attentive staff. **Cons:** pricey given the lack of facilities; no on-site parking. [$] *Rooms from: €280* ✉ *C. San Francisco 5* ☎ *952/900840* 🌐 *www.hotelclaudemarbella.com* 🛏 *6 rooms, 1 suite* ⏲ *Closed Jan. 7–Feb. 14* 🍴 *Breakfast.*

$$ HOTEL 🏨 **La Morada Mas Hermosa.** On one of Marbella's prettiest plant-filled pedestrian streets (on the right just up Calle Ancha), this small hotel has a warm, homey feel, and the rooms are lovely. **Pros:** a hotel with real character; quiet street, yet near the action. **Cons:** some rooms accessed by steep stairs; no parking. [$] *Rooms from: €105* ✉ *C. Montenebros 16A* ☎ *952/924467* 🌐 *www.lamoradamashermosa.com* 🛏 *6 rooms, 1 suite* ⏲ *Closed mid-Dec.–mid-Feb.* 🍴 *Breakfast.*

$$ HOTEL 🏨 **Lima.** Two blocks from the beach and a short walk from the historic center stands this midrange option, which has appealing though slightly generic rooms. **Pros:** downtown location is good for town and beach; beach towels are provided so you don't have to sneak the fluffy white ones out from the bathroom; open all year. **Cons:** room sizes vary considerably. [$] *Rooms from: €96* ✉ *Av. Antonio Belón 2* ☎ *952/770500* 🌐 *www.hotellimamarbella.com* 🛏 *64 rooms* 🍴 *No meals.*

$$$$ HOTEL Fodor's Choice ★ 🏨 **Marbella Club.** The grande dame of Marbella hotels offers luxurious rooms (all refurbished in 2013–14), tropical grounds, and sky-high rates. **Pros:** classic hotel; superb service and facilities. **Cons:** a drive from Marbella's restaurants and nightlife; slightly stuffy; extremely expensive. [$] *Rooms from: €700* ✉ *Blvd. Principe Alfonso von Hohenlohe at Ctra. de Cádiz, Km 178, 3 km (2 miles) west of Marbella* ☎ *952/822211* 🌐 *www.marbellaclub.com* 🛏 *84 rooms, 37 suites, 14 bungalows* 🍴 *No meals.*

$$$ HOTEL Fodor's Choice ★ 🏨 **The Town House.** In a choice location in one of old town Marbella's prettiest squares, this former family home is now a luxurious boutique hotel. **Pros:** upbeat design; great central location. **Cons:** no parking; street-facing rooms are noisy on weekends. [$] *Rooms from: €160* ✉ *C. Alderete 7, Pl. Tetuan* ☎ *952/901791* 🌐 *www.townhouse.nu* 🛏 *9 rooms* 🍴 *Breakfast.*

NIGHTLIFE

Casino Marbella. This chic gambling spot is in the Hotel Andalucía Plaza, just west of Puerto Banús. Shorts and sports shoes are not allowed, and passports are required. It's open daily from 8 pm to 4 am (9 pm to 5 am in August). ✉ *Hotel Andalucía Plaza, N340* ☎ *952/814000* 🌐 *www.casinomarbella.com.*

La Sala. One of Marbella's most popular night spots for "older" clubbers, i.e., those out or nearly out of their twenties. Dine in before you dance to the live music. ✉ *C. Belmonte, near bullring, Puerto Banús* ☎ *952/814145.*

Olivia Valére disco. Marbella's most famous nightspot is decorated to resemble a Moorish palace. To get here, head inland from the town's mosque (it's easy to spot). Doors open at midnight (daily in July and

August; weekends only from September to June), and it closes at 7 am. ✉ *Ctra. de Istán, Km 0.8* ☎ *952/828861.*

Fodor's Choice ★ **Puerto Banús.** Much of the nighttime action in Marbella revolves around the Puerto Banús—the marina—in bars like Sinatra's and Joy's Bar.

Tablao Ana María. At this popular flamenco venue in the center of town, there are performances every evening in summer, starting around 11 pm. Off-season, October through May, the shows start at 10:30 and are held Wednesday through Sunday. Group bookings are available at other times. ✉ *Pl. de Santo Cristo 5* ☎ *952/771117.*

OJÉN

10 km (6 miles) north of Marbella.

For a contrast to the glamour of the coast, drive up to Ojén, in the hills above Marbella. Take note of the beautiful pottery and, if you're here the first week in August, don't miss the **Fiesta de Flamenco** (August), which attracts some of Spain's most respected flamenco names, including the Juan Peña El Lebrijano, Miguel Póveda, and Marina Heredia. Four kilometers (2½ miles) from Ojén is the **Refugio del Juanar,** a former hunting lodge in the heart of the Sierra Blanca, at the southern edge of the Serranía de Ronda, a mountainous wilderness. A walking trail takes you a mile from the Refugio to the **Mirador** (lookout), with a sweeping view of the Costa del Sol and the coast of North Africa.

GETTING HERE AND AROUND

Approximately eight buses leave from the Marbella main bus station for Ojén on weekdays and Saturday with just four on Sunday.

WHERE TO STAY

$ B&B/INN 🏨 **La Posada del Angel.** With friendly Dutch owners and rooms with lots of traditional Andaulusian features and even a few Moroccan touches, this hotel makes a perfect rural retreat. **Pros:** good service; chance to sample Andalusian village life. **Cons:** could be too quiet for some. [$] *Rooms from: €79* ✉ *C. Mesones 21* ☎ *952/881808* 🌐 *www.laposadadelangel.net* 🛏 *15 rooms* 🍴 *Breakfast.*

$ HOTEL 🏨 **Refugio del Juanar.** Once an aristocratic hunting lodge (King Alfonso XIII came here), this secluded hotel and restaurant was sold to its staff in 1984 for the symbolic sum of 1 peseta and is a world apart from the glamour of Marbella, just 30 minutes' drive away. **Pros:** superb for hikers; traditional Andalusian looks. **Cons:** can seem very cut off; some rooms are a little tired. [$] *Rooms from: €80* ✉ *Sierra Blanca s/n* ☎ *952/881000* 🌐 *www.juanar.com* 🛏 *21 rooms, 4 suites* 🍴 *Breakfast.*

ESTEPONA

17 km (11 miles) west of San Pedro de Alcántara, 22 km (13 miles) west of Marbella.

Estepona is a pleasant and relatively tranquil seaside resort, despite being surrounded by an ever-increasing number of urban developments. The beach, more than 1 km (½ mile) long, has better-quality sand than the Costa norm, and the promenade is lined with well-kept, aromatic flower gardens. The gleaming white **Puerto Deportivo** is packed with bars and restaurants, serving everything from fresh fish to Chinese food. Back from the main Avenida de España, the old quarter of cobbled narrow streets and squares is surprisingly unspoiled.

GETTING HERE AND AROUND

Buses run every half hour from 6:30 am to 11 pm from Marbella to Estepona. The town is compact enough to make most places accessible via foot.

ESSENTIALS

Bus Contact Bus Station ✉ *Av. de España.*

Visitor Information Estepona ✉ *Av. San Lorenzo* ☎ *952/802002.*

EXPLORING

Casa de la Juventud. Right in the heart of Estepona's old quarter in the flower-filled Plaza de las Flores is one of the eastern Costa del Sol's cultural treasures—a private art collection containing more than 300 paintings and sculptures, belonging to actor and comedian Ángel Garó. It's on display in this 19th-century mansion, which is itself a museum piece. Highlights include paintings and sketches by Picasso, Dalí, and the poets Lorca and Alberti, as well as an 18th-century *Madonna and Child* by Maella, and more modern works, including Walt Disney drawings. You need to show your passport on entry. ✉ *Pl. de las Flores* 🎫 *Free* 🕓 *Tues.–Fri. 9–2 and 5–8, Sat. 9–2.*

BEACHES

El Saladillo. Something of a Costa del Sol secret, this quiet 4-km (2½-mile) beach of gray sand has long, empty stretches with plenty of room for towels, even in high summer, making it a great place to relax, walk, or swim. The water's safe for swimming when waves are low, but watch out for the undertow when it's windy. Located between San Pedro and Estepona, and flanked by residential developments, El Saladillo is dotted with the occasional beach bar, including Pepe's Beach, one of the first on the Costa del Sol and still a popular seafood spot. **Amenities:** food and drink; lifeguards (mid-June to mid-September); showers; toilets; water sports. **Best for:** solitude; sunset; walking. ✉ *A7, Km 166–172.*

WHERE TO EAT AND STAY

$$$ INTERNATIONAL Fodor's Choice ★

🍴 **Alcaría de Ramos.** José Ramos, a winner of Spain's National Gastronomy Prize, opened this restaurant in El Paraíso complex, between Estepona and San Pedro de Alcántara. It gained an enthusiastic and loyal following as his two sons followed in his culinary footsteps. Try the *carpaccio de solomillo de cerdo ibérico con morcilla* (Iberian pork steak carpaccio with black pudding) followed by *rodaballo con salsa de almejas* (skate with clam sauce). Portions are very generous, but if you can, leave room for the chocolate soufflé or the equally delicious Pavlova. Reservations are a good idea on weekends and in summer. [$] *Average main: €18* ✉ *Urbanización El Paraíso, Ctra. N340, Km 167* ☎ *952/886178* 🌐 *www.laalcariaderamos.es* 🕓 *Closed Sun. No lunch.*

$$$ MEDITERRANEAN

🍴 **Puro Beach.** This luxurious beach club and restaurant has all the trendy trappings: white canopied beach beds, "nomad" tents, exotic Oriental theme, a glossy marbled spa, hip young waitstaff, and chill-out

DID YOU KNOW?

Casares is one of the most atmospheric of the pueblos blancos and is becoming increasingly more of a tourist destination.

background music. Try the daily dawn yoga ritual or one of the massages within the "Global Treats" program. The restaurant serves seafood dishes and meatier fare, including the popular Puro burger and chicken satay. Cocktails are a specialty: the classic Puro piña colada is a deliciously frothy concoction. $ *Average main: €19* ⊠ *Laguna Village, Pl. El Padrón* ☎ *952/800015* ⊕ *www.purobeach.com* ⊘ *Closed Mon. and Tues. Nov.–Feb. No dinner mid-Sept.–mid-June.*

$$$ 🏨 **Hotel Fuerte Estepona.** The beach hotel, part of the local Fuerte chain,
HOTEL sits to the west of Estepona right on a tranquil beach, which you have almost to yourself outside high season. **Pros:** tranquil location; spacious rooms. **Cons:** out of town; may be too quiet for some. $ *Rooms from: €150* ⊠ *Ctra. A7, Km 150, Arroyo Vaquero* ☎ *900/343410* ⊕ *www. fuertehoteles.com* ⇱ *210 rooms* ⊘ *Closed roughly Nov.–mid-Mar.* ❑*No meals.*

$$$$ 🏨 **Kempinski Hotel Bahía.** This luxury resort, between the coastal high-
RESORT way and the sea, looks like a cross between a Moroccan casbah and a take on the Hanging Gardens of Babylon, with tropical gardens and a succession of large swimming pools meandering down to the beach. **Pros:** great beachside location; excellent facilities. **Cons:** so-so beach; no shops or nightlife within walking distance; expensive. $ *Rooms from: €350* ⊠ *Playa El Padrón, Ctra. A7, Km 159* ☎ *952/809500* ⊕ *www. kempinski-spain.com* ⇱ *132 rooms, 15 suites* ❑*Breakfast.*

CASARES

20 km (12 miles) northwest of Estepona.

Fodor's Choice   The mountain village of Casares lies high above Estepona in the Sierra
★ Bermeja, with streets of ancient white houses piled one on top of the other, perched on the slopes beneath a ruined but impressive Moorish castle. The heights afford stunning views over orchards, olive groves, and woods to the Mediterranean sparkling in the distance.

WHERE TO EAT AND STAY

$$ ✕**Arroyo Hondo.** Tucked in one of the many bends on the road from
ECLECTIC Estepona, Arroyo Hondo is a favorite with local expats and tourists. The rustic interior, in ocher tones with a log fire, make for cozy meals, and the terrace and poolside tables are perfect for alfresco dining with panoramic vistas. Food is a fusion of Mediterranean, Japanese, and Thai cuisines. Start with chicken *karaage* (deep-fried Japanese-style) or ruby fig salad with Roquefort, Serrano ham and arugula, then follow with five-spice duck with pumpkin curry or beef with porcini and truffle butter. Vegetarian options include a truffle-scented mushroom tart. The three-course set menu is a sound option. Reservations are advised in the summer and on weekends. $ *Average main: €16* ⊠ *Ctra. de Casares, Km 10* ☎ *952/895152* ⊕ *www.arroyo-hondo.com* ⊘ *Closed Mon. No dinner Sun., or Tues. and Wed. Oct.–May.*

$ 🏨 **Cortijo el Papudo.** Michael and Vivien Harvey, expats from the United
B&B/INN Kingdom, have given this *cortijo* (country house) a delightful, homey feel. **Pros:** wonderful breakfast; gorgeous gardens. **Cons:** 30 km (19 miles) from Casares proper; may be too quiet for some. $ *Rooms from: €75* ⊠ *Secadero, San Martín de Tesorillo, San Roque* ✛ *Turn right at*

pharmacy in Secadero and drive for 1 km (½ mile) ☎ *952/854018* ⤵ *11 rooms* ⦿| *Breakfast.*

$$$$
RESORT
⌂ **Finca Cortesín.** If you're looking for a luxury option on this side of the coast, then this suites-only hotel, on a 532-acre estate adjacent to an 18-hole Cabell Robinson golf course, will probably exceed your expectations. **Pros:** luxury standards and service; tranquil surroundings. **Cons:** pricey; some distance from resorts. $ *Rooms from:* €450 ✉ *Ctra. de Casares Km 2* ☎ *952/937800* ⊕ *www.fincacortesin.com* ⤵ *67 suites* ⦿| *Breakfast.*

TARIFA

74 km (46 miles) southwest of San Roque.

Fodor's Choice
★
Tarifa's strong winds helped keep it off the tourist maps for years, but now it is Europe's biggest center for windsurfing and kiteboarding, and the wide, white-sand beaches stretching north of the town have become a huge attraction. Those winds have proven a source of wealth in more direct ways, also, via the electricity created by vast wind farms on the surrounding hills. This town at the southernmost tip of mainland Europe—where the Mediterranean and the Atlantic meet—has continued to prosper. Downtown cafés, which not that long ago were filled with men playing dominoes and drinking *anís,* now serve croissants with their café con leche and make fancy tapas for a cosmopolitan crowd.

ESSENTIALS
Visitor Information Tarifa ✉ *Paseo de la Alameda s/n* ☎ *956/680993.*

EXPLORING
Fodor's Choice
★
Baelo Claudia. Ten kilometers (6 miles) north of Tarifa on the Atlantic coast stand the impressive Roman ruins of Baelo Claudia, once a thriving production center of garum, a salty, pungent fish paste appreciated in Rome. The visitor center includes a museum. Concerts are regularly held at the restored amphitheater during the summer months. ☎ *956/106797* ⬚ €1.50 ☯ *June 16–Sept. 15, Tues.–Sun. 10–5; Sept. 16–June 15, Tues.–Sat. 10–6:30, Sun. 10–5.*

Castle. Tarifa's 10th-century castle is famous for the siege of 1292, when the defender Guzmán el Bueno refused to surrender even though the attacking Moors threatened to kill his captive son. In defiance, he flung his own dagger down to them, shouting, "Here, use this," or something to that effect (they did indeed kill his son). The Spanish military turned the castle over to the town in the mid-1990s, and it now has a **museum** on Guzmán and the sacrifice of his son. ✉ *Av. Fuerza Armadas* ⬚ €2 ☯ *June–Sept., Tues.–Sat. 11–1:30 and 6–8, Sun. 11–1:30; Oct.–May, Tues.–Sat. 11–1:30 and 4–5:30, Sun. 11–1:30.*

BEACHES
Playa Los Lances. This part of the Atlantic coast is home to miles of white and mostly unspoiled beaches. Los Lances, to the north of Tarifa and the town's main beach, is one of the longest. Backed by low-lying scrub and lagoons, the beach is also close to the odd campsite, kite-surfing school, and boho-chic hotel. Its windswept sands make for perfect

kite-surfing: the beaches at Los Lances and Punta Paloma (just up the coast) are where you'll see most sails surfing the waves and wind. Amenities are concentrated at the Tarifa end of the beach, where there are a few bars and cafés, usually open mid-June through mid-September; this is naturally where the crowds congregate in the summer. Otherwise, most of the beach is deserted year-round. Swimming is safe here, except in high winds, when there's a strong undertow. **Amenities:** food and drink (mid-June to mid-September only); lifeguards; showers; toilets. **Best for:** solitude; sunset; walking; windsurfing.

WHERE TO STAY

$
B&B/INN
⛅ **Convento de San Francisco.** The rooms here are comfortable and attractive, with exposed-stone walls and arches, but the main draw is the setting: a restored 17th-century convent in the spectacular village of Vejer, overlooking the coast. **Pros:** great location in the center of the village; friendly owners. **Cons:** rooms rather bare; nearest parking a five-minute walk away. $ *Rooms from: €67* ✉ *La Plazuela, just west of Tarifa, Vejer* ☎ *956/451001* ⊕ *www.tugasa.com* ⇴ *25 rooms* ❍| *No meals.*

$$$
HOTEL
⛅ **Hurricane Hotel.** Surrounded by lush subtropical gardens and fronting the beach, the Hurricane is one of the best-loved hip hotels on this stretch of coastline, famous for its Club Mistral wind- and kite-surfing school, and its horse-riding center. **Pros:** fun and sophisticated; excellent restaurant. **Cons:** 6 km (3½ miles) from Tarifa proper; rooms are quite plain. $ *Rooms from: €156* ✉ *Ctra. 340, Km 78* ☎ *956/684919* ⊕ *www.hotelhurricane.com* ⇴ *28 rooms, 5 suites* ❍| *Breakfast.*

GIBRALTAR

20 km (12 miles) east of Algeciras, 77 km (48 miles) southwest of Marbella.

The Rock of today is a bizarre anomaly of Moorish, Spanish, and—especially—British influences. There are double-decker buses, "bobbies" in helmets, and red mailboxes. Millions of pounds have been spent in developing its tourist potential, and a steady flow of expat Brits comes here from Spain to shop at Morrisons supermarket and other stores. This tiny British colony—nicknamed "Gib" or simply "the Rock"—whose impressive silhouette dominates the strait between Spain and Morocco, was one of the two Pillars of Hercules in ancient times, marking the western limits of the known world and commanding the narrow pathway between the Mediterranean Sea and the Atlantic Ocean. The Moors, headed by Tariq ibn Ziyad, seized the peninsula in 711, preliminary to the conquest of Spain. The Spaniards recaptured Tariq's Rock in 1462. The English, heading an Anglo-Dutch fleet in the War of the Spanish Succession, gained control in 1704, and, after several years of local skirmishes, Gibraltar was finally ceded to Great Britain in 1713 by the Treaty of Utrecht. Spain has been trying to get it back ever since. In 1779 a combined French and Spanish force laid siege to the Rock for three years to no avail. During the Napoleonic Wars, Gibraltar served as Admiral Horatio Nelson's base for the decisive naval Battle of Trafalgar, and during the two world wars, it served the Allies well as a naval and air base. In 1967 Franco closed

Windsurfing at Tarifa

the land border with Spain to strengthen his claims over the colony, and it remained closed until 1985.

There are likely few places in the world that you enter by walking or driving across an airport runway, but that's what happens in Gibraltar. First you show your passport; then you make your way out onto the narrow strip of land linking Spain's La Linea with Britain's Rock. Unless you have a good reason to take your car—such as loading up on cheap gas or duty-free goodies—you're best off leaving it in a guarded parking area in La Linea, the Spanish border town. Don't bother hanging around here; it's a seedy place. In Gibraltar you can hop on buses and take taxis that expertly maneuver the narrow, congested streets. The Official Rock Tour—conducted either by minibus or, at a greater cost, taxi—takes about 90 minutes and includes all the major sights, allowing you to choose where to come back and linger later.

In 2013, tensions between Gibraltar and Spain ramped up yet again, and as a result, lines for leaving the colony, both via car and on foot, are long—it can take up to three hours to cross the border into Spain. This is likely to continue, as there's little sign of any progress on any sort of joint Anglo-Spanish sovereignty, which the majority of Gibraltarians fiercely oppose.

When you call Gibraltar from Spain or another country, prefix the seven-digit telephone number with 00–350. Gibraltar's currency is the Gibraltar pound (£), whose exchange rate is the same as the British pound. Euros are accepted everywhere, although you will get a better exchange rate if you use pounds.

GETTING HERE AND AROUND

There are frequent day tours organized from the Costa del Sol resorts, either via your hotel or any reputable travel agency.

ESSENTIALS

Visitor Information Gibraltar ⊠ *Grand Casemates Sq., Gibraltar* ☎ *200/45000.*

EXPLORING

TOP ATTRACTIONS

Apes' Den. The famous Barbary Apes are a breed of cinnamon-color, tailless monkeys (not actually apes, despite their name) native to Morocco's Atlas Mountains. Legend holds that as long as they remain in Gibraltar, the British will keep the Rock; Winston Churchill went so far as to issue an order for their preservation when their numbers began to dwindle during World War II. They are publicly fed twice daily, at 8 and 4, at Apes' Den, a rocky area down Old Queens Road near the Wall of Carlos V. Among the monkeys' talents are their grabbing of food, purses, and cameras, so be on guard.

Fodor'sChoice ★ **Cable Car.** You can reach St. Michael's Cave—or ride all the way to the top of Gibraltar—on a cable car. The car doesn't go high off the ground, but the views of Spain and Africa from the Rock's pinnacle are superb. It leaves from a station at the southern end of Main Street, which is known as the Grand Parade. ⊠ *Grand Parade* ⛺*£10.50 round-trip* ☉ *Apr.–Oct., daily 9:30–6:45; Nov.–Mar., daily 9:30–5:45.*

Gibraltar Museum. Often overlooked by visitors heading to the Upper Rock Reserve, this museum houses a beautiful 14th-century Moorish bathhouse and an 1865 model of the Rock; the displays evoke the Great Siege and the Battle of Trafalgar. There's also a reproduction of the "Gibraltar Woman," the Neanderthal skull discovered here in 1848. ⊠ *Bomb House La.* ☎ *200/74289* ⊕ *www.gibmuseum.gi* ⛺*£2* ☉ *Weekdays 10–6, Sat. 10–2.*

Gibraltar Town. The dignified Regency architecture of Great Britain blends well with the shutters, balconies, and patios of southern Spain in colorful, congested Gibraltar town. Shops, restaurants, and pubs beckon on Main Street; at the Governor's Residence, the ceremonial Changing of the Guard takes place six times a year, and the Ceremony of the Keys takes place twice a year. Make sure you see the Anglican Cathedral of the Holy Trinity; the Catholic Cathedral of St. Mary; and the Crowned Law Courts, where the famous case of the sailing ship *Mary Celeste* was heard in 1872. ⊠ *Main St.*

Great Siege Tunnels. These tunnels, formerly known as the Upper Galleries, were carved out during the Great Siege of 1779–82 at the northern end of Old Queen's Road. You can plainly see the openings from which the guns were pointed at the Spanish invaders. They form part of what is arguably the most impressive defense system anywhere in the world. The privately managed World War II Tunnels, which are nearby, are also open to the public but are less dramatic. ⊠ *Old Queen's Rd.*

Moorish Castle. The castle was built by the descendants of the Moorish general Tariq ibn Ziyad (670–720), who conquered the Rock in 711.

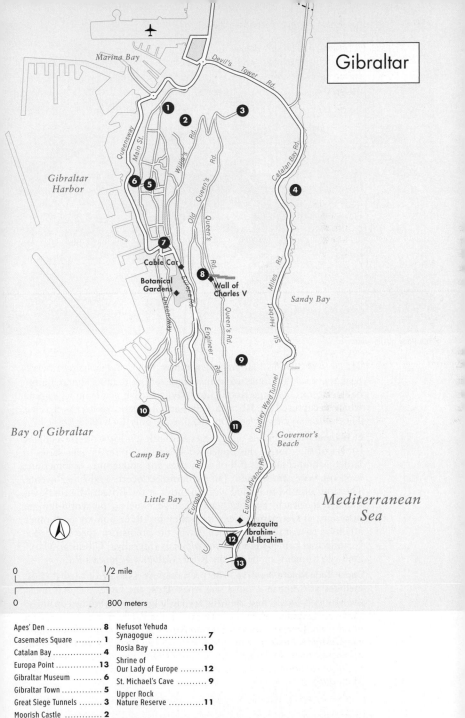

Gibraltar

Marina Bay

Devil's Tower Rd.

Gibraltar Harbor

Queensway

Main St.

Willie's Rd.

Old Queen's Rd.

Queen's Rd.

Catalan Bay Rd.

Cable Car

Botanical Gardens

Wall of Charles V

Europa Rd.

Engineer Rd.

Queen's Rd.

Sir Herbert Miles Rd.

Sandy Bay

Queensway

Dudley Ward Tunnel

Governor's Beach

Bay of Gibraltar

Camp Bay

Little Bay

Europa Rd.

Europa Advance Rd.

Mezquita Ibrahim-Al-Ibrahim

Mediterranean Sea

0 — 1/2 mile

0 — 800 meters

The Rock of Gibraltar

The present Tower of Homage dates from 1333, and its besieged walls bear the scars of stones from medieval catapults (and later, cannonballs). Admiral George Rooke hoisted the British flag from its summit when he captured the Rock in 1704, and it has flown here ever since. The castle may be viewed from the outside only. ⊠ *Willis's Rd.*

St. Michael's Cave. This is the largest of Gibraltar's 150 caves; a visit here is part of the tour of the Upper Rock Nature Preserve. This series of underground chambers full of stalactites and stalagmites is sometimes used for very atmospheric (albeit damp) concerts and other events. The skull of a Neanderthal woman (now in the British Museum) was found at the nearby Forbes Quarry eight years before the world-famous discovery in Germany's Neander Valley in 1856; nobody paid much attention to it at the time, which is why the prehistoric species is called Neanderthal rather than *Homo calpensis* (literally, "Gibraltar Man," after the Romans' name for the Rock, *Calpe*). ⊠ *Queen's Rd.*

Upper Rock Nature Preserve. The preserve, accessible from Jews' Gate, includes St. Michael's Cave, the Apes' Den, the Great Siege Tunnels, the Moorish Castle, and the Military Heritage Center, which chronicles the British regiments that have served on the Rock. ✢ *From Rosia Bay, drive along Queensway and Europa Rd. as far as Casino, above Alameda Gardens. Make a sharp right here, up Engineer Rd. to Jews' Gate, a lookout over docks and Bay of Gibraltar toward Algeciras* ⌂ £10 *for all attractions, plus £2 per vehicle* ◷ *Apr.–Oct., daily 9–7:15; Nov.–Mar., daily 9–6:15.*

WORTH NOTING

Casemates Square. Gibraltar's social hub is on this pedestrian-only square in the northern part of town, where there are plenty of places to sit with a drink and watch the world go by. The Gibraltar Crystal company, where you can watch the glassblowers at work, is worth a visit. ✉ *Grand Casemates Sq.*

Catalan Bay. This fishing village founded by Genoese settlers is now a resort on the eastern shores. The massive water catchments once supplied the colony's drinking water. ✥ *From Rock's eastern side, go left down Devil's Tower Rd. as you enter Gibraltar.*

Europa Point. From here, take a look across the straits to Morocco, 23 km (14 miles) away. You're now standing on one of the two ancient Pillars of Hercules. In front of you is the lighthouse that has dominated the meeting place of the Atlantic and the Mediterranean since 1841; sailors can see its light from a distance of 27 km (17 miles). ✉ *On coast road, at the Rock's southern tip.*

Nefusot Yehuda Synagogue. One of the oldest remaining synagogues on the Iberian Peninsula, Nefusot Yehuda dates back to 1798. Guided tours, which include a short history of the Gibraltar Jewish community, must be reserved by phone. ✉ *Line Wall Rd.* ☎ *200/76477.*

Rosia Bay. There are fine views to be had if you drive up above Rosia Bay. The bay was where Nelson's flagship, HMS *Victory,* was towed after the Battle of Trafalgar in 1805. On board were the dead, who were buried in Trafalgar Cemetery on the southern edge of town—except for Admiral Nelson, whose body was returned to England, preserved in a barrel of rum. ✥ *From Europa Flats, follow Queensway along Rock's western slopes.*

Shrine of Our Lady of Europe. To the north of the lighthouse, along the Rock's southern tip, stands this shrine, on the site of a mosque. The small Catholic chapel, venerated by seafarers since the 14th century, has a small museum with a statue of the Virgin from 1462. 🎟 *Free* 🕒 *Mon. and Fri. 10–1, Tues.–Thurs. 10–1 and 2:30–6, Sat. 11–1.*

WHERE TO EAT AND STAY

$ MEDITERRANEAN 🍴 **Café Solo.** Enjoying an ace position with a sprawling terrace on Casemates Square, this place specializes in Mediterranean cuisine. Daily specials might include seafood risotto; char-grilled chili and garlic squid; or penne with roast chicken, mushroom, and pancetta. The interior is edgily modern. Across the square is the Solo Express branch, which specializes in tasty takeout wraps and similar choices. [$] *Average main: £10* ✉ *Grand Casemates Sq., Gibraltar* ☎ *200/44449.*

$ BRITISH 🍴 **Sacarello's.** Right off Main Street, this busy restaurant is as well known for its excellent coffee and cakes as it is for the rest of its food. There's a varied salad and quiche buffet, as well as stuffed baked potatoes and daily specials, which could include fish-and-chips, or brandy-pork stuffed with cheese and bacon. Top your meal off with a specialty coffee with cream and vanilla. The restaurant has several warmly decorated rooms with cozy corners, dark-wood furnishings, and low-beamed ceilings, and the whole place has an old-fashioned English feel. [$] *Average* *main: £10* ⊠ *57 Irish Town* 🕾 *200/70625* ⊕ *www.sacarellosgibraltar. com* ⊗ *Closed Sun. No dinner.*

$$　✕**Waterfront.** Easily distinguished by its flags and located right at Queens-
INTERNATIONAL　way Quay, this restaurant is a favorite with locals, especially for the
Sunday Carvery. It was refurbished in 2014; navy and white are the
colors that predominate among the cane furniture and the various Med-
iterranean touches. In addition to the upstairs and downstairs dining
inside, there's also a generous terrace and several tables that sit perched
on the quay, allowing for views over the marina and to the mountains
in Spain. The menu is distinctly international, with à la carte special-
ties such as steaks (aged on the premises), and British staples such as
bangers and mash (sausages with mashed potatoes and onion gravy).
Service is efficient and comes with a smile. Ⓢ *Average main: £15* ⊠ *4/5
Ragged Staff* 🕾 *200/45666* ⊕ *www.gibwaterfront.com.*

$$$$　🏛 **O'Callaghan Eliott.** If you want to stay at the slickest and most modern
HOTEL　of the Rock's hotels, try this one, in the center of town. **Pros:** views of
either marina or the Rock; well-located for pubs and restaurants; good
amenities. **Cons:** very business-oriented; fee for Wi-Fi. Ⓢ *Rooms from:
£150* ⊠ *2 Governor's Parade* 🕾 *200/70500* ⊕ *www.ocallaghanhotels.
com* ↪ *113 rooms, 10 suites* ¶◎¶ *No meals.*

$$$　🏛 **The Rock.** This hotel overlooking the straits first opened in 1932, and
HOTEL　although furnishings in the rooms and restaurants are elegant and col-
orful, they still preserve something of the English colonial style, with
bamboo, ceiling fans, and a terrace bar covered with wisteria. **Pros:**
old-fashioned, excellent service; magnificent Gibraltar bay views. **Cons:**
inconvenient for shopping; Barbary apes are sometimes unwelcome
visitors. Ⓢ *Rooms from: £130* ⊠ *3 Europa Rd.* 🕾 *200/73000* ⊕ *www.
rockhotelgibraltar.com* ↪ *101 rooms, 2 suites* ¶◎¶ *Breakfast.*

NIGHTLIFE

Lord Nelson. A restaurant during the day and a lively bar at night, the
Lord Nelson has karaoke on Saturday nights and jam sessions and live
music during the week. A wide selection of ales is available on tap.
⊠ *Grand Casemates Sq.* 🕾 *200/50009.*

SPORTS AND THE OUTDOORS

Bird- and dolphin-watching, diving, and fishing are popular activities
on the Rock. For details on tours and outfitters, visit the Gibraltar
government tourism website (⊕ *www.visitgibraltar.gi*) or call the local
tourist office (🕾 *200/45000*).

VOCABULARY

	ENGLISH	SPANISH	PRONUNCIATION
BASICS			
	Hello	Hola	**oh**-la
	Yes/no	Sí/no	see/no
	Please	Por favor	pohr fah-**vohr**
	May I?	¿Me permite?	meh pehr-**mee**-teh
	Thank you (very much)	(Muchas) gracias	(**moo**-chas) **grah**-see-as
	You're welcome	De nada	deh **nah**-dah
	Excuse me	Con permiso/perdón	con pehr-**mee**-so/ pehr-**dohn**
	Pardon me/ what did you say?	¿Perdón?/Mande?	pehr-**dohn/mahn**-deh
	Could you tell me . . . ?	¿Podría decirme . . . ?	po-**dree**-ah deh-**seer**-meh
	I'm sorry	Lo siento	lo see-**en**-to
	Good morning!	¡Buenos días!	**bway**-nohs **dee**-ahs
	Good afternoon!	¡Buenas tardes!	**bway**-nahs **tar**-dess
	Good evening!	¡Buenas noches!	**bway**-nahs **no**-chess
	Goodbye!	¡Adiós!/ ¡Hasta luego!	ah-dee-**ohss/** ah-stah-**lwe**-go
	Mr./Mrs.	Señor/Señora	sen-**yor**/sen-**yohr**-ah
	Miss	Señorita	sen-yo-**ree**-tah
	Pleased to meet you	Mucho gusto	**moo**-cho **goose**-to
	How are you?	¿Cómo está usted?	**ko**-mo es-**tah** oo-**sted**
	Very well, thank you.	Muy bien, gracias.	**moo**-ee bee-**en**, **grah**-see-as
	And you?	¿Y usted?	ee oos-**ted**
	Hello (on the phone)	Diga	**dee**-gah
DAYS OF THE WEEK			
	Sunday	domingo	doh-**meen**-goh
	Monday	lunes	**loo**-ness
	Tuesday	martes	**mahr**-tess
	Wednesday	miércoles	me-**air**-koh-less
	Thursday	jueves	hoo-**ev**-css
	Friday	viernes	vee-**air**-ness

	Saturday	sábado	**sah**-bah-doh

NUMBERS

1	un, uno	oon, **oo**-no
2	dos	dohs
3	tres	tress
4	cuatro	**kwah**-tro
5	cinco	**sink**-oh
6	seis	saice
7	siete	see-**et**-eh
8	ocho	**o**-cho
9	nueve	new-**eh**-veh
10	diez	dee-**es**
11	once	**ohn**-seh
12	doce	**doh**-seh
13	trece	**treh**-seh
14	catorce	ka-**tohr**-seh
15	quince	**keen**-seh
16	dieciséis	dee-**es**-ee-**saice**
17	diecisiete	dee-**es**-ee-see-**et**-eh
18	dieciocho	dee-**es**-ee-**o**-cho
19	diecinueve	dee-**es**-ee-new-**ev**-eh
20	veinte	**vain**-teh
21	veinte y uno/ veintiuno	**vain**-te-oo-noh
30	treinta	**train**-tah
32	treinta y dos	train-tay-**dohs**
40	cuarenta	kwah-**ren**-tah
50	cincuenta	seen-**kwen**-tah
60	sesenta	sess-**en**-tah
70	setenta	set-**en**-tah
80	ochenta	oh-**chen**-tah
90	noventa	no-**ven**-tah
100	cien	see-**en**
200	doscientos	doh-see-**en**-tohss
500	quinientos	keen-**yen**-tohss
1,000	mil	meel
2,000	dos mil	dohs meel

USEFUL PHRASES

Do you speak English?	¿Habla usted inglés?	**ah**-blah oos-**ted** in-**glehs**
I don't speak Spanish	No hablo español	no **ah**-bloh es-pahn-**yol**
I don't understand (you)	No entiendo	no en-tee-**en**-doh
I understand (you)	Entiendo	en-tee-**en**-doh
I don't know	No sé	no seh
I am American/ British	Soy americano (americana)/ inglés(a)	soy ah-meh-ree-**kah**-no (ah-meh-ree-**kah**-nah)/in-**glehs**(ah)
My name is . . .	Me llamo . . .	meh **yah**-moh
Yes, please/ No, thank you	Sí, por favor/ No, gracias	**see** pohr fah-**vor**/ no **grah**-see-ahs
Yesterday/today/ tomorrow	Ayer/hoy/mañana	ah-**yehr**/oy/mahn-**yah**-nah
This morning/ afternoon	Esta mañana/tarde	**es**-tah mahn-**yah**-nah/**tar**-deh
Tonight	Esta noche	**es**-tah **no**-cheh
This/Next week	Esta semana/ la semana que entra	**es**-tah seh-**mah**-nah/lah seh-**mah**-nah keh **en**-trah
This/Next month	Este mes/el próximo mes	**es**-teh mehs/el **prok**-see-moh mehs
How?	¿Cómo?	**koh**-mo
When?	¿Cuándo?	**kwahn**-doh
What?	¿Qué?	keh
What is this?	¿Qué es esto?	keh es **es**-toh
Why?	¿Por qué?	por **keh**
Who?	¿Quién?	kee-**yen**
Where is . . . ?	¿Dónde está . . . ?	**dohn**-deh es-**tah**
the train station?	la estación del tren?	la es-tah-see-**on** del **train**
the subway station?	la estación del metro?	la es-ta-see-**on** del **meh**-tro
the bus stop?	la parada del autobus?	la pah-**rah**-dah del oh-toh-**boos**
the bank?	el banco?	el **bahn**-koh
the hotel?	el hotel?	el oh-**tel**
the post office?	la oficina de correos?	la oh-fee-**see**-nah deh-koh-**reh**-os
the museum?	el museo?	el moo-**seh**-oh
the hospital?	el hospital?	el ohss-pee-**tal**
the bathroom?	el baño?	el **bahn**-yoh

Here/there	Aquí/allá	ah-**key**/ah-**yah**
Open/closed	Abierto/cerrado	ah-bee-**er**-toh/ ser-**ah**-doh
Left/right	Izquierda/derecha	iss-key-**er**-dah/ dare-**eh**-chah
Straight ahead	Todo recto	**toh**-doh-**rec**-toh
Is it near/far?	¿Está cerca/lejos?	es-**tah sehr**-kah/ **leh**-hoss
I'd like . . . a room the key a newspaper a stamp	Quisiera . . . una habitación la llave un periódico un sello	kee-see-**ehr**-ah **oo**-nah ah-bee-tah-see-**on** lah **yah**-veh oon pehr-ee-**oh**-dee-koh **say**-oh
How much is this?	¿Cuánto cuesta?	**kwahn**-toh **kwes**-tah
A little/a lot	Un poquito/ mucho	oon poh-**kee**-toh/ **moo**-choh
More/less	Más/menos	mahss/**men**-ohss
I am ill	Estoy enfermo(a)	es-**toy** en-**fehr**-moh(mah)
Please call a doctor	Por favor llame un médico	pohr fah-**vor ya**-meh oon **med**-ee-koh
Help!	¡Ayuda!	ah-**yoo**-dah

ON THE ROAD

Avenue	Avenida	ah-ven-**ee**-dah
Broad, tree-lined boulevard	Paseo	pah-**seh**-oh
Highway	Carretera	car-reh-**ter**-ah
Port; mountain pass	Puerto	poo-**ehr**-toh
Street	Calle	**cah**-yeh
Waterfront promenade	Paseo marítimo	pah-**seh**-oh mahr-**ee**-tee-moh

IN TOWN

Cathedral	Catedral	cah-teh-**dral**
Church	Iglesia	**tem**-plo/ee-**glehs**-see-ah
City hall, town hall	Ayuntamiento	ah-yoon-tah-me-**yen**-toh
Door, gate	Puerta	poo-**ehr**-tah
Main square	Plaza Mayor	plah-thah mah-**yohr**
Market	Mercado	mer-**kah**-doh

Neighborhood	Barrio	**bahr**-ree-o
Tavern, rustic restaurant	Mesón	meh-**sohn**
Traffic circle, roundabout	Glorieta	glor-ee-**eh**-tah
Wine cellar, wine bar, wine shop	Bodega	boh-**deh**-gah

DINING OUT

A bottle of . . .	Una botella de . . .	**oo**-nah bo-**teh**-yah deh
A glass of . . .	Un vaso de . . .	oon **vah**-so deh
Bill/check	La cuenta	lah **kwen**-tah
Breakfast	El desayuno	el deh-sah-**yoon**-oh
Dinner	La cena	lah **seh**-nah
Menu of the day	Menú del día	meh-**noo** del **dee**-ah
Fork	El tenedor	ehl ten-eh-**dor**
Is the tip included?	¿Está incluida la propina?	es-**tah** in-cloo-**ee**-dah lah pro-**pee**-nah
Knife	El cuchillo	el koo-**chee**-yo
Large portion of tapas	Ración	rah-see-**ohn**
Lunch	La comida	lah koh-**mee**-dah
Menu	La carta, el menú	lah **cart**-ah, el meh-**noo**
Napkin	La servilleta	lah sehr-vee-**yet**-ah
Please give me . . .	Por favor déme . . .	pohr fah-**vor deh**-meh
Spoon	Una cuchara	**oo**-nah koo-**chah**-rah

MENU GUIDE

STARTERS
aguacate con gambas avocado and prawns
caldo thick soup
champiñones al ajillo mushrooms in garlic
consomé clear soup
gazpacho chilled soup made with tomatoes, onions, peppers, cucumbers, and oil
huevos flamencos eggs with spicy sausage and tomato
judías con tomate/jamón green beans with tomato/ham
sopa soup
sopa de ajo garlic soup
sopa de garbanzos chickpea soup
sopa de lentejas lentil soup
sopa de mariscos shellfish soup
sopa sevillana soup made with mayonnaise, shellfish, asparagus, and peas

OMELETS (TORTILLAS)
tortilla de champiñones mushroom omelet
tortilla de gambas prawn omelet
tortilla de mariscos seafood omelet
tortilla de patatas, tortilla española Spanish potato omelet
tortilla francesa plain omelet
tortilla sacromonte (in Granada) omelet with ham, sausage, and peas

MEATS (CARNES)
beicón bacon
bistec steak
cerdo pork
lomo de cerdo pork tenderloin
cabrito roasted kid
chorizo seasoned sausage
chuleta chop, cutlet
cochinillo suckling pig
cordero lamb
filete steak
jamón ham
jamón de York cooked ham
jamón serrano cured raw ham
morcilla blood sausage
salchicha sausage
salchichón Spanish salami (cured pork sausage)
solomillo de ternera fillet of beef
ternera veal

POULTRY (AVES) AND GAME (CAZA)
conejo rabbit
cordonices quail
faisán pheasant
jabalí wild boar
oca, ganso goose
pato duck
pato salvaje wild duck
pavo turkey
perdiz partridge
pollo chicken

ORGAN MEATS
callos tripe
criadillas bull's testicles (shown on Spanish menus as "unmentionables")
hígado liver
lengua tongue
mollejas sweetbreads
riñones kidneys
sesos brains

FISH (PESCADOS)
ahumados smoked fish (i.e. trout, eel, salmon)
anchoas anchovies
anguila eel
angulas baby eel
atún, bonito tuna
bacalao salt cod
besugo sea bream
boquerones fresh anchovies
lenguado sole
lubina sea bass
merluza hake, whitefish
mero grouper fish
pez espada, emperador swordfish
rape angler fish
raya skate
salmón salmon
salmonete red mullet
sardina sardine
trucha trout

SHELLFISH AND SEAFOOD (MARISCOS)
almeja clam
calamares squid
cangrejo crab
centolla spider crab
chipirones, chopitos small squid
cigalas crayfish
concha scallops
gambas prawns, shrimp
langosta lobster
langostino prawn
mejillones mussels
ostra oyster
percebes barnacles
pulpo octopus
sepia cuttlefish
vieiras scallop (in Galicia)
zarzuela de mariscos shellfish casserole

VEGETABLES (VERDURAS)
aceituna olive
aguacate avocado
ajo garlic
alcachofa artichoke
apio celery
berenjena eggplant
berza green cabbage
brécol/bróculi broccoli
calabacín zucchini
cebollo onion
calabaza pumpkin
champiñon mushroom
col cabbage
coliflor cauliflower
endivia endive
escarola chicory
ensalada salad
ensaladilla rusa potato salad
espárragos asparagus
espinacas spinach
espinacas a la catalana spinach with garlic, raisins, and pine nuts
garbanzos chickpeas
guisantes peas
habas broad beans
judías dried beans
judías verdes green beans
lechuga lettuce
lenteja lentil
palmitos palm hearts

patata potato
pepinillo gherkin
pepino cucumber
pimientos green/red peppers
puerro leek
seta chanterelle
tomate tomato
verduras green vegetables
zanahoria carrot

FRUIT (FRUTAS)
albaricoque apricot
ananás, piña pineapple
cereza cherry
chirimoya custard apple
ciruela plum
frambuesa raspberry
fresa strawberry
fresón large strawberry
grosella negra black currant
limón lemon
manzana apple
melocotón peach
melón melon
naranja orange
pera pear
plátano banana
sandía watermelon
uvas grapes
zarzamora blackberry

DESSERTS (POSTRES)
bizcocho, galleta biscuit
bizocho de chocolate chocolate cake
buñuelos warm, sugared, deep-fried doughnuts, sometimes cream-filled
con nata with cream
cuajada thick yogurt with honey
ensalada de frutas, macedonia fruit salad
flan caramel custard
fresas con nata strawberries and cream
helado de vainilla, fresa, café, chocolate vanilla, strawberry, coffee, chocolate ice cream
melocotón en almibar canned peaches
pastel cake
pera en almibar canned pears
pijama ice cream with fruit and syrup
piña en almibar canned pineapple

postre de músico dessert of dried fruit and nuts
la tarta de queso cheesecake
tarta helada ice-cream cake
la tartaleta de frutas fruit cake
yogur yogurt

MISCELLANEOUS

a la brasa barbequed
a la parrilla grilled
a la plancha grilled
aceite de oliva olive oil
al horno roasted, baked
arroz rice
asado roast
azúcar sugar
carbonade pot roasted
churros: baton-shaped donuts for dipping in hot chocolate, typically eaten at breakfast.
crudo raw
espaguettis spaghetti
fideos noodles
frito fried
guisado stewed
huevo egg
mahonesa mayonnaise
mantequilla butter
mermelada jam
miel honey
mostaza mustard
pan bread
patatas fritas french fries
perejil parsley
poché poached
queso cheese
relleno filled, stuffed
sal salt
salsa sauce
salsa de tomate catsup
vinagre vinegar

DRINKS (BEBIDAS)

agua water
agua con gas carbonated mineral water
agua sin gas still mineral water
blanco y negro cold black coffee with vanilla ice cream
café con leche coffee with cream
café solo black coffee (espresso)
caliente hot
caña small draught beer
cava, champán sparkling wine, champagne
cerveza beer
chocolate hot chocolate
cuba libre rum and coke
fino very dry sherry
frío/fría cold
gaseosa soda
granizado de limón (de café) lemon (or coffee) on crushed ice
hielo ice
horchata cold summer drink made from ground nuts
jerez sherry
jugo fruit juice
leche milk
limonada lemonade
manzanilla very dry sherry or camomile tea
sidra cider
té tea
con limón with lemon
con leche with milk
vaso glass
un vaso de agua a glass of water
vermut vermouth
vino wine
vino añejo vintage wine
vino blanco white wine
vino dulce sweet wine
vino espumoso sparkling wine
vino rosado rosé
vino seco dry wine
vino tinto red wine
zumo de naranja orange juice

TRAVEL SMART
SPAIN

GETTING HERE AND AROUND

▮ AIR TRAVEL

Flying time from New York to Madrid is about seven hours; from London, it's just over two hours.

Regular nonstop flights serve Spain from many major cities in the eastern United States; flying from other North American cities usually involves a stop. If you're coming from North America and want to land in a city other than Madrid or Barcelona, consider flying a European carrier.

There are a few package-flight options for travel to and within Spain. Iberia, for example, offers the Iberia Plus Internet club, which can offer exceptionally low fares.

The Europe By Air E-Flight Pass offers the lowest-fare tickets within Europe to more than 170 destinations on 18-plus airlines. There are no blackout dates, no charge for reservation changes, and no fare zones, but be aware that these passes are nonrefundable.

In the past few years there has been a sharp rise in the number of low-cost flights from the United Kingdom to Spain on carriers such as Monarch (⊕ *www.monarch. co.uk*) and flybe (⊕ *www.flybe.com*). They provide competition to the market's main players, easyJet (⊕ *www.easyjet. com*) and Ryanair (⊕ *www.ryanair.com*). All these carriers offer frequent flights, cover small cities as well as large ones, and have very competitive fares. Attitude Travel (⊕ *www.attitudetravel.com/ lowcostairlines*), Skyscanner (⊕ *www. skyscanner.net*), and Wegolo (⊕ *www. wegolo.com*) are comprehensive search sites for low-cost airlines worldwide.

Contacts Air Europa ☎ *800/2387672 in U.S., 902/401501 in Spain* ⊕ *www.air-europa. com.* **E-Flight Pass** ☎ *866/478–1810* ⊕ *www. europebyair.com.* **Iberia** ☎ *870/772–4642, 902/400515 in Spain* ⊕ *www.iberia.com.*

Transportation Security Administration. Answers for almost every transportation question that might come up. ⊕ *www.tsa.gov.*

AIRPORTS

Most flights from North America land in, or pass through, Madrid's Barajas (MAD). The other major gateway is Barcelona's El Prat de Llobregat (BCN). From the United Kingdom and elsewhere in Europe, regular flights also touch down in Málaga (AGP), Alicante (ALC), Palma de Mallorca (PMI), and many other smaller cities. Many budget airlines flying from the United Kingdom to Barcelona land at Girona airport, 90 minutes north of Barcelona.

GROUND TRANSPORTATION

Sagalés runs a shuttle-bus service between Girona's airport and Barcelona's North Station (Estació Nord), timed for arrivals and departures of Ryanair flights.

Airport Information Barcelona–El Prat de Llobregat ☎ *902/404704* ⊕ *www.aena. es.* **Girona** ☎ *902/404704.* **Madrid–Barajas** ☎ *902/404704* ⊕ *www.aena.es.* **Shuttle Buses Sagalés Buses** ☎ *902/130014* ⊕ *www.sagales.com.*

FLIGHTS

From North America, Air Europa flies to Madrid; American Airlines, part of the Oneworld Alliance, Iberia, and US Airways fly to Madrid and Barcelona; Delta flies direct to Barcelona. Note that some of these airlines use shared facilities and do not operate their own flights. Within Spain, Iberia is the main domestic airline, but Air Europa flies most domestic routes at lower prices. The budget airline Vueling heavily promotes its Internet bookings, which are often the country's cheapest domestic flight prices. The further from your travel date you purchase the ticket, the more bargains you're likely to find. Air Europa also has flights from Spain to other destinations in Europe. Air Europa and Iberia Express also serve destinations within Spain and elsewhere in Europe.

Iberia runs a shuttle, the Puente Áereo, offering flights just over an hour long between Madrid and Barcelona, every 30 minutes (more often during peak travel times) 6:45 am–9:45 pm. You don't need to reserve; you can buy your tickets at the airport ticket counter upon arriving or book online at ⊕ *www.iberia.com*. Passengers can also use the self-service check-in counters to avoid the line. Puente Áereo departs from Terminal T1 in Barcelona; in Madrid, the shuttle departs from Terminal 4.

Airline Contacts Air Europa ☎ *800/238–7672 in U.S., 902/401501 in Spain, 807/505050 in Spain* ⊕ *www.aireuropa.com.* **American Airlines** ☎ *800/433–7300* ⊕ *www. aa.com.* **Delta Airlines** ☎ *800/221–1212 for U.S. reservations, 800/241–4141 for international reservations* ⊕ *www.delta.com.* **Iberia** ☎ *870/772–4642* ⊕ *www.iberia.com.* **Iberia Express.** Flies to seven mainland destinations, the Balearic and Canary Islands, and to Athens, Berlin, Copenhagen, Dublin, Frankfurt, Naples, and Stockholm. ☎ *902/100424* ⊕ *www. iberiaexpress.com.* **United** ☎ *800/864–8331* ⊕ *www.united.com.* **US Airways** ☎ *800/428–4322* ⊕ *www.usairways.com.*

Within Spain Air Europa ☎ *902/401501* ⊕ *www.air-europa.com.* **Iberia** ☎ *902/400515* ⊕ *www.iberia.com.* **Vueling** ☎ *807/200100 (premium rate charged)* ⊕ *www.vueling.com.*

▌ BIKE TRAVEL

Taking bikes on Spanish intercity trains is restricted to overnight trains (bikes go under your bunk and must be packed in a special bike bag with the pedals off). Short-range daytime trains normally accept bicycles, although the conductor may decide that the train's too crowded and bump you and your bike. The very expensive alternative is to courier them. Cycling on freeways is against the law. For bike rentals, contact local tourist offices or check with rural hotels; we list some in individual cities.

▌ BOAT TRAVEL

Regular car ferries connect the United Kingdom with northern Spain. Brittany Ferries sails from Plymouth and Portsmouth to Santander and Bilbao. Trasmediterránea and Balearia connect mainland Spain to the Balearic and Canary islands.

Direct ferries from Spain to Tangier leave daily from Tarifa on FRS and from Algeciras on Trasmediterránea. Otherwise, you can take your car either to Ceuta (via Algeciras, on Balearia) or Melilla (via Malaga, on Trasmediterránea)—two Spanish enclaves on the North African coast—and then move on to Morocco.

Contacts **Balearia** ☎ *902/160180* ⊕ *www. balearia.com.* **Brittany Ferries** ☎ *0871/244–0744 in U.K., 902/108147 in Spain* ⊕ *www. brittany-ferries.com.* **FRS** ☎ *956/681830* ⊕ *www.frs.es.* **Trasmediterránea** ☎ *902/454645* ⊕ *www.trasmediterranea.com.*

▌ BUS TRAVEL

Within Spain, a mix of private companies provides bus service ranging from knee-crunchingly basic to luxurious. Fares are almost always lower than the corresponding train fares, and service covers more towns. Smaller towns don't usually have a central bus depot, so ask the tourist office where to wait for the bus. Note that service is less frequent on weekends. Spain's major national long-haul bus line is ALSA.

For longer trips, you can travel to Spain by modern buses (Eurolines/National Express, for example) from European destinations such as London, Paris, Rome, Frankfurt, Prague, and other major European cities.

Although it may once have been the case that international bus travel was significantly cheaper than air travel, new budget airlines have changed the equation. For perhaps a little more money and a large saving of travel hours, flying is increasingly the better option.

Most of Spain's larger companies have buses with comfortable seats and adequate legroom; on longer journeys (2 hours or more), a movie is shown on board, and earphones are provided. Except on smaller, regional lines, all buses have bathrooms on board; most long-haul buses also usually stop at least once every two to three hours for a snack and bathroom break. Smoking is prohibited on board.

ALSA has two luxury classes in addition to its regular seating. Clase Supra includes roomy leather seats and onboard meals; also, you have the option of *asientos individuales,* individual seats (with no other seat on either side) that line one side of the bus. The next class is the Clase Eurobus, with a private waiting room, comfortable seats, and plenty of legroom. The Clase Supra and Clase Eurobus usually cost, respectively, up to one-third and one-fourth more than the regular seats.

If you plan to return to your initial destination, you can save by buying a round-trip ticket. Also, some of Spain's smaller, regional bus lines offer multitrip passes, which are worthwhile if you plan to move back and forth between two fixed destinations within the region. Generally, these tickets offer a saving of 20% per journey; you can buy them at the station. The general rule for children is that if they occupy a seat, they pay full fare. Check the bus websites for *ofertas* (special offers).

At bus station ticket counters, most major credit cards (except American Express) are accepted. If you buy your ticket on the bus, it's cash only. Big lines such as ALSA encourage online purchasing. Once your ticket is booked, there's no need to go to the terminal sales desk—it's simply a matter of showing up at the bus with your ticket number and ID. The smaller regional services are increasingly providing online purchasing but will often require that your ticket be picked up at the terminal sales desk.

During peak travel times (Easter, August, and Christmas), it's a good idea to make a reservation at least a week in advance.

Contacts ALSA ☎ *902/422242* ⊕ *www. alsa.es.* **Eurolines/National Express** ☎ *0871/781–8178* ⊕ *www.eurolines.co.uk.* **Eurolines Spain** ☎ *902/405040, 93/367–4400* ⊕ *www.eurolines.es.*

▌ CAR TRAVEL

RENTAL CARS

Alamo, Avis, Budget, Europcar, Hertz, and National (partnered in Spain with the Spanish agency Atesa) have branches at major Spanish airports and in large cities. Smaller, regional companies and wholesalers offer lower rates. The online outfit Pepe Car has been a big hit with travelers; in general, the earlier you book, the less you pay. Rates run as low as €15 a day, taxes included—but note that pick-ups at its center-city locations are considerably cheaper than at the airports. All agencies have a range of models, but virtually all cars in Spain have manual transmission. ▌TIP➜ **If you don't want a stick shift, reserve weeks in advance and specify automatic transmission, then call to reconfirm your automatic car before you leave for Spain.** Rates in Madrid begin at the equivalents of $65 a day and $300 a week for an economy car with air-conditioning, manual transmission, and unlimited mileage, plus 21% tax. A small car is cheaper and prudent for the tiny roads and parking spaces in many parts of Spain.

Anyone age 18 or older with a valid license can drive in Spain, but most rental agencies will not rent cars to drivers under 23.

Major Agencies Atesa ☎ *902/100101 in Spain* ⊕ *www.atesa.es.* **Avis** ☎ *800/331–1084, 902/135531 in Spain* ⊕ *www.avis.com.* **Budget** ☎ *800/472–3325, 902/110291 in Spain* ⊕ *www.budget.com.* **Europcar** ☎ *902/503010 in Spain* ⊕ *www.europcar.es.* **Hertz** ☎ *800/852–3879, 915/097300 in Spain* ⊕ *www.hertz.com.* **Pepe Car** ☎ *807/414243 premium call charge* ⊕ *www.pepecar.com.*

Your own driver's license is valid in Spain, but U.S. citizens are highly encouraged to obtain an International Driving Permit (IDP). The IDP may facilitate car rental and help you avoid traffic fines—it translates your state-issued driver's license into 10 languages so officials can easily interpret the information on it. Permits are available from the American Automobile Association.

Driving is the best way to see Spain's rural areas. The main cities are connected by a network of excellent four-lane divided highways (*autovías* and *autopistas*), which are designated with the letter *A* and have speed limits—depending on the area—of between 80 kph (50 mph) to 120 kph (75 mph). If the artery is a toll highway ("toll" is *peaje*) it is designated *AP*. The letter *N* indicates a *carretera nacional*: a national or intercity route, with local traffic, which may have four or two lanes. Smaller towns and villages are connected by a network of secondary roads maintained by regional, provincial, and local governments, with an alphabet soup of different letter designations.

Spain's network of roads and highways is essentially well maintained and well marked, but bears a lot of traffic, especially during the vacation season and long holiday weekends. Crackdown campaigns on speeding have reduced what used to be a ghastly annual death toll on the roads—but you still need to drive defensively. Be prepared, too, for heavy truck traffic on national routes, which, in the case of two-lane roads, can have you creeping along for hours.

GASOLINE

Gas stations are plentiful, and most on major routes and in big cities are open 24 hours. On less-traveled routes, gas stations are usually open 7 am–11 pm. Most stations are self-service, although prices are the same as those at full-service stations. At night, however, you must pay before you fill up. Most pumps offer a choice of gas, including unleaded (*gasolina sin plomo*), high octane, and diesel, so be careful to pick the right one for your car. Prices vary little among stations and were at this writing €1.40 a liter for unleaded. A good site to monitor prices is ⊕ *www.energy.eu.* Credit cards are widely accepted.

PARKING

Parking is, almost without exception, a nightmare in Spanish cities. Don't park where the curb is painted yellow or where there is a yellow line painted a few inches from the curb. No-parking signs are also fairly easy to recognize.

In most cities, there are street-parking spaces marked by blue lines. Look for a nearby machine with a blue-and-white "P" sign to purchase a parking ticket, which you leave inside your car, on the dashboard, before you lock up. Sometimes an attendant will be nearby to answer questions. Parking time limits, fees, and fines vary. Parking lots are available, often underground, but spaces are at a premium. The rule of thumb is to leave your car at your hotel unless absolutely necessary.

ROAD CONDITIONS

Spain's highway system includes some 6,000 km (3,600 miles) of well-maintained superhighways. Still, you'll find some stretches of major national highways that are only two lanes wide, where traffic often backs up behind trucks. Autopista tolls are steep, but as a result these highways are often less crowded than the free ones. If you're driving down through Catalonia, be aware that there are more tolls here than anywhere else in Spain. This can result in a quicker journey but at a sizable cost. If you spring for the autopistas, you'll find that many of the rest stops are nicely landscaped and have cafeterias with decent but overpriced food.

Most Spanish cities have notoriously long morning and evening rush hours. Traffic jams are especially bad in and around Barcelona, Madrid, and Seville. If possible, avoid the morning rush, which can last until noon, and the evening rush, which lasts from 7 to 9. Also be aware that at the beginning, middle, and end of July and August, the country suffers its worst traffic jams (delays of 6 to 8 hours are common) as millions of Spaniards embark on, or return from, their annual vacations.

ROADSIDE EMERGENCIES

The rental agencies Hertz and Avis have 24-hour breakdown service. If you belong to AAA, you can get emergency assistance from the Spanish counterpart, RACE.

Emergency Service RACE ☎ 900/100992 *for info, 900/112222 for assistance* ⊕ *www. race.es.*

RULES OF THE ROAD

Spaniards drive on the right and pass on the left, so stay in the right-hand lane when not passing. Children under 12 may not ride in the front seat, and seat belts are compulsory for both front- and backseat riders. Speed limits are 30 kph (19 mph) or 50 kph (31 mph) in cities, depending on the type of street, 100 kph (62 mph) on national highways, 120 kph (75 mph) on the autopista or autovía. The use of cell phones by drivers, even on the side of the road, is illegal, except with completely hands-free devices.

Severe fines are enforced throughout Spain for driving under the influence of alcohol. Spot Breathalyzer checks are often carried out, and you will be cited if the level of alcohol in your bloodstream is found to be 0.05% or above.

Spanish highway police are increasingly vigilant about speeding and illegal passing. Police are empowered to demand payment on the spot from non-Spanish drivers. Police disproportionately target rental-car drivers for speeding and illegal passing, so play it safe.

■ CRUISE SHIP TRAVEL

Barcelona is the busiest cruise port in Spain and Europe. Other popular ports of call in the country are Málaga, Alicante, and Palma de Mallorca. Nearby Gibraltar is also a popular stop. Although cruise lines such as Silversea and Costa traditionally offer cruises that take in parts of Spain and other Mediterranean countries such as Italy and Greece, it is becoming increasingly common to find package tours wholly within Spain. Two popular routes consist of island hopping in the Balearics or around the Canary Islands. Among the many cruise lines that call on Spain are Royal Caribbean, Holland America Line, Norwegian Cruise Line, and Princess Cruises.

■ TRAIN TRAVEL

The chart here has information about popular train routes. (⇨ See Experience Spain for a map of the country, with train routes.) Prices are for one-way fares (depending on seating and where purchased) and subject to change.

International trains run from Madrid to Lisbon (10 hours 40 minutes, overnight), Barcelona to Paris (6 hours 30 minutes), and Madrid to Paris (10 hours).

Spain's wonderful high-speed train, the 290-kph (180-mph) AVE, travels between Madrid and Seville (with a stop in Córdoba) in 2½ hours; prices start at about €52 each way. It also serves the Madrid–Barcelona route, cutting travel time to just under three hours. From Madrid you can also reach Lleida, Huesca (one AVE train daily), Málaga, Toledo, and Valladolid.

The fast Talgo service is also efficient, but other elements of the state-run rail system—known as RENFE—are still a bit subpar by European standards, and some long-distance trips with multiple stops can be tediously slow. Although some overnight trains have comfortable sleeper cars, first-class fares that include a sleeping compartment are comparable to, or more expensive than, airfares.

Most Spaniards buy train tickets in advance at the train station's *taquilla* (ticket office). The lines can be long, so give yourself plenty of time. For popular train routes, you will need to reserve tickets more than a few days in advance and pick them up at least a day before traveling. The ticket clerks at the stations rarely speak English, so if you need help or advice in planning a more complex train journey, you may be better off going to a travel agency that displays the blue-and-yellow RENFE sign. A small commission (e.g., €2.50) should be expected. For shorter, regional train trips, you can often buy your tickets from machines in the train station.

You can use a credit card for train tickets at most city train stations, but in smaller towns and villages it may be cash only. Seat reservations are required on most long-distance and some other trains, particularly high-speed trains, and are wise on any train that might be crowded. You need a reservation if you want a sleeping berth.

The easiest way to make reservations is to go to the English version of the RENFE website (⊕ *www.renfe.com*—click on "Welcome" on the top line) or use the RenfeTicket smartphone app (to buy tickets using the app, you need to register and to have bought a RENFE ticket with your credit card). Go to Timetables and Prices, but be aware that the site can often be wonky, with unpredictable broken links. Input your destination(s) and date(s), and the site will indicate seat availability; book earlier if you're traveling during Holy Week, on long holiday weekends, or in July and August. (The site allows you to make reservations up to 62 days in advance, which is important in qualifying for online purchase discounts. ⇨ *see below*.) When you've completed your reservation, you can print out a PDF

TRAIN TRAVEL TIMES	
Madrid to Barcelona: From €40 to €213	AVE rapid trains make the trip in 2 hours 30 minutes
Madrid to Bilbao: From €20 to €65.20	Semi-express Alvia train time is 4 hours 57 minutes
Madrid to Málaga: From €47.70 to €160.80	Fastest AVE trains take 2 hours 20 minutes
Madrid to Seville: From €52 to €127.20	Fastest AVE trains take 2 hours 20 minutes
Madrid to Granada: From €41.05 to €88.90	Running time about 4 hours 25 minutes
Madrid to Santander: From €24.95 to €64.90	Semi-express Alvia is 4 hours 25 minutes
Madrid to Valencia: From €39.10 to €122	Fastest AVE trains take 1 hour 38 minutes
Madrid to Santiago de Compostela: From €21.70 to €70.50	Fastest time about 5 hours 30 minutes
Barcelona to Bilbao: From €26.15 to €85	Running time about 6 hours 20 minutes
Barcelona to Valencia: From €22.50 to €73.90	Fastest time 2 hours 59 minutes
Seville to Granada: From €29.55	Running time about 3 hours 10 minutes

version of your ticket, with the car and seat assignment; you will also get a confirmation by email with a *localizador* (locator number) that you can use, in case you can't access the PDF file, to pick up the tickets at any RENFE station (most major airports have a RENFE booth, so you can retrieve your tickets as soon as you arrive in Spain); central stations in most major cities have automated check-in machines. You'll need your passport and the credit card you used for the reservation. You can review your pending reservations online at any time.

Caveats: You cannot buy tickets online for certain regional lines or for commuter lines (*cercanias*). Station agents cannot alter your reservations; you must do this yourself online. The RENFE website may not work with all browsers, but it does accept all major credit cards, including American Express.

DISCOUNTS

If you purchase a ticket on the RENFE website for the AVE or any of the Grandes Lineas (the faster, long-distance trains, including the Talgo) you can get a discount of anywhere from 20% to 60%, depending on how far ahead you book and how you travel: discounts on one-way tickets tend to be higher than on round-trips. Discount availabilities disappear fast: the earliest opportunity is 62 days in advance of travel. If you have a domestic or an international airline ticket and want to take the AVE within 48 hours of your arrival but haven't booked online, you can still get a 10% discount on the AVE one-way ticket and 25% for a round-trip ticket with a dated return. On regional trains, you get a 10% discount on round-trip tickets (15% on AVE medium-distance trains).

■ TIP→ If there are more than two of you traveling on the AVE, look for the "4M" symbol (in a navy square) quoting the price per person for four people traveling together and sitting at the same table. If you select the price, it tells you how much the deal is for one, two, and three people. You have to buy all the tickets at the same time, but they're at least 20% cheaper than regular tickets.

RAIL PASSES

If you're coming from the United States and are planning extensive train travel in Europe, check Rail Europe for Eurail passes. Whichever pass you choose, you must buy it before you leave for Europe.

Spain is one of 24 European countries in which you can use the Eurail Global Pass, which buys you unlimited first-class rail travel in all participating countries for the duration of the pass. If you plan to rack up the miles, your best bet might be a Select Pass, which allows you to travel on as many as 15 days of your choice within a two-month period, and among up to five bordering countries. Note, however, that France isn't included in the five, so travel between Spain and Italy must be via ferry between Barcelona and Livorno (discounted fares apply with the Select Pass). Prices (for passengers 26 or older) range from $632 to $1,478, depending on the number of travel days and countries you select.

If Spain is your only destination, a Eurail Spain Pass allows three days of unlimited train travel in Spain within a two-month period for $320 (first class) and $257 (second class); for 10 days of unlimited travel within two months, the passes are $650 and $484, respectively. There are also combination passes for those visiting Spain and Portugal, Spain and France, and Spain and Italy.

Many travelers assume that rail passes guarantee them seats on the trains they wish to ride: not so. Reserve seats even if you're using a rail pass.

Contacts Eurail ⊕ *www.eurail.com.* **Rail Europe** ☎ *800/622–8600 in U.S., 800/361–7245 in Canada* ⊕ *www.raileurope.com.* **RENFE** ☎ *902/320320 for info, 902/109420 for tickets* ⊕ *www.renfe.es.*

ESSENTIALS

▮ ACCOMMODATIONS

By law, hotel prices in Spain must be posted at the reception desk and should indicate whether the value-added tax (I.V.A. 10%) is included. Note that high-season rates prevail not only in summer but also during Holy Week and local fiestas. In much of Spain, breakfast is normally *not* included. *Prices in the reviews are the lowest cost of a standard double room in high season.*

Most hotels and other lodgings require you to give your credit-card details before they will confirm your reservation. If you don't feel comfortable emailing this information, ask if you can fax it (some places even prefer faxes). However you book, get confirmation in writing, and have a copy of it when you check in.

Be sure you understand the hotel's cancellation policy. Some places allow you to cancel without any kind of penalty— even if you prepaid to secure a discounted rate—if you cancel at least 24 hours in advance. Others require you to cancel a week in advance or penalize you the cost of one night. Small inns and bed-and-breakfasts are most likely to require you to cancel far in advance.

APARTMENT AND HOUSE RENTALS

If you are interested in a single-destination vacation, or are staying in one place and using it as a base for exploring the local area, renting an apartment or a house can be a good idea. However, it is not always possible to ensure the quality beforehand, and you may be responsible for supplying your own bed linens, towels, etc.

Contacts Holiday Lettings ⊕ *www. holidaylettings.co.uk.* **Home Away** ☏ *877/228–3145, 512/782–0805 international* ⊕ *www. homeaway.com.* **Interhome** ☏ *954/791–8282, 800/882–6864* ⊕ *www.interhomeusa.com.* **Villas and Apartments Abroad** ☏ *212/213–6435* ⊕ *www.vaanyc.com.* **Villas International**

☏ *415/499–9490, 800/221–2260* ⊕ *www. villasintl.com.*

HOSTELS

Youth hostels (*albergues juveniles*) in Spain are usually large and impersonal (but clean) with dorm-style beds. Most are geared to students, though many have a few private rooms suitable for families and couples. These rooms fill up quickly, so book at least a month in advance. Other budget options are the university student dorms (*residencia estudiantil*), some of which offer accommodations in summer, when students are away.

▮TIP→ Note that in Spain hostales are not the same as the dorm-style youth hostels common elsewhere in Europe—they are inexpensive hotels with individual rooms, not communal quarters.

Contacts Hostelling International—USA ☏ *240/650–2100* ⊕ *www.hiusa.org.*

HOTELS AND BED-AND-BREAKFASTS

The Spanish government classifies hotels with one to five stars, with an additional rating of five-star GL (Gran Lujo) indicating the highest quality. Although quality is a factor, the rating is technically only an indication of how many facilities the hotel offers. For example, a three-star hotel may be just as comfortable as a four-star hotel but lack a swimming pool.

All hotel entrances are marked with a blue plaque bearing the letter *H* and the number of stars. The letter *R* (standing for *residencia*) after the letter *H* indicates an establishment with no meal service, with the possible exception of breakfast. The designations *fonda* (F), *pensión* (P), *casa de huéspedes* (CH), and *hostal* (Hs) indicate budget accommodations. In most cases, especially in smaller villages, rooms in such buildings will be basic but clean; in large cities, these rooms can be downright dreary.

When inquiring in Spanish about whether a hotel has a private bath, ask if it's an *habitación con baño*. Although a single room (*habitación sencilla*) is usually available, singles are often on the small side. Solo travelers might prefer to pay a bit extra for single occupancy of a double room (*habitación doble uso individual*). Make sure you request a double bed (*cama de matrimono*) if you want one—if you don't ask, you will usually end up with two singles.

There's a growing trend in Spain toward small country hotels and agri-tourism. Rusticae (⊕ *www.rusticae.es*) is an association of more than 170 independently owned hotels in restored palaces, monasteries, mills, and estates, generally in rural Spain. Similar associations serve individual regions, and tourist offices also provide lists of establishments. In Galicia, *pazos* are beautiful, old, often stately homes converted into small luxury hotels; Pazos de Galicia (⊕ *www.pazosdegalicia.com*) is the main organization for them. In Cantabria, *casonas* are small to large country houses, but as they don't have individual websites, it is necessary to check the regional tourist office websites. If you're headed for Andalusia, the Asociación de Hoteles Rurales Andalucia (AHRA ⊕ *www.ahra.es*) is a useful resource.

A number of *casas rurales* (country houses similar to B&Bs) offer pastoral lodging either in guest rooms or in self-catering cottages. You may also come across the term *finca,* for country estate house.

Many *agroturismo* accommodations are fincas converted to upscale B&Bs.

PARADORES

The Spanish government operates nearly 100 *paradores*—upscale hotels often in historic buildings or near significant sites. Rates are reasonable, considering that most paradores have four- or five-star amenities, and the premises are invariably immaculate and tastefully furnished, often with antiques or reproductions. Each parador has a restaurant serving regional specialties, and you can stop in for a meal without spending the night. Paradores are popular with foreigners and Spaniards alike, so make reservations well in advance. (⇨ *See the Paradores: A Night with History feature, in the Experience chapter, for more details.*)

Contact Paradores de España
☎ 902/547979 in Spain, 800/634–1188 in U.S.
⊕ *www.parador.es or www.eparadors.com.*

▌ COMMUNICATIONS

INTERNET

Internet cafés are most common in tourist and student precincts. If you can't find one easily, ask at either the tourist office or a hotel's front desk. The most you're likely to pay for Internet access is about €3 an hour.

Migration to the country's bigger cities means the demand has skyrocketed for *locutorios* (cheap international phone centers), which double as places to get on the Internet.

Internet access in Spanish hotels is now fairly widespread, even in less expensive accommodations. In-room dial-up connections are gradually getting phased out, in favor of Wi-Fi; some hotels will still have a computer console somewhere in the lobby for the use of guests (either free or with a fee), but Wi-Fi hot spots are common.

Contacts Cybercafes. Lists more than 4,200 Internet cafés worldwide. ⊕ *www.cybercafes.*

com. **Gonuts4free** ⊕ *www.gonuts4free.com/ yellow/internetcafes.*

PHONES

The good news is that you can now make a direct-dial telephone call from virtually any point on earth. The bad news? You can't always do so cheaply. Calling from a hotel is almost always the most expensive option; hotels usually add huge surcharges to all calls, particularly international ones. In some countries you can phone from call centers or even the post office. Calling cards usually keep costs to a minimum, but only if you purchase them locally. And then there are cell phones, which are sometimes more prevalent—particularly in the developing world—than landlines; as expensive as cell phone calls can be, they are still usually a much cheaper option than calling from your hotel.

Spain's phone system is efficient but can be expensive. Most travelers buy phone cards, which for €5 or €6 allow for about three hours of calls nationally and internationally. Phone cards can be used with any hotel, bar, or public telephone and can be bought at any tobacco shop and at most Internet cafés.

Note that only cell phones conforming to the European GSM standard will work in Spain. If you're going to be traveling in Spain for an extended period, buying a phone often turns out to be a money saver. Using a local cell phone means avoiding the hefty long-distance charges accrued when using your own cell phone. Prices fluctuate, but offers start as low as €20 for a phone with €10 worth of calls.

A cheap and usually free alternative to using a phone is calling via your computer with a VOIP provider such as Skype or FaceTime, or installing a free messager–call app on your cell phone such as LINE. The country code for Spain is 34. The country code is 1 for the United States and Canada.

CALLING WITHIN SPAIN

International operators, who generally speak English, are at 025.

All area codes begin with a 9. To call within Spain—even locally—dial the area code first. Numbers preceded by a 900 code are toll-free in Spain; however, 90x numbers are not (e.g., 901, 902, etc.). Phone numbers starting with a 6 or 7 belong to cellular phones. Note that when calling a cell phone, you do not need to dial the area code first; also, calls to cell phones are significantly more expensive than calls to regular phones.

You'll find pay phones in individual booths, in local telephone offices (locutorios), and in many bars and restaurants. Most have a digital readout so you can see your money ticking away. If you're calling with coins, you need at least €0.50 to call locally and €1 to call a cell phone or another province. Simply insert the coins and wait for a dial tone. Note that rates are reduced on weekends and after 8 pm during the week.

CALLING OUTSIDE SPAIN

International calls are awkward from coin-operated pay phones and can be expensive from hotels. Your best bet is to use a public phone that accepts phone cards or go to the locutorios. Those near the center of town are generally more expensive; farther from the center, the rates are sometimes as much as one-third less. You converse in a quiet, private booth and are charged according to the meter.

To make an international call, dial 00, then the country code, then the area code and number.

The country code for the United States is 1.

Before you leave home, find out your long-distance company's access code in Spain.

General Information AT&T ☎ *800/331– 0500* ⊕ *www.att.com.* **MCI** ☎ *800/444–3333 for US, 800/955–0925 for international* ⊕ *www.mci.com.* **Sprint** ☎ *888/211–4727* ⊕ *www.sprint.com.*

LOCAL DO'S AND TABOOS

GREETINGS

When addressing Spaniards with whom you are not well acquainted or who are elderly, use the formal *usted* rather than the familiar *tú*.

DRESS

Some town councils are cracking down on people wearing swimsuits in public spaces. Use your common sense—it's unlikely you'd be allowed entry in a bar or restaurant wearing swimming attire back home, so don't do it when overseas. Be respectful when visiting churches: casual dress is fine if it's not too revealing. Spaniards object to men going bare-chested anywhere other than the beach or poolside.

OUT ON THE TOWN

These days, the Spanish are generally very informal, and casual-smart dress is accepted in most places.

DOING BUSINESS

Spanish office hours can be confusing to the uninitiated. Some offices stay open more or less continuously from 9 to 3, with a very short lunch break. Others open in the morning, break up the day with a long lunch break of two to three hours, and then reopen at 4 or 5 until 7 or 8. Spaniards enjoy a certain notoriety for their lack of punctuality, but this has changed dramatically in recent years, and you are expected to show up for meetings on time. Smart dress is the norm.

Spaniards in international fields tend to conduct business with foreigners in English. If you speak Spanish, address new colleagues with the formal *usted* and the corresponding verb conjugations, then follow their lead in switching to the familiar *tú* once a working relationship has been established.

LANGUAGE

One of the best ways to avoid being an Ugly American is to learn a little of the local language. You need not strive for fluency; even mastering a few basic words and terms is bound to make chatting with the locals more rewarding.

Although Spaniards exported their language to all of Central and South America, Spanish is not the principal language in all of Spain. Outside their big cities, the Basques speak Euskera. In Catalonia, you'll hear Catalan throughout the region, just as you'll hear Gallego in Galicia and Valenciano in València (the latter, Mallorquín in Mallorca, and Menorquín in Menorca are considered Catalan dialects). Although almost everyone in these regions also speaks and understands Spanish, local radio and television stations may broadcast in their respective languages, and road signs may be printed (or spray-painted over) with the preferred regional language. Spanish is referred to as Castellano, or Castilian.

Fortunately, Spanish is fairly easy to pick up, and your efforts to speak it will be graciously received. Learn at least the following basic phrases: *buenos días* (hello—until 2 pm), *buenas tardes* (good afternoon—until 8 pm), *buenas noches* (hello—after dark), *por favor* (please), *gracias* (thank you), *adiós* (good-bye), *sí* (yes), *no* (no), *los servicios* (the toilets), *la cuenta* (bill/check), ¿*Habla inglés?* (Do you speak English?), and *No comprendo* (I don't understand). If your Spanish breaks down, you should have no trouble finding people who speak English in major cities and coastal resorts, but you won't necessarily be able to count on the bus driver or the passerby on the street. It's much more likely that you'll find an English-language speaker if you approach people under age 30.

CALLING CARDS

Pay phones require phone cards (*tarjetas telefónicas*), which you can buy in various denominations at any tobacco shop or newsstand. Some phones also accept credit cards, but phone cards are more reliable.

MOBILE PHONES

If you have a multiband phone (some countries use different frequencies than those used in the United States) and your service provider uses the world-standard GSM network (as do T-Mobile, AT&T, and Verizon), you can probably use your phone abroad. Roaming fees can be steep, however: 99¢ a minute is considered reasonable. Overseas you normally pay the toll charges for incoming calls. It's almost always cheaper to send a text message than to make a call, as text messages have a very low set fee (often less than 5¢). If you just want to make local calls, consider buying a new SIM card (note that your provider may have to unlock your phone) and a prepaid service plan in the destination. You'll then have a local number and can make local calls at local rates. If your trip is extensive, you could also simply buy a new cell phone in your destination, as the initial cost will be offset over time.

■ TIP→ If you travel internationally frequently, save one of your old cell phones or buy a cheap one on the Internet; ask your cell phone company to unlock it for you and take it with you as a travel phone, buying a new SIM card with pay-as-you-go service in each destination.

Contacts Cellular Abroad. Rents and sells GMS phones and sells SIM cards that work in many countries. ☎ 800/287–5072, 310/862–7100 for international calls, 800/3623–3333 in Spain (toll-free) ⊕ www.cellularabroad.com. **Mobal.** Rents cell phones and sells GSM phones (starting at $29 a week) that will operate in 190 countries. Per-call rates vary throughout the world. ☎ 888/888–9162 ⊕ www.mobal.com. **Planet Fone.** Rents cell phones at $21 a week, but discounts can cut that fee by 10%. ☎ 888/988–4777 ⊕ www.planetfone.com. **Telestial.** Sells Spanish SIM cards online for $15, which includes $5 worth of calling credit. ☎ 213/337–5560 ⊕ www.telestial.com.

▌ EATING OUT

Sitting around a table eating and talking is a huge part of Spanish culture, defining much of people's daily routines. Sitting in the middle of a typical bustling restaurant here goes a long way toward building understanding of how fundamental food can be to Spanish lives.

Although Spain has always had an extraordinary range of regional cuisine, in the past decade or so its restaurants have won it international recognition at the highest levels. A new generation of Spanish chefs—led by the revolutionary Ferran Adrià—has transformed classic dishes to suit contemporary tastes, drawing on some of the freshest ingredients in Europe and bringing an astonishing range of new technologies into the kitchen.

As of 2010, smoking has been banned entirely in all eating and drinking establishments in Spain.

MEALS AND MEALTIMES

Outside major hotels, which serve morning buffets, breakfast (*desayuno*) is usually limited to coffee and toast or a roll. Lunch (*comida* or *almuerzo*) traditionally consists of an appetizer, a main course, and dessert, followed by coffee and perhaps a liqueur. Between lunch and dinner the best way to snack is to sample some *tapas* (appetizers) at a bar; normally you can choose from quite a variety. Dinner (*cena*) is somewhat lighter, with perhaps only one course. In addition to à la carte selections, most restaurants offer a daily fixed-price menu (*menú del día*), consisting of a starter, main plate, beverage, and dessert. The menú del día is traditionally offered only at lunch, but increasingly it's also offered at dinner in popular tourist destinations. If your waiter does not suggest it when you're seated, ask for it— "*¿Hay menú del día, por favor?*"

Mealtimes in Spain are later than elsewhere in Europe, and later still in Madrid and the southern region of Andalusia. Lunch starts around 2 or 2:30 (closer to 3 in Madrid) and dinner after 9 (as late as 11 or midnight in Madrid). Weekend eating times, especially dinner, can begin upward of an hour later. In areas with heavy tourist traffic, some restaurants open a bit earlier.

Most prices listed in menus are inclusive of 10% value-added-tax (I.V.A.), but not all. If I.V.A. isn't included, it should read, "10% I.V.A. no incluido en los precios" at the bottom of the menu. Unless otherwise noted, the restaurants listed in this guide are open daily for lunch and dinner. *Prices in the reviews are the average cost of a main course or equivalent combination of smaller dishes at dinner or, if dinner is not served, at lunch.*

PAYING

Credit cards are widely accepted in Spanish restaurants, but some smaller establishments do not take them. If you pay by credit card and you want to leave a small tip above and beyond the service charge, leave the tip in cash. (⇨ *See Tipping, for guidelines.*)

RESERVATIONS AND DRESS

Regardless of where you are, it's a good idea to make a reservation if you can. In some places, it's expected. We only mention them specifically when reservations are essential (there's no other way you'll ever get a table) or when they are not accepted. For popular restaurants, book as far ahead as you can (often 30 days), and reconfirm as soon as you arrive. (Large parties should always call ahead to check the reservations policy.) We mention dress only when men are required to wear a jacket or a jacket and tie.

WINES, BEER, AND SPIRITS

Apart from its famous wines, Spain produces many brands of lager, the most popular of which are San Miguel, Cruzcampo, Aguila, Voll Damm, Mahou, and Estrella. Jerez de la Frontera is Europe's

largest producer of brandy and is a major source of sherry. Catalonia is a major producer of *cava* (sparkling wine). Spanish law prohibits the sale of alcohol to people age 18 or younger.

▌ ELECTRICITY

Spain's electrical current is 220–240 volts, 50 cycles alternating current (AC); wall outlets take Continental-type plugs, with two round prongs.

Consider making a small investment in a universal adapter, which has several types of plugs in one lightweight, compact unit. Most laptops and cell-phone chargers are dual voltage (i.e., they operate equally well on 110 and 220 volts) and require only an adapter. These days the same is true of small appliances such as hair dryers. Always check labels and manufacturer instructions to be sure. Don't use 110-volt outlets marked "For Shavers Only" for high-wattage appliances such as hair dryers.

▌ EMERGENCIES

The pan-European emergency phone number (☎ 112) is operative in all of Spain, or you can dial the emergency numbers here for the national police, local police, fire department, or medical services. On the road, there are emergency phones marked "SOS" at regular intervals on autovías and autopistas. If your documents are stolen, contact both the local police and your embassy. If you lose a credit card, phone the issuer immediately.

Foreign Embassies and Consulates
U.S. Embassy ✉ *Calle Serrano 75, Madrid* ☎ *91/587–2200 for international, 91/587–2240 for US citizen emergencies* ⊕ *spanish.madrid.usembassy.gov* ✉ *Paseo Reina Elisenda 23, Barcelona* ☎ *93/280–2227* ⊕ *barcelona.usconsulate.gov.*

General Emergency Contacts Fire department ☎ *080.* **Local police** ☎ *092.* **Medical service** ☎ *061.* **National police** ☎ *091.*

▮ HEALTH

The most common types of illnesses are caused by contaminated food and water. Make sure food has been thoroughly cooked and is served to you fresh and hot; avoid vegetables and fruits that you haven't washed (in bottled or purified water) or peeled yourself. If you have problems, mild cases of traveler's diarrhea may respond to Imodium (known generically as loperamide) or Pepto-Bismol. Be sure to drink plenty of fluids; if you can't keep fluids down, seek medical help immediately.

Infectious diseases can be airborne or passed via mosquitoes and ticks and through direct or indirect physical contact with animals or people. Some, including Norwalk-like viruses that affect your digestive tract, can be passed along through contaminated food. Condoms can help prevent most sexually transmitted diseases, but they aren't absolutely reliable and their quality varies from country to country. Speak with your physician and check the CDC or World Health Organization websites for health alerts, particularly if you're pregnant, traveling with children, or have a chronic illness.

SPECIFIC ISSUES IN SPAIN
Medical care is good in Spain, but nursing can be perfunctory, as relatives are expected to stop by and look after patients' needs. In some popular destinations, such

as the Costa del Sol, there are volunteer English interpreters on hand at hospitals and clinics.

In the summer, sunburn and sunstroke are real risks in Spain. Even if you're not normally bothered by strong sun you should cover yourself up, slather on sunblock, drink plenty of fluids, and limit sun time for the first few days. If you require medical attention for any problem, ask your hotel's front desk for assistance, or go to the nearest public **Centro de Salud** (day hospital); in serious cases, you'll be referred to the regional hospital.

OVER-THE-COUNTER REMEDIES
Over-the-counter remedies are available at any *farmacia* (pharmacy), recognizable by a large green cross outside. Some will look familiar, such as *aspirina* (aspirin), and other medications are sold under various brand names. If you get traveler's diarrhea, ask for an *antidiarréico* (antidiarrheal medicine); Fortasec is a well-known brand. Mild cases may respond to Imodium (known generically as loperamide) or Pepto-Bismol. To keep from getting dehydrated, drink plenty of purified water or herbal tea. In severe cases, rehydrate yourself with a salt-sugar solution—½ teaspoon salt (*sal*) and 4 tablespoons sugar (*azúcar*) per quart of water, or pick up a package of oral rehydration salts at any local farmacia.

If you regularly take a nonprescription medication, take a sample box or bottle with you, and the Spanish pharmacist will provide you with its local equivalent.

▮ HOURS OF OPERATION

The ritual of a long afternoon siesta is no longer as ubiquitous as it once was. However, the tradition does remain, and many people take a postlunch nap before returning to work or continuing on with their day. The two- to three-hour lunch break makes it possible to eat and then snooze. Midday breaks generally begin at 1 or 2 and end between 4 and 5, depending on the city and the sort of business.

The midafternoon siesta—often a half-hour power nap in front of the TV—fits naturally into the workday cycle, since Spaniards tend to work until 7 or 8 pm.

Traditionally, Spain's climate prompted the creation of the siesta as a time to preserve energy while afternoon temperatures spiked. After the sun began to set, people went back to working, shopping, and taking their leisurely *paseo* (stroll). In the big cities—particularly with the advent of air-conditioning—the heat has less effect on the population; in the small towns in the south of Spain, however, many still use a siesta as a way to wait out the weather.

Until a decade or so ago, it was common for many businesses to close for a month in the July–August period. When open, they often run on a summer schedule, which can mean a longer-than-usual siesta (sometimes up to 4 hours), a shorter working day (until 3 pm only), and no Saturday-afternoon trading.

Banks are generally open weekdays from 8:30 or 9 until 2 or 2:30. From October to May the major banks and savings banks open on Thursday until 6:30 or 7:30. Currency exchanges at airports, train stations, and in the city center stay open later; you can also cash traveler's checks at El Corte Inglés department stores until 10 pm (some branches close at 9 or 9:30). Most government offices are open weekdays 9–2.

Most museums are open from 9:30 to 2 and 4 to 7 or 8, every day but Monday. Schedules are subject to change, particularly between the high and low seasons, so confirm opening hours before you make plans. A few large museums, such as Madrid's Prado and Reina Sofía and Barcelona's Picasso Museum, stay open all day, without a siesta.

Pharmacies keep normal business hours (9–1:30 and 5–8), but every midsize town (or city neighborhood) has a duty pharmacy that stays open 24 hours. The location of the nearest on-duty pharmacy is usually posted on the front door of all pharmacies.

When planning a shopping trip, remember that almost all shops in Spain close from 1 or 2 pm for at least two hours. The only exceptions are large supermarkets and the department-store chain El Corte Inglés. Most shops are closed on Sunday, and in Madrid and several other places they're also closed Saturday afternoon. Larger shops in tourist areas may stay open Sunday in summer and during the Christmas holiday.

HOLIDAYS

Spain's national holidays, observed countrywide, are New Year's Day on January 1 (*Año Nuevo*), Three Kings Day on January 6 (*Día de los Tres Reyes*), Good Friday (*Viernes Santo*), Labor Day on May 1 (*Día del Trabajo*), Assumption on August 15 (*Asunción*), Columbus Day on October 12 (*Día de la Hispanidad*), All Saints Day on November 1 (*Todos los Santos*), Constitution Day on December 6 (*Día de la Constitución*), Immaculate Conception on December 8 (*Immaculada Concepción*), and Christmas Day on December 25 (*Navidad*). Holidays observed in many parts of Spain, but not all, include Father's Day on March 19 (*San José*, observed in Madrid and some regional communities*)*, Maundy Thursday (*Jueves Santo,* observed in most of Spain except Catalunya, Valencia, and the Balearic Islands), Easter Monday (*Día de Pascua,* observed in Catalunya, Valencia, and the Balearic Islands), St. John's Day on June 24, with bonfire celebrations the night before (*San Juan,* observed in Catalonia, Valencia, and the Balearic Islands), *Corpus Christi* (June), St. Peter and St. Paul Day on June 29 (*San Pedro y San Pablo*) and St. James Day on July 25 (*Santiago*). In addition, each region, city, and town has its own holidays honoring political events and patron saints.

Many stores close during *Semana Santa* (Holy Week—also sometimes translated as Easter Week), the week that precedes Easter.

If a public holiday falls on a Tuesday or Thursday, remember that many businesses also close on the nearest Monday or Friday for a long weekend, called a *puente* (bridge). If a major holiday falls on a Sunday, businesses close on Monday.

▌ MAIL

Spain's postal system, or *correos,* does work, but delivery times vary widely. An airmail letter to the United States may take from four days to two weeks; delivery to other destinations is equally unpredictable. Sending your letters by priority mail (*urgente*) or the cheaper registered mail (*certificado*) ensures speedier and safer arrival.

Airmail letters to the United States cost €0.90 for up to 20 grams (¾ ounce). Letters within Spain are €0.37. Postcards carry the same rates as letters. You can buy stamps at licensed tobacco shops; post offices no longer sell stamps, but stamp mail with the correct amount.

Because mail delivery in Spain can often be slow and unreliable, it's best to have your mail held at a Spanish post office; have it addressed to "Lista de Correos" (the equivalent of *poste restante*) in a town you'll be visiting. Postal addresses should include the name of the province in parentheses, for example, Marbella (Málaga).

SHIPPING PACKAGES

When time is of the essence, or when you're sending valuable items or documents overseas, you can use a courier (*mensajero*). The major international agencies, such as FedEx, UPS, and DHL, have representatives in Spain; the biggest Spanish courier service is Seur. MRW is another local courier that provides express delivery worldwide.

Express Services Correos ☎ *902/197197* ⊕ *www.correos.es.* **DHL** ☎ *902/122424 for air, 902/123030 for ground* ⊕ *www.dhl.es.* **FedEx** ☎ *902/100871* ⊕ *www.fedex.com/ es_english.* **MRW** ☎ *902/300400* ⊕ *www.mrw.*

es. **Seur** ☎ *902/101010* ⊕ *www.seur.com.* **UPS** ☎ *902/888820* ⊕ *www.ups.com.*

▌ MONEY

Spain is no longer a budget destination, even less so in the expensive cities of Barcelona, San Sebastián, and Madrid. However, prices still compare slightly favorably with those elsewhere in Europe.

Prices throughout this guide are given for adults. Substantially reduced fees are almost always available for children, students, and senior citizens.

▌TIP➜ Banks never have every foreign currency on hand, and it may take as long as a week to order. If you're planning to exchange funds before leaving home, don't wait until the last minute.

ATMS AND BANKS

Your bank will probably charge a fee for using ATMs abroad; the foreign bank you use may also charge a fee. Nevertheless, you'll usually get a better rate of exchange at an ATM than you will at a currency-exchange office or even when changing money in a bank, and extracting funds as you need them is a safer option than carrying around a large amount of cash.

▌TIP➜ PINs with more than four digits are not recognized at ATMs in Spain. If yours has five or more, remember to change it before you leave.

You'll find ATMs in every major city in Spain, as well as in most smaller towns. ATMs will be part of the Cirrus and/or Plus networks and will allow you to withdraw euros with your credit or debit card, provided you have a valid PIN.

Spanish banks tend to maintain an astonishing number of branch offices, especially in the cities and major tourist destinations, and the majority have an ATM.

CREDIT CARDS

It's a good idea to inform your credit-card company before you travel, especially if you're going abroad and don't travel internationally very often. Otherwise, it might put a hold on your card owing to unusual activity—not a good thing halfway through your trip. Record all your credit-card numbers—as well as the phone numbers to call if your cards are lost or stolen—in a safe place, so you're prepared should something go wrong. Both MasterCard and Visa have general numbers you can call (collect if you're abroad) if your card is lost, but you're better off calling the number of your issuing bank, since MasterCard and Visa usually just transfer you to your bank; your bank's number is usually printed on your card.

If you plan to use your credit card for cash advances, you'll need to apply for a PIN at least two weeks before your trip. Although it's usually cheaper (and safer) to use a credit card abroad for large purchases (so you can cancel payments or be reimbursed if there's a problem), note that some credit-card companies *and* the banks that issue them add substantial percentages to all foreign transactions, whether they're in a foreign currency or not. Check on these fees before leaving home, so there won't be any surprises when you get the bill.

■TIP→ Before you charge something, ask the merchant whether he or she plans to do a dynamic currency conversion (DCC). In such a transaction the shop, restaurant, or hotel (not Visa or MasterCard) converts the currency and charges you in dollars. In most cases you'll pay the merchant a 3% fee for this service in addition to any credit-card company and issuing-bank foreign-transaction surcharges.

DCC programs are becoming increasingly widespread. Merchants who participate in them are supposed to ask whether you want to be charged in dollars or the local currency, but they don't always. And even if they do offer you a choice, they may well avoid mentioning the surcharges. The good news is that you *do* have a choice. And if this practice really gets your goat, you can avoid it entirely thanks to American Express; with its cards, DCC simply isn't an option.

Reporting Lost Cards American Express ☎ *800/528-4800 in U.S., 336/393-1111 collect from abroad ⊕ www.americanexpress. com.* **Diners Club** ☎ *800/234-6377 in U.S., 514/877-1577 collect from abroad ⊕ www. dinersclub.com.* **MasterCard** ☎ *800/627-8372 in U.S., 636/722-7111 collect from abroad ⊕ www.mastercard.com.* **Visa** ☎ *800/847-2911 in U.S. ⊕ www.visa.com.*

Use these toll-free numbers in Spain. **American Express** ☎ *900/814500.* **Diners Club** ☎ *900/801331.* **MasterCard** ☎ *900/971231.* **Visa** ☎ *900/991124.*

CURRENCY AND EXCHANGE

Since 2002, Spain has used the European monetary unit, the euro (€). Euro bills come in denominations of 5, 10, 20, 50, 100, 200, and 500; coins are worth 1 cent of a euro, 2 cents, 5 cents, 10 cents, 20 cents, 50 cents, 1 euro, and 2 euros. Forgery is quite commonplace in parts of Spain, especially with 50-euro notes. You can generally tell a forgery by the feel of the paper: counterfeits tend to be smoother than the legal notes, and the metallic line down the middle is darker than those in real bills. Local merchants (even those with counterfeit-spotting equipment) may refuse to accept €200 and €500 bills.

At this writing the dollar was weak against the euro and other currencies, although analysts expect it to strengthen: it stands at €0.75 to the U.S. dollar.

■TIP→ Even if a currency-exchange booth has a sign promising no commission, rest assured that there's some kind of huge, hidden fee. (Oh . . . that's right. The sign didn't say no fee.) And as for rates, you're almost always better off getting foreign currency at an ATM or exchanging money at a bank.

■ PASSPORTS AND VISAS

Visitors from the United States need a passport valid for a minimum of six months to enter Spain.

■TIP→ Before your trip, make two copies of your passport's data page (one for someone at home and another for you to carry separately). Or scan the page and email it to someone at home and yourself.

VISAS

Visas are not necessary for those with U.S. passports valid for a minimum of six months and who plan to stay in Spain for tourist or business purposes for up to 90 days. Should you need a visa to stay longer than this, contact the Spanish consulate office nearest to you in the United States to apply for the appropriate documents.

▌ RESTROOMS

Spain has some public restrooms (*servicios*), including, in larger cities, small coin-operated booths, but they are few and far between. Your best option is to use the facilities in a bar or cafeteria, remembering that at the discretion of the establishment you may have to order something. Gas stations have restrooms (you usually have to request the key to use them), but they are more often than not in terrible condition.

The Bathroom Diaries. This website is flush with unsanitized info on restrooms the world over—each one located, reviewed, and rated. ⊕ *www.thebathroomdiaries.com.*

▌ SAFETY

Petty crime is a huge problem in popular tourist destinations. The most frequent offenses are pickpocketing (particularly in Madrid and Barcelona) and theft from cars (all over the country). Never leave anything valuable in a parked car, no matter how friendly the area feels, how quickly you'll return, or how invisible the item seems once you lock it in the trunk. Thieves can spot rental cars a mile away. In airports, laptop computers and smartphones are choice prey.

Distribute your cash and any valuables (including your credit cards and passport) between a deep front pocket or an inside jacket or vest pocket. Don't wear a money belt or a waist pack, both of which peg you as a tourist. When walking the streets, particularly in large cities, carry as little cash as possible. Men should carry their wallets in their front pocket; women who need to carry purses should strap them across the front of their bodies. Leave the rest of your valuables in the safe at your hotel. On the beach, in cafés and restaurants, and in Internet centers, always keep an eye on your belongings.

Be cautious of any odd or unnecessary human contact, verbal or physical, whether it's a tap on the shoulder, someone asking you for a light, someone spilling a drink at your table, and so on. Thieves often work in teams, so while one distracts your attention, another swipes your wallet.

As different countries have different worldviews, look at travel advisories from a range of governments to get more of a sense of what's going on out there. And be sure to parse the language carefully. For example, a warning to "avoid all travel" carries more weight than one urging you to "avoid nonessential travel," and both are much stronger than a plea to "exercise caution." A U.S. government travel warning is more permanent (though not necessarily more serious) than a so-called public announcement, which carries an expiration date.

Consider registering online with the State Department (⊕ *travelregistration.state.gov/ibrs*), so the government will know to look for you should a crisis occur in the country you're visiting.

The U.S. Department of State's website has more than just travel warnings and advisories. The consular information sheets issued for every country have general safety tips, entry requirements (be sure to verify these with the country's embassy), and other useful details.

▌ TAXES

Value-added tax, similar to sales tax, is called I.V.A. in Spain (pronounced "*ee-vah*," for *impuesto sobre el valor añadido*). It's levied on both products and services, such as hotel rooms and restaurant meals. When in doubt about whether tax is included, ask, "*¿Está incluido el I.V.A.?*" As of February 2014, the I.V.A. rate for hotels and restaurants is 10%, regardless of their number of stars. A special tax law for the Canary Islands allows hotels and restaurants there to charge 7% I.V.A. Menus will generally read at the bottom whether tax is included ("*I.V.A. incluido*") or not ("*más 10% I.V.A.*").

Although food, pharmaceuticals, and household items are taxed at the lowest rate (4%), most consumer goods are now taxed at 21%. A number of shops participate in Global Refund (formerly Europe Tax-Free Shopping), a V.A.T. refund service that makes getting your money back relatively hassle-free. You cannot get a refund on the V.A.T. for such items as meals or services such as hotel accommodations or taxi fares.

When making a purchase that qualifies for Global Refund, find out whether the merchant gives refunds—not all stores do, nor are they required to—and ask for a V.A.T. refund form. Have the form stamped like any customs form by customs officials when you leave the country or, if you're visiting several European Union countries, when you leave the EU. After you're through passport control, take the form to a refund-service counter for an on-the-spot refund (which is usually the quickest and easiest option), or mail it to the address on the form (or the envelope with it) after you arrive home. You receive the total refund stated on the form, but the processing time can be long, especially if you request a credit-card adjustment.

Global Blue is a Europewide service with 225,000 affiliated stores and more than 700 refund counters at major airports and border crossings. The refund form, called a Tax Free Check or Refund Cheque, is the most common across the European continent. The service issues refunds in the form of cash, check, or credit-card adjustment.

V.A.T. Refunds Global Blue ☎ *866/706–6090 from U.S., 00800/3211–1111 in Spain (toll-free, weekdays 8–6)* ⊕ *www.globalblue.com.*

▌ TIME

Spain is on Central European Time, six hours ahead of Eastern Standard Time. Like the rest of the European Union, Spain switches to daylight saving time on the last weekend in March and switches back on the last weekend in October.

Time Zones Timeanddate.com. Helps you figure out the correct time anywhere. ⊕ *www.timeanddate.com/worldclock.*

▌ TIPPING

Aside from tipping waiters and taxi drivers, Spaniards tend not to leave extra in addition to the bill. Restaurant checks do not list a service charge on the bill but consider the tip included. If you want to leave a small tip in addition to the bill, tip between 5% and 10% of the bill (and only if you think the service was worth it), and leave less if you eat tapas or sandwiches at a bar—just enough to round out the bill to the nearest €1.

Tip taxi drivers about 10% of the total fare, plus a supplement to help with luggage. Note that rides from airports carry an official surcharge plus a small handling fee for each piece of luggage.

Tip hotel porters €0.50 a bag and the bearer of room service €0.50. A doorman who calls a taxi for you gets €0.50. If you stay in a hotel for more than two nights, you can tip the maid about €0.50 per night, although it isn't generally expected

Tour guides should be tipped about €2, barbers €0.50 to €1, and women's hairdressers at least €1 for a wash and style. Restroom attendants are tipped €0.50.

▌TOURS

SPECIAL-INTEREST TOURS

Madrid and Beyond. An array of customized private luxury tours (no two are the same) are offered by this company, focusing on culinary, cultural, and sports-related themes. ☎ *91/758–0063* ⊕ *www.madridandbeyond.com* ✉ *Prices available on application.*

Toma Tours. This company provides personalized and small-group tours with the focus on discovering Andalusia's culture, landscape, and gastronomy beyond the guidebook. ☎ *956/066815, 650/733116* ⊕ *www.tomatours.com* ✉ *From €1,669.*

ART

Atlas Cruises and Tours. Based in the United States, this company offers a range of tours with accents on art, cultural history, and the outdoors. ☎ *888/942–3301* ⊕ *www.escortedspaintours.com* ✉ *From $950.*

Heritage Tours. Based in New York, this company helps arrange customized cultural tours based on your interests and budget. Guides are drawn from a network of curators, gallery owners, and art critics. ☎ *800/378–4555, 212/206–8400* ⊕ *www.htprivatetravel.com* ✉ *From $3,500.*

Ole Spain Tours. This guide offers art and historical tours to Spain. ☎ *91/551–5294* ⊕ *www.olespaintours.com* ✉ *From €300.*

BIRD-WATCHING

Discovering Doñana. In the Coto Doñana National Park in Andalusía, this company offers some of the best guided bird-watching tours and expeditions in Spain. ☎ *620/964369* ⊕ *www.discoveringdonana.com* ✉ *From €30.*

CULINARY AND WINE

Artisans of Leisure. This company offers personalized food-and-wine and cultural tours to Spain. ☎ *800/214–8144, 212/243–3239* ⊕ *www.artisansofleisure.com* ✉ *From $9,500.*

Cellar Tours. Based in Madrid, Cellar Tours offers a wide array of wine and cooking tours to Spain's main wine areas. ☎ *91/143–6553 in Spain, 310/496–8061* ⊕ *www.cellartours.com* ✉ *From €2,400.*

GOLF

The following Spain-based companies offer golf tours and information.

HIKING

Spain Adventures. This company offers biking and hiking around Spain as well as unusual tours such as yoga and cookery. ☎ *772/564–0330* ⊕ *www.spainadventures.com* ✉ *From $3,400.*

LANGUAGE PROGRAMS

Go Abroad. This is one of the best resources for language schools in Spain. ☎ *720/570–1702* ⊕ *www.goabroad.com.*

VOLUNTEER PROGRAMS

Go Abroad. This is the best resource for volunteering and finding paid internships in Spain. ☎ *720/570–1702* ⊕ *www.goabroad.com.*

ONLINE TRAVEL TOOLS

ALL ABOUT SPAIN

For more information on Spain, visit the Tourist Office of Spain at ⊕ *www.spain.info.* Also check out the sites ⊕ *www.red2000.com/spain* and *www.idealspain.com;* the latter focuses more on living, working, or buying property in Spain. A useful Craigslist-type site listing everything from vacation rentals to language lessons is ⊕ *www.loquo.com/en_us.* For a virtual brochure on Spain's paradores and online booking, go to ⊕ *www.parador.es.*

INDEX

PHOTO CREDITS

Front cover: Wolfgang Thieme/dpa/Corbis [Description: Guggenheim Museum, Bilbao]. 1, Hidalgo & Lopesino / age fotostock. 2-3, Alvaro Leiva / age footstock. 5, JLImages / Alamy. Chapter 1: Experience Spain: 10-11, Carsten Leuzinger / age fotostock. 12, Minerva Bloom, Fodors.com member. 13 (left), Sandra Balboa, Fodors. com member. 13 (right), J.D. Dallet/age fotostock. 14, Nicki Geigert, Fodors. com member. 15 (left), Larondel, Fodors.com member. 15 (right), Wojtek Buss/age fotostock. 17, Factoria Singular/age fotostock. 20, Robert DiPietro, Fodors.com member. 21 (left), Juan Manuel Silva/age fotostock. 21 (right), Rafael Campillo/age fotostock. 22, Peter Forde, Fodors.com member. 23, jitna Bhagani, Fodors.com member. 24 (left), Brian Maudsley/Shutterstock. 24 (top center), aguilarphoto/ Shutterstock. 24 (bottom center), Foucras G./age fotostock. 24 (right), Javier Larrea/age fotostock. 25 (top left), Atlantide S.N.C./age fotostock. 25 (bottom left), Victor Kotler/age fotostock. 25 (bottom center), Paco Gómez Garc.a/age fotostock. 25 (right), José Fuste Raga/age fotostock. 26, EllenS, Fodors. com member. 27 (left), love2explore, Fodors.com member. 27 (right), J.D. Dallet/age fotostock. 28, dalbera/Flickr. 29, ezio bocci/age fotostock. 30, Matt Trommer/Shutterstock. 31, Alan Copson/age fotostock. 38, Howard/age fotostock. 39 (left), Juan Manuel Silva/age fotostock. 39 (right), Ken Welsh/ age fotostock. 40, Pedro Salaverría/age fotostock. 41 (left), J.D. Dallet/age fotostock. 41 (right), Alberto Paredes/age fotostock. 44, Carlos Nieto/age fotostock. 45, Javier Larrea/age fotostock. 46 (top), Pictorial Press Ltd/ Alamy. 46 (bottom), The Print Collector / Alamy. 47 (top), Paradores de Turismo de España, S.A. 48, Fernando Fernandez/age fotostock. Chapter 2: Madrid: 49, Factoria Singular/age fotostock. 50, Duncan P Walker/iStockphoto. 51 (left), E.M. Promoción de Madrid, S.A.(Paolo Giocoso). 51 (right), VICTOR PELAEZ TORRES/iStockphoto. 52, Peter Doomen/Shutterstock. 53 (left), jlstras/ wikipedia.org. 53 (right), Patty Orly/Shutterstock. 54, Graham Heywood/iStockphoto. 68, Alan Copson / age fotostock. 71, Doco Dalfiano / age fotostock. 72, Alberto Paredes / age fotostock. 77, José Fuste Raga / age fotostock. Sergio Pitamitz / age fotostock. 82, Peter Barritt / Alamy. 83, David R. Frazier Photolibrary, Inc. / Alamy. 84 (top), Factoria Singular/age fotostock. 84 (bottom), REUTERS/Susana Vera/Newscom. 86, HUGHES Herv. / age fotostock. 87, rubiphoto/Shutterstock. 88 (top), Mary Evans Picture Library / Alamy. 88 (center and bottom), Public Domain. 89 (all), Public Domain. 90 (top), Public Domain. 90 (2nd from top), Peter Barritt / Alamy. 90 (3rd from top), A. H. C./age fotostock. 90 (bottom), Tramonto/age fotostock. 94, E.M. Promoción de Madrid, S.A. (Paolo Giocoso). 108, Paul D. Van Hoy II / age fotostock. 123, Berchery/age fotostock. 124, imagebroker / Alamy. 125, G.Haling/age fotostock. 126 (center), Charles Sturge / Alamy. 126 (top), Paco Ayala. 126 (bottom), Jean Du Boisberranger/ Hemis.fr / Aurora Photos. 127, Vinicius Tupinamba/Shutterstock. 131, Chris Seba / age fotostock. 137, E.M. Promoción de Madrid, S.A.(Carlos Cazurro). Chapter 3: Toledo and Trips from Madrid: 145, José Fuste Raga/age fotostock. 146, J.D. Dallet/age fotostock. 147, Juan Carlos MuÓoz/ age fotostock. 148, M. Angeles Tomás/iStockphoto. 149 (left), zordor/Flickr. 149 (right), Boca Dorada/ wikipedia.org. 150, jms122881, Fodors.com member. 160, Ivern Photo / age fotostock. 165, José Antonio Moreno/age fotostock. 169, Jose Fuste Raga / age fotostock. 180, Josep Curto / age fotostock. 183, PHB.cz (Richard Semik)/Shutterstock. 190, Jeronimo Alba / age fotostock. 193, Alan Copson / age fotostock. 195, Ioseba Egibar/age fotostock. 196, Javier Larrea/age fotostock. 198 (top left), Daniel P. Acevedo/age fotostock. 198 (bottom left), Sam Bloomberg-Rissman/age fotostock. 198 (right), Javier Larrea/age fotostock. 199, J.D. Dallet/age fotostock. 200 (top), PHB.cz (Richard Semik)/ Shutterstock. 200 (2nd from top), Javier Larrea/age fotostock, 200 (3rd from top), Jakub Pavlinec/Shutterstock. 200 (4th from top), J.D. Dallet/age fotostock. 200 (5th from top), Fresnel/Shutterstock. 200 (6th from top), J.D. Dallet/age fotostock. 200 (bottom), Marta Menéndez /Shutterstock. 201 (top left), Mauro Winery. 201 (top 2nd from left), Cephas Picture Library/Alamy. 201 (top 3rd from left), Alvaro Palacios Winery. 201 (top right), Mas Martinet Winery. 201 (bottom), Mike Randolph/age fotostock. 211, Kevin George/ age fotostock. 218, M. A. Otsoa de Alda / age fotostock. 224, José Antonio Moreno/age fotostock. 231, Richard Semik / age fotostock. 232, José Fuste Raga/age fotostock. Chapter 4: Galicia and Asturias: 237, Francisco Turnes/Shutterstock. 238, Alberto Paredes/ age fotostock. 239 (left), plazas I subiros/Shutterstock. 239 (right), Alan Copson/age fotostock. 240, Alberto Paredes/age fotostock. 241 (left), scaredy_kat/Flickr. 241 (right), M. Angeles Tomás/iStockphoto. 242, lheitman, Fodors.com member. 244, Juan Carlos MuÓoz / age fotostock. 255, José Carlos Pires Pereira/iStockphoto. 261, imagebroker/ Alamy. 262, Schütze Rodemann/age fotostock. 263 (left), Visual Arts Library (London) /Alamy. 263 (right), John Warburton-Lee Photography / Alamy. 264 (top), Javier Larrea/age fotostock. 264 (bottom), R. Matina/age fotostock. 265, J.D. Dallet/age fotostock. 266 (left), Toño Labra/age fotostock. 266 (center), Anthony Collins / Alamy. 266 (right), Ian Dagnall / Alamy. 267 (left), Javier Larrea/age fotostock. 267 (right), Miguel Angel Munoz Pellicer / Alamy. 270, SOMATUSCANI/ iStockphoto. 278, Phooey/iStockphoto. 286, Cantabria tradicional / age fotostock. 291, Aguililla & Marín/age fotostock. 298, Alberto Paredes/ age fotostock. 300, Javier Larrea / age fotostock. Chapter

5: Bilbao and the Basque Country: 303, Jeronimo Alba / age fotostock. 304, Javier Larrea/age fotostock. 305 (top), Juan Carlos Muñoz/age fotostock. 305 (bottom), Javier Larrea/age fotostock. 306, OSOMEDIA / age fotostock. 307 (left),Patty Orly/Shutterstock. 307 (right), Núria Pueyo/wikipedia. org. 308, Javier Gil/Shutterstock. 310, Adriaan Thomas Snaaijer/Shutterstock. 316, Gonzalo Azumendi / age fotostock. 321, Atlantide S.N.C./age fotostock. 324, John Miller / age fotostock. 333, BER-NAGER E./age fotostock. 334 (left and right), Javier Larrea/age fotostock. 335 (left), Le Naviose/age fotostock. 335 (bottom right), Mark Baynes /Alamy. 335 (top right), Robert Fried / Alamy. 335 (bottom), Mark Baynes / Alamy. 336, Mark Baynes/Alamy. 343, Toño Labra / age fotostock. 348-49, FSG / age fotostock. 348 (bottom), Jon Arnold Images / Alamy. 350 (top), Tim Hill / Alamy. 350 (2nd from top), mediacolor's / Alamy. 350 (3rd from top), Ramon grosso dolarea/Shutterstock. 350 (bottom), Peter Cassidy/age fotostock. 351 (left), Kathleen Melis/Shutterstock. 351 (top right), Mark Baynes / Alamy. 351 (2nd from top right), Alex Segre /Alamy. 351 (3rd from top right), Peter Cassidy/ age fotostock. 351 (bottom right), Frank Heuer/laif/Aurora Photos. 359, Graham Lawrence / age fotostock. 362, Wojtek Buss / age fotostock. 367, Brigitte Merz / age fotostock. Chapter 6: The Pyrenees: 371, GUY Christian/age fotostock. 372, Bryan Brooks, Fodors.com member. 373 (left), Jule_Berlin/ wikipedia.org. 373 (right), Matyas Arvai/Shutterstock. 374, Gonzalo Azumendi / age fotostock. 375 (left), Leser / age fotostock. 375 (right), Toniher/wikipedia.org. 376, Gustavo Naharro/wikipedia.org. 378, Matyas Arvai/Shutterstock. 388, Gonzalo Azumendi/age fotostock. 394, Alfred Abad / age fotostock. 403, P. Narayan / age fotostock. 406, Tolo Balaguer/age fotostock. 408, Javier Larrea/age fotostock. 415, horrapics/Wikimedia Commons. 419, Hugo Alonso / age fotostock. 423, Marco Cristofori / age fotostock. Chapter 7: Barcelona: 429, Rafael Campillo / age fotostock. 432, Peter Holmes / age fotostock. 433 (left), Tamorlan/wikipedia.org. 433 (right), diluvi/wikipedia.org. 434, Mikhail Zahranichny/ Shutterstock. 435 (left), Philip Lange/Shutterstock. 435 (right), Regien Paassen/Shutterstock. 436, Vinicius Tupinamba/Shutterstock. 447, BORGESE Maurizio / age fotostock. 455, Ken Welsh / age fotostock. 456, Ruben Olavo / age fotostock. 464, Petr Svarc / age fotostock. 474, Oso Media/Alamy. 475, Sandra Baker/Alamy. 476 (top left), Public Domain. 476 (bottom left), Alfonso de Tomás/Shutterstock. 476 (top right), Zina Seletskaya/Shutterstock. 476 (center right), Amy Nichole Harris/Shutterstock. 476 (bottom right), Luis M. Seco/Shutterstock. 477 (left), Iwona Grodzka/Shutterstock. 477 (top right), zvonkomaja/Shutterstock. 477 (center right), Public Domain. 477 (bottom right), Smackfu/wikipedia. org. 478 (top left), synes/Flickr. 478 (bottom left), rubiphoto/Shutterstock. 478 (right), Solodovnikova Elena/Shutterstock. 479 (top), Quim Roser/age fotostock. 479 (bottom),Jan van der Hoeven/Shutterstock. 483, Factoria Singular / age fotostock. 485, Jordi Puig / age fotostock. Chapter 8: Catalonia, Valencia, and the Costa Blanca: 531, Hermes/age fotostock. 532, VRoig/Flickr. 533, Helio San Miguel. 534, Patty Orly/Shutterstock. 535 (left), Ana Abadía/ age fotostock. 535 (right), Mauricio Pellegrinetti/ Flickr. 536, Helio San Miguel. 544, Oscar García Bayerri / age fotostock. 548, Carlos S. Pereyra / age fotostock. 551, B&Y Photography Inc. / age fotostock. 553, Oscar García Bayerri / age fotostock. 557, José Fuste Raga / age fotostock. 562, Helio San Miguel. 565, Alberto Paredes / age fotostock. 571, Isidoro Ruiz Haro / age fotostock. 576, Nils-Johan Norenlind/age fotostock. 581, Igor Gonzalo Sanz / age fotostock. 586, Charles Bowman / age fotostock. 588, Hidalgo & Lopesino/age fotostock. 590, Alan Copson/age fotostock. Chapter 9: Ibiza and The Balearic Islands: 593, Stuart Pearce / age fotostock. 594 (left), Factoria Singular/age fotostock. 594 (right), Casteran/age fotostock. 595 (top), Szymaniak/iStockphoto. 595 (bottom), mayla, Fodors.com member. 596, Bartomeu Amengual / age fotostock. 597 (left), Rafael Campillo/ age fotostock. 597 (right), Laurie Geffert Phelps, Fodors.com member. 598, GARDEL Bertrand / agefotostock. 599 (left), Anibal Trejo/Shutterstock. 599 (right), Salvador & lvaro Nebot/age fotostock. 600, Karolina Ksiazek/ Shutterstock. 610, Stuart Pearce/age fotostock. 620, Skowron/Shutterstock. 624, Katja Kreder / age fotostock. 630, Hubertus Blume / age fotostock. 637, Martin Siepmann/age fotostock. 639, snap foto-design / age fotostock. 648, Gonzalo Azumendi / age fotostock. Chapter 10: Andalusia: 653, José Fuste Raga/age fotostock. 654, Hayal, Fodors.com member. 655, Mariana Sacramento, Fodors.com member. 656, Seiffe / age fotostock. 657 (left), ampFotoStudio/Shutterstock. 657 (right), Carmen Martínez Banús/iStockphoto. 658, riverside, Fodors.com member. 659 (left), csp/Shutterstock. 659 (right), José Francisco Ruiz/age fotostock. 660, Christine B. Patronick, Fodors.com member. 668, MOIRENC Camille / age fotostock. 675, José Antonio Moreno / age fotostock. 679, Johnny Stockshooter/age fotostock. 685, Doug Scott/age fotostock. 686, Marina Spironetti / Alamy. 687, Kimball Hall / Alamy. 688, Profimedia International s.r.o. / Alamy. 689 (top), amjad el-geoushi / Alamy. 689 (left), Felipe Trueba / Alamy. 689 (right), Redferns Music Picture Library / Alamy. 690, christina wilson/ Alamy. 697, lbuchanan, Fodors.com member. 705, Alessandra Sarti / age fotostock. 709, S Tauqueur / age fotostock. 712, Travel Pix Collection/ age fotostock. 714, Francisco Barba / age fotostock. 717, Ken Welsh/age fotostock. 726-27, Sylvain Grandadam. 731, Lucas Vallecillos / age fotostock. 738, Thomas Dressler / age fotostock. 744, Juergen Richter / age fotostock. 755

ABOUT OUR WRITERS

 Lauren Frayer is the Madrid correspondent for National Public Radio and the *Los Angeles Times*. Before moving to Europe, she spent nearly 10 years reporting for the Associated Press in Washington, Jerusalem, Cairo and Baghdad. Lauren updated the Toledo chapter.

 Born and raised in Madrid, economist Ignacio Gómez spent three years living and working in New York, then rode the online journalism wave in Madrid, writing about technology, leisure, and travel for various publications. He is now the director of strategy and innovation for the interactive media department of RTVE, the Spanish broadcasting corporation. He updated the Madrid chapter.

 Jared Lubarsky is a teacher and freelance travel writer who has been writing for Fodor's since 1997, first on Japan, where he lived for thirty years, and more recently on Spain—having relocated to Barcelona in 2005. He still wonders how it took him so long to discover that eminently livable city. Lubarsky has written for *Travel & Leisure, National Geographic Traveler,* the *New York Times Magazine,* and a variety of inflight publications. He updated Ibiza and the Balearic Islands; Catalonia, Valencia, and the Costa Blanca; and contributed to Barcelona for this edition.

 Originally from the north of England, Elizabeth Prosser has lived in Barcelona since 2007. When she is not indulging in her passion for travel around Spain and beyond, she works as a freelance writer covering a range of topics including travel, leisure, food and technology for a range of publications. Elizabeth updated the Pyrenees, and Galicia and Asturias chapters.

 Joanna Styles is a freelance writer and author based in Marbella, Andalusia, where she has lived for more than 20 years. Her writing covers a range of topics including everything and anything about Spain, particularly Andalusia, her favorite region in this very varied country. She updated the Experience Spain, Andalusia, Costa del Sol and Costa de Almería, and Travel Smart Spain chapters.

 Steve Tallantyre is a British journalist and copywriter. He moved from Italy to Barcelona in the late 1990s, just in time to witness Spain's rise as a global culinary superpower. Married to a Catalan native, with two "Catalangles" children, Steve writes about the region's recipes, restaurants, and food culture for a number of international publications. He also owns a popular blog about Barcelona cuisine (⊕ *www.foodbarcelona.com*) and works as a consultant for several travel companies. Steve updated Where to Eat in Barcelona.

 Originally from Australia, Suzanne Wales arrived in Barcelona in 1992 and immediately became captivated with the city's rich architecture, sunny weather, and strong coffee. She regularly writes travel and arts features, generally with a focus on design and architecture, for top European and U.S. publications between leading tours on the city's most original shops and design destinations. Suzanne updated Shopping and Nightlife and the Arts in Barcelona, as well as the Bilbao and the Basque Country chapter.